D - F

### THE SURREY INSTITUTE OF ART & DESIGN

Farnham Campus, Falkner Road, Farnham, Surrey GU9 7DS

**Return on or before the last date stamped below**
**Fines will be charged on overdue books**

| | | |
|---|---|---|
| 20. MAY 97 | -3. DEC 1998 | - 9 OCT 2000 |
| | 11 JAN. 1999 | |
| 12. JUN 97 | 1 5 FEB 1999 | 1 6 FEB 2005 |
| 13. NOV 97 | | 2 9 MAY 2007 |
| 27. NOV 97 | 2 MAR 1999 | |
| 16. FEB | 23. APR 99 | 1 1 JAN 2010 |
| | 10. MAY 99 | 1 9 NOV 2010 |
| 28. APR | 18. MAY 99 | |
| 12. MAY 98 | 16. JUN 99 | |
| 02. JUN | 11. JUN 1999 | |
| | 16.6.99 | |
| 18. JUN | - 6 JUN 2000 | |
| 09. OCT | 1 5 JUN 2000 | |

# MARKETING

# McGRAW-HILL SERIES IN MARKETING

# MARKETING

## SECOND EDITION

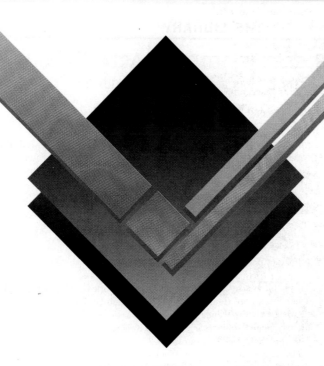

### COURTLAND L. BOVÉE
C. Allen Paul Distinguished Chair
Grossmont College

### MICHAEL J. HOUSTON
Research Professor of Marketing
University of Minnesota

### JOHN V. THILL
Chief Executive Officer
Communication Specialists of America

**McGraw-Hill, Inc.**
New York ▪ St. Louis ▪ San Francisco ▪ Auckland ▪ Bogotá ▪ Caracas ▪ Lisbon ▪ London ▪ Madrid ▪ Mexico City
Milan ▪ Montreal ▪ New Delhi ▪ San Juan ▪ Singapore
Sydney ▪ Tokyo ▪ Toronto

MARKETING

4 5 6 7 8 9 0 VNH VNH 9 0 9 8 7 6 5

ISBN 0-07-006879-8

This book was set in Century Old Style by York Graphic Services, Inc.
The editors were Bonnie K. Binkert and Bob Greiner;
the designer was Wanda Lubelska;
the production supervisor was Paula Keller.
The photo editor was Susan Holtz.
Collages were drawn by Roy Weimann;
line art was done by Fine Line Illustrations, Inc.
Von Hoffmann Press, Inc., was printer and binder.


Library of Congress Cataloging-in-Publication Data

Bovée, Courtland L.
    Marketing / Courtland L. Bovée, Michael J. Houston, John V. Thill.
    —2d ed.
        p.      cm. — (McGraw-Hill series in marketing)
    Includes bibliographical references and index.
    ISBN-0-07-006879-8
    1. Marketing.      I. Houston, Michael J.      II. Thill, John V.
    III. Title.     IV. Series.
    HF5415.B6213        1995
    658.8—dc20                                      94-12132

# CONTENTS IN BRIEF

# CONTENTS

## PART II MARKET ANALYSIS AND TARGET MARKETING 105

# PART III PRODUCT STRATEGY 237

## PART IV PRICING STRATEGY AND MANAGEMENT 327

# PART V DISTRIBUTION STRATEGIES 391

## PART VI PROMOTION STRATEGY 513

# PART VII  MARKETING IN TODAY'S GLOBAL ECONOMY  611

# PREFACE

## CONTINUES TO LEAD THE WAY INTO THE TWENTY-FIRST CENTURY

As an art and a science, marketing is undergoing dramatic and exciting changes, and the field promises to be just as dynamic in the years ahead. Marketing has emerged as the most critical function in today's international business climate; even the smallest firms are now using innovative marketing techniques to compete globally. The second edition of *Marketing* continues in the ground-breaking tradition of the first edition by pioneering important emerging topics that promise to join the core of contemporary marketing. In the first edition, *Marketing* introduced quality and customer service into the marketing principles curriculum. The key innovation in the second edition is intercultural marketing, a strategy being adopted by an increasing number of marketing firms. Chapter 20, "Intercultural and International Marketing," emphasizes the importance of both concepts and explains how they are related.

*Marketing* also continues with its extensive integration of vital topics that reflect the evolution of the marketing profession. More than ever, nonprofit organizations are harnessing marketing strategies to help achieve their objectives, and marketing in the service sector continues to grow in both importance and sophistication as this sector of the economy grows. Contemporary marketers reap the benefits of advanced technology in creating new products and new ways to distribute these products, but they also face increasing pressure to market in socially and environmentally responsible ways. *Marketing* successfully introduces students to all of these major trends. We've integrated international marketing, nonprofit marketing, services marketing, and ethics throughout the book, in addition to addressing them in dedicated sections or chapters.

Of course, content is only one aspect of an effective marketing text. *Marketing* presents both fundamentals and emerging trends in a lively and engaging style that reflects our enthusiasm for the profession. And students not only read about marketing; they get to experience it firsthand through the many involvement activities we present. A quick look at the pedagogy in *Marketing* reveals a much richer set of exercises and learning experiences than is offered by any other text in the field. In addition to learning objectives, key term definitions, chapter summaries, and other traditionally available features, we provide role-playing case studies, primary and secondary research activities, experiential exercises on a wide range of topics, decision-making opportunities on ethical dilemmas, and numerous possibilities for class discussion. This unmatched collection of teaching tools makes the classroom experience much more interesting for students and frees instructors from the burden of creating their own exercises.

For all these reasons, *Marketing* meets the needs of today's marketing students and instructors. Here's a closer look at the features and benefits of this text.

## PROVIDES A BALANCED, INTEGRATED INTRODUCTION TO MARKETING

Marketing is a discipline that cannot be fractured and compartmentalized without losing some of its meaning. For example, services marketing can't be covered in isolation. It requires focused treatment, which we provide in Chapter 10, "Service and Nonprofit Marketing." But for students to truly grasp the challenge of services marketing, they need to encounter it throughout the course as well. For instance, we introduce the concept of the goods-service continuum early in the first chapter on product strategy. This helps students understand from the beginning that all products have tangible and intangible components. We then integrate services throughout the entire book, and we do the same with nonprofit marketing, ethics, and international marketing—all important themes that cannot be treated adequately in isolation.

In addition to this high level of integration, *Marketing* provides balance. Marketing texts historically have had a strong bias toward packaged consumer goods. Even though packaged goods are clearly important, many students will spend part or all of their careers in consumer services, industrial goods and services, advanced technology products, nonprofit enterprises, and government agencies. Not every graduate will market potato chips or blue jeans; many will find themselves working in semiconductors, commerical banking, industrial chemicals, health care, computer integration services, agricultural equipment, government services, or other products outside the consumer mainstream. To help students prepare, and to make the course material more interesting, we provide a balanced treatment of the many types of marketing challenges they are likely to encounter.

## PUTS STUDENTS ON THE CUTTING EDGE OF CONTEMPORARY MARKETING

Three key themes emerge as we look at the marketing landscape in the mid-1990s. First, marketers that have embraced quality and customer services as cornerstones of the marketing concept continue to succeed, while those who don't by and large struggle. Businesses, government agencies, and nonprofit groups around the world are caught up in the quest for quality and customer service. Considering the amount of attention these subjects are receiving from both academics and practitioners, it was puzzling when we prepared the first edition that textbooks then gave them so little coverage. Other texts have begun to emphasize these subjects since then, but not nearly with the degree of comprehensiveness that *Marketing* offers. We present quality and customer service as major themes in contemporary marketing. We define quality in its varied aspects, discuss the effect it has on an organization's marketing efforts, and describe the role that marketers play in the pursuit of higher quality. Similarly, we give students a new perspective on customer service, explain how customer service and marketing are related, and present a plan for providing superior customer service. The essence of Chapter 21, "Quality and Customer Service," is that satisfied customers are the foundation of success through the marketing concept.

Second, while researchers and practitioners continue to argue the merits of globalized strategies in international marketing, an intriguing phenomenon has emerged both here and in other countries. Marketers are discovering that not only are there significant cultural differences from country to country, but that pockets of cultural uniqueness exist inside many countries. The United States is a prime example of this, with its long and continuing tradition of receiving immigrants from all over the globe. As a result of this growing recognition of cultural diversity in the marketplace, more and more marketers are searching for effective ways to identify and target specific cultural segments. Marketing to African-Americans is perhaps the most visible example of this in the United States, but microcultures exist in the various Hispanic-American and Asian-American segments, as well as in segments of consumers who trace their roots back to Western and Eastern Europe. In addition to this important and exciting development in marketing, we've expanded our international marketing chapter to include a section on intercultural marketing. The two subjects are covered in one chapter as a way to highlight the similarities between crossing cultural borders and crossing national borders. (As one expert in the field has pointed out, intercultural marketing is like international marketing inside your own borders.)

Third, marketers realize they can no longer afford to execute marketing programs in isolation from one another. The trend toward integrated marketing communication (IMC), which we introduce in Chapter 1, is the most visible response to this realization. But even for all its potential value, IMC is only the first level of marketing integration. Throughout the book, we continually tie pieces of the marketing puzzle together so students get an integrated perspective. For example, Chapter 11 (the first of two pricing chapters) links price with the other elements in the marketing mix. Students learn that successful marketers not only integrate their communications, they integrate all aspects of the marketing process.

In addition to these major content enhancements, *Marketing* introduces students to a number of leading-edge marketing topics not found in most other texts. For example, Chapter 7 describes database marketing and the goal of "individualized" marketing, outlining the efforts being made to target smaller and smaller groups of customers. Chapter 8 explains brand equity and the reasons smart marketers place such a high economic value on strong brands. Chapter 13 introduces the concept of value-added resellers, an important marketing channel in the computer industry. Chapter 21 discusses the emergence of relationship marketing and the emphasis that leading marketers place on long-term partnerships with their customers. These and other important new trends prepare students for contemporary marketing in a way that no other text can.

## BUILDS A SOLID FOUNDATION OF MARKETING FUNDAMENTALS

Pedagogy and coverage of emerging issues set *Marketing* apart, but not at the expense of the fundamentals. We examined and reconsidered the traditional coverage of every important issue at the heart of marketing. Here's a brief sample of how we've approached some of the major topics:

- *Positioning.* Positioning is perhaps one of the most misunderstood aspects of marketing management. Using examples as diverse as Infiniti automobiles and rock guitarist Joe Satriani, we explore the meaning of positioning and its influence on the marketing mix. And to give students the proper strategic perspective on the power of positioning, we introduce it early in the book as part of the definition of marketing strategy, then reinforce the concept throughout the chapters on product strategy, pricing, distribution, and promotion.

- *Pricing.* Is there any area of marketing more challenging than pricing? Students are expected to grasp a bewildering array of concepts, from arcane legislation to price elasticity, which present opportunities for confusion at every turn. To promote a successful learning experience, we carefully organized the pricing material into a logical process flow. Students start with the most general strategic concepts and gradually work toward the specifics of pricing while exploring examples from Sears, American Airlines, Burroughs Wellcome, Komatsu, and a host of other organizations. By adding each successive layer to the pricing foundation in a methodical fashion, *Marketing* transforms pricing from a complex jumble of terms and theories to a clear and vital part of the marketing management process.

- *Wholesaling.* Too often, wholesaling is treated solely from the producer's or the retailer's perspective. This view is of course important, but the strategic marketing management of the wholesaling function itself is frequently overlooked. However, the wholesaling sectors employ hundreds of thousands of people in the United States alone, and many of them work in marketing capacities. Using examples from Super Valu, McKesson, Semiconductor Specialists, and other successful wholesalers and industrial distributors, we show what it's like to manage the business of wholesaling. As a result, *Marketing* addresses wholesaling from all three vantage points: production, retailing, and wholesaling itself.

## EXPLORES TODAY'S MOST IMPORTANT ETHICAL ISSUES

Unlike some texts, *Marketing* draws a clear distinction between ethical dilemmas and ethical lapses, which helps students understand the difference between unresolved ethical questions and behavior that is simply unethical. This text covers ethics in three ways: in a dedicated section in Chapter 2, in 12 "Ethical Dilemma in Marketing" boxes, and in shorter examples placed throughout the book. Students get the point that nearly every aspect of marketing presents ethical questions. Here's a sampling of the ethical dilemmas we highlight in the text:

- *Can Adults Learn Ethical Behavior?* Examines the current controversy over whether colleges and companies should try to teach ethics.

- *Your Right to Privacy vs. the Marketing Databases* Describes the growth in database marketing and explains the controversy between a marketer's right to promote its products and the consumer's right to privacy.

- *Can Market Segmentation Be Hazardous to Your Health?* Explores the issue of identifying target customers based on their likelihood of purchasing cigarettes, using the Dakota and Uptown incidents as examples.

- *Is Skim Pricing Ethical?* Discusses skim pricing and the pricing of significant medical products in particular, using the current controversy over AZT pricing.

- *How Far Can We Go in Marketing to Kids?* Examines the controversy over the amount of advertising aimed at children and the effect this may have on family consumption patterns.

Every Ethical Dilemma box ends with two "What's Your Opinion?" questions that encourage students to think about the issue presented and to draw their own conclusions. These questions can form the basis of class discussions, homework assignments, or student projects.

On the subject of ethics and social responsibility, we present an evenhanded view of marketing. We work hard to fire students' enthusiasm and respect for the profession (our upbeat coverage of personal selling in Chapter 19 is a good example), but we don't pretend that marketing in the 1990s is without its problems or its critics. By pointing out ethical dilemmas and reminding students of the responsibilities that accompany the rights of free enterprise, *Marketing* helps prepare the next generation of conscientious marketing professionals.

*Marketing* has no examples of alcohol promotions. We certainly support companies' rights to market legal products, but considering that many students taking this course are not of legal drinking age and that alcoholism among college students is a continuing social concern, we believe that an emphasis on alcoholic products in a textbook is inappropriate. *Marketing* also avoids tobacco examples (other than those cases in which tobacco products are the subject of ethical dilemmas). The trade literature offers thousands of other great marketing examples that students can relate to, and we've taken advantage of those.

## BRINGS THEORY TO LIFE WITH PRACTICAL EXAMPLES

Anybody who has tried to implement marketing theory knows that real life doesn't always work the way textbooks say it should. To help students prepare for their professional responsibilities, we point out those areas in the field of marketing where practice doesn't follow theory. For instance, all texts explain the relationship between price and demand, but few mention that managers rarely have reliable data on market demand when they set prices. We not only point that out, but we go a step beyond and explain a variety of methods marketers can use to compensate for the lack of hard data. Other areas in which we offer a realistic assessment include channel selection, forecasting, and portfolio management. All of these combine to give students a more accurate view of the challenges facing today's marketers.

To further help students relate the text material to their future careers in marketing, we provide a number of concise studies of how various concepts are implemented by today's marketers. In highlight boxes entitled "Techniques for Marketing Success," we show how to get the job done. Examples of these boxes include the following:

- *Lighthouse for the Blind: A Nonprofit Marketing Success.* How to use marketing strategies to meet the unique objectives of nonprofit marketers, such as providing stable employment for disadvantaged workers.
- *Facing an Uncertain Future: How to Reduce the Risk.* How to prepare for the future when you can't rely on traditional forecasting methods.
- *When the News Isn't Good.* How to minimize damage when communicating bad news to the press.
- *How to Keep Customers Coming Back.* Steps that business-to-business marketers can take to build customer loyalty.

In addition, Component Chapter A, "The Marketing Plan," discusses the goals and content of a marketing plan and presents a sample plan from a T-shirt company. By anchoring the theories and concepts with practical, how-to discussions, the text provides yet another way for students to grasp the material.

## OFFERS UNPARALLELED, PEDAGOGICAL SUPPORT

Rich pedagogy sets *Marketing* apart, and we include a number of unique elements.

### Facing a Marketing Challenge

These unique case studies put the student into the marketer's shoes to explore a number of decisions related to the chapter material. Each chapter opens with a short slice-of-life vignette that draws students into the chapter by vividly portraying a marketing challenge faced by a real executive. Each chapter concludes with a section entitled "A Case for Critical Thinking: Meeting a Marketing Challenge," which describes the actions taken by the featured executive and analyzes the results in light of the concepts presented in the chapter. Then the student takes over, playing a role in the executive's organization by making marketing decisions in four carefully chosen scenarios. The 22 marketing challenges include such intriguing cases as these:

- The U.S. Postal Service using qualitative research to explore the relationships between customers and letter carriers and to build on that knowledge in a new ad campaign
- Sears looking for a way out of its pricing trap, stuck between discounters on the low end and upscale retailers on the high end
- Hewlett-Packard trying to make a cultural shift from dozens of divisions marketing independently to a more highly coordinated centralized marketing focus
- Saturn trying to build an image as a new kind of U.S. car company
- Starbucks Coffee entering the Los Angeles market relying primarily on public relations to build awareness of its gourmet coffee offerings

### Sharpen Your Marketing Skills

These assignments offer students the opportunity to practice or analyze a particular marketing skill covered in the chapter. Examples include conducting simple price elasticity research, evaluating product designs, assessing promotional tactics, finding ways to take market share from a larger competitor, and identifying customers who would be interested in a line of natural cosmetics. By solving real-life marketing problems such as these, students develop a much stronger grasp of the material presented in the text. The exercises include both decision-making and communication components, two of the most important skills students will need in their careers.

### Keeping Current in Marketing

These library research exercises ask students to find and analyze a recent article about a particular company that relates to the material in the chapter, such as an article dealing with government regulation of an industry or with the reasons behind the success or failure of a new product. This exercise not only keeps the student up to date on important issues, but it reinforces research and analysis skills.

## Highlight Boxes

We have included four types of boxes in this book: the "Ethical Dilemma in Marketing" and "Techniques for Marketing Success" boxes described earlier, along with "Marketing in Action" and "Exploring Global Marketing" boxes. Marketing in Action features extended examples of how one company or organization applied the concepts presented in the chapter. Exploring Global Marketing highlights companies that are attempting to market goods and services internationally. All four boxes provide additional opportunities for class discussion, homework assignments, and student projects.

## Integrated Cases

Each of the seven parts in the book provides an in-depth case study of the marketing strategies and tactics used by a particular organization. All of these cases are right out of today's headlines, including Snapple's efforts to build nationwide sales while fending off PepsiCo and Coca-Cola, Compaq's attempt to revolutionize the personal computer market by introducing top-of-the-line products at unheard-of low prices, and Nestlé's use of database marketing techniques to build close relationships with consumers in the French baby food market. Every case includes four discussion and analysis questions, including one ethics question and one international question.

## Video Cases

Video provides a powerful and engaging learning experience—as long as the material is relevant, well produced, and clearly tied to the text. To ensure that our videos meet these criteria, we searched for the best possible tapes on each subject and then adapted the videos to *Marketing* by including a customized introduction at the beginning of each tape. This will make the viewing experience more meaningful for the student and easier to manage for the instructor. Here's a selection of the video cases we offer:

- SAS planning its strategy in the face of deregulation of the European air travel industry.
- General Motors using marketing research in the United Kingdom to increase market share for its Vauxhall and Bedford product lines.
- Chrysler reinventing its product development process to stay competitive in an increasingly tough auto market.
- McKesson building a nationwide distribution powerhouse by employing the latest advances in technology.
- Campbell reorganizing to address the increasingly fragmented U.S. consumer market.

## Important Additional Features to Help Students Learn

This text includes numerous other student-oriented features:

- Learning objectives in every chapter guide the learning effort, and the chapter summary is keyed by objective to help students measure their progress.
- The margin glossary quickly reinforces concepts from the text; for easy reference, the entire glossary is repeated at the end of the book.
- Each chapter features a map identifying a country that is covered in the text; these 22 maps enhance the student's sense of geography and highlight the need for a global perspective.
- Over 1,000 examples illustrate the marketing decisions of hundreds of organizations to show students how marketing works.
- "Questions for Discussion" at the end of each chapter are structured so that students apply what they've learned, rather than simply reviewing the concepts.

What are the benefits of having so many instructional features? Students grasp concepts and terminology more completely because they have the opportunity to learn in several ways: experience, analysis, review, and application. Also, the instructor's preparation time is reduced because discussion questions, activities, and homework possibilities are all here and ready to be used. Instructors won't have to spend their limited time searching out ways to involve students in the course. And finally, the pedagogy is sufficient for instructors to teach the course term after term without exhausting the text's rich resources. By not limiting chapter pedagogy to just a case study and some simple review questions, *Marketing* contains enough material to keep the course fresh and interesting for both instructors and students.

## RELIES ON EXTENSIVE, UP-TO-DATE RESEARCH

*Marketing* provides up-to-date coverage, both in terms of examples and emerging concepts. The thoroughness of the research is evidenced by the number and currency of endnotes in each chapter—more than any other leading text and two to three times more than many textbooks. To illustrate every concept, we collected a number of possible examples and then carefully selected the one or two instances that best illustrated the material. For every article and book reference you see in the notes, many more were reviewed and not included. This careful preparation produced such positive confirmation as this comment from one reviewer: "This is the best retailing chapter I have ever read."

A quick scan of any chapter or of the index will show how many real-life examples are included. These examples cover both large and small organizations in the commercial, nonprofit, and government sectors. We include well-known, extensively studied organizations such as IBM, American Express, and Coca-Cola, and we cover numerous other organizations such as the Manitoba Goatmilk Cooperative, Kenetech, and Perrigo.

## CATCHES STUDENTS' ATTENTION WITH LIVELY WRITING

The best textbook in the world is of little value if nobody reads it. From the beginning of this project, we placed an emphasis on lively, interesting prose that invites students to read. As one reviewer put it: "The writing style is clear and provocative. The authors avoid overly complex definitions in favor of clarity. Expressing definitions and concept descriptions clearly and supporting them with examples have to lead to ease of learning."

Without sacrificing academic integrity, *Marketing* communicates and informs with a light touch. We believe that the careful use of intelligent humor is a great way to keep students interested and involved. Communicating to students that marketing is not only a respectable and vital profession but also an enjoyable profession is the best way we know to inspire interest in the field.

## ENHANCES LEARNING WITH AN ATTRACTIVE, EFFECTIVE DESIGN

The visual appeal of a textbook has a lot to do with the success of the student's learning efforts. Every element of *Marketing* is part of an integrated instructional design. Every exhibit includes a complete caption and is closely integrated with the related text. Advertisements and photos were carefully chosen to support the text, rather than to simply entertain the reader. The open, attractive layout complements the lively writing to ensure a high level of interest and retention. In this edition, we've made the design even cleaner and more accessible by moving all margin exhibits into the text column.

## SUPPORTS THE INSTRUCTIONAL PROCESS

Obviously, the textbook is only a part of the overall instructional package. To meet the challenges of large classes, heavy teaching loads, and limited preparation time, instructors need a complete program of pedagogical resources and support features. And the multitude of demands on the student's time call for a textbook that makes the learning process both efficient and effective. Here are the ways in which *Marketing* supports both groups.

## Instructor Supplements

- *Instructor's Resource Manual.* Each chapter in the Instructor's Manual contains annotated learning objectives, key terms, chapter outline, lecture notes (with references to specific overhead transparencies), and answers to all questions and exercises. We've provided the information instructors need, without slowing them down with extra supplements of questionable value.

- *Acetate Transparency Program.* This set of 245 transparencies presents exhibits that aren't in the text, including comparative ads (two different ads illustrating a common marketing theme) and informative diagrams that illuminate text material. Each transparency is supported by a cover sheet that outlines the learning objectives for that transparency, the major points that should be emphasized, and several discussion questions specific to each transparency, along with answers. A special pack of 25 intercultural and international transparencies was created for this edition to complement the new coverage in the text.

- *Test Bank.* This manual is organized by text chapters and include a mix of 140 true/false, multiple choice, matching, fill-in, and short essay questions for each chapter—more than 3,000 questions in all. The questions are coded by level of difficulty, question type, and text page. The test bank has been carefully screened by reviewers to ensure that questions and answers are correct, relevant, and appropriate for this course. The test bank is available both in hard copy and on disk (both IBM and Macintosh formats).

- *Computerized Test Bank.* A powerful microcomputer program allows the instructor to create customized tests using the questions from the test bank, self-prepared items, or a combination. This versatile program incorporates a broad range of test-making capabilities, including editing and scrambling of questions to create alternative versions of a test. This program is available for both Apple and IBM computers.

- *Customized Test Service.* Through its Customized Test Service, McGraw-Hill will supply adopters of *Marketing* with custom-made tests consisting of items selected from the test bank. The test questions can be renumbered in any order. Instructors will receive an original test, ready for reproduction, and a separate answer key. Tests can be ordered by mail or by phone, using a toll-free number.

- *Classroom Management Software.* This program helps with grading and recordkeeping.

## Student Supplements

- *Study Guide.* Each chapter in the Study Guide includes a quick summary of the text chapter, a chapter outline, discussions of major concepts, a checkpoint test (to give the student an indication of how much more studying is needed), key-term matching, a checklist for applying chapter material on the job, an extra practice sheet that can also be assigned as homework, and several supplemental exercises. The Study Guide provides an effective learning experience that makes the most of the student's time.

- *Spreadsheet Exercises.* These computer-based exercises present a set of Lotus 1-2-3 spreadsheets that support the learning experience by bringing decision making to life for the students, using the same tools that marketing managers use.

- *Computer Simulation.* A simulation game called SHOES lets student teams manage athletic-shoe companies and compete with each other using the concepts they've learned in the book and in class.

## REFINEMENTS TO KEEP *MARKETING* ON THE LEADING EDGE

To meet the goal of providing the most effective and most up-to-date marketing text available, we solicited feedback from numerous professors and reviewed every chapter of *Marketing* in detail. In addition to hundreds of minor improvements and updates throughout the text, major enhancements that have been made in the second edition include:

- Introducing students to intercultural marketing strategies and the importance of recognizing cultural variations in a market

- Explaining the reasons behind the trend toward everyday low pricing

- Describing the shift away from mass marketing to targeted marketing that tries to build one-on-one relationships with customers

- Expanding the discussion of competitiveness and competitive analysis

- Simplifying and unifying the coverage of positioning statements and strategies

- Combining coverage of domestic and international environmental elements to give students an integrated perspective

- Clarifying discussions of marketing strategy development

- Adding a section on assessing market opportunities

- Reframing the consumer and organizational market chapters in the context of the decision-making process

- Adding coverage of nonrational decision making

- Simplifying the material on consumer learning and adding information about consumer knowledge structures

- Revising the segmentation chapter to emphasize the three-stage process of segmentation, targeting, and positioning

- Aligning the services and nonprofit marketing chapter with the two product strategy chapters

- Adding direct marketing to the channel strategy chapter

- Simplifying the coverage of retailing to focus more on strategies and less on definitions

- Expanding discussion of setting promotional objectives

- Adding a discussion of integrated marketing communication

- Revising the chapter on marketing organization, implementation, and control to give it greater emphasis on marketing management

## ACKNOWLEDGMENTS

*Marketing* is the product of the concerted efforts of a number of people. A heartfelt thanks to our many friends, acquaintances, and business associates who contributed to this textbook.

A very special acknowledgment to George Dovel for his remarkable talents. His wisdom, communication skills, and unique insights were invaluable, and his wealth of real-world experience gives this book an added dimension of reality.

We also extend our deep gratitude to Marian Burk Wood, whose creativity, rich experience, and sound advice were invaluable.

Our thanks to Terry Anderson, whose communication abilities and organizational skills ensured the clarity and completeness of this project. She aided us admirably throughout the preparation of this textbook. We are also grateful to Randy Stevens for his specialized knowledge and expert assistance.

Deep gratitude is extended to Marie Painter for her expertise in word processing and her work beyond the call of duty.

We also feel it is important to acknowledge and thank the American Marketing Association, an organization whose meetings and publications provide a useful forum for the exchange of ideas and for professional growth.

We are grateful for the valuable suggestions of David M. Andrus, Kansas State University; Donald J. Bowersox, Michigan State University; M. Bixby Cooper, Michigan Iona College; Sanford B. Hillman,

Middlesex Community College; Kathleen A. Krentler, San Diego State University; Priscilla Ann La Barbera, New York University; William Locander, University of Tennessee–Knoxville; Kent Monroe, University of Illinois; William L. Moore, University of Utah; Keith B. Murray, Northeastern University; Dennis A. Pitta, University of Baltimore; Bert Rosenbloom, Drexel University; Michael L. Rothschild, University of Wisconsin; F. Kelly Shuptrine, University of South Carolina; Donald E. Siemsen, California Polytechnic State University–San Luis Obispo; Harlan P. Wallingford, Pace University; and Valarie Zeithaml, Duke University.

We also appreciate the constructive comments of the reviewers of the second edition: Ronald Adams, University of North Florida; M. Wayne Alexander, Moorhead State University; Linda Anglin, Mankato State University; Arnold Bornfriend, Worcester State College; Gul Butaney, Bentley College; William Darley, University of Toledo; Robert Gwinner, Arizona State University; Hari Hariharan, University of Wisconsin–Madison; Lynn Harris, Shippensburg University; Denise Johnson, University of Louisville; Joe Jones, Clarkson University; Gail Kirby, University of Santa Clara; Geoff Lantos, Stonehill College; Kenneth Lord, SUNY Buffalo–NY; Keith Murray, Bryant College; Kimberly Pichot, Andrews University; Robert Quade, Centenary College; Margaret Sheehy, Bradford School; Fred Stephenson, University of Georgia; Martin St. John, Westmoreland Community College; Michael Swenson, Brigham Young University; Neville Webster, Andrews University; and Timothy Wilson, Clarion University.

We also want to extend our warmest appreciation to the very devoted professionals at McGraw-Hill. They include Gary Burke, Bonnie Binkert, Dan Loch, Susan Holtz, and the outstanding McGraw-Hill sales representatives. Finally, we thank editor Bob Greiner for his dedication and expertise, and we are grateful to copyeditor Gretlyn Cline and designer Wanda Lubelska for their superb work.

*Courtland L. Bovée*
*Michael J. Houston*
*John V. Thill*

# MARKETING

# PART I
# UNDERSTANDING MARKETING TODAY

# 1

# The Foundations of Marketing

**After studying this chapter, you will be able to**

**1.** Explain the exchange process and its importance in the marketing of all products

**2.** Define the four economic utilities that marketers can offer customers

**3.** Discuss the three categories of products

**4.** Identify the two types of organizations that practice nonprofit marketing

**5.** Describe marketing myopia and explain the risks inherent in a myopic approach to marketing

**6.** Outline the process of developing a marketing strategy

**7.** Describe the marketing mix and its major components

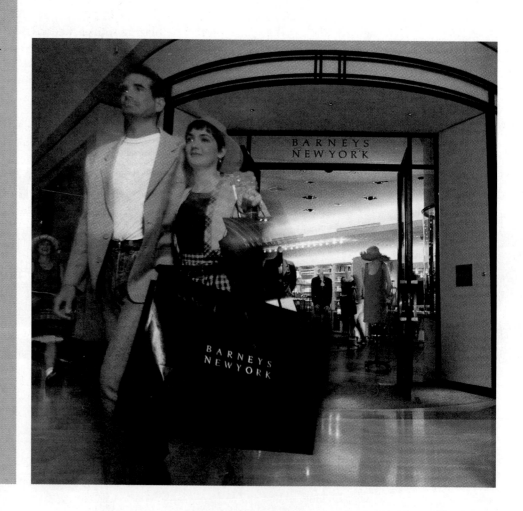

## *Running a Race That Never Ends*

Manufacturers of athletic shoes are running their own race, a race that never seems to end. Nike was named after the Greek goddess of victory for a good reason: the company has no intention of letting the competition run away. Started by former collegiate sprinter Philip Knight and his University of Oregon coach, Bill Bowerman, Nike stressed technology and high-performance products from the very beginning. An experiment with urethane rubber and a waffle iron got it all started, and serious runners loved the new waffle-soled shoes. By 1981 Knight and his company controlled about half the U.S. athletic shoe market, outpacing established overseas competitors such as Adidas and Puma.

In the 1980s, Nike offered over 140 models of shoes. As the running boom of the 1970s faded, Knight knew he had to look beyond high-performance running shoes to expand the company's sales. He identified target segments in the sports market, including basketball and tennis players. Then with products designed specifically for these athletes, Nike continued to prosper.

The 1980s brought a new twist to the market, however. Serious athletes weren't the only people interested in athletic shoes. Capitalizing on the aerobic exercise boom, younger rival Reebok boldly poured on the speed, taking the lead by 1986 on the strength of its innovative aerobics shoes. Two years later, Reebok's share of the market was 27 percent, and Nike's share had tumbled from around 50 percent to 23 percent. Then the aerobics fad was followed by another important change in the U.S. shoe market. Athletic shoes became fashionable footwear. People who had no intention of being serious athletes, or even serious exercisers, adopted athletic shoes as their favorite footwear. Again, Reebok was ahead of Nike in responding to this shift. First, actress Cybill Shepherd arrived at the Emmy Awards ceremony wearing an elegant evening gown and blazing orange Reeboks. Then, on a poster for his hit movie *Back to the Future,* Michael J. Fox dashed through time wearing Reeboks. What started as a product for dedicated runners had turned into a product for dedicated followers of fashion.

Despite impressive technology, its own series of celebrity endorsements, and award-winning advertising, Nike lost its footing in the late 1980s, and Reebok streaked ahead. By 1988 Reebok was selling 75 million pairs of shoes annually, compared with Nike's 50 million. However, the scrappy Knight fought back with new products and an emphasis on style and fashion. Nike regained the lead and has held it by a slim margin into the mid-1990s.

The race continues. If you were Phil Knight, what would you do to keep Nike on top? How would you help Nike meet the ever-changing demands of consumer tastes and advances in shoe technology? How would you define your market and identify areas of potential growth? What message would you want to communicate to your audience and how would you get that message across? How would you make your shoes available to more diverse groups of customers?[1]

# CHAPTER OVERVIEW

Nike puts something of value (shoes) on customers' feet and is rewarded with something of value in return (money). This exchange represents the basic function of marketing. Businesses, individuals, governments, and nonprofit organizations all develop products and exchange them with customers. This chapter gives you an expanded notion of *product* and *customer,* and it helps you see that many interactions between people are actually marketing exchanges. This chapter explains how marketing has evolved in the twentieth century and how today's successful marketers approach the task. You then get a quick look at the major elements of marketing strategy and tools marketers use to foster exchanges with their customers. The chapter concludes with a look at the future of the marketing profession.

# MARKETING DEFINED

Marketing is everywhere in our economy, and it touches everyone. Consider a few of the activities we take for granted, like riding a bus, shopping for clothes, reading a newspaper, or watching television. All of these rely on marketing. For example, the bus company encourages you to climb aboard, tells you about schedules, sets prices, tries to reach as many people as possible, and might offer special services such as providing vans or special buses for people using wheelchairs. Each of these activities is the result of a marketing decision, and these decisions are based on the principles you'll learn about in this course.

It's tough to imagine contemporary life without marketing. You're on the customer side of marketing when you shop at a 7-Eleven, pay your tuition, or go to a movie (see Exhibit 1.1). You're on the marketer side of the transaction when you advertise for a roommate, convince friends to lend you their cars, or interview for a job.

In the last two examples you're marketing yourself and your credibility. Job applicants use résumés as marketing tools to gain interviews with potential employers and then use the interviews to demonstrate what desirable "products" they are. Similarly, models and actors use photographs to market themselves; artists and writers supply samples of their work. Some applicants for the position of "director of romance" at Korbel Champagne Cellars took the self-marketing process a bit further. They sent the company flowers, balloons, videotapes, poems, and other items to demonstrate their romantic capabilities.[2] The search for creative, innovative ways to communicate is a key theme in marketing today.

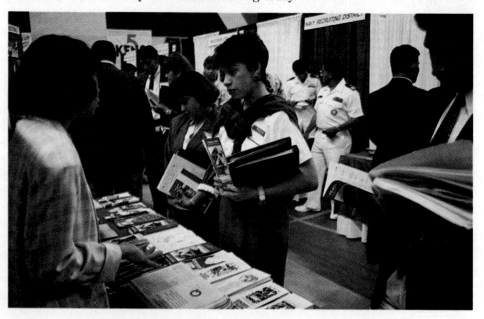

**Exhibit 1.1
MARKETING: IT'S ALL AROUND YOU**
Marketing plays a part in many of the activities we human beings engage in, whether it's satisfying our needs as consumers or promoting ourselves to prospective employers.

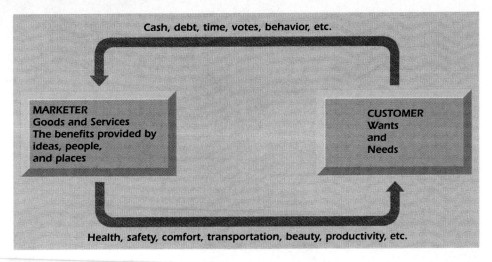

Cash, debt, time, votes, behavior, etc.

**MARKETER**
Goods and Services
The benefits provided by ideas, people, and places

**CUSTOMER**
Wants
and
Needs

Health, safety, comfort, transportation, beauty, productivity, etc.

**Exhibit 1.2  THE EXCHANGE PROCESS**
In the exchange process, marketers offer elements of value, including goods and services and the benefits provided by ideas, people, and places.

You can see by these examples that marketing is more than just a business activity. It's something everyone does quite often, acting as either the customer or the marketer. Even in the commercial realm, "companies" aren't the only marketers, and "goods" aren't the only items marketed. Dentists market their services when they mail reminder cards to their patients. Baseball teams market themselves when they give hats, team photos, and other premiums to their fans. The gas company markets itself when it encloses a newsletter with residential bills. Nonprofit groups also market what they do, be it medical research or political action, when they solicit contributions of time and money or try to influence people's behavior.

For decades two misleading notions generated confusion over the definition of marketing. The first was that only businesses market products, and the second was that selling and marketing are virtually the same thing. Although marketing was once little more than selling, the marketing function has changed, and the marketing manager's role has evolved. In 1985 the American Marketing Association cleared up much of the confusion when it redefined **marketing** as "the process of planning and executing the conception, pricing, promotion, and distribution of ideas, goods, and services to create exchanges that satisfy individual and organizational objectives."[3] This definition clarifies the concept of marketing because it encompasses all the diverse activities in marketing and highlights the central marketing function, the exchange process. When today's successful companies and organizations implement marketing, however, they expand this functional definition to include the ongoing process of fostering long-term relationships with customers.

## The Exchange Process

A central part of any definition of marketing is the **exchange,** which is giving something of value in return for something of value (see Exhibit 1.2). When you buy a pair of Nike shoes, you give value (money) to get something of value (the benefits provided by shoes). The shoes are valuable to you, and you're willing to pay the retail price to own them.

Even though the exchange is the core element of marketing, it's important not to focus heavily on the exchange process at the expense of long-term customer relationships. As a marketer, you might be able to maximize short-term profits by cutting corners on product quality and customer service and by hard-selling every customer. However, you'll lose customers to the competition. In this sense, the exchange is part of a partnership between the marketer and the customer, not simply a way for the marketer to extract money from the customer.

A **product** is anything customers will exchange something of value for, usually because it satisfies a need. Marketers divide products into three categories: (1) **goods,** or physical items; (2) **services,** or activities that provide some value to the recipient; and (3) **ideas,** or concepts that provide intellectual or spiritual benefits to

**marketing**
The process of developing and exchanging ideas, goods, and services that satisfy customer and organizational needs, using the principles of pricing, promotion, and distribution

**exchange**
The transfer between two or more parties of tangible or intangible items of value

**product**
A good, service, or idea for which customers will exchange money or something else of value

**goods**
Tangible products that customers can evaluate by touching, seeing, tasting, or hearing

**services**
Intangible products that offer financial, legal, medical, recreational, or other benefits to the consumer

**ideas**
Concepts, philosophies, or images that can be exchanged in the marketplace

*"This is the support of business."* Continent Bank.

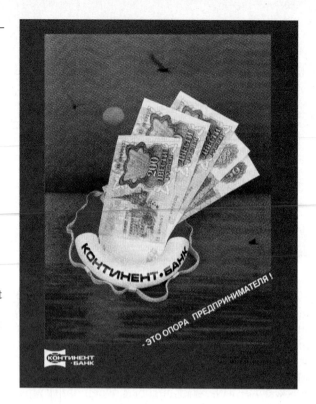

**Exhibit 1.3**
**MARKETING INTANGIBLE PRODUCTS**

This ad for Russia's Continent Bank uses a life preserver (a tangible symbol) to represent the safety and security of the bank's financial services (which are of course largely intangible).

the customer. People (such as political candidates) and places (such as cities trying to attract new businesses) are the two other major categories of products. Note that most people are used to saying "products and services," but this is a misleading notion for a marketer. Anything that can be exchanged for something of value is a product, whether it's lumber or legal services.

Bicycles and books are goods. Housekeeping, hair styling, and tax preparation are services. Publishers and broadcasters also provide a service when they sell advertising space and time. Ideas include musical compositions and lyrics, visual images, fictional characters and plots, computer software, business plans, and other creative works. Religious and political beliefs are also ideas.[4] Evangelists try to sell you on salvation, and political groups market ideas ranging from animal rights to anarchy.

Clothing, carrots, pencils, and other goods are *tangible* products. This means you can touch, see, measure, or otherwise sense them. On the other hand, services and ideas are *intangible* products—they don't have a physical dimension. It's easy to show people the attractive appearance of a blouse or the smooth ride of a car. But you can't test drive a movie. Marketers of intangibles must convey the product's benefits without a physical example of the product. Many products have both tangible and intangible components, such as an automobile and the service that the dealer offers along with it.

Intangible products require some special marketing techniques that promote the *outcome* of buying the service (see Exhibit 1.3). To sell a Jamaican vacation package, for example, travel agents can't display the product physically because travel is intangible. However, they can describe the island's friendly residents, its beautiful beaches and sunsets, the food and music, and other attractions. For the consumer, the outcomes of using this service include a reduced stress level, a replenished energy level, and so on. Likewise, when a university markets its educational services to students, it may emphasize the quality of its faculty and the prestige of earning a degree from that particular school. Alternative approaches include promoting campus size or beauty and the help the school offers graduates who are hunting for jobs. Here the outcomes include an enriching college experience and preparation for a fulfilling career. You'll learn about marketing intangible products in Chapter 10.

In any marketing exchange, the driving force for both marketers and customers is the desire to increase their own well-being. Customers strive for improved physical, intellectual, social, emotional, financial, or spiritual status. Commercial marketers aim to boost profits, and nonprofit marketers attempt to better serve clients, patients, congregation members, constituents, or the general public. When you're trying to market a product, the more your potential customers view your product as offering increased well-being, the more successful you'll be.

You are probably most familiar with monetary exchanges, but currency isn't always exchanged between marketers and their customers, even when a profit motive exists. For example, when buying industrial products from U.S. firms, companies in developing countries sometimes pay partially in goods as diverse as shoes, fish meal, and barbed wire.[5] In such countries, these goods are often more readily available than cash.

Nonprofit marketers frequently offer exchanges that have nothing to do with money. When Australia's Transport Accident Commission tries to convince people to stop drinking and driving, it is in essence saying to its customers (the public), "in exchange for not drinking and driving, we will offer you and everyone around personal safety on the highway." Of course, the exchange isn't always stated in such explicit terms. One of the commission's ads had this to say: "If you drink, then drive, you're a bloody idiot."[6] Beneath this rather blunt message is the offered exchange; give up something of value (the freedom to drive after you drink), and we'll give you something of value in return (life and health).

Regardless of the nature of the exchange, certain conditions must exist before an exchange will occur. At a minimum, the following five conditions are necessary:

- At least two parties must be involved.
- Each party must have something that interests the other party.
- Each party must be able to communicate and deliver.
- Each party must be free to accept or reject any offer from the other party.
- Each party must consider it desirable, or at least acceptable, to deal with the other party.[7]

The absence of even one of these conditions can cause the best strategies and plans to fail (see Exhibit 1.4). For instance, what would happen if Nike were unable

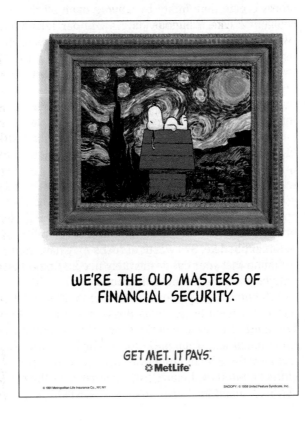

**Exhibit 1.4   THE CONDITIONS NECESSARY FOR A MARKETING EXCHANGE**
Creating an exchange in the insurance industry means more than just offering an attractive policy at a competitive rate. Buyers want to know that the company is stable and trustworthy, the message MetLife works to convey in this ad.

to deliver its products to the people trying to buy them? Or if customers believed Nike to be a bad company to do business with? Or if Nike's products didn't meet customers' needs? The answer is simple: no marketing exchanges would occur. Marketing campaigns to stop drunk driving and drug abuse aren't always successful because the target customers don't think the marketer has anything of interest or value to offer. If you think you can drive safely after drinking, you think you've already got what the marketer is offering (your safety).

## Needs, Utility, and Demand

Marketing exchanges work, in part, because customers have needs they are trying to fulfill, and marketers produce the goods and services to meet those needs. From a marketing perspective, **needs** are disparities between customers' actual conditions and their desired conditions. When you're hungry, you experience a disparity between your actual condition (physical discomfort) and your desired condition (physical comfort). This need creates a motivation to seek satisfaction. Without needs and the motivation to fulfill them, there would be no exchanges and no need for marketing.

Marketing steps into the spotlight when people have choices to make about fulfilling their needs. When you're hungry, you probably have lots of options to satisfy that hunger—your college cafeteria, a coffee shop, a nearby convenience store, an upscale restaurant off campus, or the fruitcake in the back of your closet that your aunt and uncle sent six months ago. The choice you make depends on how attractive an available exchange seems each time you make the decision to eat. **Wants** are the consumption choices people make to satisfy their needs.[8] You *need* food; you *want* a cheeseburger, oysters on the half shell, spinach salad, or that ancient fruitcake. Wants exist when you have a desire for a specific means of satisfying a need.

The degree to which a product meets customer needs (and therefore the degree to which potential buyers are likely to want it) can be defined in terms of its utility. **Utility** is the product's inherent ability to satisfy a customer's needs. Raw materials gain **form utility** when they are transformed into useful products. For example, Baskin-Robbins turns cream, sugar, fruit, and other ingredients into ice cream. Products have **time utility** if they are available when customers want them. Convenience stores create time utility by staying open all day, every day, and some direct-mail retailers create it by providing a 24-hour telephone-order service. Products have **place utility** if they are available in the places customers prefer. If your marketing professor followed you to the beach and lectured while you played volleyball or worked on your tan, he or she would be creating significant place utility. Finally, products offer **possession utility** when buyers are allowed to use or abuse products as they see fit. For example, the purchaser of a white T-shirt is free to dye it purple, cut off the sleeves, or wear it just as the manufacturer produced it.

These four utilities are examples of *economic utility,* which is a useful measure of a product's practical value. However, economic utility is inadequate when it comes to explaining many of the purchase choices people make. Economics can't explain why you choose one brand of perfume over another brand of equal price or why you might spend your last $15 on a compact disk when you should logically be spending it on gas to get to work or something else "useful." Think of utility in a broader sense, as a measure of a product's ability to meet your needs. Half an hour before a big date, $75 worth of roses may have more utility for you than the $75 water pump that your car desperately needs. Emotions can play a bigger role than economics in many purchase decisions.

Whether it's a rose or a water pump, a product will be purchased only if someone has a need for it and it possesses acceptable utility (in the broadest sense). **Demand** is a measure of the desire that potential customers have for a product and their ability and willingness to pay for it.[9] Marketers don't usually have much control over the demand for entire product categories (such as the demand for cars or clothes), but they do have some control over the demand for specific products (such as the demand for Range Rovers or Levi's).

---

**needs**
Differences between customers' actual conditions and their desired conditions; the driving forces behind all purchases

**wants**
The particular choices (including the type of product and the specific brands) that people make to satisfy their needs

**utility**
The ability of a product to satisfy the customer's wants or needs

**form utility**
The value created by shaping raw materials and components into products

**time utility**
The value of providing products when customers want them

**place utility**
The value of providing products where customers want them

**possession utility**
The value of owning a product and controlling its use

**demand**
The degree to which potential customers have an interest in, and the financial ability to buy, a product or class of products

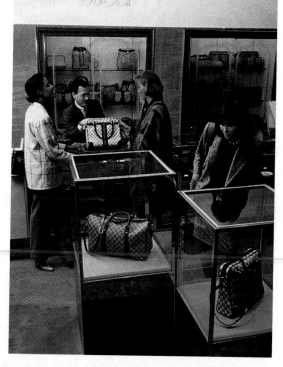

Can marketers create artificial demand? Some critics charge that marketing (and advertising in particular) makes people buy things they don't need. After all, nobody "needs" $50,000 cars or 100 pairs of shoes. However, when we reexamine the distinction between needs and wants, we understand that basic transportation is not the need that causes someone to choose the $50,000 Range Rover over the less expensive Ford Explorer. Both vehicles fulfill the basic *transportation* need, but when Range Rover buyers make their costlier purchases, they are fulfilling a different set of *psychological* and *social* needs than Explorer buyers. Marketers don't create these needs; they simply give buyers a greater range of options for satisfying their wants (see Exhibit 1.5).

Moreover, some critics charge that advertising manipulates people or somehow forces them to buy things they don't need. If that were the case, we'd all own hundreds of cars, hold dozens of life insurance policies, eat every kind of food imaginable, and travel to every conceivable vacation spot. Just think about all the ads you're exposed to in a typical day; if advertising were as effective as critics say it is, we'd all be buying every advertised product we could afford and quite a few we couldn't. The fact that the majority of new products fail is another clear indication that marketers can't force people to buy products they don't want. These critics probably give consumers too little credit and advertising too much credit.[10]

## Nonprofit Marketing

As its name implies, **nonprofit marketing** seeks to meet marketing objectives that don't involve financial return. This includes the marketing of ideas, causes, places, persons, and organizations. Political candidates market themselves to voters. Countries hoping to lure foreign investment market their people and resources to businesses in other countries. Many organizations market causes; AIDS research, gun ownership rights, and environmental protection are prominent examples. All of these marketers are similar in one important aspect: They are trying to change consumer behavior, but not in the interest of realizing a profit.

Two types of organizations practice nonprofit marketing. The first group markets goods and services, often in direct competition with for-profit companies, but it doesn't seek profit. Minnesota Public Radio markets a variety of products through direct-mail catalogs, but its objective is to raise money for public radio and televi-

**nonprofit marketing**
Marketing with objectives that don't involve financial return; includes the marketing of ideas, causes, places, persons, and organizations, as well as goods and services sold without profit motives

**social marketing**
Nonprofit marketing that aims to change attitudes and behaviors on various social and personal issues

sion broadcasting.[11] The second group pursues social goals. **Social marketing,** or *idea/cause marketing,* is the persuasive communication of ideas with the ultimate goal of changing attitudes, beliefs, and behavior. Regardless of the objective, successful nonprofit marketing uses the same basic rule as for-profit marketing: Understand what you need to offer people in order to convince them to take some desired action.

Throughout the course you'll study various other differences between for-profit and nonprofit marketing. If you keep in mind the definitions of exchange, needs, utility, and demand, it will be easy to see how nonprofit organizations of every type can benefit from marketing.

# THE EVOLUTION OF MARKETING

The fact that marketing is virtually everywhere in today's free-market economies is a dramatic change from a few decades ago. Marketing emerged as a discrete discipline in the early 1900s, but it didn't affect most companies right away.[12] The business world has gone through several phases on its way to becoming marketing oriented. In general, business was first driven by production, then by sales, and finally by marketing, as seen in Exhibit 1.6. The eras shown in the exhibit are generalizations, of course; some companies have been driven by marketing concerns and customer needs for decades, and others are still driven by production or sales goals.

## The Production Era

**production era**
The period extending from the Industrial Revolution to about 1930, during which companies focused on perfecting their manufacturing techniques

**sellers' markets**
Market conditions in which the demand for products exceeds the supply, giving sellers an advantage in the exchange process

The Industrial Revolution of the eighteenth century was the beginning of the **production era,** which generally lasted until the late 1920s. During this period, companies focused on the manufacturing process. They looked for ways to produce their goods faster and more efficiently. The production era had **sellers' markets** in many industries, meaning that demand for products exceeded supply. During this era, manufacturers could afford to focus on production because demand was assured. Desire for their products was so strong, in fact, that they needed to streamline production methods just to meet existing demand. Pillsbury was the classic example of a production era firm when it started business in 1869. Charles A. Pillsbury had two things on his mind back then: wheat and water power. Production, not marketing, was his main concern. This orientation was typical for the time, and it worked—for a while.[13]

## The Sales Era

**sales era**
The period from approximately 1930 to 1950, during which companies focused on promoting and distributing their products

Following on the heels of the production era and extending roughly from the 1930s into the 1950s was the **sales era,** during which manufacturers believed business success lay in outselling the competition. The question they usually asked was not "What does the customer want?" but "How can we get them to buy what we make?" Companies emphasized product promotion, formed direct sales forces, and established relationships with dealers and other firms that could push their products into the market. Advertising also took on new importance during this time.

**Exhibit 1.6 THE EVOLUTION OF MARKETING**
Companies began to make marketing a priority in the 1950s and are still learning to put customers first.

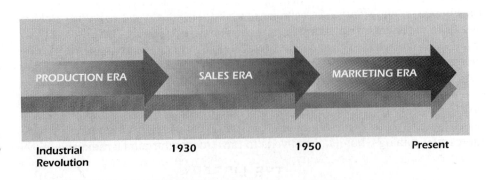

| PRODUCTION ERA | SALES ERA | MARKETING ERA |

| Industrial Revolution | 1930 | 1950 | Present |

## LIGHTHOUSE FOR THE BLIND: A NONPROFIT MARKETING SUCCESS

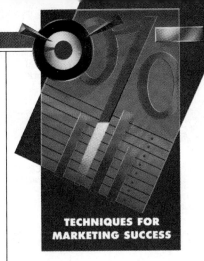

TECHNIQUES FOR MARKETING SUCCESS

Successful nonprofit organizations market their goods, services, and ideas using many of the same techniques used by commercial businesses. The Lighthouse for the Blind, in Duluth, Minnesota, is an example of how a nonprofit organization can succeed by using a good marketing strategy. The organization partially funds its rehabilitation services by selling goods and services produced in its sheltered workshop, a special facility that's adapted to the capabilities of the visually disabled workers employed there.

Until the mid-1980s, the Duluth Lighthouse's workshop produced textile goods for various agencies of the federal government. Although these customers represented an assured long-term market for the Lighthouse's products, they weren't an ideal market. The agencies couldn't predict their future need for the Lighthouse's goods, and that interfered with production planning at the workshop, creating a boom-or-bust cycle and workshop layoffs.

This forced the Lighthouse to re-examine two of the fundamental variables in the marketing process: its target market and its marketing mix. Its original target market, the federal agencies, didn't represent stable demand. The Lighthouse solved this problem by diversifying its product line and by marketing to nongovernment customers. Using grants from two private philanthropic foundations, the Lighthouse branched out into producing specialty sporting goods and converting documents to microfilm. It chose these products partly because distribution channels for them were well established. Such goods and services are labor-intensive, which helps the sheltered workshop keep a large number of assembly workers on the payroll.

The Lighthouse's first sports product was a molded-wood goose hunting decoy. The organization later expanded into snowshoes and snowshoe bindings by buying the assets of a company that manufactured those goods. The move strengthened its position in the specialty sporting goods market because the acquired snowshoe manufacturer had captured a significant share of that market. Using a similar strategy, the Lighthouse consolidated its strength in the microfilm services market by acquiring the assets of its only competitor.

Armed with a new understanding of products and markets, the Lighthouse once again took on the federal government as a customer. However, this time the product was toilet tissue, which represented a predictable demand. Revenue from this project alone boosted the Lighthouse's annual sales by $4 million. Before implementing the diversification strategy, the organization had total annual sales of only about $1 million.

The Duluth Lighthouse's successful turnaround is just one example of how Lighthouse organizations around the country are benefiting from nonprofit marketing strategies. The San Antonio, Texas, Lighthouse has marketed products as diverse as sweatpants, mechanical pencils, and paper fasteners. The Seattle Lighthouse makes parts for Boeing aircraft and Paccar trucks. Moreover, activities go beyond selling goods and services. The Columbia Lighthouse (Washington, D.C.) sponsors a day camp for sight-impaired children and a road race in which sighted drivers receive directions from blind or visually impaired navigators using Braille maps. Whether the Lighthouses are selling products or simply helping members of the community, they rely on marketing techniques to select target markets and establish marketing mixes.

### APPLY YOUR KNOWLEDGE

**1.** Would Lighthouse for the Blind select the same target markets if it were a for-profit company? Why or why not?

**2.** What role does price play in the Lighthouse's market mix?

---

During the 1930s, Pillsbury grew to appreciate both the grocers who sold its products and the consumers who bought them. Realizing it could use information about customer likes and dislikes to create advertising that would stimulate demand, the company formed a research department to collect market data. Also recognizing the importance of strong relationships with grocers, Pillsbury nurtured these relationships to assure a smooth flow of Pillsbury products from the mill to the customer.

## The Marketing Era

The 1950s were the start of the **marketing era,** during which companies began to practice marketing in its current form. The development of efficient production tech-

**marketing era**
The period that began in the 1950s and continues today, during which companies formed marketing departments, began to pay attention to customer wants and needs, and started to implement the marketing concept

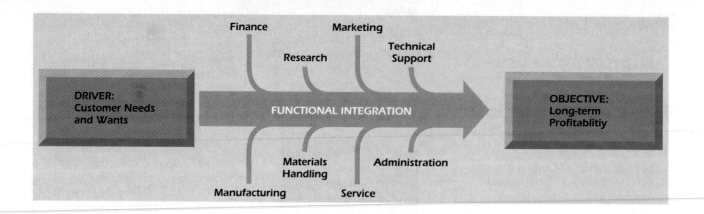

**Exhibit 1.7 THE MARKETING CONCEPT**
The marketing concept combines functional integration with customer satisfaction and long-term profitability.

**buyers' markets**
Market conditions in which supply exceeds demand

niques earlier in the century had already laid the groundwork for plentiful supplies of most products. This led to **buyers' markets** in many cases; that is, supply exceeded demand. These buyers' markets created two important forces that define the essence of marketing today: the marketing concept and vigorous competition. As the marketing era progressed, the method of conducting business shifted from pushing products on customers to finding out what buyers wanted and then filling that need.

Pillsbury's marketing orientation grew during the 1950s, a decade in which the firm learned to value customer opinions. Rather than concentrating on how much it could produce or sell, the company focused on meeting customer needs and wants with new and enhanced products. During the 1950s, Pillsbury expanded its advertising department into a marketing group responsible for satisfying both current and future needs of customers. The company, now part of the U.K.-based Grand Metropolitan conglomerate, sells more than $6 billion worth of baked goods, pizza, vegetables, refrigerated fresh dough, and flour every year. Its Jolly Green Giant and Pillsbury Doughboy characters are among the best-recognized promotional devices in the world. It continues to stay in touch with and respond to changing customer needs through extensive marketing research and such programs as the Pillsbury Bake-Off baking competition.[14]

## THE MARKETING CONCEPT

**marketing concept**
The idea of maximizing long-term profitability while integrating marketing with other parts of the company and meeting customer needs and wants

The notion of marketing continued as businesspeople began to talk about the **marketing concept,** stressing not only customer needs and wants but also long-term profitability and the integration of marketing with other functional units within the organization.[15] The marketing concept came into existence in the 1960s and continues to develop and expand. To apply this concept, marketers meet customer needs, achieve and maintain long-term profitability, and integrate marketing with the other functions in the company (see Exhibit 1.7). Here's a quick look at these three elements.

SENSITIVITY TO CUSTOMER NEEDS AND WANTS   A conscious dedication to meeting customer needs is at the core of the marketing concept. This dedication requires two steps: understanding what customers expect and then meeting those expectations better than your competitors. Some needs are obvious. For instance, drivers need cars that are safe and dependable, and most would like cars that are stylish, comfortable, and quiet. On the other hand, some customer expectations may not occur to you right away: certain terms included in a warranty, a pleasant shopping experience, the comfort of being addressed by either first or last name, easy parking, ethical treatment of employees—any number of varying expectations that customers might have. Companies that place a premium on satisfying their customers are said to have a **customer orientation.**

**customer orientation**
A management philosophy in which the customer is central to everything the company does

## FOR SPIKE LEE, THE RIGHT THING INCLUDES MARKETING

Millions of people recognize Spike Lee's talents as an actor and as a director of movies and television commercials. Now they are starting to see another talent emerge: marketing. He has become quite adept at marketing himself, his company's products, and the products of other companies as well.

Artists, athletes, and politicians share an important marketing challenge: they are products themselves. More to the point, their public images are products that are created and managed like any other product, and Spike Lee knows this. His carefully crafted public image as an ultrahip urban wise guy gains praise from marketing experts. According to Philip Dusenberry, chairman of BBDO, a major ad agency, Lee is "a shrewd self-promoter."

After the release of his first movie, *She's Gotta Have It,* Lee began selling merchandise related to his films. Things really picked up with the release of *Do the Right Thing* in 1989. The film pulled in $28 million and brought the young filmmaker widespread recognition. That awareness now helps sell $50,000 worth of *Do the Right Thing* T-shirts and other mail-order merchandise every month. Lee's popularity has continued to rise with such hits as *Jungle Fever* and *Malcolm X.* When mail-order customers started showing up at Lee's studio trying to buy merchandise, he opened a retail store called Spike's

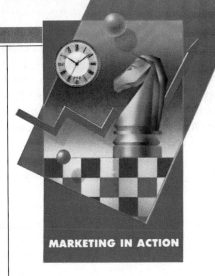

**MARKETING IN ACTION**

Joint. Next to his studio in Brooklyn, the store is both a thriving retail operation and something of a tourist attraction.

Lee's marketing talents aren't reserved for his own products. He directed and co-starred (with former basketball great Michael Jordan) in the Air Jordan television commercials, which Nike credits with helping

increase market share against Reebok. Lee is skilled at presenting images, and he applied those skills to the $20 million television campaign for Levi Strauss that aired in mid-1990. The public's awareness of the Mars Blackmon character he portrayed in some commercials and his effectiveness at creating winning advertising appeals should open many companies' eyes when it comes time to select their next celebrity spokesperson. There's a good reason it's called show business, and Spike Lee is well on his way to becoming a master of both the artistic and commercial sides of the entertainment industry. As a scriptwriter, director, book author, promoter, actor, advertising specialist, and retailer, Lee has just about the right combination of talents to make it big.

In addition to his own success, Lee continues to influence the movie industry, the advertising industry, and society in general. His commercial success and critical endorsement have helped open doors for other African-American filmmakers. Moreover, some observers think he sets a positive example for young people. In the words of Georgetown University basketball coach John Thompson, "A role model of somebody who makes money honestly and aggressively is very valuable."

### APPLY YOUR KNOWLEDGE

**1.** How does Spike Lee use the marketing concept?
**2.** Is there an inherent conflict between a product orientation and a marketing orientation in the film industry?

LONG-TERM PROFITABILITY    The second component of the marketing concept is maintaining acceptable profit levels year after year while meeting customer needs. Even when companies are well aware of customer needs and are motivated to meet them, doing so is not always easy. Marketing research, product design, manufacturing, promotion, and customer service all require money. Companies have to perform all these functions, meet customer needs, and still generate enough revenue to have some profit left over.

The emphasis on *long-term* profitability is the key here. Companies that focus on short-term profits are less inclined to invest in research laboratories, support personnel, repair facilities, and other elements needed to satisfy customers. This may save money in the short term, but it usually leads to customer defections, followed by reduced sales and reduced profits. In contrast, companies that want to be financially healthy long into the future realize that they need to make these investments.

The concept of profitability should be considered by nonprofit marketers as well. Profit may be interpreted as the group's ultimate goals or as the benefits it gives to its membership.[16] Greenpeace's goal, for example, is to safeguard the environment. The group markets its political action to contributors and "profits" by being able to carry out its mission of protecting the environment. It generates money along the way by collecting contributions and membership dues, but money is simply a means to an end.

FUNCTIONAL INTEGRATION    The marketing concept's final component is integrating the marketing department with other functional groups, such as research and development (R&D), manufacturing, and finance. Cooperation among these functional groups greatly increases a firm's chances of success. One study of new-product development projects showed that in cases where "severe disharmony" existed between marketing and R&D, 68 percent of the projects failed and only 11 percent were commercially successful.[17]

To foster better working relationships between marketing and other departments, some companies have developed programs in which financial and technical people call on customers, just as the salespeople do. By walking a mile in their colleagues' shoes, the nonmarketers gain some marketing insights and, ideally, some sympathy for their peers in sales and marketing. Moreover, the interaction helps marketers understand the challenges faced by their counterparts in engineering, production, and finance. The result is better communication and more productive relationships.[18]

Just as important as integrating marketing with the other business functions is integrating the various activities inside the marketing function. Large companies employ hundreds of marketing people to perform a wide variety of marketing activities. To be as effective as possible, these activities have to be coordinated, especially when communicating with customers so that they don't get confusing or conflicting messages. For instance, make sure your salespeople communicate the same message carried by your advertising. An increasingly popular way to ensure this is **integrated marketing communications (IMC),** a strategy of coordinating and integrating all of your communications and promotions efforts with customers.[19] You'll learn more about IMC and the general concepts of integrated marketing at several points throughout the course.

**integrated marketing communications (IMC)**
A strategy in which marketers try to coordinate and integrate all of their communications and promotions efforts with customers

## COMPETITIVENESS

Contemporary marketing requires marketers to be more competitive. When you think about it, at the same time that you're trying to satisfy customer needs, so are your competitors. Although successful marketers still keep their primary focus on the customer, they must keep an eye on their competitors as well (see Exhibit 1.8).

The nature of competition varies dramatically from market to market and from situation to situation. A gas station 50 miles from the nearest town might have little competition; if you need gas, you're going to buy it there and pay whatever price the place charges. In contrast, a busy intersection in town might have two or three gas stations competing fiercely for your business. Some industries have unique rules of competition. If you want to market software for IBM-compatible personal computers, you have to follow the design standards set by Microsoft, the company that makes the basic operating system used in most personal computers. Customers won't be interested if you don't. You'll learn more about the nature of competition in Chapter 2 and more about the competitive strategies marketers use in Chapter 3.

**marketing culture**
A corporate culture geared toward customer satisfaction through marketing concepts and procedures

## MARKETING CULTURE

By embracing the marketing concept and responding to increased competition, companies try to adopt a **marketing culture,** a corporate style and value system that

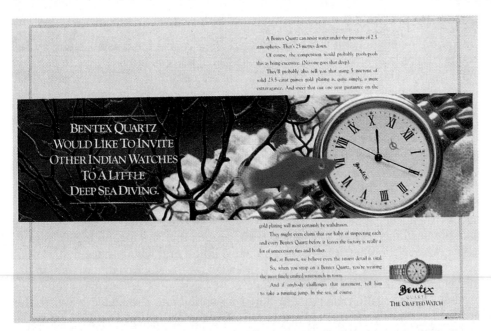

puts the customer first and emphasizes market-sensitive management. Central to the formation of a marketing culture at DuPont was the creation of an internal "marketing community" that includes everyone in the company. To provide employees in all departments with the point of view of a marketer, DuPont trains everyone in the principles of marketing and customer relations. Top management led the change, challenging "every employee to become market oriented, to think first about customer needs, and then to find ways DuPont could meet those needs better than anyone else in the industry."[20]

The competition that emerged among airlines when the industry was deregulated in the late 1970s forced Scandinavian Airlines System (SAS) to abandon its production orientation. According to Jan Carlzon, SAS president and CEO at the time, "In that situation you can't be production driven any more. You can't focus on controlling the cost side as if the revenue side were a given." So SAS developed a marketing culture to attract and keep business travelers. The firm is now praised as one of the world's most customer-oriented companies. To enhance customer relations, SAS encourages employees to use whatever resources they must to correct service problems. In one instance, a delay left an SAS purser without enough snacks and coffee for the passengers on her flight. When the company's catering supervisor refused to fill her order because it wasn't standard procedure, the purser got 60 cookies and cups of coffee through the purser on a flight of Finnair, one of SAS's competitors. SAS senior management later applauded her unorthodox actions.[21] Because SAS had a marketing culture in place, the employee had both the motivation and the flexibility to meet customer needs.

Fashion designers Dana Buchman and Karen Harman provide another great example of a competitive, marketing-oriented firm. Other top designers in New York, Paris, and Milan have a reputation for following their own artistic whims when it comes to product design, as you can see in the often unusual and sometimes outlandish clothes they produce. These designers more or less make what they want to make, without asking for input from customers. What these designers are no longer making is money; many of the top names are in financial trouble. However, this is not the case with Buchman and Harman, the creative forces behind the Dana Buchman division of Liz Claiborne. They make sure their clothes match the needs (and budgets) of professional women. Not only do they personally visit stores to talk with retailers and consumers, they employ seven full-time marketing consultants to analyze customer needs and market trends. This customer-oriented approach is unusual for the fashion industry—and so are the sales and profit figures at the Dana Buchman division.[22]

**marketing myopia**
Product orientation without
regard for customer benefits

One of the foundations of living by the marketing concept and establishing a marketing culture is a clear understanding of just what it is you provide your customers. For instance, although utility companies market natural gas and electricity, what they really supply is the comfort and convenience provided by gas furnaces and electric lights and appliances. When a pet store sells a kitten, puppy, or canary, it's really supplying companionship, not just animals.

Meeting customer needs sounds simple enough, but many companies seem to have trouble with it. Rather than looking at what they do from the buyer's point of view, in terms of customer benefits, they see themselves strictly as producers. Marketing professor Theodore Levitt came up with a name for the product orientation that many marketers use to define their business: **marketing myopia,** the situation when companies view themselves as supplying products rather than as fulfilling customer needs and wants. Levitt argues that the U.S. railroads, for example, lost out to other transportation modes in the first few decades of the twentieth century because of this attitude. Railroad executives believed they were in the railroad business rather than the transportation business.[23] Automobiles and other forms of transportation emerged in the same period and responded better to the needs of various types of travelers. If the railroads had defined their business as *transportation* rather than *railroading,* they would have been more flexible and in a better position to compete with automakers, trucking companies, airlines, and other transportation marketers (see Exhibit 1.9).

As director of personal products at software developer Intuit, Mari Baker understands the clear distinction between the means (products) and the ends (what you do for customers). Even though Intuit's Quicken is the world's leading software product for personal financial management, Baker emphasizes that "Intuit's mission is to automate financial tasks. There's nothing in our mission statement that has anything to do with software." In other words, helping people manage their money—not selling software—is Intuit's goal, and if satisfying customers means going beyond software, Baker and company are ready to do it. This antimyopic vision has led to such unique moves as a special Visa card account that customers can access through their Quicken software.[24]

# MARKETING STRATEGY AND ELEMENTS OF THE MARKETING MIX

**marketing strategy**
The overall plan for marketing
a product that includes selecting and analyzing a target
market and creating and
maintaining a marketing mix

To coordinate and control the marketing effort, managers define a **marketing strategy,** which outlines where and how the organization will compete. The "where" part of strategy involves the customers you've chosen as your *target market,* and the "how" part involves the *position* you hope to achieve in that target market and the

## Exhibit 1.9  MARKETING MYOPIA

| Marketers | The Good Old Days Before Television | The Introduction of Television | Television Becomes the Dominant Medium |
|---|---|---|---|
| Radio broadcaster #1 | "We provide radio programs." | "TV doesn't apply to us; we do radio." | "Hey! What happened to our sales?" |
| Radio broadcaster #2 | "We meet people's desire to be entertained." | "People now want to be entertained on TV as well; we'll start offering TV programs too." | "Our sales are just fine, thank you." |

Marketers suffer from marketing myopia when they view their business as providing products, rather than as meeting customers' needs. Myopic companies are extremely vulnerable to changes in their marketing environment. Imagine two radio broadcasting companies in the days before television.

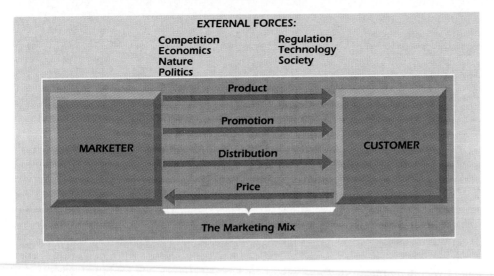

**EXTERNAL FORCES:**

Competition    Regulation
Economics    Technology
Nature    Society
Politics

Product
Promotion
Distribution
Price

MARKETER    CUSTOMER

**The Marketing Mix**

**Exhibit 1.10   THE MARKETING MIX**
The marketing mix is a combination of product, price, distribution, and promotion; remember that external forces play a role in the definition and management of your marketing mix.

*marketing mix* you'll use to persuade customers to buy. Here's an overview of these three fundamental elements of marketing strategy:

- *Target market.* Effective marketing springs from a firm grasp of who your customers are. A **market** includes all the customers and potential customers who have a want or need in common and who would exchange money or something else of value to satisfy it.[25] A **target market** is the part of a market (a group of customers) that you've chosen to be the focal point of your marketing efforts. You separate the target market from the overall market because it consists of the customers most likely to buy products. For instance, both the Ford Explorer and the Range Rover are sport/utility vehicles with four-wheel drive and the space to haul cargo. However, the Range Rover costs twice as much as the Explorer, so the two vehicles are aimed at different target markets.
- *Market position.* As a consumer, you keep a place in your mind for each product category that you're aware of, and in each place, you rank individual products. Think of luxury cars, basketball shoes, and rock guitarists. What specific product did you think of in each category? Say you listed Infiniti, Nike Air, and Joe Satriani. If Infiniti represents the ultimate luxury car to you, it occupies the primary **position** in the luxury car category in your mind. When you think of luxury cars, you think of Infiniti. The companies and products that hold these primary positions have a powerful advantage over their competitors. When Infiniti tries to entice you with a new car, you're already leaning in that direction. Your most successful marketing strategies start with a clear idea of the position you would like to achieve in your target market.
- *Marketing mix.* Once you've identified your target market and chosen the position you want to occupy in it, the next step is to create the **marketing mix,** your marketing toolkit: product, price, distribution, and promotion. (These elements are often referred to as the four Ps, when *distribution* is called *place.*) As you can see from Exhibit 1.10, the marketing mix has to work in the context of your marketing environment, which means that you take a wide range of factors into account when designing your mix.

Because the four elements of the marketing mix are the focus of both what you'll learn in this course and what you'll do as a professional marketer, it's important to understand what each element means to today's marketers.

**market**
The customers and potential customers who want or need a product and who are willing and able to exchange something for it

**target market**
The market you've selected as the focus of your marketing program; it covers the potential customers you think are most likely to need or want your product

**position**
The spot that a product holds in the minds of current and potential customers, relative to competitive products

**marketing mix**
The four key elements of marketing strategy: product, promotion, distribution, and price

## Product

The first element of the marketing mix is product. As already mentioned, a product can be a good, a service, an idea, a place, or a person. Astute marketers realize that

**product value**
A measure of the value that
products represent to customers; equal to the benefits a
product provides minus the
costs of acquiring and owning it

a product is actually a "bundle of value" that meets customers' expectations. For example, when you buy a pair of Nike shoes endorsed by a basketball star, you get more than leather, rubber, and laces. You buy a little piece of the star's image. **Product value** is the benefits a product provides minus the costs of acquiring and owning it. A machine that did your homework offers an attractive benefit; it would be a good value at $5, but not such a good value at $5,000,000. Similarly, a $12,000 car that requires frequent repairs is less valuable to customers than an otherwise identical $12,000 car that never breaks down.

The value that companies deliver to their customers often encompasses more than just the basic product. It can include consulting, training, manuals, installation, and other tangible and intangible components. As competition grows more intense in many industries, and as products start to look more and more alike, these extra features and benefits become important criteria for customers deciding which product to buy. British Airways used to have a reputation for quality of service that one executive described as "about as pleasurable as downing a shot of cod liver oil." Not surprisingly, the company was losing money by the millions. Then the company's chief executive officer, Sir Colin Marshall, led a marketing revitalization that examined all aspects of the company's products. Recognizing that airline service is more than just moving people and cargo from place to place, Marshall overhauled everything from ground crew operations to dinner selections in first class. A decade later, frequent travelers consider British Airways one of the best in the sky, and the company's growing sales and profits are witness to the product improvements.[26]

Product development is an intriguing aspect of the marketing job because you get involved with so many aspects of the total business operation, including sales, service, research and development, package design, finance, and manufacturing. You'll get a closer look at this process in Chapters 8, 9, and 10.

## Price

**price**
The value, usually in monetary terms, that sellers ask in
exchange for the products
they are offering

The second element of the marketing mix is **price,** the amount a marketing organization charges for its product. A powerful component of the marketing mix, price is often expected to do more than just generate revenue. For example, a high price helps build an exclusive image for a product. A low price can take sales away from competitors, increase overall demand in a market, and create an image of good value. Carefully managed prices help airlines keep a certain percentage of passengers in the more expensive business and first-class seats. Temporary price reductions help movie theaters shift demand from busy times of the week to slower times. The thought process behind pricing covers a wide spectrum, from black-and-white financial analysis to complex and uncertain buyer emotions.

Setting prices is one of the most difficult tasks facing the marketing professional. First of all, competitors and customer expectations can put a ceiling on the range of possible prices, which limits your flexibility. Customers won't buy the product if they don't believe it's worth the price. So you have to offer something really special if your prices are significantly higher than those of competitors.

A manufacturer must also consider its costs to buy raw materials, to convert them into products, and to put the finished goods in customers' hands. Service providers need to track the amount of time it takes to perform services, as well as the materials and equipment that may be required. A product's price usually covers these costs, but products may be priced at a loss. One objective of such a strategy would be to build market acceptance for the product; however, underpricing can also happen by accident. Dartington Crystal, a British glassmaker, discovered that the prices on its best-selling products weren't covering costs, but only after a new chief executive officer started examining the details of the business.[27]

Government regulation and ethical standards also affect pricing decisions. Regulatory commissions preside over utility rates, and the federal government limits marketers' authority over their own product prices. For instance, federal law prohibits marketers from setting artificially low prices if the aim is to destroy competition. The government also watches companies to make sure they aren't charging too much. A recent example of this occurred in 1990, when both Congress and former President George Bush expressed concern over the amount that oil companies increased prices after Iraq invaded Kuwait.

High prices can help create a top-of-the-line image. Some marketers of luxury products even advertise their high prices. A Piaget ad campaign touted the product as "the most expensive watch in the world."[28] The same approach can be used to position a relatively inexpensive product at the high end of its category. L'Oréal promotes its Preference hair products by emphasizing their high price. Actresses such as Cybill Shepherd sell Preference on TV by admitting the products cost a lot but then emphasizing, "I'm worth it."

In contrast, low price can be the focal point of the marketing strategy. Companies that vigorously promote their low prices are typically out to undercut the competition with lower prices while keeping operating costs at a minimum. Amstrad, an English computer and consumer electronics company, sells on price. Founder Alan Sugar has summarized the Amstrad philosophy as "pile 'em high and sell 'em cheap."[29] Chapters 11 and 12 give you more information on pricing concepts and techniques.

## Distribution

The third marketing mix element is **distribution,** the various methods used to move products from the producer to the customer. This involves selecting marketing channels, which are the people and organizations (including wholesalers and retailers) who help get products to customers (see Exhibit 1.11). Managing product transportation, arranging storage, processing orders, and keeping track of finished-product inventory are also distribution activities.

A poorly conceived distribution strategy can spell disaster. When Etak first went to market with its innovative electronic roadmap, it made the mistake of trying to sell the $1,430 product to consumers through car-stereo shops. The strategy flopped because the product's sophistication and price didn't mesh with the distribution channel. Etak finally retrenched, focusing on the industrial market. It began selling its product in volume to organizations such as Coca-Cola, Frito-Lay, Hertz, and *The Los Angeles Times*. The new strategy helped propel the company into profitability for the first time.[30] Chapters 13, 14, 15, and 16 cover the details of the distribution process.

**distribution**
The process of moving products from the producer to the consumer, which may involve several steps and the participation of multiple companies

## Promotion

The fourth element of the marketing mix is **promotion,** which encompasses a wide variety of techniques you can use to communicate with your target market. The main categories of promotion are advertising, personal selling, public relations, and sales promotion; Exhibit 1.12 lists some common examples of each type. You are certainly aware of advertising, being exposed to hundreds of advertising messages every day, on everything from TV to T-shirts. Personal selling plays a big role in many major purchases, from automobiles to airlines. Marketers use public relations

**promotion**
A variety of techniques, including advertising, sales promotion, public relations, and personal selling, that are used to communicate with customers and potential customers

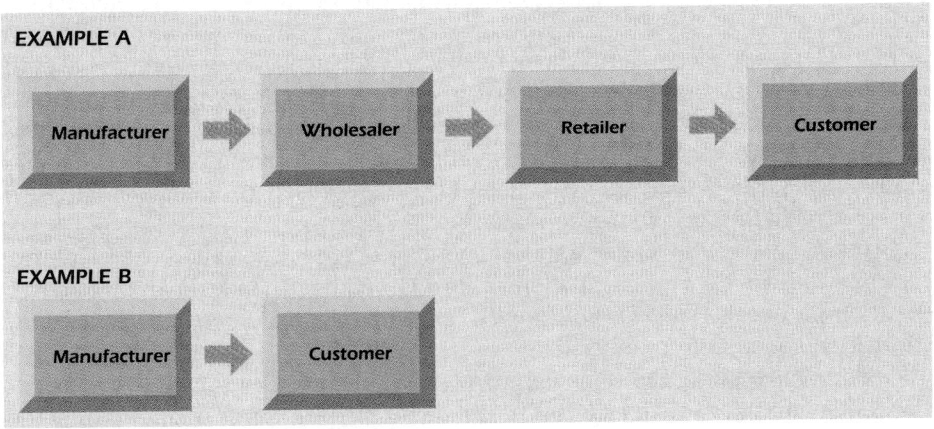

**EXAMPLE A**

Manufacturer → Wholesaler → Retailer → Customer

**EXAMPLE B**

Manufacturer → Customer

**Exhibit 1.11
MARKETING
CHANNELS**
Marketing channels, also called distribution channels, move products from producers to consumers; two examples are shown here.

**Exhibit 1.12  COMMON PROMOTIONAL TECHNIQUES**

| Category | Examples |
|---|---|
| Advertising | Radio |
| | Television |
| | Billboards |
| | Stadium signs |
| Sales promotion | Coupons |
| | Sweepstakes |
| | Frequent flyer programs |
| | Free samples |
| Public relations | Press conferences |
| | Press releases |
| | Sponsorship of sporting events |
| Personal selling | Corporate sales |
| | Door-to-door sales |
| | Telemarketing |
| | Seminars |

Marketers can choose from a range of promotional vehicles to reach various audiences. Each method has advantages and disadvantages; in many cases, you'll want to use more than one method.

in a variety of ways, including press conferences and support for cultural events. Sales promotion is a major force in marketing today; coupons, rebates, and free samples are some of the techniques that fall into this category.

Marketers combine the various elements of promotion to communicate aspects of their organizations and products to customers, employees, shareholders, and other important audiences. For example, the promotional strategy for a new cake mix from General Mills might include such diverse elements as advertising, coupons, a consumer sweepstakes, and premiums in every box of product. General Mills might use a press tour featuring a home economist spokesperson (not Betty Crocker, however; she doesn't really exist). On the other hand, Nike might rely heavily on the endorsement of a popular professional athlete to promote a new shoe in television commercials.

Industrial marketers also rely heavily on promotion. A machine-tool marketer can use magazine advertising, a dealer sales-incentive contest, trade shows, and press releases to promote products. IBM, Hewlett-Packard, and other computer suppliers combine extensive personal selling with advertising and public relations. For expensive, complex products and systems, close interaction between buyer and seller is often required, which leads to a lot of personal selling in such markets.

In the services area, some family therapists use personal selling to get on the referral lists of health maintenance organizations. Others use direct-mail advertising to bring themselves to the attention of divorce lawyers, thus gaining patient referrals. Some group therapists even offer prospective patients a free trial session.[31] All of these activities—sales calls, advertising, and free sessions—are elements of promotion.

Marketers' selection of advertising media reflects their overall promotional strategy for a product. For instance, to create an image for Nutri-Grain as a health-enhancing cereal, Kellogg initially relied heavily on health-conscious "lifestyle" magazines rather than on the company's traditional use of television.[32] When Black & Decker wanted to reach younger consumers, it advertised on the late-night television programs they are known to watch.[33]

Industrial marketers may advertise in a range of specialized and general-interest business magazines. To reach potential buyers, building-supplies marketers advertise their products in *Professional Builder, Building Design & Construction, Qualified Remodeler,* and a score of other magazines. Meanwhile, to advertise its image as a good corporate citizen, the same company might choose TV programs like "Nightline" and publications such as *Business Week* and *The Wall Street Journal.* Marketers in many other industries enjoy a similar range of media options. You'll get a closer look at promotion in Chapters 17, 18, and 19.

Although this four-part classification of the marketing mix is quite common in both academic and professional circles, it has been criticized as conflicting and incomplete. For instance, the technique known as direct marketing (where you bypass retail stores and sell directly to customers) fits in both the distribution and the promotion categories. Similarly, a discount coupon could be classified as a promotional technique or as a pricing technique. A number of alternative classifications have been proposed. In a classification scheme proposed by Dutch professors Walter van Waterschoot and Christophe Van den Bulte, sales promotion can be used with all four marketing mix categories, which they define as product, price, distribution, and communication.[34]

## MARKETING IN THE FUTURE

Marketing continues to grow in both importance and complexity. As a result, the marketing profession will be even more challenging in the years ahead. Here's a quick look at several key trends that marketing people can expect to encounter.

Information is already a mixed blessing for marketers. On one hand, the amount of marketing data available and the technologies to manage it will continue to increase. You'll be able to pinpoint buyers and their buying habits more accurately than ever before, which should open the door for more efficient marketing because less money is wasted talking to people who aren't listening. On the other hand, you'll have to be more sensitive to the information overload suffered by your weary customers.

In many industries, *mass marketing* is gradually being replaced by *target marketing* as companies target groups of customers that are smaller and more focused. For example, some years ago everybody wore plain old sneakers; the big choice was whether to buy high-top or low-top. In either case, they were made of black or white canvas, period. Now consumers can choose shoes specifically designed for walking, jogging, running, aerobic exercising, and so on. However, a multitude of slightly different products does not guarantee that customers are being satisfied. Successful marketers will define and select their target markets carefully and aim products at particular targets, rather than simply creating dozens of product variations.

The international and intercultural dimensions of marketing are becoming increasingly important. Marketers are crossing national borders in search of new customers, and global competition is forcing marketers to improve their skills. In addition to learning foreign languages, you'll be learning about various cultures, business practices, and government influences in countries all over the world. Moreover, you'll be learning about cultural differences within each country, including your own. You may not have the time or the talent to master one or more languages, but your knowledge of cultural subtleties and legal forces will be essential.

Marketers will have some impressive new promotional tools at their disposal. Interactive television will let viewers talk back to their TV sets, allowing them to select specific commercials, receive coupons, and order products without having to reach for the phone. Advertisers could test potential commercials and ask for viewers' opinions right on the spot. In addition, the home computer has already turned into an advertising platform. The Prodigy service, a joint venture of IBM and Sears, scrolls advertisements along the bottom of your computer monitor while you're sending electronic mail messages, reading the on-line version of *Consumer Reports,* or scanning the current U.S. weather map.[35]

Quality and customer satisfaction have become significant competitive forces in most industries. As competition and customer expectations increase, marketers will have to do a better job of providing quality products and making sure their customers are satisfied. Consistently delivering first-rate quality and customer service allows a company to build competitive barriers, increase customer loyalty, and lower marketing costs.

The United States has a multi-billion-dollar annual trade deficit with Japan, a tribute in part to the strength of Japanese marketing skills.

As part of improved quality and customer satisfaction, successful marketers will be the ones who emphasize long-term relationships with their customers. If you're a car dealer, for instance, you'll focus on customer satisfaction long after each car leaves your showroom. You'll want customers to come back three or four or five years from now, when they're ready for another car. You'll also want them to tell family and friends how satisfied they are doing business with you. Building lasting relationships may take more effort in the short term, but it is ultimately more efficient because you don't have to work so hard to make new sales.

In addition to these professional topics, an increased awareness of ethical issues will be on every marketer's agenda. This includes both an understanding of what constitutes unethical marketing and a grasp of ethical dilemmas that pit the desires of companies against interests of individual consumers or society as a whole. Moreover, you will experience increasing pressure to consider the effects on society as a key element in your marketing plans, in addition to customer satisfaction and profitability. Known as the **societal marketing concept,** this view of marketing urges companies to act in ways that help, or at least don't hurt, the societies in which they do business.

**societal marketing concept**
An expanded view of marketing urging companies and organizations to act in ways that contribute to society's wellbeing

Companies such as Ben & Jerry's Homemade and Body Shop International are among the most visible marketers who have successfully integrated social interests with their own corporate interests.[36] Social responsibility is far more prevalent in the business world than outside observers realize. Mainstream corporate giants such as Hewlett-Packard, Ford, and AT&T routinely donate millions of dollars to schools, social organizations, and other nonprofit groups every year. These firms also help directly in so many ways, including loaning managers to United Way, providing internships for students, and setting up recycling and pollution-control programs.

The marketing professional in the twenty-first century will have the analytical capacity to handle increasing amounts of data, the creative talents to define products and develop messages for a crowded marketplace, and the social awareness to navigate in complex global markets. Add a strong dose of technological knowledge and ethical sensitivity, and you end up with a pretty good idea of what the marketing challenge will be like in the next century.

# SUMMARY OF LEARNING OBJECTIVES

**1. Explain the exchange process and its importance in the marketing of all products.**

An exchange—giving something of value in return for something of value—is the primary objective of marketing. Exchanges redistribute resources between marketers and customers, helping marketers accomplish their profit and nonprofit objectives and helping customers meet their personal or organizational wants and needs. Regardless of the products, circumstances, or motivations, an exchange is at the core of marketing.

**2. Define the four utilities that marketers can offer customers.**

Utility represents the value that is transferred from the buyer to the seller during a marketing exchange. Form utility is the economic value a marketer provides by shaping raw materials into products. Place and time utilities are the economic values the marketer provides by making goods and services available where and when customers want them. Possession utility is the value that comes with owning and controlling a product.

**3. Discuss the three categories of products.**

There are three types of products. Goods are tangible products that buyers can examine by touching, seeing, hearing, smelling, or tasting. Services, on the other hand, are intangible and provide benefits without the transfer of anything tangible. Ideas are also intangible and deliver any of a variety of spiritual, emotional, or intellectual benefits.

**4. Identify the two types of organizations that practice nonprofit marketing.**

The first group markets goods and services, often in direct competition with for-profit companies, but it doesn't seek profit. The second group pursues social goals using social marketing, or idea/cause marketing. This is the persuasive communication of ideas with the ultimate goal of changing attitudes, beliefs, and behavior. Regardless of objective, successful nonprofit marketers use the same basic rule as for-profit marketers: Understand what you need to offer people in order to convince them to take some desired action.

**5. Describe marketing myopia and explain the risks inherent in a myopic approach to marketing.**

Marketing myopia is an orientation toward products rather than toward customer needs. Companies that suffer from marketing myopia see themselves providing products rather than providing benefits or solving customers' problems. Myopia carries an enormous risk: Customer needs can change, and if you concentrate on doing what you've always done, instead of changing with your customers, you could find yourself trying to sell products that people no longer want.

**6. Outline the process of developing a marketing strategy.**

The marketing strategy outlines where and how the organization will compete. Deciding where to compete involves defining and selecting target markets, or smaller portions of the overall market on which you'll concentrate your marketing efforts. Deciding how to compete involves choosing the position you'd like to occupy in your target market and defin-

ing the marketing mix you'll use to persuade customers to buy.

**7. Describe the marketing mix and its major elements.**

The marketing mix represents the resources you have as a marketer to encourage exchanges with customers. There are four elements of the marketing mix: product, pricing, distribution, and promotion. Products involve more than just the obvious features of goods or services; they can also include customer service, warranties, repair, prestige, and other components of value. Pricing serves the obvious function of generating revenue and profit, but it is also used to stimulate timely purchases, create specific images for products, and build competitive advantage. Distribution gets products from producers to final customers and includes the efforts of wholesalers, retailers, and other organizations. Finally, promotion is the process of communicating with customers and other members of the public, using a variety of techniques and media.

---

## KEY TERMS

buyers' markets (12)
customer orientation (12)
demand (8)
distribution (19)
exchange (5)
form utility (8)
goods (5)
ideas (5)
integrated marketing communications (IMC) (14)

market (17)
marketing (5)
marketing concept (12)
marketing culture (14)
marketing era (11)
marketing mix (17)
marketing myopia (16)
marketing strategy (16)
needs (8)
nonprofit marketing (9)

place utility (8)
position (17)
possession utility (8)
price (18)
product (5)
product value (18)
production era (10)
promotion (19)
sales era (10)
sellers' markets (10)

services (5)
social marketing (10)
societal marketing concept (22)
target market (17)
time utility (8)
utility (8)
wants (8)

---

## APPLYING WHAT YOU'VE LEARNED

Taking what you learn in a marketing course and applying it to the real world can sometimes be a challenge. Practicing your new skills on a real company's marketing situation is a good way to prepare, and each chapter in this book gives you that opportunity. You'll read about the company's situation at the beginning of the chapter in a vignette called "Facing a Marketing Challenge." For example, at the beginning of this chapter, you read about the challenge Nike faced as it tried to deal with some aggressive competitors. After reading the vignette, think about the company's marketing problem as you read through the chapter and learn the various concepts presented there.

At the end of the chapter is an innovative simulation called "Meeting a Marketing Challenge." In each simulation, you'll play the role of a marketing person at the company introduced in the vignette, and you'll face the situation you'd face on the job. The simulation starts by explaining what the company actually did and whether it worked. Then the simulation presents four marketing scenarios, each with several possible courses of action, and you recommend one course of action from the available choices. These simulations let you explore various marketing ideas and apply the concepts and techniques you learn about in the chapter.

The simulations weren't designed as tests, but as a means to stimulate your thinking about various marketing concepts. In fact, some of the questions have more than one acceptable answer, and some have no really satisfactory answers. That's how it happens for marketing people on the job, too. The point is to consider the concepts you learn in each chapter, apply your own judgment, and then pick the answer that you think is best. Consider each possible answer carefully, and think about why each one is either a wise or an unwise choice. The company chosen for each simulation uses the same principles you're studying. Your instructor may assign the simulations as homework, as teamwork, as material for in-class discussion, or in a host of other ways.

Now you're ready for your first simulation. Because you've just started learning about marketing, this simulation is a little different from the rest. It relies primarily on your experience as a consumer to give you the insight needed to answer the questions. As you tackle each question, think about the material you covered in this chapter, and consider your own experience at the purchasing end of marketing transactions. You'll probably be surprised to discover how much you know about marketing already.

## Meeting a Marketing Challenge at Nike

Phil Knight's company was facing a formidable challenge launched by Reebok, an upstart company in a newly emerging market segment. The high-fashion world of aerobic exercise .was quite different from Nike's world of high-performance athletics. Reebok's chairman, Paul Fireman, was among the first to spot the trend, and he had his designers create a unique shoe for aerobics workouts. But even Fireman wasn't prepared for what happened next. As running and sport shoes caught on as fashionable footwear, Reebok's sales shot past those of its older competitor.

The result was that Nike slipped into the runner-up position in 1986, and Knight knew he had to act. He examined the company's marketing mix and made key adjustments in products, distribution, and promotions. Before taking drastic action, however, he made the all-important decision to improve his understanding of his target customers. One of the key insights he gained was that, although technology and performance were vitally important to customers, so too were fashion and style.

As a result, Nike fine-tuned its product strategy by adding stylish accents and more colors. This move soon helped it compete more effectively against Reebok and newcomer L.A. Gear, both successful in combining fashion and technology. Performance remained a top priority for many customers, so Knight poured money into product research and development. A key result was the Nike Air technology, soon featured in many Nike shoes.

Knight had always been adept at using promotion effectively, but this element became even more important as competition heated up. The slogan "Just Do It," which first appeared in ad campaigns in 1989, has become the cornerstone of the company's advertising strategy. Nike ads have been winning industry awards for years, and they catapulted a once-obscure Portland, Oregon, ad agency to prominence. In fact, Wieden & Kennedy's former creative director, Dan Wieden, says that Nike taught him and partner David Kennedy how to advertise.

Knight also raised the stakes on celebrity endorsements, the industry's major marketing technique. Ever since Adidas and Puma pioneered the concept, success in the athletic footwear industry has depended on attaching the image of a sports star to a line of products. Nike's endorsers include many of the top names in professional sports, including former basketball star Michael Jordan, runner Joan Benoit Samuelson, hockey player Wayne Gretzky, and tennis pro Andre Agassi. Knight explains that you can't say much in a 60-second commercial, but "when you have Michael Jordan, you don't have to."

As the new products and new ads drew new customers, Knight learned how important it is to maintain good relations with members of the distribution channel. Back when aerobics shoes were all the rage, Nike accumulated mountains of unsold running shoes. But when the company turned to discount stores to empty its warehouses, it alienated the 12,000 sporting goods dealers and department stores that carried Nike's regularly priced shoes. Fortunately for Knight, he was able to win the retailers back with Nike Air.

Reebok wasn't sitting still all this time, of course, and its moves included introducing The Pump technology in 1989 and signing the NBA's newest superstar, Shaquille O'Neal, as an endorser. But Nike learned well from its past challenges and today maintains the lead over Reebok. Nike's sales are around $4 billion a year, with the help of expanded product offerings (most notably clothing) and growing markets in Asia and Europe. The race goes on.

**Your mission:** You have joined Nike as a marketing specialist with a mandate to increase sales of children's shoes. Use your knowledge of the marketing mix and your experience as a consumer to identify winning strategies.

1. Most kids are intensely interested in fashion and brand names, which seems to smooth the way for an established name such as Nike. But traditional children's shoe specialists claim to have the edge. Market leader Stride-Rite points to its reputation for fit, quality, and service. Which of the following advertising strategies would you recommend for Nike?
   a. Focus on Nike's strengths in adult athletics. Emphasize that Nike was founded by a sprinter and a track coach, and ask who would know more about footwear than these two people. Remind parents that their children will get the benefit of Nike's years of research in adult shoe technology.
   b. Focus on fashion statements that come with wearing Nike shoes. Point out the famous people who wear Nikes, and pay these celebrities to mention in public that they think Nikes are the coolest shoes.
   c. Combine the messages from (a) and (b).
2. Phil Knight wants to showcase the firm's interest in the welfare of younger children through local projects and national efforts. Which of the following ideas would most effectively generate goodwill while building potential sales of Nike kids' shoes?
   a. Start a model day-care center for children of Nike employees and open the center to other parents in the neighborhood. Emphasize physical fitness and outdoor activities that involve shoes of the type made by Nike for children. Invite day-care officials from major cities to tour this model center and speak with teachers, children, and Nike executives about the program.
   b. Sponsor annual "young olympics" competitions so that local teams can compete for state and regional championships in such sports as softball and running. Hold a final round of competition for the finalist teams; include press coverage, and feature the winners in Nike kids' shoe ads.

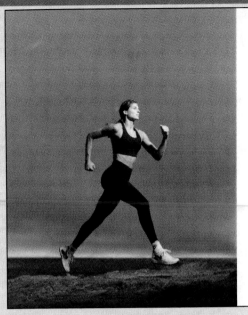

c. Negotiate contracts with young television stars to endorse Nike kids' shoes. Arrange autograph sessions in shoe and department stores around the country so that children can see the stars wearing Nike shoes. Hand out autographed photos of the stars wearing Nike shoes, and arrange for the stars to visit children's wards in nearby hospitals.

3. When you asked parents of young children to describe their experiences with children's shoes, one parent made the following comment:

My kids outgrow or destroy their shoes so fast, I seem to be buying new shoes almost every month. That's a lot of shoes in a short time.

You sense that there might be a marketing opportunity here. Which of the following strategies makes the most sense? Be sure to consider how well it addresses the parents' needs and how it will affect Nike's image.

a. Make a line of cheaper shoes that look more or less like regular Nikes, but use cheaper materials and less rigorous quality control.

b. Point out to parents that Nikes are built to last, so you can take care of at least half the problem. You can't do anything about the rate at which children's feet grow, but neither can any other shoe company.

c. It's too risky to make cheap shoes because it could damage the Nike image. If customers start to wonder whether the Nike product they're about to buy is a cheap version or a regular version, they may avoid the confusion by buying Reeboks or some other brand. It's best to ignore the problem.

4. To get new products out in front of adult audiences, Nike uses a network of professionals, such as aerobics trainers, who are given shoes free in exchange for appearing at trade shows and for other promotional duties. Consumers frequently ask these professionals for advice on athletic

shoes, and the fact that these pros wear Nikes themselves influences purchases as well. You would like to have a similar panel of people who are in a position to recommend Nike kids' shoes to purchasers. Which of the following groups of people would have the most influence on children's shoe purchasers?

a. Podiatrists, doctors who specialize in care and treatment of foot problems, would be your best choice. They understand feet, and parents will trust their opinions.

b. Scholarship winners from local schools would make the best spokespersons. They will be respected for their scholastic achievements, so parents and children will put faith in what these students have to say.

c. Young celebrities would make the best representatives because children look up to them. Young athletes, musical performers, and television and movie stars will have the visibility to grab the children's attention and get their loyalty.

## SPECIAL PROJECT

Children's shoes are marketed differently in various retail outlets. Visit your neighborhood shopping center and compare how casual shoes for kids are displayed and sold in a department store (such as Sears or J.C. Penney), a full-line shoe store (such as Kinney's or Stride-Rite), and a discount store (such as Kmart or Wal-Mart). For example, are brand names for children's sneakers promoted through in-store materials, such as posters, customer brochures, demonstrations, dissected shoe models, and so forth? Are the shoes offered in discount stores the same brands as those offered in full-price stores? Do they cost the same? For each type of retail outlet, describe briefly how each of the four elements of the marketing mix is used in presenting and selling sporty children's shoes.[37]

# McDonald's Turns Up the Heat on Fast Food

Although McDonald's is the house that beef built, it's not just burgers anymore. Today's menu will get you through the day, starting with breakfast goodies such as Egg McMuffin and continuing through lunch and dinner with Chicken McNuggets, prepackaged green salads, and Big Macs. The chain that dishes out nearly one-third of all the burgers and about a quarter of all the french fries eaten in the United States is now the number two chicken retailer in the country, and CEO Michael R. Quinlan is continuing the search for menu selections that will keep McDonald's on top.

Quinlan is in the food fight of his life, reflecting a variety of marketing challenges that are much more complex than those faced by founder Ray Kroc, back when a hamburger cost just 15 cents. For one thing, McDonald's, with its 8,000 units across the United States (12,000 worldwide), is no longer the only burger business on the block. Traditional rivals include Burger King, the second largest fast-food chain, with 6,000 U.S. outlets; and Wendy's, number three with 3,500 U.S. restaurants. Furthermore, the competitive arena includes thousands of outlets specializing in pizza, fried chicken, roast beef sandwiches, and various ethnic foods.

That's not all. Some big food producers are taking aim directly at McDonald's target market. Campbell Soup and Oscar Mayer (part of the Kraft General Foods conglomerate) are but two of the consumer goods marketers that are searching for ways to compete with fast-food chains. Individually packaged meals sold in grocery stores, such as the Lunchables combos of meat, cheese, and crackers, are designed to entice consumers who would normally grab a burger and fries at lunch.

McDonald's also faces the problem of satisfying changing consumer tastes and concerns. For example, an increasing number of customers are interested in lighter, healthier food. For these people, a healthy meal is not two all-beef patties, special sauce, lettuce, cheese, pickles, and onions on a sesame seed bun, so McDonald's has gone beyond beef to attract these potential customers. In 1987 the chain introduced the prepackaged salad, an item that now accounts for 7 percent of total sales and that has the potential to open the door to a whole new target market. Also, bowing to public pressure, McDonald's switched to healthier cooking oil, which should make french fry devotees feel a little better about indulging.

Distribution is a key marketing element, so Quinlan is opening more restaurants than ever. Although the best urban and suburban locations have already been snapped up, McDonald's is using NASA photographs to find attractive sites near busy intersections in smaller towns. Quinlan is also pushing to open McDonald's outlets inside hospitals, museums, airports, military installations, and big retail stores such as Wal-Mart and Home Depot. Like McDonald's founder Ray Kroc, Michael Quinlan is never satisfied, and he'll use every marketing angle he can find to keep the heat on his fast-food competitors.

1. Assume that McDonald's is going to launch a new Mexican-style salad and wants to promote the introduction with a joint marketing partner. The target market is health-conscious consumers who like Mexican food. Would you suggest teaming up with a salad dressing supplier such as Wishbone or with a Mexican-food producer such as El Paso? Why?

2. McDonald's is prepared to meet a variety of international marketing challenges because of the close working relationship with franchise owners who run the local McDonald's restaurants in 50 countries. For example, the McDonald's on the Champs Elysées in Paris offers wine because it's traditional for French diners to enjoy a glass with lunch or dinner. On the other hand, it's increasingly important for McDonald's to present a consistent image to the world, no matter where the individual restaurant may be located. To what degree should the chain enforce menu consistency worldwide? Why?

3. From dawn until way after dark, McDonald's is beckoning hungry customers with a variety of breakfast, lunch, and dinner items, about 41 at the typical U.S. outlet. In fact, some critics warn that the menu is becoming unmanageable. Nevertheless, Quinlan needs to keep the per-outlet productivity high, and he wants to maintain customer traffic throughout the day. Should he call a new-product moratorium and add a new product only to replace an older product that's pulled from the menu? Or should he test new products and then add them at a steady pace, regardless of how large the menu becomes?

# QUESTIONS FOR DISCUSSION

1. What is the value provided by the following products?
   a. Soccer game
   b. Drug-abuse awareness campaign
   c. Lumber
   d. French fries
2. Assume you're managing the marketing group at a Von's grocery store; how could you figure out the wants and needs of your customers?
3. Which of the four economic utilities do the following products provide?
   a. Home-study course
   b. Pizza delivery service
   c. Cake mix
   d. All-night deli
4. Think about the Nike story presented at the beginning of the chapter; was Nike guilty of marketing myopia when it missed the aerobics trend?
5. What is the target market for Nintendo games?
6. Humana Corporation, with dozens of hospitals across the country, and the Sisters of Mercy both operate health-care facilities. One organization (Humana) seeks a financial profit, but the other (Sisters of Mercy) doesn't. How might their marketing programs differ?
7. Can you think of any marketers who can still get away with a product orientation?
8. Assume you're managing a McDonald's franchise; how can you foster a marketing culture?
9. What is the function of price in the advertising headline "The Most Expensive Perfume in the World"?
10. Name a good advertising medium for reaching the following audiences:
    a. Children
    b. College students
    c. College professors
    d. Farmers

# SHARPEN YOUR MARKETING SKILLS

You're in charge of the marketing department at McCormick & Company, the century-old spice maker. The last decade has been a tough one. American consumers now use 20 percent less spice than they did in 1980, and your share of that shrinking market has dropped from 40 to 35 percent. To make matters worse, you're battling the product orientation reflected in the company's motto: "Make the best. Someone will buy it." Well, you're still making the best, in over 200 varieties, but all those someones aren't buying like they used to.

Your research shows that the spice market is changing. Working couples and single professionals are moving toward convenience foods. Also, people who still cook from scratch say they don't experiment with spices unless they're cooking exotic or complicated dishes.

**Decision:** Knowing what you know about McCormick, decide how you could best convince the company to adopt a more market-driven philosophy.

**Communication:** Write a brief letter (one page or less) to the company's president, explaining why McCormick needs to drop its product orientation and outlining how you would change its marketing mix to respond to its changing market.

# KEEPING CURRENT IN MARKETING

A number of issues face marketers intent on success in today's markets. Choose one of the issues listed here; then find one or more articles in the business press that relate to how one company is dealing with the issue you've chosen.

- Overcoming marketing myopia
- Choosing target markets
- Assessing market opportunities
- Focusing on the customer
- Staying in touch with reality
- Building on strengths
- Integrating the marketing mix

After you've collected your research material, answer as many of the following questions as you can, based on the information in the article(s).

1. What changes occurred within the company as a result of its focus on the issue? Over what period of time? What effect has this focus had on marketing operations? On other operations within the company?
2. How successful would you say the company has been at addressing the issue you've selected? Have the changes brought about by focusing on the issue produced the results the company set out to achieve? How do you know?
3. What forces were at work that persuaded the executives of the company to tackle this specific marketing issue? For example, was the new focus precipitated by a crisis? New competition? Changing consumer wants and needs? The arrival of new management?

**2**

# Environmental Forces and Marketing Ethics

**After studying this chapter, you will be able to**

**1.** Discuss the importance of environmental scanning and environmental analysis

**2.** List the seven major elements of the marketing environment

**3.** Cite the four phases of the business cycle and discuss the nature of consumer behavior in each

**4.** Outline the types of competition and the various competitive structures that markets can exhibit

**5.** Explain how government regulations can affect your marketing plans

**6.** Describe how technology can change both the products you sell and the way you market them

**7.** Discuss how changes in social values and attitudes affect marketing

**8.** Describe the role of ethics in marketing and distinguish between ethical dilemmas and ethical lapses

## *Making Headlines across the Country*

Critics called it "McPaper," ridiculing its bite-size news stories and flashy graphics. Nonetheless, *USA Today* changed the industry forever, becoming the first successful major newspaper introduction in 40 years, because founder Allen H. Neuharth took advantage of key elements in the marketing environment.

*USA Today* was started by the Gannett Company in September 1982, when many daily papers were struggling just to stay alive. Only *The Wall Street Journal* was distributed nationally then. Conventional wisdom held that newspapers were a hometown business, but Al Neuharth, Gannett's chairman, believed the time was right for a new, nationwide paper. To be successful, Neuharth had to pay close attention to his marketing environment, which presented both opportunity and risk.

First, the country was on the move. Nearly 1 million people were flying each day, and 2 million were staying in hotels or motels. Neuharth reasoned that these travelers would want a timely news snapshot of the nation and of their home states. He figured that these busy, on-the-go people would appreciate news packaged in a concise, easy-to-read format.

Second, advances in technology made it possible to send news stories, color graphics, and photos to printing sites thousands of miles away in minutes. Using satellite transmission, *USA Today* could be printed every night at Gannett plants across the United States (even around the world) in time for the morning rush hour.

Third, political and regulatory forces allowed Neuharth to distribute his paper using eye-catching vending machines, which cost more than $30 million to construct. Because widespread placement of the machines would be controversial, Neuharth had to be sure he was on solid ground both legally and politically—and his careful planning paid off.

The weekend before the newspaper's 1983 New York City debut, the *USA Today* team bolted 3,000 machines to the city's sidewalks. On Monday morning, angry competitors and local politicians threatened to have the machines removed. However, the members of Neuharth's team had done their homework and discovered that the First Amendment protects newspaper vending machines as vehicles for distributing news. The machines stayed on the sidewalks and played a crucial role in the successful launch in New York: They put the product right in front of the target audience, making it hard to miss the new paper. This move was particularly important in an urban area such as New York City, which was already served by several major newspapers.

Economic factors presented another problem. Ad revenues are vital to newspaper profitability, but *USA Today* had difficulty attracting advertisers in significant numbers. Companies were reluctant to advertise in the new paper, in part because they were unsure about customers buying yet another newspaper and substituting *USA Today* for their regular paper.

The positives outweighed the negatives, and by 1987 *USA Today* had a higher paid circulation than any general-interest U.S. daily. Even with this success, Neuharth couldn't afford to slow down, not even with 2 million subscribers. If you were Neuharth, how would you capitalize on your marketing environment in order to keep *USA Today* competitive? How would you shape *USA Today*'s next innovations by using social, economic, legal, and technological changes to the best advantage?[1]

# CHAPTER OVERVIEW

Executives at *USA Today* know that every marketer is influenced by a number of external elements. Known collectively as the **marketing environment,** these elements include competition, economics, nature, politics, regulation, technology, and society. They are beyond the marketer's direct control, but they can have a profound effect on marketing success. These external forces affect the products that can be sold, how they are sold, and who can buy them. This chapter explains how marketers respond to their environment and, in some cases, how they influence it. The final section is devoted to two topics very much in the public eye today: marketing ethics and social responsibility.

# ANALYSIS OF THE MARKETING ENVIRONMENT

As a marketer, every move you make is affected by—and has some effect on—your marketing environment (see Exhibit 2.1). This happens on a small scale, such as between a manufacturer and a retailer, and on a larger scale involving entire industries and governments. Changes in the environment create new opportunities and eliminate old ones, and the marketing environment is always changing. These changes can be exciting, frustrating, confusing, irritating, and invigorating. They can establish entire industries and drive companies into bankruptcy.

Consider the effect on U.S. business of one major change in the marketing environment: the Clean Air Act Amendments of 1990. Manufacturers, dry cleaners, oil refineries, gas stations, bakeries, and a host of other businesses have to reduce harmful emissions. The result will be a healthier planet, but these changes cost U.S. business an estimated $25 billion every year, Some of that $25 billion comes out of

**marketing environment**
The general atmosphere in which marketers operate and are influenced by such external elements as competitors, economics, nature, politics, regulations, technology, and society

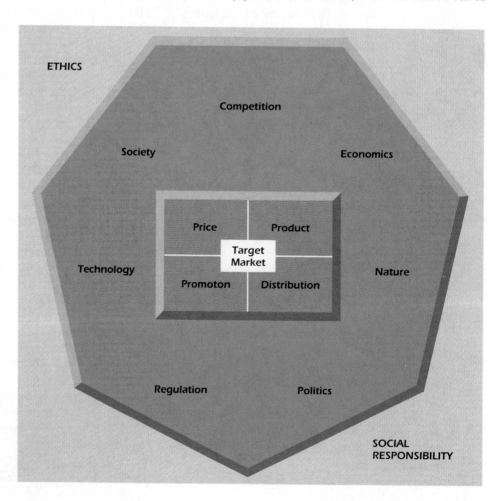

**Exhibit 2.1**
**THE MARKETING ENVIRONMENT**
The marketing environment includes the four marketing mix elements (product, distribution, price, and promotion) as well as seven environmental elements (competition, economics, nature, politics, regulation, technology, and society), all set within the context of ethics and social responsibility.

30

salaries, profits, and the other financial rewards of being in business; some of it comes out of consumers' pockets in the form of higher prices.[2]

On the other hand, thousands of companies stand to benefit. For instance, companies like Enviroplan and Ecotech Autoworks market goods and services that help polluters meet the new regulations. Their sales are booming. Natural gas suppliers such as Pacific Gas & Electric hope to increase their sales as carmakers look for cleaner alternatives to gasoline.[3] All of these losses and gains result from a change in the marketing environment.

The process of gathering information on various aspects of your marketing environment is called **environmental scanning.** You can collect this information from customers, salespeople, dealers, distributors, suppliers, government agencies, magazines, publications, newspapers, and books. **Environmental analysis** is the interpretation of all this information. Marketers evaluate the data collected in environmental scanning with an eye to their own businesses, considering how the various trends could affect them both now and in the future. Their goal is to create marketing strategies adapted to the dynamic marketing environment.

When the shoe manufacturer Timberland pondered the U.S. market in the late 1980s, it saw a dramatic increase in the number of lower-cost overseas suppliers (along with corresponding factory shutdowns and bankruptcies among U.S. firms) and population growth patterns that showed slow increases in the mainstream market but much larger increases in the affluent market. Rather than trying to compete with the lower-cost suppliers, Timberland went after the high end. The careful monitoring and analysis of the environment paid off; sales turned around and net income grew from $552,000 to nearly $8 million in just four years. Timberland's sales exploded again in the early 1990s, as outdoorsy footwear became mainstream fashion. Sales climbed past $400 million, and income nearly tripled to $21 million in 1993.[4]

**environmental scanning**
The process of gathering data on the marketing environment from people and publications

**environmental analysis**
The interpretation of data generated in environmental scanning

# ELEMENTS OF THE MARKETING ENVIRONMENT

All marketers face controllable and uncontrollable environmental elements. **Controllable elements** are those internal factors over which marketers have a high degree of control, specifically their own pricing, promotion, distribution, and product selection. **Uncontrollable elements** are external factors such as currency exchange rates, consumer tastes, and political shifts. You might be able to influence these factors, but you cannot control them.[5] Note that a given component of the marketing mix, such as pricing, is controllable in some industries and largely uncontrollable in others. For example, the government doesn't regulate the prices set by hairdressers, but it does control the prices set by public utility companies.

As noted earlier, marketers are influenced by the competitive, economic, natural, political, regulatory, technological, and social elements of the marketing environment. Not only are these elements in a constant state of change, but they are interdependent and often shape one another. For example, cigarette marketers now face opposition in multiple areas of the marketing environment because the antismoking sentiment in the social area is fueling similar attitudes in the legal and regulatory areas. As social attitudes have turned against public smoking, the U.S. Congress has banned smoking on commercial airline flights between cities in the 48 contiguous states, and some cities have passed ordinances forcing restaurants to maintain nonsmoking sections.[6] Here's a closer look at the elements of the marketing environment.

**controllable elements**
Internal factors over which marketers have a high degree of control, specifically their own pricing, promotion, distribution, and product selection

**uncontrollable elements**
External factors such as currency exchange rates, consumer tastes, and political shifts, over which the marketer has no control (although some elements may be subject to influence)

## Competitive Elements

One of the most important aspects of the overall marketing environment is **competition,** the rivalry among marketers approaching the same set of customers, each trying to increase sales, market share, or profits. Competitive elements can be categorized, both in terms of products and in terms of overall market structure.

**competition**
The rivalry among sellers trying to increase sales, profits, or market share while addressing the same set of customers

## TYPES OF COMPETITITION

There are three types of product competition. The first is direct competition between marketers of similar products. British Petroleum and Chevron compete directly, marketing gasoline to motorists. *USA Today* competes with local newspapers, and Johnson & Johnson competes directly with store brands in the shampoo market (see Exhibit 2.2). One of the most important trends in contemporary marketing is global competition between directly competing products. Consider Procter & Gamble, long the powerhouse in several dozen product categories in the U.S. market. P&G now faces growing competition both at home and abroad from the likes of Unilever (a Dutch-English company), Henckel (a German company), Shisedo (a Japanese company), and L'Oréal (a French company).

The second type of competition occurs between marketers whose products can be substituted for one another. Pretzels and potato chips are not identical products, but both are snacks, and consumers often substitute one for the other. In the same way, fax machines offer a partial substitute for express delivery services, and baking soda can take the place of toothpaste as a dentifrice.

The third type of competition is even more general. It exists between marketers of dissimilar goods and services who are all competing for consumer dollars and preference. Customers enjoy a virtually endless list of purchasing choices. The marketing challenge is to persuade them to choose a specific type of product and a particular brand at least some of the time. In this broadest competitive arena, motorcycle marketers compete with movie theaters, clothing boutiques vie with restaurants, airlines are in competition with publishers, and on and on.

## THE COMPETITIVE STRUCTURE OF MARKETS

**monopoly**
A competitive structure in which one marketer controls the supply of a product that has no direct substitutes

As industries have evolved, several competitive structures have arisen that dictate the relationships between businesses. A **monopoly** is a competitive structure in which one marketer completely controls the supply of a product for which there are no exact substitutes. An example of a company in a monopoly position is Spain's Telefonica, which was recently granted 30 years of protection from competition in the Spanish telephone service market.[7] Though the U.S. government restricts monopolies, some have survived. Regional utilities such as gas and electric companies are monopolies, and so are companies holding unexpired patents for unique products. Typically, organizations can't enter a monopoly market because equipment, training, product development, and sales cost too much or because governmental regulations prevent newcomers from joining. For example, the staggering cost of buying and maintaining electricity-generating equipment, combined with strict regulations, makes it almost impossible to compete with an electricity monopoly.

**barriers to entry**
Competitive conditions that make it expensive, illegal, or otherwise difficult to enter a market as a competitor

Such costs and regulations are called **barriers to entry;** that is, they keep potential competitors out of the industry. Product benefits and features that can't be imitated also erect a barrier to entry. For example, if MCI, Sprint, and other newcomers to the long-distance telephone market had been unable to provide static-free phone service, they would never have gained acceptance in the marketplace. This entry barrier would have left AT&T in a virtual monopoly position despite the deregulation of long-distance service. Relationships between marketers and their customers, resellers, and suppliers can also be barriers to entry. Established connections can give existing marketers an advantage over would-be competitors when it comes to buying production materials and distributing finished goods.

**oligopoly**
A competitive structure in which a small number of competitors control the market

In an **oligopoly,** a few competitors control the market, particularly the element of pricing. In addition, the barriers to entry are so high that few new competitors can join the fray. It's difficult to get into the air-transportation business, for example, because aircraft and terminal facilities are so expensive. Consequently, a handful of airlines now control most of the commercial air traffic in the United States.[8] The presence of even a few competitors can make for lively marketing, as the U.S. automotive, tobacco, and textiles industries (also oligopolies) have shown. Unlike marketers in a monopoly, those in an oligopoly do not enjoy complete freedom in

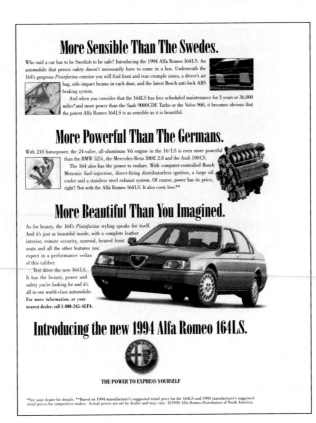

**Exhibit 2.2
COMPETITION
BETWEEN SIMILAR
PRODUCTS**
Marketers with products that
are similar to those offered by
the competition often have to
explain why their products
are more desirable. In this ad,
Alfa Romeo compares the
164LS with other cars.

establishing their marketing mix. The presence of several competitors forces each marketer to develop strategies and tactics aimed at gaining an advantage over the others.

**Monopolistic competition** refers to a competitive structure that includes many marketers, each with a relatively small share of the market and products that are unique to at least a small degree.[9] To capture market share, marketers try to differentiate their offerings from those of the competition by varying their marketing mixes. Restaurants, auto mechanics, clothing marketers, publishers, and many others operate within the constraints of monopolistic competition, striving to make their goods and services unique in the eyes of consumers. A mechanic may do that by specializing in BMWs, Volvos, and Jaguars, and by providing patrons with free loaner cars. The majority of industries in developed countries, including the United States, operate in monopolistic competition.

**Pure competition** describes an ideal competitive structure in which many organizations market a product that cannot be differentiated on anything other than price. The advantage of pure competition is that all the marketers are on the same footing, selling the same product for similar prices through the same channels of distribution. The disadvantage is that the lack of differentiation keeps everyone's profit margins slim. In the United States and other industrialized countries, agricultural commodities are about the only products sold in a pure competition structure. Chapter 3 explores the techniques marketers can use to analyze their competitors and develop strategies in response.

**monopolistic competition**
A competitive structure in which many marketers compete to sell similar products and in which marketing strategies typically emphasize product differentiation

**pure competition**
The ideal competitive structure in which many marketers compete to sell the same undifferentiated product

## Economic Elements

The economy affects marketers and consumers alike. The major **economic elements** of the marketing environment include business cycles, consumer income, and customer willingness to spend. You can't control these economic factors, but they certainly affect your business. For instance, companies that seem to be doing everything right can simply vanish if the economy slows down. This is of particular concern to companies that produce nonessential goods and services, which consumers and businesses are likely to stop purchasing if money gets tight. On a more

**economic elements**
Factors in the marketing environment that are shaped by, or are part of, the economic climate, such as consumer wealth, buying power, and income

**Exhibit 2.3**
**RESPONDING TO ENVIRONMENTAL CHANGES**
In recognition of the growing demand for small-business computer solutions, Microsoft targeted small companies with its Works product and promoted it with ads such as this one.

positive note, your sales can really take off during times of economic growth, provided you sense the growth that's coming and prepare for it.

For example, when marketers realized that one of the fastest-growing segments of the U.S. economy was small business, they started altering their strategies by targeting that segment to ensure their own growth. Between 1970 and 1987 the number of Americans starting their own businesses grew 50 percent; between 1982 and 1984 small companies created 74 percent of new jobs. Responding to these changes in the economic environment, companies such as Price Waterhouse, AT&T, Microsoft, and American Express started targeting small companies as prospective customers for everything from financial services to computer software. To attract small firms, these marketers designed products and advertising that addressed the problems and concerns of small businesses, offered lower prices, and gave small-business training and other specialized services.[10] (See Exhibit 2.3.)

In addition to influencing how marketers do business, the economic elements affect consumers. In a depressed economy, customers tend to think twice before buying the commercial marketer's products, and they may even hesitate to support nonprofit organizations. On the other hand, when the economy is booming, consumers are confident about the future and more likely to spend their earnings.

**buying power**
The consumer's ability to purchase products

**effective buying income (EBI)**
The consumer's total income after taxes

**buying power index (BPI)**
A measure of various geographic regions' collective purchasing power, based on population, effective buying income, and retail sales

**income**
The consumer's financial gain from all sources, usually specified over some time interval

BUYING POWER

One way to predict how the economic elements are affecting consumers is to monitor consumer **buying power,** or purchasing ability. Because buying power ebbs and flows with changing prices and consumer income, marketers track these fluctuations to predict demand for their products and to develop appropriate marketing strategies.

Many marketers use two buying power indicators: effective buying income and the buying power index. **Effective buying income (EBI)** reflects consumers' total after-tax income including wages, tips, interest, and dividends. The **buying power index (BPI)** shows the collective purchasing power of geographic regions based on population, EBI, and actual retail sales. The BPI is useful for comparing various regions' buying power. The higher the region's BPI rating, the more buying power it enjoys.

INCOME    As EBI and BPI illustrate, marketers must evaluate consumer income levels to assess buying power. **Income** is the consumer's total financial gain over a defined period of time, including salary, wages, government assistance, pensions, dividends, interest, and other sources. Consumers use their income to buy products

**34**

and to pay taxes, and they often save part of it. Exhibit 2.4 shows the distribution of household income in the United States.

Two more measures of buying power are disposable and discretionary income. **Disposable income,** like effective buying income, is what's left after taxes. Consumers use their disposable income to pay for necessities such as food, clothes, and housing. **Discretionary income** is the amount of disposable income left after necessities are paid for. Consumers use it to buy nonessentials such as televisions, jewelry, toys, vacations, and movie tickets. If you're marketing a product that is normally purchased with discretionary income, you need to pay close attention to the economy. When people think hard economic times are approaching, they often respond by reducing their discretionary purchases.

CREDIT  Another indicator of buying is credit, which allows customers to obtain goods and services on the understanding that they'll pay for them later. Consumers obtain credit through automotive finance companies, banks, credit card providers such as American Express, and department stores. In essence, credit enhances consumers' current buying power while it decreases their future buying power.

Interest rates and the size of down payments and monthly payments affect consumers' inclination to use credit, and marketers can take advantage of this by offering attractive rates or payment plans. For example, automakers frequently use low- or no-interest financing to stimulate car purchases during periods of slow sales.

WEALTH  Another measure of buying power is **wealth,** or accumulated financial resources. Wealth is related to income if the individual got wealthy by earning a large salary or by saving his or her earnings over the years. But people also gain wealth through inheritance, gambling, gifts, theft, and luck. In addition to cash, wealth includes stocks and bonds, real estate, jewelry, art and antique collections, and other investments. Wealth increases buying power by providing ready cash for purchases and by increasing a person's ability to qualify for credit.

## WILLINGNESS TO SPEND

Marketers not only monitor buying power but also evaluate consumer willingness to spend money, which affects some marketers more than others. For example, companies marketing basic food items such as bread and milk are less likely to be endangered when consumer willingness to spend drops. Willingness to spend is affected largely by economic considerations that may reflect either current conditions or expectations for the future. Higher wages, improved health benefits, and larger government subsidies—or the expectations of these improvements—increase consumer willingness to spend. Anticipated product shortages and fears of price hikes also increase short-term willingness to spend.

**disposable income**
Income the consumer retains after paying taxes

**discretionary income**
The portion of disposable income the consumer retains after paying for food, shelter, and other necessities

**wealth**
Total financial resources accumulated over time

## Exhibit 2.4  INCOME LEVELS FOR HOUSEHOLDS HEADED BY 35- TO 54-YEAR-OLDS

| Income Range | Number of Households in Thousands | | | |
| | 1986 | 1990 | 1995 | 2000 |
|---|---|---|---|---|
| Under $10,000 | 3,557 | 3,660 | 3,963 | 4,074 |
| $10,000 to $19,999 | 4,943 | 5,046 | 5,418 | 5,521 |
| $20,000 to $29,999 | 5,889 | 6,007 | 6,434 | 6,534 |
| $30,000 to $39,999 | 5,494 | 5,845 | 6,488 | 6,781 |
| $40,000 to $49,999 | 3,982 | 4,608 | 5,460 | 6,006 |
| $50,000 to $59,999 | 2,803 | 3,148 | 3,782 | 4,331 |
| $60,000 to $74,999 | 2,165 | 2,767 | 3,545 | 4,214 |
| $75,000 and over | 2,266 | 3,186 | 4,618 | 6,205 |
| Total households | 31,099 | 34,267 | 39,708 | 43,666 |
| Median income | $32,110 | $34,140 | $36,230 | $38,410 |

Between 1986 and 2000, as the "baby boomers" mature, significantly more U.S. households will have incomes of $40,000 or more. (Note: Households are in thousands, and income is for previous year, shown in 1985 dollars.)

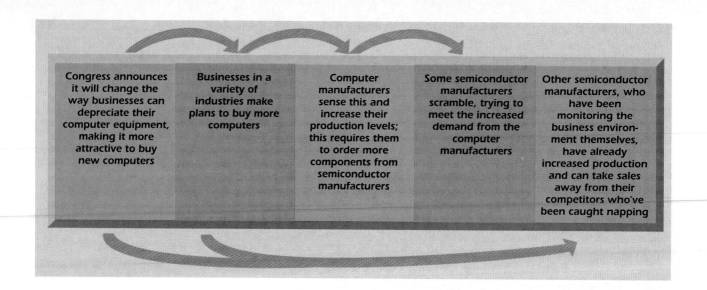

| Congress announces it will change the way businesses can depreciate their computer equipment, making it more attractive to buy new computers | Businesses in a variety of industries make plans to buy more computers | Computer manufacturers sense this and increase their production levels; this requires them to order more components from semiconductor manufacturers | Some semiconductor manufacturers scramble, trying to meet the increased demand from the computer manufacturers | Other semiconductor manufacturers, who have been monitoring the business environment themselves, have already increased production and can take sales away from their competitors who've been caught napping |

**Exhibit 2.5
THE EFFECT OF
WILLINGNESS
TO SPEND**
When one group in the economy changes its willingness to spend, the effect often ripples through to other groups.

**business cycle**
A predictable economic fluctuation that gives rise to four stages: prosperity, recession, depression, and recovery

**prosperity**
The stage of the business cycle in which consumers enjoy high income, willingness to spend, and low unemployment

**recession**
The stage of the business cycle in which unemployment rises and consumer buying power drops

On the other hand, rising unemployment rates and expectations of job layoffs suppress willingness to spend. Prices that seem high compared to the prices on substitute products have the same impact. Sometimes changes in the marketing environment can increase consumer willingness to spend on some products and decrease it on others. For example, a trend toward larger families would have a mixed effect. Growing families are more willing to spend money on basics such as food and shelter but are less willing to spend it on exotic vacations, electronic toys, and other diversions.

Willingness to spend is a common economic measure in consumer marketing, but businesses, governments, and other organizations also exhibit various levels of willingness to part with their money. For example, if Chrysler thinks its auto sales will drop this year, it might postpone purchases of land, buildings, or equipment. This creates a ripple effect back through all the companies that supply Chrysler. Because of this, companies that market to other companies often have to look past their own customers and see how their customers' customers are faring economically. This effect is illustrated in Exhibit 2.5.

THE BUSINESS CYCLE

Consumer willingness to spend and consumer buying power are greatly affected by the **business cycle,** a pattern of economic fluctuation that includes four scenarios:

- *Prosperity.* The period that combines low unemployment, high income, and strong willingness to spend is called **prosperity.** Prosperity often brings low interest rates as well as high buying power. Buyers are confident about the economy, relatively insensitive to high prices, and more willing to buy luxury items. Marketers typically expand their product lines, promotional budgets, and distribution channels; they may also raise prices.

- *Recession.* During a **recession** unemployment rises, overall buying power falls, and buyer confidence drops. Major purchases such as new-home construction, auto sales, and factory expansions decrease. Between 1920 and 1993 the United States experienced about 16 recessions, 6 of them between 1948 and 1976. During those six, unemployment rose to between 6 and 9 percent.[11] In a recession, consumers have limited buying power and tend to base purchasing decisions on price and value; prices can drop considerably in some markets. In the recession of 1992–1993, exotic carmaker Lotus dropped the price of its top-end Esprit Turbo model by $20,000.[12]

- *Depression.* **A depression** is characterized by extremely high unemployment, low buying power and wages, minimal disposable income, and a general lack of confidence in the economy. The only depression experienced by the United States in the twentieth century spanned 1929 through 1933. During that time, the U.S. gross national product dropped from $104 billion to $56 billion, and unemployment exploded, ultimately reaching 25 percent.[13] Because of a depression's devastating effect on businesses and individuals alike, the government acts to avoid it with antidepression policies that incorporate tax incentives, currency-supply controls, and changes in government spending.

- *Recovery.* The phase of the business cycle in which the economy moves from recession or depression toward prosperity is called **recovery.** Unemployment drops, disposable income increases, willingness to spend returns, and businesses and consumers become more confident about the future. Because it's difficult to judge how quickly a recovery will turn the corner into prosperity, companies must plan their marketing strategies carefully during a recovery.

**depression**
A more intense form of recession in which unemployment peaks, buying power drops dramatically, and consumers lose faith in the economy

**recovery**
The stage of the business cycle in which the economy moves from depression or recession toward prosperity

## LEVEL OF ECONOMIC DEVELOPMENT

A country's level of economic development is an important environmental indicator of potential markets. One of the statistics commonly used to measure economic development is a country's *gross national product (GNP),* which refers to the market value of all the goods and services produced during a given period. When GNP is divided by a country's total population, the resulting figure is *per capita GNP.* This is more meaningful to marketers because it gives a general indication of the income of individual members of a nation's population.

The World Bank, an agency associated with the United Nations, uses per capita GNP to classify countries according to five levels of economic development, ranging from preindustrial to postindustrial (as shown in Exhibit 2.6). Countries with a low per capita GNP will not provide the best market for luxury goods or many personal and business services.[14] In contrast, low per capita GNP markets such as China represent tremendous future promise for marketers who get in on the ground floor. However, low per capita GNP figures must be interpreted case by case. India's per capita GNP is only slightly more than $300, but the country has a rapidly growing and prosperous middle class eager to buy consumer goods and services. For instance, in 1978 Indians bought only 150,000 TVs, but 10 years later they bought 6 million.[15]

Exhibit 2.7 gives a thumbnail sketch of what real-life income and expenses look like in nine major cities around the world. Although income is closely related to a country's level of economic development, what people actually pay for goods and services is less predictable. For example, bus drivers in Bangkok earn less than one-fifth of what bus drivers in Frankfurt earn, but they have to pay nearly twice as much for an apartment. Some managers in Hong Kong earn four times what their counterparts earn in São Paulo, but they pay less than half as much for a business suit.

## Exhibit 2.6   STAGES OF MARKET DEVELOPMENT

| Category | Per Capita GNP | Number of Countries in Each Category |
|---|---|---|
| Preindustrial countries | $400 or less | 32 |
| Less-developed countries | $401–1,635 | 48 |
| Developing countries | $1,636–5,500 | 42 |
| Industrialized countries | $5,501–10,000 | 14 |
| Postindustrial countries | $10,001 or more | 24 |

The World Bank divides countries into five stages of market development, an environmental factor that should play a key role in any international marketer's plans.

**Exhibit 2.7  A SNAPSHOT OF LIVING STANDARDS**

| Expense | Bangkok | Frankfurt | Hong Kong | London | New York | Paris | São Paulo | Seoul | Tokyo |
|---|---|---|---|---|---|---|---|---|---|
| **Costs** | | | | | | | | | |
| Apartment rent, 3 rooms, per month | $950 | $496 | $2,136 | $1,244 | $1,680 | $966 | $1,365 | $1,694 | $6,123 |
| Color TV | $636 | $550 | $356 | $820 | $577 | $1,079 | $528 | $859 | $1,427 |
| Business suit | $212 | $275 | $214 | $303 | $352 | $260 | $488 | $240 | $536 |
| Eggs, one dozen | $.79 | $1.99 | $1.04 | $2.32 | $1.15 | $2.24 | $.83 | $1.05 | $1.43 |
| Gasoline, 1 liter | $.36 | $.54 | $.60 | $.69 | $.36 | $.80 | $.70 | $.91 | $1.06 |
| Hairdresser, ladies' | $1.90 | $18.20 | $8.60 | $20.80 | $32.90 | $23.20 | $18.70 | $14.00 | $29.80 |
| Taxi fare, 5 km | $1.83 | $7.71 | $2.85 | $10.44 | $8.12 | $4.91 | $4.70 | $1.82 | $9.11 |
| **Earnings** | | | | | | | | | |
| Bus driver | | | | | | | | | |
| After-tax earnings | $2,971 | $15,658 | $11,119 | $15,764 | $20,959 | $15,967 | $4,207 | $9,404 | $25,049 |
| Hours worked | 2,731 | 1,915 | 3,018 | 1,841 | 1,916 | 1,841 | 2,346 | 3,110 | 2,175 |
| Department manager | | | | | | | | | |
| After-tax earnings | $10,769 | $46,773 | $30,878 | $26,127 | $37,303 | $20,885 | $5,871 | $17,663 | $52,741 |
| Hours worked | 2,428 | 1,909 | 2,486 | 1,792 | 1,995 | 1,814 | 2,149 | 2,312 | 2,114 |

Living standards around the world vary significantly and are an important consideration when developing marketing strategies.

INFRASTRUCTURE

**infrastructure**
A nation's energy (gas and electric utilities), transportation, and communication systems

Closely related to a country's level of economic development is the adequacy of its **infrastructure,** which includes systems for energy, transportation, and communication. If a country's infrastructure is poorly developed, you'll have to adapt marketing strategies accordingly. Marketers of electrical products, for example, must make sure that energy is affordable and compatible with the products to be marketed. If a company's potential customers are contacted primarily by phone, a country's telephone system must be reliable. In addition, if a product is promoted through print advertising, there must be adequate circulation of newspapers and magazines and a sufficient level of literacy.

## Natural Elements

**natural elements**
Factors in the marketing environment that are not human-made, such as natural resources, weather, and geologic and astronomical events

The availability of natural resources such as land, water, and minerals significantly affects everyone in the economy, marketers as well as consumers. The **natural elements** of the marketing environment include natural resources, weather conditions, geologic events such as volcanic eruptions and earthquakes, and astronomical events such as eclipses. Changes in the natural environment can seriously affect marketers, both positively and negatively.

Major natural disasters can damage and even destroy companies, as U.S. marketers discovered after major hurricanes and flooding in 1992 and 1993. Even when the company survives physically intact, it may still fall victim to supply disruptions or customers who've been wiped out financially. On the other hand, even less dramatic weather patterns affect marketing. When an unusually stormy summer hit the Pacific Northwest in 1993, many businesses that cater to outdoor activities watched sales drop sharply. George McConnell of McConnell's Boat House in Mukilteo, Washington, says that even wind affects his boating and fishing equipment business. When the wind blows boats away from people's favorite fishing spots, they give up and go home.[16] Even the smartest marketing strategies can be outsmarted by Mother Nature.

**political elements**
Factors in the marketing environment related to domestic and international politics and governmental policies

## Political Elements

**Political elements,** the domestic and international political events and government policies that shape economic conditions and trade relationships, are some of the most powerful environmental forces. They can put a stop to even the best-designed marketing plans, but they can also create tremendous opportunities.

Political changes, whether they are gradual trends or dramatic upheavals, can create, destroy, or alter marketing opportunities. The opening of Eastern Europe and the end of the Cold War created great opportunities for marketers (see Exhibit 2.8). For example, anticipating growth in the number of business and recreational travelers to Poland, Marriott opened a 520-room hotel in Warsaw and was looking into building similar hotels in Prague and Budapest.[17] Digital Equipment Corporation (DEC) and General Electric (GE) both gained footholds in the region via Hungary. DEC set up a joint venture to build minicomputers there, and GE bought a 50-percent stake in Tungsram Company, a formerly state-owned Hungarian light-bulb concern.[18]

Operating in global markets means adjusting to disruptions created by governmental actions. For example, the Chinese government decreed several years ago that canned beverages are wasteful and must be banned from all state functions and banquets. To say the least, the decision was troublesome for companies such as Coca-Cola, PepsiCo, and Continental Can, all of which have operations in China. In addition, China doubled tariffs on aluminum and other materials imported for producing cans, and then announced plans to impose a new tax on canned-drink consumption.[19]

Governmental attitudes toward international marketing vary significantly from one country to another and are reflected most visibly in the degree to which they restrict trade. The most common barriers to trade include tariffs, quotas, and standards.

- *Tariffs.* A **tariff** is a tax imposed by a government on goods entering its borders. Tariffs are used to generate revenue, to discourage the importation of goods, and to penalize uncooperative trading partners. For example, when U.S. government officials believed that the European Union was discriminating against U.S. citrus fruit, they retaliated with a 25 to 40 percent increase in the duties on $30 million worth of pasta being imported from Europe. The U.S. Tariff Code now contains more than 8,000 rates on items from vitamin A to color TVs.[20] Tariffs require constant monitoring and analysis.

- *Import quotas.* An **import quota** is a limit placed on a particular product coming into a country. Products limited by quotas may be subject to tariffs as well. How-

**tariff**
A tax imposed by a government on goods entering its borders

**import quota**
A monetary or quantity limit placed on a product coming into a country

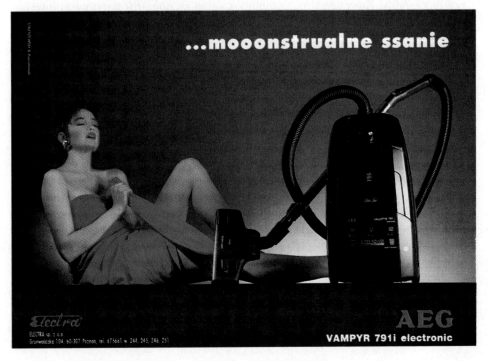

...monster suction.
Vampire 791i.

**Exhibit 2.8**
**REACHING NEW MARKETS IN EASTERN EUROPE**
The German manufacturer AEG targeted the growing consumer market in Poland with this ad for a vacuum cleaner.

## MARKETERS CATCH THE "GREEN" WAVE

Like the other elements of the marketing environment, social values change over time. To ensure continued success, marketers and their products must change along with society. In the late 1980s, social values converged to support preservation of nature and its resources. In response, many consumer and industrial marketers started modifying existing products and creating new, more environmentally safe products. Customers increasingly concerned about pollution, the deteriorating ozone layer, overflowing landfills, and indiscriminate logging welcomed these so-called green products.

That change in attitudes and purchasing behavior had serious consequences for marketers of packaging materials, particularly plastics. Demand for plastics waned as con-

**MARKETING IN ACTION**

sumers migrated to other kinds of packaging. To bring customers back, plastics processors started developing products that environmentally conscious consumers would buy, such as biodegradable and recyclable plastics. Warner-Lambert Company, for one, has invented a plastic made with vegetable starch for faster decomposition.

The changed attitude toward packaging also affected Procter & Gamble, whose products and packaging are responsible for 1 percent of the solid waste in the United States. The company started packaging its Spic and Span cleanser in bottles made of recycled plastic. It also reformulated its Downy fabric softener for packaging in a refillable carton that requires 25 percent as much packaging as the traditional formulation.

New-product development is particularly important for marketers of products perceived as environmentally dangerous. For marketers of Freon cooling compound (a chemical believed harmful to the ozone layer and widely used in refrigeration equipment and air conditioners), developing substitutes became a top priority. Competitors in the Freon market—Du Pont, Allied-Signal, and Pennwalt Corporation—all launched research-and-development programs. Du Pont, inventor of Freon, was the

---

ever, quotas tend to increase prices even more than tariffs, and once a quota is filled, the product may be unavailable at any price.

- *Standards.* Governments establish various standards to protect health, safety, and product quality. However, they sometimes serve as nontariff barriers to international marketing (both intentionally and unintentionally). Sales of everything from jams to pharmaceuticals to cars can be controlled by government standards. For instance, the postal and telecommunications administrations in the European Union (EU), a group of European nations that have formed an economic union to promote trade and industry among themselves, are developing uniform standards for equipment that could create new trade barriers for other countries. Even a relatively small detail (such as a battery cable specification) could prevent a foreign-made product from being sold in the EU.[21] Like tariffs and import quotas, standards change continuously, so they're another key environmental factor that marketers must monitor.

## Regulatory Elements

**regulatory elements**
Factors in the marketing environment, specifically laws and regulations, that govern pricing, distribution, promotion, and product decisions

One of the most complex parts of the marketing environment is the area influenced by **regulatory elements,** which include laws and regulations on pricing, joint marketing agreements, distribution and product labeling, packaging, branding, liability, and other marketing issues. As Exhibit 2.9 shows, a number of federal laws restrict marketing activities in the United States. Marketers are subject to the control and scrutiny of federal, state, and local bodies through thousands of regulations that have evolved over many decades of lawmaking. Through the years, layers and lay-

first to patent an environmentally safe substitute. Now, the marketing challenge for Du Pont and others in the Freon market is to move buyers from Freon to substitutes without losing customer confidence or market share.

*The Deja Shoe is made from recycled materials.*

For all the good it promises, green marketing has had some controversies. Some companies attempted to capitalize on consumer interest in the environment without actually doing much for the environment. Consumers grew suspicious of environmental claims. In one survey, more than a quarter of the respondents said environmental claims in advertising weren't believable, and another two-thirds said the claims were only somewhat believable. Some environmental claims in advertising have even drawn the legal attention of governmental regulators. New York City's consumer affairs office calls its cases "green collar" fraud, and has accused several advertisers of making environmental claims that were misleading or false. Prosecutors at the state and federal levels have slapped makers of diapers, trash bags, and aerosol products with consumer fraud lawsuits.

Even the best-intentioned green marketers were running into problems with terminology. Consumers weren't exactly sure what all the terms meant, and many marketers weren't either. The FTC recently helped everyone by issuing more precise definitions for such common terms as *recyclable* and *biodegradable*. With consistent terms in place, manufacturers now have a better idea of what they can and can't say, and consumers will have a better idea of what the terms mean.

## APPLY YOUR KNOWLEDGE

**1.** How did changing consumer attitudes about the natural environment affect plastics marketers?

**2.** How can you be sure that a company's interest in the environment isn't just a marketing gimmick?

## Exhibit 2.9    KEY MARKETING LEGISLATION

| Act | Year | Application |
|---|---|---|
| Sherman | 1890 | Prohibits monopolization and unreasonable restraint of trade |
| Clayton | 1914 | Outlaws anticompetitive activities such as exclusive dealing and the tying of a sale to the purchaser's promise not to buy competitive products |
| Federal Trade Commission | 1914 | Prohibits unfair competition and deceptive practices in interstate commerce |
| Robinson-Patman | 1936 | Amends the Clayton Act to prohibit price discrimination under various circumstances |
| Wheeler-Lea | 1938 | Prohibits unfair and deceptive practices regardless of whether competitors are damaged |
| Celler-Kefauver Antimerger | 1950 | Prohibits stock purchases and corporate acquisitions that reduce competition |
| Fair Packaging and Labeling | 1967 | Mandates that consumer-product labels identify the product, the supplier's name and address, and (when relevant) the serving size |
| Truth in Lending | 1968 | Requires financial institutions to disclose loan terms and regulates advertising of terms |
| Fair Credit Reporting | 1970 | Controls the kinds of information placed in credit reports and how credit-reporting agencies may use the reports |
| Consumer Product Safety | 1972 | Creates the Consumer Product Safety Commission, which sets safety standards for many consumer products |
| Consumer Goods Pricing | 1975 | Prohibits certain pricing agreements between retailers and manufacturers |
| Nutrition Labeling and Education Act | 1990 | Requires uniformity in nutrition labeling by food manufacturers |

Certain pieces of legislation have had a significant impact on marketing. These are a few of the most prominent.

ers of regulations have sprung up, with individual regulations uncoordinated at best and contradictory at worst. Dozens of governmental agencies, often with overlapping authority, enforce the regulations, adding to marketers' confusion about their regulatory responsibilities.

Although the complexity of the regulatory elements makes it tough to honor all the relevant regulations, marketers must strive for compliance. It's not uncommon for companies to stray accidentally, but as with any law, ignorance is no excuse. The consequences for blunders might be as slight as public embarrassment for the marketing company or as serious as prison terms for the marketing executives who authorized the breach. Therefore, it's extremely important to understand the regulatory environment and meet its demands. Also, marketers doing business in other countries must adhere to the local rules, laws, and regulations. For example, the EC Commission accused Coca-Cola of anticompetitive practices because it was giving Italian restaurant chains special rebates for selling its soft drinks exclusively. Though Coca-Cola insisted it had not broken the law, it did finally agree to alter its European marketing practices.[22]

Regulations may be an expensive headache at times, but marketers often welcome them because they prevent unscrupulous competitors from gaining unfair advantages. When the Chinese government imposed rules for accuracy and scientific supportability on medical advertising in 1992, legitimate marketers were pleased. Kenny Ho of the Dentsu, Young & Rubicam ad agency explained that the new rules will help stop dishonest advertising and allow his clients to compete more effectively.[23]

## REGULATORY EVOLUTION IN THE UNITED STATES

The tangled web of regulatory elements has evolved gradually. The easiest way to study the evolution is to look at four major eras of U.S. regulation that have unfolded in the last century. The first era, lasting from 1890 through 1914, created a wave of federal antimonopoly laws that included the Sherman Act, the Clayton Act, and the Federal Trade Commission Act. The vision behind such laws was to keep powerful marketers from restraining trade, putting competitors out of business, and generally monopolizing industries.[24]

The second regulatory era, which coincided with the Great Depression of the 1930s, spawned the Robinson-Patman Act and other laws that fortified independent retailers against the growing strength of retail chains. Enacted by the federal government in 1936, Robinson-Patman made it illegal for marketers to sell the same product to two customers at different prices if that would stand in the way of free competition.

From the 1950s through the 1970s, the third era of lawmaking took yet another tack, focusing on consumer protection. Laws enacted in this era include the Fair Packaging and Labeling Act, which mandates specific product and supplier information on consumer-goods labels, and the Fair Credit Reporting Act, which regulates how reporting agencies collect consumer credit information and prescribes how they may use it.[25]

The final, ongoing era in the evolution of regulation started in the late 1970s. Its central theme is deregulation, something that has dramatically changed the financial services, telecommunications, and transportation industries. In the telecommunications business, for instance, the federal government broke up AT&T in 1982 to allow other companies to compete for long-distance telephone business. Companies such as MCI and Sprint quickly entered the market, and price emerged as a key competitive issue.[26] But deregulation wasn't all bad for AT&T; it allowed AT&T to enter the market for computers and other goods at the same time that it lost its monopoly on long-distance phone service (see Exhibit 2.10).

The government's position on regulation is largely a response to pressure from consumers, businesses, and other interested parties. Marketers should anticipate changes in the government's regulatory stance if public opinion is changing. The

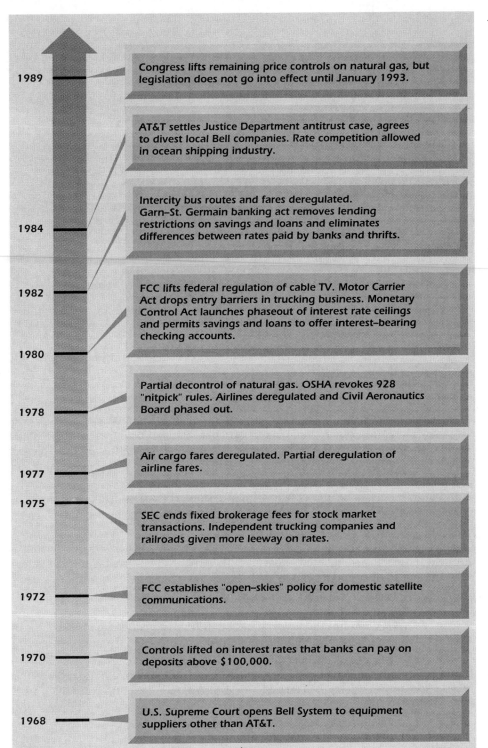

1989 — Congress lifts remaining price controls on natural gas, but legislation does not go into effect until January 1993.

AT&T settles Justice Department antitrust case, agrees to divest local Bell companies. Rate competition allowed in ocean shipping industry.

1984 — Intercity bus routes and fares deregulated. Garn–St. Germain banking act removes lending restrictions on savings and loans and eliminates differences between rates paid by banks and thrifts.

1982 — FCC lifts federal regulation of cable TV. Motor Carrier Act drops entry barriers in trucking business. Monetary Control Act launches phaseout of interest rate ceilings and permits savings and loans to offer interest–bearing checking accounts.

1980 —

1978 — Partial decontrol of natural gas. OSHA revokes 928 "nitpick" rules. Airlines deregulated and Civil Aeronautics Board phased out.

1977 — Air cargo fares deregulated. Partial deregulation of airline fares.

1975 — SEC ends fixed brokerage fees for stock market transactions. Independent trucking companies and railroads given more leeway on rates.

1972 — FCC establishes "open–skies" policy for domestic satellite communications.

1970 — Controls lifted on interest rates that banks can pay on deposits above $100,000.

1968 — U.S. Supreme Court opens Bell System to equipment suppliers other than AT&T.

**Exhibit 2.10**
**THE DEREGULATION TIME LINE**
Between the late 1960s and 1990 the U.S. government gradually deregulated the telecommunications, transportation, and finance industries.

Nutrition Labeling and Education Act of 1990 (which wasn't finalized until 1994) forced food marketers to adopt standardized nutrition labels (see Exhibit 2.11). It cost manufacturers millions of dollars but created a business bonanza for food-test laboratories; one lab president referred to the new law as the "National Laboratories Employment Act."[27] U.S. airlines have lost billions of dollars in recent years as price became their primary competitive weapon and fare wars drove many deep into the red. TWA chairman William Howard urged the government to reconsider some form of minimum fares to prevent desperate competitors from dragging the entire industry down.[28]

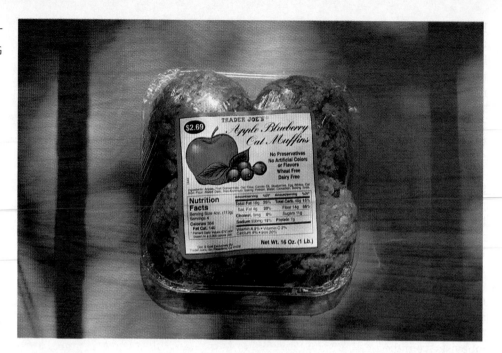

**Exhibit 2.11
NEW LABELING
REGULATIONS**
Recent changes in U.S. food-labeling regulations required marketers to provide standardized nutrition information on their products.

## REGULATORY AGENCIES

Innumerable regulatory agencies dictate how marketers may produce, price, promote, and distribute their products. Some of these agencies make decisions that affect many industries; others hone in on particular kinds of businesses. The Federal Trade Commission (FTC) is an agency with cross-industry authority over promotional claims. It can act against any marketer that uses unfair or deceptive methods, including false advertising and misleading labeling and pricing.

In contrast, the Food and Drug Administration (FDA) controls only three industries: food, drugs, and cosmetics. The agency monitors packages and labels for these products to ensure truth in marketing, and it can also authorize recalls of these products.[29] Also, the FDA has considerable power over new food, drug, and cosmetic product development. Pharmaceutical companies cannot market a new drug without FDA approval, and in some cases, they must gain approval to change dosages.[30] Here are a few more federal agencies that influence marketing:

- The Federal Communications Commission (FCC) regulates communication by wire, radio, and television and influences the prices of local telephone service plus some aspects of broadcast advertising
- The Environmental Protection Agency (EPA) enforces antipollution standards that can affect product design, production, and distribution.
- The U.S. Patent and Trademark Office grants exclusive marketing rights to marketers of original products.

Companies must also keep up with rulings and directives from various state and local agencies. These offices frequently regulate the sale and marketing of utilities, alcoholic beverages, and financial services. State laws cover antitrust, franchisor-franchisee relations, advertising claims, hours of operation, product labeling, and other marketing issues.[31]

## THE IMPACT OF MARKETING ON REGULATIONS

Marketers don't have to sit passively and let these regulatory (and political) forces affect their businesses. They can become active participants in the process. Businesses and nonprofit organizations see three main reasons for developing close ties to elected and appointed officials. First, a politician is unlikely to vote for laws that hurt important constituents such as the companies that supported his or her election campaign or that employ large numbers of voters. Second, politicians wield a lot of power over trade relations, so they can create a favorable environment for international marketing. Third, elected officials influence government spending and may influence the awarding of contracts for items ranging from weapon systems, which the Defense Department buys, to light bulbs, which the General Services Administration purchases in massive amounts. Developing ties to government officials is a touchy ethical issue, and both marketers and officials need to make sure that ethical standards are not violated.

In the domestic arena, marketers use several methods to influence the regulatory elements of the marketing environment. They contribute to candidates' campaign funds, endorse candidates who have supported their industry's interests in the past, and sometimes even run political ads for favorite candidates. Another way marketers try to influence regulation is by lobbying against proposed laws that could hurt their businesses and by lobbying for efforts to revise or strike existing laws that seem to threaten their industry.

International marketers also lobby politicians and government officials in other countries. Members of the European Union tried to throw international franchisors a curveball recently. A proposed rule would have eliminated corporate control over the franchisees' product selection, use of corporate logos, and suppliers. In response, lobbyists from the International Franchising Association (IFA) and U.S. franchisors such as Pizza Hut and Midas Muffler persuaded EC officials that franchisors must control some aspects of their franchisees' business.[32]

## NONGOVERNMENTAL REGULATION

Despite the many federal, state, and local rules, marketing issues periodically fall between the cracks of governmental regulation. That's where trade associations and public service groups step in. For example, the Council of Better Business Bureaus (BBB), which includes member-supported bureaus across the United States, promotes honest marketing practices and arbitrates consumer complaints. Meanwhile, the National Advertising Review Board (NARB), a related group, monitors advertising and tells the public and the FTC when it finds false or misleading claims in national ads.

The BBB and NARB monitor many industries, but other groups set standards solely for their own industry. **Self-regulation** occurs when trade groups promote certain marketing methods or approaches for companies in their business. The National Association of Securities Dealers (NASD), for example, requires its members to reveal which mutual funds charge extra fees when dealers list the funds in newspaper tables.[33] Self-regulation has also reined in the marketing of legal services, such as when the American Board of Trial Advocates came out against lawyers using direct-mail advertising.[34]

**self-regulation**
A form of nongovernmental regulation in which industry groups or leaders promote specific marketing approaches

## INTERNATIONAL REGULATORY ELEMENTS

The regulatory aspect of international marketing is three-dimensional, encompassing U.S. law for companies operating in other countries, international regulations, and host-nation law. International marketers spend a great deal of time and energy trying to stay current on these regulations, which differ from country to country.

U.S. LAW    When a U.S. company sets up operations or markets outside the United States, it is not necessarily exempt from U.S. law. Three primary issues can subject U.S. companies to legal restrictions on international marketing activities: national security, antitrust matters, and bribery.

National security issues include any activity that threatens the security of the United States. In an international marketing situation, that can mean restricting the sale of certain goods to unfriendly nations. For example, during the Cold War years, Caterpillar Tractor waited for over a year to get permission from the U.S. government to sell pipe-laying equipment to the Soviet Union.[35] A number of high-technology products, including certain types of computers, communications gear, and signal-measuring instruments, remain on restricted export status to countries such as Iraq.

The U.S. government is particularly careful about U.S. companies forming partnerships with foreign companies that already compete in the United States. If officials determine that a pending partnership between a foreign company and a U.S. company would create an economic giant that could monopolize the U.S. market, it will prohibit the transaction. Some international marketers believe U.S. antitrust laws put them at a disadvantage in the global marketplace. W. B. Seaton of American President Companies, for example, is convinced that U.S. freight transport companies such as his could become more competitive with Japanese companies if antitrust laws would permit U.S. competitors to join forces and attack the foreign market together.[36]

Bribery is one of the most troublesome issues affecting international marketing because it is considered ethical in some cultures and freely practiced in some countries as a means of gaining influence and closing sales. In 1977 the United States passed the Foreign Corrupt Practices Act (FCPA), making it illegal for companies from the United States to bribe officials in foreign countries. However, since bribery is still a commonly accepted business practice in some parts of the world, U.S. companies believe that the FCPA puts them at a competitive disadvantage.

INTERNATIONAL TREATIES AND AGREEMENTS    Although no enforceable body of global law exists, certain treaties and agreements are respected by a number of countries and influence international business operations. These include the *Friendship, Commerce, and Navigation (FCN) treaties* and the *General Agreement on Tariffs and Trade (GATT)*. An FCN agreement defines the rights of firms doing business in the host country. The GATT treaty provides an international forum in which countries can negotiate trade barriers. For instance, among the most contentious issues facing GATT negotiators in recent years are government-provided agricultural subsidies that let farmers compete at artificially low prices. Other countries trying to compete in subsidized markets complain that the subsidies put them at a disadvantage. GATT talks continue from year to year, as negotiators try to iron out old issues and find solutions for new issues that affect marketers.

One of the newest international agreements to affect marketing is the North American Free Trade Agreement (NAFTA), which went into effect in 1994. NAFTA was designed to make trade between Canada, the United States, and Mexico easier and more efficient. Supporters hope that by removing restrictions on imports and on the flow of investment into manufacturing and service businesses, the agreement will help the economies of all three countries.[37]

HOST-NATION LAW    When marketers do business in other countries, those host nations have numerous laws that affect the entry of goods, pricing, joint ventures and licensing agreements, product development, and promotion. Many of these are similar to U.S. laws, but many countries have specific variations. In Germany, for instance, advertisements cannot claim a company's products are the best, because such claims violate a German law that forbids discrediting competitors.[38] Many countries arbitrarily establish laws and regulations that often take international marketers by surprise. For example, when Venezuela ran short of foreign currencies, it ordered domestic companies to extend payments on their foreign debt for several years. Union Carbide was owed $8 to $10 million by its Venezuelan customers at the time but received only interest payments for four or five years.[39]

The *lack* of laws in host countries can also be a problem. United States patents and copyrights, for example, are not observed in some Asian and Latin American countries. In particular, software and pharmaceutical companies lose millions of dollars in sales because foreign competitors are allowed to pirate their technologies and produce duplicate versions of their products, which are sold at lower prices.

The North American Free Trade Agreement (NAFTA) helped create a common market across Canada, the United States, and Mexico.

# Technological Elements

An exciting and rapidly changing aspect of the marketing environment involves advances in **technology,** the application of scientific and engineering developments to specific problems. Technological changes have completely recast the world in just the last century, bringing both significant new benefits and serious new problems to humanity.

Technology has brought us vaccines against polio, measles, the flu, and dozens of other diseases that, until fairly recently in human history, could wipe out or cripple an entire generation. Thanks to advances in aviation, we can fly safely and quickly to other cities and countries. We can use our telephones and fax machines to communicate with faraway businesses, friends, and relatives. And developments in computers have increased our efficiency in areas ranging from banking to engineering to advertising.

On the downside, technology has brought us acid rain, air and noise pollution, contaminated waterways, overflowing landfills, and animal exploitation in product testing. There are so many chemicals in the typical U.S. home that some people are allergic to their own houses and furnishings. In Eastern Europe, things are even worse. Doctors believe air pollution causes as many as 10 percent of all deaths in Hungary, and in Poland pollution has sent the heart disease and infant mortality rates soaring.[40]

All these changes, positive and negative, hold serious consequences for marketers. Technology creates new products but also renders some products obsolete. Some advances in technology are so complicated that promotions have to emphasize education so that potential customers know what the product is about. Here are the major ways technology affects the elements of the marketing mix.

**technology**
The result of applying scientific and engineering knowledge to practical problems

## TECHNOLOGY AND THE PRODUCT ELEMENT

The element of the marketing mix that technology affects most visibly is the product. Technology affects products in two ways: by changing the way marketers design and make their products, and by changing the products themselves. Marketers of goods ranging from microprocessors to evening gowns now use computer software to design their products, and automated systems have radically changed manufacturing.

The same technologies that make these changes possible have created entirely new product categories. Microsoft founder Bill Gates took advantage of the advent of personal computing, and his company now produces software used by millions of people around the world. Truly new technologies, such as broadcasting and personal computing, don't erupt often, but when they do they create revolutionary products such as televisions and personal computers, and markets for such products develop quickly.[41]

More commonly, technology fuels the development of evolutionary products that erode demand for existing products. For example, marketers of high-performance plastics sell their products to automakers as an alternative to steel. Similarly, superconductive materials will gradually start competing with materials currently used to build supercomputers, medical scanners, radar systems, and other high-tech products.[42] In the consumer-goods arena, video games emerged as a substitute for traditional toys. Sales of video games and other high-tech toys have been growing much faster than low-tech toys for nearly a decade.[43]

## TECHNOLOGY AND THE PRICING ELEMENT

Technology is changing pricing as well. In the last few decades, marketing managers have replaced their adding machines with calculators and then with computers, which crunch out supply, demand, and competitive pricing numbers and even establish prices for their products.

Distribution intermediaries such as retailers also use technology to manage pricing. For example, some grocery stores display product prices on liquid-crystal screens attached to the shelves. The liquid-crystal screens and the store's cash registers are linked to the store's main computer. When the grocer updates prices in the computer, the liquid-crystal screens and cash registers instantly reflect those changes. The interconnected system updates prices more quickly, eliminates price-label switching by consumers, and reduces employee pricing errors.[44]

## TECHNOLOGY AND THE DISTRIBUTION ELEMENT

Technological advances are streamlining distribution and, in some cases, creating entirely new channels of distribution. Transit companies and department stores are starting to use automated teller machines to distribute fare tickets and gift certificates.[45] Citicorp distributes financial services to residential customers with its "enhanced telephone," a combination phone and computer terminal with which customers can pay bills, move funds between accounts, obtain loans, and conduct other transactions.[46] Meanwhile, videotex services, on-line computer databases, and 900 phone numbers have emerged as new distribution channels in the marketing of information. *USA Today* can achieve its goal of being a nationwide daily newspaper because the technology exists to transmit the newspaper electronically across the country every day.

Products using new technologies also change things for retailers and other distribution intermediaries. These changes can be particularly dramatic for retailers that focus on narrow product categories, because one small advance in technology can affect most or all of their business. For example, as point-and-shoot cameras became popular, camera shops' sales of interchangeable lenses and add-on flashes dropped because the newer cameras don't need such accessories. To make up for the lost business, many shops started selling video equipment and other nontraditional goods and services.[47]

## TECHNOLOGY AND THE PROMOTION ELEMENT

The availability of laptop computers greatly changed personal selling for marketers of products such as pharmaceuticals, insurance, and food. Rather than calling customers back later with important information, salespeople can use their laptops to quote prices and check the status of orders while sitting in the customer's office. The result has been significant time savings and happier customers.

For instance, to market food to institutional customers such as corporate cafeterias, J. P. Foodservice has equipped its sales representatives with laptops to enhance field sales. The rep uses the laptop while with the customer to check the order against J. P.'s inventory. If an item is unavailable, the computer finds a substitute automatically, saving time for both the sales rep and the customer.[48]

Advertising has also benefited from technological advances. Radio and television offered new ways to entertain people, but they also provided new advertising media. More recently, video technology has created a new ad medium: marketers distribute videocassettes touting their products or, more commonly, place commercials on videotapes of movies. Meanwhile, cable technology has spawned shopping by TV. The development of interactive television promises yet another medium (see Exhibit 2.12).

Marketers are using technology to design narrowly focused sales promotions. Quaker Oats, for example, gains product-preference information on specific customers by tracking their coupon-redemption patterns. The company mails consumers coupons coded with household identification numbers, and when a customer redeems a coupon, the supermarket's electronic scanner notifies Quaker. Armed with information on which products particular households buy, Quaker makes follow-up mailings of coupons, each tailored to the household's purchasing habits.[49]

**Exhibit 2.12
PROMOTIONS TAKE
ADVANTAGE OF NEW
TECHNOLOGY**
Interactive technologies such
as the system used at Levi
Strauss stores provide new
ways to promote products and
deliver information to buyers.

## Social Elements

Society plays an important role in the marketing process. **Social elements** are the characteristics of contemporary society that influence how consumers perceive, purchase, and use products. Social elements can swiftly change a market's dynamics, creating and destroying opportunities along the way. These elements include values, beliefs, traditions, cultural identities, and lifestyles.

**social elements**
Factors in the marketing environment that correlate with social trends, including changes in consumer values and tastes

### SHIFTING DEMOGRAPHICS

The most straightforward way to quantify social trends is through **demographics,** describing a market using variables such as age, gender, occupation, education, religion, race, nationality, income, and household type. Changes in demographics reveal shifts in the average consumer's age, income, or education level and in the concentration of consumers in regions and occupational categories. The three most significant topics in U.S. demographics in recent years are the baby-boom generation, the aging of the U.S. population, and the changing roles of women and men.

**demographics**
A system of describing a population's objective attributes such as age, income, education, and marital status

BABY BOOMERS    A major demographic change in the post–World War II era was the **baby boom,** a period of rapid population expansion that lasted from 1945 through 1964. During those years, 79 million babies were born in the United States.[50] As they grew up, product markets matured along with them. During the late 1940s and early 1950s, marketers of strollers, cribs, toys, diaper services, and infant clothes and furniture thrived. Book publishers also found a ready market for child-rearing manuals written by experts like Dr. Benjamin Spock. By the 1960s the boomers had grown into teenagers, and the markets for record albums, denim jeans, education, and other teen-oriented products exploded. In the 1990s, middle-aged boomers are stimulating the markets for major items such as houses, cars, and appliances. And their children are once again fueling the markets for child and teen products.

**baby boom**
The increase in births that started in 1945, when World War II ended, and extended into the early 1960s

AGING AMERICA    Combined with a low birth rate and improved health care in recent years, the aging of the baby boomers has gradually increased the average age of people in the United States. In the 1980s, the number of 25- to 44-year-olds jumped 30 percent, the number of 10- to 24-year-olds dropped 12 percent, and the number of people 65 or older grew 23 percent.[51] Just as the demographic baby bulge fueled demand for diapers and other infant-care products in the 1950s, the growing number of elderly will cause a spike in the demand for health and elder care, financial planning, and tourism in the first decades of the twenty-first century.[52]

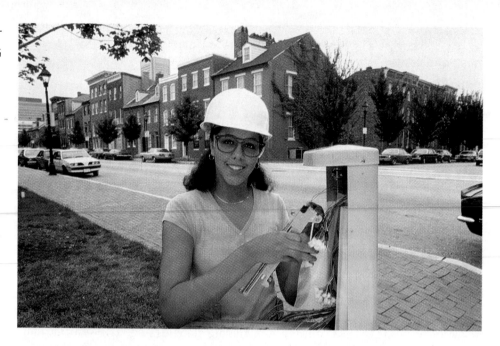

**Exhibit 2.13
RESPONDING TO
LIFESTYLE SHIFTS**
As more and more women appear in jobs and other roles once held exclusively or predominantly by men, marketers need to adjust their plans and strategies to accomodate these lifestyles.

ROLES OF WOMEN AND MEN    Another critical demographic shift is the movement of women into the work force. Projections indicate that by the turn of the century, 65 percent of women aged 16 to 68 and 90 percent of women with children younger than 6 years of age will work outside their homes. The shift has had a profound effect on marketers of both consumer and organizational products, driving up the demand for child care and for products that save time in cooking, housecleaning, washing, ironing, and other homemaking tasks. Day-care centers have sprung up. Supermarkets have installed salad bars to help harried working parents save time, and food companies have come up with quick-to-fix frozen and boxed entrees. Marketers of cleaning products have developed their own time-saving products, including formulations that require less-frequent bathroom and kitchen cleaning (see Exhibit 2.13).[53]

Meanwhile, the advancement of women to positions of purchasing power within their companies has changed some organizational marketers' priorities. In 1990 women held more than 39 percent of management, executive, and administrative positions in the information and service industries. Women represented 30 percent of the marketing executives at Procter & Gamble, 30 percent of the managers at Apple Computer, and 40 percent of Apple's professionals.[54] At the same time, women were starting their own businesses at unprecedented rates.

## GROWING CULTURAL DIVERSITY

Another important social element in the United States is the continuing growth of ethnic minority groups. For example, between 1985 and 2000, the percentage of Americans with Hispanic origins is projected to grow from 7.2 percent to 9.4 percent. Between 2000 and 2080 the percentage will increase further, to 20.4 percent.[55] Other groups continue to immigrate as well. Between 1980 and 1990, for instance, the Asian population of the United States increased 65 percent.[56]

The country's changing cultural texture creates marketing opportunities. According to Ed Escobedo, an expert on marketing to Hispanic consumers, "People have to start realizing that these new immigrants have a lot of buying power." Hispanic grocery shoppers in Los Angeles, for example, spend an average of $20 more per week on groceries than other customers. Realizing what a lucrative segment the Hispanic market is, the Mars Market in suburban Los Angeles hired Spanish-speaking employees and started hosting mariachi fiestas and other promotions to attract Hispanic families. The store also changed its product selection to appeal more to Hispanic tastes, replacing London broil with Mexican *biftec* and offering freshly baked tortillas. "The payoff is that we have built credibility with these people over all these years," said the market's owner. His strategy was so successful in drawing Hispanic shoppers that Mars's competitors, the chain supermarkets, are now deploying their own strategies to lure these shoppers to their stores.[57]

## CHANGING VALUES

Values are among the most intriguing and dynamic social elements. As demographics shift and the ethnic balance realigns, the way consumers think and live changes. As the average age rises, more people are concerned about basic issues of family, health, and spirituality. The health and fitness consciousness of the 1980s prompted many changes for marketers of food, beverages, cigarettes, and sports and recreation products. In 1989 alone, food marketers introduced 218 new products containing oat bran, an additive thought at the time to reduce blood cholesterol levels. By the end of that year, consumers could buy oat bran–laced licorice, beer, potato chips, pasta, pretzels, tortilla chips, waffles, and, of course, cereals and muffins. Health concerns about fried food prompted Kentucky Fried Chicken to change its public name to KFC in 1991, and then to begin offering roasted chicken in 1993.[58]

Another health issue, cigarette smoking, emerged as an important social issue in the 1980s. The negative publicity surrounding smoking, together with antismoking regulations, clearly hurt U.S. tobacco sales. The volume of cigarettes manufacturers shipped to distributors declined steadily during the 1980s.[59] However, smoking is still on the rise in Eastern Europe, and the recently opened markets in those countries presented U.S. and British tobacco firms with an opportunity for growth.[60]

The condom market is another good example of how social values affect marketing. For many years, most publishers and all broadcasters refused to carry condom advertising because of the product's sexual nature. However, when the AIDS epidemic broke out, attitudes about sex and health changed so much that many magazines and even some radio and TV stations now accept condom ads. Carter-Wallace, which markets Trojan condoms, has responded to the social shift with an aggressive marketing campaign that includes skywriting and educational programs in schools.[61] Changing social values also affect nonprofit marketers, as groups involved with AIDS, abortion, gun control, family planning, and drug-abuse education have discovered in recent years (see Exhibit 2.14).

**Exhibit 2.14**
**ADVERTISING AND CHANGING SOCIAL STANDARDS**
Advertising reflects society's changing values; smoking is viewed by fewer and fewer people as an acceptable health risk.

TEENAGE BOYS ARE SMOKING IN THE BOY'S BATHROOM AT SCHOOL. ONE OF THE BOYS HAS A GAS MASK ON AND IS READING FROM A CIGARETTE PACKAGE.
BOY WITH GAS MASK: "You know, smoking causes a wide array of damage to the human body. Here's just a partial list of the side effects: number one, lung cancer; number two, heart disease; number three, emphysema. I mean, asthma, stroke, bronchitis, pneumonia, *death*."
ONE OF THE SMOKERS TAPS HIM ON THE SHOULDER: "Hey man, can I bum a smoke?"
BOY WITH GAS MASK: "Birth defects."
BOY THROWS CIGARETTE PACKAGE ON THE FLOOR AND LEAVES IN DISGUST. SMOKER PICKS IT UP LOOKING FOR A CIGARETTE BUT THROWS IT DOWN WHEN FINDS NONE.

These examples clearly illustrate how powerful values are as a social element. The next section examines ethics and social responsibility in the context of the marketing environment. You'll see how the values of an individual, a company, and an entire society play a role in the marketing profession.

## ETHICS AND SOCIAL RESPONSIBILITY IN THE MARKETING ENVIRONMENT

Individual citizens and marketers have a responsibility to act within legal and ethical constraints. Unlike laws, which are a matter of public record, ethics are situation-specific and impossible to define precisely. Although ethics and laws are often related, it is possible to behave in ways that are legal, yet unethical. Broadly speaking, ethics implies the establishment of a system of conduct that is recognized as correct moral behavior. **Marketing ethics** is the application of ethical evaluation to marketing strategies and tactics. To help their employees make the right ethical choices, many companies have created formal codes outlining what management views as ethical—and unethical—behavior. These codes often cover conflicts of interest, the giving and receiving of business gifts, and other scenarios marketing managers face. Penalties for disobeying the codes range from a warning to police arrest.[62] Some trade associations have written their own codes of ethics, including the American Marketing Association (see Exhibit 2.15). Marketers who violate the AMA code risk losing their membership in a prestigious and influential association.

Social responsibility is closely related to marketing ethics and, like ethics, is integral to the marketing environment. **Social responsibility** is the marketing organization's commitment to the welfare of its customers and the general public. Here are some criteria that marketers use to differentiate their products as socially responsible:[63]

**marketing ethics**
The moral sensibility that guides marketing choices and activities

**social responsibility**
Marketers' duty to enhance the welfare of customers and the general public through their products

- Ecological impact (nonpolluting)
- Social impact (healthy and safe)
- Product performance
- Product extensions, such as packaging and service
- Product information
- Product design
- Product embellishment, including advertising and personal selling approaches

Ultimately the marketer must weigh both profit potential *and* the various aspects of social responsibility to create an optimal marketing mix.

### Marketing Ethics

Consider two categories of ethics topics. The first is the *ethical dilemma,* which consists of two conflicting, but arguably valid, sides to an issue. Such dilemmas can be particularly difficult in international marketing if the ethics and values of one country clash with those of another country. A classic marketing dilemma is whether tobacco companies should be allowed to advertise a legal product. Allowing them to do so exposes people to unhealthy products, but banning advertising violates their freedom of speech and ability to do business.

The second category of marketing ethics covers a variety of *ethical lapses,* instances when companies have made unethical and sometimes illegal decisions. It is important not to confuse ethical dilemmas, which are unresolved interpretations of ethical issues, with ethical lapses, which are simply cases of unethical behavior. For example, a beer company's desire to advertise a product that can result in alcoholism is an ethical dilemma, but a defense contractor's deceptive pricing on a Pen-

**Exhibit 2.15    AMA CODE OF ETHICS**

Members of the American Marketing Association (AMA) are committed to ethical professional conduct. They have joined together in subscribing to this Code of Ethics embracing the following topics:

**Responsibilities of the Marketer**
Marketers must accept responsibility for the consequences of their activities and make every effort to ensure that their decisions, recommendations, and actions function to identify, serve, and satisfy all relevant publics—customers, organizations, and society. The marketer's professional conduct must be guided by

1. The basic rule of professional ethics: not knowingly to do harm
2. The adherence to all applicable laws and regulations
3. The accurate representation of their education, training, and experience
4. The active support, practice, and promotion of this Code of Ethics

**Honesty and Fairness**
Marketers shall uphold and advance the integrity, honor, and dignity of the marketing profession by

1. Being honest in serving consumers, clients, employees, suppliers, distributors, and the public
2. Communicating in a truthful and forthright manner
3. Not knowingly participating in any conflict of interest without prior notice to all parties involved
4. Establishing, equitable fee schedules, including the payment or receipt of compensation only for usual, customary, and/or legal marketing exchanges

**Rights and Duties of Parties in the Marketing Exchange Process**

Participants in the marketing exchange process should be able to expect that:

1. Products and services offered are safe and fit for their intended uses
2. Communications about offered products and services are not deceptive
3. All parties intend to discharge their obligations, financial and otherwise, in good faith
4. Appropriate internal methods exist for equitable adjustment and/or redress of grievances concerning purchases

It is understood that the above would include, but is not limited to, the following:

**In the Area of Product Development and Management**

- Disclosure of all substantial risks associated with product or service use
- Identification of any product component substitution that might materially change the product or have an impact on the buyer's purchase decision
- Identification of extra-cost added features

**In the Area of Promotions**

- Avoidance of false and misleading advertising
- Rejection of high-pressure manipulations, or misleading sales tactics
- Avoidance of sales promotions that use deception or manipulation

**In the Area of Distribution**

- Not manipulating the availability of a product for the purpose of exploitation
- Not using coercion in the marketing channel
- Not exerting undue influence over the reseller's choice to handle a product

**In the Area of Pricing**

- Not engaging in price fixing
- Not practicing predatory pricing
- Disclosing the full price associated with any purchase

**In the Area of Marketing Research**

- Prohibiting selling or fundraising under the guise of conducting research
- Maintaining research integrity by avoiding misrepresentation and pertinent omission of research data
- Treating outside clients and suppliers fairly

**Organizational Relationships**
Marketers should be aware of how their behavior may influence or impact on the behavior of others in organizational relationships. They should not demand, encourage, or apply coercion to obtain unethical behavior in their relationships with others, such as employees, suppliers, or customers. Marketers should

1. Apply confidentiality and anonymity in professional relationships with regard to privileged information
2. Meet their obligations and responsibilities in contracts and mutual agreements in a timely manner
3. Avoid taking the work of others, in whole or in part, and representing this work as their own or directly benefiting from it without compensation for or consent of the originator or owner
4. Avoid manipulating to take advantage of situations to maximize personal welfare in a way that unfairly deprives or damages the organization or others

Any AMA member found to be in violation of any provision of this Code of Ethics may have his or her Association membership suspended or revoked.

The American Marketing Association developed this list of guidelines to help its members behave ethically in their work.

## CAN ADULTS LEARN ETHICAL BEHAVIOR?

Throughout this book, you'll get to tackle many of the ethical dilemmas facing today's marketers. Before getting into specific issues, though, here's a topic that is of immediate interest: Is it even possible to teach an adult how to behave ethically? If so, how should it be done?

Two schools of thought on this subject can be found. The first maintains that ethical behavior is learned as a child at home and in religious institutions, so any attempt to teach ethics to adults is doomed. The idea behind this position is that a person's value system and resulting behavior are shaped primarily by parents. The second group insists that ethics can

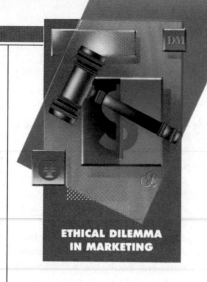

**ETHICAL DILEMMA IN MARKETING**

indeed be taught to adults and that college is a good time to do so.

The assumption that adults can learn ethical behavior raises several points. First, to make any difference in the way you'll conduct your business and your life, your ethical train

ing has to focus on changing *behavior.* Learning about ethical dilemmas and ethical lapses might be interesting and perhaps entertaining, but it doesn't do much good if it doesn't lead to ethical behavior.

Second, some ethical questions are so tangled up in specific marketing and business issues that it's difficult to understand the ethical dilemma if you don't understand the underlying business problem. Although the case-study method is recommended for in-depth analysis of ethical dilemmas, it is sometimes a challenge to grasp the management situation in which the ethical issue is buried. (The ethical dilemmas in this book all address fundamental issues and so don't require detailed understanding of business operations.)

Third, when you have to make a

tagon contract is an ethical lapse. The following sections take a look at the question of ethical dilemmas and then describe some of the more common ethical lapses that show up in marketing today.

### ETHICAL DILEMMAS

Marketers face a number of ethical dilemmas. For example, when doing business in a country where bribes are common, should you play the game too and offer bribes to potential customers or influential officials? Should marketers be allowed to disguise promotions as entertainment, as happens in many children's television shows? Is it deceptive to have products shown in movies, when the viewers are expecting commercial-free entertainment? Should marketers of alcohol, tobacco, and firearms be allowed to advertise at all? Why should people protest tobacco ads when hamburgers, ice cream, and fast cars can also be unhealthy? These are some of the issues you'll learn more about in the special features on ethics that are provided throughout this book.

Ethical dilemmas are not easy to resolve because they often involve trading off the rights or interests of one group for those of another. One example: For many years Virginia Slims sponsored a professional tennis tour for women, even in the face of growing evidence that cigarette smoking causes health problems. Other tobacco marketers and numerous alcoholic beverage marketers sponsor sporting events as well. The government's dilemma is whether to prohibit the sponsorship or to allow the sponsorship to continue. If the government were to prohibit these companies from sponsoring sporting events, the companies would lose a powerful promotional tool and, conceivably, some of their sales revenue. But if the sponsorship is allowed to continue, more and more young people will be exposed to the promotions for decidedly unhealthy products.

How then should you go about addressing an ethical dilemma? Your value system and the collective values of your company will play a big role in how the decision is made. Moreover, the welfare of your customers is always a primary concern.

judgment call, whose value system are you going to use? For example, some countries consider bribery to be standard operating procedure, simply a way to make the wheels of business turn a little faster. But U.S. companies find themselves at a distinct competitive disadvantage in this situation because bribery is considered unethical by most U.S. businesspeople and is, in fact, illegal in the United States. A hot topic in international marketing is the Foreign Corrupt Practices Act, which prohibits U.S. citizens from offering bribes to anybody, even in countries where the practice is accepted. An entire value system is at the center of this law, but some people argue that it is irrelevant in other countries.

Fourth, some of the material written about ethics clouds the issue by failing to draw a distinction between ethical dilemmas and ethical lapses. Ethical lapses and illegal behavior may be difficult to control, but they aren't difficult to understand. The tough issues are the ethical dilemmas, when you are forced to choose between two arguably valid positions.

Regardless of the approach, several goals are important to the teaching of business ethics:

**1.** To help you realize that ethics are an important part of business

**2.** To help you recognize ethical dilemmas and issues

**3.** To relate your sense of moral obligation to marketing dilemmas

**4.** To develop the skills needed to analyze ethical dilemmas

**5.** To reduce ambiguity and disagreement surrounding common dilemmas

**6.** To understand the business issues intertwined with ethical issues

In the dilemmas you'll encounter in this course, you'll have the chance to test your ethical decision making on real-life problems affecting today's marketing professionals.

## WHAT'S YOUR OPINION?

**1.** Can you learn ethics as an adult? If not, what should we do about all the adults with weak ethics who are already working in the business world?
**2.** Do you think ethics should be taught separately or integrated with all relevant college courses?

To help guide you in ethical decision making, you can apply three tests to ethical problems. The first test, based on the principle of utilitarianism, considers a decision by asking, Which course of action will produce the greatest amount of good for the greatest number of people? The second test judges whether a course of action would violate someone else's rights. And the third test judges whether all parties affected by a decision are treated fairly.[64]

Consider the dilemma facing T. E. Haigler, Jr., president of Burroughs Wellcome, the company that markets the antiviral drug AZT to AIDS patients. AZT is one of the most expensive drugs ever sold, with an initial price of $8,000 for a year's supply (recently dropped to around $2,400). Haigler has to balance his firm's need to maintain some level of profit and fund ongoing research with the responsibility of making the drug available to patients. So far, AIDS activists and leaders in Congress think Wellcome has not made the correct ethical choice because the drug is still so expensive. Many people think Wellcome would do more good for a greater number of suffering people if it lowered its price.[65]

## ETHICAL LAPSES

Marketing is not a rigid process in which you do things the same way every time. You're likely to come across situations in marketing research, product development and packaging, distribution, promotion, and pricing that require you to make ethical choices. The choices covered in this section are not ethical dilemmas; you aren't choosing between two defensible positions but between ethical behavior and unethical behavior. You need to be aware of these potential problems because they appear frequently in marketing, and companies don't always make the right choices.

- *Ethical lapses in marketing research.* A common ethical problem occurs in marketing research when outside researchers uncover data that the customer isn't prepared for. The researcher may be tempted to distort the research findings to make them say what the client wants to hear, in the hopes of keeping that customer's business. This is a misrepresentation of the facts and clearly unethical. It can also hurt business by leading the client to kill potentially successful products during test marketing or to launch products that no one will buy. Unethical field-research tactics are also used all too often. For example, researchers sometimes pose as graduate students doing thesis research when they're actually marketers on the prowl for competitive information. With this trick, the researcher gets competitors to reveal information they'd never knowingly tell someone from a competing company.[66]

- *Ethical lapses in product development.* Marketing researchers aren't the only marketing professionals to face potential ethical problems. People involved in product development, packaging, and branding regularly tackle questions of right and wrong. Marketers are ethically bound to provide a basic level of product quality and to meet customers' product specifications. Ethical behavior also dictates the use of brand names that communicate honestly about the product, the use of packaging that realistically portrays product size, and safe and ethical product development techniques.

- *Ethical lapses in distribution.* Like the other elements of the marketing mix, distribution holds its own ethical pitfalls. Fortunately, many of the potential ethical problems involved in distribution are now covered by laws such as those contained in the Robinson-Patman Act. However, producers still force each other off the shelves in retail stores, either directly or indirectly, and products are still transported in dangerous or unhealthy ways (such as hauling toxic chemicals in trucks that also carry food products).

- *Ethical lapses in promotions.* Promotion is the area of marketing in which ethical mistakes are most visible, and perhaps most damaging. Ethics issues play a key role in advertising, personal selling, and other promotional activities because these are the primary methods for disseminating product information. Misleading advertising and false claims by salespeople may be legal in some cases, but they are certainly not ethical. More blatant examples of unethical promotional tactics include bribing purchasing agents with "gifts" in return for purchase orders and creating advertising messages that exploit children, pensioners, or other vulnerable groups. Perhaps because of past errors, advertisers face an increasingly skeptical public: 80 percent of consumers responding to a recent survey characterized advertising as a "deceptive persuader," up from 54 percent in the 1964 version of the survey.[67]

- *Ethical lapses in pricing.* Ethical problems in pricing are a bit easier to avoid because virtually anything that is unethical in pricing is also illegal. The defense industry provides many examples of marketers making unethical, or ethically questionable, pricing choices. One of the largest defense contractors in the nation, General Dynamics, was accused by the secretary of the Navy of systematic pricing fraud. Indictments were handed down against four executives, and the company was banned from government contracts until it proved it could clean up its act.[68]

Companies need to take an active role in preventing ethical lapses. Employees sometimes feel pressured to make unethical choices because they believe their managers want them to, so managers need to make it very clear that unethical behavior will not be tolerated. Of course, top management of the company must first set a good example through its own ethical behavior. Some companies train their employees in ethical decision making and provide handbooks and telephone hotlines to help employees deal with tough issues. General Dynamics took all three of these steps in its efforts to clean up its pricing problem.

## Social Responsibility

The subject of social responsibility is closely allied with marketing ethics. As participants in society, marketers bear a responsibility to serve and protect the general public and the various groups that make it up. That responsibility does not invalidate the profit motive, it simply adds another layer to the process of strategy development. In fact, the cost of social responsibility may be viewed as an investment in the marketer's future success.[69]

Social responsibility differs from ethics in that the motivation for socially responsible deeds is irrelevant. Whether the company recalls a faulty product because it cares about consumers or because of a court order doesn't matter; the recall is socially responsible. On the other hand, an action is ethical only if it's motivated by the desire to do the right thing.[70] Social responsibility also differs from ethics in that it tends to change more quickly. Many of the ethical positions we hold have remained the same for years, but the measures of social responsibility change with the social climate.

For example, the emergence of ecological consciousness among consumers has redefined social responsibility. Many consumers now care whether the products and services they buy cause global warming, air and water pollution, landfill expansion, or depletion of natural resources. Recognizing the connection between this change in awareness and social responsibility, marketers started changing the way they produced and packaged their products, and some even altered their product mix.

McDonald's was under attack for some time from environmental groups for using nondegradable packaging. By 1990 the chain was trashing 1.5 billion cubic feet of polystyrene hamburger cartons and coffee cups annually. Recognizing the social irresponsibility of adding so much plastic to already overburdened landfills, and responding to tremendous outside pressure, the chain decided to drop its familiar polystyrene packaging in favor of paper boxes (even though it had begun a recycling program for the polystyrene and even though some question remains about whether paper or plastic is better for the environment). Some other major chains, notably Burger King, have always used paper.[71]

The same year, General Motors Corporation tacitly acknowledged the social irresponsibility of marketing cars that cause air pollution by announcing its intention to add nonpolluting electric cars to the GM product line. According to a GM executive, the company's goal is to be "the first automobile company since the early days of the auto industry to mass-produce an electric car. We are taking a major step toward helping our country meet its transportation needs and environmental goals."[72]

Two examples vividly illustrate how differently marketers may view social responsibility. The first, a classic case of doing the right thing, comes from Johnson & Johnson. In the early 1980s, that company and seven of its customers were the victims of a criminal who put poison in bottles of Tylenol capsules while the product sat on retail shelves. The seven consumers died. Even though the company was not responsible for the deaths, it spent $50 million to recall all Tylenol capsules. Johnson & Johnson also started a campaign to promote voluntary tamper-evident packaging for over-the-counter pharmaceuticals.

The second example illustrates the other end of the social responsibility spectrum and comes from Ford Motor Company, which was involved in a tragedy of even greater proportions. The design of Ford's Pinto rendered the car vulnerable to collision from behind; upon impact, the fuel system could rupture and cause a fire. The flawed fuel system was linked to dozens of deaths. Ford knew of the design problem even before the accidents occurred. On another fuel-tank safety issue, the company decided not to correct a known problem and to simply settle legal claims as they arose; a cost analysis showed it would be cheaper that way.[73]

The marked difference in how Ford and Johnson & Johnson handled their problems pointedly illustrates the range of possible actions that companies can take to meet their social responsibilities. Profit is an important consideration for any commercial marketer, but to be socially responsible, customers' health, welfare, and certainly their lives come first.

## Consumerism

Because some marketers don't take their social responsibility seriously (or not seriously enough, in the eyes of some consumer advocates), consumers have banded

**consumerism**
A social, economic, and political movement that seeks to protect the safety and rights of consumers

together to pressure them into meeting their responsibility. The **consumerism** movement emerged as a powerful force in the 1960s, focusing attention on consumer rights and business responsibilities. In 1962 President John F. Kennedy summarized the goals of consumerism in a "consumer bill of rights":

- The right to safety
- The right to be informed
- The right to choose
- The right to be heard

These rights entitle consumers to a selection of safe products, to information about them, and to forums in which they can complain about products or simply ask questions. The consumer bill of rights has stood the test of time and is as applicable now as it was in the 1960s. Marketers who respect these basic consumer rights enjoy a double benefit: the moral satisfaction that goes with social responsibility and the competitive advantage of satisfied customers.

## SUMMARY OF LEARNING OBJECTIVES

### 1. Discuss the importance of environmental scanning and environmental analysis.

Environmental scanning is the process of gathering data on your marketing environment. Scanning activities include reading magazines and newspapers, interviewing the public, listening to salespeople, and keeping in touch with government activities and plans. Environmental analysis interprets the data you collect in the scanning process. Together, environmental scanning and analysis help you become more responsive to marketing opportunities and challenges. Without these two activities, your chances of missing opportunities are greatly increased.

### 2. List the seven elements of the marketing environment.

First, the competitive element is made up of the companies that compete with you for the attention and dollars of the same set of target customers. Second, economic factors of interest to the marketer include business cycles, consumer income, and consumer willingness to spend. Third, the natural elements of the marketing environment include natural resources, natural events and conditions (such as the weather), and natural disasters. Fourth, political forces affect marketing both domestically and internationally. Fifth, regulatory forces, usually the result of social and political forces, affect every element of the marketing mix. Sixth, technology creates both opportunities and problems for marketers; it affects both the products you market and the way you can market them. And seventh, social forces can profoundly shape the marketing environment.

### 3. Cite the four phases of the business cycle and discuss the nature of consumer behavior in each.

The four phases of the business cycle are prosperity, recession, depression, and recovery. Prosperity is a period of low

unemployment, high income, and a strong willingness to spend. During a recession, consumers are less optimistic, unemployment rises, and buying power falls. As a result, willingness to spend starts to drop. In a depression, the characteristics seen in a recession are intensified; unemployment is high, disposable income is minimal, and many consumers lose confidence in the economy. In a full-scale depression, willingness to spend is extremely low. Finally, the recovery phase occurs when the economy is struggling back from a recession or depression. During such times, customers start to spend more freely, especially as their confidence in the economy improves.

### 4. Outline the types of competition and the various competitive structures that markets can exhibit.

Competition can occur at three levels. The first is direct competition between similar products, such as Campbell's soups and Progresso soups. The second is between products that are not identical but that can be substituted in many cases. For instance, you might consider a Stouffer's frozen dinner to be a substitute for Campbell's soup, in which case the two products would be in competition. The most general type of competition is between a given product and all the other products in the world vying for the customer's attention. In this sense, Campbell's soups compete with *Time* magazine, Ford automobiles, and Club Med vacations because they are all trying to reach the consumer's pocketbook.

Markets also exhibit various competitive structures. In a monopoly, one company controls the supply of products and doesn't have any competition. In an oligopoly, a small group of competitors control the market, and other companies find it very hard to enter the market. Most business in developed economies such as the United States occurs in monopolistic competition, in which numerous competitors can potentially gain advantage by differentiating their products, price, promotion, and distribution. In cases of pure competition, the only way to differentiate yourself is on the basis of price.

**5. Explain how government regulations can affect your marketing plans.**

Governments control many aspects of marketing. In the product element, regulations often dictate contents, ingredients, usage, and labeling. In pricing, a number of federal and state regulations influence price levels, discounting, and the way prices are advertised. The distribution function falls under legal guidelines as well, ranging from control of marketing channels to the manner in which some products can be transported. Finally, many laws apply to promotions, including truth in advertising and restrictions on the advertising of certain products.

**6. Describe how technology can change both the products that you can sell and the way in which you market them.**

Technology enables the development of entirely new categories of products, as well as dramatic improvements to old ones. For instance, the development of semiconductor electronics created opportunities for many new types of products, such as video cameras and compact disk players. This technology also improved existing products; the addition of electronic engine controls to automobiles is a good example. When it comes to marketing products, technology also helps. In promotions, technology allows new methods for promotion (such as computer-based advertisements) and more efficient use of existing methods (such as computer databases that do a better job of focusing direct-mail efforts). Technology also provides new ways of distributing products. The automated teller machine, which lets banks extend the time and place utility of their services, is a good example.

**7. Discuss how changes in social values and attitudes affect marketing.**

Changes in social values and attitudes alter the market's dynamics, making certain products and marketing tactics acceptable or unacceptable. For example, at one time it was perfectly acceptable to advertise cigarettes on television. But as social values turned against smoking, tobacco advertisers were forced off the air. Conversely, condom ads weren't accepted by most media in years past, but increased social concerns changed the standards.

**8. Describe the role of ethics in marketing and distinguish between ethical dilemmas and ethical lapses.**

Ethics provides the basis for evaluating marketing strategies and selecting morally acceptable options. Ethical issues fall into two categories: Ethical dilemmas are unresolved questions of ethical judgment in which some validity exists on both sides of the question. Ethical lapses, on the other hand, are clear-cut cases of unethical behavior. Just about every aspect of the marketing profession involves ethical issues, and today's successful marketers are aware of the effects of their ethical choices.

## KEY TERMS

baby boom (49)
barriers to entry (32)
business cycle (36)
buying power (34)
buying power index (BPI) (34)
competition (31)
consumerism (58)
controllable elements (31)
demographics (49)
depression (37)

discretionary income (35)
disposable income (35)
economic elements (33)
effective buying income (EBI) (34)
environmental analysis (31)
environmental scanning (31)
import quota (39)
income (34)
infrastructure (38)

marketing environment (30)
marketing ethics (52)
monopolistic competition (33)
monopoly (32)
natural elements (38)
oligopoly (32)
political elements (38)
prosperity (36)
pure competition (33)

recession (36)
recovery (37)
regulatory elements (40)
self-regulation (45)
social elements (49)
social responsibility (52)
tariff (39)
technology (47)
uncontrollable elements (31)
wealth (35)

## KEEPING CURRENT IN MARKETING

Find an article that describes how a federal regulatory agency (such as the Food and Drug Administration, the Federal Trade Commission, or the Federal Communications Commission) is attempting to influence the marketing behavior (such as advertising, sales tactics, or pricing) of one company.

1. What steps is the agency taking to change the company's behavior? What is the goal of these steps? Is it to promote competition, protect competitors, regulate marketing tactics, deregulate an industry, protect consumers, or something else? How might this goal impede the company's marketing efforts?

2. What steps is the target company taking in response to the agency's actions? Do you think the steps you identify will strengthen or weaken the company's marketing efforts?

3. Whose interests or needs is the government agency serving? The target company itself? Society at large? Special interest groups? One or more competitors? The international business community? Some other group? Was the federal agency right to take the steps it did? Why or why not?

## *Meeting a Marketing Challenge at Gannett*

From no readers to 6.6 million of them—*USA Today* became a publishing powerhouse in less than a decade. Gannett chairperson Allen Neuharth dreamed of establishing a national daily paper, and by studying the marketing environment, he turned his dream into reality.

To understand the competitive elements of the marketing environment, Neuharth sent Gannett executives out to talk to people in the industry. His team learned that, among others, *The New York Times* and *The Washington Post* were considering national general-interest newspapers. As a result, Neuharth kept his plans confidential, confirming rumors of the new paper's launch only a short time before its first issue.

By analyzing the social elements, Neuharth came up with ideas for designing a newspaper with broad appeal. This generation had grown up with television, and Neuharth knew that *USA Today* had to be special to keep their attention. Bright colors and clever charts and graphs were Neuharth's answer. He even had vending machines designed to resemble television sets and had front-page layouts jazzed up to attract the pedestrian's eye.

Neuharth also considered economic elements. Would advertisers buy space in *USA Today?* Gannett people heard again and again that national advertisers (who controlled large ad budgets) typically shunned newspapers because they couldn't get quality color reproduction. Neuharth reacted by upgrading all printing sites to a new, more precise color process.

Neuharth was told that it was hard for big-city advertising executives to take *USA Today* seriously because of Gan-

nett's small-town newspaper image. Most advertisers wanted proof that the paper was being purchased and read by as many people as Neuharth claimed. Without verifiable circulation figures, advertisers weren't sure their pitches were reaching the projected number of people.

The big break came during the 1984 Summer Olympics in Los Angeles. Advertisers were hunting for new ways to reach the millions of Americans excited by this international event, and readers were hungry for standings and photos. *USA Today* attracted a record number of ads, including major new advertisers such as Federal Express, Mutual of Omaha, and Nissan Trucks.

A reader survey later revealed that *USA Today*'s audience had above-average incomes. Combined with the steadily growing readership, this gave the paper more ammunition for signing additional national advertisers. Neuharth went even further, commissioning million-dollar media campaigns to show *USA Today*'s readership strengths. Patrick Ewing, Chris Evert, Willard Scott, and other celebrities appeared in *USA Today* ads.

Neuharth exploited technological elements as well. First, satellite delivery established *USA Today* in cities across the United States. Then, Gannett began transmitting a specially prepared mix of news to overseas locations. The result was *USA Today International,* now available in Europe and Asia. Technology also enabled Neuharth to move Gannett beyond traditional news media into related fields of information delivery. USA Today Decisionline, a news database produced by Gannett News Media Services, allows news buffs with personal computers to tap into a database through GE In-

formation Services, The Source, and other on-line services.

Having reinvented the newspaper, Neuharth retired, to be succeeded by John J. Curley. Curley must now make Gannett's $600 million investment in "the nation's newspaper" pay off. *USA Today* passed a major milestone in 1993 when it became profitable for the first time. Curley admitted in January 1994 that it took a long time to prove the viability of a national daily, but those critics who voiced their skepticism early and often may finally have been proved wrong.

**Your mission:** As a summer intern working at Gannett's headquarters, you have been assigned to a special project team at *USA Today*. Your team is reviewing the paper's marketing environment, and your goal is to recommend programs that will increase readership and advertising revenues.

1. Increasing daily nationwide readership will raise revenues from newspaper sales while helping *USA Today* marketing representatives sell more advertisements. Your project team has been asked to think of cost-effective ways to boost readership. Which of the following ideas would be effective?
   a. Talk to airlines and hotels about buying large quantities of *USA Today* at a discounted price, to be offered free as a service to their customers. Place large stickers on the front page of each newspaper, identifying the name of the sponsor, such as "Compliments of Air North-South."
   b. Lower the price to 5 cents below competing publications, and print the price in very large type on the front page. Put up banners at every newsstand to announce the price break, and mention that *USA Today* is the lowest-priced newspaper of all major dailies.
   c. Start a campaign to sign up advertising executives as *USA Today* subscribers. This will introduce ad people to the newspaper, make them more familiar with the reporting and with the other advertisers who use *USA Today*, and increase subscription revenues.

2. Gannett has asked your group to analyze several ideas for reaching potential advertisers. Choose the proposal that has the best chance for success.
   a. Send the top 25 national advertisers a box breakfast (juice, croissant, an orange, and coffee) every day for a week, with each day's issue of *USA Today* packed on top of the box. Include the business card of the paper's local advertising representative, who will call for an appointment.
   b. Commission a limited-edition Rand McNally atlas of the United States to be sent to potential advertisers. On the maps inside, indicate the markets served by *USA Today* and include circulation data for each market. Under each city's name, show the name and phone number of the local ad representative.

   c. Send a direct-mail package to the ad managers of the leading national advertisers, comparing the circulations and ad rates of *USA Today*, *The New York Times*, *Newsweek*, and other general-interest news publications.

3. John Curley recognizes that *USA Today* has several categories of competition. Which of the following overall competitive strategies makes the most sense?
   a. You need to establish *USA Today* as a serious newspaper and shed the "McPaper" image. To do this you should compete head-to-head with respected names in the news media, such as *The New York Times*, *Newsweek*, and CNN.
   b. You need to pick your target first. *USA Today* wasn't designed to compete with *The New York Times*; it was designed to meet travelers' needs for daily news of home and nation. Analyze the news-reading habits of travelers, and make sure you're doing everything possible to reach them with your product.
   c. The people who care about news are already reading, so it won't do you any good to preach to the converted. The competition you need to worry about is from the dissimilar products. You should try to redirect some of the money spent on hot dogs, telephone calls, and clothes to *USA Today*.

4. Although it is currently legal to print cigarette ads in newspapers and magazines, some publications (including *Reader's Digest*) refuse to accept such ads. Given the significant ad revenues at stake, what should *USA Today* do about this issue? Discuss the pros and cons of each of the following options, and then select the most attractive one.
   a. Accept only small cigarette ads, not full-page ads.
   b. Insist that manufacturers increase the size of the surgeon general's warning before *USA Today* will print the ad.
   c. Stop printing cigarette ads immediately.

**SPECIAL PROJECT**

Due to competitive and economic pressures, various publications are available at different newsstands. Visit a newsstand at a train or bus station, in a supermarket, at a candy store, at a hotel, in a drugstore, and on a downtown street corner, if possible. Also check the vending machines you may find on downtown streets, at the train or bus station, or in front of public buildings.

Which daily and weekly newspapers do you find at each location? Are the issues current? Are the prices at each location the same as shown on the publication's front page? How are the papers displayed at each location? Look for *USA Today* at each location and check for any promotional displays. Summarize briefly which papers you feel *USA Today* is competing with at each location, and describe what types of customers are typical at each location.[74]

## Rerouting SAS for Success

For a clear lesson in the benefits of analyzing the marketing environment, consider how Jan Carlzon, former CEO of Scandinavian Airlines System (SAS), pulled his company out of a nose dive caused by shrinking demand and mushrooming fuel costs. SAS started in 1946 as an airline owned jointly by government and private investors in Denmark, Norway, and Sweden. Early on, consumer demand for air travel outstripped supply at a time when fuel prices were very reasonable. To make money, management simply had to roll out the planes. By concentrating on flying an ever-increasing number of passengers, SAS delivered handsome profits for 17 consecutive years.

However, during the 1970s and 1980s, the environment was changing. In the United States and around the world, the airline industry was deregulated. For example, rather than following rigid pricing guidelines controlled by government regulators, airlines now had to compete on the basis of price. At the same time, oil prices rose sharply, and demand for air travel leveled off.

SAS adjusted slowly to these changes. Saddled with an aging fleet, the airline finally ordered technologically advanced Airbuses with larger passenger and cargo capacity. In fact, each Airbus could carry more than double the number of passengers that one of the airline's DC-9 planes could handle. However, after the new planes were delivered, management realized fuel prices were so steep that the Airbuses were not economical unless full, and demand was dropping. Further, SAS posted a multimillion-dollar loss in 1981. When the president resigned, SAS's multinational owners turned the top job over to Jan Carlzon, who had successfully revitalized an SAS subsidiary.

Carlzon assessed the environment and came up with immediate marketing priorities. He recognized the oversupply problem, and he realized that intense competition was keeping profits low. To reverse course, SAS needed a new focus. Carlzon's analysis revealed a lucrative market that wasn't getting the attention it deserved: the business traveler.

Business travelers tend to be less price sensitive because their travel plans are dictated by business de-

mands rather than the need to save money. In fact, businesspeople are generally willing to pay full fare if they can get to their destinations on time with the least amount of hassle. So Carlzon resolved to make SAS the preferred airline for the frequent business traveler.

Next, Carlzon set aside special sections in each aircraft for business travelers and beefed up onboard service and amenities. He also set punctuality objectives, so SAS developed a reputation for on-time performance. Tying it all together, he launched a training program that encouraged everyone to make customer needs the top priority.

By scanning the environmental horizon and implementing an effective marketing strategy, Carlzon made SAS profitable in just over a year. In 1983 his airline won the *Air Transport World*'s Airline of the Year award; in 1986 SAS won that magazine's Passenger Service award. However, the turbulent times that struck nearly every air carrier in the early 1990s brought an end to Carlzon's accomplishments at SAS, and he left the company. With passenger traffic and revenues down worldwide, airlines are still fighting for profitability in an extremely challenging business environment.

1. SAS is concerned about how the 1992 economic unification of Europe will affect the company. Should SAS concentrate its environmental scanning on Europe and the trans-Atlantic air-travel market, or should the company include the worldwide air-travel market?

2. Imagine that SAS marketers believe a recession will ground the airline's hopes for higher profits next year. To keep businesspeople flying SAS, should they step up promotions to the corporate travel market, emphasizing service and schedules? On the other hand, should they go for the broader travel market by lowering fares to draw price-conscious vacationers?

3. Smoking on airplanes has become a controversial topic with social responsibility implications, in part because of health concerns and in part because of safety issues. Should SAS ban smoking on all flights, regardless of length or destination, or should the company ban smoking only in accordance with legislation in countries where SAS operates?

# QUESTIONS FOR DISCUSSION

1. How can environmental scanning and analysis help a marketer of sports equipment?
2. Does your college compete with the U.S. Army? Why or why not?
3. Assume you're in Kmart's marketing department; what are some of the things you could do to keep track of your competitors?
4. What are some possible barriers to entry in the following markets?
   a. Aircraft manufacturing
   b. Cable television
   c. Minerals
   d. Genetically engineered medicines
5. How might changes in consumer buying power affect marketers of the following products?
   a. Flour, sugar, salt, and other basic food products
   b. Racing bicycles
   c. Overseas vacations
   d. Local vacations
6. How would a shortage of petroleum affect companies that aren't in the petroleum business?
7. Consider the progress of the baby-boom generation, from birth through retirement; what effect did they have on automakers, what effect are they having now, and what effect will they have in the future?
8. How might changing social values affect the marketing efforts of Planned Parenthood?
9. Would you characterize each of the following issues as an ethical dilemma or an ethical lapse?
   a. Donating to the campaign of a public official and then asking for helpful legislation in return
   b. Raising prices of heating oil during a harsh winter, in response to the increased demand
   c. Eliminating cigarette advertising
   d. Touching up photos of products shown in advertisements
10. What are the ethical issues that might be faced by a marketer of alcoholic beverages?

# SHARPEN YOUR MARKETING SKILLS

The changing role of women is readily apparent in the computer market. For instance, Zenith Data Systems recently learned that 65 percent of the people planning to buy laptops were women. A survey conducted for *Working Woman* magazine revealed that 75 percent of the female executives polled played a role in the purchase of company computers. Moreover, computers are big business for the magazine itself: It sold over a million dollars' worth of computer advertising in 1989.

Clearly, women are using and buying computers, but computer makers aren't completely sure how to market their products to women. Qume Corporation tried laser printers with pastel colors on control buttons and special handles and knobs that accommodated longer fingernails. The effort didn't pay off in increased sales, however. Other makers concentrate on featuring women in their ads.

**Decision:** Talk to several women who use computers, and ask them what they think computer marketers should be doing. Based on your discussions, what recommendations would you make to a company trying to market hardware or software to women? Be sure to consider the question of whether the company should do anything different for women versus men.

**Communication:** Draft a three-minute speech to a computer-industry convention, suggesting why efforts to target women haven't worked in the past and outlining your suggestions for future efforts.

# 3

# Strategic Marketing Planning

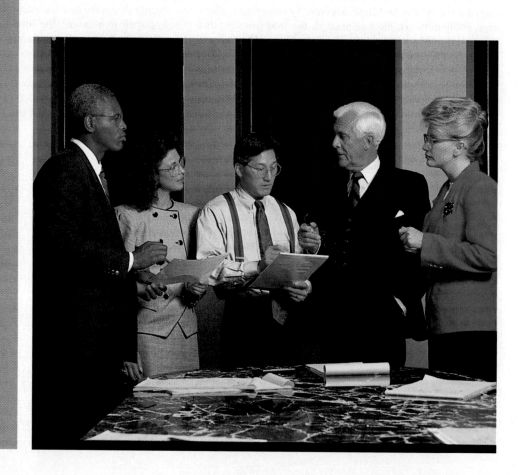

### Putting the Joy Back into Joysticks

Your assignment: Bring a devastated, neglected world back to life. Those who came before you suffered terrible losses. The same dangers are waiting for you, and there's no guarantee you won't meet the same fate. You'll have to rely on your skill at finding clues, piecing together evidence, formulating a strategy, and preparing for global battle.

A scene from the latest hit video game? No, this was real life for Minoru Arakawa, head of Japan's Nintendo in 1985. The once-booming U.S. home video game market had nearly been destroyed. From a high of $3.2 billion in 1982, sales had plummeted 97 percent to $100 million in 1985, and well-known companies were deserting the market as fast as they could pack their bags and turn the lights out in their factories.

Led by Atari in 1979, the first wave of video games saw sales double each year until 1982. By that time, more than a dozen U.S. companies sold game systems. To provide their systems with as many games as possible, these companies let anybody who had the software expertise create games. The game cartridges were available just about everywhere, from the downtown retailer to the corner convenience store. In 1982 the video game seemed as integral to the U.S. family room as the sofa and the TV. However, it didn't last.

In 1985 Atari released 4,500 employees, including its president. The company had lost $539 million, and things were so bad that truckloads of game cartridges had to be buried in a New Mexico landfill. Retailers couldn't give away games that used to cost as much as $35, and some even fired the buyers who had plunged them so deeply into the video game business.

So what had happened? Children are a noto-riously volatile market, explained marketing experts. A huge hit today will disappear tomorrow if kids get bored or if a new fad arrives on the scene. Remember when people would swim deep rivers and climb tall mountains to find one of Coleco's Cabbage Patch dolls? Who would have imagined that Coleco would end up filing for bankruptcy when the Cabbage Patch rage quickly died down? Well, this time those fickle kids had simply outgrown video games.

But Nintendo's Arakawa didn't agree. Kids were still pouring streams of quarters into arcade video games. At the arcade, detailed graphics and complex scenarios held the kids' attention for hours. However, when the kids ran out of money and went home to play, they were faced with crude graphics, monotonous sound, and simplistic variations on familiar themes. No, kids hadn't abandoned all video games, only the boring home versions.

Nintendo knew it could produce better home games, but company leaders realized they needed more than just a better product. The collapse of the video game market had destroyed the confidence of several important groups, so, to put together a winning strategy, Nintendo had to address the special concerns of each one.

It was Minoru Arakawa's task to bring the U.S. video game market back to life, but was the task feasible? What was the competition doing? How could Arakawa restore the confidence of software developers, retailers, and customers? Would anyone ever have faith in the video game market again? Also, if Arakawa did manage to reenergize the market, how could he protect Nintendo from the inevitable rush of competitors once the market looked promising again?[1]

**strategic marketing planning**
The process of exploring marketing opportunities, investing time and money to pursue those opportunities, and predicting the outcome of those investments

**marketing plan**
A formal document that details your objectives, your situation analysis, your marketing strategy, and the elements of your marketing mix

**reactive marketing**
An approach to marketing in which you view environmental forces as uncontrollable and simply try to adjust to changes after they occur

**proactive marketing**
An approach to marketing in which you try to anticipate changes in the marketing environment and perhaps even try to influence future changes

# CHAPTER OVERVIEW

Like Nintendo, companies from around the world must plan for success, outlining not only the daily operations but also the long-term strategies that will guide the company's direction for years to come. This chapter defines strategic marketing planning and outlines the three stages of the planning process: (1) assessing your marketing performance using portfolio analysis and other techniques; (2) assessing marketing opportunities and your ability to capitalize on them; and (3) designing the marketing strategy by selecting target markets, staking out a desired position, and defining a marketing mix. The chapter concludes with a look at the nature and importance of sales forecasting, which provides vital information for use in the strategic planning process.

# STRATEGIC PLANNING CONCEPTS

Companies that live by the marketing concept realize that marketing efforts are more successful when they are carefully planned. **Strategic marketing planning** is the process of examining a company's market opportunities, allocating resources to capitalize on those opportunities, and predicting the market and financial performance that is likely to occur.[2] The purpose of marketing planning was summed up nicely by British marketing professor Malcolm MacDonald: The overall purpose of marketing planning is to help you identify and create competitive advantage.[3]

The results of strategic marketing planning are documented in the **marketing plan,** which summarizes the current situation, states your objectives, and outlines strategies and programs designed to help the organization reach those objectives. As marketing manager of a strategic business unit at AC Rochester (a parts division of General Motors), Mary Kulpinksi believes that the marketing plan "links customer opportunities and competitive threats with organizational realities."[4]

Component Chapter A (which follows this chapter) presents a sample marketing plan and describes the information that is commonly found in strategic marketing plans. The following sections introduce three fundamental planning issues: the two approaches to planning, the dimensions of planning, and the levels at which planning takes place.

## Approaches to Strategic Planning

All marketers can employ the basic concepts of marketing strategy, but they don't always approach strategy in the same way. **Reactive marketing** views environmental forces as uncontrollable and simply tries to adjust to them. In contrast, **proactive marketing** tries to anticipate changes in the marketing environment and makes plans to capitalize on future market conditions. Moreover, as a proactive marketer you take steps to influence those future conditions to make them conducive to your plans (see Exhibit 3.1).

Consider how the two approaches differ. Confronted with new legislation banning some of their products, reactive marketers might define a strategy to simply abandon those offerings and concentrate on developing new products in unregulated areas. The proactive marketer would probably have anticipated the forthcoming changes and would already have new products in place. In addition, this marketer would probably join an industry coalition to lobby Congress and raise public support for the industry's point of view.

However, you don't always have a choice. Sometimes you're affected by a sudden change in the marketing environment, and you're left with no alternative but to react. Study as you might, you can't always predict the behavior of nature, governments, competitors, or customers. Even so, every little bit helps. By understanding the nature of your marketing environment and by playing an active role in your industry, you stand less chance of being at the mercy of outside forces.

**Exhibit 3.1**
**REACTIVE VERSUS PROACTIVE MARKETING**
The National Rifle Association, one of the most powerful lobbying organizations in the country, takes a proactive stance in its marketing efforts.

## The Dimensions of Strategic Planning

Strategic planning differs from other planning efforts in two important ways. First, the scope of strategic planning is broad. It considers all the products a company offers and all the markets the company serves. Strategic planning considers both environmental factors on the outside and organizational factors on the inside. Because the marketing concept implies functional integration, so does strategic planning. It incorporates production, research, finance, and the other organizational elements necessary for success.

Second, strategic planning looks beyond immediate circumstances, trying to project market conditions 5 or 10 years into the future. It's important for marketers to be prepared for changes in the marketing environment, whether the changes are political, cultural, technological, or economic. Marketers who look only 6 or 12 months down the road run the risk of being caught off guard and of being unable to respond to environmental changes before their competitors do.

There is another side to this long-term perspective. As a strategic marketer, you'll not only consider where the world is going to be in 5 or 10 years, you'll weigh the long-term consequences of the decisions you make today. This might mean that you'll skip an immediate market opportunity that will box you in later on, or perhaps you'll forgo short-term profits to invest in long-term technologies. Unfortunately, too many companies still look for short-term results, a fault that's particularly common with U.S. and European firms. For instance, 87 percent of the British firms in a recent study listed profit maximization as their primary objective, whereas 80 percent of the Japanese firms said that increasing the size of their customer base was their primary objective.[5] Expanding your customer base is usually considered a long-term strategy, unlike profit maximization, which tries to make as much money as possible as soon as possible.

Of course, you can still find non-Japanese firms making long-term decisions. For example, Oscar Denis of Allen-Bradley convinced his division managers to make an investment that made no sense in the short run. Until his idea came along, electronic products were constructed of printed circuit boards, rigid cards that carry the components and wiring. The disadvantage of these boards is that they require a lot of space, often too much space for products such as telephones and automobile dashboards. Denis designed molded circuit boards (MCBs), which can be shaped to fit irregular, cramped spaces. In the short run, these products don't have

Although a profit maximization objective is often maligned as short-term thinking, the majority of British firms list this as their number one priority. This objective is common with U.S. and European firms but is not as popular with Japanese firms.

much of a market; MCBs contributed only 3 percent of the division's $80 million of revenues in 1989, even after many years and millions of dollars of development.

So why hasn't Allen-Bradley pulled the plug on this project? The reason is that management doesn't foresee much growth for the division's other products, and they realize they need to invest in future opportunities. The company expects MCBs to pull in a third of its revenues by the mid-1990s. Managers could have taken the easy route, limiting investments to increase current profits, but the strategic planning process led them to spend money today in the hopes of a greater payback tomorrow.[6]

## Levels of Planning

**tactical planning**
Planning typically undertaken by middle management to examine the performance over a relatively short period of time of specific products in a firm's marketing portfolio

Strategic planning doesn't happen in isolation at the top layer of an organization. It's supported by planning and execution throughout the organization. **Tactical planning** is of narrower scope and shorter time frame than strategic planning (see Exhibit 3.2), and it is usually the responsibility of middle management. Tactical planning looks at the performance of specific markets or products over a shorter period of time than strategic planning, although it must be closely tied to strategic planning. The Woodworker's Store, a retail supplier of tools and hardware for cabinetmakers and other people working with wood, saw the need to expand its product offerings in the mid-1990s as the needs of its customers changed. In 1994 the company added large selections of materials and tools for building European-style cabinets and computer furniture, two increasingly popular classes of woodworking projects. The products are sold through the same retail stores and mail-order catalogs as the company's other products, and they're related to the company's other product lines, so this doesn't represent a major strategic shift. Instead, it's an effort to increase sales in the near future by responding to customer needs.[7]

**operational planning**
Planning that is engaged in by supervisory managers and that focuses on activities of narrow scope and short duration

Moving closer to the customer, supervisory managers engage in **operational planning,** which of all the formal planning activities of the business is narrowest in scope and concerned with matters of the shortest duration. Operational planning focuses on meeting objectives such as immediate improvement of the market position of a particular brand of product or improvement of the current period's sales of a single product.

Businesspeople use the terms *top-down planning* and *bottom-up planning* to refer to planning processes that start at the top and at the bottom of the organization, respectively. There are advantages to both approaches. Top-down plans are usually developed by the people in the organization with the broadest perspective and the

**Exhibit 3.2 LEVELS OF PLANNING**
There are three levels of marketing planning. Operational planning looks at the shortest time frame and the narrowest scope, and strategic planning takes the longest and broadest view; tactical planning falls between the two.

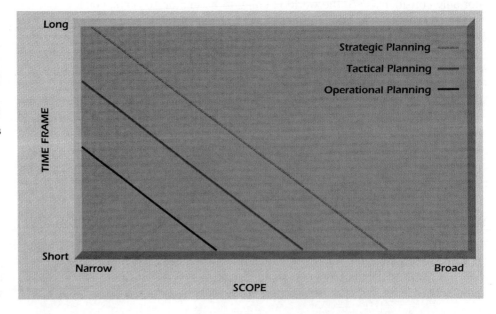

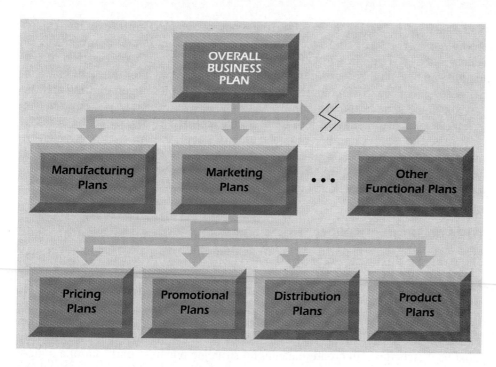

**Exhibit 3.3**
**THE PLANNING HIERARCHY**
Marketing plans fit in a hierarchy of plans that address each level in the organization.

most experience. On the other hand, bottom-up planning, which is started by people on the "front line" of the organization, has the advantage of being close to the action. For instance, people in sales and customer service positions, who interact most frequently with customers, have the best idea of what customers are thinking and doing. The ideal planning process combines both the top-down and bottom-up approaches, which results in plans that take advantage of an organization's experience and that respond to customer needs and expectations.

Of course, marketing is just one of a number of departments in the typical organization. The marketing plan is one of several functional plans that are part of the hierarchy of plans shown in Exhibit 3.3. For the firm to be successful, all the departments must be coordinated by an overall strategic business plan. Therefore, the other departments will have planning processes analogous to the one in marketing. For instance, the finance department needs to engage in broad, long-range planning to make sure the company stays financially healthy from year to year. It takes the combined teamwork of all these groups to make an organization successful.

## THE STRATEGIC MARKETING PLANNING PROCESS

Strategic marketing planning is a three-stage process that assesses current performance and opportunities, then defines the marketing strategies, and designs marketing programs. Once the plans are in place, the marketing programs are implemented and the results are monitored. If everything works, performance feedback provides the good news. On the other hand, if the marketing program doesn't meet expectations, feedback helps marketers adjust the process. Strategic marketing planning is a continuing process, not a one-time event, and continuous monitoring and feedback is the best way to stay in touch with dynamic market conditions.

### Assess Your Current Performance

The first stage in planning for the future is to figure out where you are today. A new company with popular products in growing market segments faces a situation far different from that of an older company whose sales are slowing down or whose markets have stopped growing. In addition, an honest assessment of how well you've performed in the recent past is the only way to fix problem areas and exploit strengths. Maybe you'll find that your products are strong but your advertising or selling skills aren't up to par. On the other hand, maybe you're fairly good at selling but you haven't had the right products or weren't going after the right markets. Self-assessment requires looking at both the products you've been offering and the way you've been marketing them.

Unless your firm is new, it has some products. If it's a large company, it might be involved in quite a number of businesses. A good strategic marketing plan requires that you periodically assess the performance of these products and businesses. To do so, you should be aware of several concepts, starting with the strategic business unit and portfolio analysis.

## THE STRATEGIC BUSINESS UNIT

**strategic business unit (SBU)**
A unit of the firm that can be considered a separate entity for planning purposes; it may be a single product, a product line, a division, or the entire company

The **strategic business unit (SBU)** is the basic unit of the firm for strategic planning purposes. An SBU might be the entire company, a division, a product line, or even a single product as long as the unit can be considered a separate entity for planning purposes. This generally means that it must have its own management, its own access to resources, its own competitors, and its own customers. Sometimes when a firm's management reviews its strategic plans, it finds that the company must be restructured to create meaningful strategic business units out of a hodge-podge of divisions that compete with one another. When the Monsanto Agricultural Company (an SBU that is part of Monsanto) decided to pursue an opportunity in the consumer market, it created a new SBU called the Lawn and Garden Business Unit. This allowed the firm to manage its commercial farm and home markets as separate efforts.[8]

General Electric was a pioneer in this activity, setting up several dozen SBUs, each of which had its own mission within the company, an identifiable market with a unique customer base, and all its own major business functions—manufacturing, engineering, finance, and marketing.[9] GE continues to refine its structure by concentrating its operations in what it feels it knows best, buying firms that complement its strengths and selling off SBUs that don't meet GE's goal of being first or second in their respective markets. Among its better-known moves were selling its small-appliance division to Black & Decker, buying the Radio Corporation of America (RCA), and selling its consumer electronics division (including part of the newly acquired RCA) to Thomson-CSF of France.[10] Johnson & Johnson is another successful user of the SBU concept, giving its business units the freedom—and funding—to pursue business opportunities.[11]

## BUSINESS PORTFOLIO ANALYSIS

How do companies like GE decide which of their operating units to keep and which to dispose of? How do they know which acquisitions will be good for them and which to avoid? Many use a form of **portfolio analysis,** which provides a framework for categorizing each of the company's SBUs. Categorizing your various business efforts helps you design an individual strategy for each business unit.[12] General Electric shouldn't manage its major appliance business in the same way it manages its broadcasting business—and portfolio planning helps the company define the right strategies for each business.

**portfolio analysis**
One of several techniques for categorizing a firm's SBUs for purposes of investment, development, or divestiture

**growth/share matrix**
A portfolio analysis technique developed by the Boston Consulting Group that categorizes SBUs for investment based on their current market share and the prospects for growth of their market

One of the most widely known portfolio analysis schemes is the model pioneered by the Boston Consulting Group (BCG) in the early 1970s.[13] BCG's **growth/share matrix** looks at two variables: the relative market share held by an SBU (the market share relative to its largest competitor) and the rate at which the market is growing (see Exhibit 3.4).

The BCG matrix plots relative market share and rate of market growth of each of the firm's SBUs. This results in four quadrants. SBUs with high relative market

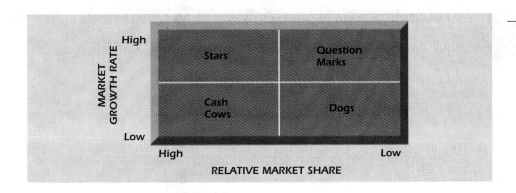

share in rapidly growing markets are called *stars*. Those with low shares in rapidly growing markets are characterized as *question marks* because you don't know whether they'll turn into stars. *Cash cows* are those having large shares of slowly growing markets. These SBUs are called cash cows because you no longer invest much in them, but you can continue to "milk" profits. Finally, SBUs having only a small share of a slowly growing market are branded *dogs*. The strategy you formulate for one type of SBU is different from the strategy you create for the others.

Some general guidelines exist for designing a strategy based on the growth/share matrix. For example, as the name suggests, dogs usually don't warrant much investment and, in many cases, marketers look for ways to remove them from the firm's portfolio. On the other hand, cash cows are milked of profit dollars—preferably to finance SBUs in high-growth categories. Stars are pampered because they usually produce significant income, and their market is a growing one. A good strategy with SBUs in this category is investing development funds to assure continued growth. Finally, what do you do with a question mark? You must decide whether to invest more money for future growth or abandon the SBU. Since many question marks consume more money than they produce, the answer to this question often depends on the financial well-being of the company.

Like all marketing models, the growth/share matrix must be used with careful interpretation and judgment. First, it's based on the assumption that high market share leads to greater profitability. Although a strong relationship exists between market share and profit, you can't assume that high market share is the only way to survive or succeed. In fact, many businesses do quite nicely with low market shares.[14] Second, the decision to enter or leave markets or to add or drop products is more complex than the growth/share matrix implies. For example, the existence of patents, government regulations, complex customer applications, and significant investment requirements can all influence your decisions.

BCG and others have since refined the portfolio model concept. The two axes in the revised BCG matrix, for example, are (1) the number of ways you can achieve a competitive advantage and (2) the sales growth potential if you can achieve an advantage. In a *stalemate* situation, you have few ways to achieve competitive advantage, and even if you do, your sales potential isn't great. In a *volume* situation, you also have few ways to gain advantage, but you have the opportunity to sell in high volumes if you can get an advantage. In a *specialization* situation, you have a number of ways to gain advantage, and each one has the potential for high-volume sales. In a *fragmentation* situation, you have a number of ways to gain advantage, but each one represents a fairly small sales volume.[15] Understanding the situation you're in with each SBU is key to formulating successful strategies, since your marketing options change from one situation to the next.

General Electric is another pioneer in portfolio management techniques. Together with McKinsey & Company, a consulting firm, GE developed an alternative model. To evaluate markets, the GE/McKinsey **market attractiveness/business position model** uses multiple criteria that summarize how attractive a given opportunity seems to be and your ability to capitalize on that opportunity.[16] In doing

**Exhibit 3.4 THE BCG GROWTH/SHARE MATRIX**
The Boston Consulting Group's growth/share matrix pioneered the idea of portfolio planning. Other strategists and BCG itself have since improved on the concept.

**market attractiveness/ business position model**
Developed by General Electric and the consulting firm of McKinsey & Company, this portfolio analysis model evaluates market attractiveness and business position in terms of multiple criteria

**Exhibit 3.5   CRITERIA IN THE MARKET ATTRACTIVENESS/BUSINESS POSITION MODEL**

| Criteria | Market Attractiveness | Business Position |
|---|---|---|
| Market factors | Size of market<br>Market growth rate<br>Diversity of market segments<br>Sensitivity to price and promotional actions | Firm's share of market<br>Firm's growth rate<br>Firm's participation in diverse segments |
| Competitive factors | Types of competitors<br>Number of competitors<br>Levels and types of integration | How the firm compares with competitors—its strengths<br>Firm's level of integration |
| Financial and economic factors | Contribution margins<br>Leverage through scale<br>Barriers to entry | Firm's contribution margins<br>Firm's leverage and scale economies<br>Barriers to firm's entry |
| Technological factors | Maturity and volatility<br>Patents and copyrights<br>Required technology | Firm's ability to handle change<br>Firm's patents and copyrights<br>Firm's technology level |

The market attractiveness/business position model analyzes the factors that make markets attractive targets and the factors that enable a business to succeed in those markets.

so, this model presents a more realistic characterization of the decisions that marketers make, as you can see from Exhibit 3.5.

The best SBUs are those in the most attractive markets and most consistent with the business position—the strengths—of the firm. The results of the evaluation allow planners to position an SBU on a grid indicating whether that SBU is to receive investment, for what purposes, and how much (see Exhibit 3.6). Segments in the three cells labeled "attractive" or "very attractive" are destined to receive investment for the purposes illustrated. Those labeled "acceptable" will be selectively supported to maintain their position, and the "unacceptable" segments will be used to generate cash flow or will be divested.

Like the growth/share matrix, the market attractiveness/business position model is not a perfect tool for decision making. Depending on the factors you choose and the way you scale them, an SBU might look perfectly attractive in one model but unacceptable in a second model.[17] You never base decisions strictly on these (or any other) models. They are used to help diagnose your current situation and to support your judgment—not to replace it.

In addition, not all firms have such a broad portfolio that they can afford to drop all their dogs and develop a stable of all-star SBUs.[18] A dog (or its equivalent) is an established product with a history of sales, or it wouldn't be in your portfolio in the first place. Many dogs are old products that are no longer needed for their original use or have been made obsolete by newer technology, but such products can often be rejuvenated.[19] It may be possible to find new markets for them by finding new uses. In some cases, new markets can be found for their original use. If either of these can be done, a dog in one market stands a chance of becoming a star in another.

THE PIMS PROGRAM

**Profit Impact on Marketing Strategy (PIMS)**
A database developed by the Strategic Planning Institute that is used to compare strategies with marketplace performance and thereby isolate reasons for marketing success

To give marketers a better understanding of why companies and products fail or succeed, a nonprofit organization called the Strategic Planning Institute started a program in the early 1970s to get a better grasp of the factors that lead to business success. This effort, the **Profit Impact on Marketing Strategy (PIMS)** program, has collected data on strategy and performance from over 3,000 business units of several hundred companies. By comparing strategies and plans with actual sales performance, the PIMS program attempts to isolate general principles that affect marketing success. Some of the program's conclusions include the following:

- Greater perceived product quality leads to higher profitability.
- Larger market share usually leads to higher profitability. (Although, as noted earlier, this conclusion has been disputed by some researchers.)
- Businesses that require a lot of investment tend to be less profitable.
- The dog, question mark, and cash cow labels are frequently misleading. For example, 24 percent of the so-called cash cows in the PIMS database actually lose money.

Because PIMS helps you assess the strength of individual business units, it is sometimes considered a variation of portfolio planning. However, PIMS differs in two key respects: It takes a much more comprehensive view of the factors that lead to marketing success or failure, and it contains an extensive database of real-world business experiences. Portfolio models can help you describe an SBU's current status, but PIMS can go beyond that to help you explain why an SBU is performing a certain way.[20]

In addition to models, you can use a number of other yardsticks to gauge how well you've been performing in your marketing efforts. Sales, profits (sales revenue minus your costs), and scores in customer satisfaction surveys are ways to measure different aspects of your marketing efforts. Performance assessments can be quick and easy for companies with few products and few target markets, but not so with larger, diversified companies. Whichever method you employ, the key points are to assess your performance objectively and to understand why you're performing at this level.

## Assess Your Opportunities

Now that you have an idea of where you are, the obvious question is "What's next?" Where should you spend your time, money, and energy in the future? This is another question that can range from the very simple to the very complex. If you run the corner grocery store, you probably face questions such as whether to expand your hours, which product lines to carry, and how much to charge for each product. If you're Nintendo, your choices might include developing new game products for interactive television, expanding sales in Europe, or investigating telecommunications services. If you're General Electric or Hewlett-Packard, with dozens of SBUs and hundreds or thousands of products, you're facing many individual decisions that need to take place in the context of an overall company strategy. You may decide to pull out of some markets, move into others, drop some products, improve some existing products, and so on. You can see how marketing planning can easily turn into a full-time job.

Assessing your opportunities involves three steps: (1) analyzing the marketing environment to uncover possible opportunities; (2) recognizing your capabilities, re-

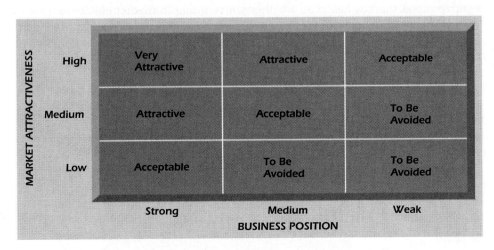

**Exhibit 3.6  MARKET ATTRACTIVENESS/ BUSINESS POSITION MODEL**
This model ranks segments on a scale from unacceptable to highly attractive.

sources, and limitations relative to those opportunities; and then (3) weighing the potential risks and rewards.

## ANALYZING THE ENVIRONMENT

Chapter 2 introduced you to the major forces in the marketing environment. You put that knowledge to use in strategic planning when you analyze the environment to find marketing opportunities. The ability to spot market opportunities and capitalize on them first is one of the most important attributes of a successful marketing organization. Following is a sample of the ways marketers discover potential opportunities:

- Shifts in demographics can affect your product, promotion, and price elements. Marketers around the world are scratching their heads, trying to figure out how to market to the increasingly affluent U.S. teenagers. The average U.S. boy now spends over $6 a week on clothes, and the average girl spends nearly $11 (the boy compensates with over $10 worth of snacks). Overall, teen spending has increased to more than $50 billion annually, and companies from Nike to Nintendo want a piece of the action.[21]
- Impending changes in government regulations can create opportunities, as the Clean Air Act did for pollution-control companies and the Nutrition Labeling and Education Act did for food-testing laboratories.
- "Gap analysis" can isolate groups of customers who aren't being served adequately by existing suppliers. With this technique, you methodically scan market segments to see whether any gaps exist between customer needs and the products those customers are currently buying.
- The success of a competitor can alert you to an opportunity. Bandag is an Iowa company that sells retreaded truck tires and has enjoyed dominant market share and continued growth for years. Unfortunately for Bandag, its success recently caught the attention of Goodyear Tire and Rubber, a company more than 20 times Bandag's size. (To its credit, Bandag countered Goodyear's entry into the retread market with superior customer service, which should help offset Goodyear's size advantage.)[22]
- Your customers can bring opportunities to your attention. As your customers grow and change, they may need new goods and services, which can open new markets for you.
- Other sources of information, including consultants, marketing research firms, the news media, and government agencies, can bring opportunities to your attention.

Successful marketers routinely scan the environment looking for new opportunities, which can appear in several forms (as seen in Exhibit 3.7). The Ansoff matrix categorizes opportunities based on whether you're going to market existing products or develop new ones and whether you'll continue to pursue your existing target markets or go after new ones. Thus the Ansoff matrix involves four types of marketing opportunities:[23]

**Exhibit 3.7   GROWTH STRATEGIES**
The Ansoff matrix outlines four possible growth strategies, employing different combinations of product and market development.

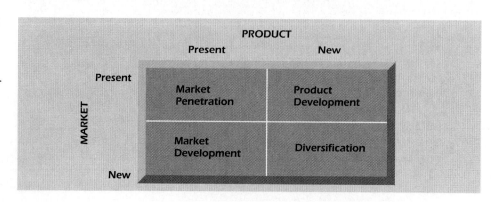

## A COMPANY THAT KNOWS ALL ABOUT STRATEGIC WINDOWS

Rough economic times present marketers with some special challenges. Customers often shift to cheaper sources or stop buying altogether. Then, as sales slow down, marketers are tempted to cut back on their promotional efforts to save money. Many marketers just try to ride out the storm, waiting for economic recovery to bolster sales.

However, a number of successful companies shun this batten-the-hatches approach during recessionary periods. A good example is Marvin Windows, a manufacturer of commercial and residential windows based in Warroad, Minnesota. In fact, Marvin looks at a recession as a strategic window in which an aggressive marketer can gain ground from retrenching competitors.

The reasoning is straightforward: When competitors are reducing their marketing budgets, every dollar you spend is that much more powerful. Also, if you *increase* promotions while the others are cutting theirs, your relative strength grows even more. According to vice president Susan Marvin, a second advantage to strong marketing during a recession occurs when the competition is running for cover; you have the opportunity to pursue customers that you might not be able to reach during good times.

**MARKETING IN ACTION**

Marvin learned its approach during the 1981–1982 recession. Prior to this economic downturn, the company aimed for the middle of the market, offering "a good window at a fair price." The windows were purchased primarily for the construction of new homes, but the new home market dried up during the recession. Fortunately, the consumers who couldn't afford new homes were remodeling the ones they had, which opened a strategic window for Marvin. Customers in the remodeling market often wanted unique, top-of-the-line products built to individual specifications, so the company shifted its sights upward and began to make such products.

The popularity of historic preservation also grew during this period, thanks to generous tax credits for homeowners who remodeled historic houses in the original style. This market required customized windows as

well, and Marvin was able to take advantage of another strategic window. Because competitors were retrenching, Marvin had a better shot at influential customers such as architects and preservation specialists. As a result of both strategic windows, Marvin nearly doubled its sales from 1981 to 1983, emerging from the recession as an important player in the national window market.

In the early 1990s, the U.S. economy tumbled into another recession, and Marvin repeated its strategy from a decade earlier. For instance, while competitors instituted hiring freezes or layoffs, Marvin increased its staff both in marketing and in production. The company also increased its advertising budget by 20 percent. In addition, Marvin expanded the services it offered to building-supply wholesalers, making them more receptive to selling Marvin products. By vigorously pursuing opportunities while the competition is running for cover, Marvin Windows has developed a knack for prospering during hard times.

### APPLY YOUR KNOWLEDGE

**1.** What kind of strategic windows might Marvin find during prosperous times?
**2.** In your opinion is aggressive marketing during a recession a dependable strategy? Will it always work?

---

1. *Existing products in existing markets.* When you seek opportunities to sell more of your current products to the customers you already have (or to customers who are similar to your current customers) you are using the **market penetration strategy.** This approach involves increasing the intensity of your marketing effort. A typical penetration strategy includes actions such as increasing the advertising budget, employing additional sales representatives, or increasing the number of outlets that offer your products.

2. *New products in existing markets.* When you seek opportunities to serve your current customers better by developing new products for them, you are using the **product development strategy,** in which you work to improve present products or develop new ones for your current markets. The people at Disney World have proven themselves masters of the technique. Their property in central Florida has been a developing product for two decades. New attractions are constantly being opened, and this will continue well into the twenty-first century. The first attraction was a replication of Disney's West Coast success, the Magic King-

**market penetration strategy**
A growth strategy based on increasing the intensity of the firm's marketing effort in its current markets with current products

**product development strategy**
A growth strategy that improves present products or develops new ones for the firm's current markets

dom; then EPCOT was unveiled, followed by the MGM–United Artists theme park. A fourth park is in the works now. In addition to the theme parks, the Walt Disney World Corporation continues to develop hotels and resorts on the property and other attractions such as Pleasure Island (a combination shopping, dining, and night club area that was opened in 1989) and Typhoon Lagoon (a water park that was opened in 1990). Even so, over 90 percent of the available land at Disney World remains unused at this time.[24]

3. *Existing products in new markets.* When you enter new markets with existing products, you are following a **market development strategy.** The Coca-Cola Company aggressively pursues this strategy, especially in the international market, seeking to gain a foothold in places where Coke doesn't have significant market share, such as the People's Republic of China.[25] Market development is often an expensive, time-consuming strategy because you usually need to educate consumers about your products and their benefits.

4. *New products in new markets.* When you've exhausted the opportunities in the first three scenarios, or when you've spotted demand for a new product in a different market than you now serve, you may have to take the most extreme approach. When you either develop the new product yourself or buy a company that already provides it you are using the **diversification** strategy. The opportunities in this strategy are usually the riskiest and the most expensive to pursue, simply because you have to do everything from scratch. The record of success for most companies is not encouraging. Many companies such as Quaker Oats, which began a diversification effort in the 1980s, are scaling back to focus on the products and customers they know best. Quaker moved into unrelated areas when it bought Joseph A. Bank Clothiers, a seller of traditional men's and women's clothing and accessories; Brookstone, a company that sells hard-to-find tools and hardware by mail and in its own retail stores; Herrschners, a mail-order needlecrafts firm doing business in the United States and Canada; and Eyelab, an eyewear chain selling both prescription and nonprescription items. Quaker has since sold many of these organizations.[26]

As a general rule, pursue opportunities in the order listed. In other words, try to do a better job of marketing your existing products to your current customer base before developing new products. The simple reason for this is because product development is usually more expensive than additional marketing effort. When you've done everything you can to satisfy your current customers, start looking for different kinds of customers in new markets. This is a judgment call that may differ from situation to situation. In other words, it might be better to find new customers for your existing products (category 3) before trying to develop new products for your current customers (category 2). It all depends on (1) how expensive and risky it will be to develop the new products and (2) your chances of breaking into the new markets. Since market positions and customer relationships are often harder to build than new products, opportunities in category 2 are usually easier to pursue.

## RECOGNIZING YOUR CAPABILITIES, RESOURCES, AND LIMITATIONS

You probably can't pursue every opportunity you dig up in the market. A good strategic plan capitalizes on your company's strengths and seeks to minimize the effects of your weaknesses. The things you do better than everyone else in the market are called **distinctive competencies** or *core competencies,* and they can be the foundation for a successful marketing strategy. For example, Wal-Mart developed a distinctive competency in distribution, which allowed it to address small-town markets cost-effectively. Wal-Mart's technique of building its stores in concentric rings around regional distribution centers cut its transportation and storage costs in half. By the time the competition recognized the savings, Wal-Mart had claimed enough store sites to make it impossible for competitors to employ the same technique.[27] Sometimes a company has a single unique advantage that forms the basis of its suc-

---

**market development strategy**
A growth strategy that involves entering new markets with existing products

**diversification**
A broad growth approach in which a firm enters new markets with new products

**distinctive competencies**
Things you do better than everyone else in the market, such as customer service or product design

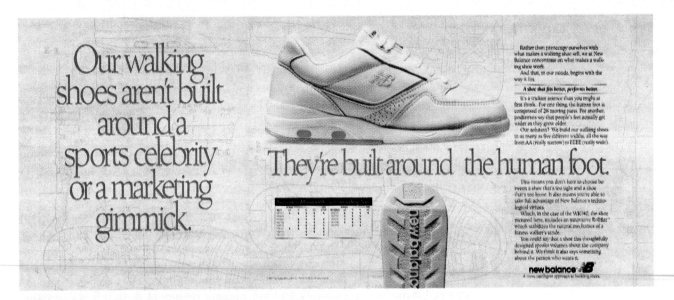

**Exhibit 3.8   MARKETING A UNIQUE ADVANTAGE**
While other shoe companies promote pumps, air bags, and other features that are supposed
to make shoes fit better, New Balance tries to convince consumers that it offers a unique advantage: shoes that fit better in the first place.

cess. Southwest Airlines boasts lower operating costs than rivals such as American
and United, and it uses that advantage to build market share with lower prices.[28]
New Balance survives in the ferocious athletic shoe business by offering a greater
selection of shoe widths (and thereby offering better fit) than huge rivals Nike and
Reebok (see Exhibit 3.8).[29]

In addition to building your distinctive competencies, you also need to consider
the resources at your disposal. Even a brilliant marketing strategy is of little value
if the company doesn't have the time, money, or skills required to pull it off. For instance, Avanti, a small manufacturer of luxury cars, would never try to compete directly with the huge engineering teams at Lexus or Mercedes. That's a battle Avanti
simply couldn't win—so it competes on the basis of unique styling. In recognition
of its small role in the luxury market, Avanti established appropriate objectives: just
1 percent of the market.[30]

Timing is also an important element in marketing planning. The term **strategic
window** identifies a limited period of time during which the characteristics of a market and the distinctive competencies of a firm fit together well, thus reducing the
risk.[31] Strategic windows can open when customer needs evolve, new technologies
emerge, government regulations change, or other elements in the marketing environment change. Windows can close for the same sorts of reasons. In one instance,
Power Test Corporation, which operates a chain of service stations, took advantage
of a strategic window when a competitor (Texaco) was forced to sell off some stations to avoid monopoly charges. Power Test had to be prepared to move quickly
when the stations were put up for sale; the strategic window would close if somebody else bought the stations.[32]

**strategic window**
A limited period of time during which the characteristics
of a market and the distinctive
competencies of a firm fit together well and reduce the
risks of seizing a particular
market opportunity

## WEIGHING THE RISKS AND REWARDS

When you identify a potential target market, there are several tests to apply before
proceeding. First, make sure the market is *big enough* to justify the effort needed
to enter it. Look for a *need* within the market for a product that you are capable of
delivering. Be certain a potential exists for *growth* within the market. Finally, make
sure the *structure of demand* gives you a reasonable chance of making a profit. Un-

less people are willing to buy a sufficient quantity of your product each time they make a purchase, think twice about entering the market.

How difficult is it for a market to pass these tests? That depends, of course, on the individual company. L. F. Deardorff and Sons makes cameras and sells about 300 of them a year. The company has been in business since 1921, and business has never been better. Yet 300 sales are just a drop in the bucket to most firms. What's the difference? L. F. Deardorff and Sons is one of the world's four producers of 8-by-10-inch sheet-film cameras. A Deardorff negative is 57 times as large as a 35-millimeter negative, providing much better picture quality. Deardorff cameras cost upward of $3,000 each and are used mainly by portrait, architectural, and catalog photographers, whose work must be as clear as possible. By Deardorff's standards, this market is very attractive, as it has been for the last 70 years.[33]

It's also important to understand the risks that an opportunity presents. Many types of risk exist in marketing. For example, if you spend $100 million developing a new headache medicine, only to find that the government won't approve the product, you've lost a risky gamble. On the other hand, you sometimes run the risk of being so successful that you invite competition. If other companies sense that you've uncovered a market opportunity and are making money at it, they'll try to figure out some way to share in the spoils.

Marketers often combine several stages of examination in a technique called *SWOT analysis,* from an acronym for strengths, weaknesses, opportunities, and threats. Once they've analyzed both themselves and their competitors using SWOT analysis, they have a good idea of what their strategic objectives should be—and what their competitors' objectives might be.

Applying SWOT analysis to your competitors is part of a larger effort known as **competitor intelligence,** which is a systematic process of understanding competitors and their influence on your markets. Analyzing your competitors involves uncovering four pieces of information about them:[34]

**competitor intelligence**
The systematic collection and analysis of data about a firm's competitors, with the goals of understanding the competitors' positions in the market and of formulating strategies in response

- *Their goals.* The goals of a company like Subway (which is focused on rapid worldwide expansion) are quite different from Next (which has retreated from the computer hardware business and is trying to carve a niche for itself in software) and from Ben & Jerry's Homemade (which places a significant emphasis on social goals in addition to financial goals). Knowing a competitor's goals is crucial to predicting how it will respond to changes in the marketing environment. For instance, a small company that wants to be the leader in a given market is likely to behave differently than a larger company that wants to protect its sales revenue and maximize the return for shareholders.

- *Their assumptions.* The strategic moves that a company makes are based on one or more assumptions about their marketing environment, both present and future. If a drug company like Merck assumes that the U.S. government will eventually establish price controls on prescription medicine, it might decide to abandon development of an expensive new drug or pursue development of more low-cost drugs. When Communist governments fell in Eastern Europe, western advertising agencies began setting up offices in the region on the assumption that free-market economies would need advertising services.

- *Their current strategies.* The strategies your competitors have established to reach their goals are driven by their goals and assumptions, and they also shed light on their capabilities and weaknesses. If you owned a discount department store and found out that arch-rival Wal-Mart was building a massive warehouse and distribution facility in the next state, you might surmise that the company is planning to build more stores in the region.

- *Their capabilities.* The first three items tell you what a competitor might do; this one tells you whether the competitor might be able to do it. Say you're in the telecommunications business and need to know which of several competitors is most likely to introduce video telephones at a cost most households can afford. Your analysis shows that one competitor holds several key patents in video transmission technology, and it also has the most efficient production facilities. You might safely conclude that this is the competitor to be most concerned about.

Clear analysis of your competitors enables you to select which competitors you might want to take on and which you might want to avoid. An attractive market opportunity might look a lot less so when you discover that a major global corporation has targeted the same opportunity. On the other hand, discovering that no one else seems to have noticed your opportunity can give you the green light to go ahead with your plans.

## SETTING OBJECTIVES

With this analysis completed, you're ready to set the objectives that will guide your marketing strategies and plans. Marketing planning is part of a hierarchy of planning that begins with your overall strategic business plan. That plan grows out of your **organizational mission,** a statement of the role your firm plays in the market and the way you want to be perceived by customers (see Exhibit 3.9). From this high-level vision, you can form the rest of the links in the chain—strategic, tactical, and operational marketing planning.

Consider the central theme of the mission statement used by Verbatim Corporation, a manufacturer of computer disks. It states that the company wants to be a

**organizational mission**
A statement of the firm's desired role in its sphere of business, often stated in terms of long-term goals and objectives

> growth organization, known worldwide for the quality of its products, its marketing expertise, and its ability to develop new products to serve the needs of its customers. Verbatim will manufacture its products worldwide at the lowest costs in the industry.[35]

This statement says a lot about what Verbatim wants to be and—just as important—what it doesn't want to be. The company wants to spend time and money to design and manufacture products with high quality at low cost. On the other hand, the mission statement doesn't say anything about being the world's biggest producer of disks or being the first with product innovations.

Nonprofit organizations develop mission statements for the same reason that their profit-seeking counterparts should: to focus the organization's energy, time, and money on the right problems and opportunities. For example, Head Start, a government program designed to help poor children overcome educational disadvantages, has a mission statement that identifies the market need being addressed and the solution being offered:

> For the child of poverty there are clearly observable deficiencies in the processes that lay the foundation for a pattern of failure . . . special programs can be devised for these children that will improve both the child's opportunities and achievements.[36]

**Exhibit 3.9   NOT ALL MARKETING GOALS INVOLVE GROWTH**
Amnesty International's marketing efforts flow from its mission of freeing political prisoners worldwide.

**VO:** This man is just one of tens of thousands of people who have been imprisoned or tortured because of the peaceful expression of their beliefs, the color of their skin, their religion, or even their sex.

Since 1961 Amnesty International has worked on behalf of over 42,000 such prisoners. By putting pressure on governments worldwide, Amnesty members are giving prisoners like him not just hope but freedom.

Raise your voice. Call 1-800-55-AMNESTY.

**market share**
An organization's portion of
the total sales in a given market, expressed as a percentage

Once the mission statement is developed, marketers need to establish objectives that are specific, measurable, and challenging. Establishing a goal to "increase sales in the future" is not a good objective; it doesn't say by how much or by what date. On the other hand, a goal to "increase sales 25 percent by the end of next year" provides a clear target and a reference against which progress can be measured. A common marketing objective is to achieve a certain level of **market share,** which is a firm's portion of the total sales in a market. Nintendo, for instance, might establish a market share goal of 70 percent at a certain level of profit, to be achieved over the course of five years. Portland General Electric, in contrast, would like its customers to use less of its product (electric power), so it runs ads encouraging people to conserve.[37] Making the objective challenging but still attainable is a great way to motivate people for peak performance. As Mitchell Leibovitz of the Pep Boys auto parts chain says, "If you want to have ho-hum performance, have ho-hum goals."[38]

With an overall business objective in place, each functional area in the organization can then set objectives that support the top-level objective. Each objective is accompanied by a strategy for meeting it, which leads to a hierarchy of objectives and strategies, similar to the hierarchy of plans shown in Exhibit 3.3. For Nintendo to meet its market share objective, for instance, each part of the company will have to do its part. Manufacturing will have an objective and a strategy for meeting the objective, as will finance, personnel, and marketing. The next section explains how to develop a marketing strategy once your marketing objectives are established.

## Develop Your Marketing Strategy

With an objective to guide your efforts, you're ready to define a marketing strategy. As discussed in Chapter 1, marketers engage in three activities to develop a marketing strategy: (1) selecting a target market, (2) staking out a desired market position, and (3) developing a marketing mix. This section gives you an overview of these three activities. In Chapter 7, you'll explore the detail of selecting a target market and staking out a position. In Chapters 8 through 19, you'll see how to develop a marketing mix.

### SELECT A TARGET MARKET

Selecting a target market is a matter of identifying the group of potential customers who are most likely to respond to your marketing efforts. This leads to an obvious question: Why not try to market your products to everyone and anyone? In some cases, this is in fact the best approach. If you market gasoline, potatoes, electricity, or some other product that most people need, it makes sense to market far and wide. Arco, for instance, would be happy if everyone bought the company's gasoline. However, in many situations, it doesn't make sense to market a particular product to every person on the planet. If someone isn't a likely customer, you'll waste both time and money trying to convince him or her to buy.

Spreading your reach far and wide also creates the risk of spreading yourself too thin. As a leader in the grand piano market, Yamaha had developed expertise in bending and laminating wood. The company then tried to leverage that expertise into a variety of related and unrelated markets, from guitars to skis to furniture. Profits plunged in the early 1990s as the company lost focus. In an effort to turn things around, president Seisuke Ueshima is refocusing on high-end musical instruments and now demands that the company examine each new market very carefully before plunging into it.[39]

In recognition of the fact that various groups of people often want different products, many marketers choose to develop products in more than one style, size, or level of quality—then they market each product to a different target market. Marriott did this with hotels and resorts when it realized that the market was really composed of a number of submarkets with differing needs. The company has created lodging products to meet the needs of five distinct groups of travelers:

- Marriott Hotels and Resorts offer traditional hotels aimed at the upscale business, leisure, and convention markets.
- Marriott Suites hotels offer two-room suites with first-class hotel services. The company created this product to meet the needs of frequent business travelers.
- Courtyard by Marriott offers small, moderately priced hotels for travelers who want attractive, functional hotel rooms, quality service, and amenities such as a restaurant and swimming pool.
- Residence Inn offers lodgings with moderately priced suites that include full kitchens. This product was designed for the "long-term stay" traveler.
- Fairfield Inn offers rooms-only economy lodging designed for budget-conscious travelers who want a nice room but don't need many amenities.[40]

The decision to focus on particular target markets as Marriott does or to go after the entire market as Arco does is one of the most important marketing decisions you make.

## STAKE OUT A MARKET POSITION

Smart marketers do everything possible to achieve the top position in the customer's mind. Think of business newspapers and you probably think of *The Wall Street Journal,* although a British student is more likely to think of the London-based newspaper *Financial Times*—different products can hold the top position in different markets (see Exhibit 3.10). For travelers checks, you might think of American Express, or of Steinway for pianos. These products achieved these positions through a careful combination of product qualities, advertising, and other aspects of marketing. The process of achieving a desired position in the mind of the market is called **positioning.**

Obviously, only one product can hold the top position in your mind. What about everybody else? To begin with, not everybody will agree with the positions in your mind. Some people will think Mercedes is the top luxury car, some will think Lexus, some BMW, some Cadillac, and so on. Even if Infiniti holds the top position in your mind, other carmakers shouldn't give up and go home. Perhaps you can't afford the

**positioning**
The process of achieving a desired spot in the minds of customers and potential customers; you can position your company, your products, your technologies, or any other entity that commands customer attention

(excerpts) How many more seconds till my date with Mathilde? How fast does my heart beat for Mathilde?

**Exhibit 3.10**
**STAKING OUT A MARKET POSITION**
In this unusual and humorous way, Casio tries to stake out its position as a supplier for highly functional watches that tell a lot more than just the time.

Infiniti, or maybe it isn't available in your area. On the other hand, Infiniti might make a mistake, and one of its competitors might seize the opportunity to take over. If you played king of the hill as a child, you have a good idea of what positioning is all about—achieving a position, then defending it against your competitors.

Establishing a strong market position has its advantages, to be sure, but there is some risk as well. If you decide to try for a different position, you may have trouble changing the market's mind. For instance, what do you think of when you hear "Fruit of the Loom"? You probably think of underwear, but Fruit of the Loom is trying to change that image because the company is moving into casual clothes. Fruit of the Loom envisions competing with The Gap someday, but time will tell whether the firm can achieve this new position.[41] Because positioning is such a fundamental part of marketing, you'll be encountering it throughout this course.

Everyone would like to be first in the minds of their target segments, but the simple fact is that most companies aren't first. What should you do if you're not at the top? You have three choices. First, you can try to dislodge the leader. For example, the makers of Infiniti don't say their cars are cheaper than BMWs; they want you to think that Infiniti automobiles are *better* than BMWs. Second, you can acknowledge that the leader already has that position and try to find a comfortable position lower down the chain. Price is a common way to do this, presenting yourself as a lower-cost alternative to the leader (see Exhibit 3.11). Third, you can try to change the way the market thinks about the product category. For example, mouthwashes have traditionally competed on the basis of effectiveness, but some brands have started to tout plaque-removal capabilities, which might make consumers change the way they think about mouthwashes.

Although you can do a wide variety of things to achieve a desired position, it is the market that ultimately decides the position you occupy. Positioning is a lot like romance; you can influence someone's thoughts and feelings, but you can't force anyone to fall in love with you. In both positioning and romance, your job is to be consistent, dependable, and persuasive. If you do the right things long enough, if you've targeted the right audience, and if the competition hasn't beaten you to the punch, you should eventually achieve your desired position.

It's important to define the position you want to occupy before proceeding with

**Exhibit 3.11
POSITIONING
RELATIVE TO A
MARKET LEADER**
Promoting yourself as a less expensive alternative to the market leader is common positioning strategy. Zeos challenged top computer makers by offering quality products at competitive prices. In ads such as this one, the company used quotes from industry experts who say that its computers are as good as or better than those from market leaders IBM and Compaq, at significantly lower prices.

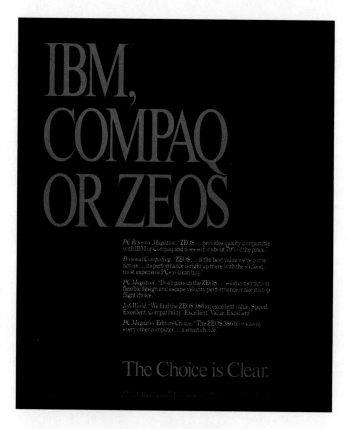

product development and other activities. Nissan didn't design the Infiniti only to look around and say, "Hey, why don't we position this thing as a luxury product?" The company chose the position it wanted to occupy and then set out to develop the marketing mix that would help it achieve that position. This raises an important point: Everything you do, intentionally or otherwise, can affect the position you hold in the mind of the market. Advertising is an important tool in the positioning process, but advertising isn't the only significant factor. Product quality, customer service, philanthropic activities, the trash in your parking lot, labor relations—everything you do influences the way people think about you. Finally, recognize that you need to position more than your products. You can also apply the concept of positioning to your company, your technologies, your sales force—any entity that holds a place in the minds of customers.[42]

## DEVELOP A MARKETING MIX

If the analysis of a potential market is promising enough to make it a good target, develop a marketing mix that will appeal to this market. Assemble a combination of product characteristics that closely matches what the customers in the target market are looking for. Create a structure of prices that will make product purchase feasible for market members. Put together a distribution system that assures goods are made available where and when they are wanted. Finally, assemble a promotional mix of advertising and other tools that will communicate the benefits of what you have to offer.

Karsanbhai K. Patel, for example, is an Indian entrepreneur who knows how to appeal to the needs of his customers. His detergent, Nirma, contains few perfumes or whiteners, is sold in plastic bags with crudely printed labels, is carried by thousands of tiny independent stores, and sells for 9.25 rupees (about 58 cents U.S.) per kilogram, half the price of other, more conventionally packaged and distributed products in the same geographic area. Although it might not sound like a strong product, Nirma holds 30 percent of the Indian laundry detergent market because it meets the needs of its customers. The majority of the people in India simply need a basic product that is available close to home at a low price.[43]

# SALES FORECASTING

Good strategic planning rests on a foundation of good sales forecasting. The **sales forecast** is an estimate of the firm's sales for a specified future period. It is an essential tool in developing new products, scheduling production, determining necessary inventory levels, and creating a distribution system. Based on estimates of **market potential,** the amount that the entire industry can sell during a specified future period, the sales forecast serves as the reference point for marketing control efforts.

## The Nature of Forecasting

Forecasting is one of the most challenging, intriguing, and frustrating aspects of marketing. Mistakes in either direction can be costly. A forecast that is too high can lead a company to invest too much money and produce too much inventory, thus wasting money and reducing profitability. On the other hand, a forecast that is too low can also hurt. If demand is higher than expected, delivery times will increase, customer support might suffer, and other aspects of quality become vulnerable as the company races to meet demand. Gillette won over a lot of men with its recent introduction of the Sensor razor, but it underestimated demand. Many stores were stuck without products to sell. Some customers switched to Sensor but then couldn't find replacement blades.[44] As far as marketing problems go, underestimating demand isn't such a bad problem to have, but be aware that it isn't always a painless situation.

**sales forecast**
An estimate of a firm's sales volume in dollars or units for a specified future period

**market potential**
The amount of product, in dollars or units, that a firm's entire industry can be expected to sell during some specified future period

## FACING AN UNCERTAIN FUTURE: HOW TO REDUCE THE RISK

A big part of marketing planning lies in making assumptions. For example, if you were going to publish a marketing textbook, you would have to assume that a certain percentage of college students will take marketing courses and that paper supplies will be adequate. Perhaps you would assume that other publishers will come out with competitive books within a year or two of yours. You can't arrive at a forecast until you make these assumptions.

But what if some element in your marketing environment is just too difficult to predict accurately? Maybe you heard a rumor that the U.S. De-

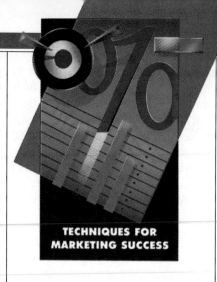

**TECHNIQUES FOR MARKETING SUCCESS**

partment of Education might mandate that all marketing textbooks cover ethics; your book doesn't, and you can't predict the government's decision. Perhaps labor unrest is rising in the printing business; if strikes hit the industry, you won't be able to print

enough books to meet demand. Each of these situations might be very hard to predict, and a wrong assumption on your part could seriously hurt your business. You can't eliminate risk from business decisions, but a technique known as *scenario planning* can help you understand and cope with uncertainty.

Scenario planning involves four steps. First, identify all the possible future conditions in your marketing environment. For the printing labor situation, you might identify three scenarios: no labor unrest, isolated work stoppages, and an industrywide strike. These scenarios will be the basis of your plans and forecasts.

The second step is to develop a deeper understanding of each potential scenario. Identify the factors in the market that could lead to each possible outcome. In the printing la-

Forecasts are of two types: those you can base on historical data and those you can't. As an example of forecasts based on historical data, say you're the manager of a Target store, and you want to forecast sales for October. You might use a process like this:

1. Compute the average sales data from previous Octobers; this gives you a good starting point.
2. Consider this year's sales trend; for instance, if sales so far this year are 5 percent better than last year, increase your forecast by 5 percent.
3. Take into account other factors—weather, sporting events, teacher strikes, and the like—that might affect sales. For example, if history tells you that sales increase 10 percent during rainy months, adjust your forecast accordingly.

Naturally, you can't have complete confidence in the forecast that results from a process like this (What if a surprise snowstorm hits?), but you can feel pretty good about it. Your projection is based on solid historical data, and if you've taken all important factors into account, chances are good that your forecast will be reasonably accurate.

The second type of sales forecasting is a different matter entirely. What if you don't have extensive past sales data? What if this is your store's first month of operation? What if you're introducing a product the world has never seen? In such cases, you have to rely on a combination of methods, including judgment, analogy, and common sense.

Finally, forecasting has both broad and narrow applications. On one hand, executives at General Motors would like to know the transportation needs of people around the world 10 or 20 years from now. On the other hand, a GM dealership in Denver needs to know how many cars it can sell this year, this month, even this week. Both situations require a forecast of sales in the future.

bor situation, list factors that either cause or predict a strike. These include the level of union recruiting activity, the growth or decline of union members' buying power, labor unrest in related industries, and certain conditions in labor negotiations.

The third step in scenario planning is to develop a contingency plan for each possible scenario. Because you can't be sure which scenario will come true, you need to be prepared for all of them. This requires extra work, but preparation is the best way to face an uncertain future.

The fourth step is to continually monitor the factors that lead up to each scenario. When it looks like a particular scenario is starting to unfold, put the plan for that scenario into action. If union activity is up, or negotiations aren't progressing well, you might decide that the strike scenario

is about to happen and manage accordingly.

A classic case of scenario planning that brought this technique to the attention of many people is the way Royal Dutch/Shell handled the Arab oil embargo in 1973. In the years before the embargo, competitors had built their business plans based on specific assumptions about crude oil supply. However, Royal Dutch/Shell had constructed several scenarios, including one in which oil supplies were severely disrupted. After they studied that possible scenario, company managers decided to take a more conservative approach to investing in their various businesses. While competitors charged full speed ahead, assuming oil would always be available, Royal Dutch/Shell's scenario planning helped it anticipate the embargo and the resulting shift of power from the

oil companies to the oil-producing nations. When the embargo did hit, Royal Dutch/Shell was the only major oil company to avoid significant financial damage.

## APPLY YOUR KNOWLEDGE

1. If you were the superintendent of a public school district, what data could you collect to help identify possible scenarios of student population patterns 10 years into the future?
2. Your company is designing an electric car, and your job is to forecast sales when the car is introduced five years from now. What are the possible demand scenarios for this product, and how should your company get ready for each scenario?

## Forecasting Techniques

When it's time to forecast, you have quite an array of techniques to choose from. The choice depends on the availability of data, budget, time, and the range of your forecasting skills and experience. Here's a quick look at the most common techniques, which can be divided into *qualitative* and *analytical* methods. Put simply, qualitative forecasting is based primarily on judgment and experience, whereas analytical forecasting is based primarily on data.

QUALITATIVE FORECASTING

Qualitative forecasts have some distinct advantages and disadvantages. On the positive side, people with experience in a market segment can often predict sales with surprising accuracy, based on their understanding of market dynamics. In addition, qualitative forecasts are inexpensive, which no doubt makes them some of the most commonly used methods. On the negative side, qualitative forecasts are only as good as the people making them. A forecaster with poor judgment or no experience in a market stands a good chance of making an inaccurate qualitative forecast. Two popular techniques rely on human judgment: the jury of executive opinion and the Delphi technique.

EXECUTIVE JUDGMENT    The **jury of executive opinion** is a method of forecasting that asks top executives of the firm to give their predictions of the future. These predictions are then combined and averaged to produce a picture of the executives' expectations for company performance. Cheap and quick to do, this method works best for short-run forecasts. Its major flaws are (1) the executives have a vested interest in the company, so their forecasts might be biased; and (2) the amount of information each executive uses may be limited by the time he or she has to research the market before making a prediction.

**jury of executive opinion**
A method of forecasting that averages the predictions of top executives of the firm to create a sales forecast

**85**

**Delphi technique**
A forecasting method that
uses the averaged opinions of
inside and outside experts
who are allowed to change
their predictions after learning the overall results of a
first-round forecast; the revised estimate becomes the
final forecast

THE DELPHI TECHNIQUE    Similar to the jury of executive opinion, the **Delphi tech-nique** uses experts (often from outside the company) and features multiple passes. The process starts with each expert making a prediction. Then the researcher averages these results and sends them back to the experts. The experts are asked for a second prediction, taking into account the results of the first pass. Knowing the results of the first round, the forecasters are free to revise or stick by their original judgments. This method tests the conviction of the predictors by telling them what the group's combined prediction was the first time through. The idea is that receiving the group's consensus may cause some experts to change their predictions one way or the other. How good is this method? Naturally, its accuracy depends on the expertise of the people involved. As one example, American Hoist and Derrick Company is fortunate to have qualified experts. After one year of using the Delphi method to make short-term forecasts, the error of the forecasts has been less than 1 percent.[45] Remember, though, executive opinion and the Delphi technique are only as good as the people who participate in them.

## ANALYTICAL FORECASTING

Judgment can be a powerful forecasting tool, but it doesn't always offer accurate answers. The alternative is analytical forecasting, which takes advantage of data to give you answers that are more acceptable from a statistical perspective. Numerous analytical methods range from simple surveys to complex computer models.

SURVEYS OF BUYING INTENTIONS    One direct way to build a sales forecast is to come right out and ask potential customers whether they intend to buy. A *survey of buying intentions* indicates the percentage of the target market that is likely to buy your products. These surveys make the most sense when you have a small number of potential customers. The most common technique is to ask them to rate their likelihood of purchase, from 0 to 100 percent, within a given time frame. This technique has the advantage of being directly in touch with the potential purchasers. On the other hand, it is measuring *intent,* not actual purchase *behavior.* For instance, people might say they intend to buy, but then change their minds later. Obviously, the longer the time frame, the less accurate buying-intention surveys become. These surveys can be either qualitative or quantitative, depending on whether the people you ask truly represent the overall market.

You can complement a customer survey by polling your sales force. These people are closer to the customers than anyone else in the company, but there are two potential problems with their answers. First, each respondent can answer only for his or her territory; you must avoid the temptation to extrapolate individual answers to the entire market. Second, sales reps have a personal interest in the forecast,

**Exhibit 3.12  SALES HISTORY OF HYPOTHETICAL PRODUCT**
Using these data as a starting point, you can compare the three common techniques in time-series analysis (see Exhibits 3.13 through 3.15).

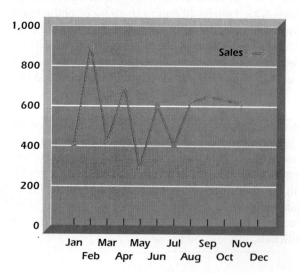

which might influence the numbers they give you. For example, many salespeople earn additional commission when they exceed 100 percent of their sales goals, so they might be tempted to give you a lower forecast number—this makes it easier for them to reach 100 percent. In spite of these drawbacks, sales force surveys can still provide a good cross-check for other forecasting methods.

TIME-SERIES ANALYSIS    One of the most widely used forecasting techniques is **time-series analysis,** which is based on the assumption that the past can be used to predict the future. Take a look at the sales data in Exhibit 3.12. Sales of this hypothetical product started at 400 in January, jumped to 900 in February, then bounced between 300 and 675 units per month. Looking at these 11 months of sales history, what do you think December's sales are going to be?

You could take a very simple approach and assume that December's sales will be equal to November's, but history tells you that one month doesn't necessarily follow another's pattern. Perhaps an average of the previous months' sales would be more appropriate. The average sales figure so far this year is 571 units a month. However, there might be a trend in the data, in which case a simple average wouldn't be appropriate.

You can check these data for trends with a technique called **trend analysis.** This method looks at sales history for possible long-term movements in the direction of the data. The simplest trend analysis uses a math technique called *linear regression analysis* to arrive at the straight line that best fits the data points. Exhibit 3.13 shows the linear trend for our sales data over the past 11 months. Average sales show a slight increase from month to month. Using trend analysis, you can extend the trend line to December, which yields a forecast of 615 units.

Questions already exist. What if market conditions have changed over the course of the year? For instance, perhaps a new competitor appeared in September, which started a three-month decline in your sales. In this case, computing the trend over the entire year probably isn't appropriate. If you compute the trend over the last three months, as in Exhibit 3.13, a dramatic decline in sales is evident, with a December projection of around 600 units. You can see that selecting the time frame over which you figure trends is critical; the long-term trend in these data is upward, but the short-term trend is downward. You need to know what is happening in the market before you try to choose the amount of data.

If your market seems to grow and ebb as a matter of course, projecting trends might not be the best idea. An alternative is a **moving average,** which averages the data over short periods of time. The moving average picks up new data and discards old as you move along in time. For example, to compute a three-month moving av-

**time-series analysis**
A collection of forecasting methods that predict future sales by analyzing historical sales patterns

**trend analysis**
A time-series forecasting method that creates an equation to describe the expected behavior of sales in the future using sales data accumulated over some period in the past

**moving average**
A forecasting method that averages inside a moving window of fixed duration; for instance, a three-month moving average averages three months of data at a time and then adds the newest month and discards the oldest month to compute the next data point

**Exhibit 3.13    TREND ANALYSIS**
Simple trend analysis indicates that sales have gradually increased over the past 11 months, leading to a December projection of 615 units. However, a trend line computed over just the last three months tells a different story.

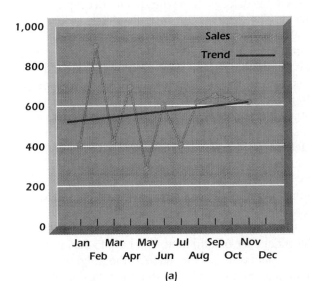

(a)

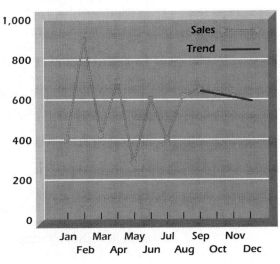

(b)

## Exhibit 3.14
## MOVING AVERAGE FORECASTING

Moving averages ignore older data, presenting you with projections based only on the most recent data. Longer averaging windows tend to flatten out peaks and valleys in the data.

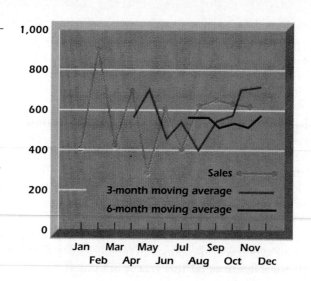

## Exhibit 3.15
## EXPONENTIAL SMOOTHING

Exponential smoothing is an alternative to simple trend projections and moving averages; it keeps all the data but lets you choose how much emphasis to put on new data versus old. A high emphasis on new data yields a forecast that tends to track recent sales.

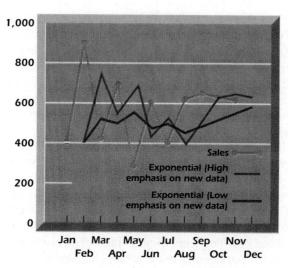

**exponential smoothing**
A time-series analysis method that assigns weights to the sales data used in the forecast; you can give newer data either a high or low weighting, depending on how much you want to emphasize them

erage, you take sales data for the last three months and project them as the forecast for the next month. Exhibit 3.14 shows a three-month and a six-month moving average for our hypothetical sales data. You can see that the three-month average tends to track short-term variations in the data, whereas the six-month average tends to flatten out the peaks and valleys. The three-month formula yields a December forecast of 650, compared with 593 for the six-month formula.

Some forecasters aren't comfortable with either trend analysis or moving averages. They don't like ignoring some of the data, but they don't want to let old data bias their projections. In these situations, the technique of choice is **exponential smoothing,** which is a weighted average that lets you place greater importance on parts of the data. With exponential smoothing, you can decide how much more important the new data are, and assign a weighting factor accordingly. Exhibit 3.15 shows two exponentially smoothed curves for our sales data. One placed a high emphasis on new data, producing a December forecast of 632. Contrast this with the other curve in Exhibit 3.15, which placed a low emphasis on new data and ended up with a forecast of only 576—the lowest of all six attempts. (The table in Exhibit 3.16 provides the data points from these forecast examples.)

Perhaps you've noticed something interesting about these so-called analytical methods—they all require a substantial dose of judgment. You have to decide which method to use, which data to include, and other factors such as the weighting in exponential smoothing. This highlights an important point about forecasting, regardless of the method: You cannot feed data into your computer blindly. Experience and good judgment are always essential aspects of the forecasting process.

To improve the precision of their forecasts, marketers often apply several correction techniques to their projection. The first of these is **cycle analysis,** which isolates larger economic effects and removes them from the time-series analysis. For instance, if your entire industry is in a slump, as the housing industry was in the early 1990s, you might want to remove the effects of the slump from your data analysis. This will give you an idea of how well your marketing programs are working, apart from the overall economic conditions.

Another common adjustment technique is to remove **seasonality,** the annual patterns that many businesses experience in their sales. For instance, formal wear shops, vacation facilities, and apartment complexes often experience seasonal fluctuations that are tied to school schedules. Business-to-business marketers frequently see seasonal shifts tied to their customers' fiscal years, which affects the timing of large purchases. Because these fluctuations are fairly predictable, it's easy to remove them from the overall data.

Finally, when no other approaches can explain fluctuations in the data, marketers use a third correction technique. **Random factor analysis** covers one-time events that affect sales but that don't occur in regular patterns. Strikes, wars, factory fires, and passing fads are some of the events that fall into random factor analysis. Of course, you can't do anything to forecast these occurrences, but they can help you explain the historical record. And the better you understand your sales history, the more accurately you can project future sales.

CORRELATION ANALYSIS    In some cases, you can use the sales of other products to help guide your own forecasts. For example, yearly production of steel is a fairly accurate predictor of yearly sales of limestone, coke, and alloy metals. **Correlation analysis** is a forecasting technique that predicts the sales of an item on the basis of the sale, use, or availability of one or more other items. The object of correlation analysis is to find a variable or group of variables that will accurately predict the behavior of another variable. However, it is important to rule out coincidence and to make sure that a true correlation exists between the predictor product and the product you're trying to forecast.

SIMULATED TEST MARKETING    One of the more advanced forecasting techniques is **simulated test marketing,** in which you attempt to measure customers' buying behavior without having them actually make purchases in a real-life setting. You will find two ways to do this. The first is with laboratory experiments such as the mock supermarkets that some consumer-goods marketers use. Representative consumers

**cycle analysis**
A time-series correction technique that adjusts forecasts for movements in the overall economy

**seasonality**
The effect exhibited by recurring annual fluctuations in sales data; seasonality is caused by such events as school schedules, weather cycles, holidays, and crop-growing seasons

**random factor analysis**
Analysis of unexplained differences between predicted and actual sales behavior; usually due to such random occurrences as strikes, wars, and factory fires

**correlation analysis**
A forecasting method that predicts the sales of an item on the basis of the sale, use, or availability of one or more other items

**simulated test marketing**
A forecasting method that gathers data for predicting a product's likely market performance by marketing it in artificial settings

**Exhibit 3.16   FORECAST DATA**

| Month | Actual Sales Data | Trend Analysis (long) | Trend Analysis (short) | 3-Month Moving Average | 6-Month Moving Average | Exponential Smoothing (high) | Exponential Smoothing (low) |
|---|---|---|---|---|---|---|---|
| January | 400 | 535 | — | — | — | — | — |
| February | 900 | 542 | — | — | — | 400 | 400 |
| March | 425 | 550 | — | — | — | 750 | 500 |
| April | 700 | 557 | — | 575 | — | 523 | 485 |
| May | 300 | 564 | — | 675 | — | 647 | 528 |
| June | 600 | 571 | — | 475 | — | 404 | 482 |
| July | 400 | 579 | — | 533 | 554 | 541 | 506 |
| August | 610 | 586 | — | 433 | 554 | 442 | 485 |
| September | 675 | 593 | 675 | 537 | 506 | 560 | 510 |
| October | 650 | 600 | 650 | 562 | 548 | 640 | 543 |
| November | 625 | 608 | 625 | 645 | 539 | 647 | 564 |
| December forecasts | | 615 | 600 | 650 | 593 | 632 | 576 |

This table shows the data resulting from the example forecasts.

are asked to go shopping in this laboratory setting, choosing from the available products. By watching how people shop and tallying the results, you can predict sales in the real world with some degree of accuracy. The second approach is based on the same concept but uses simulations instead. Simulations can be created both with catalogs of real and planned products and with computer software that presents various products and features on the screen.

**test marketing**
Marketing products on a small scale in order to test sales potential and the various elements of the marketing mix before paying for a full-scale introduction

TEST MARKETING    The next step is to get out in the marketplace and see how well your product will sell. **Test marketing,** as the name implies, involves testing the potential of a product by marketing it on a limited scale. For some radically innovative products, this may be the only way to predict market reaction. The scope of the test is much more limited than a full-scale introduction would be, often involving only a few cities or towns. The performance of the product in the smaller market should be a good predictor of its performance in the larger market if the test sites have been well chosen. Test marketing is expensive, though, and some costs related to production and marketing are almost as large as if full-scale marketing had been undertaken. In cases where the costs to develop the product far exceed the costs of marketing it, companies usually skip test marketing. These companies have already spent the big money, and their only choice now is to market the product as aggressively as possible.

### COMBINING METHODS

Firms often make predictions of sales performance by combining two or more of the techniques discussed in this section. The process of sales analysis might begin with a jury of executive opinion and move to a customer survey, continue with some time-series and correlation analysis, followed by test marketing. These methods are not mutually exclusive. They all seek to improve a firm's ability to see into the future, and as long as the budget and schedule can handle it, the more methods used the better.

## Forecast Evaluation

Forecasts that are simple judgment calls and those based on complex computer models share an important attribute: They can't foresee the future with complete accuracy. Forecasting should support your judgment, not replace it. Therefore, when you've finished your forecast, review what you've done. Ask yourself the following questions:

1. *Are your assumptions reasonable?* When you're developing forecasts, you often have to make assumptions about future events, so make sure these assumptions are reasonable. For instance, McDonald's can safely assume that the U.S. hunger for fast food won't go away overnight. However, unreasonable assumptions, particularly about the adoption of new technologies, have been the downfall of many forecasts. Personal helicopters, artificial beef, plastic houses, and undersea hotels are just some of the products that would have required enormous changes in customer behaviors and attitudes, and forecasters mistakenly assumed that people would want to change. At the same time, many companies once assumed that radial tires, automatic coffeemakers, paperback books, semiconductors, digital watches, disposable diapers, and overnight delivery services were silly ideas that would never catch on.[46]
2. *Have you used consistent definitions?* This seems like an obvious point, but it can hobble the best of forecasts. Verify that everyone involved is using the same definitions of markets, market share, profit, customer needs, competition, and other factors that play into the forecast.
3. *Where did you get your data?* Whether you have two bits of data or a closetful, verify both the source and the accuracy of your data. For example, if you're assuming that 5 percent of the people of Milwaukee will visit your new store, do you have an accurate count of the city's population from a reliable source?

4. *Does it make sense?* Step back from the numbers you've generated and consider their logic. Marketers often apply a "reality check" to make sure a forecast makes sense. The factors to consider vary from situation to situation, but common sense should be your guide. For instance, does your sales forecast indicate a market share that just seems unbelievable? Never take the word of a computer, a consultant, or any expert if it doesn't make sense to you.[47]

At this point, you have a brilliant strategy in place and a forecast that predicts success. You just sit back and wait for orders to roll in, right? Unfortunately, the real world doesn't work this way. The biggest challenge in marketing isn't usually strategic planning or forecasting—it's implementation, the art and science of making things happen. The rest of the book shows you the details of putting a marketing mix together.

# SUMMARY OF LEARNING OBJECTIVES

**1. Identify the two primary dimensions of strategic marketing planning.**

The two most important dimensions of the strategic planning process are (a) a broad scope and (b) a long-term perspective. Strategic planning considers all the products a company offers and all the markets the company targets, as well as environmental and organizational factors. Strategic planning also looks beyond immediate circumstances and tries to project market conditions 5 or 10 years into the future.

**2. Discuss the levels at which planning takes place in an organization and the types of plans that are made at each level.**

Planning occurs at three levels in the organization. Strategic planning is the highest level; as such, it is conducted by a firm's top management. At the middle-management levels, brand managers and marketing directors engage in tactical planning, which is narrower and of shorter time frame than strategic planning. The shortest and narrowest planning is operational planning, which is done by first-level supervisors and nonmanagement professionals.

**3. Outline the activities that take place in the process of developing strategic objectives.**

To develop strategic objectives, first, understand and monitor the environment in which your firm operates. This helps you recognize opportunities and risks. Second, recognize your capabilities, resources, and limitations. The best strategy in the world is of little value if you don't have the means to make things happen. Third, identify your opportunities and risks and those of your competitors.

**4. Explain portfolio analysis and its strengths and weaknesses.**

Portfolio analysis refers to a variety of techniques that categorize strategic business units so that you can apply specific strategies to each SBU. Two of the most common models are the growth/share matrix and the market attractiveness/business position model. The growth/share ranks SBUs by market growth and market share, whereas the market attractiveness/business position model uses a richer set of variables that do a better job of characterizing the decisions

marketers actually make. Portfolio analysis has two major disadvantages. First, it doesn't always take into account all the factors that can affect the attractiveness of a target segment and your ability to access that segment. For instance, the growth/share matrix ignores every factor except market share and growth, and it's based on the presumption that cash flow is your primary objective. Second, models tend to stress big market shares, but many firms with small market shares continue to prosper.

**5. Discuss the process of designing marketing strategy.**

When designing a particular marketing strategy, you need to make three choices. The first of these is the position that you are shooting for in the target market. Second is the growth approach that will be most appropriate: intense, diversified, or integrated growth. Third is the marketing program approach, whether undifferentiated, differentiated, or concentrated.

**6. Describe the nature of sales forecasting and list the most common methods of creating forecasts.**

Sales forecasting is one of the most important tasks in marketing, but it is far from an exact science. Forecasting techniques can be divided into two categories: judgmental and analytical. The judgmental techniques rely on human judgment; the two most common are the jury of executive opinion and the Delphi technique. The analytical techniques are based on analysis of data, either from surveys of purchase intent or historical sales records. Three common methods are based on sales data: trend analysis, moving averages, and exponential smoothing. In addition, some marketers opt for simulated or actual test marketing to determine sales potential.

**7. List the steps you can take to evaluate sales forecasts.**

You can ask a series of questions to help evaluate your sales forecasts. First, are your assumptions reasonable? Second, have you used consistent definitions of such items as markets, market share, profit, customer needs, and the competition? Third, did your data come from reliable sources? Fourth, aside from what computers and experts tell you, does the forecast make intuitive sense?

### Meeting a Marketing Challenge at Nintendo

When most companies looked at the U.S. home video game market in the mid-1980s, they saw only the remains of past failures. However, Nintendo's Minoru Arakawa saw a strategic window waiting for the company with the right marketing strategy. Arakawa realized that poor quality had caused the market to fall apart the first time. Home games were slow and simplistic, and no one was controlling the quality or quantity of game software. Companies that wanted to create high-quality games were caught in a price war and couldn't afford to spend the time to develop superior software. The result was a flood of poor-quality home systems that drove kids back to the arcades.

Nintendo was in a unique position to reignite the U.S. market. Its parent company in Japan already claimed 95 percent of the market in that country with a high-quality product called the Famicom. Nintendo adapted Famicom for the United States, renaming it the Nintendo Entertainment System (NES). NES accepted software game cartridges (called Game Paks) designed by Nintendo and a network of handpicked software developers. Arakawa was ready for the U.S. market with a product that was already a proven winner.

He needed more than a great product, however, to overcome the skepticism of U.S. retailers and consumers. It was crucial for Nintendo to introduce the NES with a bang and demonstrate there was new life in video games. To achieve quick success, Arakawa chose a strategy of concentrated marketing. He decided to initially target only young boys and introduce the NES in one local market, the New York City area. This allowed Nintendo to focus its resources and increase the chance of success. By combining intensive local advertising with a wide variety of retail channels, Nintendo reached a large audience quickly. Consumers responded to the quality of the new system, and as the news spread, Nintendo moved nationwide.

Price control was a big factor in Nintendo's success. Software developers chosen by Nintendo are the only other companies authorized to develop games for the NES. As part of this arrangement, Nintendo controls manufacturing, pricing, and distribution of all games. No one is able to undercut prices, so Nintendo maintains strong profit margins and avoids a price war. The profits enjoyed by its game developers also help Nintendo keep innovative software companies in the family.

Promotion is another powerful component of the marketing mix. The centerpiece is *Nintendo Power,* a bimonthly magazine that promotes new games and helps players win the hottest games. Television advertising builds awareness for the system and its most popular games. Also, a variety of cooperative marketing projects, from breakfast cereal to posters, keep the Nintendo name in front of millions of consumers.

Nintendo's distribution strategy relies on a wide range of retail outlets, including department and discount stores, toy stores, and consumer electronics outlets. Whether a family shops at a discounter such as Kmart or a premium retailer like FAO Schwarz, it has access to Nintendo products. And Nintendo provides strong support to the stores that carry its products, ranging from attractive in-store displays to a telephone support center that relieves stores of the expensive customer support burden.

From a low of $100 million, Nintendo pushed U.S. sales of home video games back up to over $3 billion in only four years. Along the way, it captured about 80 percent of the rejuvenated market. Nintendo's success is striking proof of how strategic marketing planning can turn even the most discouraging situations into opportunities. In the mid-1990s, Nintendo faces mounting competition from traditional rivals such as Sega, the growing presence of home computers, and new possibilities such as multimedia technologies. The company remains optimistic about its future, and given its track record so far, that optimism certainly seems reasonable.

**Your mission:**  As Minoru Arakawa expected, the rebirth of the home video game market brought a number of competitors back into the ring. These companies have access to the same technologies Nintendo uses, so Nintendo can't maintain its lead based on technology alone. As assistant to Peter Main, Nintendo of America's marketing vice president, you must track changes in the market and suggest corrections for Nintendo's marketing strategy.

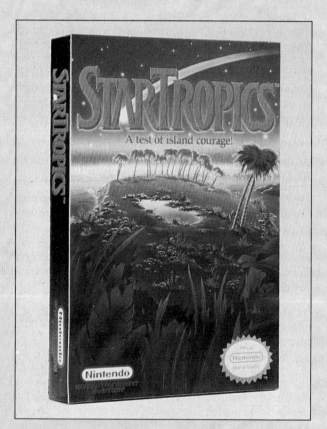

1. The Software Publishers Association started a promotional campaign to tell families about the advantages of home computer-based games. The organization says children and their parents should look to computer games instead of video games for several reasons. First, computer games are now as action-packed as video games. Second, computer games can offer a level of interaction that is unheard of in video games (with some software packages, players can create their own characters and modify storylines as games progress). Third, computer games offer a big advantage for parents because there is a much greater emphasis on education. How should Nintendo respond?

   a. Continue with your current strategy of selling fun and excitement. It's best to ignore the computer challenge and concentrate on your core business of video games in order to fend off Sega and Atari.

   b. Create ads that show the computer as a boring business machine meant for parents. Children may respond to this and turn away from the computer. Tell parents that if they have a stack of Nintendo games in the house, the kids will leave the computer alone and let the parents get real work done.

   c. Continue to sell fun and excitement but gradually expand into more education-oriented games if the threat from PC software continues to grow. This will give concerned parents an option without having to take away their kids' video systems.

2. Phone calls to your U.S. headquarters in Redmond, Washington, indicate that players are starting to sense too much similarity in games. Sports games simply copy the real-world sports without adding anything new. Combat games use the same "good guy versus bad guy" theme, and everybody is a karate expert. Boredom is Nintendo's worst enemy; you must convince the market there is a never-ending supply of fresh games and fresh characters. Suggest the best way to revitalize the product offering.

   a. Start designing an adapter for Atari and Sega games. This device would let players plug competitive games into the Nintendo system, thereby letting them play all the popular games.

   b. Continue your product development efforts, providing accessories that work with your games. These include the Power Pad, the Power Glove, and other control devices. Create new accessories that your competitors may have difficulty duplicating and feature these in *Nintendo Power*.

   c. Involve players in the design process. Meet with groups of players and let them critique game outlines before programming starts. Offer rewards for customers who bring in fresh game ideas. Ask them to submit both original ideas and ideas from movies, television, and books.

3. Nintendo executives have decided the company's heavy reliance on video games makes it too vulnerable to declines in that market. Headquarters in Japan has asked Nintendo of America to suggest extensions of the company's product mix to give it a more stable revenue base. Which of the following proposals would you support?

   a. Move into home computers. You're a known force in the home electronics market, so it's a logical step for you to make. Parents are already familiar with the Nintendo name, so they'll accept the "NIntendo PC."

   b. Move into nonelectronic games. Take advantage of your visibility by basing board games and travel games on popular Nintendo characters. Market them as less expensive alternatives to Nintendo games.

   c. Stick to the video game business; expansions into other market areas are too risky. Broaden your offering of accessories, and increase promotions of the Power Glove, Power Pad, joysticks, and other add-ons.

4. Nintendo headquarters wants an updated competitive analysis. What's the best way to analyze your competitors and present your findings to company management?

   a. Interview retailers and summarize their comments. The retailers have the best view of what's happening in the market and will be able to tell you how the various products are doing. Retailers are particularly interested in maintaining good relationships with Nintendo, so you'll get their full cooperation.

   b. Examine the actions of major competitors and try to uncover their underlying strategies. Learn how to predict their potential behavior when facing a given situation. Compare how they'll respond to how Nintendo will respond, and see who has the strongest strategy. Include a summary of sales and your best estimates of the capabilities of each competitor.

   c. Focus your attention on the largest competitor, since that company is your biggest threat. Report on that company's sales, as well as your best estimate of its strategy. Try to uncover its engineering, manufacturing, and marketing capabilities so that you'll have a better chance of projecting its future moves.

**SPECIAL PROJECT**

Assume that a potential problem just turned into a real problem: Atari Games won its antitrust suit against Nintendo. You are now forced to let any software developer write game software for the Nintendo system. Peter Main reminds the Nintendo marketing staff of how a flood of poor-quality software choked the market in the mid-1980s. Not only do you no longer have control over the quality of all games, you've lost control of prices as well. Main has asked for your thoughts on a revised competitive strategy. The rules of the game have changed drastically; how will you respond?[48]

## Marriott Serves Up Strategic Moves

"Success is never final," says J. W. (Bill) Marriott, Jr., chairman of Marriott, and that's especially true in the hospitality business. With revenues approaching $10 billion, Marriott has succeeded by taking some daring risks—but not without careful strategic planning and a clear-cut corporate mission to guide the process.

J. Willard Marriott, Sr., started in 1927 with an A & W root beer stand in Washington, D.C. To spark demand during the winter, Marriott added food and later changed the name to the Hot Shoppe. Eyeing the growth in automobile use, he then opened the East Coast's first drive-in restaurant, and sales sizzled. Five years later, Marriott spotted another opportunity: feeding airline passengers. He approached Eastern and American airlines and arranged to provide on-board meals. For the next decade, catering was the company's main focus.

Marriott kept watching the trends, including a big increase in car ownership, and he believed that there were opportunities beyond food service. In 1957 he opened a huge motel in Virginia, and the company has been in the lodging business ever since. Today, Marriott holds 4 percent of all U.S. lodging rooms, making it the nation's largest hotel/motel operator.

However, the environment for food and lodging has been getting dicier as supply swells and demand shrinks. Hotel operators kept on building even as many corporations clamped down on business travel. By 1989 more than half the hotels in the country were operating at a loss. In this hotly competitive environment, Marriott, like others in the industry, is reviewing its strategies, including a plan to split the company in two (isolating hotels from the company's other interests).

Marriott's strategic planning process is guided by an overall corporate vision: to create the best lodging and food service in the world. Tom Curren, senior vice president for corporate planning and business development, explains, "In each business, we look to become (1) the preferred employer with the best management team, (2) the preferred provider and (3) the most profitable." Marriott also sets financial goals for growth: Each business must earn at least a 15 to 20 percent annual return on equity.

The company conducts planning at the business-unit level and at the corporate level. To support its plans, Marriott develops forecasts on a three- to five-year time frame and examines markets in North America and other continents. As the result of strategic planning, Bill Marriott has in his time made some tough decisions that have changed the course of the company. For example,

the restaurant division was the heart of the business for many years. However, in 1989 Marriott announced it would sell Roy Rogers and its other restaurants. By that time, the restaurants were serving up a mere 13 percent of Marriott's revenues, and Marriott believed that the restaurants would grow too slowly to meet corporate expectations.

Another tough choice was the decision to enter the residential life-care business. Marriott marketers considered four alternatives in the retirement market: a community geared to leisure activities; a community oriented toward health care; a community with on-site nursing; and a full-service community with leisure and medical facilities. After looking at population forecasts and assessing the needs of potential users, they settled on the full-service concept.

One risk Marriott faced was that healthy retirees would be reluctant to sign up for the new residences because they wouldn't want to admit the possibility of serious illness or incapacitation. However, Marriott decided to bank on the firm's reputation as a quality hotelier to win over potential residents. He committed more than $1 billion to develop 150 retirement communities across the country. Eighty percent of the units in the first two developments were snapped up on the first day of business. As population patterns change over time, Marriott will continue to seek out new opportunities and develop marketing strategies in the pursuit of growth.

1. Imagine that Marriott has decided to pursue a market penetration strategy to fill those hotel rooms left empty by the glut in lodging. Should the chain contract with major cities to temporarily house local homeless families at a reduced rate, or should it contract with large corporations and government agencies to provide employees with overnight accommodations at a reduced rate?

2. Could Bill Marriott better leverage his firm's current positioning by developing and managing golf resorts or by developing and managing day-care facilities for children?

3. Assume that Marriott wants to expand its reach in the university cafeteria management business. Should it adopt a position as the caterer that feeds more college students than any other food service marketer, or should it position itself as the best-quality full-service food supplier?

# KEY TERMS

competitor intelligence (78)
correlation analysis (89)
cycle analysis (89)
Delphi technique (86)
distinctive competencies (76)
diversification (76)
exponential smoothing (88)
growth/share matrix (70)
jury of executive opinion (85)

market attractiveness/business position model (71)
market development strategy (76)
market penetration strategy (75)
market potential (83)
market share (79)
marketing plan (66)
moving average (87)
operational planning (68)

organizational mission (79)
portfolio analysis (70)
positioning (81)
proactive marketing (66)
product development strategy (75)
Profit Impact on Marketing Strategy (PIMS) (72)
random factor analysis (89)
reactive marketing (66)
sales forecast (83)

seasonality (89)
simulated test marketing (89)
strategic business unit (SBU) (70)
strategic marketing planning (66)
strategic window (77)
tactical planning (68)
test marketing (90)
time-series analysis (87)
trend analysis (87)

# QUESTIONS FOR DISCUSSION

1. Would the owner of a small flower shop use strategic planning, tactical planning, or operational planning? Explain your answer.
2. How might environmental influences affect market opportunities and risks for the following organizations?
   a. British Airways     c. Waste Management
   b. Frito-Lay           d. United Way
3. What are the distinctive competencies of your college or university?
4. What is the difference between long-term planning for a fashion retailer and long-term planning for an electric energy utility?
5. What are the dangers faced by an insurance company that relies exclusively on the growth/share matrix to select its target markets?
6. Ferrari and General Motors both manufacture cars; should they use the same strategic business unit structure?
7. Should McDonald's and Tiffany pursue growth using the same approach? Why or why not?
8. How would you describe the market position of each of the following firms? Why?
   a. AT&T
   b. Von's
   c. MTV
   d. Boeing
9. You're trying to forecast next year's sales for *The New York Times;* which of the following sources of information would be most valuable to your project?
   a. Newsstand operators
   b. Sales history for the *Detroit Free Press*
   c. Population patterns in the New York City area
   d. Projected literacy rates in North America
10. Assume you've been in business for three years, a new competitor entered the market several months ago, and your sales are subject to numerous whims of fashion; which time-series analysis technique should you use, and how many years of data should you include in your computation?

# SHARPEN YOUR MARKETING SKILLS

Browse the aisles of the nearest supermarket and find evidence of a company that expanded by developing new products for existing markets. Look for a well-known brand name that has been applied to a new product. Some examples of this expansion technique include a new cold medicine from the makers of Alka-Seltzer, Diet Coke, and Kleenex diapers.

**Decision:** Sometimes this sort of expansion is successful, sometimes not. Do you think it is appropriate for the company you discovered? Make a list of other possible products that this company could develop for existing markets, using one of its established brand names.

**Communication:** Write a one-page memo explaining (1) why you think the brand extensions you saw in the supermarket are a good idea or a bad idea and (2) why the possibilities you've identified would be a good fit for the company.

# KEEPING CURRENT IN MARKETING

Choose one or more articles describing a successful small local or regional company that is planning to expand its marketing to the national level.
1. Describe how the company is executing the four-step strategic marketing planning process. For example, what specific objectives does the company have?
2. What aspects of the marketing environment have been identified that will influence the ability of the company to serve a national market profitably? Which of these can the company's executives influence? Which are beyond their control?
3. Which forecasting method would you recommend as most appropriate? Why? How does your recommendation differ, if at all, from the one the company is using?

# A Sample Marketing Plan

The results of the strategic marketing planning process are presented in a marketing plan, a document that guides your marketing efforts and helps you strike a balance among all the competing demands for resources. This component chapter starts by explaining why you need a marketing plan and then describes the scope of typical marketing plans. After that, you'll see the basic elements that make up a marketing plan. Finally, you can examine a plan from a hypothetical T-shirt company, The Shirt Off My Back, to get an idea of what a real marketing plan looks like.

If you're thinking about career advancement, pay close attention to the marketing plan—it usually represents a great opportunity to show your skills to upper management. Brand and product managers are frequently assigned the task of preparing the plans, which are then reviewed by higher levels of management. This is your chance to demonstrate your grasp of marketing concepts, your understanding of the company's business, and your talent for making things happen.

## WHY YOU NEED A MARKETING PLAN

Developing a marketing plan takes time, money, and energy, but it is well worth the effort. Here are the major benefits of a good marketing plan:

- Highlights important problems and opportunities
- Focuses resources on the right tasks
- Establishes targets by which you can measure performance
- Makes marketing more efficient
- Coordinates everyone's efforts (particularly important as more companies try to integrate all of their marketing activities)

Too many companies spend time and money creating a marketing plan, only to watch the plan sit on a shelf when it's finished. Responding to daily interruptions can divert your attention from the strategies and tactics outlined in your plan. However, long-term success is rarely the result of a mad scramble from one day to the next. To achieve your goals, you need to operate according to a plan—your marketing plan.

## THE SCOPE OF THE MARKETING PLAN

Marketing plans fall into two general categories. The first focuses on specific products, whereas the second covers the company's entire product offering. Each type has advantages and disadvantages. Product-oriented plans can go into greater tactical detail because they can focus on one product. They are particularly helpful when you're introducing a new product, a process that requires a lot of coordination and control. However, the overall plans do a better job of keeping the company's marketing efforts in harmony. By avoiding too much detail, the overall plans can also concentrate on higher-level strategic issues. A good compromise is to have one marketing plan for the company (or strategic business unit), complemented by individual product-oriented plans.

Another important aspect of marketing plans is the time frame they cover. A common planning horizon for marketing is one year. Companies don't usually develop formal plans for periods shorter than a year, although a shorter time frame can be helpful in selected situations such as product introductions. On the other hand, many companies go beyond a year with their planning cycles. Sometimes one document covers both short- and long-term plans; sometimes the one-year plan is accompanied by a separate plan with a longer perspective, such as five years. Keep in mind, however, that with rapidly changing market conditions, long planning horizons can become impractical.

# WHAT'S IN A MARKETING PLAN

The marketing plan answers three important questions:

- Where are you now?
- Where do you want to be in the future?
- How are you going to get there?

The basic components of the marketing plan address these questions. First, *situation analysis* describes where you are now. Then *objectives* state where you want to be. Finally, the *action plan* outlines how you can get there. Other common sections are the executive summary, which presents a quick overview of the plan, and a variety of appendixes containing such information as risk analysis, financial data, and product details. A complete operational plan includes budgets, activity assignments, schedules, and all the supporting data required by the marketing team to get the job done.

The specific outline an organization uses depends on its market situation and the information needs of decision makers in the organization. For example, here's the outline used to develop a marketing plan for specific products at Fidelity Bank in Philadelphia:

- Management summary (brief overview of plan)
- Economic projections (What factors in the economy will affect this product?)
- The market—qualitative (Who are the potential customers?)
- The market—quantitative (How many potential customers are there?)
- Trend analysis (Based on history, what does the future hold for this service?)
- Competition (Who are our competitors, and how are we positioned?)
- Problems and opportunities (What problems need to be solved in order to be successful? What opportunities can we pursue with this product?)
- Objectives and goals (What sales volume and profit do we expect to achieve? How will this product affect our organization?)
- Action programs (What must we do to meet our objectives?)

You can see that even though this plan uses different terminology, it still addresses the three basic questions required in a marketing plan. To give you a better feel

for the content and tone of the marketing plan, the following sample was developed.

# SAMPLE MARKETING PLAN

The Shirt Off My Back (TSOMB) is a hypothetical T-shirt producer in Denver, Colorado. The company buys plain T-shirts from clothing manufacturers and prints its own unique designs on them. The completed shirts are sold to various retailers, who then sell them to consumers. TSOMB has grown quickly during its two-year history, and in 1994 the company sold 250,000 shirts. The challenge now facing founder Sue Scheeren and her staff is to expand beyond the Denver market. Here's a look at a plan that Scheeren's marketing manager might have put together to guide this expansion. The plan presented here is shorter and contains less detail than a typical marketing plan, but it does show you the key points successful plans address. Note that all figures in this plan are fictional, with the exception of population statistics.

## Situation Analysis

TSOMB has enjoyed phenomenal growth during its first two years in business. Exhibit A shows the market share we've achieved. Our nearest competitor is

**Exhibit A   DENVER-AREA T-SHIRT MARKET (1994 MARKET SHARE DATA)**
This pie chart shows the market share of the major T-shirt companies in Denver, Colorado.

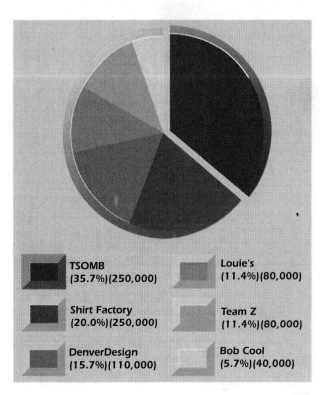

TSOMB (35.7%)(250,000)

Shirt Factory (20.0%)(250,000)

DenverDesign (15.7%)(110,000)

Louie's (11.4%)(80,000)

Team Z (11.4%)(80,000)

Bob Cool (5.7%)(40,000)

## Exhibit B  INCOME STATEMENT

| The Shirt Off My Back<br>Summary Income Data, 1994 | | |
|---|---:|---:|
| Sales revenue | | $3,500,000 |
| Cost of plain shirts<br>(average $4.00/shirt) | $1,000,000 | |
| Cost of adding designs<br>(average $1.50/shirt) | 375,000 | |
| Administrative costs | 457,550 | |
| Salaries | 883,200 | |
| Other expenses | 168,800 | |
| Total expenses | | 2,884,550 |
| Income before taxes | | $ 615,450 |
| Taxes | | 92,318 |
| Net income | | $ 523,132 |

This report shows TSOMB's income, expense, and profit data for 1994.

Shirt Factory, which has just over half our share. In addition, TSOMB has achieved healthy profitability, as seen in Exhibit B. We sold 250,000 shirts in 1994, at an average price of $14 each, for total 1994 revenue of $3,500,000. From this, we have to subtract $2,884,550 in expenses, for a pretax profit of $615,450. This gives us an attractive profit of well over $2 per shirt.

The typical TSOMB customer is 25 to 45 years old and has an interest in outdoor activities such as hiking, organized athletics, winter sports, and photography. Annual income levels range from $25,000 to well over $100,000; the common factor among these people is an interest in quality and attractive clothing. We sell quite a few children's shirts every year, but our research shows that the buyer in almost all these cases is a parent or adult relative. Our customers tend to be informed of and involved in current events, including the environment, politics, business-society relationships, and education.

Our current marketing mix is based on several varieties of T-shirts, including several styles of children's shirts (which typically sell at retail prices of around $10) and several styles of adult shirts (which sell for as much as $20). Unlike most of our competitors, we avoid short-term fad themes and stick with lasting images of Colorado landscapes, winter sports, and wildlife. Admittedly, we miss some sales opportunities by not pursuing fads, but we also avoid the risks of getting stuck with inventory when fads die out. In addition, our customers don't accumulate shirts that go out of style long before they wear out. DenverDesign is the only competitor that is trying a product strategy similar to ours, and it is starting to show some success.

Our pricing strategy supports our position in the market as a supplier of high-quality, long-lasting products. As such, we lean toward the high end of the price scale in the Denver market, but the extra revenue allows us to hire top artists and production people. In addition, an above-average price helps communicate a message of quality to prospective buyers.

TSOMB shirts are sold through department stores and other retailers. Because our shirts are more expensive than the average T-shirt, we target customers who see the value in a high-quality shirt that won't go out of style in a short time. These people shop for their clothes in upscale department and specialty stores, so those are the retailers we use as well.

Up to this point, our promotional strategy has relied primarily on the products themselves. When consumers see their friends or relatives wearing our shirts, many are inclined to ask what brand they are and which stores carry them. Our logo is worked into each design to make sure potential buyers always know which company produces the shirts that caught their attention. We use personal selling to promote our shirts to retailers. The salespeople also serve as our customer support arm, helping retailers design displays and perform other tasks needed to successfully sell our shirts.

This marketing mix has produced great success in Denver. Unfortunately, our marketing research shows that the Denver market is approaching saturation. Based on sales histories from other markets, we believe that sales growth begins to level off when the per capita ownership of fashion T-shirts approaches 0.4. With a metropolitan-area population of 1,861,000 and 1994 sales of 700,000 fashion T-shirts, Denver is currently at 0.38. Once a market reaches saturation, most sales come from people who are replacing outgrown or worn-out shirts, rather than from people who are buying fashion T-shirts for the first time. In other words, we don't think we can continue our current rate of growth if we confine ourselves to the Denver market.

## Objectives

This marketing program is designed to meet three major objectives. First, we want to maintain a level of profitability that is close to the level we currently enjoy in the Denver market. This means we must avoid markets in which we can't compete with our premium prices or where the costs of doing business would eat into profits. We expect to see temporary declines in profit as we invest in new markets, but profit should recover and return to its current level.

Second, we want to finance our expansion ourselves as much as possible. In other words, we don't want to incur a significant amount of debt while trying to reach new markets. Borrowing money to finance marketing programs is not in itself bad, of course, but we believe our company's long-term interest is best served by remaining as debt-free as possible. The consequences of this objective are that we'll have to be especially creative in designing a low-cost marketing mix.

Our third goal is to quadruple sales by the end of

1997. This means an additional 750,000 T-shirts sold per year. We realize this is an aggressive goal, but we believe it is attainable with the right products and the right marketing programs. A detailed look at our sales force is included in the following section, where we identify the target markets we'll pursue.

## Marketing Strategy

We realize that a successful marketing strategy rests on (1) a clearly defined target market and (2) an effective, efficient marketing mix. Here's a brief look at both components, followed by a representative schedule for entering new markets.

### TARGET MARKETS

We examined a number of variables when selecting target markets for expansion. We decided early on to stick with the same demographic market we sell to in Denver. This leaves us with the geographic variable: Which cities should we pursue? When choosing cities, we looked at demographic profiles, to assure a sufficient number of the kind of people we target. After that, we looked for cities with low per capita sales of fashion T-shirts, which is a rough indication of untapped market opportunity. We looked at dozens of cities around North America; Exhibit C presents the data on ten selected cities. Based on the theory that low per capita sales are a good indicator, Albuquerque and Des Moines look like great places for TSOMB to enter. In addition, Phoenix and Boston are good choices, with per capita figures below 0.25. At the other end of the scale, Memphis and Honolulu appear to be even more crowded than Denver, with per capita figures over 0.4.

We've limited ourselves to the four low-per-capita markets because success there would mean reaching our goal of 750,000 additional shirts. This forecast is based on the assumption that we can attain the same market share we have in Denver (35 percent) and that each of the four cities will eventually reach per capita T-shirt sales of 0.3. Research we've done in the four markets indicates that consumers would be willing to buy more fashion T-shirts, but they currently don't see

**Exhibit C  T-SHIRT SALES IN SELECTED METROPOLITAN AREAS**

| Area | Population (1,000) | T-Shirt Sales (1,000) | Per Capita T-Shirt Sales |
|---|---|---|---|
| Albuquerque | 486 | 80 | 0.16 |
| Des Moines | 385 | 75 | 0.19 |
| Phoenix | 1,960 | 450 | 0.23 |
| Boston | 4,093 | 1,000 | 0.24 |
| Atlanta | 2,657 | 750 | 0.28 |
| Chicago | 8,147 | 2,500 | 0.31 |
| Las Vegas | 600 | 225 | 0.38 |
| Denver | 1,861 | 700 | 0.38 |
| Memphis | 972 | 400 | 0.41 |
| Honolulu | 831 | 350 | 0.42 |

This table indicates fashion T-shirt sales in 10 selected metropolitan areas. You can see that Denver is among the most saturated of these markets.

a lot of shirts that interest them. By entering the markets and providing the products people are looking for, we believe we can increase the overall size of the markets and reach a dominant share in each city as well.

As Exhibit D shows, if we can achieve 35 percent of the market in each city, and if per capita sales reach 0.3, these four new markets will yield a total sales volume of 728,000 shirts. This is roughly equal to the sales increase we need to meet our sales objective. We expect sales will continue to increase in Denver at a modest rate, so our combined sales in all five cities will exceed 1 million shirts.

Of course, sales in each new city won't jump from zero to forecast volume overnight. We expect each market to take about a year to generate sufficient consumer awareness and retailer activity. Sales will probably build slowly in each market, as word gets around about the new shirts. We think it will take three to four months until sales really pick up; then they'll take off for the next six months or so, eventually reaching expected volume after a year. Exhibit E shows what this buildup looks like for each of the four cities. (To make comparison convenient, we've shown all four cities starting simultaneously. However, as we explain in the

**Exhibit D  SALES OBJECTIVES IN FOUR NEW MARKETS**

| Market | Population (1,000) | Per Capita Sales Goal | Total Market Sales Goal (1,000) | TSOMB Share Goal | TSOMB Sales Goal (1,000) |
|---|---|---|---|---|---|
| Albuquerque | 486 | 0.30 | 146 | 35.0% | 51 |
| Des Moines | 385 | 0.30 | 116 | 35.0% | 41 |
| Phoenix | 1,960 | 0.30 | 588 | 35.0% | 206 |
| Boston | 4,093 | 0.30 | 1,228 | 35.0% | 430 |
| Totals | 6,924 | | 2,078 | | 728 |

Based on our per capita sales goal of 0.30 and market share goal of 35 percent in each market, our total sales objective for these four new markets is 728,000 shirts.

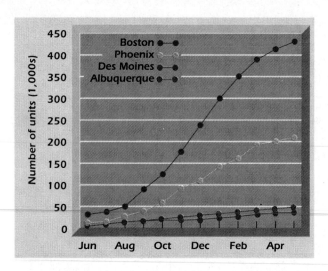

**Exhibit E**
**PROJECTED SALES GROWTH IN FOUR NEW MARKETS**
We think we'll need about a year to establish sales volumes in each new market; this graph shows how sales are likely to build over the first year.

following section, we plan to stagger our introductions over the course of two years.)

MARKETING MIX

The marketing mix we'll use in each of the four new cities is based on the mix we've used successfully in Denver for the last two years. In order to ensure our success in new markets, however, we'll research local tastes, which will give us a better idea of the types of designs to develop for each market. Much of our success in Denver stems from our creative images of Colorado scenery. Obviously, these designs won't be in heavy demand in other cities and states, but by researching local tastes, we can identify desirable images for each new market.

Pricing also requires some research to make sure we identify price ranges in each market. We want to continue our position as an upscale supplier of premium products, but we don't want to price ourselves out of a given market because we've misread local economics. Our initial research shows that each of the four markets we've targeted will support the prices we've used in Denver. In fact, we're considering raising prices for the Boston market, which has shown a generally higher price structure than the other markets.

Not surprisingly, the distribution aspects will require a great deal of attention. We'll start by identifying key retailers in each market, which are those stores that attract our target customer. The next step is to understand the needs of these retailers so that we can effectively present our products and support services to them. After that, we make our presentation to each target retailer and then negotiate selling arrangements with those retailers who opt to pick up our products.

Once we've established these marketing relationships, we go to work helping these retailers get ready for our launch in the given market.

The promotion element is the area in which we'll make the greatest changes from the approach we use in the Denver market. Because we want to build sales as quickly as possible in these new cities, we believe we need a stronger promotional campaign. However, we don't have a lot of money to spend on promotions because the research and product development required to enter these new markets will consume most of the cash we have on hand. Consequently, we're looking for clever, low-cost ways to put our products in the public eye.

One of the most important things we can do is create bold display advertising for retailers to use in their stores. These displays will catch the attention of shoppers and help sell TSOMB products. In addition, we're currently exploring all possible avenues for getting the message out, including appearances at local fairs, musical events, and sports contests. In a related effort, we'll contact local sports teams to offer TSOMB shirts to team members for wear before and after games. Finally, we'll contact the local media in each market immediately prior to our launch date, with the hope of generating some news coverage of our entry into the market.

INTRODUCTION PLANS

Entering these new markets won't be a simple task. It will take the coordinated efforts of everyone at TSOMB and several months of planning to make it happen. However, by mapping out a logical chain of events and then following that schedule closely, we're confident we can enter the new markets successfully.

Exhibit F is a schedule of events leading up to our introduction in the Des Moines market. Programs in the other three cities will follow similar schedules. The research and planning phase takes approximately five months, which covers January through May in the case of Des Moines. As the schedule indicates, the introduction program is divided into four simultaneous efforts, each one corresponding to an element of the marketing mix. We've assigned product, price, distribution, and promotion specialists to pursue their respective elements of the mix in all four cities, to make sure we're doing the best job possible.

We'll enter the four markets in a staggered fashion, which allows us to spread our people and money more evenly. We'll allow six months to plan and prepare for each city—five months for the process outlined in Exhibit F, plus one month in case we need to keep the marketing team focused on that city. This results in the following timetable:

**Jan. 1, 1995:**   Begin planning for Des Moines introduction

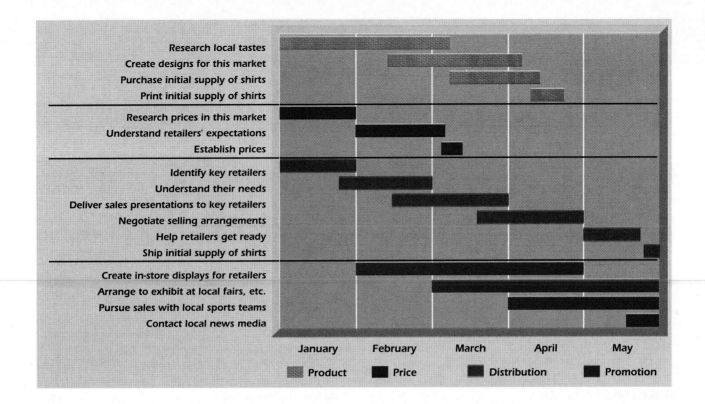

| | January | February | March | April | May |
|---|---|---|---|---|---|
| Research local tastes | | | | | |
| Create designs for this market | | | | | |
| Purchase initial supply of shirts | | | | | |
| Print initial supply of shirts | | | | | |
| Research prices in this market | | | | | |
| Understand retailers' expectations | | | | | |
| Establish prices | | | | | |
| Identify key retailers | | | | | |
| Understand their needs | | | | | |
| Deliver sales presentations to key retailers | | | | | |
| Negotiate selling arrangements | | | | | |
| Help retailers get ready | | | | | |
| Ship initial supply of shirts | | | | | |
| Create in-store displays for retailers | | | | | |
| Arrange to exhibit at local fairs, etc. | | | | | |
| Pursue sales with local sports teams | | | | | |
| Contact local news media | | | | | |

■ Product   ■ Price   ■ Distribution   ■ Promotion

**June 1, 1995:** Introduce in Des Moines

**July 1, 1995:** Begin planning for Albuquerque introduction

**Dec. 1, 1995:** Introduce in Albuquerque

**Jan. 1, 1996:** Begin planning for Boston introduction

**June 1, 1996:** Introduce in Boston

**July 1, 1996:** Begin planning for Phoenix introduction

**Dec. 1, 1996:** Introduce in Phoenix

With the projected one-year sales buildup in each market, the last market we enter, Phoenix, will be at full sales volume by the end of 1997. At that time, with some continued growth in Denver, we should be selling over 1 million shirts per year, which supports our goal of quadrupling sales from their current level.

**Exhibit F**
**THE SHIRT OFF MY BACK:**
**DES MOINES INTRODUCTION SCHEDULE**
The Des Moines introduction schedule is representative of the schedule we'll follow in each new market. We'll need about five months to plan and prepare for each introduction.

**APPLY YOUR KNOWLEDGE**

**1.** What are some of the risks in TSOMB's plans? How would you reduce these risks?
**2.** If TSOMB decided to use magazine advertising to build awareness among potential buyers, which magazines would you suggest the company advertise in?
**3.** How would you improve the accuracy of TSOMB's sales forecasts?
**4.** What elements of the marketing environment might affect TSOMB's success?

## AT&T Rings Up Marketing Successes

Ma Bell. The phone company. AT&T used to be easy to figure out. It was practically synonymous with telephone service in the United States. It made the telephones, owned the long-distance wires, and owned most of the local phone business around the country as well. In short, when you picked up the phone, you were most likely dealing with AT&T. The government kept other companies out of AT&T's markets, and the company grew into a huge, unresponsive monolith that many considered the very antithesis of entrepreneurial capitalism.

### Becoming a World Technology Leader

Fast-forward to the 1990s. AT&T is now one of the world's top advanced-technology companies, making entrepreneurial efforts in voice recognition, computers, video conferencing, telephone-computer hybrids, semiconductors, cellular phone networks, portable systems that will let you send a fax from the beach, and even advanced video game technologies. It is also the second-largest issuer of credit cards in the United States (after Citicorp). Even though AT&T still processes 140 million phone calls a day, top managers spend a lot of time thinking about computers, video, and other nontelephone opportunities.

What happened to boring old Ma Bell? One of the most important lawsuits in U.S. history, that's what. The U.S. government had been after AT&T for decades, worried that its control of both telephone manufacturing and local and long-distance phone service was restraining competition. In 1968 the Justice Department succeeded in stripping AT&T's protected monopoly in telephone equipment and in 1969 began allowing other companies to provide long-distance service. (This is when MCI got its start.)

## The Beginning of the New AT&T

Then in 1984 came the biggest blow. The government forced AT&T to sell its seven giant regional Bell companies, which provided service for most of the United States. (You're probably served by one of these "Baby Bells," which now go by such names as Nynex, Bell Atlantic, and Pacific Bell.) On the bright side, the Justice Department allowed AT&T to enter new businesses, such as computers.

Looking back a decade after this monumental decision, AT&T CEO Robert Allen argues that the twin hits from the Justice Department weren't really blows after all. In fact, he says the government did AT&T a favor by jolting the sleepy giant and forcing it to learn how to compete and innovate. Allen and his team have been doing just that, with streamlined operations, energetic research into new technologies and new products, and dedication to the marketing concept.

Listen to what Jerre Stead, one of AT&T's top executives, has to say to employees about customer orientation: "If you're in a meeting, any meeting, for 15 minutes, and we're not talking about customers or competitors, raise your hand and ask why. If it goes on for half an hour, leave!" Hardly the attitude of a sleepy, unresponsive monopoly.

## Learning to Compete

The dual theme of customers and competition is evident in AT&T's approach to marketing long-distance services. As you can tell from the barrage of advertising in this business, AT&T is locked in vigorous competition with MCI and Sprint. Having lost 30 percent of the market it once controlled as a monopoly, AT&T is not about to give away any more territory without a fair fight. The marketing program is based on three promises to customers. First, they won't pay significantly more than competitors charge. This doesn't mean that AT&T will always have the lowest price, but it will always be close, and AT&T hopes customers always find greater value in the AT&T service offering. Second, AT&T rewards customer loyalty with discounts and other special offers. If you keep calling with AT&T, they'll return the favor by giving you a break on your phone bill. Third, AT&T will strive to offer the best mix of goods and services for each customer's individual needs. For instance, residential customers who make a certain number of long-distance calls in the evening qualify for a special discount on calls made during that time of the day.

You'll recognize this three-part promise as part of a clear dedication to the marketing concept described in Chapter 1. In addition to this sensitivity to customer needs, Allen stresses long-term profitability for each of the company's strategic business units. Products such as the VideoPhone and the Hobbit microprocessor weren't expected to generate quick returns, but they established beachheads in significant markets where the company expects to reap rewards over the long haul. In terms of functional integration, not only does AT&T expect divisions and departments to work together, it expects entire business units to help each other succeed. With the VideoPhone, for instance, the Communications Products Group is expected not only to succeed with its own product but to provide more business for the core telecommunications business (since videophones operate on the company's long-distance phone lines).

The AT&T of the 1990s is clearly a different kind of company. With a new attitude about customers and competitors and a focus on fast-moving technologies, it is positioned to be perhaps the major player in the increasingly intertwined telecommunications/computing industry.

## Questions

1. If someone described AT&T's long-distance business in terms of telephones and wires, would you consider this a case of marketing myopia? Why or why not?

2. Did AT&T's position in the market change as it went from a regulated monopoly to a less regulated competitor, even though it remained the dominant provider of telephone service? Explain.

3. Since the name AT&T was derived from American Telephone & Telegraph, should the company operate under a different name if it tries to offer phone service in other countries? Why or why not? Do you think BT (British Telecom) or NTT (Nippon Telegraph and Telephone) would have trouble using their names in this country?

4. Do phone companies and other utilities have an ethical obligation to offer service to people in remote areas, even if that service is far more costly to deliver? Why or why not?

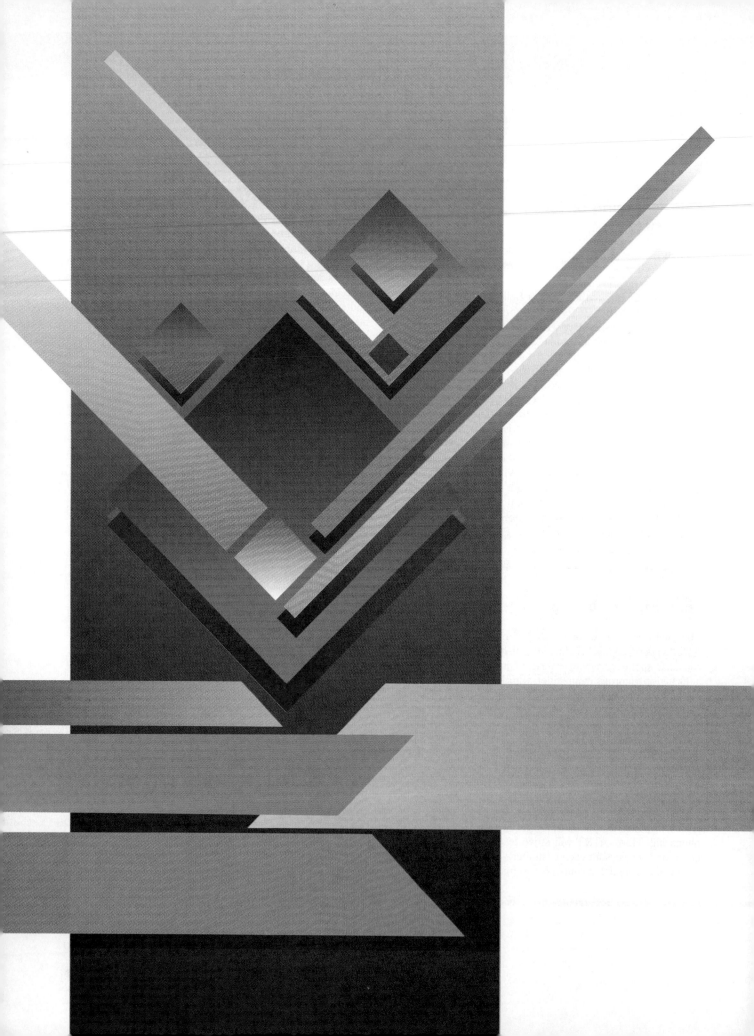

# PART II
# MARKET ANALYSIS AND TARGET MARKETING

# 4

# The Consumer Market

**After studying this chapter, you will be able to**

**1.** Describe how involvement affects the consumer decision process

**2.** Differentiate among routine, limited, and extensive problem solving

**3.** Explain how perceived risk relates to the consumer's information search process

**4.** List the five stages of the consumer decision process and briefly explain what occurs at each stage

**5.** Discuss the psychological factors that influence consumer buying behavior

**6.** List the cultural and social factors that influence consumer buying behavior

**7.** Identify the situational factors that influence consumer buying behavior

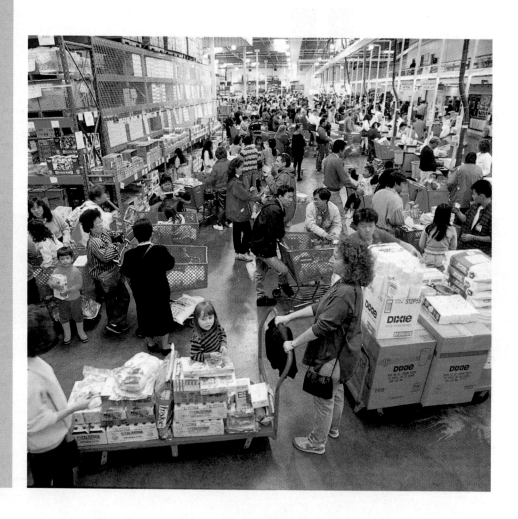

## Double Cheese in Double Time

A University of Michigan undergraduate bought a pizzeria in 1960 and went on to change the world's pizza-buying behavior with a simple formula: delivery in less than 30 minutes. Thomas C. Monaghan's guaranteed delivery formula was the key to building Domino's, his international empire of more than 5,000 pizza outlets, with yearly sales in excess of $2 billion.

The market wasn't exactly ready and willing when Monaghan first made his move in the pizza business, however. Back when Monaghan bought his first pizza place, only students in dorms were accustomed to dialing for dinner. Families and young working adults were unfamiliar with telephone ordering, let alone delivery to the doorstep. These consumers viewed pizza as a snack, not as a real meal, and home delivery was generally unavailable.

During the 1960s and 1970s, changes in the social and economic environments started altering consumer demand and buying behavior. More women were working and family income was increasing. Mealtimes—even the meals themselves—were changing as lifestyles became more active than ever. Also, the giant hamburger and chicken chains were expanding rapidly, spending millions to promote fast food as an easy alternative to eating at home. Casting a sharp eye around the U.S. market, Monaghan recognized that time and convenience were powerful elements in consumer attitudes and buying behavior. He also found that he didn't have to offer every possible type of pizza in every conceivable size to keep customers satisfied. "During a rush one night," he explains, "I got mad and told people not to take any more orders for six-inch pizzas. Sales jumped 50 percent that night, we dropped the smaller pies and suddenly made money for the first time."

Success didn't come overnight to the would-be prince of pizza. As Monaghan expanded his chain, he came to the brink of financial disaster more than once. However, through all the ups and downs, he kept experimenting with the ingredients of time and convenience until 1972, when he cooked up his ultimate recipe for success: guaranteed home delivery within 30 minutes. This guarantee was the cornerstone of Domino's strategy for the next two decades.

That guarantee proved to be the key influence on the consumer's purchasing decision. Sales took off, and Monaghan's chain went on to capture a significant share of the U.S. pizza market. Domino's dominates the home-delivery segment it created, even increasing its share of pizzas delivered in the United States from 48 to 54 percent in only five years. At the same time, Monaghan's success in helping modify consumer buying habits didn't escape the attention of his competitors. As these companies realized how many consumers want pizza to arrive on the doorstep, home delivery became the hottest battleground of the giant pizza chains.

In such a market, Domino's needs smart marketing to keep its share. If you were Tom Monaghan, which influences on consumer behavior would you pay closest attention to? How would you use the consumer decision process to boost your pizza sales? Which customer groups would you focus on, and what marketing approaches would you use? What would you do to keep a step ahead of your competitors, who are sure to imitate just about any service innovation you can cook up?[1]

# CHAPTER OVERVIEW

The success of Domino's Pizza stems from the company's ability to understand and influence consumer behavior. This chapter introduces the elements of consumer behavior to consider when designing and implementing marketing programs, starting with a general model of consumer decision making. The chapter then explores the five sets of factors that determine consumer behavior: psychological influences, personal influences, cultural influences, social influences, and situational influences. By examining these reasons for behavior, you'll gain a better understanding of how consumers will respond to your marketing efforts.

# CONSUMER BEHAVIOR AND THE MARKETING MIX

**Consumer behavior** encompasses all the actions involved in selecting, purchasing, using, and disposing of goods and services. Whenever you watch a commercial on television, buy a new pair of shoes, read a book, or recycle soft drink cans, you are engaging in consumer behavior. **Consumer buying behavior** refers specifically to the actions consumers take when they decide what to buy and make the actual purchase.

**consumer behavior**
Selecting, seeking, purchasing, using, and disposing of goods and services

**consumer buying behavior**
Deciding what goods or services to buy and then obtaining them

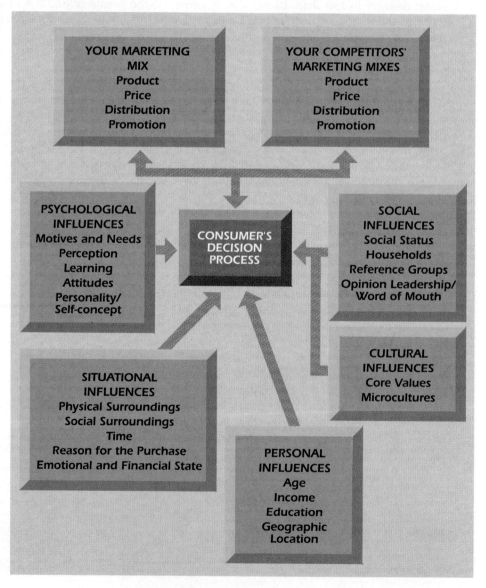

**Exhibit 4.1**
**INFLUENCES ON THE CONSUMER DECISION PROCESS**
The consumer decision process is influenced by psychological, personal, cultural, social, and situational factors —as well as by the marketing mixes of you and your competitors.

The consumer's decision process is influenced by a number of forces, as Exhibit 4.1 illustrates. Your marketing mix and those of your competitors influence purchase behavior. The influences of your mix can be strong or weak, positive or negative, depending on how well you understand the consumer and how effectively you can design a marketing mix based on that knowledge. Note that not only does the marketing mix influence the consumer's decision process but the process influences the marketing mix as well. On one hand, the consumer influences you because you design a mix based on your marketing research and your understanding of consumer behavior. On the other hand, you hope that your marketing efforts have a positive influence on the consumer's behavior.

## CONSUMER DECISION MAKING

Because consumers are individuals and because they buy a wide variety of goods and services, no two purchases are exactly alike. However, it's useful to make some generalized assumptions about the consumer decision-making process in order to learn how to influence the choices people make. As seen in Exhibit 4.2, people can go through up to five steps in the **consumer decision process.** The process can be lengthy and time consuming, or it can be fast and simple. You probably spent weeks or months gathering information about colleges and making your decision, but when you grab a candy bar or a copy of *TV Guide* while standing in line at a supermarket checkout, you spend only a few seconds and very little thought on the decision.

**consumer decision process**
A five-step process consumers go through when making a purchase

### Consumer Involvement

The complexity of the decision-making process depends greatly on the consumer's **involvement** with the product, which is the degree of personal importance or relevance accompanying the product and brand choice in a particular situation.[2] The more involved the person is in the decision, the more important making the right choice becomes. Involvement is highest when the product has personal or symbolic meaning to the individual, when it is related to centrally held values, when risk is involved in its purchase or use, and when it has high hedonic value.[3]

The greater the amount of involvement, the greater the extent of consumer problem solving. Thus, if involvement is minimal, as when consumers pick up their usual brand of toothpaste, decision making is minimal, and consumers engage in what is known as **routine problem solving (RPS).** They simply shift into automatic and buy on the basis of habit, with no consideration of alternatives.

If the usual brand is out of stock and consumers have to choose from what's on the shelf, they go into the **limited problem solving (LPS)** mode, an approach that is used when they have no firmly established preferences, must choose between a select group of brands, and have low involvement with the product. LPS is often influenced by in-store displays, free samples, and other promotional inducements to try something new. In these cases, consumers consider only a handful of alternatives and judge them on the basis of only a few attributes (see Exhibit 4.3).

**Extensive problem solving (EPS)** occurs with only a minority of purchase decisions, such as shopping for a new car, and entails high involvement and complex evaluation of a number of alternatives. (The stages shown in the consumer decision-making model represent EPS.)

**involvement**
The degree of personal importance or relevance a decision has for a consumer

**routine problem solving (RPS)**
Automatic buying behavior

**limited problem solving (LPS)**
Choosing between a small number of alternatives using only a few criteria

**extensive problem solving (EPS)**
Complex evaluation of a number of alternatives

**Exhibit 4.2 THE CONSUMER DECISION-MAKING PROCESS**
Consumers go through a decision-making process that can include up to five steps.

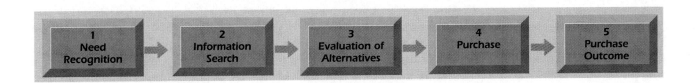

| 1 Need Recognition | 2 Information Search | 3 Evaluation of Alternatives | 4 Purchase | 5 Purchase Outcome |

**Exhibit 4.3   COMPARISON OF LIMITED AND EXTENSIVE PROBLEM SOLVING**

| Extensive Problem Solving (EPS) | Limited Problem Solving (LPS) |
|---|---|
| **Need recognition** | |
| 1. High involvement and perceived risk | 1. Low involvement and perceived risk |
| **Information search** | |
| 1. Strong motivation to search | 1. Low motivation to search |
| 2. Multiple sources used, including media, friends, and point-of-sale communication | 2. Exposure to advertising is passive, and information processing is not deep |
| 3. Information processed actively and rigorously | 3. Point-of-sale comparison likely |
| **Evaluation of alternatives** | |
| 1. Rigorous evaluation process | 1. Nonrigorous evaluation process |
| 2. Multiple evaluative criteria used, with some more salient than others | 2. Limited number of criteria, focus on most salient |
| 3. Alternatives perceived as significantly different | 3. Alternatives perceived as essentially similar |
| 4. Compensatory strategy where weakness on given attributes can be offset by others | 4. Noncompensatory strategy, eliminating alternatives perceived to fall short on salient attributes |
| 5. Beliefs, attitudes, and intentions strongly held | 5. Beliefs, attitudes, and intentions not strongly held |
| | 6. Purchase and trial can be a primary means of evaluation |
| **Purchase** | |
| 1. Will shop many outlets if needed | 1. Not motivated to shop extensively |
| 2. Choice of outlet may require a decision process | 2. Often prefer self-service |
| 3. Point-of-sale negotiation and communication often needed | 3. Choice often prompted by display and point-of-sale incentives |
| **Purchase outcome** | |
| 1. Doubts can motivate need for postsale reassurance | 1. Satisfaction motivates repurchase because of inertia, not loyalty |
| 2. Satisfaction is crucial, and loyalty is the outcome | 2. Main consequence of dissatisfaction is brand switching |
| 3. Motivated to seek redress if there is dissatisfaction | |

Limited problem solving and extensive problem solving vary at each stage in the consumer decision process.

## Consumer's Buying Process

Understanding the decision-making processes of your target customers is very important when planning marketing strategy and programs because you need to make sure that your marketing efforts are aligned with the consumer's buying behavior. For instance, if H&R Block discovers that many people who are considering a tax-preparation service look for a second opinion from periodicals such as *Money* and *Forbes*, it might decide to advertise heavily in those magazines. In a case like this, the consumer is searching for information in a handful of publications, and the marketer is aligning its efforts with the consumer's behavior. Here's a closer look at the steps in the consumer's buying process.

RECOGNIZE A NEED

The first step in the consumer buying process is recognizing that one has a need to fulfill or a problem to solve. Recognizing a need means noticing a discrepancy between a desired state and an actual state that is significant enough to activate the decision process.[4] It can be sudden ("Uh oh, the garbage disposal just died"), or it can evolve over time ("If I'm going to be doing a lot of traveling this year, I should probably get some new luggage").

Need recognition may be triggered either by dissatisfaction with one's actual state or by changes in one's conception of the ideal state. Among the many factors that can contribute to need recognition are availability of products, normal depletion, brand performance, family changes, financial status, and a marketer's promotional efforts. Thus, the need to replace the family car might be triggered by its poor performance, by a change in family size, by an increase in family income, by a desire to have a car that's in style, or by a need for better gas mileage (resulting from increased gas prices).

As a marketer, you should base your strategy on identifying consumer needs, determining how your product can fill those needs, activating need recognition (by altering consumers' desired state, altering their perception of their actual state, or emphasizing an existing discrepancy between the two), and then convincing consumers to consider the benefits your product offers. For example, many people need eyeglasses but hate to go through multiple visits to an optometrist, first having their eyes tested, then waiting weeks for the lenses to come in, and then having the frames adjusted. Companies such as LensCrafters have had great success because they identified this need and met it by offering glasses in about an hour at shopping malls throughout the country.

## SEARCH FOR INFORMATION

Once a need has been recognized, the consumer's next step is to seek out information on potential solutions. This information search is both internal and external. The internal search reviews existing knowledge about the need: What worked last time? What store did I pass the other day that specializes in this sort of thing? If the internal search does not produce a satisfactory solution, the consumer begins an external information search: consulting relatives, friends, or co-workers; checking independent sources such as *Consumer Reports;* reading ads and sales literature; calling or visiting retailers; and examining product labels (see Exhibit 4.4).

The extent of the information search in a particular decision-making process depends on the characteristics of the individual consumer (attitudes, knowledge and experience, motivation, involvement), market characteristics (the number of alternatives, price range, information availability), and situational characteristics (time constraints, financial pressure). Another important factor at this stage is **perceived risk,** or uncertainty about the purchase and concern about the potential losses that will result from making a wrong choice. People worry about financial risks, safety

**perceived risk**
Uncertainty about a purchase decision and concern about the potential losses from making the wrong choice

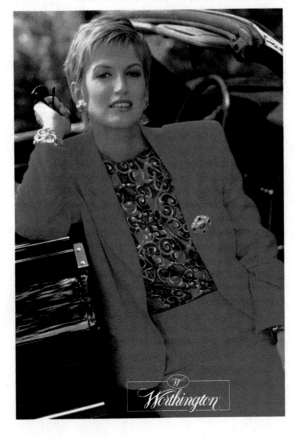

**Exhibit 4.4**
**GETTING INFORMATION FROM ADVERTISING**
Advertising is a major source of information for consumers. In this ad, for instance, consumers learn that J.C. Penney offers a certain style of clothing.

risks (to themselves and to the environment), time risks, psychological and social risks (such as to self-image), and product performance risks. Perceived risk is highest with goods or services that are expensive, conspicuous, intangible, or complex. You can reduce consumers' perceived risk in purchasing your product by offering money-back guarantees, warranties, and other assurances and by building a reputation for quality and customer service.

Conducting an extensive information search before making a decision can cost a lot of money and take a long time. It can also result in information overload and stress (such as battling crowds, driving from retailer to retailer, reading or viewing too many ads, and feeling frustrated in search efforts). However, the payoff from such an extensive search is finding just the right thing at the desired price, which reduces risk and increases satisfaction. For many people, the information search is rewarding in itself. In fact, most consumers engage in an ongoing external search process, gathering information that will be useful in future decisions.

As a marketer, determine the relative importance of various consumer information sources so that you can adapt your promotion and distribution methods to typical searching and shopping habits. For instance, if you were planning a promotional strategy to attract volunteers for the Peace Corps, you would choose advertising vehicles that young people are likely to encounter, such as MTV, campus newspapers, and fast-food packaging.

### EVALUATE ALTERNATIVES

**evoked set**
The group of alternatives that a consumer actually considers before making a choice

Out of all the available brands of a product, the consumer will be aware of only a portion, and of those, he or she will consider only a few: these few are called the **evoked set** (see Exhibit 4.5). From the evoked set, one brand will eventually be purchased, and the rest (the *inert set*) will be rejected. Consumers exclude products from their evoked sets for several reasons. The price might be too high or the quality too low. Obviously, one of your jobs as a marketer is to make sure your product gets into the evoked set of your target consumers. When buyers are more inclined to select one particular brand over all others, they are said to have *brand loyalty* to that product; this concept is covered in more detail in Chapter 8.

The attributes, features, and standards that consumers use when comparing various alternatives are known as *evaluative criteria,* which might include price (the consumer usually has a range in mind), convenience, brand reputation, and product characteristics. For example, a consumer considering various brands of VCRs

**Exhibit 4.5
EVOKED SET**
The evoked set, or the collection of brands considered in a decision, is a subset of all brands in a product class.

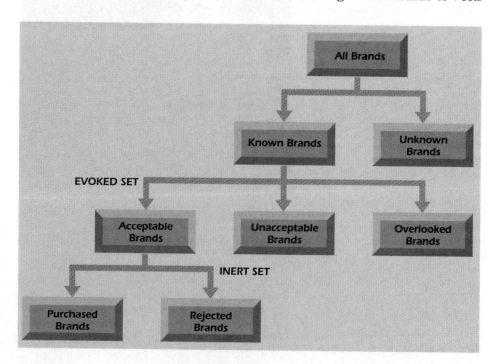

would use such criteria as price, brand image, design/appearance, and features (from basic to sophisticated).[5] Alternatively, a consumer choosing a physician or dentist would consider the person's courtesy, competence, reputation, availability, and interpersonal skills.[6]

The number of criteria considered varies with the product, as does the importance of each criterion. Furthermore, consumers focus on various criteria, depending on their motives, personality, and lifestyle. Criteria can even vary from situation to situation. For instance, consumers have one set of requirements for a snack food when they're at the movies and another set when they're having company at home.

When a particular product is difficult to judge, people usually rely on price, store image, and brand image as indications of quality. When it comes to products such as cosmetics, consumers tend to equate a higher price with higher quality, but for products such as cold remedies they rely on established brand names to ensure safety and quality. Another indicator used with certain products is country of origin—consumers generally expect high quality from German cars, Japanese electronics, Belgian chocolates, and so on.

Determine which criteria are of greatest importance to people in your target audience and emphasize those criteria in your advertising. For example, stressing that a brand of catsup is lower in calories than competing brands would be futile if consumers' main criterion is price or taste; most people use such small servings of catsup that the calorie difference would be insignificant.

## MAKE THE PURCHASE

The consumer might first choose a particular brand and then a place to buy it (retail outlet, catalog, phone order), might first choose the place and then the brand, or might choose both simultaneously (when seeing a shirt in a store window). Choice of a retail outlet depends on the store's location, assortment, prices, personnel, services, ambiance, clientele, and advertising, as well as on the consumer's particular shopping orientation and perceived risks.

The great majority of purchases are not planned far in advance; most decisions are made right in the store.[7] These in-store purchase decisions share one or more of the following characteristics:

- *Spontaneity.* These purchases are often stimulated by in-store advertising materials or salespeople, and the consumer gets the urge to buy immediately.
- *Excitement.* Consumers often get a thrill from impulsive buying decisions.
- *Compulsion.* For some consumers, the excitement outweighs all other considerations.
- *Disregard for consequences.* Often to their eventual dismay, consumers sometimes make impulse purchases without considering the consequences.[8]

Regardless of the nature of the purchase, marketers can add value to their offerings by making the purchase process easier. That's the secret behind Domino's success: simply making it easier to buy pizza. No longer do customers have to pile the family into the car, fight traffic, and then sit in a crowded restaurant. Now they can just pick up the telephone. This concept of purchase convenience applies to every business, whether you're selling pizza or power plants.

## EVALUATE THE PURCHASE

After consumers make purchases, they frequently evaluate the choice they made. Does it live up to their expectations? If so, they'll be satisfied; if not, they'll be dissatisfied. In the United States, one-third of all households have had trouble with a purchase, and roughly one-quarter of all purchases result in dissatisfaction.[9]

As a marketer, you can increase the chances of customer satisfaction by creating realistic expectations for your products, regularly monitoring customer satisfaction, taking complaints seriously, ensuring quality control in production, providing suffi-

**postpurchase dissonance**
A feeling of discomfort or
doubt following a purchase

cient information on product use, and offering service after the sale. Chapter 21 covers customer satisfaction in more detail.

After making a purchase, some consumers experience **postpurchase dissonance** (also called *buyer's remorse*), a psychological discomfort or doubt that arises from the knowledge that unchosen alternatives also had desirable characteristics. The consumer wonders, Did I really make the best choice? Dissonance is more likely to occur when the decision has been important, difficult, and hard to undo, such as choosing a college or buying a house. You can help consumers reduce their dissonance by stressing the superiority of the chosen product in manuals or on the package, using advertising to bolster pride in ownership, and contacting buyers after the sale to see whether they are satisfied and to ask whether you can do anything to help.

## Rational versus Nonrational Decision Making

Not all purchases are as rational as this model suggests. In fact, many purchases seem downright illogical to an outside observer, and it's important to understand how these nonrational elements affect decision making and responses to advertising. Here are some factors that can affect purchasing behavior and cause it to be less than totally logical:[10]

- *Feeling and intuition.* Particularly when competing products are close in terms of price and quality, decisions can be swayed by how confident the buyer is in the seller. A feeling that deserves special attention is fear, which can range from physical safety to social acceptance.
- *Acting on imperfect information.* Consumers often make decisions when they either don't have enough information or are so bombarded with advertising that they tune out most marketing messages. In other words, they don't act on perfect information, as the rational decision-making model suggests. They rely on perceptions formed by bits and pieces of information they've gathered here and there, rather than on coherent, complete messages.
- *Postdecision rationalization.* Buyers have often made up their minds before they even begin a "buying process." They continue through the steps of collecting and evaluating information, often to confirm their initial hunches or to sell their ideas to family or friends.

Harley-Davidson is a good example of an advertiser that recognizes the nonrational side of consumer behavior. In fact, the company's ads even play up the idea. One print ad showed a new, exquisitely polished Harley parked next to an old, tiny trailer house. The obvious conclusion was that this person spent a lot more on the Harley than on the house, not a choice that all consumers would make. The headline said it all: "It's Not a Rational Decision."

## Decision Making in Nonprofit Marketing

Understanding customer behavior is just as crucial for nonprofit marketing programs. Particularly with social marketing, getting inside your customers' heads and hearts means the difference between success and failure. For example, telling people to avoid crack cocaine because it leads to personal ruin will not be a universally successful way to modify behavior, at least not for everybody. Antidrug campaigns need to understand that some people don't like to be told how to conduct their lives, some aren't convinced (in spite of the overwhelming evidence) that crack will hurt them personally, and some use drugs to gain peer group approval or to escape emotional desperation. The decision is much more complex than "just saying no."

Social marketing seeks to change behavior in ways that are frequently personal and often difficult. Social marketing exists because social problems exist, and making desired changes in behavior can be much more difficult than taking a trip to a store and spending money on a product. Convincing people to stop drinking when they drive or to start practicing safe sex isn't easy, as evidenced by continuing problems in both areas. All persons and organizations pursuing social goals need to recognize that changing personal behavior is a challenging objective that requires skilled application of marketing concepts and techniques.

# INFLUENCES ON CONSUMER DECISIONS

The remainder of the chapter explores the factors that influence consumer decision making. Keep in mind as you study these sections that the decision-making model is a simplified version of reality. Consumers are complex creatures, and marketers are still learning how people make purchase decisions.

## *Psychological Influences*

Each person's actions and choices are influenced by a variety of internal forces. **Psychological influences** include a person's needs and motives, involvement with a decision, perceptions, learning experiences, attitudes, and personality characteristics. Such psychological influences affect all behavior, including consumer behavior.

### NEEDS AND MOTIVES

When you buy a product, you do so to fulfill some kind of need, a discrepancy between your actual state and your desired state (see Chapter 1). For instance, in the recent past you were just dying to know all about marketing; you had a need for knowledge. In response to that need, you signed up for this course. In other words, you were *motivated* to expand your knowledge of marketing. **Motives** are internal factors that activate and direct behavior toward some goal. They drive people to act, whether that action is eating, working, playing, sleeping, or buying products.

An early and influential way of looking at human needs and motives was provided by psychologist Abraham Maslow.[11] He classified needs into five main categories: physical needs, safety, love, esteem, and self-actualization. He argued that there is a natural hierarchy to these needs, as seen in Exhibit 4.6. According to Maslow, people must satisfy needs at the bottom of the hierarchy (the needs for biological survival and physical safety) before they can worry about pursuing the needs at higher levels.

As a marketer, you can promote products more effectively if you know where in the hierarchy they are most likely to appeal to consumers (see Exhibit 4.7). Consider Schlage dead bolts and Mont Blanc fountain pens. The Schlage product keeps the consumer safe and secure, but it won't add much in the way of love or self-esteem. For perhaps ten times as much money, though, the consumer can have (or give as a gift) a Mont Blanc pen, which conveys a feeling of success and importance to the person who owns it. Given these distinctly different appeals, how would you market these products? You'd probably promote the dead bolt on its ability to increase the consumer's personal safety and promote the fountain pen on its ability to convey a sense of self-esteem. People don't buy locks because they're looking for love, and they don't buy $200 fountain pens to improve their health or safety. Understanding motives is a vital step in creating effective marketing programs. (When you think about the motives behind consumer purchases, seemingly illogical choices begin to make more sense; people are simply trying to fulfill different needs.)

Researchers who followed Maslow have questioned some of the assumptions he made (such as the rule that people try to fill needs in order from lowest to highest), but his model is a useful way to begin studying needs and motives. Another useful way of looking at needs is to categorize them as being utilitarian or hedonic. Products that meet **utilitarian needs** are functional and provide material benefits. When you buy Bayer aspirin, you're looking for functional benefits. Products that meet **hedonic needs** provide pleasure or a means of self-expression. Examples in-

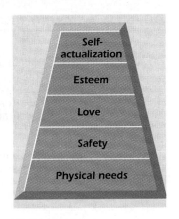

**Exhibit 4.6
MASLOW'S NEEDS HIERARCHY**
Abraham Maslow identified a hierarchy of human needs, with physical needs being the most fundamental. Many elements of consumer marketing are based on this model.

**psychological influences**
Characteristics within the individual that influence consumer behavior

**motives**
Internal factors that activate and direct behavior toward some goal

**utilitarian needs**
Needs that fulfill a functional purpose

**hedonic needs**
Needs for pleasure or personal expression

**115**

**Exhibit 4.7  MARKETING PRODUCTS BASED ON THE NEEDS HIERARCHY**

### Physiological

| | |
|---|---|
| Products: | Limited in the United States. Generic foods, medicines, special drinks, and foods for athletes. |
| Specific themes: | Raisins—"Thank goodness I found a snack kids will sit for. And mothers will stand for." Kellog's All-Bran—"At last, some news about cancer you can live with," with copy that stresses the role of fiber in the diet. |

### Safety

| | |
|---|---|
| Products: | Smoke detectors, preventive medicines, insurance, social security, retirement investments, seat belts, burglar alarms, safes. |
| Specific themes: | Sleep Safe—"We've designed a travel alarm that just might wake you in the middle of the night—because a fire is sending smoke into your room. You see, ours is a smoke alarm as well as an alarm clock." Alka-Seltzer—"Will it be there when you need it?" |

### Love

| | |
|---|---|
| Products: | Personal grooming, foods, entertainment, clothing, and many others. |
| Specific themes: | Atari—"Atari brings the computer age home," with a picture of a family using an Atari home computer. J.C. Penney—"Wherever teens gather, you'll hear it. It's language of terrific fit and fashion. . ." |

### Esteem

| | |
|---|---|
| Products: | Clothing, furniture, hobbies, stores, cars, and many others. |
| Specific themes: | Sheaffer—"Your hand should look as contemporary as the rest of you." Cadillac—". . . those long hours have paid off. In recognition, financial success, and in the way you reward yourself. Isn't it time you owned a Cadillac?" |

### Self-actualization

| | |
|---|---|
| Products: | Education, hobbies, sports, some vacations, gourmet foods, museums. |
| Specific themes: | U.S. Army—"Be all you can be." Outward Bound School—"Challenges, adventure, growth." |

Maslow's hierarchy of needs can be applied to marketing strategy; these marketers created their promotional messages after considering the type of needs their products could fill.

clude hair styling and ice cream. To some degree, consumers are more likely to use deliberate, rational decision-making processes based on objective product attributes when making purchases that satisfy primarily utilitarian needs. Conversely, they are more likely to use decision processes based on subjective, emotional factors when making choices that satisfy primarily hedonic needs.[12] Consumer choices that are most likely to be emotional are those involving products that give sensory and aesthetic pleasures, such as arts and crafts, entertainment (movies, concerts, records, books), fashion, and perfumes.[13]

Many experts believe that in the past few decades consumer researchers have placed too much emphasis on utilitarian needs and rational decision-making processes and have neglected the importance of hedonic needs and symbolic meanings. However, because such needs and meanings are difficult to identify and assess, you face a tough task when you try to take this type of consumer motivation into account.

## PERCEPTION

**perception**
Reception and interpretation of sensory stimuli

Before consumers can buy a product, they must be aware that it exists. **Perception** is the process of being *exposed* to the stimuli that represent a particular product, *attending* to these stimuli, and *interpreting* them. Here's a look at each of those steps.

EXPOSURE   The first step in perception is exposure to the stimulus, such as seeing a *TV Guide* display at the supermarket checkout counter or hearing a Marriott hotel commercial on the radio. To some extent the stimuli to which people are exposed are actively chosen—people select the television channels to watch, the store to go to, the magazines to read. Other exposure is somewhat random—by simply driving down the street people are exposed to billboards, ads on buses and taxis, and so on.

Advertisers try to increase the chances that consumers will be exposed to one of their ads. As a result of their efforts, people can now see ads on shopping carts, videocassettes, church bulletins, and athletes. Credit card bills often contain fliers from other companies selling a variety of products. The packaging for mail-order purchases often includes advertisements for other products. All of these efforts represent attempts by advertisers to increase exposure.

ATTENTION    Mere exposure to a stimulus doesn't guarantee that consumers will pay attention to it. Most people live in an environment that is filled with sensory stimuli, but their capacity to handle this information is limited. Therefore, they must actively choose which stimuli to attend to, a phenomenon that is called **selective attention.** For example, it has been estimated that people notice less than 15 percent of the ads they are exposed to.[14]

**selective attention**
Choosing to attend to only a small portion of the stimuli to which you are exposed

How can you capture the consumer's attention amid the clutter of ads and products clamoring to be noticed? It is helpful to know that attention is influenced both by external stimuli and by factors unique to each individual. People are more likely to attend to a stimulus when it is

- Particularly relevant to them
- Novel or unexpected
- Larger or more intense than other stimuli
- In the center of their perceptual field
- Isolated
- Colorful
- In motion
- In contrast to other stimuli around it

For instance, when you approach most shopping malls in December, you'll see and hear a volunteer for the Salvation Army. You can't miss this person: he or she stands out from the crowd because of the sound of the bell, location at the front doors, and perhaps a bold Santa costume. How many donations would the Salvation Army get if its people sat quietly in a remote corner of the parking lot?

As a marketer, you can control the attributes of stimuli you send to your audience. What you cannot control are the individualized factors that affect attention: the person's needs and motives, involvement, attitudes, expectations, and ability to tune out stimuli. As a result, someone who is not hungry is less likely to notice ads for Taco Bell, a man will usually ignore ads for nail polish, and someone who believes that U.S. cars are superior will screen out ads for Toyota and Volkswagen.

INTERPRETATION    Even if consumers pay attention to your message, they may not interpret its meaning accurately. In fact, misinterpretation of marketing communications is quite common. An average of 30 percent of television communications (both commercial and noncommercial) were miscomprehended.[15]

Among the variables that influence interpretation of a stimulus are the consumer's needs and motives, past experiences, and expectations; the context or situation; the learned symbolic meanings for the stimulus; and the order in which related stimuli are received. Expectations are particularly important: people will often perceive what they expect to perceive, such as "their" brand of cola tasting better than other colas (even if the labels have been switched and they are drinking something different). Because of these variables, it's often hard for you to know whether a product is being perceived accurately, which is why you conduct research on consumer perceptions of your product category and specific brand.

As with attention, the aspect of perceptual interpretation over which you have the greatest control is the stimulus itself. You can take advantage of some basic stimulus characteristics to present your products in ways that will enhance consumer perception:

- People tend to organize perceptions into simple patterns, so you should keep messages and images simple.
- People tend to focus on a single aspect of a situation and treat the rest as background, so advertisers must ensure that the audience will focus on the product and not on the scenery, a celebrity, or some other element.
- People tend to relate things that are close together physically or temporally, so try to associate your products with people or situations that have an appropriate image and avoid inappropriate connections. Coca-Cola, for example, does not advertise on TV news shows for fear of associating its upbeat products with the bad news inevitable on such programs.[16]
- People tend to fill in missing parts in a perceptual stimulus, a phenomenon called closure, and advertisers can capitalize on this tendency by using gaps or substitutions in images or by leaving out words in jingles or slogans for the consumer to mentally fill in, thereby making the consumer an active participant in the ad.

Whatever methods you use to increase consumer perception of your products, you must be careful not to create an inappropriate interpretation. A loud radio ad with a catchy jingle and funny voices may be great for selling soft drinks to teens, but it would present the wrong image for marketing financial services to senior citizens.

## LEARNING

**consumer learning**
The way people acquire the knowledge and experience they apply to consumer behavior

**Consumer learning** is the way people acquire the knowledge and experience they apply to buying and using products.[17] Most consumer behavior is learned, not innate, and this learning falls into two general categories: *behavioral learning* (in which people learn by responding to the external events that happen around them or to them) and *cognitive learning* (in which people learn by thinking about problems and reaching conclusions). In addition, memory plays an important part in learning and in consumer behavior.

**classical conditioning**
Learning to associate a stimulus with a response

BEHAVIORAL LEARNING    Behavioral learning happens in two ways: The first is called **classical conditioning,** or *association learning,* in which a person learns to associate a stimulus with a response. This type of learning applies primarily to automatic responses—things we have little control over, such as blinking, blushing, or reflexes. Emotions are automatic responses that are subject to association learning. Marketers try to associate their products with situations and people that are likely to arouse positive feelings in consumers. That's why you see cute little puppies, adorable children, and other positive images in so many advertisements. Advertising expert Hal Riney uses this "feel good" approach extensively in his agency's work for such clients as See's Candies, Saturn automobiles, and Dreyer's Ice Cream. Unlike the "in your face" approach taken in other ad campaigns, Riney uses a softer, quieter approach to encourage positive feelings about the product.[18]

**reinforcement**
Strengthening behavior as a result of rewards

A second type of conditioning, explored extensively in the work of B. F. Skinner, involves voluntary rather than automatic responses. According to the principle of **reinforcement,** responses that are rewarded are likely to be repeated, whereas responses that go unrewarded are unlikely to be repeated. Because successful marketing is closely tied to repeat purchase behavior, providing reinforcement for desired behavior is crucial.[19] In marketing, the main source of reinforcement is good performance by the product—the cold remedy relieves the sufferer's symptoms, the laundry detergent gets clothes clean, and so on. Other marketing methods for providing consumer reinforcement include rebates, premiums, and praise for having made "the right choice."

Marketers also apply other basic conditioning principles from psychology in their

Guess what Penn is coming out with next?

The all new ProPenn tennis shoe. Timeless styling with high-tech construction, from the world's largest manufacturer of tennis balls. Available exclusively through pro shops and selected tennis specialty stores.

*Penn*

**Exhibit 4.8**
**GENERALIZING A**
**BRAND NAME**
To appeal to the positive associations customers have with
an established brand, marketers frequently introduce
new products with the same
brand name. In this example,
Penn is introducing a line of
tennis shoes, while capitalizing on the strength of its
name as a supplier of tennis
balls and other tennis equipment.

packaging and promotional efforts. For example, according to the principle of **generalization,** people will learn to respond in the same way to similar stimuli. Generalization is the basis for "family branding": if a familiar brand name that has provided rewarding products in the past now appears on a new, related product,
consumers may buy it in anticipation of being reinforced (see Exhibit 4.8). Thus,
satisfied consumers of Lifesavers candies might buy Lifesavers-brand frozen treats
expecting similar satisfaction. On the other hand, according to the principle of **discrimination,** people will learn to differentiate between two very similar products
when one turns out to be rewarding and the other doesn't. Thus, some consumers
prefer Diet Coke whereas others prefer Diet Pepsi, and many insist they can tell the
difference between the two brands. The task for many marketers is to help the consumer learn to discriminate between their product and similar competitive products.

**generalization**
The tendency to respond
in the same way to similar
stimuli

**discrimination**
The ability to distinguish between similar stimuli

COGNITIVE LEARNING    In contrast to behavioral learning, *cognitive learning* occurs
when people think their way through situations and actively solve problems. This
happens either when consumers make their own decisions or when they watch others make decisions and observe the outcomes. Much of our learning, especially in
childhood, comes from observing other people. We learn how and when to use products—and which products to use—by watching others. If we see someone benefit
from using a product, we are much more likely to choose that product ourselves, a
process referred to as **modeling.** Early in life, parents are our most important models; later, our friends become significant models.

   You can capitalize on modeling by showing people (celebrities, attractive people,
happy families, or people representative of the target market) being rewarded for
using your product. One of Dry Idea's competitors, Sure antiperspirant, used models in stressful situations who pulled through without sweating. Sometimes marketers even show models being punished or going unrewarded for using competing products. One of the more blatant examples of this technique was a TV commercial for Prestone antifreeze that showed a young boy left stranded on a downtown
street corner because his parents hadn't purchased Prestone and the family car had
broken down.[20] Modeling is also used to demonstrate how or where to buy a product and how to use it, especially if that process isn't simple.

**modeling**
Learning behaviors by ob-
serving others

**knowledge structure**
An arrangement of related bits of information in a consumer's mind

MEMORY AND CONSUMER BEHAVIOR   Of course, the learning that consumers do doesn't always take place during the actual purchase process. Memory plays a major role in consumer behavior and is therefore a key issue for marketers. The information the consumer collects when preparing for a purchase decision is combined with information already stored in memory.[21] When Saab advertises its cars, the company knows that most consumers won't be in the actual process of buying cars. What Saab hopes is that its message will stick in consumers' minds and still be persuasive when the time comes to buy a car.

Consumer memory is important in another key aspect. When you communicate a promotional message to consumers, chances are they have already formed a **knowledge structure,** that is, they've already stored information about your product or products like it. The way consumers interpret and respond to your incoming message depends on how the information fits with such knowledge structures.[22] This is one reason the coordinated, cohesive messages promised by integrated marketing communications (see Chapter 1) are so valuable. Consumers hear about your products from your ads, your salespeople, their neighbors, magazine articles, and various other sources; if new information conflicts with stored information, consumers will be confused and your marketing will be less effective.

A knowledge structure is more than just brand names and product types, however; it can include celebrities, family and friends, personal experiences, and various other bits and pieces of information (see Exhibit 4.9). In the hypothetical knowledge structure pictured, you can see various associations related to perfume. What if you tried to position a perfume called "Cher" as something associated with youth or wealth? What if you introduced a new perfume and tried to associate it with being both "sexy" and "rich"? You might not succeed because consumers aren't making such associations in their memories.

**Exhibit 4.9**
**KNOWLEDGE STRUCTURES**
Consumers store information in knowledge structures, networks of related and connected bits of information.

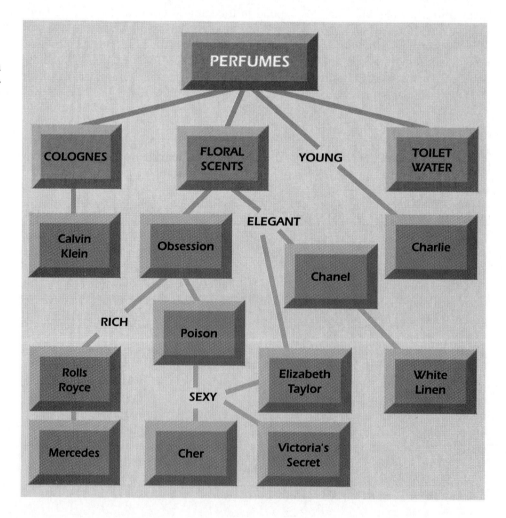

An **attitude** is a person's enduring positive or negative inclination toward a product, person, place, idea, or issue. Attitudes tend to be generalized (I don't like health food) and lasting (I've never liked health food and never will).[23] This is an important topic for marketers because many consumer behaviors are related to attitudes.[24] For instance, if you have a positive attitude about Fireman's Fund life insurance, you're not only likely to purchase that product yourself but also recommend it to friends, relatives, and business associates. The job for the marketer is to understand attitudes and then learn how to influence those attitudes through the marketing mix.

It is often useful to segment markets by consumers' attitudes; this helps you design marketing mixes that align closely with the feelings in each segment. As an example of this sort of segmentation, researchers in the Netherlands recently measured the attitudes of Dutch women toward traditional and nontraditional roles for women. Researchers identified five segments, ranging from conservatives (who are satisfied with their traditional roles and who reject nontraditional roles) to pioneers (whose attitudes are just the opposite). Some of the implications for marketers? The conservatives are rarely interested in new products, and they watch a lot of television. Pioneers, on the other hand, look for new products and read more newspapers and magazines.[25] Such clues are valuable when selecting target segments and designing marketing mixes.

Attitudes have three components: the cognitive, the affective, and the behavioral. The *cognitive component* is the easiest to understand, consisting of the particular beliefs or knowledge that a consumer has about something. An example of a belief is "potatoes are high in calories" or "plastic containers damage the environment." A belief can be accurate or inaccurate, positive or negative. Consumers have beliefs about the marketplace (that smaller stores carry expensive merchandise or that January is the best time to buy sheets and towels) and about their own skills ("This camera is too complicated for me to operate"), as well as about products ("Computers are too hard to use").

An attitude's *affective component* encompasses the consumer's positive and negative feelings; that is, it refers to how strongly a person likes or dislikes something. People can differ in their affective responses to the same belief. For example, the belief that a store such as Sharper Image carries expensive merchandise or that a salad dressing is low in calories may cause some people to respond negatively and others to respond positively. The person driven by a need to lose weight won't respond to the salad dressing the same way as a person who cares primarily about taste.

Finally, an attitude's *behavioral component* consists of any action a consumer takes on the basis of his or her beliefs and feelings. The behavior may take the form of buying or shunning a product, using it, recommending it to others, and so on. Of course, simply having a positive attitude toward a product doesn't mean that a person will rush out to buy it; he or she may not need it, may not be able to afford it, may have other priorities, or may have to take other household members into consideration ("Sure, Dad thinks that Porsche is a great car and would love to own one, but . . . ").

Marketers can try to change consumer attitudes by directing their efforts at each of the attitude components. To emphasize the cognitive component, they can try to change beliefs about the brand's attributes (as Domino's did when it convinced consumers that pizza could be a real meal), alter the relative importance of brand attributes (emphasizing butter's "naturalness" over its caloric content), add new beliefs (pointing out beneficial new-product features, such as Clorox bleach now smelling of lemons), or change consumer beliefs about the ideal attributes of the product (emphasizing convenience over price, such as the ease of preparing LeMenu frozen dinners). Taking another tack, they can also try to change beliefs about competitors' products, putting their own products in a better light. For instance, as it battled to improve its service image, Northwest Airlines ran ads with this bold headline: "Northwest beats the top five U.S. airlines in on-time performance."[26]

**attitude**
Enduring positive or negative inclinations toward objects, people, ideas, or products in a particular way

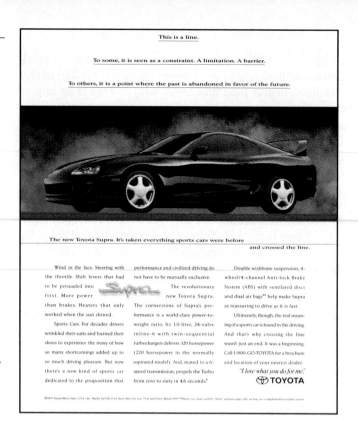

**Exhibit 4.10**
**APPEALING TO THE**
**SPIRIT OF**
**ADVENTURE**

In this ad for the 320-horse-power Supra sports car, Toyota appeals to those who view driving as something a little more exciting than just moving from point A to point B.

Attempts to change the affective component might involve using likable ads that increase pleasant feelings toward the company or product (the "reach out and touch someone" commercials from AT&T). Or you might increase the amount of exposure to the product (based on the idea that familiarity enhances liking or attraction). Why does McDonald's keep advertising, when every person in the solar system is aware of the company and can probably give you directions to a half-dozen McDonald's restaurants? McDonald's keeps advertising because it doesn't want you to forget for even a moment that McDonald's is there to serve you. Through persistent advertising, Domino's slowly built acceptance for the idea of phone-order pizza; now most people think nothing of picking up the phone and ordering dinner.

Marketers attack the behavioral component by getting people to try the product (through a free sample, a test drive, or a price reduction, for example) in hopes that product use will lead to satisfaction and thus positive beliefs and feelings. Samples of products such as Irish Spring soap have been sent through the mail, and samples of food drenched in Masterpiece BBQ sauce have been offered in grocery stores. Taking the direct approach, Nissan recently offered to pay people $100 if they purchased a Toyota or Honda after test driving a Nissan.

The relationship of attitude and purchase behavior is important, but it is by no means straightforward. You can ask five classmates about their attitude toward Ferraris, and you'll probably get fairly positive answers. Does that mean these five people are going to buy Ferraris anytime soon? Probably not. To predict Ferrari sales, ask the people whether they intend to buy that brand of automobile. Such measures of *purchase intent* are a better predictor of purchase behavior than simple attitude measurements. But even purchase intent isn't always reliable. For instance, perhaps one of your classmates can't afford a Ferrari, even though she indicated the intent to buy one. Other people might change their minds between the time of your survey and the time of their purchases. You can understand why marketers need to be careful when measuring consumer attitudes.

**personality**
A person's evaluation of a product, person, place, idea, or issue

## PERSONALITY AND SELF-CONCEPT

**Personality** refers to a person's consistent way of responding to a wide range of situations. Perhaps you meet life with energy and passion whereas your roommate hides under the blankets. Marketers are interested in personality as a way to target consumers. Are people with particular personalities more likely to buy certain products? This question has intrigued consumer researchers for quite a while, but so far they've come up with few conclusive answers.

Over the years personality theorists have tried to categorize people according to a discrete number of personality "types" or separate them on the basis of having specific personality "traits." However, researchers have found little relationship between such categories and buying behavior—with one or two exceptions. For instance, people who are particularly susceptible to interpersonal influence have a need to enhance their image through buying and using certain products and brands, are willing to conform to the expectations of others regarding purchase decisions, and tend to learn about products by observing others and seeking information from others.[27] Because these individuals tend to have low self-esteem and low self-confidence, they rely more on others when they have to make decisions. Another personality variable that seems to be related to buying behavior is risk taking. High risk takers, estimated to be about 25 percent of the population, have a higher-than-average need for stimulation. They are bored easily and seek out adventure—a characteristic that can be exploited by marketers of travel services, sports equipment, and other such products[28] (see Exhibit 4.10).

As a consumer, you naturally buy goods and services that fit your **self-concept**, which consists of your perceptions, beliefs, and feelings about yourself. It encompasses both your private self (how you see yourself), your public self (how others see you), your actual self (how you really are), and your ideal self (what you would like to be).[29] Some purchases and possessions, such as clothing, cars, furniture, and houses, are more involved with self-concept than others because they become extensions of yourself.[30] Marketers of products that contribute strongly to self-image (hairstyling, shoes, perfume, jewelry, eyeglasses) need to assess the self-concepts (especially the social and ideal self-concepts) of their target customers and develop brand images that maintain or enhance those self-images (see Exhibit 4.11).

Self-concept is also important to marketers because it serves as the internal basis of lifestyle.[31] Your **lifestyle** consists of all your interests, activities, likes and dislikes, and consumption patterns. It is how you spend your time and money. Although you consciously choose your lifestyle to some extent, it is also a function of your social class, age, income, education, and similar factors. Analyzing markets on the basis of lifestyles is explored in greater detail in Chapter 7.

**self-concept**
Your perceptions, beliefs, and feelings about yourself

**lifestyle**
A person's interests, activities, likes and dislikes, and consumption patterns

(left) Her Schulthess was given to her by her husband.
(right) She bought one for her husband.

**Exhibit 4.11**
**MARKETING TO A CONSUMER'S SELF-CONCEPT**
Schulthess, a maker of home appliances, understands the ways in which self-concepts have changed over the years.

# Personal Influences

The elements that define every consumer also affect purchase choices. These include such factors as age, income, education, and geographic location. Obviously, senior citizens rarely shop for skateboards, low-income individuals don't buy mink coats, uneducated people are less likely to join book clubs, and desert dwellers aren't a good market for umbrellas. Marketers are constantly looking for useful factors to help them identify and reach attractive market segments. It's important to remember that these personal influences (and the cultural, social, and situational influences described in the following sections) work through the psychological influences, not as separate forces. The psychological influences ultimately determine a person's behavior, but those factors are themselves influenced by the personal, cultural, social, and situational factors.

## AGE

Age affects people's needs, interests, tastes, purchasing ability, and preferences. It also determines to some extent the stage of the household life cycle and the type of household a person is in, two other influences that are examined later in this chapter. The focus here is on two large consumer groups that are based on age: baby boomers and the mature market.

**baby boomers**
The generation of people who were born in the United States between 1946 and 1964

BABY BOOMERS    The term **baby boomers** refers to the generation of people who were born in the United States between 1946 and 1964. This huge postwar generation (77 million people) has been a favorite target market for decades, not only because of its size but because of its penchant for consumption and its ability to set trends. In the 1990s the baby boomers are hitting middle age, and their buying power is at its all-time peak.

Baby boomers are better educated and wealthier than average, and they buy more and save less than other generations. Now in their thirties and forties, their main concerns are starting and raising families, upgrading their homes, and making the most of their leisure time. As one group of experts put it, baby boomers want "quality products that are aesthetically pleasing, personally satisfying, natural, and if possible, noncaloric."[32] They also want to obtain these products quickly and easily. They are more likely to shop by catalog and to use credit cards than any other age group, and they show strong loyalty to the stores they shop in.[33] How can you keep boomers happy? Here are some tips:

- Boomers read fine print and tend to be suspicious, so give them the straight facts about your product.
- Convenience and comfort are important to them, so show them how your product will make life easier.
- As they grow older, many boomers are becoming more interested in life-enhancing experiences rather than material possessions, so indicate how your product will enrich their lives.
- Boomers are concerned about the environment and safety, so assure them that your products, packaging, and manufacturing processes are nonhazardous.[34]

THE MATURE MARKET    The mature market (people age 50 and over) in the United States is growing rapidly as people stay healthier and live longer. More than 25 percent of the people in the United States are now in this age group, and similar trends are occurring in Canada, Britain, Germany, Japan, and France.[35] People 85 and older make up the fastest-growing segment of the U.S. population.[36] Overall household income may be lower than that of younger people, but fewer people are in the household and expenses are reduced, so more of this group's income is discretionary. Although a significant percentage of the people in the 50-plus age group still work, most are retired, and they have lots of time for travel, hobbies, and social activities (see Exhibit 4.12).

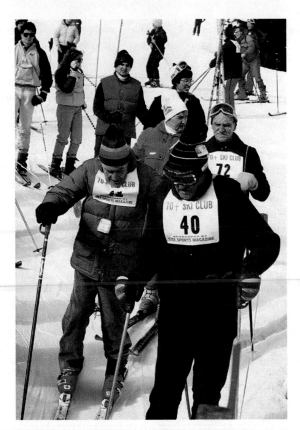

**Exhibit 4.12**
**THE MATURE MARKET**
**ISN'T WHAT IT USED**
**TO BE**
Many people over age 50 simply don't fit the old stereotypes anymore; they are healthier and more active than ever before, and their growing number presents one of today's most significant marketing opportunities.

Seniors tend to be less price conscious than younger people and are willing to pay more for quality products. They also rely more heavily on the mass media for consumer information, especially television and radio. They often enjoy shopping and are increasingly spending time at enclosed shopping malls for entertainment and recreation as well as for shopping. Despite what you might expect, seniors are not too concerned with special amenities for the elderly, such as larger print on labels or delivery services. Of particular importance to marketers is that seniors do not like to be reminded of their age and often perceive themselves as being younger than they really are.[37]

The growing mature segment has also affected the nonprofit sector. Membership in organizations such as the American Association of Retired Persons (AARP) continues to increase as the number of older people increases. And more retired people with newfound free time are helping at hospitals and community centers around the country.[38] Both for-profit marketers selling products to senior citizens and nonprofit marketers recruiting volunteer help need to reconsider the way people's daily routines change after retirement.

## INCOME

The amount of money consumers make obviously affects how they spend it. Only one-third of U.S. households have money left over for nonessential purchases. Not surprisingly, marketers are particularly interested in the consumers who have the most discretionary income, primarily the affluent. Defined as having an income of over $60,000 a year, affluent people are predominantly in the 35 to 49 age group. The affluent market is one of the fastest growing, constituting a quarter of the adult population.

What do affluent consumers spend their money on? They are the biggest purchasers of electronics and home entertainment, home furnishings, cars, services, travel, and alcoholic beverages. However, they are not the materialistic, conspicuous consumers that rich folks were in times past. Today's affluent consumers are more concerned with quality and value; "status items" are less important.[39]

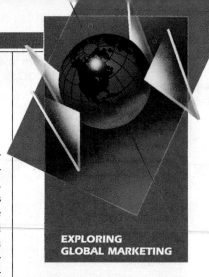

## THE GLOBAL CONSUMER: HOW ALIKE ARE WE?

**EXPLORING GLOBAL MARKETING**

Whether we live in Baltimore or Bangkok, we all need food, clothing, various household items, transportation, and lots of other goods and services to make it through the day. How alike are we, from country to country and culture to culture? This is more than a point of idle curiosity for multinational marketers trying to reach consumers around the globe. MTV, Levi's, Coke, and many of the same brands you're familiar with here in the United States are also quite popular in other countries, and the popularity results from marketers doing their consumer behavior homework.

The question appears both at the global level and at the regional level,

with Europe as a key testing ground. The nations of Europe represent a larger consumer market than the United States, so consumer marketers of every stripe want to know how to succeed there. If a single type of "Euroconsumer" existed, things would certainly be easier, since you

could reach them with a single marketing mix. The cost advantages could be significant because companies would no longer have to maintain product variations for different countries, create different ads, and so on.

Depending on which marketers you ask, the Euroconsumer (1) doesn't exist and never will; (2) definitely does exist and is already buying standardized products; or (3) may or may not exist, we're not really sure yet, or may exist only to a degree and only for certain products. Some people scoff at the idea of a Euroconsumer, but more than a few marketers are betting that such a person exists. Mars, the giant U.S. candy company, is betting that the Euroconsumer does indeed exist. Its recent moves include changing the brand name of its Marathon and Raider candy bars to the names you'll probably recog-

Not every marketer is interested in the affluent consumer, however. A number of companies specifically target low-income consumers. For instance, when managers from the Family Dollar discount store chain look for locations to open a new store, they even go so far as to check parking lots in the vicinity for oil stains. The people they target are low-income adults who typically drive old, leaky cars.[40]

### EDUCATION

A person's level of education influences his or her buying and consumption patterns to some extent. The main differences that have been identified are those between college-educated and less educated households. College-educated consumers are much more likely to buy services (such as dry cleaning and baby sitting); travel; eat out; attend movies, concerts, and plays; and read books, magazines, and newspapers. Although they make up less than half the population, they account for nearly 60 percent of the clothing market.

Even though college-educated consumers tend to have a high average income and thus many of the characteristics of affluent consumers, the two groups are not identical. In particular, highly educated affluents are better informed and take more factors into account when making consumer decisions than do less educated affluents. Marketers trying to reach college-educated consumers strive to fill their information needs and cater to their desire for services.[41]

### GEOGRAPHIC LOCATION

Whether urban or rural, warm or cool climate, the Midwest or the South, geography plays a part in consumer behavior and creates a need for varying marketing strategies. For instance, western men tend to consume more cottage cheese, vitamins, and regular coffee than easterners or southerners. Consumers in the South and Midwest prefer soft (white) bread, whereas those on the East and West coasts nize from the U.S. market: Snickers and Twix.

The appliance maker Whirlpool has been working for several years to build pan-European demand for a consistent set of products. The conventional wisdom has always said that people in different countries want different kinds of appliances, such as top-loading washing machines in one country but front-loading machines in another country. In other words, these country-to-country differences have always existed and always will.

Whirlpool discovered, however, that everyone was interested in a washing machine that does a good job, consumes less electricity, and cuts down on repair bills. The product variations were more a matter of habit than steadfast tradition. For instance, people in France have top-loading washing machines simply because that's the way washing ma-chines have been made and marketed for years in that country. But as Whirlpool's Alex Vente explained, "Europeans are a lot less set in their ways than many people believe." The secret is to understand what really drives their purchase decisions and then to offer them attractive products.

Other marketers aren't so sure. Food is a good test case, since it does appear to be one of the harder things to get consumers to change their habits over. The degree of sweetness, spiciness, and other taste factors varies dramatically from country to country. Visit a Thai restaurant, a French restaurant, and a Mexican restaurant on three consecutive nights and you'll get a clear reminder of this fact. However, the fact that these cuisines have managed to travel around the world indicates that consumers do like variety and are willing to experiment. Young people are becoming increasingly important in this global consumer question, because they are more likely to consider themselves "European" over "Italian," "German," or "French." Their parents may cringe at the thought, but MTV, Levi's, and other global marketers couldn't be happier.

### APPLY YOUR KNOWLEDGE

**1.** What changes would you make to this textbook before trying to market it in England? In France? Explain your answer.

**2.** Consider the last imported product that you or a member of your family purchased. Do you think this product was adapted to appeal to U.S. consumers? Why or why not?

---

prefer firmer breads (rye, whole wheat, French, Italian).[42] Regional differences have also been found in fashion tastes, wine drinking, and musical preferences. Such differences can, of course, be found all across the globe. Winter clothes in Finland are distinctly different from winter clothes in Morocco. Not surprisingly, you need to study consumers in target areas to identify any differences in the buying behaviors related to your particular product category.

## Cultural Influences

**Culture** encompasses all the beliefs, values, and objects that are shared by a society and passed on to succeeding generations. The important characteristics of culture are that (1) it is learned; (2) it is shared through social institutions (such as family, religious institutions, schools, and the media); (3) it rewards socially appropriate responses; and (4) it changes with the times.[43] U.S. culture in the 1990s is very different from what it was in the 1890s; it is also different from Japanese culture, Scandinavian culture, and Arab culture.

As U.S. companies continue to search for markets in other countries, an understanding of cultural nuances is vital to success. Cultural mistakes tend to fall into two categories. The first is the U.S. tendency to treat dissimilar groups of people as parts of one larger group. This mistake is probably made in Europe most often, but it can also happen in Asia and Africa. For instance, people in Great Britain, France, Germany, and Italy certainly have a lot in common, but they do not usually view themselves as Europeans first and citizens of their own countries second. Just by taking a look at advertising in the various countries you can sense differences of both substance and style. British advertisers tend to rely on humor, whereas their French counterparts use sex and high style as the more common appeals. Coldly factual German ads stand in contrast to shouting, singing, splashy ads from Italy.[44]

The second type of cultural blunder assumes that everyone in the world is basically the same and that they all think, feel, and act like people in the United States.

**culture**
The beliefs, values, and objects shared by a group and passed on to succeeding generations

Sometimes the mistakes are tactical errors, such as PepsiCo's attempt to export its "Come Alive with Pepsi" theme around the world, only to learn that in Thailand it became "Bring your ancestors back from the dead with Pepsi." In other cases, the differences affect the very way you conduct business. For example, businesspeople in Indonesia have a term that is roughly translated as "rubber time." This means that time is elastic and unstructured; if a local festival overlaps with a business meeting, you cancel the business meeting. Hard-driving U.S. businesspeople often have trouble adjusting to this concept.[45]

This isn't to say that there are no cross-cultural markets. The point is that you have to do your homework so that you truly understand your markets. For instance, the Japanese teenager listening to a Walkman and wearing Levi's while eating in a Burger King shares many of the buying habits of teenagers in California, Iowa, Denmark, and Australia. In fact, global teenagers often have more in common with each other than they have with their own parents. But don't assume anything about cultural influences: research is absolutely necessary.[46]

The culture we live in determines the language we speak, the foods we eat, the clothing we wear, and the activities we engage in. Obviously, culture is a complex topic to cover in detail. Consider two aspects of particular concern to marketers: core values and microculture.

## CORE VALUES

**values**
Beliefs about what is good or desirable

**core values**
Pervasive and enduring values within a culture

**Values** are beliefs about what is good or desirable. The **core values** of a culture are shared values that are pervasive and enduring. A culture's core values define how products are used, determine whether products are seen negatively or positively, and define how market relationships are set up.[47] In the United States, for example, core values include an emphasis on the following:

- Material comfort and well-being
- Achievement and success
- Efficiency and practicality
- Progress
- Individualism
- Freedom of expression and choice
- External conformity
- Activity and involvement
- Egalitarianism
- Humanitarianism

Some people hold particular values more strongly than other people do, and some of the values may actually conflict, such as freedom of expression versus external conformity. Always keep in mind that people in other countries have different value systems.

Core values evolve and change over time. For example, some U.S. core values that seem to be emerging in the 1990s include the following:

- Greater emphasis on the environment and other living things
- Greater emphasis on fitness and health
- A shift from a national viewpoint to a more global viewpoint

Researchers in the Netherlands identified five attitude segments among Dutch women, in terms of traditional versus nontraditional roles for women; these segments range from very conservative to very progressive.

As society changes and values are altered, needs in the marketplace change, calling for a change in marketing strategy. A prime example is the changing nature of sex roles. In response to changing views of men and women, marketers are redesigning many of their products to eliminate previous sex typing. Thus, the previously "masculine" Swiss army knife now comes in a variety of colors and is considered a handy item to keep in your pocket or in your purse. Marketers are also realizing that women are making more and more buying decisions in traditionally male areas. For example, women now buy 50 percent of new cars and influence 80

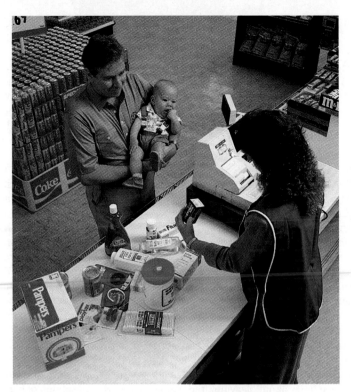

**Exhibit 4.13**
**THE CHANGING ROLES OF WOMEN AND MEN**
Some of the most significant changes in consumer behavior in recent decades have been the changing roles of women and men, as more women work outside the home and many men now participate in shopping, child care, and housework. Marketers respond to these changes with new strategies for retailing and promotion.

percent of new-car purchases. Their car-buying criteria are often quite different from men's criteria.[48] At the same time, as more women join the work force, more men are participating in housework, cooking, child care, and shopping (see Exhibit 4.13). In response, retail outlets such as supermarkets are learning to adapt to the needs of male shoppers by adding specialty departments for hardware and automotive supplies and by offering later store hours, since men prefer to shop when stores are less crowded.[49] Another recent change is the growing interest mainstream marketers have shown in the gay and lesbian market. The Gap, Eurodollar Rent-A-Car, and Benetton are among the companies that have set their sights on this segment's above-average income.[50]

Of course, such changes occur at different rates around the world. For instance, *The Economist,* a prominent British news magazine, still refers to businesspeople as "businessmen," and male employees in South Korea are served tea by silent, uniformed women. Race relations also vary from country to country. In Asia, for example, the Darkie brand of toothpaste, with blatantly racist African caricatures, was available until quite recently.[51]

## MICROCULTURES

Consumer behavior is influenced not only by the general culture in which people live but also by the microculture to which they belong. A **microculture** is a group of people who exist within a larger culture and who share beliefs, values, and customs that differ, at least in some respects, from those of the larger society. We are all members of microcultures. A microculture may be based on ethnic or national origin, religion, physical attributes (such as skin color), geographic location, or some other aspect that sets a group of people apart and contributes to identifiable behavior patterns.

According to one estimate, by the year 2000 one-third of U.S. children will belong to minority groups, primarily because of high birth rates among minorities and the contribution of immigration to U.S. population growth.[52] As minorities make up more and more of the population, it's important to learn more about these growing consumer groups. Be aware of variant buying behaviors and attitudes among microcultures, both to appeal to these groups and to avoid offending them.

**microculture**
A group of people who share beliefs, values, and customs different from those of the larger culture

## HOW FAR CAN WE GO IN MARKETING TO KIDS?

Marketing to children has taken off in a big way in the past few years. And we're not just talking about breakfast cereals, candy, or toys. Crest for Kids, the Polaroid Cool Cam, My Own Meal microwave dinners, Kachoos children's tissues, Kids Deli luncheon meats, *Sports Illustrated for Kids,* and the Young Americans Bank are but a few of the latest products that have been developed specifically with kids in mind. And big-time marketers such as Burger King, Delta Air Lines, Sears, Nike, Seven-Up, and Heinz are going after kids in a big way as well.

Why kids? For one thing, they have money. By some estimates, U.S. preteens have $15 billion to spend. For another thing, kids are doing more and more of the family food shopping because both Mom and

**ETHICAL DILEMMA IN MARKETING**

Dad work. Third, kids are exerting greater influence on household buying decisions, from picking a fast-food restaurant for dinner to choosing the family car. Some parents are just too busy to make such decisions on their own, while others—feeling guilty about leaving the kids alone so much—give in easily to their children's demands for anything from new clothes to stereo equipment. Fi-

nally, today's kids are tomorrow's adult consumers, so many marketers think it's never too early to begin building brand recognition.

To reach this lucrative market, advertisers have gone beyond television—the medium of choice—to specialized kids' magazines, direct mail, and now even the schoolroom. The extent of this last approach was brought into focus in 1990 with the advent of Channel One, a closed-circuit TV broadcast developed for school classrooms by Whittle Communications. Whittle provides schools (primarily high schools) with free video equipment in exchange for airing daily 12-minute news broadcasts that include 2 minutes of commercials. Other inroads of marketing into the schools include distribution of free ad-bearing textbook covers, sponsorship of high school athletics, product sampling, and provision of educational materials such as wall posters and magazines.

To see how microculture can affect consumer behavior, the following sections focus on three cultural groups that have received the attention of consumer researchers: African-Americans, Hispanic-Americans, and Asian-Americans. These examples are taken from the United States, but remember that ethnic microcultures exist in many countries, such as the Maoris in New Zealand, transplanted Indonesians in the Netherlands, and ethnic Russians in Estonia.

AFRICAN-AMERICAN CONSUMERS    Some 26 million African-Americans make up 12 percent of the U.S. population and 50 percent of the minority population. A disproportionate number (as many as one-third) are in the low-income bracket.[53] Nevertheless, they still represent significant buying power: an estimated $150 billion a year.

Do African-American consumers vary in any significant way from other consumers? Researchers have found some notable differences, many of which are attributable to the socioeconomic disadvantages that African-Americans have traditionally experienced. When such things as income are adjusted for, many of the differences in buying behaviors disappear. Experts are quick to point out, however, that middle-class African-American consumers are not identical to middle-class white consumers, and although some marketing will appeal to both, this is not always the case. Many upscale African-Americans identify with black culture and resent marketers who do not realize this fact.[54] Cross Colours, a clothing firm, has been successful selling clothes in the traditional African colors of green, yellow, and black. Mass marketers such as Kmart and J. C. Penney have also targeted the African-influenced clothing market.[55]

A marketer targeting African-Americans should know that their families tend to be larger, younger, and more mobile than average; their households are more likely to be headed by females and to be single parent; and they are more likely to live in urban areas, especially central cities. African-American consumers are less likely to buy generic products but are more price conscious than other consumer groups.

Adults alarmed by all this marketing aimed at children worry that kids are being exploited and that impressionable youngsters are being manipulated by unscrupulous advertisers. Among the most vocal critics of promotions targeted to children is Consumers Union, publishers of *Consumer Reports* and *Zillions*, a consumer magazine for kids. According to Consumers Union, "Educators and parents should object to promotions that exploit the inexperience and vulnerability of children or that fail to identify themselves clearly as advertising." Consumers Union decries the proliferation of free "educational" materials containing advertising messages that students will construe as facts.

Consumers Union is also critical of licensing deals that create kids' TV shows based on toys or that encourage children to buy products for the simple reason that they are related to a popular movie or character. Other critics denounce promotions for tobacco or alcohol that will lead kids to believe these products are desirable. Also of concern are ads that encourage kids to consume costly or unhealthful products and ads that use role models such as athletes and rock stars to push products for their status appeal.

Marketers who are concerned about the most ethical ways to market to children should follow the guidelines provided by the Council of Better Business Bureaus. These guidelines include the following:

- Take into account the level of knowledge, sophistication, and maturity of the primary audience. Younger children are less able to evaluate the credibility of what they see, and they often don't distinguish fact from fiction.
- Be as truthful and accurate as possible, recognizing that children may learn practices from advertising that can affect their health and well-being.
- Wherever possible, include positive social images, such as kindness, justice, generosity, and respect for others.

## WHAT'S YOUR OPINION?

**1.** Several state legislatures are considering banning Channel One from classrooms. Financially strapped school districts, on the other hand, resent this interference and welcome corporate funding of classroom equipment and materials. Which side do you agree with? Why?

**2.** What should teachers do when offered free educational materials by corporations? What can corporations do to ensure that such classroom materials are ethically produced and distributed?

---

They are also more likely to watch television and listen to the radio and less likely to read newspapers than other consumers. Because half of all African-American consumers are single heads of households, most of whom are working mothers, they have needs for child care, one-stop shopping, fast food, and stores that offer a wide selection at low prices.[56]

HISPANIC-AMERICAN CONSUMERS    The term *Hispanic* encompasses a number of groups whose major link is the Spanish language. Hispanics include Mexican-Americans, Puerto Ricans, Cuban-Americans, and various groups from Central and South America. Altogether they make up some 20 million people, concentrated primarily in urban areas.

Although each Hispanic subgroup has distinctive characteristics, all tend to emphasize strong bonds with their original culture and with the Catholic church. Hispanic cultures are built around the family, and the family often shops as a group. Hispanic consumers are highly loyal to favorite brands and tend not to experiment. One study indicates that only 35 percent can be lured away from their regular brands with competitive discount offers.[57] They are least likely to use coupons or buy generic products (it is a matter of pride to be able to pay full price), they buy less frozen food than the general population, and they consume half the convenience packaged mixes that non-Hispanic consumers do.[58] They are a good market for big-ticket items because family members often pool their resources to buy cars and other expensive products.

You can best serve Hispanic customers by showing an interest in their community, using their own language, and catering to their specific needs. According to one study, more than 40 percent of Hispanics buy products from companies that show genuine interest in the Hispanic consumer.[59] Among marketers who have gained a strong identity among Hispanic consumers are McDonald's, Coors, PepsiCo, and Coca-Cola, all of which have sponsored major Hispanic art or music events. Sponsorship of church fund-raising events and promotion of sporting events, especially amateur soccer, have created great visibility among Hispanic consumers for companies such as Ford.[60]

ASIAN-AMERICAN CONSUMERS    Asian-Americans constitute the fastest-growing ethnic minority in the United States. This cultural group includes people who have come from China, Japan, the Philippines, India, Pakistan, Korea, Vietnam, Laos, and Cambodia. Asian-Americans represent almost half of all U.S. legal immigrants, and their population is growing at 14 times the U.S. average growth rate.[61] Asian-Americans have above-average education and household incomes.

Quality is the number one concern of Asian-American consumers. They tend to be traditional, conservative, and highly loyal to premium brands. They are less likely than other groups to use coupons or to shop by catalog.[62]

Like members of other minority groups, Asian-Americans respond well to companies and businesses that recognize their needs and treat them with respect. In fact, this is the key to marketing to all microcultures. As noted in *Inc.* magazine: "Targeted advertising, bilingual salespeople, and special events all help to break down barriers. But their long-term value is to confirm for minorities that they are genuinely welcome and valued not just as consumers, but as people—and as Americans."[63]

Even though this section discusses broad groups of people, remember that the terms *African-American, Hispanic-American,* and *Asian-American* include many different people. For instance, just as you wouldn't assume that all Asians are alike, don't assume that all Asian-Americans are alike.

## Social Influences

In addition to cultural influences, consumer decisions are also influenced by a variety of social elements. These include a person's current or desired social status, the impact of other members in the household, the influence of people and groups the consumer would like to identify with, and the effects of word-of-mouth communication.

### SOCIAL STATUS

**social classes**
Stratified groups in society made up of people with similar values, lifestyles, interests, and behaviors

Every society can be seen as stratified into a number of **social classes** made up of people who share similar values, lifestyles, interests, and behaviors. Social class is determined primarily by occupation but is also based on income, education, possessions, personal success, social skills, community participation, and other factors.[64] Exhibit 4.14 shows the U.S. population broken down into seven social classes.

Social class influences many aspects of consumer behavior: the quality and style of clothing people wear, their home furnishings, their use of leisure time, their choice of media, where and how they shop, and their saving, spending, and credit patterns. It is important for you to realize that income and social class are separate influences on consumer behavior and that the two are not necessarily related. For example, people who consider themselves to be middle class or even working class may have very high incomes, especially if they are in two-earner households, but what they spend that income on will differ from what upper-class people spend their money on.

### HOUSEHOLDS

**household**
All the people who occupy a housing unit

Another important social influence of interest to consumer marketers is the **household**—all the people, related or unrelated, who occupy a housing unit. From a market planning point of view, the basic unit of consumption is not the individual person but the household. A household is not the same as a family; a household can consist of a single person, two or more unmarried or unrelated persons, a stepfamily, or the traditional family.

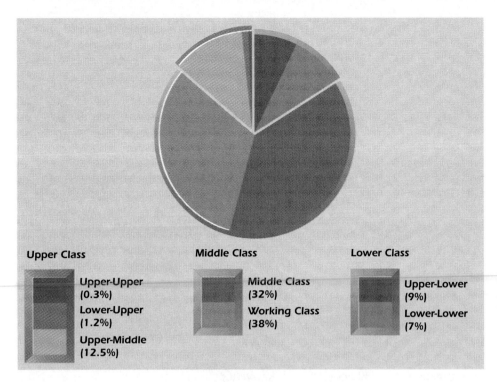

Upper Class

Middle Class

Lower Class

| | |
|---|---|
| Upper-Upper (0.3%) | |
| Lower-Upper (1.2%) | |
| Upper-Middle (12.5%) | |

| | |
|---|---|
| Middle Class (32%) | |
| Working Class (38%) | |

| | |
|---|---|
| Upper-Lower (9%) | |
| Lower-Lower (7%) | |

**Exhibit 4.14**
**U.S. SOCIAL CLASSES**
Social classes in the United States are divided into three main categories; however, any classification like this must be interpreted carefully.

The average household size in the United States has dropped to an all-time low: 2.62 persons. People living alone make up 25 percent of all U.S. households. The traditional family household, a married couple with their own children, is now in the minority and declining. The largest increases have been in stepfamilies (which will be the most common kind of family by the year 2000) and in single-parent families.[65] In London, fewer than 30 percent of households have children.[66]

Fast-food marketers are among those who have responded to the changes in families. When they realized that fewer and fewer people were sitting around the breakfast table in the morning with their families, McDonald's, Burger King, and Jack-in-the-Box added breakfast foods to their menus, which was a successful move. In the last decade, consumption of breakfast in restaurants has grown much faster than consumption of lunches or dinners.[67]

THE HOUSEHOLD LIFE CYCLE    The structure of most households changes over time. Exhibit 4.15 shows the stages that households can go through as people age. (Note the many variations on the "traditional" view of the household, with a married couple and their children.) Each stage in this life cycle presents problems for decision makers in the household and opportunities for marketers. Young singles, for example, need to furnish their first residence and tend to be fashion- and recreation-oriented. They want to look good and have fun on relatively low incomes. However, the lifestyles of young parents with children are very different. Their focus is on child-care products, home maintenance, and tight budgeting. As the family ages and household income rises, the emphasis shifts toward school activities and services such as music lessons, recreation equipment, and time-saving appliances. Successful marketers are those who are able to identify a particular type of household and related lifestyle and then build a strategy around meeting the needs of this defined market. For example, a financial services firm such as Merrill Lynch can offer one set of services for people just starting their careers and another set for people nearing retirement, because the needs of these two groups are vastly different.

DECISION MAKING IN HOUSEHOLDS    Individuals within households fulfill many roles in consumer behavior, from information gatherer and influencer to decider, purchaser, and user. One family member may express a need for a product, another may decide on the brand, a third may make the actual purchase, and all members

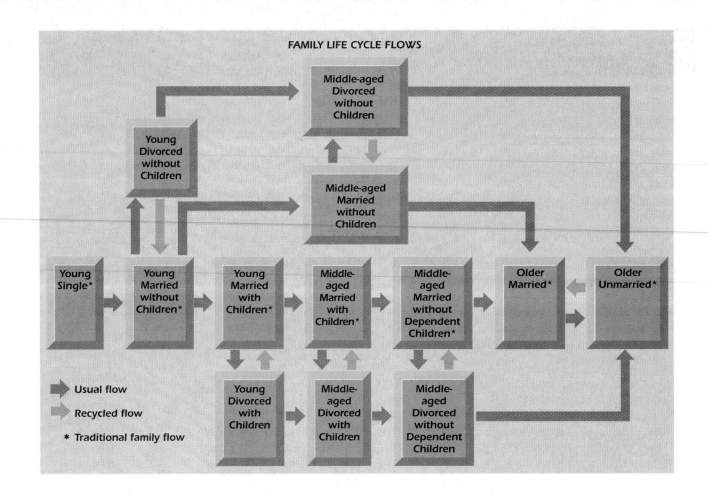

FAMILY LIFE CYCLE FLOWS

**Exhibit 4.15**
**THE MODERN FAMILY LIFE CYCLE**
Today's family life cycle can take many paths compared with the traditional family life cycle, and marketers must consider these changes when assessing their markets.

may use it. Often the principal user of a product is not the person who buys it; for example, women are major purchasers of men's underwear, and men are big spenders on perfume.

Marketing research can help you identify the individuals in a household who have the most influence on the decision process. Who has a say in the decisions about a particular product type? Who finally decides? Each household member has unique needs and a unique perspective and thus may evaluate different attributes of a product or brand. Whereas Billy may want a camcorder with lots of special-effects capabilities, Mom may be interested primarily in price and warranty, and Dad may be concerned with the unit's ease of operation. However, marketers need to be careful when trying to influence family purchasing behavior by advertising to children; not everyone thinks this is an ethically acceptable practice.

## REFERENCE GROUPS

**reference group**
A group that has an influence on a particular consumer

The fifth important influence comes from all the groups to which a consumer belongs. Any group that influences consumer decisions is considered a **reference group,** which may be one to which the consumer belongs (such as a family, a club, or a microculture), one to which he or she aspires to belong (and thus identifies with), or one that he or she shuns. Reference groups influence people's decisions by providing information, by pressuring them to conform to group norms, or by offering a set of values for people to identify with and express.[68] Individuals are more likely to rely on reference groups when making consumer decisions under certain conditions:

• They lack information about or experience with the product.
• They are particularly committed to the group.
• The reference group is particularly credible, powerful, or attractive.

- The product is conspicuous (publicly consumed).
- The product is a luxury rather than a necessity.
- The product is particularly relevant to group function.

American Express cards are great examples of products that appeal to people who want to identify with groups known for their financial success. Most anybody can get a Visa or MasterCard, but you have to be somebody to qualify for an American Express card—at least that's the idea American Express promotes. Visa and MasterCard offer convenience and credit, but holding an American Express card tells people that you've arrived.[69]

By the mid-1980s the credit card market was just about saturated, and the average cardholder had seven credit cards.[70] Indeed there were so many American Express cards out there that the card had lost some of its special appeal. Looking for a new way to increase the number of its cards in circulation by creating even more-exclusive groups, American Express introduced the Gold Card, followed by the Platinum Card. Now you are special if you have the original green card; you are really special if you qualify for the Gold Card; and you are really, really special if you are *invited* to apply for the Platinum Card. More than any other credit card, the Platinum Card appeals to people who want to feel that they are part of the world's financial elite.

### OPINION LEADERSHIP AND WORD OF MOUTH

The final social influence is **word-of-mouth communication**—obtaining consumer information from other consumers rather than from mass media or sales personnel. People often consult with their friends and family members before making purchases, and they consider this word-of-mouth information to be particularly credible. Word of mouth is one of the more powerful forms of communication in both a business and a nonbusiness environment. Word of mouth influences many purchase decisions, but it can be particularly strong with services. Because word of mouth can have such a strong influence over purchase decisions, it's important to understand how it operates in your target segments.

Those individuals who exert a great deal of influence on purchase decisions through word of mouth are considered to be **opinion leaders.** Such people tend to have a great amount of involvement with and knowledge of a particular product category; to actively seek out product information; to try new products; to make greater use of the media, particularly special-interest publications; and to be self-confident, gregarious, and outgoing. Opinion leadership is more likely to occur when the opinion leader and the consumer have similar backgrounds and attitudes, when the consumer has high involvement with the product but low product knowledge, when the product is complex and difficult to evaluate, and when the opinion leader is easily accessible.

Negative word of mouth should be of particular concern to marketers; many studies have shown that unfavorable information has a stronger impact on consumer buying behavior than favorable information does. The most common types of negative word of mouth are consumer complaints and rumors. Effective handling of complaints and public relations efforts focused on providing accurate and truthful information are important means of avoiding or neutralizing negative word of mouth.[71]

## Situational Influences

Various aspects of the communication, purchase, and usage situation can influence consumer buying behavior. **Situational influences** are factors within a particular time or place, independent of the consumer's or the product's characteristics, that affect consumer decision making. By understanding the following situational influences, you can start to make adjustments to help bring about desired consumer responses:[72]

**word-of-mouth communication**
Transmission of consumer information from person to person

**opinion leaders**
Individuals who exert influence on consumer decisions through word of mouth

**situational influences**
Factors within a particular time or place that influence consumer behavior

- *Physical surroundings.* The location, weather, sounds, aromas, lighting, decor, and so on make up the physical situation in which consumers encounter products, purchase them, or use them. Of special concern are such things as information load (Is the consumer given too much to choose from? Too little?), background music, odors, store layout, product location, color schemes, and displays.

- *Social surroundings.* Very often, other people are present when the decision is made. For example, while watching television or listening to the radio, family members may comment on commercials and influence each other's perceptions. Similarly, shopping is a social activity for many consumers, and the people they shop with can have a significant influence on both what they buy and where they buy it.

- *Time.* Time influences purchasing not only because of the time available for consumers to learn about, shop for, or use a product but also because of the time of day or time of year, the amount of time since the product was last used, the amount of time until next payday, and so on. You also need to consider the ever-increasing time constraints on today's consumers. In particular, 55 percent of U.S. residents under age 50 complain of a lack of leisure time, and the percentage is even higher for two-income families.[73] People are willing to pay more to make the best use of their leisure time, which means spending money on products that save time (microwave foods, lawn maintenance services) or on those that improve the quality of leisure time (recreation equipment, travel services). Savvy marketers are catering to both types of time expenditures. In addition, people who are in a hurry will not spend a lot of time gathering information about alternatives, will limit the number of alternatives they consider, and will tend to stick to the tried-and-true solutions that have worked in the past.

- *Reason for the purchase.* The reason a consumer is making a particular purchase affects the choice he or she makes. For example, customers might buy paperback books for themselves but a hardbound copy of the same title as a gift. Also, the kinds of items chosen as gifts will depend on the situation (wedding gifts tend to be more practical than birthday gifts) and on the relation of the recipient to the giver (a woman might buy silk pajamas for her husband but not for her boss).

- *Emotional and financial state.* The state of a person's mind and finances at the time of purchase is also important. Moods can influence the consumer's ability to process and retrieve information, the shopping process, and consumption behavior. Some people go out to the mall if they are feeling bored or depressed, go to a fancy restaurant or expensive stores if they've come into some extra cash, and make other such decisions based on monetary states.

# SUMMARY OF LEARNING OBJECTIVES

**1. Describe how involvement affects the consumer decision process.**

Involvement is the degree of personal importance or relevance a product holds for the consumer. The more involvement the consumer has, the more extensive the decision process and the greater the consumer's commitment to the chosen item. Low-involvement products are those that require relatively little planning and don't elicit strong emotions, such as routine purchases of school supplies or gasoline. On the other hand, high-involvement purchases require significant planning, and the products under consideration mean a lot to the consumer.

**2. Differentiate among routine, limited, and extensive problem solving.**

With routine problem solving, decision making is automatic and minimal, often based on habit or convenience. In limited problem solving, the consumer chooses among a limited number of alternatives using only a few criteria. In extensive problem solving, the consumer engages in a complex evaluation of multiple alternatives, and involvement is high. When designing a marketing strategy, you do well to understand the type of problem solving consumers are likely to engage in while purchasing a given product.

**3. Explain how perceived risk relates to the consumer's information search process.**

Perceived risk is the consumer's amount of uncertainty about a purchase and concern about potential losses that might result from making a wrong choice. The greater the perceived risk regarding a particular product, the greater the information search. Risk can take several forms, including personal safety, financial risk, environmental risk, and social risk.

**4. List the five stages of the consumer decision process and briefly explain what occurs at each stage.**

The five stages of the consumer decision process are (a) need recognition, in which the consumer experiences a discrepancy between a desired state and an actual state; (b) information search, in which the consumer conducts an internal search and an external search to learn about available solutions to the problem; (c) evaluation of alternatives, in which the consumer applies evaluative criteria to items in the evoked set of potential solutions; (d) purchase, in which the consumer selects a brand and an outlet; and (e) purchase outcome, in which the consumer experiences satisfaction or dissatisfaction with the product.

**5. Discuss the psychological factors that influence consumer buying behavior.**

The main types of psychological factors that affect consumer buying behavior are needs and motives, perception, learning, attitudes, personality, and self-concept. Needs and motives define the underlying reasons for consumers to buy anything. The elements of perception that interest marketers include being exposed to stimuli, attending to those stimuli, and interpreting them to form perceptions. The consumer learning process underlies the way consumers acquire knowledge about products; the two major methods are conditioning and social learning. Attitudes express the emotions that consumers have toward products; the components of attitude are the cognitive (what you believe), the affective (how you feel), and the behavioral (how you act). Finally, although personality hasn't proven to be a good general indicator of purchase behavior, self-concept has, because it drives consumer lifestyles.

**6. List the cultural and social factors that influence consumer buying behavior.**

A culture is composed of the beliefs, values, and objects that are shared by a society. The primary cultural factors discussed are core values and microcultures such as Asian-Americans and African-Americans. The major social factors are social status, household status, reference groups, opinion leadership, and word of mouth. The study of social status tries to identify groups of people who share similar values, lifestyles, interests, and behaviors. Because social status influences many aspects of behavior, smart marketers work to understand the status of their target consumers. An understanding of household dynamics is important in consumer marketing because the household is the basic unit of consumption. You need to understand both the life-cycle stage and the decision-making processes of your target households. Reference groups play an important role in consumer marketing; many consumer purchases are influenced by groups that the buyer wants to identify with. Opinion leadership and word of mouth, which greatly influence purchasing behavior, demand the marketer's close attention as well.

**7. Identify the situational factors that influence consumer buying behavior.**

The main types of situational factors that affect consumer buying behavior are physical surroundings, social surroundings, time, reason for the purchase, and emotional and financial states. Physical surroundings include everything from the weather to the decor inside a retail store. The social surroundings, on the other hand, consist of the people present while the consumer plans for or makes a purchase. Time influences purchase behavior in more than one way, including time of the year and of the day, the amount of time until payday, and the amount of time consumers have to shop for and use products. Consumers make purchases for different reasons, such as buying products for personal use versus buying them as gifts, and these reasons affect their purchase choices. The final situational factor is the consumer's mood and circumstances prior to making purchases.

## KEY TERMS

attitude (121)
baby boomers (124)
classical conditioning (118)
consumer behavior (108)
consumer buying behavior (108)
consumer decision process (109)
consumer learning (118)
core values (128)
culture (127)
discrimination (119)

evoked set (112)
extensive problem solving (EPS) (109)
generalization (119)
hedonic needs (115)
household (132)
involvement (109)
knowledge structure (120)
lifestyle (123)
limited problem solving (LPS) (109)
microculture (129)

modeling (119)
motives (115)
opinion leaders (135)
perceived risk (111)
perception (116)
personality (122)
postpurchase dissonance (114)
psychological influences (115)
reference group (134)
reinforcement (118)

routine problem solving (RPS) (109)
selective attention (117)
self-concept (123)
situational influences (135)
social classes (132)
utilitarian needs (115)
values (128)
word-of-mouth communication (135)

## Meeting a Marketing Challenge at Domino's

Sizzling pizza fresh from the oven to your door in just 30 minutes: that's the promise that catapulted Domino's to the lead in the home-delivery pizza segment. However, if you look at all pizzas sold in the United States, not just pizzas delivered to the door, you'll see Pizza Hut, the PepsiCo subsidiary, in the number one position. How is Tom Monaghan's pizza empire striking back at market leader Pizza Hut and other competitors? Domino's does it by understanding, shaping, and responding to the buying behavior of pizza purchasers.

For 29 years, the Domino's menu was stripped down to keep preparation and delivery within the 30-minute time limit. When you called to order a pizza, you could have your pick of 2 pizza sizes, 11 toppings, and 1 soft drink. In the meantime, consumers developed a taste for pan pizza, a deep-dish variety that now accounts for about half the pizzas sold in the United States. Rival Pizza Hut introduced pan pizza in 1981 and added hand-tossed pizza in 1988; the two products now outsell that chain's original thin-crust pizza by four to one. Monaghan recognized that consumer buying behavior had changed to include variety—and Domino's needed to respond quickly to stay in the game.

Faced with this competitive environment, Domino's began testing pan pizza in 1988. Monaghan wanted to be sure his stores could make a quality pan pizza that could still be delivered within the 30-minute time limit. The test was successful, and Domino's added pan pizza to its menu in 1989, one of the last pizza chains to offer this increasingly popular item. By expanding the menu to include pan pizza, Domino's is taking advantage of changes in consumer buying behavior to reach a larger audience. In 1992 the company added a premium pizza (with more cheese and toppings) to counter advances being made by Pizza Hut. That same year, Domino's also started giving customers the option of picking up pizzas, rather than waiting to have them delivered. In 1993 the chain began test marketing such new items as chicken wings and submarine sandwiches. That same year saw another major change in Domino's operations, when the company decided to drop the 30-minute delivery guarantee. Safety concerns about drivers racing to meet the deadline had been brewing for some time, and a $78 million settlement paid to the family of a woman who died in a collision with a Domino's driver was enough to convince the company to change the policy.

Monaghan knows that quality and service are the keys to reinforcing pizza customers' brand loyalty, and he's trying to stay one step ahead of his competitors by maintaining a tight grip on these areas. In one of his quality-control programs, two mystery shoppers per store each order at least

one Domino's pizza per month and then rate the store on service and customer satisfaction. That's 10,000 mystery pizza buyers buying 120,000 pizzas every year, giving Monaghan a lot of information on how customers view his pizza and his service. Domino's uses these evaluations to monitor chainwide performance and also bases individual store manager compensation, in part, on how mystery buyers rate the stores.

Because consumer buying behavior is changing and competitors are spicing up their menus and expanding delivery services, Domino's is also extending its target audiences and advertising messages. One segment now targeted by Domino's is the Hispanic market, which has not received much attention from the pizza chains, even though it's been courted with success by McDonald's. With the ad theme "Domino's Pizza entrega" ("Domino's Pizza delivers"), the company is reaching out to Hispanic customers in the Southwest, in south Florida, and on the West Coast.

**Your mission:** As a member of Domino's marketing staff, you have been asked to take part in a week-long planning meeting to identify and suggest solutions for key marketing problems facing the company. Use your knowledge of consumer buying behavior to respond to the challenges Tom Monaghan presents during the sessions.

1. Monaghan starts by describing two demographic trends: The number of households with a single parent and at least one child under the age of 18 is increasing, and a surprising number of people return to live with their parents after finishing college. With these two trends in mind, which of the following target market descriptions would you recommend?
   a. Working parents who have no time to cook after work and want their families to get a hot meal in a hurry.
   b. College graduates living at home who are trying to save money and want an inexpensive, fast meal that won't interfere with their active lifestyle.
   c. Young professional couples who frequently entertain business associates.
2. The next challenge Monaghan presents is the search for a Domino's spokesperson. The firm wants to maximize its promotional efforts by selecting someone who can be a believable opinion leader or represent a desirable reference group for a large number of potential Domino's purchasers. Considering the groups that might be influenced by the following spokespersons, which would you recommend for Domino's? Why?

a. Heavyweight boxer George Foreman
b. Cartoon characters The Teenage Mutant Ninja Turtles
c. Author Danielle Steel

3. Ernest Higa, a Japanese entrepreneur who helped Domino's break into Japan, meets with the marketing team to discuss his strategies and plans. He recognizes that cultural differences between countries can affect consumer behavior, but he also wants to differentiate Domino's from other chains now operating in Japan. For instance, although market research reveals that tomato and cheese flavors are not particularly pleasing to the Japanese palate, Higa thinks this might be a way to stand apart from the competition. Which of the following marketing strategies would you recommend?

a. To emphasize that Domino's in Japan is part of the mainstream, open restaurants in downtown areas next to restaurants that serve only traditional Japanese food.

b. Leave the tomato and cheese toppings off, but add other toppings that score well on local market research, and

offer local soft drinks. Stress the speed of home delivery because this will differentiate Domino's from other food-delivery firms.

c. Add a variety of Japanese foods such as noodles to the home-delivery menu as well as other Italian-style foods such as calzones. Focus advertising on the wide range of Italian and Japanese foods available for home delivery from Domino's.

4. As your final task, Monaghan asks your group's help in addressing a growing consumer concern: the nutritional value of fast foods. Lifestyles are becoming more hectic, and because more information about health hazards has become available, consumers are looking more closely at what they eat. One result may be that all fast foods will be lumped together in the public consciousness and considered unhealthy because some fast foods are high in cholesterol and other undesirable elements. Which of these approaches would you suggest that Domino's adopt in order to deal with this issue?

a. Perform nutritional tests privately on Domino's pizza as well as other fast foods, including hamburgers, hot dogs, and tacos. If the results are good for Domino's, release the news to the media as proof that Domino's pizza is better for consumers' health than other fast foods.

b. Organize a letter-writing campaign among Domino's employees to petition the government to change the minimum daily requirements of key nutritional elements to be more in accordance with current dietary trends, which include more frequent servings of fast food.

c. Sponsor a fitness contest in the major urban areas where Domino's has a presence, offering all contestants free Domino's pizzas as part of their training for the competition. Run ads featuring the winners eating Domino's pizza and saying how pizza makes them feel fit and healthy.

### SPECIAL PROJECT

Domino's wants to capitalize on the investment in its delivery system by delivering other products. However, Monaghan knows that customers will always associate Domino's with pizza. In addition, there is a limited range of food products that customers are accustomed to ordering for home delivery. Make a list of products you think Domino's could deliver along with pizza. For each product, explain how you would take consumer beliefs, emotions, and behaviors into account.[74]

## Grattan Looks at the Bits and Bytes of Buying Habits

How do catalog marketers learn about their customers' buying behavior? Grattan, a British catalog firm (which in turn is owned by the German catalog firm Otto Versand), has been facing this challenge for decades. Because Grattan markets by mail and by telephone, it's difficult to find out consumers' needs and wants. Grattan's managing director, Michael Bottomly, and his predecessor, David C. Jones, have been sensitive to this problem and aggressively pursued a high-tech approach to discovering clues to consumer purchasing patterns: the computerized customer database.

Grattan's database, like all customer databases, includes a variety of information about each customer. Grattan collects some demographic data, such as customer name and address, by asking where to ship the merchandise. Then the firm hires outside suppliers who "overlay," or add, other data, giving Grattan a rounder picture of its customers. Overlaid information is generally developed on the basis of where a customer lives, rather than on direct knowledge of a specific customer's circumstances.

These overlays include a brief socioeconomic description of where the customer lives, the types of homes, the size of families, and other details. Because people of similar socioeconomic standing tend to cluster in the same neighborhood, have homes of comparable size, and have households of roughly similar size and life-cycle stage, Grattan gains valuable insights into each customer's lifestyle by learning about where he or she lives.

If Grattan has a large concentration of customers in one particular area, for example, it's reasonable to believe that the catalog would appeal to noncustomers who live in that same neighborhood. Therefore, the firm can seek out new customers by mailing to noncustomers who live near current customers. Further, the cataloger can make some good assumptions about the kinds of products these customers need or don't need, based on the lifestyle that the overlays indicate. That's why Grattan doesn't send its gardening catalog to people who live in high-rise apartments.

Another key element in the database is product purchase history. Because Grattan's customers order by mail or by telephone, Grattan can easily keep track of every item they buy. Then the firm can fit future offers to the customer's specific needs by mailing smaller specialty catalogs only to those people who have purchased similar or related products in the past.

It's costly to print and mail a catalog, so Grattan needs to zero in on the customers who are most likely to buy.

In many cases, mail-order retailers send their catalogs to a subset of the entire customer base rather than to everyone on the list. Who should get which catalog? That's another area where the customer database comes in handy.

Catalogers usually select customers for a specific mailing on the basis of recency, frequency, or monetary value. Recency refers to how long ago customers placed their last orders; mail-order retailers typically skip over people who have not purchased for many months. Frequency is a measure of how often the customer has made a purchase; customers who buy often are valuable indeed. Finally, monetary value is obtained by totaling how much each customer has spent in a given period (generally a year). By examining recency, frequency, and monetary value, it's possible to make a reasonable guess about the customers who will buy in the future.

Grattan has found that its customer database is crucial to pinpointing the right target customer for expensive items sold by mail. The company decided to offer two styles of grandfather clocks selling for the equivalent of nearly $2,000. After mailing 30,000 brochures, Grattan sold 60 clocks. On the other hand, it learned the exact profile of a customer who buys a costly clock by mail. So Grattan searched its database and mailed offers to other customers with similar characteristics—and sold every clock. That's the kind of consumer behavior every marketer wants to see.

1. If Grattan wanted to expand catalog sales beyond Great Britain to France, Italy, and Germany, would it do better to translate the current catalog and mail it to those countries, or should it start with small specialty catalogs featuring products that are hard to find in each of those countries?

2. Like most marketers, Grattan would like to generate positive word of mouth. Which would generate the most productive word-of-mouth campaign before a new catalog is mailed: sending fashion apparel to editors of the leading women's magazines or sending copies of the apparel patterns to sewing classes in high schools?

3. Assume that Grattan is producing a new cookware specialty catalog and needs a strategy to ensure that potential customers include Grattan in the evoked set of alternatives. Would Grattan do better to emphasize low price and extensive selection, or would it have more success stressing high quality and unusual, imported products?

# QUESTIONS FOR DISCUSSION

1. How could Maslow's hierarchy be used to develop a marketing strategy for a new brand of multivitamins? For a brand of running shoes? For a cruise line?
2. Consider your most recent purchase of a snack food. How was it influenced by perceptual processes? How was it influenced by learning processes?
3. If you wanted to develop favorable attitudes among college students toward nonalcoholic beer, would you focus on the cognitive, affective, or behavioral component? Why?
4. What cultural values might affect the purchase of cigarettes? Of bacon? Of motorcycles?
5. How would you describe yourself as a consumer, using the factors described in this chapter? Think of a recent purchase. How did these factors affect this purchase?
6. Choose two stages from the household life cycle. How would you market a sporting goods store to the households in each of these two stages? How would your marketing strategy change if both were upper-class households? Working-class households?
7. Give an example of a consumer decision you made recently that was influenced by various reference groups. Was this influence in the form of providing information, pressuring you to conform, or offering you a set of values that you could identify with and express?
8. Describe a recent purchase for which you consulted an opinion leader. Did this person have the characteristics of a product enthusiast?
9. How might each of the situational influences play a role in your purchase of new clothes to wear at a party this weekend?
10. Give examples from your own experience of purchases that involved routine, limited, and extensive problem solving. What was your level of involvement in each purchase? What was the amount of perceived risk? How long did each step take in extensive problem solving? Did you experience dissonance after the purchase?

# SHARPEN YOUR MARKETING SKILLS

South Korea finds itself in an interesting consumer predicament. For several decades, the country has been struggling to join the international business mainstream, and the results have been impressive. You can find Korean products sold in countries all over the world: Daewoo construction equipment, Hyundai cars, Gold Star stereos and TVs, and Samsung semiconductors are just a few examples. Korea's rising status as an international manufacturing powerhouse has raised the living standards of many people in Korea, especially in the upper class. Recently, these people in the upper class have taken to enjoying their discretionary income in a decidedly conspicuous manner.

Among developed nations, Korea boasts one of the most even distributions of wealth, but the gap between the upper class and everyone else is starting to grow. As the affluents' income grows, so does the resentment of the middle and lower classes. A reporter for *The Wall Street Journal* recently interviewed a construction worker who was watching wealthy people stroll through the trendy and spendy Apkujongdong district of Seoul. The worker said he'd like to "beat them up" and would do so if given the opportunity.

**Decision:** What advice would you give to retailers in Seoul (or in any other city) who are trying to reach the upper class without offending everyone else? (You'll have to use some creative thinking here; how would you as a consumer respond to this situation?)

**Communication:** Write a one-page summary that outlines the steps a company should take to market high-end products without angering consumers who can't afford those products.[75]

# KEEPING CURRENT IN MARKETING

Find articles that describe the failure of several products or even entire companies. Limit your search to consumer goods and services. Try to find instances of companies that didn't understand what consumers believe, how they feel, or how they behave. If possible, get examples from both for-profit and nonprofit organizations.

1. In each case, were there competitors who did a better job of understanding their customers? If so, did the competition benefit from the mistakes made by the companies you researched?
2. How did consumers respond to each company's marketing efforts? Were they angry? Confused? Did the marketing messages ever reach the right people?
3. Do your examples of failure have anything in common? Can you draw any conclusions about consumer behavior from these examples?

# 5

# The Organizational Market

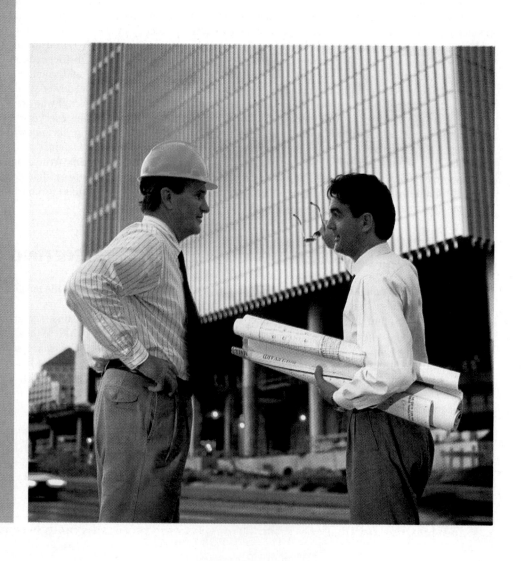

## Can the Industry Leader Deliver over the Long Haul?

The world's first overnight delivery service was born in a Yale student's imagination in the 1960s, at a time when even high-priority deliveries took three business days. Frederick W. Smith developed his revolutionary idea in a paper for an economics class. The professor found it an interesting but utterly impossible dream and gave him a C. However, by 1973 Smith was ready to give his wild idea a try. He used his $4 million inheritance and $80 million in venture capital to launch Federal Express, known as FedEx by its customers. The company today handles more than 45 percent of the overnight deliveries in the United States, with sales of over $5 billion.

FedEx's high-efficiency service turns on an ingenious hub-and-spoke arrangement that requires relatively few planes and trucks to get the job done. Packages are hauled to one of FedEx's superhub distribution centers, where they're sorted and flown out by 4:30 A.M. At the next airport, they're sorted again and dispatched to their final destinations.

Although it ranks well ahead of its nearest domestic rivals, UPS and the U.S. Postal Service, FedEx was anything but an overnight sensation. By the end of the first year, the company had handled just over a million shipments and was losing $1 million a month. FedEx continued to sputter along until the government deregulated the air cargo industry in 1977. After that, the sky was the limit.

In the beginning, FedEx had no real competition, so the company's biggest problem was devising a marketing strategy that would make or-

ganizational buyers think about purchasing a service they'd never considered before. Initially, FedEx used magazine advertising aimed at shipping executives. The company soon realized that the benefits of overnight delivery would appeal to anyone in the customer's organization who needed a package sent, so it switched to TV advertising in order to reach everyone from secretaries to CEOs. Its famous theme "When it absolutely, positively, has to be there overnight" was an instant hit because it focused on its customers' greatest need. The slogan soon became a promise that made FedEx's name synonymous with dependable overnight delivery, and the company's sales volume doubled every two years.

Naturally, this success attracted competition. Shrewd customers began to win huge price-breaks as they consolidated their companies' shipping business by using fewer couriers. At one point, the competition became so cutthroat that Airborne Express landed a three-year deal with IBM by discounting prices as much as 84 percent below FedEx's rates.

Smith knows, however, that organizational buyers demand more than just low prices. If you were CEO of Federal Express, which organizational market opportunities would you explore for profitable new business? How would you identify these markets and measure their potential? If you plan to sell your service to large corporations, which people inside the target companies would you talk to? What marketing strategies would you use to reach them?[1]

**organizational market**
Group that buys goods and services for use in its operations, for resale, or as raw materials or components for other products

**business-to-business marketing**
The process of marketing goods and services to nonconsumer customers

**industrial/commercial market**
The portion of the organizational market made up of companies that produce goods and services to be sold to other businesses or to consumers

# CHAPTER OVERVIEW

Fred Smith and his company face the challenging task of marketing to organizational customers. For some companies, this sort of marketing involves products that everyday consumers never see, such as semiconductors, crude oil, and robotic welding systems. For other companies, such as Federal Express, the products are sold to both consumer and organizational markets. However, even when the product is identical, the process for marketing to organizations differs greatly from the process for marketing to individual consumers. This chapter introduces you to the organizational market, which includes industrial customers, institutions such as colleges and hospitals, government agencies, and companies engaged in wholesaling and retailing. The chapter compares the consumer and the organizational markets, building on the concepts you learned in Chapter 4. Following that is a discussion of the organizational buying process. This process is similar in some respects to the consumer buying process, but it also differs in some important ways. The chapter concludes with a look at the factors that influence the buying process, which range from related demand in consumer markets to personalities and office politics.

# THE ORGANIZATIONAL MARKET

As a consumer, you already have a basic understanding of the products and processes in the consumer marketing environment. However, if you pursue a career in marketing, chances are that you'll work in organizational marketing. The majority of people graduating from business schools in this country are employed by companies that sell to other companies, not to consumers.[2]

The **organizational market** consists of all groups that purchase goods and services for use in operations, for resale to others, or as raw materials or components for their own products. Put simply, the organizational market consists of all buyers other than final consumers. This market is huge. In the United States alone, it employs over 100 million people and buys over $5 trillion worth of goods and services every year. The organizational market includes manufacturers, banks, insurance companies, wholesalers, department stores, restaurants, schools, hospitals, police departments, federal agencies, and so on—nearly 19 million organizations in the United States. Add in the millions of additional businesses around the world, and you have an enormous market.[3]

## Types of Organizational Markets

The terms *organizational market* and *industrial market* are often used interchangeably because industry is perhaps the most visible component of the organizational market. However, the organizational market has four distinct groups: industrial/commercial firms, resellers (retailers and wholesalers), governments, and nonprofit organizations. Exhibit 5.1 shows the number of establishments in each of the first three categories, which represent nearly all of the organizational market. The process of marketing goods and services to nonconsumer customers is usually called **business-to-business marketing.**

### THE INDUSTRIAL/COMMERCIAL MARKET

The **industrial/commercial market** is made up of for-profit organizations that market goods and services to other businesses or to consumers. Exhibit 5.1 lists the major categories in this market in the United States. As you can see from the exhibit, these organizations number in the millions, with over half in the service area. These companies spend billions of dollars a year on raw materials, equipment, machinery, component parts, supplies, and services, which they transform into their own products. For example, a textbook publisher buys office supplies, computer

| Market | Number of Organizations |
|---|---|
| **Industrial/Commercial Market** | |
| Agriculture, forestry, fishing | 579,000 |
| Mining | 253,000 |
| Construction | 198,000 |
| Manufacturing | 642,000 |
| Transportation, public utilities | 735,000 |
| Finance, insurance, real estate | 2,519,000 |
| Other services | 7,095,000 |
| TOTAL INDUSTRIAL/COMMERCIAL | 12,021,000 |
| **Reseller Market** | |
| Wholesalers | 641,000 |
| Retailers | 2,658,000 |
| TOTAL RESELLER | 3,299,000 |
| **Government Market** | |
| Federal government | 1 |
| State governments | 50 |
| Local governments | |
| Counties | 3,042 |
| Municipalities | 19,200 |
| Towns and townships | 16,691 |
| School districts | 14,721 |
| Special districts* | 29,532 |
| TOTAL GOVERNMENT | 83,237 |
| **TOTAL ORGANIZATIONAL MARKET** | 15,403,237 |

*Includes port authorities, water districts, and other specialized agencies and organizations.

The organizational market includes industrial and commercial companies, resellers, and government agencies.

equipment, telecommunications equipment, writing services, art services, photography, paper, printing, binding, and so on to produce the books that are then sold to you.

U.S. organizational markets tend to be concentrated in certain areas of the country, particularly in the northeastern states, around the Great Lakes, and across the Sunbelt states. See Exhibit 5.2 for the top 10 states in terms of number of manufacturing facilities. Over 200,000 of the manufacturing sites in this country are found in these 10 states. In addition, specific industries tend to be clustered geographically. Car manufacturers, for example, are centered in Detroit, tire makers in Akron, brewers in St. Louis, and software developers around Seattle and California's Silicon Valley. Internationally, certain regions, countries, and cities specialize in various industries. Germany, for instance, is a major manufacturing country, and London is a dominant center of international financial services.[4]

As you can see in Exhibit 5.2, the service segment of the U.S. market is spread across the country in much the same manner as the manufacturing segment. These same 10 states are home to nearly 60 percent of the more than 1.2 million service businesses in the United States.[5] It shouldn't come as much of a surprise that the concentrations of business establishments tend to follow the country's population profile. These numbers are important to organizational marketers because personal selling is often important in this market, and marketers need to have salespeople located where the customers are.

## THE RESELLER MARKET

**Resellers** are businesses that buy products to resell either to other businesses or to consumers. They include retailers (department stores, specialty stores, mail-order companies, and so on) and wholesalers (companies that distribute to retail-

**resellers**
Establishments in the organizational market that help move goods and services from producers to consumers

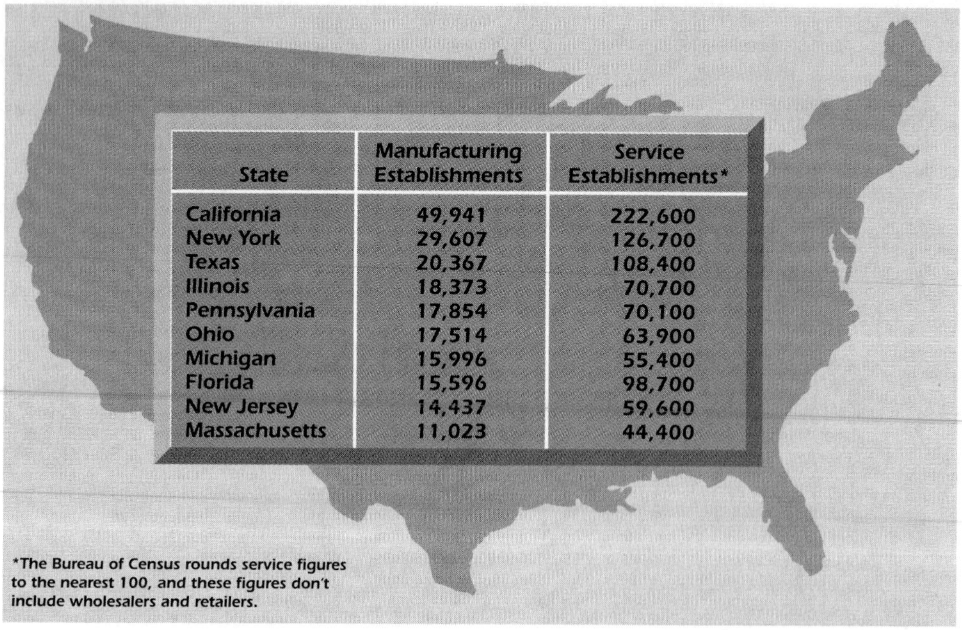

**Exhibit 5.2
MANUFACTURING
AND SERVICE
BUSINESSES IN THE
UNITED STATES**
Nearly 60 percent of the manufacturing and service establishments in the United States are found in just 10 states.

| State | Manufacturing Establishments | Service Establishments* |
|---|---|---|
| California | 49,941 | 222,600 |
| New York | 29,607 | 126,700 |
| Texas | 20,367 | 108,400 |
| Illinois | 18,373 | 70,700 |
| Pennsylvania | 17,854 | 70,100 |
| Ohio | 17,514 | 63,900 |
| Michigan | 15,996 | 55,400 |
| Florida | 15,596 | 98,700 |
| New Jersey | 14,437 | 59,600 |
| Massachusetts | 11,023 | 44,400 |

*The Bureau of Census rounds service figures to the nearest 100, and these figures don't include wholesalers and retailers.

ers and to other business customers). These resellers range in size from independent businesspeople to multibillion-dollar wholesalers such as Super Valu and McKesson. Also, an important part of the reseller market is product rental and leasing, which covers everything from aircraft to garden tools to party furniture.

From a manufacturer's standpoint, resellers are vital business partners for two reasons. First, many companies that produce goods and services designed for consumers don't have the ability to reach those consumers. For example, General Motors, Toyota, Volkswagen, and the other automobile manufacturers can't possibly sell cars directly to every person in the country. For this service, they rely on more than 26,000 new-car dealers. In addition, many products that are sold to organizational customers travel through resellers as well. In the electronics industry, for instance, resellers handle most of the components and parts that manufacturers build into stereos, computers, and other such products (see Exhibit 5.3). Second, resellers themselves constitute a large market for equipment, supplies, vehicles, shelving, displays, cash registers, business forms, and such services as telecommunications, consulting, accounting, interior design, and maintenance.

## THE GOVERNMENT MARKET

**government market**
Federal, state, local, and foreign governments that buy goods and services

The **government market** consists of agencies at the federal, state, and local levels that purchase goods and services. Governments at all levels spend more than $1.5 trillion every year on the machinery, equipment, facilities, supplies, and services needed by the military, schools, hospitals, law enforcement agencies, public utilities, and so on.[6] Half this spending is done at the federal level, and as you can guess, federal agencies receive a lot of marketing attention from companies in the United States.

Selling to government markets at any level requires going through a bidding process or negotiating a contract. For most routine items, the government buyer issues specifications and solicits bids; usually the lowest bid must be accepted. In some cases, the agency will use the bidding process to develop a list of approved suppliers for regularly purchased items. For nonstandardized items, especially expensive ones like submarines, the purchase may involve a negotiated contract that outlines the project. Often these contracts spell out detailed specifications as well.

Because of the tangle of regulations and policies, extensive paperwork, multiple purchasers, and varying degrees of buyer expertise, selling to the government market can be complex, time consuming, and expensive. Even so, many government contracts are lucrative enough to make it well worth the marketer's time and effort to master the intricacies of bidding and negotiation. In fact, some companies cater exclusively to the government market. One such company, Infocel in Raleigh, North Carolina, specializes in producing information systems for local governments, a sizable market.[7] Also, some of the most well-known companies in the United States, including McDonnell Douglas, Boeing, Hewlett-Packard, and General Electric, receive sizable portions of their revenues from government markets. Many of these companies with both government and private-sector customers create a separate department to deal exclusively with government sales because they require such specialized expertise.

The U.S. Government Printing Office (GPO) publishes a number of guidelines for selling to the federal government, including the *Federal Acquisition Regulations* as well as specialized publications such as *Selling to the Military.* The GPO also issues *The Commerce Business Daily,* which lists federal bid invitations, subcontracting leads, and foreign business opportunities. Companies needing advice on how to do business with the federal government can contact the Government Service Administration's Business Service Center in Washington, D.C., or one of its branch offices in major U.S. cities. Many state and local governments and trade associations also offer publications to help potential suppliers identify sales opportunities and understand bidding procedures.

Foreign companies and governments also represent significant markets for goods and services. As CEO of General Electric, Jack Welch has been spending a lot of his time in China, India, Indonesia, and Mexico—markets that he sees as the growth opportunities for the future. These countries don't have nearly the established base of customers that GE finds in the United States, Japan, Germany, and other industrialized nations, of course, but growth has slowed in all the major economies, leaving small but growing economies as the best hope for sales increases. GE's marketing activities in these growth markets include the first commercial lending operation in China, jet engine sales and service centers in China and Indonesia, medical equipment in India and Thailand, and plastics factories in Singapore and Mexico.[8]

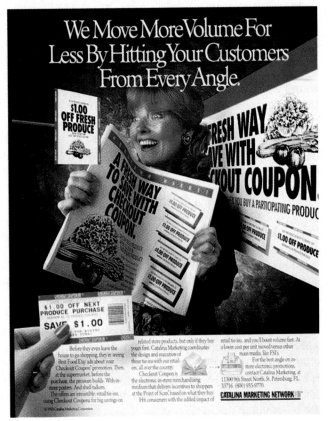

**Exhibit 5.3  THE IMPORTANCE OF THE RESELLER MARKET**
The reseller market is important both for its value as a distribution channel and for the products that resellers buy and use themselves. In this ad, Catalina Marketing Network promotes its Checkout Coupon system and other services that retail stores can use to promote products.

**ETHICAL DILEMMA IN MARKETING**

The products sold to organizations in other countries are much the same as those purchased by their U.S. counterparts, with some exceptions. Certain categories of products are under export restrictions imposed by the U.S. government, including weapons, surveillance equipment, high-performance computers, nuclear energy materials, and a variety of communications gear. Depending on the product and the country, marketers may have to apply for special export licenses, or they might not be able to make the sale at all. The *Commodity Control List,* published by the U.S. Department of Commerce, provides the details of these restrictions.[9] In general, restrictions are on military products, commercial products that can be used in military applications, and materials and components that can be used to build military goods.

## OTHER ORGANIZATIONAL CUSTOMERS

In addition to the three main market categories just discussed, a number of organizational customers are found in the nongovernment, nonprofit sector, including religious institutions, private hospitals, museums, private universities, civic clubs, charities, foundations, and political parties. These institutions may be organized at the international, national, state, or local level. They buy a wide variety of goods and services, from fixtures and supplies to insurance and advertising. To put on an annual convention, for example, a nonprofit organization such as the American Medical Association might spend money to rent convention facilities and exhibit booths, print programs, hire security guards, rent audiovisual equipment, compensate guest speakers, and pay for many other goods and services. In addition, the organization probably owns telephone equipment, computers, office furniture, and a variety of other products.

The People's Republic of China is one of several countries around the world for which U.S. companies must have special licenses in order to export goods with potential military application.

gases for chemical warfare. If you stretch your imagination a little, you can see that even basic construction materials and office supplies could be put to military use. Are fears of national security enough to justify a ban on the export of any product that might conceivably be used for military purposes?

The situation would be complicated enough if it involved only the United States. However, many of our largest trading partners face the same dilemma. For example, the German government cracked down on a number of companies that supplied Iraq with weapon-building capability. As many as 170 German companies were believed to be involved in projects that included a 150-meter-long "supercannon" and a variety of poison gas facilities. However, it appears that many of these exports were legal under German laws at the time.

Finally, a third component of this export dilemma concerns the issue of final destination. As a U.S. marketer, how can you be sure that your products won't be reexported to a country that doesn't see eye-to-eye with the United States? For instance, the Amsterdam office of a U.S. electronics company once received an order for a very precise atomic clock, which can be used in military research. However, the company trying to buy the device identified itself as an accounting firm, and there is no conceivable reason for an accounting firm to buy an atomic clock. Because the potential customer refused to say what the clock would be used for, the employees at the electronics company refused to sell it. They suspected that the deal was an attempt to circumvent U.S. export laws.

Export control promises to remain a sticky ethical issue. On one hand, there seems to be little reason to restrict exports of products that are being used for legitimate civilian purposes—particularly to countries that are currently on friendly terms with each other. On the other hand, can you be absolutely certain that your products won't be adapted to military use? Should the United States ever allow military products to leave its borders, even when they were developed by private companies?

## WHAT'S YOUR OPINION?

**1.** Should U.S. companies voluntarily halt their exports of military equipment until the federal government straightens out the export control situation?

**2.** Should the government ban all exports of commercial products that can also be used in military applications? Is this fair to the companies involved?

## Characteristics of the Organizational Market

The organizational market differs from the consumer market in several ways that affect how products are promoted, priced, and sold. These differences can be broken down into three categories: (1) the kinds of products marketed and how they are purchased, (2) the nature of the buyer-seller relationship, and (3) the nature of organizational demand.

### DIFFERENCES IN PRODUCTS AND PURCHASING

The products sold to organizational markets include both raw materials (grain, steel, fabric) and highly technical and complex products (printing presses, telecommunications systems, management consulting). Between these two extremes, organizations buy many products also found in consumer markets: food, paper products, cleaning supplies, and landscaping services are some examples. Federal Express, for instance, sells its services to both organizational customers and individual consumers. However, even though the products may look the same, the quantities purchased and the buying processes are different.

Many organizational products are designed specifically for individual customers, especially production machinery and component parts for the customer's own products. For example, Sonoco Products, an industrial and consumer packaging supplier in Hartsville, South Carolina, actively surveys its customers to learn of specialized needs. When one customer expressed a need for more innovative packaging to differentiate a consumer product, Sonoco came up with a reclosable cap, a plunger system for dispensing the package, and improved print quality on the label so that the package would look more vibrant.[10]

Many organizational products are purchased in massive quantities—often by the ton or truckload (Exhibit 5.4). Also in contrast to consumer buying, purchases tend to have a large dollar value. Even the average consumer's biggest purchases, such as a home, can pale in comparison to the sorts of purchases that organizational giants make, from blast furnaces to skyscrapers.

Because orders are large, organizational purchases tend to be made less frequently. In addition, the purchase planning period is longer. A consumer who decides to buy a new toaster simply goes to the store and picks one up, but an organizational buyer in need of machine tools usually has to get input from various departments, select both product and supplier, negotiate the deal, place a purchase order, arrange for delivery, and so on. In complicated situations, the buying process can stretch out over several years. Moreover, organizational buyers can employ a wide variety of negotiation and bargaining techniques that marketers must be able to recognize and respond to.[11]

Consumers don't normally have much contact with sellers after a purchase, but organizations often rely heavily on postpurchase service from suppliers. Buyers of heavy industrial equipment, telecommunications systems, computers, and so on require technical assistance for installing and using the equipment and expect the supplier to provide regular maintenance and repair.

The motivations behind consumer and organizational purchases are also different. In a general sense, consumer purchases are driven by a desire for personal satisfaction, whereas organizational purchases are driven by economic motives (see Exhibit 5.5). As a consumer, you purchase airline tickets to visit relatives or to escape to the beach during spring break. As a businessperson, you purchase airline tickets so that you can make sales calls, service customers' equipment, negotiate with suppliers, or perform a variety of other business functions—all of which are motivated by economics.

Finally, many organizational purchases entail much greater risks to the buyer than consumer purchases do. Choosing the wrong equipment or suppliers can cripple a business. Critical purchase decisions involve the commitment of huge amounts of money, affect the daily operations of the company, and influence the long-term profitability and survival of the business. For instance, if you choose a United Airlines flight for a visit home, and it turns out to be late, the consequences aren't usually disastrous. On the other hand, if United chooses the wrong computers for its reservations and ticketing system, it could lose millions of dollars. Because of this risk, organizational buyers make more of a commitment to the major products and suppliers they select.[12]

**Exhibit 5.4   THE UNIQUE NATURE OF MANY ORGANIZATIONAL PRODUCTS**
In addition to purchasing products that consumers generally never see, organizational customers frequently buy in large quantities, as this shipment of rubber from Shell indicates. These large purchases often involve complicated buying and selling processes.

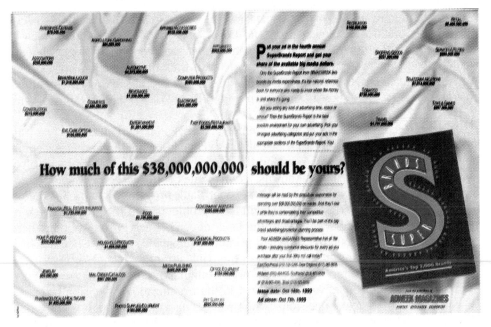

**Exhibit 5.5
ECONOMIC
MOTIVATIONS IN
ORGANIZATIONAL
BUYING**
*Brandweek* makes an obvious
appeal to its readers' eco-
nomic interests in this ad.

## DIFFERENCES IN THE BUYER-SELLER RELATIONSHIP

Unlike households, many organizations have people specially trained to make informed purchases. They have a title such as "purchasing agent" and may be certified by a professional organization. Because there are far fewer organizational buyers than consumer buyers, they are often approached individually, rather than
through mass marketing. These buyers are often constrained by standardized purchasing procedures and by company guidelines concerning suppliers, prices, and
negotiations.

Once established, relationships between organizational buyers and their suppliers tend to be stable and long term. Most buyers will choose two or three suppliers for a frequently purchased item. That way, the buyer ensures a smooth, regular supply and price competition while preventing overdependence.[13] Buyers who
prefer to stick with tried-and-true suppliers (as long as those sources continue to
perform up to expectations) are practicing **source loyalty**. Such loyalty results in
part from the amount of time and effort that goes into choosing a supplier, especially if the buyer has made a major commitment by modifying plant equipment (in
order to use the supplier's product), by training employees on the equipment, or by
taking other risks. Source loyalty may also stem from the fear of taking new risks
or from the lack of desire to make an effort to locate new sources.[14] Source loyalty
benefits the buyer with improved communication flow, better customization of products (adapting a product to fit a single customer's needs), and preferred status
in case of shortages or other crises.[15] Of course, consumers can also have long-
lasting relationships with some of their suppliers.

Consider the relationship between the Hamilton Standard Division of United
Technologies and Bamber Tool Supplies. Hamilton, an aerospace systems manufacturer, has relied on Bamber's cutting tools for nearly four decades, and the two
companies have developed a close relationship during that time. In fact, when Hamilton decided to require all its suppliers to test product quality before shipment, the
company sent technicians to work with Bamber's people, teaching them how to conduct the tests. In addition, the president of Bamber spent time in Hamilton's test
labs, learning more about tool quality.[16]

Savvy marketers such as Bamber Tool Supplies work hard to establish and maintain long-term relationships with buyer organizations because loyal customers can
be highly resistant to switching. Source loyalty maintains a built-in market for "in"
suppliers but makes it difficult for "out" suppliers to gain a foothold, even if they offer higher quality, better service, or lower prices than current suppliers.

**source loyalty**
An organizational customer's
commitment to continue buying from its current suppliers

**reciprocity**
The practice of buying
products from one's own
customers; it is illegal if
the arrangement restricts
competition

Another unique aspect of the organizational buyer-seller relationship is **reciprocity,** the practice of buying from one's own customers. For example, given a choice of several otherwise equal maintenance services, a chemical supply house would choose a service that buys its products. In the automotive industry, Borg-Warner manufactures transmissions, which it sells to General Motors, among other customers. Then, to equip its own employees, Borg-Warner buys GM cars and trucks.[17]

*Informal* reciprocity is a relatively common and accepted marketing practice, but *formal* reciprocity agreements may be considered anticompetitive (therefore illegal) by the Federal Trade Commission and the Justice Department.[18] Reciprocity also has the potential for ethical breakdowns, as when one company coerces another into buying its products. New York–based Chemical Bank provides a good example of how a company can avoid both ethical and legal problems with reciprocity. When it reviews bids from potential suppliers, the bank doesn't check to see whether each bidder is a Chemical customer. If fact, a printing company owned by Chemical has to compete with other printers for most of the bank's printing business.[19]

A final significant difference between organizational buying and consumer buying is that many more people are involved in the organizational decision process. Whereas consumers make decisions by themselves or with the input of a few other household members, as many as 50 organizational members may contribute to a single buying decision. This *multiple buying influence* is perhaps the key aspect of organizational purchasing behavior.

## THE NATURE OF ORGANIZATIONAL DEMAND

**derived demand**
The fact that the demand for
organizational products is
driven by the demand for
consumer products

When organizational marketers forecast future sales, they can often take clues from consumer product demand. This is based on the idea of **derived demand;** that is, the demand for most organizational goods is derived from the demand for consumer goods. Even if a company sells strictly to manufacturers and institutions, its customers, in turn, sell directly to consumers or to other companies that sell to final consumers. (One notable exception to derived demand is military goods; in this case demand is driven by government policy and international politics.)

This means that to gauge the market for extruded plastics, for example, manufacturers of such plastics must study the consumer market for the final products made with extruded plastic. Dow Chemical got caught off guard when it expanded a division whose products are employed, among other places, in the products used to perm hair. The division expanded in the late 1980s and early 1990s, but women's hair fashions went in a different direction, reducing the demand for perms.[20]

**acceleration principle**
The idea that a small change
in consumer demand can lead
to a major change in organizational demand

Marketers also need to be aware of the **acceleration principle** (see Exhibit 5.6), which implies that a small change in consumer demand for a product can cause a

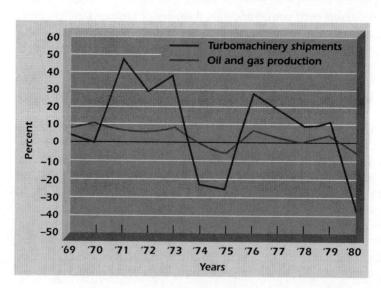

**Exhibit 5.6   THE
ACCELERATION
PRINCIPLE**
In the 1970s relatively small
changes in consumer demand
for oil and gas led to major
fluctuations in the demand for
the turbomachinery used to
produce oil and gas products.

**Risky Business**

In today's competitive business climate, product development is a perilous journey. One slip can mean lost opportunity... or worse. You've got to plan intelligently, execute on time, and use the best available technology. If you don't, your competitors undoubtedly will.

Why put up with risks and shortcomings associated with obsolete power technologies... bulky, one-of-a-kind designs; program delays; agency approval cycles; last minute surprises; and unproven field reliability. Vicor's power component approach has been proven by thousands of users to be the fastest and most predictable path to successful power system development. And Vicor's complete line of "plug and play" power system building blocks offer unprecedented design flexibility and result in smaller, cooler, more cost-effective products.

Tired of power development cliffhangers? The solution is right at your fingertips... just give us a call.

*Component Solutions For Your Power System*

**VICOR**
23 Frontage Road Andover, MA 01810
TEL: (508) 470-2900 • FAX: (508) 475-6715

**Exhibit 5.7
EMOTION IN
ORGANIZATIONAL
BUYING**
Although the buying process in organizational markets often centers on economic and technical factors, marketers such as Vicor know that emotional factors can play a big role. The analogy between slipping off the cliff and missing business opportunities taps a strong emotion in target buyers.

major change in the demand for the goods and services that go into the product. This change can be an increase or a decrease. A sharp increase in demand can lead to a shortage in materials, production capacity, and labor, whereas a decrease can lead to shutdown of production lines, layoffs, and other cutbacks.[21] Similarly, when consumer demand is high, manufacturers will buy large quantities of raw materials and components and may expand production facilities, but when demand is low, they will curtail spending. A good example is what happened to the demand for turbomachinery in the 1970s in light of fluctuations in the consumer demand for oil and natural gas. In 1974 a 5 percent drop in the demand for fossil fuels led to a 30 percent drop in the demand for the turbomachinery equipment used to produce the fuels. Similarly, a 10 percent increase in consumer demand in 1970 resulted in a more than 40 percent increase in turbomachinery shipments.[22]

## Similarities between Consumer and Organizational Purchasing

Even though the organizational market is unique in many ways, much of what you learned about consumer purchasing behavior applies to organizational purchasing. Several concepts overlap the two markets:

- *Rational versus nonrational decision making.* Organizational purchasing is generally much more rational and logical than consumer decision making, but it's a mistake to think that emotion and other nonrational forces don't play at least a small role (see Exhibit 5.7). Purchases such as computer systems, management consulting, and office space can affect a company's financial health and the satisfaction level of employees. The people who make these decisions can face tremendous pressure.
- *Buyer involvement.* As discussed in Chapter 4, the consumer's level of involvement determines how complex and formal the buying process is. As discussed later in this chapter, that same concept applies to organizational buying.

**TECHNIQUES FOR MARKETING SUCCESS**

## HOW TO KEEP CUSTOMERS COMING BACK

Source loyalty—buying from tried-and-true vendors—is becoming less common today. Instead, more and more organizational buyers are shopping around for new suppliers. Why are buyers so willing to change their sources? One big reason is poor customer relations, or "a failure to build an enduring bond with those we hope will buy our products and services," in the words of one consultant. Too many marketers are emphasizing new sales at the expense of cultivating current customers, even though maintaining current accounts is one of the best ways to increase sales over time. What can marketers do to keep customers satisfied and loyal? Here are eight handy tips:

- *Let your customers know why they are smart to do business with you.* Reinforce the idea that they have made the right choice in selecting your product or company. One easy way to do so is to send your customers copies of positive product reviews and published articles about your company.
- *Educate your customers.* Tell your customers everything they need to know about all your products. An informative newsletter is a good vehicle for customer education. To make your newsletter a valuable source of information, include features on your customers and on useful applications of your products.
- *Give customers ideas on how to improve their business operations.* Because salespeople observe operations in a number of companies, they can often pick up ideas and techniques helpful to other customers. They can make referrals along the lines of "Company X had a similar problem. Why don't you give them a call to see how they solved it?"
- *Say "thank you" regularly.* Let customers know you appreciate their business by contacting them through phone calls, thank-you notes (if, for example, the customer has given you a referral), and sales promotion items (such as coffee mugs or pens with your logo).
- *Project a leadership image for your company.* Your company should have a distinctive image that clearly separates it from competitors. Keeping on top of industry trends and informing customers about them also enhances your status in the field.
- *Show a continuing interest in your customers.* Keep an up-to-date mailing list and do regular mailings, whether of articles that might be of interest to specific customers, reminders to check supplies for possible reorder, or other messages that let customers know you care about them.
- *Ask your customers for their opinions.* Giving people an opportunity to express their views shows that you value their ideas.
- *Make your customers feel important.* Offering congratulations for successes and positive comments about a business makes people feel good about what they do and gives them a boost they won't forget.

### APPLY YOUR KNOWLEDGE

**1.** What are some possible disadvantages that organizations might experience by sticking with regular suppliers?

**2.** What additional steps might a vendor take to ensure customer satisfaction?

- *Perception, learning, and attitudes.* The ways that people perceive ads and products, learn about new products, and form attitudes about products and suppliers are largely similar in consumer and organizational markets.
- *Personal influences.* The personal influences on consumers (such as age, income, and so on) are replaced in organizational buying by company characteristics, such as number of employees, sales volume, and so forth.
- *Social influences.* As in consumer buying, social influences also play a role in organizational buying, although such influences are of a different nature (see this chapter's section on the buying center).
- *Opinion leadership and word of mouth.* Just as consumers look to trendsetters and experts for guidance, so do organizations in some cases. Corporate buyers often talk about their purchasing experiences with other buyers (and potential buyers). Trade shows, professional conferences, and computer networks are among the most common gathering places.

# THE ORGANIZATIONAL BUYING PROCESS

The **organizational buying process** encompasses the steps an organization follows as it makes a purchase. This dynamic decision-making and communication process involves the interaction of various organization members and their relationships with suppliers.[23] Like the consumer buying process described in Chapter 4, organizational buying goes through a series of stages that depend on the complexity of the purchase. If the purchase is routine, the buying process is simple; if the purchase is complex, important, or different from anything the company has dealt with before, the buying process can become long and drawn out. In general, organizational purchasing is a more obvious "process," with forms to be filled out, approval signatures from various managers, and other formal elements. The more expensive a purchase is, and the more risk it represents to the organization, the more formal and rigid the purchasing process becomes. The following section explores the six steps of the organizational purchasing process (see Exhibit 5.8).

**organizational buying process**
The steps that organizations go through to purchase goods and services

## Recognize a Need

The first step in the organizational buying process is recognizing a problem or need that can be resolved by purchasing a good or service. As in consumer buying, problem recognition occurs when a discrepancy between an ideal state and the actual state is realized. Equipment may break down, wear out, or become outdated. The company may be developing a new good or service for which it needs components, materials, or advice. Current suppliers may have gone out of business or discontinued a particular component. Existing machinery may be inefficient or overly expensive to run. All these situations create a need.

Anyone in the company may recognize the problem, from workers on the assembly line on up to top management. Problem recognition can also come from external sources, such as articles in trade magazines pointing out new trends in an industry, trade show displays of state-of-the-art equipment (see Exhibit 5.9), advertising, and salespeople demonstrating new products. Marketers need to become familiar enough with an organization's operations to point out problems and offer solutions—such as ways to increase efficiency, save money, improve quality, or ensure safety. For example, Guy Milner, chief executive officer of Norell, saw a need in the health-care industry for temporary workers. Now his company provides

**Exhibit 5.8   THE ORGANIZATIONAL BUYING PROCESS**
In new-task situations, organizational buying goes through six stages.

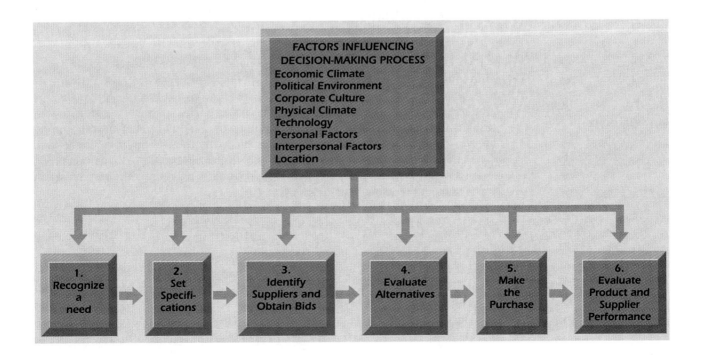

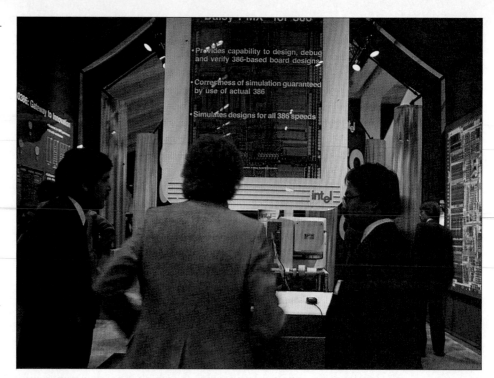

**Exhibit 5.9**
**HELPING CUSTOMERS IDENTIFY NEEDS**
Smart marketers can help customers recognize needs by pointing out new ideal states. Here Intel points out the benefits of a design system for computer engineers.

temps for hospitals and home-health firms to the tune of $200 million in annual sales, constituting 25 percent of the company's revenues.[24]

## Set Specifications

**make/buy decision**
The choice organizations (and consumers) face between making a product themselves and buying it from an outside supplier

Once the need is recognized, the next question might be the **make/buy decision:** "Can we make what we need to solve the problem, or do we need to buy something?" If the decision is to buy, the company must then determine the characteristics of the desired item—its dimensions, materials, performance, and so on. (Note that consumers often face the same decision: Should I pay someone to paint the house or take the time to do it myself?) It is often up to the engineering department to produce detailed specifications for technical items. Suppliers can work with the client to develop these specifications. A few years ago, for instance, a supplier of glass bottles suggested a redesign of Heinz catsup bottles that reduced costs, improved yields on the bottle-filling line, reduced shipping costs (because of the bottle's lighter weight), and saved labor besides.[25]

**value analysis**
A comparison of the cost of a potential purchase and the benefits it promises

Once the specifications are written, the purchasing department may prepare a **value analysis** to compare the costs of the potential purchase with the benefits the good or service will provide. This appraisal notes the costs of the design, materials, components, production process, and similar factors. The analysis may include suggestions for some alternative approaches that would be more economical. For example, a design for a book may call for expensive cloth covering in a 7-by-10-inch size. The purchasing department might suggest a different cover material (that serves the purpose but costs less) and might propose a slightly different size (that would make more economical use of paper).

## Identify Suppliers and Obtain Bids

The third step in the organizational buying process is to search for potential suppliers of the desired item and, if appropriate, request *bids*. The organization learns of possible suppliers from sales representatives, conferences and trade shows, advertising, catalogs, industry directories, yellow pages, and word of mouth. Buyers often investigate potential suppliers to see whether they can indeed supply the desired product. The criteria used for adding suppliers to an approved bidders' list include production capacity (especially for large orders), location (close suppliers help reduce shipping costs), and quality of production.[26] As a marketer, you need to make sure that your company is positioned as a viable supplier, or you may never be considered for sales that you're perfectly capable of handling (see Exhibit 5.10).

Having narrowed down the list of potential suppliers, the company commonly sends out a **request for proposal (RFP)** (also called a *request for quotation*) outlining the product specifications and indicating the quantity desired, the date needed, and so on. Suppliers then submit bids for fulfilling the company's needs. Bidders that are most likely to get strong consideration are those that respond on time, provide as much information as possible, and quote a competitive price—in addition to proving they can fulfill the customer's needs.

**request for proposal (RFP)**
A document sent to potential suppliers, outlining requirements and requesting bids

## Evaluate Alternatives

In the fourth step, proposals are evaluated by one or more people in the customer organization, each of whom may use different criteria. Although price is often a key concern, especially when there is little differentiation between products, buyers usually have many other criteria as well, among them product quality, the supplier's past performance, technical services offered, tooling costs, contract terms, warranties, and delivery schedule. At some companies, engineering or production staffs will conduct a technical study of the proposals to determine whether bidders can meet specifications. Personal interaction remains an important factor, however, even when written proposals and bids are involved. A study of the behavior of purchasers of business consulting services showed that personal sources of information (such as meeting in person with the consulting firm) were used twice as much as impersonal sources (such as written proposals).[27]

An important consideration at this stage is the amount of perceived risk involved in making the choice. *Perceived risk* relates to the uncertainty of the situation and to the buyer's concern over losses that might be incurred by making the wrong choice. In general, organizational buyers have a tendency to avoid risk. That is, they prefer products they've used before to unknown products that may be of higher quality or lower price.[28] However, keep in mind that risk aversion is a personal trait, so some buyers are more willing than others to go out on a limb to try new products or suppliers.

Factors that increase buying risks include high price tags, unproven products (because buyers in many fields don't want to be guinea pigs for experimental designs), product complexity, uncertainty about product performance, the need for

**Exhibit 5.10
PROMOTING
YOURSELF AS A
VIABLE SUPPLIER**
Digital Equipment promotes itself as a reliable and capable supplier of computer systems.

extensive training to use the product, and substantial investment in retooling or other start-up costs.[29]

How can new suppliers help reduce these risks? They can demonstrate that their products are reliable, show a track record of on-time delivery and prompt service, and provide performance guarantees as part of their proposal. They can also reduce uncertainty by supplying as much information as possible about the product and by being willing to accept a small initial order or only a portion of the account.

## Make the Purchase

**single sourcing**
Using only a single supplier for a particular product

Once a buying decision has been made, it's up to the purchasing department to place the order and negotiate terms such as delivery and payment method. The buyer may decide to purchase from several suppliers or from just one. Using only one supplier for a particular item is called **single sourcing.** From the buyer's perspective, the advantages of single sourcing are improved flow of information, significant cost efficiencies, and better quality control. Some corporate buyers also say they get the latest technology if they cultivate a close relationship with a single leading-edge supplier.[30] The disadvantages are reduced bargaining power and potential shortages if anything disrupts the supplier's production. On the supplier's side, single sourcing improves operating stability, increases volume, and reduces unit costs.[31] Among products that are sometimes single sourced are transportation services, hardware, motors, electronic components, textiles, chemicals, cement, pipe, fiberglass, lighting, solvents, computers, leather, and paper. The purchasing manager for Shaw-Walker, a Michigan office products manufacturer, says he single sources plastic parts, packaging, and aluminum extrusions because the company gets better pricing on a higher volume and has lower shipping costs, more clout with the suppliers, and better control over colors. On the other side of the coin is the buyer for Klipsch and Associates, makers of loudspeakers; he feels that having multiple sources "keeps everyone on their toes."[32]

## Evaluate Product and Supplier Performance

**vendor analysis**
Formal evaluation of suppliers

Did the supplier deliver as promised? Did the product meet specifications? Did it solve the problem as expected? Because the answers to these important questions will determine future purchases, many organizations have a formal process for evaluating suppliers. Ford Motor Company, for example, uses performance criteria to evaluate all its key suppliers. Such supplier evaluation, or **vendor analysis,** may consist of various departments rating the supplier as excellent, fair, or poor in appropriate categories. On the other hand, it may be based on a weighted-point system, in which suppliers are rated on performance factors such as price, quality, and service, with each factor being given a weight reflecting its importance. Alternatively, a cost-ratio method may be used, with plus points given for positive performance and minus points for deficiencies; the final score must be above a certain standard to be considered satisfactory.

Smart marketers know that customer satisfaction is the key to repeat purchases. They therefore make a special effort to attend to customer needs and provide consistent and valuable services. Norell, for example, has instituted a "45-minute callback" policy, guaranteeing that clients will know within 45 minutes whether the company can provide them with the temporary workers they need. Norell regional and local managers also work closely with clients to help them find the most qualified people for temporary jobs. Such policies have greatly increased both customer satisfaction and Norell's revenues.[33]

## Buying Situations

**buyclasses**
Types of organizational buying situations, including straight rebuys, modified rebuys, and new-task purchases

As pointed out in Chapter 4, consumer decision making can range from limited to extensive problem solving. Similarly, organizational purchasing spans three kinds of buying situations referred to as **buyclasses:** straight rebuy, modified rebuy, and new-task purchase.[34]

**Exhibit 5.11  BUYING SITUATIONS**

**159**
Chapter 5
THE ORGANIZATIONAL
MARKET

| Characteristics | Straight Rebuy | Modified Rebuy | New Task |
|---|---|---|---|
| Time required | Little | Average | Much |
| Size of buying center | Small | Medium | Large |
| Information needs | Minimal | Moderate | Maximum |
| Alternatives considered | None | Few | Many |
| Novelty | None | Average | High |
| Decision complexity | Low | Medium | Medium-high |
| Frequency | Often | Recurring | Infrequent |

Straight rebuy, modified rebuy, and new-task situations result in different organizational purchasing behavior.

In a **straight rebuy,** the same product that has been purchased in the past is routinely reordered from a regular supplier. The straight rebuy is the most common purchasing situation. It occurs when the organization is experienced in buying the product, has an ongoing need for the product, and has regular vendors that supply the product. Office supplies are an obvious example. At many companies the straight rebuy is automated, using a computerized reordering system.

A **modified rebuy** occurs if some aspect of a routine purchase changes. If the desired item has been discontinued or changed by the supplier, if prices have changed, if the supplier has a new product, or if the buyer's needs have changed, members of the buying center will need to consider this new information and make a decision. In a modified rebuy, the organization is willing to consider alternatives to the usual choices. Among modified rebuy items identified in one study of six large manufacturers were hydraulic-drive motors, fuel oil, parts for lift trucks, electrical cables, coal, and acids.[35] A modified rebuy may also occur subsequent to a new-task purchase.

A **new-task purchase** occurs when the buyer has little or no experience purchasing a particular product. Most new-task situations introduce an element of risk; as a result, the buying center tends to be larger, the information search is more extensive, and many alternatives may be considered. Solving a problem is often a top priority, rather than simply getting the best price. Therefore, technical personnel such as engineers are more influential than purchasing agents in new-task situations. In contrast, buying centers in straight and modified rebuys tend to be smaller, more concerned about price and supply, and more influenced by purchasing agents.[36] Exhibit 5.11 compares the three types of buying situations.

As a marketer, determine where a particular purchase falls in the buyclass continuum and then tailor your efforts accordingly. It is often difficult for new suppliers to get in on straight rebuys, unless current suppliers are unable to deliver—in which case the buyer must consider alternatives, and the situation becomes a modified rebuy. It is up to the "in" suppliers to keep customers satisfied by meeting delivery dates, providing proper maintenance, and so on. "Out" suppliers, on the other hand, should be alert to signs of buyer dissatisfaction with current suppliers and should be ready to point out the advantages of their own goods and services.

In new-task situations, smart marketers focus on helping members of the buying center develop specifications and offer their own solutions to the organization's problem. In short, the supplier acts as a consultant.[37] Such a role entails finding out which members of the buying center have the most influence in this particular type of buy in order to provide useful information to these individuals. Furthermore, keep in mind that two decisions are actually made: what product to buy and whom to buy it from. Thus, you might target engineering or production personnel with product information while calling on the purchasing department with pricing and similar data.[38]

Buying situations vary in their novelty, complexity, and importance—three factors that also affect participation and influence in the buying center.[39] *Novelty* is the amount of experience (or lack thereof) that the organization has had with this type of purchase. The more novel it is, the greater the number of individuals included in

**straight rebuy**
An organizational buying situation in which the purchaser automatically reorders the same item from the same supplier

**modified rebuy**
An organizational buying situation in which the purchaser considers a limited number of choices before making a decision

**new-task purchase**
An organizational buying situation in which the purchaser is unfamiliar with the product and must use an extensive decision-making process to arrive at a choice

the buying center. Those who seem most knowledgeable about the product area are likely to have the most influence. In the early days of overnight package delivery, Federal Express probably had to explain the concept and procedures to some companies, but seemingly everyone in business today ships packages overnight without a second thought.

*Complexity* refers to the amount of information that must be gathered before a decision can be made, the number of people included in the buying center, and the extent to which the decision will require changes in the organization, such as alterations in procedures or a need for training. Switching laser printer paper isn't a big deal, but changing production line robots is. The more complex the situation, the longer the decision process will take, the greater the number of people involved, the higher the risk, and the greater the amount of communication within the buying center. The individuals who are able to amass the most information about the decision are likely to be the most influential.

*Importance* is the ultimate effect of the purchase on the organization. The greater the impact, the greater the risk. The most important decisions will take the longest time and will have the largest buying centers. Assess the novelty and importance of a purchase decision and then provide adequate and appropriate information to the right people. If the product is highly technical, such as high-speed fiber-optic multiplexers for telecommunications, engineers and their managers are a good target. If the product is manufacturing equipment, such as a drilling machine, plant managers might be targeted. If you don't identify the right buying influences up front, you run the risk of having a sale canceled later in the process by someone whose needs aren't being met.

# INFLUENCES ON ORGANIZATIONAL BUYING

As with consumer buying, a number of factors can influence the organizational buying process. Successful marketers work to understand these influences and to structure their marketing strategies accordingly. The influences can vary dramatically from one customer organization to the next, which is one of the primary reasons business-to-business marketers emphasize personal selling in their marketing mixes.

## The Buying Center

**buying center**
The group of individuals involved in making a particular buying decision within an organization

Although one person may be responsible for making the actual purchases for a company, in reality many people play a role in deciding what to purchase and from whom. Thus, marketing efforts must be targeted toward a group of people, referred to as the buying center. Also called the *decision-making unit,* the **buying center** consists of all those people within an organization who are significantly involved in the buying process for a particular good or service. The buying center is not a formalized group or location; rather, it is a communication network that varies from purchase to purchase, evolves during the purchasing process, and differs from organization to organization.[40]

To get an idea of how complex an organizational purchase can be, consider the organization represented in Exhibit 5.12. Say that this company is purchasing an electronic mail system; the exhibit shows just some of the questions this customer will have. For instance, the operations people want to know how much work the system will create for them, the financial group wants to know how much this system will cost to operate, and the marketing people want to know whether they can use it out in the field. If you're trying to sell them a system, you'll need to understand all of their individual needs, and you'll have to answer all of their questions. Don't forget, you'll still need to satisfy the purchasing agent, who is responsible for making the deal happen. Taken together, all these people make up the buying center.

To analyze the complexity of an organization's purchasing process, you can view the interactions within the buying center along five dimensions. Understanding these dimensions is an important part of planning a sale to organizational customers because it helps you prepare for sales calls and other marketing efforts.[41]

- *The number of management levels.* A number of levels of the organization are represented within the buying center, from top management down to production workers.
- *The number of departments or divisions represented in the decision-making process.* For large-scale purchases such as factory equipment you may have to make a sales presentation to nearly every department in the company.
- *The number of individual people involved.* This can range from as few as one person to several dozen in the most complex purchasing situations. If you picture yourself as a salesperson calling on a large commercial customer, you can imagine how complex your job might be if 10 or 20 people have a say in the purchase decision.
- *The degree of interaction among buying center members.* For some purchases, the members of the buying center may work together as a team, such as when a group of accountants and their manager try to choose a temporary agency to handle work overflow. In other cases, the buying center is less connected; perhaps its members are even in different geographic locations.
- *The importance and role of the purchasing agent.* Depending on the nature of the purchase, the purchasing agent's role can range from being the most important member of the buying center to being more of a contract administrator who simply implements the decision made by other people.

Identifying all the players is often the most challenging part of the sales effort. For a particular company and product, marketers determine how many levels of the

**Exhibit 5.12  THE COMPLEXITY OF ORGANIZATIONAL PURCHASING**
Imagine that this company is purchasing an electronic mail system; many people in the organization will be affected by the decision, and each of them has specific questions and concerns.

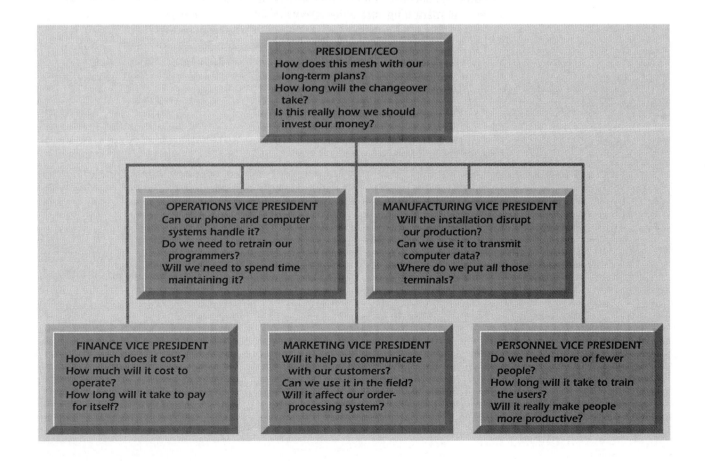

organization's hierarchy are involved, since these factors affect the ability of the buying center to process information quickly and accurately. It's also important to know the role of the purchasing agent; if this person's influence is low, the marketer must seek out the more influential members of the buying center.

## ROLES IN THE BUYING CENTER

In each purchase decision, members of the buying center assume general social roles in the buying process. If you can identify the role each member is playing, you can do a better job of satisfying each one and taking advantage of his or her influence on the buying decision. Six such **buying center roles** have been identified:

**buying center roles**
Roles assumed by various members of the buying center, including initiator, influencer, decision maker, gatekeeper, purchaser, and user

- The *initiator* is the person who identifies a problem or need that could be resolved by purchasing a good or service. It may be a hospital stock clerk who notes that the supply of patient gowns is low or a manager who sees a new robotic welding system at a trade show and thinks it will fill the company's needs.
- *Influencers* are people who have input into whether a purchase is made, what will be bought, and who it will be bought from. Influencers can include board members and stockholders if the purchase is a major one, but they are often engineers or production managers who want to make sure that the purchased item fits their specifications and needs. Influencers can come from any department or level or may even be outside consultants, such as when organizations contract with computer specialists to select and purchase hardware and software products.
- *Decision makers* are those who make the actual yes-or-no decision about the purchase and who choose or approve the product and supplier. In many cases, the initiator and the decision maker are not the same person, a fact you must keep in mind when marketing to such companies. One study found that the key decision makers in the purchase of an automatic drilling machine for an industrial safety products manufacturer were the vice president for manufacturing and an engineer, whereas the main decision maker for buying vending machine service for a paper products company was the personnel manager.[42]
- *Gatekeepers* are individuals who control the flow of information in the buying center. A receptionist who screens salespeople acts as a gatekeeper, as does a purchasing agent who invites bids from suppliers. To a large extent, gatekeepers determine which products and suppliers will actually be considered by members of the buying center.
- The *purchaser* is the person who actually orders the good or service. He or she may have little to say in the actual choice but is expected to negotiate the best deal possible with chosen suppliers. This is usually the purchasing agent, or the buyer in some companies.
- *Users* are the ultimate customers of the good or service. They are the production workers who operate the machinery, the secretaries who use the office equipment, the employees who use the telephone system. Although users may be the initiators of a purchase, they often have little say in the eventual decision.[43]

An alternative to identifying buying influences in a customer organization according to social roles is identifying them based on their needs in the purchase. In this scheme, the three main influences are the economic buyer, the technical buyer, and the end-user buyer. Each person has different needs. The *economic buyer* is making a decision that is primarily financial, such as return on investment, payback time, or effect on profit. When you're marketing to this person, speak his or her language. Endless lists of technical features don't matter to this buyer; talk financial impact. On the other hand, technical features matter very much to the *technical buyer,* who is typically an engineer or other technically oriented employee. Finally, the *end-user buyer* is the person who will have to use the products when they are installed. End-user buyers include secretaries, bank tellers, store clerks, and air-traffic controllers. These people may not have much influence on the buying decision, but the product won't be successful long term unless these people are satisfied.

The involvement and influence of buying center members varies at each stage. The purchasing department, for example, usually has the greatest involvement when the organization is identifying suppliers and obtaining bids, making the purchases, and evaluating product and supplier performance. Its involvement is lower when technical specialists set specifications or evaluate alternative products. Furthermore, the value of the purchase affects the extent to which departments other than purchasing are involved at each stage. In general, the higher the value, the greater the number of levels and departments that will want to have a say.[44]

In some cases, especially for small and routine purchases, one person may fill many or all of these roles. In other cases, especially with large purchases, one role might be filled by several individuals. Which role has the most influence in the buying center? That depends on the product, the buying situation, and the stage in the buying process.

## Buying Methods

Organizational purchase behavior can also change depending on the type of product. For instance, a hospital doesn't buy 100 new beds in the same way that it buys a new laser scalpel or a major management consulting project, even though all three products might cost about the same. Organizational buyers typically use one of four methods to make a purchase:

- *Inspection,* or examining each item to be purchased, is used when the product is not standardized, such as buildings, vehicles, or livestock. The buyer must look at, choose, and perhaps even bid against competitors for the item. In many cases, this requires the involvement of technical specialists.
- *Sampling,* or looking at representative samples from a lot, is used when a large quantity of something with uniform quality is being bought, such as a grade of lumber or paper. The paper for this book, for example, was chosen on the basis of a sample.
- *Description,* or buying on the basis of written specifications, is used with standardized items such as office supplies. The buyer usually orders from a catalog or brochure, choosing those items that have the desired characteristics.
- *Negotiated contracts* are used when a customized product is ordered; the contract outlines the general specifications but the details are often left to be worked out during the course of the project. Negotiated contracts are common in construction and in federal defense projects.

## Operational and Situational Influences

A variety of other influences can affect organizational purchasing patterns. Such factors as the economic climate tend to affect business buyers in all industries; other factors, such as new government regulations, may affect only certain industries or even individual companies. Be sure to research and understand the particular influences in each marketing situation you encounter, since there is no generic list that applies in all cases. Here are the more common operational and situational influences:

- *The economic climate.* Buying may increase or decrease depending on the condition of the overall economy and of the particular industry. Trends such as recession, inflation, and high interest rates affect inventories and put financial constraints on purchasing. Thus, successful marketers keep a finger on the nation's economic pulse, as well as a close eye on target industries.
- *The political and regulatory situation.* Deregulation, environmental impact, international trade agreements, government spending cuts—all can have a significant

effect on buying behavior. Take the case of Telco Systems, a successful supplier of automatic dialers to MCI and U.S. Sprint back when customers had to dial 10-digit access codes to make calls. Then the FCC ordered regional phone companies to give callers the same access to MCI and Sprint as they had to AT&T. The sudden drop in demand for Telco's main product forced the company to diversify to stay in business.[45]

- *Corporate culture.* Organizations vary in the extent of formalization and centralization in their buying and in specific buying policies, which affects the kinds of purchases made and the choice of suppliers. Organizations also differ in their objectives and therefore in the criteria they use for buying decisions.

- *Location.* A company's geographic location affects its access to labor resources, raw materials, available transportation, and so on.

- *Technology.* Some fields—telecommunications and medicine, for example—change rapidly because of technological advances, requiring great flexibility in purchasing choices and procedures.

- *Personal and interpersonal factors.* Organizations are made up of people who have individual needs, motives, perceptions, and attitudes. Conflicts, power struggles, ethical standards, and other interpersonal factors can complicate buying center choices. Furthermore, buyers vary greatly in their experience, communication abilities, negotiation skills, and personality. Marketers need to be aware that buyers want to make wise choices and also want to look good in the eyes of their organization. Many want to impress others in the organization with having made the wisest choices at the lowest risk. Anything a marketer can do to help such purchasers enhance their image will increase the marketer's appeal.

When you consider all the personal and organizational aspects of marketing to businesses, nonprofit groups, and governments, you can see that marketing to these customers takes time and careful planning. Marketers who do a good job of understanding their customers have a definite advantage in the organizational marketplace.

## SUMMARY OF LEARNING OBJECTIVES

### 1. Identify four types of organizational markets.

The three dominant types of organizational markets are industrial/commercial, resellers (wholesalers and retailers), and governments. The industrial/commercial market encompasses all the for-profit businesses that produce goods and services ranging from small, entrepreneurial firms to the largest multinational corporations. The reseller market includes organizations that help move products from producers to consumers; it is made up of wholesalers and retailers. The government segment includes the federal government, state governments, and local governments, as well as their counterparts in other countries. A fourth group is made up of nongovernment, nonprofit organizations, such as political parties, trade unions, professional associations, charities, and environmental groups.

### 2. Describe the differences between organizational and consumer buying behavior.

Organizational buying differs from consumer buying in that products purchased range from raw materials to highly technical or complex items, many products are custom designed, products are purchased in massive quantities and for a large

dollar value, purchases are made less frequently, the purchase planning period is longer, postpurchase service is more extensive, purchases often entail greater risks to the buyer, buyers tend to be specially trained, relationships between buyers and sellers tend to be stable and long term, buyers maintain loyalty to their sources, reciprocity occurs between buyer and seller, and more people are involved in the decision process.

### 3. Explain how derived demand affects organizational buying.

Because organizations buy products with the ultimate aim of serving consumers, consumer demand affects all organizational buying. Furthermore, because of the acceleration principle, small changes in consumer demand can have amplified effects on organizational demand.

### 4. Outline six stages in the organizational buying process.

Particularly for new tasks, organizational buying proceeds through six stages: (a) recognizing the problem, (b) setting objectives and specifications, (c) identifying suppliers and obtaining bids, (d) evaluating alternatives, (e) making the purchase, and (f) evaluating product and supplier performance.

## 5. Differentiate three types of organizational buying situations.

Buying situations range from straight rebuys (routine reorders) to modified rebuys (in which limited choices are considered) to new-task rebuys (which usually require an extensive decision-making process). Successful marketers understand the type of purchase each customer is making because the buying behavior differs in each case.

## 6. Explain the concept of the buying center and describe its composition.

The buying center consists of all those individuals within the organization who are involved in a particular buying decision. The buying center has five dimensions: the number of levels of the organization that participate, the number of depart-ments that participate, the number of individuals who participate, the degree of interaction among participants, and the extent to which the purchasing manager is involved in communications.

## 7. Identify six main roles in the buying center.

Among roles assumed by individuals in the buying center are initiator, influencer, decision maker, gatekeeper, purchaser, and user. The initiator is the person who recognizes the organization's need and brings it to the attention of people in the buying center. An influencer is anyone who can affect the outcome of the purchase decision, including whether a purchase is made, which product will be purchased, and who the supplier will be. The decision maker is the person who actually makes the final decision. A gatekeeper is someone who controls the flow of information into the buying center. The purchaser is the person who orders the product and deals with the supplier. Finally, the users are the people who ultimately consume the good or service purchased, such as truck drivers, receptionists, designers, and writers.

## KEY TERMS

acceleration principle (152)
business-to-business
    marketing (144)
buyclasses (158)
buying center (160)
buying center roles (162)
derived demand (152)

government market (146)
industrial/commercial
    market (144)
make/buy decision (156)
modified rebuy (159)
new-task purchase (159)

organizational buying
    process (155)
organizational market (144)
reciprocity (152)
request for proposal (RFP)
    (157)

resellers (145)
single sourcing (158)
source loyalty (151)
straight rebuy (159)
value analysis (156)
vendor analysis (158)

## QUESTIONS FOR DISCUSSION

1. You are the marketing manager for a company that makes office carpeting. Would all four subgroups in the organizational market represent potential customers? Explain your answer.

2. Your company makes high-end video equipment for industry. Top management is considering getting into the government marketplace. How would you research potential government markets and procedures before trying to sell to them?

3. As a manufacturer of photographic chemicals and papers, how would you market them to businesses (such as photo labs) and to consumers (individual photographers)?

4. Think of an organization to which you belong—a club, a business, or whatever—that has made a major purchase. Who initiated the purchase? Who played the other five roles in the buying center?

5. As purchasing agent for a steel manufacturer, you plan to buy a coke oven, a plant janitorial service, and a new supply of rubber gaskets. Which of these purchases would be a straight rebuy, a modified rebuy, or a new-task rebuy? Explain your answers.

6. You are a representative of a company that makes fax machines. One of your biggest clients is a paper manufacturer. In this situation, what would be the advantages and disadvantages of reciprocity—of using your client as a major paper supplier for your company?

7. A fast-food company decides to add pizza to its menu. What steps would the members of the buying center take in the decision-making process for purchasing pizza ovens for 100 fast-food outlets?

8. How might a manufacturer of printing presses reduce the perceived risk of buying one of its new state-of-the-art, high-speed color presses?

9. What criteria might a construction company use in a supplier analysis of window manufacturers?

10. What are some of the organizational markets that are likely to experience sales declines if college enrollment drops?

## Meeting a Marketing Challenge at Federal Express

During the late 1970s, when a shipment "absolutely, positively, had to be there overnight," organizational buyers had little choice; they called Federal Express, the pioneer in the overnight shipping business. Today that's all changed. By the early 1980s, competitors had copied FedEx's system, so the skies have become crowded with competition, much of it priced lower than FedEx. Fred Smith's company must now find ways to remain the industry leader.

Aside from FedEx's technical superiority, the company's major competitive edge is its renewed commitment to serving the demanding organizational market. Smith understands that as organizational buying patterns change, couriers must offer their customers maximum flexibility. He also recognizes the growing importance of time-certain delivery as a marketing tool. "Distribution has become a primary means of product and service differentiation," he says. "How I get a product to you may well become as important as what I get to you."

Smith has taken a number of steps to keep FedEx competitive, including establishing hundreds of retail outlets for greater customer convenience. The company developed its own weather forecasting system, which has helped it achieve a 98.8 percent on-time flight record. Perhaps the most important innovation is FedEx's pioneering effort in electronically tracking and tracing items in transit. With the introduction of the company's highly sophisticated Digitally Assisted Dispatch System, customers have become even more confident that FedEx will deliver as promised.

With small-package delivery becoming more competitive and less profitable, FedEx looked for new markets as well. Delivering heavier cargo—especially overseas—seemed to hold great promise, so in 1988 FedEx bought Flying Tiger, the world's largest heavy-cargo airline. That gave Smith the established international routes that he hopes will eventually allow the company to offer two-way service between most cities around the globe.

To avoid competing on price alone, FedEx has continued to diversify in order to offer organizational customers still more services. For example, a growing number of high-tech companies are shifting from traditional warehouses to faster, more flexible distribution systems. So in 1990, the company instituted a Business Logistics Services program that handles every warehouse function from inventory management to bookkeeping. For some customers, says Smith, "Federal Express has actually become a 50- to 500-mile-an-hour warehouse." He believes that as high-speed delivery grows in importance, FedEx's unique array of services will keep the company a step ahead of the competition.

**Your mission:** You are a marketing manager for Federal Express, and Fred Smith has asked you to explore ways to increase the company's business in the organizational market. In each of the following situations, choose the alternatives that would be most effective in helping you meet your company's goals.

1. In devising a strategy to guide Federal Express's growth in coming years, you've decided to focus on one primary competitive advantage. Assuming that you could claim the best position on the following three points, which do you think would be most important to customers? Keep in mind the reasons businesses and government agencies want to use express delivery services.
   a. *Price.* You need to make sure that you offer the cheapest service.
   b. *Warranties.* In the event of poor performance, your customers will want to know that you will refund the price they paid.
   c. *Quality of service.* Customers will want to know how often pickups will be made, whether deliveries are made on time, whether packages arrive in good condition, and so forth.

2. You realize that not all organizations expect the same level of service, and that focusing on most likely segments will help you succeed. Which of the following segments would you approach first?
   a. *High-tech industries that manufacture computers and related products.* These companies are likely to need a courier that's capable of providing express delivery service and maintaining inventory for them.
   b. *Private health-care facilities.* Because life itself may sometimes hang in the balance, fast, dependable delivery service is particularly important in this sector of the institutional market.
   c. *Toy retailers.* These firms need express delivery services because their business depends on having the right products in the marketplace at the right time; otherwise their customers will go elsewhere.

3. Because FedEx's various markets overlap to some extent, you decide to analyze the differences between consumer and organizational buying patterns. This will help ensure that you develop the proper marketing and sales strategies. Which one of the following differences would be the most important to keep in mind as you put your plans into action?
   a. Because of the amount of money involved, more than one person will usually participate in the buying process.

b. Every large organization employs at least one professional buyer who's been specifically trained to carefully consider all the facets of every significant purchase.

c. Organizational purchases are made relatively infrequently and usually only after an extended planning period. Also, once the buying decision has been made, it often marks the beginning of a long-term relationship between buyer and seller.

4. Which of the following is most important to consider as you begin to help your salespeople present FedEx's services to the organizational market?

a. Because organizations often buy only from approved vendors, make it your business to get on the proper list of bidders used by each company you target. After all, you'll never get to make a sales presentation if you're not in the lineup.

b. Many organizations use the buying center concept to make significant purchases; therefore identify and contact all the individuals participating in the buying center. You can then tailor your presentation to appeal to each person's vested interest.

c. Make every effort to determine exactly what the target company is looking for in an express delivery service. Also verify the exact specifications that will be used when evaluating alternatives. You'll then know what to stress and what to eliminate in your marketing strategy.

## SPECIAL PROJECT

You are the new industrial salesperson for FedEx, and Fred Smith has asked you to write a proposal that can be used to sell FedEx's overnight delivery services to a company that manufactures components for commercial aircraft. Begin your proposal with a paragraph that briefly introduces FedEx to the target company's purchasing agent, as well as the buying center as a whole. Following that, explain how FedEx's wide range of services can meet the unique needs of the company president or division manager, production manager, personnel manager, and finance manager. Make up whatever data or circumstances you need to complete this project, and keep it under two pages. When the proposal is completed, write a one-page memo to Smith outlining how you plan to reach the purchasing agent within the target company.[46]

# How NCR Rings Up Organizational Sales

From hand-cranked cash registers to automated teller machines, NCR has been selling to the organizational market for more than 100 years. Based in Dayton, Ohio, and headed by Charles E. Exley, Jr., the company racks up $6 billion in annual sales by selling to banks, retail stores, and other businesses. However, rapidly changing technology and a heated battle with IBM threatened to ring up a "No Sale" for Exley's organizational marketing efforts not long ago.

By the late 1960s, NCR had built a commanding lead in cash registers, accounting equipment, and large mainframe computers. However, the acceleration of computer technology caused a major shift in demand for banking equipment and cash registers. Retailers, for example, were clamoring for more sophisticated sales terminals that could keep track of inventory, approve credit purchases, and speed sales transactions. NCR's profits tumbled from $50 million in 1969 to $2 million in 1971.

Top management steered a course toward electronic cash register systems, automated teller machines (ATMs) for banks, and smaller computer systems. NCR was making headway by 1984, when Charles Exley, Jr., became CEO. But Exley's review of the market revealed that rival IBM had a lock on 70 percent of the mainframe computer market. Therefore, rather than waste time butting heads with Big Blue, Exley withdrew NCR from the large-scale computer business and redoubled efforts to sell transaction-processing equipment to NCR's best markets: banks and retailers.

A straight rebuy of a product as complex and expensive as an ATM is rare, so Exley knew that NCR had to dig into its market to get a better understanding of customer needs. At the NCR plant in Dundee, Scotland (where ATMs are produced), managers began a series of customer meetings, inviting a different customer to visit the plant every working day of the year. Meanwhile, the plant manager traveled the world, talking with customers about the features they wanted and about their relationships with their own customers.

Next, the ATM team in Dundee set out to fulfill the needs they had uncovered. Because reliability was a key element in the buying decision, NCR engineers built an ATM that was three times as reliable as competing machines. Customers also wanted ATMs that were easy to service if they broke down, so NCR overhauled the design to make it modular for more convenient servicing.

In addition, customers wanted the ability to hook up ATMs installed overseas to a variety of telecommunications networks. NCR developed an ATM with 17 data languages that would be compatible with virtually every international network.

All these changes added up to a steady increase in competitive advantage, and as more customers placed ATM orders, NCR's market share grew. By 1989 NCR was the undisputed leader in ATMs with a 20 percent share of the world's sales. More important, Exley's strategy had brought NCR to the forefront at the expense of its old opponent, IBM. Once boasting a worldwide share of 22 percent, IBM was struggling to cling to a 9 percent market share by the end of the decade. Charles Exley has since retired, and NCR has been purchased by new corporate parent AT&T. With its record of product innovation, NCR promises to be a strong performer for years to come.

1. Now that IBM and Diebold have joined forces to market ATMs, NCR must take a careful look at its own strategy for organizational sales. Should NCR use a value strategy and lower prices to increase market share, or should it use a solution strategy and emphasize the availability of a customized system for every user's needs?

2. When looking at the environment for electronic cash registers in supermarkets, NCR marketers realized that fewer teenagers will be entering the work force in coming years, Thus, supermarket managers will have a smaller labor pool from which to select, and it will be harder to attract people with the skills necessary to operate sophisticated electronic registers. Should NCR support its electronic cash register sales with a series of free training courses for supermarket cashiers? Or should NCR develop more highly automated checkout devices to reduce the labor necessary to help customers pay for groceries?

3. Given the increased competition in ATMs, NCR may find that its valued status as a single source is fading. To shore up NCR's position as a single-source supplier, should it promote the availability of a complete line of related items such as receipt paper and ink cartridges for ATMs? Or should it promote the benefits of excellent customer service and customization to keep buyers on the hook?

It's not as if Lynn Shostack hasn't faced challenges before. When she entered the Harvard Business School in 1969, only 26 women were in her class. After graduating, one of her first jobs was to help launch Greenwich Associates, now a highly respected consulting firm. Her next major accomplishment was the definition of Citibank's strategy for targeting affluent individuals, and she is credited with creating the field of private banking. Next she moved to Bankers Trust, where she put together the entire business strategy for that bank's consumer business.

Today, Shostack is back on the organizational marketing side of things, and she's facing another big challenge. Several years ago she was hired to turn around Joyce International, an office furniture manufacturer that was losing money. Although Shostack has pulled Joyce back up to profitability, she knows the job is far from finished. For starters, Joyce is a small player in a market dominated by Steelcase. When customers think of office furniture, they're likely to think of Steelcase.

**Decision:** How can Joyce overcome the problem of being a small supplier? Knowing what you know about organizational behavior, what are the top three things Shostack and her company can do to win sales from organizational customers who are accustomed to doing business with Steelcase?

**Communication:** You've run into Shostack in the elevator in her office building. You'd like to impress her with your knowledge of buyer behavior in the hopes of landing a summer intern job at her company. Quickly describe your three points and the behavioral concepts on which you based your decision. (You may be interested to know that professional salespeople often apply the "elevator test" to their sales presentations, making sure they can deliver the essential sales message in the time it takes to ride in an elevator. This is a good way to ensure that you can make a quick, concise sales pitch that clearly states the benefits for the customer.)[47]

# KEEPING CURRENT IN MARKETING

Find articles that describe a company's strategy for marketing to organizational customers. It doesn't matter whether the company's efforts have been a success or a failure, but find a company that has gone beyond the planning stage and has actually implemented its marketing plan.

1. What did the company do to understand the nature of its organizational customers? Does it have an ongoing program to analyze customer behavior or does it operate from a standard model? What are some specific things the company did in its marketing program that were based on its understanding of buyer behavior?

2. If the strategy failed, what were the reasons? Was it because of poor understanding of buyer behavior? Did any competitors do a better job of understanding customers? Can the company turn things around by changing its strategy or tactics?

3. If the strategy has been successful, can you identify the reasons for success? Did a good understanding of organizational behavior play a role? How much of the company's success is due to luck, in your opinion?

# 6

# Marketing Research and Analysis

**After studying this chapter, you will be able to**

**1.** Define marketing research and marketing intelligence

**2.** Describe the four steps in the marketing research process

**3.** Discuss the use of exploratory research, descriptive research, and causal research

**4.** Outline the advantages and disadvantages of primary and secondary data

**5.** Compare the two major classes of sampling techniques used in marketing research

**6.** Describe the three data collection techniques used in primary research

**7.** Explain how questionnaire design affects research results

**8.** Discuss the ethical issues in marketing research

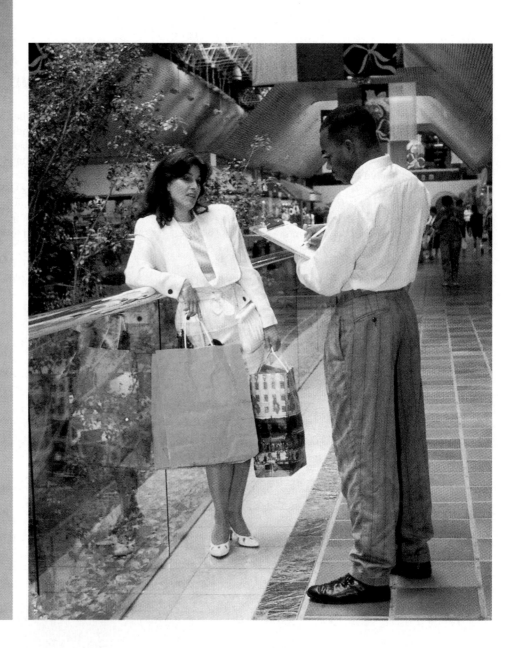

### Stamping a New Image in the Public's Mind

You wouldn't have to tell John Wargo or his colleagues at the U.S. Postal Service that they need to get more from their marketing and advertising efforts. As assistant postmaster general in charge of marketing, Wargo describes their efforts as trying to "position ourselves as modern and caring and not necessarily as old fashioned." He knows that many consumers and businesses view the U.S. Postal Service as rather bureaucratic, impersonal, and even incompetent to a degree. His goal would be to have people "walk away feeling something positive is going on in the Postal Service," and he wants advertising to play a key role in this transformation.

Image and perception are not the only issues facing Wargo and his organization, however. Although it has a government-mandated monopoly on the regular delivery of letters, it does not have a competitive barrier when it comes to overnight mail or package delivery services. This market has been cut into dramatically by hungry competitors, including such giants as Federal Express and United Parcel Service as well as smaller regional and local delivery and courier services. The U.S. Postal Service was the first to offer overnight express service, more than two decades ago, but even postal executives admit that Federal Express has "taken the overnight business to its heights."

Although a government operation, the Post Office functions like a business in many respects, including identifying new products and promoting them to the public. The Elvis Presley stamp, introduced on the King's birthday (January 8) in 1992, was a major commercial success. By letting the public vote on which of two versions to produce, the Post Office not only generated a great deal of publicity but also captured the names and addresses of the 800,000 people who voted. These consumers then received direct-mail advertising for various products related to the Elvis stamp, resulting in Elvis sales in the neighborhood of $20 million.

Wargo also notes that beyond image, competition, and special products, the U.S. Postal Service has an educational mission. Using the mail is no longer as simple as licking a stamp and dropping your letter in the mailbox. In some cases, the education effort is as easy as telling consumers when they need to mail packages in time for Christmas delivery. In other cases, the story is more complex; for example, helping direct marketers who want to send millions of odd-sized envelopes and need to know the best way to automate the process.

What should John Wargo do to make his organization's advertising as successful as possible? If you were in his position, what steps would you take to better understand consumers and businesses? How could you discover their thoughts and feelings about the U.S. Postal Service? How would you translate such knowledge into effective advertising?[1]

# CHAPTER OVERVIEW

John Wargo and the other marketing people at the U.S. Postal Service recognize the importance of marketing information, whether it comes in the form of vast databases or a single expert's knowledge. This chapter introduces marketing research and marketing information systems. It starts by emphasizing the importance of marketing information and explaining the meaning of marketing research. Next it describes the marketing research process, which includes defining the problem; designing the research; collecting the data; and analyzing, interpreting, and presenting the research findings. The chapter concludes with a look at the two biggest ethical issues in marketing research: deceptive practices and invasion of privacy.

# THE ROLE OF MARKETING INFORMATION

Whenever marketers get ready to launch or change products, create or modify marketing programs, or identify or evaluate consumer needs, they face a decision-making process that leads to either profit or loss. In today's fast-paced, high-stakes business environment, even small mistakes can add up to big losses. The risk is especially high for the growing number of global marketers venturing into new overseas territories.[2]

How do marketers improve the odds of making the right decisions? They do so by getting the information they need when they need it. See Exhibit 6.1 for the many ways marketing research can support decision makers throughout the marketing process. Campbell Soup knows how important information can be. In the early 1980s, Campbell's marketers were studying research on family patterns when they noticed that the number of people per household was steadily dropping. This trend coincided with an increase in the number of mothers joining the work force, which prompted Campbell to take a closer look at the needs of people in smaller households where mealtimes don't always include the entire family. As a result, Campbell introduced Great Starts, a line of single-serving frozen breakfasts aimed at the new lifestyles of today's families. Riding the crest of the boom in single-serving frozen breakfasts, Campbell now claims 17 percent of this fast-growing market.[3] No matter how large the organization, or how small, the right information at the right time can make the difference between marketing success and marketing failure. Research specialist Tim Powell summed up the value of information nicely when he compared it to insurance: "Its value is most painfully apparent when you don't have it."[4]

## Marketing Research Defined

**marketing research**
The systematic collecting, recording, and analyzing of information to support marketing decision making

One of the most powerful tools available to marketers is **marketing research,** traditionally defined as the systematic gathering, recording, and analyzing of information to help managers make marketing decisions. This definition implies that marketing research professionals play only a supporting role in the marketing process, a role confined to collecting and processing data. However, marketing research in the 1990s is becoming an integral part of the decision-making process, so this definition has been expanded to reflect the wider role that researchers play. The American Marketing Association now defines marketing research as

> the function that links the consumer, customer, and public to the marketer through information—information used to identify and define marketing opportunities and problems; generate, refine, and evaluate marketing actions; monitor marketing performance; and improve understanding of marketing as a process. Marketing research specifies the information required to address these issues; designs the methods for collecting information; manages and implements the data collection process; analyzes the results; and communicates the findings and their implications.[5]

This definition gives marketing research a broader perspective, touching every aspect of marketing, because marketers need information to make decisions about all these areas.

It's important to distinguish between data and information. **Data** are recorded statistics, facts, and views, whereas **information** is material that's relevant in a particular marketing situation and that can help the marketer reach a decision. The process of analyzing data produces information. Information on trends and forces in the marketing environment is called **marketing intelligence.**[6] In the same way that military strategists gather intelligence and use it to plot their campaigns, marketing strategists gather intelligence to help them select target markets, define market positions, and develop marketing mixes.

Marketers usually keep a large amount of data on hand to use in a variety of marketing research situations, so they often utilize a **marketing database,** a data storage and retrieval system specifically designed to serve the information needs of the company's marketing managers. Although databases are usually computerized, manual databases are fine for many smaller companies. Whether they're using a computerized or manual database, marketers can retrieve data as needed for specific marketing research studies, and at that point, they are turning the data into information.

Data for marketing research come from a wide variety of sources. You can find some data easily by examining sources inside your company, including the number of products you sold last year or your profit margin on individual products. However, some data may be harder to get, including an understanding of why consumers prefer one brand over another or which of your advertisements attracts the most attention. Such data generally come from sources outside the company. Over a period of time, you'll find that various kinds of data are essential, both internal and external. Moreover, you'll discover that in order to be useful, your raw data will have to be organized and converted into information.

**data**
The statistics, facts, and opinions that market researchers record and store

**information**
Data that are useful in a specific marketing situation to help marketers make a decision

**marketing intelligence**
Information on trends and forces in the marketing environment

**marketing database**
A computerized system to store and retrieve data as needed by marketers

## Exhibit 6.1   USING RESEARCH THROUGHOUT THE MARKETING MANAGEMENT PROCESS

| Phase 1<br>Setting Goals and Establishing Strategies | Phase 2<br><br>Developing a Plan | Phase 3<br><br>Putting the Plan into Action | Phase 4<br><br>Evaluating the Plan's Effectiveness |
|---|---|---|---|
| Research can monitor: | Research can: | Research can monitor: | Research can provide: |
| Dissatisfactions and needs in relevant market segments | Identify key market segments by product category | Total industry and product class sales | End of period compilation and aggregation of operating data to present an accurate picture of performance. Summary of survey findings on consumer awareness, trial, attitudes, preferences, repurchase rates, and so on |
| Demand size and trend | Identify market segment attitudes toward present products, promotions, and advertising | Firm's sales, by product and market | |
| Industry/market structure and composition, competition, market shares, and profitability | | Product availability in retail stores, shelf space, retailer support, and so on | |
| | Test the appeal of potential product attributes | | |
| Technological and materials innovations | Test the effectiveness of advertising and promotion | The costs and effectiveness of the firm's marketing efforts, by product and market and by advertising, promotion, and so on | |
| Supply conditions and prices | | | |
| | Evaluate the needs and attitudes of channel members | Awareness and trial in relevant market segments | |
| Distribution, environmental and legal developments | | | |
| | | Changes in competitive spending levels and strategies, including price, package, promotion, and so on | |
| Media trends | | | |

Marketing research provides vital information for management decisions throughout the marketing process.

**marketing information system (MIS)**
An established series of procedures and methods to collect, sort, analyze, store, and distribute marketing information on an ongoing basis

# Marketing Information Systems

As a marketer, you'll face marketing information problems at both extremes: not enough data and too much data. Some of the material may be data that are irrelevant to today's decisions but that may be important tomorrow or the next day. Successful marketers have an ongoing process for finding and holding the information necessary for making marketing decisions now and in the future. A **marketing information system (MIS)** is an organized set of procedures and methods designed to capture, sort, analyze, store, and distribute the continuous information flow from inside and outside the company.

A good MIS can transform data into information by defining the relationship between two or more pieces of data, calculating trends, or identifying patterns.[7] For example, if Kellogg's MIS reported that cereal shipments to Chicago supermarkets totaled 10,000 cases last month, that would be one piece of data. But if the MIS indicated that Kellogg's shipments to Chicago supermarkets rose 10 percent last month, that would be information because it would alert Kellogg's marketers to the upward trend in the Chicago market.

As powerful as it can be, an MIS doesn't run itself; managers must determine what they want out of it before they can select what to put into it. At Hallmark Cards, for example, the MIS includes information about every card produced in the preceding five years. The system analyzes why the card did or didn't sell, and it shows where the card was a big seller. One advantage of this system is that the company can now track, down to a specific neighborhood, exactly where certain types of cards sell best. In one case, Hallmark learned that engagement cards sell best in the Northeast, where engagement parties are a tradition, so now the company makes it a point to be sure that Northeast stores receive enough of these popular cards.[8] On the other hand, if the information gathered by the MIS isn't accurate, meaningful, or timely, the company's marketing decisions will suffer. That's why Hallmark and other firms that use an MIS are careful to keep their systems up-to-date and loaded with the details they need.

# Marketing Decision Support Systems

**marketing decision support system (MDSS)**
A computerized system of accessing and handling MIS data and other data so that marketers can apply analysis and modeling methods and immediately see the results

For a growing number of marketers, working with an MIS is the first step in managing the data they need to make informed decisions. They also use a **marketing decision support system (MDSS),** a computerized system that integrates data

**Exhibit 6.2**
**APPLYING MARKETING RESEARCH**
The Visionary Shopper system creates a simulated shopping environment that lets researchers test consumer reactions to packaging and other marketing variables.

from the MIS and other sources with analysis and modeling techniques to allow marketers to see immediately the results of manipulating data in a variety of ways. Marketers can access the MDSS via personal computer terminals to review trends, pose and solve hypothetical problems, and gather whatever additional data they need to support their marketing decisions. For example, marketers at the pharmaceutical company Glaxo use their MDSS to fine-tune product marketing plans and allocate product samples more precisely. Chevron Chemical uses its MDSS to compare monthly sales forecasts to actual sales, examine profitability for each product line, and evaluate the share of business for each product line on a regional basis.[9]

Using MDSS offers several advantages. First, you have the flexibility of combining large quantities of data drawn from a variety of sources. Second, you're able to evaluate a larger number of scenarios in a short time, using a wide spectrum of methods. Third, you can get immediate answers to your questions because the data and the analysis methods are computerized and readily available.

On the negative side, assembling such a comprehensive system of data and analysis tools can be expensive and complicated; only about 20 percent of the companies in a recent survey reported using an MDSS.[10] However, this number is sure to grow as more organizations recognize the benefits of using an MDSS and are willing to invest the time and money needed to implement such a system.

## Applications of Marketing Research

Marketing research is a key element throughout the marketing process. Marketers rely on research when they set goals for market share, product profitability, or a program's sales results. They also use marketing research when developing new products, identifying profitable target markets, and planning future marketing programs (see Exhibit 6.2). During a marketing campaign, marketers use research to monitor the program's effectiveness by answering questions concerning how many people have seen a particular ad, how many consumers are using a product, and how many consumers buy a product more than once. They also use marketing research to keep an eye on the competition.

Understanding customer satisfaction has become a hot area for marketing research. For example, Nissan hires a research agency to call customers who buy cars at Nissan dealerships and ask about their purchase experience. Ford regularly hosts meetings with car buyers to discuss car quality.[11] Of course, research on customer satisfaction is also important to any service or nonprofit marketer. In addition, marketers use research after a marketing campaign is complete to evaluate how effective the program was. Then the cycle starts over again, using marketing research to help plan the next program and forecast its results.

However, if you don't use marketing research appropriately, you may risk the loss of more than just sales. Before launching New Coke, Coca-Cola conducted extensive taste tests to find a cola taste consumers liked better than traditional Coke and Pepsi. In 1985 the company introduced the new formula as New Coke, replacing the 100-year-old Coca-Cola formula. New Coke simply didn't sell, and Coca-Cola had to mount an expensive marketing effort to salvage the new brand. At the same time, the public outcry drove the company to bring back the original formula, renamed Coke Classic. What happened? Marketers had focused their marketing research only on taste and had failed to look at the emotional attachment consumers had to the traditional Coke soft drink. By changing a product many consider to be a part of our culture, Coca-Cola stirred up strong feelings in its customers, who reacted by shunning the new Coke and demanding the return of the original. If the company had used marketing research to investigate how consumers felt about losing Coke—not just which taste they prefer—the rocky course of New Coke's introduction might have been smoother.[12] When doing marketing research, remember the advice of renowned mathematician John Tukey, who noted that it is far better to have an approximate answer to the right question than a precise answer to the wrong question.[13]

Obviously, marketing research can be applied to nearly every marketing activity, and most companies use research in a variety of ways. However, research, even when aided by advanced technology such as an MDSS, can't happen without guidance from marketing experts. Your own involvement as the marketer is an essential part of applying marketing research for better decision making.

# THE MARKETING RESEARCH PROCESS

Before you begin a marketing research project to uncover what you need to know, you'll want to consider your personal role. Whether you conduct the research yourself, work with your internal marketing research department, or hire an expert to conduct the research, you'll find that your information needs, knowledge, and insights are an integral part of the process.

Marketing research helps take the guesswork out of marketing decisions, but it's also important for marketers to use their own experience and common sense when they plan and apply marketing research. When people rely on experience, personal knowledge, and feelings about a subject, they are using **intuition.** Frequently, before marketers start the marketing research process, they use intuition to outline the information needed, likely sources, and possible results.

However, the design and execution of the actual marketing research must be based on the **scientific method,** a process of systematically collecting, organizing, and analyzing data in an unbiased, objective way. One of the considerations in applying the scientific method to marketing research is whether the research will have **reliability,** meaning that you could repeat the same study over and over again and produce the same results each time. Keep in mind, though, that if you do the study a second time and the results are not exactly the same as they were the first time, it doesn't necessarily mean that the research lacks reliability. The circumstances may have changed since your first study, and that change may have had an effect on your results. Reliability means that the research will be repeatable under identical environmental conditions.

In general, reliability is important because research must be both objective and accurate to provide useful information for marketing decisions. Just to be able to replicate the results is not enough. The research must also have **validity;** that is, the research must actually measure what it was designed to measure, telling researchers exactly what they need to know.[14] Only when research is both valid and reliable can marketers trust the results and use them as the basis for decision making.

Generally, the scientific method dominates the research project, although intuition can make all the difference in some cases. Intuition is what inspired Akio Morita, chairman of Sony, to approve production of the incredibly successful Walkman. Sony's marketing research had indicated that consumers would not buy tape players that lacked a "record" feature. Despite the research, Morita felt strongly that the Walkman, which would only play and not record, was going to be a hit. Morita trusted his intuition, disregarded the research, and put the Walkman on the market. Clearly, Morita's intuition was right: the Walkman's worldwide sales skyrocketed.[15] Of course, you can't always trust intuition over research, but intuition is one of the tools you use.

Marketers plan and conduct marketing research by following four basic steps: they define the problem, design the research, collect the data, and interpret the findings for presentation to management. As a market researcher, to come up with the kind of thorough, accurate information needed to make better decisions, follow all four steps in order (see Exhibit 6.3).

## STEP 1: Define the Problem

Before doing anything else, define the problem. **Problem definition** is a precise statement of the marketing problem you're going to investigate. You know a prob-

**intuition**
The personal beliefs, experiences, and views of a marketer

**scientific method**
The process of methodically gathering and organizing data in an objective way

**reliability**
One of the aspects of the scientific method requiring repeated studies to produce the same result every time

**validity**
The ability to design marketing research that will measure specifically what researchers need to know

**problem definition**
A clear description of the marketing problem being researched

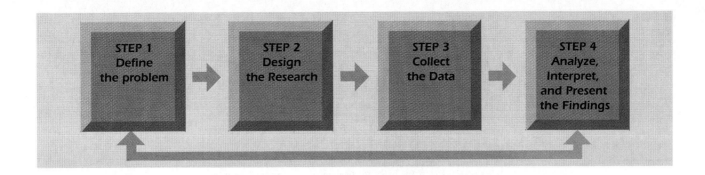

**Exhibit 6.3 THE MARKETING RESEARCH PROCESS**
Marketers follow four steps, in order, as they plan and implement any marketing research project.

lem must be solved when you undertake marketing research, but before beginning, narrow your focus to the specific question you will explore. Suppose you're an electric appliance manufacturer and you see your hairdryer sales dropping rapidly. You decide to use marketing research to uncover the reason for falling sales, so you try defining your problem several ways. You could ask, "What's wrong with the advertising for my hairdryers?" or "What's wrong with my packaging?" Each problem definition would lead you to design your marketing research with a different focus. If your packaging is not a problem, but your advertising is at fault, you might not uncover this if your problem definition doesn't include advertising. That's why problem definition is an important road map, showing you the direction to take when conducting your marketing research. Marketers often conduct some preliminary research just to find out what it is they should be researching in greater detail.

In academic research in particular, a possible step to take after defining the problem is formulating a **hypothesis,** a tentative explanation about the solution to the problem, which will be proved or disproved by the marketing research. Sometimes you can develop more than one hypothesis about a given problem. Going back to the example of your appliance manufacturing company, if you defined your problem as "What's wrong with the advertising for my hairdryers?" then you might come up with a hypothesis such as "The advertising message is not effective for my target audience." As a result of developing this hypothesis, you might come up with another to prove or disprove at the same time, such as "The advertising is appearing in the wrong magazines." The second hypothesis stems directly from the first, and there is a clear relationship between your two hypotheses and the problem definition. You were able to formulate your hypotheses only because your problem definition was so precise.

**hypothesis**
The marketer's untested assumption about the probable solution to the marketing problem

## STEP 2: Design the Research

Now that you've defined the problem, you can design the actual marketing research in preparation for collecting the data. The three parts to this process are determining the type of research you'll need, identifying the sources of data, and designing the sample.

### DETERMINE THE TYPE OF RESEARCH

Naturally, the type of research you conduct depends on what you expect to get out of the project. When you first set out to get a better picture of your situation, your preliminary research is generally exploratory, which is a *qualitative,* or nonstatistical, type of research (see Exhibit 6.4). On the other hand, once you've defined your objectives more precisely, you use either descriptive or causal research, or a combination, to collect your data because these methods are more *quantitative,* or statistical in nature. The following sections examine these three types of research in more detail.

EXPLORATORY RESEARCH    When you need a better definition of what to study, you'll often use **exploratory research,** which is a series of initial research steps that help

**exploratory research**
A type of research conducted to clarify the problem definition and prepare for additional research to prove or disprove the hypothesis

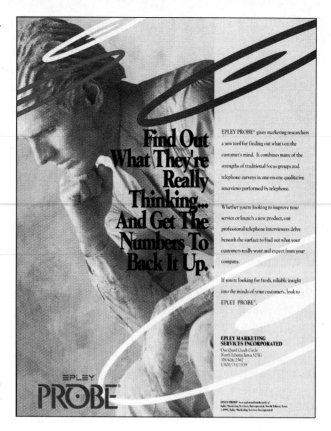

**Exhibit 6.4
QUALITATIVE
RESEARCH**
Epley Marketing Services promotes its qualitative interviewing services.

clarify the problem definition and lay the groundwork for more extensive marketing research. Sometimes exploratory research consists of looking at information in your own marketing database or reviewing magazine and newspaper articles on the subject. Then you might approach experts inside and outside your organization to discuss the problem in greater depth. You might also talk with customers or prospects in focus group interviews as a way of getting insight into your situation or as a way to pinpoint a hypothesis more precisely (see Exhibit 6.5).

Arm & Hammer used exploratory research to find a way to boost sales of baking soda, a trusty old product whose sales had leveled off. The company was searching for new product uses, so researchers talked with groups of consumers and showed some of the early print ads for the product, including one that promoted the use of baking soda to clean the inside walls of the refrigerator. As these consumers started to talk about freshening the refrigerator, the marketers suddenly realized that they could get more mileage out of positioning baking soda as a way to keep the refrigerator smelling clean.

To test the power of this positioning, Arm & Hammer ran a television ad on the West Coast and measured the number of households reporting that they had used baking soda to deodorize their refrigerators. The research showed that after the ad had been running for over a year, more than three times the number of households on the West Coast were using baking soda in the refrigerator than were using it before the ad. Moreover, sales had skyrocketed with subsequent reports of bare shelves all over the West Coast. Exploratory research helped Arm & Hammer turn baking powder into gold.[16]

**descriptive research**
A type of preliminary research that allows marketers to better describe the marketing problem

DESCRIPTIVE RESEARCH    Another type of research used in the design phase is **descriptive research,** which helps describe the nature of a marketing problem. This type of research often follows exploratory research because a good understanding of the problem is essential for conducting research that will describe it in greater detail. When you use descriptive research, you're trying to literally describe what is going on in a particular market, for example, or to establish the characteristics

**Exhibit 6.5**
**FOCUS GROUPS**
Focus groups are a popular data collection method, although researchers must always be careful not to treat the results as hard statistical evidence.

of consumers who use or don't use your product. In fact, the majority of marketing research can be called descriptive because it helps marketers get a better picture of their customers and their markets so that they can use the elements of the marketing mix more effectively (see Exhibit 6.6).

For example, when the U.S. Travel and Tourism Administration (USTTA), a division of the U.S. Department of Commerce, wanted to stimulate pleasure travel to the United States, it commissioned descriptive research to survey vacationers in Great Britain, Germany, and France. The purpose was to identify the characteristics of people who travel internationally for pleasure, estimate the U.S. market share of international vacation travel, and learn how potential travelers view the United States and its attractions relative to competing destinations. From this research, the USTTA learned that tourists from various countries generally have differing views of the United States as a travel destination, and they also tend to have different priorities when planning vacations. Moreover, the research convinced the USTTA to

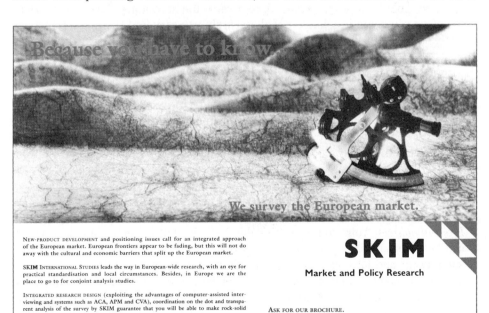

**Exhibit 6.6**
**DESCRIPTIVE RESEARCH**
SKIM International, a research firm based in the Netherlands, is one of a number of firms offering descriptive research services for the European market.

**causal research**
Research that helps marketers identify a specific factor that causes an effect in the marketplace

**independent variable**
The marketplace factor that, when manipulated, affects a dependent variable

**dependent variable**
The marketplace factor that is affected when another factor is changed

**secondary data**
Data that have been collected for other purposes, not specifically for the research being conducted

vary its marketing mix on a country-by-country basis because of these varying perceptions and interests.[17]

CAUSAL RESEARCH    The third type of research is **causal research,** developed to identify the factor that causes a particular effect in the marketplace. You would use causal research, for example, when you want to understand what could happen to sales if you lower prices or how a heavier advertising schedule might affect customer awareness of your product. In these examples, the price and the advertising are the **independent variables,** the factors being manipulated. The sales level and the awareness are the **dependent variables** that will be affected when the independent variables are changed.

Causal research helps you confirm that the dependent variable is affected when you change the independent variable. If Kellogg offers a 25-cent coupon to stimulate short-term sales of Corn Flakes, it can then monitor data from supermarket checkout scanners to see whether consumers are responding. This type of cause-and-effect relationship provides valuable information for decision making, but use causal research with care: No one can predict with certainty that a change in one part of the marketing mix will definitely cause a particular effect. Did your sales go up because of the lower prices, or was it because a major competitor stopped producing a similar product? Did customers notice your product because of the increased advertising, or was it because a local environmental group endorsed the product as being especially safe? You cannot control every factor in the marketplace, so you must use caution when looking at the results of causal research.

## IDENTIFY SOURCES OF DATA

Now that you have determined the type of research to conduct, the next step is to pinpoint the sources of your data. The following sections examine the two kinds of data you can use in your research: secondary data and primary data.

SECONDARY DATA    **Secondary data** have been collected previously, not specifically for the current research project. Census records, sales invoices, and reports from investment analysts are common examples of data that can be "reused" for marketing research. You might use secondary data when you want to research a problem quickly and inexpensively; secondary data are generally less expensive and more accessible than primary data. Also, review the secondary data that are available before you commission additional research; you may find information that can help pinpoint the problem, refine your hypothesis, or specify the data you want to collect.

However, consider some of the disadvantages of secondary data. At times, secondary data may be too old to be relevant for the current research project, or may be in a form that's not useful for the current study. Moreover, secondary data may not be as accurate as needed for a particular study, or the methodology used may not be appropriate for the current purpose. In addition, your competitors usually have access to the same secondary sources you do (except for data collected from your own firm's records, of course). Despite the drawbacks, check secondary data sources before spending time and money on additional research. You can locate secondary data from both internal and external sources.

- *Internal sources.* Your company probably has files full of secondary data, which can be a treasure trove for marketers. Company budgets, sales forecasts and results, profit and loss statements by product or department, and even customer billing statements show product cost, expected and actual sales, profitability, and customer purchasing patterns. If you or your colleagues have conducted other research studies in the past, these are also an excellent source of secondary data. Don't overlook the company's own marketing database, which is full of data that your competitors generally don't have access to.

- *External sources.* When looking for secondary data outside the company, you have to know where to look. When you find it, external secondary data can be very useful. Marketers will find secondary data in private databases, consumer and business publications, and government studies. A **database** is a system for holding and retrieving various types of data. Private computerized databases include LEXIS, with over 3 million legal cases and documents; NEXIS, with the full text of more than 8 million articles from 125 periodicals around the world; and PAT-SEARCH, with information and designs of more than 1 million U.S. patents filed since 1975. To provide convenient access to the wide variety of databases currently available, companies such as Dialog can connect you to hundreds of databases with a simple phone call. Syndicated data services also offer access to their private databases. For example, the National Purchase Diary Panel gathers monthly records from 13,000 families who keep diaries about their purchases in 50 distinct categories.

**database**
A computerized system that stores and retrieves a variety of data

The list of consumer and business publications that are good sources of secondary data is quite long, ranging from periodicals to encyclopedic industry guidebooks. Here are just two examples: *Million Dollar Directory,* a thick volume with details about the products, locations, sales, and employment numbers of companies with assets over $500,000; and *Directory of Mailing List Houses,* which lists sources of mailing lists for research and other marketing functions. Also available are indexes to newspaper and magazine articles, listings of books by subject, and a wide range of other published sources.

The list of government studies is also very lengthy. You probably know about many of the national surveys—the census, unemployment figures, the Consumer Price Index—but marketers can also seek out state and local data and even international data. Prepared annually by the U.S. Department of Commerce, the 1,000-page *Statistical Abstract of the United States* packs an extensive collection of statistics on social, economic, and political subjects. Each state publishes employment and economic data, and each local government has tax records and other information available for inspection. In short, the list of external sources for secondary data is long.[18] The only time you're likely to find less secondary data than you'd like is when you're researching small markets, particularly the markets for specialized technical products.

An important type of secondary data for many marketers is **single-source data,** so called because it combines data about product sales, brand sales, coupon usage, and television advertising exposure into a single database.[19] The data on product and brand sales and on coupon usage are collected through the use of supermarket checkout scanning devices, and the ad exposures are collected through devices in each participating household's television set. Developed during the 1980s, single-source data help marketers measure the direct impact of advertising and promotions on consumer purchasing behavior. Information Resources Inc. (IRI) is a leading single-source data supplier.[20]

**single-source data**
A technique of gathering and storing data about product and brand sales, coupon redemption, and television advertising, in a single database

PRIMARY DATA    In contrast to secondary data (which have been previously collected) **primary data** are collected directly from subjects or through on-site research for a particular marketing research project. Primary data have a number of advantages over secondary data: they fit the research project exactly, they are generally the most up-to-date data possible, are sometimes the only data available, and your competitors don't usually have access to the same data. On the other hand, gathering primary data can be expensive, time consuming, and difficult, as you will see in the section on collecting data.

**primary data**
Data that are gathered directly from the subjects or through on-site research for a specific marketing research program

## DESIGN THE SAMPLE

If you (or your research suppliers) need to collect primary data, the next step is to identify the appropriate **population,** which includes all the people, places, or things

**population**
The universe of people, places, or things to be investigated in a specific research study

**census**
A survey of every person or
item in the population

**sample**
A portion of a population that
represents the whole in a research study

**sampling error**
A measure of the discrepancy
between the results of surveying a sample and the expected
results of surveying the entire
population

that are of interest in a particular study. To define the population, decide not only who or what you want to study, but also where and when. Suppose you were study-ing the market in New England for restaurant stoves and your hypothesis was that the majority of chefs prefer natural gas stoves over electric stoves. The population for your research would be people who are currently restaurant chefs in the New England states.

Now that you know who to ask about restaurant stoves and where to find these people, it should be easy just to go out and call chefs, right? Not really. It's difficult to conduct a **census,** a survey of every member of the research population. You'd have to track down every last chef in New England and get each one to answer your questions. If you marketed your product nationally or internationally, you'd need even more time and money to take a census. When the U.S. government conducted a census in 1990, it tried to count each and every person living in the United States on Sunday, April 1. The objective was to get a complete and accurate picture of the demographic makeup of the country. The cost was a mind-numbing $2.6 billion, but the 1990 census still failed to count a significant percentage of the estimated 250 million people who live in the United States.[21] (See Exhibit 6.7 for a sample of the census studies conducted by the U.S. government and Exhibit 6.8 for a description of the key research variables in the census.)

Because most marketers don't have a budget as large as the U.S. government's, they rarely use the census technique unless the population is very small and reach-able. Instead, they select a **sample,** a subset of a population that is intended to rep-resent the whole. Selecting the right sample is important because it will be used to project the reactions, attitudes, and behavior of the entire population and because marketers will make decisions on the basis of this projection. That's why marketers look at the **sampling error,** the difference between the results of surveying a sam-ple of the population and the results that could have been expected if a census of the entire population had been conducted. The term *error* refers to the level of pre-cision in using a sample instead of taking a census. Samples can't be expected to yield exactly the same results as a census, and some sampling techniques have higher (worse) sampling errors than others. In general, the larger the sample, the lower the sampling error and the greater the precision.[22]

When choosing the type of sample to use, look at the size of the possible sam-pling error, the feasibility of each sampling technique, and the cost of gathering the research. Sampling techniques fall into two general categories, each of which in-

## Exhibit 6.7 SELECTED U.S. GOVERNMENT CENSUS STUDIES

| Census | Focus of Study | Frequency |
|---|---|---|
| Census of Population and Housing | Counts the population; looks at household composition and other demographic factors | Every 10 years in years ending in 0 |
| Census of Retail Trade | Counts the number of establish-ments and firms, employees, and sales levels | Every 5 years in years ending in 2 and 7 |
| Census of Service Industries | Counts the number of establish-ments and firms, employees, and sales levels | Every 5 years in years ending in 2 and 7 |
| Census of Governments | Counts the number of employees, payroll, taxable property values, and revenues for federal, state, county, municipal, township, school district, and other governmental bodies | Every 5 years in years ending in 2 and 7 |

In an attempt to provide a complete and detailed picture of the economy and the country, the U.S. Department of Commerce Bureau of the Census conducts a series of censuses, some of which are described here.

1. Age:
    Under 5, 5–12, 13–17, 18–24, 25–34, 35–44, 45–54, 55–64, 65–74, 75–84, 85+
   Sex:
    Male, female

2. Race/ethnicity:
    White
    Black
    Asian
    Hispanic (may be of any race)
    Other (includes Native Americans)

3. Household types:
    Families:
       Married couple with children under age 18
       Married couple with no children under age 18
       Other family (includes single parents)
    Nonfamilies:
       Persons living alone
       Unrelated persons sharing living quarters

4. Household ownership:
    Single-family, owner-occupied
    Two+-family, owner-occupied
    Condominium or coop
    Rented unit
    Mobile home or trailer
    Other (includes houseboats, etc.)

5. Educational attainment:
    Not high school graduate
    High school graduate
    Some college (1 to 3 years)
    College degree
    Advanced degree (master's degree, doctorate, etc.)

6. Employment status and occupation:
    Employed full-time
    Employed part-time
    Not employed
    Retired
   If employed:
    Professional worker, executive/administrative/managerial
    Clerical/sales/technical
    Craft/repair/equipment operator
    Service worker (food service, etc.)
    Other

7. Household income:
    Under $10,000
    $10,000–$24,999
    $25,000–$34,999
    $35,000–$49,999
    $50,000–$74,999
    $75,000+

This list includes some of the more significant variables collected during the U.S. census.

cludes a variety of specialized techniques. **Probability samples** are samples in which every individual in the population has a known chance, or probability, of being selected. In some probability samples, each member of the population has an equal chance of being sampled, whereas in other probability samples, the chance of being sampled is not equal. However, in all probability samples, the likelihood of being included in the sample can be calculated, and it is not zero. **Nonprobability samples** are chosen on the basis of convenience or according to the researcher's judgment, so the members of the population included may not be representative of

**probability samples**
Samples in which every member of the population has a known, nonzero chance of being chosen to be surveyed

**nonprobability samples**
Samples in which items are selected from the population according to convenience, a quota, or the researcher's judgment

the population overall. In contrast to probability samples, the likelihood of being included in a nonprobability sample cannot be calculated. For this reason, nonprobability samples are less objective than probability samples. Because the probability of being selected cannot be measured, the sampling errors of nonprobability samples cannot be statistically measured. Researchers use nonprobability samples most often in exploratory research where the ability to measure sampling error may be less important than the discovery of insights that will help refine the problem definition.

## STEP 3: Collect Data

At this point in the marketing research process, you've defined your problem and designed your research. Next, collect the data. You can collect primary data in one of three ways: by observation, by surveys, and by experimentation.

OBSERVATION

**observation**
The recording of consumer actions or marketplace events as they occur

Have you ever seen a guard standing in a museum lobby with a counter in hand, clicking it each time someone enters the building? To gather primary data about the number of museum visitors, the guard is using **observation,** the record of behavior or events as they are witnessed (Exhibit 6.9). In some situations, the speed of an event or the number of events being recorded may make mechanical or electronic observation more desirable than stationing a person to observe and record. For instance, a retailer can use electric eyes to count the number of people entering and leaving the store. Companies such as New York–based Envirosell specialize in monitoring, filming, and analyzing the behavior of store shoppers.[23] A disposable diaper manufacturer can use videotapes of diaper changing at a day-care center to gather data for redesigning diapers.[24] Some marketers use an invisible beam of infrared light to track consumer eye movement and collect information about which packages attract the consumer's attention. This method of electronic observation helps grocery product manufacturers improve their package designs.[25]

Marketers like observation because it shows them what customers actually do, rather than what customers say they do. Only through observation can marketers be sure they are seeing exactly how consumers act in particular situations. How-

**Exhibit 6.9
MEASURING
CONSUMER RESPONSE
TO ADVERTISING**
Collecting data with super-market checkout scanners is a common form of observation research.

## Exhibit 6.10  THE COST PER COMPLETED INTERVIEW FOR SELECTED MARKETING RESEARCH METHODS

| Method of Communication | High | Cost Range Low | Typical |
|---|---|---|---|
| Mail | $  15 | $  4 | $  8 |
| Telephone | 25 | 6 | 12 |
| Personal—shopping center | 40 | 8 | 15 |
| Personal—home | 100 | 25 | 40 |
| Per focus group (5–12 people) | 3,000 | 1,000 | 1,800 |

Because costs for various methods vary widely, marketers think about their budgets and their needs when deciding which survey method to use.

ever, observation alone may not explain why consumers behave as they do, so some marketers talk with consumers as well as record their behavior. That's how one researcher found out that people who love chocolate hide their favorite bars in peculiar places (under a chair, in the freezer, or in an underwear drawer, for example) to keep other people away from their special treats. This information helped one advertising agency propose a television commercial for a chocolate manufacturer.[26] Watching people use products in their natural environment (such as their homes) is a special observation technique borrowed from anthropology called *ethnography.*[27]

## SURVEYS

A **survey** is a research technique in which data are systematically collected directly from the people being studied by using a questionnaire. A survey is a good research method to use when marketers want to discuss a product directly with customers or find out how employees feel about specific issues. Marketers can use surveys to collect a wide range of data, including descriptive factors such as educational level or home ownership, consumer attitudes toward certain companies or products, or purchase behavior or intentions.[28]

**survey**
A method of gathering data directly from consumers via a questionnaire

You can conduct surveys by mail, by telephone, or in person. You can select among three types of surveys by considering the accuracy, the timing, and the cost of the research. See Exhibit 6.10 for an overview of survey costs and Exhibit 6.11 for a brief comparison of the three methods.

MAIL SURVEYS    Mail surveys are a popular choice for a number of reasons. First, mail is an economical way to reach large groups of people and people in far-flung geographic locations. Second, mail surveys are best when the questions pertain to information that people must look up before answering or that is quite personal. Third, mail surveys can result in more objective answers because the person answering the questions isn't influenced by the presence of a researcher. On the downside, mail surveys can take weeks or sometimes months, so you have to allow time for the questionnaires to be mailed and responses to be returned; also, many people won't bother to return the questionnaire.

TELEPHONE SURVEYS    A telephone survey is a good technique to use when you need immediate responses, particularly from a large group of people. Today, asking ques-

## Exhibit 6.11  COMPARING THREE SURVEY METHODS ON SELECTED FACTORS

| Factor | Mail | Telephone | Personal |
|---|---|---|---|
| Quantity of information | Limited | Limited to good | Good |
| Suitability for complex questions | Limited | Limited | Good |
| Turnaround time | Slow | Fast | Slow to moderate |
| Versatility | Limited | Limited to good | Good |

Although cost is a major factor, marketers also consider other elements when selecting an appropriate survey method.

tions by telephone is cheaper than ever because of discounted telephone rates and WATS lines. Also, telephone surveys take less effort to respond to than mail surveys, so people may be more willing to participate. For example, when Eurasia, a Chicago restaurant serving European-Asian food, wanted to know why business wasn't better, the owner hired a researcher to survey customers by phone. The research revealed that customers wanted more traditional Oriental foods at lower prices. When the restaurant overhauled its menu and cut prices, its popularity soared.[29]

However, telephone surveys do have some drawbacks. You can't show a product or even a picture to the people being surveyed. Also, some people do not have telephones, and others have unlisted telephone numbers. Most significant, an increasing portion of the U.S. population—as much as 25 percent or more in some segments—simply refuses to participate in telephone surveys. Resentment of long interviews, pushy or rude interviewers, and the growth of telemarketing sales calls are among the key factors in these rising refusal rates.[30]

PERSONAL SURVEYS   When marketers want to discuss questions in great depth, they generally use personal surveys, which are face-to-face interviews conducted with one person or a group of people at one time. Personal surveys can be longer and more detailed than other types of surveys, allowing you to explore complex or emotional issues and display products or advertising copy. On the other hand, personal interviews are the most expensive type of survey, and often the most difficult to get people to participate in, because they take longer than other types of surveys. Also, people being surveyed, who are known as *respondents,* may inadvertently be influenced by the interviewer, which can distort the results. Of course, the interviewer may misinterpret what the respondent says, which can also distort the results.

Marketers have also begun to use computers for personal surveys. In computer-administered questioning, the respondent sits in front of a computer screen and types in answers in response to questions on the screen. Some researchers believe this technique removes the possibility of the interviewer influencing the results. However, researchers are still investigating whether the results of computer-administered questioning differ from the results of research conducted without computers.[31] The computer-based interview has two significant advantages. First, the computer can compile and sort the data during the interview, which allows you to see results immediately. Second, computer surveys can adapt themselves while the interview is in progress. You can use interviewing software to build a profile of each respondent at the beginning of the interview and then ask only those questions that pertain to each individual. This saves time for the respondent, reduces errors, and allows you to probe for additional information when necessary.[32]

The Lake Stevens Instrument Division of Hewlett-Packard uses a new twist on computerized surveys. One of the products it markets is a computer-based system for analyzing communication systems. If customers have comments about the system while they are using it, they simply press the "Product Feedback" key, and a survey form pops out of the printer (see Exhibit 6.12). They write down their comments and questions and then fax the form back to Hewlett-Packard.[33]

Personal surveys include mall intercepts, in-home or in-office interviews, and focus group interviews.

- *Mall intercepts.* A large percentage of all personal surveys are conducted in shopping centers. This type of survey is called a mall intercept because people are flagged down while shopping in a mall and asked to participate. Many marketing research firms have special research centers set up in shopping centers, ready to test everything from food products to hosiery. When properly conducted, mall intercepts are as good a research technique as telephone surveys, according to some researchers.[34] However, others are skeptical because they believe that only people who are not very busy or who are intrigued by research will agree to be interviewed.[35]

**PRODUCT FEEDBACK FORM**

MAIL TO: Lake Stevens Instrument Division      FAX TO: (206) 335-2828
Hewlett-Packard Company
Customer Support Department      MS40
8600 Soper Hill Road
Everett, WA 98205-1298, USA

Product          : HP 3587S
Serial Number    : 2529A99238
Version          : A.01.00 [DEMO]
Revision:        : built: mikeg@labmgg, Wed July 7 11:14:50 PDT 1993
HP-UX Version    : B.09.00 B 9000/382 08000932663f
HIL Loop         : [X]Keyboard  [X]Mouse  [X]Knob Box  [X]Button Box
E1485 DSP Mod    : Serial Number:3200AA3C1  DSP's:5  Capture
                   RAM:8388608
E1430 A/D Mod    : Serial Number: _____

Your Name:_____

Position:_____

Company Name:_____

Division:_____ Mail Stop:_____

Street:_____

City: _____State or Province:_____

Postal Code:_____Country:_____

Telephone: (_____)_____

Fax: (_____)_____

   Enhancement Request [ ]     Defect Report [ ]     Other [ ]

_____
_____
_____
_____
_____
_____
_____
_____
_____
_____
_____
_____
_____
_____
_____
_____

**Exhibit 6.12
SOLICITING
FEEDBACK FROM
CUSTOMERS**
When customers press a button on a Hewlett-Packard communications test system, this form prints, allowing them to provide immediate feedback to the company's marketing and engineering teams.

- *In-home interviews.* In-home or in-office interviews are personal surveys conducted by researchers who visit the respondent's home or office. Interviewers are able to ask detailed questions and then follow up to probe for the motivation behind the answers. Such interviews also allow the researcher to observe the circumstances in which the customer uses the product. In some situations, a big drawback to in-home and in-office interviews is the difficulty of reaching the right people.
- *Focus group interviews.* Increasingly popular, **focus group interviews** are personal surveys involving a number of people, perhaps 6 to 12, brought together in a room with a moderator. The moderator presents questions in a way that encourages focus group members to answer in their own words and discuss the issues with each other. The reactions of these individuals are helpful to marketers who want to gain insights into customer motivation. Frequently, marketers and advertising agency personnel sit behind a one-way mirror so that they can see

**focus group interview**
A personal survey technique that involves interaction between a small group of people and a moderator

the group without being seen. (The respondents are usually told they are being observed.) By watching how people interact and by listening to their comments, marketers hope to come away with valuable information for decision making, or at least uncover the need for additional research on specific topics. That's why focus groups are often used in exploratory research and to help identify new product ideas.[36]

When American Express wanted to attract new cardholders while increasing purchases made by current cardholders, it used focus group interviews to help pinpoint which new card benefits would interest customers. The focus groups helped American Express narrow the possibilities from 10 to just a handful. Additional marketing research helped the firm select just one: a buyers' assurance program that extends the warranties on products charged on the American Express card. With this new benefit in place, American Express was able to increase both the number of people who used their cards and the amount each person typically charged on the card.[37]

QUESTIONNAIRES   Once you've selected the kind of survey method that meets your needs, your next step is to frame the right questions. Creating questionnaires is both an art and a science: The questions must be reasonably simple to be understood; at the same time, the questions should lead people to express their reactions in enough detail so that you can use the data to make marketing decisions.

When creating questionnaires, you should take care to avoid several pitfalls. One pitfall is phrasing questions in a way that might bias the person answering. For example, if asked, "You do care about health, don't you?" you'd probably give the obvious answer. Another pitfall is asking questions that cannot be answered reasonably. "How many glasses of water did you drink last week?" would be difficult for anyone to answer accurately.[38] Because writing questionnaires is a tough but critical part of the marketing research process, pretest the questionnaire by sending it to a few people to be sure they understand the questions and interpret them properly.[39]

Next time an election rolls around, take a close look at the questions the pollsters ask. A popular question during presidential elections is "Are you better off today than you were four years ago?" Presumably, an incumbent president can advertise a record of success if the majority of people say they are better off now than they were four years ago. However, think about this question for a minute. What is the relationship between the president's performance and your personal well-being? Maybe you won the lottery last year, or made a fortune in the stock market, or got a great promotion and a huge raise. You might well be better off in this case, but the president can hardly take credit for it. At the other extreme, what if the president did a great job, but you were struck by lightning, hit by a bus, and afflicted with amnesia during finals week? These unfortunate events would have a lot to do with your sense of well-being but very little to do with the president's performance.

The effectiveness of your survey also depends on the type of question you use to gather information. Survey questions can be categorized in three ways: open-ended, dichotomous, and multiple-choice.

- *Open-ended questions.* Open-ended questions are questions that allow people to answer in their own words and express any ideas they think are pertinent.[40] "How many sisters and brothers do you have?" and "What are your career plans?" are examples of open-ended questions. Surveys that include open-ended questions tend to take longer than surveys with other types of questions because answers may be lengthy and must be accurately recorded. Moreover, open-ended questions add to the expense of the research because of the difficulty of collecting and interpreting the data. However, open-ended questions remain popular and are often used in public opinion polls. Although some researchers have expressed concern that not everyone is articulate enough to answer open-ended questions, some studies conclude that open-ended questions do not damage the results of these polls.[41]

In Saudi Arabia and some other Arab countries, interviews with women are extremely difficult to arrange, especially in the home. The culture prevents women from interacting with men they don't know, and women are unlikely to hold jobs as research interviewers.

- *Dichotomous questions.* Dichotomous questions are also known as two-way questions because people are asked to choose between only two answers. These are the most frequently used types of questions because they are easy for people to answer and easy for researchers to total. "Did you have pizza for dinner yesterday?" is an example of a dichotomous question to which the response can only be yes or no. Another example is "Do you prefer a two-door car or a four-door car?" However, researchers sometimes offer a third answer ("I don't know," "Neither," or "I don't have any opinion") when asking a dichotomous question such as "Do you prefer pink or coral lipstick?" This allows a respondent to indicate that neither of the two alternatives is applicable. The third response option is crucial in situations where forcing respondents to choose one of two options would generate misleading answers.
- *Multiple-choice questions.* Multiple-choice questions offer people a number of answers from which to select. Marketers sometimes ask people to choose only one answer and sometimes ask them to choose as many as they wish. Here are two examples of multiple-choice questions:

  1. How often do you brush your teeth?
     a. Less than once a day
     b. Once a day
     c. Twice a day
     d. Three times a day
     e. More than three times a day
  2. What do you like about this textbook?
     a. The illustrations
     b. The size
     c. The colors
     d. The writing style
     e. The case studies
     f. The organization
     g. The margin glossary

Multiple-choice questions, like dichotomous questions, are easy for the respondent to answer, and the answers are easy for the researcher to count and interpret.

## EXPERIMENTS

Another technique you can use to collect data is the **experiment,** a structured type of research that involves altering one or two variables while keeping all others constant and then measuring the results. Experiments are causal research: Your objective is to learn what will happen to the dependent variable when you manipulate the independent variable. You can conduct experiments in the field or in the laboratory.

In **field experiments,** the research is conducted in the real world—in the store, in the bank, on the street, wherever the product is usually sold or used. Field experiments can be expensive, but they are a good way to learn how consumers will react to new products, changes in distribution, and other variations in the marketing mix. **Test marketing** is a field experiment in which a marketer selects a geographic area in which to try a new product and measure sales or usage results. Before General Foods (now known as Kraft General Foods) introduced Maxim freeze-dried instant coffee nationally, it used test marketing for nearly four years to learn how consumers would respond when price and other marketing elements were varied. Certain cities, including Tulsa (Oklahoma), Charleston (West Virginia), and Midland (Texas), have become favorites for test marketing because they are not too large or too small, they have representative demographic compositions, and they are easy locations in which to control marketing variables.[42]

Another type of experiment is the **laboratory experiment,** where the setting is not the real world but a highly controlled environment. A laboratory experiment

**experiment**
Research in which one or more variables are changed while others are kept constant so that the results can be measured

**field experiment**
An experiment conducted in the real world rather than in a laboratory

**test marketing**
Field experiments in which marketers select a geographic area in which to try a new product and measure sales or usage results

**laboratory experiment**
An experiment set in an environment where all the factors can be controlled

## TEST MARKETING, EUROPEAN STYLE

In today's increasingly global economy, test marketing on an international level has become a more important challenge for marketers. That's especially true as marketers eye opportunities in the new European Union, 350 million consumers strong. But how can a marketer go about selecting places to test market a product bound for the European market? After all, a product that sells in Spain may not necessarily do well in France, so it's hard to use a single test market to predict new-product sales elsewhere on the continent. Europe is a diverse collection of countries characterized by many varieties of language, culture, and media. What's a marketer to do?

One thing marketers cannot do is select test markets the same way they do in the United States. When companies choose U.S. test markets, they look for cities where they can narrowly target their promotions using local media and where they can then easily measure the results. However, in Europe, television and newspapers are frequently national in scope rather than local, so it's difficult to isolate just a few cities (even within a single country) to compare various advertising or promotional campaigns.

Still, marketing research experts say ways are available to marketers so that they can cope with the complexities. Marketers are trying segmentation strategies that break up the European market into segments that make sense for their particular products. With that in mind, here are some ways marketers can test in Europe:

- *Look for areas that have an international population.* Many marketers like to test market in Brussels, because it provides access to three separate cultures: French, Flemish, and Germanic.
- *Look for areas that are isolated.* For example, Northern Ireland is isolated enough so that a marketer can test a product and then read the results. That's why the area is a favorite for laundry detergent marketers.
- *Look for areas that have local media.* To create a test market environment, GFK Test Market Research, a German firm, acquired its own local cable television station in Hassloch, a small town in Germany. Now GFK offers marketers a test market opportunity that includes targeted local media. Moreover, the firm has recruited 3,000 local families and signed up local retailers who will provide GFK with checkout scanner data (showing families' purchase histories so that marketers can see consumer reaction to various configurations of the product marketing mix). Next the firm will create local test markets in France and the United Kingdom.
- *Conduct a minitest.* Marketers can choose to sample a smaller group of people and then use a computer model to analyze the test's results and determine whether the product will succeed. When Tetley wanted consumer reaction to its new round tea bag, it brought some consumers to a local hotel and showed them the product. A few days later, Tetley conducted in-home interviews with the same consumers and then ran the results through a computer model. The minitest gave the company the feedback it needed, and it kept the new product away from the prying eyes of competitors long enough for Tetley to retool its factories and produce the product.
- *Consider nonbroadcast media.* Holland is a favorite test market for marketers who can use print advertising and direct mail. Its tenth largest city, Amersfoort, has a major newspaper that reaches a large audience in and around the urban area, and the city itself has a mix of residents that's fairly representative of the country as a whole.

Europe is an attractive market and one way or the other, marketers will figure out how to conduct test marketing to support their new products. Certainly, the increasing sophistication of European marketing research can only help as marketers continue their search for the best test markets.

### APPLY YOUR KNOWLEDGE

**1.** If you were test marketing a new soft drink in Amersfoort prior to rolling it out across Europe, what risks might you face?

**2.** Suppose you were marketing Borden's ReaLemon lemon juice concentrate in Europe and had already successfully introduced the product in Belgium. How would you conduct a minitest to gauge consumer reaction in Switzerland, your product's next destination?

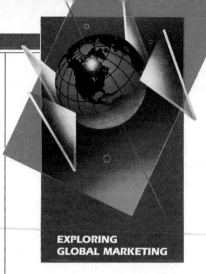

EXPLORING
GLOBAL MARKETING

allows marketers to control everything about the situation, whereas in a field experiment many factors, including the competition and the weather, are beyond the control of the marketer. Manufacturers of consumer goods often use simulated supermarkets and other laboratory conditions to collect data about how changes in packaging or displays can affect consumer behavior. MarketWare's Visionary Shopper uses virtual reality techniques that let people sit at computer terminals and "shop" in simulated stores.[43]

When you're ready to collect data, you can choose to conduct the research using people in your own organization, or you can hire another firm to handle the research. Many large organizations that have their own marketing research departments design the research and then hire outside researchers to collect the data. The advantage of using internal marketing research professionals is that they have a good understanding of the needs of your organization and can gear the research specifically to the type of decisions you face. Also, some marketers believe they have better control over the project when they do the research themselves. Exhibit 6.13 shows the types of research conducted by companies, the percentage that do research internally, and the percentage that contract with outside research firms.

## Exhibit 6.13 INTERNAL AND EXTERNAL MARKETING RESEARCH

| Type of Research | Companies Conducting Research | Research Conducted Internally | Research Conducted by Outside Firm |
|---|---|---|---|
| **Business, economic, corporate** | | | |
| Industry/market trends | 83% | 72% | 14% |
| Acquisition/diversification | 53 | 50 | 8 |
| Market share analyses | 79 | 70 | 11 |
| Internal employee studies | 54 | 44 | 14 |
| **Pricing** | | | |
| Cost analysis | 60 | 55 | 3 |
| Profit analysis | 59 | 54 | 2 |
| Price elasticity | 45 | 43 | 5 |
| Market potential | 74 | 69 | 39 |
| Sales potential | 69 | 65 | 4 |
| Sales forecasts | 67 | 62 | 3 |
| Competitive pricing analyses | 63 | 62 | 4 |
| **Product** | | | |
| Concept development/tests | 68 | 56 | 17 |
| Brand name generation/tests | 38 | 35 | 14 |
| Test market | 45 | 42 | 10 |
| Product test/existing products | 47 | 42 | 10 |
| Packaging design studies | 31 | 29 | 11 |
| Competitive product studies | 58 | 49 | 11 |
| **Distribution** | | | |
| Plant/warehouse location studies | 23 | 23 | 5 |
| Channel performance studies | 29 | 27 | 5 |
| Channel coverage studies | 26 | 24 | 5 |
| Export/international studies | 19 | 21 | 5 |
| **Promotion** | | | |
| Motivation research | 37 | 32 | 14 |
| Media research | 57 | 39 | 22 |
| Copy research | 50 | 35 | 21 |
| Advertising effectiveness | 65 | 49 | 22 |
| Competitive advertising studies | 47 | 36 | 14 |
| Public image studies | 60 | 44 | 23 |
| Sales force compensation studies | 30 | 29 | 6 |
| Sales force quota studies | 26 | 28 | 3 |
| Sales force territory structure | 31 | 33 | 3 |
| Studies of premiums/coupons, etc. | 36 | 33 | 7 |
| **Buying behavior** | | | |
| Brand preference | 54 | 40 | 19 |
| Brand attitudes | 53 | 40 | 19 |
| Product satisfaction | 68 | 57 | 17 |
| Purchase behavior | 61 | 48 | 17 |
| Purchase intentions | 60 | 48 | 16 |
| Brand awareness | 59 | 44 | 20 |
| Segmentation studies | 60 | 48 | 18 |

(Total of percentage of "research conducted internally" and "research conducted by outside firm" is greater than "companies conducting research" because some firms have studies done internally and externally.)

Although they often use their own research departments, some organizations use external marketing research suppliers to handle specialized studies, such as those that examine buying behavior.

Other organizations prefer to hire external research firms to take the research project from start to finish. This may be less costly than maintaining an internal marketing research department, and it allows you to choose from among a number of suppliers that have expertise in a variety of industries or research methodologies. See Exhibit 6.14 for a list of the largest U.S. marketing research firms.

Sometimes it makes sense to assign employees to some projects and hire outside firms to manage others. When Caterpillar, the heavy-equipment manufacturer, set out to make a new tractor, the process took the better part of seven years and relied on findings from a variety of marketing research projects, some conducted by outside research firms and some conducted by Caterpillar employees. An independent research agency handled the initial study of farmers' tractor needs, using mail surveys and personal interviews. Meanwhile, Caterpillar managers fanned out to personally interview dealers and to understand their sales and service requirements for the new product. Later, Caterpillar put prototypes into the field to test their operation and sent its own technicians and product development team into the field to visit the test sites. The technicians interviewed users in person and by phone, and they videotaped field tests at dozens of locations. When the product was finally launched, it was very successful, thanks to the extensive marketing research and attention to customer needs.[44]

When hiring an external marketing research organization, you can choose from a variety of firms, including full-service research suppliers, limited-service research suppliers, and syndicated data services. As their name implies, full-service suppliers offer a complete range of research services, from research strategies through data collection and analysis, across several industries or product categories. Limited-service suppliers, in contrast, specialize in particular markets or individual stages of the research process. For instance, Plaza Research specializes in focus group research, whereas Survey Sampling specializes in sample design. The French firm Pierre Audoin Conseil is a good example of a market specialist; it researches the services segment in the French computer industry.[45]

**syndicated data services**
Marketing research firms that regularly collect data on a variety of issues by following a standardized format

**Syndicated data services** are organizations that follow a standardized research format year after year, asking consumers about a variety of issues in which marketers are interested. The syndicated services conduct these studies regularly and then make the data available for purchase by any company. You can contract with syndicated data services to buy data weekly, monthly, or yearly for your marketing information systems, or you can ask the services to extract data according to the requirements of a particular marketing research project.

A. C. Nielsen is the world's largest syndicated data service. The company makes most of its money from tracking the movement of consumer product goods into and out of retail stores as a way to measure market share in particular product categories. However, Nielsen is probably best known for its Nielsen Television Index, which measures how many television sets are tuned to a particular show. Often television programming is shuffled and advertising fees go up or down on the basis of

**Exhibit 6.14   THE LARGEST MARKETING RESEARCH FIRMS IN THE UNITED STATES**

| Firm | Annual Research Revenue |
| --- | --- |
| 1. Nielsen | $ 1.3 billion |
| 2. IMS International | $586 million |
| 3. Information Resources | $276 million |
| 4. The Arbitron Company | $178 million |
| 5. Westat | $114 million |
| 6. Walsh/PMSI | $ 87 million |
| 7. Maritz Marketing Research | $ 70 million |
| 8. The NPD Group | $ 57 million |
| 9. The M/A/R/C Group | $ 54 million |
| 10. NFO Research | $ 47 million |

These marketing research suppliers lead the industry in revenues and are among the many external firms that marketers can use to conduct marketing research.

Nielsen ratings. Although founder A. C. Nielsen once said he was not happy about the power his company's ratings wield, many marketers use Nielsen data to support decision making about the shows their companies will sponsor.[46]

## STEP 4: Analyze, Interpret, and Present the Findings

The fourth step in the marketing research process is to analyze, interpret, and present the findings to management. This is the moment of truth for the researcher: Has the study produced the information needed to help management make the marketing decision?

### ANALYSIS AND INTERPRETATION

At this point in the process, you probably have a lot of data waiting to be turned into information. You (or your research supplier) start by **tabulating** the data, calculating the responses question by question, and summarizing. Then you analyze the data in a variety of ways, using software packages if the data are computerized. This analysis helps you understand the relationship between factors in the research and identify patterns and details.

When analyzing quantitative results, marketers use **statistical interpretation,** methods designed to show statistically how some data are different from the average in the study and how others are close to the average. By comparing data to the averages in each study, marketers are able to interpret the results with greater insight. Also keep in mind the sampling error and other measures of error when interpreting statistics so that you know how close to the real results a survey would have been if it had been conducted by census instead of by sampling. Although statistical interpretation is based on the scientific method, intuition does play a part. For example, if the results of your survey of telephone usage showed a high incidence of calls placed on December 25 compared with the number of calls placed on an average day, you might use your intuition to interpret this as people calling with Christmas greetings.

**tabulating**
Calculating the answers to survey questions and then summarizing for interpretation

**statistical interpretation**
Using statistical methods to learn how some data differ from the study's averages and how some data are similar to the study's averages, and the reasons for these deviations

### PRESENTATION

The last step in the process is also the one that determines the next step management will take in making the marketing decision. That's why you should present the findings in a concise, complete way that is understandable to the people who must make the decision. Whether made in person or in written form, the report should explain clearly what the results showed and should draw conclusions about the meaning. Most important, the report should tell management the implications of the research and make specific recommendations about the decisions they face. For example, when restaurant researcher Allen H. Kelson undertook a survey about Don & Charlie's American Rib & Chop House in Scottsdale, Arizona, he found that customers considered the restaurant dirty. Although Kelson didn't see any dirt, he reported the findings to the owners. Don Carson, one of the owners, realized that customers were complaining about the outside of the restaurant, which needed painting, and the parking lot, which needed repaving. Carson had been postponing the repairs because they were costly, but Kelson's research convinced him that the work was necessary. When Kelson surveyed customers again after the repairs were completed, they rated the restaurant high on cleanliness.[47]

## RESEARCHING IN INTERNATIONAL MARKETS

Research is a challenging part of the marketing process under the best of conditions. When marketers try to conduct research in other countries, they frequently run into enormous obstacles, ranging from the difficulty of reaching people at home or work to the shortage of many things that U.S. researchers take for granted, such as dependable and widespread telephone service or plentiful shopping malls for snaring passing consumers. In spite of these problems, however, international research is a large and growing part of the research business. In fact, the 50 largest research firms based in the United States get more than a third of their combined revenue from work done in other countries. Research efforts are growing worldwide; nearly two-thirds of the money spent on research is spent outside the United States.[48] Here are the major challenges that researchers can encounter in the international arena:[49]

- *Language and meaning.* Researching in markets where people speak a different language is an obvious challenge, but that's not the only language issue. Words don't always mean the same thing, even when translated correctly. The word *family,* for instance, usually means one or two parents and their children in the United States, but it usually means the extended family (including grandparents, cousins, and aunts and uncles) in Latin America. Language often provides a window into cultural differences that affect research, but researchers need to know where and how to look for differences.
- *Sample design.* The names of consumers and organizations in the United States are compiled into thousands of lists, making it fairly easy to design research samples. However, other countries may have no census data, accurate telephone directories, or other tools that U.S. marketers are accustomed to using.
- *Access to respondents.* Whether it's by phone, mail, mall intercept, or office visit, respondents in the United States are comparatively easy to reach. (Top executives are one big exception, but even they are easier to reach in the United States than in most other countries.) In some countries, women may not consent to interviews at all, especially if the researcher is male. In others, researchers are viewed with great suspicion; potential respondents may worry that the researcher is actually a competitor or government agent.
- *Availability, reliability, and comparability of secondary data.* Secondary data that marketers take for granted in the United States are often unreliable or simply unavailable in other countries. For instance, data on U.S. population, income, and business establishments are readily available, but not for most other countries. Moreover, when such data are available, they often aren't accurate, current, or in a form that can be readily compared with data from around the world. For example, researcher Rena Bartos checked U.S. census data and learned that 55 percent of U.S. women work outside the home. A similar check in Brazil showed that only 27 percent of Brazilian women have outside jobs. Can we assume that U.S. women are twice as likely to work outside the home? Definitely not, Bartos cautions, because the U.S. census defines a woman as any female over the age of 16, whereas the Brazilian census defines a woman as any female over the age of 10. Furthermore, a standard secondary data handbook on Latin America uses *every* woman, regardless of age, in its calculation.[50]

International research poses great challenges. On the other hand, the shortage of good information presents a competitive opportunity to marketers who can do a better job of piecing together their own information. Unlike the United States, where marketers often have access to the same data, or at least data of similar quality, other countries present marketers with a chance to build competitive advantage through effective marketing research.

## THE ETHICS OF MARKETING RESEARCH

As mentioned at the beginning of this chapter, the everyday decisions a marketer makes have an important impact on the company's future. At times, you are faced with critical decisions about marketing research, decisions that pose ethical questions. Some of the issues revolve around deception or fraud, and some revolve around invasion of privacy.

## YOUR RIGHT TO PRIVACY VS. THE MARKETING DATABASES

Right now, even as you're reading this, your name and your life are part of dozens and dozens of databases. Your school knows the courses you take, the grades you get, and your home address. Your bank knows your account balance, your former bank, and maybe even your mother's maiden name (it's requested on most account applications). Your government knows how much money you made last year, the kind of car you own, and how many speeding tickets you've gotten. The list goes on and on: video stores, libraries, doctors, dentists, insurance companies, and many others keep records on your behavior and activities.

Nothing about maintaining a database is unethical, and certainly nothing about using a computer to manage the database is unethical. The dilemmas arise when marketers buy, borrow, rent, or exchange information, usually without your knowledge or permission. Computers make it so fast and simple to mix and match databases that the process is usually invisible. Most of the time, you won't even know that your records are being seen or used by others—people you never imagined would or should be able to build a file on your life.

That's dilemma number one: Who should have the right to see your records? Should the government have the right to ask your employer to turn over your employment records? Should a marketer selling low-cost long-distance telephone service be allowed to look at your telephone records? In the 1980s, the Selective Service Administration wanted to find men of draft age who hadn't yet registered. Among other databases, they

**ETHICAL DILEMMA IN MARKETING**

bought a list of names and birthdays from an ice cream parlor, a list developed as a promotion to recognize children's birthdays in some special way. In the outcry that followed, the Selective Service gave back the list. But the dilemma remains: Who should see your records?

Dilemma number two: Should you have the right to know who wants your records and be able to refuse access? Say you've been getting all kinds of unsolicited mailings lately, and you're tired of having your mailbox filled with offers for magazine subscriptions, computer software, or ski parkas. You can ask that mailers not use your name and address by writing to the Direct Marketing Association. However, that's the easy part. What happens when you apply for health insurance and you're asked to sign a statement that allows the insurer to search a medical records database for your history and provide information on you to others? In some cases, such as when the government wants to verify your eligibility for welfare, you must be notified for a response before the government makes a move on a negative decision. Should you have the right to know when people want your records? Should you have the right to allow some people to see your records and refuse others?

Dilemma number three: What information should or should not be disclosed? In the United States, at least five major federal laws concern privacy, dealing with credit data, governmental data, bank files, videotape movie rentals, and computerized matching of government data. Despite some state laws, a lot of personal information about U.S. citizens can still be disclosed, information that may embarrass people or in some other way have a negative impact on their lives. Denmark has strict laws that prohibit marketers from exchanging information about substance abuse, criminal activities, or sexual inclinations. Who decides what should or should not be allowed to be disclosed?

A debate is raging between marketers and those who are concerned about privacy. On the one hand, privacy advocates argue that people should have the right to be left alone. On the other, marketers argue that they should have the right to freedom of speech, the right to inform customers about their offers. Thus the ultimate dilemma: Does a marketer's freedom of speech outweigh the consumer's right to privacy? Some argue that although the freedom of speech is guaranteed in the United States Constitution, the right to privacy is not. As the number of comprehensive databases continues to grow, this issue promises to be a central topic in marketing.

### WHAT'S YOUR OPINION?

**1.** Should research companies be allowed to collect, store, or sell information about you or your company?
**2.** Are voluntary ethical guidelines adopted by marketers sufficient or are laws necessary to protect consumers' privacy?

## Deceptive or Fraudulent Research Practices

A lot of seemingly small decisions actually pose large ethical dilemmas in marketing research. For example, should the questionnaire be secretly marked even if respondents have been promised anonymity? If you don't want to reveal the company's name during the research, should you use a fake name? If the research really takes an hour to complete, should respondents be told it will take a half hour because otherwise no one would participate?[51]

When sales efforts are disguised as marketing research, the issue becomes even stickier. Is it ethical to pose as a marketer conducting research when you are actually gathering information for a sales pitch? Many people will cooperate with legitimate research, but when the "research" turns out to be a sales call, they feel misled. Worse, these people may be reluctant to cooperate in the future with a marketing researcher because they don't want to be deceived again. The entire profession is discredited in the eyes of people who have been exposed to sales posing as research. A related problem is fund-raising under the guise of research, a problem that nonprofit organizations must be careful to avoid.

## Invasion of Privacy

A second category of ethical issues has to do with the invasion of privacy. For example, should researchers conduct studies without the consent of those being studied? When one-way mirrors, videotape recorders, and other devices are used without warning or permission, people being studied may feel their privacy has been invaded. When researchers ask respondents to answer questions about family, friends, or neighbors, are they invading the privacy of those not present? As another example, should respondents be allowed to have their answers removed from the study if they decide they don't really want to participate after they've completed the questionnaire?

Do companies have the right to privacy? An entire industry has grown up around competitive intelligence to help firms find out virtually anything about their competitors. Whether it's pricing, market share, new products, costs, or manufacturing processes, competitive intelligence will reveal to one company what another probably thinks should remain private. This is another ethical issue marketers face in today's hotly competitive environment.

Several professional organizations, including the American Marketing Association (AMA) and the Marketing Research Association, have adopted codes of ethics for their members to follow. The Marketing Research Council of the AMA recently adopted the ethics code established by the European Society for Opinion and Marketing Research (ESOMAR), giving the industry an increasingly global set of standards to follow.[52] By spelling out exactly what the ethical standards of the industry should be, these organizations are sending a clear signal that ethical decisions are important and must be made with great care.

## SUMMARY OF LEARNING OBJECTIVES

**1. Define marketing research and marketing intelligence.**

Marketing research is the process of gathering data from inside and outside the company to help make better marketing decisions. Marketing intelligence is information about trends and forces in the environment, information that has been extracted from the data collected through marketing research.

**2. Describe the four steps in the marketing research process.**

Marketing research consists of four steps that are followed in order. The marketer defines the problem, designs the re-

search, collects the data, and interprets the findings for presentation to management. None of the four steps can be skipped if the marketing research is to be thorough and accurate enough to help marketers make sound decisions.

**3. Discuss the use of exploratory research, descriptive research, and causal research.**

In the design phase of the marketing research process, marketers determine which one or more of these three types of research they will use, making their selection on the basis of their research objectives. Exploratory research is used to help clarify the problem definition and to specify more extensive research to prove or disprove a hypothesis (if one has been established). Often following exploratory research, descriptive research helps describe the nature of the marketing problem. Causal research helps identify factors that cause particular effects in the marketplace.

### 4. Outline the advantages and disadvantages of primary and secondary data.

One of the advantages of primary data is that the data are timely and have been collected for the current research project. However, in some cases you'll collect primary data simply because the data are not available any other way. Also, primary research gives you data that none of your competitors have. The disadvantages of collecting primary data include expense, time, and difficulty. The advantages of secondary data include speed and availability (in most markets) and a lower cost. The disadvantages of secondary data include the likelihood of their being obsolete or outdated, in a form that isn't useful, inaccurate, and collected with a methodology that may not be appropriate for the current research. In addition, assume that all of your competitors have access to the same secondary data that you use.

### 5. Compare the two major classes of sampling techniques used in marketing research.

In probability samples, every individual in the population has a known chance of being selected. In some probability samples, each member of the population has an equal chance of being sampled, whereas in other probability samples, the chance of being sampled is not equal. In nonprobability samples, subjects are chosen on the basis of convenience or according to the researcher's judgment, so the members of the population included may not be representative of the population overall.

### 6. Describe the three data collection techniques used in primary research.

You can collect primary data in one of three ways: by observation, by surveys, and by experimentation. Observation is a technique in which you record behavior or events as they are happening so that you can see what consumers will actually do, rather than what they say they will do. Surveys are a way to systematically gather data via questionnaires. Three types of surveys are mail, telephone, and in-person interviews. Finally, an experiment is a structured type of research that measures what will happen when you change one or two variables and keep the others constant. You can conduct experiments in the field or in the laboratory.

### 7. Explain how questionnaire design affects research results.

Marketers develop questionnaires with great care because answers must be accurate and objective to provide good data for marketing decisions. When a question appears biased or asks for information that cannot be recalled by the respondent, the survey will not provide reliable or valid results. Finally, questionnaires must encourage people to answer with enough detail for marketers to analyze and interpret the data.

### 8. Discuss the ethical issues in marketing research.

Marketing researchers face two types of ethical issues. Deceptive or fraudulent practices are actions that mislead the people being surveyed. For example, misrepresenting a one-hour survey as a half-hour survey would be a deceptive practice. Another example is posing as a marketing researcher when the purpose is really to sell. The other type of ethical issue is invasion of privacy. For example, asking people to talk about friends who are not present would violate the friends' privacy. Whether competitive intelligence is an invasion of a company's privacy is often debated.

## KEY TERMS

causal research (180)
census (182)
data (173)
database (181)
dependent variable (180)
descriptive research (178)
experiment (189)
exploratory research (177)
field experiment (189)
focus group interview (187)
hypothesis (177)

independent variable (180)
information (173)
intuition (176)
laboratory experiment (189)
marketing database (173)
marketing decision support system (MDSS) (174)
marketing information system (MIS) (174)
marketing intelligence (173)
marketing research (172)

nonprobability sample (183)
observation (184)
population (181)
primary data (181)
probability samples (183)
problem definition (176)
reliability (176)
sample (182)
sampling error (182)
scientific method (176)
secondary data (180)

single-source data (181)
statistical interpretation (193)
survey (185)
syndicated data services (192)
tabulating (193)
test marketing (189)
validity (176)

## QUESTIONS FOR DISCUSSION

1. If you were a manufacturer of stuffed animals, what kind of information could you extract from the following data? Why?

a. Birth rates
b. Production of polyester batting for stuffing
c. Price of thread

## Meeting a Marketing Challenge at the U.S. Postal Service

In the face of a negative public image and aggressive competition, Assistant Postmaster General John Wargo knew his organization needed to meet the needs of its customers and create effective advertising to communicate the benefits of using the U.S. Postal Service. First, Wargo and his organization had to discover and understand customer needs. A research technique employed by the Postal Service's advertising agency, Young & Rubicam, uncovered an important element of customer attitude that formed the basis of much of the service's subsequent advertising.

The agency used an observational method of research called *ethnography,* watching people in action and then exploring the reasons they feel and behave as they do. As Margaret Mark of Young & Rubicam explained, ethnography uncovered an interesting paradox with small business customers. While watching businesspeople interact with their letter carriers, researchers realized that the standard notion of negative perceptions regarding the post office didn't tell the whole story. Although many of these people in fact had neutral or negative feelings about the organization as a whole, they often had positive interpersonal relationships with their individual letter carriers. Many of the businesspeople treated their carriers as friends and neighbors.

Recognizing a great advertising opportunity, Wargo and the agency translated this important new insight into a series of television commercials that featured the individual efforts of letter carriers. One spot showed a carrier trudging through snow to deliver a graduate-school acceptance notice to an

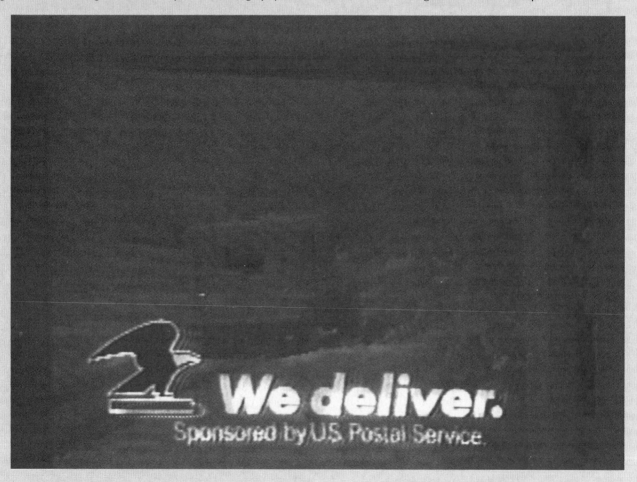

We deliver.
Sponsored by U.S. Postal Service.

elated young man. The knowledge the research yielded led to the new slogan "We Deliver," which has become the umbrella theme for all the U.S. Postal Service's advertising.

**Your mission:** You've recently joined the U.S. Postal Service as its new director of marketing research. Building on the successful research efforts that helped produce the "We Deliver" campaign, you want to continue using advertising research wherever and whenever it can help. Consider the following research situations and pick the best answer in each case.

1. In your role as the director of research, you are responsible for approving all requests for research projects submitted by various marketing staffers throughout the organization. You are working with all these people to help them use research effectively and efficiently. From the following three problem definitions submitted for your approval, which one would you hold up as an example of a well-defined research problem?
   a. In recognition of the time and expense that any marketing project involves, we must make sure that every new campaign is based on thorough qualitative and quantitative research.
   b. We plan to identify the top three reasons some corporate customers choose Federal Express (or other commercial services) over the U.S. Postal Service for overnight document delivery.
   c. We want to find out what people think about our current advertising campaign and compare this to what they thought about our previous campaign.
2. The "We Deliver" theme and its associated campaigns have been running for several years now, and you periodically check to see how well these advertising efforts are working. If you want to see whether the ads aimed at small businesses prompted them to spend more with the U.S. Postal Service, which of the following 1,000-subject samples would you use?
   a. The business telephone directory for your metropolitan area. It lists roughly 12,000 businesses, so you can pick every twelfth listing to get a sample of 1,000 companies.
   b. The list of businesses that have purchased bulk mail permits. You can select the 1,000 customers that have mailed the smallest volume in the last year.
   c. A nationwide database. You can first select the com-

panies that fit your definition of *small businesses* and then randomly select 1,000 from that list.
3. Say that earlier research has indicated that some consumers don't like the service they've received at post offices, and you want to know whether those negative experiences are hurting business. Which of the following questions would yield the most reliable information?
   a. Please list all the reasons why you don't visit your local post office more often.
   b. Wouldn't you conduct more business at the post office if the experience were less negative?
   c. Isn't the fact that you were able to buy the goods and services you needed at your local post office more important than the way you may have been treated?
4. The U.S. Postal Service recognizes that it competes not only with Federal Express and other delivery services, but with fax machines, electronic mail on computers, and even basic telephone services. Which of the following research methods would you use to find out whether increases in postage rates prompt consumers to send fewer letters and make more telephone calls? Assume that the last postal rate increase was three weeks ago.
   a. Select several dozen post offices around the country and, over the course of two weeks, have clerks at those locations ask each customer whether he or she started using the telephone more after postal rates went up the last time.
   b. Ask consumers the same question as in (a), but contact a nationwide sample via telephone instead.
   c. Go back through the U.S. Postal Service's pricing records, looking for the date of each postage increase. Compare this data with nationwide telephone-volume trends to see whether the price changes increased telephone usage (assume that you can get the data you need on telephone usage).

### SPECIAL PROJECT
You know from sales records that many people buy certain stamps as collector's items, with no intention of actually using them to mail letters. You'd like to take advantage of this consumer behavior to help the post office increase its sales revenues. The challenge is to figure out what kind of collector stamps to issue. Should you go with more celebrities? Historical figures? Animals? How would you research this question? Outline the steps you would take to address this puzzle.[53]

# VIDEO CASE

## General Motors Gets Mileage from U.K. Market Research

To car buyers in the United Kingdom, the brand names Vauxhall and Opel are as familiar as Chevrolet and Pontiac are to U.S. car buyers. However, the initials GM are less familiar to U.K. consumers, and the connection between GM and Vauxhall and Opel is even more remote. As the U.K. arm of Detroit-based GM, would General Motors Ltd. prosper by publicizing the fact that it owns Vauxhall and Opel? That's what GM executive Eric Fountain set out to discover when he began researching GM's image in the United Kingdom.

GM officials also wondered whether the corporate name would boost sales for Vauxhall, Opel, and the other GM companies, including AC Spark Plug, Delco Products, Fisher Body, and Bedford. Finally, the GM managers wanted to find out whether there might be any disadvantages to openly linking the U.K. companies with their U.S. parent. Eric Fountain knew that the marketing research results would be used in several ways: to formulate corporate strategy, as a baseline against which to measure the impact of any corporate communications campaigns, and to help shape marketing programs.

Fountain hired an external research supplier, the British Market Research Bureau (BMRB), to plan a three-pronged approach to the marketing research. Phase I was exploratory qualitative research designed to determine how GM was perceived by the general public and by people with influence in or knowledge of the automotive field. During this phase, BMRB researchers talked with motorists, people who live near a GM plant, car and truck dealers, union leaders, government officials, journalists, and others. In phase II, the research supplier tested its survey questionnaires and prepared for the extensive quantitative phase of the research. Then, in phase III, BMRB surveyed a sample of the general population in the United Kingdom, a sample of people living near GM plants, local opinion leaders, fleet operators, dealers, repair shops, GM employees, and others. After seven months of data collection from over 3,500 respondents, the researchers analyzed the results and reported the findings to Fountain and his colleagues at GM.

The researchers reported that the level of awareness of GM in the United Kingdom was very low, far below that of two competing car manufacturers. Further, few people were aware that Vauxhall, Opel, and Bedford were GM companies. Those who had heard of GM simply had the impression that it was a "big American motor manufacturer." The researchers also found that attitudes toward U.S. ownership of U.K. firms were generally positive and that attitudes toward the specific issue of GM ownership of Vauxhall and Bedford were quite positive.

Even among people who said that they would buy only British cars, the researchers learned, a car manufactured by the U.K. subsidiary of a U.S. company—with parts made and assembled in Britain—would be considered a British-made car. Overall, the researchers concluded, the U.K. companies would probably benefit by playing up their membership in the international family of GM companies.

On the basis of this research, each GM operating company developed its own strategies to take advantage of the association with the GM name. The marketers started conveying the GM connection in their promotional campaigns. On the corporate level, GM marketers arranged to sponsor sports and cultural events to heighten awareness of the GM name and its presence in the United Kingdom. For Eric Fountain and the marketers in GM's subsidiaries, the findings revealed a clearer path to competing more effectively in the United Kingdom.

1. To gather data about the extent of car buyers' knowledge of the features and options available on GM cars in Great Britain, the researchers must zero in on the right population for this study. Should they survey people who've purchased GM cars in the past two years or should they talk to people who own other makes of cars but say they would be interested in buying a GM car in the next two years?

2. Imagine that the GM researchers defined a new marketing problem: Vauxhall cars labeled with the GM corporate name do not sell as well in Scotland as in England. Which of the following would be a reasonable hypothesis?
   a. The Ford name is better known than the GM name in Scotland.
   b. Scottish car buyers prefer to buy other cars rather than Vauxhall cars.

3. Looking ahead to next year when a large British distribution company plans to buy a new fleet of trucks, GM wants to find out what its truck drivers think of the cab layout in a particular model of Bedford truck. Should GM use a field experiment and bring a truck out to the distribution center to have the drivers inspect it, or should GM use a laboratory experiment in GM's corporate offices and set up a simulated cab layout for drivers to inspect?

2. Even a small business can set up and run an efficient MIS without a computer or any sophisticated equipment. What data would you recommend be included in an MIS for a small housecleaning service? What source(s) would you suggest be used to gather these data?

3. Which sampling technique, probability or nonprobability, would be most appropriate for conducting research to answer each of these marketing questions? Why?
   a. A drug manufacturer wants to know how many people suffer from migraine headaches.
   b. A bank wants to find out what its customers think about its service.
   c. A university dean wants to learn how high school seniors select the colleges they apply to.

4. Assume you own a veterinary hospital and you're interested in opening a branch office for walk-in treatment. To find out whether your services would be used for routine veterinary care, you decide to do research among the people who own the animals you're currently treating. How would you define your problem?

5. Assume you're marketing a pocket calculator and you suspect that fewer people are aware of your brand than one year ago. How would you use exploratory research to help define your marketing problem?

6. How would you use descriptive research and causal research to better understand your pocket calculator marketing problem from question 5?

7. How well would observation work as a technique for collecting primary data when trying to prove or disprove each of these hypotheses?
   a. Most babies sleep with their mouths open.
   b. People generally compare rates on savings accounts before opening one.
   c. All senior citizens like tapioca.
   d. Women buy more pencils than men buy.

8. What type of survey would be the most effective to use in researching each of these hypotheses? Why?
   a. Retailers sell fewer gasoline-powered lawn mowers when the price of gasoline rises.
   b. College students dread writing term papers.
   c. People drink more than one brand of soft drink.

9. Assume you've done some research into the demand for a wristwatch telephone, and the results indicate that 90 percent of the U.S. population would buy such a product. How would you react to such a finding?

10. Assume you work for McDonald's and you want to find out about Burger King's plan to test pizza in selected outlets and then expand to other outlets if the test proves successful. You want to know about the price, the size, the toppings, and the hours pizza will be served in those outlets. Would it be unethical to pose as a customer and go to a Burger King to research these issues? Why or why not?

## _____ SHARPEN YOUR MARKETING SKILLS _____

Marketing decision support systems (MDSSs) promise a lot of power. They can help you quickly analyze sales patterns, competitive moves, and other market variables. With these analyses, you can presumably make better decisions faster. The MDSS at Frito-Lay, for example, compiles checkout scanner data from supermarkets every day, searches for patterns and clues, and then alerts management to opportunities and threats. Frito-Lay can do such things as monitor how many bags of Tostitos are sold in a specific store each week, and sound an alarm if sales drop unexpectedly. However, praise for such systems is not universal. Critics such as Jonathan Copulsky of the consulting firm Booz, Allen & Hamilton say that these systems distort the strategic planning process by encouraging managers to focus on short-term sales. Copulsky expresses concern that an MDSS will give managers a "quick-fix orientation" rather than the long-term vision needed for continued success in the marketplace.

**Decision:** What kind of commonsense advice would you give to Frito-Lay's CEO about the careful and responsible use of the company's MDSS?

**Communication:** Draw up a brief list of policy guidelines to make sure that this powerful tool helps Frito-Lay in the long run.[54]

## _____ KEEPING CURRENT IN MARKETING _____

Find some articles that describe two or three product failures. These can come from any industry and cover any type of product.

1. Why did the products fail? Which part of the marketing mix was to blame in each case? Are there any similarities among the failures?

2. What role did marketing research play in these situations?

Did the companies research their target markets adequately before designing the products? How would you have done the research differently?

3. Do you think you could have foreseen any of the failures? Do any of the product ideas strike you as so obviously off the mark that anybody should have known the product would fail? If so, why do you think the company involved went ahead with the idea?

# 7

# Segmentation, Targeting, and Positioning

**After studying this chapter, you will be able to**

**1.** Discuss the role of market segmentation and targeting

**2.** List the criteria for determining whether a segment is meaningful

**3.** Discuss the variables used to segment consumer and organizational markets

**4.** Describe a market segmentation matrix and explain how marketers use the matrix to help define their target markets

**5.** Describe the four target marketing options

**6.** List the options you have for positioning products relative to the competition

**7.** Define the positioning statement and identify its purpose

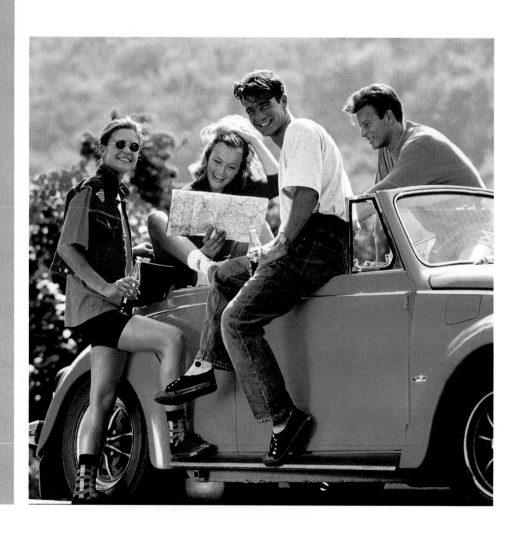

## More Boomers than Babies

A g-r-r-e-a-t market gone soggy: That's what many were saying about the ready-to-eat cereal market when William E. LaMothe became chairman of Kellogg in 1979. With over 92 percent of U.S. households already eating cereal, and with more than four cereal packages in every kitchen pantry, there seemed to be little hope of industry growth. However, LaMothe, a veteran of Kellogg's research-and-development group, was able to look beyond cartoons and sugar to cook up a fresh recipe for success: nutritious cereals for a new generation of health-conscious adults.

In a big-stakes industry where one percentage point in market share means $63 million in sales, Kellogg was stumbling. It was still the market leader, but its share had dropped from 42.6 percent in 1976 to 41.5 percent in 1979, on its way to 38.5 percent in 1983. General Mills, number two and gobbling up share, shot from 20.8 percent in 1976 to 22.2 percent in 1979, and up to 23.2 percent by 1983.

A close look at demographics and lifestyles convinced LaMothe to think older and healthier. The baby bust among baby boomers was fast leading to a drop in the biggest cereal market: school-age kids. Not only were youngsters a barely growing population, but their cereal consumption, always the largest of any age group, was sliding.

America is aging: The median age, now passing 30, will be over 35 by the year 2000. The number of adults, particularly those 25 to 55, is increasing at a double-digit rate. Though LaMothe's critics insisted that 80 million boomers jog for fitness, watch their calories, and skip breakfast, Kellogg's chairman knew the market was too important to ignore.

Focusing on differing adult tastes and lifestyles with a health and nutrition banner, Kellogg single-handedly created the grown-up breakfast market. A hefty investment in product development, an infusion of innovative manufacturing technology, and an abundance of marketing savvy helped Kellogg become the tiger of the adult cereal niche it started, ringing up half the 1987 annual adult sales of $2 billion. Among Kellogg's successes are Nutri-Grain, a product without sugar or preservatives; All-Bran, which offers health benefits tied to cancer prevention; Crispix, a unique two-grain cereal; Raisin Squares, fruit wrapped in cereal; and Müeslix, an upscale European-style cereal.

Increasingly, this highly competitive market comes with a dauntingly high price tag. In November 1987, Kellogg spent $33 million to launch Müeslix in the largest product introduction by Kellogg to that point—an industry record. Despite big budgets, some product introductions have fizzled, including Pro-Grain, backed by a $30 million promotion budget. However, the firm has more new products simmering in development as it remembers its roots—promoting the health benefits of cereals for adults in the tradition of founders W. K. Kellogg and Dr. John H. Kellogg in the 1890s.

New CEO Arnold G. Langbo faces a competitive crunch as other cereal manufacturers jump on the bandwagon to offer new, nutritious adult breakfast choices. His job is to be sure that Kellogg keeps finding the customers of tomorrow and knows how to set the table with cereals that whet grown-up appetites. If you were Langbo, how would you start looking for new cereal eaters? What would you do to find out what is important to people who eat cereal? How would you select a group of people and develop a cereal for their tastes and interests?[1]

**mass marketing**
The practice of covering an entire market with one marketing mix

**target marketing**
The practice of identifying desirable segments in a market and developing special marketing mixes to meet the needs of those segments

# CHAPTER OVERVIEW

Kellogg recognizes the importance of segmentation and targeting in today's increasingly crowded markets. By identifying clear targets, segmentation helps you increase the effectiveness of nearly every aspect of your marketing efforts. This chapter opens with a look at the reasons for not going after the entire consumer or organizational markets, including the ever-increasing fragmentation in both sectors of the economy. Following that, the chapter explores the first of three significant marketing topics: market segmentation. You'll explore the techniques used to segment consumer and organizational markets and the special segmentation issues in nonprofit marketing. Next, you'll look at the target market selection process, in which marketers look over the segments they've identified and choose the ones in which they want to focus their time, energy, and money. The chapter concludes with the process of positioning products in those selected target segments.

# FOCUSING IN TODAY'S FRAGMENTED MARKETS

How does it feel to be a target market? Because you're a college student, you're part of a major market that many companies want to reach. The college market holds as much as $45 billion in disposable income—and an increasing number of marketers want a piece of it. Textbooks are at the top of the collegiate shopping list, followed by clothes and then health and beauty aids. But American Express, Chase Manhattan Bank, Sony Corporation, Plymouth, PepsiCo, and lots of other firms are also wooing you, as you can tell from the marketing materials at your campus bookstore, in your mailbox, on bulletin boards, and even at the beach during spring break.[2]

College students are only one example of a group that can be identified for marketing purposes. Increasingly, marketers find that they must target specific markets because customers display too many differences to treat the whole world as a single market. After all, college students are certainly different from high school students, who are different from junior high school students. Each group has its own needs and wants and will therefore respond to marketing efforts differently.

**Mass marketing,** the practice of blanketing the country or the world with one marketing mix, was popular in the past when companies manufactured in large quantities for the broadest possible market. Henry Ford's first Model T was aimed at the mass market, a market that wanted an automobile for basic transportation and initially cared little that a choice of model or color wasn't available. However, those days are long gone for the automotive industry; today car manufacturers use **target marketing** to identify desirable segments and then to develop and sell cars that meet the needs of those segments. General Motors targets larger families with its Chevrolet, Oldsmobile, and Pontiac minivans. Mazda targets smaller families and individuals with its 323 and Protege models. (These marketers don't confine themselves to one segment, but create multiple marketing mixes for the multiple segments they've identified.) Exhibit 7.1 compares the mass marketing and target marketing approaches.

This chapter helps you decide whether mass marketing or target marketing makes more sense in each situation you face. Marketers who use target marketing successfully find that it delivers important advantages:

- *Efficient use of marketing resources.* By using target marketing, you can deploy your resources efficiently to create variations of the marketing mix that fit only the most attractive market subsets. For instance, the bookstore chain Barnes & Noble has 750,000 customers in its database, but it can identify some segments that are as small as several hundred customers. The company can promote specific selections of books to various segments based on their interests and buying habits.[3] The result is more efficient marketing, which saves money and increases sales.

• *Better understanding of customer needs.* It's difficult to try to understand customer needs in a large and diffuse market. Through market segmentation, you divide your markets into segments whose needs are easier to define. Then you can gear your efforts to satisfy those needs (see Exhibit 7.2). In Michigan, the East Lansing State Bank knows that students care very much about the cost of their checking accounts. Thus, the bank designed an account that lets students write up to five checks for a low service charge of $1 per month. If a student goes to a teller window to transact business, this costs 50 cents every time; tellers are an expensive resource for the bank. On the other hand, students aren't charged for using an automated teller machine because that is less costly for the bank. By fo-

**Exhibit 7.1**
**MASS MARKETING AND MARKETING SEGMENTATION**
These GM ads demonstrate the choice between aiming at a mass market (most consumers would like to earn 5 percent on a new car or truck) and aiming at a segment of the market ("Get an Edge" will catch the eye of people who are into outdoor action and adventure).

**Exhibit 7.2**
**FOCUSING ON MARKET SEGMENTS**
In its attempt to move past Nintendo in the video game market, Sega is focusing much of its efforts on older, hipper consumers.

# CAN MARKET SEGMENTATION BE HAZARDOUS TO YOUR HEALTH?

Cigarette manufacturers face some tough marketing challenges. They cannot advertise on television, and they must include health warnings in every advertisement and on every package. Moreover, the antismoking movement in the United States gets stronger every day. To get ahead in the $36 billion industry, the tobacco companies have increasingly turned to market segmentation as a way of reaching people who smoke. However, market segmentation is now under fire as cigarette marketers are accused of unethical behavior.

R. J. Reynolds Tobacco is a case in point. Late in 1988, RJR found that its Salem menthol brand was losing market share to competitor Lorillard's Newport, with its milder menthol taste. Salem was RJR's best-selling brand among African-Americans, and the company was concerned because African-American smokers are considered a particularly important market: African-Americans are dropping the smoking habit at a slower rate than whites. RJR decided to stop the defections by developing a lighter menthol cigarette, to be called Uptown. By early 1990, the company was ready to test market the new brand and made the decision to test market Uptown exclusively among African-American smokers. Internally, RJR faced an ethical dilemma: Should the company come out and say the brand was aimed at African-Americans, or should it be more subtle? Because RJR didn't want to be accused of deception, it decided to take the straightforward approach, and it scheduled Uptown for test marketing in Philadelphia, expecting some controversy.

Before the brand even made it to test marketing, critics took issue with the targeting. First, African-American community leaders spoke out; then, during a speech at the University of Pennsylvania, Health and Human Services Secretary Louis W. Sullivan de-

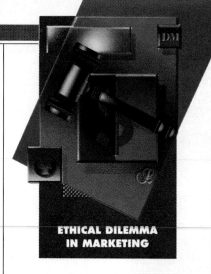

**ETHICAL DILEMMA IN MARKETING**

nounced RJR for "promoting a culture of cancer" among African-Americans. "Uptown's message is more disease, more suffering and more death for a group already bearing more than its share of smoking-related illness and mortality," Sullivan told the audience. The very next day, RJR canceled Uptown's test marketing, and Peter Hoult, executive vice president for marketing, told reporters, "This represents a loss of choice for black smokers and a further erosion of the free enterprise system."

Targeting African-American smokers as part of an overall strategy that also includes whites is nothing new. Cigarette marketers have wooed African-Americans using outdoor signs in African-American neighborhoods, ads in magazines of special interest to African-Americans, and sponsorship of African-American cultural events. However, Uptown provoked charges of unethical behavior because it was the first time a manufacturer had aimed a brand specifically at African-Americans, who are more likely to smoke than whites. Whereas about 29 percent of all American adults smoke, among African-Americans the proportion of smokers is above 34 percent. The higher smoking rate is a major reason that African-Americans experience "higher rates of lung cancer, other cancers, heart disease and stroke, compared with whites," Sullivan wrote in a letter to RJR.

Although RJR withdrew Uptown, it was back in the news a month later with a new cigarette, Dakota, its answer to rival Philip Morris's Marlboro, the top brand in the world. Ac-

cording to published reports, RJR originally planned to target Dakota to a market segment of blue-collar women 18 to 24 years of age with only a high school diploma, who tend to be Marlboro smokers. Once again, critics cried foul, because lung cancer has become the leading cause of death among women as a result of increased smoking. Also, opponents were concerned that underage smokers would be attracted.

RJR denied that young women were Dakota's current target, saying the strategy had been broadened to include men and women over 18 who smoke Marlboros. Despite protests from local health groups, Dakota entered its test markets in Houston and Nashville on schedule, and the company started a newspaper ad campaign geared specifically to the interests of each regional market. In Nashville, the ads referred to gracious hospitality and steel guitars; in Houston, ads touted wide-open spaces and great barbecues. In both test markets, the first ads featured only men.

The House Subcommittee on Transportation and Hazardous Materials has begun looking into how cigarette marketers use segmentation, calling for legislation to protect certain groups from cigarette advertising. The Association of National Advertisers, a trade group that represents 80 percent of American national and regional advertisers, is fighting the move. The ANA says that banning target marketing would amount to censorship and would violate advertisers' constitutional rights under the First Amendment. As long as cigarette smoking is legal—as long as cigarette marketing is legal—the controversy will continue to smolder.

## WHAT'S YOUR OPINION?

**1.** How narrowly should cigarette marketers such as RJR be allowed to target their segments?

**2.** Is it unethical to base segmentation on unhealthful behavior, regardless of the product involved?

cusing on the student segment, East Lansing State Bank was better able to understand student needs and design a package of benefits and services that fulfill those needs.[4]

- *Better understanding of the competitive situation.* Marketers who target individual marketing segments can see more clearly who their competitors are and the tactics each uses in that segment. For instance, Family Dollar is a retailer based in North Carolina that targets the low-income shopper. Only a few retailers are in this segment: Dollar General Corporation and Stuarts Department Stores are competitors. Kmart was once also a competitor, but it has since changed its strategy and now targets more affluent customers by offering more upscale products. So Family Dollar is no longer competing directly with Kmart. Family Dollar is able to watch its few competitors and compete successfully because it understands the needs of this segment.[5]
- *Accurate measurement of goals and performance.* By defining your marketing goals segment by segment, you'll be able to measure your performance more precisely. For instance, if you manage a recording company and define separate segments for rap, grunge, blues, classical, and other musical styles, it'll be easier to see how you're doing relative to each of your competitors.

Again, not all marketers should use target marketing, but when it makes sense, the payoff can be considerable. The following section explores the first step, identifying market segments.

# IDENTIFYING MARKET SEGMENTS

**Market segmentation** is the process of dividing a large market into smaller segments of consumers or organizations that are similar in characteristics, behavior, wants, or needs. Each of these marketing segments can then be targeted using variations of the marketing mix. McDonald's doesn't see just one big market for its fast-food restaurants. Yes, everyone has to eat, but McDonald's knows that not everyone eats at McDonald's, and not everyone who eats there does so for the same reason. For children, the reason may be the prize in the Happy Meal box. For young adults, the reason may be the grand prize in the latest contest. For families, the reason may be the convenience of eating out. On the other hand, health-food fans and vegetarians might find little reason to eat at McDonald's, so any time and money spent on marketing to these segments will probably be wasted.

Market segmentation allows a marketer to take a **heterogeneous market,** a market consisting of customers with diverse characteristics, needs, wants, and behavior, and carve it up into one or more **homogeneous markets,** which are made up of individuals or organizations with similar needs, wants, and behavioral tendencies. For example, Porsche doesn't try to market its cars to every driver in the United States. In producing a recent direct-mail promotion, it analyzed the 80 million car-owning households in this country and identified the small group of people whose incomes and lifestyles made them most likely to purchase a Porsche.[6] Were you among the lucky 300,000 who received an invitation for a test drive?

Segmentation involves more than just thinking up a segment to target. The point of using market segmentation is to end up with segments in which marketing can be conducted more efficiently and effectively. However, if the segments don't deliver on this promise, then the market segmentation is not meaningful. Here are some important areas to consider when evaluating whether a segment will be meaningful:

- *Definition.* Sometimes a marketer tries to define a market segment so narrowly that it's not practical to actually track down members of that segment. For instance, how would you put together a market of women who are shorter than average and wear taupe pantyhose only when they have a tan? Because that market can't really be found, the definition is not meaningful for market segmentation.

**market segmentation**
A way of dividing a large market into smaller groupings of consumers or organizations in which each subset has a common characteristic such as needs, wants, or behavior

**heterogeneous market**
A market in which people or organizations have differing characteristics

**homogeneous market**
A market in which people or organizations have similar characteristics

Marketers must also be sure that the defined segments are themselves homogeneous while being different from each other. You might define your pantyhose market for women who are shorter than average by using specific heights, so that women under 5 feet tall would compose one marketing segment and women 5 feet to 5 feet 3 inches would make up another. In this way, separate variations of the marketing mix can be used to appeal to each segment.

- *Sales potential.* Say that you could define a segment of shorter-than-average women who wear taupe pantyhose only when they have a tan, and say you found 250 women in the segment. Even if your pantyhose sold for $100 per pair, it probably wouldn't be profitable to market only to this segment. However, measuring the sales potential of a segment is relative. The sports drink segment is only one-eightieth of the entire soft drink industry, and Coca-Cola's PowerAde brand, its answer to Gatorade, aims for a piece of that tiny segment. Small it may be, but the sports drink segment swallows $500 million in sales each year, compared with $40 billion in sales for all soft drinks. Clearly, Coca-Cola thinks this segment is big enough to justify some marketing muscle.[7]

- *Accessibility.* A segment is meaningful only if it can be reached with a marketing program. Say you've discovered that students who prefer colleges with modern architecture are more likely to buy your product than students who prefer a more classical-looking campus. That's great—but how will you ever reach just those students? On the other hand, if you've discovered that students who live in states east of the Mississippi are more likely to buy your product, it's easy to reach these customers. You simply sort your addresses by state and toss out all the names living on the west side of the river.

- *Response.* Marketers spending money to find and reach segments are interested in how these segments will respond. For instance, the American Savings & Loan Association of California targeted senior citizens with a seniors club and other special benefits; then it created television, print, and direct-mail advertising to reach the segment. The segment responded: The bank received $30 million in new accounts in a single day after airing one 30-second television commercial featuring seniors. However, when a baby-food manufacturer tried marketing "adult baby food" for seniors who wear dentures, the segment didn't respond. Seniors just didn't want to be seen buying food that announces their denture wearing to the world.[8]

## Segmentation in Consumer Markets

As you saw earlier, Kellogg reaches out to a large and diverse group of consumers, but even this huge company organizes its marketing efforts according to segments defined by specific variables. These include geographic, demographic, psychographic, geodemographic, and behavioral variables. In many cases, marketers use more than one type of segmentation (geodemographics is in fact a multivariable approach).

### GEOGRAPHIC SEGMENTATION

**geographic segmentation**
A way to separate large markets into smaller groupings according to country, region, state, city, community, or block divisions

When marketers define their segments according to where they will market, they are using **geographic segmentation.** With geographic segmentation, you can identify one or more countries, regions, states, cities, communities, even individual blocks, to divide the consumer market into meaningful subsets. Marketers consider a wide variety of elements when they use geographic segmentation. Population patterns, transportation, climate, growth patterns, and government are just a few examples. These elements are important because they influence and sometimes dictate the marketing mix for a given geographical area. You wouldn't market snowblowers in Key West, just as you wouldn't market surfboards in Kansas City. Also, consumers in some countries have a preference for one type of product over another, as Whirlpool discovered when it set out to market washing machines in Europe. The French use mostly top-loading washers; other Europeans use mostly front-loaders. So Whirlpool had to match its product to the tastes of consumers in each country.[9] Geographic variables can help you segment your market into groupings of areas that have a need for your product and groupings that have no need for your product.

Geographic segmentation can also be used in other ways. Campbell Soup uses geographic segmentation to divide the country into 22 regions so that it can consider the taste buds of each region separately. Because western and southwestern palates crave spicier foods, Campbell puts many more jalapeño peppers into the nacho cheese soup it markets in these regions. Chrysler also uses geographic segmentation but hasn't always been successful. When the automotive manufacturer introduced its California K car in the early 1980s, it targeted California buyers by adding pinstripes and special paint. The product sold poorly because Chrysler had incorrectly assumed that Californians cared more about appearance than performance. A few years later, Chrysler created another model specifically for the California market: the Dodge Lancer Pacifica, which included a better suspension system and a higher-quality radio. This time, the car took off, selling well over forecasted numbers in the first six months.[10]

Often, geographic areas cannot be defined by state or city lines or other boundaries. For example, New York City is separate from its suburbs of Long Island and Westchester and from nearby Connecticut and New Jersey. Yet the city is tied, economically and socially, to these neighboring regions. Therefore, the city and its surrounding areas are generally referred to as the *New York metropolitan area*. The U.S. Bureau of the Census first set up formal guidelines for defining metropolitan areas in 1949, and the definitions are used to help track and analyze regional population trends. Because these standardized definitions are used in a wide range of marketing situations, from buying advertising space to hunting for secondary research about consumer buying patterns, it's important to understand what they represent. Since 1983 the bureau's three standard definitions have been the metropolitan statistical area, the primary metropolitan statistical area, and the consolidated metropolitan statistical area. Exhibit 7.3 shows examples of these census areas in the state of Texas, and here's a quick look at their definitions:

**Exhibit 7.3**
**EXAMPLES OF METROPOLITAN AREAS**
This map of Texas shows that state's MSAs, PMSAs, and CMSAs. For companies targeting urban consumer markets in Texas, these population areas make more sense than city boundaries.

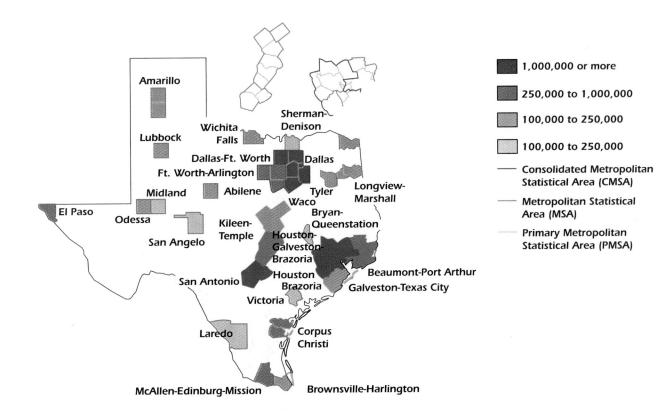

■ 1,000,000 or more

■ 250,000 to 1,000,000

■ 100,000 to 250,000

□ 100,000 to 250,000

— Consolidated Metropolitan Statistical Area (CMSA)

— Metropolitan Statistical Area (MSA)

— Primary Metropolitan Statistical Area (PMSA)

- *Metropolitan statistical areas (MSAs)* are geographic areas containing at least one city of 50,000 or more inhabitants *or* an urbanized area of at least 50,000 inhabitants, *and* a total population of 100,000 or more (75,000 in New England). For example, all of Midland County in Texas (including the city of Midland) is defined as the Midland, Texas, MSA. More than 77 percent of the U.S. population was living within an MSA in 1989, although only 16.3 percent of the country's land area was considered part of an MSA that year.[11]
- *Primary metropolitan statistical areas (PMSAs)* are metropolitan areas that have 1 million or more residents or are part of a CMSA. The Seattle, Washington, PMSA consists of all of King County and all of Snohomish County, for a total of 1.86 million residents.[12]
- *Consolidated metropolitan statistical areas (CMSAs)* are geographic areas containing more than one PMSA. The Milwaukee-Racine, Wisconsin, CMSA consists of the Milwaukee PMSA (which includes four counties and a population of 1.4 million) and the Racine MSA (with one county and a population of 174,000). There are 267 MSAs, 73 PMSAs, and 21 CMSAs in the United States.[13]

International marketing is an obvious point to consider when discussing geographic segmentation. If it makes sense to consider Midland and Seattle as separate markets, it probably makes sense to consider Paris and Lyon, France, as separate markets or France and Germany as separate markets. Of course, it's not as simple as basic geography, as you'll see in the discussion of international marketing in Chapter 20. The fundamental segmentation issue in international marketing is whether to treat each country or each region of the world as a distinct segment or treat the world as one giant market. Opinion is divided, with marketers such as M&M/Mars, Coca-Cola, and Holiday Inn treating the world as one giant market (with obvious adaptations such as language), while other marketers treat each country as a distinct segment.

## DEMOGRAPHIC SEGMENTATION VARIABLES

**demographic segmentation**
A way to divide large markets into smaller groupings according to the elements of size, composition, and distribution of the population

Marketers use **demographic segmentation** when they market on the basis of information about the size, composition, and distribution of a population, including age, sex, race, religion, national origin, family size, marital status, occupation, social class, income, and education. You could, for example, segment the market for young women's lipstick by using demographic variables such as sex (female) and age (13–19). Information about demographic variables is generally available to marketers through government studies and other sources, making demographic segmentation a practical way of looking at the market. Many products can be naturally and realistically targeted for segments defined by demographic variables. Of course, people are moving targets whose demographics are constantly changing, and it's important to keep up with these changes. Ideally, you would forecast any changes in an effort to be ready with marketing mixes that fit the demographic trends of today and tomorrow. The household life cycle (see Chapter 4) shows the sequence of events in adult lives starting with the unmarried stage and moving through such stages as marriage, children, divorce, and remarriage. Marketers can target specific needs that customarily arise in each stage of the family life cycle, from wedding invitations to diapers to legal advice to college loans. Kodak's "life stages" strategy aims products and promotions at the youth, new-parent, and senior segments.[14]

Would you treat Switzerland as part of one global market, or as its own segment? What about the four language divisions in Switzerland (German, French, Italian, and Romansh)— should each of these be a market segment as well?

Who uses demographic segmentation? Kellogg, you will remember, found that the number of school-age children was shrinking, threatening the cereal giant's traditional market for packaged cereals. By studying the population shift toward people 25 and older, Kellogg was able to target new cereals to adults. And Kellogg isn't the only marketer using age to segment the market. The First Women's Bank has a division called The First Children's Bank (inside New York City's upscale FAO Schwarz toy store), offering bank accounts to youngsters. Teens are the exclusive target of Dallas-based Gadzooks, a retail chain selling fashion clothing for young men and women. Even colleges are using marketing techniques because of the drop in the number of children approaching college age. In fact, the fastest-growing segments in the college market are people over 25 and women. Therefore, Adelphi University in New York offers "Adelphi-On-Wheels," an outreach program of business courses taught on commuter trains. Age is a factor in the segmentation strategies of Levi Strauss, which uses men around 40 in commercials for its Dockers line of apparel, and of Denny's restaurant chain, which targets people over 55 with specially selected menus and prices.[15]

Demographic segmentation also involves looking at the American melting pot, which holds a changing group of people; the number of Asian-Americans, Hispanic-Americans, and African-Americans in the United States has increased significantly since 1980. Asian-Americans now make up 3 percent of the population; Hispanic-Americans, 8 percent; and African-Americans, 12 percent. Toyota has targeted African-American car buyers. The manufacturer sponsors a leadership award for African-American athletes and joined hair products marketer Soft Sheen for the Sportin' Waves Toyota MR2 Sweepstakes, in which five cars were given away. Coca-Cola, Domino's Pizza, Burger King, 7-Eleven, and Mazola are just some of the firms taking aim at the growing Hispanic population in America. American Express has featured prominent Hispanic-Americans in its Miami media campaigns, and Citibank is targeting several segments by fitting its New York City automated teller machines with software that permits the user to choose instructions in English, Spanish, or Chinese.[16]

Demographic segmentation variables are put to use in international marketing as well, whether it's understanding a particular country or comparing two or more countries. Say that you're looking for future growth markets in Europe. Demographic data will tell you that the population of Turkey will double in the next 30 years or so, while the population of France won't double for more than 150 years. Similarly, comparative demographic data will tell you that the average Austrian is roughly seven times richer than the average Hungarian, which may indicate that Austrians have more money to spend on consumer goods or that Hungarians are more likely to emigrate to Austria than vice versa.[17]

## PSYCHOGRAPHIC SEGMENTATION VARIABLES

Marketers use **psychographic segmentation** when they divide their markets according to lifestyles, activities, opinions, and beliefs, seeking to group people with similar lifestyles or interests. Kellogg used psychographics to tap into the health-conscious market segment and launch Nutri-Grain and All-Bran. It also used psychographics to find a segment that would respond to its European-style packaged cereal Müeslix. In Canada, food-distributing giant Loblaw targets issue-conscious consumers with its Nature's Choice line of foods and household products. For example, its gardening products, endorsed by a Canadian environmental group, are aimed at the market segment interested in reducing pollution. Nature's Choice baking soda is a case of an old product in a new segment. It's not just for baking anymore; Loblaw is aiming the baking soda at the segment interested in an environmentally safe cleanser. As concern for the environment grows throughout the 1990s, psychographic segmentation to reach consumers interested in this area will become an important tool for more marketers.[18]

Some products get more mileage from psychographic segmentation than other products. The type of car you buy expresses your lifestyle more than, say, the brand of toothpaste you use. However, psychographics is also a moving target, so marketers need to stay abreast of the rapid changes. At one time, owning a personal computer implied a certain status, but today personal computers are so commonplace they no longer convey the status they once did. The winds of psychographic change convinced the editors of *Apartment Life* to move away from a focus on alternative home furnishings and toward more stylish interior design features. In fact, the magazine changed its name to *Metropolitan Home* because most readers no longer rented but owned their residences.[19]

A number of researchers and organizations have developed systems for lifestyle

**psychographic segmentation**
A way of dividing large markets into smaller groupings according to consumer lifestyles, activities, opinions, and beliefs

segmentation. VALS 2 (values and lifestyles), developed by the Stanford Research Institute, attempts to profile consumers by grouping them into three "self-orientation" categories (depending on whether they're motivated primarily by principles, status, or action) and splitting these three categories again according to the resources (money, physical assets, and so on) the people have at their disposal (see Exhibit 7.4). This creates six lifestyle segments, plus special segments at the top and bottom of the resource spectrum. The *actualizers* at the top have enough resources to indulge in any of the self-orientations (for instance, an actualizer would have the time and money to get involved in politics or go on an African safari). The *strugglers,* by contrast, are so urgently focused on immediate health and safety needs that self-orientation options don't really apply.[20]

A typical application of the VALS 2 model, combined with product usage data from another research supplier, showed that actualizers are heavy users of ibuprofin pain relievers but that Nuprin has relatively low sales to this lifestyle segment. If you were Nuprin's advertising agency, your next step would be to devise an improved message to do a better job of reaching this important segment.[21] Keep in

**Exhibit 7.4
SEGMENTING BY
LIFESTYLE**
The VALS 2 system is a well-known model for segmenting consumers according to lifestyle.

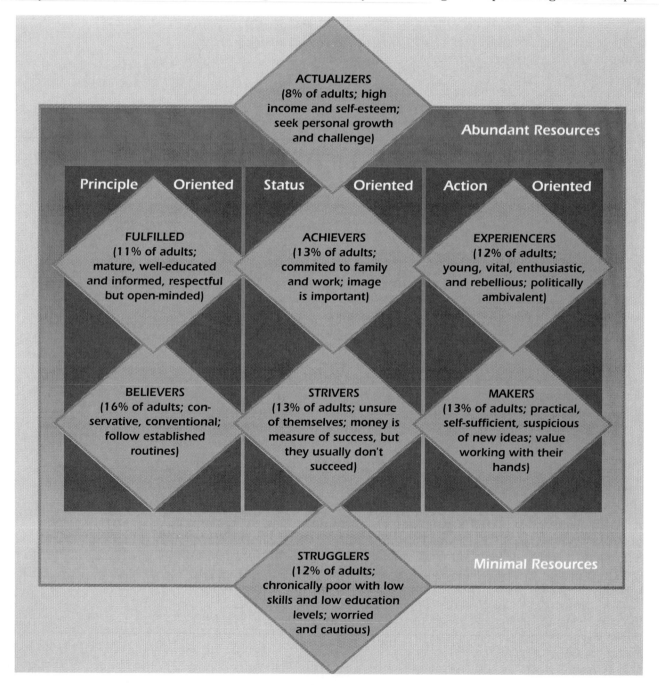

ACTUALIZERS
(8% of adults; high income and self-esteem; seek personal growth and challenge)

Abundant Resources

Principle Oriented    Status Oriented    Action Oriented

FULFILLED
(11% of adults; mature, well-educated and informed, respectful but open-minded)

ACHIEVERS
(13% of adults; commited to family and work; image is important)

EXPERIENCERS
(12% of adults; young, vital, enthusiastic, and rebellious; politically ambivalent)

BELIEVERS
(16% of adults; conservative, conventional; follow established routines)

STRIVERS
(13% of adults; unsure of themselves; money is measure of success, but they usually don't succeed)

MAKERS
(13% of adults; practical, self-sufficient, suspicious of new ideas; value working with their hands)

STRUGGLERS
(12% of adults; chronically poor with low skills and low education levels; worried and cautious)

Minimal Resources

mind that VALS 2 and other segmentations are models, and as such are simplified views of reality. VALS 2 doesn't claim to encompass every type of consumer or to be applicable to every product. The variety of segmentation programs is growing as marketers increasingly turn to psychographic variables as a powerful way to segment their markets.[22]

## GEODEMOGRAPHIC SEGMENTATION

By combining data from the first two consumer segmentation methods, marketers can produce results that look similar to those of the third segmentation method. **Geodemographic segmentation** averages demographic data inside geographic segments. The resulting profiles, which are at the neighborhood level, can be remarkably accurate predictors of values and lifestyles. The demographic data in each geographic segment are usually enhanced with survey data covering purchase behavior, media choices, attitudes, opinions, and other psychographic variables. Even though the results often look like psychographic segmentation, geodemographic segments are defined primarily by demographic data that are organized geographically.[23]

**geodemographic segmentation**
A segmentation approach in which you average demographic data inside geographic segments; the resulting profiles can be remarkably accurate predictors of values and lifestyles

Geodemographic segmentation operates on the theory that people with similar demographic and psychographic profiles tend to live in clusters (in fact, geodemographic segmentation is often called "clustering"). Whether it's a rural area with scattered farmhouses or an urban center full of high-rise apartments, people within a given neighborhood usually share quite a few consumer characteristics. Researchers have found similar clusters spread across the country. As one investigator put it, except for the palm trees, Fairfield, Connecticut, and Pasadena, California, are really the same place.[24] In other words, consumers in Fairfield and Pasadena behave in much the same way and are more like each other than consumers in cluster types that are physically much closer.

The pioneering geodemographic system is the Potential Rating Index by Zip Markets (PRIZM) system developed by Claritas Corporation. It defines 40 neighborhood types that range from "Blue Blood Estates" (characterized by the nation's highest incomes, vacations in exotic locales, subscriptions to *Gourmet,* and so on) to "Public Assistance" (poor inner-city neighborhoods with poverty rates five times the national average).[25] In between are the 38 other neighborhood types, each defined by particular demographic and psychographic patterns. Exhibit 7.5 lists the clusters and shows the percentage of U.S. households living in each. In Phoenix, Arizona, for example, PRIZM labels ZIP code 85254 a "Furs & Station Wagons" cluster where residents tend to be country club members, read *Gourmet,* and vote Republican. In Revere Beach, Massachusetts, ZIP 02151 is called "Old Yankee Rows," where residents are inclined to drink beer, join fraternal clubs, and vote Democratic.

The National Symphony Orchestra in Washington recently profiled its subscribers, comparing the concert attendance patterns of the single adults common in "Money & Brains" neighborhoods with the attendance of the affluent suburban families in "Furs & Station Wagons" neighborhoods. The symphony discovered that four times as many "Money & Brains" residents attended concerts. The next promotional campaign focused on these "Money & Brains" neighborhoods, and subscriptions increased by 25 percent in some clusters.[26] (As you probably guessed, children are the key demographic difference between the two categories, making it harder for "Furs & Station Wagons" people to attend concerts.) Major companies using geodemographic systems include American Express, Time, General Motors, 3M, and Gannett.[27]

Clearly, not everyone in a "neighborhood" as large as a ZIP code area exhibits precisely the same lifestyle and consumption tendencies, but the averages that define PRIZM clusters have been extremely helpful for advertisers trying to pinpoint target markets for media selection, store location, and other marketing tasks. To get over the generalizations inherent in any average, some researchers recommend supplementing PRIZM-type segmentation with psychological studies that probe deeper into neighborhoods.[28]

**Exhibit 7.5   AMERICA'S 40 NEIGHBORHOOD TYPES**

| Cluster | Thumbnail Description | Percentage of U.S. Households |
|---|---|---|
| Blue Blood Estates | America's wealthiest neighborhoods, including suburban homes and one in ten millionaires | 1.1 |
| Money & Brains | Posh big-city enclaves of townhouses, condos, and apartments | 0.9 |
| Furs & Station Wagons | New money in metropolitan bedroom suburbs | 3.2 |
| Urban Gold Coast | Upscale urban high-rise districts | 0.5 |
| Pools & Patios | Older, upper-middle-class, suburban communities | 3.4 |
| Two More Rungs | Comfortable multiethnic suburbs | 0.7 |
| Young Influentials | Yuppie, fringe-city condo and apartment developments | 2.9 |
| Young Suburbia | Child-rearing, outlying suburbs | 5.3 |
| God's Country | Upscale frontier boomtowns | 2.7 |
| Blue-Chip Blues | The wealthiest blue-collar suburbs | 6.0 |
| Bohemian Mix | Inner-city bohemian enclaves à la Greenwich Village | 1.1 |
| Levittown, U.S.A. | Aging, post–World War II tract subdivisions | 3.1 |
| Gray Power | Upper-middle-class retirement communities | 2.9 |
| Black Enterprise | Predominantly black, middle- and upper-middle-class neighborhoods | 0.8 |
| New Beginnings | Fringe-city areas of singles complexes, garden apartments, and trim bungalows | 4.3 |
| Blue-Collar Nursery | Middle-class, child-rearing towns | 2.2 |
| New Homesteaders | Exurban boom towns of young, midscale families | 4.2 |
| New Melting Pot | New immigrant neighborhoods, primarily in the nation's port cities | 0.9 |
| Towns & Gowns | America's college towns | 1.2 |
| Rank & File | Older, blue-collar, industrial suburbs | 1.4 |
| Middle America | Midscale, midsize towns | 3.2 |
| Old Yankee Rows | Working-class rowhouse districts | 1.6 |
| Coalburg & Corntown | Small towns based on light industry and farming | 2.0 |
| Shotguns & Pickups | Crossroads villages serving the nation's lumber and breadbasket needs | 1.9 |
| Golden Ponds | Rustic cottage communities located near the coasts, in the mountains, or alongside lakes | 5.2 |
| Agribusiness | Small towns surrounded by large-scale farms and ranches | 2.1 |
| Emergent Minorities | Predominantly black, working-class, city neighborhoods | 1.7 |
| Single City Blues | Downscale, urban, singles districts | 3.3 |
| Mines & Mills | Struggling steeltowns and mining villages | 2.8 |
| Back-Country Folks | Remote downscale farm towns | 3.4 |
| Norma Rae-Ville | Lower-middle-class mill towns and industrial suburbs, primarily in the South | 2.3 |
| Smalltown Downtown | Inner-city districts of small industrial cities | 2.5 |
| Grain Belt | The nation's most sparsely populated rural communities | 1.3 |
| Heavy Industry | Lower-working-class districts in the nation's older industrial cities | 2.8 |
| Share Croppers | Primarily southern hamlets devoted to farming and light industry | 4.0 |
| Downtown Dixie Style | Aging, predominantly black neighborhoods, typically in southern cities | 3.4 |
| Hispanic Mix | America's Hispanic barrios | 1.9 |
| Tobacco Roads | Predominantly black farm communities throughout the South | 1.2 |
| Hard Scrabble | The nation's poorest rural settlements | 1.5 |
| Public Assistance | America's inner-city ghettos | 3.1 |

The Claritas Corporation uses these 40 neighborhood types to segment the entire United States.
(Household percentages are based on 1987 census block groups and estimated to the closest 0.1 percent.)

The United States isn't the only market in which researchers are applying geo-demographic segmentation. Marketers in the United Kingdom, for example, have been using geodemographics for a variety of target marketing efforts. The neigh-borhoods in U.K. geodemographic systems can be identified at the postcode (the British equivalent to a ZIP code) level, which is about 15 households on average, or at the census district level, which is about 150 households on average. Retail stores are among the most active users of geodemographics in the United Kingdom, us-ing the technique's ability to pinpoint customers for such key tasks as selecting store locations.[29]

## BEHAVIORAL SEGMENTATION

When marketers use people's behavior toward a product to segment the market, they are practicing **behavioral segmentation.** Behavioral variables include prod-uct usage, consumer needs for certain benefits, price sensitivity, brand loyalty, and other characteristics. For example, sports equipment manufacturers can apply us-age elements of behavioral segmentation to cut three broad paths in the market: people who will use equipment, people who might use it, and people who will never use it. Each of these broad segments has subsegments that are identified by the de-gree of usage and additional subsegments that are keyed to the individual sport. None of these segments could be identified by psychographic, demographic, or geographic segmentation because consumer behavior is not measured by those variables.[30]

**behavioral segmentation**
A way of dividing large mar-kets into smaller groupings according to consumer be-havior

Brand loyalty and usage have become strategic weapons in the cola wars. Royal Crown Cola, a distant third in the cola market behind first-place Coke and second-place Pepsi, has shifted its market segmentation to concentrate on young adults, even though teens are the heaviest cola chuggers. Royal Crown thinks the cola in-dustry's frequent price promotions have undermined brand loyalty and believes a growing number of people are now willing to switch brands. The company found that the heaviest concentration of brand switchers is in the segment of adults aged 18 to 34, so that's where RC is putting its advertising dollars in a campaign to en-tice switchers to try RC. Also, this strategy helps RC sidestep the teen market bat-tleground where Coca-Cola and PepsiCo slug it out using expensive advertising and promotion.[31] Although usage is very important, and marketers need to target seg-ments that will use their products, too often the segment with the heaviest usage is also the segment that gets the most attention from competing firms.

**Benefit segmentation** is a type of behavioral segmentation in which the mar-keter divides the market according to the benefits consumers seek from a product or product category. Some researchers say that benefit segmentation variables de-termine consumer behavior more accurately than demographic or usage segmen-tation variables; the benefits that people seek are the real basis for their response to a product. For example, research conducted by Colgate-Palmolive identified three distinct segments in the bar soap market. The first was men who wanted a lightly fragrant soap, the second was women who wanted a gentle soap that also had a mild fragrance, and the third was mostly men who wanted a strong fragrance with re-freshing deodorant capabilities. The company's Irish Spring brand was selling well in the third segment, but the marketers involved thought there might be an oppor-tunity to appeal to the second segment as well. To pursue this opportunity, they re-formulated the product and changed their ads to stress a family appeal that reached out to both men and women.[32]

**benefit segmentation**
A form of behavioral segmen-tation that divides the market according to benefits sought by consumers

## Segmentation in Organizational Markets

Organizational marketers often face many of the same challenges that consumer marketers face, including a large and diffuse market with diverse needs. By aiming at specific market segments and fulfilling their needs, organizational marketers can gain the benefits of market segmentation mentioned earlier. The goal of organiza-

## COURTING AFRICAN-AMERICAN UNDERGRADS

For 120 years, Morgan State has been a cultural and educational beacon in Baltimore, providing a quality college education to thousands of African-American students. Morgan earned a reputation for preparing students for graduate and professional schools and for graduating dozens of athletes who became professional sports stars. One of America's 100 African-American colleges and universities, Morgan had, at its peak, 6,000 undergrads. But during the 1970s, white universities began to compete for the same target market—African-American students—and Morgan found that its traditional strengths weren't enough to meet this new challenge.

The integrated University of Maryland in College Park was attracting African-American scholars and African-American athletes, two student groups that Morgan customarily wooed. State legislators supported the integrated schools, so the African-American college received less state funding, which in turn meant that Morgan couldn't afford to keep its campus or its buildings in tip-top shape. Even the college teams, once a source of intense pride, suffered as opponents triumphed over Morgan's weaker rosters.

By the time Earl S. Richardson be-

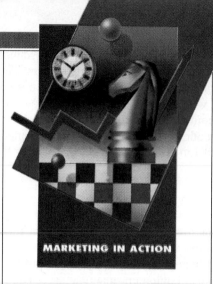

**MARKETING IN ACTION**

came president in 1985, enrollment had dropped to 3,300. He found the school in a state of physical neglect and almost immediately began to lobby the legislature for additional funding. Although Dr. Richardson's plan included a multimillion-dollar program to rebuild the university, he knew that sprucing up the campus wasn't enough. He revitalized the academic side as well, installing a new honors program with enriched courses for the top 10 percent of the freshman class. To appeal to students who were profession-bound, Dr. Richardson also beefed up the school's business, engineering, and computer science resources.

The next step was mounting a new marketing program to reach out to the target market segment, and for this, Dr. Richardson turned to alumni: "I say to our alumni, either give us your money or your influence." So

pop singer Deniece Williams, a Morgan graduate, has appeared on campus, generating media coverage. Joe Black, a Morgan alum who had pitched for the Brooklyn Dodgers, asked his friend Bill Cosby to lend a hand. Cosby responded by appearing on his television show one week in a Morgan T-shirt. The publisher of *Black Enterprise* magazine, Earl Graves, class of 1958, stars in Morgan's student recruiting videotape, *Success Begins at Morgan.*

African-American colleges have now turned the trend around and are gaining ground. Other African-American public universities, such as Tennessee State in Nashville and Norfolk State in Virginia, have seen enrollments stabilize. At Morgan, enrollment is up to 3,900 and expected to go even higher. Dr. Richardson's new marketing approach is aggressive, but he knows that's the only way Morgan State will succeed in today's competitive market.

### APPLY YOUR KNOWLEDGE

**1.** If you were recruiting freshmen for Morgan State, which segments of the African-American high school student population would you target? Why?

**2.** What risks do you see in the student segments you selected in question 1?

---

tional segmentation is the same as the goal for consumer segmentation: to identify homogeneous market segments with similar needs, wants, and response characteristics. The three major segmentation methods involve geographic, demographic, and operational variables.

## GEOGRAPHIC SEGMENTATION

In the same way that consumer marketers select market segments according to where consumers are located, organizational marketers select market segments according to where customers are located, do business, or are concentrated. For example, a wood finish marketer who sells to furniture manufacturers in the United States would find that many are clustered in the Southeast. A marketer selling industrial sewing machines would find many clothing manufacturers in the garment district in New York City. An electronic cash register manufacturer would find many retailers located in shopping centers across the country.

Organizational marketers must also consider their distribution strategy when they use geographic segmentation. If your company uses personal selling and installation (as it might when offering a complex, expensive product such as a copying machine), then you might want to target only specific geographic areas in which you have sales and installation coverage. However, if buyers use a catalog or price list to call in their orders, then you would be able to target a broader geographic area.[33] The U.S. Bureau of the Census publishes volumes of statistics about various industries and the trends in various locations. These reports provide data for the entire country and often provide detailed data for states, MSAs, counties, and cities. Organizational marketers can thus use the standard government geographic definitions as well as traditional geographic boundaries to segment their markets.

## DEMOGRAPHIC SEGMENTATION

Organizational marketers use a variety of demographic segmentation variables, including sales revenues of the business, number of employees, age of the business, and type of business. (Exhibit 7.6 compares a sampling of the types of variables used to segment organizational markets and those used to segment consumer markets.) One of the most common is a categorization scheme established by the U.S. government. The **Standard Industrial Classification (SIC)** system assigns codes to industries based on various product categories, as seen in Exhibit 7.7. SIC codes have anywhere from two to seven digits, although four is the most commonly used arrangement. The value of the SIC system is that it gives you an easy way to find organizational customers.

**Standard Industrial Classification (SIC)**
A system devised by the U.S. government that assigns codes to industries based on various product categories

**Exhibit 7.6   A SAMPLE OF BUSINESS DEMOGRAPHICS COMPARED WITH CONSUMER DEMOGRAPHICS**

| Category | Business Demographics | Consumer Demographics |
|---|---|---|
| Market size | Number of potential customers<br>Number of stores/locations/ plants for a firm<br>Number of employees in a company | Population<br>Number of households or families<br>Family or household size |
| Age and stage | Number of years firm has been in business<br>Stage of product/industry life cycle firm is in | Age distribution<br>Family life cycle |
| Monetary factors | Financial factors (revenues sales volume, profits)<br>Type of business (products and services)<br>Management style/structure | Income<br>Occupation<br>Education |
| Ownership factors | Own building/property vs. lease<br>Type of establishment (storefront, office, plant, warehouse)<br>Length of time at facility | Homeowner vs. renter<br>Type of dwelling<br>Household mobility/ stability |
| Social class (Industry stature) | Market/Industry position | Lower-lower to upper-upper<br>Cluster approach |

When segmenting industrial markets, organizational marketers use business demographics that are somewhat different from consumer demographics.

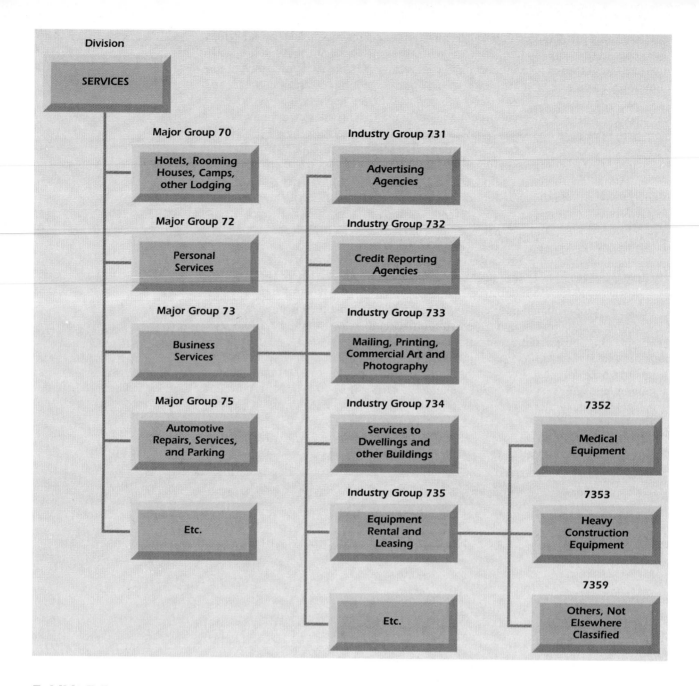

Division

SERVICES

Major Group 70

Hotels, Rooming Houses, Camps, other Lodging

Major Group 72

Personal Services

Major Group 73

Business Services

Major Group 75

Automotive Repairs, Services, and Parking

Etc.

Industry Group 731

Advertising Agencies

Industry Group 732

Credit Reporting Agencies

Industry Group 733

Mailing, Printing, Commercial Art and Photography

Industry Group 734

Services to Dwellings and other Buildings

Industry Group 735

Equipment Rental and Leasing

Etc.

7352

Medical Equipment

7353

Heavy Construction Equipment

7359

Others, Not Elsewhere Classified

**Exhibit 7.7**
**THE STANDARD INDUSTRIAL CLASSIFICATION CODES**

The SIC system categorizes organizations at several levels; this example shows the three company groups (7352, 7353, and 7359) that make up Industry Group 735 (equipment rental and leasing), which is part of Major Group 73 (business services), which is part of Division I (services).

The SIC system is used extensively in government and business publications as a basis for organizing data about companies. Among the publications that use this system are the federal government's *Census of Business, Census of Manufacturers,* and *County Business Patterns,* along with Dun & Bradstreet's *Market Identifiers,* Standard & Poor's *Register,* and *Sales & Marketing Management's Survey of Industrial and Commercial Buying Power.* These references help marketers target potential organizational buyers by indicating the locations and sizes of industrial firms, the rate of growth in particular industries, major producing areas for specific products, and so on. For example, a marketer wanting to reach the hotel, and motel industry in Arizona would find listings of potential clients under SIC code 701 in the *County Business Patterns* volume for that state. In addition, the previously mentioned mailing lists (bought or rented from various companies) can also be sorted by ZIP codes, making it easy to pinpoint target businesses in specific geographic areas.

The SIC system is not an ideal solution for all marketers, however. To begin with, SIC categories are only updated every 10 or 15 years (the last update was in 1987), so they aren't always recent enough to suit marketers in certain industries. This is an acute problem in dynamic high-technology industries, which can be transformed in just a few years. Second, some classifications include too many types of businesses, making it difficult to pinpoint segments precisely.[34] Third, each company is assigned one SIC code, even though many companies are engaged in numerous and diverse business activities. This can be misleading when you're dealing with a company such as General Electric, which is involved in broadcasting (it owns NBC), medical equipment, aircraft engines, semiconductors, light bulbs, plastics, and a variety of other businesses. Any company that has more than one strategic business unit is likely to present this problem. Finally, only U.S. companies are classified under the SIC system, so it can't help with international marketing.

To overcome these difficulties, some private companies have developed their own classification schemes. The directories published by CorpTech, for instance, define markets with much greater detail than the SIC system. As you can see from Exhibit 7.8, directories like this get into fine detail. These directories are updated frequently to keep track of new industries and new companies. CorpTech also provides information on each business unit of the companies it profiles, giving precise marketing targets. Also, depending on the country and the industry, various directories are available for marketers to use when analyzing international markets. Two examples are the *Japan Trade Journal* and the *International Electronics Directory: Guide to European Manufacturers, Agents, and Applications.*

## OPERATIONAL SEGMENTATION

Operational segmentation variables help define customers based on such attributes as organization type, power structure, customer capabilities, and purchasing policies. Many large commercial banks, for example, segment according to the way their target market businesses are organized. For segments consisting of large firms with centralized finance and banking functions, the bank assigns a national account team to handle the business. For segments with local firms or firms having decentralized finance and banking functions, the bank assigns a regional account team or

### Exhibit 7.8 ALTERNATIVES TO THE SIC SYSTEM

| CorpTech Code | Technology/Product | SIC Code |
| --- | --- | --- |
| AUT-RO-R | Robots | 3569 |
| AUT-RO-RA | Autonomous robots | 3569 |
| AUT-RO-RB | Bang-bang robots | 3569 |
| AUT-RO-RC | Continuous path robots | 3569 |
| AUT-RO-RD | Controlled path robots | 3569 |
| AUT-RO-RE | Supervisory controlled robots | 3569 |
| AUT-RO-RF | Pedestal robots | 3569 |
| AUT-RO-RG | Gantry robots | 3569 |
| AUT-RO-RI | Robots for specific applications | 3569 |
| AUT-RO-RJ | SCARA robots | 3569 |
| AUT-RO-RK | Sensory controlled robots | 3569 |
| AUT-RO-RL | Pick & place robots | 3569 |
| AUT-RO-RM | Servo robots | 3569 |
| AUT-RO-RN | Space robots | 3569 |
| AUT-RO-RO | Cylindrical motion robots | 3569 |
| AUT-RO-RP | Point-to-point robots | 3569 |
| AUT-RO-QR | Cartesian robots | 3569 |
| AUT-RO-RR | Rectilinear robots | 3569 |
| AUT-RO-SR | Spherical coordinate robots | 3569 |
| AUT-RO-RT | Teleoperator robots | 3569 |
| AUT-RO-XR | Record-playback robots | 3569 |
| AUT-RO-RZ | Other robots | 3569 |

SIC codes do not provide adequate detail for segmenting many high-technology markets. For example, the SIC code 3569 lumps together many different kinds of factory automation manufacturers. CorpTech, one of the private coding systems developed in response to SIC shortcomings, provides far greater detail, as you can see from this listing of codes for robot manufacturers.

Where else can a parent earn college credit during nap time?

As her toddlers doze peacefully, a mother of three hears the pounding of Confederate cannons. And the compelling strains of an old country fiddle.

She is quietly completing part nine of Ken Burns' epic series "The Civil War." One of 62 telecourses offered in Public Television's unique Adult Learning Service.

A program that reaches out, each year, to over a quarter of a million people (many with family responsibilities and full-time jobs). In homes. Hospitals. Offices. Even in prisons. Providing educational opportunities that might otherwise be unavailable to them.

Through courses that cover a canvas of subjects from principles of marketing management to exploring the universe.

Each demands the discipline of reading, writing, researching and taking exams. (Just like on campus.)

And accordingly, each rewards its students with credit towards a college degree. Along with skills, knowledge and a healthy measure of self-assurance.

In other words, just about everything needed to succeed both in life and the work force.

Except, of course, a baby-sitter.

**PUBLIC TELEVISION**
Keep us in mind.

**Exhibit 7.9
SEGMENTATION IN
NONPROFIT
MARKETING**
The Public Broadcasting System (PBS) recognizes that several segments exist in the college education market. In the ad, the target segment consists of people who want the benefits of college courses but for one reason or another can't participate in the traditional classroom environment.

branch manager to handle the business. Organizational marketers also look at the power structure of market segments. If a potential customer has a powerful engineering department that influences equipment purchases, then an equipment supplier might want to prepare a technical marketing approach. However, if the company has a powerful accounting and finance department, the supplier might prepare detailed price sheets instead.

Another operational variable is customer capabilities: A company may be strong or weak in specific operating, technical, or financial abilities. For example, Digital Equipment Corporation has traditionally targeted its minicomputers to companies capable of writing their own software, but IBM has always been known for extensive computer and software support and for going after market segments in which companies require those added services. Also, organizational marketers can use purchasing policies to segment their markets. Although some companies prefer to lease equipment, for example, others want to purchase, and this distinction can help organizational marketers identify appropriate segments. It's also important to know whether companies prefer to purchase from large, established businesses or are willing to do business with new or small companies. Naturally, a new firm shouldn't waste time marketing to businesses that prefer large suppliers. Another related twist is to segment according to personal influence on business purchases. Coverage Concepts, Incorporated (CCI), an insurance agency on Long Island, New York, was able to segment the market for commercial clients by finding clients who already owned personal policies through CCI but also exerted influence over commercial insurance purchases.[35]

## Segmentation for Nonprofit Marketers

Successful nonprofit marketers realize that they can also benefit from segmentation. When the Red Cross features Paul Schaefer or Carly Simon in an ad (see Exhibit 7.9), the organization is trying to reach people who are fans of those particular entertainers. The National High Blood Pressure Education Program (NHBPEP) discovered several segments when it researched attitudes among people with high blood pressure. Older people tended to take the condition more seriously than younger people. In contrast, younger people were less willing to share news of their condition with other people, and they reacted more negatively when experts told them what to do. Needham Porter Novelli, the firm that did the research, recommended that NHBPEP address younger people with a separate promotional campaign that could deal with the "macho" attitude and encourage these people to take their condition seriously.[36]

# SELECTING TARGET SEGMENTS

Once you've identified the variables you'll use to segment the market and identified homogeneous segments, it's time to narrow the possibilities in order to find the most attractive segments. For some products, you may need only one variable to segment the market. If you were marketing lipstick, you could use the demographic variable of sex to separate the larger market into two marketing segments, men and women. However, most markets cannot be segmented quite so easily. For example, to market home security systems in the metropolitan New York area, you might use the demographic variable of income to separate the whole market into three segments (such as annual household income below $25,000; income between $25,000 and $50,000; and income over $50,000), on the assumption that higher-income residents will have greater interest in security systems. However, marketers usually use two, three, or even more variables because this allows them to define narrower, more meaningful segments. The security system company could use a psychographic variable such as fear of crime (worried/not worried) and a geographic variable such as residence (New York City/Westchester/Long Island) in addition to household income. Although using more variables makes the segmentation process more complex, it also defines segments more precisely.

One tool that marketers use to get a better picture of the segments being considered is a **market segmentation matrix,** a grid showing two or more segmentation variables and the segments they form within a market. Using a market segmentation matrix, marketers can spot which segments contain **prospects,** people or businesses that are potential purchasers of the product, and **nonprospects,** people or businesses that are not potential purchasers. This way they can rule out segments of nonprospects and then select the most appropriate segments to target from the remaining segments of prospects. Just like gold miners looking for riches, marketers looking for customers refer to this process as *prospecting.*

Consider the home security system. The market segmentation matrix in Exhibit 7.10 shows three variables (household income, fear of crime, and geography) for a total of 18 segments in the grid. If you are offering a very sophisticated, expensive system, the first step might be to rule out the six segments with household income below $25,000 because they would be unable to afford your system and would therefore be nonprospect segments. Also, perhaps the system is not yet in stores on Long Island; then you would temporarily rule out the remaining four Long Island segments because they, too, represent nonprospects. That would leave eight segments:

**market segmentation matrix**
A grid that illustrates the marketing segments formed when two or more segmentation variables are applied to a market

**prospects**
Consumers or organizations that are potential customers

**nonprospects**
Consumers or organizations that are not potential customers

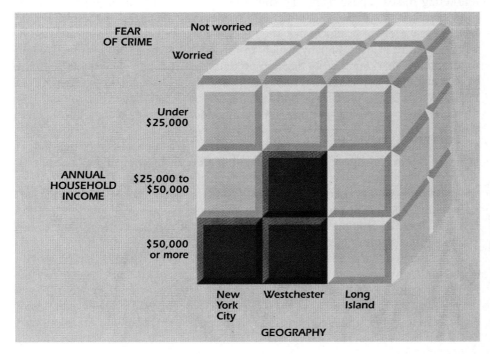

**Exhibit 7.10**
**A MARKET SEGMENTATION MATRIX**
Marketers use a marketing segmentation matrix to graphically examine the various segments created when they apply more than one segmentation variable to a particular market.

four New York City resident segments and four Westchester resident segments. You could then use the concepts presented in the following sections to further narrow your targets.

## Target Marketing Options

Once you've uncovered the best segments, you are faced with a variety of ways to implement your marketing programs. You can choose to market to all the target segments, to some of the target segments, or to just one. Taking target marketing to the extreme, you might choose to treat every customer as an individual market segment.

### UNDIFFERENTIATED MARKETING

**undifferentiated marketing**
A strategy in which you sell only one product or product line and offer it to all customers in a single marketing mix; another name for mass marketing

At one extreme is **undifferentiated marketing,** in which you sell only one product or product line and offer it to all customers in a single marketing mix. This is simply another term for mass marketing. Until the recent introduction of its brand of Bloody Mary Mix, McIlhenny offered only one product, Tabasco Sauce, and marketed it the same way everywhere. The only option you have as a customer is size: Tabasco comes in 1/8 ounce, 2 ounces, 12 ounces, and of course the handy gallon. Such limited offerings are becoming fewer and fewer in today's marketplace as firms become more conscious of the opportunities they can seize if they customize their marketing mixes and aim for chosen groups of possible customers.

Firms that use an undifferentiated strategy are often aware of distinct groups of people who use their products. However, they try to cover the whole spectrum as broadly as possible, relying on the product's versatility or lack of competition for success. They often knowingly risk their strategy backfiring if a competitor creates a product that is specialized for one of the groups in which they have an interest. The specialized product may offer more benefits to that group, in which case the undifferentiated marketer may lose out. On the other hand, an undifferentiated strategy allows for substantial economies of scale in production and marketing.

### DIFFERENTIATED MARKETING

**differentiated marketing**
A strategy in which you offer many products or product variations aimed at specific segments, using marketing mixes adapted for each segment

Companies that have decided to abandon undifferentiated marketing because it's no longer effective enough can adopt **differentiated marketing,** which offers many products or product variations aimed at specific market segments, using various marketing mixes. These firms are still attempting to satisfy a large proportion of the total market, but instead of doing it with one product offered one way, they market a wide variety of products designed to appeal to well-defined subgroups of the whole. The Coca-Cola Company, which for most of its 100-year history practiced undifferentiated marketing of its flagship product, has changed approaches and now offers caffeine-free Coke, Diet Coke, caffeine-free Diet Coke, and even Cherry Coke in addition to Coca-Cola Classic and "new" Coke. A Coca-Cola for everyone—or so the company hopes—each with its own promotional program designed for its own market.

Also, companies that use differentiated marketing can balance their markets to avoid risks that may develop in one segment. If a firm is in two markets, one shrinking while the other is growing, the marketer can alter the marketing mixes to stress the growing segment. Because the market for major appliances has been nearly stagnant in America for years, appliance manufacturers are adding markets abroad. General Electric's Hotpoint appliance division is continuing to market in the United States but has also targeted Europe as a segment.

Differentiated marketing can help a firm exploit emerging trends that create new segments within segments. Hearst Magazines targeted its home magazines primarily to women, starting with *House Beautiful,* introduced in 1896. Next, Hearst introduced *Colonial Homes,* aimed at older, more affluent women. Then came *Country Living,* developed in response to a trend that sentimentalized the American past, and *Victoria,* which harked back to nostalgic Victorian times. In 1990 Hearst began publishing *American Home* for younger homeowners and *Countryside* for people at the top end of the affluent market, who own two homes.[37]

## CONCENTRATED MARKETING

The two previous options for marketing assume that you are pursuing large national or multinational markets. However, many firms shoot for narrow niche markets or segments of national markets. The approach to use in these cases is **concentrated marketing,** which targets a single market segment with a single product or limited line of products. The basic reasons you might choose this strategy are two: either the structure of the market makes the other approaches impractical, or you don't have the resources to pursue the other strategies. For example, a broad, national market for buggy whips doesn't exist anymore. In fact, only one narrow niche is left: harness racing. Westfield Whip Manufacturing concentrates on this market for a simple reason: it's about the only group of buggy whip customers in existence.[38] At the other end of the sophistication scale, medical equipment is marketed with concentration strategies because the target market is so specialized.

> **concentrated marketing**
> A strategy in which you target a single market segment with a single product or limited line of products

Can concentrated marketing pay off? If the segment is sizable, the answer is a resounding yes. California-based Gymboree has built a multimillion-dollar business catering to parents of toddlers. Parents of preschoolers aged 3 months to 4 years can take their tots to any of the more than 350 Gymboree centers across the country to participate in physical fitness activities. Gymboree even has stores where the company targets the same market, using an expanded marketing mix that includes play equipment and toddler apparel.[39]

## INDIVIDUALIZED MARKETING

If you pursue segmentation to its extreme, you might reach the conclusion that every single customer is a distinct market segment. This is already the case for many large organizational customers, whose financial importance is so great that suppliers can't afford not to give them special treatment. Take the biggest customer of them all, the U.S. government; it is indeed a segment of one. At the other end of the economic spectrum, the neighborhood grocery store or barbershop, where the proprietor knows every customer by name and offers individualized service, has, in effect, segmented its market down to the individual customer.

What about all the marketers and customers in between? A national or international company like Chevrolet or Levi Strauss, with millions of customers, can't simply identify each customer and treat him or her individually, right? Not any more. *Individualized marketing,* as consultants Stan Rapp and Tom Collins refer to it, holds promise for many industries, including large consumer marketers. Have you ever read through a magazine you subscribe to and realized that half the articles and many of the ads didn't apply to you? Publishers don't like these mismatches any more than you do, and they're turning to individualized marketing to avoid them. *Farm Journal* led the way in this effort by customizing its content to match reader profiles. A typical issue is now printed in 2,000 to 3,000 different versions—the record is 8,896 versions of one issue. Readers like the system because they don't have to wade through articles and ads that don't apply to them, and advertisers like it because they can pinpoint audiences much more precisely. Taking this idea a step further, Time Warner has indicated it might custom-assemble editions based on several of its magazines. Therefore, you might, for instance, someday get a copy of a magazine that is part *Time,* part *Sports Illustrated,* part *People,* and part *Money.*[40]

## Criteria for Selecting Segments

How do you choose between market segments when deciding where you should focus your efforts? In some cases, the answer will be obvious, such as when you don't have the necessary technological skills or financial power to enter a market segment. In other cases, you'll have the resources to compete in a number of segments, but not enough resources to compete in all of them. Marketers use criteria such as these to choose the most attractive segments:[41]

- *Sales and profit potential.* How many units can you theoretically expect to sell in each segment, and at what profit? As stated earlier, sales potential is one of the criteria for determining whether a marketing segment is meaningful. At the outset, you determine whether sufficient sales potential to segment the market exists and then select variables and perform the segmentation. When you're ready to select attractive segments, sales potential is used again, this time to actually measure the size of the market in each segment. By assigning a unit sales or sales revenue and profit estimate to every prospect segment, you can see which segments offer the most potential. In the security systems example, you'll determine that you have less sales and profit potential in the segments with incomes of $25,000 to $50,000 and more sales and profit potential in the segments with incomes over $50,000. Also, people who worry about crime are more likely to buy than those who do not, so the sales potential is higher in the high-worry segments.
- *Fit with company resources.* Is the segment compatible with the company's resources and strengths? If you have a warehouse in Westchester, dealers there can receive extra stock quickly, and the Westchester segments might be more compatible with the company's resources than the New York City segments. You may also ask a number of other questions. Do you have enough salespeople? Can you support customers after the sale? Can you build enough units to stock all the stores in your target market?
- *Competitive environment.* Identify how many competitors are in each segment and how aggressive they are. For instance, the aggressiveness of Coca-Cola and PepsiCo in the teen market was one of the reasons that led Royal Crown Cola to pass on that segment.
- *Cost to reach the segment.* You can't reach a market segment for free, and some segments are more expensive to reach than others. If you are selling a complicated life insurance policy, you'll be able to reach financially astute consumers easily because they understand money matters. On the other hand, if you've targeted financial novices, you're likely to spend a lot of time and money trying to educate the market before you can sell to it.
- *Growth.* Launching a marketing program is an expensive venture, and you would naturally like to find segments that will grow. A projection for slow growth in the children segment, for instance, led Kellogg to search for other segments.
- *Risks.* Risks may involve the product, the market, or the way the customer relates to the product, including economic, political, technological, environmental, legal, cultural, or competitive risks. By knowing the risks and their possible consequences, the marketer can decide to skip over certain segments or enter some segments before others. Some risks are so critical that you avoid certain segments altogether. Other risks may threaten your ability to sell or make a profit in one or more segments.

Each of these criteria plays an important role in helping the marketer evaluate the marketing segments. You've probably developed the sense that market segmentation is often a balancing act, because a segment may look attractive according to some criteria and unattractive according to others. Marketers must use their experience and judgment to weigh the findings and select the segments they will target.

## POSITIONING YOURSELF IN THE CUSTOMER'S MIND

Regardless of the segmentation and targeting selections you make, your next step will be to stake out the position you'd like to occupy in each market you're pursuing. How can marketers position their products, their distribution channels, their technologies, even their company's corporate identity? The answer, of course, is by using the four elements of the marketing mix. Once marketers identify the position they would like to occupy in the market, they design a unique marketing mix that will support that position by reaching the target market and meeting its needs. Product, price, distribution, and promotion all combine to support the firm's positioning and to differentiate it from competitors in the same segment. When they decide to position their products differently for various segments, marketers change the marketing mixes to make them unique to each segment.

As discussed in Chapter 3, positioning is the process of achieving a desired place in the mind of your target market. To determine the best position for a particular product, you can investigate which factors are most meaningful to customers, how customers perceive competitive products with respect to those factors, and how customers perceive your product with respect to the same factors.[42]

Then you can plot a **perceptual map,** a diagram that shows how customers perceive products in the market according to the most important attributes. Of course, features help create perceptions; for example, leather seats and a premium sound system contribute to the perception that a car is a luxury model. However, when you use a perceptual map, you are looking at perceptions rather than features; you're trying to understand how customers perceive your products and your competitors' products. The perceptual map also shows exactly where consumers prefer a product to be positioned.[43] Part of the marketing challenge is to make sure customer perceptions are accurate and favorable.

Using the perceptual map, you can find any gaps where customers have a need that is unfulfilled by existing products. These gaps can be a desirable position for new or existing products. L'Eggs filled a gap in convenience and distribution, becoming the first pantyhose that consumers could buy in their local supermarkets. Campbell Soup's Casera brand spaghetti sauce filled a gap for Caribbean-style spaghetti sauce aimed at Hispanic consumers.[44] If no such gap exists, it may be because competitors have already positioned products appropriately. So you can also look at the perceptual map to understand where customers believe competing products to be positioned.

## Competing for the Best Position

Sometimes competitors are literally all over the map, and sometimes several competitors are clustered in the same area. Suppose you were a marketer investigating how consumers view pain-relieving products. Exhibit 7.11 shows pain relievers on a perceptual map that represents positioning in terms of long-lasting effectiveness and gentleness to the stomach. The three pain-reliever products shown in the lower left-hand quadrant are perceived as relatively similar in terms of being less effective on pain and being less gentle. Excedrin is perceived to be the most effective

**perceptual map**
A diagram that shows how customers perceive products in the market according to the most important attributes

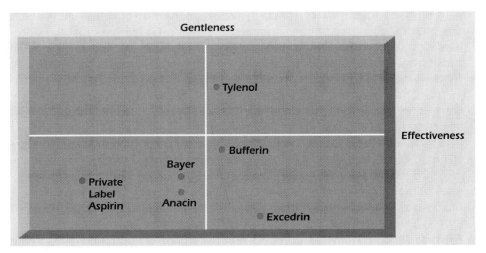

**Exhibit 7.11**
**PERCEPTUAL MAP OF THE PAIN-RELIEVER MARKET**
Marketers use perceptual maps to gain a better understanding of how consumers perceive the products on the market in terms of key benefits or attributes.

product. As you can see, no pain reliever is positioned in the top left-hand quadrant, which represents less effective but gentle products.

You know that if your product is perceived as both gentle and effective it will be more attractive to consumers. Among the products on the map, the only one in this position is Tylenol, which is perceived as very gentle but only somewhat effective. What do you do when another product has the best position on the map? You could give up on pain relievers, but that's not a good idea if your company just spent a lot of money to develop a new product. Your second option is to try to displace the competitor that's sitting in the best position. It's difficult to do, and it takes both time and money, but it is possible in some cases. Your third option is to try to reposition the competitor who's in the position you covet. This approach is frequently used in high-tech markets where marketers position their new products as, say, faster or better suited to a particular application. By altering the way consumers view the market, high-tech marketers change the way consumers perceive current products—and the way they perceive the new product. Your final option in the pain-reliever market might be to come up with a new extra-strength pain reliever that's both gentle to the stomach and more effective than Tylenol.[45]

The definition of the ideal position can depend on both the culture and the country in which you're marketing a product. In the United States, for instance, General Foods successfully positioned Tang as a breakfast drink that was a substitute for orange juice. But this positioning didn't make sense in many Latin American countries, where few people sit down to a breakfast that includes orange juice. General Foods eventually positioned Tang in these countries as a "fun drink" that people could enjoy with their friends.[46]

## Choosing a Positioning Approach

You can choose from a number of positioning approaches, depending on the strengths of your product, the factors that are important to customers, and the actions of your competitors.[47]

- *By product differences.* One of the strongest positioning approaches is based on some feature, or combination of features, that your product has but that your competitors' products don't. Of course, the difference must be truthful and it must be meaningful to customers in order to have any impact. Embassy Suites Hotels are positioned as the hotels where every room is a two-room suite that's offered at about the same price as the single bedroom of a typical hotel. The two-room suite is a key feature that sets Embassy Suites Hotels apart from competitors.
- *By product benefits.* This approach identifies a product attribute or benefit that is meaningful to customers and then bases a positioning strategy around it (see Exhibit 7.12). Campbell Soup's Home Cookin' canned soups are positioned as ready to serve, with no preservatives, which appeals to two needs: convenience and health. Lower price is another benefit often used in positioning. For example, Budget Gourmet frozen dinners are positioned as gourmet-style at bargain prices.[48] The Sierra Club, a nonprofit environmental organization, realizes that the calendars its sells have the obvious benefits that all calendars provide as well as the added bonus of making the buyer feel good about protecting the environment.[49]
- *By product users.* This sounds a bit like targeting, but explicitly identifying a target market in an ad can be a good way to position a product. The Eagle Vision, one of a new line of cars introduced by Chrysler in 1992, used the theme "Not intended for the general public" in its ads. Why would someone say that a product isn't for everybody? In order to position it as something special. When you buy an Eagle Vision, part of what you get is the feeling that you're somebody unique, somebody who wouldn't buy just any old car. Of course, as *Advertising Age* columnist Bob Garfield pointed out, "95 percent of all consumers regard themselves as the 5 percent of consumers who are above the 95 percent of all consumers," so every Vision owner can feel special about the purchase.[50]
- *By product usage.* The ways a product is used can provide positioning opportuni-

The protection you need in the colors you want.

You'll find an entire spectrum of the strongest colors in the world in Sally Hansen Hard As Nails with Nylon. Its unique patented formula helps nails grow longer and stronger, while it prevents chipping, splitting and breaking. No wonder the number one name in nails is Sally Hansen. Why trust your nails to anything less?

*Sally Hansen*
The most trusted name in nail protection.

**Exhibit 7.12**
**POSITIONING BY PRODUCT BENEFITS**
This Sally Hansen ad positions the nail polish on its ability to protect fingernails.

ties as well. A classic case is Arm & Hammer baking soda, which has been going strong for decades because the company continues to position it as a refrigerator deodorizer, as a toothpaste substitute, and in a variety of other ways. Nyquil is the nighttime cold medicine, a position based on two aspects of usage, having a cold and taking medicine at night. As a result, consumers have come to associate products such as Nyquil with a particular occasion, time, or place of usage. Another good example is General Foods, the makers of Jell-O, which came up with the idea for Jell-O Jigglers. These Jell-O shapes are created with cookie cutters, positioning the product as another option for holiday treats.[51]

- *Against a particular competitor.* Sometimes the most effective way to move into a potential customer's mind is to compare yourself with a known competitor and try to explain why you are the better choice. Alfa Romeo took this approach with a recent ad that claimed, "It's like a BMW that's been to driving school," asserting that its 164S model handled better than the BMW 525i.[52]
- *Against an entire product category.* Marketers sometimes find themselves competing against an entire category of products, particularly when they are offering to solve a problem that customers are used to solving with other types of products.
- *By association.* This approach involves associating your product with some other entity, in the hope that some of that entity's positive image will rub off on your product. When you see a product being called "the Cadillac" of something or other, the attempt is to position it by association.

## Repositioning Your Products

From time to time, marketers use **repositioning** to change the way existing products are perceived by consumers. Repositioning a product is often a good strategy when you want to expand your potential market. For instance, product repositioning sweetened the market for NutraSweet's Equal, which was originally positioned as a good-tasting nonsaccharin sweetener. Competing with Sweet 'N Low, the product was seen mainly as a dietetic sweetener for coffee and tea. Later, NutraSweet marketers repositioned Equal to appeal to a larger market by emphasizing its use as a sugar substitute in other foods. To support this new position, the company changed Equal's packaging. The new packages featured "usage vignettes" (pictures of Equal being sprinkled on cereal, coffee, iced tea, fruit salad, and strawberries) and gave the well-known NutraSweet brand name more prominence.[53] Volvo is

**repositioning**
An attempt to change the way existing products are perceived by consumers; the term is also applied to one marketer's efforts to change the perceived position of a competitor's product

in the middle of a repositioning effort, trying to present a sportier, performance-oriented image. Most consumers still perceive the company's cars as safe and reliable, but not terribly exciting to drive.[54]

## Writing the Positioning Statement

Once you have a good understanding of what's important to customers, how competing products are perceived, and where you want your own product to be positioned, you develop a formal statement of your proposed position. A *positioning statement* is a concise statement of the position you want the product to achieve. Positioning statements describe the position in terms of the factors that are most important to consumers, and they stress specific features or benefits of the product that are different from—usually superior to—the competition. For example, a radio manufacturer offering build-it-yourself kits might discover through marketing research that ease of assembly and sound quality are most important to hobbyists, the consumer segment being targeted. Using a perceptual map, the manufacturer sees that other kits are perceived as being easy to assemble, but none is perceived as having good sound. Thus, the manufacturer might write this positioning statement for its own radio kit: "An easy-to-build radio for the hobbyist who wants high-quality sound."

The positioning statement sounds a little like a headline from an ad, but it isn't necessarily. Even if your company never runs a single ad, it still needs a positioning statement. You may end up using or adapting the actual positioning statement in your promotional program, but its primary purpose is to guide all your marketing efforts, starting with product design.

A product is often positioned in various ways for distinctly separate market segments, so you must develop a positioning statement for each individual segment. For instance, a manufacturer of jeans might position its products as fashion items for the general consumer and as sturdy work clothes for people who work in carpentry and other trades. Whatever the market, and the position, write the positioning statement so that it focuses on what customers feel is most important, stressing why customers should buy this product rather than its competitors.[55]

## Executing the Positioning Plan

With the positioning statement completed, you can communicate that position to the people who will execute the plan. A wide variety of people play a role in executing the positioning plan, shaping the way customers and prospects perceive the product. Many of these people are inside the company, but outsiders are also involved.

- *Inside the company.* Communicate the positioning plan to numerous company insiders, including product designers, marketing researchers, finance and accounting staff, marketing and sales personnel, public relations and investor relations staff, customer service representatives, and others.
- *Outside the company.* People outside the company who need to be aware of the positioning plan include the firm's advertising agency, public relations agency, consultants, and writers and editors who cover the industry.[56] Some of these groups, such as the ad agency, need to know your positioning plan before the product is introduced so that they can help develop marketing materials. Others, including the writers and editors, generally learn about your positioning objectives when you introduce the product.

The positioning plan guides you in developing a complete marketing plan, which specifies how the product will be developed, managed, promoted, distributed, and priced. When you have more than one product, each has a positioning plan to deal with its individual target markets, and each has an individual marketing plan. This way, you can manage your product mix most effectively.

**1. Discuss the role of market segmentation and targeting.**

Market segmentation is the process of dividing a large market into smaller groupings of consumers or organizations sharing similar characteristics, needs, wants, or behaviors. People and businesses have extremely diverse needs, and it isn't usually advisable to treat everybody as part of one big market. That's why marketers use market segmentation to select just those markets whose needs they can understand and fulfill. Each market segment can then be targeted using a specific variation of the marketing mix. Market segmentation helps marketers use their resources more efficiently, identify markets and understand their specific needs, gain a better understanding of the competitive environment, and set sales goals and measure performance more accurately.

**2. List the criteria for determining whether a segment is meaningful.**

For a segment to be meaningful, it must meet four criteria. First, the segment must be definable. Second, the segment must have significant sales potential. Third, the segment must be accessible. Fourth, the segment must be responsive to marketing approaches.

**3. Discuss the variables used to segment consumer and industrial markets.**

Consumer marketers use geographic, demographic, psychographic, geodemographic, and behavioral variables to segment their markets. Geographic variables can be used to divide the market into segments according to countries, regions, states, cities, communities, and neighborhoods. Other geographic variables include population patterns, transportation, climate, growth patterns, and government. Demographic variables are used to divide the market according to information about the size, composition, and distribution of a population, including age, sex, race, religion, national origin, family size and life cycle, marital status, occupation, social class, income, and education. Psychographic variables are used to divide the market according to lifestyles, activities, opinions, and beliefs. Geodemographic variables combine demographic information with geographic segments to produce lifestyle segmentations. Behavioral variables are used to divide the market according to product usage, needs for specific benefits, price sensitivity, and brand loyalty. Organizational marketers can use much the same set of variables, substituting operational variables such as purchasing policy and customer capability for the psychographic variables.

**4. Describe a market segmentation matrix and explain how marketers use the matrix to help define their target markets.**

A market segmentation matrix is a grid that shows the segments created when a market is divided according to two or more segmentation variables. Using a market segmentation matrix, you can easily see which segments contain prospects and which contain nonprospects. Once the prospect segments have been identified, you eliminate any segments judged to be too risky and then evaluate the remaining prospect segments to find the most attractive targets. You can construct a market segmentation matrix for every product, using the individual variables that are most important for each market and for each product.

**5. Describe the four target marketing options.**

When you choose undifferentiated marketing, you've decided that you have only one meaningful segment. In differentiated marketing, your analysis shows two or more segments, and each needs to be approached with a marketing mix. In concentrated marketing, you select one segment, make sure it's big enough to support your company profitably, and then pour all your resources into it. In individualized marketing, you try to treat each individual customer as a unique market segment.

**6. List the options you have for positioning products relative to the competition.**

The positioning options discussed in the chapter are positioning by product differences, by product benefits, by product users, by product usage, against a particular competitor, against an entire product category, and by associating your product with some other entity (such as a celebrity or well-regarded product).

**7. Define the positioning statement and identify its purpose.**

A positioning statement is a concise statement of the position you want a product (or company or other entity) to achieve in the minds of current and potential customers. Positioning statements describe the position in terms of the factors that are most important to consumers, and they stress specific features or benefits of the product that are different from—usually superior to—the competition.

# KEY TERMS

behavioral segmentation (215)

benefit segmentation (215)

concentrated marketing (223)

demographic segmentation (210)

differentiated marketing (222)

geodemographic segmentation (213)

geographic segmentation (208)

heterogeneous market (207)

homogeneous market (207)

market segmentation (207)

market segmentation matrix (221)

mass marketing (204)

nonprospects (221)

perceptual map (225)

prospects (221)

psychographic segmentation (211)

repositioning (227)

Standard Industrial Classification (SIC) (217)

target marketing (204)

undifferentiated marketing (222)

## Meeting a Marketing Challenge at Kellogg

Kellogg's cereals have been poured into breakfast bowls for 100 years, establishing the ready-to-eat cereal industry in America with Wheat Flakes in 1894 and Corn Flakes in 1898. The overall market today has expanded to a $6 billion business, and U.S. consumers eat well over 20 billion bowls of cereal each year.

Little wonder—cereal offers a lot of convenience: no cooking; the choice of eating it dry or with milk, sugar, or fruit; and an easy way to satisfy some daily nutritional needs, all at literally pennies per day. The price of a bowl of Corn Flakes and milk is about one-quarter the cost of a plate of bacon and eggs. Cereal adds up to a great bargain for parents with young mouths to feed.

Yet the market in the 1970s showed almost no growth, mirroring the flat growth in the youth age groups. Moreover, other challenges threatened to change the way the industry operated. In the early 1970s, consumer groups began pressing for tighter regulatory control of children's television advertising, causing the Federal Trade Commission to set limits on the commercials shown on kids' shows. Then the FTC launched a lawsuit against Kellogg and other manufacturers, charging the existence of a shared monopoly (or oligopolistic market condition) in ready-to-eat cereal. By the time the FTC dropped its action in 1982, Kellogg executives found they had been distracted by the regulatory battles and had allowed market share to tumble nearly four percentage points. Chairman William LeMothe knew he could reclaim ground, but not using traditional kid cereals.

Competitors tried to escape the stagnant cereal market of the 1970s by gobbling up businesses in unrelated markets: toys and fashion, to name just two. In time, many of those diversified lines were sold off as the glamour faded along with profits. In contrast, when the Battle Creek giant made acquisitions, it stayed close to the kitchen: Mrs. Smith's pies, Eggo waffles, Whitney yogurt, Salada teas.

However, Kellogg is clearly committed to cereal, the source of more than 75 percent of its annual sales volume. Under former CEO William LaMothe, the company embarked on the largest single capital expenditure in its history, spending $100 million to expand and improve cereal manufacturing plants. The investment paid off in productivity: Sales per employee skyrocketed from $70,000 in 1976 to $192,000 in 1986. Production averaged 81,000 pounds per employee in 1976, and that figure grew to 108,000 pounds 10 years later. On top of impressive increases in ad spending and product development budgets during the 1980s, it's clear that Kellogg is serious about cereal.

Kellogg's marketing strategy now includes a focus on key market segments, and an effort to reposition cereal in innovative ways. The firm has set its sights on the adult market and on the no-breakfast segment. For instance, to entice this no-breakfast segment to eat something, Kellogg offers Smart Start cereal bars, a product line that combines nutrition and great taste in a foil-wrapped bar.

Not all its marketing innovations are met with enthusiasm. Kellogg unveiled an anticancer positioning for its All-Bran cereal in 1984, sparking controversy among industry, medical, and regulatory groups. Five years later, the debate raged again with Kellogg's introduction of Heartwise, which contains psyllium, a super-high-fiber ingredient. However, Kellogg tried a different approach, proposing a new industry standard that would distinguish specific product claims from more general messages about the benefits of a healthy diet. "It is in the consumer's best interest to allow food manufacturers to communicate health messages," LaMothe said at the time. "On the other hand, any statement regarding a specific food that goes beyond the concept of a total diet . . . should be subjected to the Food and Drug Administration's regulatory approval process."

Aside from health-related issues, Kellogg's latest market efforts have been a smashing success. After three consecutive years of declines, sales picked up in 1992, and the company got back to the 40 percent market share it enjoyed in the 1980s. With the exception of Rice Krispies, every one of Kellogg's core brands is enjoying renewed sales growth.

**Your mission:** As the marketer in charge of Kellogg's Raisin Bran, you have been asked by Arnold Langbo to consider the audience for this established brand and come up with new ways to market the product. You are to examine current sales trends, look at potential new customers, and propose methods for increasing sales.

1. You know ethnic groups in the United States continue to grow and now represent significant consumer segments. You'd like to increase sales of Raisin Bran in these markets. Which of the following segmentation and marketing strategies would be most effective?
   a. Let's face it; cereal is cereal. People eat it because it's inexpensive and easy to prepare. There is nothing to be gained by trying to break down the cereal market along ethnic lines, so just continue with your current marketing mix.
   b. Before you do any segmentation, understand your market well enough to know what is important to each group. You may discover that you don't have to do anything. Or you may find that one group prefers food products from companies that hire a significant percentage of employees from a particular ethnic background. Once you've done this level of research, the amount of segmentation needed will be obvious.
   c. The only change to make is to translate advertisements into each group's native language.
2. As you think about potential customers, you believe a more focused way of segmenting the market would open the door to new sales opportunities. For example, you see a wide variety of kids' cereals being introduced, using age as the market segmentation factor. Which of the following would be a sensible target marketing strategy for Raisin Bran?

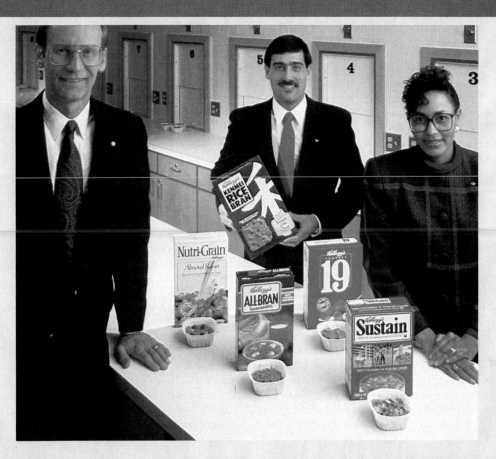

a. Adapt the product's flavor regionally to appeal to various tastes around the country.

b. Package the cereal in diverse ways for various end-users, with single-serving packages for restaurants and schools and with giant packages for large families.

c. Change the ads to show how Raisin Bran is good for various age groups, including retired people and preschoolers.

3. You are about to draft a memo suggesting ways Raisin Bran might be positioned as a snack for various market segments. Which of the following would you tell Langbo are good ways to advertise Raisin Bran as a snack treat?

a. Have a college student rush into her dormitory room, pour a bowl of Raisin Bran, and quickly begin to eat while she explains that cereal is a convenient between-meal snack on a busy school day.

b. Present a fashion model taking a break from a photography session and nibbling on a handful of cereal. She tells viewers that Raisin Bran is a healthy way to stay slim and still get the nutrition she needs to look good all the time.

c. Start the commercial with two preteen children coming into the kitchen after dinner. They find cookies in the cabinet but decide to have Raisin Bran instead because they see raisins on the cereal package. They talk about how they like the natural sweetness of raisins.

4. To help you better understand consumer behavior, your marketing research department arranged several focus groups around the country. A dominant theme in these discussions was consumers' frustration over lack of time. Working parents in particular said they just didn't have enough time to ensure that they and their children always ate well-balanced meals. You think the time-pressured consumer might be an attractive market segment for Kellogg. Which of the following approaches would be the best way to determine whether this segment really exists?

a. Launch a major TV and radio advertising campaign that focuses on how quick and easy cold cereals are. If consumers respond, you'll know the segment exists.

b. Count the number of people in your focus groups who said they felt time pressure and then project that number across the total U.S. population. This will tell you how many people are in this market segment.

c. Conduct another round of research in which you collect more information on the time pressures that consumers feel and ask people whether the benefits of easy preparation would lead them to purchase more cereal.

## SPECIAL PROJECT

Kellogg is considering moving its existing products into new market segments. Take demographics, psychographics, and behavior patterns into account when contemplating such a move. Management's current primary market is the business traveler who eats Kellogg's products at home but can't always get them while traveling. Identify all the situations in which these consumers might eat cereal and then state how to modify the marketing mix in each case.[57]

## American Express Charges into Segmentation

If you're American Express CEO Harvey Golub, you don't leave home without it. Traveling the world to preside over his financial services empire, Golub is sure to pack his American Express card when visiting the firm's divisions, which include Travel Related Services, IDS Financial Services, the American Express Bank, and the Information Services Company. All the divisions are heavy hitters in their respective fields, but the unit that put the company on the map—and the card in Golub's wallet—is Travel Related Services. When you add up the contribution of the 33 million American Express cards and other products in Travel Related Services, it becomes clear why he considers this group his core business: The division delivers about one-third of American Express's revenues and two-thirds of its profits.

However, competition in the card arena has become incredibly fierce, and Travel Related Services has to defend its share of wallet against a variety of challengers including Visa, MasterCard, Diner's Club, Sears Discover Card, and the JCB card (in the Japanese market). Faced with escalating competition and fragmented markets, Travel Related Services is fighting back using differentiated market segmentation strategies.

First, the company recognizes that it's marketing a feeling of exclusivity in addition to financial services. Each of the three upscale cards is positioned as a prestige product, corresponding to a unique target audience, and each has a marketing mix to support its positioning. For example, the Green Card appeals to people who want to be part of the elite, with a greater degree of financial success than people who rely on ordinary bank credit cards. So ads for the Green Card feature celebrities such as Mary Steenburgen, Wayne Gretzky, and Yo-Yo Ma to encourage Green Card customers to feel like they belong to the same exclusive club as these personalities and to prompt people who aspire to membership to apply for the card. The Gold Card is positioned as more luxurious than the Green Card, and the Platinum Card is even more luxurious than the Gold Card, with appropriate marketing mixes to support these positionings. Optima is positioned to complement the other cards, providing a way for cardholders to repay their charges over a period of time.

Next, American Express marketers look inside the target market for each card product to identify smaller segments that warrant special attention. Within the universe for Green Cards, marketers are courting women and students, and within the universe for the Corporate Card, the small-business market has become a priority. In all, the company has identified 15 separate groups to be targeted within the total customer base.

To find and reach all the targets in their market, the company segments the market using a combination of geographic, demographic, psychographic, and behavioral variables. For instance, it analyzes prospects according to ZIP codes, block groups, and census tracts to decide where to market the Green Card within the United States. Among the demographic parameters used are sex, home ownership, and car ownership; lifestyle orientation is one of the psychographic factors used, and propensity to respond is one of the behavioral factors.

In the United States, card companies have already issued more than 250 million cards, so you might think that growth opportunities in this market are limited. However, as long as Travel Related Services continues to wield its powerful segmentation tools, the company will continue to attract people who won't leave home without their American Express cards.

1. Optima, the credit card that allows customers the choice of repaying in full or in part, has been positioned as an adjunct to the existing American Express cards: Only customers who have the Green, Gold, or Platinum card can qualify. Considering the increased competition from bank cards that offer the same partial repayment option, should Travel Related Services widen its net to include non–American Express prospects, especially consumers who hold premium Visas or MasterCards?

2. Would it be meaningful for American Express to further segment the Corporate Card market beyond the groupings of big business and small business? Why or why not?

3. Although American Express has been successful in segmenting the market for new card customers, it may not be able to continue the cards' growth on the same scale in the future. Given the competitive situation domestically and internationally, should the company shift emphasis and stimulate current customers to use the card more often? Or should it pursue prospects by using even more aggressive techniques that position American Express cards as superior to the competition?

# QUESTIONS FOR DISCUSSION

1. Would market segmentation be meaningful if you were marketing the following products?
   a. Hand-bound reproductions of an eighteenth-century English dictionary
   b. Quart-size plastic bags
   c. Pencils that write through grease and water
   d. Computer connecting cables
2. How would a Japanese manufacturer of portable cassette players use demographic and geographic segmentation variables to market its products?
3. How would this Japanese manufacturer of portable cassette players use psychographic and behavioral segmentation variables to market its products?
4. You're marketing paper for computer printers. Does target marketing make sense? Why or why not?
5. What segment risks might you face as an international marketer of artificially sweetened candy for children?
6. How well would targeted marketing work for each of these products?
   a. Postage stamps
   b. Ski goggles
   c. College savings accounts
   d. Airplanes for rent
7. What are the advantages and disadvantages of using mass marketing to market solid milk chocolate candy bars?
8. Assume you're starting an accounting firm that will specialize in handling tax and financial reporting for small businesses that operate only in Canada. What factors would you consider when selecting a desired position in your market?
9. You're marketing subscriptions to a new magazine, *Macintosh Computers on Campus,* which is positioned as the magazine that helps college and grad students use their Macintosh computers more effectively. How would you use your marketing mix to support this position?
10. If Henry Ford had wanted to change his strategy for the Model T from mass marketing to target marketing, what problems might he have faced?

# SHARPEN YOUR MARKETING SKILLS

Not every business owner can list Sting and Princess Diana as avid supporters, but then Anita Roddick is no ordinary business owner. She's the co-founder of The Body Shop International, a company that is known both for its natural cosmetics and its passionate pleas for various environmental and social causes. The Body Shop has become something of an international phenomenon. Roddick and her husband started it in England in 1976, and it is now a leading symbol of corporate concern for the environment. Its appeal is so strong in the United States that 2,500 people wrote Roddick asking for franchises—before the company had even set foot on U.S. soil.

Roddick doesn't target the traditional segments in the cosmetics market. She's not interested in selling glamour or promises of instant beauty. She wants you to be healthy, and she wants the planet to be healthy.

**Decision:** This brings us to an interesting segmentation question: How can she identify customers who want the same things from their cosmetics? What are three ways that Roddick could reach her target segment? How can you identify people based on an attribute as intangible as social and environmental concern?

**Communication:** Pretend that you have Roddick's ear during a short cab ride between two of her stores. Explain how you would convince her that you have the right idea for reaching the target audience.[58]

# KEEPING CURRENT IN MARKETING

Read several articles describing competition in one of the following industries:

Pharmaceuticals
Bank credit cards
Airline travel
Snack foods
Farm machinery

1. How are the markets for the products segmented? Characterize the consumers in each segment.

2. Does each supplier of products go after all market segments? How do the various competitors decide which segment(s) to go after?
3. Forecast the potential of each segment in five years. Ten years. Twenty-five years. Will segment size grow, shrink, or remain unchanged? Why? What factors will influence the change you foresee?

## Nestlé Targets Success by Targeting Consumers

Here's a challenge: See how many days you can go without consuming a product marketed by Nestlé, the giant Swiss food conglomerate. From more than 400 factories in 60-plus countries, the firm churns out tons of candy bars (including Butterfinger, KitKat, and Baby Ruth), bottled water (Calistoga, Poland Spring, and Perrier), coffee (Hills Brothers, Nescafé, and Taster's Choice), and a wide variety of other offerings, ranging from Lean Cuisine frozen dinners to Mighty Dog pet food. With a pile of cash in the bank and an eye on expansion, the company continues to build its portfolio of worldwide brand names.

### Choosing Not to Compete on Price Alone

Like everyone else in the food business, Nestlé finds itself facing increased competition and consumers who have many product choices. The company's chief marketing strategist, Peter Brabeck, figured Nestlé had three options: aggressive discounting to capture customers with frequent sales and promotional offers, everyday low pricing to permanently lower prices on most goods, or more effective communication with target customers. Not wanting to get in an endless cycle of coupons and discounting or to give up profits as everyday low pricing might require, Brabeck opted for better marketing communications. A closer look at how this strategy was applied to one Nestlé product line in one particular market will show the wisdom of Brabeck's plan.

In most segments of the consumer-goods business, gaining a few points of market share is usually considered a success. Gain 5 or 10 points, and you're really on a roll. How, then, would you label Nestlé's recent surge, when it picked up an astounding 24 share points in the French baby food market? Gains this large are almost unheard of in consumer products. Nestlé doesn't compete with a bunch of light-

weights, either. Market leader Boussois Souchon Neuvesel (BSN) is one of Europe's most respected companies and France's largest food company. (You probably recognize such BSN brands as Dannon yogurt and Evian bottled water.) BSN's Bledina brand had long been the dominant line of baby food in France.

## Dislodging an Entrenched Market Leader

Nestlé's Sopad-Nestlé division based its move on Bledina with a plan to become known to parents as a company that cared about their needs and wanted to make the often challenging job of raising a baby just a little easier. The strategy of more effective communication starts with a database of 220,000 new mothers. The names and addresses are initially taken from public birth records, and Sopad-Nestlé initiates contact with the new parents by sending a card that essentially asks permission to keep the names in the database. The card also gathers information about the family, allowing Sopad-Nestlé to continually fine-tune its consumer profiles. When a mother sends her card back, Sopad-Nestlé follows up with six direct-mail packages filled with product samples, coupons, and health-care information. For Mother's Day, the company delivers special cards and roses. Consumers certainly seem to like the program; 97 percent of mothers in a recent survey approved of the direct-mail program.

Sopad-Nestlé doesn't rely on direct-mail alone to reach parents, however. Knowing that driving anywhere with young children can be a challenge, the company operates a number of care centers for children at rest stops along main highways. During the summer months, when a large portion of France's population is on the road for vacation, parents can pull into *Le Relais Bébé* (The Baby Service Station) and be assured of a clean place to change diapers, feed the baby, or simply take a quick break from the car. Not only that, but Sopad-Nestlé provides free disposable diapers and samples of their baby food products. Traveling parents appreciate having a safe, clean place to stop, and the company gets an average of 20 minutes of quality time per family to build and solidify a relationship with its consumers. Most consumer-goods marketers rarely come in contact with consumers at any level (other than for research, naturally), but in *Le Relais Bébé,* employees are on the spot, helping parents feed and care for their children. It's a superb opportunity to build a bond with parents and to get instant feedback about the

company and its products. To these parents, Sopad-Nestlé is no faceless, multinational conglomerate; it's a group of people who help them bring up the baby.

## Why Nestlé's Program Works

Fabienne Petit, Sopad-Nestlé's marketing director, lists four reasons her operation's efforts have been so successful. First, the mailings are written in a personal, caring tone that respects the joys and challenges new parents experience. Second, the message evolves over the two-year life of the mailing as the baby grows through different stages. Third, Sopad-Nestlé stresses helpful information over product promotion, so parents view the mailings as more than just advertising. For example, information cards that pediatricians helped develop explain the changes their babies will go through as they grow. This helps parents know what to expect; first-time parents in particular often need reassurance that their children are healthy and happy. Fourth, through both the mailings and *Le Relais Bébé,* the company provides help and companionship at important times in the lives of both parents and children.

Nestlé's success highlights the importance of understanding consumers, targeting them accurately (notice how the company not only targets new parents but at specific points in the lives of their new babies), and building one-on-one relationships with customers.

## Questions

1. What role does information about the consumer play in Nestlé's success in the French baby food market?

2. Describe the bond that Nestlé is building with its customers with *Le Relais Bébé.* Would this approach work with any of the company's other products?

3. Is it ethical for Nestlé to have this much personal information about new parents? Will parents feel that the company is invading their privacy? What steps could the company take to address their concerns without hampering the effectiveness of its marketing programs?

4. What, if any, steps should Nestlé take before it tries to use this marketing program in other countries?

# PART III
# PRODUCT STRATEGY

237

# 8

# Product Concepts

## Personality with a Pop

It's a funny name for a food product, but Orville Redenbacher is laughing all the way to the bank since his Orville Redenbacher Gourmet Popping Corn surpassed 82 brands to become the market leader. "Gourmet" popcorn did not exist before Orville Redenbacher. In fact, before Redenbacher energized the entire category, popcorn production in the United States had languished under 350 million pounds a year. It popped up to over 675 million pounds after Redenbacher's product became a hit.

As a boy, Redenbacher had grown corn for popping as part of a 4-H project to devise a better strain. He majored in agronomy (soil management and field crops) at Purdue University in the 1920s and after graduation served as an agricultural agent. Then he managed a large Indiana farm where he became involved in growing hybrid corn and processing popcorn seed. That's when Redenbacher met Charlie Bowman, who ran a seed program at Purdue. In 1951 the two entrepreneurs bought a small company that raised and sold corn seed; they renamed it Chester and started to experiment with popcorn seed.

Bowman handled grain storage and irrigation systems for the company, and Redenbacher worked with corn-breeding experts to invent a better corn hybrid. By 1965 he had crossbred 40 generations of corn and come up with what he considered the consummate corn for popping. The new corn popped up fluffier than other varieties, and a higher percentage of individual kernels popped. Redenbacher's secret? He harvested and stored the hybrid corn on the cob, drying it at a controlled temperature to maintain a specific moisture level in each kernel.

Redenbacher now faced the challenge of producing and marketing his newfangled snack. Farmers weren't exactly lining up to grow the new corn. It cost more to harvest than other popping corns, and yields were lower per acre than with traditional corns. Also, retailers weren't eager to stock the new popcorn, which had been dubbed Red Bow. Over and over again, merchants told Redenbacher that people just wouldn't pay more for a new popcorn, even popcorn that was of higher quality.

Redenbacher realized he needed a different approach. He traveled to Chicago to meet with a team of marketing specialists and spent hours talking about popcorn. He was astonished when they advised calling the product Orville Redenbacher's Gourmet Popping Corn. To the onetime farm boy who had spent his life in the cornfields, this idea seemed awfully farfetched, to say the least. But that wasn't all. The marketers wanted Redenbacher to put his own picture on the label. They also suggested the new popcorn be positioned as unabashedly upscale, packaged appropriately, and tagged with a premium price.

Although he was skeptical, Redenbacher decided to get his money's worth and try these marketing ideas. Put yourself in Redenbacher's shoes. How would you create and support the new brand? What packaging and labeling decisions would you have to make as you introduce the new product? How would you encourage retailers to open up space on their crowded shelves for your new product? How would you encourage people to try your popcorn, then buy it again? How would you sustain sales after the product was established?[1]

# CHAPTER OVERVIEW

The marketers helping Orville Redenbacher had to grapple with some important issues when they dreamed up the concept of gourmet popcorn. This chapter introduces you to fundamental product concepts, beginning with a broad definition of "product." Following that, the chapter explains how marketers classify the products they deal with, which is a vital step in designing your marketing strategy. Next you'll look at the elements that make up a product, including features, branding, labeling, and supporting elements. The chapter concludes with several special product issues, including safety, standards, compatibility, and the idea of selling a complete solution instead of an individual product.

# WHAT IS A PRODUCT?

If you were asked to name three popular "products" off the top of your head, you might think of Snickers, Levi's, and Pepsi—or three similar products. You might not think of the Boston Celtics, Disneyland, or a popular television show. That's because when we're on the buying end of an exchange, we tend to think of products as *tangible* objects that we can actually touch and possess. Basketball teams, theme parks, and TV programs provide an *intangible* service for our use or enjoyment, not for our ownership; however, they are products just the same.

As defined in Chapter 1, a product is anything offered for sale for the purpose of satisfying a want or need on both sides of the exchange process. This includes tangible objects that marketers refer to as *goods,* as well as intangible services, ideas, persons, places, or organizations—or any combination of these.

In fact, most products encompass a bundle of attributes that can be heavy on the tangible side, heavy on the intangible side, or anywhere in between, as reflected in the product continuum presented in Exhibit 8.1. Salt is overwhelmingly tangible, whereas education is predominantly intangible. The products offered by a fast-food restaurant such as Burger King fall somewhere in the center of the product continuum because they have both tangible attributes (the food) and intangible attributes (the service of preparing the food for you). Products that are predominantly intangible—services—present some special marketing challenges, and these issues are addressed in Chapter 10.

When you purchase a product, you expect more than just the basic product features. When you visit Burger King you want more than a hamburger bun with some beef and assorted extras. The various ingredients in the burger itself are important, of course, but you want more. You want it to satisfy your hunger, you want to have fun while you're eating it, and you want to avoid the hassle of cooking it yourself. This leads us to one of the most important concepts in the field of marketing: Customers expect *benefits* from the *features* they're paying for. Features are important only to the extent that they provide benefits. Therefore, the essence of good product design is understanding the benefits customers are looking for and then creating the features that provide those benefits. From the customer's perspective, the product includes all the features and all the benefits.

**Exhibit 8.1
THE PRODUCT
CONTINUUM**
Products contain both tangible and intangible components; predominantly tangible products are called goods, and predominantly intangible products are considered services.

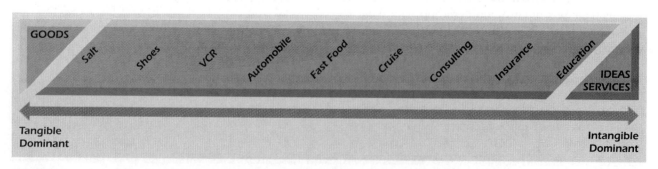

| GOODS | | | | | | | | IDEAS SERVICES |
|---|---|---|---|---|---|---|---|---|
| Salt | Shoes | VCR | Automobile | Fast Food | Cruise | Consulting | Insurance | Education |

Tangible
Dominant

Intangible
Dominant

Apply this concept to the last expensive meal you ate. Assume for a moment that the food could have been prepared to your satisfaction by any number of restaurants, including some that would have charged you far less. However, the meal you pay for in an exclusive, upscale restaurant is just not the same product as the meal you pay for at a less expensive establishment—even if the food is identical. This is true for two reasons: First, the expensive restaurant offers more intangible product features, such as better service, valet parking, coat checking, and possibly other features such as live music. Second, you get benefits from the expensive restaurant you simply cannot get at the cheaper place. You can be seen eating there, you can impress your dinner companions, you can run into influential people, and you can feel better about yourself.

It doesn't matter what the product is; this concept of features and benefits still applies. For instance, Kinko's, a nationwide chain of copy shops, understands that its customers are buying more than photocopying. When people go to Kinko's, they're thinking in terms of getting a job interview from a professional-looking résumé, having access to a computer in the middle of the night, impressing a client with a beautifully bound report, or making it to class on time instead of waiting in line for copies. Therefore, Kinko's marketers develop product strategies that address a broad range of customer needs and expectations, not just the simple need to make photocopies.

Product strategy for nonprofit organizations that deliver goods and services is similar to strategies developed by for-profit firms. However, in social marketing, the concept of product must be reconsidered. The idea or the cause becomes the product in these cases, and sometimes just defining the product can be difficult. For instance, Thailand's Population Development Associates markets contraceptive devices, but its real product is the cause of population control.

## PRODUCT CLASSIFICATION

The variety of products offered in today's marketplace is almost mind-boggling. Take the average U.S. supermarket, which stocks some 10,000 or more individual products or brands. Then consider Biggs in Cincinnati, which stocks 60,000 products. When it comes to prescription drugs, doctors have at least 100,000 to choose from—enough to give anyone a headache.[2] Television viewers used to have only a handful of channels to watch; now scores of channels are competing for our attention, and systems with several hundred channels are on the way.

Every year, product choices increase as companies introduce new products of all types. In a typical year, for example, the 1,500 companies listed on the New York Stock Exchange introduce more than 5,000 significant new products, not to mention thousands of less important products. In addition, at least 5 million other U.S. corporations have their own array of products.[3]

Marketers have devised various product classification systems. By classifying products according to certain criteria, marketers can develop strategies that are more closely attuned to specific customer wants and needs or that can even change preconceived ideas customers may have about certain products. Marketers distinguish between goods, services, and ideas; between durable and nondurable goods; and between consumer and organizational products.

### Durable and Nondurable Goods

**Durable goods** are used or consumed over a long period of time, usually at least three years. They include products such as major home appliances, video cameras, furniture, building materials, and jet airplanes. **Nondurable goods** are used or consumed over a short period of time, or after one or a few uses. Nondurable goods include products such as grocery items, gasoline, and office supplies.

When putting together marketing strategies for goods, first consider whether

**durable goods**
Goods that are used or consumed over a long period of time, usually at least several years; examples include houses and automobiles

**nondurable goods**
Goods that are used or consumed over a short period of time or after one or a few uses; examples include food and office supplies

your good is durable or nondurable, because customer needs and perceptions are different for the two groups. Many people view the purchase of durable goods as investments, and they worry about operating costs, resale value, and other long-term parameters. If they don't think about these elements, you can encourage them to do so, if that would present your products in a better light. Say you're marketing home appliances. Your products are more expensive than the competition's, but because they last longer you can promote them as better values. For example, Maytag washers and dryers typically carry premium price tags, but they are marketed as better values because they don't break down as often as lower-priced alternatives. On the other hand, you can't usually position nondurable goods as better investments because consumers don't consider them investments in the first place.

## Consumer Products

Marketers in the consumer sector find it useful to classify goods and services by the amount of time, money, and risk involved in the purchase decision. The time required for a purchase includes the time spent searching for and evaluating alternatives in addition to the time spent making the actual purchase. The money aspect naturally includes the purchase price, but it also includes the cost of searching for and evaluating alternatives as well as the cost of owning a product (such as maintenance, repair, and storage fees). The risk involved in making a purchase can take several forms: (1) the consumer's peer group might not approve of the purchase (social risk), (2) the product might not perform adequately (functional risk), (3) the consumer might end up wasting money on a bad purchase (financial risk), (4) the consumer might buy a product that is unhealthy or unsafe (physical risk), or (5) the consumer might buy a product that doesn't provide emotional or intellectual satisfaction (psychological risk).

The classification scheme based on these factors provides a great start toward effective marketing strategies. Once you know how consumers buy a given product, you'll have a basic idea of how it should be marketed. Using the variables of time, effort, and risk produces three common categories: convenience products, shopping products, and specialty products.

**convenience products**
Relatively inexpensive products that buyers or users choose frequently with a minimum of thought and effort

**Convenience products** are relatively inexpensive goods and services that are purchased with a minimum of thought and effort. Step into a 24-hour convenience store, and you'll get a clear picture of convenience products. These stores are designed to carry products that consumers want to buy in a hurry, without spending much time or energy in the process. One of the reasons these products are purchased without much thought is that the purchase represents very little risk to the consumer.

**shopping products**
Products that are more costly and involve more risk than convenience products, thereby causing buyers and users to invest more time and effort when making the selection

**Shopping products** are more costly and involve more risk than convenience products, thereby causing buyers to invest more time and effort in making the selection. For instance, you usually don't buy the first blouse or jacket you see in a store; you spend some time examining various brands and styles. For example, if you dragged your parents (or vice versa) all over the country, visiting and comparing college campuses, you know all about how much effort shopping products involve.

**specialty products**
Unique or specialized products that are the most costly and that are unique or so specialized that buyers and users are willing to expend great effort to seek out and acquire them

**Specialty products** are the most costly, involve significant risk, and are unique or so specialized that buyers and users are willing to spend a great deal of time and money to acquire them. Consumer specialty products can include expensive sports cars or antique cars, events such as the Olympics or the Super Bowl, the Mayo Clinic, and custom-made furniture. Customers are willing to wait for weeks if necessary for a specialty product, and they are reluctant to accept substitutes.

These categories don't apply in every case for every customer, of course; what one person considers a convenience product might be a shopping product or even a specialty product for someone else. Some people buy the cheapest coffee in the grocery store, while others travel to specialty shops to buy small bags of gourmet beans.

The purpose of classifying products in this manner is to provide a frame of ref-

**Exhibit 8.2
RETAILING
STRATEGIES FOR
CONVENIENCE
PRODUCTS**
*People* magazine and other
convenience products placed
near the checkout stand in
this grocery store are in this
particular spot because consumers usually buy them on
impulse, and the retailer
wants to bring the products to
the consumers' attention
while they are standing in line
with nothing else to do.

erence for developing product, promotion, pricing, and distribution strategies. This
gives marketers two important advantages. First, by understanding how consumers
perceive and purchase products, they can design marketing programs that fit customer behavior. For instance, look around next time you're standing in line at a grocery store checkout (see Exhibit 8.2). *People* magazine, Wrigley's gum, Duracell batteries, and all the other goods staring at you while you wait are put there for one
important reason: These are products that you often buy on impulse, without any
planning. While you're standing there, you remember that you need batteries, you
think that some gum might taste good, or you contemplate slipping the *People* magazine inside a textbook next time you're supposed to be reading in class. These marketers know how you buy their products, and they market them accordingly.

The second reason for classifying consumer products is to help marketers reposition them. This is particularly important for products that don't seem to be much
different from their competitors, such as home-repair materials, paper, meat, and
spices. As a marketer, if you can move your product up a notch in the customer's
eyes, you'll increase your competitive advantage. Also, shifting your product upscale
often allows you to charge higher prices. For instance, the physical difference between Evian and plain old water isn't all that much, but consumers pay more for
Evian because it is positioned as something better. Of course, positioning doesn't
always mean moving a product upscale. At times, marketers do just the opposite,
positioning a product as something that a wide target market can afford.

Exhibit 8.3 shows how the three consumer-product categories relate to each other
in terms of the risk associated with product selection, the customer's level of effort
in choosing a product, and the scope of strategies needed to gain a competitive advantage. In addition to these three types, certain products are considered *unsought
products* because consumers don't normally think about buying them. Marketers of
life insurance, roof cleaning, and many charitable contributions fall into this category. If you're marketing such products, you usually have to work extra hard just
to convince people they even need what you're selling.

## Organizational Products

As you might expect, organizational customers buy a wide variety of products that
allow them to create their own products. Canon must buy furniture, computers, manufacturing equipment, telephones, buildings, vehicles, and office supplies before it

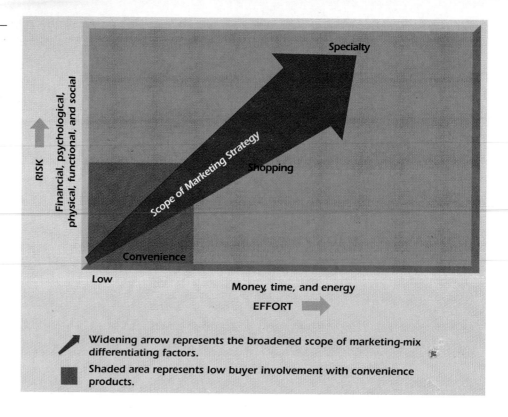

**Exhibit 8.3
A STRATEGIC
CLASSIFICATION OF
PRODUCTS**

Classifying products according to customer perception and behavior helps you develop more effective marketing strategies.

can start selling copiers. In addition, it might buy a number of services as well, from janitors, lawyers, accountants, marketing research firms, and advertising agencies. It also purchases electricity, water, and a variety of fuels. With all these products in place, Canon then purchases the metal, plastic, glass, and electronic components that it will transform into copying machines. Organizations of all types, including your college, the 7-Eleven on the corner, the Internal Revenue Service, the Red Cross, and Ford Motor Company, spend a lot of time and money buying the products they need to produce their own goods and services.

As with consumer products, marketers classify organizational products to provide more insight into customer behavior and potential marketing strategies. Over the years, a classification system has evolved for organizational products that is different from the consumer system. Knowing the terminology used in organizational markets is helpful because these terms have become the standard language for organizational buyers and sellers. Here's a quick look at the various categories of organizational products.

- *Raw materials.* Manufacturing and processing companies have to buy a variety of raw materials, ranging from iron ore and crude petroleum to lumber and chemicals. Although these products are often rather simple, customers usually buy in vast quantities, so the total purchase price can run into thousands or millions of dollars.
- *Components.* In addition to raw materials, most manufacturers also buy components, which are parts that go into the manufacturers' final products. For instance, Boeing might buy seats, radios, serving carts, tires, and other components from a variety of manufacturers, and then assemble all these parts into a finished aircraft.
- *Supplies.* Organizational customers of all types need supplies to keep their operations going. A common term for supplies is **MRO items,** referring to maintenance, repair, and operating items. Depending on the customer, supplies can mean anything from pencils to nails to floor wax. Supplies are consumed during the creation and delivery of products, but unlike raw materials and components, they don't become part of the finished product.

**MRO items**
Consumable industrial supplies categorized specifically as maintenance, repair, and operating supplies

- *Equipment.* Even if it's only a desk and a telephone, organizational customers need equipment. For a small service provider, such as an independent consultant, the equipment needs are fairly modest. At the other extreme, the U.S. government, Citicorp, and General Motors have mammoth equipment needs, ranging from robots, computers, and vehicles to thousands of pieces of office furniture. **Capital equipment** refers to equipment that produces goods, provides services, or otherwise supports the operation of an organization. The largest pieces of equipment are often considered installations, the next organizational product category.

- *Installations.* Installations are among the most complicated organizational goods. They are composed of buildings and large stationary equipment such as production lines, milling machines, and semiconductor fabrication machinery. Some examples of complete installations include factories, power plants, airports, and mainframe computer systems. Such major purchases hold a great deal of risk for the buyer because things can go wrong in so many ways. In addition, the location itself is an important part of an installation. Various cities, states, and countries promote themselves as ideal places to build factories and other business facilities. For instance, the French Industrial Development Agency advertises in U.S. magazines, hoping to catch the attention of companies looking to expand their European operations.[4]

- *Business services.* Business services range from simple and fairly risk-free services such as landscaping and cleaning to complex services such as management consulting and auditing, which can strongly affect an organization's success or failure. Examples of some of the big names in business services include Price Waterhouse (accounting), Bain (management consulting), UPS (package delivery), CSX (shipping and rail transportation), and ServiceMaster (cleaning and maintenance). Even though some of these services are relatively simple, the purchase process can be complicated because the total price is significant in many cases.

**capital equipment**
Industrial machinery, office and store equipment, or transportation vehicles that are purchased infrequently and are used to produce goods, provide a service, or support the day-to-day operation of an organization

## Limitations of Product Classification Models

As important as they are, the product classification models presented here aren't without limitations. First, many products are sold to both consumers and organizations, so they can't be put into either group exclusively. The reason a product is purchased determines its categorization; personal computers, for instance, can be purchased for both consumer and organizational use. Second, customer behavior isn't always rational and can't always be neatly categorized. A person who spends an hour debating the relative merits of eating at Pizza Hut versus Godfather's on another occasion might walk past a Brooks Brothers store, pop inside, and lay down an American Express card for a suit on display in the window. The $12 pizza starts to look like a shopping product, and the $800 suit flew out the door like a convenience product. Third, customers don't always categorize products in the same manner. A pair of Reebok Pumps might be the dream product for one consumer, who shops for months and compares competing models from Nike, Adidas, Etonic, and New Balance. Somebody else might be strolling through the mall and buy a pair without thinking twice. Fourth, some inexpensive products that involve little risk can become specialty products anyway because of exceptionally strong loyalty to the brand name. Coca-Cola Classic is a good example.[5]

Even with these limitations, product classification schemes are a helpful tool for designing marketing strategies. Just be careful when you apply them, and don't worry if products don't seem to fit the scheme perfectly. Now take a closer look at what actually constitutes a product.

## ELEMENTS OF A PRODUCT

The elements that make up a product include features, branding, packaging, labeling, and supporting elements. Each of these elements applies to all categories of products, but the way that marketers treat them can vary significantly from one product to another. In fact, one of the primary goals of many marketers is to differentiate their products from competing products by developing unique strategies for each product element. On the other hand, some marketers purposely strive to develop "me-too" versions of the most popular products. Here's a closer look at each element.

## Features

Saying that any product must provide the features that customers need and want sounds obvious, but too often marketers either misjudge customer needs or think they have something customers will be sure to love as soon as they hear about it. In general, the most successful products address well-defined customer needs, whether the need is more efficient processing of iron ore, more durable lipstick, or better-tasting french fries. Many products get started when someone observes or experiences a problem of some kind. When management consultant Bernie DeKoven saw clients wasting time (and therefore money) in meetings, he designed the Meeting Meter. This software program keeps a running total of the cost of tying people up in a meeting, which encourages faster, more efficient meetings. Clients ranging from American Airlines to Eastman Kodak to the FBI use it to keep meetings as short as possible.[6]

Marketers often come up with unique ideas for products and assume that customers will find the products irresistible. Unfortunately, it rarely works that way. Most successful products evolve through a process of discovering what specific features members of the target market find desirable or acceptable, then merging that information with what makes the most sense technically and financially. Wind-powered electrical generators have been around for decades now, but are only now becoming financially acceptable alternatives to coal, gas, hydro, and other power-generation technologies. Luz Technologies went bankrupt trying to sell wind generators in the late 1970s, but in the mid-1990s, Kenetech and other producers offer efficient systems that are catching on with customers worldwide.[7]

In addition to a specific technology, the many aspects of product features to consider include the product's physical form or design, level of quality, durability, environmental impact, and ease of use. These considerations apply to tangible products as well as intangible products. Sometimes marketers focus their efforts and attention on one or two aspects of a product because they are convinced those features are most important to customers, even when successful competitors are taking a different approach.

Although product features are one of the most important marketing considerations, they do not necessarily dictate how other marketing strategies will be handled. Sometimes factors such as promotion, pricing, and distribution dictate product features. For instance, many consumers complain about the taste of commercially grown produce. Perhaps you've purchased a beautiful tomato or apple only to find that the taste just didn't live up to its great looks. One reason for this is that producers have developed new strains of fruits and vegetables that are designed to

**Exhibit 8.4
THE BRAND NAME
SPECTRUM**
All brand names fall somewhere along this spectrum, with free-standing names being the strongest (as far as legal protection is concerned) and descriptive names being the weakest.

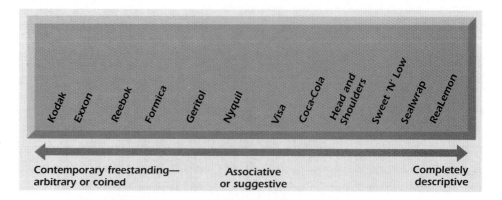

travel well and look good in the grocery store—sometimes at the expense of taste.

Just because customers like certain product features one day doesn't mean they will forever. Customer wants and needs change continually. Marketers regularly evaluate their products and the marketplace to keep pace with customer expectations.

## Branding

For centuries businesspeople have been devising ways to identify their wares and distinguish them from those of competitors. In the early years, they used pictures because many potential customers were illiterate. Then shopkeepers started using their own names to distinguish their shops from others. Eventually marketers coined product names like Kodak, which George Eastman created in 1888.[8] Today brand names range from utterly meaningless to minutely descriptive, as seen in Exhibit 8.4. With the world's increasing clutter of products all clamoring for recognition, the process of branding is more important and challenging than ever.

Branding involves much more than simply choosing a product name. A **brand** can encompass a name, a word, a phrase, a design, a symbol, or any combination of these elements in order to distinguish one product from another. A **brand name** is the portion of a brand that can be spoken, including letters, words, or numbers, such as Kellogg's Product 19, Acura, IBM, and Blockbuster Video. A **brand mark** is the portion of a brand that cannot be expressed verbally, such as a graphic design or symbol. Some of the most widely recognized brand marks are the Mercedes-Benz three-pointed star within a circle, the McDonald's golden arches, and the NBC peacock. A brand mark is sometimes referred to as a logo; however, a **logo** can also refer to a distinctive type style such as Coca-Cola's elegant script.

Many companies offer several brands under one company name. The legal name under which a company or organization operates is referred to as its **trade name.** For example, the trade name for the company that sells Kodak products is Eastman Kodak Company. When the owner of a brand or portion of a brand registers it with the U.S. government for exclusive use by the brand owner, the brand is then referred to as a **trademark.** A **service mark** is the same as a trademark, but it refers to a service rather than a good. Good luck coming up with an effective trademark that hasn't already been used: the U.S. Patent and Trademark Office received 125,237 trademark registration applications in 1992 alone.[9]

### THE VALUE OF BRANDING

A brand is often an organization's most valuable asset because it provides customers with a way of recognizing and specifying a particular product if they want to choose it again or recommend it to others. A brand also enables marketers to develop specific images and interrelated marketing strategies for a particular product. In addition, a brand can command a premium price in the marketplace, and it is often the only element of a product competitors can't copy. Agricultural specialists may eventually be able to duplicate Orville Redenbacher's popcorn, but they'll have to search far and wide for a name that could match his. Rather than building brands from scratch, some firms simply buy established brand names. Highly successful brands can be worth millions of dollars. Cadbury Schweppes, for example, calculated that the $220 million it paid for Hires and Crush included $20 million for physical assets and $200 million for "brand value."[10] This notion of the value of a brand is also called **brand equity,** which indicates a brand's overall strength in the marketplace. The concept of brand equity and its definition are still evolving, but one useful definition breaks it down into five components: brand loyalty, brand awareness, perceived quality, brand associations, and other proprietary brand assets.[11]

**Brand loyalty** refers to the level of commitment that customers have for a specific brand. The primary benefit of brand loyalty is that it provides insurance against significant market share loss when a new competitor appears on the scene. Another company may have a much larger base of customers to begin with, but if they are "nonloyal" customers, they are more easily lured away by competitors.[12]

**brand**
A name, term, phrase, design, symbol, or any combination of these chosen by an individual or organization to distinguish a product from competing products

**brand name**
The portion of a brand that can be expressed verbally, including letters, words, or numbers

**brand mark**
The portion of a brand that cannot be expressed verbally, such as a graphic design or symbol

**logo**
A unique symbol that represents a specific firm or organization, or a brand name written in a distinctive type style

**trade name**
The business name under which an organization operates

**trademark**
A brand or portion of a brand that is legally registered with the U.S. government for exclusive use by the owner of the brand

**service mark**
A trademark that represents a service rather than a tangible good

**brand equity**
The overall strength of a brand in the marketplace and its value to the company that owns it; composed of brand loyalty, brand awareness, perceived quality, brand associations, and other proprietary brand assets

**brand loyalty**
The level of commitment that customers feel toward a given brand, as represented by their continuing purchase of that brand

Some marketers are putting a renewed emphasis on image advertising to strengthen brand loyalty. A small but growing number of companies are also trying to instill greater loyalty by offering catalogs, magazines, and membership clubs to brand users.[13] Experts say that in a tight race for brand loyalty, victory can be assured by three elements: (1) swift management response both to the press and to the marketplace, (2) the ability to create a perception of quality, and (3) maximized spending on marketing.[14]

**brand awareness**
A measure of the percentage of the target market that is aware of a brand name

The second element of brand equity is **brand awareness,** a measure of how many potential buyers know about a brand. A common strategy in marketing and advertising is increasing the level of awareness (see Exhibit 8.5). Naturally, people can't buy products they don't know about, but familiarity is also a powerful purchase influence (assuming the other elements associated with the brand are positive, of course). Buyers are more comfortable with known products than with unknown products.[15]

The third element is *perceived quality.* Part of a buyer's image of a brand is based on actual facts and experiences—the type of steel used in a saw blade, the reliability ratings that *Consumer Reports* gives to cars, and so on. However, another part of that image is based on perceptions born out of a company's reputation, word of mouth, media coverage, and other indirect sources of information. For instance, someone who has never owned, shopped for, or even ridden in a Mercedes-Benz is still likely to perceive it as a quality automobile.

*Brand associations* are perceptions and images that people link with particular brands. If you saw Hershey's and Drost brands of chocolate milk in the supermarket, which would you associate with chocolate? Most U.S. consumers would go with Hershey's, since that name has a strong association with chocolate. Drost is also a

**Rose:** The Minnesota Orchestra is putting on this opera called *Falstaff*—a really wonderful opera.

**Todd:** I would rather be dropped into a mountain of road salt. I would rather be dragged by a team of wild horses through burning hot desert sands. I am not an opera kind of person. I like to have a few beers.

**Rose:** So does Falstaff, Todd.

**Todd:** Have a few laughs.

**Rose:** Falstaff is very funny. Falstaff is an easy-to-love, light Italian opera about a fat, beer-swilling middle-aged guy. Who do you think that's starting to remind me of, Todd?

**VO:** Falstaff. A funny opera complete with English supertitles projected above the stage. See it Wednesday, November 7 and Friday, November 9 at Orchestra Hall. Call 371-5656 for tickets.

**Exhibit 8.5**
**BUILDING BRAND AWARENESS**
The Minnesota Orchestra used this humorous radio commercial to build awareness of both opera in general and its particular product offering.

brand of chocolate, quite well known in Europe. Note that brand associations can also be negative, and these detract from a brand's equity. Companies that have been linked to scandals, environmental disasters, and poor quality also have strong brand associations—but not the kind likely to increase sales.

The final element is a catch-all category for other assets owned or held by the marketer. Branding expert David Aaker includes in this list such elements as patents, trademarks, and relationships with distribution channels. Frito-Lay and Procter & Gamble are well-known consumer-goods marketers with strong channel relationships.[16] The more of these assets a brand holds, the greater its equity will be.

You can see that brands offer potentially great value to the people and companies who own them, but brand owners aren't the only ones who benefit from branding. For buyers, brand names simplify shopping. Imagine how confused consumers would be after a day of visiting car showrooms if none of the vehicles had identifying names or symbols. In addition to making shopping easier for consumers, brands also protect them from repurchasing products that they don't like or that have problems.

For example, Hyundai lost potential customers when its first wave of Excel compacts developed a multitude of annoying mechanical problems at 35,000 to 45,000 miles. Sales dropped dramatically from the peak of 264,000 units sold in 1987.[17] Even though new models have proven to be of better quality, Hyundai is still struggling to regain its stature in the minds of consumers.

What are the best brands around? Total Research of Princeton, New Jersey, conducts an annual survey of U.S. consumers' favorite brand names, and the same outfit—Disney World/Disneyland—has been at the top for three years running. The other top brands are Kodak, United Parcel Service, Hallmark Cards, Fisher-Price, and AT&T.[18]

## TYPES OF BRANDS

Three types of brands are manufacturer brands, private brands, and generic brands. A **manufacturer brand** is designated, owned, and used by the manufacturer or producer of the product. Examples of manufacturer brands include Goodyear, L.A. Gear, Xerox, Nike, Liz Claiborne, Ralph Lauren, Jockey, and Black & Decker. Because they are usually marketed nationwide, manufacturer brands are often referred to as *national brands.*

**manufacturer brand**
A brand that is designated, owned, and used by the manufacturer of the product

A **private brand** is designated, owned, and used by a wholesaler or retailer; it's sometimes called a *private label* or *store brand*. Nearly every large supermarket chain has its own private brands for many popular products ranging from cold medicine to sandwich bags to dandruff shampoo. Private brands are promoted to a limited extent by the wholesaler or retailer, but they don't achieve the national recognition that manufacturer brands do—with some exceptions. The Sears Diehard is the leading brand in car batteries.

**private brand**
A brand that is designated, owned, and used by a wholesaler or retailer

The relationship between national brands and private brands has been changing in recent years. Stop and think about why a national brand would be attractive in the first place: It supposedly offers the consumer the security of going with a recognized, high-quality supplier, rather than some obscure local supplier (the awareness component of brand equity). However, in many product categories, the perceived difference between national and private brands has narrowed, prompting more and more consumers to make the switch to often-cheaper private brands. In just two years, for example, private brands' share of the disposable diaper market jumped from 21 to 31 percent. Perrigo, a company that specializes in producing private-label nonprescription drugs that are the functional equivalent of well-known brands, watched sales grow nearly 300 percent in a recent five-year period. This significant shift in consumer behavior is prompting major national marketers such as Procter & Gamble to work hard to reduce their manufacturing and marketing costs in order to get on more even pricing ground with private brands.[19]

The trend isn't confined to the United States, either; private brands now account for 24 percent of all supermarket sales in France and 32 percent in Great Britain. Aggressive cost reductions on private-label brands in Japan in recent years have caused many consumers to switch from well-known U.S. and Japanese national brands.[20]

The attack of the private labels has not been universally successful, however. In such product categories as toothpaste, canned tuna, baby food, and shaving cream, private labels have either failed to make much headway or are falling back from earlier gains. Experts point to a combination of competitive pricing by national brands and doubts about private-label quality as the reasons. An explanation from a shopper in Minneapolis says a lot about which categories offer a better chance to private labels. For paper towels and bread, he said, "They all work. Why pay for a name?" However, when it came to baby food, the same shopper's response was, "For something like that, you want to make sure you get the good stuff. I don't know anything about Elmer Fudd baby food, but I know Gerber."[21]

**generic brand**
A nonbranded product that is identified only by its product category

A **generic brand** is actually a nonbranded product that is identified only by its product category, such as "paper towels." Unlike private brands, which look almost like competing manufacturer brands when it comes to packaging, generic brands have a plain look. Over 75 percent of all U.S. supermarkets are now offering at least some generic items in their stores.[22] Generic drugs are also becoming increasingly prevalent as patents expire on branded drugs, opening the way for other drug corporations to legally manufacture the generic version.

Manufacturers who produce private and generic brands sometimes make nearly identical products that compete directly with their own brands. Manufacturers make competing private and generic brands for several reasons. If manufacturers have excess production capacity, making private and generic brands provides a means of achieving a better return on the company's assets. Producing private and generic brands also helps manufacturers generate a more predictable cash flow, since orders tend to be placed on a regular basis at a contracted price. Another benefit is that manufacturers don't have to bear the cost or expend the effort to promote, distribute, and guarantee the product. Finally, if manufacturers decide *not* to produce a private or generic brand (hoping to stifle additional competition), competing manufacturers will simply get the business instead.

Retailers who sell private and generic brands realize several advantages. First, the retailer has complete control over the product's quality, how it's promoted, and how it's priced. Second, private- and generic-brand products can generate a better profit because the promotion costs are not usually as high as those for a manufacturer brand. Third, when customers develop brand loyalty to private and generic brands, the retailer gets all the benefit because the product cannot be purchased at any competing store. The Limited, for example, is a fashion specialty chain that has achieved impressive growth because of its popular private-brand merchandise. In fact, The Limited's Forenza and Outback Red brands make it number three in sales of women's apparel in the United States.[23]

## KEY BRANDING ISSUES

Once marketers decide to offer a branded product (whether they're producers offering their own brand or retailers offering a private brand), three primary issues are considered: (1) brand selection, (2) brand protection, and (3) brand extension versus individual branding.

BRAND SELECTION    Selecting a brand is one of the most important decisions a marketer has to make because the brand name is key to a product's personality. However, many successful brands have emerged from unimaginative company trade names. Perdue Chicken Farms, for example, got its name from founder Frank Perdue. When he decided to build brand loyalty, Perdue Farms became the brand name, and the strategy has been successful. Other commodity items such as coal, beef, and lumber aren't usually branded. However, branding commodities is a growing trend.

When you choose a brand name, consider issues such as ease in pronouncing, writing, and remembering the name; the image you want the brand to reflect; any negative or controversial overtones that it may have; how it translates into a foreign

Even though its symbol wasn't created for religious purposes (it's the inverse of the Swiss flag), the International Red Cross must use a red crescent in Islamic countries such as Turkey because the cross is an unacceptable religious symbol in those countries.

language (if it will possibly be marketed internationally); any geographic limitations (if it sounds too local); and whether new additions to the product line can use the same brand. Crayola, for example, may mean crayons to most of us, but Hallmark Cards (which now owns the Crayola brand name) has introduced a line of children's clothing under the Crayola name.[24]

BRAND PROTECTION   Marketers can protect a brand in two ways: by using it and by legally registering it. Registering a brand offers the most protection because an unregistered brand has no rights in many countries outside the United States—even if it has been used for years.

To register a brand for exclusive use by the owner, it must be legally protectable. According to the Lanham Act of 1946, it should not contain generic words in common usage such as *perfect, premium,* or *fantastic.* If a brand is being used, or has already been registered by someone else, it cannot be registered by another person unless its use is for an entirely different category of products, such as Hallmark Cards, Hallmark Circuits, and Hallmark Financial Services.

Once a brand is registered, the owner can help ensure that it remains protected by using it regularly and renewing the registration when necessary. To avoid any doubt of ownership, use the ® symbol following the trademark or service mark. If a brand is awaiting registration, use the ™ symbol to identify it as your exclusive property. A trademark is always capitalized, and the spelling is never changed or modified. Trademark experts also suggest that owners (1) keep records of total sales of products bearing the trademark or service mark and (2) make sure that the trademark or service mark appears on invoices.[25]

Some trademarks that have been in common use for years run the risk of becoming generic terms and losing their protection. For example, words such as *thermos, zipper,* and *aspirin* were once brand names but have since been ruled by the courts to be generic terms. When it comes to fighting for proprietary rights to a trademark, Coca-Cola heads the list. The soft drink company files 40 to 60 trademark suits every year to prevent its various trademarks from becoming generic words, which would depreciate nearly 100 years and millions of dollars of investment in its identity.[26] Xerox (see Exhibit 8.6) and Styrofoam are two other brand

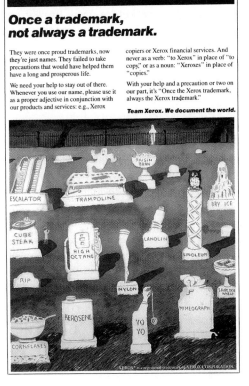

**Exhibit 8.6**
**PROTECTING BRAND NAMES**
A well-established brand name is a valuable asset, and companies whose brands have become nearly synonymous with their product categories often find themselves struggling to keep their brands from becoming generic terms. Xerox is worried that it might lose the ability to keep its trademark if public misuse transforms "Xerox" into a generic verb for photocopying.

names that have fallen into common use, and their respective owners are trying to convince people to treat their brands with a little more respect.

**brand extension**
Assigning an existing brand name to a new product in the same product line or in a different product line

BRAND EXTENSION VERSUS INDIVIDUAL BRANDING    **Brand extension** refers to the practice of assigning an existing brand name to a new product either in the same product line or in a different product line. In 1992 Gillette introduced the ClearGel clear deodorant technology in the Gillette Series line of men's toiletries. In 1993 and 1994, it added ClearGel to other brands, creating Right Guard ClearGel, Soft & Dri ClearGel, and Dry Idea ClearGel.[27] No universal rule for brand extension exists, however; sometimes it works, and sometimes it doesn't. It worked for Diet Coke but not for Sara Lee frozen dinners.[28]

**family brand**
A brand assigned to an entire line of product items

The most common form of brand extension is family branding. A **family brand** is assigned to an entire line or mix of product items. Campbell makes Campbell's Pork & Beans, Campbell's Soup, and Campbell's Tomato Juice. Orville Redenbacher makes several flavors and types of popcorn, all under the founder's name. Even sequels to hit movies use the family brand extension concept to get additional mileage out of popular brand names. A powerful name, however, is no guarantee that family branding will succeed. Xerox tried to extend its powerful brand name to computers and computer printers but failed. Scott hung its name on so many household products during its 20-year strategy of brand extension that the name began to lose any specific meaning it might have once had.[29]

**individual brand**
A separate brand assigned to an individual product item within a product line

An **individual brand** is a separate brand assigned to an individual product item within a product line. Mars offers Three Musketeers, M&M's, Snickers, and Milky Way. Snickers, however, started its own family of brands when it introduced the Snickers Ice Cream Bar. Using an individual branding strategy has one important advantage: if customers don't like a new product, the negative impact isn't likely to affect the company's other products. In addition, individual branding allows companies to expand into new, unrelated product areas without confusing customers.

Some companies use a combination of family brands and individual brands. Kellogg, for example, combines its companywide brand name with individual product identifiers to create such names as Kellogg's Rice Krispies and Kellogg's Special K. This gives each product its own distinct image while allowing it to take advantage of the well-known company name.

Using family branding and employing well-known brand names when creating new products can be an effective strategy, but doing so isn't without risks. Marketing experts caution that going too far with brand spinoffs poses a threat to product innovation. If marketers grow to rely on leverage from their past successes, they may lose the sparks of creativity that made them successful in the first place. Without innovative new products, a company can severely damage its long-term prospects.[30]

## Packaging

In addition to the obvious purpose of containing products, packaging gives you a way to present your product to potential buyers. Nearly all products are packaged in one way or another. Even intangible services, ideas, people, and places are packaged for particular markets. The packaging of politicians and entertainers is big business.[31]

### PACKAGING FUNCTIONS

Packaging performs two important functions that interrelate with the rest of the marketing mix: facilitating promotion and facilitating distribution.

FACILITATING PROMOTION    The packaging of consumer products always seems to get more attention than the packaging of industrial and organizational products, perhaps because of the sheer volume of consumer packaged goods displayed in gro-

**Exhibit 8.7**
**PROMOTING WITH PACKAGING**
Both the product packaging and the display rack help promote Topol toothpaste in this situation.

cery stores, department stores, and other retail outlets. However, packaging does play an important role in facilitating the promotion of many industrial products, especially in the area of services.

One way packaging facilitates promotion of organizational products is by creating and supporting a particular image. Financial institutions, car rental firms, and retailers that cater to businesses work hard to create an image that carries out the firm's promotional message. For example, a computer retailer that caters to the needs of businesses might create store interiors that look like a professional office. The stores' clerks and salespeople would dress and act like executives, and perhaps the technicians would even wear ties. All these efforts would be part of "packaging" the store.

Of course, when it comes to consumer packaged goods, few companies can afford to sell image alone. One way packaging facilitates promotion of consumer products is by enhancing identification. TV advertisers usually give the package a starring role in commercials to reinforce consumer identification.[32]

Another important function of consumer-product packaging is providing in-store promotion (see Exhibit 8.7). Smartfood, for example, designed a striking package for its cheese-coated popcorn. In fact, shoppers accustomed to seeing row upon row of look-alike potato chip packages can't help noticing Smartfood's jet-black bag with its bright green and yellow ear of popping corn. Even unexciting auto parts sell better when they're displayed in attractive packages. Toyota USA, for instance, convinced its parent company to toss the plain cardboard boxes and adopt colorful hanging packages with plastic windows.[33]

Packaging can also enhance product appeal for customers who have specific needs and preferences. For example, buyers for single and small households often find small and single-serving packages more appealing than large economy packages. Many buyers also prefer plastic squeeze bottles, pump dispensers, and packages that can be easily opened and resealed.

FACILITATING DISTRIBUTION    Packaging can facilitate distribution in several ways. The most obvious is by providing protection for tangible products such as food, drugs, toys, appliances, and computers. With protective packaging, consumers need not risk purchasing products that have been tampered with, are damaged, or are

## TAKING YOUR BRANDS INTERNATIONAL

**EXPLORING GLOBAL MARKETING**

When you market products internationally, consider two important factors of branding. The first concerns the culture in your target markets, particularly language and symbolism. Logo symbols that work well in the United States don't always work elsewhere. One company that used a red circle in its logo had to adjust in some Asian markets, where people said it reminded them of the Japanese flag. In Mexico, a company whose trademark included yellow flowers discovered that yellow symbolizes death or disrespect in that country. The International Red Cross, the Geneva-based organization whose symbol was created by reversing the Swiss flag, uses a red crescent in certain Islamic countries because a cross is not an acceptable religious symbol in those countries.

Standard Oil of New Jersey made an embarrassing linguistic discovery when it tried to develop a single brand name for the global marketplace. It had been using the brand name *Esso,* but for legal reasons it couldn't use that name in all countries. So the company switched to *Enco,* because the word was easy to remember and pronounce in most languages. While the brand change was under way, the company discovered that *Enco* described a sewage disposal truck in Japan, which wasn't exactly the image the company had in mind. It therefore tossed out *Enco* and switched to *Exxon,* the name we all know it by today.

The second consideration is the legal environment in various countries. This includes both protection for your brand names and legal restrictions on the use of some elements of branding. Shoppers in several Asian countries, notably Taiwan, don't have to look far to find counterfeit goods sold under such well-known brand names as Rolex and Louis Vuitton. Until recently, brand piracy wasn't even a crime in Taiwan, and entre-preneurs got rich selling fake Reeboks and $33 copies of $9,000 Swiss watches. However, now that Taiwan is developing products that are vulnerable to piracy (such as computer software), the Taiwanese government is trying to clean up the country's reputation and create a safer market for business.

Diet Coke provides a good example of the legal restrictions on branding. In some languages *diet* has a medical connotation, and labeling products as such means they can be sold only in pharmacies—clearly not a good distribution strategy for a soft drink. Therefore Coca-Cola changed the name to Coca-Cola Light in all non–English-speaking countries.

### APPLY YOUR KNOWLEDGE

**1.** Have you seen any import brand names that strike you as confusing or inappropriate for a U.S. audience? If so, what would you do to change them without destroying the awareness marketing has built up in the brand?

**2.** As a U.S. marketer going international, what sort of policy would you put in place to make sure your company avoids international marketing blunders?

---

spoiled. A recent survey showed that 84 percent of food-product buyers and 92 percent of over-the-counter pharmaceutical buyers felt "tamper-evident" features were important to packaging.[34]

Protective packaging is especially important to mail-order companies like Williams-Sonoma, a San Francisco–based firm that sells gourmet cookware and garden accessories. After switching to Dow Chemical's Mold-A-Pac system, Williams-Sonoma estimated a savings in packing materials of more than a dollar per package. In addition, its superior protection capabilities allowed Williams-Sonoma to offer customers a greater variety of fragile items.[35]

Another recent development in packaging has been the aseptic package that keeps food free from oxygen and moisture. (Although these packages have been around a while in Europe, they are fairly new in the United States.) Fruit drinks such as Hi C are being packaged in aseptic containers that reduce the need for refrigeration and provide long shelf lives—a benefit to both the retailer and the consumer.[36] Packaging also helps meet the needs of intermediaries by facilitating transportation and handling. In an attempt to solve the problem of transporting fresh fruits and vegetables, for instance, a Delaware chemical and aerospace company named Hercules developed a package that keeps fresh produce in its just-picked condition for weeks.[37]

In addition to the functional purposes of packaging, marketers must consider three other aspects of packaging: the safety of the package, the package's environmental impact, and the cost of the package.

SAFETY   Improper and dangerous packaging materials can create a serious risk for manufacturers, intermediaries, and customers. For example, high-value products such as computers are often encased in flammable packaging and then stockpiled in warehouses. When Digital Equipment Corporation realized that the company faced substantial risk from fire in its warehouses, it replaced the highly flammable packaging material. This move avoided potential disaster and saved the company money on fire equipment and inventory insurance.[38]

Another type of packaging that has caused concern are microwave-food wrappers that contain thin, metalized plastic-film strips. These strips are used to enhance the cooking of certain foods, such as pizza. However, the strips release chemicals that some health experts consider to be cancer-causing. Fortunately, several companies are developing alternative types of microwave packaging that do not expose consumers to potential health hazards.[39]

ENVIRONMENTAL IMPACT   The amount and type of solid waste that packaging generates is a concern for both consumers and marketers. A recent survey covering 17 packaging types indicated that consumers would like to see nearly half of them replaced out of concern for the environment.[40] As these concerns grow, new ways of packaging consumer goods are being developed and old packaging methods are being revived. For example, a Canadian subsidiary of Du Pont is selling a flexible pouch for milk that consumes much less landfill space than existing containers. Old-fashioned cellophane is making a comeback because it degrades better than current plastic wraps.[41] When Stephanie Glass wanted her new company, Bio Pure, to be environmentally friendly, she had her shampoos and conditioners packaged in recyclable paperboard cartons.[42] Entrepreneur Jerry Smith scored an environmental double when he introduced his BCD brand of environmental cleaner. The product itself is biodegradable and free of synthetic dyes or perfumes, and the package is a flat pouch that uses 70 percent less plastic than traditional cleaner packages.[43]

Recyclability tends to get the most attention when it comes to packaging and the environment, but such a narrow interpretation of environmental concerns often oversimplifies the situation. The aseptic drink boxes mentioned earlier are a good example. They are not yet as recyclable as other materials; however, the fact that they don't need refrigeration—and all the energy consumption and air pollution that refrigeration systems involve—may in fact make them more environmentally sensitive than other packages.

COST   Last but certainly not least is the matter of packaging cost. Although consumers want products packaged in a way that is safe for themselves and the environment, marketers must consider whether consumers will pay for the added costs. Some studies have found that consumers don't mind paying more as long as the cost is within reason. On the other hand, overpackaging that is perceived as adding unnecessarily to a product's cost can turn consumers off, especially for cosmetics, toys, sports items, and gifts. Therefore, the challenge for marketers is to provide packaging that meets the wants and needs of the producer, the customer, and the intermediaries without jeopardizing company profits (see Exhibit 8.8).

## Labeling

In addition to packaging, many consumer and organizational goods must also have labels. Labels can range from a thumbnail-size sticker on a bunch of bananas to a full-page label outlining refrigerator features. Many labels are an absolute necessity;

others are optional. In either case, labeling is an important product element that deserves careful consideration.

## LABELING FUNCTIONS

The primary functions of labeling are to help promote the product, provide information for buyers and intermediaries, and meet regulatory requirements.

- *Promotional support.* Whether visible or hidden, labels play an important role in a company's promotional efforts. Consider designer labels inside clothing. They don't exactly serve as eye-catching enticements, and no one sees them except the buyer, but when discount stores cut them out, the value of the clothing drops immediately. The labels on food products, however, play a key role in enticing customers to buy. If a label is poorly designed, sales can suffer no matter what the product's price. Nasoya Foods, for example, was having difficulty getting shelf space for its tofu-based mayonnaise, but then it redesigned the jar label and sales jumped 50 percent.[44]
- *Information for buyers and intermediaries.* Product labels can contain as many as a dozen or more items of information, including the brand name; the generic name; pictures and logos; the name of the manufacturer; quantity; size; contents or ingredients; nutritional information; instructions for using, consuming, storing, or caring for the product; certification; warnings; and sometimes even the history behind the product or its creator. Label information that is important to wholesalers and retailers includes the expiration date and the **universal product code (UPC),** which is the bar code assigned to products that indicates price, weight, and inventory number. When stores use optical scanners to read the UPC, they are able to reduce customer checkout time as well as their administrative expenses. Furthermore, scanner data collected from the UPC labels are a great source of marketing research data.
- *Regulatory compliance.* Government agencies in the United States (such as the Federal Trade Commission, the Food and Drug Administration, and the Consumer Product Safety Commission) and their counterparts in other countries have various regulations requiring that product labels include certain types of information. Clothing labels, for example, must include fiber content. Information about potential hazards must be spelled out on labels for products such as paints and sol-

**universal product code (UPC)**
A type of bar code assigned to products, which indicates price, weight, and inventory number and can be read by optical scanners at store checkout counters

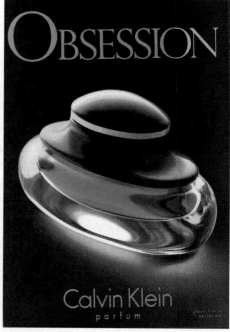

**Exhibit 8.8**
**PACKAGING MUST MEET MULTIPLE DEMANDS**
The bottles used for Obsession perfume and cologne not only have to present the product in an appealing way, but they must meet the needs of retailers and consumers in a cost-effective manner as well.

vents. Nutritional value must be included on various food-product labels. Prescription drugs, health remedies, and electrical appliances are among the many products that must include information on correct usage.

## DESIGN CONSIDERATIONS

Like packaging, labels often communicate with customers during the purchase decision, and they must communicate their promotional messages within a very short period of time. Therefore, the design of the label is often a critical element in the total marketing strategy. Even so, successful marketers understand that customers generally recall only three to five items of information on a label. The three most commonly recalled items are the brand name, the generic name, and pictures and logos.[45]

To help ensure that labels are appealing and eye-catching, remember the following suggestions (which apply to packaging as well as labeling):

- *Avoid trying to look trendy.* Fads fade, but good designs can last for years, often with little or no change.
- *State the product's benefit in simple terms.* Stress the product's two or three major selling points in no more than one or two sentences. Save the small print for the back of the label or package.
- *Keep it clean.* Visual clutter reflects indecision. Simplicity reflects confidence.
- *Be consistent.* Repeat the design in advertisements, on letterhead, on business cards, on trucks—everywhere.[46]

## Supporting Elements

Most products include some type of supporting elements. These include related products; a warranty or guarantee; maintenance and repair services; and installation, training, and consulting services. Such product support not only serves as a selling point but in many cases helps generate additional revenue for the firm.

Related products can include reference manuals that come with computer software, flight bags and snacks that airlines give to their passengers, and souvenirs sold at baseball games. In fact, souvenirs are key supporting products for all types of sporting events and a major source of revenue growth in professional sports. In 1992 alone, combined retail sales of licensed logo merchandise for major league baseball, the National Football League, the National Basketball Association, and the National Hockey League hit $6.6 billion. Sales are booming outside the United States and Canada as well. Basketball-crazy fans in Turkey, Taiwan, Mexico, and other countries buy millions of dollars' worth of NBA merchandise.[47]

A **warranty** is a statement specifying what the producer of a product will do to compensate the buyer if the product is defective or if it malfunctions. Warranties are important selling points for products in many industries, from cars to plumbing fixtures (see Exhibit 8.9), because they help calm the nerves of prospective buyers. A **guarantee** is an assurance, written or implied, that a product is as represented and will perform satisfactorily. Guarantees usually mean that the purchase price will be refunded, a credit issued, or the product replaced if it fails to perform as represented. A Seattle ad agency, for example, offers a money-back guarantee on its service fees if it doesn't meet client goals. Gregg Rapp, owner of the agency, said, "It was the only way to prove we were different."[48]

Companies may offer maintenance and repair services as part of a warranty program, as a way to increase customer satisfaction, or as a means of generating additional revenue. Car dealers, for example, began looking at repair services as crucial to their long-term survival when auto prices started climbing and owners stopped trading cars as frequently. Sewell Village Cadillac in Dallas was particularly successful in implementing a comprehensive maintenance and repair program. Each customer is assigned a personal service adviser whose sole job is to take the has-

**warranty**
A statement specifying what the producer of a product will do to compensate the buyer if the product does not live up to its promised level of performance

**guarantee**
An assurance, written or implied, that a product is as represented and will perform satisfactorily

Moen has your style.

Traditional style faucets, classic complements to any decor, are now available from Moen. Select from two styles of spouts, available in antique brass, chrome, and polished brass finishes. Add a cross-handle or lever-handle in chrome, white, and antique or polished brass finishes to complete the look.

Moen faucets. Timeless yet contemporary design and Moen's exclusive Lifetime Limited Warranty against leaks and drips, truly an exceptional value.

To learn more about these and other fine Moen products, just call us at 1-800-347-6636.

Moen. Faucets for a lifetime.

**Exhibit 8.9
PROMOTING A
PRODUCT WARRANTY**
To support its positioning as a quality product supplier and to give substance to the phrase "Faucets for a lifetime," Moen takes special care to point out its warranty to potential customers.

sle out of maintaining and repairing the customer's automobiles. These little extras add up; Sewell is one of the leading Cadillac dealerships in the country, in terms of both sales and customer satisfaction.[49]

Many companies add value to their products by providing installation, training, consulting, or other related services. For instance, when a company such as GE Medical sells patient-monitoring equipment to a hospital, it offers to train the nurses and other people who use the equipment. Services like this help differentiate a product from its competitors and lead to greater customer satisfaction.

## SPECIAL PRODUCT ISSUES

In addition to the basic product concepts, consider several special product issues that can have a significant impact on your marketing efforts. Four of the most important issues are safety, standards, compatibility, and the concept of solutions versus products.

## Product Safety

Product safety is one of the most worrisome and potentially costly issues businesses face. It is also an important ethical issue for both businesses and consumers. Unsafe products expose the producer or seller to **product liability,** which is a product's capacity to cause damage or injury for which the producer or seller would be held responsible. Product liability lawsuits cost business owners as much as $80 billion annually.[50] In our litigious society, all businesses are vulnerable to lawsuits. In addition, companies are forced to carry liability insurance, which can significantly increase the cost of doing business.

Unfortunately, the current confusion in the judicial and regulatory realms makes product liability issues difficult to sort out. The only general guideline you can apply to the situation is to design products carefully and responsibly, taking every conceivable customer usage scenario into account and clearly explaining risks to customers.

**product liability**
A product's capacity to cause damage or injury for which the producer or manufacturer is held responsible

## IS PRODUCT LIABILITY GETTING OUT OF HAND?

**ETHICAL DILEMMA IN MARKETING**

An Illinois man, Robert Loitz, injured a thumb when his 12-gauge shotgun exploded during a trapshooting contest. He sued the gun manufacturer, Remington Arms Company, and a state jury awarded him $1.5 million in punitive damages. For Loitz, who had incurred only $5,000 in expenses for medical bills and lost wages, the award was like winning the state lottery. Fortunately for Remington, the Illinois Supreme Court rescinded the award, leaving Loitz with an award of $75,000.

In the last decade, the number of product liability claims filed in the United States has tripled, with increasing numbers of consumers seeking the kind of riches initially bestowed upon Loitz. Between 1975 and 1986, the number of million-dollar damage awards rose 85 percent, with the average award quadrupling to $1.8 million. The result is that insurance costs for U.S. businesses have skyrocketed, and consumers have a smaller range of product choices at higher prices. In fact, in a 1988 survey of 500 CEOs, 39 percent reported deciding against introducing new products, and 47 percent discontinued product lines altogether because of adverse effects of litigation experience (both actual and anticipated).

At the same time, the survey revealed equal numbers of CEOs who redesigned product lines and improved product usage and warnings because of litigation experience. When it comes to safety innovation, consumer advocates are convinced that the fear of litigation forces manufacturers to think safety first, thereby creating mechanisms previously ignored. Thanks to product liability suits we now have air bags, explosive-resistant fuel tanks, roll bars, and thousands of other safety features on products that otherwise might never have been introduced.

But the bottom line is that our current product liability system is costing all of us a bundle in one way or another, and the penalties get worse from year to year. Who's to blame? Greedy consumers who take advantage of deep-pocketed corporations? Greedy attorneys who encourage their clients to file outrageous claims? Greedy businesspeople who cut corners to make bigger profits? Naive businesspeople who unknowingly market defective or unsafe products?

Even though infallible defenses are nonexistent, you can reduce the likelihood of facing a product liability lawsuit—and especially the likelihood of losing one. Some of the most important steps include thinking of everything that could possibly go wrong when someone uses the product, striving to eliminate defects, providing specific instructions and warnings, advising distributors to sell only to targeted consumers, testing component parts manufactured elsewhere, testing the finished product under the toughest conditions it is likely to encounter, and documenting your testing efforts. According to Leonard M. Ring, former president of the Association of Trial Lawyers of America, "The law doesn't require a perfect product—the idea is to make it as safe as can reasonably be done for the foreseeable use."

### WHAT'S YOUR OPINION?

**1.** If you are marketing hair-care products to professional beauticians, what steps might you take to limit liability exposure?

**2.** Who should be responsible if a customer is injured after unintentionally misusing a product? After intentionally misusing a product? Why?

## Standards

As new technologies emerge and prove useful, standardization becomes necessary in order to fulfill their true potential. For instance, railroads were a wonderful innovation 150 years ago, but each railroad had a different track width. It took 55 years to standardize them so that goods could move easily among geographic regions.[51] Many products in today's marketplace, including data transmission networks, radio and TV equipment, computers, and telephones, are designed to meet specific standards. These standards are controlled by professional associations and government agencies such as the American National Standards Institute, the National Institute of Standards and Technology, and various international bodies. As an example, think of the tones you hear when you dial a touchtone telephone. The frequencies of those tones are controlled by a standard, so if you're designing telephone accessories, your equipment must meet the standard. If your gadget doesn't generate or respond to the correct tones, it won't work with your customers' phone systems.

## Compatibility

In addition to the official issue of standards, many product categories have to deal with compatibility. For instance, a manufacturer of computer equipment called Practical Peripherals advertises that its modems are "Hayes-compatible." But Hayes is one of Practical Peripherals' biggest competitors—why would you boast that your product is compatible with that of the competition? In this case, Hayes was the first major supplier of modems, so the software that controls modems is written to work with Hayes products. Therefore, if you want to sell a modem, it has to work with the buyer's software, which means it has to act like a Hayes.

Compatibility issues aren't limited to high-tech products, however. What would happen if you decided to market bologna slices that were 8 inches in diameter? They would be incompatible with everybody's bread, that's what. Compatibility means designing to meet customers' expectations, which is good practice in any case.

## Solutions versus Products

Have you ever had this experience? You're buying something relatively complicated, such as a home entertainment system. Perhaps you get a Sony receiver, a Technics cassette deck, a Magnavox CD player, and Boston Acoustics speakers. You take all the boxes home and get ready for music. You discover you need speaker stands, a cabinet for all the components, and maybe additional wires and cables. Then you sit for hours, reading four separate manuals, trying to get all the pieces to play together. Now imagine that you're a production manager at General Motors. You just paid $10 million for a bunch of robots, computers, and assembly lines to paint your cars, and you're having the same experience, running back to suppliers for extra bits and pieces, and then trying to make the whole thing work.

The frustration you feel in both cases stems from the fact that you haven't bought a solution to your problems—you've bought a bunch of individual products. So you are responsible for transforming these pieces into something that meets your needs. Many customers, particularly in the organizational sector, are tired of the extra work this entails. Smart marketers respond to this frustration by putting together *total*

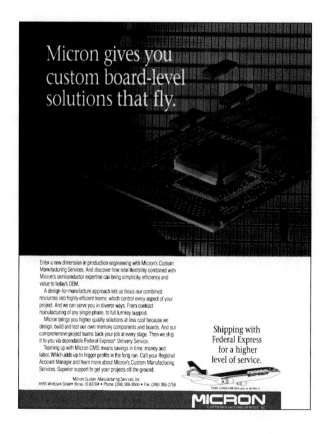

**Exhibit 8.10 MARKETING COMPLETE SOLUTIONS** Micron Custom Manufacturing Services tells potential customers that it offers complete solutions to their needs, not just the basic service of contract manufacturing.

*solutions* instead of collections of individual products. These total solutions start with the basic products and add all the other goods and services needed to solve the customers' problems completely (see Exhibit 8.10). Whether you're offering a supercomputer, a home sprinkler system, or a set of library shelves, you can gain competitive advantage by offering the complete solution. Like designing for compatibility, selling solutions isn't a dramatic shift in your thinking; it's just good marketing.

# SUMMARY OF LEARNING OBJECTIVES

## 1. Explain the role of tangible and intangible features in products.

Most products encompass a bundle of both tangible and intangible attributes. Products that are entirely or predominantly tangible are considered goods, whereas predominantly intangible products are services. Many products have significant elements of both, however, and successful marketers include both sides to satisfy their customers.

## 2. Describe the various classifications of consumer and organizational products.

You can classify products in several useful ways. The first is to distinguish between goods and services, or between products that are predominantly tangible and those that are predominantly intangible. Within the goods category, products can be split into durable and nondurable. An important distinction also exists between consumer and organizational products. Consumer products are classified as convenience, shopping, or specialty, depending on the effort required by the consumer to purchase the product. Organizational products can be classified as raw materials, supplies, components, equipment, installations, and business services.

## 3. Explain the value of branding and discuss typical branding strategies.

Branding helps distinguish one product from another and provides a way for customers to recognize and specify a particular product if they want to choose it again or recommend it to others. Branding also helps marketers give a product a distinct personality by creating an image and interrelated marketing strategies for the branded product. Over a period of time, a brand can become a company's most valuable asset. Three primary branding strategies are manufacturer brands, private brands, and generic brands. Manufacturer brands are owned by the producer or manufacturer (such as Coca-Cola and Liz Claiborne), whereas private brands are owned by the wholesaler or retailer (such as Sears's Kenmore and Craftsman products). Customers can develop strong brand loyalty to either manufacturer or private brands. Generic brands are unbranded products that manufacturers produce for retailers as a way of generating additional revenue.

## 4. Analyze the two primary functions of packaging.

The two primary functions of packaging are to facilitate promotion and to facilitate distribution. Packaging facilitates promotion by tying the product to the promotional program, by providing in-store promotion, and by enhancing the product's appeal to customers who have specific needs and preferences such as small packages, large packages, packages that are easier to use, and packages that can be resealed.

The promotional function of packaging is particularly important in the retailing environment, where the advertising contained on the packaging can be one of the most significant influences on the customer's purchase decision. Packaging facilitates distribution by protecting the product from damage, spoilage, or tampering, which is important to intermediaries who transport the products, to the retailers who stock and display the products, and especially to the customers who buy the products.

## 5. Discuss the three primary functions of labeling.

The three primary functions of labeling are to provide promotional support by incorporating attractive graphics and wording that catches the buyer's attention; to give buyers and intermediaries important information such as the product's content, usage, size, quantity, and manufacturer; and to comply with regulatory requirements.

## 6. Describe the important elements of product support.

Product support elements can include related products such as software reference manuals, accessories, and souvenirs sold at sporting events; product warranties and guarantees that let buyers know they won't be left holding the bag if a product does not perform as represented; and maintenance and repair services that can be a feature of the warranty program or that are provided as an extra service. For many complex products, particularly in organizational markets, product support can include other services as well, such as system design, site preparation, installation, training, and regularly scheduled maintenance programs. Product support elements not only serve as important selling points but also help generate additional revenue for many companies.

## 7. Explain why individual products may not be enough to satisfy customers.

For many customers, a single product or a collection of individual products may be unsatisfactory because customers are looking for integrated solutions to their problems. Smart marketers respond by providing total solutions, which can include training, accessories, and other goods and services.

## 8. Explain the significance of product safety.

Product safety is a critical issue for marketers because an unsafe product can expose a company or organization to liability for any damages the product might cause. To protect themselves from costly lawsuits, most companies carry liability insurance. However, the best protection is for companies to make certain their products are as safe as possible and to clearly communicate any potential dangers to the right people.

# A CASE FOR CRITICAL THINKING

## *Meeting a Marketing Challenge at Orville Redenbacher*

Popcorn marketers divide time into two distinct eras: pre-Redenbacher and post-Redenbacher. The pre-Redenbacher period stretches back centuries. At the first Thanksgiving celebration in Plymouth, Native Americans treated the colonists to the taste of corn popped over the fire. In the years to come, people sometimes popped corn in a wire basket held over the fire in the fireplace, but popcorn never even came close to being a food fad.

The popcorn business started to heat up late in the nineteenth century, when agricultural experts discovered how to grow hybrid corns that produced better-tasting, fluffier popcorn. By the turn of the century, the industry had its first brand name product. The pioneer was Cracker Jack, the caramel-washed popcorn-and-peanut confection packaged with a prize inside. In the twentieth century, unflavored pop-at-home corn products appeared regionally on store shelves, primarily in the South and the Midwest. Products such as Jolly Time used modest claims, usually trumpeting their low number of unpopped kernels. Then Orville Redenbacher popped up in 1970 with his namesake brand, Orville Redenbacher's Gourmet Popping Corn, and the post-Redenbacher period began.

Even after changing the name from Red Bow, Redenbacher wasn't sure his product would be a hit because consumers still thought of popcorn as a stodgy convenience good. The challenge was to encourage people to think of his product as a specialty good so that they would ask for it by name and pay a premium price. Thus Redenbacher differentiated his product in a variety of ways, such as packaging his corn in glass jars that were vacuum-sealed to keep the kernels fresh. Another twist was in the labeling. The label sported a picture of Redenbacher himself, portraying the folksy co-founder as sincere and convincing.

Redenbacher also went to work on distribution and promotion. He decided that Marshall Field's, the illustrious Chicago department store, would be an appropriate retail outlet. So he sent a case of his popcorn to the manager of the gourmet food department, waited a month, then called to ask if he liked it. The manager was very enthusiastic and placed an order immediately. Redenbacher drove his truck to the store's loading dock and hung around, offering to autograph jars for purchasers. That was the start of a promotional strategy that worked wonders for the fledgling product. Marshall Field's ran newspaper ads about the product and the offer, and Redenbacher signed countless jars over the course of three days, while television reporters recounted the story of the popcorn with a personality.

Next Redenbacher drove a shipment up to Byerly's, an upscale Minnesota supermarket, and looked for other retailers who wanted fancier foods. By this time the product was catching on, bolstered by the personal promotion, and Redenbacher and his partner Charlie Bowman could barely keep up with the flood of orders. In late 1971 Redenbacher turned over distribution in the South and the Southeast to Blue Plate Foods, a subsidiary of Hunt-Wesson foods. The following year, when Blue Plate launched Orville Redenbacher's Gourmet Popping Corn across the country, Reden-

bacher traveled almost nonstop for six months to promote his product.

Redenbacher's strategy was paying off: More people were buying the notion of a gourmet popcorn—and buying his brand. The product sold 365,000 pounds in 1970–1971, 1 million pounds in 1972–1973, and more than 5 million pounds in 1975–1976. In 1976 Redenbacher and Bowman sold their product to Hunt-Wesson, and Redenbacher agreed to continue his popcorn pilgrimages. To promote its popcorn sensation, new parent Hunt-Wesson promptly plunked down $6 million, a figure that was ten times larger than the annual ad budgets of all competitors combined. This advertising onslaught cemented Redenbacher's fate as the most famous name—and face—in popcorn.

The post-Redenbacher boom continues, with newer products such as microwavable popcorn capturing the imagination and the pocketbooks of consumers everywhere. The Orville Redenbacher brand is the best-selling popcorn brand in the world, and Hunt-Wesson intends to keep it that way, no matter how competitors try to turn up the heat.

**Your mission:** You're the marketing manager for Orville Redenbacher's Gourmet Popping Corn product. Hunt-Wesson wants you to consider additional ways to increase the product's appeal. Use your knowledge of product concepts to select the answers that will best support your product in the following situations.

1. As the product manager, you are responsible for recommending new-product ideas. Marketing research tells you that the Orville Redenbacher brand is the best-known name in the popcorn business, thanks to your extensive advertising and the personal promotion efforts of Redenbacher himself. You are thinking about using the brand loyalty your customers feel for Orville Redenbacher's Gourmet Popping Corn to create new products under the same brand name. You've checked out your competitors, and you've also gone into the field to take a look at other snacks and related products. Of the brand extension ideas you got when you were doing your research, which of these would you recommend? Why?
   a. A line of Orville Redenbacher salty snacks, including pretzels and potato chips.
   b. A line of Orville Redenbacher popcorn accessories, including popcorn popping oil, popcorn butter, and popcorn salt.
   c. A line of Orville Redenbacher popcorn appliances, such as hot-air poppers.
2. Supermarket shelves are overflowing with premium home-popping competitors such as Borden's Cracker Jack Extra Fresh Popping Corn, Old Capital Popcorn, and Yoder's T. T. Popcorn. Although Orville Redenbacher sales have been going up steadily, the pace of growth has slowed. You suspect that the rate of adoption for all gourmet popcorns has increased as consumers learn more about this type of product, but you also suspect that increased competition is cutting into the sales momentum for your own

product. In effect, gourmet popcorns have become a convenience product because the novelty has worn off. How can you persuade consumers to see the Orville Redenbacher product as a shopping product and buy by brand, while keeping competitors in the convenience product category?

a. Remove Orville Redenbacher popcorn from supermarkets and distribute the product only through gourmet food shops, mail-order fancy-food catalogs, and upscale department stores.

b. Hold in-store demonstrations of Orville Redenbacher popcorn being popped alongside the leading brands. Prove to consumers that your brand pops up fluffier, tastes better, and produces more popcorn per jar than any competitor.

c. Change the packaging and the label. Use a classier-looking label in black and gold foil that emphasizes the premium nature of the product, and put the popcorn into a jar that's shaped like a champagne glass. This will convey upscale quality to the consumer.

3. One of your major concerns has been consistent quality. Your product is vacuum-packed to seal the right amount of moisture in the corn kernels, but lately you've been worried about the length of time it takes the product to travel from your warehouse to the distributors' warehouses and then out to the store shelves. Also, you don't really know how long the product sits in the store before it's purchased or how long it sits in the pantry before the consumer uses it. You can't afford to let the quality slip, but you're not certain how to reassure consumers that Hunt-Wesson stands behind its Orville Redenbacher popcorn. After all, if your popcorn fails to pop or if it tastes stale, your customers may switch to other brands. Which of these ideas should you adopt?

a. Promote your interest in quality by printing a toll-free telephone number on the label. Invite customers to call with any questions, comments, or complaints. Then monitor their feedback to determine whether quality is deteriorating.

b. Institute a money-back guarantee. If every last corn kernel doesn't pop, consumers can get their money back by soaking the label off the jar and mailing it back to Hunt-Wesson along with the sales receipt. Ask that consumers tell you how many kernels didn't pop.

c. Run an advertising campaign that shows spokesperson Orville Redenbacher popping his own corn and describing the special care he takes in growing and selecting the corn, then packaging it to preserve the quality. He should stress that no one else uses the hybrid corn he grows and that no one else has been making popcorn as long as Orville Redenbacher.

4. In a discussion with Orville Redenbacher, you learn that making good popcorn is as much an art as it is a science. Slight variations can make the difference between good popcorn, great popcorn, or burned popcorn, no matter which method you use. Perhaps you can incorporate these tips into your product support to help as many consumers as possible. You've been giving the matter some thought and have come up with a list of three ideas to be further explored. When you submit your final report to the marketing manager, which one of the three should you recommend?

a. Train a group of popcorn experts to go into stores and demonstrate good popcorn-making technique across the country. They can use a variety of popcorn appliances and use only Orville Redenbacher–brand popcorn in their demonstrations.

b. Offer a video of Orville Redenbacher demonstrating how to make good popcorn. Advertise the video on product labels and in ads. Ask consumers to send in one label from any Orville Redenbacher product plus $4.95 and they will receive a 10-minute videotape that will help them make the best-tasting popcorn they've ever had.

c. Inside every Orville Redenbacher jar, pack a tiny booklet that gives tips on how to make the best popcorn. Use Orville Redenbacher's face on the booklet and write it from the point of view of a private lesson from the king of popcorn.

## SPECIAL PROJECT

Hunt-Wesson has a responsibility to its consumers to protect product purity and guard against product safety problems. For example, if the corn didn't pop because it was stale, that would have a negative effect on consumer confidence in the premium quality of the product. However, if the oil in Orville Redenbacher's microwave popcorn product was inadvertently contaminated, that would pose a safety hazard, and might leave Hunt-Wesson open to liability actions. At the same time, consumers have become increasingly aware of the environmental impact of product packaging. Sometimes manufacturers package a product to protect its purity, but end up using materials that are unkind to the environment.

In this assignment, you are to team up with another student and tackle these safety issues. One student should describe, in two or three paragraphs, the major product purity and safety issues that confront the Orville Redenbacher Gourmet Popping Corn product. The other student should then answer, in two or three paragraphs, how Hunt-Wesson can address those issues in an environmentally responsible way. Keep in mind that product features, packaging, and labeling are the key elements to consider, and make your issues and answers as realistic as possible, given budget and time constraints.[52]

## Goodyear Tire Products on the Fast Track

In the race for market share in the worldwide tire business, Goodyear is accustomed to being a lap ahead. However, former Chairman Tom H. Barrett and his recent successor Stanley Gault have been glancing nervously into the rearview mirror as two international challengers gain on the company. One contender for the lead is Michelin, the French tire manufacturer that invented the radial tire. The other is Bridgestone, the Japanese firm that took over Firestone's tire business. It has become a close race, with Goodyear holding 20 percent of the international tire market, Michelin in second place with 18 percent, and Bridgestone third with 16 percent. Goodyear can't afford any mistakes in its product strategy for the 1990s.

From its earliest days, Goodyear has showcased its tire technology on the racetrack. Car racing demands top-performing tires, and drivers are constantly pushing for breakthroughs that will give them an edge. Of course, tires that help the racers get ahead also get lots of attention from innovators and early adopters in the racing audience. In 1989 some 79 percent of the winners in major car races won with Goodyear racing tires.

Building on the innovations used in its racing tires, Goodyear launched the Eagle product line. Eagles are designed for the dual benefits of speed and handling, and each product in the line has features fitted to a specific application. For example, Goodyear worked closely with General Motors to equip the Corvette with Eagle tires that fit that car's specific performance capabilities. Now Goodyear supplies Eagle tires to be sold with new Berettas, Lotus Esprit Turbos, Mazda RX-7s, and many other high-performance cars. In fact, Goodyear Eagles are sold with nearly 9 out of 10 new American high-performance cars and have even begun to appear on selected models of imported luxury cars such as Lexus and Audi. By arranging to have its tires sold as original equipment on new cars, Goodyear boosts brand awareness and increases the odds that car owners will put new Goodyear tires on when the old ones wear out.

Another major Goodyear product line is its Tiempo all-weather radial tires. Back in the 1970s, Michelin created the radial tire design, which became so popular that American tire manufacturers were left in the dust. Determined to catch up, Goodyear invested heavily over a period of 10 years to modernize plants and switch from manufacturing bias-ply tires to making radial tires. The company also experimented with improved versions of the radial tire until it had developed a new type of radial tire to be used in any weather, and it mounted a successful marketing effort to communicate this product line's benefits to the target audience. Going beyond car tires, Goodyear also struck back at Michelin in the lucrative market for radial truck tires. Goodyear's share of this segment in the United States zoomed past 25 percent, squeezing Michelin's market leadership position down from 60 percent to about 30 percent.

Goodyear continues to put technology to work in the search for better tire products. Significant developments include a tire that can continue to be used even if punctured, eliminating the need for spare tires and allowing carmakers to use the added space for larger fuel tanks. In the years ahead, you can be sure that Gault will keep driving hard to maintain Goodyear's leadership pace in a product development race that never ends.

1. In the past, Goodyear gave away racing tires to entrants in top-name races in exchange for the promotional opportunity. However, profitability has become a major issue, so this practice is being reexamined. Should Gault continue this form of product promotion, or should he start charging (perhaps at discounted prices) for the tires he provides?

2. Bridgestone is one of Goodyear's most aggressive competitors, yet Bridgestone makes most of the tires that Gault sells under the Goodyear brand name in Japan. Should Gault continue this private brand arrangement or should he begin to supply the Japanese market by expanding his own production in plants in the Far East?

3. According to Goodyear's market research, outlet, brand, and price are key elements in the consumer's tire purchasing decision. To sell high-performance tires, which tend to be more expensive than ordinary tires, should Gault limit distribution to relatively few specialty outlets and car dealerships that cater to car enthusiasts and will carry the Goodyear brand exclusively? Or should he widen distribution to a broader spectrum of tire outlets so that he can reach out to consumers who want to trade up when they buy replacement tires?

# KEY TERMS

brand (247)
brand awareness (248)
brand equity (247)
brand extension (252)
brand loyalty (247)
brand mark (247)
brand name (247)

capital equipment (245)
convenience products (242)
durable goods (241)
family brand (252)
generic brand (250)
guarantee (257)
individual brand (252)

logo (247)
manufacturer brand (249)
MRO items (244)
nondurable goods (241)
private brand (249)
product liability (258)
service mark (247)

shopping products (242)
specialty products (242)
trade name (247)
trademark (247)
universal product code
  (UPC) (256)
warranty (257)

# QUESTIONS FOR DISCUSSION

1. What strategies might you use to convert a convenience product such as a fruit-flavored seltzer into a shopping product?
2. What would be the advantage of converting a specialty product to a shopping product, and how would you change your marketing strategies to accomplish such a move?
3. How would you determine what special features to include in a new computer software program that you want to market?
4. What are some steps you might take to build greater brand loyalty for a fitness center?
5. Suggest some good and bad brand names for a new perfume. Why is each good or bad?

6. What are the advantages and disadvantages of giving a new product the same brand name as a well-established product that you are currently marketing?
7. If you had to create a package for a toddler toy, what are some of the packaging issues you would need to consider?
8. How could product packaging help market a new line of gourmet cheese?
9. If you owned a chain of print shops, what types of warranties or guarantees might you offer to your customers?
10. How might a musical instrument retailer provide complete solutions to its customers' needs, rather than individual products? (Think about both tangible and intangible components.)

# SHARPEN YOUR MARKETING SKILLS

Karen Zehring plays to a tough audience. Her magazine, *Corporate Finance*, reaches only 54,000 readers, but they are some of the most powerful people in the corporate world. Her readers don't have time for a magazine that doesn't help them manage their businesses, so Zehring has to work constantly to make sure that *Corporate Finance* is a useful product for high-level executives.

**Decision:** How can Zehring make sure she's providing the right product features to her readers? If you were called in as a consultant to help her out, what steps would you recommend and why?

**Communication:** Write a one-page memo describing the process she should use to define and refine her product.[53]

# KEEPING CURRENT IN MARKETING

Find an article that describes the marketing of an idea by a nonprofit organization, and find a second article that describes the marketing of a tangible good by a for-profit company.

1. What are the features and benefits of each product? Given what you know about customer behavior, which product will be more attractive in the eyes of its target customers?

2. How did the nonprofit organization arrive at the definition of its product? How does this compare with the way the for-profit company defined its product?

3. How do the marketing mixes differ for the two products? How much of the difference is due to the fact that one marketer seeks a profit? How much is due to the difference between a tangible good and an intangible idea?

# 9

# Product Management

**After studying this chapter, you will be able to**

**1.** Define the product mix and its role in marketing strategy

**2.** Describe how marketers manage the product mix by introducing products, discontinuing products, and modifying products

**3.** Define the four stages of the product life cycle

**4.** Identify the four types of new products

**5.** Discuss how marketers use the marketing mix to manage products throughout the product life cycle

**6.** Outline the six steps in new-product development

**7.** Discuss the major reasons for the success of new products

## Canon Tries to Copy Its Success

Like players on a sports team who try to outperform each other, divisions in a company try to outdo each other as well. Executives in Canon's Copier Division had seen Canon's Camera Division score a major-league success with the Canon AE-1, a sophisticated single-lens reflex camera. Now the copier people wanted to develop their own breakthrough product.

They started by examining the copier market carefully. Two types of copiers were on the market at the time: plain-paper copiers, which used regular bond paper, and coated-paper copiers, which used specifically treated paper (like that still used in most fax machines). Companies with high-volume copying requirements generally used one of the massive and expensive plain-paper copiers, which produced high-quality copies. Companies that couldn't afford plain-paper copiers and those that didn't make many copies at a time turned to the smaller, less expensive coated-paper copiers, which produced poorer-quality copies.

On the surface, it appeared that any firm needing a copier already had one, and many firms had more than one. Canon questioned whether the market for plain-paper copiers was completely saturated. However, looking below the surface, the Copier Division discovered other needs and other users. First, small offices had coated-paper copiers because they couldn't afford the higher-priced plain-paper copiers. Second, even larger firms with a main copier might need smaller copiers for immediate or occasional use. Third, the Canon managers foresaw a growing market for copiers in home offices. Combined, the three segments made an attractive market, and Canon decided to make a play for their copier business. Executives came up with a plan for their breakthrough product. The personal copier would be developed and positioned specifically for a seemingly lucrative but unproven market.

The personal copier project was turned over to Hiroshi Tanaka, then the director of Canon's Reprographic Products Development Center. Asked to create a copier product that would meet the needs of the identified market segments, Tanaka coined the slogan "Let's make the AE-1 of copiers!" to help rally his troops, and he set up a companywide task force to work on the challenge.

Developing a breakthrough new product such as a personal copier is a challenge, to say the least. The road from initial idea to successful launch in the market is a long one indeed. In many cases, technological obstacles present problems, a situation that was certainly true for Tanaka and company. Financial worries are a constant companion of new-product teams, as they race to complete their designs without going over budget. Every organization has its own special culture and norms, and a product team has to pursue its vision while operating in the larger context of the organization. In addition to the team fitting into the organization, the new product has to fit with the company's current product lines, adding to overall sales without eating into the sales of existing products. Then, of special importance is the fundamental issue of understanding customer needs: How can you be sure that you're developing a product that people will actually want to buy?

Tanaka knew it wouldn't be easy to bring the new product from concept to reality. If you were Hiroshi Tanaka, how would you analyze the new product and determine its potential? What steps would you take to develop a copier that has the technical capabilities the market demands? And what marketing mix would you use to introduce the new product?[1]

**product line**
A group of closely related product items

**product mix**
A company's complete assortment of product lines and items

# CHAPTER OVERVIEW

Hiroshi Tanaka and his team at Canon were facing one of the most important and challenging aspects of marketing: defining and introducing a new product. This chapter opens with the task of managing the product mix, which includes determining which products you'll carry and how you'll manage them through the product life cycle. Next you'll get a look at the new-product development process and the steps companies go through to generate, screen, analyze, develop, test, and commercialize new-product ideas. The final section in this chapter considers the intriguing issue of predicting the success of new products and discusses some common reasons products succeed or fail.

# MANAGING THE PRODUCT MIX

To meet the needs of their customers, and to stay ahead of their competitors, most companies eventually market more than one product. In some cases, companies have hundreds or thousands of products. For example, Rubbermaid, a maker of plastic household items, introduced 700 new products in one five-year period.[2] In order to develop effective marketing strategies for numerous product items, companies group their products into categories. A group of closely related product items is referred to as a **product line.** The Walt Disney Company, for example, has a line of theme parks, a line of filmed entertainment, and a line of consumer goods.[3] A company's complete assortment of product lines and items is referred to as its **product mix** (see Exhibit 9.1).

Whether the company has only a few products or hundreds of products, marketers manage the product mix in similar ways. They consider not only how their products are positioned in the market but also how they relate to other products in the line and to other products in the mix. However, the larger the company is, the more complex product management becomes. Imagine the challenge faced by mar-

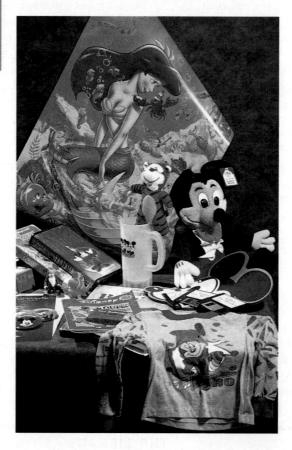

**Exhibit 9.1**
**THE PRODUCT MIX AT DISNEY**
Disney's product mix includes theme parks, movies, and a variety of licensed merchandise.

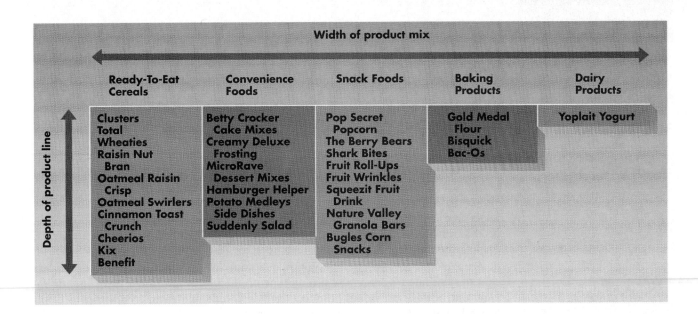

**Width of product mix**

| Ready-To-Eat Cereals | Convenience Foods | Snack Foods | Baking Products | Dairy Products |
|---|---|---|---|---|
| Clusters | Betty Crocker | Pop Secret | Gold Medal | Yoplait Yogurt |
| Total | Cake Mixes | Popcorn | Flour | |
| Wheaties | Creamy Deluxe | The Berry Bears | Bisquick | |
| Raisin Nut | Frosting | Shark Bites | Bac-Os | |
| Bran | MicroRave | Fruit Roll-Ups | | |
| Oatmeal Raisin | Dessert Mixes | Fruit Wrinkles | | |
| Crisp | Hamburger Helper | Squeezit Fruit | | |
| Oatmeal Swirlers | Potato Medleys | Drink | | |
| Cinnamon Toast | Side Dishes | Nature Valley | | |
| Crunch | Suddenly Salad | Granola Bars | | |
| Cheerios | | Bugles Corn | | |
| Kix | | Snacks | | |
| Benefit | | | | |

*Depth of product line*

keters at Kraft as they manage their many consumer product lines, which include refrigerated products, grocery products, frozen foods, and dairy products. That's only the start: The company also offers food service and ingredients for the commercial sector, and it has an international foods division as well. Although Kraft is well known for its popular Velveeta and Philadelphia Cream Cheese brands, cheese accounts for just one-third of its sales overall; the product mix as a whole is quite diverse. Obviously, Kraft wants to make the most efficient use of all its resources, including advertising, sales, and distribution budgets, but each product line requires its own level of staff and funding. Several years ago, the merger of Kraft and General Foods, both major food producers, created an even more complicated product mix. That's why multiproduct companies must use the product portfolio concept, defining and managing their product mixes by understanding how each product fits into the product line and into the product mix.

## Defining the Product Mix

The **product portfolio** is a combination of products and product lines balanced to achieve the company's profit objectives overall while satisfying the needs of its target markets. The portfolio concept helps marketers consider individual products within the context of the entire line and the complete mix, allocating more money to products and lines that have attractive current or future sales or that are competitively strong. At the same time, the portfolio concept helps marketers avoid problems that can arise from overreliance on particular products or lines. For example, if sales of some products grow slowly—a situation Kraft faced several years ago in its grocery business—the company can look to its other products (such as frozen foods) to help bolster profits. Also, marketers adjust their product portfolio when they see shifts in the marketing environment, changing the emphasis on individual products or lines accordingly. When consumers became more health conscious and began changing their eating habits, Kraft shifted its portfolio away from high-fat, high-cholesterol products toward lighter foods such as prepackaged salads and diet mayonnaise.[4]

Marketers also consider the number of product lines in the product mix and the number of products in each line. **Product line width** refers to the company's total number of product lines, whereas **product line depth** refers to the number of products in each line (see Exhibit 9.2). A narrow product line allows the company to concentrate on just the products it knows best, which may help the firm develop a reputation as a specialist in the product category. However, a narrow line may also limit the firm's ability to increase sales and profits once the products are established.

**Exhibit 9.2**
**PRODUCT MIX WIDTH AND DEPTH**
Selected General Mills products illustrate a wide product mix, with product lines varying in depth.

**product portfolio**
A combination of products and product lines balanced to achieve the company's profitability goals and satisfy the needs of the target market

**product line width**
The number of product lines in a company's product mix

**product line depth**
The number of products in each product line

Also, distributors may prefer to deal with companies that carry wider product lines or that offer related products. On the other hand, a wider product line helps the company reach more consumers, spreading its resources across many more products for higher potential profits. The company may benefit from a position as a full-line supplier. However, having a wide product line can also mean extra expenses, which may stretch the firm's resources too thin. Borden recently decided it had too many products—2,800 snack products alone—and is working to narrow its offerings.[5] Also, competitors with a narrower product line may be perceived more favorably as specialists when compared with marketers that offer a wider product line.

Toymaker Mattel has a relatively narrow product line consisting mainly of two lines: Barbie dolls and Hot Wheels toy cars, which account for 76 percent of its sales. However, the product lines have been getting deeper, especially since Mattel introduced Barbie Style accessories for dolls and children in 1990. Gillette has five main product lines, including stationery products, Braun electric appliances, toiletries, dental products, and razors and blades. Even with a wide product line, Gillette's profits are concentrated in one line, the razors and blades, which accounts for 32 percent of sales and 62 percent of profits. The product lines are rather deep; among razors and blades, individual products include disposable razors such as the Good News brand, Atra and Trac II shavers and blades, and the high-tech Sensor razor introduced early in 1990.[6]

As you manage the product mix, you can modify products, discontinue products, and add products. This results in a dynamic product mix in which some products are new, some have been on the market for a while, some are being repositioned, and some have been taken off the market. How you treat an individual product depends on your company's profit and market share objectives and on changes in the marketing environment.

## Modifying Products

Faced with new products introduced by competitors, or with changes in the marketing environment that have occurred since products were introduced, you may decide to modify existing products. Other common reasons for modifying products include solving safety problems, decreasing vulnerability to product liability suits, and reducing manufacturing cost. You can modify products by changing their features or adding new features. You can also modify the quality (by increasing durability, for example, or by beefing up service). Also, you can modify the sensory appeal of a product (by changing the color, style, shape, packaging, name, or brand). All these modifications contribute to the product's repositioning, and all are aimed at increasing the product's sales or defending market share. Even moving from an unbranded product to a branded one is a way to modify your product offering.

Take the case of toothpaste, a century-old invention that's spawned a $1.5 billion market. Fluoride was the big news in the 1960s, followed by antiplaque and antitartar formulations; but today, no one knows when the next big breakthrough will hit the store shelves. In the meantime, Colgate and Procter & Gamble have been modifying products as they fight for market share. In the mid-1980s, Colgate introduced the pump dispenser, a modification that P&G's Crest then adopted. A recent development in the market is the addition of baking soda (see Exhibit 9.3). In the disposable diaper market, manufacturers are trying to boost sales by modifying products with extra features. Kimberly-Clark's Huggies brand leads the pack in the U.S. disposable diaper market, and to defend its turf, the company has attached a leakage-control shield and made diaper waistbands softer and more stretchable. Procter & Gamble has upgraded its Luvs brand with colors and additional padding where appropriate for each gender.[7]

Restaurants can modify their products by offering speedier service. Bennigan's began its "Express Lunch" program, promising to serve lunch within 15 minutes—or patrons eat free. To boost its lunch business, Pizza Hut pledged a second pizza free if the first one ordered wasn't served within five minutes. These product modifications help the restaurants compete with McDonald's, Burger King, and other

General Foods discovered that a positioning that succeeds in one country doesn't necessarily succeed in others. In Argentina, it had to change the positioning of Tang from a breakfast orange juice substitute to a "fun beverage" that people could drink with their friends any time of the day.

You read ingredient labels.

You avoid chemical additives in your food.

You appreciate nature.

Is your toothpaste consistent with that thinking?

**What we make:**

Just because your toothpaste has baking soda doesn't mean it's natural.

Take a look at the package of baking soda toothpaste you're using now. If you find saccharin, dyes, artificial flavors or preservatives, you may find it out of step with today's world.

Now take a look at Tom's of Maine Natural Baking Soda Toothpaste. It's the only baking soda toothpaste that has fluoride, but doesn't contain saccharin or any other artificial additives. We use natural peppermint oil for flavor, and calcium and baking soda to clean away plaque.

Just what you need for a naturally refreshing taste and clean, healthy teeth. Nothing more.

**SAVE 75¢**
on Tom's of Maine Natural
Toothpaste for Children and Adults.

AVAILABLE AT SUPERMARKETS, DRUGSTORES AND HEALTH FOOD STORES.

**What we believe:**

We live and work by a mission which all of us helped create. At the heart of it is the belief that people and nature deserve our respect.

We continually seek ways to reduce and recycle our packaging, support recycling in our community, and reduce water consumption in manufacturing.

We believe it's important to look beyond profit and attend to the Common Good, of the community, the environment and one another. We donate 10% of profits to these causes and encourage employees to use 5% of their paid work time for volunteering.

It's Time for Tom's.

**Exhibit 9.3
MODIFYING
PRODUCTS**

Tom's of Maine is one of several toothpaste manufacturers that have tried to boost sales by adding baking soda.

fast-food chains that gobble up a giant share of the lunch business. The beef industry has turned to product modifications in the wake of changes in consumer tastes that have made red meat the outsider in lower-fat, lower-cholesterol diets. The U.S. Department of Agriculture has traditionally graded red meat according to the level of fat in its lean sections. Prime meat was labeled as the highest quality because of its high-fat content, followed in order of quality by choice meat and then good meat. Fine restaurants advertised their prime steaks; supermarkets carried choice meat. However, in 1987 the U.S.D.A. renamed the good grade, calling it "select" to give this leaner cut of meat a more positive image. When research found that consumers considered well-trimmed beef to be more appealing, meat retailers started trimming fat to about one-quarter inch around the meat, compared with the previous one-half inch of fat. Although these sound like small modifications, they helped boost beef's popularity.[8]

## Discontinuing Products

Despite the boldest attempts to save them, products must sometimes be discontinued. Perhaps new technology has made the product obsolete, or heavier costs have started eroding profits. The product may have become the victim of changes in consumer tastes or competitive pressures. Whatever the reason, when a product reaches the decline phase of its life cycle and sales dip seemingly irreversibly, consider discontinuing the product so that you can maintain an efficient product mix. Discontinuing a product is a difficult decision to make because dropping even a single product will alter the product line and the product portfolio. So that a single product's demise will not hurt the company, marketers balance their product portfolios carefully to guard against reliance on any one product or line. Yet some companies dis-

## CONVERTING A COMMODITY INTO A BRAND NAME

Robinson Brick is not the flashiest brand name around, but it has a certain rock-solid quality about it. F. George Robinson, Jr., was convinced that he could turn the brick company his great-grandfather founded into a household name, so he mapped out a plan to make it happen.

Robinson's first step was to come up with a differentiation strategy that would make his company and its products stand apart in a mature, crowded market. He decided Robinson Brick would stand for highest quality, fashion colors, and responsive service. The hope was that people would call for Robinson bricks by name, much as they specify Andersen windows or Levolor blinds. However, Robinson wasn't quite sure about what to say. "Our bricks are better" would be seen as puffery, he thought, and no money was available for a celebrity endorser. Then he hit on the idea of playing up the fact that Robinson bricks meet the strict quality standards established by the American Society for Testing and Materials. That was his first move.

The second step was to get the word out. Since Robinson couldn't af-

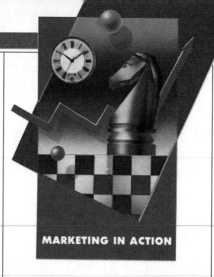

**MARKETING IN ACTION**

ford the hefty prices charged to advertise directly to consumers in magazines such as *Architectural Digest,* he decided to focus all his attention on brick distributors. However, a majority of the distributors were turned off by the higher cost of Robinson bricks. Fortunately, a handful of distributors, more out of curiosity than anything else, were willing to let Robinson set up a display in their showrooms. To the surprise of many, the bricks sold.

Robinson and his distributors learned that customers who were spending $300,000 and up for a house didn't mind paying a $1,500 premium to get the exact color and delivery date they wanted. Knowing that the choice of color and speed of delivery were more important than price to his

customers allowed Robinson to further define his marketing strategy. He increased the available colors to 47 and still promised to ship within 48 hours of receiving the order.

Since his market isn't particularly price sensitive, Robinson even increased his rates a couple of percentage points over inflation. However, the company still had virtually no marketing budget, so Robinson continued to recruit one distributor at a time. The cost of setting up a new distributor was just $8,000, including a salesperson's expenses, and he considered it one way to reach consumers, builders, and architects.

However, Robinson knows it takes a long time to build national distribution one supplier at a time. Also, if the idea of premium bricks begins to catch on, a far larger competitor could create a premium line of its own and blow Robinson Brick away overnight. But Robinson says, "I suppose we're vulnerable, but we'll continue what we're doing." After all, that's what it takes to build a brand name.

### APPLY YOUR KNOWLEDGE

**1.** Would Robinson's strategy have been necessary in a new and growing market? Explain your answer.
**2.** What is Robinson's product, and how does it differ from other bricks?

---

continue product lines and then grow considerably, often because they can concentrate on the remaining core products. Hunt-Wesson, for example, increased sales eightfold in 11 years even as it pruned its product lines from 33 to 3.[9]

In a classic example of needing to modify a product mix, IBM recently faced a no-growth market for its Selectric line of typewriters. Once a familiar fixture in American offices, the Selectric was the most popular typewriter ever made, and 15 million were sold in 29 years. However, by the mid-1980s, computerized word processors were becoming the new office standard. Although IBM tried to resuscitate the Selectric by adding a spelling checker, a digital display, and other features, the venerable typewriter simply couldn't compete with newer technology. Also, IBM's own line of PCs was gaining ground in the word-processing market. In 1990 IBM decided to discontinue the Selectric, and the company sold off its typewriter business entirely.[10]

## Adding Products

Marketers modify and discontinue products to keep the product mix healthy and to maintain a balanced product portfolio. They also add products to help build the business for the long term. As you can see from IBM's experience with the Selectric, even consistently successful products sometimes hit a sales plateau or a decline.

Thus, companies must have the next potential winner on the drawing board to keep sales energy high. Companies introduce new products for a variety of reasons. They want to support the quest for future sales and profits, and they need to replace products that are discontinued. Also, new products help marketers stay on top of changes in the marketing environment, including shifts in consumer tastes and competitive changes that create attractive markets or opportunities.

Every year, thousands and thousands of new products are introduced. In recent years, the annual total has been 15,000 products or more.[11] In fact, nearly 20 percent of the brands on grocery store shelves that achieve sales of $1 million or more were not even on the market in 1970, making new products a major contributor to sales. Is each product added to the product mix really a *new* product? Some new products are truly innovative, creating entirely new product concepts. A good example is the Sony Walkman. Some new products are brand extensions. General Foods used brand extension to successfully introduce Jell-O Pudding Pops, a product with a familiar brand name in an entirely new food category, frozen pudding on a stick.[12]

Marketers can also launch a new product through a **product line extension,** in which additional products are introduced into an existing product line. For example, candy king Mars is using product line extension to add Peanut Butter M&M's to its ever-popular line of M&M's chocolates (as if trying to decide between Plain and Peanut wasn't hard enough already).

**product line extension**
A method of adding products to the product mix by introducing products into an existing product line

Product line extensions are probably the most frequently used technique of adding products because marketers can depend on the consumer's familiarity with the other products in the line. However, if the new product doesn't fit the consumer's perception of what the product line stands for, the new product can fail, possibly damaging the image of the rest of the line. Finally, some companies with existing product lines in a particular category introduce more products or more product lines under separate brand names. Borden does this in the potato chip market where it makes three national brands (Wise, New York Deli, and Krunchers!) and a bagful of regional brands (Buckeye, Guy's, Laura Scudder's, and others).[13]

## Managing through the Product Life Cycle

People go through various stages in life, and products tend to do the same. Marketers use the term **product life cycle** to represent the phases a product or product category goes through from the time it is introduced to the time it is taken off the market (see Exhibit 9.4). The life cycle is an important concept because your marketing strategy and tactics are adapted to each stage.

**product life cycle**
A model that describes the stages that a product or a product category passes through, from its introduction to its removal from the market

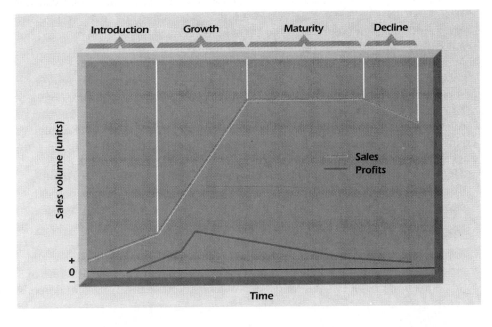

**Exhibit 9.4
THE PRODUCT
LIFE CYCLE**
The product life-cycle model shows four stages that products and product categories move through.

## PRODUCTS IN DECLINE: GOING, GOING, BACK AGAIN?

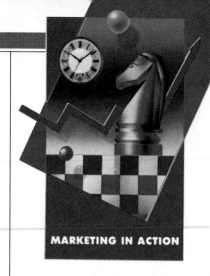

**MARKETING IN ACTION**

Your old standby product is finally showing its age as it sinks into the decline stage doldrums. It's tempting simply to scrap the product and start the new-product development process all over again. But hold on! At a time when product introductions often cost megabucks, it's even more important to get just a little bit more from a product that's near the end of its life cycle. Think about one of these two ideas: Sell the product, brand name and all, to a company that wants to keep it going, or sell your leftover merchandise to a company that specializes in finding new distribution channels.

If you're marketing something sweet, you might sell your product to Leaf, a company that breathes new life into candies from a bygone era.

In their heydays, some of the products Leaf has salvaged had a respectable following. Good & Plenty was a licorice-flavored treat for baby-boomer youngsters, and Pine Bros. cough drops soothed many a sore throat. However, as time passed, these older brands were dwarfed by newer, more powerful names in candy that were supported by much larger promotional budgets. With an aging customer base and a dwindling ad budget, the end seemed near. Then Leaf came to the rescue.

Based in Bannockburn, Illinois, Leaf buys niche candy brands that other companies dump and then nurtures them with nostalgic promotion. Since 1989 Leaf's strategy generates a half billion dollars in sales every year, giving it a major share in the U.S. candy market. Its products include Chuckles jellies, purchased from Chuckles; Pay Day, Zero, Milk Shake, and Butternut candy bars, purchased from the Hollywood Brands division of Sara Lee; and a bagful of other confections, including Milk Duds, Heath English Toffee Bar, and Rain Blo bubblegum.

Leaf has revitalized some products by reprising their original tag lines and advertising themes in a bid to recapture the fond memories that consumers may have about enjoying the

---

**introduction phase**
The first phase of a product's life cycle when sales growth is slow and profits are low or nonexistent

1. *Introduction.* During the **introduction phase** the product first appears on the market. You try to stimulate demand through heavy promotion while building distribution, and product development may still be ongoing. Because of these three activities, you're not usually making any money on the product at this point. Some companies find the introduction phase to be a major financial challenge as they try to come up with enough money to effectively launch their products. On the positive side, you occasionally have very little competition at this stage, especially if you've introduced a truly innovative product.

**growth phase**
The second phase of a product's life cycle when sales increase rapidly and when profits peak and begin declining

2. *Growth.* The **growth phase** is the second stage of a product's life cycle; sales increase rapidly and prices stabilize as more suppliers become involved. During the growth phase, a much larger group of customers adopt the new product, but aggressive competitors begin to appear on the scene as well. Although the competition can help stimulate demand, it usually forces you to make a greater investment in promoting your product. Marketers may begin to add supporting services and enhance their product in other ways to stay ahead of the competition. Increased competition can also force prices down. During the early part of the growth stage, profits usually grow because manufacturing costs are dropping. However, at some point the effects of competition turn things around, and profits start to decline.

**maturity phase**
The third phase in a product's life cycle when sales level off and profits decline

3. *Maturity.* When sales level off, the product has entered the **maturity phase.** Profits generally continue to decline as low price becomes the major competitive parameter. However, companies that can control their costs do quite well financially. They can cut back on their marketing expenses, continue to serve loyal customers, and reap reasonable profits. In other cases, marketers decide to reenergize mature products, giving them a boost of marketing support. Cheez Whiz, for example, reached the mature phase, and sales began to decline at a rate of 3 to 4 percent a year. However, the Cheez Whiz marketers at Kraft General Foods

candies when they were younger. When Leaf reincarnated spokescharacter Choo-Choo Charlie to push Good & Plenty candy, for example, sales jumped. However, if the brands are to grow, not just survive, Leaf knows that it must hook the next generation. So the company reformulated its venerable Milk Duds brand, adding pure milk chocolate, and reintroduced the product. Then Leaf followed up with a new campaign, including a baseball promotion that promised children tickets to baseball games in exchange for Milk Duds candy wrappers.

Suppose, however, that rather than marketing candy you're marketing television video games. Your product seems glued to store shelves. What can you do? You can hire Tradewell Industries, the New York–based remarketer that can help a company put some energy into mature products. Tradewell has worked its remarketing magic for more than 45 clients, including Norelco,

Richardson-Vicks, and International Playtex, and its magic is exploiting new distribution channels.

For example, Magnavox turned to Tradewell when one of its television video games wasn't selling very well. Tradewell arranged to advertise the game on Duncan Hines cake mix packages, and consumers snapped it up for $11.95—plus three box tops. Several years ago, when consumers didn't come running for Keds high-top sneakers, Tradewell overhauled the product, cutting off the tops to create a tennis sneaker. Newly altered, the sneaker sold.

Tradewell makes its deals in advance, up to 18 months before a product is produced. If the product flops after it's introduced, Tradewell then buys the leftovers at or near the wholesale price and proceeds to remarket the inventory. The key to Tradewell's approach is its unique way of selling a product through creative distribution channels. The company was asked to

step in one time when a kitty litter product made of paper pellets didn't do well with cat owners. Tradewell's solution was to sell it to horse stables to use as a substitute for sawdust.

If you have a product that's hit bottom and can't drag itself out of the decline stage, you do have alternatives. In fact, you might use the methods of Leaf and Tradewell and give your product one last chance.

## APPLY YOUR KNOWLEDGE

**1.** If you were Leaf, would you advertise the fact that a newly acquired brand was "under new management"?

**2.** Why would marketers rather have Tradewell handle their slow movers than sell the products themselves at cost just to clear the shelves?

decided not to let their product fade into the sunset. With the help of a $6 million advertising budget they began promoting Cheez Whiz as a cheese sauce for the microwave oven, and sales subsequently climbed 35 percent.[14]

4. *Decline.* When sales begin to drop off, a product has entered the **decline phase.** A new technology or changing trends in the marketplace can cause a product to decline. When a product begins to decline, marketers react in various ways. Some cut the promotional budget and simply phase out the product. Others decide to give the product another shot at stardom. Most marketers agree, however, that deciding which products to revive and which are too far gone is a tricky judgment call. The safest bet is to revive only the products that generate positive memories among customers and that still have at least a small group of devoted fans.[15]

**decline phase**
The fourth phase in a product's life cycle when both sales and profits decline

## LIMITATIONS OF THE LIFE-CYCLE MODEL

Like most models, the product life cycle has a few quirks you should be aware of. First, if tends to apply more accurately to product categories than to individual products. Not too long ago, many college students were equipped with slide rules, once the standard tool for personal calculation. As advances in technology made the pocket calculator affordable, the popularity of slide rules declined so that they are now little more than a curiosity. Calculators took off vigorously and are now a well-established mature product. This example fits the model well. On the other hand, the life cycle can't always explain why individual products flourish or wither. Some products never get off the ground, some turn around in the growth stage and decline rapidly, and some decline and then come back to life again.

The second potential problem with the life cycle model is that it can lead marketers into thinking that products are born with a predetermined life span—that they will sell for a period of time and then inevitably go into decline. However, well-managed products can live for decades. Take Procter & Gamble's Ivory soap; it was introduced in 1879 and is still one of the leading brands today. By adapting the marketing mix as market conditions changed, Procter & Gamble kept the brand healthy for over 100 years, and as long as it's marketed intelligently, Ivory should have no reason ever to decline. In summary, marketers should use the product life cycle to *describe* the behavior of their products in the market, rather than *predict* that behavior.

## PRODUCT DIFFUSION AND THE LIFE-CYCLE CONCEPT

**product diffusion process**
The acceptance of new products by various segments of a market

The **product diffusion process** describes how products work their way into markets. In general, diffusion starts when a few customers, known as *innovators,* try a new product. In the consumer market, innovators are usually the trendsetters in a given product category. In the organizational sector, they are usually companies that need the latest technologies in order to improve quality, productivity, or some other aspect of their business.

Once the innovators show that the new product is viable, the *early adopters* move in. These are customers who want the latest and greatest but aren't willing to take risks like the innovators; they want somebody else to test the product first. Following the early adopters, the majority of the market steps forward. These are divided into the *early majority* and the *late majority.* Finally, *laggards,* as their name implies, are the very last customers to jump on the bandwagon. Based on normal statistical distribution, marketers assume that 2.5 percent of the potential customers in a market segment are innovators, 13.5 percent are early adopters, 34 percent are in the early majority, 34 percent are in the late majority, and 16 percent are laggards.[16]

When you're introducing a new type of product, aim for the innovators and early adopters, who make up only 16 percent of your market. Research can help you identify these groups, in both the consumer and organizational sectors. Reaching these two groups first is important because they will help spread your products through the market. For many customers in the majority categories, word of mouth from the innovators and early adopters and the examples they set have more influence on the purchase decision than any advertising you can do. After you've captured the first two groups you can move on to the majority groups.

## STRATEGIES THROUGHOUT THE LIFE CYCLE

As a product or product category goes through its life cycle, you manage differently in each phase. The product life cycle varies from product to product and category to category, and no two products or categories have the same cycle. This means that you have to be in tune with the life cycles of your own products and categories, watching the market carefully so that you can plan for and react to evolving changes. As you manage your products, you face specific challenges in each phase of the product life cycle (see Exhibit 9.5).

INTRODUCTION   For marketers who have developed an innovative product, introduction is a time of pioneering, a time to spend money to educate the consumer about the product's unique qualities and then anxiously watch the sales results. For marketers who follow another firm's lead by introducing a *me-too* product (which is very similar to one already on the market), product introduction is less risky and often less expensive. During the introductory phase, marketers are seeking sales; the quest for profits will come later. They want customers to have access to their products, buy them, and try them, so the emphasis is on distribution and promotion. Introduction can be quite costly: By one estimate, a major food manufacturer has to ring up first-year sales nationally of $25 million to $30 million just to break even with a new product. At the same time, some categories (such as ice cream specialties for children) have extremely short life cycles, with the average product lasting less than 12 months. Therefore, the introductory phase is especially important for marketers who need to grab market share early and hang on until the profits start coming in.[17]

Much of the hoopla in the marketing world can be traced to product introductions. Look at the introduction of the Sensor shaving system, the single most costly product Gillette has ever launched. The product itself cost an estimated $200 million to develop; advertising in the United States, Canada, and Europe added another $110 million to the tab. The product was important to Gillette because the company had been losing market share to disposable razors made by Bic and other rivals. Gillette's objective in the introduction phase was to convince consumers to try the razor, which was positioned as a new shaving technology. In the first month, Gillette sold 5 million Sensors, and if the company can get a lot of repeat business, it will be sitting pretty because Sensor razor cartridges carry a higher profit margin than other Gillette cartridge products.[18]

## Exhibit 9.5  MANAGING THE PRODUCT MIX THROUGHOUT THE PRODUCT LIFE CYCLE

| Effects and Responses | Stages of the Product Life Cycle | | | |
| --- | --- | --- | --- | --- |
| | Introduction | Growth | Maturity | Decline |
| Competition | None of importance | Some emulators | Many rivals competing for a small piece of the pie | Few in number with a rapid shakeout of weak members |
| Overall strategy | Market establishment; persuade early adopters to try the product | Market penetration; persuade mass market to prefer the brand | Defense of brand position; check the inroads of competition | Preparations for removal; milk the brand dry of all possible benefits |
| Profits | Profits are negligible because of high production and marketing costs | Profits reach peak levels as a result of high prices and growing demand | Increasing competition cuts into profit margins and ultimately into total profits | Declining volume pushes costs up to levels that eliminate profits entirely |
| Retail prices | High, to recover some of the excessive costs of launching | High, to take advantage of heavy consumer demand | What the traffic will bear; need to avoid price wars | Low enough to permit quick liquidation of inventory |
| Distribution | Selective, as distribution is slowly built up | Intensive; employ small trade discounts since dealers are eager to store | Intensive; use heavy trade allowances to retain shelf space | Selective; slowly phase out unprofitable outlets |
| Advertising strategy | Aim at the needs of early adopters | Make the mass market aware of brand benefits | Use advertising as a vehicle for differentiation among otherwise similar brands | Emphasize low price to reduce stock |
| Advertising emphasis | High, to generate awareness and interest among early adopters and persuade dealers to stock the brand | Moderate, to let sales rise on the sheer momentum of word-of-mouth recommendations | Moderate, since most buyers are aware of brand characteristics | Minimum required to phase out the product |
| Consumer sales and promotion expenditures | Heavy, to entice target groups with samples, coupons, and other inducements to try the brand | Moderate, to create brand preference (advertising is better suited to do this job) | Heavy, to encourage brand switching, hoping to convert some buyers into loyal users | Minimal, to let the brand coast by itself |

Each stage of the product life cycle presents a different set of challenges and opportunities to which marketers must respond.

People who watched much of the country get swept up in the "Achy Breaky Heart" dance craze in 1992 might've asked themselves how it all happened. How did the then-unknown country singer Billy Ray Cyrus turn into an overnight sensation, with the first debut country album ever to hit the charts right at the top? (The album, "Some Gave All," stayed at number one for four and a half months.) Who came up with that dance, anyway? Well, marketing executives at Cyrus's record company came up with the idea, along with the rest of the launch strategy for Cyrus and his music. The marketing team headed by Steve Miller, now the vice president of marketing for Mercury Nashville, thought the dance would be a great publicity generator. He filmed people doing the made-up dance at a Cyrus concert, then sent tapes to dance clubs around the country for release on Valentine's Day. With dance contests and instructional videos, and careful timing of the release of the regular music video, the single, and finally the album, Miller and company orchestrated a carefully planned assault on the nation's eyes, ears, and feet. In the process they created an instant celebrity.[19]

Even as they launch a new product, smart marketers begin to think about the next product development project. That's because a company can count on only so many months or years until a product grows and reaches maturity. As the first product moves toward maturity and decline, the next product must be ready for introduction to keep up sales momentum.[20]

GROWTH    In this phase, sales grow faster than during the introduction; the product starts to break even and then achieves profitability. Marketers are concerned with meeting demand for the product through adequate or expanded distribution, and with maintaining product quality as well as quantity. By now, competitors have noticed the product's impact and are launching counterattacks to get a piece of the action. Many a product has been challenged by me-too competitors in the growth stage, so you can't afford to let up on promotion.

Sometimes a company can suffer from growth that occurs too fast. Rapid growth nearly destroyed Snugli, a small company founded as a cottage industry by Ann Moore, a former Peace Corps volunteer. Following her service in Togo, West Africa, Moore designed a soft corduroy baby pouch for carrying infants against the parent's chest, and she started a mail-order business. After the introduction phase, the company began growing at a 40 percent rate and kept up that breakneck pace for years. Then a positive review in *Consumer Reports* magazine brought a torrent of orders, and Moore had to rethink the company's strategy. To meet demand, she switched from hand-sewn carriers to mass-production techniques, building a factory and hiring 50 workers. However, the company ran into labor problems and found itself with a pile of back orders and a rising number of defective carriers. Moore needed capital to keep up with the growth and finally accepted a buyout offer from a subsidiary of Huffy, the bicycle manufacturer. Growth had yielded a hot product but had turned the company into a buyout target; Snugli continued into the maturity phase, but without its founder.[21]

MATURITY    The majority of products in the marketplace are in their maturity phase. In this phase, sales slow down in comparison to the growth phase, and profits are probably starting to slip. Supply easily keeps up with demand, and marketers must continue promoting the products in order to empty their warehouses. In fact, some manufacturers begin to manufacture private-label products to take advantage of their excess capacity. However, the product now faces competition from many challengers, and often the only way to increase sales is by stealing market share from someone else, so price and promotion become critical in this phase. Still, marketers try to find new sales potential by modifying products, changing the marketing mix, or seeking out new market segments (see Exhibit 9.6).

Even the hottest craze cools, as Nintendo of America discovered. Nintendo's home video games were incredibly successful in the 1980s, but as the 1990s began, the product category had reached maturity in the United States. Competitors Sega Enterprises and NEC were coming on strong with new, sophisticated technology.

Take two and call us in the morning. Healthcare professionals have been taking Polaroid pictures with very healthy results.

Polaroid film is used to enhance written documentation of wounds for more consistent treatment. And, to easily and instantly

record microscopic specimens. We've even created a dry imaging system that's revolutionizing radiology departments every-

where. If your business needs to document information

stat, call 1-800-348-5287, ext.410 for a free brochure.

Until you know what we can do for you, business, you haven't seen the whole picture. **Polaroid**

**Exhibit 9.6**
**SEARCHING FOR NEW SALES**
Polaroid encourages health-care professionals to use film as part of their documentation and recordkeeping procedures.

In 1990, for the first time ever, Nintendo cartridge players experienced a sales drop, and pressure was mounting for newer, more sophisticated games to challenge skilled players. It was a whole new game for Nintendo, which responded by beefing up its ad budget to $30 million and spending another $60 million on retail displays and other promotions. Firms that market game cartridges for Nintendo players also began spending heavily, to the tune of nearly $150 million.[22]

DECLINE   Sales and profits continue to slacken in the product's decline phase. The decline can occur either suddenly or slowly, but when a product enters this phase, marketers face tough choices. Some marketers choose to discontinue products rather than spend money to promote or reposition them, especially if the products have become obsolete. When the marketing environment changes drastically, some marketers believe that discontinuing the product is the most sensible move. Other marketers decide to "harvest" the product, keeping it in production but cutting back on expenses. In this situation, the marketer limits distribution and lowers or eliminates the product's ad budget. If marketers want to keep their products on the market during this phase, they reexamine pricing to be sure they're achieving profitability. However, sometimes marketers want to sell what they have and then discontinue the product, so they lower the price and change the marketing mix to emphasize the bargain. Regardless of the situation, discontinuing a product is a difficult decision that can affect a company's work force, its relationship with its customers, and its position in the marketplace.

If the product is particularly well known, you may decide to rejuvenate it. You can reach out to past and present customers with a new promotion or a modified product. You can search out new customers by refocusing your marketing efforts on new segments. Or you can reposition the product (modified or not) for a new audience. Tic-Tac mints were originally targeted for children. However, the candy went into a tailspin during the 1970s, dropping to a 2 percent market share in 1979. Tic-Tac tried to reverse the declining trend by targeting the candy for weight-watching adults. Tic-Tac advertised its candy as having fewer calories than Velamints, the leading competitor. The revival worked: Adults bought the candy, tripling its market share in just two years.[23]

### HOW TO EXTEND THE PRODUCT LIFE CYCLE

As you can see, marketers face choices that can change the product's course in every phase of the product life cycle. By manipulating the product, the promotion, the pricing, and the distribution, you can give your product at least a temporary sales boost. No product life cycle is preordained, and you can extend the product life cycle for decades if you pay close attention to the marketing environment. Even products that have been discontinued can make a comeback. For example, G.I. Joe was once a hero in Hasbro's toy line. However, by 1977 G.I. Joe was becoming more expensive to produce and competing action figures had begun to crowd toy store shelves. Moreover, antimilitary sentiment was strong in the wake of the Vietnam War. Hasbro discontinued the doll, putting it out of sight but not out of mind. Five years later, Hasbro reintroduced a less expensive G.I. Joe, and a new generation discovered the toy. By 1985 G.I. Joe was the leading toy for boys, and Hasbro had extended its life cycle through product modification and careful timing.[24]

Consider orange juice, a category that's been stuck in the mature phase for years and years. Three manufacturers' brands (led by Coca-Cola's Minute Maid) are the market leaders, but private-label juices account for more than half the category's sales. Sales of fruit beverages overall are barely growing, and frozen orange juice is getting a smaller slice, so price has become the main battleground for marketers seeking to increase share. To breathe some life into the market, the branded marketers have turned to a subcategory of refrigerated, ready-to-serve orange juice that's not made from concentrate. Convenience has become increasingly important to consumers, and the new niche has helped orange juice marketers extend the product life cycle.[25]

Another way to extend the life cycle is to position the product for other uses or other audiences. That's how Kraft extended Velveeta's life cycle. Market share was high and brand recognition was solid, but marketing research showed that consumers associated the brand with cooking, not with snacking or with sandwiches. The company responded by introducing Velveeta Slices and backed the launch with television advertising that emphasized the convenience of the slices. Initially, the sliced version was promoted as a new product, but gradually the company began to promote the slices as a more convenient form of Velveeta. Kraft was able to prolong Velveeta's life cycle by giving current customers another reason to buy the brand and by showing it off to a new group of consumers who had never tried the product.[25]

# DEVELOPING NEW PRODUCTS

New products are among the most important concerns of nearly every marketing organization. In dynamic industries in particular, such as fashion, entertainment, and computer software, companies that can't produce a continuing stream of new products usually can't stay competitive. A company's products may still be perfectly useful and usable, but if customers don't perceive them to be the latest and greatest, they'll usually turn to other suppliers.

Some products are discovered by accident; others, like the Canon personal copier, are the result of a careful, methodical process of product development, such as the process seen in Exhibit 9.7. In step 1, marketers generate ideas by looking inside and outside the company. In step 2, marketers screen the ideas and then pick the most promising for further analysis. In step 3, the best ideas are analyzed further to define the product concept, to understand how the new product would relate to other products in the line, and to determine how much of the company's resources it would require. In step 4, marketers begin to develop the product, which can be

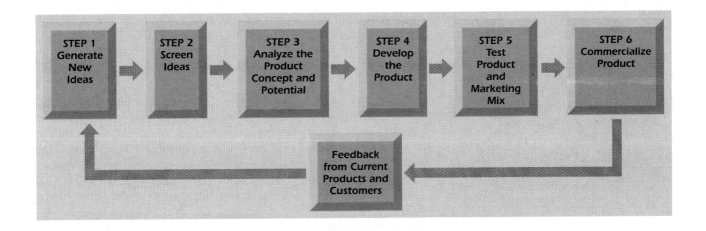

an internal or external activity. In step 5, the new product is test marketed, and a variety of marketing mixes are evaluated. Finally, in step 6, marketers commercialize the product by starting production and implementing the preferred marketing mix. Keep in mind that this is a general-process model that doesn't apply in all cases. For instance, some products are designed to meet specific customer needs in certain ways and, thus, require little need to fish around for new-product ideas.

**Exhibit 9.7**
**THE NEW-PRODUCT DEVELOPMENT PROCESS**
Marketers can follow a six-step process to develop new products, although not all situations require all six steps.

## STEP 1: Generate Ideas

Marketers are constantly on the prowl for new-product ideas. As you have seen, the marketing environment is dynamic, and new ideas can bubble up at any time. Also, an idea that seems unattractive at one point can look more appealing just a short while later. Marketers use a wide variety of sources to generate ideas (see Exhibit 9.8).

- *Internal sources.* Inside the company, you can gather new ideas from research-and-development staffers; from people in sales, marketing, or planning; from engineers; from production people; and from top management and board members.
- *External sources.* Noncompany sources of new ideas include customers and prospects, distribution channel members, government agencies, consultants, scientists and inventors, competitors, college teachers and students, advertising and public relations firms, trade shows, the news media, and suppliers.

**Exhibit 9.8    SOURCES OF NEW-PRODUCT IDEAS IN 40 COMPANIES**

| Source of Ideas | Number of Companies |
|---|---|
| **Internal sources** | |
| Research and engineering | 33 |
| Sales, marketing, and planning | 30 |
| Production | 12 |
| Other executives and board of directors | 10 |
| **External sources** | |
| Customers and prospects | 16 |
| Contract research organizations and consultants | 7 |
| Technical publications | 4 |
| Competitors | 4 |
| Universities | 3 |
| Inventors | 3 |
| Unsolicited sources | 3 |
| Advertising agency | 2 |
| Suppliers | 2 |
| Government agencies | 2 |

Companies use a wide variety of sources when generating ideas for new products.

To generate new-product ideas, companies use a variety of techniques, such as brainstorming, contests, marketing research, and employee suggestion boxes. They keep an open mind because the goal at this stage is to encourage a free flow of ideas, not to criticize or prematurely reject an idea. Take the case of Tagamet, SmithKline Beecham's trade name for the antiulcer drug cimetidine. Scientists had theorized that the stomach wall contained *receptor sites* that could be manipulated to stop the flow of stomach acid, and they had also generally agreed that this theory could not be proved. Nevertheless, James Black, a pharmacologist at a SmithKline subsidiary, stubbornly continued to try. It took a decade and cost $10 million, but Black finally proved that receptor sites exist. Then he and a team of chemists created a drug, Tagamet, to take advantage of this breakthrough. Had Black rejected the idea of receptor sites or given up his quest, Tagamet would never have been brought to market.[27]

Sometimes an accident may yield a new-product idea. A lab technician at 3M spilled a chemical solution on her tennis shoes and then tried to wash it off. The chemical repelled the water, and the technician realized that the chemical formulation would help protect textiles from stains. That's how Scotchgard fabric protector became a new-product idea.[28]

Like their for-profit counterparts, nonprofit marketers must also generate new-product ideas. For instance, when polio was widespread, the March of Dimes's product was research and research support that would lead to a cure. Once use of vaccines controlled the disease, the organization needed a new product, so it switched its efforts to the reduction of birth defects.[29]

## STEP 2: Screen Ideas

In the next step of product development, companies screen the pool of ideas to determine which are impractical or inappropriate and which should be further analyzed. (Exhibit 9.9 shows how Johnson Wax screens new-product ideas.) For example, when DePaul University wanted to expand its offerings to residents in the greater Chicago area, it screened a list of five possible educational service extensions and ended up with one (a new adult degree program).[30] You can screen ideas in a variety of ways. Some marketers use informal screening, applying their own judgment to determine which ideas should be abandoned. More often, marketers use a formal screening process consisting of a checklist, rating system, economic analysis, or other method. To screen out ideas that aren't appropriate, marketers look at the fit with current company operations, the size of the potential market, the competitive environment, the technical and production requirements, the financial impact, and the legal issues.[31]

Firms also consider whether a product idea seems to have a strong differential advantage, is truly innovative, has a technological edge, or will help the firm achieve or maintain a leadership position. Another consideration is whether the idea can be protected by a patent or copyright. Obviously, the screening process takes time and effort, but it can save the company from a costly flop or prevent a seemingly wild idea from being rejected too quickly. Companies often assemble task forces or committees to help screen the ideas so that people with diverse backgrounds, such as engineering and finance, can lend their expertise to the process.[32]

## STEP 3: Analyze the Product Concept and Potential

Once marketers have narrowed the number of new-product ideas, they analyze the product concept for each remaining idea, examine its fit within the product line, and understand its sales potential. (This step is sometimes referred to as the *business analysis* stage.) To start, marketers define each new-product concept in specific terms. They may conduct marketing research to understand what consumers want in this product category, and they often construct a perceptual map to help define the product. Once marketers have defined the concept, they ask consumers in the target audience what they think of the idea. **Concept testing** is a form of market-

**concept testing**
A type of marketing research in which marketers describe a new product and ask consumers to react to the concept

## Exhibit 9.9 THE JOHNSON WAX CHECKLIST FOR SCREENING NEW-PRODUCT IDEAS

| Element | Yes | No |
| --- | --- | --- |
| 1. The idea represents high value-added products, not commodity-type products. | | |
| 2. It requires consumer-oriented development and presentation of products utilizing existing marketing capabilities. | | |
| 3. The idea has high advertising or promotional content that allows for intensive communication of products. | | |
| 4. It's not a major capital investment for the consumer (such as appliance or motor home). | | |
| 5. There is opportunity for logical extensions to be developed. | | |
| 6. The product offers a significant "plus" that is discernible by a large majority of consumers. | | |
| 7. There is an opportunity to expand into many overseas markets. | | |
| 8. The idea ties in with existing key Johnson's functions—technology, marketing, sales force. | | |
| 9. Labor will be of average or lower intensity relative to national norms. | | |
| 10. Capital will be of average or lower intensity relative to national norms. | | |
| 11. The product is compatible with Johnson's physical packaging capabilities. | | |
| 12. The product is preferably nonperishable. | | |
| 13. The idea is related to entomology, microbiology, polymer chemistry, emulsion or film formation, or substrate technology. | | |
| 14. The product utilizes existing distribution channels. | | |
| 15. There is an extended product life cycle; that is, years versus months. | | |
| 16. The product can be a building block for a multiproducts line or business. | | |

Marketers at Johnson Wax use this checklist to see how well a new-product idea fits with the company's strengths and capabilities.

ing research in which consumers evaluate new-product ideas by examining written, verbal, or pictorial descriptions; this helps marketers find out whether their ideas make sense and whether they appeal to the target market (see Exhibit 9.10). If the product is particularly complex, you can present a prototype of the proposed product to help customers envision what it is and what it can do.[33]

When Mary Anne Jackson was considering whether to launch her own line of children's entrées, she used a questionnaire to test her concept and had a diaper service deliver the survey to 2,000 families. After analyzing the responses, she discovered that parents preferred chicken and turkey over beef, wanted a nutritious children's meal without additives or preservatives, and expected to pay less than $3 for the product. Encouraged by the positive reaction of her target market, Jackson went on to produce My Own Meals, pioneering a new category of shelf-stable, microwavable meals for children.[34] Her successful idea caught the attention of competitors, however, and giants Tyson Foods, ConAgra, and Hormel jumped on the bandwagon. The competitors were so worried that some allegedly resorted to throwing her products into the damaged-food bins at grocery stores. However, opportu-

## Exhibit 9.10   A CONCEPT TEST QUESTIONNAIRE

**Face-to-face interview**

(The respondent is asked to look over the proposed product concept or concepts . . . a written description, or a sketch or drawing, etc.)

1a. First, what's your reaction to the proposed product? You can answer using this 0-to-10 scale, where 0 means very negative and 10 means very positive. (Show him/her the scale.)

| Very negative | 0 | 1 | 2 | 3 | 4 | 5 | 6 | 7 | 8 | 9 | 10 | Very positive |
|---|---|---|---|---|---|---|---|---|---|---|---|---|

1b. Why so positive (or negative)? _____

2a. How interested are you in the concept? (Show response category scale.)

| not interested at all | not too interested | somewhat interested | quite interested | very interested |
|---|---|---|---|---|

2b. Why did you answer the way you did? _____

3a. To what extent do you like the proposed product? Please answer on this 0-to-10 scale, where 10 means "like very much" and 0 means "don't like at all."

| Don't like it at all | 0 | 1 | 2 | 3 | 4 | 5 | 6 | 7 | 8 | 9 | 10 | Like it very much |
|---|---|---|---|---|---|---|---|---|---|---|---|---|

3b. Why did you like/not like it? _____

4a. What is the likelihood that you would buy this product at a price of $XX?

| definitely not | probably not | maybe | probably yes | definitely yes |
|---|---|---|---|---|

4b. Why or why not? _____

5a. What do you see as the product's main strengths? _____

5b. Its main weaknesses? _____

5c. Would you like to see anything changed? What are your suggestions? _____

Marketers use concept testing to determine consumer reaction to new-product proposals; surveys like this one are important tools at this stage.

nity knocked again in the early 1990s when Jackson scored a hit with Jewish travelers and military personnel. These people couldn't find shelf-stable kosher meals, but Jackson adapted her technology and now counts the U.S. military as a major customer.[35]

Jackson didn't have an existing product line, but marketers who do are usually concerned about the effect the new product might have on the others. They worry about **cannibalization,** a situation in which a new product takes market share or sales away from existing products in the line. When marketers at root beer king A&W were evaluating cream soda as a new product, they found out through marketing research that the cream soda would barely cannibalize their root beer sales. After further analysis and testing, A&W rolled the product out nationally, and it has become a major ingredient in the product line.[36]

At this point, marketers also ask another key question: What is the sales potential for this product? Having already guessed at the market for each idea, they now try to come up with a dollar figure; then they decide whether the company has the resources to make the product successful. If the market for a new product is large enough and the company can support it through product development, launch, and beyond, marketers give it the go-ahead. Mary Anne Jackson used a computer model to size the market for My Own Meals. She purchased secondary marketing information, looked at demographic trends, and then applied what she had learned from her concept test. She sliced off the 45 percent of American families with annual in-

**cannibalization**
A situation in which a new product steals sales or market share from other products in the existing product line

comes below $20,000, reasoning that they wouldn't spend extra on children's food. Another 5.5 percent was eliminated because that percentage of respondents in her survey said they wouldn't buy. Multiplying the number of times per month that respondents said they would serve My Own Meals by the average number of children per household by the average meal price of $2.30 and by the number of families in the market, Jackson calculated the potential retail market at $500 million in annual sales—large enough for Jackson to proceed with rounding up investors and moving on to the next step.[37]

## STEP 4: Develop the Product

In this step, the new product is actually designed and produced, often a time-consuming process. First, marketers decide on the *product specifications,* the characteristics that should be included in the product. Product specifications include the size, weight, materials, performance requirements, and other details. They also specify the design elements of the new product.

Design helped Ford differentiate its Taurus and Sable cars from competing cars. For example, Ford design engineers listened when consumers griped about the lack of backseat legroom in the new cars, and they angled the floor underneath the front seats to give rear passengers more room. Sometimes the market changes, so the design must be changed to meet new needs. Ford started developing the Taurus in 1979; by 1981 the designers believed that car buyers in 1985 would want larger cars. Thus the engineers enlarged the car's dimensions to meet these newly perceived needs. Reacting to another change in the marketing environment, the push for recyclability, London-based Great British Kettles ordered its new U Kettle teapot designed so that the plastic parts could be recycled.[38]

At this point, marketers decide whether to use the company's internal resources or to look outside for support. Many firms have their own departments for research and development, groups of researchers, engineers, or scientists who investigate the technical aspects of product development and design the products. However, independent R&D organizations are qualified to handle many assignments, either bringing the product from the specification and design phase all the way to completion or managing just one aspect. Also, rather than taking the time and money to develop technical capabilities in their own R&D departments, marketers can choose **technology licensing,** a form of licensing that allows a company to use technology developed by another company. For example, Merck, the drug manufacturer, licenses the antiulcer drug Losec from Astra, a Swedish company. Another drug company, Glaxo Holdings, licenses a variety of drugs, primarily antibiotics, to Schering-Plough and other companies. Technology licensing is also widespread in the computer industry: Some software products may be adopted as industry standards, and these can be licensed by firms that need to incorporate the technology into their own products. For example, the UNIX system created by AT&T (and now owned by Novell) is licensed by a wide variety of computer manufacturers, including Honeywell, Data General, and Motorola. Digital Equipment Corporation (DEC) treats technology as an asset that should be managed like cash, stocks, real estate, and anything else of value. DEC recently established a department charged with licensing its computer technology.[39]

To learn how to make the product and to be able to show a working model to consumers, marketers build a prototype. Kodak's Sayett Technology division brought a prototype of its new Kodak Datashow to an industry convention and listened as potential customers discussed the features they preferred in this computer-driven enhancement for overhead projectors. Within weeks, Kodak's engineers had redesigned the product to incorporate a number of these new features, and the strong response from showgoers produced several thousand orders by the end of the year.[40]

With the product built, the marketer uses the positioning statement and the marketing plan to focus each element of the marketing mix. As discussed in Chapter 8, product decisions run the gamut from branding and packaging to labeling and sup-

**technology licensing**
A type of licensing arrangement in which one company sells its technology to other companies

**brand licensing**
A type of licensing arrangement in which one company sells others the right to use one or more of its brand names

port services. This part of the process is as important as the physical development of the product itself because customer perceptions are shaped by all these product elements. Branding, in particular, can be vital to a new product's success, and an increasing number of marketers are choosing **brand licensing,** a form of licensing in which one company pays for the privilege of using a brand that is owned by another company. The Walt Disney characters are some of the most popular brands licensed. More than 3,000 companies license such characters as Donald Duck and Goofy. However, cute and cuddly products aren't necessary to get licensing deals. Nickelodeon's decidedly rude comic pair, Ren & Stimpy, already have their names on clothes, video games, puppets, and other items (see Exhibit 9.11).[41]

## STEP 5: Test Product and Marketing Mix

Marketers now take the new product and put it out in the world to gauge consumer reaction. Then they can judge which configuration of elements in the marketing mix gives sales the best boost, and they can decide whether the results are encouraging enough to launch the product on a wider scale. This is also the time when marketers may uncover flaws in the product and still have time to fix them before launching the product.

Test marketing is generally conducted in the field, in an environment that is representative of the target market. However, some marketers measure the reaction to new products by using *simulated test markets* (such as test labs set up to imitate a retail store environment) before going to the trouble and expense of test marketing. That's how Campbell Soup determined that its spaghetti sauce Prego showed enough promise to be put into field tests, and that's why Sara Lee decided to bake its Sara Lee Hearty Fruit Muffins for the frozen food section. However, simulated test marketing doesn't give marketers a true fix on how competitors might react. In reality, Pillsbury jumped into the frozen muffin market right behind Sara Lee. Luckily, the product category caught on so quickly that Sara Lee was able to stay on top, with sales exceeding the company's projections.[42]

**Exhibit 9.11**
**BRAND LICENSING**
Delrina licensed the Opus and Bill cartoon characters for a computer software product.

Putting the new product into a test market and fiddling with the marketing mix is usually the best way to figure out what works and what doesn't. However, traditional test marketing can be very expensive, time consuming, and risky because the product is out on public display and available to competitors. Therefore, marketers are looking at other ways to test-market, hoping to keep costs in check, to keep rivals at bay, and to speed up the results. Kraft General Foods tested its Bull's Eye barbecue sauce in two test markets and enlisted the aid of a single-source data service to measure results as marketers manipulated various elements in the marketing mix, including price and promotion. In a test that lasted just 24 weeks, the company found that it could achieve the market share it was seeking. It also discovered that the higher price didn't hurt sales and, in fact, appeared to support the product's premium positioning. In addition, higher ad spending had a minimal effect on purchasing patterns, a finding that could save the company a bundle on promotions.[43]

Sometimes the product doesn't live up to expectations, or problems arise with the product, the rest of the marketing mix, or the competition. Then marketers may make changes to the marketing mix and prolong the testing period to see how customers and competitors react. On the other hand, they may withdraw the product and look at alternatives. After six months of test marketing, the Louis Rich division of Oscar Mayer realized that its Dark Roast of Turkey product wasn't flying off the shelves. In fact, when it was tested without advertising support, virtually no one bought the product; with advertising, consumers tried the product but few came back for more. So the company yanked the product and began testing another. Of course, if a product achieves or exceeds the level of sales that marketers expect during the test-marketing period, it advances to the final step of the product development process, commercializing.[44]

As helpful as test marketing can be, it isn't used with every new product. In some cases, marketers opt to proceed without a test because they're worried that the competition will beat them to market. In other cases, they simply don't have the money to finance the test-market project, or they're so desperate for revenue that they launch the product as soon as possible. Often, marketers believe that they have enough insight into their target markets and that test marketing won't teach them enough to justify the time and expense.

Test marketing makes the most sense when the cost to market a product far exceeds the cost required to develop it. For instance, if you've spent $10 million to develop a product, and you know you'll need to spend $80 million to market it, test marketing makes sense. If the product doesn't look like it will fly, you can keep it off the market and lose only your $10 million. However, with some industrial and high-technology products, the cost to develop the product far exceeds the cost to market it, so once the product is ready to sell, there is usually no turning back. Test marketing can be used to tune price, promotion, or distribution in these situations, but the decision to go ahead and launch the new product was essentially made long before you had the chance to conduct test marketing. In cases where much of the manufacturing and distribution capacity is already in place from other products, skipping test marketing is not as risky as it might seem, although you can never eliminate the element of risk.

## STEP 6: Commercialize the Product

When you have all the pieces in place, introduce the product. This is called **commercialization;** companies start to produce the product in quantity and decide where and when it is to be launched. Commercializing a product often requires both a hefty investment in plant and equipment for manufacturing (or for service-delivery facilities for service products) and an investment in up-front marketing support. Up to the last minute, marketers have some flexibility to change their minds if, for example, they see competitive threats or shifts in the marketing environment that appear likely to endanger the product's successful introduction. Then the product may be modified or even discontinued, depending on the nature of the threat the

**commercialization**
The part of the product development process in which the new product is launched beyond the test markets into the full target market and is supported by the preferred marketing mix

marketer perceives. Once the product has been introduced, the marketer monitors its progress and makes management decisions throughout its product life cycle.

Companies such as car manufacturers traditionally unveil new models nationwide at the start of the new model year. However, many marketers opt to *roll out* a new product on a market-by-market basis rather than release the product simultaneously across one entire region. Caterpillar introduced its Cat Challenger 65 tractor in only a few states at first so that it could gear up to meet demand. This slower start also enabled the manufacturer to learn more about the postsale service needs that new buyers might experience. Because farmers generally don't have backup tractors and usually plant and harvest on a tight schedule, fast repair service is essential. A national or international introduction might have slowed Caterpillar's ability to react quickly to service demands. Following this limited rollout, the company launched the new tractor throughout North America less than a year later.[45]

# PREDICTING NEW-PRODUCT SUCCESS

During the idea-generation stage, dozens or even hundreds of ideas start the journey toward new-product development. However, few of the new products proposed ever make it to the commercialization stage, and just because a product is commercialized doesn't automatically guarantee success. Apple's Lisa computer never caught on; Polaroid's Polavision instant home movie system didn't make it into too many homes; and Yabba Dabba Dew was a soft drink that the public simply didn't swallow. As you can see, not every product ends up a winner. However, a company has ways to get closer to predicting which products will succeed and which will fail.

## Why Products Succeed

A new product may succeed for a variety of reasons. For starters, nearly everyone agrees that if a product has the backing of top management, it has a greater chance of success than if it lacks that endorsement. Beyond that, the various reasons for a product's success can be classified into four categories: the product, the positioning and the rest of the marketing mix, the product development process, and the marketing environment.

THE PRODUCT

Marketers can look at the product itself for clues to why it should succeed. Some of the main reasons are as follows:

- The product offers an advantage over competing products. For example, Pizza Hut's personal pan pizza is tasty and fast and is served at the customer's table in 5 minutes or less, compared with 20 minutes or more for a conventional pizza.[46]
- The product is innovative in fulfilling real customer needs. American Cyanamid's Combat roach-bait tray fulfilled a real need—to get rid of roaches—and was innovative because it didn't harm people or pets, and it was convenient to use.[47]
- The product's benefits fulfill the needs of the target market better than the benefits of other products on the market. Mattel's Barbie is a perennial best-seller because 3- to 11-year-old girls enjoy the doll's glamour and fantasy (see Exhibit 9.12).[48]
- The product's features are more appealing to the target market. The IBM Selectric enjoyed a long period of success because its features were attractive to busy typists. For example, typists could change fonts merely by snapping out the round typing element.[49] Electronic word processors and then personal computers gradually became even more appealing, however, and IBM chose to get out of the typewriter market.

## THE POSITIONING AND THE REST OF THE MARKETING MIX

The new product's positioning and every element in its marketing mix can contribute to its success. The following are some of the key reasons for a product succeeding because of its positioning or marketing mix:

- The company owns a powerful position. Xerox made its name in plain-paper copiers, and today the Xerox brand is nearly synonymous with photocopying.[50] Future Xerox copiers will be greeted by a market that already accepts Xerox products.
- The product is priced reasonably in relation to the value perceived by consumers. For instance, the Budget Gourmet microwavable frozen dinners promise a good meal at a low price.[51]
- The product's packaging is unusually appropriate, attractive, or functional relative to the product and the target market. Colgate introduced the pump dispenser for its toothpaste in the 1980s, and consumers found the packaging convenient and easy to use; it even offered a way to give kids a little fun at toothbrushing time.[52]
- The promotion program effectively communicates the product's benefits and advantages (see Exhibit 9.13). Budget Gourmet's ads emphasize taste and price, two compelling reasons for consumers to buy the product.[53]
- The distribution places the product exactly where the target market wants or needs it. Women who buy pantyhose responded well when L'Eggs hit the supermarket shelves because they realized they wouldn't have to make a special trip to a department store or hosiery shop to make this purchase.

## THE PRODUCT DEVELOPMENT PROCESS

The product development process contributes to new-product success in two ways:

- The ideas are well screened and thoroughly analyzed before development. Hershey Foods carefully evaluates each new-product idea to be sure the ideas fit the company's strengths in research, development, and marketing.[54]
- The marketer moves through each step of the process in order and does not skip any steps. Mary Anne Jackson used a textbook approach to developing My Own Meals and methodically worked her way through each of the six steps before launching the new product, which spawned a hot new category. However, *TV-*

### Building Industries

**WENN SIE DAS VERLEGT
HABEN, KÖNNEN DIE ANDEREN
RUHIG PUTZ MACHEN.**

Sauber und fachgerecht ist alles verlegt und verputzt.
Und an Europas meistverlegten Installationsrohre
sucht's nicht lagen, wenn ein Kunde eigenhändig
Putz macht wegen Wasserschaden. SANCO Kupfer-
rohre sind wirksam geschützt gegen Lochkorrosion

**Exhibit 9.13
CLEARLY PROMOTING
PRODUCT BENEFITS**
SANCO promotes the
strength and reliability of its
pipe products.

*Once this has been installed
the others can rabble-rouse as
much as they like.*

*Cable Week* was never test-marketed and ended up being discontinued just 25 weeks after it was introduced.[55] As noted earlier, however, some products have to charge ahead without the benefit of test marketing, and many of these are still successful.

### THE MARKETING ENVIRONMENT

Although the marketing environment is not something a marketer can easily change, you can hit a product home run by handling the environment properly or by being on the lookout for an opportunity:

• The first product into a category establishes a reputation as a pioneer or a leader. Although early growth wasn't spectacular, Federal Express was the first overnight package delivery company, and when the product caught on, no one else could catch up.[56]
• The product that is carefully positioned takes advantage of changes in the environment. Walt Disney saw that its traditional family moviegoing market was changing and that the new Disney films weren't doing well. The company launched a new brand, Touchstone Pictures, to make other types of movies.[57]
• When competitors make mistakes, the product has a window of opportunity. JVC is the Japanese manufacturer that originated the VHS video standard, and it succeeded because rival Sony made a mistake with its Beta VCR format: Beta could accommodate only a one-hour recording. JVC's VHS format was introduced 18 months later and let consumers record for as long as six hours.[58]

## Why Products Fail

As you can see, new products succeed for a wide variety of reasons, some of which are controllable and some of which are not. Similarly, new products fail for many reasons, and not all are within your control. Even so, a smart marketer can anticipate many of these situations and maneuver the new product into a trend or out of harm's way.

Obviously, products can fail for reasons that are directly opposite to the reasons products succeed. However, experts also point to other reasons for product failure:

- The company doesn't understand the product, the category, or the technology. In 1975 Exxon strayed from the oil business and tried to crack the market for electronic office systems. Ten years and $500 million later, Exxon dropped the line, which had proved to be quite different from its main business.[59]
- The product suffers from poor quality. A camera named the Wristmatic failed because the mechanism tended to jam, the quality of the photos was poor, and the camera wasn't very durable. Similarly, the Adam home computer had technical problems and, although the problems were later fixed, the product couldn't overcome the initial perceptions of poor quality.[60]
- The target market doesn't really exist. That's what the makers of the Solar Rover doghouse found out. Solar Rover was a doghouse designed to use solar energy to keep the dog warm during cold winter nights. However, there weren't nearly enough people willing to plunk down $800 for the product.[61]
- The new product meets unexpectedly strong competition. When General Mills test-marketed a new liquid chicken-batter product, Crisp 'N Tender, it found itself staring down the gun barrel of category leader General Foods, maker of Shake 'N Bake. General Foods stepped into the fray with its own liquid batter product, Batter 'N Bake, and finally forced Crisp 'N Tender off the market. Soon afterward, General Foods discontinued its liquid batter product so that it wouldn't steal share from its own category-leading Shake 'N Bake.[62]
- Government regulations can hurt. In 1967 Canada Dry was test-marketing its new Sport caffeine-free cola when it found the product in hot water with the government. The Food and Drug Administration ruled that Sport wasn't a cola because it didn't meet the technical definition. Because Canada Dry was removing the caffeine that occurred naturally in the cola nut, it was told that the new drink couldn't legally be labeled a cola. Sport had to be pulled from store shelves. Today, of course, both Coca-Cola and PepsiCo have their own no-caffeine colas, and Canada Dry's former president, David Mahoney, charged in a 1988 book that these two formidable competitors ganged up and urged the government to use regulations to kill Sport back in 1967.[63]

## SUMMARY OF LEARNING OBJECTIVES

**1. Define the product mix and its role in marketing strategy.**

A company's assortment of products is referred to as its product mix. In order to develop effective marketing strategies for numerous product items, marketers group their products into categories. These groups are called product lines. The product mix is the foundation of the marketing mix and is therefore the key element in the marketing strategy.

**2. Describe how marketers manage the product mix by introducing products, discontinuing products, and modifying products.**

As you manage the product mix, you have the choice of modifying products, discontinuing products, or adding products. The goal is to create a product mix that meets the needs of the target audience, with new products, existing products, and repositioned products. How you treat individual prod-

ucts depends on your company's profit and market share objectives. Also, when deciding whether to add, modify, or discontinue a product, you monitor changes in the marketing environment, such as emerging technology, competitor actions, and shifting consumer tastes. When a product moves into the decline phase of its life cycle and sales go down with no sign of rebounding, you consider modifying the product, discontinuing it, or adding a new product in its place.

**3. Define the four stages of the product life cycle.**

During the introduction phase, products first appear on the market. This phase can be a major financial challenge as companies try to launch marketing activities while still paying for product development and manufacturing start-up. The second phase is growth, during which sales increase rapidly and prices stabilize as more suppliers become involved. More customers adopt the new product, but aggressive competitors begin to appear on the scene as well. When sales growth levels off, the product has entered the maturity phase, during which profits generally begin to decline as low price becomes the major competitive parameter. Last, if sales begin to drop off, a product has entered the decline phase, during which marketers have to decide whether to try to revive the product or remove it from the market.

### 4. Identify the four types of new products.

The first type of new product is the innovative product, which creates an entirely new product concept and often a new category. The second type is a brand extension, which is a new product that has been branded with the name of an existing product line. The third type is a product line extension, or additional products that are introduced into an existing product line. The fourth type is a product or line of products introduced under a new brand name in a product category where the company has other brands.

### 5. Discuss how marketers use the marketing mix to manage products throughout the product life cycle.

In the introduction phase, the product has already been developed and produced, so you are concerned with distribution, promotion, and pricing. This is the part of the life cycle in which you must make the product available, tell customers about the product, and price it for trial and repeat business.

In the growth phase, you seek to expand distribution and promotion to support increased sales. Also, you are concerned with product output and quality during this phase. In the maturity phase, supply may outstrip demand, so you must change your pricing and promotion to keep sales momentum high. Also, manufacturers may produce the product under private-label branding to take advantage of excess production capacity. In the decline phase, you typically limit distribution and keep promotional expenses to a minimum. To postpone the decline phase, some marketers modify their products or target additional market segments. If the product is discontinued, you frequently drop the price to sell off inventory; if the product is kept alive to generate income for other marketing programs, you price it for profitability. You can try to revive products that slump into the decline phase by modifying the product, finding a new audience for the promotion, or using the entire marketing mix to reposition and relaunch the product.

### 6. Outline the six steps in new-product development.

You start the new-product development process by generating ideas. In this step, you search for new-product concepts by looking inside and outside the company for ideas. The second step is screening the ideas. Review all the ideas, eliminate those that seem inappropriate or impractical, and then select the most promising for further analysis. The third step is analyzing product potential by defining the product con-

## A CASE FOR CRITICAL THINKING

### *Meeting a Marketing Challenge at Canon*

When Hiroshi Tanaka took on the challenge of developing a new copier, it was cameras, not copiers, that dominated Canon's sales figures. The company had been in the copier business for years, but copiers contributed only 24 percent to Canon's overall sales, whereas cameras accounted for 46 percent of the company's sales. To tip the scales in its direction, Canon's Copier Division wanted to develop a blockbuster product that would become the AE-1 of the copier industry. Senior management had already generated the idea of a personal copier, and now it was up to Tanaka's task force to analyze the product and its potential, define the product concept, test the new product, and then successfully commercialize the new copier.

To analyze the product potential, Tanaka and his team had to look at the market in an entirely new way. Traditionally, the market had been divided into three segments: high-speed copiers, medium-speed copiers, and low-speed copiers. Instead, the Canon group segmented the market in terms of number of employees. They defined five segments: offices with 300 or more employees, offices with 100 to 299 employees, offices with 30 to 99 employees, offices with 5

to 29 employees, and offices with fewer than 5 employees. Plain-paper copiers were established in the four largest market segments, but no one was selling plain-paper copiers to businesses with 4 or fewer employees. Just within Japan, more than 4 million small offices fit this definition, so it was a sizable segment.

Next the Canon team looked at the way businesspeople work. To make a copy, people had to leave their desks and go to the copy room. Since the calculator can be on the desk, and the telephone can be on the desk, why can't the copier be right on the desk? If Canon could sell firms on the convenience of putting a personal copier on each employee's desk, the market would be immense. In Japan alone, nearly 9 million employees worked in the 4 million small-business offices. It was an entirely new product concept, and it also defined a plain-paper copier market in which Canon would be the only player.

Of course, Canon faced formidable competition in the copier industry, including industry colossus Xerox. The low-speed market was served by a variety of coated-paper copier manufacturers, including 3M and Pitney Bowes. None of the cept, estimating demand, and examining the resources necessary to develop and market the product. Also, consider whether a new product will cannibalize sales from existing products. The fourth step is designing and developing the product internally or externally, including any necessary research and development. In this step, you may license brands or technology for your new product. The fifth step is test-marketing the product to see how various configurations of the marketing mix affect sales. The sixth step is commercializing the product by starting production and implementing the chosen marketing mix.

## 7. Discuss the major reasons for the success of new products.

Marketers can attribute the success of new products to the product itself, to the positioning and the rest of the marketing mix, to the product development process, or to the marketing environment. Considering the product itself, success is often achieved when it has a differential advantage, it is innovative in fulfilling needs, its benefits meet the target market's needs better than competitors, or its features are more appealing. From the viewpoint of positioning and the product marketing mix, a product succeeds when it preempts a key position, is priced according to perceived value, is packaged appropriately, is distributed through appropriate channels, or is promoted effectively. Marketers can use the product development process to support successful products by screening and analyzing all ideas thoroughly before proceeding to develop any. In the marketing environment, the successful product is often the first in its category, carefully positioned to take advantage of environmental changes, or able to take advantage of competitive stumbles.

## KEY TERMS

brand licensing (286)
cannibalization (284)
commercialization (287)
concept testing (282)
decline phase (275)

growth phase (274)
introduction phase (274)
maturity phase (274)
product diffusion process (276)

product life cycle (273)
product line (268)
product line depth (269)
product line extension (273)

product line width (269)
product mix (268)
product portfolio (269)
technology licensing (285)

plain-paper competitors had yet targeted the low-end market, so Canon would gain a valuable head start in this segment.

The next challenge was to understand target market needs. Price was the major issue. Canon's top executives had set a hypothetical top selling price of $1,000. To fit on a desk, size and weight would be important, so Tanaka aimed for a weight of 20 kilograms (44 pounds) or less. The copies would have to be clear and high quality, and the copier would have to be maintenance-free, a departure from traditional plain-paper copiers, which required regular service visits.

Thus, Tanaka's team settled on a basic product concept: a low-priced, high-quality, low-maintenance, lightweight copier. Next they set out to develop a product that was reliable and at the same time affordable. The task force learned that 90 percent of copier problems were related to the drum, a basic copier component, so they made a revolutionary proposal: They suggested that the copier's drum and ink supply be discarded after a certain number of copies had been made, to be replaced by a new drum and ink cartridge. The customer would simply pull out the special cartridge and re-

place it with a new one. This would solve the maintenance problem, and it would allow the machine to be uncomplicated, smaller, and lighter. No competitor could match the convenience of this new technology, or the price. Canon protected its technology with 594 patents.

Moving through the product development, testing, and commercialization stages, Canon was able to launch two personal copiers, the PC-10 and the PC-20, by late 1982. The PC-10 had a suggested retail price of $995, and the PC-20 had a suggested price of $1,295 because of its more expensive automatic paper-feeding feature. From 1982 to 1984, Canon increased its worldwide copier sales from $1.03 billion to $1.47 billion, an astounding 43 percent increase. By 1986 the company held a commanding 28 percent share of the U.S. market in copier sales and rentals, more than double the sales and rentals of Sharp, its closest competitor. By 1987 the Copier Division was the single largest contributor to Canon's sales results. Cameras counted for 18 percent of all Canon sales, and copiers had skyrocketed to 35 percent. The achievement was even more impressive because Tanaka and his task force had created the AE-1 of copiers in only

three years. Now in the mid-1990s, Canon holds a solid position in the worldwide copier market.

**Your mission:** You're the marketing representative on Hiroshi Tanaka's personal-copier task force. You have been assigned the role of managing the product mix and implementing the marketing mix to support the introduction of Canon's personal-copier product line in the United States. You are also in charge of managing the personal copier throughout its life cycle, and you must think about how to extend the product's life cycle in the future. Use your knowledge of product development and management to choose the best marketing decisions from the alternatives you face in the following situations.

1. You've just introduced the PC-10 and PC-20, and you are thinking ahead to the product line of the future. The new products have immediately attracted competitive attention and you don't have much time before imitators flood the market. The Copier Division's top management will be meeting with you next week and has asked for your product management plans for the coming year. Which of these programs will you present?

   a. To keep sales figures high and profits growing, you decide to add features to the basic personal-copier models and gradually convince small offices to trade up to the better, more expensive models. You plan to start by introducing a new personal copier that can reduce and enlarge but costs only slightly more than the PC-20. Competitors will follow you upward, but it will be months until they can make their plays.

   b. Rather than sacrifice the positioning you've created in the small-business market, you choose to make your models even smaller and less expensive. Your new products will be aimed at the home-office market, where people have less space for equipment and less money to spend. However, the home-office market is growing like crazy, and the potential number of machines you can sell is very large. Therefore, you will strip away features, shrink the machine in size and weight, and sell a new personal copier for $500 or less.

   c. Because you see the small-business market and home-office market as interested in a variety of machines, you want to expand the product line in both directions. Therefore, you plan to manage your product mix by implementing the strategy in choice (a) to firmly ensconce Canon's name in personal copiers. Then you'll move into choice (b) when you've gobbled up the major share of the small-business market. You reason that competitors will be slower to enter the home-office market and you can establish Canon's position before others even think about trying their luck.

2. Top management of the Copier Division has decided to postpone investing in new personal-copier products. They ask you to extend the life cycle of the two current products without changing the technology. You can manipulate any elements of the marketing mix, including com-

ponents of the existing products, to give sales a boost and maintain profitability. To prevent the products from slipping into the decline phase, your goal is to keep the current target markets interested or find new audiences. You've been brainstorming with your colleagues and they have a few suggestions. Of these ideas, which would you implement?

a. Lean toward the home-office or single-proprietor business market by cutting the price on the PC-10 from $995 to $795. Emphasize the cost benefit by advertising the price break.

b. Seek out new markets by expanding your distribution strategy. Look for mail-order merchants who target small businesses, and arrange for them to feature the PC-10 and PC-20 in their catalogs. Also, place the copiers in retail outlets that carry desk accessories and office supplies, such as stationery stores and discount department stores.

c. Manufacture the personal copiers in a variety of colors, including ivory, mauve, blue, gray, and black. Then advertise that the copiers are available in colors to match any customer's office decor, and illustrate how the copiers fit into the color scheme of various offices.

3. You've been asked to prepare a report that discusses how copier customers perceive the Canon personal copier in relation to three competitors, and how Canon is differentiated from these competitors. To complete this assignment, draw a perceptual map showing the positions of Canon, Sharp, Xerox, and Minolta. Through marketing research, you learn that the two key attributes consumers consider when purchasing a personal copier are price and reliability. On your perceptual map, you put reliability on the horizontal axis and price on the vertical axis so that the highest price is at the top, the lowest price is at the bottom, the highest reliability is at the right, and the lowest reliability is at the left. Your research shows that customers perceive Xerox and Minolta to be in the top right quadrant (high priced and very reliable), whereas they place Sharp in the bottom right quadrant (low priced and very reliable). Canon is also in the lower right quadrant, just a bit more reliable than Sharp. You realize that the ideal position is at the farthest point in the bottom right, very reliable and very inexpensive. How can you differentiate Canon copiers from Sharp copiers by convincing consumers that your product is closer to the ideal?

a. Extend the warranty on the personal copiers and offer free on-site service for any needed maintenance during the entire warranty period. This will reinforce the perception that Canon copiers are very reliable and that consumers can depend on Canon.

b. Make the Canon personal copier even smaller than the Sharp model, and introduce the new product as a product line extension. Position the new product as smaller but just as reliable as the original Canon.

c. Price the Canon products 10 percent below the Sharp products, no matter how low the Sharp copiers are priced. This will position Canon as less expensive than Sharp, even when Sharp copiers are on sale.

4. As the personal-copier products move from the growth stage to the mature stage of their life cycle, you decide that the home-office market represents the segment with the most potential for the next 12 to 18 months. However, people who run businesses from their homes have purchasing patterns that differ from those of people who run office-based businesses or of purchasing agents who buy copiers for the larger firms. You therefore create a slightly different positioning statement for this segment: "Canon personal copiers deliver the features you need and the convenience you demand at a price you can afford." You want to step up advertising to communicate with this segment, and Dentsu Young & Rubicam (your ad agency) develops a number of advertising packages for your consideration. Of these alternatives, which do you think would be most effective in reaching the home-office market?

a. Focus on people who are moonlighters, using their home offices only at night and on weekends. Use the Sunday edition of local newspapers and ads on local radio news programs to reach these people during their leisure time. Stress the low cost and the convenience of having a copier in your home office.

b. Target entrepreneurs with an ad campaign that uses up-scale consumer magazines such as *Travel & Leisure* and *Money* along with business magazines such as *Forbes* and *Inc.* Hammer away at the personal copier's cost effectiveness and features.

c. Focus on anyone who has a home office and needs the convenience of a personal copier at a low price. Use mass media such as television commercials during major sports events and popular national news programs to reach a broad audience. Also advertise during local early evening and late evening news programs.

## SPECIAL PROJECT

Plain-paper personal copiers have become a big segment in the duplicating industry. Canon no longer has the field to itself, and others have crowded in to take advantage of the market that Canon pioneered. The market is mature, but not yet in decline. Everyone, Canon included, is scrambling to keep sales and profits high. For this assignment, scan newspapers and magazines looking for advertisements from Canon and from competing manufacturers. Visit an office supply store (or a department store) to look at Canon copiers and competitive models. Note how the competitive products are positioned and marketed, compared with Canon's personal copiers. Select two competitors, write a brief summary of the positions they appear to be occupying, and describe how their marketing mixes support those positions.[64]

# VIDEO CASE

## Chrysler Drives Back into the Black

Chrysler certainly knows how to make the headlines. The company was all over the front page in 1979, when it had to ask the U.S. government for loan guarantees to stay afloat. The loans and outspoken CEO Lee Iaccoca helped Chrysler regain its footing in the early 1980s, only to plunge into big losses again in the early 1990s. The company lost $665 million in 1991. More headlines, more bad news.

True to form, Chrysler was back in the news in the mid-1990s. Only this time, the news was surprisingly positive. To understand how Chrysler got out of trouble, one first has to understand how the company got into trouble. In the early days of the auto industry, a group of engineers did it all for a company, from designing and building the cars to designing and building the factories. As companies grew and technology grew more complex, however, people began to specialize in particular functions. Some engineers specialized in product development; others in production. Other people specialized in production planning, purchasing, finance, and marketing. Among the development engineers, some even began to specialize in particular parts of the car, such as the engine. Formal organizations gradually became cemented in place, and without anyone really intending for it to happen, walls—both physical walls and barriers to effective communication—began to take shape between the different groups involved in the design and production of cars.

The result was bad for the company and bad for consumers. With no single group of people in charge of a car's quality, for instance, quality slipped. Developing new products consumed mountains of time, money, and people, as groups separated by distance and culture struggled to work together. For instance, the K-car family from the early 1980s required the efforts of 2,000 technical specialists over four and a half years.

To get back on track, Chrysler reinvented the way it develops new products. Rather than having isolated functional groups work on different phases from design through production, the company now uses *platform teams* made up of specialists from marketing, design, research, engineering, sales, and production planning. (A "platform" in the auto business is the basic chassis and drive train used for a family of vehicles, such as small cars, midsize cars, and Jeeps/trucks.)

The new approach raises quality and cuts development time and staffing. The Dodge Viper, with its radical styling and muscular V-10 engine, is a good example. A team of 85 technical experts designed the Viper in three years. It took just three years and three months for 740 people to develop the three midsize LH platform cars, the Dodge Intrepid, Eagle Vision, and Chrysler Concorde—15 months faster than the K-cars and one-third the staff.

Creating products that consumers want certainly pays off. While many of its previous models barely broke even (if they broke even at all), the popular minivans pull in more than $5,000 of profit on each vehicle (and Chrysler sells more than half a million of them every year), and the Jeep Grand Cherokees net more than $8,000 per vehicle. The new midsize sedans are selling well against such tough competition as the Ford Taurus and Honda Accord. The Neon, Chrysler's 1995 entry into the small car segment, looks like a competitive winner, and the first profitable U.S. economy car in years. It's no coincidence that the Neon cost less than half the amount other automakers spend to develop a new car.

1. Why is it important to get new products on the market as soon as possible?
2. How could a small, growing company learn from Chrysler's experience over the last two decades?
3. As a marketer, what kind of training and education would you need to succeed at the new Chrysler?

1. What are the pros and cons of a narrow product line? Should a marketer such as Snapple expand beyond its current product offerings in bottled juices and iced tea?
2. Should your college automatically drop classes for which enrollment has fallen below specified levels? Think of this decision in the larger context of attracting students when you explain your answer.
3. Which stage of the product life cycle do you think the following product categories currently occupy?
   a. Automobiles
   b. Electric automobiles
   c. Health food
   d. Videophones
4. If you were the brand manager of the Elmer's line, which includes Elmer's Glue-All, which of these proposed product line extensions would you approve? Why?
   a. Masking tape
   b. Rubber cement
   c. Paint remover
   d. Spackle
5. Which of the four new-product types does each of the following products represent?
   a. Disneyland
   b. Kodacolor Gold 400 film
   c. Kellogg's Kenmei Rice Bran cereal
   d. Maytag dishwashers
   e. Reynolds Plastic Wrap
6. How could you modify apple juice, certainly a mature product, to extend the product life cycle?
7. Say you're in the marketing department of Fox Broadcasting and you watch the popularity of "The Simpsons" start to drop precipitously. What are the advantages and disadvantages of discontinuing this product?
8. Assume you're working for KFC (Kentucky Fried Chicken) and you're looking for new-product ideas that you can use to expand your menu. What sources would you consult to generate new-product ideas?
9. Would it be a good idea for General Mills to license its Betty Crocker brand trademark to a cooking magazine? Is it a good idea for General Mills to license its Micro-Rave microwave dessert mix technology to a fast-food restaurant? Defend your answers.
10. Imagine you've developed a new video arcade game called "King Kong's Environmental Rampage." What are the pros and cons of test marketing your new product in the highly volatile video game industry, where hits can come and go almost monthly?

# SHARPEN YOUR MARKETING SKILLS

Concern for the natural environment has become an increasingly important aspect of product design. Some examples: General Mills now requires the use of recycled paper for all its cereal boxes, Kodak plans to recycle disposable cameras, and H. J. Heinz pledged to stop buying tuna from fish suppliers whose nets trapped dolphins. Furthermore, an overwhelming majority of people in the United States now consider themselves environmentalists and claim they have changed their buying and living behavior in order to protect the environment.

**Decision:** Pick a product category such as paint, pesticides, or automotive fluids, and visit a retail outlet that sells such products. Examine the packaging, labeling, and product design. In what ways are the manufacturers of these goods changing their products to better meet environmental concerns?

**Communication:** For one of the products you've identified, create a simple magazine ad that highlights its environmental sensitivity. Don't worry about polished graphics or precise layout, but provide a rough sketch, a headline, and supporting body copy.[65]

# KEEPING CURRENT IN MARKETING

Find articles that describe a company's decision to remove a product from the market. It doesn't matter what product category or markets are involved; just be sure that the product has already been taken off the market.

1. How did the company come to the decision to delete the product from its portfolio? Did it have a replacement product ready to introduce?

2. Were competitors able to take advantage of the company's decisions? Did they do anything differently as a result?
3. How did the decision affect customers of the obsolete product? Did the company help them make the transition to other products? Was such a transition necessary?

# Service and Nonprofit Marketing

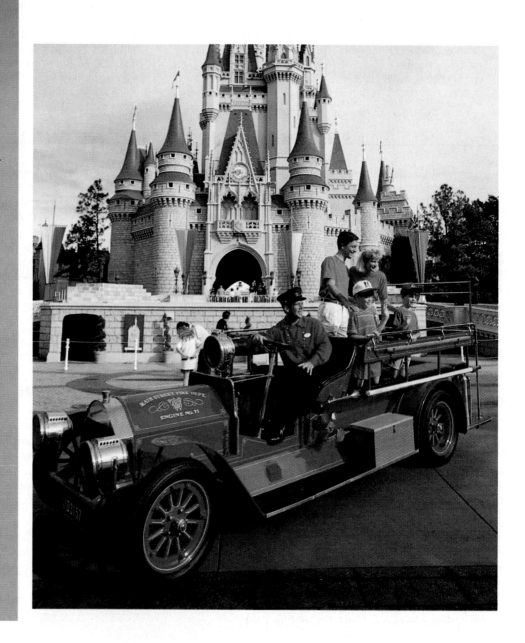

# FACING A MARKETING CHALLENGE AT WMX TECHNOLOGIES

## One Person's Trash Is Another Person's Treasure

Next time you throw away a piece of trash, stop and think: What happens now? Multiply your personal trash output by the several billion people on the planet. Now add in the millions of large and small businesses and other organizations that generate everything from computer printouts to toxic chemicals. Who takes care of the trash we all leave behind?

The waste generated by today's industrialized economies is by itself staggering, but that's just the beginning. As countries in Eastern Europe, Asia, and other parts of the world crank up their economic engines, the amount of trash in need of disposal just grows and grows. This colossal mess looks like nothing but trouble to most people, but to Dean Buntrock and his colleagues, it looks like a business opportunity.

Buntrock is the chairman and CEO of WMX Technologies, a group of companies engaged in the collection, processing, recycling, and disposal of a wide variety of wastes from residences, office buildings, factories, power plants, and other creators of trash. The company's services range from picking up household trash to disposing of low-level radioactive waste.

The fact that WMX markets services, rather than goods, presents Buntrock with a unique set of marketing challenges. For instance, compare the challenge of marketing neighborhood trash pickup (a service) with the challenge of marketing trash cans (a good). The trash can marketer could make a few thousand cans, store them in a warehouse, and sell them through retail stores that are open whenever it's convenient for consumers to shop. This marketer would be happy to make as many trash cans as people can buy. However, Buntrock faces an entirely different situation. He can't sell the trash collection service whenever consumers want to buy; this would be like allowing consumers to call in for trash pickup whenever they feel like it. With millions of customers, the inefficiency of personalized pickup would make the service wildly expensive. Moreover, Buntrock may not always want to sell as much of his product as possible because he has to do something with all the trash he picks up. If he's running out of landfill space, he may want customers to buy *less* of his product, not more.

These and other challenges are common to nearly all service marketers, but the waste business presents a special twist of its own. Waste is a problem that everyone would like to see just go away. Of course, it won't just go away, so companies such as WMX play a crucial role in keeping the wheels of contemporary life turning day after day. People want the comforts of a consumer-oriented economy (with all the manufacturing, distribution, and packaging waste that it entails), but they aren't always happy with the way WMX and others take care of the mess that this economy leaves behind. Waste companies are frequent targets of protests, lawsuits, and government regulators. The chairman of WMX competitor Browning-Ferris Industries summed up the situation perfectly when he remarked, "People are very willing to have us pick up their trash; they just don't want us to put it down." Not only does Buntrock have to deal with the challenges of marketing a service, he has to market a service that many people don't understand or appreciate.

If you were Dean Buntrock, what kind of marketing strategies would you like to see in place at WMX? How would you address the intangibility of your product? How would you respond to the extensive government regulations that drive your business? What steps could you take to make the public feel more comfortable with your company and your services?[1]

# CHAPTER OVERVIEW

Like all marketers of services, WMX Technologies faces a special marketing challenge because of the nature of service products. Most of the marketing concepts you've learned so far apply to services; however, some additional considerations are unique to services. This chapter starts by emphasizing the importance of services in the U.S. economy and then describes the unique attributes of service products. Following that is a discussion of the various ways you can classify services, which is an important step in designing a service marketing strategy. Next is a section on understanding the market for services (including service buyers and the service environment), which is followed by a discussion of marketing strategies and tactics. The final part of the chapter covers marketing for nonprofit organizations, with a description of the unique aspects of nonprofit marketing and a discussion of the importance of nonprofit marketing in our society and economy.

# DEFINING SERVICE MARKETING

A service is a performance that delivers some combination of benefits to the buyer. A service can be provided by a machine (automatic teller), a person (consultant), or a combination of both (mechanic). A service can be directed toward the buyer (dental checkup) or toward the buyer's possessions (roof repair). All government agencies are service providers, as are schools, hospitals, and transportation systems.

As discussed in Chapter 8, most products are a combination of tangible and intangible attributes. **Goods-dominant products** are more tangible and rely primarily on the exchange of physical goods to fulfill customer needs. On the other hand, **service-dominant products** are less tangible because the majority of the exchange is a service. Although we talk about "goods" and "services" as separate categories, you can see that many products include elements of both.

## The Importance and Growth of Services

Service occupations now account for more than 75 percent of the U.S. national income. Every recent economic recovery gained momentum from the **service sector,** the segment of the economy that delivers services rather than goods. The service sector has created over 44 million jobs in the last three decades. Many of these new jobs went to women and minorities entering the work force.[2] Looking to the future, most of the new jobs created in the United States by the end of the century will be in services, although a frequent complaint about these service jobs is that they often don't pay as well as manufacturing jobs. Experts foresee 107.4 million service jobs in the year 2005, compared to 25.2 million in manufacturing (see Exhibit 10.1).[3]

Why does the service sector continue to grow? First, economic prosperity increases the demand for services. Baby boomers have entered their peak earning years, and 76 million of them live in the United States alone. Moreover, the number of households with incomes over $60,000 a year doubled from 1985 to 1990. These consumers find themselves with more disposable income and look for services to help them invest, travel, relax, and stay fit. Similar trends are taking place in other parts of the world. For example, people over age 35 are crowding into exercise centers, sports clubs, and sporting goods stores across Europe, trying to get in shape and feel better about themselves.[4]

Second, population patterns in the United States continue to change, with more elderly people, more single people living alone, and fewer traditional families. The number of women in the work force grew 213.7 percent in the four decades after World War II, compared to a 51.5 percent increase in the number of working men.[5] As a result, more two-career households exist than ever before. This creates op-

**goods-dominant products**
Products for which the main benefits to customers are derived from goods

**service-dominant products**
Products for which the main benefits to customers are derived from services

**service sector**
That portion of the economy whose output is services, as opposed to goods

300

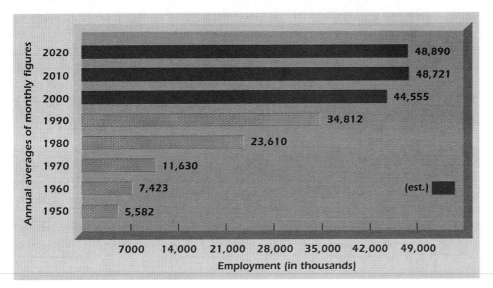

**Exhibit 10.1
GROWTH OF THE
SERVICE SECTOR**
The service sector has grown
dramatically in recent
decades, and this trend is expected to continue into the
next century.

portunities for service companies that can help couples with all the tasks they no longer have time for, including lawn maintenance, food service, and child care. Nationwide, 60,000 to 70,000 day-care centers have been established. Bright Horizons Children's Centers is an example of the new upscale facilities that target professional couples. Its flagship center in Cambridge, Massachusetts, is operating at full capacity with a long waiting list. The nation's largest chain, Kinder-Care Learning Centers, provides on-site day-care facilities for a number of large companies. Kinder-Care has over 1,000 centers and expects to grow 10 to 15 percent annually to the turn of the century.[6]

Third, the number and complexity of goods needing service are increasing. Computers, VCRs, CD players, recreational vehicles, and security systems are examples of products that can require specialized installation, repair, or user training. In the office, products ranging from laser printers to fax machines need expert attention. Factories use robots, automated test equipment, and computer-controlled production lines that require extensive support services.

The need for business services continues to change and expand for several reasons. First, corporate restructurings can leave firms without adequate internal services; free-lance promotional writers, for example, will flourish in the 1990s as many companies put a squeeze on their marketing staffs.[7] Second, the continued growth of global marketing and manufacturing requires more international support services.[8] United Parcel Service and Federal Express, among others, are expanding their international package delivery services to take advantage of the increase in global business operations.[9] Finally, the business of business just keeps getting more complicated, and the number of consultants who can help with complex problems in finance, marketing, engineering, and global operations will continue to grow.

## The Unique Aspects of Service Marketing

The most important lesson to learn about service marketing is that it is not the same process as goods marketing. Many of the concepts and techniques are similar, but you must approach service marketing differently. You can begin to understand the special nature of service marketing by examining four attributes that set services apart: intangibility, inseparability of production and consumption, perishability, and heterogeneity.

### INTANGIBILITY

Scooters, skateboards, and spacecraft are tangible products. Buyers determine whether the products are acceptable based on physical observation and evaluation.

On the other hand, haircuts, therapy, and accounting classes are predominantly intangible. The **intangibility** of services means that buyers cannot make judgments based on sensory evaluation (taste, touch, sight, smell, or hearing). Buyers rely instead on whatever cues they can find to assess quality, including the appearance of the service provider and the physical environment in the service firm. A recent study of restaurant customers, for instance, indicated that the manner in which employees treat customers is a key purchase decision factor.[10]

**intangibility**
The characteristic of services that prevents customers from evaluating products according to sensory criteria

To overcome intangibility, service marketers often add tangible elements to symbolize the qualities and benefits of their services. Dentists give patients brushes and floss, which represent quality dental care. The chocolate left on your hotel room pillow symbolizes the personal attention of the hotel staff.

Intangibility also leads to a special management challenge. Service marketers can't rely on normal measures of product quality to make sure they're offering the right level of performance. Instead, service marketers often use customer satisfaction surveys to monitor and maintain control over product quality. Customer satisfaction is discussed further in Chapter 21.

## INSEPARABILITY

**inseparability**
The attribute of services that denotes the inability to separate production from consumption

The second unique aspect of services is **inseparability;** because you can't store services, you can't separate production from consumption. You can't mail someone a haircut or drop off a TV repair job on a customer's front porch. Services don't follow the "normal" model of first production, then sale, then consumption; they are sold first, then usually produced and consumed simultaneously.

Inseparability has a special meaning in many service industries. In some cases, a particular provider is so closely identified with a service that substitute providers will simply not suffice. If you pay to be entertained by Garth Brooks, a performance by Billy Ray Cyrus just won't do. Your marketing professor is probably so good that you would be deeply disappointed if you got stuck with a substitute instructor. In many service fields, in fact, the service provider's major objective is to establish this kind of exclusivity. Medical specialists, lawyers, writers, entertainers, consultants, chefs, and designers frequently work to make customers believe they can't get the same service from anybody else.

## PERISHABILITY

**perishability**
The quality of services that prevents the creation or storage of inventory

Another result of intangibility is that services cannot exist before or after the actual performance. You can bake six loaves of bread and sell them one at a time, but you can't cut one customer's hair six times in one day and save the other five haircuts in case a basketball team walks in. This **perishability** of services means that you can't store the capacity to perform a service for future use.

What problems can perishability create? Put yourself in the boots of the manager at a ski resort such as Sun Valley. You can sell skiing time only when customers are available, weather conditions are cooperating, your lifts are operating, and your staff is trained and on the job. If any one of these pieces of the puzzle is missing, you can't sell skiing—and you can't store your capacity to sell skiing for some later date when you've got it all together. You can train your staff all summer long, tune up your lift engines, hope for snow, and use effective marketing to pull in a steady stream of customers, but you're still at the mercy of perishability because you can't store skiing time for future use.

## HETEROGENEITY

**heterogeneity**
The inconsistency in the performance of services that causes variations in quality

Consistency and quality need close attention with all products, but they are of particular concern with services. Services are most often performed by people, and people don't always offer consistent performances. **Heterogeneity** is the variation in service quality caused by inconsistencies of performance. Several factors con-

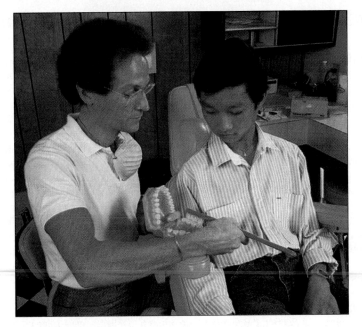

**Exhibit 10.2
CUSTOMER
COOPERATION IN
HEALTH CARE**
Dentists can't promise healthy
teeth unless patients share
the responsibility for service
quality.

tribute to heterogeneity, including customer cooperation, employee morale, and company work load.

- *Customer cooperation.* Any hairstylist who has tried to make a squirming child look great knows all about customer cooperation. Jenny Craig diet centers can't promise the same results to everyone because the customer has at least as much control over the outcome of the service as the provider has. Similarly, dentists can't promise healthy teeth to patients who won't take responsibility for personal dental hygiene (see Exhibit 10.2).

- *Employee morale.* The best system in the world for delivering quality service will fall apart if employees aren't motivated to serve customers. A delicious restaurant meal just isn't quite as special if you have to tangle with a waiter who's in a bad mood. Motivated employees make the difference. For an inspiring example of motivation that leads to superior service, check out the National Park Service guides as they give tours of Civil War battlefields in the sweltering southern summer. They not only overlook their own discomfort, they have an extra margin of patience to deal with hot, grumpy tourists.

- *Company work load.* Quality suffers if employees and equipment are overloaded. Maintaining enough resources to handle peak loads without creating too much idle capacity during off-peak times becomes a balancing act for the service provider. AT&T, MCI, and other telephone services struggle to maintain this balance. Telephone lines and switching equipment are expensive, and extra capacity just sits idle when calls aren't being placed. However, the phone companies try to have enough extra lines available to handle the deluge at Christmas, Mother's Day, and other peak times. When you try to call home and hear "We're sorry; all circuits are busy," you've experienced a breakdown in service quality because of resource overload.

## The Major Service Classifications

Now that you understand how services differ from tangible products, the next step is to separate them into groups of similar service types. Classification is important because it gives you a greater understanding of the value you provide customers. This understanding in turn provides the insight needed to create effective marketing strategies.[11]

## WHO IS RESPONSIBLE FOR SERVICE QUALITY?

In many service industries, the provider has complete control over the final quality of service. However, in some cases the customer's actions influence the quality of the service. For example, when a doctor puts you on a specific diet regimen to help you recover from surgery, whether or not you follow the diet might determine how well you recover. How can you be sure that the surgery was a success and that the diet was correct? Marketing consultants and marketing research firms face similar situations frequently. In fact, one of the nation's largest marketing research vendors, Yankelovich Skelly & White, recently found itself in the middle of a controversy over responsibility for quality.

Beecham Products had spent two years developing its Delicare cold-water detergent and was ready to take a run at market leader Woolite (marketed by American Home Products Corporation). Woolite held a commanding 90 percent of the market. To make sure it had a winner before investing millions in a national introduction, Beecham hired Yankelovich to test Delicare's market potential.

Yankelovich informed Beecham that Delicare could grab from 45 to

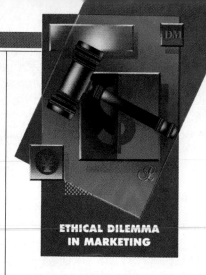

**ETHICAL DILEMMA IN MARKETING**

52 percent of the market, provided Beecham spent $18 million to promote the product. Based on this projection, Beecham introduced Delicare, spending more than $6 million in the second quarter alone. Alas, reality failed to cooperate with marketing projections. Delicare never gained more than a 25 percent share.

Beecham's response? The company sued Yankelovich, alleging negligence and professional malpractice. Of course, Yankelovich denied the charges, and legal experts say that Beecham will have to prove that Yankelovich's mistakes caused Delicare to fail. From a marketing perspective, the problem of proof is obvious: How can anyone be sure that Delicare failed because of Yankelovich's advice and not because of the way the product was marketed?

Beecham claims that Yankelovich was in a state of turmoil while this project was being conducted. Yankelovich had been acquired not long before by the world's largest advertising agency, Saatchi & Saatchi, and was later merged with another Saatchi & Saatchi acquisition to become Yankelovich Clancy Schulman. Beecham also claims that Yankelovich made a serious error while building a model to project Delicare's sales: According to Beecham, rather than using 30 percent as the portion of households that purchase fine-fabric detergents, Yankelovich used 70 percent. Yankelovich has declined to comment on the case.

Regardless of who is to blame, this case raises important questions. How can we judge the quality of marketing research when the only way to know for sure is to go ahead with the marketing program? Doctors and lawyers are already familiar with malpractice insurance; perhaps it will become an issue for marketing services firms as well.

### WHAT'S YOUR OPINION?

**1.** Is it ethical for a company to advertise quality services if it can't absolutely guarantee 100 percent quality?

**2.** What is a company's responsibility if a customer causes service quality to be less than perfect?

---

You can classify services according to several variables: profit objective, customer type, labor and equipment needs, customer contact, and skill level. Refer to Exhibit 10.3 to see how some common services can be defined by these variables. Note that classification isn't always clear cut; for example, a carpenter can provide one service that is labor-based (such as installing a new roof) and another that is largely equipment-based (such as creating custom millwork). Also, you can use a wide range of variables to classify services; the five described here are the most common.

### PROFIT OBJECTIVE

A major distinction among service providers is whether or not they seek financial profit. Consider the case of hospitals. Profit-seeking hospitals make strategic marketing decisions based on potential return on investment. Their locations, services, equipment, and target patient groups are all chosen with an eye to making a profit.

On the other hand, Wheaton Franciscan Services, one of the top Catholic hospital systems in the United States, makes strategic decisions based on religious and humanitarian goals.[12] Wheaton may locate a hospital where it can help the greatest number of homeless people, for example. Its product mix might emphasize services that address the health and diet needs of the poor rather than cosmetic surgery or other services aimed at more affluent patients. For-profit and nonprofit hospitals both practice marketing in all its various forms, and they often compete with each other, but their objectives remain quite different.

## CUSTOMER TYPE

Service firms sell to both consumers and organizational customers. The services are identical in some cases, but different marketing strategies are required for the two types of customers. For example, personal selling might make sense for a carpet-cleaning service targeting large office buildings, but the cost for selling the same service to individual homeowners would be prohibitive (at least in person; carpet cleaners often sell their services over the telephone). Of course, many services are sold only to one customer type or another. As the global economy grows ever more complex, marketers of business services are looking for new opportunities to provide specialized services in training, import/export consulting, international finance, and other growing areas.

## LABOR AND EQUIPMENT NEEDS

As the name implies, **labor-based services** rely primarily on the activities of people, whereas **equipment-based services** rely primarily on the functions of equipment. For example, the performance of management consultants depends almost entirely on their knowledge, skill, and experience. On the other hand, the service you receive during a long-distance telephone call relies on an extensive communication and computer network; if you use direct dialing, you won't involve any operators in the transaction.

Equipment-based services tend to be more consistent than labor-based services because they reduce or eliminate the influence of human variability. Automation can also let you service more customers more cost-effectively. AT&T's long-distance network handles millions of calls daily, which would swamp the company if it had to rely exclusively on human operators. However, basing service delivery on equipment presents two potential drawbacks. First, if your equipment fails, you lose your ability to deliver the service. Second, relying too heavily on automation could prevent you from providing personalized service. If AT&T eliminated all its operators,

**labor-based services**
Services that are delivered primarily by people

**equipment-based services**
Services that are delivered primarily by equipment

**Exhibit 10.3
A CLASSIFICATION
MODEL FOR SERVICES**
Marketers can gain strategic insights by classifying services.

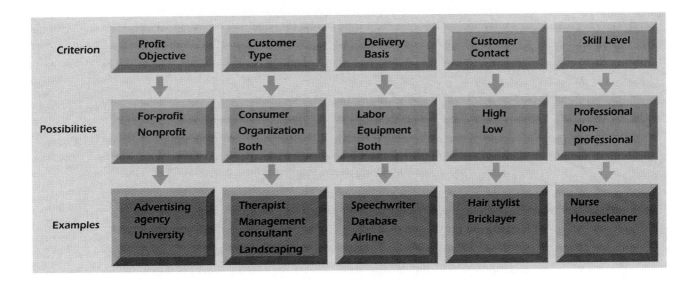

| Criterion | Profit Objective | Customer Type | Delivery Basis | Customer Contact | Skill Level |
|---|---|---|---|---|---|
| Possibilities | For-profit Nonprofit | Consumer Organization Both | Labor Equipment Both | High Low | Professional Non-professional |
| Examples | Advertising agency University | Therapist Management consultant Landscaping | Speechwriter Database Airline | Hair stylist Bricklayer | Nurse Housecleaner |

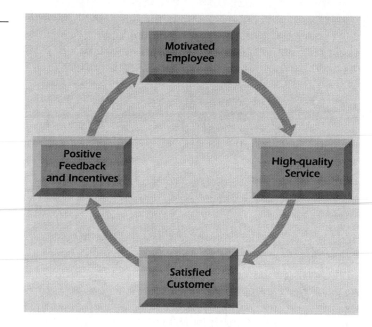

**Exhibit 10.4**
**THE CYCLE OF SATISFACTION IN HIGH-CONTACT BUSINESSES**
Quality and satisfaction build on each other in service firms.

you couldn't call for directory assistance, refunds for wrong numbers, or help with calls that don't go through. Even though it relies on a complex, automated system to handle the bulk of its traffic, AT&T realizes it must also provide the personalized service available only from human operators.

## CUSTOMER CONTACT

**high-contact services**
Services in which customers experience a high degree of involvement with the service providers

**low-contact services**
Services in which customers experience a low degree of involvement with the service providers

Another useful way to classify services is by the amount of customer involvement. **High-contact services** entail considerable personal contact and usually involve actions directed toward individuals. On the other hand, **low-contact services** are usually directed toward objects, and the customer may not need to be present. Two examples of high-contact services are health care and transportation. Your veterinarian can't examine your cat unless the two of them get together. British Airways can't transport you to London unless you get on one of its planes. Stereo repair and landscape maintenance are low-contact services, which don't require the customer's presence and involvement. Some services are a combination of high and low contact. Free-lance writers spend part of their time meeting with clients to define projects and present results. During other phases of a project, clients aren't involved.

The degree of customer contact has important marketing implications (see Exhibit 10.4). For example, physical surroundings may not be of much concern in low-contact services, but in high-contact businesses, physical surroundings contribute to the image you want to project. They can also affect both the reality and the perception of service quality. That's why Virgin Atlantic Airways offers on-board massages and Continental furnishes its BusinessFirst cabins with high-tech reclining seats.[13] Also, interpersonal skills are crucial in high-contact services because personal interaction heavily influences customer satisfaction.[14] This can be particularly important in countries that value courtesy and friendliness. However, don't ignore the importance of interpersonal skills even in low-contact services. Given a choice between two equally competent auto mechanics, most consumers will pick the one who makes the exchange more satisfying on a personal level.

Good interpersonal skills are important in the delivery of services, particularly in countries that value friendliness, such as Australia.

## PROVIDER SKILL LEVEL

Finally, you can classify services according to the level of skill required of the service provider. Services based on high levels of skill present several marketing challenges. For one thing, skill may be hard to prove, even after the service is performed. Maybe your financial adviser turned your inheritance into a small fortune, but another adviser might have turned it into a large fortune. Another challenge is customer education, since the benefits of some skilled services may be unclear to consumers. Service providers in health care, law, repair, consulting, advertising, and design all face the need to educate customers at times. Finally, services involving higher skill levels usually encounter more regulation and oversight from professional organizations. Health professionals, for example, are regulated by the government and influenced by such groups as the American Medical Association.

# UNDERSTANDING THE MARKET FOR SERVICES

Since services have unique characteristics, it isn't surprising that the market for services has some unique attributes as well. This section discusses the buyers of services and the environment in which services are marketed.

## Understanding Service Buyers

Intangibility and inseparability affect the attitude and behavior of service buyers. Consumers respond to a service's intangibility in whatever manner it increases their level of comfort. One of these responses is equating the service with the provider. You don't say that a *physical examination* concluded that you are healthy; you say that *your doctor* concluded you are healthy. Another common response is picking up quality cues from anything tangible associated with the service provider. You wouldn't place much confidence in your doctor if you saw a copy of *Teach Yourself Brain Surgery* on the desk. On the other hand, you probably would trust the doctor after you saw the diploma from Johns Hopkins University hanging on the wall.

Intangibility also influences the way consumers think about risk. They generally perceive service purchases as riskier than the purchases of tangible goods. You can help lower buyer apprehension in several ways (see Exhibit 10.5):

### Lotte, The VIP's Choice

## "The service mainly. It's impeccable."

We're pleased that a good and growing number of our guests come back to stay with us.

Why? As Mr. Moore of Asia Pacific Marketing, explains, it's the "impeccable service" they appreciate most. "Discrete and unobtrusive," in Mr. Moore's words.

While the reasons vary from one return guest to the next, they all share an uncompromising taste for excellence.

At Hotel Lotte they find excellence in service and facilities.

Shouldn't the Lotte be your hotel in Seoul?

HOTEL LOTTE
SEOUL KOREA

**For Reservations:** New York (201) 944-1117, **Toll Free 800-22 LOTTE**, LA (310) 540-7010, **Toll Free 800-24 LOTTE**
**Hotel Lotte:** C.P.O.Box 3500 Seoul Tel. (02) 771-1000, Telex: LOTTEO K23533/4, Fax (02) 752-3758, Cable HOTELLOTTE

**Exhibit 10.5
REDUCING BUYER
APPREHENSION**
A positive comment from a fellow traveler can be reassuring to people who might be considering the Hotel Lotte in Seoul.

- Start by making sure you're positioned as a quality supplier.
- Provide plenty of information about the service.
- Use testimonials from past customers.
- Offer warranties and guarantees whenever possible.

**search qualities**
Product attributes that can be objectively evaluated prior to purchase

**experience qualities**
Product attributes that can be evaluated only after consumption of the product

**credence qualities**
Product attributes that cannot be evaluated, even after consumption

The way buyers evaluate products depends on where the products fall on the product continuum. Products with tangible attributes are high in **search qualities,** attributes that can be evaluated prior to purchase, and consumers feel confident about purchasing them. On the other hand, **experience qualities** can only be assessed after the product has been consumed. Because they are performances, most services are high in experience qualities. Finally, the group of product attributes known as **credence qualities** can't be evaluated even after purchase and consumption. Consumers are forced to place their trust in products with high-credence qualities. Nurses, for example, frequently supply services that are high in credence values and must be accepted partly on faith by consumers. Because they can't inspect the product prior to purchase and can't always be sure that treatment is working, health-care buyers pay for the promise of performance. Exhibit 10.6 uses a number of common products to illustrate the concepts of search, experience, and credence qualities.

## Understanding the Service Environment

The economic, competitive, regulatory, social, and technological elements discussed earlier generally affect the marketing of goods and services in the same manner. However, a few special considerations apply only to services.

### ECONOMIC ELEMENTS

As national and global economies grow more complex, the demand for services continues to increase. For example, a manufacturing company that wants to expand its market by selling in other countries may need the services of international freight handlers, export consultants, translators, and government lobbyists in each country. The beginning of this chapter pointed out several other changes that affect the economic landscape for services: increased affluence, changing demographic patterns, and more goods requiring service.

Economic interdependencies are another important factor to consider. Changes in one area of the economy can ripple through other areas and affect the demand for goods and services. For instance, when venture capital is in short supply, management consultants who target start-up companies find less demand for their services. Consider the car rental business; even though it was started back in 1916, it didn't really take off until air travel became common about two decades ago.[15]

### COMPETITIVE ELEMENTS

Services compete at several levels. First is the competition with similar services, such as the heated competition between Nielsen and Information Resources, the two biggest suppliers of marketing research data to consumer marketers such as

**Exhibit 10.6
SEARCH, EXPERIENCE, AND CREDENCE QUALITIES**
Services tend to be high in experience and credence qualities, whereas most goods are high in search qualities.

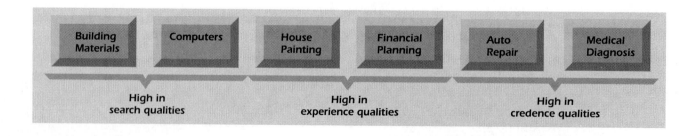

Procter & Gamble. Another level is indirect competition between services that can replace other services. When you have to choose between spending money on season tickets for baseball or basketball, you find that both of these services are competitive forms of entertainment that vie for your purchase. Major league baseball, in fact, has become acutely aware of this competition in recent years, as it finds itself losing fans to other sports. The percentage of U.S. residents who call baseball their favorite pro sport slipped from 23 percent to 18 percent between 1985 and 1993. In comparison, pro basketball doubled from 6 percent to 12 percent. (Pro football stayed constant at 24 percent.) Baseball's marketing minds are now engaged in a search for ways to lure fans back from other sports.[16]

Service providers can also find themselves competing with companies that are outside the service sector. A common source of competition is from goods. Movie theaters compete with VCRs for your entertainment budget. Unit volume in movie tickets hasn't increased since 1960, but videocassette purchases and rentals have increased for more than a decade. By 1996 U.S. consumers are expected to spend $15 billion a year on the rental and purchase of videocassettes.[17] Another twist on goods-service competition comes from leasing and rental companies. For example, firms that rent construction equipment compete with firms that sell the same equipment.

Government agencies and nonprofit organizations also compete with service providers. Public schools, public hospitals, and the U.S. Postal Service all compete with private companies. Savings bonds offered by the U.S. government compete with the investment opportunities offered by your bank. Nonprofit groups market services in areas that compete with for-profit firms; two big examples are education and health care.

Your customers might be your biggest competitors. The chance of this happening increases as the skill level decreases. For example, a residential architect won't get much competition from potential customers; the job is too complex. On the other hand, a window-washing service will frequently compete with homeowners, most of whom are perfectly capable of washing their own windows.

## REGULATORY ELEMENTS

Local, state, and federal governments of course play a major role in the management of all companies. International marketers have to observe laws in each of the countries in which they operate. Service providers are particularly affected by regulation because governments regulate many services to ensure consistency and reliability. This regulation can be as simple as licensing service providers (private investigators) or as invasive as controlling prices and professional practices throughout an entire industry (insurance). At any level, regulation tends to reduce marketing flexibility as well as the range of competition. Industries subject to extensive regulation need to keep a close eye on governmental proceedings to predict and perhaps influence the regulation of services.

Regulation affects competitive forces in two important ways. First, the range of marketing options is usually restricted, so competitive differentiation is more difficult to achieve. Until 1986, for example, commercial banks and savings and loan institutions couldn't offer more than 5.5 percent interest on savings accounts. Since the major product feature was equal for everybody in the market, banks had to search for other ways to set themselves apart from the competition. Second, the range of competition is reduced. For instance, in the United States, you can't provide radio or television broadcasts without a license from the Federal Communications Commission, which restricts the number of stations on the air. In contrast, the FCC doesn't restrict the number of manufacturers of radios or television sets.

Marketing has been restricted in some service professions. Lawyers, for example, were not allowed to advertise until 1977.[18] In addition to government rules, some professional associations regulate and influence their members. In addition to attorneys, doctors and accountants are restricted by their peers. However, an over-

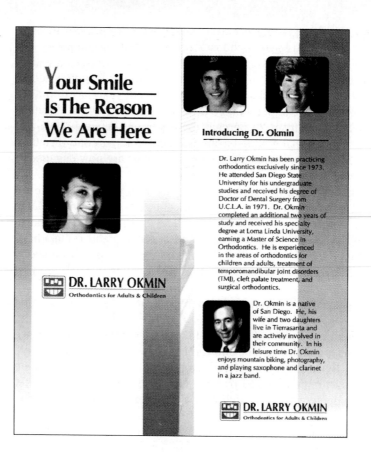

Your Smile
Is The Reason
We Are Here

**Introducing Dr. Okmin**

Dr. Larry Okmin has been practicing orthodontics exclusively since 1973. He attended San Diego State University for his undergraduate studies and received his degree of Doctor of Dental Surgery from U.C.L.A. in 1971. Dr. Okmin completed an additional two years of study and received his specialty degree at Loma Linda University, earning a Master of Science in Orthodontics. He is experienced in the areas of orthodontics for children and adults, treatment of temporomandibular joint disorders (TMJ), cleft palate treatment, and surgical orthodontics.

Dr. Okmin is a native of San Diego. He, his wife and two daughters live in Tierrasanta and are actively involved in their community. In his leisure time Dr. Okmin enjoys mountain biking, photography, and playing saxophone and clarinet in a jazz band.

**DR. LARRY OKMIN**
Orthodontics for Adults & Children

**Exhibit 10.7 PROFESSIONAL SERVICES MARKETING**
Professional service providers, particularly in law and medicine, traditionally have not advertised their services. In recent years, however, more and more professionals are advertising to consumers.

supply of service providers in some sectors has induced providers to push for changes and caused them to break with the old professional cultures.[19] Not everyone is happy about the brave new world of professional service marketing. Some professional groups continue to frown on marketing in general and advertising in particular (see Exhibit 10.7).[20]

## SOCIAL ELEMENTS

Social forces can play a big role in service marketing. To start with, the public's acceptance, skepticism, or rejection of a profession affects demand. Mental health offers a compelling example. In 1972 revelations that he had seen a psychiatrist cost Thomas Eagleton the vice presidential nomination. By the 1980s, however, the stigma of seeking psychiatric help began to vanish, and demand for such services increased. Over the last three decades, the number of Americans visiting mental health professionals increased tenfold. In the last dozen years, the number of centers specializing in the treatment of phobias has grown from 2 to 50.[21]

Marketers continue to respond as consumer attitude and outlooks change. As more people expressed interest in looking good and feeling good, exercise and diet services grew. Safety concerns and growing apprehension about crime spurred the growth of personal and home security services. Lifestyle enhancements such as travel, higher education, and cultural involvement have partially replaced material goods as symbols of achievement. Because all these lifestyle elements are service-based, demand for services has grown.

## TECHNOLOGICAL ELEMENTS

In the old days, college students used telephone or mail services to ask Mom and Dad for more money. Now you can have the neighborhood copy center fax the message for you, or you can use electronic mail from the computer in your dorm, and you may soon use videophones to make a deeply stirring plea. Firms that provide these services have responded to changes in their technological environment.

Advancements in science and technology create many opportunities to improve service quality and productivity. Computerized reservation systems help hotels, airlines, and car rental firms process customers faster and with fewer mistakes. New procedures and specialized equipment help medical professionals improve treatment and rehabilitation of patients. Manufacturers increasingly use robots and other automated machinery for jobs that require precision and consistency.[22] The application of technology and manufacturing techniques to services is known as **industrialization of services.**[23]

**industrialization of services**
The application of technology and manufacturing techniques to services

# PLANNING STRATEGY AND TACTICS FOR SERVICE MARKETING

Services need marketing strategies and tactics that are different, sometimes radically different, from those used to market goods (see Exhibit 10.8). The major reason for this is intangibility.[24] The following sections point out several issues to consider when you formulate strategies and tactics for services: differences in buyer behavior, differences in marketing approaches, and ways to differentiate service products. As you learn about pricing, distribution, and promotion in future chapters, you'll get more insight into the specifics of designing marketing programs for services.

**Exhibit 10.8**
**SERVICES MARKETING DOESN'T HAVE TO BE SERIOUS TO BE EFFECTIVE**
As this television commercial for the Norwegian airline Braathens SAFE demonstrates, services marketing can be entertaining, even when price is the most significant marketing variable.

**SFX:** Jolly Norwegian folk music.

A MAN COMES HOME FROM WORK. HE UNLOCKS THE DOOR OF HIS APARTMENT. HAVING BARELY STEPPED INTO THE HALL, HE STARTS UNDRESSING. COMPLETELY "STARKERS," HE HURRIES OVER TO THE LIVING ROOM DOOR AND GAZES THROUGH THE KEYHOLE AT THE OBJECT OF HIS DESIRE (HIS WIFE). NOTHING CAN HOLD HIM BACK NOW.

HE STICKS A ROSE BETWEEN HIS TEETH AND BURSTS INTO THE LIVING ROOM TO FIND HIS WIFE HAS BEEN JOINED BY HER OUT-OF-TOWN PARENTS. HIS DRAMATIC APPEARANCE IS GREETED BY STONY SILENCE.

**Superscript:** Warning: We're flying your in-laws at half price! Braathens SAFE. The Norwegian airline.

## Differences in Buyer Behavior

When you market a service, you are in effect selling the promise of a performance. In addition, many services are loosely defined by their nature, such as legal advice and management consulting. The result is that customers switch the focus of evaluation from the product to the provider. For instance, when people are buying cars from Ford, they probably aren't all that interested in the people who created them. They want to evaluate the cars. If they are buying accounting services from Price Waterhouse, however, they are interested in the qualifications of the people who'll be performing the service.

Also, because service customers usually can't "test-drive" services, they may need greater motivation to switch suppliers. This need for motivation results from the relationships that many service providers build with their customers. If your favorite gas station raises its prices, what's to stop you from driving past to the next station? However, if your tax accounting firm raises its rates, you may be reluctant to change immediately, since you know you'll have to train another accounting firm in your financial situation. The time it takes to change suppliers may not offset the cost savings.

Just as customers might be extra picky when choosing service providers, service providers are sometimes picky when choosing their customers. The reason for this unusual approach to segmentation and targeting is that different customers tend to generate roughly the same profit when they buy goods, but not when they buy services. Insurance companies and bank loan departments want customers who are low risks. Restaurants usually want patrons who eat, smile, pay, and leave; customers who linger for hours occupy additional service capacity without paying extra for it.

## Differences in Marketing Approaches

**interactive marketing**
Marketing situations in which the customer is actively involved in the production/ performance and delivery of products

The unique attributes of service products also determine many aspects of your marketing approach. To begin with, service distribution involves **interactive marketing;** that is, the provider interacts significantly with the buyer. Service marketers make sure their service providers have excellent interpersonal skills, and they support those providers with policies that put top priority on customer satisfaction.

As you'll see in the rest of the course, the marketing mixes for services are defined differently from those for goods. For example, because they usually can't get concrete evidence of the service itself, buyers search for tangible evidence related to the service. Physical surroundings, printed materials, and personal appearance all give consumers visual cues about service quality. Even though these attributes may have nothing to do with the actual delivery of a service, they are in effect a part of your product offering.

**service capacity management**
The process of smoothing demand fluctuations and responding to fluctuations that cannot be smoothed

The pricing element of the services marketing mix is an important tool for **service capacity management,** the process of matching service supply to market demand. Since you can't store services in inventory, forecasting demand and responding to demand fluctuations are critical for profitable operation. Therefore, service providers often adjust prices to help smooth demand. For example, movie theaters reduce prices to stimulate purchases during times of lower demand, a practice known as **off-peak pricing.**

**off-peak pricing**
The practice of using lower prices to stimulate demand during times of low demand

Intangibility can make services difficult to promote effectively, for two obvious reasons. First, you can't demonstrate certain services without giving them away. For instance, you can't show customers how well you can cut their hair without actually cutting their hair. Second, advertising depends heavily on graphic images, and you don't have a tangible product to show off. You can easily convey the power of a Caterpillar tractor in a photo, but you'll find it difficult to show the intelligence and experience of your accounting firm. Satisfied customers are a key way to help you overcome the inability to demonstrate your service.

## Techniques for Differentiating Services

In a crowded marketplace, you need to be creative to stand out from the competition. The following techniques of differentiation are an essential part of any service marketing strategy.

- *Divergence and complexity.* Divergence and complexity are two important dimensions of differentiating services.[25] Divergence indicates the degree of standardization in the service you offer. In some cases, standardization is important to maintain speed and quality and to meet customer expectations. Domino's Pizza relies on standardized menu offerings to provide quick service. In other cases, divergence or flexibility can help you establish a position apart from your competition. Dallas travel agency Sargent & Strong differentiates itself by going to amazing lengths to provide clients with unusual trips managed down to the last important detail. Owner Nancy Strong has taken such steps as making sure Hong Kong cab drivers know her clients' favorite activities, faxing up-to-the-minute baseball scores to passengers on cruise ships, and introducing clients who will be traveling together to give the people a feeling of camaraderie before they even leave home.[26]

  Complexity is a measure of the number and variety of services you offer. Photocopy centers can now offer fax services, laser printing, desktop publishing, and photo-typesetting services. On the other hand, low complexity may help you maintain a clear position in a crowded market. By emphasizing your focus on one or two services, you can more easily convince consumers that you are an expert in your field. KFC uses its focus on one type of food to support its claim that "we do chicken right." A combination strategy might be best in some cases. For example, a medical clinic that combines several specialists in complementary fields can offer high complexity without sacrificing the appearance of expertise. For a more detailed example, Exhibit 10.9 shows some of the decisions restaurants must make when choosing to increase or decrease complexity and divergence.

- *Service policies.* Most service providers use guidelines and policies that define how they interact with customers and help maintain productivity and profit levels. These policies sometimes have the unintentional effect of turning off customers, however. A dry cleaner that posts a large sign disclaiming any responsibility for damage to garments is not going to inspire customer confidence or loyalty. It might make superficial financial sense not to accept responsibility, but it doesn't make marketing sense. A dry cleaner that automatically repairs damaged garments and offers to replace destroyed articles—and follows these actions with sincere apologies—is likely to gain customers for life.

  Remember the classic little sign, "We reserve the right to refuse service to anyone"? Service providers (and all businesses, for that matter) must continually remind themselves that every consumer also carries an invisible sign: "I reserve the right to take my business elsewhere."

- *Warranties and guarantees.* Services with high experience and credence qualities can differentiate themselves through warranties and guarantees. For example, a free-lance writer might agree to keep rewriting until the document satisfies the client. Contracts often contain performance clauses to make sure service

**Exhibit 10.9   COMPLEXITY AND DIVERGENCE DECISIONS FOR A RESTAURANT**

| Decision to Be Made | Lower Divergence/ Complexity | Higher Divergence/ Complexity |
|---|---|---|
| Reservations | None | Specific table |
| Menu variety | Few choices | Many choices |
| Seating process | Self-seating | Guided by maître d' |
| Payment options | Cash only | Choice of methods, including house accounts |

Complexity and divergence decisions can help differentiate a service from its competitors.

## AARP'S SUCCESS— AND CONTROVERSIES— WITH NONPROFIT MARKETING

The American Association of Retired Persons (AARP) is the second largest membership organization in the United States. Its 34 million members in 1993 made it second only to the Roman Catholic Church (at 53 million). With nearly 20 percent of the voting public on its rolls, AARP catches the eye of politicians at every level of government. Its headquarters takes up half a block on K Street in Washington, D.C., putting its team of lobbyists within close range of the federal government. Using a scheme called the "telephone tree" (the telephone equivalent of a chain letter), AARP can reach thousands of members

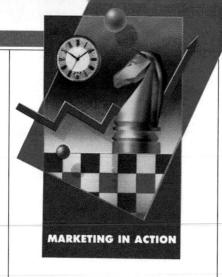

**MARKETING IN ACTION**

quickly and have them flood Congress with calls whenever AARP's lobbyists think it would help influence votes.

As a nonprofit marketer of goods and particularly of services, AARP's record is impressive. After paying a small membership fee, people who join get discounts on magazines, pre-

scriptions, tours, and health insurance. As *Money* magazine put it, "Low dues bring prospects through the door, and the direct-mail maestros move in from there." AARP typically sends 50 million pieces of mail a year. Its flow of incoming mail is so great that AARP was assigned its own ZIP code. Nonprofit status allows AARP to pump out 74 percent more mail per dollar than a for-profit firm is able to.

AARP's bimonthly magazine for members, *Modern Maturity,* averages a higher circulation than any other magazine in the country. The organization's pharmacy service is the second largest private mail-order supplier of prescription medicine. The AARP Group Health Insurance Program is the largest in the nation. In all, eight businesses gather under AARP's nonprofit umbrella, generating about $10 billion in annual revenues.

providers fulfill customer expectations in a timely and satisfactory manner. For instance, builders sometimes agree to pay lodging costs for families if new-home construction falls behind schedule.

You simply can't guarantee some services, of course. A surgeon can't guarantee that a particular operation will be 100 percent successful and without complications. A lawyer can't guarantee the outcome of a case. Where appropriate, some service providers and their customers agree to pay-for-performance compensation. Lawyers in liability cases, for example, frequently charge a percentage of the amount awarded to the plaintiff.

- *Follow-up and complaint resolution.* Taking the extra step can be an important way to differentiate a service business. For instance, the management consultant who checks in with clients after they've tried to implement his or her recommendations will win points for caring about clients' success. Also, the manner in which a business handles complaints can mean the difference between losing a customer or improving a relationship. The worst customer dissatisfaction problems result from not resolving service mistakes.[27]

- *Service quality.* Just as with tangible products, the quality of a service product, in terms of both real and perceived quality, can be a major factor in a customer's choice of supplier. Service quality means more than just doing the job correctly, however. It includes those extra touches that make the experience enjoyable for the customer as well. Both Sheraton and Marriott can put a roof over your head, but the people who work in each hotel can make a difference by the way they treat guests. Service expert Christian Grönroos divides quality into two parts. *Technical quality* is the measure of how well you did the job the customer expected you to do. *Functional quality* is the style or manner in which the service is performed.[28]

The driving force behind AARP's conception was Ethel Percy Andrus, a retired schoolteacher who wanted to achieve better living conditions for retired persons. The financial force, however, came from Leonard Davis, an insurance broker who saw an organization of senior citizens as an attractive market for services such as health insurance. He provided $50,000 in seed money to get the organization off the ground and then founded his own insurance company to provide policies to AARP's members. The offer of health insurance was appreciated by members; at the time, few companies would sell elderly people health insurance. More than 30 years after its founding, AARP still collects a large portion of its revenues from insurance services.

Not everyone is an unqualified fan of AARP, however. Some members complain about the nonstop flow of direct mail. Pitches for insurance arrive as frequently as three times a month. Observers question the influence wielded by the group's outside lawyers, as well as the amount AARP pays them yearly. Harriet Miller, a former executive director of AARP, accused the leadership that ousted her of turning the organization into a cover for enriching the insurance broker who provided the original financing. At one point, *Consumer Reports* judged AARP's Medicare supplement policy as providing the worst protection among 16 tested. (The organization later changed insurance suppliers.)

Perhaps the biggest controversy is AARP's influential and highly visible role in the intergenerational struggle for shares of government budgets. Young parents, children, and college students are some of the groups that have begun to protest the clout AARP has in Washington. In a world of finite budgets, money that goes to one group obviously can't go to another, and some young people are wondering if retired people are getting more than their fair share. By 1995 federal spending on the elderly is expected to be four times greater than federal spending on children. The issue is clearly not simple, nor is it going to get any easier, since the number of elderly people continues to grow. You can expect AARP to continue to play a major role in the nation's political system.

## APPLY YOUR KNOWLEDGE

**1.** What are the various types of marketing AARP is engaged in? How might this confuse role expectations among its members?

**2.** Does AARP compete with for-profit marketers?

- *Branding.* As the number of competitors in a service category increases, branding can mean the difference between pulling ahead and getting lost in the pack. Building brand awareness is just as important for services as it is for goods.[29] Think about the strength of the Federal Express brand—many people say they're going to "Fed Ex" a package, even when they're using one of Federal Express's competitors.

  When two companies perform essentially the same service, it can be difficult to establish separate identities, and that's where service branding comes in. Accountants and market research firms increasingly brand their services. Although the services provided may be based on common industry practices, firms can add their own twists and packaging to create brands and achieve independent market positions.

- *Peripheral services.* Finally, you can differentiate your business through **peripheral services,** services that complement the core service you offer. These increase your competitive advantage by enhancing the value you deliver to customers. For example, your university's graduate placement office offers an important service in addition to the university's core business of providing an education. The placement service requires a substantial investment in training, office space, and management time, but it enables the university to increase the value it offers to students, parents, and company recruiters.

**peripheral services**
Services performed by a company in support of its core service offering

# DEFINING NONPROFIT MARKETING

Although commercial ventures and nonprofit groups usually have differing goals, nonprofit firms market their products just like for-profit companies do. Public bodies such as the U.S. Internal Revenue Service, the Pennsylvania Department of Public Assistance, and the New York City Police Department are nonprofit marketers. Private groups such as the American Red Cross, United Way, the Christian Children's Fund, and the Teamsters are also nonprofit marketers. These groups have different goals but are alike in that they all market their people, ideas, places, or organizations.

A political party markets its people and its ideas. It produces candidates with distinct political points of view, and it promotes them through a variety of advertising techniques. The target market is registered voters, and the marketing goal is to sell voters on the politician and the kind of representation he or she would provide. The price is a vote.[30]

Chambers of Commerce, visitor and convention bureaus, and similar agencies typically market places—cities, states, countries, and regions. The Irish Export Board, for example, markets Ireland to U.S. businesses by promoting the country's experience in European trade and its educated, English-language work force.[31]

Nonprofit organizations dedicated to changing public views on issues of health, education, politics, safety, and human rights also market their ideas. The National Rifle Association markets ideas on gun control, gun safety, and other gun-related issues. The National Audubon Society markets its ideas about the natural environment. The Ribbon Project, started by a group of New York artists to show support for victims of AIDS, has had phenomenal success in persuading celebrities and the general public alike to wear the now-ubiquitous red lapel ribbon.[32] These organizations develop and promote ideas, asking for money, time, legislation, or changes in public or private behavior (see Exhibit 10.10).

## The Importance of Nonprofit Marketing

Many aspects of human activity rely on nonprofit marketing, with its focus on social, political, and economic goals. Both the University of Michigan and the American Lung Association seek social goals; that is, education and health are goals that reflect society's desire to improve life for some or all members. However, in order to attract enough students to maintain adequate financing, the university may employ marketing techniques that don't appear to reflect social goals. Even so, its guiding objective remains one of serving society through education. Similarly, when the

**Exhibit 10.10
NONPROFIT
MARKETING
EXCHANGES**

Even though there is no money involved in the two marketing exchanges represented by this ad, they are still marketing exchanges. The National Association of Atomic Veterans reaches out with an offer to help victims of government nuclear testing, and it tries to get people to commit the time and energy to write letters to the government.

Lung Association solicits donations, its final goal isn't collecting money but informing people about the dangers of smoking and other unhealthy behavior.

When the Democratic or Republican National Committee markets a candidate, or when your local school board promotes a bond issue, marketing is being used to pursue political goals. An advocate of a particular piece of legislation promises certain benefits, tangible or intangible. Social goals are often pursued through political action, where the political goal facilitates the social goal.

Cities, states, and entire countries use marketing to achieve broad economic goals. They may desire business investment, tourism, or new homeowners. The government of Scotland, for instance, promotes the country to business leaders in the United States and other countries, hoping they will build factories in Scotland and employ Scottish citizens. The U.S. government's Overseas Private Investment Corporation seeks to stabilize the economies of developing countries by encouraging U.S. companies to invest in those locations.[33] As with social goals, economic goals are frequently pursued through political channels.

Religions, trade unions, and professional associations all market themselves to potential members. While money in the form of dues may be part of the exchange, seeking profits is not the primary goal of these groups. Organizations throughout the country are recognizing the need to improve their marketing. For example, the Ladies Professional Golf Association realizes that it has the potential to reach a much larger audience, so it is working hard to improve its marketing skills.[34]

## The Unique Aspects of Nonprofit Marketing

Most of the concepts you'll learn in this course apply to both for-profit and nonprofit marketing, but nonprofit marketing has a few of its own special twists, including the following:

- *Nonfinancial exchanges.* Nonprofit marketing frequently involves nonfinancial exchanges, in which the marketer is not asking the target audience to exchange money for goods or services. For example, AIDS awareness programs seek to change people's sexual behavior. Various programs try to stop people from drinking and driving. Aside from fund-raising efforts, most political marketing involves nonfinancial exchanges.
- *Indirect exchanges.* The exchanges in nonprofit marketing aren't always of the direct "you give me something and I'll give you something" variety. The Nature Conservancy solicits donations to buy land in environmentally sensitive areas. The exchange offered is your money in return for protected habitats for various species of plants and animals. You are being asked to make (through the organization's efforts) a tangible purchase: land. What you personally receive from the exchange, however is intangible: the knowledge that you've helped. The satisfaction of helping is the key benefit offered in many nonprofit marketing campaigns.
- *Controversial issues.* Few people would question the motives of a bakery or a landscaping service. Nonprofit marketers, on the other hand, occasionally find themselves promoting controversial programs. Gun control, sex education, clean-needle programs for addicts, and family planning are all causes that have been marketed and countermarketed. Profit-seeking marketers in the normal business environment worry that they'll be ignored. Nonprofit marketers, especially those marketing ideas or causes, often worry about being actively counterattacked in the marketplace of people's minds.
- *Tax-advantaged competition.* Nonprofit organizations are exempt from a variety of taxes and sometimes have other financial advantages such as free advertising that are not available to profit-seeking organizations. In some industries, nonprofit organizations compete with profit-seeking businesses, and business owners protest that the nonprofits have unfair advantages. Consulting services, nursing homes, and schools are examples of areas in which both types of organizations compete.

This conflict is likely to continue as more nonprofit organizations engage in commercial activities to supplement their other sources of income.[35]

- *Slow acceptance of marketing.* The application of marketing in the nonprofit sector is generally less advanced and less pervasive than in the for-profit sector. A recent study of health-care marketing showed that over half the hospitals surveyed didn't have a marketing department.[36] Nonprofit marketers have been doing marketing for years, but many are unaware or unconvinced they are even involved in marketing. The basic principles of marketing—even the concept of customers—are unfamiliar to many people working in the nonprofit sector. The likely cause of this slow acceptance is that most people associate marketing with making money. However, a central objective of marketing is to change public or private behavior, which is also a goal of nearly all nonprofit organizations.

# SUMMARY OF LEARNING OBJECTIVES

### 1. Highlight the unique aspects of service marketing.

Service marketing involves four major unique aspects, all stemming from the special attributes of service products. The first is intangibility, which prevents customers from evaluating products with sensory means. The second aspect is inseparability of performance and consumption, which means that the customer often has to be present at the time the product is being produced. The third factor is perishability: You can't usually store the ability to create services. And the fourth aspect is heterogeneity, or variability of performance. Most of the special challenges in service marketing are a result of intangibility.

### 2. Describe the growth and importance of services in the U.S. economy.

Services now provide the major portion of the nation's income and nonfarm employment, and this trend is likely to continue. Services have also provided most of the new jobs for women and minorities entering the work force. This growth results from three factors: economic prosperity, changing demographics, and the increasing number of goods that require service.

### 3. Differentiate the major classifications of services.

You can classify services according to several criteria: profit (for-profit or nonprofit), customer type (consumer or organizational), labor and equipment needs (labor-based or equipment-based), customer contact (high or low degree), and provider skill level (professional or nonprofessional). Classifying the services you're trying to market will help you understand the value you are offering to customers.

### 4. Point out the important elements of the service environment.

The elements of the marketing environment for services are much the same as the environmental elements for goods. The significant differences include (a) a growing demand for many types of services as national and international economies grow more complex; (b) various forms of competitive pressure from goods and from customers themselves; (c) regulatory elements, which often play a more prominent role in services, particularly in the health-care and financial services industries; (d) social elements, which have a strong influence on service marketing and include the cultural acceptance of various professions and lifestyle changes; and (e) technological elements, which affect both the need for services and the way services can be delivered to customers.

### 5. Identify the major goals of nonprofit marketing.

The general categories are social, political, economic, and organizational goals. Social goals communicate ideas with the ultimate objective of modifying private or public behavior. Political goals include both election (marketing candidates to voters) and legislation (influencing legislation by influencing decision makers). Note that political goals often facilitate actions toward social and economic goals. Economic goals involve changes in economic circumstances and frequently involve cities, states, or nations. Organizational goals include membership drives for religious, trade, and professional groups.

### 6. Explain the unique aspects of nonprofit marketing.

Nonprofit marketing often involves nonfinancial exchanges, in which no transfer of money takes place from customer to provider. Nonprofit marketers frequently handle controversial issues, such as gun control, environment versus employment, and family planning. Tax exemptions and other financial advantages are important to nonprofit groups, and these can create conflicts when nonprofit organizations compete with for-profit firms. Finally, nonprofit groups have generally been slow to adopt marketing or, in some cases, even to recognize they are involved in marketing.

### 7. Describe the exchange process in nonprofit marketing.

The exchange process—giving something of value in return for something of value—needs to be reconsidered in many nonprofit marketing situations. Nonprofit marketing often involves nonfinancial exchanges, in which the customer is asked to give something other than money. For instance, an animal rights group might ask you to spend time writing a letter to Congress. In other cases, the nonprofit marketer asks people to refrain from certain behaviors, such as polluting and drunken driving. When formulating a nonprofit marketing strategy, be sure you understand what you're asking customers to give up and what you're planning to offer them in return.

credence qualities (308)
equipment-based services (305)
experience qualities (308)
goods-dominant products (300)
heterogeneity (302)

high-contact services (306)
industrialization of services (311)
inseparability (302)
intangibility (302)
interactive marketing (312)

labor-based services (305)
low-contact services (306)
off-peak pricing (312)
peripheral services (315)
perishability (302)
search qualities (308)

service capacity management (312)
service-dominant products (300)
service sector (300)

# QUESTIONS FOR DISCUSSION

1. How would you classify the following services?
   a. Church-sponsored preschool
   b. Architectural firm
   c. Bicycle-based courier service
   d. Private psychotherapist
2. What tangible cues would you provide for customers of a financial-planning consultant?
3. Would a videotape rental store have the same capacity management challenges as a movie theater? Explain your answer.
4. What sort of problems could a marriage counselor face when using personal selling?
5. What benefits would the following three customers expect from a lawn-care service?
   a. Busy, two-career couple
   b. Homeowner concerned about the proper use of tools and chemicals
   c. Active, healthy retiree who enjoys yard work

6. How could you use divergence and complexity to build competitive advantage for a nutrition and fitness counseling service?
7. What are some potentially negative side effects of using technology to increase productivity and quality? How can you minimize the effects of these problems?
8. As the marketing director of a for-profit hospital competing with a nonprofit hospital, how would you overcome the financial advantages enjoyed by your competitor?
9. How would you improve a social marketing campaign that delivered the following message to high school students: "Leave drugs behind and join the good life?"
10. What are the potential problems you would encounter trying to solicit funds for an organization that supports gun control or one that is against gun control?

# SHARPEN YOUR MARKETING SKILLS

Collect several examples of promotions dealing with drug abuse. Some possibilities are the Just Say No campaign and D. A. R. E.

**Decision:** Did the marketer clearly define the exchange? Does the exchange promise a meaningful benefit to the target audience? Will the target audience think that the opportunity cost is reasonable? Does the promotion speak the audience's language? If you can find any information about the results of the promotions you've analyzed, do the results match your expectations? How would you improve the promotion?

**Communication:** For each example you find, write a paragraph outlining your opinion of the promotion's effectiveness. Back up your opinion with the concepts you've learned in the course so far.

# KEEPING CURRENT IN MARKETING

Find an article that describes how the competition in an industry has changed because services have taken business away from goods or vice versa. Two prominent examples include VCRs taking business away from movie theaters and microwave ovens competing with fast-food restaurants.

1. How was the new competitor able to offer better value? Is the new competitor cheaper? More effective? More convenient? Safer?

2. How is the new competitor being promoted? Must customers be educated about benefits, or are the benefits obvious? Does intangibility play a role in promotions?
3. How have customers responded? Do they convert immediately, or does the process take months or years? Will some customers stay with the old product type? If some customers won't convert, what are their reasons?

## Meeting a Marketing Challenge at WMX Technologies

It may be stretching things a bit to call trash a "treasure" for WMX Technologies, but it's not exaggeration to say that the company has profited from the waste that consumers and businesses generate. WMX's sales are pushing the $9 billion mark annually, and enough trash is available to keep 65,000 WMX employees busy worldwide. WMX owns all or part of several major players in the waste business, from the everyday pickup and landfill operations of the Waste Management subsidiary to Rust International's toxic cleanups to Wheelabrator's pollution-control technologies.

Market forces (including population growth and increasing industrialization around the world) created the opportunities that WMX has capitalized on so far, and those forces continue to present opportunities. The deplorable environmental conditions in Eastern Europe, largely due to historically inadequate waste management, provide another big opportunity. Subrata Chakravarty, a senior editor at *Forbes* magazine, claims that, "As the world begins dealing with that giant problem, few companies are better placed to help than WMX Technologies."

Market forces have not been as kind to the Chem Waste subsidiary, however. In the early to mid-1990s, a recession forced governments and private companies to slow spending for chemical cleanup projects. A longer-term concern is that the market for chemical disposal might diminish as companies learn how to produce goods and services with less waste. However, Chem Waste says it is ready to change along with the market, selling its expertise through consulting and other services.

Capacity management is a major concern for Buntrock and each of his companies, and the issue differs from company to company. For handling waste chemicals, for instance, capacity management means having plants with enough space to accept the outputs of the factories and facilities that have contracted for WMX's services. Waste Management International's new hazardous-waste facility in Hong Kong's Victoria Harbor (the largest such facility in the world) handles all of Hong Kong's hazardous chemical waste. Capacity management means something entirely different for the trash-hauling business in the Waste Management unit. To keep the operation efficient and the costs low, the company has to dictate terms to its customers. Trash is picked up when it is efficient for the company to bring a truck around, not when it is convenient for the customer.

New and stricter government landfill regulations being phased in during the mid-1990s are hammering ill-prepared competitors, while WMX is profiting from its foresight. Long before the new rules came into place, Buntrock predicted that governments would grow more sensitive to everything

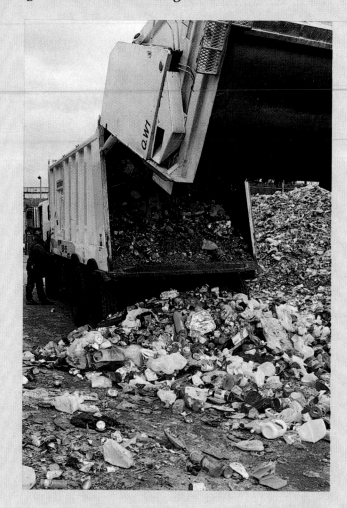

from the soil geology under landfills to odor emissions. He began buying up suitable sites, constructing landfills in a way that would meet stricter regulations, and simply saving the sites for future use. The strategy cost dearly at the time, but WMX is in great shape now, as competitors scramble to fix outmoded landfills and buy increasingly scarce (and increasingly expensive) sites for new landfills.

WMX continues to serve the world's waste-management needs with an evolving mix of services (and goods in some cases, such as air scrubbers for factory smokestacks). Its range of services includes every phase of the business, from redesigning factories to hauling away the trash at the other end. The company finds an increasing part of its business outside the United States, in such far-flung locales as New Zealand and Saudi Arabia. Waste handling is a growing and universal concern, and WMX has demonstrated the marketing talent that should keep it in the lead.

**Your mission:** You've recently signed on as a marketing adviser for all the companies in the WMX Technologies family. The solutions you help the various companies create must take into account the special nature of the waste-management business as well as the general concepts of service marketing.

1. Some of WMX's services for industrial customers come with multimillion-dollar price tags. Clearly, no business will make a purchase this big without knowing what it's getting into. However, for a service such as redesigning a factory to reduce toxic emissions, customers won't know how good the product is until after they have already made the purchase decision (in other words, this product is high in experience qualities). Which of the following strategies would you use to overcome this aspect of service intangibility?
   a. Run an advertising campaign that emphasizes WMX's experience and expertise in this field.
   b. Establish a program in which potential customers can talk to your current customers. This will assure the prospects that you really can and do follow through on your promises.
   c. Offer pay-for-performance pricing, in which your fee is tied to how well you do the work. The more you reduce the customer's waste output, the more you earn.
2. Residential waste haulers usually contract with local governments to provide exclusive service, so consumers don't have a choice of which waste service to buy. However, WMX's image and reputation with consumers is crucial to its overall success because of the influence consumers have on politicians and government regulators. Which of the following image ads would you recommend?
   a. An ad that encourages people to look beyond their own trash cans and ponder the larger issue of waste disposal. The ad would feature a burly garbage collector in action, with the headline, "Hey, where do you think all your trash goes, anyway?"
   b. An ad that lays out the choice between innovative waste management and the alternative of doing little or nothing. Show a photo of a disastrous garbage dump in a developing country beside a photo of WMX's Settler's Hill project in Geneva, Illinois, where a golf course has been built on top of a closed section of the landfill. The headline would say, "I never thought of it that way before."
   c. An ad that confronts the image problem head-on. A photo would show a healthy-looking reclaimed area that had once been a hazardous-waste site. The headline would say, "What business do we have saying we help the environment? That *is* our business."
3. Because services are intangible, you know that it is sometimes difficult to foster the right image of a service in the minds of potential customers. However, by using a tangible object to represent the nature and quality of your service, you can "borrow from" the image of that object and assign it to your intangible service. For industrial customers who are concerned about the safe handling of their toxic wastes, which of the following photographs would you use in a brochure?
   a. A truck designed especially for transporting chemical wastes.
   b. An inside shot of a chemical processing plant, showing advanced technology and well-managed operations.
   c. A wild animal walking through a pristine mountain meadow.
4. Assume that one of Waste Management's landfills is reaching capacity sooner than anticipated. The local management team needs to encourage consumers and businesses to reduce their trash output until it can arrange an alternative storage site. Which of the following strategies would be most effective?
   a. Use an ad campaign that plays to the customer's sense of guilt for generating so much trash. This will shame people into generating less trash.
   b. Use an ad campaign with the message. "We're all in this together." Offer suggestions on reducing trash.
   c. Keep prices reasonable for basic trash collection services, such as $15 a month for one large can per week for each single-family household. Institute steep "excess trash" fees whenever people exceed these preassigned limits. This will encourage people to recycle more and find ways to generate less trash.

## SPECIAL PROJECT

Through library or in-store research, find a product or technology that might affect sales of WMX services. This can range from products that are marketed with less packaging material (meaning less waste for WMX to collect and process) to applications for a new technology such as photographic film that reduces the toxic chemicals that film processing labs must dispose of (meaning lower volumes of waste for WMX treatment plants). In a brief report (no more than one page), summarize the product or technology, its potential impact on WMX sales, and the moves that WMX might be able to take to protect its sales.[37]

## H&R Block Serves Up Tax Help

Federal income tax forms have been an annual companion for U.S. citizens since 1913, but the tax preparation industry didn't exist until Henry and Richard Bloch stumbled across the opportunity after World War II. The brothers were handling individual tax returns as a sideline to their accounting service for smaller companies. Then a customer suggested they could build tax-return volume if they tried advertising their low-priced services. Although skeptical, the brothers agreed to test the idea. They placed newspaper ads offering to do taxes for $5 and quickly found themselves swimming in a sea of tax returns.

The Blochs sold the accounting firm so that they could concentrate on the new business, which they called simply H&R Block (with a "k" instead of an "h" to avoid mispronunciation). They targeted ordinary people and heavily promoted the reasonable price, steadily building market share. They also recognized that customers view tax preparation as a very personal service, so they decided that Henry Bloch should appear in their advertising, personifying the concern that H&R Block's owners feel for clients. Over the years, Bloch appeared in so many company commercials that he became the recognized "face" of the tax preparation business.

H&R Block now holds a commanding lead in the race for market share. With 7,000 offices across the country and $500 million in tax-related revenues, the company completes 20 percent of all professionally prepared tax forms. Competitors such as Jackson Hewitt, Mr. Tax, and Triple Check want to grab a piece of the tax action, but all three combined can't catch H&R Block's coattails.

When Congress passed the Tax Reform Act in 1987, however, the company's bright future suddenly dimmed. Block's real competitors are people who fill out their own tax forms, and the new, simplified rules seemed to give more taxpayers the encouragement they needed to complete their own returns.

To transform this potential disaster into an opportunity, Henry Bloch again turned to advertising. His nationwide television campaign in 1988 hammered away at the problems of trying to adjust to the new tax laws without professional help. H&R Block appeared knowledgeable, experienced, and interested in the plight of the ordinary citizen. The tactic worked: Bloch was able to steer his firm away from the brink and into its best year ever. However, he knew the company needed to find additional target audiences and position its services with benefits that suited their needs. He and his management team studied the market and came up with several segments that would respond to specialized services.

One segment consisted of filers who are entitled to tax refunds but don't want to wait months for their money. For this group, Bloch created a product called "Rapid Refund." Taking advantage of a recent IRS plan that allows tax preparers to submit customer tax forms electronically, H&R Block could file for the refund and then advance that amount to the customer; the government would pay the refund directly to Block. Rapid Refund is priced higher than regular tax services, but it has become popular because it gives customers faster access to their refunds.

Ironically, tax reform created a segment of people who ended up with a more complicated tax situation. Because of the new laws, they now needed more than basic tax preparation. Bloch created "Executive Tax Services" for this group, offering an upscale decor, service by appointment, and more sophisticated tax preparation programs.

Despite the challenges of marketing an intangible product, H&R Block found a way to stay on top of the industry it created four decades ago. By continuing to pay close attention to customers and their needs, the company should be able to keep its healthy lead for many April 15s to come.

1. Demand for tax preparation services increases as April 15 nears. Say that Bloch wants to try to smooth demand slightly and encourage customers to file earlier by establishing a new pricing policy. Should he increase his prices from April 1 to April 15, or should he offer a discount before March 1?

2. When Henry Bloch became the firm's spokesperson, his objective was to let customers know a real person was behind the service, a person who cares about his customers. Suppose Bloch wants to bow out as spokesperson. Should he have several of his tax preparers appear in the new ads or should he hire a celebrity like Phil Donahue, who conveys a feeling of honesty and believability?

3. In services marketing, a guarantee can go a long way toward lowering buyer apprehension, but guarantees can backfire if companies have to pay off too often. If Bloch wants to institute a guarantee, would he do better to offer customers their money back if not satisfied or offer money back and a free tax return the following year?

# Sony Has Designs on the Future

The next time you enjoy music from a personal stereo, say a word of thanks to Masaru Ibuka. He was the person who came up with the idea to package a tape recorder so small that you could clip it on your belt, toss it in a backpack, or even slip it in your pocket. Through the years, he also dreamed up a transistor radio small enough to fit in your pocket, the home VCR, and the camcorder.

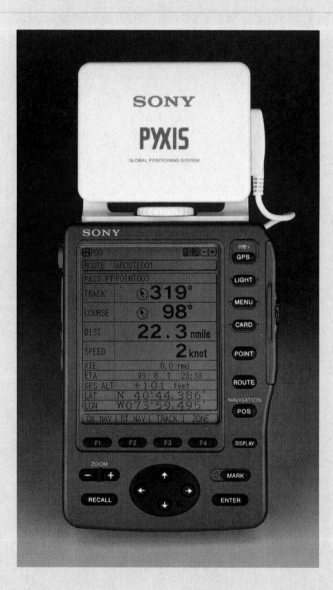

## A Half Century of Creative Engineering

Ibuka co-founded (with Akio Morita) Sony Corporation in a bombed-out Tokyo department store just after World War II. The two infused the company with a knack for creating new products, for working tirelessly to find new ways to satisfy consumers, and for going out on a limb to develop new markets. In the five decades since, Sony has become not only one of the largest companies in the world (with annual sales in excess of $30 billion), but also one of the most innovative.

Sony engineers are considered among the most productive in the world, cranking out an average of 1,000 new products every year. The majority, around 80 percent, are variations and improvements on existing products. You've no doubt seen or owned several types of Walkman personal stereos, for instance. The company makes inexpensive players that offer only tape or radio as well as top-of-the-line units that are waterproofed for outdoor use and that sport digital radio tuners and alarm clocks.

The other 20 percent of Sony's new-product effort is aimed at breaking barriers and creating new markets. The Walkman is a classic example. Before Sony came out with the idea, people simply didn't walk around with tape players attached to their belts and lightweight headphones on their heads, as unbelievable as that may seem in the mid-1990s. Now personal stereos are a multimillion-dollar market, and running around with a Walkman (or a look-alike from another company) seems almost as natural as, well, running around.

## Always on the Lookout for New Ideas

The secret to Sony's continuing success with new products lies in the attitudes Ibuka and Morita fostered in all the company's engineers. They are always on the lookout for new ways to make life more enjoyable and more productive (primarily for consumers, but increasingly for businesses as well). Ibuka describes the creative process as "looking for the unexpected and stepping outside your own experience."

One of the most important ways that product designers can step outside their own experience is to get out of the lab and into the "real world" to see how customers actually use products. Tomoshi Hirayama is a Sony software engineer who wanted to learn more about how customers use computers. He requested a temporary transfer from Japan to England, where he spent two years in customer support. As he helped people use Sony computers, he learned more about design changes that could make his company's products easier to use and more valuable to buyers. He returned to Tokyo with a rough design of the Sony PalmTop, an innovative handheld computer that helps businesspeople manage their time more productively.

Creativity in product design doesn't always mean million-dollar breakthrough products, of course. Sometimes an existing product can benefit from a bit of clever engineering or design. In cassette tapes, for instance, the quality of sound recording and playback depends heavily on how stable the tape is as it passes over the record/playback heads (the electromagnetic elements in the tape player that "read" and "write" the sound on the tape). This means that the tape is vulnerable to vibration. The small electric motor that winds and unwinds the tape generates vibration as it spins, and the tape itself generates vibration as it passes through the player and the tape case. Sony engineers solved the problem by making the tape case from a sturdy resin material, and by inserting dual plastic windows that absorb much of the vibration. On the strength of product innovations such as this, Sony's share of the cassette market increased from 20 to 25 percent during a three-year period when the market actually shrank.

## Learning from Experience

Innovation of any form is not without risks, of course, and the bigger the gamble the bigger the potential loss. Sony has had its share of disappointments, starting with a pair of home appliances that nearly bankrupted the company soon after it was founded. Later, it lost a high-stakes battle when it tried to market a VCR tape format (Beta) that was incompatible with the format that eventually took over most of the market (VHS). Sony executives say they learned from the experience not to push something that runs counter to market demands and expectations.

As Sony pushes for the twenty-first century, its engineers and executives face a fresh set of challenges. Facing a weak consumer electronics market and a pack of low-price competitors, the company is under pressure to generate profits and deliver the next round of fresh product innovations. Expect to see the company in new types of video games, personal digital communicators, and other computer, audio, and video products that the rest of us can only imagine at this point.

## Questions

1. How can Sony predict whether a new product idea will be a success? In the consumer audio market, what are several factors that Sony managers could look for when they evaluate a new-product proposal?

2. What might be some of the risks of imposing a structured screening and approval process on Sony's most innovative new-product ideas? What would be the advantages? What steps could Sony take to make sure that measures taken to minimize the occurrence of unsuccessful products don't stifle creativity at the same time?

3. Do you think Sony should be held liable if a consumer is injured after intentionally misusing a Sony product (say that hearing is damaged by playing a Walkman too loud)?

4. Which of the following products would be easiest for Sony to market globally: a Walkman with cassette tape only, a Walkman with tape and radio, or a karaoke machine? Why?

# PART IV
# PRICING STRATEGY AND MANAGEMENT

327

# Pricing Strategy

**After studying this chapter, you will be able to**

**1.** Explain the meaning of price and its role in the marketing mix

**2.** Outline the pricing process, from analyzing market conditions to adjusting prices in response to dynamic marketplace conditions

**3.** Describe demand curves and elasticity and relate how marketers use these concepts to establish ranges of possible price points

**4.** List the primary aspects of price sensitivity and explain its importance to marketers

**5.** Explain how to analyze competitors' pricing moves and compare the categories of competitive pricing strategies

**6.** Identify the constraints that affect pricing decisions and the effect that each constraint can have on the pricing process

**7.** List the major pricing objectives and explain the purpose behind each type

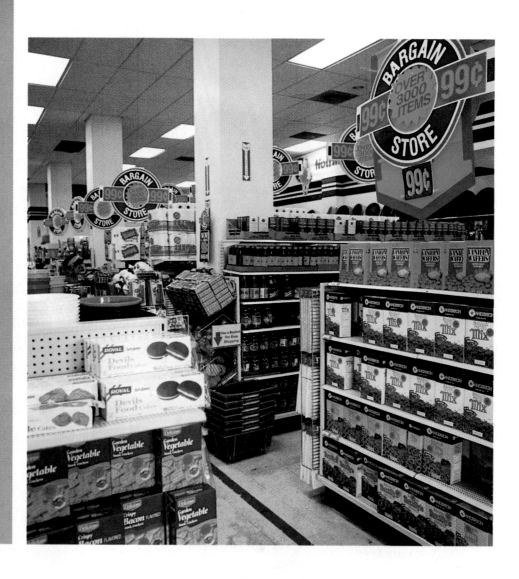

## FACING A MARKETING CHALLENGE AT SEARS

### *Big Retailer with a Big Pricing Problem*

Imagine figuring out the best way to price a pair of shoes, a chainsaw, and a skirt. Now imagine that you have a large department store packed with thousands of items. Also imagine that you have over 800 of these stores, employing nearly half a million people and pulling in billions of dollars annually. That's the challenge Michael Bozic faced when he was chairman of the Sears Merchandise Group.

However, Bozic's job wasn't nearly this simple. The vast U.S. middle class that used to shop at Sears for everything from blouses to bolt cutters had grown restless. Those with a little extra money and an image to worry about defected to upscale department stores such as Nordstrom and the thousands of specialty shops sitting next door to Sears in shopping malls all over the country. On the other hand, customers looking for the best deals looked to a growing number of discount retailers, including Wal-Mart, Target, and Kmart. Sears was also under attack from big specialty retailers such as Toys 'R' Us and Circuit City. Is it any wonder that Sears's market share declined steadily for a decade?

Competition wasn't Sears's only challenge. Retailers knew that customers were losing patience. Many suspected that retailers raised "regular" prices just so they could lower them when it was time to have a sale. The cycle of high prices, followed by sales on selected items, followed by a return to high prices had customers frustrated. Retailers weren't happy with this kind of pricing either. It raised their advertising costs (to promote the frequent sales), forced them to carry more inventory on sale items, and often hurt regular-priced products that were similar to sale products. On the other hand, Sears had been pricing this way for more than 100 years and sold much of its merchandise at sale prices.

Customers were changing more than just their attitudes; they were changing the way they shopped. Increasingly, they went to malls to shop for clothes. (More than 70 percent of revenue in U.S. malls is now generated by clothing sales, and over 75 percent of the clothes hanging in women's closets come from stores in shopping malls.) Putting it bluntly, to survive in shopping mall retailing, companies have to be successful at selling women's clothes. Sears was in shopping mall retailing in a big way—more than two-thirds of its stores are located inside malls—but the big retailer was having a hard time selling women's fashion clothing.

To make matters worse, Sears's selling and administration costs were among the highest in the industry, eating up 30 cents of every dollar Sears took in (compared to 23 cents at Kmart, for instance). Sears's corporate staff numbered 6,000, compared to 2,500 at Wal-Mart. Moreover, Sears's major presence in shopping malls had a big downside: Mall space is more expensive than space on the outside, where Kmart, Wal-Mart, Toys 'R' Us, and the rest are usually located. Toys 'R' Us and other aggressive discounters set up shop close to malls to catch the mall traffic, so Sears got stuck with the bill for attracting shoppers; unfortunately, the shoppers were stopping at the competition.

How would you use the pricing element in Sears's marketing mix to help the big retailer? Would you stick with the policy of frequent sales? Would you slide prices up to give Sears an upscale image? Would you slide prices down to compete better with the discounters? Do you need a completely new approach to pricing?[1]

# CHAPTER OVERVIEW

Sears executives know that pricing is one of the most interesting and challenging aspects of marketing. To arrive at the figure on the price tag, they must take many variables into account, ranging from government regulations to company image. This chapter discusses pricing from a strategic planning perspective, starting with a look at how customers perceive price and how it affects their purchase behavior. The chapter goes on to examine pricing constraints, the forces that limit how high and how low you can set prices. The chapter concludes by discussing the pricing objective, which drives every move you make regarding pricing. Chapter 12 continues with the tactical aspects of pricing and includes the special pricing issues encountered by nonprofit and service marketers.

# THE ROLE OF PRICE IN THE MARKETING MIX

Three of the marketing mix elements—product, promotion, and distribution—are concerned with delivering value to the customer. Price, on the other hand, attempts to get something of value back from the customer. Strategic pricing appears to be a late bloomer in the management of marketing mixes. As late as the 1970s, many companies let the finance department set prices, based on a simple calculation of internal costs and desired profit levels. However, when the measurement of marketing success began to emphasize profit and other financial variables, marketing managers developed a strong interest in pricing. By the end of the 1980s, many executives ranked pricing as the second most critical element that marketers had to manage, up from sixth place in a 1964 study. (Product was ranked first.)[2] One important result of this changed perception is a more powerful array of pricing techniques, which allows companies to select prices that will help them meet their business objectives.

## Price in Today's Economy

Prices can take on a number of assumed names. The *fare* you pay a cab driver, the *admission* you pay at a theater, and the *toll* you pay when exiting the Pennsylvania Turnpike are all forms of price. Similarly, the *tuition* you and your parents pay to your college, the *rent* you hand over to your landlord, and the *user's fee* required for entry to a national park are also prices. Regardless of the situation or the terminology, price represents the seller's estimate of the value customers are likely to place on the good or service being offered (see Exhibit 11.1).

There's more to price than the price tag. Whether they consciously consider other costs or not, buyers frequently pay more than the figure on the price tag. For example, when firms in the aerospace industry purchase computers and instruments to help them test aircraft and spacecraft, they usually have to spend a considerable amount of time connecting the equipment and programming the computers. The cost of this time (in terms of salaries) can be as much as 10 times the cost of the equipment they purchased. This illustrates the concept of **cost of ownership,** which includes the original price paid plus all the costs involved with installing, maintaining, and repairing the products. For a more down-to-earth example, when you compare the price of two cars, you consider operating, repair, insurance, and depreciation costs because all these things add up to the real cost of owning a car. In its broadest sense, price includes time, frustration, and anything else that the buyer has to give up to obtain and use a product.

Prices in every industry fluctuate in response to buyer demand, national economies, personal income, business profitability, population shifts, and other factors. However, a fundamental change seems to have occurred in the first half of the 1990s. Consumers and businesses normally watch their budgets more carefully during re-

**cost of ownership**
The total cost of acquiring and owning a product; it includes the search costs, the purchase price, and any other expenses related to installation, maintenance, service, and replacement

cessions, then expand spending as the economy improves. However, a combination of factors, including the rise of private-label goods and ferocious price wars in many industries, seems to have convinced many buyers that they no longer have to pay top prices for top-quality products. Whether pricing disposable diapers, credit card interest rates, or luxury cars, marketers are feeling the pressure. When Procter & Gamble announced in 1992 that it would lower prices on a variety of products, including its Luvs and Pampers diapers, competitors Chesebrough Ponds and Kimberly Clark had little choice but to follow suit. Researchers working on the Discover card say they've uncovered a "deep-rooted change in the consumer psyche." And when Lexus, Infiniti, and Acura began luring luxury car buyers away with lower prices (relatively speaking, of course), European carmakers had to respond. Jaguar lowered the price of its 1993 XJS flagship sedan by a monstrous 18 percent, and Mercedes-Benz is thinking the unthinkable—an economy car.[3]

## Price in the Marketing Mix

Every element in the marketing mix must be coordinated to support an overall strategy, and price is certainly no exception. The relationships between price and the other elements of the mix are addressed throughout this chapter and the next, but here are some important points that highlight the interdependence of price, product, promotion, and distribution.

PRICE AND PRODUCT

Price and product are closely interrelated. For example, the price that marketers can command in the market for a given product will determine how much they can afford to spend producing that product. When the Kosta Boda factory in Sweden produces a vase, it can afford to hire the talent of top designers, glassblowers, and painters, because the price for that vase will support a relatively high cost of production. On the other hand, a mass-produced vase from a discount store can't command much of a price at all, so the manufacturer can spend only a small amount of money on production.

Price interrelates with the product element in other important ways. First, prices are frequently changed over the course of the product life cycle. For example, as a product category declines, marketers often have to lower the price in order to keep

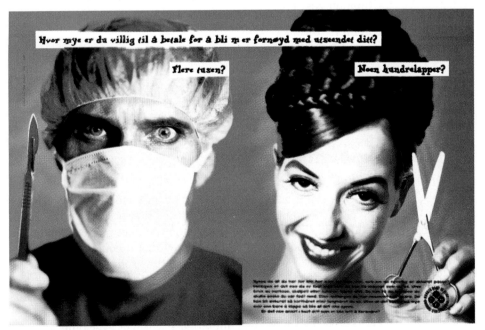

How much do you want to spend on improving your appearance? Several thousand? Or two hundred (*Norwegian kroners*)?

**Exhibit 11.1**
**SUCCESSFUL PRICES REFLECT PERCEIVED VALUE**
In this whimsical ad that compares the price of cosmetic surgery with the price of a haircut, the Norwegian hairdressers' association encourages consumers to consider the value of appearance-enhancing services.

the product competitive. A second way that price relates to product is in product line pricing, in which marketers use price to distinguish various classes of similar products. Third, price can have as much to do with customer perceptions of a product as the product's features and benefits. For example, part of what makes a car from Rolls-Royce seem so special is that everybody knows it costs a great deal.

### PRICE AND PROMOTION

Price also plays a big role in the promotion effort. A company telling its customers that it offers high-quality, exclusive products won't be bashful about a hefty price tag. In fact, some premium producers go out of their way to let customers know how expensive their products are. Rolex watches, Hermès luggage, and Joy de Jean Patou perfume are examples of products that are promoted with prices high enough to connote exclusivity for the people who buy them.

On the other hand, a vast assortment of products are promoted primarily on the basis of low price. For instance, so-called knockoff perfumes imitate the scent of expensive perfumes but are promoted on their low prices. Parfums de Coeur closely imitates the chemical composition of such premium perfumes as Opium and Ralph Lauren and sells its products at a fraction of the originals' prices. The appeal is primarily low price, so that's what the company emphasizes in its promotions. The strategy of promoting on price has certainly been effective in this case; sales of knockoff perfume grew 100 percent during a year when overall perfume sales dropped 2 percent.[4] In another example, Crown Books consistently promotes its bookstores with the phrase "If you paid full price, you didn't buy it at Crown Books." This company is sending its message loud and clear: If you want to pay less money for books, come to Crown.

### PRICE AND DISTRIBUTION

Distribution and pricing are linked for all products, but they are very closely linked for some products. Consider a bag of gardening limestone offered for sale by Nitron. Gardeners who live close to Nitron in Fayetteville, Arkansas, carry it home themselves and don't pay for shipping. A gardener in Portland, Oregon, buys the very same product and pays so much for shipping that the total price is nearly 360 percent higher.[5] The reason is distribution cost, which is a significant factor for products that are heavy, bulky, or relatively inexpensive. Many companies compensate by taking the distribution cost out of the standard price and charging customers separately for transportation.

Marketers also consider price when selecting distribution channels. Every channel costs money to operate, whether it's a budget mail-order catalog or a world-class retailer such as Harrods in London. The channel costs must be figured into the prices that final customers are expected to pay. The number and nature of the intermediaries in the channel determine the cost of distribution, which is a concern for everyone in the channel, from the manufacturer to the wholesaler to the retailer.

## Price and the Bottom Line

Setting the correct price is key to any business's survival. Poor pricing can result in financial disaster, even if the other three marketing mix elements are planned and executed effectively. Whether they're too high or too low, prices that miss hurt a company's ability to make money. If the price is lower than market conditions would support, the firm isn't bringing in all the money that it could. On the other hand, if the price is too high, the company will sell fewer products, which will reduce its revenue as well. Pricing is a balancing act, and success can be dramatic. In a classic case of great pricing, Ford introduced the Mustang, offering sports car excitement just below the price most customers were willing to pay. The result? Ford sold more Mustangs in the first year than any other car it had ever built, and the Mustang generated over a billion dollars in profit during its first two years.[6]

# OVERVIEW OF THE PRICING PROCESS

How can marketers know what price to charge? Arriving at the "correct" price involves examining a number of financial and nonfinancial variables, placing these variables in the context of the overall business environment, and finally relying on a healthy dose of experience and judgment. As Exhibit 11.2 shows, pricing includes six general steps:

1. *Analyze market conditions.* Pricing starts with an analysis of market conditions. The most important aspect of this analysis is understanding the relationship between price and demand. In some cases, changes in price can greatly influence demand; in other cases a significant change in price does little to modify demand.
2. *Identify constraints.* Accurate pricing can't happen in a vacuum. Numerous constraints limit the prices that a firm can set. Constraints such as production costs set lower limits for price. Other constraints such as customer perceptions and competitive pressure tend to set upper limits on price. For example, when Texas Instruments (TI) gets ready to price a new integrated circuit, it has to look at its own internal costs to see how much it needs to recover in order to remain profitable. Then it must look at what customers are willing to pay and at what competitors can offer. In addition, TI must consider a variety of government regulations that are supposed to prevent companies from doing such things as selling products below cost in order to eliminate competition.
3. *Establish objectives.* Like all business decisions, pricing is guided by clearly defined objectives. A firm's pricing objectives are linked with its marketing strategy and its overall business plan. Some typical marketing objectives that a pricing policy supports are generating a specified level of profit, selling a certain number of products, and capturing some share of the market. Of course, objectives can be changed over time as a company responds to both internal and external changes.
4. *Analyze profit potential.* The next step is to figure in cost, which tells the marketer how profitable a given business effort will be. Think of *price* as the amount the customer must spend to acquire a product and *cost* as the amount the producer has to spend to make and market that product. The difference between price and cost is the producer's *profit.* The four variables of demand, price, profit, and cost are closely linked. For example, if AT&T dropped the price of long-distance service to one-tenth its current level, customers would certainly place more phone calls. However, AT&T wouldn't be able to cover its cost and therefore wouldn't generate any profit. On the other hand, the company could increase the price of long-distance service to 10 times the current level and make a lot of profit on every call, but then customers would place fewer long-distance calls. In either case, the company would be making a pricing mistake by ignoring the balance required to set the right price.
5. *Determine initial price levels.* With the first four steps completed, the next step is setting the initial price level. Marketers have developed a number of techniques to help at this stage. For example, if you're about to introduce the world's first wristwatch fax machine, you'll probably start with a high price and then gradu-

**Exhibit 11.2
THE PRICING PROCESS**
Pricing generally takes six steps, starting with analyzing the market.

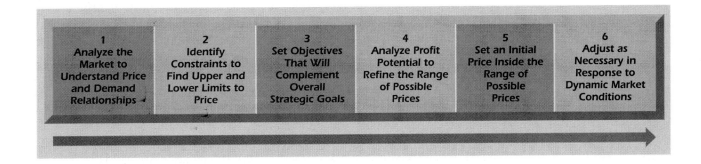

| 1 | 2 | 3 | 4 | 5 | 6 |
|---|---|---|---|---|---|
| Analyze the Market to Understand Price and Demand Relationships | Identify Constraints to Find Upper and Lower Limits to Price | Set Objectives That Will Complement Overall Strategic Goals | Analyze Profit Potential to Refine the Range of Possible Prices | Set an Initial Price Inside the Range of Possible Prices | Adjust as Necessary in Response to Dynamic Market Conditions |

# ANTIDUMPING REGULATIONS: WHO'S DOING WHAT TO WHOM?

**EXPLORING GLOBAL MARKETING**

On the surface, dumping regulations seem to make sense. To prevent overseas competitors from gaining an unfair foothold in U.S. markets, the Commerce Department increases import duties on any product it believes is being sold in this country for less than it is sold in other countries for the purpose of injuring U.S. competitors. However, the history of antidumping actions and their impact on U.S. consumers and businesses suggests that things aren't so simple.

Several factors complicate the issue. First, dumping can help as many people as it hurts. Not only do customers benefit from lower prices, but actions to stop supposed dumping can hurt businesses that need the goods in question. For example, after Torrington and other U.S. ball bearing makers filed a complaint about their overseas competitors, Caterpillar and several other U.S. companies that use ball bearings in their products unsuccessfully begged the Commerce Department not to impose antidumping duties. Caterpillar apparently didn't want to be stuck with Torrington bearings. One executive put it bluntly: "We've repeatedly slipped our production schedule to work around Torrington's string of broken promises. We have customers with Caterpillar equipment shut down in the field, waiting for replacement bearings from Torrington."

In a classic case, the U.S. steel industry successfully lobbied for *reference prices* on steel imports. These prices were set at a level that was based on the cost structure of the most efficient steel producers in the world. Any imported steel priced below the reference price automatically triggered an antidumping investigation. The result was higher prices for steel in the United States, which may have helped the U.S. steel industry, but it hurt U.S. companies that used steel in their products, and it eventually raised prices for consumers and businesses.

Second, at least from other countries' perspective, the United States has a reputation for pursuing dumping cases with overaggressive zeal. A Taiwanese firm was convicted of dumping after a factory burned down and prevented executives from answering all the questions in a 100-page questionnaire it received from Department of Commerce officials. The department convicted a Hong Kong sweater producer because the company made only a 2 percent profit margin on sweaters it sold in the United States, even though many companies in the United States operate at similar profit levels. Overall, the Department of Commerce's conviction rate on dumping cases it investigates is 97 percent.

Third, the vague wording of both U.S. and international dumping regulations makes it easy for regulators to implement *protectionism* under the guise of antidumping enforcement. Protectionism, a hotly debated topic in many countries, is an effort by one country to protect its domestic industries from competitors in other countries—even if the domestic industries can't compete with their foreign rivals in the open market. Protectionism tends to raise prices for customers, and it can insulate domestic firms from the real world, removing any incentive to becoming better competitors.

As the U.S. trade deficit with Japan continues to loom in the minds of regulators, legislators, and the public, you can expect lots of discussion and numerous lawsuits about dumping. Also, antidumping efforts are spreading: Japan recently filed its first claims, against 100 mineral producers from China.

## APPLY YOUR KNOWLEDGE

**1.** Is it fair to regulate dumping, even if it helps some U.S. customers?
**2.** Do you think predatory pricing should be illegal in general? Would you agree that it is just another aspect of competition?

---

ally bring the price down over time. If customers need a wristwatch fax machine, and you're the only one who has it, you have some extra latitude in setting your price. On the other hand, if you have a number of established competitors and your objective is to capture significant market share as soon as possible, you might pick a low price to give customers a good reason to leave your competitors. Depending on the price-demand-profit relationships, your pricing objectives, and the constraints you've identified, you have various techniques available to guide you toward the best price.

6. *Adjust and manage prices.* The final step is to adjust and manage prices in response to particular situations or changing marketing conditions. The range of possible actions here is wide and includes such modifications as discounts, geo-

graphical adjustments to cover transportation costs, and price changes to accommodate maturing products. These pricing modifications often play a key role in building or maintaining competitive advantage.

# PRICING STRATEGY

This overview gives you a basic understanding of the six steps of the pricing process. Moreover, it serves as a quick reference guide as you finish this chapter and progress through the next one. The remainder of this chapter covers the first three steps in more detail. These steps make up the planning necessary before actually setting prices. The last three steps, covered in Chapter 12, address the details of setting and managing prices.

## STEP 1. Analyze Market Conditions

Marketers must first understand customer demand and competition when setting prices. Unfortunately, customer demand and competitive behavior can be difficult to measure and predict. In practice, marketers rely on a combination of analysis, judgment, and in some cases, plain old guesswork.

### ESTIMATING DEMAND

How many people will buy the next model of the Chevrolet Corvette? How many will buy a Corvette if it is priced at $25,000? $35,000? $45,000? What will happen to sales if Texaco raises the price of unleaded gasoline by 20 percent? Uncovering the relationship between demand and price is one of the most important tasks you'll face in the pricing process. The fundamental tool used here is called the **demand curve,** which is a graph that shows how many units can be sold across a range of possible prices.

For example, Exhibit 11.3 shows the relationship of price and demand for a brand of pancake syrup. The vertical axis shows the percentage of the market that would purchase this brand at the five price points shown along the horizontal axis. The demand curve for this product shows several interesting pricing aspects. First, lowering the price 25 percent, from $2.00 to $1.50, nearly doubles the number of people who would buy the product. Second, the relationship between price and demand doesn't make as much sense as you might think at first; the price increase from $2.00 to $2.25 *raises* demand rather than lowering it. Third, the demands at $2.00 and $2.50 are nearly identical, implying that this product could be sold at the higher price with no loss in sales volume and (probably) a significant increase in profit. Also note that this demand curve is *nonlinear;* that is, changes in price don't always cause proportional changes in demand. *Linear* demand curves always show the same demand change for a given price change, but such curves are found more often in textbooks than in real life.

PRICE ELASTICITY OF DEMAND    If customer demand for a product changes as the price changes, customers are clearly sensitive to price. **Price sensitivity** is the indicator of how much demand will change for a given change in price. Economists refer to this as the **price elasticity of demand,** which is usually expressed as the following ratio:

$$\text{Elasticity} = \frac{\text{\% change in quantity purchased}}{\text{\% change in price}}$$

The terms *sensitivity* and *elasticity* are interchangeable in the marketing context; if you want to sound more like an economist, say *elasticity*. Also, keep in mind that quantity and price are interdependent: A change in one might cause a change in the other. If the price of Häagen-Dazs ice cream jumped to $10 a scoop, demand

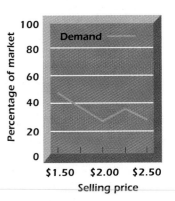

**Exhibit 11.3
DEMAND CURVE FOR PANCAKE SYRUP**
The results of a test-market laboratory experiment for a brand of pancake syrup show that lowering price won't always increase demand.

**demand curve**
A graph that plots the relationship between demand and price; it indicates the sensitivity of buyers to various selling prices

**price sensitivity**
An indication of the effect price has on buyers' intentions to purchase a given product or class of product; if buyers are considered price sensitive, changes in price will cause definite changes in their buying behavior

**price elasticity of demand**
The measure of price sensitivity, expressed as the ratio of percentage change in demand to percentage change in price

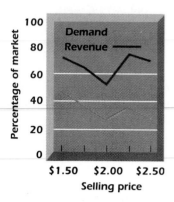

**Exhibit 11.4
COMPARING SALES
AND REVENUE
CURVES**
Demand and total revenue
don't always peak at the same
price points, which can complicate pricing decisions; the
price you would pick in this
case depends on your pricing
objectives.

**inelastic demand**
A price-demand relationship
in which a decrease in price
decreases total revenue

**elastic demand**
A price-demand relationship
in which a decrease in price
increases total revenue

**perfectly inelastic demand**
The most extreme case of inelastic demand, in which
changes in price have no effect on demand; this applies
to products that people can't
or won't live without

**perfectly elastic demand**
The case when changes in demand have no effect on price;
the opposite of perfectly inelastic demand

would probably drop. On the other hand, if 150 million people suddenly decided they couldn't live without Häagen-Dazs every day, the company could raise its prices because the demand would support such a move.

ELASTICITY AND TOTAL REVENUE    Understanding elasticity is a critical step in setting prices because it is strongly related to total revenue. Reconsider the pancake syrup data from Exhibit 11.3; if you compute total revenue by multiplying demand (sales) by price, you'll get a revenue curve like the one seen in Exhibit 11.4. By compar-ing the two curves, you can see that demand and revenue peak at different price points. From these data, if you wanted maximum market share (in terms of num-ber of packages sold), you'd pick the $1.50 price; if you wanted maximum revenue, you'd pick $2.25.

These data show two kinds of demand elasticity. **Inelastic demand** means that total revenue decreases as price decreases. This effect is seen in Exhibit 11.4 be-tween $2.25 and $2.00, where dropping the price decreases the total revenue. The opposite type of elasticity is **elastic demand,** in which a decrease in price increases total revenue. This is seen in Exhibit 11.4 at several points; dropping the price from $2.50 to $2.25, for instance, increases total revenue from $70 to $74. Data like these emphasize a crucial point in pricing: You can't always assume that dropping the price will help either sales or total revenue. This is especially important to remember in times of poor sales because it's easy to surrender to the price-cutting temptation, even though price may not be the cause of your sales trouble.

The extremes of elastic and inelastic demand provide interesting cases of pric-ing. At one end, **perfectly inelastic demand** implies that changes in price will not affect demand at all. This is the case for products that people can't or won't live with-out, such as drugs, medical services, and the necessities—heating oil, gasoline for driving to work, basic food, and so on. Naturally, people can't stay insensitive to price forever; drastic increases in price will eventually curtail demand when some people can no longer afford even the essentials. At the other end of the spectrum, **per-fectly elastic demand** occurs when changes in demand don't (or can't) cause any change in price. For example, this happens when prices are locked in contractually, such as when farmers agree at the beginning of the season to sell crops for a set price at harvest time. Of course, most pricing situations fall between these two extremes.

Another key element of elasticity is the effect that the price of one product (or product category) has on the demand of another product (or product category), a phenomenon known as *cross elasticity.* Consider the relationship of new cars and used cars. From 1977 to 1992, the price of the average new car sold in the United States jumped from around $6,000 to nearly $18,000, increasing at a significantly faster rate than household incomes. People still need to drive, but the higher prices are convincing many that they don't need to drive new cars. As a result, demand for used cars is climbing. Every year since 1989, franchised auto dealers (those who sell both new and used cars) have sold more used cars than new cars.[7]

## JUDGING PRICE SENSITIVITY INFLUENCES

The pancake syrup data used to discuss price sensitivity were based on a market research laboratory experiment. Unfortunately, many marketers don't have access to this sort of information, and they are forced to rely on a less scientific combina-tion of judgment and experience. Why don't more companies use elasticity data? To begin with, the type of research required to get elasticity data is generally expen-sive and time consuming. Also, price sensitivity is a complex and subtle topic, and not all the managers in a position to pay for elasticity studies believe they're worth the time and money. A recent study of industrial marketing managers showed that only a third of the companies regularly collected elasticity data, and that was only on their major products.[8] However, marketers continue to push for new ways to cre-ate viable demand curves. One promising breakthrough is the amount of data pro-vided by supermarket checkout scanners. These systems can easily track changes in price and demand, helping marketers assess the effect of price changes and thereby helping them build demand curves.

When they don't have *quantitative* elasticity data, marketers can rely on the following *qualitative* measures to help them evaluate price sensitivity:[9]

- *Customer expectations*. One of the most important factors is simply what customers *expect* to pay for your product. These expectations are set by such factors as the last price paid, perceptions of what is a "fair" price, the price of a favorite brand, self-image ("How much should a person like me pay for this?"), and individual notions of maximum allowable price (beyond which the customer will choose not to buy anything).[10] If a price is within the expected range, the customer may not think twice about it, and price will essentially disappear as a factor in the purchase. If the price is above or below this, price can become a major issue. If your price is above the customer's expected price, for example, you'll have to explain why your product is worth more than the customer expected to pay for it.

- *Unique value*. If customers believe that a product offers value that can't be found in other products, they are willing to pay more. Extreme cases of this can be found in the art market. For example, Vincent Van Gogh sold exactly one painting while he was alive, for about $80. A hundred years or so later, his painting *Portrait of Dr. Gachet* sold for $82.5 million, and the buyer was quite pleased to get it at that price.[11] Van Gogh died a pauper and probably never envisioned the extremely inelastic prices his paintings would command in the future.

- *Substitute awareness*. If customers are aware of viable substitutes, they will usually be more sensitive to price changes. For example, customers are very aware of substitutes when it comes to air travel, so they're intensely price sensitive. When a low-price supplier such as Southwest Airlines enters a market, it quickly gains sales.[12]

- *Difficult comparison*. When customers have difficulty comparing products, they're usually less sensitive to price. For example, when you're comparing bicycles, you can look at the various features, give the bikes a try, and generally get a good picture of what each product offers. On the other hand, if you're trying to decide between two doctors, it might be hard for you to make comparisons, and price will be less important (within a reasonable range, of course). In this case, the doctors' reputations, manner, and experience are likely to be more important than their fees. As you'll recall from the discussion of intangibility in Chapter 8, products high in experience and credence qualities are hard to evaluate before purchase. In response, customers tend to compare prices as a way of comparing perceived quality.

- *Total expenditure*. The size of the check the customer has to write also affects price sensitivity. For instance, a 10 percent discount on a candy bar isn't going to motivate many consumers to choose one product over another, but a 10 percent discount on a car might. The total expenditure effect is particularly common in organizational markets, where customers may be laying out millions of dollars for a purchase. Be careful with this effect in consumer markets, however, because the consumer's income level relative to the total expenditure also influences sensitivity. A wealthy family, for instance, spends a lot more on clothes than a poor family does, but the wealthy family might be less sensitive to changes in price because they have greater income.

- *Contribution to overall benefits*. This effect is most relevant when you're marketing to industrial customers. Say you're selling steel to both Steelcase (a manufacturer of office furniture) and Samsonite (a maker of luggage). A steel desk and briefcase both contain some steel, but the proportion is much higher for the steel desk. Consequently, Steelcase is going to be more sensitive to the price of your steel than Samsonite is. Even if the people who buy desks and briefcases are equally sensitive to the prices of those finished products, the desk customers will indirectly be more sensitive to the price of steel because it affects the price of desks more than it affects the price of briefcases. What does this mean for you as a marketer of steel? It means that your prices might have a ripple effect. For instance, if you decide to charge Steelcase more for your product and Steelcase then loses sales because its own products are now more expensive, you'll end up cutting your own sales volume.

- *Shared cost.* If a customer isn't responsible for the total price of a product, he or she will be less sensitive to its price. This shared cost effect continues to plague health insurance providers, for instance. If customers don't have to pay for all of their health-care costs, they are likely to visit doctors more often, for ailments and complaints that they might just live with if forced to pay for health care themselves. If an insurance company requires preapproval before surgery, the shared cost effect is the reason. The insurer wants to be certain it's paying only for necessary health-care costs.

- *Sunk investments.* When you engage the services of a lawyer or an accountant, part of the money you spend pays for the time and effort that service provider spends to get familiar with your situation. For example, the accountant will have to review your personal or business finances before evaluating your investment opportunities and tax liability, and part of the fee you pay goes for this learning period. This investment is considered "sunk" because you can't get it back. It will tend to keep you loyal to this accountant because you don't want to pay a second accountant just to get familiar with your finances. Even if that second accountant's hourly rate is lower, you're liable to stay with your current accountant; this sunk investment effect has increased your insensitivity to the price of the second accountant (see Exhibit 11.5).

- *Price-quality associations.* Sometimes customers equate higher price with higher quality. That's why the sales of some products increase after a price increase. For example, one brand of car wax didn't sell well at $.69 but took off when its price was raised to $1.69. This isn't always the case, however; extensive research into the price-quality relationship hasn't shown conclusive, generalized proof that customers will automatically assume a product with a high price is of high quality. In any event, other variables in the marketing mix also play an important role in the perception of quality and its relationship with price sensitivity; marketers need more than just a high price to establish the perception of quality.[13] However, it's

**Exhibit 11.5**
**DEALING WITH THE SUNK INVESTMENT EFFECT**

The makers of Approach database software know that they couldn't give their software away if the product required customers to give up their investment in existing databases.

The EPSON Stylus™ 300 Ink Jet
is the best value in its class.

**EPSON Stylus 300 Thermal Ink Jet**

If you want great quality printing
and a great value, you want the
EPSON Stylus 300. It's the latest addition
to our award-winning EPSON Stylus
line of ink jet printers. The
EPSON Stylus 300 delivers printing so clean
and crisp, you'll be amazed it's so
affordable. In fact, of all the low-cost thermal
ink jets, including HP's DeskJet 500 and
Canon's Bubble Jet 200, there's no
better value than the EPSON Stylus 300. And
nothing else in its class has the worldwide
EPSON reputation for reliability.

The EPSON Stylus™ 800
is in a class by itself.

**EPSON Stylus 800 Piezo Ink Jet**

If you want the finest ink jet technology ever
offered, there's only one choice. Step up to the
extraordinary EPSON Stylus 800. The
Piezo-powered EPSON Stylus 800 is a major
breakthrough in printing technology.
EPSON's Piezo technology, featuring our
exclusive Multi-Layer Actuator Head, enables
the EPSON Stylus 800 to print the sharpest,
clearest images ever formed by a personal ink jet.
Better than any personal thermal ink jet. And
no other personal ink jet does it at a lower cost per
page*. The Piezo-powered EPSON Stylus 800
is clearly in a class by itself.

All printers in the EPSON Stylus line of ink jets are backed by a solid two year warranty, and by the EPSON Connection toll-free help line. For information about the EPSON

line of ink jet printers, or our complete line of scanners, laser and dot matrix printers, call the EPSON Connection at 1-800-BUY-EPSON (1-800-289-3776).

**EPSON**

*Based on an independent test comparing the standard printing modes for the Canon BJ-200, the HP DeskJet 500 and the EPSON Stylus 800. All company and/or product names are trademarks and/or registered trademarks of their respective manufacturers, including Canon, which is registered by Canon Inc. and HP, which is registered by Hewlett-Packard Co.

EPSON disclaims any and all rights in those marks. EPSON is a registered trademark of Seiko EPSON Corp. ©1994 EPSON America, Inc., 20770 Madrona Ave., Torrance, CA 90503. For dealer referral or warranty details, call 800-BUY-EPSON (800-289-3776). In Canada, call 1800-GO-EPSON. For Latin America, 305-265-0092.

**Exhibit 11.6**
**PROMOTING THE LINK AMONG PRICE, QUALITY, AND VALUE**
Epson demonstrates two approaches to the promotion of value; one product leads with price, and the other leads with quality.

important not to assume that even when people do perceive higher quality they'll be willing to pay higher prices. Particularly in tough economic times and in countries with developing economies, people are often more interested in savings than in lasting quality (see Exhibit 11.6). A recent study in the former Czechoslovakia (now composed of the Czech Republic and Slovakia) indicated that more than half the households there say they simply buy the cheapest products on the market.[14]

## UNDERSTANDING DEMAND CURVE CHANGES

Demand curves and price sensitivity are not static; they are affected by changes in consumer tastes and trends, technology, government regulations, and a variety of other factors. For instance, as more companies introduced clones of IBM's personal computer, prices in the industry dropped an average of 20 percent a year.[15] In other words, increased competition shifted the demand curve in the direction of lower prices. Think about the Van Gogh painting that sold for $82.5 million, a million times more than the single painting the artist sold while he was alive. Changes in consumer taste did some radical rearrangement of that demand curve. When consumers grew tired of mediocre home video games in the early 1980s (the pre-Nintendo days), games that once sold for $30 couldn't be given away. These examples highlight one of the basic rules of pricing: When you finally get some insight into price sensitivity, your work has just begun, because market conditions are bound to change.

## ANALYZING COMPETITION

The other important aspect of understanding market influences on price is to understand the effect of competition. At the very least, analyze competitors to see how they price, what level of discounts they're willing to offer, and so forth. At the next level, predict how they might behave in a given situation. It's important to realize that the presence of strong price competition can dramatically change the demand curves and sensitivity variables just discussed. For example, if you drop prices by 10 percent to try to gain market share and your competitors match your price, you haven't made any progress, at least not relative to your competitors. Before making any pricing moves, try to anticipate your competitors' responses and the effect these responses will have on demand and price relationships. The most advanced level of competitive price analysis is to be able to influence the pricing behavior of your competitors. If you're managing prices at Safeway and want to lower the price of lettuce, do you know how your counterpart at Kroger is going to react? If you want Kroger to react in a certain way, what do you do? These questions aren't easy to answer, but they're too significant to ignore.

ANTICIPATING COMPETITIVE PRICING MOVES   You can get a handle on possible competitive responses by examining four general categories of price competition. Once you understand the nature of the price competition you're facing, you have a better chance of anticipating the next move. The four general categories of price competition are cooperative, adaptive, opportunistic, and predatory:[16]

- *Cooperative pricing.* In oligopoly markets, which are markets controlled by a small number of suppliers, competitors often engage in cooperative pricing. They can't explicitly agree on pricing; that's illegal. However, they can respond to each other's pricing moves in a way that benefits the group. When the price leader in the market raises prices, for example, the others in a cooperative pricing situation will follow suit. This benefits all competitors. The price increases in the overnight package delivery industry are a good example of cooperative pricing; Federal Express, United Parcel Service, and Airborne Express aren't interested in dragging each other's profit down with aggressive pricing, so they tend to cooperate now that they have significant control of the market.
- *Adaptive pricing.* Smaller competitors are more likely to be in an adaptive situation, in which they have to respond to the pricing moves made by their larger competitors. For example, oil-producing countries such as Great Britain that are not members of the Organization of Petroleum Exporting Countries (OPEC) tend to follow OPEC's lead in pricing.[17]
- *Opportunistic pricing.* Opportunistic pricing is even less cooperative than adaptive pricing. Competitors in this situation look for opportunities to initiate price cuts or to delay price increases after competitors increase their prices. In other words, they're looking for chances to keep their prices below their competitors'. Sometimes opportunistic pricing moves are disguised as giveaways or added services, but they have the same effect of offering more value for the money.
- *Predatory pricing.* When companies set prices at very low levels with the intent of inflicting damage on competitors, they are practicing **predatory pricing.** In some cases, predatory pricing is used to "educate" competitors if they aren't cooperating or adapting in a way that satisfies market leaders. Shell Oil once used this tactic in response to the opportunistic pricing of independent gas stations in southern California. The independents tried to lower their prices dramatically to take business away from Shell, but the oil giant dropped its prices as well, and it continued to match any decrease made by the independent stations. As a result, everybody involved suffered low profits, but the independents were less capable of long-term survival under these conditions. They eventually realized that they had no choice but to cooperate with Shell, which meant they could no longer price opportunistically.[18] The extreme case of predatory pricing is sometimes referred to as cutthroat pricing, in which the objective is not to damage competitors but to destroy them.  Cutthroat pricing is fairly rare, particularly because it is illegal. On the other hand, if your intent is only to cause temporary pain for a competitor, rather than to run it out of business, aggressive underpricing is legal.

**predatory pricing**
The practice of lowering prices to a point where they inflict financial damage on competitors: the extreme case of predatory pricing seeks to drive competitors out of business entirely and is illegal

Monitoring and responding to competitive pricing moves is a tricky business. When a competitor lowers prices, for example, this could signal an aggressive move to gain market share, supported by strong financing that the company will rely on to stay afloat while it sells at lower profits. It could also mean that the company is in serious financial trouble and is trying to stimulate sales with a price cut. On the other hand, it could mean that the company has found a new way to reduce its production or marketing costs. Each of these competitive moves has a different implication, so try to understand *why* competitors are doing what they're doing.[19]

INFLUENCING COMPETITIVE PRICING MOVES   In many cases you can influence the pricing moves made by your competitors. The first step is to assess the amount of influence you might possibly have. Generally, if you have enough market share to catch the attention of your competitors, or even the perceived potential to gain enough share, you can probably exert some influence.

The fundamental theme behind influencing competitors' pricing behavior is to influence the perceptions they have of your own pricing moves. For instance, if they think you're raising prices because customers see new value in your products, they'll respond in a different way than if they think you're just temporarily digging for more profit. Pricing experts use the term **signaling** to describe the messages that a company sends to its competitors about pricing intentions. You can send messages to competitors through all the promotional channels that you normally use for communicating with customers. For example, when Delta Airlines publicly announced during a period of intense price competition that it would not be undersold, competitors got the message that Delta was serious and had the financial strength to stand behind its word. Delta was trying to send a signal that it wouldn't do a competitor any good to cut prices because Delta would just cut its own prices even further. When Goodyear announced to the business press that its new low-cost, automated plant in Oklahoma would allow it to dominate the market for radial tires, creditors foreclosed on two of the company's competitors, and a third, Goodrich, began diversifying outside the tire industry.[20]

One competitive response that most marketers try hard to avoid is a **price war,** a fierce competition in which competitors quickly beat each other's low prices in an attempt to maintain low-price leadership in the market. Price wars frequently lead to a serious loss of profit for some or all competitors involved; in some cases, only those competitors with deep pockets or paper-thin cost structures can survive (see Exhibit 11.7).

Some industries that have lived through price wars in recent years include fast food, soft drinks, computers, and air travel. For example, Pepsi and Coke frequently find themselves in a price war that hurts each other's profits when prices in retail stores fall to unbelievably low levels. A grocery store in Tempe, Arizona, recently had a six-pack of Coke on sale for 59 cents, less than the cost of a single can in some vending machines. Some people wonder whether the two soft drink giants will ever be able to pull prices back up to reasonable levels.[21] Two things are certain: Consumers are benefiting in the meantime, and smaller soft drink competitors without the financial strength of Pepsi and Coke are surely hurting. What effect can price

**signaling**
Sending a message to competitors about your pricing intentions; this includes both genuine messages and "bluffs"

**price war**
A market situation in which competitors constantly try to beat each other's prices; a frequent result is that prices are driven down so low that companies sell at a loss

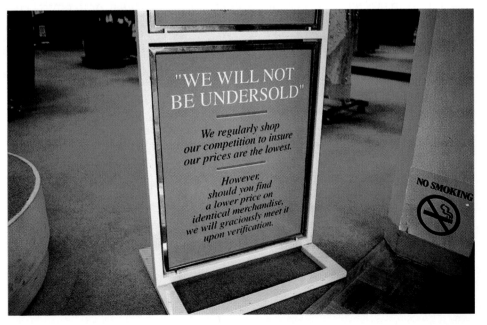

**Exhibit 11.7**
**THE RISK OF PRICE WARS**
Retailers who promise to beat any price in town risk triggering price wars; if competitive retailers take the same approach, the result could be a downward price spiral in which the retailers continually try to underprice each other.

wars have on an industry? In the three-year period from 1990 through 1992, the U.S. airline industry lost more than enough money to wipe out the cumulative profits made since the beginning of commercial aviation more than half a century ago.[22]

## STEP 2: Identify Pricing Constraints

Many forces place limits on the range of possible prices. Some of these (such as cost) are internal forces, whereas others (such as government regulations and competition) are external forces that affect pricing decisions. Exhibit 11.8 shows the major pricing constraints.

### COSTS

The price a company gets for its product must cover the cost of production and marketing, plus a variety of other expenses, and still leave enough for profit. As you'll see in the next chapter, identifying costs isn't always as simple as it might seem at first. Some costs are directly related to the materials and wages involved in the production of goods, but other costs come from licensing fees, taxes, investments in research, business services, and other areas. For instance, costs for insurance companies such as State Farm are tied to accident rates, weather, and the general behavior of their customers. State Farm was able to reduce its rates at one point in 1988 simply because fewer than normal hurricanes and other catastrophes had reduced its costs of doing business.[23] (However, rates can turn around quickly when nature loses its temper, as in the San Francisco earthquake of 1989; hurricanes Hugo, Iniki, and Andrew; and other events since then.) Regardless of the type of business, these expenses add up, and smart marketers know that they must identify all these costs to ensure that enough money will be generated by the prices the company plans to charge.

### GOVERNMENT INFLUENCES

The U.S. government plays a big role in pricing, as do the governments of many other countries. Sometimes this role makes perfect sense, as in the laws that forbid deceptive pricing. Sometimes it's harder to fathom. Consider milk pricing in the United States. Stacks of convoluted regulations that few people understand include this one: The minimum price that can be charged for milk is based in part on the dairy farm's distance from Eau Claire, Wisconsin. The farther you are from Eau Claire, the more valuable your milk supposedly is.[24]

In efforts to protect consumers, to encourage fair competition, or to protect certain industries, the government has enacted a variety of price-related legislation over the years, and all successful marketers are aware of legal ramifications. Unfortunately, these laws can be confusing, and they are subject to changes in judicial in-

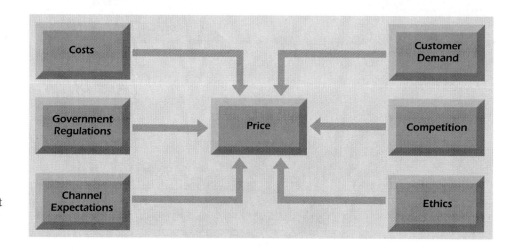

**Exhibit 11.8**
**PRICING**
**CONSTRAINTS**
A variety of constraints limit the range of possible prices for every product.

## FAST-FOOD PROFITS DON'T LOOK SO APPETIZING ANYMORE

"When elephants start fighting, ants get killed." That's how Murray Riese describes the pain his company, National Restaurants, is feeling. National owns a string of fast-food franchises, including Pizza Hut and Roy Rogers outlets. Riese and others in his shoes have good reason to feel like ants under the feet of battling elephants.

Many of the McDonald's, Burger King, and other fast-food restaurants in the United States are owned by independent businesspeople. Some own just one or two restaurants; others own sizable networks of restaurants. (These independent operators are called *franchisees,* and the companies such as McDonald's are called *franchisors.*) The franchisors establish operating procedures for the franchisees, and one of these procedures is pricing.

The big franchisors have been locked in a price war for several years, catching franchisees like Riese in the crossfire. Pizza restaurants now frequently offer two-for-one specials, and sandwiches can be had for half-price all over the place. The result is incredible pressure on profits. A Burger King operator in Omaha says his company has to serve 15 to 20 percent more customers just to keep revenues at the same level as before the price war. "It's almost as if you're doing extra work just to give away the food," he adds. Discounting used to be a regular tactic during the winter as restaurants tried to stimulate de-

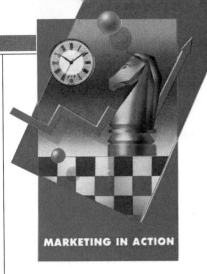

MARKETING IN ACTION

mand, but by 1989 discounting turned into a year-round marketing activity.

How did this happen? Why would otherwise sane companies engage in unhealthy discounting and lead themselves into a price war? Many believe they have no choice. Some areas have so many fast-food outlets that the only way to grow is to take away somebody else's customers. Also, many customers don't perceive enough value difference between a Big Mac and a Whopper, or a Big Mac and a pizza for that matter, to pay much of a premium for one product over another. It seems that price is the only variable left to compete on.

Customers don't seem to mind. Some restaurants report that customers are so used to discounts and other promotional tactics that they won't walk in the door if they have to pay full price. Conditioning customers to expect low prices is a danger any time you run discount programs frequently, and the fast-food industry appears to be the victim of its own marketing tactic.

Why don't franchisees like Riese just say no? That sounds reasonable: If you're running a discount promotion that's ruining your business, just retreat and crank your prices back up. However, the franchisees feel trapped, for three reasons. The first is simple competition: Each restaurant is afraid to raise prices unless everybody else does, too. The second reason is the relationship with the franchisor: Operators try not to upset the franchisor, for fear of losing favorable treatment in the future. The third reason comes from government regulations: Even if an operator discovers it is losing money on a discount promotion, the franchisor can force it to continue the program, to avoid accusations of deceptive pricing.

The future doesn't look terribly bright for some franchisees. An executive at McDonald's said things aren't all that gloomy, but that opinion isn't shared by all franchise operators. The new strategy did bring in more customers, however. Analysts and some industry insiders predict that the larger franchise networks can ride the storm out, but some smaller independents might get squeezed out of business altogether.

### APPLY YOUR KNOWLEDGE

**1.** When does it make sense for a company to engage in the kind of aggressive discounting that can lead to a price war?

**2.** Nobody wants to get caught in a price war, but how do you avoid it? If all your competitors are going crazy with discounts, what should you do?

---

terpretation. Marketers must navigate these legal waters carefully or risk facing lawsuits from the government, their competitors, or their customers. The safest and simplest route is to learn what pricing practices the courts have considered illegal in the past and then avoid these or similar tactics.[25] The government monitors pricing in four areas: price fixing, price discrimination, deceptive pricing, and dumping.

PRICE FIXING    When two or more companies supplying the same type of products agree on the prices they'll charge or on the formulas they'll use to set prices, they are engaging in a practice known as **price fixing**. For instance, Pepsi and Coke bottlers in Norfolk, Virginia, were convicted of price fixing after regulators discovered

**price fixing**
An illegal collaboration between two or more competitors who agree on the prices they'll charge for products in the same category

the bottlers had shared confidential price information and conspired to fix the whole-sale price of soft drinks during the mid-1980s. The result, according to prosecutors, was to inflate prices to consumers and restrict the sales of smaller competitors.[26] In nearly all cases, price fixing is illegal; two exceptions are when the government it-self fixes prices or when regulated public utilities set prices for their services (which they can do only with government approval).[27]

Price fixing can appear in several forms. Since 1958 the Ivy League universities (Harvard, Yale, Brown, Columbia, Cornell, Dartmouth, Princeton, and Penn), MIT, and a number of other schools had been meeting regularly with the intent of elim-inating price competition for desirable scholarship applicants, according to a find-ing issued by a federal court in Pennsylvania. The court found that by using a com-mon method to determine financial need, sharing financial information on students, and agreeing not to award merit scholarships, the universities denied students the ability to compare prices. The Ivy League schools chose not to defend themselves against the charges (admitting guilt, in effect). MIT lost its case and was convicted in 1992 of price fixing in violation of the Sherman Antitrust Act.[28]

Another variation involved the U.S. airline industry and its shared computer reser-vation system. The Justice Department filed suit against eight major U.S. airlines in 1992, accusing them of using the industry's reservation system to fix prices.[29] The issue was the practice of one airline announcing proposed fare changes on the sys-tem, then waiting to see if competitors responded. For instance, if an airline wanted to raise its Phoenix-to-Denver coach price by $40, it would post the fare increase on the computer system. If competitors on the route then posted similar increases, the airline would go ahead with the price change. If competitors didn't, the first airline would withdraw the proposed increase. The Justice Department's contention is that the airlines were in effect collaborating on price levels.

**resale price maintenance**
The effort of manufacturers to suggest and potentially influ-ence the prices charged by re-tailers carrying their products

A special case of potential price fixing is **resale price maintenance,** in which manufacturers suggest and sometimes try to enforce the prices that are charged by the distributors and retailers of their products. When you see a price tag that says "manufacturer's suggested retail price," that is the price the manufacturer would like to see the retailer charge. However, the courts have disallowed attempts by manufacturers to coerce retailers into charging those prices. When Russell Stover Candies refused to sell to retailers that didn't charge its suggested retail price, the Federal Trade Commission required the candy maker to include the following state-ment with any communication to retailers about prices: "This retail price is sug-gested only. You are completely free to determine your own price." Resale price maintenance remains an unclear legal area because of inconclusive judicial stands on the issue. Marketers should proceed with caution.[30]

**price discrimination**
The practice of offering attrac-tive discounts to some cus-tomers but not to others for the same product; usually ille-gal

PRICE DISCRIMINATION   One of the most important pieces of pricing-related legisla-tion in the United States is the Robinson-Patman Act. A key part of this legislation outlaws **price discrimination,** the practice of unfairly offering attractive discounts to some customers but not to others. Price discrimination applies only to tangible goods of the same grade and quality, sold to customers who compete with each other. Furthermore, the difference in prices has to be proven to adversely affect that competition. Robinson-Patman was originally passed to protect small retailers unable to command the same discounts from food producers as their large chain-store competitors could; nearly all the defendants in Robinson-Patman cases are large companies.[31]

Robinson-Patman is bound to provoke an opinion from anyone who has ever en-countered it. Among other things, it has been called (1) the most basic pricing law the marketing executive must deal with, (2) one of the most confusing and complex laws ever enacted by Congress, and (3) completely ineffective in protecting anyone. The details of Robinson-Patman are indeed more than most marketers are trained to handle. One marketing professor's general advice seems particularly astute here: If you have a question about pricing and the law, seek the advice of your company's lawyers.[32]

DECEPTIVE PRICING    The Federal Trade Commission (FTC) has the authority to investigate and stop pricing schemes that it considers misleading; the term normally used in such cases is **deceptive pricing.** The problem in this case is not so much a pricing issue, but the way prices are promoted. The FTC's guidelines describe five situations considered deceptive pricing:

- *Comparison with former prices.* You can't legally claim that an item is on sale and compare the sale price to the former price unless (1) the old price was in effect for a substantial length of time and (2) you actively tried to sell the item at the old price. This prevents companies from artificially jacking prices up temporarily, just so they can turn around and put the item on "sale."

- *Comparison with prices that aren't really being charged.* Advertising that your prices are lower than "the competition's" (without naming specific competitors) is a great way to attract customers, but this is legal only if a substantial number of your competitors actually charge higher prices. If only a few specialty shops in an affluent part of town are charging higher prices, for instance, and everybody else charges prices similar to yours, then you can't claim to have prices lower than "the competition's." However, if you identify the competitive companies by name and make specific, head-to-head comparisons, you're on safe legal ground.

- *Comparison with suggested retail prices.* You also can't advertise that your retail price is below the manufacturer's suggested retail price unless some retailers actually charge the suggested price. For example, the FTC ordered Regina Corporation to stop providing retailers with suggested prices on its floor polishers and vacuum cleaners because retailers were using those suggested prices to make their actual selling prices seem like great deals (see Exhibit 11.9).

- *Bargains with strings attached.* Sales that promise two items for the price of one, a second item for 1 cent more, or other such promotions are legal only if the first item is sold at its normal price. If the price is cranked up just for such promotions, or if lower-quality products are substituted for either the first or second purchase, the FTC considers the pricing arrangement illegal.

- *Other misrepresentations.* The FTC continually tries to uncover pricing schemes that are misleading to customers. For example, it is illegal to advertise a price as a "wholesale price" unless it is in fact the price paid by retailers when they purchase the goods in question from wholesalers. Just because your price is sub-

**deceptive pricing**
Pricing and promotional tactics that disguise the true price customers must pay for a good or service

**Exhibit 11.9**
**ETHICS IN PRICING**
This ad demonstrates a common tactic in the magazine industry that some people might construe as misleading, even though the ad is honest in terms of the facts involved. The issue is the "Save 63%" offer. This sounds like a great bargain, but this is compared with the cost of buying 12 issues at the cover price. It is not a 63 percent discount off the normal subscription price. You would realize the promised savings only if you had planned to buy every issue from the newsstand and then decided to subscribe instead.

stantially lower than everybody else's doesn't qualify it for the wholesale price label. Other deceptive pricing schemes include (1) "limited-time offers" when the company has no intention of eventually raising the price and (2) low prices advertised for "seconds" if the products aren't clearly identified as being of lower quality.[33]

Laws against deceptive pricing are common throughout the world. Among other countries, Germany, France, Japan, Finland, New Zealand, Norway, Sweden, Switzerland, and the United Kingdom all have laws that regulate the promotion of prices. In many countries concern is growing about the way prices are advertised, so all marketers operating internationally must be aware of the price regulations of each country in which they do business.[34]

**dumping**

The combination of price discrimination and predatory pricing in international marketing situations; this occurs when a company tries to sell products below cost to customers in another country

DUMPING   A special case of international pricing occurs when a firm exporting its products to the United States is accused of both price discrimination and predatory pricing. The term **dumping** refers to the practice of selling imported goods at prices so low as to injure local competition; the price discrimination occurs because the supplier sells its products for different prices in various countries.[35] Dumping has been an issue in the semiconductor industry, for instance, as Japanese firms try to build market share in the United States. Of course, dumping isn't bad news for everybody; most customers are more than happy to buy dumped goods at attractive prices.

In addition to these four areas of explicit regulation, governments can exert their influence in less direct ways. For example, in response to growing consumer complaints about drug prices, Congress and President Bill Clinton pressured pharmaceutical manufacturers to keep prices in check. After a study found that the prices of some popular medicines more than doubled from 1987 to 1992—and up against the threat of government price controls—the manufacturers agreed to voluntary restraint.[36]

## CHANNEL EXPECTATIONS

The expectations of all the organizations in the marketing channel also place constraints on pricing. For instance, when a product moves from the producer to a wholesaler to a retailer, costs are incurred at each stage, and the final price has to be high enough to support those costs. In addition, depending on the type of organizations in a particular marketing channel, the final price also has to cover fees, commissions, and profits for each channel member. Various industries have evolved their own cost structures and expectations; when you enter these marketing channels, make your prices meet the needs of all the members in the channel.

Pricing through the distribution channel can be a delicate balancing act. Imagine a can of Dole pineapple you just bought from a neighborhood grocery store. At least three companies owned this can before you: Dole, a wholesaler, and the grocery store. Each of these companies makes a profit when it sells the pineapple. Dole wants to make a profit selling to the wholesaler, who wants to make a profit selling to a retail store, who wants to make a profit selling to you. These individual profit objectives can lead to pressure among the companies involved as each tries to buy low and sell high.

Denmark is one of many countries with strict laws concerning deceptive prices; before Danish retailers can say that a product is "on sale," they must be able to prove the product has been previously sold from the same location at a higher price.

## CUSTOMER DEMAND

Customer demand is obviously an important aspect of pricing. When Nintendo released its long-awaited Super Mario Brothers 3 video game cartridge, retail prices were as high as $70, which is anywhere from $20 to $40 higher than most Nintendo games. Even at that price, however, retailers still ran out of the game. Customers wanted that particular product, and they were apparently willing to pay almost any price to get it. Nintendo was aware of customer demand and, together with retailers, priced the game at a level they felt the market would support. When environ-

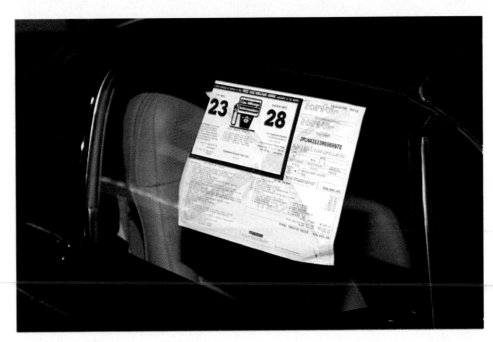

**Exhibit 11.10
PRICE INCREASES
IN RESPONSE TO
BUYER DEMAND**
If consumer demand is high
relative to product supply, car
dealers sometimes increase
prices beyond the suggested
retail price.

mental concerns cut the supply of logs from Pacific Northwest forests, lumber prices jumped 82 percent from September 1992 to March 1993.[37]

As customer demand grows or shrinks, prices often need to be adjusted. During the introduction stage, for instance, a price may be raised to temporarily increase profit. This is possible only if demand is significant, of course (see Exhibit 11.10). On the other hand, if people aren't exactly lining up in anticipation of your new product, you may have to lower prices initially to encourage people to try your product. Also, as new competitors enter the market or as fashions change, pricing can be adjusted to maintain desired sales levels. Sometimes temporary surges in customer demand prompt suppliers to raise prices dramatically; just ask anyone who has tried to get a hotel room in a city hosting the Super Bowl, a World's Fair, or some other event that stimulates increased demand for lodging.

## COMPETITION

As you might expect, competitive forces are usually a major pricing constraint, and the more emphasis customers put on price, the more powerful the competitive constraint becomes. For example, when students try to decide between two colleges, they might not put a lot of emphasis on price differences. However, when students' parents enter the discussion, chances are pretty good that competitive prices become an issue. From the marketer's perspective, then, the presence of price competition can place firm limits on the range of possible prices. However, remember that competition involves more than price. **Nonprice competition** refers to all the elements of competition other than price that companies can use to differentiate their products. Some of these attributes are quality, service, warranties, performance, and image.

For example, sellers of generic drugs face a significant nonprice competition challenge. Generic drugs are substitutes for brand name prescription drugs, and generics are usually much cheaper (anywhere from 50 to 80 percent cheaper). Pharmacists frequently have the option of offering customers either the name brand or the generic substitute, but a surprisingly low percentage of pharmacists typically offer the generic alternative. Researchers looked into the problem and learned that the customer-perceived risk from generic drugs far outweighed the price advantages. Even though the generics have been extensively tested and approved by the Food and Drug Administration, customers place a lot of importance on brand name. In the case of antibacterial drugs, for example, even though the brand name drug

**nonprice competition**
Competition that occurs on factors other than price, such as quality, image, convenience of distribution, and performance

Macrodantin is more than twice as expensive as the generic nitrofurantoin, over half the customers choose to stay with it.[38] It's crucial for generic drug marketers to understand the relatively low importance customers put on price before they attempt to define a marketing strategy; raising customer confidence would appear to be a quicker path to increased sales than lowering prices.

Price competition remains popular for many marketers for the simple reason that it is often easier to implement than nonprice competition. For instance, redesigning products to make them more competitive can take months or years, but in most cases, marketers can change prices as quickly as they can enter numbers in a computer.

As markets grow and mature, the nature of price competition frequently changes. For example, in the overnight delivery service business, prices were held fairly low for a period of time because a number of new competitors were jockeying for position and stimulating attractive price cuts. However, as the market matured and the big players (Federal Express, United Parcel Service, and Airborne Express) either bought up smaller competitors or drove them out, prices began to move up.[39] With fewer players in the market, competition started to look more oligopolistic, and the small number of suppliers remaining were less threatened and therefore less likely to keep prices low.

## ETHICS

Finally, ethical considerations play a role in the pricing decision. Although a number of unethical pricing moves are illegal and monitored by various government agencies, gray areas exist in which the ethical choice is left up to the marketer. In addition, the opportunities for illegal pricing outnumber the government watchdogs. Even if a company doesn't think it will get caught, it should still manage its business, including pricing, by acceptable standards of conduct.

Questionable pricing practices are not unheard of, however. For example, pricing in the travel industry is so complicated that even professional travel agents can't always figure out the true price customers have to pay. Moreover, airlines have been accused of advertising attractive low fares that had so many restrictions they were nearly impossible for any passenger to take advantage of. A more ethical approach might be to establish and advertise the prices that most people will actually end up paying.[40]

Another pricing tactic that raises eyebrows is highlighting an attractive price that might not tell the whole story. The car rental industry has been the target of acute criticisms in recent years. For example, various companies have been accused of quoting prices that don't mention severe restrictions, offering "special" rates to corporations that are actually higher than what people right off the street are paying, and selling collision insurance to people who don't need it. In some cases, customers are threatened with large blocks on their credit cards (which prevent them from using some of their available credit) if they don't buy the insurance. Industry leaders and law enforcement officials agree that it's time to clean up the industry, although not much has been done so far.[41]

## STEP 3: Establish Pricing Objectives

Price is an important component in the marketing mix, and companies have devised various strategies for taking advantage of price to help them pursue their marketing goals. Because the pricing objective has such a profound effect on the entire organization, the people responsible for establishing it must work closely with the other functional areas in the company to ensure a coordinated effort. For example, if the marketers at an automaker such as Hyundai attempt to grab market share with attractive prices, their counterparts in production need to be ready to build enough cars to support that strategy. On the other hand, marketers at Lamborghini and other premium car companies must maintain an image of exclusivity and quality, so they might be less concerned with the speed at which they produce cars.

They're more worried about building a car that will help them keep that premium image and that breathtaking price tag.

As you read about pricing objectives, keep in mind that even though the objectives are discussed individually, marketers often have more than one pricing objective and will seek to maintain balance between them. For instance, it's common to have both profit and sales volume objectives; the profit objective helps the company maintain its financial health, and the sales volume objective helps it maintain or increase market share. The five general categories of pricing objectives are profitability, sales, competition, positioning, and survival.

## PROFITABILITY OBJECTIVES

Pricing objectives are frequently expressed as some variation of profitability. For example, a firm can aim for a certain percentage profit, say 25 percent. This means that for every dollar of product sold, 75 cents will be consumed by design, production, marketing, and all other costs, leaving 25 cents for profit. The 25 percent figure is called the firm's **profit margin,** which is the ratio of profit to sales.

Another form of profitability objective is **return on investment (ROI),** which is the ratio of profit to the capital invested in the company. A related way to express profit is **return on equity,** which is the ratio of profit to the amount of equity held by the owners of the company. For instance, Alcoa's chief executive has set a goal of 15 percent return on equity for the big aluminum producer.[42]

American firms are frequently criticized for an unhealthy focus on short-term profits, and yet the very structure of American business often encourages it. All U.S. companies that sell shares of their stock to the public are required by the government to file quarterly reports listing sales and profit numbers. These short-term reports are often used to measure a manager's ability to run the firm. As a result, managers sometimes use pricing tactics and other marketing moves that make the profit numbers look as good as possible every quarter, even when those actions aren't in the companies' best long-term interest.

What is the driving force behind the short-term focus? Frequently mentioned are the stockholders with ownership in U.S. firms who want quick returns on their investments. They don't want to sit through months or years of low returns while the company invests in new technologies or new products. To make matters worse, the compensation plans for many executives are tied to quarterly performance, so they're motivated by short-term results themselves.[43] This is in sharp contrast to many Japanese managers and investors who tend to be satisfied with lower profit margins and longer periods of return.

## SALES OBJECTIVES

The second category of pricing objectives centers on a target level of sales. This is expressed either as an absolute number of products sold over some unit of time or as a percentage of market share. Companies are interested in market share because of the strong relationship between market share and profit. As seen in Exhibit 11.11, companies with large shares of their markets often enjoy higher levels of profit, although no guarantee exists. In addition to increasing profitability, dominant market share helps suppliers control distribution channels and product standards. For example, in the personal computer software market, Microsoft's market share is so great that it controls the standards for key aspects of product design.

Note that a change in sales and a change in market share don't necessarily go hand in hand. A company's sales may increase just because the market is growing, not because of any action on the company's part. For this reason, firms usually monitor both absolute sales levels and market share in order to chart their progress along both lines. A final note about market share: In many market segments, companies find it difficult to get an accurate measurement of either their market share or the overall size of the market. This is particularly true of segments that are too small to justify extensive tracking research, either by the companies themselves or

**profit margin**
The amount of profit left over after expenses have been accounted for, expressed as a percentage or revenue

**return on investment (ROI)**
A measure of profitability; specifically, the ratio of profits to overall investment

**return on equity**
A measure of profitability that is similar to ROI but indicates profit as a percentage of the owner's equity in the company

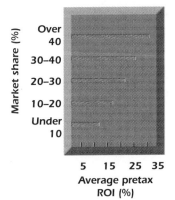

**Exhibit 11.11
THE RELATIONSHIP OF MARKET SHARE AND RETURN ON INVESTMENT**
A strong relationship exists between market share and return on investment as illustrated by these data from the PIMS program.

by outside research firms. For example, an independent gas station may not have access to precise market share data and will tend to rely on sales figures.

## COMPETITIVE OBJECTIVES

The third category of pricing objectives is setting prices in relation to those of the competitors. Toys 'R' Us founder Charles Lazarus uses a low-price strategy to keep competitors at bay, or in his words, Toys 'R' Us attempts to "sell at such low prices that no one will even try to compete." Every aspect of Toys 'R' Us is designed to help meet the objective of lower-than-everybody-else prices, from automated ordering systems to store locations (close enough to malls to catch traffic but not in malls where store space costs are steep).[44]

**price leadership**
The position in a given market held by the company that takes the lead in raising or lowering prices

Another aspect of competitive pricing is **price leadership,** which exists when one firm in an industry tends to influence the direction of prices. Such a firm is usually the first to raise or lower prices, and other companies in the industry follow suit in order to remain competitive. For example, Southwest Airlines, with its below-average cost structure, usually serves as the price leader in air travel markets in which it competes. Of course, price leadership can be an important factor in pricing only when a market has a dominant supplier and when customers are concerned about price.

## POSITIONING OBJECTIVES

In this category of pricing objectives, companies use price as a means of positioning their products in the minds of potential customers. High prices are associated with quality, prestige, or exclusivity, and companies use premium prices to foster those images. For instance, Tiffany & Company, the ever-so-pricey supplier of jewelry and other luxuries, realizes that any association with budget or bargain will hurt the image of the entire company. When Avon owned Tiffany (for a six-year period), it nearly destroyed the Tiffany brand by selling cheap merchandise that people just didn't associate with the high-prestige store. During Avon's last year of ownership, Tiffany lost millions. Today Tiffany is positioned back where it belongs, complete with a $7 million necklace in the entryway of its store on New York's Fifth Avenue, and the company is extremely profitable as a result.[45]

On the other hand, a company sometimes needs to lower prices in order to obtain a desired positioning. Apple Computer did this when it dropped the price of its biggest seller at the time, the Macintosh Plus. The company realized that many small-business owners perceived the Mac as an expensive machine that was suitable only for their larger, richer corporate cousins.[46]

Some marketers have recently experienced difficulty in maintaining a midrange position on price, and in response, some have developed separate product lines to address the upper and lower segments. Ramada now operates a low-end motel chain called Rodeway Inns and a more upscale chain called Renaissance. In the restaurant business, Marriott Corporation found that its three chains of casual restaurants, Bob's Big Boy, Allie's, and Wag's, weren't gracious enough to provide a nice dining atmosphere, but on the other hand, they weren't cheap enough to compete with fast-food restaurants. Marriott said it was "sandwiched in the middle" and decided to get out of the restaurant market.[47]

## SURVIVAL OBJECTIVES

The final class of pricing objective is simply survival. Firms that are in trouble will try to find whatever price points will pull in enough sales to keep the company operating. Survival pricing means that firms try to beat the prices of competitors, even if that means selling for no profit or for negative profit. For example, much of the U.S. steel-producing industry has been using this approach in recent years, as international competitors with lower costs and comparable quality have begun to capture more and more sales. Clearly, survival pricing should be adopted only as a temporary strategy, until the company is able to reduce its production costs or until competitors are forced to raise their prices.[48] Sustained survival pricing inevitably leads to financial collapse.

## A LOOK AHEAD

This chapter has addressed the first three stages of the pricing process: analyzing market conditions, identifying constraints, and establishing objectives. At this point, you have an idea of the amount of planning that goes into pricing. The remaining three stages—analyzing profitability, setting initial price levels, and adjusting and managing prices—are covered in Chapter 12. By the time you've finished these two chapters, you'll have a good understanding of the challenging, sometimes confusing, but always interesting pricing task that faces marketing professionals.

## SUMMARY OF LEARNING OBJECTIVES

**1. Explain the meaning of price and its role in the marketing mix.**

In its broadest sense, price encompasses everything that the buyer has to give up in order to obtain and use a product. Although price is primarily a financial measure, it also includes time, frustration, and so forth. The role of price in the marketing mix, and in the company's overall operation, is both important and influential. It affects products by setting limits on the investment that suppliers can make in designing, producing, and marketing products. For example, price interacts with promotion because both low and high prices are often used as the theme in promotional campaigns. Also, price affects distribution both in the cost of getting products to customers and in the cost and profit expectations of channel members. Setting the correct price can mean success or failure to a business. Setting prices too low prevents companies from generating all the profit they could. However, setting prices too high prevents companies from selling as many products as they could. Ranked by many as the second mix, pricing is a balancing act that successful marketers in any industry must master.

**2. Outline the pricing process, from analyzing market conditions to adjusting prices in response to dynamic marketplace conditions.**

The pricing process covers six general steps: (1) analyzing market conditions; (2) identifying constraints (which include cost, competition, customer demand, government regulations, channel expectations, and ethics); (3) establishing pricing objectives; (4) analyzing profit potential; (5) setting initial price levels; and (6) adjusting and managing prices in response to special situations and marketplace dynamics.

**3. Describe demand curves and elasticity and relate how marketers use these concepts to establish ranges of possible price points.**

The demand curve illustrates the relationship between customer demand and selling price. Marketers construct demand curves to get an idea of the demand they can expect at particular prices. Lowering prices doesn't always increase demand, so it's important to get some idea of how demand and price are related in each market segment. Elasticity, which measures this demand-price relationship, is computed by dividing the change in demand by the change in price. Marketers don't always have reliable elasticity data at their disposal, so judgment and experience are critical.

**4. List the primary aspects of price sensitivity and explain its importance to marketers.**

The most important aspects of price sensitivity include the perception of unique value, the awareness of substitutes, the difficulties of comparison, the total expenditure involved, a product's contribution to overall customer benefits, the effects of shared costs if the customer isn't fully responsible for the purchase price, the sunk investment effect that tends to make customers insensitive to price once they've invested significantly in one supplier, and the price-quality associations that can lead some customers to equate a higher price with higher quality. It's important to understand the individual components of price sensitivity because you don't always have reliable elasticity data to guide your decisions, and you'll often rely on judgment.

**5. Explain how to analyze competitors' pricing moves and compare the categories of competitive pricing strategies.**

You can start analyzing competitors' pricing moves by classifying their pricing behavior. Cooperative pricing occurs when the major sellers in a market avoid dragging down profit margins for the industry and tend to price at similar levels. Adaptive pricing is the response of smaller competitors who have no choice but to respond to pricing moves that affect them. Opportunistic pricing is used by competitors who are looking for ways to stay a step ahead of the market in terms of lower price. Finally, predatory pricing is used to inflict financial damage on competitors, although it is illegal if the intent is to drive competitors out of business. By placing a competitor in one of the categories, you'll have a better chance of understanding why it behaves as it does. Always look below the surface of competitive pricing behavior, and try to understand why various moves were made.

**6. Identify the constraints that affect pricing decisions and the effect that each constraint can have on the pricing process.**

The constraints that affect pricing decisions can be grouped into six areas. The first category is the cost required to design and produce products and then to get them to customers. Costs include a variety of elements, ranging from materials and labor to taxes and technology licensing fees. The second group includes government influences at both the state and federal levels. The major regulatory areas that affect pricing include price fixing, price discrimination, deceptive pricing, and predatory pricing. Third, the needs and expectations of the wholesalers, retailers, and others in the marketing channels place constraints on pricing, both in terms of price levels and in the way discounts and other pricing tasks are managed. The fourth constraint is customer de- mand, which affects both sales volume and price. Fifth, the presence of price competition can severely limit a company's pricing flexibility, and this is further influenced by the type of price competition in a given market. Sixth, ethics should always be a major consideration in pricing strategies and tactics. A number of pricing moves are definitely illegal, but even situations that are legal can be ethically unclear, and these are left up to the marketers making the pricing decisions.

**7. List the major pricing objectives and explain the purpose behind each type.**

The major pricing objectives can be divided into five categories. First, profitability objectives establish a target level of profit, expressed in profit margin, return on investment, or return on equity. Second, sales objectives aim for a certain level of sales volume, measured either in unit sales or in market share. Third, competitive objectives are focused on

---

# A CASE FOR CRITICAL THINKING

## Meeting a Marketing Challenge at Sears

Michael Bozic and his colleagues at Sears took a long, hard look at the market dynamics that were putting them in a tight squeeze: the changing nature of mall shopping with its increased emphasis on clothing, the growth of upscale department and specialty stores, the growth of both full-line and specialty discounters, and the growing frustration of customers with retailers' pricing schemes. Bozic knew that many of his competitors had already switched to some form of stable pricing, in which regular prices were lower with less emphasis on sales.

Thus, Sears decided to change its pricing strategy. In a move considered one of the most dramatic in the history of retailing, Sears stepped off the regular-price/sale-price roller coaster and announced "everyday low prices." For a 42-hour period starting at 6:00 P.M. on February 27, 1989, Sears closed all its stores to reprice the inventory. Out went regular prices and in came new low prices; some prices were cut as much as 50 percent.

However, Bozic knew it would take more than just low prices; changes in other areas were needed as well. For example, merchandise had to be jazzed up in several categories, particularly women's clothing, to pull in the people who had left in search of a little more style. Costs had to be cut, which Sears tried to do by simplifying its organizational structure and making its distribution system more efficient. Finally, Sears had to get the message of everyday low prices out to the millions of customers and potential customers that the big retailer desperately needed to pull in.

Sears got the message out in a big way indeed. During the week of February 27, it ran 700 television commercials, 1,300 radio spots, and full-page ads in more than 900 newspapers. It also sent 13 million catalog customers a new price list. In addition, ABC, NBC, CBS, and CNN featured the pricing change in their newscasts.

The country's reaction in February and March was encouraging. Local newspapers around the country carried photos of long lines forming outside Sears stores. Some people came out of curiosity; others were looking for big savings. People did start to spend more money at Sears. In March revenue was up nearly 10 percent over March 1988, and April was up almost 7 percent. Customers seemed to be pleased with the prices. Magazines and newspapers printed headlines such as "Sears Awakes with Vengeance" and "Sears' Legendary Move." It looked like the old giant had pulled it off.

However, the days of happy customers and breathless media attention didn't last long. Consider how the headlines changed in just over a year:

February 1989: "Sears Cutting Prices by as Much as 50% in a Shift of Strategy"
March: "Shoppers Line Up to Check Out New Low-Pricing Policy at Sears"
May: "Skeptics Seek More Evidence of Long-Term Turnaround"
June: "Consumers Are Confused by Sears' New Policy"
August: "Now Sears Has Everyday Low Profits, Too"
September: "Slow Start for Pricing Strategy"
January 1990: "Sears' Plan on the Ropes"
May: "Its Earnings Sagging, Sears Upgrades Line of Women's Apparel"

Clearly, something was going wrong with Sears's grand plan of everyday low prices. The company started running sales within a month of the new pricing announcement, maintaining prices that are at, above, or below those of the competition, depending on the circumstances. Fourth, positioning objectives try to use price to help position products. This is most commonly done at the two extremes: using a high price to position a product as exclusive and of high qual-

ity, or using a low price to position a product as the best available bargain. Fifth, basic survival pricing, can be a valid objective if it's temporary; pricing low enough to stay alive will lead to financial ruin if it forces you to sell at or below cost for a long period of time.

## KEY TERMS

cost of ownership (330)
deceptive pricing (345)
demand curve (335)
dumping (346)
elastic demand (336)
inelastic demand (336)
nonprice competition (347)

perfectly elastic demand (336)
perfectly inelastic demand (336)
predatory pricing (340)
price discrimination (344)
price elasticity of demand (335)

price fixing (343)
price leadership (350)
price sensitivity (335)
price war (341)
profit margin (349)
resale price maintenance (344)

return on equity (349)
return on investment (ROI) (349)
signaling (341)

which served to confuse customers. A study in June 1989 indicated that, in spite of $110 million in advertising, consumers weren't convinced about the new low prices. Over half the customers surveyed believed that Sears had full prices or full prices with frequent sales. This confusion began to show up at the cash register. In July, for instance, revenue was down 2.4 percent over the same month in 1988. Sears's sales in December were only 3.6 percent higher than in the previous December, whereas Kmart's sales were up 11.8 percent and Wal-Mart's were up 22 percent. In January 1990, *Advertising Age* announced that Sears's everyday-low-price plan was on the way out. A new strategy, relying less on low prices and more on upscale merchandising, would be phased in during 1990 because the 1989 plan just wasn't working. Michael Bozic didn't last much longer than the new pricing strategy. In August 1990 he was replaced by his manager, Ed Brennan, who stepped into Bozic's job to try to increase sales and bring costs under control. Brennan replaced himself in 1992 with department store veteran Arthur Martinez.

What happened to Sears? Once the largest retailer in the United States, Sears promised customers everyday low prices; why didn't they respond more enthusiastically? Two reasons seem to be the key. First, Sears just wasn't successful at convincing shoppers it was the place to go for great bargains. (New York's Attorney General wasn't convinced, either; he filed suit on December 21, 1989, claiming that the promise of lower prices was deceptive. The suit is still unresolved.) Second, by the end of 1989, it seemed that every store on the planet was promising everyday low prices or guaranteed lowest prices. Consumers began to go numb from the barrage of identical messages; one more message with the same theme simply fell on deaf ears.

Sears now finds itself in the mid-1990s as the nation's third-largest retailer, having been passed by both Wal-Mart and Kmart. Martinez's strategy is now to cede those gains to the two discounters and focus instead on midrange, mall-based competitors such as J. C. Penney and May Company. Efforts continue to position Sears as a desirable retailer of clothes, cosmetics, and other products that people typically shop for in malls. Profits have begun to improve, but only time will tell whether the once-mighty Sears can pull off the transition to twenty-first-century retailing.

**Your mission:** As chairman of Sears Merchandising Group, you're responsible for the overall operation of Sears's retailing efforts. You're well aware the big retailer is facing some tough times, and like all retailers these days, you're racking your brain to come up with the right pricing strategy. Consider the following scenarios, and decide how you will react.

1. You think it's time to try a policy of guaranteed lowest prices. The idea would be that customers have only to show an advertised price from any competitor, and your sales clerks are authorized to beat it on the spot. You realize that this might have some effect on the rest of the marketing mix and store operations overall. Which of the following scenarios is most likely?

a. It will force Sears to change its product offerings because consumers will buy only those goods that are cheaper at Sears than anywhere else.
b. It will have very little impact on anything because most consumers don't like to haggle about prices.
c. It will decrease customer service to the point that some customers quit shopping at Sears. Clerks will have to spend so much time handling the on-the-spot price changes that checkout time will increase, and clerks won't have time to help customers with other problems.

2. Competitive pricing doesn't seem to be working. You want to try to move Sears's image up and use price and the other marketing mix variables to accomplish this. It's easy enough to raise prices, but what do you do with the rest of the mix? Consider this question primarily in terms of women's clothing, which remains a point of weakness for your stores.

a. Obviously, you need the sort of merchandise that will support a higher price, such as designer labels and premium fabrics.
b. A classy promotional campaign is the answer. Get prominent actresses or other entertainers to be spokesmodels for your clothes. When consumers see such women in Sears clothes, they'll overcome that "Sears" problem and be willing to pay the higher prices.

## QUESTIONS FOR DISCUSSION

1. What are some of the elements of total cost of ownership for the following products?
   a. Home computer
   b. Car
   c. Haircut
   d. Air travel
2. How might price affect the marketing mix for these products?
   a. Pencils
   b. Diamond earrings sold by Tiffany & Company
3. Assume you're the marketing manager for K2 skis, and your company has just decided to shift its pricing objective from market share to premium positioning. How will this change the way you set prices?
4. Your restaurant is experiencing price and quality competition at both ends. Low-cost, family-oriented restaurants are taking away the budget-conscious eater, and an increasing number of expensive establishments are attracting the people who want an elegant night on the town. What should you do with your prices? Explain your answer.
5. Your manager asked you to submit a plan to increase sales revenues by charging consumers more for your paper products than you charge your organizational customers. How should you respond?

6. What is an example of a company in each of the following types of markets, and how does being in such a market affect its pricing?
   a. Monopoly
   b. Oligopoly
   c. Pure competition
   d. Monopolistic competition
7. What are some of the possible explanations for the nonlinearity of the demand curve in Exhibit 11.3?
8. You've just conducted a price study, and the data seem to imply that if you lower prices slightly, you'll see an increase in overall revenue. Before you make this move, what factors should you think about?
9. What sort of price sensitivity is represented by each of these purchase situations?
   a. A one-of-a-kind antique desk you just discovered in a shop in London
   b. Conflicting investment advice from two financial advisers
   c. The decision whether to buy a new car or to pour another $500 into the one you own, on which you've already spent $2,000 in repairs
   d. Your choice of colleges when a rich aunt has agreed to pay 90 percent of your costs, regardless of which school you pick

c. Some combination of (a) and (b) is required, along with better merchandise and some sort of image surgery.

3. Consider the following dilemma. Several of your competitors in the power tool segment have dropped prices on table saws by removing important accessories from the standard price and charging extra for each one. This allows them to advertise very attractive prices for the basic saw; in fact, they're undercutting the price on your best-selling saw by 25 percent. However, one of the better-known competitors, Delta, has decided not to join in with this new pricing strategy. Half your staff wants to switch to the new pricing tactic, but the other half considers it unethical and says you should emulate Delta. Unfortunately, Delta hasn't been noticeably successful so far. What should you do?

   a. The new pricing tactic isn't illegal; thus, Sears has no reason to avoid it.
   b. You should stay on the high road; stick with your current tactics.
   c. When you promote your saw, point out that the price is for a complete package, and encourage consumers to take a close look at what the competition is really offering.

4. You've decided that you can't drop your prices far enough to compete primarily on price. You ask your staff to come up with three proposals for a strategy based more on non-price competition. Take a look at these proposals and decide which one makes the most sense.

   a. Borrow a page from the Nordstrom manual and provide superb customer service. Provide personal shoppers, no-hassle returns, free delivery, and whatever else you can do to make shopping at Sears more enjoyable. Keep prices as low as possible, however.
   b. Make the same customer service changes as in (a), but raise prices high enough to cover the additional cost of providing these services.
   c. Assess the entire inventory and drop your low-end, low-cost products.

## SPECIAL PROJECT

Sears's top management has decided to add motorcycles to the company's product offering. Competition is fierce in this market, and most firms are scraping along with low profit margins. Management wants to add motorcycles because they make a good strategic fit with the rest of Sears's sporting goods, but they're not sure what sort of pricing objective the company could pursue. They ask you to consider a profit margin objective, a market share objective, and a premium positioning objective. You respond that more data are required. Briefly list the type of data necessary to evaluate the three potential objectives you've been given.[49]

---

10. Assume that you work for Ford and that General Motors recently announced some unsettling news at a press conference. Your longtime competitor claims that its new models in the Saturn line have achieved such a level of assembly automation that the company can afford to sell them at prices 10 percent below the prices of comparable cars on the market today. What are some of the possible messages that GM is trying to send you?

---

## SHARPEN YOUR MARKETING SKILLS

Tired of reading this book? Good. Your next assignment is to go out and sell it to somebody. Actually, you're just going to ask people whether they want to buy it. The object is to build a simple demand curve for your textbook. Team up with three or four other people so that you can spread out the interviewing task. Ask 24 people whether they would buy your book. Divide your subjects into four groups of six people. Ask the first group whether they would buy it at $50, the second group at $40, the third group at $30, and the fourth group at $20. For example, you might end up with numbers like these:

| Price | People Who Said They Would Buy |
|-------|-------------------------------|
| $50 | 3 |
| $40 | 2 |
| $30 | 5 |
| $20 | 6 |

When you're finished, plot your data on a simple graph (a pencil sketch is fine). Show the price points along one axis and the number of respondents who said they'd buy along the other axis. What does your demand curve look like?

**Decision:** Is the demand for this textbook elastic or inelastic? How much money would you make if you could sell the quantity indicated at the $50 price? At the $20 price? Is the demand curve linear or nonlinear? What are the weaknesses of the research technique you just used?

**Communication:** In a memo no longer than one-half page, explain the research you did and the strengths and weaknesses of this approach to measuring price sensitivity.

# VIDEO CASE

## Are You Paying a Fair Price for College Textbooks?

Are textbook publishers and college bookstores getting rich at your expense? It seems that way when you spend $250 or more on texts each year. Fifteen years ago, one anatomy and physiology text carried a $16.50 price tag; today, the updated version of that same book sells for $47.95. That's an increase of nearly 200 percent. However, inflation increased only 120 percent over the same 15 years, which raises a tough question: What are publishers and college bookstores doing with textbook prices?

Publishers and college bookstores have different perspectives on textbook pricing. First, look at textbook pricing from the publishers' viewpoint. They must pay the author; edit the manuscript; pay for the manuscript to be reviewed; design and illustrate the book; then typeset, proofread, print, and bind the book. To market the text, the publisher sends salespeople out to meet with faculty members, mails brochures, displays texts at academic conventions, and advertises in academic journals. Tack on the administrative costs to manage the whole project, and the result is a significant investment in just one textbook.

Although publishers can easily determine their costs, analyzing market conditions is trickier. When college enrollment swells, as it did during the 1970s, textbook demand also rises. However, when enrollment plateaus, as it did during the 1980s, demand stagnates. Moreover, every book is a gamble because the publisher cannot estimate demand until instructors have seen the book and have determined whether it meets their requirements.

From the bookstores' perspective, the process can be risky as well. For example, instructors sometimes select a book too late to have the bookstore stock it in time. When the books finally come in, students may have bought elsewhere.

College bookstores traditionally order texts from publishers at a discount of 20 percent off the suggested retail price. But the bookstores' costs for staff, utilities, and other overhead keep rising, so maintaining profitability is a struggle. Plus students resent shelling out higher prices for new texts when they have shelves of texts from prior terms. These factors gave bookstores an opportunity to start a brisk trade in used textbooks.

Today, used texts are a big business. Bookstores buy texts back at 25 to 50 percent of the original price and then resell for as much as 75 percent of list. Even some national companies specialize in marketing used texts. Naturally, publishers are concerned, because demand for used books reduces demand for new books. Therefore some publishers now discount their new texts by 23 or 24 percent, giving bookstores the choice of higher profits or lower prices. And a growing movement away from suggested retail prices allows bookstores to set prices based on profitability goals, market conditions, and other factors.

You've seen the pricing dilemma from the point of view of the publisher and the bookstore. But as a consumer, all you really care about is the price. Or do you? For example, the costs of developing these video cases and having access to the videotapes were factored into the price of this textbook. Of course, videos are an entertaining way to bring education to life. Rather than requiring you to buy a text or watch a video, your instructor could have sent you to the library to learn about marketing. However, to get the equivalent amount of information found in an average text, you'd have to wade through hundreds or thousands of magazines and newspaper articles and hundreds of books. By saving you time and trouble, a textbook is an efficient, one-stop guide to the subject.

1. College bookstores that give their profits to the college administration to defray other expenses sometimes face a pricing dilemma when deciding what to charge for textbooks. Should they put a high price tag on textbooks so that they can raise as much money as possible for the college, or should they charge a lower price so that students get a break even though the college receives less money because profits are lower?

2. Suppose you're a textbook publisher introducing a marketing text with new features not found in competing texts. Because numerous marketing textbooks are available, would it be reasonable for you to compete on the basis of price, or would you do better to use nonprice competition strategies?

3. Imagine you're the manager of an independent college bookstore and you learn that the giant book retailer Barnes & Noble plans to blanket your area with a direct-mail and telemarketing campaign offering new textbooks by mail at discount prices. Should you promote your bookstore's nonprice advantages, such as the timeliness of having textbooks and study guides immediately and the availability of used texts at reasonable prices? Or should you match the low discount prices offered by Barnes & Noble to avoid losing sales, even if this means cutting back on customer service?

Companies use the price element to accomplish more than just generating income. Find an article about a company that used some aspect of pricing to accomplish one of the following marketing objectives:

- Achieve a desired position in the market
- Attack a competitor
- Fix a problem in the distribution channel
- Reach new customers
- Reduce demand for a product
- Increase acceptance or trial use of a new product

After you've read the article, answer as many of the following questions as you can.

1. How did the company use the price element? How did this move differ from the company's normal pricing policy?
2. What effect did this move have on the company's financial position? Did the company think the move was a success or a failure from a profit perspective?
3. Why did the company use price to accomplish this objective, rather than one of the other elements in the marketing mix? How were the other elements used?

# 12

# Pricing Management

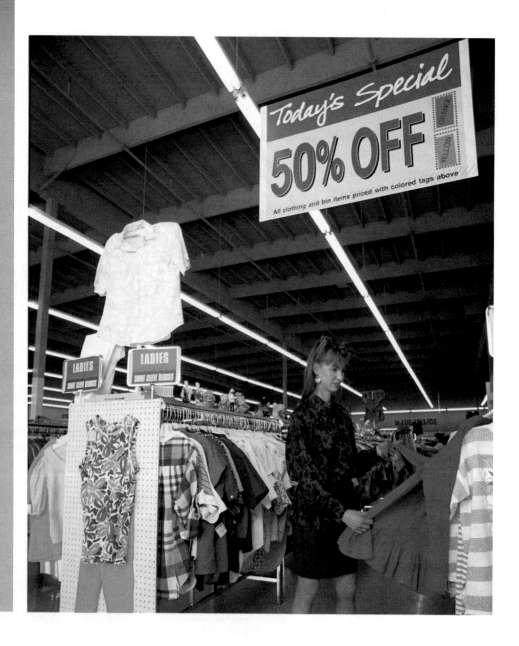

## Flying through a Competitive Storm with Innovative Pricing

What a nice, comfortable business running an airline used to be. The Civil Aeronautics Board (CAB), an agency of the federal government, decided which airlines would be in the air and where they would fly (including routes the government said needed service). Airlines enjoyed healthy profits and healthy salaries; they were assured of a stable marketplace and steady incomes.

The flying public, however, didn't feel very healthy at all; it was paying sky-high prices for tickets. Therefore, the government decided to come to the public's rescue. As part of the wave of deregulation that washed over U.S. industries in the 1970s and 1980s, the cozy world of the airlines started to crumble. The 1978 Airline Deregulation Act gave the operators more freedom to choose when and where they wanted to fly. By December 31, 1982, the government had also phased out controls on ticket prices.

The airlines were forced to compete, and compete they did. In the 10 years following deregulation, more than 100 new airlines were started. The number of passenger-miles certainly increased during that time, but not fast enough to support that many airline companies. The result was inevitable: mergers, bankruptcies, and for the survivors, price wars.

Both established companies and start-ups knew the public was hungry for affordable air travel. The growing number of competitors started to pull prices down as new low-fare operators began to carve out market share. The industry was unaccustomed to competing on price (or much else, for that matter), and profits were squeezed in major ways.

This was the situation facing Robert Crandall, CEO of American Airlines. First, he had to keep his company's planes as full as possible. With the number of planes increasing faster than the number of passengers, airline operators were particularly worried about getting enough passengers to make each flight profitable. Whether an American plane flies with 300 passengers or 3, the flights cost essentially the same to operate. Each of Crandall's flights has a minimum passenger load below which it loses money.

His second challenge was to shift some of the demand to off-peak travel times. A problem related to keeping the airplanes full is trying to balance the load on his people and equipment. If all American's customers wanted to leave Dallas at 8:00 A.M. and return at 6:00 P.M., there would be a horrible crunch at those times, while planes would sit idle the rest of the day. Crandall had to find ways to convince people to spread their arrival and departure times throughout the day and evening.

Third, Crandall had to figure out how to compete with the low-fare airlines such as Southwest Airlines, one of the few carriers making much money in the 1990s. The well-established airlines also had well-established overhead costs, and they found it difficult to lower prices to compete.

Fourth, Crandall had to minimize defections from high-fare to low-fare tickets. One way to compete on price while staying profitable was to offer some of the tickets at higher prices and some at lower prices. However, if too many customers switched from the high-fare to low-fare seats, profits would slip. On the other hand, if too many people were enticed to upgrade from coach to business, business class might get overcrowded and lose its appeal to the people who traditionally buy those tickets.

What sort of price structure and pricing management system could possibly help American fly through this storm? How can Robert Crandall keep the planes full without destroying profits? How can his company survive the nonstop price pressure in the air travel industry?[1]

# CHAPTER OVERVIEW

For American Airlines and its competitors in the air travel industry, careful attention to price is vital to success. Chapter 11 discussed the planning aspects of pricing: analyzing market conditions, identifying constraints, and establishing the pricing objective. These are the first three steps of the pricing process. This chapter continues the discussion of pricing by covering the tactical aspects of price management, which make up the last three steps of the process: analyzing profit potential, setting initial prices, and adjusting and managing prices as necessary. This chapter also addresses some special pricing issues, including competitive bidding, international pricing, the special pricing challenges faced by nonprofit organizations, and price testing.

# PRICING TACTICS

Once you've analyzed the market's perception of price and the relationship between price and demand, the next step is to analyze costs. These two variables—the price you charge customers and the cost of making and marketing products—determine your company's profit. This simple but all-important relationship is expressed by the *profit equation*:

$$\text{Profit} = \text{revenue} - \text{cost}$$

Revenue is equal to price times the number of products you sell, and cost is the sum of all the expenses it takes to design, manufacture, and market your products. Chapter 11 showed you how to estimate revenue based on price sensitivity, and the following section completes the picture by including cost.

## STEP 4: Analyze Profit Potential

In order to analyze profit potential, marketers estimate profit by combining price sensitivity data with cost data. In Chapter 11, you arrived at a demand curve (either through quantitative measurement or through qualitative judgment), which gave you some idea of the prices that would lead to certain sales volumes. The next step was to calculate total revenue by multiplying the price and demand figures at each point in the curve. Now, bring cost into the picture, which will lead you to profit. For many companies, cost is a complex topic that requires more thought than you might expect.

COST ANALYSIS

To create goods and services and then deliver them to customers, businesses have to spend a certain amount of money (see Exhibit 12.1). These expenses are often surprisingly complicated, particularly in large organizations, with products that require a complex manufacturing process, and with some services. For example, when a company sets out to build a personal computer, the costs of purchasing parts and paying employees to assemble the computers are obvious. Other expenses include real estate payments, taxes, payments on the machinery and equipment needed for assembly, and a variety of other overhead costs that range from managers' salaries to landscaping services.

Look outside the factory when you're analyzing costs. This is especially true for complicated industrial products that require a lot of customer support. Also, some customers cost more to serve. For example, an aggressive customer who demands frequent attention and special consideration costs more to serve than a passive customer who buys your products quietly and then uses them in peace.[2]

The careful management of costs can give a company powerful competitive advantages. For example, Houston-based Southwest Airlines has a cost structure much lower than average for the airline industry. At a time when the industry average was 7.5 cents per passenger-mile, for example, Southwest could boast a much leaner 5.8 cents per passenger-mile. When somebody wants to get in a fare war, Southwest just smiles and waits until the competitor is forced to give up. Prices are so low that Chairman Herb Kelleher says that in many cases his main competition isn't other airlines, but automobile travel.[3] Manufacturers can keep their costs under control by picking a target cost for each new product before development begins, a technique commonly used by such Japanese firms as Sharp and Toyota. By designing to meet a cost goal, rather than designing first and analyzing costs later, you can build in a competitive advantage when you set your prices.[4]

To get a better handle on their costs, companies divide them into two categories. The first category, **fixed costs,** includes those expenses that remain constant regardless of the number of products produced. For example, whether a PolyGram compact disk factory produces 1 CD or 1,000,000 CDs a month, the company makes the same monthly payment for the property the factory is sitting on. To help evaluate the costs of individual products, businesses often calculate the **average fixed**

**fixed costs**
The portion of a company's production and marketing costs that remains constant regardless of the level of production

**average fixed cost**
The amount of fixed cost attributed to each unit produced; equal to total fixed costs divided by the number of units

| AT THE FACTORY | | AT NIKE | | AT THE RETAILER | |
|---|---|---|---|---|---|
| Labor | $ 2.25 | Payment to factory | $17.50 | Payment to Nike | $32.50 |
| Materials | 4.95 | Sales and administration | 4.59 | Costs (salaries,leases,etc.) and profit | 32.50 |
| Overhead | 1.80 | Advertising and endorsements | 2.93 | | |
| Other expenses and net income | 8.50 | Research and development | 2.00 | | |
| | | Taxes | 1.82 | | |
| | | Interest payments | 0.33 | | |
| | | Net income | 3.33 | | |
| **TOTAL** | **$17.50** | **TOTAL** | **$32.50** | **TOTAL** | **$65.00** |

**Exhibit 12.1**
**WHERE DO COSTS COME FROM?**
The price you pay for a pair of Nikes has to cover costs and profits for several business entities. This exhibit shows you how the costs add up, from the factories in Asia, to Nike, and on to the retailer. (The retail price used here, $65, is the average retail price of Nike shoes in the United States.)

**variable costs**
The portion of a company's production and marketing costs that are dependent on the level of production

**average variable cost**
The amount of variable cost attributed to each unit produced; equal to variable costs divided by the number of units

**average total cost**
The sum of average total and average variable costs; represents the average expenses required to make one unit

**total cost**
The sum of variable costs and fixed costs; represents all the expenses required to make a specified number of units

**marginal cost**
The expense required to produce one more unit; the incremental cost of increasing production by one unit

**cost,** which is total fixed costs divided by the number of units produced. For instance, if PolyGram's monthly fixed costs are $200,000 and it produces 400,000 CDs in August, the average fixed cost for that month is $200,000/400,000, or 50 cents per disk.

The second category is **variable costs,** costs that change as production quantities change. In PolyGram's case, the plastic used in the disks, the artists' royalties, some of the energy used in the production process, and possibly some of the labor costs are examples of variable costs. For instance, some electricity is used for heating and lighting, which will remain constant regardless of production quantity. This part of the electric bill would be a fixed cost. However, part of the factory's electricity will be used for pressing machines, labeling machines, and other equipment that is used to produce the disks. As more disks are produced, more electricity will be consumed; this portion of the electric bill, then, is a variable cost. As with fixed costs, the **average variable cost** is computed by dividing the total variable costs by the number of units produced.

The sum of average fixed and average variable costs is called **average total cost,** and it represents the average cost of making one unit. **Total cost,** then, is equal to average total cost multiplied by quantity. The equations for these cost variables are as follows:

$$\text{Average fixed cost} = \frac{\text{fixed costs}}{\text{number of units produced}}$$

$$\text{Average variable cost} = \frac{\text{variable costs}}{\text{number of units produced}}$$

$$\text{Average total cost} = \text{average fixed cost} + \text{average variable cost}$$

$$\text{Total cost} = \text{average total cost} \times \text{number of units produced}$$

The final cost variable to be familiar with is **marginal cost,** which is the incremental total cost incurred to produce one more unit. Marginal cost becomes an important figure when you're trying to determine the most profitable number of products to produce, as you'll see in the following discussion.

The hypothetical data for a compact disk manufacturer in Exhibit 12.2 show all these cost figures. Exhibits 12.3 and 12.4 provide graphs of these data to give you a visual feel for this example of cost analysis. Exhibit 12.3 shows the average cost data, based on a fixed cost of $5. (Real fixed costs will be in the thousands or millions of dollars, of course.) You can see how the average fixed cost quickly drops as quantity increases. The average variable cost data in this example were chosen to illustrate two common effects of variable costs. First, the average variable cost

**Exhibit 12.2   COST DATA FOR COMPACT DISK MANUFACTURER**

| Quantity Produced | Fixed Cost | Average Fixed Cost | Average Variable Cost | Average Total Cost | Total Cost | Marginal Cost |
|---|---|---|---|---|---|---|
| 1 | 5.00 | 5.00 | 15.00 | 20.00 | 20.00 | — |
| 2 | 5.00 | 2.50 | 14.00 | 16.50 | 33.00 | 13.00 |
| 3 | 5.00 | 1.67 | 13.00 | 14.67 | 44.00 | 11.00 |
| 4 | 5.00 | 1.25 | 12.00 | 13.25 | 53.00 | 9.00 |
| 5 | 5.00 | 1.00 | 11.00 | 12.00 | 60.00 | 7.00 |
| 6 | 5.00 | 0.83 | 10.00 | 10.83 | 65.00 | 5.00 |
| 7 | 5.00 | 0.71 | 9.00 | 9.71 | 68.00 | 3.00 |
| 8 | 5.00 | 0.63 | 10.00 | 10.63 | 85.00 | 17.00 |
| 9 | 5.00 | 0.56 | 11.00 | 11.56 | 104.00 | 19.00 |
| 10 | 5.00 | 0.50 | 12.00 | 12.50 | 125.00 | 21.00 |

Manufacturers need data like these to analyze their costs and predict potential profit; these hypothetical numbers were used to generate the graph in Exhibits 12.3 and 12.4. (All costs are in dollars.)

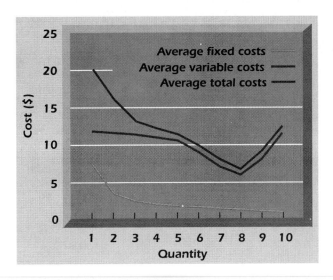

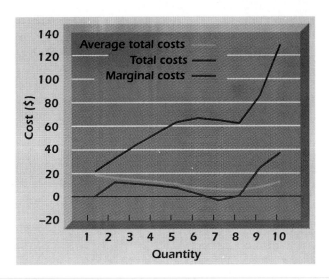

decreases from 1 through 8 units (which could be the result of quantity discounts the company received on the plastic, for instance). But then average variable costs increase from 8 to 10 units (which might, for example, represent the extra expense of having to pay overtime wages to get these additional units produced). Exhibit 12.4 continues the analysis of these data, showing the total cost and the marginal cost. (The average total cost line is repeated in this graph to help you establish the relationship of average total cost, total cost, and marginal cost. Remember, these are the same average total cost data shown in Exhibit 12.3, but the vertical scale has been expanded to show the total cost lines.) Marginal cost is of particular interest here because it is the basis of marginal analysis, a common technique for profit analysis.

## MARGINAL ANALYSIS

The technique of **marginal analysis** identifies profit potential by comparing marginal cost with **marginal revenue,** which is the additional revenue generated by the sale of one more unit. The concept of marginal analysis is quite simple: You get maximum profit when marginal cost equals marginal revenue. This can be demonstrated for the compact disk manufacturer. First, assume that the demand curve for these disks looks like the one shown in Exhibit 12.5. Then take a look at the mar-

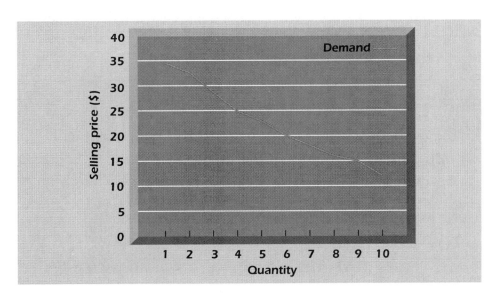

**Exhibit 12.3 (Left)
AVERAGE COSTS FOR
COMPACT DISK PLANT**
This graph shows how quickly average fixed costs can decrease with increased volume, whereas average variable costs may rise with increased volume.

**Exhibit 12.4 (Right)
MARGINAL COSTS
FOR COMPACT
DISK PLANT**
Based on the cost data from Exhibit 12.2, this graph shows the relationship of average total costs, total costs, and marginal costs.

**marginal analysis**
A method of cost analysis that identifies maximum potential profit by showing when marginal cost is equal to marginal revenue

**marginal revenue**
The revenue generated by selling one additional unit; this figure is used in marginal analysis to help identify maximum potential profit

**Exhibit 12.5
DEMAND CURVE FOR
COMPACT DISKS**
After you've calculated the most profitable level of demand, you can use a demand curve like this one to identify the appropriate price.

### Exhibit 12.6   MARGINAL REVENUE FOR COMPACT DISKS

| Selling Price | Total Revenue | Marginal Revenue | Profit per Unit | Total Profit |
|---|---|---|---|---|
| 35 | 35.00 | 0 | 14.60 | 14.6 |
| 33 | 66.00 | 31 | 16.80 | 33.6 |
| 29 | 87.00 | 21 | 14.33 | 43 |
| 25 | 100.00 | 13 | 11.50 | 46 |
| 23 | 115.00 | 15 | 10.40 | 52 |
| 20 | 120.00 | 5 | 9.17 | 55 |
| 18 | 126.00 | 6 | 8.86 | 62 |
| 16 | 128.00 | 2 | 8.00 | 64 |
| 15 | 135.00 | 7 | 5.11 | 46 |
| 12 | 120.00 | –15 | –0.80 | –8 |

These data show the marginal revenue and total profit for the compact disk manufacturer, and they are used to generate the graph in Exhibit 12.7.

ginal cost, marginal revenue, and total profit in Exhibits 12.6 (data) and 12.7 (curves). You can see that profit is indeed maximized when marginal cost and marginal revenue are equal. Below this point, each additional dollar spent generates more than one dollar in revenue, so the marketer should keep on spending. After the point at which marginal cost and marginal revenue are equal, however, each additional dollar spent yields less than a dollar of revenue. By looking back at the demand curve in Exhibit 12.5, you can get the optimum price: $16. With this set of data, then, $16 is the price that should yield maximum profit.

Marginal analysis has some limitations. First, as stated in Chapter 11, demand curves are not always available, and even when they are, you can't always have complete confidence in their validity. Second, the necessary cost variables aren't always available in the right format. For example, let's say your marketing department provides technical assistance to field salespeople who call in for help on your ten products. To accurately perform marginal analysis on each of these, monitor the time spent by the technical assistance people and divide it among the ten products. Finally, marginal analysis is sometimes difficult to perform on new products that you haven't yet manufactured at full capacity because you haven't confirmed the necessary cost variables.

**breakeven analysis**
A profit analysis technique that identifies the sales volume at which total cost is equal to total revenue; you'll make a profit if sales exceed this level and suffer a loss if they don't reach this level

## BREAKEVEN ANALYSIS

Another important technique for profit analysis is **breakeven analysis,** which shows the minimum number of units that must be sold at a given price for the company to break even. "Breaking even" means that the company recoups all its costs

**Exhibit 12.7
MARGINAL ANALYSIS
OF COMPACT
DISK PRICES**
Here is a graphic presentation of the marginal revenue data from Exhibit 12.6.

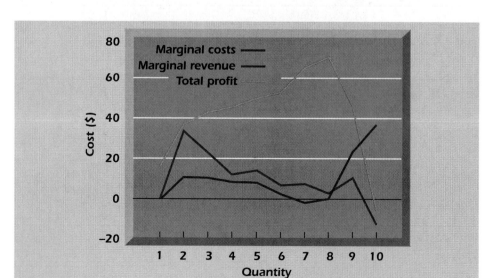

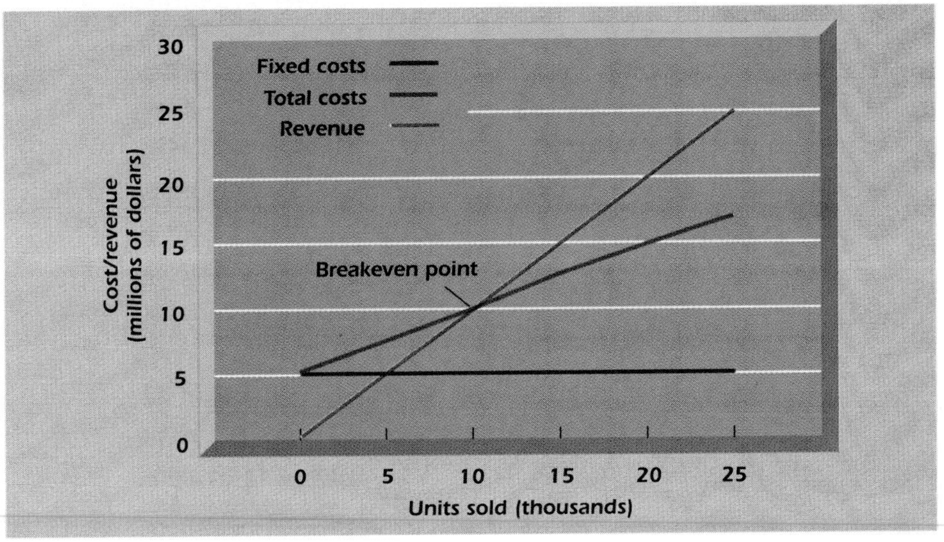

30

25

20

Cost/revenue
(millions of dollars)

15

10

5

0

Fixed costs ▬▬▬
Total costs ▬▬▬
Revenue ▬▬▬

Breakeven point

0    5    10    15    20    25

Units sold (thousands)

**Exhibit 12.8
BREAKEVEN
ANALYSIS FOR
TUXEDOS**
Breakeven analysis shows the
sales level at which revenue
equals total costs; sales above
that level will result in profit,
whereas sales below it will result in a loss.

but doesn't earn any profit. The sales level required to break even is called the
**breakeven point.** If sales are below the breakeven point, the company will operate at a loss. In particular, new-product forecasting is often something of a guess-
ing game, and breakeven analysis helps by telling you the minimum number you
will need to sell.

**breakeven point**
The sales volume at which a
company breaks even

Breakeven analysis plots the total cost line against the revenue curve, as seen in
Exhibit 12.8, for a hypothetical tuxedo business. Here are the data used for this
analysis:

Price: $1,000
Fixed costs: $5,000,000
Average variable cost: $500 (assumed to be the same for all levels of demand)

The point at which the two intersect is the breakeven point, identifying the number
of tuxedos that must be sold to break even (10,000 units in this case). You can also
compute the breakeven point directly, without building a graph:

$$\text{Breakeven point} = \frac{\text{total fixed costs}}{\text{price} - \text{average variable costs}}$$

So for this example:

$$\text{Breakeven point} = \frac{\$5,000,000}{\$1,000 - \$500}$$

$$= \frac{\$5,000,000}{\$500} = 10,000 \text{ tuxedos}$$

Breakeven analysis involves some interesting variations, including figuring in a desired profit amount before computing the breakeven point and calculating the market share required to break even.[5] For example, to achieve a desired profit of
$750,000 for your tuxedo business, the breakeven point would have to move up to
11,500 units:

$$\text{Breakeven point} = \frac{\$5,750,000}{\$500} = 11,500 \text{ tuxedos}$$

Conversely, if you wanted to stick with a forecast of 10,000 units and determine how
low to drive variable costs in order to achieve that same profit of $750,000, you'd
first figure that your per unit profit would be $75 (that is, $750,000/10,000). You
could then include that $75 amount in the denominator of the equation, and you
would discover that your average variable cost must drop to $425:

$$\text{Breakeven point} = \frac{\$5,000,000}{\$500} = \frac{\$5,000,000}{\$75 + \$425} = 10,000$$

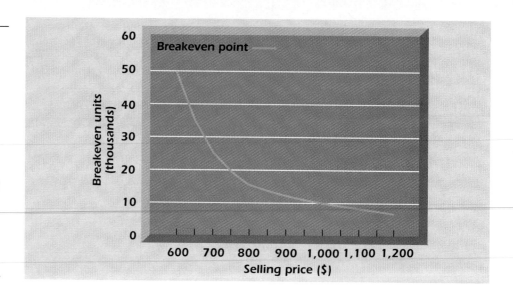

**Exhibit 12.9**
**EFFECT OF PRICE ON**
**BREAKEVEN POINT**
Selling price dramatically affects the breakeven point; it doesn't take much of a discount to double or triple the sales required to break even.

Breakeven analysis highlights the effect that selling price has on profitability. Assume your tuxedo business got into a price war with the competition. You believe that you must also drop your prices, but you're not sure what effect this will have on your ability to earn a profit. The effect is dramatic, as illustrated in Exhibit 12.9. For example, dropping the price just 25 percent, to $750, *doubles* the breakeven point. You'd have to sell twice as many tuxes at the lower price just to break even. A 40 percent price cut, to $600, raises the breakeven point to 50,000 units.

You can see that breakeven analysis provides an important data point, but make sure you don't fall into the trap of using it to forecast sales. It doesn't tell you how many units you *will* sell; it tells you only how many you *need* to sell at a given price to start turning a profit. Furthermore, breakeven analysis often simplifies the cost picture as well. Fixed costs aren't always really fixed. If you increase the production in your skateboard factory from 100 to 1,000 boards a month, you may have to add more machinery and factory space. This is a fixed cost that wouldn't show up in simple breakeven analysis. To make your analysis more accurate, include a true picture of these "semifixed" costs.[6]

With an understanding of costs and profit potential, you're ready to set prices. This is done in the final two steps of the pricing process: determining initial price levels and making adjustments as necessary.

## STEP 5: Determine Initial Price Levels

Marketers have developed quite an array of pricing techniques to help set initial price levels. These fall into three categories: demand-based, cost-based, and competition-based. Now you're probably thinking that isolating the elements of demand, cost, and competition in the pricing decision is a mistake, and you're right. The most effective pricing policies take all three into account. As you study each of the following techniques, keep in mind this need for an integrated approach to setting prices. Also, remember that whatever combination of techniques you choose, your pricing policy relates directly to your pricing objectives.

DEMAND-BASED PRICING TECHNIQUES

The first group of price-setting techniques is based primarily on an analysis of customer perceptions and needs. These techniques are considered demand-based because some aspect of customer demand is the theme behind each one. Marketers often try to base prices on the value that customers place on products. If you think it's worth $19 to have someone else get filthy changing the oil in your car, then someone could charge you $19 for the service. Demand pricing is especially powerful when a company's product is perceived by customers to have greater value than alternatives. Also, this approach is most achievable when customers are less sensitive to price, either because they perceive the value to be unique or because they aren't aware of alternatives. Consider this comment from a customer who had just paid $22 and $28 for one-day passes to Walt Disney World: "Disney World could probably get away with charging even more—$30, $40, even $50 a day. People might complain, but they'll pay for it. They're over a barrel." The customer was right on the money, so to speak. Several years later, one-day passes rose to $30 and $37. If you want to go to Disney World, you don't have many alternatives, and although this customer clearly wasn't crazy about the prices, he offered a classic case of demand-based pricing. In fact, the revenue pulled in at Disney's theme parks increased nearly 75 percent in a recent three-year period during which attendance increased only about 25 percent (see Exhibit 12.10). Disney realized that it was underpricing its product relative to the value that people placed on it, so it eventually raised prices.[7]

How will buyers react if you try to charge as much as the market will bear, even if that puts buyers in a financial bind? Economists suggest that buyers will eventually come back to punish companies that tried to take advantage of them. When Hurricane Andrew devastated parts of South Florida in 1992, sheets of plywood became precious, as home and business owners needed them to patch over damaged walls and roofs. Demand-based pricing would tell lumber stores to raise prices as high as possible. However, Home Depot, the largest building supplies retailer in the region, teamed up with manufacturer Georgia Pacific to *lower* prices after the storm. Their theory was that people will remember—both the companies that gouged them and the companies that tried to cut them a little slack.[8]

VALUE PRICING   Strong price competition hit many industries in the early 1990s, and the term **value pricing** has been applied to any pricing strategy that lowers prices while maintaining perceived value. In the fast-food market, Taco Bell started the revolution by dropping prices to as low as 39 cents, a move that triggered value pricing across the industry. This phenomenon is more than an isolated price war; today's consumers want bargains everywhere: vacations, cars, clothing—the list goes on. Many marketers are worried, since value pricing feeds on itself. If shoppers assume that prices will eventually come down, they tend to delay purchases. If buyers delay long enough, marketers get desperate and lower prices so they can sell something, even at reduced profits. The new lower prices reinforce the consumer belief that prices will continue to drop, and the cycle starts all over again.[9]

Value doesn't necessarily mean the lowest price, however. For a certain segment

**value pricing**
A somewhat vague term often used to describe the practice of adopting a lower price while maintaining the product's basic value

**Exhibit 12.10**
**PRICING INSIGHTS AT WALT DISNEY WORLD**
Visiting Disney World is a unique experience, a fact that allows the Disney company to charge higher prices than it could if other companies offered identical products.

of customers, a $45,000 Lexus may seem like a better value than a far less expensive car that doesn't provide the desired features and benefits. Value includes service, selection, product quality, and other desirable attributes—along with a price that is competitive.[10]

**skim pricing**
A variation of value pricing for new products in which you attempt to recover a high level of profit for a limited period of time, based on the unique value that you're offering the market

SKIM PRICING    When you introduce a product, you may choose to apply **skim pricing,** also called skimming, in which you charge a high price for an innovative or unique new product. The term skimming comes from *skimming the cream*, implying that you're trying to get only the best. When competition catches up, you lower prices to retain or improve market share, but as long as you're the only choice you can plan to keep prices high. For example, when Motorola introduced its innovative pocket cellular phone in 1989, the device carried a price tag of around $3,500; by 1990, it could be purchased for about $1,300.[11] By 1993, cellular telephone companies were occasionally giving phones away (or selling them for $100 or less) to entice people to sign up for cellular service.

Also, skim pricing is often more than just simple "price gouging," as some people call it. New products frequently require a great deal of investment before companies ever see any revenue, and skim pricing allows companies to recoup that investment. However, skim pricing has its critics, particularly in such cases as new drugs and medical services. For example, for-profit hospitals have been faulted by some observers for entering markets with prices so high that poor people are unable to buy the care they need.[12] Whether or not such criticisms are justified, they highlight the fact that high prices for vital goods and services are bound to generate controversy.

**penetration pricing**
A value-pricing technique in which you set prices aggressively low in order to gain as much market share as possible; the opposite of skim pricing

PENETRATION PRICING    When companies want to increase their presence in a given market, they often use **penetration pricing,** which sets a lower price with the specific intention of gaining market share (as in "penetrating the market"). Microsoft used this technique in 1992 and 1993 to build market share for its new Access database software. Introducing it at a limited-time price of $99, the company sold hundreds of thousands of copies before raising the price to $495.[13]

Low prices can be an effective method in some cases, but not in others. The generic drug pricing situation discussed in Chapter 11 is a great example of the limitations of penetration pricing. Even though they are often significantly cheaper than branded prescription drugs, the generics aren't purchased as often as one might think, and the reason seems to be a perception of risk. It all comes back to price sensitivity; if customers aren't sensitive to price, penetration pricing won't be terribly effective. Another area in which this tends to hold true is large, national customers of organizational marketers. These customers often tend to stick with established suppliers, even if prices appear to be higher on the surface. They fear interruptions of supply, quality problems, or other potential risks that can be dispelled only through experience. This customer mindset often frustrates new competitors trying to use aggressive pricing to grab market share.[14]

**prestige pricing**
A technique that attempts to use a high price to establish an image of quality or exclusivity

PRESTIGE PRICING    As you saw in Chapter 11, you can use price to help you position a product as high quality or exclusive; the pricing technique used to accomplish this is known as **prestige pricing.** You can see prestige pricing with clothes, cars, jewelry, luggage, and other products; it also shows up in some unlikely places. For instance, the Pet Foods Division of Quaker Oats Company recognizes that people tend to "transfer their own wants and desires to their pets." As a result, upscale dog and cat owners generally buy their pets expensive "gourmet" pet foods. These high-class pet foods come with premium prices and, consequently, higher profit margins. Quaker's premium dry dog food, Tender Chops, doesn't cost much more to produce than the company's regular dog food, but it sells for 12 percent more.[15] This higher price creates the image that Tender Chops is an exclusive brand of pet food that upscale dogs deserve.

How valid is the basis for prestige pricing? That is, do higher prices mean higher quality? This question remains a point of controversy in the marketing profession,

## IS SKIM PRICING ETHICAL?

In a few short years, Burroughs Wellcome has seen a significant product achievement turn into a public relations nightmare. In 1986 the company proudly introduced AZT, a life-prolonging drug for AIDS patients. The product was hailed as the first major breakthrough in the fight against AIDS. However, public perception of the company changed radically in the next few years. In September 1989, AIDS activists demonstrated in San Francisco, London, and New York, calling Burroughs Wellcome and its British parent, Wellcome PLC, corporate extortionists. Five protesters chained themselves to a balcony in the New York Stock Exchange and yelled at traders to sell Wellcome stock. Other protesters put stickers on other Wellcome products in pharmacies, accusing the company of being an "AIDS profiteer."

The protests and accusations stem from the price Burroughs Wellcome charges for AZT. When the drug was introduced, it cost $10,000 for a year's supply—for one patient. The price was subsequently dropped to $8,000, but the protest continued because many AIDS patients just can't afford the treatment. The U.S. government stepped in to help, but it has spent several hundred million dollars on AZT and is starting to question the price as well.

Steep initial prices for new drugs are not uncommon. At an average cost of $250 million to develop a new drug, the companies that do so usually feel forced by simple financial pressure to charge high prices in order to recoup their investments. However, patients and the public can't always tell whether a drug company is really just trying to recoup its investment or whether the company is squeezing as much money as possible from people who have no other choice. That's the ethical question at the center of the AZT controversy: Is Burroughs Wellcome charging a high price because the drug is ex-

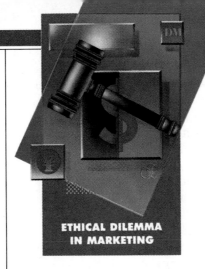

**ETHICAL DILEMMA IN MARKETING**

pensive to produce, or is the company charging a high price because it has the only drug on the market that can prolong the lives of AIDS patients?

"There is a myth out there that we're robber barons, ripping people off." That's how David Barry of Burroughs Wellcome sees the controversy. He points to the enormous cost of pushing the drug through clinical trials, the cost of giving the drug free to 5,000 AIDS patients before it was available for sale, and the $80 million the company has invested in raw materials and a new plant to produce the drug in larger quantities.

The company's critics point out two facts in response to the company's self-defense. First, the market for AZT is turning out to be much larger, unfortunately, than people originally anticipated. People outside the company, including Representative Henry Waxman of California, contend that the company should therefore be able to spread its costs out over a greater number of sales. Second, the drug wasn't really developed by Burroughs Wellcome. It was created over 20 years ago by a researcher looking for a cure for cancer. The original formulation proved ineffective against cancer, and the researcher didn't bother to patent it. Following his efforts, other scientists investigated possible uses for the drug. Much of the work needed to understand AZT's potential for AIDS patients was done by scientists at the government-funded National Institutes of Health (NIH). NIH eventually turned its compound over to Burroughs Wellcome for final develop-

ment. (As a result of the AZT controversy, at least one change has already been made in the arrangements for drugs that are codeveloped by the government and private companies. The NIH now makes companies sign a special agreement before they take over drugs that started in government labs. The agreement forces companies to charge reasonable prices once their drugs are introduced.)

Burroughs Wellcome isn't doing much to silence the critics. It refuses to release figures showing how much it actually spent to get the drug ready for market. Barry claims that people will just use the numbers to make "false and misleading calculations." However, playwright Larry Kramer is among those demanding to know why the company won't release the numbers. He emphasizes that he and other protesters aren't going to accept the company's word at face value. Furthermore, the company's profits doubled in the three years following AZT's introduction, due in no small part to the estimated $100 million in profit AZT generated in 1989, which further undermines its moral position in the eyes of its critics.

The controversy doesn't promise to subside any time soon. Burroughs Wellcome insists that it has been compassionate, by distributing the drug in the free trial program and by starting a program to help uninsured patients get the drug. (Critics, however, claim that the program is so hard to use that it has helped only 300 people so far.) Several days after the protest in September 1989, the price was dropped again, to $6,400 per patient per year. By 1993 it was still around $2,400. That is a large expense for most patients, and the activists say the price has to come down still further before the majority of AIDS patients can afford treatment.

### WHAT'S YOUR OPINION?

**1.** Where should companies in Burroughs Wellcome's situation draw the line on profits?

**2.** Should the government force the company to sell AZT at a lower price?

but sufficient analytical data to support a consistent link between high price and high quality seem to be lacking. For example, in one study, researchers tried to find a connection between the prices of 679 food brands and the quality ratings those foods were given by Consumers Union, publisher of *Consumer Reports*. The study concluded that the "correlation between quality and price for packaged food products is near zero."[16] This raises a challenging ethics dilemma: If a product isn't substantially better than its competitors, is it honest to charge a higher price just to create an image of higher quality? Are you implying a level of quality that doesn't exist?

Although prestige pricing and skim pricing both result in high prices, the two methods differ. First, the objectives of these methods are different. Prestige pricing aims to use price as a component of the product's overall image, whereas skim pricing has the specific objective of generating high profit levels. Second, prestige pricing is a long-term strategy, whereas skimming is usually a short-term technique to reap profits until the competition shows up.

**odd-even pricing**

A pricing technique that uses specific numbers chosen for their supposed psychological effect on customers; the most common approach is prices that end in 9, just below a round number

**psychological pricing**

A general term encompassing all techniques that attempt to evoke a certain reaction based on price; applies both to prestige and to odd-even pricing

ODD-EVEN PRICING    Ever wonder why an item is priced at $9.99 instead of a nice even $10.00? The marketer who set the price figured that you would see $9.99 as cheaper than $10.00. This is a common pricing technique called **odd-even pricing,** which assumes that customers will perceive an odd-numbered price slightly below some even-numbered threshold to be significantly cheaper.

Prestige and odd-even pricing represent a class of pricing known as **psychological pricing,** so called because the prices are designed to stimulate certain reactions from potential buyers. The use of odd-even pricing is supported by little evidence, but that doesn't stop thousands of companies from using it. One study that supports the case for odd endings to price tags compared the sales of Parkay-brand margarine at regular price, discounted prices, and "odd" discount prices. With Parkay, for instance, dropping from the regular price of 83 cents to the discount price of 63 cents sales increased 194 percent. However, when the price was dropped to 59 cents, sales increased 406 percent over sales at the regular price. (It would have been interesting to test a price below 59 cents, say 56 cents, to verify that it was indeed odd-even pricing and not some other price sensitivity effect at work here.) Neither case is supported by much evidence, but discount retailers tend to use odd prices, whereas full-price retailers tend to use round numbers.[17]

**price lining**

The establishment of a limited number of price levels that cover an entire product line

PRICE LINING    When a business has more than one product in a related area, it can use **price lining,** which establishes a limited number of price points that are used for all the company's products. For example, Crown Books prices bargain books at around $1, around $2, and so on. If you want to spend a certain amount of money for a book, you go to the appropriate shelf and see what's available at that price. Establishing price levels across a product line helps you differentiate your various products from one another. It can also help you achieve a balanced profit picture by lowering prices on price-sensitive products and raising them on others.

**uniform pricing**

An extreme case of price lining in which all products are sold for one price

The extreme case of price lining is **uniform pricing,** which is simply charging one price for all the products a company sells (see Exhibit 12.11). Although not a common approach, it is used with dramatic success in some cases. For example, the One Price Clothing Stores charge an even $6 for everything they sell, including sportswear, blouses, and skirts. Customers respond to both the low price and the simplicity of shopping there. The formula certainly seems to work: Sales and profits have climbed every year since the store opened, and the more than 400 stores in the chain bring in well over $100 million in annual revenue.[18]

**unit pricing**

Prices that are calculated in terms of some common standard of measurement, such as ounces, to make price comparisons easier for consumers

**bundle pricing**

The practice of including several products together for one price; the objective is to persuade buyers to buy more by offering an attractive price for a group of products

OTHER DEMAND-BASED PRICING TECHNIQUES    Companies in various industries use several other demand-based pricing approaches. For example, groceries are often marketed with **unit pricing,** which simplifies the consumer's shopping task by showing the price of some standard unit of measure. If you see a 16-ounce bottle of salad dressing selling for $1.69 and a 12-ounce bottle selling for $1.49, can you compute in your head which one is a better buy? In response to pressure from consumer groups, many retailers now do the calculation for you, and you can see the price per ounce on the shelf label. **Bundle pricing** allows a company to offer a package price

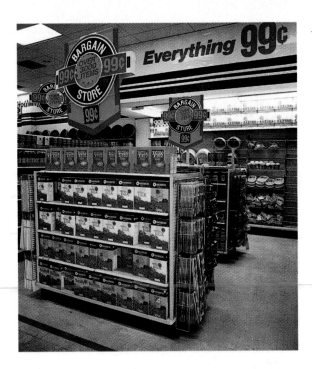

**Exhibit 12.11**
**UNIFORM PRICING IN THE EXTREME**
With everything selling for 99 cents, this store is a good example of uniform pricing.

for a group of related goods and services. Perhaps you've purchased a vacation package that included airfare, hotel rooms, and other services such as bus fare or entertainment tickets. Industrial goods are frequently sold this way as well; a computer maker such as AST, for instance, includes the MS-DOS operating system from Microsoft in the price of its personal computers. Finally, to help select prices that meet the needs of wholesalers and retailers, manufacturers sometimes use **demand-backwards pricing**. This starts with an assessment of the price customers are willing to pay, takes into account the profit or commission required by each intermediary in the market channel, and then arrives at the price the manufacturer will be able to charge.

    If none of these demand-based techniques seems to work for you, you might consider using the pricing approach of Jerome Rowitch, owner of the Sculpture Gardens restaurant in Venice, California. He invited a selected group of affluent residents to dine at his restaurant and told them to pay whatever price they felt their meals were worth. Did it work? The 100-plus diners who took Rowitch up on the deal paid an average of $33, about 30 percent higher than the prices he would normally charge.[19]

## COST- AND PROFIT-BASED PRICING TECHNIQUES

Cost- and profit-based techniques are discussed together because they share an important attribute: They don't take external forces such as competition and customer perceptions into account. Therefore, if used by themselves, these techniques can lead to prices that are too high for the market to accept or too low to capture all the potential revenue. In this respect, these techniques are usually considered rather weak, and companies that rely on them exclusively are occasionally subject to criticism by marketing observers. Generally speaking, use a combination of techniques to make sure you have considered both the internal forces (such as cost) and the external factors (such as customer perceptions). However, in some cases the choice of cost- or profit-based pricing makes a lot of sense.

    Two common cost-based techniques are cost-plus and standard markup pricing. **Cost-plus pricing** means that the seller arrives at the price by starting with the cost and then adding a certain percentage of the cost:

$$\text{Selling price} = \text{cost} + (\text{cost} \times \text{desired markup})$$

For example, if a pair of basketball shoes costs the seller $20, and the seller wants

**demand-backwards pricing**
An approach that starts with a price the market will support and backs up through the marketing channel, subtracting the profits and fees needed by retailers and wholesalers, until it arrives at the price the manufacturer can charge

**cost-plus pricing**
A simple pricing technique that calculates price by adding an acceptable profit level to average total costs

a markup of 25 percent, the price would be set at $20 + ($20 × 25%). Although this method has some obvious shortcomings, including a lack of insight into demand, competition, and profit, it does have the very important advantage of being simple to manage.

In the world of wholesaling and retailing, cost-plus pricing is usually called **standard markup pricing** because wholesalers and retailers in some industries simply add a fixed percentage to the prices they pay in order to arrive at the selling price. This technique is frequently used when the number or variety of products to be priced is so large that considering the market situation for every single product would be impossible. The supermarket manager faced with 30,000 or 40,000 items needs some way to quickly set and change prices, and standard markups provide a reasonable answer. This technique isn't completely devoid of market sensitivity, however: Price-sensitive products will be assigned lower standard markup percentages, whereas other products will be given higher markups.

## COMPETITION-BASED PRICING TECHNIQUES

The third category of pricing techniques looks primarily at the competition and then sets prices relative to their prices. Note that the price you wind up with might be above, below, or equal to the competition. These techniques are distinguished by the fact that you arrive at your price by looking at the competition and not at demand or costs.

LEADER PRICING    Some companies use an attractive price on one product to pull customers away from the competition and stimulate demand for other products, a technique known as **leader pricing**. (This is not the same concept as price leadership discussed in Chapter 11.) The leader is intentionally priced below the point of optimum profit, with the hope that sales of other products will make up the difference. For instance, grocery stores such as Lucky and Safeway run specials on various items and advertise them aggressively. By offering prices on selected items that are below those offered by competitors, the stores stand a better chance of getting you to walk through the door. They are usually interested in making money on the sale items, of course, but they also want to pull customers into the store to buy other products. If these other products are held at their normal prices, the overall profit earned by the store remains strong.

The most extreme case of leader pricing is when a company prices a leader product so low that it doesn't generate any profit on that particular product; the leader product is then called a **loss leader**. However, if the mix of products purchased by the average customer offsets the profit forgone on the loss leader, the technique can be successful. For example, Toys 'R' Us sells diapers and infant formula at cost and popular toys at low markups. Charles Lazarus is straightforward about his company's motivation to sell baby supplies at cost: "How can you not [also] buy your baby a toy when you are out there?" It seems to work; the company shuns normal promotional sales events and has still grown to dominate toy retailing.[20] Loss leaders can be a powerful marketing technique, but be aware that some states have laws concerning minimum markups, which can restrict your ability to use loss leaders.

POSITIONING AND PRICING    The final pricing technique is used to position products relative to the competition. This notion was introduced earlier with prestige pricing, but when you're considering competitive pricing and positioning, you may also want to position your product as less expensive or at the same price. For example, Subaru positions roughly half its models as low-priced and promotes its lowest-priced model, the Justy, with the phrase "Inexpensive and built to stay that way." Subaru has chosen not to follow its fellow Japanese automakers in building upscale cars such as Toyota's Lexus line. When you think low-priced cars, Subaru wants you to think Subaru and only Subaru, and it uses price to position its brand that way in your mind.[21]

The first five steps in the pricing process define the overall pricing agenda so that you can establish a general price level. Now take a look at the ongoing administrative aspect of pricing, which is adjusting and managing prices in response to marketplace changes and specific customer and competitive situations.

Most of this involves making changes to the **list price,** which is the price you'll see published in price lists, catalogs, and other marketing materials. You can consider this the product's "official" price. The **market price,** which is the actual selling price, is frequently different from the list price; in some cases it is radically different. One of the most common reasons for this difference is the use of discounts and allowances.

## DISCOUNTS AND ALLOWANCES

Marketers frequently use both discounts and allowances to encourage consumers to try new products, to stimulate demand, to clear out excess inventory, and to entice customers to make larger purchases. **Discounts** are direct reductions from the list price, such as a 10-percent-off sale. **Allowances,** on the other hand, are indirect reductions from the list price, such as rebates and trade-ins.

With either discounts or allowances, a carefully designed program that considers customer buying patterns and competitive behavior can significantly strengthen a company's long-term market position. To be successful, the program must fit in with the overall pricing objective and not be just a series of reactions to short-term market pressures. Here are the major types of discounts, followed by a look at allowances:[22]

- *Trade discounts.* Manufacturers grant discounts to wholesalers and other marketing channel partners, and these price breaks are called **trade discounts.** (The wholesaling and retailing functions are often referred to as "the trade.") Trade discounts are based on the services that those channel partners are expected to perform. For example, a distributor of electronic components, such as Marshall Electronics, needs to receive a healthy trade discount on microprocessors and other products that might require a lot of customer support.
- *Quantity discounts.* A frequently used discounting device is the **quantity discount,** which gives customers a break on price if they purchase specified quantities of goods or services. The marketer doesn't necessarily lose money on these discounts, since larger orders from fewer customers reduce its selling, administration, and shipping costs.[23]
- *Timing discounts.* Customer demand for some goods and services is not consistent over time, and companies can respond to this by offering discounts for purchases at specific times. For example, resort hotels typically reduce their rates during the off-season to balance demand and to keep facilities and employees occupied. Another form of timing discount is the matinee prices at theaters; by offering lower prices during off-peak times, the theater owners try to shift excess demand away from evening performances and thereby encourage even more people to attend overall.
- *Cash discounts.* A **cash discount** is a billing scheme that offers customers a discount if they pay within a certain time frame. For example, you might see a price quoted as $1,000, 2/10, net 30. This shorthand means that the price is $1,000 and that the customer can deduct 2 percent from this price if the bill is paid within 10 days; otherwise the entire amount is due in 30 days. Many sellers prefer this method because it speeds up the flow of money after they've completed a sale; buyers often take advantage of it because the savings can be significant.
- *Promotional discounts.* The last category of discounts is **promotional discounts,** which are temporary price reductions that are designed to stimulate customers to try new products, to increase the purchase of mature products, and generally

**list price**
The "official" price of a product, even if the product is sold at that price only occasionally

**market price**
The actual price at which a product sells (to consumers and organizational customers other than resellers); equal to list price minus discounts and allowances

**discounts**
Direct reductions from the list price

**allowances**
Indirect reductions from list price in which part of the list price is effectively returned to the customers, such as with a rebate

**trade discounts**
Discounts at which products are sold to wholesalers and retailers; trade discounts allow these marketing intermediaries to recover their costs and generate profits

**quantity discount**
A discount based on the number of products purchased or on the total value of the purchase

**cash discount**
A discount given in return for paying a bill within a certain number of days

**promotional discounts**
Discounts given as part of promotional programs, such as when products are put on sale to increase traffic in a retail store

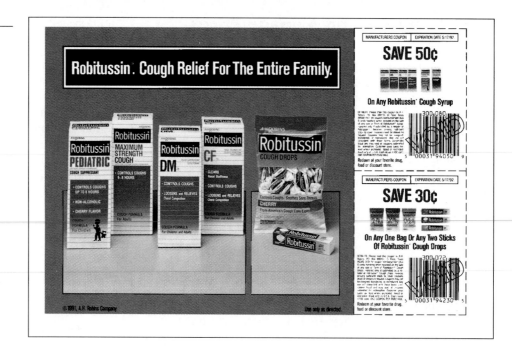

**Exhibit 12.12
PROMOTIONAL
DISCOUNTS**

Companies frequently use promotional discounts to induce customers to try new products or to increase traffic in retail stores, as A. H. Robins did with these coupons for some of its cough medicine products.

to make products more competitive (see Exhibit 12.12). Promotional discounts are used instead of permanent price reductions when the seller thinks that price sensitivities might change over time, such as after consumers adopt a new product and no longer demand the price break in order to purchase it. The hundreds of billions of coupons distributed in the United States every year are a type of promotional discount as well, although some marketers are trying to cut down on couponing because it encourages a bargain-hunting mentality among consumers, making them unwilling to buy items at regular prices.[24]

Sometimes marketers use allowances rather than discounts to stimulate purchases. Two common allowances are trade-ins and rebates. *Trade-ins* are typical in the automobile business, but they can be used whenever a seller thinks such a program would be an advantage. For example, IBM used a trade-in program to get customers to give up their old IBM PCs and purchase IBM PS/2 computers.[25]

Use of *rebates* has grown dramatically in recent years, and the auto industry has come to rely on such programs. Even Jaguar, the manufacturer of premium English autos, felt it had to resort to rebates in the soft U.S. car market in recent years. However, like coupons, rebates have gotten out of hand, or so many marketers think. An understandable phenomenon in pricing explains this: When buyers grow accustomed to frequent sales, coupons, rebates, or other promotional devices, they eventually expect them and refuse to pay full price. If customers believe they can get a better deal by waiting for your next promotional program, they are increasingly willing to delay their purchases. Furthermore, rebates have the potential to damage the image of prestige brands and to frustrate customers who'd rather just pay a lower price and avoid the hassle.[26]

Trade discounts have become a major force in consumer marketing in recent years. Attempts to bring the situation under control are upsetting more than a few established practices. Manufacturers see two big negatives in excessive trade discounting. First, it encourages retailers to buy extra stock when discounts are in effect, then stop buying when the discounts are taken away, a practice known as *trade loading* from the manufacturer's perspective and *forward buying* from the trade's perspective. If a discount is set to run for a month, for instance, a retailer might buy two or three months' worth of inventory at the discounted price, then buy nothing for the two months after the discount is removed. This can throw a manufacturer into chaos as it tries to stop and start production in response to ever-fluctuating demand. Discontinuous manufacturing flows like this are also more expensive than smooth, continuous flows. Loading gives the manufacturer a short-term sales boost but creates tremendous inefficiencies and waste throughout the distribution system, costing U.S. consumers an estimated $20 billion a year.[27] Second, a new subindustry has sprung up to take advantage of trade discounts that are offered in one region of the country but not in others. In the practice of *diverting*, intermediaries buy goods in one region and sell them to retailers in other regions, often foiling the manufacturer's pricing strategy.[28]

Packaged goods giant Procter & Gamble (P&G) is trying to bring some sense to this whole arena of discounting, using the increasingly popular strategy of **everyday low pricing (EDLP).** Rather than shelling out millions of dollars in trade and consumer discounts, P&G has shifted most of its product lines to EDLP. The idea is to keep prices at consistent levels, day in and day out, avoiding the cycle of regular prices interrupted by frequent sale prices. The initial backlash from retailers was severe; some stopped advertising P&G products and others even stopped carrying some products. Supermarkets initially fought EDLP, since trade discounts were a major source of their profits, but most have since joined the effort as a way to compete at the retail level.[29]

How well is EDLP working for P&G and others who have tried it? That depends on whom you ask, when you ask, and whether you're talking about manufacturers or the trade. Smoothing out production schedules alone might save P&G as much as $175 million a year, and the reduced discounting (along with other cost-cutting efforts such as dropping less profitable products) should boost profits even more. The net result is increased competitiveness: Chairperson Edwin Artzt says P&G can now cut list prices on many products while maintaining profit margins.[30] On the other hand, the company's market share (in dollars) dropped from 1992 to 1993 in most categories.

From the retailer's perspective, "everyday low pricing may not be the marketing panacea believed," says Mary Purk of the University of Chicago. She managed an experiment that monitored EDLP in Chicago-area grocery stores and concluded that, at the retail level at least, EDLP yielded slightly higher revenues but significantly lower profits. Another result of the study was that many consumers find the high-low cycle of traditional pricing more interesting than EDLP. Specials and other discounts seem to add a bit of zip to what is the otherwise dreary task of grocery shopping.[31] One marketer summed up the current situation as "chaotic," a description that may well apply for the foreseeable future, as manufacturers and the trade try to adapt in an ever-changing marketing environment.[32]

## GEOGRAPHIC PRICING

For some products, shipping costs can be a significant portion of the price paid by the customer. This is particularly true for natural resources and materials that don't have a lot of manufactured value added to them. Because shipping costs vary according to the distance of the customer, the true cost of serving customers varies. Depending on customer expectations and competitive practices, a company can choose whether or not it wants to include shipping charges in the price of its products.

If shipping charges are not included, the company is using a scheme called **origin-point pricing,** in which the price applies to the product at its point of origin, not at the customer's location. Origin-point prices are usually quoted with the acronym FOB (free on board) followed by a city. For example, American Machine & Tool Company lists its prices as "FOB Royersford, Pennsylvania," where the company is located. When a customer places an order, the freight charges for that particular order are calculated and added to the total price.[33] Origin-point prices have the advantage of allowing companies to advertise lower prices because they don't include freight costs. On the other hand, origin-point pricing means higher prices for distant customers, which might be a competitive disadvantage.

The second scheme of geographic pricing is called **delivered pricing,** in which prices do include shipping charges. You can use several methods to incorporate these costs into the selling price. With **single-zone pricing,** all customers pay the same amount; an average freight charge has already been figured into the price. If

**everyday low pricing (EDLP)**
A strategy of keeping prices at consistent levels, day in and day out, rather than setting a comparatively high price and running frequent sales

**origin-point pricing**
A class of geographic pricing that doesn't include shipping charges in the selling price; also called FOB pricing

**delivered pricing**
A class of geographic pricing in which shipping charges are included in the selling price

**single-zone pricing**
Delivered pricing that charges each customer an average shipping charge based on the seller's total shipping expenses; customers end up paying more or less than the actual shipping cost

**multiple-zone pricing**
A modification of single-zone pricing that uses more than one zone and calculates an average shipping charge for each zone

**freight-absorption pricing**
A form of delivered pricing in which the seller agrees to return freight costs to the buyer in the form of a discount

**basing-point pricing**
A form of delivered pricing that sets shipping charges based on delivery from one or more locations, even if the shipment never actually moved through those locations

this average charge is so high that it makes the price uncompetitive in markets close to the producer, **multiple-zone pricing** is a good alternative, splitting customers into a number of zones and charging average prices inside each zone. **Freight-absorption pricing** is a third alternative, in which the seller agrees to absorb freight costs, allowing the customer to subtract shipping charges from the list price. This method can be helpful when you're trying to expand your geographic coverage or when you're in close price competition with another supplier. The fourth method is **basing-point pricing,** which charges customers freight from one or more locations, called basing points, even if the goods never actually passed through those locations.[34]

## PRICE CHANGES

Price changes often require a careful touch, to avoid confusing or upsetting customers and to keep from triggering undesirable reactions from competitors. The first step in making a price change is to stop and ask yourself whether the change is really necessary. Companies are often tempted to cut prices when sales decline, but that might not be the best answer, because small reductions in price can cause large reductions in profit. On the other hand, if you're about to raise prices, several steps are available to make the change as painless as possible, including training your sales force and channel partners thoroughly, discussing increases in advance with big customers, and working with customers to see whether you have nonprice options that can help compensate for the burden of higher prices.[35]

Should you follow or lead the competition when prices across the market are changing? The answer depends on the position you hold in the market. Generally speaking, certain companies should follow when prices are going down and lead when prices are going up:[36]

- Firms with high market share
- Firms with high production and marketing costs
- Firms whose products lead the competition
- Firms that are using most of their production capacity

Conversely, certain companies should lead when prices are going down and follow when prices are going up:

- Firms with relatively lower market share
- Firms with relatively lower production and marketing costs
- Firms whose products are not as strong as the competition's
- Firms that are not using most of their production capacity

By considering each of these attributes, you can see that the basic idea is to minimize the profit loss (or maximize profit gain) in the event of price changes. Of course, these are general guidelines, and you should consider all the market dynamics before making price changes.

## SPECIAL PRICING ISSUES

The pricing function takes on some intriguing variations as you move into various marketing environments. The basic concepts already discussed still apply, but consider also the issues of bidding and negotiated prices, transfer pricing, barter arrangements, filtered pricing, international pricing, pricing for services, and pricing for nonprofit organizations.

### Competitive Bidding and Negotiated Prices

When customers have a need that can't be filled with a standard product or when they are buying large quantities of standard products, they frequently ask two or more suppliers to submit *competitive bids*. Some customers routinely ask for com-

HERE YOU'LL FIND THE WORLDS GREATEST BARGAINS, BUT YOU'LL HAVE TO BARGAIN FOR THEM.

**Exhibit 12.13**
**NEGOTIATED PRICES**
Negotiations between buyer and seller are quite common in many countries, as this ad promoting tourism in Singapore attests.

petitive bids, regardless of the quantity. For example, the U.S. government sends out a Request for Proposal (RFP) when it needs any of a variety of products, ranging from office supplies to missile guidance systems. The RFP specifies every aspect of the desired product, including documentation, training, and other support services. Companies with the ability to respond will submit their proposals, including the price they intend to charge, and the government will pick the proposal with the best combination of price and conformance to the specifications in the RFP. (In times of tight budgets, however, the government might simply pick the cheapest alternative.)

With *negotiated pricing,* the buyer and seller work out a price that is acceptable to both, rather than relying on a published list. Price negotiation happens at all levels of product expense and complexity. Negotiating the prices of consumer goods and services isn't common in this country, but it is an everyday aspect of commerce in many countries (see Exhibit 12.13). For example, when you walk through the Itaewon district of Seoul, South Korea, you have the chance to do business with vendors selling everything from toys to suits. These vendors quote a price, but they accept, even expect, a counteroffer in which you name a lower price, and the process continues back and forth until a price is agreed on. This same process can happen, with perhaps a little more formality, on products as complex and expensive as bridges, roads, and power plants.

## Transfer Pricing

If you go to work for a company that produces products in more than one location or organization, you may run into the phenomenon of *transfer pricing,* which sets the prices that one part of a company charges another part of the same company. For instance, the division of Hewlett-Packard that manufactures personal computers sells them to other divisions in the company, and it charges a transfer price rather than normal list price.

You might find it surprising that companies have to struggle to figure out how much to charge themselves, but transfer pricing can turn into something of an accounting nightmare. The problem is finding a price that both the buyer and the

## SUBSIDIES: WHEN GOVERNMENTS GET INVOLVED IN PRICING

When French farmers dump manure and burn hay in the middle of a busy Paris street, the protest may seem thousands of miles away. However, it's part of a contentious global pricing issue that affects virtually every U.S. taxpayer and consumer and their counterparts in more than a hundred other countries.

The issue is *government subsidies,* payments made to help a business or an entire industry stay profitable and competitive. Let's say it costs you 20 cents to produce and market a pound of sugar. However, producers in other countries can put a pound of sugar on the market for 10 cents. Maybe you can get help from your government.

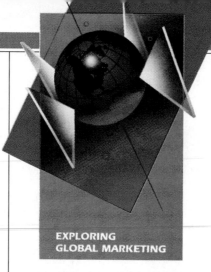

EXPLORING GLOBAL MARKETING

One form of help would be limits on sugar imports. Another option would be for the government to guarantee you 20 cents of revenue for each pound of sugar you produce, even if the market price is 10 cents. Therefore, you'd produce your sugar for 20 cents, sell it for 10 cents, and collect the other 10 cents from the govern-

ment. On the other hand, the government could combine the two: limiting imports to keep domestic prices at 20 cents, while pitching in the 10 cents you need to sell overseas in more competitive markets. Consumers in this country would pay more for sugar, and competitors overseas would have to contend with a supplier who's backed by U.S. tax dollars; you get the best of both worlds. This might sound a little crazy, but it is going on all over the globe, with products as diverse as aircraft, grain, and honey.

Subsidies can have bizarre effects. The U.S. government has been subsidizing honey producers since 1949. The program (which lets producers take out no-interest loans using their honey as collateral) was originally an attempt to keep the bee population from dropping so low that crops

---

seller consider fair and that helps each part of the company achieve its own goals and performance measures. Although it is largely an accounting problem, the marketing department is involved at least peripherally because whatever pricing method is being employed has to take transfer pricing into consideration. If the number of products sold internally is a significant portion of your total sales, the internal sales might have a big effect on both your cost and profitability analyses.

## Barter Arrangements

**barter**
An exchange that is not based on monetary prices

An alternative to a monetary exchange is **barter,** in which goods or services of equal value are exchanged. The barter system preceded monetary systems, but it hasn't faded away entirely. In fact, barter has been in the news recently as Western firms conduct an increasing amount of business with Russia and other countries in Eastern and Central Europe. Because many of the purchasers in these countries, both consumer and organizational, don't yet have convertible currency, they often agree to trade domestic goods for Western goods. In Russia, for instance, PepsiCo exchanges soft drinks for Stolichnaya vodka. Bartering is also used by a variety of firms domestically, when normal financial exchanges are impractical or impossible. For example, Borg-Warner Corporation trades its chemicals for supplies it needs, and Shell Oil once traded 5 million pest control gadgets for a load of unrefined sugar from a Caribbean resort.[37] Even though no money changes hands in these transactions, barter partners are very conscious of the equivalent financial value of the goods they trade.

## Filtered Pricing

Some companies realize that various customers represent different levels of potential profit. This happens for two reasons. First, some customers cost more to keep happy than others. For instance, smaller orders can be proportionately more expensive to process, and some customers require higher levels of support. These problems can be addressed by linking the price you charge each customer to the would no longer be pollinated. In the 1980s, however, the market price plunged below the government's guaranteed price, and many producers simply let the government keep their honey. The government wound up with nearly three-quarters of the U.S. honey production one year. Foreign competitors jumped in to fill supermarket shelves (since the U.S. government gave most of its honey to the poor). Not only did the subsidy give foreign producers a shot at the U.S. market, it costs U.S. consumers many millions of dollars.

Why the worry over subsidies? One source estimates that U.S. consumers pay an average of $360 more a year to cover the costs of subsidies in all industries. Consumers in the 12-member European Union are hit even harder, paying an average of $450 annually. The hardest hit among the three groups are Japanese consumers, who shell out an estimated $600 per year. Also, because subsidies are usually applied to the most basic consumer goods, such as sugar and rice, the poorest consumers suffer proportionately the most.

The protest by French farmers is particularly important because it threatens to upset some complex trade negotiations that have been progressing slowly and shakily for years. The United States and other countries are demanding that France reduce the subsidies it pays its farmers. The farmers, with strong support from French consumers (who value the tradition of family farms, even though most of the subsidy funds go to large corporate farms), are threatening to wreak political and economic turmoil if their subsidies are taken away. The French situation is hardly unique, however; import restrictions and subsidies to Japanese farmers keep rice prices in that country four or five times higher than they would be otherwise. The United States protects a number of industries, from sugar to textiles, with various combinations of subsidies and other maneuvers. Pricing is indeed a complex part of international marketing, and the ever-changing government arena promises to keep it that way for years to come.

## APPLY YOUR KNOWLEDGE

**1.** What effect might subsidies eventually have on an industry's ability to compete in the global market?
**2.** Why might consumers be willing to support subsidies, aside from the notion of tradition and sentiment?

---

cost of serving that customer. For example, you can charge relatively higher prices for small orders, and you can charge for support services.

The second reason potential profit differs from one customer to the next is that customers exhibit differing degrees of price sensitivity, even on identical products. Although Jack might go ahead and pay full list price for that pail of water, Jill might demand a discount before she'll buy it. Which price should you then charge? Keep the list price, and Jill won't buy; offer a discount, and you'll be selling to Jack at a lower price than necessary.

Marketers have developed an interesting pricing technique to address this situation. Known as **filtered pricing,** this method allows you to offer discounts only to those customers who won't buy without them. Coupons, mail-in rebate offers, and special prices available only to new customers are a common means of implementing filtered pricing.[38] Customers who will buy at full price are free to ignore the offer and go ahead and pay list price. However, the price-sensitive customers can effectively get a lower price by redeeming coupons at the time of purchase or applying for rebates after purchasing at full price. These programs allow you to address both sets of customers and still get the highest possible level of total profit.

Restricted consumption is another use of filtered pricing; airline fares are a good example.[39] For instance, when American Airlines offers attractive fares that passengers can take advantage of only under certain circumstances, the company is using a form of filtered pricing. The most price-sensitive customers will live with the restrictions necessary to get the lower price, but price-insensitive customers who won't or can't live with the restrictions will go ahead and pay higher prices. By using this technique, American can serve a greater universe of passengers without completely sacrificing profit.

Two difficulties are inherent in filtered pricing, however. The first is identifying and targeting the sensitive and insensitive segments. The cost of the research and the administrative hassles might outweigh the increased profits generated by the pricing strategy. Second, the program must be structured in a way that discourages the insensitive segment from taking advantage of the discount. If the discount is so easy to achieve that nearly everyone exploits it, the marketer might as well skip the work involved in filtered prices and simply offer a standard discount.

**filtered pricing**
A strategy of variable pricing that tries to restrict discounts and allowances to only those customers who probably won't buy without them

# International Pricing

International pricing, like the rest of the global marketing function, can be quite a challenge. Legal constraints, competition, and customer expectations vary from country to country, and you've got to stay on top of these details to remain effective. The study of international pricing is a rather large undertaking, but here are the main points:

- *Costs of doing business.* Even the most simple costs of operating your business get complicated once you leave the United States. For instance, expanding your market to include France is considerably more expensive than expanding it to include Texas. You'll suddenly be faced with a host of new expenses, ranging from translated and reprinted marketing materials to an additional set of tax attorneys to deal with the French government.

- *Currency fluctuations.* The best pricing strategies can be frustrated by changes in currency valuations. For example, exchange rates have played a big role in the continuing competition between Caterpillar, which is based in the United States, and Komatsu, which is based in Japan. These two industrial giants compete head-to-head in many segments of the construction equipment market. The dollar/yen rate first favored Komatsu, whose prices were up to 40 percent lower than Cat's. Then the scale tipped the other way as the dollar declined relative to the yen, making U.S. products cheaper in Japan and Japanese products more expensive here. As a result (helped by some very impressive cost-cutting moves at Cat), Cat's prices in the United States during most of the 1980s rose only 9.5 percent, while Komatsu's jumped as much as 20 percent.[40] Monitoring exchange rates and making pricing decisions based on them are increasingly important activities for international marketers.

**protectionism**
A country's attempt to protect its own industries by imposing high tariffs on competitive imported goods

- *Protectionism.* A very large political issue affecting international pricing is **protectionism,** which is the use of import tariffs that are high enough to make imported products significantly less competitive with local products. Protectionism affects U.S. companies in both directions: They can face protective tariffs as they try to export to other countries, and they can be protected from imports by this country's own tariffs. As in the case of dumping discussed in Chapter 11, protectionism remains a sticky political and economic issue with winners and losers on both sides of the argument.

- *Regulations.* Laws affecting pricing in the United States are challenging enough by themselves, and you'll face another set in every country in which you do business. However, countries try to coordinate their regulatory efforts in several areas to make international business easier and more efficient. The General Agreement on Tariffs and Trade (GATT), an international organization with dozens of member countries, tries to reduce or eliminate trade barriers such as import quotas and protective tariffs. The consolidation of trade regulations among member nations in the European Union is another example of international cooperation that helps the pricing process.

Protectionism can take some strange twists, as PepsiCo discovered when the Indian government forced it to rename all of its products, just before they were scheduled to be introduced in the country.

## Pricing Strategies for Nonprofit Organizations

Although it might not be apparent at first glance, pricing is very important for nonprofit organizations. Many of them are directly involved with selling goods and services, and others rely on effective pricing to help with fund-raising efforts. Keep in mind that price isn't always a monetary consideration. If you think back to the definition of the marketing exchange, in which the customer gives up something of value in exchange for something else of value, the entity given up can be a behavior, an attitude, or time (see Exhibit 12.14).

Much of the pricing information covered in these two chapters applies to nonprofit pricing; the biggest area of difference is in establishing pricing objectives (the third step). Here are the most common objectives established by nonprofit organizations:[41]

SMOKING STINKS.

Smoking makes your breath stink. Smoking makes your hair and clothes stink. Smoking is an addiction that will take your money, your looks and your health. And while some people want to brush aside the facts, smoking can cost you your life. That really stinks. Don't smoke. If you do, call **1-800-537-5666** for helpful information on quitting.

**Michigan Department of Public Health**


**Exhibit 12.14 PRICE ISN'T ALWAYS MEASURED IN MONEY**
The price in a nonprofit exchange doesn't have to be measured in money. In this appeal by the Michigan Department of Health, the price the marketer asks is giving up the smoking habit.

- *Generating profit.* The term *nonprofit* applies to an organization's primary purpose; a nonprofit organization might still pursue profits on specific projects or products. For example, political parties often host fund-raising dinners with price tags of $100 or $1,000 per plate. These groups are very much interested in turning a profit on the sales of these dinners. Financial profit serves as a means to achieve nonprofit ends, such as helping the homeless, healing the sick, and electing political candidates.
- *Recovering costs.* Rather than generate an explicit profit, many nonprofit groups seek only to recover their costs. In other words, they want to make sure that they remain self-sustaining. For example, the U.S. Postal Service sets prices at a level designed to recover costs. In other cases, the income from goods and services is sometimes used in conjunction with fund-raising to help recover costs. This is the cost-recovery approach of many colleges and universities.
- *Increasing market size.* Some nonprofit organizations want to increase the number of people who take advantage of their services. Therefore, they will set prices as low as possible. This objective might be in direct conflict with the cost-recovery objective, however. For example, an AIDS counseling clinic would want to help as many people as possible while still making enough money to keep the door open; its prices would have to combine elements of both objectives.
- *Striving for social equity.* Striving for social equity is related to increasing market size. Some organizations implement this objective by charging customers according to their ability to pay. This has the effect of shifting money from those customers with more money to those customers with less.
- *Influencing behavior.* Price can also be used as a mechanism for influencing public behavior, particularly when it is used as a deterrent. For instance, the government body in charge of San Francisco's Golden Gate Bridge wanted to reduce the number of cars crossing the bridge, so it used a pricing policy that charged single-occupant cars the most and full car pools the least. This had some effect on creating more car pools, thereby reducing the amount of traffic on the bridge.

## PRICE TESTING

Even after you've followed all the guidelines from setting objectives to offering discounts, how can you be sure that you've really selected the best price? You might be selling at forecasted levels, but how do you know that a lower price wouldn't have yielded more sales and total profit, or that a higher price wouldn't generate higher profit without hurting total sales? Unfortunately, the answer is that you can never be sure. Most markets involve too many variables, are affected by too many subtle influences, and go through too many changes for you ever to feel completely confident about pricing decisions.

However, all is not lost; pricing uncertainties can be greatly reduced. This is done through a variety of marketing research techniques that help you identify price levels and test them in both laboratory and real-world settings. What you're basically trying to measure is price sensitivity: How will demand change at various price points? Here are some of the more common research methods that are most applicable to testing the elements of price:

- *Analysis of sales data.* A relatively easy way to get some insight into price sensitivity is to examine historical sales data. By looking at sales data over a period of months or years, you can see whether changes in demand coincide with changes in price. The word *coincide* was used for a reason: In uncontrolled situations like this, you can't say with any confidence that a change in price caused the change in demand. You may have raised prices at the same time a competitor entered the market; how can you separate the two influences? Still, analysis of sales data can supplement other techniques and your own judgment; just be sure that you don't read more into the data than is really there.

- *Direct questioning.* The simplest way of collecting data about customers is to come right out and ask. Show customers the product and ask whether they would purchase it at price A or price B, for example. This technique is attractive because it is simple. Its biggest drawback is that you are not really measuring their purchase behavior; you're measuring what customers *say* about their purchase behavior.

- *Simulated shopping.* One possible way to measure price sensitivity is through simulated shopping. With this technique, you let a group of representative customers make purchase decisions in a simulated store. By analyzing their purchase behavior, you can get some idea of the best price to charge.

- *Test marketing and in-market testing.* Test marketing a new product is a good way to test price sensitivity because you can keep the rest of the marketing mix constant and measure various price points. In-market testing, or conducting pricing tests after you've introduced the product, goes one step beyond test marketing. Because it is happening in the real world, not in a test-market situation, in-market testing gives you the highest confidence results. Marketers who sell through catalogs have been using in-market testing for decades, given the ease of distributing catalogs with different prices to different sets of customers.[42]

- *Conjoint analysis.* One technique that has quickly gained popularity for testing product attributes, including price, is conjoint analysis. Its unique strength is that it breaks down the total value that customers place on a product into the component values they place on individual product features. This helps you design products that offer the most valuable features at optimum prices. It is also called trade-off analysis because it forces customers to emulate the trade-offs they make in their real-world purchase decisions. For example, conjoint analysis won't allow a customer to say, "I want a luxury, high-performance car, and I want to pay only $5,000." By forcing them to choose various levels of luxury, performance, and acceptable price, conjoint analysis gives you valuable insights into the importance that customers place on price.

## SUMMARY OF LEARNING OBJECTIVES

**1. Delineate the role of cost in the pricing process.**

Cost is a fundamental element in the pricing process because of the nature of the profit equation. Profit is equal to revenue minus expenses, so cost affects both profit and selling price. Cost therefore constrains the lower boundary of possible prices. However, as important as cost is, it isn't the only fac-

tor considered in pricing. To set prices most effectively, successful marketers also take into account customer demand and competitive pressure.

**2. Describe what breakeven analysis can and cannot do.**

Breakeven analysis provides a valuable piece of data by identifying the number of units you have to sell in order to break even. This point occurs when total cost equals total revenue. If you sell more than this number of products, you'll realize a profit; if sales don't achieve the breakeven point, you'll face a loss. What breakeven analysis doesn't tell you is whether you stand a chance of selling enough units to reach the breakeven point. Therefore, it must not be used as a forecasting technique.

### 3. Highlight the most common demand-based pricing strategies.

About a half dozen demand-based pricing strategies are in common use. Value pricing uses the value customers place on a product as the primary factor in determining price. Skim pricing, or skimming, as it is also called, can be considered a special, temporary case of value pricing that is popular with significant new products. If a new product brings unique value to the market, and customers are willing to pay more for that value, you can use skim pricing to charge a higher introductory price. Skim prices are usually lowered as competition enters the market and your unique value is diluted. Penetration pricing is the exact opposite of skimming; you use an aggressively low price to gain market share. Prestige pricing is the method of choice when you want to use a high price to help create an image of quality or exclusivity. Odd-even pricing is a commonly used technique, especially in retailing, that sets odd-numbered prices (e.g., $1.99) that are just under some round threshold (e.g., $2.00). The last common technique is to establish a limited number of price levels and then align all your merchandise with these levels, a technique called price lining.

### 4. Contrast the limitations and advantages of cost- and profit-based pricing strategies.

Because they don't take demand or competition into account, cost- and profit-based pricing strategies suffer by using an incomplete picture of the forces that shape product sales. A price derived strictly from cost may be so far above the competition that the product won't sell. On the other hand, a cost-based price might also be too low, in which case it won't bring in all the revenue it is capable of generating. Both possibilities apply to profit-based strategies as well. However, these techniques are attractive in one important respect: They are very easy to administer. This is particularly important for marketers with a vast number of products to manage, a situation faced by many retailers and wholesalers.

### 5. Identify the major tasks involved in adjusting and managing prices.

In general, adjusting and managing prices involves adjustments made to list prices in response to specific market situations. The first task is to define discounts and allowances, which is done for a variety of reasons, such as encouraging trial of new products, stimulating demand, clearing out excess inventory, and providing incentives for wholesalers and retailers. The second task is to make adjustments because of geographic dispersion of your customers. This is especially important when shipping costs represent a high portion of the total cost of production and marketing. Finally, when you are preparing to change a price, consider the situation in the marketplace and your competitive position first. This analysis will help you pick the right time to change prices and the best way to communicate the change to your customers.

### 6. Summarize the risks involved in relying heavily on discounting and allowances.

Relying heavily on discounting to move products (in other words, not being able to sell a product successfully at its regular price) runs the risk of "training" buyers to buy only at the discounted price. If people think that a product might go on sale soon, they'll wait to make their purchases. This has the eventual outcome of effectively lowering prices (and usually profits). Trade discounts and allowances present a host of other potential problems, including forward buying (retailers buying more than they need in the immediate future while a product is on manufacturer's special, then stockpiling the excess to sell when the manufacturer removes the discount) and diverting (intermediaries buying and selling products across regions that have different pricing and discounting arrangements, thereby undermining the manufacturer's pricing intentions).

### 7. Point out the unique pricing situation faced by nonprofit organizations.

Nonprofit organizations use many of the same pricing techniques as their profit-seeking counterparts. The major difference is in the pricing objective. The most common objectives used in the nonprofit sector are generating profit for use in financing programs and services, recovering costs, increasing market size, achieving social equity, and influencing public behavior by encouraging or discouraging certain actions or lifestyles.

## KEY TERMS

allowances (373)
average fixed costs (361)
average total cost (362)
average variable cost (362)
barter (378)
basing-point pricing (376)
breakeven analysis (364)
breakeven point (365)
bundle pricing (370)
cash discount (373)
cost-plus pricing (371)
delivered pricing (375)

demand-backwards pricing (371)
discounts (373)
everyday low pricing (EDLP) (375)
filtered pricing (378)
fixed costs (361)
freight-absorption pricing (376)
leader pricing (372)
list price (373)
loss leader (372)

marginal analysis (363)
marginal cost (362)
marginal revenue (363)
market price (373)
multiple-zone pricing (376)
odd-even pricing (370)
origin-point pricing (375)
penetration pricing (368)
prestige pricing (368)
price lining (370)
promotional discount (373)
protectionism (379)

psychological pricing (370)
quantity discount (373)
single-zone pricing (375)
skim pricing (368)
standard markup pricing (372)
total cost (362)
trade discounts (373)
uniform pricing (370)
unit pricing (370)
value pricing (367)
variable costs (362)

## Meeting a Marketing Challenge at American Airlines

The price management system adopted by American Airlines represents some of the most complex pricing techniques in use today. Most of the major carriers use similar techniques as well. Known generally as a *yield management system,* it is a powerful combination of pricing policies and computer horsepower designed to maximize the profit of every single flight. Ever sit next to someone on a flight and discover that the two of you paid different, sometimes dramatically different, amounts for your tickets? Well, you experienced a yield management system. Robert Crandall must manage three important variables in his pricing system.

The first is cost, the key measure of which is the cost required to move one seat 1 mile. With the exception of food service and some slight increase in fuel, moving an empty seat costs nearly the same as moving a full seat. Obviously, American would like to see that seat filled with a paying passenger; in fact, it needs to fill an average of 57.9 percent of the available seats on every flight just to break even.

The second problem Crandall faces is that when the plane takes off, the seats go with it. If a seat flies empty, that is a lost revenue opportunity that can never be recovered. Another way of saying this is that American always produces the product (the seat moving from one place to another), even if nobody buys it.

Third, airlines recognize the existence of a cross elasticity between full-fare demand and discount-fare demand. It works like this: Crandall knows there are two fairly distinct groups of airline passengers. One group places a premium on convenience and freedom, whereas the other group places a premium on low price. The first group will pay more to avoid restrictions (such as 90-day advance purchase requirements; business travelers often need to travel on very short notice). The second group, on the other hand, will live with restrictions if the price is low enough, and lower prices will increase demand. American and the other airlines take advantage of this by offering two distinct products: a full-fare ticket and a discount-fare ticket. It can charge more for the full-fare ticket because the buyers are involuntarily insensitive to price. They are not completely insensitive to price, however, so the question is, how high can the airlines raise the price of full-fare tickets without increasing demand for discount fares? In other words, how much are the full-fare passengers willing to tolerate before they decide to swallow the restrictions and step down to the discount fares? The airlines refer to this elasticity relationship as "diversion," and it turns out to be fairly predictable.

Based on these and other variables, yield management systems take five general steps for a given flight:

1. *Determine the flight's capacity.* Obviously, you start with the number of seats available on the aircraft that will be used on this particular flight. This is trickier than it sounds since airlines sometimes have to switch planes at the last minute because of mechanical problems.
2. *Forecast full-fare demand.* Using the airline's historical database for this flight, you forecast how many full-fare passengers to expect. You also compute the probability that a given flight will have this level of demand.
3. *Assign seats to full-fare classes.* On the basis of the full-fare forecast, you set aside a certain percentage of the seats for full fare. Based on the potential variance to the forecasted amount, you select a certain percentage of possible demand that you want to be able to satisfy, such as 90 percent or 95 percent. You then set aside the appropriate amount of seats for full fare.
4. *Assign seats to discount classes.* This step is easy; subtract the full-fare allocation from the total seats in the aircraft and you'll get the number of seats to make available for discount fares.
5. *Determine discount fare and restrictions.* Here is the tricky part: determining how far to lower the discount fares and what restrictions you'll place on those fares. Remember to push the figure low enough to attract the discount passenger without tempting too many full-fare passengers into diverting. The yield management system can simulate various combinations of restrictions and discounts and then pick the one that maximizes profit for that flight.

Powerful pricing techniques like this give Crandall some great tools to help American run at a profit, but the last several years have been times of struggle in the industry. A worldwide economic slowdown has cut travel demand and continuing fare wars have devastated profits. Things got so bad by 1993 that a presidential commission was established to find ways to help the industry. Crandall is pushing to reduce American's cost structure as well as the industry's overall tax burden. The company knows how to manage prices as long as the prices are in a range that yields a profit; it may take more than great strategies to keep prices in that range, however.

**Your mission:** As Robert Crandall's vice president in charge of passenger marketing, your job is to manage prices in the face of dynamic market conditions. Review each of the following situations and decide on the best response. Keep these factors in mind as you consider each scenario: price elasticity, cost, customer service, and competition.

1. Like every organization, American might find it difficult to analyze its true costs. Consider these variables: food, fuel, plane maintenance, personnel, gate space at airports, and airplanes. Which of the following four combinations is the most accurate reflection of variable, fixed, and semifixed costs? Be prepared to explain the reasoning behind your choice.
   a. Variable costs: food, fuel, maintenance
      Fixed costs: personnel, gate space, airplanes
      Semifixed costs: none
   b. Variable costs: food
      Fixed costs: personnel, gate space, airplanes
      Semifixed costs: maintenance, fuel

c. Variable costs: fuel, food
   Fixed costs: maintenance
   Semifixed costs: personnel, gate space, airplanes

2. Since deregulation, airline pricing has been dominated by competition-based techniques. However, Crandall wants you to take a look at other techniques to see whether they could be implemented instead. Which of the following analyses seems most sensible to you?
   a. Skim pricing would work every time you start flying a new route because this is essentially the same as introducing a new product.
   b. Cost-based pricing should be used in an industry that is so sensitive to costs. American should focus its management time and financial investments on every effort possible to reduce operating costs, which is the only way to achieve acceptable profits over the long term.
   c. Value pricing is the best idea, with the goal of always undercutting the competition.

3. Although business travelers make some discretionary purchases, such behavior is much more prevalent among nonbusiness customers. For example, IBM doesn't have much choice when it is time to train its salespeople (within limits, of course), but college students do have a choice whether or not to fly south for spring break. Consequently, discounting moves on your part will tend to influence demand to a greater extent in the nonbusiness market. Which of the following discount packages will generate the greatest increase in nonbusiness travel?
   a. Offer special discounts during the times that nonbusiness travelers are likely to want to fly, such as Christmas, Thanksgiving, and summer vacation.
   b. Offer special discounts to selected groups. One example could be a spring break special you offer college students, to make it easier for them to invade Palm Springs, Fort Lauderdale, and other Sunbelt cities.
   c. Simply ask people when they make reservations whether they are flying on business or pleasure, then give the pleasure travelers an on-the-spot discount.

4. Your marketing research manager would like to get a better grip on price sensitivity in the airline market. She outlines three possible research plans. Which one would you approve?
   a. A fairly simple survey will yield the data you need.

Construct a questionnaire that lists several routes of common interest to air travelers, and ask them whether they would fly those routes at a variety of price levels. For example, on the Nashville to Raleigh-Durham run you could pose the question as follows:

Please check the highest price you would be willing to pay for a one-way ticket from Nashville to Raleigh-Durham:

$95
$125
$149
$198

The particular prices you test aren't important; you're only trying to judge overall price sensitivity. When you analyze the answers, you'll be able to see the price points on each route at which demand starts to drop off.
   b. Plot your sales figures for the last several years and superimpose your cost changes. This will tell you what effect price changes had on sales volume. For example, if on January 1, 1993, you raised prices 15 percent on the Dallas-Chicago route and sales in January were 25 percent below sales in December, you know that customers on this route are very price sensitive.
   c. The best way to measure sensitivity is to try it right there in the real world. Plan ahead to conduct this study to make sure that all other variables in the marketing mix are held constant, particularly promotions. When you're ready, raise or lower prices on one or more routes and then sit back and see what kind of response you get.

## SPECIAL PROJECT

Frequent business travelers have a small complaint. These people perceive, with considerable justification, that airlines are financing their price wars in the discount-fare category with higher prices in the full-fare category. Business travelers are stuck; when they have to fly, they have to fly. And airlines take advantage of this involuntary price insensitivity by charging stiff fares for short-notice travel. Recognizing that Robert Crandall has established customer satisfaction as a primary goal for American Airlines, how would you respond to the business travelers' complaint?[43]

1. Are the following expenses fixed or variable?
   a. Cookie dough at Mrs. Fields
   b. Cookie ovens at Mrs. Fields
   c. Factory expansion at Deere & Company to cover increased production needs
   d. Property tax at a Burger King franchise
2. You're a concert promoter, and your next show features a hot new group called the Stapleheads. As you set the ticket price, what are some of the costs you need to consider?
3. Would penetration pricing work for an automaker introducing a minivan in 1996? Explain your answer.
4. What sort of pricing technique would you use when introducing a new personal computer that is radically easier to use than existing computers and is easy to copy?
5. Do you think prestige pricing would be effective for each of the following products? Why or why not?
   a. All-natural breakfast cereal
   b. Yacht
   c. Premium office furniture
   d. Precision robot for manufacturing applications
6. Would a penetration pricing strategy be effective for a company trying to compete with Aston-Martin, the ultraluxury British carmaker?
7. What questions should an obstetrician consider when approaching the price-setting task?
8. How could the following nonprofit organizations use price to help them meet their goals?
   a. State governor who is strongly opposed to smoking
   b. Recycling center
   c. Family planning agency
9. You're the product marketing manager for a stereo equipment manufacturer, and you know that part of your target market is fairly sensitive to price but part of it isn't. What sort of filtered pricing programs could you dream up to reach both groups while keeping your average profit as high as possible?
10. What is wrong with the following plan for testing price sensitivity?
    - Product: high-performance Italian sports car
    - Possible price: $185,000
    - Test audience: random sample of college graduates, between 22 and 30 years old
    - Survey method: describe car and ask whether the price seems reasonable

# SHARPEN YOUR MARKETING SKILLS

Assume you're about to start a company. Pick one of the following: bakery, bicycle repair shop, or community newspaper. Now make a list of all the costs you'll encounter as you launch this new enterprise. Remember to consider both fixed and variable costs. Your fixed costs might include such expenses as office space, equipment leases, real estate taxes, and management salaries. Your variable costs will include newsprint (the paper newspapers are printed on), flour, sugar, oil (both for the baker and the bicycles), and other supplies.

**Decision:** Once you've compiled a list of all the costs you can think of, identify those that would be most sensitive to a drastic reduction in your sales volume. For example, if sales dropped by 50 percent at your bakery, which of your cost elements is going to cause pain the soonest? Will it be the salaries that you have to keep paying, commitments to flour mills and other suppliers, or your advertising budget? How would you respond to such a situation?

**Communication:** Write a one-paragraph policy statement for your business, describing how you'll address cost problems in the event of a sharp decline in sales.

# KEEPING CURRENT IN MARKETING

Find an article about a company that got into pricing trouble. Here are several possibilities:

- The company priced its products too high and lost sales.
- The company priced its products too low and lost potential profits.
- The company's cost structure was too high when prices were coming down in the market, leaving the company with no way to sell its products at a profit.
- The company misjudged the value that potential customers would place on its products.

Any other pricing problems that you can dig up will work as well. Be sure to consider both consumer and organizational products.

1. Why did the company get into trouble? Did it see the problem coming, or was it taken by surprise? Did anybody inside the company try to warn management that the company was headed for trouble? What happened to the company as a result?
2. Were competitors able to take advantage of the company's problems? How? Did any competitors make the same mistake or encounter the same difficulty?
3. What was the effect on customers? Did they come out ahead as a result of the company's actions, or did they suffer in some way as well?

## British Rail Puts Pricing Back on Track

Talk about a pricing headache: Sir Bob Reid has to worry about setting fares for a massive railroad network that runs 15,000 trains a day, covering 23,500 miles of track and 2,500 stations. Since 1990 Sir Bob has been chairman of British Rail, the national railroad serving England, Scotland, and Wales, and he is responsible for getting the railroad's financial house in order. Because of the complexity of the system—about 5 million possible station-to-station combinations—pricing is a difficult but vital marketing element that must be carefully managed.

Pricing was considerably less complex when Britain's first passenger train took to the rails in 1825. Back then, railroad travel was priced by the mile, a holdover from the days of stagecoach travel. Under this pricing system, a journey of 200 miles was twice as expensive as a journey of 100 miles. Although the fare system was simple to understand and easy to administer, it had no relation to the cost structure of a railroad. However, this system was continued until the 1960s, when British Rail began to reconsider its station-to-station ticket prices. Looking at the quality of service between stations in different parts of the country, the railroad decided to vary its fares. For the first time, passengers taking a 100-mile trip in one direction did not necessarily pay the same fare as passengers taking a 100-mile journey in another direction. This was a radical departure from rail ticket pricing practices on the European continent, where even today trips are generally priced according to the length of the journey.

Picking up steam, the railroad's marketers began to examine the market for train service, targeting three main market segments. The first was the business market for long-distance train service, the second was the commuter market for daily trips to urban centers, and the third was the leisure market for nonbusiness travel. Next they identified the competition: air shuttles for the business market and automobiles for the other markets. Considering their costs, their competition, and the demand in each of their three markets, British Rail executives decided to introduce three fare categories: Standard, Cheap Day, and Saver. Cheap Day and Saver are both capacity management pricing tactics aimed at smoothing out demand peaks and encouraging people to travel at times and on days when the trains are less busy. Moreover, British Rail offers a timing discount on the Saver ticket to help balance demand, so travelers willing to take the train during off-peak periods save even more.

British Rail also used market research to understand customer perceptions and to gauge reaction to pricing in various parts of the country. In this way, the marketers discovered that travelers riding the rails from London to Manchester were less price-sensitive than travelers making the trip from Manchester to London. Capitalizing on this recognition, the railroad was able to set rates higher for journeys originating in London and lower for trips originating in other parts of the country.

With Sir Bob on board, British Rail has become even more aggressive in profitability, seeking out and fulfilling customer needs. Rail service to outlying areas will soon boast not only speedier and more spacious trains but also such customer amenities as food service and on-board telephones. On the long-distance InterCity rail network, British Rail already operates state-of-the-art trains that travel at speeds up to 140 miles per hour. British Rail boasts that InterCity is the only profitable mainline railroad system in the world. For this distinction, Sir Bob can thank shrewd pricing tactics and a marketing campaign that's aimed at derailing the major competition, the air shuttles.

1. Imagine that British Rail wants to set up a high-speed train service linking London with the France-to-England channel tunnel. To test pricing for such a route, should Sir Bob launch the service with in-market price testing to determine how demand responds to varying price points? Or should he use conjoint analysis to help determine the services target customers want and the prices they are willing to pay?

2. Suppose that fuel price hikes forced the airlines and gasoline providers to significantly increase their prices. Should British Rail lead the round of price increases and advertise to explain the impact of fuel costs on rail fares? Or should the railroad follow its competitors in raising prices and advertise the relatively lower costs of traveling by rail rather than by air or by car?

3. If Sir Bob wanted to attract international train travelers without affecting the profitability of domestic train travelers, would he accomplish this more effectively by offering special discounts that are available only in the traveler's home country or by lowering the prices on major tourist routes that originate in London and other cities where international travelers begin their travel through Great Britain?

## Compaq: From Premium Supplier to Price Competitor

Bite into a cheeseburger and think about this pricing scenario. The cheeseburgers you market are priced at, say, $5 each. You make the best burgers in town, and customers are happy to buy. Think ahead 18 or 24 months and imagine that the top price you can convince people to pay is now only $1.50 or so, and for this, your customers demand not a cheeseburger but lobster and caviar. Even worse, if you can't satisfy the demand, a hundred competitors have popped up who will.

Sounds a little improbable, doesn't it? However, that's just about what happened in the personal computer market in the early 1990s. Compaq, the first serious competitor to IBM (in the IBM-compatible segment of the market), had earned a reputation for making top-quality machines and charging a premium for them. Businesses and other buyers who wanted the best usually bought Compaq and paid the price. The company prided itself on the quality of its machines; the price tag seemed a natural result of that devotion to always building the best.

### Inviting the Competition

However, Compaq unintentionally sent an invitation to hundreds of potential competitors. The market Compaq had helped develop was growing quickly, and Compaq's prices were high enough to allow scrappy new competitors to slip into the market with lower prices. These newer, smaller players didn't have Compaq's brand image or much hope of beating Compaq on product quality by any sizable margin, so price became their major competitive weapon. With so many hungry competitors ready to drop prices, the inevitable result was a price war. Throw in a sudden slowdown in the economy as the United States and most of the world slipped into a recession, and the personal computer market quickly changed from a fairly easy place to make money to a ferociously competitive arena in which few suppliers were making any money at all.

By late 1991, Compaq's sales had slowed considerably, and the company posted its first quarterly loss ever. In the

view of the board of directors, founder Rod Canion was failing to adapt to the market's growing emphasis on low prices. Canion insisted that as soon as the economy picked up, so would Compaq sales. The board disagreed, however, and Canion was pushed out of his own company in October of that year.

## Becoming a Low-Cost Leader

Canion's replacement was Eckhard Pfeiffer, who had been in charge of the company's European operations. Compaq quickly took on a new personality under Pfeiffer's leadership. Convinced that prices were headed down permanently, he set about transforming Compaq into a low-cost producer. Various moves to improve efficiency helped lower manufacturing costs, as did an order to run the factories around the clock.

Compaq also changed its long-standing policy of assembling all its computers by itself. Realizing that it was less expensive to subcontract parts of the assembly process, Pfeiffer and his team changed course. This was a major cultural change for Compaq, and changes this dramatic often wreak havoc in large corporations. As one Compaq executive put it, however, "I don't think change is stressful; I think failure is stressful."

Within a year of taking the wheel from Canion and instituting these changes, Pfeiffer dropped prices by as much as one-third. The price gap between Compaq and lesser-known brand names became so small that many buyers switched. In the first six months of 1993, for instance, Compaq's sales more than doubled. Compaq successfully made the switch from a premium supplier (with premium prices to match) to a competitor that can compete aggressively on price while still maintaining its top-of-the-line image. The emphasis on efficiency and cost control also means that Compaq is one of the few computer manufacturers in a position to make any kind of profit as well.

## Aftermath of the Price War

After several years of unrelenting price wars, the pricing situation in personal computers may be ready to change. As one analyst said in 1993, "Smaller vendors simply aren't making money, and they can't use price as an attack weapon the way they used to." Compaq appears to have come out of the price war in even better shape than when it went in, thanks to a fresh perspective on pricing strategy and cost controls.

At the beginning of 1994, Compaq had a 10 percent share of the U.S. personal computer market, compared to Apple at just above 12 percent and IBM at nearly 14 percent. Looking toward the future, Pfeiffer set a goal of passing IBM and Apple to become the largest personal computer company by 1996. The goal certainly seems attainable in view of the company's recent performance. Compaq benefits mightily from being in a rare position for any company: It enjoys strong brand image but also has one of the lowest cost structures in the industry. Many companies have one or the other, but combining tight cost controls and efficient operations with quality products and customer support is a feat matched by few firms in any industry.

## Questions

1. What effect might lower profit margins have on Compaq's ability to provide top-notch customer service? If the company couldn't afford to spend as heavily on customer service, how might customers feel about trading lower prices for a lower level of support? (Don't forget about market segmentation.) What options would Compaq have in this situation?

2. Does Compaq's pricing strategy conflict with its positioning as a supplier of top-quality products? Explain your answer, taking into account changes Compaq has tried to implement over the years.

3. In a market as volatile as the computer industry, prices can change dramatically in the course of a few weeks. If Compaq had to drop prices significantly to respond to competitive pressure, would it have an obligation to offer refunds to customers who paid the earlier, higher price? Why or why not?

4. International marketers often add "uplifts" to their prices when they market products overseas. The uplift covers the additional cost of doing business, including import duties, additional staff, and currency exchanges. Do you think Compaq should absorb those costs itself to be more competitive in international markets?

390

# PART V
# DISTRIBUTION STRATEGIES

# 13

# Marketing Channels

**After studying this chapter, you will be able to**

**1.** Explain the need for marketing channels

**2.** Describe the functions channels perform in the marketing mix

**3.** Define the various types of channels in use today

**4.** Outline the factors producers consider when selecting channels

**5.** Clarify the difference between conventional marketing channels and horizontally and vertically integrated marketing systems

**6.** Delineate channel cooperation, channel conflict, channel leadership, and channel power

**7.** Identify the major legal issues surrounding channel management

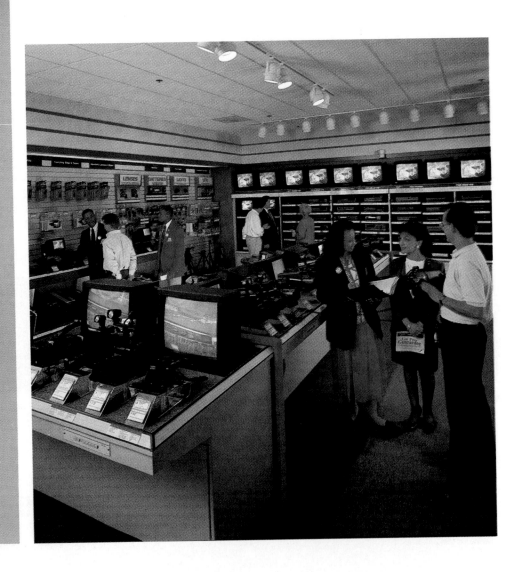

## Power Tool Maker Has a Remodeling Project of Its Own

Nolan Archibald had a bit of a mess on his hands. He had recently been promoted to chairman and CEO of 80-year-old Black & Decker, a power tool manufacturer that was having profit problems, losing market share, and generally annoying many of the wholesalers and retailers it relied on to sell products to customers.

The problem with wholesalers and retailers was particularly acute. The company was considered rather arrogant, to put it mildly. Referring to Archibald's predecessors, one former Black & Decker employee said, "Management seemed to think it had the answer to every question and would generously impart its wisdom to the masses." Such an attitude nearly got Black & Decker kicked out of Wal-Mart, now the largest retailer in the United States. Not the best plan for selling products, to say the least.

Inventory shortages plagued retailers. If a Black & Decker product turned out to be popular with the public, retailers had a good chance of running out, because Black & Decker put a lot of emphasis on meeting its internal financial goals. The company restrained production toward the end of its fiscal year, to make sure its inventory levels dropped quite low. This practice made Black & Decker's balance sheet look good, but it was driving retailers away.

To complicate matters, Archibald's predecessors had recently purchased General Electric's entire line of small household appliances (at the time, the biggest brand transfer in history). Although the new line of products provided a strong stream of revenue, it gave Black & Decker yet another marketing channel headache. Before the acquisition, most Black & Decker products were sold through hardware stores, home improvement centers, mail-order retailers, and discount stores. However, to be successful, small appliances had to be sold through department stores as well, and Black & Decker had little experience in this area. Unfortunately, the company tried to use the same approach it had used with power tools, which only served to alienate the department stores that had grown used to good treatment from General Electric.

Finally, back in the power tool division, the very foundation of the company, somebody had been asleep at the switch. While Black & Decker continued to pursue its traditional segments of low-cost "homeowner" tools and high-cost professional tools, a new market segment had developed between the two. Serious amateur woodworkers and semiprofessionals wanted higher quality than was being offered by the homeowner tools, but they didn't need the built-like-a-tank reliability of the professional tools, nor were they prepared to pay that much. Into this growing gap jumped several competitors, led by Japan's Makita. Because it worked very hard to fill a product gap that was starting to worry retailers, Makita was earning more and more shelf space. In the retail world, shelf space is absolutely vital; without adequate shelf space, manufacturers simply can't survive.

Therefore, Nolan Archibald faced quite a challenge. Now sit in his chair for a moment. How would you handle his problems? How would you repair the bad reputation that Black & Decker had gained with wholesalers and retailers? How would you combat the pressure from competitors who were trying to push you off the shelf? How would you handle the new small appliances, given your lack of experience? In short, what steps would you take to ensure Black & Decker's survival and continued success?[1]

# CHAPTER OVERVIEW

The challenge faced by Black & Decker highlights the importance of marketing channels. This chapter starts by explaining the need for marketing channels in today's competitive markets. Next, you're introduced to the most common types of marketing channels and the people and organizations that make those channels work. After that, you'll explore the strategic aspects of marketing channel selection and management, including the integrated channel systems used by many of the world's most successful companies. The chapter concludes with a look at the major legal issues that affect channel management.

# FOUNDATIONS OF MARKETING CHANNELS

The stately retail establishments along London's Regent Street and the livestock auctions in Chicago have a lot in common. They assist in the flow of products from producers to consumers. They have to invest in facilities, equipment, and people to make sure this flow continues as smoothly as possible. They also have to engage in marketing research, strategic planning, and promotion to make sure they serve the right customers profitably. Whether a customer arrives in a Bentley or a Mack truck, marketing channels are a crucial part of the marketing mix (see Exhibit 13.1).

**Exhibit 13.1**
**THE IMPORTANCE OF MARKETING CHANNELS**
This livestock auction in Montana and the art auction in London are both vital players in their respective marketing channels.

# Definition of Marketing Channels

A **marketing channel** is a system of individuals and organizations (supported by facilities, equipment, and information) for directing the flow of goods and services from producer to customer. Marketing channels are also frequently referred to as *distribution channels* because distribution is one of their primary functions. A channel can be simple and direct. For example, at the Granville Island Public Market in Vancouver, British Columbia, farmers sell fruits and vegetables directly to final consumers. The channel in this case consists of a building in which farmers rent stall space.

On the other hand, a marketing channel can be very complex. The dinner plates on which a Vancouver resident serves this farm-fresh produce might have been manufactured in a stoneware factory in Taiwan, exported by an international distributor, transported by a container cargo ship, imported by a housewares wholesaler in Vancouver, then sold by a retailer such as The Bay (a descendant of the original Hudson's Bay Company). The broccoli might have traveled 10 miles and made the trip from field to table in less than a day, whereas the plate journeyed thousands of miles and possibly spent months inside various storage facilities and transport vehicles.

## Role of Marketing Channels

Channels are a necessary component in the marketing of all goods and services, in both for-profit and nonprofit organizations. Producers need marketing channels for three important reasons. First, channels take care of the transaction aspects of marketing, including the selling, the financing, and the risk taking associated with storing products in anticipation of future sales. Second, they perform the logistical function of moving products from the point of production to the point of purchase or consumption. Third, they help producers promote goods and services.

Marketing channels also benefit customers. By giving consumers and organizations access to the right products, in the right place, at the right time, and in the right quantity, channels make products more valuable and the buying process more efficient. Say you want to share dinner with that special someone, but the college cafeteria is closed. A prominent marketing channel will come to your rescue. The 7-Eleven store around the corner carries Hostess Twinkies and Diet Coke, so it meets your requirement for having the right products. Because it is just around the corner and is open all night, 7-Eleven has the right product in the right place at the right time. Also, because it allows you to buy only the 12 Twinkies you need for dinner without requiring you to buy an entire trainload, 7-Eleven offers the products in the right quantity as well.

## Marketing Intermediaries

The people and organizations that assist in the flow of goods and services from producer to customers are called **marketing intermediaries**. Here are the common types:

- *Middleman.* An archaic but often-used term, **middleman** refers to just about anybody acting as an intermediary between producer and consumer. Obviously, many middlemen are actually middlewomen.
- *Agent or broker.* Intermediaries with legal authority to market goods and services and to perform other functions on behalf of producers are called **agents** or **brokers.** Agents generally work for producers continuously, whereas brokers may be employed for just one deal. In some cases, agents sell to other intermediaries such as industrial distributors. In addition, an agent or broker can work for the buyer rather than the seller, a situation becoming more common in real estate, for instance.
- *Wholesaler.* **Wholesalers** are organizations that buy from producers and sell to

**marketing channel**
A system designed to move goods and services from producers to customers, which consists of people and organizations supported by various facilities, equipment, and information resources

**marketing intermediaries**
People or organizations that assist in the flow of products in a marketing channel

**middleman**
An outdated term that is synonymous with marketing intermediary—a person or organization that helps producers move products through marketing channels

**agents**
Intermediaries who assist with the marketing of goods and services but who don't assume ownership of products; agents, unlike brokers, usually work long-term for producers

**brokers**
Intermediaries who assist with the marketing of goods and services but who don't assume ownership of products; brokers typically have short-term relationships with producers

**wholesalers**
Intermediaries that move goods from producers to retailers

**retailers**
Intermediaries that sell to final customers; they purchase goods from wholesalers, or in some cases, directly from producers

**distributor**
A general term usually applied in organizational markets to intermediaries that perform the equivalent functions of both wholesalers and retailers

**dealer**
Basically the same type of intermediary as a distributor, although some people distinguish dealers as those intermediaries that sell only to final customers, not to other intermediaries

**value-added reseller (VAR)**
Intermediaries that buy basic products from producers, add value by modifying or expanding the products, then resell them to final customers

**merchants**
Intermediaries that assume ownership of the goods they sell to customers or other intermediaries; merchants usually take physical possession of the goods they sell

**functional intermediaries**
Intermediaries that, unlike merchants, do not assume ownership of the products they are selling

**facilitating agents**
People and organizations that assist with the flow of products and information in marketing channels, including banking and insurance functions

other **wholesalers**, retailers, and organizational customers. The highest-revenue wholesaling system in the United States is the one serving the grocery industry, followed by the wholesalers for raw farm products and machinery.[2]

- *Retailer.* As the last link in many marketing channels, **retailers** sell directly to final customers. The most obvious form of this intermediary is the retail store, but such diverse efforts as mail order, door-to-door sales, and vending machines are also retailing.

- *Distributor.* **Distributor** is a general term applied to a variety of intermediaries. These individuals and firms perform several functions, including inventory management, personal sales, and financing. This term is more common in organizational markets, although wholesalers are occasionally referred to as distributors.

- *Dealer.* Another general term that can apply to just about any intermediary is **dealer,** although some people distinguish dealers as intermediaries that sell only to final customers, not to other intermediaries.[3]

- *Value-added reseller.* An emerging class of intermediaries, called **value-added resellers (VARs),** enhance the products they receive from producers and then sell the modified products to customers. VARs are particularly common in the computer hardware and software industries, where they buy basic products from producers, add value through such actions as writing special software or integrating several products into one system, and then sell the complete package. This process works well for producers who may not have the expertise to customize products for niche markets and for customers who can get specific solutions to their unique problems.

Intermediaries don't necessarily belong to a separate company or organization. As you'll see later in this chapter, many producers own all or part of their marketing channels and thus serve as their own intermediaries. Also, marketing intermediaries can be split into two general groups. **Merchants** assume ownership of goods and then resell them to their customers, whether to other intermediaries or final consumers. On the other hand, **functional intermediaries** do not take title to products; the producer transfers ownership directly to the functional intermediary's customers. Wholesalers, for example, are classified as either merchant or functional. Merchant wholesalers earn profits by reselling products at higher prices than they paid; functional wholesalers are compensated with fees or commissions. Agents, in contrast, don't assume ownership of the products they sell.

Finally, several other types of individuals and organizations help with the marketing and distribution process. These **facilitating agents** don't always directly participate in the flow of products; rather they add expertise or supporting functions, such as those described in the following paragraphs. In some cases, marketing intermediaries themselves perform these facilitating tasks; in other cases, the job is done by an outside firm.

- *Financial services.* An important facilitating function in many channels is extending credit to buyers. Sometimes producers opt to extend credit themselves, adding the revenue from financing to the revenue from the sale of goods. For example, General Motors Acceptance Corporation, a subsidiary of the big automaker, offers car loans and contributes a substantial portion of GM's total revenue. A second finance-related function often performed by special intermediaries is credit checks and credit ratings, which help sellers make safer choices about allowing customers to purchase on credit. TRW Information Services is one of the largest facilitators of this type in the United States, helping thousands of companies with credit history information. Finally, bill collection is an unpleasant financial task that is frequently handed over to outside companies such as Dun & Bradstreet Commercial Collections.

- *Risk taking.* Risks inherent in distribution processes include theft of goods, spoilage of perishable food products, and damage resulting from accidents and natural disasters. Occasionally, a consumer fad will die out so quickly that marketing intermediaries are stuck holding unsellable inventory, as was the case in the home video game market in the early 1980s. Although risk taking isn't always apparent in marketing channels, it is an important function.

- *Transportation and storage.* At the core of marketing channel activity is the physical movement of goods from producers to customers. Transportation and storage is a major industry in itself, and these functions also make up a significant portion of the operating costs of many manufacturing companies. The wide array of physical distribution options and decisions that affect a company's marketing efforts are covered in more detail in Chapter 16.

## BASIC CHANNEL FUNCTIONS

You can get a better grasp of the role of channels by breaking their functions into five groups: facilitating exchange processes, alleviating discrepancies, standardizing transactions, matching buyers and sellers, and supporting customers.

### Facilitating Exchange Processes

Contrary to what some people believe, marketing intermediaries generally decrease the cost of delivering products to customers. Exhibit 13.2 shows how intermediaries make the marketing of stereo equipment more efficient, for example. Assume that four manufacturers and eight customers are involved. Without intermediaries, if all customers interacted with all makers, 32 interactions would result. However, by introducing a retail store in the system, the number of interactions drops to 12. Because each interchange costs money, which shows up in the price of the equipment, lowering the number of transactions lowers the overall cost of delivering products.

In addition to directly reducing transaction costs, the presence of intermediaries allows various players in the system to specialize. This further increases cost effi-

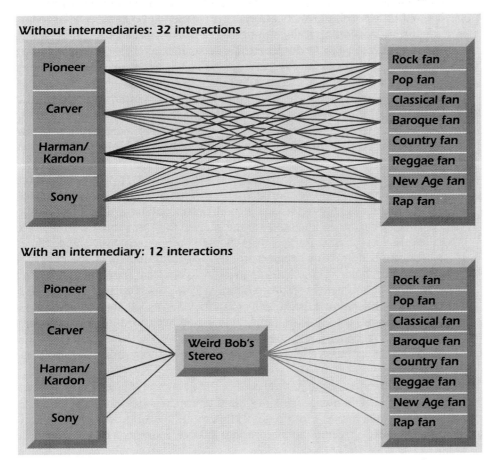

**Exhibit 13.2
INTERMEDIARIES
INCREASE EFFICIENCY**
Intermediaries increase the efficiency of marketing transactions because they decrease the number of separate interactions that must occur in a market.

ciencies because each player can make the investment needed to achieve economies of scale. For example, next time you're strolling through the nearest shopping mall, look at the names of the bookstores. You aren't likely to see Bantam, Simon & Schuster, or one of the other publishers selling its wares directly to consumers. Carrying only one publisher's line of books, such a store would probably not sell enough to stay profitable. However, B. Dalton, Waldenbooks, and other book retailers carry products from a wide variety of publishers. Thus, their wider product offerings generate enough revenue to let them operate at a profit while still maintaining reasonable prices.

## Alleviating Discrepancies

A discrepancy in distribution exists whenever a producer's offering doesn't match a customer's expectations. Channel discrepancies can be distinguished by quantity and assortment. **Discrepancies of quantity** occur when customers are unable to purchase the right amount of the desired product. For example, a refinery owned by a petroleum company such as Shell Oil can produce thousands of gallons of gasoline a day. Not too many car owners, however, need to purchase 5,000 or 10,000 gallons of gas each time they fill up. Channel intermediaries, in this case gasoline distributors and service stations, come to the rescue by selling smaller amounts to individual customers. Meanwhile, **discrepancies of assortment** exist when customers are unable to buy the right collection of goods and services. If Campbell Soup, Kellogg, Heinz, and Keebler all sold directly to consumers, you'd have to shop at four separate stores to buy soup, cereal, ketchup, and cookies. With one stop at a Safeway or Lucky food store, you can purchase all four items.

To alleviate these two discrepancies, marketing intermediaries engage in **regrouping activities,** reorganizing goods to achieve the right quantities and assortments of products. This can take up to four steps, as seen in Exhibit 13.3.[4]

- *Sorting out.* The first step, known as **sorting out,** is breaking down a diverse supply of goods into separate stocks of similar products. Weyerhaeuser, a large lumber producer, divides its products into several grades based on quality and intended use. Many agricultural products are sorted out based on quality, and packaged goods are occasionally sorted out as well. For example, L'eggs Products sorts out its "seconds," merchandise that is still functional but not aesthetically perfect, then distributes and markets them through a different channel.[5]
- *Accumulating.* The next step is **accumulating,** collecting smaller stocks of like items into a larger supply. Accumulation serves three key purposes in the marketing channel. First, it gives both buyers and sellers some protection from price fluctuations. Buyers can purchase large stocks and put them in storage if they expect prices to go up in the future. Conversely, if sellers expect prices to drop sometime in the future, they make more money by selling large accumulated quantities before prices actually decrease. Second, accumulation protects everyone in the channel (producer to customer) from interruptions in supply. For example, when Reebok accumulates a supply of its shoes in warehouses in the United States, it is protecting itself and its retailers in the event of problems at the factory in South Korea. Reebok can continue supplying retailers from warehouse stocks until the production problem is resolved. Third, accumulation of large stocks before shipping and storage reduces the per unit price of transporting goods from one intermediary to the next. For example, Jaguar couldn't afford to hire small ships to move individual cars from England to the United States. However, it can afford to collect dozens or hundreds of cars and then bring them over all at once on a large ship.
- *Allocating.* At the next stage in the process, the large accumulated stocks of similar goods are broken down into stock sizes that better meet the needs of other marketing intermediaries. This process, known as **allocating,** breaks a large bulk supply such as a petroleum tanker load into smaller, more manageable units (be-

**discrepancies of quantity**
Situations in which the quantity available doesn't match the quantity desired

**discrepancies of assortment**
Situations in which the assortment of products available doesn't match the assortment desired

**regrouping activities**
Four functions (sorting out, accumulating, allocating, and assorting) that eliminate discrepancies of quantity or assortment

**sorting out**
Dividing one heterogeneous supply into separate, homogeneous supplies

**accumulating**
Gathering individual homogeneous supplies into one large heterogeneous supply

**allocating**
Breaking accumulated supplies into smaller units that are easier for later intermediaries and customers to handle

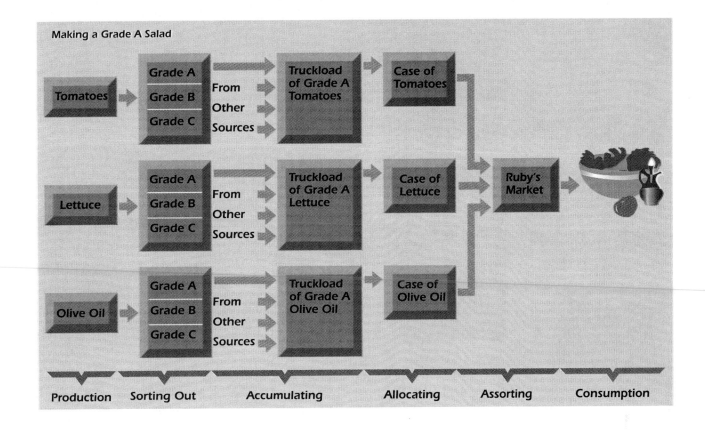

Making a Grade A Salad

Production | Sorting Out | Accumulating | Allocating | Assorting | Consumption

cause of this, allocation is often called **breaking bulk**). Individual shoe retailers like Foot Locker can't handle an entire warehouseful of Reeboks, so they are given smaller case lots.

- *Assorting.* The final step is **assorting,** in which the right assortment of goods is collected for a target group of customers. Before you went shopping for Twinkies and Diet Coke, for example, 7-Eleven created the right assortment of products to satisfy your needs. Assorting can be used to build competitive advantage as well. Safeway recognizes that its customers don't like to make several stops for common household needs, so its Safeway Super Stores carry a wide variety of housewares and supplies in addition to normal grocery stocks.

## Standardizing Transactions

The third major function of marketing channels is standardizing transactions. Think about the last time you purchased a carton of milk. Imagine how complicated the transaction would have been if you'd had to negotiate the price, the size of the container, the method of payment, and the location of the exchange. All these choices have been standardized for you in the milk market. You choose from a predetermined array of sizes, for instance, and each size has a set price that isn't negotiable, so you know in advance how much it will cost. Without these standards, even the simplest purchase would be a complicated hassle for customers. Standardization also assists intermediaries by allowing them to automate much of the buying, selling, and physical distribution required to move products through the channel. Vending machines, which can now sell anything from soda and chips to pasta and pizza, are the ultimate in standardized transactions (see Exhibit 13.4).[6]

Of course, not all markets exhibit the same degree of standardization, nor do all phases in the marketing channel. For example, when a mechanical engineering department at General Motors purchases a computer-aided design system from a vendor such as Intergraph, several elements of this transaction are likely to be negotiated. GM may want a break on prices because it is a large customer, and it might

**Exhibit 13.3
REGROUPING
ACTIVITIES IN
MARKETING
CHANNELS**
Intermediaries resolve discrepancies of quantity and assortment by performing four regrouping tasks: sorting out, accumulating, allocating, and assorting.

**breaking bulk**
Breaking accumulated supplies into smaller units that are easier to handle; synonymous with allocating

**assorting**
As the final step in the regrouping process, assorting creates the particular mix of goods required by target customers

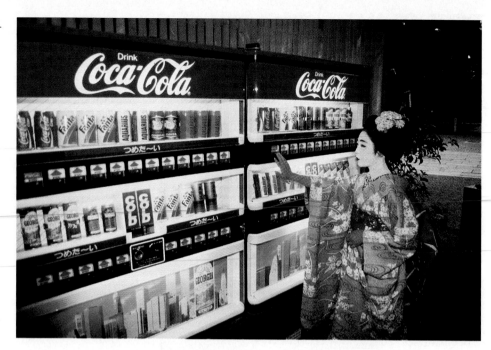

**Exhibit 13.4**
**THE ULTIMATE IN STANDARDIZED TRANSACTIONS**
Vending machines take the place of retail outlets and human cashiers. Consumers in Japan can purchase a wide variety of products from vending machines.

ask Intergraph to tailor the software for GM's specific needs. Going back to your purchase of a carton of milk, transactions farther back in the channel were probably less standardized. A large milk processor may have negotiated prices with individual dairy farmers, for instance.

## Matching Buyers and Sellers

Marketing intermediaries also provide the valuable service of matching buyers and sellers. A sculptor may not know where potential customers are located or how they can be reached, but a good art dealer will. By using the art dealer as an intermediary, the sculptor reaches a bigger audience than he or she could alone. Customers benefit as well because they don't have to peek into attic studios all over town, trying to find sculptures to buy; art dealers help with this search process.

With intermediaries carrying out this matching process, producers are able to concentrate on what they do best, which is creating products. Campbell Soup doesn't have to worry about building or managing retail outlets; it can stick to the processing and preparation of food and leave the retailing to grocery stores. Similarly, the grocer can concentrate on selling in its local markets and not on figuring out how to fill a can of soup. Campbell also benefits from grocers' close contact with final customers because it gets customer feedback from all the retailers that carry its products. Because producers are often one or more steps removed from the customers who ultimately consume their products, the market intelligence provided by intermediaries is vital if the producer is to continue to provide products that meet consumer needs.

## Providing Customer Service

Finally, marketing channels provide the critical element of customer support and service. If your Toshiba television set breaks down, you don't have to send it back to Japan for service. You're more likely to send it back to the dealer or the dealer's service representative. In addition, marketing intermediaries provide valuable support when customers attempt to use products they've purchased. If you're entranced by the sound of those home organs you hear in the mall, the dealer can help you with delivery, installation, and lessons. Providing customer service is a crucial aspect of many organizational transactions, where products often require installation, training, routine maintenance, and other forms of attention.

# TYPES OF MARKETING CHANNELS

The vast diversity of products and customers in today's markets requires a wide variety of marketing channels. **Direct channels** are the simplest channel type. The people who produce the goods and services interact directly with **customers. Indirect channels,** on the other hand, rely on one or more intermediaries between producers and customers.

## Channels for Consumer Goods

Marketing channels for consumer products can be classified by the number of intermediaries. As seen in Exhibit 13.5, consumer channels typically have from zero to three intermediaries. Here's a closer look at the characteristics of the major consumer channel types:

- *Producer to consumer.* When no intermediaries are between the producer and the consumer, the channel is direct. This type of channel is most commonly used with organizational products, but it is also used by a few well-known consumer products companies, including Avon and Tupperware. For instance, Avon and three dozen other cosmetics firms use direct channels in Thailand, where 60 percent of cosmetics are sold direct.[7] Also, nearly all services are sold through direct channels as well. Keep in mind that the absence of intermediaries doesn't mean that the job of intermediaries suddenly disappears. If the regrouping functions already described need to be performed for a given product, then the producer will have to perform these tasks. On the positive side, direct channels give producers much more control over the marketing process.
- *Producer to retailer to consumer.* The channel from producer to retailer to consumer is common when the retail establishments involved are relatively large, such as a Sears, Kmart, or Wal-Mart. In fact, Wal-Mart has pressured some of its smaller suppliers to drop their intermediaries and deal with the giant retailer directly.[8] Because these stores buy from producers in very large quantities, it often makes sense for the producers to deal directly with the retailers. However, this channel doesn't have an intermediary dedicated to storage and transportation, so either the producer or the retailer will have to perform these functions.
- *Producer to wholesaler to retailer to consumer.* The most common channel for consumer goods is from producer to wholesaler to retailer to consumer. It employs a wholesaler to take care of the shipping and transportation needs mentioned for the previous channel. In addition, wholesalers offer the accumulating and allocating functions that allow small producers to interact with large retailers, and vice versa.
- *Producer to agent to wholesaler to retailer to consumer.* In some cases, a producer

**direct channels**
Marketing channels that lack intermediaries, in which producers and customers interact directly

**indirect channels**
Marketing channels that rely on intermediaries to move products from producers to customers

**Exhibit 13.5
CHANNELS FOR
CONSUMER GOODS**
Channels for consumer goods range from a direct link between producers and consumers to a complex system involving three levels of intermediaries.

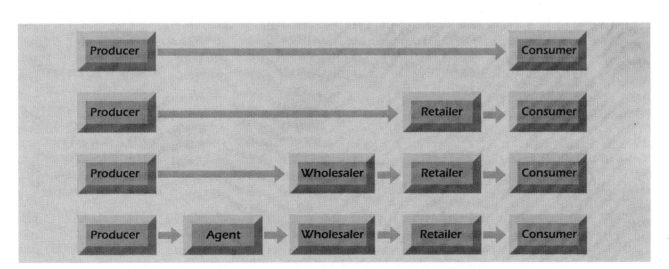

chooses to use agents to help market its goods to wholesalers. Agents are used primarily when producers lack the expertise or resources to sell their products to wholesalers. For example, small producers can engage experienced agents to help deal with large wholesalers.

## Channels for Organizational Goods

Channels for organizational goods follow the same basic concepts as those for consumer goods. A key difference is the presence of the industrial distributor in place of wholesalers (and sometimes retailers) in the consumer channel. Also, organizational channels tend to be shorter (with fewer intermediaries). Here are descriptions of the four basic organizational channels (also illustrated in Exhibit 13.6):

- *Producer to organizational buyer.* The only channel type used by about a quarter of U.S. firms engaged in business-to-business marketing is from producer to organizational buyer. Even if a firm also uses indirect channels, direct channels are the only reasonable choice for some products and some customers. Complex products that require a good deal of presale and postsale support are often best handled through a direct channel, because the manufacturer might be the only entity with sufficient expertise to help customers. Also, manufacturers frequently use direct channels with large customers because these large accounts generate enough business to support the sales effort involved and because large customers have a habit of throwing their economic weight around to demand personalized service.

- *Producer to distributor to organizational buyer.* Of all business-to-business marketers, about three-quarters use intermediaries, and of these, distributors are the most common. Distributors can be divided into general-line distributors, which sell a wide variety of goods to a large number of customers, and limited-line distributors, which specialize in one or a few high-volume goods, such as steel and chemicals. These limited-line distributors are often called jobbers.

    Marketing through distributors does have potential disadvantages. First, distributors usually want access to large customers that the manufacturer may try to keep for itself. Second, most distributors try to keep their product selections wide, which frequently means carrying competing lines. Third, distributors don't always respond to manufacturers' advice or wishes regarding promotions, pricing, and operational policies.

- *Producer to agent to organizational buyer.* Often called manufacturers' representatives or simply reps in organizational markets, agents are used by both large and small producers for two important reasons. First, agents typically have close,

**Exhibit 13.6
CHANNELS FOR
ORGANIZATIONAL
GOODS**
Like consumer goods, organizational goods are marketed through a variety of channel systems, including both direct and indirect channels.

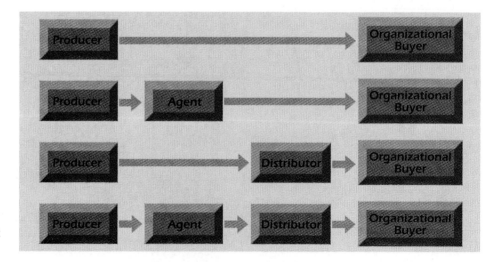

hands-on knowledge of local market areas, knowledge that can take years of persistent selling to acquire. Second, unlike distributors, agents usually don't carry competing brands of products, although a trend toward doing so does exist in some markets.[9]

- *Producer to agent to distributor to organizational buyer.* Some producers use agents to sell to distributors, who then sell to customers. This is typically done when the producer lacks the skills or resources to sell to distributors itself.

## Channels for Services

The concept of a distribution channel must be reexamined for services.[10] When you market services, you aren't moving pet food through a distribution pipeline; you're looking for ways to bring performances and customers together. Because of this, channels for services are generally simple and direct. In most cases, you have just two fundamental decisions to make regarding service distribution: where you'll provide the service and whether you'll use a channel intermediary.

The ideal service location is usually obvious. The need for specialized machinery and transportation costs may dictate that services take place at the provider's location. On the other hand, creative distribution can help you build competitive advantage. If you can save your customers time and trouble, you're a step ahead of your competition.

Channel intermediaries make sense when the number of buyers far exceeds the number of suppliers, as is the case with many travel and financial services. When you pay for dinner in a Paris restaurant with an AT&T Universal Card, you've used the credit card as a channel intermediary. It might seem a little strange, but what you've really done is get a loan from the restaurant, which then seeks payment from the bank. The bank then charges you for the convenience of borrowing money from the restaurant.

Technology can serve as an intermediary and provide indirect delivery of services. CompuServe, for example, provides access to hundreds of databases on a wide variety of topics. Subscribers can tap into this wealth of information any time they want, from anywhere in the world where appropriate telephone connections are available. The information is accessible whenever it's convenient for the customer to retrieve it. IBM and Sears are trying to go beyond CompuServe's "information junkie" audience with Prodigy, a service aimed at the general public.[11]

No matter how you deliver a service, remember that service distribution involves interactive marketing; that is, the provider interacts significantly with the buyer. The implications for marketing people are obvious and important: Make sure service providers have excellent interpersonal skills, and make sure you support them with a company that puts top priority on customer satisfaction.

## Direct Marketing

Chapter 1 points out that several areas of the marketing mix don't fit neatly into the four Ps model. The field of **direct marketing** straddles both distribution and promotion and is defined by the Direct Marketing Association as "an interactive system of marketing" that employs one or more types of advertising with the goal of creating a "measurable response and/or transaction at any location."[12] The two key words here are *interactive* and *measurable*. First, direct marketing is interactive because of the response mechanism that every target customer can use, whether a toll-free number, a postcard, a message on a computer network, or some other scheme (see Exhibit 13.7). Second, unlike other types of promotion, direct marketing allows you to measure with a high degree of precision how effectively your marketing is working. For instance, with *direct mail*, one of the most prevalent forms of direct marketing, you know exactly how many letters you send out and exactly how many responses you get in return.

Although it can be viewed as a promotional strategy, direct marketing dictates a particular set of distribution channel choices, which is why it is introduced in this

**direct marketing**
An interactive system of marketing in which producers or intermediaries communicate directly and individually with target customers

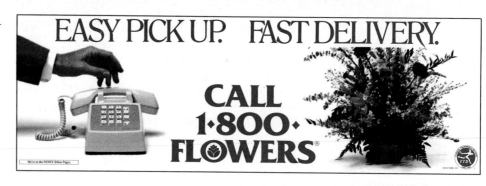

**Exhibit 13.7
DIRECT MARKETING
CHANNELS**
1-800-Flowers, the nationwide toll-free florist with the hard-to-forget name, communicates directly with its customers.

**direct selling**
Selling in which individual sellers communicate through direct contact with individual buyers

**dual distribution**
Channel systems in which more than one channel is used

**multilevel marketing (MLM)**
A hierarchical distribution system in which independent distributors sell products and recruit other distributors to work for them

chapter along with the other channel types. If the direct-marketing link is between the producer and the final customer (in either consumer or organizational markets), you're using a direct channel by definition, since no one else is involved. (The one exception to this is when the producer uses a fulfillment service to take care of shipping the products.) However, direct marketing can also occur between any two parties in any of the channel configurations. A producer can use it to reach wholesalers, wholesalers can use it to reach retailers or organizational customers, and retailers can use it to reach consumers. Chapter 18 explores the promotional aspects of direct marketing.

**Direct selling** refers to any sales situation in which one human being is selling, another one is buying, and the two come in direct, personal contact. However, direct selling isn't necessarily limited to direct channels; it can occur between producers and customers, between producers and intermediaries, and between intermediaries and customers. If one salesperson visits your office from the Apple computer factory and another visits from a retailer such as Computerland, both are engaged in direct selling, even though one is in a direct channel and the other is in an indirect channel.

## Complex Channels

The various types of channels in operation today have been presented as distinct, well-defined systems. However, this isn't always the case. Three areas show how complex marketing channels can be: multiple channels, international channels, and hybrid intermediaries.

### MULTIPLE MARKETING CHANNELS

Sometimes a manufacturer finds that it needs more than one channel to serve all its potential customers most effectively. For example, Illinois Tool Works (ITW) opted for two separate channels in order to meet the needs of two distinct customer bases. It uses a captive sales force to deal with its large customers, who require specialized attention but who aren't as cost conscious as other customers. On the other hand, the company's smaller customers want lower prices, convenient locations, and small lot sizes, so ITW uses a distributor channel to reach them. To discourage competition between its direct and indirect channels, ITW prices its products so that the large customers can't get deep discounts when buying in volume from the distributors.[13] These multichannel arrangements are often called **dual distribution,** even though they can cover more than two channels.

A variation on multiple channel arrangements is the system known as **multilevel marketing (MLM),** commonly used in such industries as cosmetics (Mary Kay), cleaners (Amway), and other home supplies. The basic structure of an MLM system involves independent distributors who both sell products and recruit other distributors to work for them. MLM is catching on in financial services, jewelry, clothing, gift items, and a variety of other areas as well. In the United States alone, more than 12 million people are engaged in MLM.[14]

As markets become increasingly fragmented and competition gets more niche-oriented, marketing channels will only get more complicated. For example, Exhibit

13.8 shows how organizational channels have grown more complicated over the last several decades. The implication of such models is that companies will have to continually search for new and different ways to reach customers. The result will be more multichannel systems, more reliance on new marketing technologies such as computer-to-computer ordering, and fewer companies that rely on simplistic, textbook-style channel systems. Computer purchasers can now pick from five major channels: smaller retailers/dealers, major chains, superstores (such as Computer City), mail-order suppliers, and computer shows.[15] IBM has used more than 18 separate channels for its diverse product family.[16] Of course, the additional cost and potential management headaches of these complicated channel systems must be considered as well. However, marketers in many industries find themselves with no other choice. As their markets fragment into collections of small niches, they need to provide each target segment with the best channel.

## INTERNATIONAL CHANNELS

International distribution adds its own set of complexities to the management of marketing channels. If a U.S. company wants to market its goods in Austria, for example, it has to abide by the export laws of the United States and the import and general business laws of Austria as well as the applicable laws of any countries the goods pass through on their way. Such legal requirements and constraints add to the differences inherent in doing business in foreign countries, ranging from language barriers to diverse government policies to local customs.

Channel patterns differ widely from country to country. Compare Colombia and Italy. Colombia has one retail store for every 56,000 people; Italy has a retailer for

**Exhibit 13.8
THE INCREASING COMPLEXITY OF CHANNEL SYSTEMS**
As markets become more fragmented and competitors concentrate on narrow market segments, marketers will increasingly adopt complex, nontraditional channel systems that use every available means to reach customers. This exhibit shows, in a general sense, how organizational channels have become more complex over the last several decades.

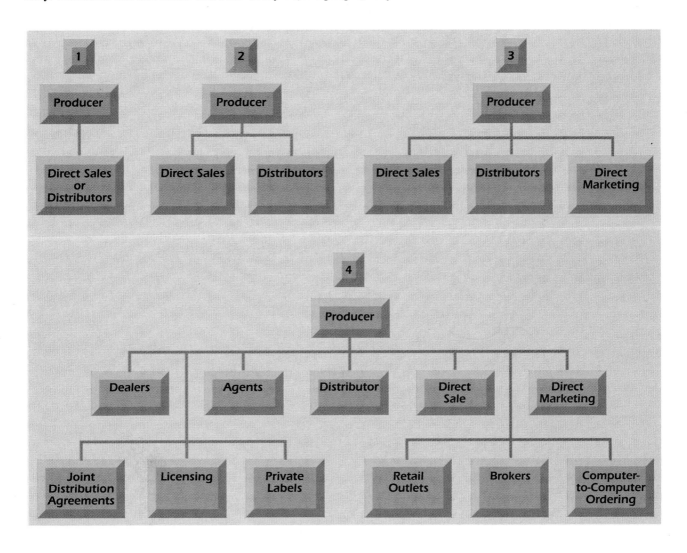

every 66 people, according to one estimate. (The figure in the United States is 127 people per store, by the way.) To reach consumers in Italy, in other words, you have to deal with a mind-boggling number of small retailers.[17]

Sometimes even the simplest assumption doesn't apply when a company considers international distribution. For instance, Doubleday Book and Music Clubs use an extensive magazinelike catalog to promote books, CDs, and other items to members. In France, customers order through the mail, just as they do with clubs such as the History Book Club here in the United States. However, in Spain, Portugal, and Italy, Doubleday relies on a door-to-door direct sales force to hand out catalogs, take orders, and deliver products. Why the different channel? The company considers the postal services in these three countries too unreliable to support mail-order sales.[18]

The marketing channel challenge faced by Kodak when it introduced a line of copier/duplicators in Europe highlights the complexity of international channels. The marketing region the company chose encompassed 18 countries with 400 million people and numerous languages and cultures. Furthermore, Kodak knew it would be competing with IBM, Xerox, and a number of European and Japanese firms. To deal with all the issues of currency, regulations, localized competition, and other market aspects, Kodak wound up establishing 13 separate companies, each with its own management and marketing channels.[19] For more insight into the challenges of international marketing, Chapter 20 covers the major aspects of doing business in multicountry, multicultural environments.

### HYBRID INTERMEDIARIES

Many intermediaries are difficult to categorize neatly because they perform more than one channel function. For example, a hot tub dealer can act as both a retailer (when the customer is a homeowner) and a distributor (when the customer is a builder who will then sell a completed house to the final customer). Is this company an industrial distributor or a consumer retailer? It's both, and one would be mistaken to categorize it exclusively as one or the other. Also, producers and intermediaries can change as they develop new business areas. North Beach Leather, a leather-goods company based in San Francisco, decided to limit its own retail chain to 10 stores and expand business beyond that by wholesaling to other retailers.[20] Again, this company is two intermediaries in one.

Now that you have a good feel for the options in marketing channels, consider channel strategies. Selecting the type, location, and number of intermediaries poses a big challenge for many firms, but if done correctly, this selection can yield formidable competitive advantages. The following section explores the important issues that marketing managers consider when they design marketing channels, including channel selection criteria and distribution intensity.

The Doubleday Book and Music Clubs prefer to conduct business through the mail, but they opted for door-to-door sales in Italy because they considered that country's postal system to be too unreliable to support mail-order business.

# CHANNEL STRATEGY DECISIONS

Marketing managers face two sets of decisions when considering marketing channels. The first set of decisions leads to a selection of one or more channels; the second set deals with the extent, or intensity, of distribution. The following section takes you through the selection criteria and examines three levels of distribution intensity.

## Channel Selection Criteria

Selecting marketing channels can be a complicated process, particularly if part of the channel is outside the producer's direct control. In addition, intermediaries aren't just sitting around waiting for producers to give them a call. Eventually, any decisions regarding channels come down to this question: Are there enough of the right kinds of intermediaries to build the desired channel? You need to find intermediaries that can handle your products capably and provide adequate service to final customers. If you're new to a market, you may find that all the best intermediaries are already in the service of your competitors, which will force you to develop alternatives.

## MARKET FACTORS

Analyzing and understanding the target market is the first step in selecting marketing channels. A thorough analysis of the market explores several factors, ranging from customer type to competitive presence:

- *Customer preferences.* Within the limits of all the other selection factors, you should try to move products to customers using the channels they most prefer. Personal computer software retailers such as Egghead Software and Babbage's, for instance, experienced explosive growth when they began selling through retail outlets in shopping malls, where many owners of PCs preferred to shop for software. As the market matured, however, customers began buying more and more software by mail. By 1993, Egghead was pondering whether it should even be in mall and storefront retailing any longer.[21] Note that consumer preferences can shift over time, and channels may need to be changed after they have been established. For example, Fuller Brush, a company long noted for its brushes and its door-to-door sales force, had to add catalog and retail store sales because many of the homemakers it sells to are now out in the work force and aren't home to answer the door.[22]

- *Consumer versus organizational customers.* As you learned in Chapters 4 and 5, organizational customers frequently have buying habits that are different from those of consumers. They can require larger quantities, bigger discounts, and special attention from suppliers. Consumers, on the other hand, have their own needs. Although an organizational buyer such as a hospital cafeteria might buy a thousand pounds of potatoes from a grocery wholesaler, most consumers can use only 5 or 10 pounds at a time.

- *Geography.* Customer location is another important factor. For instance, if your customers are small and widely dispersed, a direct sales force would be impractical. However, when customers are large and geographically concentrated, such as the computer firms in California's Silicon Valley area, direct sales might be an attractive approach.

- *Market size.* Establishing a distribution channel can require a sizable investment, so companies make sure that the market they're about to serve will return enough to make it worthwhile. A direct sales force in particular requires significant up-front investment in salaries, training, and other expenses. An agent, in contrast, requires much less investment and is a better choice for small markets and markets where you're not sure your efforts will yield sustainable sales. Also, the number of potential customers influences channel choice; a large number of customers usually dictates a large network of intermediaries. Black & Decker, for instance, wants to reach millions of consumers, and it takes a lot of retail outlets to accomplish this. Direct marketing is an exception to this, however, where you reach many customers through television infomercials or other promotional efforts, but then deliver goods from a single location. Finally, when dealing with small and potentially unprofitable markets, you may face an ethical question about whether you are obligated to make vital goods and services available to certain markets, even if those markets aren't large enough to meet your profit goals.

- *Competition.* Often a good channel choice is a channel that has been overlooked or avoided by competitors. In some cases, marketers try to duplicate their competitors' channels in order to have their products end up on store shelves next to the competitors' products.

PRODUCT FACTORS

Even products that end up at the same retail location may need different intermediaries earlier in the channel. For example, Dreyer's ice cream can't use the same distribution network as Mead's Garfield file folders because the products are vastly different. Here are the major product attributes that influence channel selection:

- *Life cycle.* A product category's stage in the life cycle can be an important factor in selecting a channel, and channels may have to be adjusted over time. Small office copiers provide a clear example of this. They were initially sold only by direct sales forces, then through office equipment dealers, and then through a wide variety of channels. Today, you can buy copiers from a manufacturer's salesperson, a mail-order supplier, a specialty office-supply store, a retailer such as Sears, and discount warehouse stores such as Staples and Office Depot. As a product becomes more common and less intimidating to customers, marketing channels add less value, and customers require less support. A wider selection of channels then starts to make sense.[23] From the intermediary's perspective, wholesalers and retailers are more inclined to accept and enthusiastically promote new and innovative products. "Me-too" products that typically appear later in the product life cycle have a harder time fighting for attention.[24] One of the main reasons is that customers are less price sensitive to new products, giving wholesalers and retailers more profit.[25]

- *Complexity.* Some products are so complicated and require so much support that producers need to stay closely involved (see Exhibit 13.9). This can mean either a direct sales force or a limited number of highly qualified intermediaries. Pharmaceuticals, large computer systems, scientific instruments, jet aircraft, and nuclear reactors are products whose complexity affects the way in which they are marketed.

- *Price.* A product's price also affects distribution choices. Items with low prices and high volume are usually distributed through large, well-established distribution networks such as grocery wholesalers. For example, Super Valu, a large grocery wholesaler, has the channel system in place for efficiently moving groceries to more than 3,000 retail stores. However, as the price of the product increases

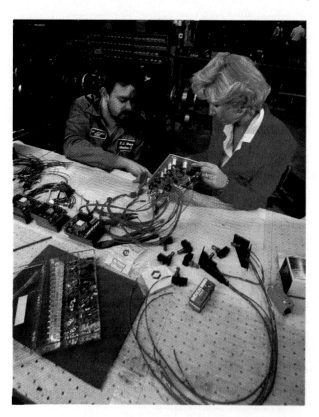

**Exhibit 13.9**
**THE COMPLEXITY FACTOR IN MARKETING CHANNELS**
Premier, a Cleveland-based supplier of electronic and industrial parts, relies on members of its sales force (sales representative Suzanne Spagnoletti is shown here) to help move its complicated products through the marketing channel.

## PC CONNECTION: CHANGING CHANNELS AND CHANGING THE RULES

Patricia Gallup and David Hall were looking for a business that would let them stay in their tiny adopted home of Marlow, New Hampshire, and they were interested in the then-new IBM PC. With these two managerial objectives in mind, they pooled $8,000, created a company called PC Connection, and started down the road to oblivion.

At least traditional marketers would've considered it the road to oblivion; PC Connection became a mail-order intermediary for software and hardware products. Dozens of companies had tried this before, and dozens had gone bankrupt trying. The traditional marketers would have said: "Just look at the market and product factors; there's no way you can satisfy computer customers with a mail-order channel." PC owners don't trust mail order, and they don't have the patience to wait weeks for a critical piece of hardware or software. Furthermore, these are complicated products early in their life cycle, so they require a lot of support from whichever marketing intermediary is brave enough to sell them.

Gallup and Hall took a look at the traditional channel rules and realized they'd have to change the rules in order to succeed. The two biggest factors seemed to be customer service and delivery time. To overcome cus-

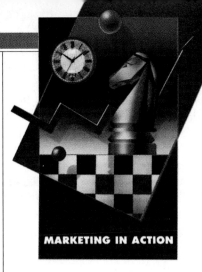

**MARKETING IN ACTION**

tomer fears that a mail-order company couldn't support them, Gallup and Hall knew they'd have to provide flawless customer support. So they built a staff of friendly experts who understand both the products they're selling and the customers they're helping.

To solve the problem of delivery time, Gallup and Hall had to turn to some important facilitators for help. They brought in five overnight package services and explained what they wanted to accomplish. Hall insisted that PC Connection's customers demanded fast service and were tired of "handling charges" and other expensive markups. When he shared some ideas for close cooperation and cost reduction, the contenders gave it a shot, and Airborne Express came up with the contract. PC Connection's customers are charged a flat $3 fee for overnight delivery, regardless of where they live or how much they order. With unsurpassed selection, service, and convenience, the company removed every reason customers

might have for not buying.

PC Connection seems to have made out just fine with its channel design choices. Through most of the 1980s, the company experienced a compound annual growth rate of 183 percent, making it one of the fastest-growing companies of any type in the United States. So what about those customers who didn't want to buy through mail order? A survey taken by a leading computer magazine gave PC Connection the top customer-service rating, with a score greater than the second- through fifth-place mail-order companies combined. In the mid-1990s, PC Connection is still considered the standard of excellence in mail-order software buying, even though many new competitors have jumped in the game in recent years. Gallup and Hall have since expanded into selling computers and producing cable TV programs on software applications. In recognition of her role in the company's success, Gallup was named one of *Working Woman's* top 50 women business owners in 1993. Not bad for a company that started out on the road to oblivion.

### APPLY YOUR KNOWLEDGE

**1.** Suppose someone at PC Connection had the idea of opening retail stores and came to you for advice; would you say go for it or not? Why?
**2.** Can you suggest another product category for which PC Connection concepts of channel management would be similarly successful? Explain your choice.

and volume drops off, channels become more selective and specialized because they deal with fewer products and often need to provide complex support tasks.

- *Size and weight.* A product with significant size and weight can face restricted distribution channel options, particularly if it is also of low value. Gardeners who need small amounts of topsoil can buy it in bags at Kmart and other garden-supply centers, but people who need larger amounts have to call on specialized topsoil suppliers. Topsoil is too heavy, bulky, and inexpensive to take up much of Kmart's retailing floor space.
- *Consumer perceptions.* The perceptions customers have of products and producers also play a role in channel decisions. From a practical perspective, a warehouse might make a great place to sell cars. It would be spacious, cheap, and

probably close to major highways. However, the prospective buyer of a Jaguar, for instance, wants a shopping experience that correlates with the ownership experience, so a classy showroom in a nice neighborhood is called for. The Jaguar dealer uses the showroom to help create and support the Jaguar image.

- *Other product factors.* Depending on the product in question, other factors may enter into the decision as well. Some of these include whether a product is fragile or perishable and whether or not it requires significant customization. For instance, Riddell, a major supplier of athletic equipment, sells football helmets both through mail-order catalogs and through in-store retail channels. With mail-order sales, however, the company explicitly states that the helmets are for use as souvenirs only and must not be worn for actual contact. The reason is that football helmets must be adjusted by a trained expert in order to provide adequate head protection, which can't be done through mail order.[26]

## PRODUCER FACTORS

Finally, several selection factors involve the producers themselves. Two firms with similar products might use different channel systems if they have different objectives and resources. Here's a look at the producer factors in channel selection:

- *Managerial objectives.* A company's overall objectives influence its marketing channel choices. A company seeking to build long-term customer loyalty by providing superior service will probably not pick the same channel system as a company trying to build market share with low prices. For example, one of Caterpillar's top marketing priorities is satisfying its customers over the long haul, so it picks dealers who can provide the level of support required, even though less capable dealers might be able to sell Cat equipment at lower prices to a larger number of people.
- *Resources.* Various distribution options require different levels of resources and investment. A direct sales force, for example, requires recruiting the right people, training them, outfitting them with the necessary equipment, and providing an administrative structure to keep it all running. Some firms that could benefit from direct sales forces simply can't afford the investment, particularly during their early stages of development.
- *Desire for control.* The need to control various aspects of the marketing process influences a producer's selection of channel system. This control can encompass pricing, positioning, brand image, customer support, and competitive presence. For example, Gotcha Sportswear, Quicksilver, Jimmy'z, and other surfing gear manufacturers are careful to avoid damage to their special images. These firms avoid mass merchandisers and national department store chains, selecting only those retail outlets that have a firm grip on being hip (see Exhibit 13.10).[27]
- *Breadth of product line.* Producers with several products in a related area face a channel situation that is different from those with one or two products. A Hewlett-Packard salesperson, for instance, can offer corporate customers several families of computers, office furniture, business software, engineering software, manufacturing software, printers, graphics plotters, and a variety of other products and services. Because one sales call could result in a very large order, it makes sense for HP to use direct sales. On the other hand, a supplier such as Epson with a more limited offering might not be able to support a direct sales force.

After a producer has selected the type of channel that makes the most sense for its products, the next step is to determine the level of distribution intensity, which specifies the number of marketing intermediaries that will carry the products.

## Distribution Intensity

The second set of decisions regarding marketing channels concerns intensity of distribution. Depending on a firm's products, objectives, and customers, different lev-

**Exhibit 13.10**
**PICKING CHANNELS THAT SUPPORT THE IMAGE**
This shop on Melrose Avenue in Los Angeles is the sort of hip retailer that hip manufacturers try to find to support the image of their products.

els of intensity make more or less sense. Also, distribution intensity is frequently modified as a product progresses through its life cycle. Marketers have three basic levels of distribution intensity to choose from: intensive, selective, and exclusive.

## INTENSIVE DISTRIBUTION

Companies that are trying to reach a wide audience usually opt for a strategy of **intensive distribution,** which seeks to put products in customers' hands whenever and wherever possible, to the greatest extent possible. For instance, Goodyear would like everyone in the country to have access to its tires. To meet this objective, the company uses three separate marketing channels. Each channel has a different cost-versus-coverage trade-off, and together they give Goodyear an optimum mix of sales volume and profitability. The first channel is Goodyear's own chain of retail stores. The second is a string of franchises called Goodyear Go Centers, which outnumber the captive retail stores and substantially increase marketing coverage. The third channel is a network of independent tire dealers who carry other lines in addition to Goodyear's. Goodyear has much less control over the marketing of its tires through the independent dealers, but this channel meets the company's objective of exhaustive market coverage.[28]

**intensive distribution**
A channel strategy that seeks to make products available in as many appropriate places as possible

## SELECTIVE DISTRIBUTION

With many consumer products, maintaining a luxury image is crucial to the product's success. In the cosmetics market, for example, Cover Girl is marketed to a wide audience, whereas Estée Lauder is aimed at a narrower, better-financed target segment. Estée Lauder knows that its customers want to avoid any association with budget outlets. That's why you can purchase Cover Girl in discount stores such as Kmart, but you'll have to visit one of a select number of upscale department stores to acquire Estée Lauder products. This strategy is called **selective distribution,** which is the practice of limiting the number of available outlets, primarily in the interest of supporting a certain image for a product.[29]

Some companies employ selective distribution for a much less glamorous reason: money. Setting up a broad distribution network is expensive, forcing many cash-hungry companies to settle for selective distribution, at least temporarily. In addition, selective distribution makes sense when the customer base is located only in selected geographic areas.

**selective distribution**
A channel strategy that limits availability of products to a few carefully selected outlets in a given market area

**exclusive distribution**
An extreme case of selective distribution in which only one outlet in a market territory is allowed to carry a product or product line

EXCLUSIVE DISTRIBUTION

At the opposite end of the universe from intensive distribution is **exclusive distribution,** in which a product is available in only one outlet in a given market area. This can be considered an extreme case of selective distribution, in which a producer is so intent on maintaining a product's image that it doesn't mind making customers work a little harder. Exclusive distribution also reduces intrabrand competition, which results from two outlets selling the same product to the same market. By eliminating competition in its own brand, a producer and its intermediaries can team up to attack other brands instead. Expensive automobiles, furniture, and major appliances are frequently given exclusive distribution. Industrial and farm equipment are also frequently distributed in exclusive arrangements, primarily to suppress intrabrand competition.[30]

# INTEGRATED MARKETING CHANNELS

In order to make marketing channels more efficient and effective, producers and intermediaries frequently join together to build integrated channel systems. For example, members in a channel system can decide who will take care of warehousing, promotion, and financing in ways that benefit all the members of the channel. In contrast, conventional channels have little or no structure and less coordination among intermediaries. Any coordination that is achieved usually happens through negotiation or bargaining. Conventional channels also tend to be unstable; members aren't united by common goals, so they feel free to enter or exit the system if it suits their individual business objectives. Integrated systems, on the other hand, are controlled to varying degrees, and members are united by common goals and, in some cases, legal contracts.[31] This section compares horizontal and vertical integration, the two ways systems can be built, and it explores several common types of vertically integrated channels.

## Horizontal Marketing Systems

**horizontal integration**
The integration of intermediaries in one level of the marketing process, such as retail outlets

**Horizontal integration** combines multiple intermediaries at the same stage in the channel under one management structure (see Exhibit 13.11). Retail chains, for example, employ horizontal integration when they purchase competitive outlets. The retail world has been in a state of near-constant change in recent years as companies integrate horizontally to build market share and fend off competitors. In the space of less than two weeks in late 1993, Price and Costco merged to form the world's biggest warehouse store chain, Wal-Mart bought most of the Pace warehouse stores from Kmart, and Kmart sold its PayLess drugstore chain to the company that owns the Thrifty drug chain.[32] Although horizontal systems can deliver

**Exhibit 13.11**
**HORIZONTAL AND VERTICAL INTEGRATION**
Horizontal integration combines intermediaries at the same level, such as retail outlets, whereas vertical integration combines intermediaries at all levels, from producer down to final intermediary.

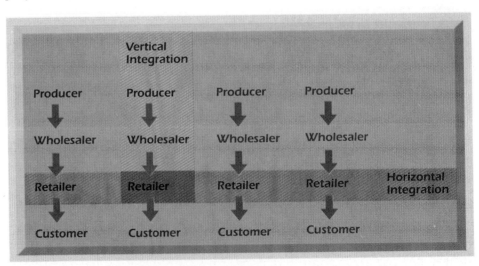

**Exhibit 13.12**
**ESTABLISHING A CORPORATE VMS**
In addition to selling through department stores, the Liz Claiborne organization also runs a corporate VMS that includes operations such as this outlet store.

significant benefits, including advertising and purchasing leverage, they can't provide the level of control over the entire channel structure that is possible with vertical marketing systems.

## Vertical Marketing Systems

A horizontal system combines multiple units of the same type, whereas a **vertical marketing system (VMS)** combines different types of intermediaries to form a cohesive chain from the producer to the last intermediary. The process of forming this chain is called **vertical integration.** A vertical marketing system can include the producing, wholesaling, and retailing functions, all acting in a more or less coordinated fashion. Consider three common classes of VMS: corporate systems, administered systems, and contractual systems.

### CORPORATE SYSTEMS

In some marketing systems, one company owns the entire chain, from producing goods and services all the way to selling them to final customers. Such an arrangement is called a **corporate marketing system** because all the elements in the channel are under the control of one corporation. For instance, Liz Claiborne sells clothing and accessories bearing the Liz Claiborne name both through department stores and through the Claiborne-owned First Issue retail chain. The First Issue channel is a corporate VMS because Claiborne owns both the production and retailing levels (see Exhibit 13.12). This system provides close control of quality, image, sales process, and customer satisfaction efforts.[33]

### ADMINISTERED SYSTEMS

The second type of VMS features a dominant company, but not the exclusive ownership of one corporation. In the **administered marketing system** one company dominates by coordinating activities in the channel. Though it has no formal orga-

**vertical marketing system (VMS)**
A channel that is integrated from producer down to final intermediary

**vertical integration**
The process of developing a marketing system that includes both the source of production and the distribution capabilities; the result of vertical integration is called a vertical marketing system

**corporate marketing system**
A type of VMS in which one company owns every player in the channel

**administered marketing system**
A type of VMS in which one player has control by way of influence and agreement but not through explicit ownership or contractual arrangement

nizational structure, an administered system has at least a minimal amount of co-operation because the nondominant members recognize the advantages of cooperating with the leader. The company that dominates the channel in these systems is usually either a large producer or a large retailer. Kraft General Foods and Corning, for instance, are producers that tend to lead many of their respective channel systems. Similarly, Sears, Montgomery Ward, and McDonald's all lead channel systems from the retailer end.

## CONTRACTUAL SYSTEMS

**contractual marketing system**
A VMS in which contracts explicitly spell out the roles and responsibilities of all members in the channel

**wholesaler-sponsored voluntary chain**
A type of contractual marketing system that is led by one or more wholesalers

**retailer cooperative**
A voluntary contractual marketing system led by a group of retailers

**franchise**
A business entity licensed to use the trademarks, operations, and other attributes of a business

The third major type of VMS falls between the other two in terms of control and coordination. **Contractual marketing systems** have formalized working relationships not found in administered systems, but they lack the controlling ownership of corporate systems, binding members by contracts specifying responsibility for each channel function. More than a dozen types of contractual systems exist; the most common ones are wholesaler-sponsored voluntary chains, retailer cooperatives, and franchises.

In a **wholesaler-sponsored voluntary chain,** one or more wholesalers pull together a group of independent retailers. The retailers benefit by getting promotions and purchasing power on a larger scale than any one of them could achieve alone. The wholesalers benefit by building loyalty among the retailers. An important wholesaler-sponsored voluntary chain is the Independent Grocers Alliance (IGA), which gives member retailers help in their competitive battles with the large grocery chains.[34]

A second voluntary group is the **retailer cooperative,** in which the retailers, rather than wholesalers, lead the group. These cooperatives have become particularly important in the retail hardware business, where they account for 35 percent of total wholesale sales. Two of the better-known systems in this category are Ace Hardware and True Value. In general, wholesaler-sponsored cooperatives have been more effective than retailer-sponsored groups because control is concentrated in the hands of fewer firms.[35]

The third contractual VMS to consider is the **franchise,** which involves the licensing of a complete business format to independent business owners. The franchise owners engage in business using the franchisor's name, brands, trademarks, and other identifiers. This arrangement also relies on standardized methods of business among all franchise owners. From the company's perspective, the benefits of franchising include rapidly expanded territorial coverage with little investment, financial assistance from franchisees to help with corporate advertising, and motivated franchise owner-managers who have a stake in the success of each outlet. On the negative side, businesses looking to franchise can face shortages of suitable franchisees, less control over operations in individual outlets, and conflict among channel partners.

Franchises involve hundreds of thousands of business entities in the United States and many other countries around the world, including more than 30,000 overseas outlets owned by U.S. firms. Some observers predict franchises will become the dominant channel form in the twenty-first century. The industries in which franchises already operate include financial services (H&R Block), weight control (DietCenter), restaurants (Burger King), clothing (The Athlete's Foot), and automotive service (Midas). Most franchises operate at the retail level, but a number operate at the wholesale level, marketing either to organizational customers or to retailers. A Caterpillar dealer, for instance, is a franchise operator marketing to organizational customers (farmers and construction firms). Soft drink firms such as PepsiCo and Coca-Cola sell drink concentrate to bottlers, who then market the finished products to retailers.

Nearly all the many franchising methods feature continuous field service and support, systemwide advertising, and centralized purchasing and record keeping. Franchisors also offer a package of start-up services including marketing research, site selection, and management training.[36]

For the potential franchise owner, franchised systems offer many of the benefits of large companies (national advertising, management training, purchasing discounts, and so forth) with some of the benefits of small business ownership (including the freedom to be your own boss and the financial rewards that come with running a successful company). However, even though a franchise might seem like a ready-made business you can jump into and start running, be sure to evaluate franchise opportunities just as you would any other marketing scenario. For example, when you add the start-up costs, your operating expenses, and the royalty payments you have to make to the franchisor, will the prices you can charge still provide adequate profit? Similarly, what kind of promotional support will the franchisor provide? Will the nationwide advertising do an adequate job of reaching your local audience? Applying sound marketing concepts can help franchisees avoid many of the hurdles and downright failures that have plagued some franchise systems.

# INTERDEPENDENCY ISSUES

The discussions of various channel topics so far in this chapter have hinted at four important issues involving relationships in marketing channels: cooperation, conflict, leadership, and power. Here is a brief look at these issues, the effects they have on channel management, and the latest trends in channel relationships.

## Channel Cooperation

Because they are collections of separate, and sometimes independent, people and organizations, marketing channels rely on cooperation from all members in order to function efficiently. If members of a channel need each other in order to survive and succeed, they should work toward common goals and provide each other with adequate support. As a first step, manufacturers must understand the needs and expectations of the wholesalers, retailers, and distributors responsible for moving products on to final customers. This was part of Black & Decker's problem described at the beginning of the chapter; it was insensitive to inventory requirements and other needs of its retailers. Intermediaries can contribute here also, by learning more about the producer's intentions and objectives.

Second, everyone in the channel needs to build solid working partnerships that are sensitive to the needs of each member. This includes developing effective communication systems, clearly signaling confidence in partners, and responding positively to marketing crises. Third, these partnerships need to be continually nurtured and managed over time. Welding equipment maker Lincoln Electric, for instance, works with its distributors to identify changing customer requirements so that both partners can respond to new market realities.[37]

## Channel Conflict

Channel conflict can occur in any number of situations, but the problem is usually rooted in one channel member placing its own success above the success of the entire channel. In an effort to increase its own market share, for instance, a producer sometimes forces intermediaries into situations that work well for the producer but not for the intermediary. Snap-On Tools uses a large network of independent dealers to sell its high-quality automotive tools to professional mechanics. It gives each dealer an exclusive territory with 200 to 300 customers, along with a sales quota of around $5,000 a week. However, one dealer sued Snap-On for pressuring him to split his territory with another dealer. The alleged motive made sense on paper: Two dealers working a territory normally considered big enough for only one would work extra hard to make sales. The result would be more sales for Snap-On but fewer for each of the two individual dealers. The dealer didn't think Snap-On's actions were fair; even though the company admitted no wrongdoing, a jury agreed with the dealer when he brought his case to court.[38]

Here are several common sources of channel conflict, along with suggested ways to minimize the problems they cause:

- *Bypassing channels.* If a producer bypasses existing channels in the hope of increasing business, conflict is inevitable. When Taco Bell opened two experimental low-cost burger chains called Hot 'n Now, Taco Bell franchisees began to worry that they'd have to compete with their own company.[39] Examples of bypassing include setting up a direct sales force that competes with your retailers and making products available through mail order when they are already selling in retail stores. A major battle has been brewing in grocery retailing over the last several years as manufacturers that have grown weary of slotting allowances and other profit-draining demands of traditional supermarkets expand into new channels. An increasing portion of U.S. grocery products gets to consumers through warehouse clubs, discount stores, and convenience stores. Not surprisingly, this creates friction between the manufacturers and their traditional allies in the supermarket channel.[40]

- *Oversaturating markets.* To avoid oversaturating markets, which is making a product available through too many intermediaries in a given market, channel members should set guidelines on the size and number of dealers or retailers and then stick to those limits. Alternatively, the dominant member in the channel can try to guide some intermediaries into market areas that don't overlap with other intermediaries. Some people who purchased franchises in the Subway Sandwich Shops chain charge that the company has sold too many operations too close to each other. Indeed, the company has grown rapidly, increasing fourfold from 1987 to 1992, and some new stores have been placed as close as 1 mile away from existing stores.[41]

- *Providing inadequate support.* In return for distributing a manufacturer's products, intermediaries expect a certain level of support. This support might include advertising, training, or managerial assistance. If intermediaries are not properly supported, they won't be content and won't be as effective as they might be. This was the case with many Burger King franchisees, who felt that the chain's previous owner, Pillsbury, had provided poor managerial support and poor advertising, among other things. Burger King's new owner, Grand Metropolitan, seems to have won over the franchisees with its improved support.[42]

- *Behaving inconsistently.* Erratic behavior is likely to disrupt life for everybody in the channel. The best way to avoid this is to establish clear guidelines and policies and make sure that discipline is maintained. When changes are necessary, they should be executed with the clear understanding and support of channel partners.[43]

## Channel Leadership

**channel captains**
The dominant players in a given marketing channel who have power over other channel members

Another crucial issue in marketing channels is channel leadership. As you saw earlier in the discussion of various marketing systems, one company or one group of companies needs to have a leadership role to make sure the system's activities are coordinated. These dominant players are called **channel captains,** or channel leaders. In a corporate VMS, the channel captain is one part of the overall company. In an administered system, the captain is the dominant player whose influence guides the actions of the other members. In a contractual system, the leadership depends on the type of arrangement; in a franchise system such as McDonald's, for instance, the franchisor (McDonald's) leads the channel.

Producers, wholesalers, and retailers have all played leadership roles in various channels. A producer such as Procter & Gamble leads many of the channels in which it markets products. Wholesalers once led a number of channels, but they no longer control as many as they used to; both producers and retailers have grown more

# WHEN DOES HEALTHY COMPETITION BECOME UNHEALTHY CONTROL?

Roses are red
Violets are blue
Go after our market share
And we'll destroy you.

Greeting card companies send some awfully sweet messages to their customers, but they're more likely to send angry letters and aggressive lawyers to each other. Sales have been more or less flat in the multibillion-dollar card market for the last several years, and competitors can increase sales only by taking market share from each other. Three giants, Hallmark Cards, American Greetings, and Gibson Greetings, control this market, with a combined share of about 80 percent. A host of smaller companies vie for share, frequently with alternative cards ranging from New Age sentiment to explicit sexual humor.

These smaller companies struggle to stay in the battle, a battle that increasingly centers around control of the distribution channel. Greeting cards are sold through a variety of retail outlets, including grocery, drug, discount, and specialty stores. None of the producers has a commanding legal authority over the channel; for instance, most of the 21,000 stores that carry Hallmark cards and sometimes bear the Hallmark name are ostensibly free to carry anybody's products. Lacking legitimate power, producers use a mixture of sweet talk and strong arm to move their goods through the channel.

Sometimes the struggle for control gets downright nasty. In a highly publicized case, Blue Mountain Arts

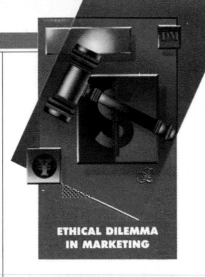

**ETHICAL DILEMMA IN MARKETING**

accused Hallmark of copying the look of its cards, pressuring retailers into dropping (and in some cases allegedly destroying) Blue Mountain cards, and then filling the vacant shelf space with products from its new Personal Touch line, which looked nearly identical to Blue Mountain cards. Blue Mountain won the first round of the legal battle when a federal judge ordered Hallmark to stop selling 83 designs until a trial could be held to sort things out. In a related bit of legal action, the prestigious Society of Illustrators recommended to a federal court that specific card styles shouldn't be monopolized, but their recommendation was tossed out when Blue Mountain lawyers discovered that Hallmark had paid the society's legal expenses and contributed a sizable amount to its scholarship fund.

In an amendment to its filing, Blue Mountain accused Hallmark of several other channel control measures that present intriguing legal and ethical issues. Prominent among the allegations: Greeting card dealers were pressured to pull Blue Mountain cards if they wanted to maintain a "beneficial business relationship" with Hallmark. Also, the smaller company alleged that Hallmark leased shopping center stores to dealers only if

they pledged not to sell Blue Mountain products. Hallmark denied all the charges. The case was settled in late 1988, with Hallmark promising to exert no pressure on retailers and to replace the product line that was similar to Blue Mountain's.

Some people complain that the power struggle hurts consumers as well because it places a greater emphasis on profit margins and shelf space than on creativity and originality. Maine Line is the first card company owned by a woman, Perri Ardman. The company specializes in humorous cards for women, and Ardman says that smaller companies with creative offerings just don't have the financial muscle to get their cards on the retailers' shelves. Ardman and her partner, Joyce Boaz, wound up selling Maine Line to a large novelty gift company with the hopes that greater financial power would let them expand their product offering and break into international markets.

Card makers continue to get some unpleasant greetings about control in marketing channels. In any industry whose competitors are clawing for shares of stagnant or slow-growth markets, fights over channel control seem inevitable. As these fights heat up, ethical issues such as shelf space control and slotting allowances are likely to consume a greater share of the marketer's time.

## WHAT'S YOUR OPINION?

**1.** Should companies be legally prohibited from buying a competitor's inventory to keep it off retail shelves? **2.** How much control should marketing intermediaries have over one another? For example, should slotting allowances be legal?

---

powerful throughout this century. Also, retailers are starting to exert more power than ever before, particularly in the area of pricing.

The rising power of retailers has come at the expense of both wholesalers and manufacturers, who find themselves bowing to demands for discounts and other concessions from retailers. One of the more extreme cases is the increasingly common use of a **slotting allowance,** which is a payment from the manufacturer or

**slotting allowance**
A specific example of the sort of power retailers can exert over producers, in which retailers refuse to grant shelf space to a product unless the producers give them some promotional money first

wholesaler in return for shelf space in retail outlets. In other cases, retailers simply want more say in product selection, pricing, or advertising campaigns. In 1992, both Oldsmobile and Infiniti considered changing ad agencies after their dealers grew restless with both companies' advertising (Olds decided to stick with its existing agency, but Infiniti switched). ConAgra, the maker of Country Pride chicken, split up its advertising budget to allow each of its major customers (retail grocery chains) to determine how the money should be spent in local markets.[44]

## Channel Power

**channel power**
The ability of the channel captain to influence or control the behavior of the rest of the channel

To achieve channel leadership, the captain obviously has to have some kind of power over the other members. This **channel power** is the relative power of the captain over the behavior of the channel. Experts consider Wal-Mart to now be firmly in control of its channels, even going to the point of proposing a plan that requires manufacturers to submit customized marketing plans and take responsibility for the success of their products.[45] Wal-Mart CEO David Glass says that his firm "is probably in a better position to determine specifically what the customer wants to buy than is the manufacturer."[46] Of course, for a member to concede power to the captain, it must have some level of dependence on the captain, such as product supply, access to customers, or financial support. Here are four types of channel power:[47]

- *Reward.* When the captain is in a position to reward members for desired actions, this is considered reward power. An example of a reward is a guaranteed price ceiling (an agreement that prices won't exceed a specified level) in return for a specified number of orders.
- *Expert.* In some cases, including the independent grocery and hardware trades, retailers grant power to wholesalers in return for expertise. IGA, for instance, advises small grocers on advertising, pricing, and other marketing issues.
- *Legitimate.* Legitimate power exists when one member believes that the captain really does have the authority to exert control. This sort of power is most obvious in corporate and contractual VMSs, where the captain might even own the other members, making lines of power rather obvious.
- *Coercive.* The one type of power that might be considered negative is coercive power, which exists when the captain has the economic power to force other members into compliance. It isn't based on the mutually beneficial transfer of power featured in the other types; members behave because they don't want to get punished. For instance, companies that supply a giant retailer such as Wal-Mart know that losing such a vast distribution channel would be a serious financial blow, so they would be more inclined to respond to Wal-Mart's demands.

Channel captains should recognize that with power comes responsibility. They have the responsibility to exercise their power in ways that are both ethical and legal. This is particularly important when small companies are at the mercy of large channel captains.

## LEGAL ISSUES

Managing marketing channels in the United States and other countries is often subject to a variety of regulations. In the United States, the Interstate Commerce and Federal Maritime commissions exert their authority over many aspects of distribution. Specific pieces of legislation, including the Sherman, Clayton, and Robinson-Patman acts, have also changed the way companies can conduct their business, for example, by limiting monopoly power and unfair pricing schemes that favor one intermediary over another. The most common channel arrangements that fall under legal scrutiny are exclusive dealing agreements, exclusive territories, and tying contracts:

- *Exclusive dealing agreements.* **Exclusive dealing agreements** prohibit intermediaries from carrying the products of two or more competing suppliers. These arrangements are usually considered legal as long as they don't appear to restrict competition. This can often be a delicate balancing act for producers who want to use exclusive distribution to protect the images of their brands.
- *Exclusive territories.* To avoid intrabrand competition among their intermediaries, many producers give each intermediary an **exclusive territory,** a designated market segment in which only one intermediary is allowed to carry the producer's products. For example, franchise owners are frequently promised an exclusive territory to ensure that other owners of the same franchise won't compete with them. However, these arrangements can be considered illegal if the producer's intent in setting up the territories is to restrain competitors or the overall business operations of intermediaries.
- *Tying contracts.* If a supplier forces customers or intermediaries to purchase products in addition to the central product in a transaction, this is considered a **tying contract** and is illegal in most cases. The only situations in which tying contracts are legal are when the supplier is the only source of the product, when the supplier is new and trying to establish distribution, or in the case of intermediaries, when the intermediary is allowed to carry competing products.

**exclusive dealing agreements**
A contract that prohibits an intermediary from carrying competing contracts; it is illegal in some circumstances

**exclusive territory**
A sales territory granted to one intermediary; granting exclusive territories can be illegal if it restrains competition

**tying contracts**
Contracts specifying that other products must be purchased along with the central product in a transaction; in most cases such arrangements are illegal

---

## SUMMARY OF LEARNING OBJECTIVES

### 1. Explain the need for marketing channels.

Channels serve three purposes for producers. First, they take care of the transaction aspects of marketing, including selling and financing. Second, they perform the logistical function of moving products to customers. Third, they help producers promote goods and services. Also, channels help customers by giving them access to the right products, in the right place, at the right time, and in the right quantities.

### 2. Describe the functions channels perform in the marketing mix.

Channels perform five basic functions in the marketing mix. First, they facilitate the exchange process, making it more efficient and more cost effective. Second, they alleviate discrepancies of both quantity and assortment. Third, they standardize transactions, which helps producers, intermediaries, and customers. Fourth, they bring buyers and sellers together. Fifth, they provide essential customer support and service activities.

### 3. Define the various types of channels in use today.

Channels fall into three general categories: channels for consumer goods, channels for organizational goods, and channels for services. Also, channels can be split by whether they are direct or indirect. Finally, several types of indirect channels each employ a different number of intermediaries.

### 4. Outline the factors producers consider when selecting channels.

These factors fall into three groups. Market factors include customer preferences, customer type, geography, market size, competition, and the nature and availability of intermediaries. Product factors to be considered are life cycle, complexity, value, size and weight, and consumer perceptions. The final group of factors surrounds the producer itself and includes managerial objectives, resources, desire for control, and size of product line.

### 5. Clarify the difference between conventional channels and horizontally and vertically integrated marketing systems.

Conventional channels aren't coordinated and controlled in the way that integrated channels are; they are an amalgam of independent producers and intermediaries loosely connected by convenience and coincident, though individual, goals. Horizontal systems exhibit close control of and cooperation among multiple entities at the same level, such as with a string of retail outlets. Vertical systems, on the other hand, are integrated from producer on down to final intermediary, covering two or more levels in the channel process.

### 6. Delineate channel cooperation, channel conflict, channel leadership, and channel power.

Channel cooperation exists when members in a given channel work together to achieve the greatest possible benefits for all the members in that channel. Channel conflict, on the other hand, results from one member's putting its individual objectives above the objectives of the channel as a whole. Channel leadership indicates the role of a dominant player in guiding and controlling the activities of the entire channel. Channel power describes the type of power that the channel captain exerts over the other members. The four major types of channel power are reward, expert, legitimate, and coercive.

### 7. Identify the major legal issues surrounding channel management.

Three significant legal issues are involved in marketing channel management. Exclusive dealing arrangements prohibit intermediaries from carrying the products of competing suppliers, which can be illegal if they restrict normal competition. Exclusive territory arrangements specify the intermediaries that are allowed to operate in specific territories, which can also be considered illegal if the producer's intent is to restrain competition or the business activities of intermediaries. Tying contracts require a customer or intermediary to purchase products in addition to the central product in the exchange, which is illegal in most cases.

## KEY TERMS

accumulating (398)
administered marketing system (413)

agents (395)
allocating (398)
assorting (399)

breaking bulk (399)
brokers (395)
channel captains (416)

channel power (417)
contractual marketing system (414)

## A CASE FOR CRITICAL THINKING

### Meeting a Marketing Challenge at Black & Decker

It's hard to say which is more impressive: The speed at which Nolan Archibald and his colleagues turned around the corporate culture, or the thoroughness of the results. Black & Decker used to be a manufacturer driven by financial measurements; it is now well on its way to being Archibald's vision of a worldwide marketing powerhouse. The company's approach to managing its marketing channels is a central component of the new Black & Decker.

The change started where it should, with strategic planning. In Archibald's own words, "You analyze the problems that are unique to the company and the industry and determine what the strengths and weaknesses are. Then you develop a plan to leverage the strengths and correct the weaknesses." Archibald and his colleagues made sure that marketing channels were a part of that strategic plan. Moreover, the new approach manages channels as a vital marketing resource, rather than simply as a pipeline for pumping products to customers.

The analysts who have observed Black & Decker's remarkable turnaround point out several aspects of channel management that have been vital to the company's success. The first change was simple, but most important: more respect for marketing intermediaries. Black & Decker had a tough act to follow when it acquired General Electric's small household appliance line. Known as "Generous Electric" in some circles, GE went out of its way to be a good supplier. This included ample support of retailer promotions, deep inventories to ensure no shortage of products in the stores, and a general level of respect for the people and organizations on the front line. Black & Decker's efforts to improve relations started by emulating this regard for retailers, a mindset surely encouraged by Kenneth Homa, a former GE executive who followed the small appliance line to Black & Decker.

Out of this new respect flowed assistance. Black & Decker made several important moves to help its channel partners.

One of these was a segmented channel strategy that focuses specialized sales assistance on the company's two major groups of customers: industrial/professional and consumer. This allows Black & Decker to give each kind of intermediary the unique help it needs. Another key move was to establish a team of retail-merchandising agents to help retailers with inventory management, purchasing, and in-store product displays. Also, the promotional budget was beefed up to help pull customers into retail stores.

The assistance is mutual. Black & Decker established a number of dealer advisory panels, which retailers can use to give the company feedback on new products customers would like to see. By using its channel as a source of marketing research information, Black & Decker benefits by getting a better picture of customer needs, and the retailers benefit by being able to deliver the right products.

Coordinated physical distribution is another change that helps both the company and its intermediaries. To better mesh its delivery systems with the needs of distributors and retailers, Black & Decker changed virtually every aspect of its physical distribution. This included new locations for distribution centers, modified transportation policies, and more powerful systems for managing and coordinating information.

Increasing the number of products held in inventory was another important step. This gives retailers the confidence that they'll be able to keep up with demand, particularly during the Christmas shopping season, when many tools and small appliances are purchased. According to Homa, Black & Decker's inventory levels have been boosted by 25 percent and "are not allowed to slip."

A final key element in Black & Decker's strategic plan is growth through acquisition, which has been tied closely to marketing channel management. The recent $2.8 billion purchase of Emhart is a good example. Some observers criticized the move, even though it gave Black & Decker a big

presence in hardware. However, the logic was clear after a second look: Some of Emhart's products fit in perfectly with Black & Decker's existing consumer-goods channels, and others mesh well with the industrial channels. The units of Emhart that didn't align with the existing marketing channels were put up for sale.

Black & Decker's dramatic turnaround is convincing evidence of the importance of effectively managing marketing channels. Its sales are growing in every channel of distribution it uses. Profits in the power tool business doubled in one year. And the company is starting to be praised as a strong marketing organization that helps create demand for retailers. Any manufacturer that hopes to succeed in today's highly competitive markets would do well to learn a lesson from Nolan Archibald and his team at Black & Decker.

**Your mission:** Nolan Archibald faces some tough issues in the selection and management of Black & Decker's marketing channels. However, he knows he can rely on you for help. In your role as the manager in charge of marketing channels, examine the following channel management situations and make your recommendations from the available choices.

1. Customer service is, of course, a vital ingredient in all successful marketing transactions. Archibald knows this and also recognizes that customer service is not all that easy to define and execute in a multichannel system like the one Black & Decker relies upon. Which of the following definitions of and approaches to customer service best fits the company's situation?

   a. Customer service efforts should focus on the final purchasers of the product. Black & Decker can do this in several ways. The first is simply to make it easier to be

*(continued on page 422)*

successful with Black & Decker products. This includes designing for ease of use, providing helpful user guides, and perhaps offering a toll-free number that customers can call with specific questions about using products. A second way to help customers might be to sponsor seminars at places like woodworking shows (for the power tool and hardware lines) and home shows (for all three lines). For organizational customers in the power tool segment, another way to help would be to send Black & Decker specialists to customer sites to help them solve specific problems.

b. Black & Decker's real customers are the thousands of marketing intermediaries that buy and then resell its tools, appliances, and hardware. These are the customers that the company should worry about servicing. The intermediaries will, in turn, satisfy the final customers. Black & Decker can help the intermediaries in a number of ways, including promotions, pricing advice, product selection, and display help.

c. The best answer would be a combination of (a) and (b). Although it is true that the intermediaries are Black & Decker's most immediate customers, the sales process really isn't complete until final customers are sold and satisfied. Therefore, Black & Decker has to pay attention to serving the intermediaries directly *and* serving final customers indirectly through the intermediaries. All the elements suggested for (a) and (b) could apply here.

2. Black & Decker's engineers have developed a new tool that cuts concrete. Unfortunately, it doesn't really fit in the marketing channels that you already have in place, so it's time for you to design a new channel. Here are some important variables to consider:

*Customer type:* Organizational, ranging in size from one-person contractors to multinational construction firms.

*Geography:* Customers are all over the place; the geographic distribution roughly mirrors the population distribution, with concentrations in large cities and widely dispersed customers elsewhere.

*Market size:* In a word, big: The saw costs around $2,000 and Black & Decker expects to sell thousands every

month; it makes sense to put a sizable investment into the distribution channel.

*Life cycle:* Tools like these are somewhere between the growth and maturity phases; most customers have a pretty good idea of how to use them and what they're all about.

*Support needs:* These customers don't need a lot of help, but they do need to be assured of fast service when things go wrong; downtime is critical, and customers would prefer on-site delivery of loaner units in the event of a breakdown.

Based on these variables, what's the best channel system for this product?

a. Consider the purchase habits of the people likely to use these products. Even though they are industrial customers, they are human beings after all, and as such, they need to do personal shopping as much as the rest of us. Because of that, the retail stores where they do their other shopping remain a good choice. That way they can combine their personal shopping with their business shopping.

b. The market is large and geographically diverse, and customers don't need much in the way of support. Therefore, mail order would be the perfect channel for this new product. It reaches every corner of the country, and its costs are lower because it needs no retail store space or salespeople.

c. This new product should be restricted to tool stores and masonry supply stores that cater exclusively to professionals. These stores should be able to deliver superior customer service, including on-site delivery of replacement and loaner units. The biggest drawback of using this channel is that these outlets are not as widespread as homeowner-oriented retail stores, but professional builders in out-of-the-way locations are accustomed to a little travel time when it comes to shopping for tools and supplies.

3. Now that you have developed the channel for your concrete cutter, do the same thing for a new product that has just been designed by the small home appliance division. This new device is a combination coffee bean grinder and

---

## QUESTIONS FOR DISCUSSION

1. Pretend you're a potato; what regrouping functions are you likely to go through as you travel through the marketing channel?
2. How do marketing intermediaries standardize transactions for producers and consumers of a Big Mac?
3. In what ways could the following intermediaries provide customer service?
   a. Retailer of lawn and garden tools
   b. Catalog (phone and mail-order) retailer of stereo equipment
   c. Distributor of surgical equipment
4. How well would a direct channel work for each of these products?
   a. Wet-mix concrete (the kind that is all mixed and ready to pour)
   b. Bubble gum

espresso machine. Here are some factors to consider when choosing a channel, and this time consider the problem of product and brand image.

*Customer type:* Consumer.

*Geography:* Again, customers are all over the place, but they are concentrated primarily in and around large cities and, for the time being, mostly on the West Coast.

*Market size:* Not terribly large because of the price, which is around $700; many people like espresso made from freshly ground coffee beans, but only the most avid connoisseurs are willing to pay that much for the quality and convenience of the combination grinder-coffeemaker.

*Life cycle:* Espresso machines have been around for years, but their move into consumer markets is fairly new; in the past most were sold to restaurants.

*Support needs:* The machine is fairly easy to use and clean, and you don't expect much in the way of repair trouble, but some customers will initially need help and advice to brew the perfect demitasse.

So what's the best channel for this product?

a. Specialty kitchen stores, particularly those that cater to upscale urban consumers, would be the best choice. These stores carry other kitchen and household products of similar quality and price, so the new espresso machine will fit in here as well. The customers who frequent stores like this enjoy buying quality products, and some like to boast that they purchase such goods only from specialty stores, never from department or discount stores.

b. Because this is a fundamentally new direction for Black & Decker, asking customers to buy directly from the company itself is a sensible choice. If you put the new machine on the retail shelves next to $19 Black & Decker toasters, its image will be tarnished beyond repair. To maintain a premium image for this product, you've got to separate it from the company's other products. The only sure way to do this is to have customers buy directly from the factory.

c. The existing channels are fine. A $700 coffeemaker might look a little out of place at Kmart, but its presence will raise the image of the entire Black & Decker product family.

4. Realizing that Black & Decker's core markets are largely mature, Archibald and his staff seek to expand the company primarily through acquisitions. The purchase of General Electric's small appliance line and the takeover of Emhart were two prominent results of this strategy. Prior to the Emhart purchase, Archibald had his sights set on Sunbeam, a major competitor in small appliances. Now the company's board of directors is considering four more acquisitions. From the perspective of marketing channel management, which of the following companies makes the most sense for Black & Decker to purchase?

a. The first candidate is a major appliance manufacturer that produces a full range of products: dishwashers, ranges, washing machines, and driers. Its products are currently sold through a network of dealers specializing in major appliances.

b. The second candidate is a bicycle and skateboard manufacturer whose products are sold through toy stores such as Toys 'R' Us, independent bicycle stores, and discount stores like Kmart.

c. The final candidate is a garden supplies manufacturer. This company specializes in organic gardening and small-scale farming supplies ranging from natural fertilizers to specialized gardening tools. Currently, these products sell through mail order, a few discount stores, and a variety of home improvement stores.

## SPECIAL PROJECT

Black & Decker is facing incredible price pressure in most of its product lines. Company leaders don't know whether they'll be able to stay competitive in the lower-priced categories, and an investigation is under way to see whether the company and its products can be shifted out of the lower- and middle-priced categories into premium categories. Archibald knows that changing an image that much is not a simple task, and to do it will require all the resources the company can muster. Your job is to figure out how marketing channels can help in this effort.[48]

---

c. Alaska king salmon

d. Nuclear reactor

5. What kind of channel would you select for premium archery equipment? (If you plan to use intermediaries, explain the role each one will play.)

6. How will market factors influence your channel selection for silk blouses?

7. Consider the silk blouses again; how will product factors affect your channel selection?

8. What level of distribution intensity would you recommend for the following products? Why?

a. Perfume ($5 a bottle)

b. Perfume ($500 a bottle)

c. Bananas

d. Personal computer software

9. As a power tool manufacturer that has traditionally marketed through a wholesaler-retailer channel, what problems might you create if you added a mail-order channel?

10. How would you minimize the effects of the problems you just created in question 9?

## Pro-Line Channels Its Products Beautifully

Comer Cottrell started his business in 1970 with only $600 in start-up capital and a borrowed typewriter, but he had firsthand knowledge of a market need and a sure-fire distribution channel. Driven by his entrepreneurial spirit, Cottrell now heads the largest African-American–owned company in the Southwest. His Dallas-based company, Pro-Line, makes beauty products for African-Americans and today rings up $35 million in annual sales.

Although Cottrell launched Pro-Line in 1970, its roots go back to the time when he was managing an Air Force PX (post exchange). The PX didn't stock grooming products for African-Americans, but 20 percent of the people on the base were African-American. Cottrell knew the demand for such hair-care products could be significant, but he couldn't convince the authorities to stock ethnic beauty products.

After leaving the service, Cottrell decided to meet this consumer need on his own. One of his first stops was a visit to Representative Gus Hawkins, an African-American congressman from California, to discuss how Cottrell could get his products stocked on military bases. Hawkins made the appropriate introductions at the Department of Defense, and soon the PX doors opened for Pro-Line.

Cottrell began to sell his first product, Pro-Line Oil Sheen, through the base stores and also to beauticians and barbers who styled African-American hair. In the first year, 72 percent of the company's $86,000 sales was to the military. However, to Cottrell's surprise, when service personnel went back to civilian life, they continued to clamor for Pro-Line products. The founder quickly followed up with a detangling spray and a holding hair spray, and his brother Jim went on the road to sell the line to hairstylists. By 1973 only 60 percent of Pro-Line's $365,000 annual sales went to the military, and Cottrell was widening his distribution network with every new product. Eventually, PX sales were eclipsed by sales through retail chains as the company edged into national retail distribution.

When his firm was five years old, Cottrell opened a distribution center in Birmingham, Alabama, and tried to place his products in local stores. But Johnson Products, the leading ethnic cosmetics firm, dominated the market. Therefore, he contacted Johnson's area manager, Isabell Paulding, a former Miss Black Alabama, and asked for help. "She wouldn't tell me anything," jokes Cottrell. "I couldn't hire her, so the only alternative was to marry her." They married a year later and the new Mrs. Cottrell joined forces with her husband to continue growing the business.

In 1977 Pro-Line launched the Kiddie Kit, a hair relaxer for children, which contributed $1 million in sales during its first year. Then in 1980 Cottrell scored even bigger with the Curly Kit, a home permanent to style hair in the Michael Jackson look. The Curly Kit pumped nearly $11 million into Pro-Line's coffers within eight months. However, Curly Kit's success came at a time when Cottrell was embroiled in a new distribution challenge.

Cottrell was nearly out of room in his Los Angeles plant, but Pro-Line's largest market was Texas, and its second largest was the Washington-Baltimore area. Moreover, Pro-Line's raw materials were supplied by East Coast vendors. Cottrell was paying to ship materials from the East, package them in the West, and then transport them to retailers in the South. So he took some of the cash generated by the Curly Kit and moved into a $4 million, 127,000-square-foot facility in Dallas, a move that saved him more than $1 million a year.

Today Pro-Line is the fourth-largest producer of ethnic beauty products in the United States, with 23 product lines and a staff of 240. As the domestic market has matured, Cottrell has targeted international markets for growth through licensing arrangements in Nigeria, Taiwan, and other overseas markets. He's still keeping a close watch on his marketing channels for the next big opportunity to increase his share of this $1.5 billion market.

1. Imagine that Cottrell wants to extend the Pro-Line brand name to a new vertical marketing system. Should he establish a new network of franchised beauty salons and barbershops, or organize a sponsored voluntary chain to help independently owned salons and barbershops purchase and promote ethnic beauty products?

2. Pro-Line now competes with both ethnic and general hair-care marketers for shelf space in retail outlets. To compete more effectively, should Cottrell use a selective distribution strategy to differentiate his products with an upscale image, or should he use an intensive distribution strategy to try to find more and more outlets?

3. If Cottrell wanted to distribute his products in Australia, should he offer his line through a local agent or wholesaler who's familiar with the country, or should he approach the larger chains without using any intermediaries?

As a producer who markets consumer products, one of your most important marketing decisions is choosing the number and nature of the retail outlets that carry your products. The factors that go into your decision include store image, customer support capabilities, and location.

**Decision:** Pick a category of consumer products, such as stereo equipment, clothes, gourmet foods, or perfume, that requires careful channel planning. Visit three stores that might be considered as possible outlets for your products and determine whether each would be a good intermediary for your company. Before you visit the stores, make sure you've identified the variables that are most important for you to consider. Why did you accept or reject each of the three stores?

**Communication:** Write a one-page memo that you could send to one of the stores, explaining why you did or didn't choose it as a channel partner. Be sure to base your conclusion on solid marketing principles.

# KEEPING CURRENT IN MARKETING

Find an article that describes conflict within one producer's marketing channels. The conflict can center around price, inventory, channel saturation, inconsistent behavior, or anything else that generated some sort of disruption.

1. What specific acts, policies, or issues created the conflict? Was it caused by the producer or by one of the marketing intermediaries?

2. What must happen for the conflict to be resolved? What additional actions would you recommend to resolve the conflict?

3. Looking ahead to the coming decade, what developments or trends are likely to occur that will have an impact on the conflict described? What new conflict issues will the developments or trends create?

# 14

# Wholesaling and Industrial Distribution

**After studying this chapter, you will be able to**

**1.** Define the role and importance of wholesalers in the marketing process

**2.** Identify the functions performed by wholesaling institutions

**3.** Distinguish industrial distribution from wholesaling aimed at retailers

**4.** Suggest ways in which wholesalers can build competitive advantage

**5.** Explain the criteria producers and retailers use to select wholesalers

**6.** Describe the major elements of strategic wholesaling management

**7.** Discuss trends in the wholesaling business

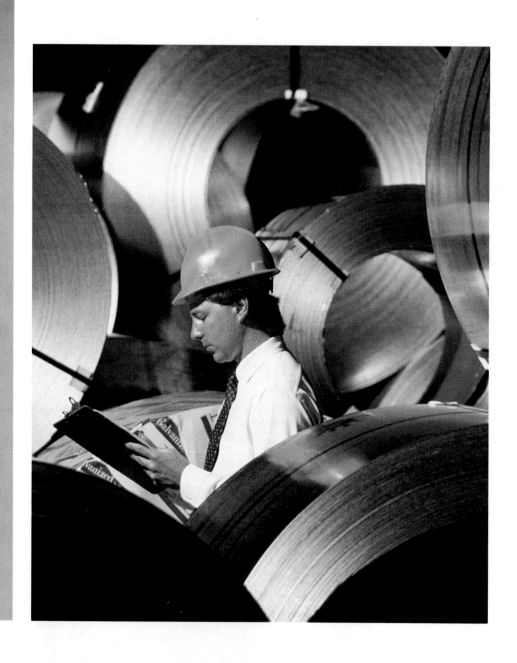

## Michael Wright Just Wants to Make People Rich

Next time you drive past a grocery store that is not a member of a large regional or national chain, ask yourself how this business can possibly compete with its huge adversaries. How can tiny Sarah's Superette or Joe's Country Mart match the advertising budgets wielded by Kroger, Winn-Dixie, and the other giants of the food retailing world? How can the independent stores learn leading-edge management techniques and technologies, when the owners can't afford to take the time—and in an industry that competes on extremely thin profit margins, no less? For over 3,000 of these small operations in more than 30 states, the answer is to get help from SuperValu, the largest grocery wholesaler in the United States.

From the wholesaler's perspective, these small stores represent a great business opportunity, but it is not a simple opportunity. One of the biggest challenges facing CEO Michael Wright at Super-Valu is the diversity of this customer base. About 50 percent of these customers are individual stores. Some are located in rural areas, some in suburbia, and a few are in and around major urban areas. Nearly half are under 10,000 square feet, compared to the average of 40,000 square feet for all grocery stores. Some SuperValu customers, on the other hand, are huge, up to 100,000 square feet or more. Whether they're superstores or small neighborhood locations, they don't have the financial muscle to compete with the big chains.

Wright knows that grocery wholesaling is not an industry for the timid or sluggish. Changing demographics dictate new approaches at the retail level, and SuperValu must be able to respond. For instance, the increase in dual-income families and single-person households has increased the demand for prepared foods. Supplying grocers with the fresh goods needed to stock in-store salad bars differs from supplying them with cases of canned goods. SuperValu's competition at the wholesaling level is intense and offers little chance for differentiating the basic products, because all wholesalers can sell pretty much the same goods. The capital investment requirements can be staggering, with multimillion-dollar ware-housing and distribution facilities.

The issue of profitability concerns every marketer, but it is particularly acute in grocery whole-saling. Wholesalers get squeezed from both sides. First, they buy from producers who, naturally, try to sell for as high a price as possible. Then they have to turn around and sell these goods to retailers, who obviously want to pay as little as possible. This leaves SuperValu and other whole-salers stuck in the middle, with profit margins typically around 1 or 2 percent and little room for error. In spite of these enormous difficulties, Wright is committed to the success of his retailer customers. As he once said, "We want to make people rich."

If you were on Wright's team at SuperValu, what sort of wholesaling strategy would you develop to support the many and varied customers who depend on SuperValu? How would you protect the paper-thin profit margins in the process while still meeting Wright's goal of making retailers rich? Could you find a way to nurture the growth of SuperValu's customers so that the wholesaler itself can continue to grow? What services would you offer to your retailers to help them compete more effectively? How would you take advantage of technological innovations to help you stay a step ahead of your wholesaling competitors?[1]

# CHAPTER OVERVIEW

Wholesaling is a vital part of the marketing process, and SuperValu is one of the best in the business. This chapter discusses the role of wholesaling and its importance in the national and international economies. You'll look at the functions that wholesalers perform as they help move products from manufacturers to retailers and organizational customers. Quite a variety of wholesaling institutions have been developed to assist producers and retailers, and you'll be introduced to the most common types. Both producers and retailers recognize how important strong wholesaling partners can be, and this chapter outlines the factors that lead up to the selection of wholesalers. After that, you'll examine the wholesaler's perspective on the marketing channel: What does it take to be a successful wholesaler? The chapter concludes with a look at the technological and economic forces that are reshaping the business of wholesaling.

# THE ROLE OF WHOLESALING

Although most consumers rarely come in contact with wholesaling, the several hundred thousand companies in wholesaling play a vital role in the marketing process (see Exhibit 14.1). One-third of the U.S. gross national product and about 70 percent of all manufactured goods travel through wholesalers on the way to final customers. This adds up to more than $2 trillion annually, split roughly 50-50 between durable and nondurable goods. Without wholesaling, many manufacturers simply couldn't get their products to market, and many retailers would be unable to maintain adequate supplies of products to be sold.[2]

Depending on their relationships with producers, other wholesalers, retailers, and organizational customers, wholesalers can provide a wide range of services that make the marketing process more efficient and cost effective. For instance, at the low end of the service scale, auction houses bring buyers and sellers under one roof and provide little else in the way of marketing services. On the other hand, a selling agent can take over a producer's entire marketing function and take care of every aspect of getting products to market.

Seeing the importance of wholesaling is easy, but arriving at a clear definition is not. Both small grain elevators and multibillion-dollar grocery distributors fall into the wholesaling category, as do rack jobbers, auction houses, petroleum terminals, export-import agents, and a multitude of other intermediaries. Although any general definition will be inaccurate in some specific cases, for our purposes **wholesalers** are marketing intermediaries that sell primarily to retailers or to organizational customers. The definition of wholesaling could easily be stretched to include every sale that doesn't involve a traditional retailer selling to a consumer customer.[3]

Wholesalers provide a variety of channel functions, ranging from marketing research to financing. Some of these services are provided to producers, whereas others are offered to retailers. Regardless of who receives the services, smart wholesalers know that, like their counterparts in every other facet of business, they must increase their attention to customer service if they hope to succeed in coming decades. In addition to the obvious roles of providing a sales channel for manufacturers and a source of supply for retailers, here are some other important wholesaling functions:

- *Providing information.* Both producers and retailers look to wholesalers for information. Producers rely on the market intelligence that wholesalers pick up during their frequent contacts with retailers and organizational customers. On the other side, retailers are demanding more information and information support services (see Exhibit 14.2).
- *Ordering, negotiating, and regrouping.* Getting the right products in the right quantities and at acceptable prices is another important service of wholesalers. A ma-

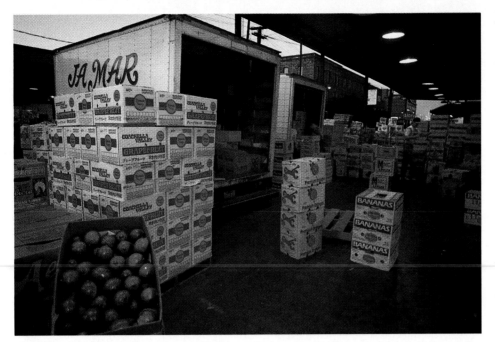

**Exhibit 14.1**
**PROVIDING TRANSPORTATION FOR PRODUCERS AND RETAILERS**
Physical distribution intermediaries transport fruits and vegetables from producers to this grocery store in Oakland, California.

jor development in this area is computer ordering. In many cases, employees no longer have to place orders with suppliers; computers at the customer location keep track of inventory and automatically place orders with computers at supplier locations when more supplies or parts are needed.

- *Storing and transporting.* Wholesalers often help their channel partners with the storage and transportation of goods. For instance, a wholesaler can keep stocks available locally to help retailers serve their customers faster. This ability to fill orders quickly is also important to organizational customers, who frequently buy critical supplies from wholesalers.[4]
- *Taking ownership, financing, and taking risks.* Some wholesalers take ownership of the goods they handle, which greatly benefits producers: They don't have to keep money tied up in inventory, and they can sell goods to wholesalers and then use these proceeds for other business purposes. Wholesalers can also provide several other forms of financial assistance: paying for storage and transportation, holding inventory, and extending credit to both retailers and organizational customers. Also, when they take ownership, wholesalers assume the risk associated with carrying that inventory, which is a valuable service for producers and retailers alike.

**wholesalers**
Intermediaries that perform a variety of marketing channel functions to move goods and services through the channel to retailers and organizational customers

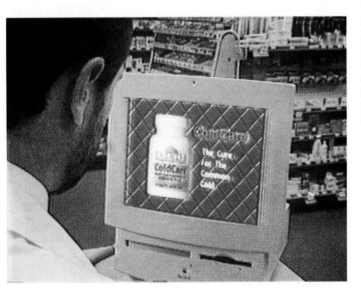

**Exhibit 14.2**
**SPECIAL SERVICES FOR RETAILERS**
Bergen-Brunswig assists pharmacists by providing this computer system that helps them select and order products.

- *Promoting and personal selling.* Wholesalers also offer valuable services in promotions and personal selling. Because they market both to other intermediaries and to organizational customers, wholesalers have developed a range of promotional skills. These skills are put to work to help the wholesalers sell to their own customers and to help retailers sell to their customers.
- *Offering special services.* Wholesalers can offer a host of other services, many of which have been developed to give them competitive advantages over other wholesalers and alternative intermediaries. These services include training of sales, support, and management staffs; advice on store layout and design; and support for accounting and inventory management operations. For instance, SuperValu handles the accounting, payroll, and tax work for the majority of the more than 3,000 stores it supplies. Marshall Electronics helps ensure the success of British-made MacLaren baby strollers by adding the brighter colors desired by U.S. consumers and seat belts that meet U.S. safety standards.[5]

**sales branches**
Manufacturer-owned selling locations that perform a variety of marketing functions; distinguished from sales offices by the fact that they carry inventory and usually fill orders from stock

**sales offices**
Manufacturer-owned selling locations that are similar in many respects to sales branches, except that sales offices don't carry inventory

**Exhibit 14.3**
**WHOLESALING INSTITUTIONS**
The three main categories of wholesalers are manufacturer-owned wholesalers, independent merchant wholesalers, and independent agent wholesalers. There are various types of wholesaling institutions in each of the three main categories.

# TYPES OF WHOLESALERS

Three major categories of wholesalers exist (see Exhibit 14.3). The manufacturer-owned wholesalers, as their name implies, are owned by manufacturers. (Actually, some retailers also own wholesalers.) The merchant and agent wholesalers, on the other hand, are independent businesses. The merchant wholesalers are further divided into full-service and limited-service institutions. The following sections describe each of the major types in greater detail.

## Manufacturers' Wholesalers

Manufacturers' wholesalers, sometimes called captive distributors, are owned and operated by manufacturers and fall into two groups: **sales branches** carry inventory and fill customer orders from stock on hand, whereas **sales offices** don't carry goods in stock and simply transmit orders to centralized warehousing facilities. With the exception of captive ownership, sales branches perform functions similar to those of merchant wholesalers; sales offices operate more like agents. Manufacturers' wholesalers are common in electrical and plumbing supplies, for instance, with Westinghouse Electric Supply Company and Crane Supply Company among the well-known firms. In the consumer-goods arena, both Procter & Gamble and Frito-Lay operate large wholesaling operations. Note that manufacturers' wholesaling operations can sell to independent wholesalers in addition to retailers and organizational customers.

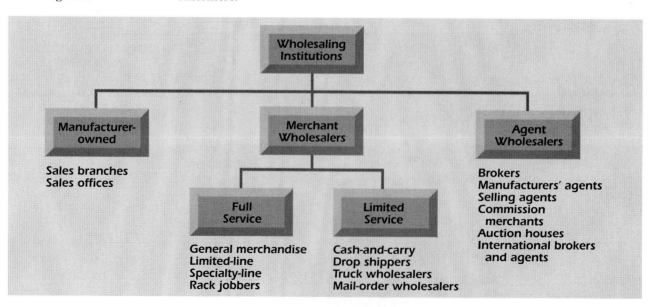

## KEEPING CUSTOMERS: A LESSON FROM BERGEN BRUNSWIG

In a world of big retail chains, independent retailers often need all the help they can get to stay competitive. Some rely on producers for help, some band together with other retailers, and others turn to their wholesalers. In the drugstore and pharmacy business, small retailers know they can count on Bergen Brunswig Drug Company. This drug and medical supplies wholesaler has long been on the leading edge of value-added wholesaling.

One of Bergen Brunswig's early pioneering achievements was to transform itself into a single-source supplier for drugs, medical supplies, and other goods carried by its customers. The change allowed retailers to fill their inventories from one wholesaler, which greatly reduced ordering, billing, and other inventory management tasks. Such benefits were particularly important for the small, independent operations, which normally can't afford to spend much time or money on the procurement process.

After organizing itself to better serve its target customers, Bergen Brunswig made its next innovation through computerization. The company relies on computer systems for all phases of its operations, including marketing and sales, and it extends the benefits of this technology to its customers. These small pharmacies and drugstores usually lack both the money and training needed to implement computer systems, so this service is a big help to them. Among the

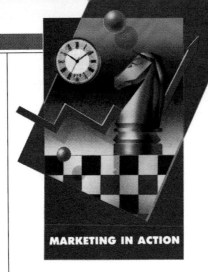

**MARKETING IN ACTION**

other services they receive are advice on sales promotions and management programs, financial and asset management assistance, automated ordering, and cooperative advertising programs.

However, technology is only part of the service solution at this innovative wholesaler. Personal service is the cornerstone of the company's continuing success. Three of the top five executives at Bergen Brunswig are trained pharmacists, so they have firsthand knowledge of the challenges and problems faced by their customers. This knowledge at the top of the company filters through every part of the organization and translates into a keen sensitivity to customers' needs and expectations. The management team stays closely involved; for example, sales vice president Leo Granucci sets himself a goal of 100 sales calls a year. His management colleagues are expected to make the same commitment to staying in touch with both customers and Bergen Brunswig's frontline employees.

One of Bergen Brunswig's cus-

tomers does a good job of summarizing why he and his fellow customers remain loyal. Richard Shapiro, owner of the independent Mel-Rich pharmacies in Santa Ana and Orange, California, says that he "stays with them because they're always there when I need them. They have the marketing information I need to be successful, and their salespeople and merchandisers are in my stores at least once a month to update me on sales promotions and management programs. It's a very close relationship."

In spite of competitors' attempts to imitate the service innovations it pioneered, Bergen Brunswig continues to grow. In the course of 10 years, its national market share jumped from 6 percent to 16 percent, and it claims as much as a 35 percent share in some regional markets. It is now the second largest drug wholesaler in the United States and in 1993 enjoyed record-breaking sales growth. Even though it focuses on small, independent businesses rather than on the large, national chains, Bergen Brunswig has built a profitable, growing business by executing the fundamental wholesaling functions extremely well and constantly searching for new ways to help its customers.

### APPLY YOUR KNOWLEDGE

**1.** What sort of training program would you establish for Bergen Brunswig's salespeople?

**2.** How else might you apply advanced technology to Bergen Brunswig's operations?

---

A manufacturer may have its own wholesaling operations for any one of four reasons. First, the complex nature of some products and applications is beyond the support capabilities of independent wholesalers, so manufacturers might stay involved to make sure customers are supported adequately. Second, intermediaries aren't always interested in the sales volume involved, either because it's too much for an intermediary to handle or because the volume is so low that it isn't profitable for an intermediary. Third, some manufacturers wish to maintain control of the marketing mix for various strategic reasons. Fourth, wholesaling sometimes presents an additional opportunity to generate revenue and profit, convincing producers to keep that business for themselves.[6]

# Merchant Wholesalers

Two categories of independently owned wholesalers are merchant wholesalers and agent wholesalers. **Merchant wholesalers** are independent business operations that buy goods from producers and then sell them to retailers or organizational customers. The difference in the prices paid and received constitutes the merchant wholesaler's margin. This can put merchant wholesalers in a tough position because producers want them to buy at high prices, whereas retailers want them to sell at low prices. Nonetheless, their growth in recent years has been quite positive.[7] Merchant wholesalers can be subdivided by range of services offered, and the two major categories are full service and limited service.

## FULL-SERVICE MERCHANT WHOLESALERS

**Full-service merchant wholesalers,** such as SuperValu, McKesson, and Bergen Brunswig (a distributor of drugs, medical supplies, and electrical equipment), provide most or all of the common wholesaling functions described earlier, and their retailer customers usually rely heavily on the services they offer. Intermediaries such as these are also called full-function merchant wholesalers to reflect the large number of wholesaling functions they perform.

The several types of full-service merchant wholesalers are grouped according to the depth and number of their product lines. **General merchandise wholesalers** carry multiple lines of unrelated items (such as foods, drugs, and office supplies) that cover most or all of the product needs of target customers. General merchandise firms usually have an advantage in economies of scale and find it easier to invest in computer systems and other efficiency equipment.[8]

**Limited-line wholesalers,** on the other hand, carry only a few product lines but typically offer a deeper selection of products than do general merchandise wholesalers. As an example, United Stationers concentrates on office supplies and focuses its attention on selling these goods to a clearly identified group of retailers. Its competitive advantages are based on superior customer service, not on multiple categories of products to a wide variety of customers.

The narrowest selection of all is offered by **specialty-line wholesalers,** which may carry only a handful of product lines or, in some cases, only one line. A good example of a specialty wholesaler is Semiconductor Specialists, which generates 90 percent of its revenue from semiconductors and microprocessors. What limited- and specialty-line wholesalers lack in selection is usually compensated for by greater depth in the product lines they do carry and increased knowledge of products and markets. This specialized technical knowledge is a requirement for success in such industries as semiconductors.[9]

A unique class of specialty-line wholesalers are the **rack jobbers,** who actually stock the display racks (which they usually own) in supermarkets and other retail outlets with selected merchandise. Rack jobbers can also be classified as limited-service wholesalers; it all depends on the number of functions they are capable of performing.

Full-service wholesaling can take on other forms as well, including wholesaling franchises and wholesaling cooperatives established by producers or retailers. Wholesaling cooperatives owned by retailers are dominant in some industries, including hardware, in which six of the top 10 wholesalers are owned by retailer groups. The largest of these is Cotter & Company, whose True Value brand accounts for nearly $2 billion in annual sales.[10]

## LIMITED-SERVICE MERCHANT WHOLESALERS

As the name implies, **limited-service merchant wholesalers** perform fewer wholesaling functions for their retailers and organizational customers than do full-service merchant wholesalers. Four common types are cash-and-carry wholesalers,

**Exhibit 14.4 SERVICES PROVIDED BY LIMITED-SERVICE MERCHANT WHOLESALERS**

| Service | Cash and Carry Wholesalers | Drop Shippers | Truck Wholesalers | Mail-order Wholesalers |
|---|---|---|---|---|
| **For customers** | | | | |
| Anticipate needs | Yes | No | Yes | Yes |
| Regroup products | Yes | No | Yes | Yes |
| Carry inventory | Yes | No | Yes | Yes |
| Deliver goods | No | No | Yes | No |
| Extend credit | No | Yes | Maybe | Maybe |
| Provide advisory services | No | Yes | Some | Some |
| Buy for their customers | No | Yes | Yes | Yes |
| Own and transfer title | Yes | Yes | Yes | Yes |
| **For producers** | | | | |
| Sell products | Yes | Yes | Yes | Yes |
| Store inventory | Yes | No | Yes | Yes |
| Help finance by buying goods | Yes | No | Yes | Yes |
| Reduce credit risks | Yes | Yes | Yes | Yes |
| Provide market information | Yes | Yes | Some | Yes |

Here are the services typically provided by various classes of wholesalers. Limited-service wholesalers provide various levels of services. Full-service wholesalers usually provide all of these services to retailers.

drop shippers, truck wholesalers, and mail-order wholesalers. Exhibit 14.4 lists the services each of these intermediaries usually provides.

- *Cash-and-carry wholesalers.* **Cash-and-carry wholesalers** earned their name by requiring customers to pay cash and to carry away their purchases themselves. Services provided by these wholesalers are limited, but these intermediaries provide ready stocks of merchandise available in small quantities, a big attraction for retailers selling to organizational customers who don't need or can't afford large quantities.

- *Drop shippers.* Natural resources such as lumber, grain, and coal are usually marketed through a class of wholesaler called **drop shippers,** who take ownership but not physical possession of the goods they handle. To contrast them with rack jobbers, drop shippers are occasionally referred to as desk jobbers because they sit at their desks and arrange deals over the telephone. Even though they don't physically possess goods, drop shippers absorb risk for producers and customers by taking ownership during various stages of transportation and storage.[11] Drop shipping is becoming more common in grocery retailing, as manufacturers begin to ship entire truckloads directly to the new, larger grocery stores.

- *Truck wholesalers.* Intermediaries that sell directly from vehicles are know as **truck wholesalers.** These intermediaries are particularly important in the fresh produce business, where they sell perishable goods directly to restaurants and food stores. Truck wholesalers can also be called wagon jobbers, although it's unlikely that many of them are still driving wagons.[12]

- *Mail-order wholesalers.* Another limited-service merchant is the **mail-order wholesaler,** which is the wholesaling counterpart of the well-known mail-order retailing function. The only significant difference between the two types is that the wholesaler version sells goods to businesses, governments, and other organizational customers, whereas the retail version concentrates on consumers.[13]

## Agent Wholesalers

The second class of independent wholesaling intermediaries includes the agents and brokers who market goods and services, usually without taking title to them. In addition, they rarely take possession of goods. The functions they do perform in-

**cash-and-carry wholesalers**
Limited-service merchant wholesalers that traditionally required customers to pay cash and then carry goods away themselves; however, some of these intermediaries are expanding their service offerings with credit, delivery, and other forms of assistance

**drop shippers**
Limited-service wholesalers that assume ownership of large shipments but don't take physical possession

**truck wholesalers**
Limited-service wholesalers that sell directly from trucks and other vehicles; they are common in tools and perishable foods

**mail-order wholesalers**
Limited-service merchants that operate in the same manner as mail-order retailers but focus on retailers and organizational customers rather than consumers

**Exhibit 14.5  SERVICES PROVIDED BY AGENTS AND BROKERS**

| Service | Brokers | Manufacturers' Agents | Selling Agents | Commission Merchants | Auction Houses |
|---|---|---|---|---|---|
| **For customers** | | | | | |
| Anticipate needs | Some | Sometimes | No | No | No |
| Regroup products | No | Some | No | Yes | Yes |
| Carry inventory | No | Sometimes | No | Yes | Sometimes |
| Deliver goods | No | Sometimes | No | Yes | No |
| Extend credit | No | No | Yes | Sometimes | Some |
| Provide advisory services | Yes | Yes | Yes | Yes | No |
| Perform the buying function | Some | Yes | Yes | Yes | Yes |
| Own and transfer title | No | No | No | Transfers only | Transfers only |
| **For producers** | | | | | |
| Sell products | Some | Yes | Yes | Yes | Yes |
| Store inventory | No | Sometimes | No | Yes | Yes |
| Help finance by buying goods | No | No | No | No | No |
| Reduce credit risks | No | No | Yes | No | Some |
| Provide market information | Yes | Yes | Yes | Yes | No |

Agents and brokers provide a diverse set of services to customers and producers; here are the services typically provided by each type.

clude promoting, negotiating, processing orders, and conducting marketing research, and they are usually paid by commission. Brokers can be distinguished from agents by the nature of their relationship with producers. Agents are generally engaged continuously, but brokers are usually employed for a limited time, sometimes for only one deal. Exhibit 14.5 lists the major services offered by agents and brokers. Here's a look at brokers and a variety of agents.

## BROKERS

The value brokers offer both producers and retailers is specialized knowledge of market segments and connections with large networks of potential buyers and sellers. Brokers are a common intermediary type in the food industry. For instance, in the cannery business a seafood broker can be engaged to sell the output of the cannery, which might be in operation for just a few months each year. The broker has the industry contacts and specialized knowledge required to move the producer's output through the appropriate marketing channels. When the year's production is sold, the formal producer-broker relationship is dissolved.[14]

## AGENTS

Numerous types of agents have evolved to address the specialized marketing needs of various businesses. Producers opt to use agents for two major reasons. First, with the average sales call costing more than $200, and with the cost of putting one salesperson in the field running as high as $150,000 annually, many producers simply can't afford captive marketing channels. Second, agents frequently have thorough, hands-on knowledge of the markets they cover, including extensive buyer contacts that would take a producer years to cultivate. Here are the most common agent intermediaries.

**manufacturers' agents**
Independent firms that perform a variety of marketing functions, including personal selling, on behalf of the manufacturers they represent; they are paid on commission, don't assume ownership, and rarely take physical possession

MANUFACTURERS' AGENTS  Manufacturers of all sizes take advantage of **manufacturers' agents** (also known as representatives or reps), which operate as independent units and whose functions are usually spelled out in explicit contracts that cover territories, services, commissions, and so forth. These intermediaries play a major role in many industrial distribution situations, although some sell to retailers as opposed to industrial/commercial customers. The commissions paid to reps usually range from 10 to 15 percent and are determined by the level and variety of services they perform for the manufacturer and the industries they serve. Agents traditionally carry noncompetitive lines of products. Increasingly, however, agents are carrying competitive lines in order to make their sales calls more productive.

Companies or divisions with annual sales less than $50 million are the most common users of reps, but larger organizations use them as well. Small producers use representatives when they can't afford their own sales forces, and larger producers use reps to enter new markets, increase market coverage, or recover from cash-flow problems. For instance, the Buffalo Tank Division of Bethlehem Steel used a team of agents to supplement its direct sales force after drastic budget cuts prevented it from addressing important target markets.[15] In contrast, Ringer Corporation, a supplier of environmentally friendly lawn and garden products, decided in 1993 to switch from agents to its own sales force. Company president Stanley Goldberg said that Ringer needed to develop closer relationships with retailers.[16]

As Ringer learned, using agents has some disadvantages. You don't have nearly as much control over agents as you do over a captive sales force. Moreover, even when agents are acting in your best interest, they usually don't work for you exclusively, so you don't have their complete attention. In some cases, you might not be able to find agents that can help you. This is particularly true with complex high-technology products. According to Douglas Juanarena, president of a Virginia-based wind tunnel and turbine engine test-systems manufacturer, "If reps aren't qualified to handle the technical details, they probably won't be able to sell the product." Even with the potential problems, agents can be a powerful part of your marketing mix.[17]

SELLING AGENTS  Sometimes a producer needs even more channel assistance from an outside partner. **Selling agents** meet this need by essentially duplicating a marketing department and offering services that encompass a wide range of marketing functions, including advertising, personal selling, marketing research, product-development guidance, and pricing. Selling agents are similar to manufacturers' agents in three ways: Typically, they don't take title, they don't carry inventory, and they operate on commission. They differ from manufacturers' agents in the amount of control and influence they have over the marketing process. In some cases, a producer decides to turn over the entire marketing/selling function to a selling agent and concentrate on research, production, or another area of specialization. For instance, Stake Fastener Company, a California producer of fasteners, uses a selling agent to market its products to industrial customers so that the company can concentrate on manufacturing.[18]

**selling agents**
Agent intermediaries that go beyond manufacturers' agents by taking control of promotion, pricing, and distribution; they are used by producers that don't want to get involved in the marketing of their own products

COMMISSION MERCHANTS  Most commonly used for agricultural products, *commission merchants* receive goods on consignment and sell them for a prearranged fee (commission). They are similar to brokers in that sense, but they differ from brokers in that they take physical possession of the products they sell. In agricultural markets, commission merchants assist small farmers by sorting out and accumulating farm products and transporting them to central markets. Their expertise is in negotiating the best possible price under given market conditions. Commission merchants are also known as *factors,* a general term that applies to any intermediary that sells goods on commission.[19] (Note that the term "factors" has a different meaning in retailing, where it refers to organizations that provide financing assistance for retailers.)

AUCTION HOUSES  The primary purpose of **auction houses** is to bring together buyers and sellers in facilities designed for bidding on selected products (see Exhibit 14.6). Auction houses are most frequently used for agricultural products (cattle and tobacco, for instance), antiques, art, real estate, oil exploration leases, used cars, and a variety of other used merchandise.[20] One big disadvantage of using auction houses is the lack of control over prices, although sellers can specify minimum

**auction houses**
Facilities designed to bring buyers and sellers together for the purpose of selling products to the highest bidder

**Exhibit 14.6
AUCTION HOUSES**
Wolf's in Cleveland is an auction house that specializes in selling collections of fine art.

**export management companies (EMCs)**
Firms that act as the international marketing arms of the manufacturers they represent; EMCs frequently operate under the names of those manufacturers in international markets

**manufacturers' export agents (MEAs)**
Firms that perform services similar to those of export management companies, except that they operate under their own names and don't always maintain long-term relationships with producers

bids in most cases. Because of the limited service they offer, however, auction houses have the lowest average operating cost of any class of wholesaling.

INTERNATIONAL BROKERS AND AGENTS    Agent wholesalers play an important role in global marketing efforts. The complexities and potential pitfalls require intermediaries with hands-on experience and knowledge of local markets. International distribution can be an exceedingly complex adventure, and a variety of international intermediaries have emerged to deal with various situations. **Export management companies (EMCs)** act as the international marketing department for the companies they represent, which are usually small and medium producers with modest international sales volumes. More than 2,000 EMCs operate in the United States, most of which specialize in particular markets or industries.[21] EMCs frequently operate under the names of producers, and customers don't usually know they're dealing with a separate company. **Manufacturers' export agents (MEAs)** are similar to EMCs, but they operate under their own names and usually have shorter relationships with producers. Finally, some producers market their products internationally by piggybacking on the established distribution channels of other manufacturers. For instance, Sony distributes the products of Westinghouse and other U.S. producers in the Japanese market.[22]

U.S. companies working with marketing intermediaries in other countries need to be aware of strict regulations concerning distribution contracts. Each country has its own legal quirks, which can cause a lot of grief for the unprepared international marketer. For instance, you can't terminate a distributor in Germany for poor sales performance unless such a provision was agreed on when you first established a working relationship. Without careful planning, you might find yourself stuck with unproductive partners.[23]

## Other Wholesaling Outlets

In addition to the wholesaling intermediaries just explored, a number of alternative outlets have been developed to perform wholesaling functions. Generally, these outlets function as marketplaces in which buyers and sellers can interact directly to move products from the producer stage on to the retailer stage (or directly to end customers, in the case of organizational customers).

- *Trade shows.* Many industries have specialized **trade shows,** which bring together buyers and sellers for a short time, allowing the sellers to display their products and provide information to buyers. Trade shows are typically held semiannually or annually and can be a major promotional emphasis in many industries. The success of new toys, for example, hinges largely on the number of retailers who agree to carry the products shown at trade shows. Another powerful attraction is low costs for sellers. One estimate claims that sales made through personal sales visits to customers are four times as expensive as comparable sales made at trade shows.[24] Some trade shows are small affairs attracting several dozen exhibitors and a few hundred customers. Others, such as the Consumer Electronics Show and the National Broadcasters Show, feature hundreds of exhibitors and tens of thousands of attendees.[25] The 1993 CeBIT computer industry show in Hannover, Germany, attracted 660,000 visitors with 3.2 million square feet of exhibit space.[26] (See Exhibit 14.7.) In addition to commercial transactions, trade shows also serve as important and influential forums for technical, political, and other issues that affect a given industry's members. (The International Exhibitors Association even sponsors a Trade Show for Trade Shows.)
- *Trade marts.* In contrast to trade shows, **trade marts** are permanent exhibitions housed in facilities designed for professional buyers from both wholesale and retail institutions. For instance, at the Homefurnishings Mart in Dallas, buyers select from displays of furniture and home decorating supplies. Similar marts for toys, gifts, computers, and other goods are located in Chicago, New York, and other cities. Trade marts are also called merchandise marts. In fact, the largest trade mart in the United States is Chicago's Merchandise Mart, which provides 1 million square feet of exhibit space for sellers in the furniture, gift, clothing, and business products industries.[27]

## Wholesalers in Service Industries

Wholesaling institutions also figure prominently in selected service-sector industries. Of course, the intangibility of service products affects the nature of services wholesaling. For instance, the wholesaling functions that deal with physical handling of products, including storage and transportation, obviously don't apply in

German law prevents you from terminating a relationship with a distributor, even for poor performance, unless your contract with the distributor contains such a clause.

**trade shows**
Exhibitions that feature a specific industry's products and bring together buyers and sellers for a short period of time; many industries use trade shows as forums for technical, political, and other issues as well

**trade marts**
Permanent facilities where wholesalers and retailers can shop for various goods, such as furniture and computer equipment; if they sell to final customers, those customers are charged higher prices

**Exhibit 14.7
TRADE SHOWS**
This computer trade show in New Orleans gives sellers a chance to show their latest products to prospective buyers.

**437**

these cases (although wholesalers often handle the supplies and equipment used to perform services). However, many of the functions discussed earlier apply equally well to services. The marketing research, promotion, ordering, and other related tasks performed by goods wholesalers are also an important part of services wholesaling. The study of services wholesaling is complicated somewhat by the complexity of some channels and the various names applied to wholesaling intermediaries in various industries.

Wholesaling can play a significant role in several service industries, including travel, financial services, health care, and cultural and social services. For instance, the travel industry relies very heavily on travel agents, hotel representatives, and automated reservation systems. The lodging industry alone has marketing channel systems that can involve up to half a dozen intermediaries operating in various degrees of cooperation and competition. Exhibit 14.8 illustrates the potential complexity of these channel arrangements. Depending on the transaction, these intermediaries can function as either wholesalers or retailers. In financial services, insurance and investment firms also make frequent use of agent wholesalers, in the form of both agents and brokers. In some situations, agents or brokers are engaged by both the buyer and seller. Finally, cultural services channels can employ various combinations of intermediaries, including personal managers, booking agents, and arts councils. For instance, musicians use agents to arrange concerts and negotiate recording contracts. This allows the musician to concentrate on music while the agent sells the musician's services. As with the travel industry, the channel role played by these intermediaries depends on the situation at hand.

**Exhibit 14.8
COMPLEXITY IN SERVICES WHOLESALING**

The travel industry uses channel systems that can be extremely complex; some intermediaries perform both wholesaling and retailing functions.

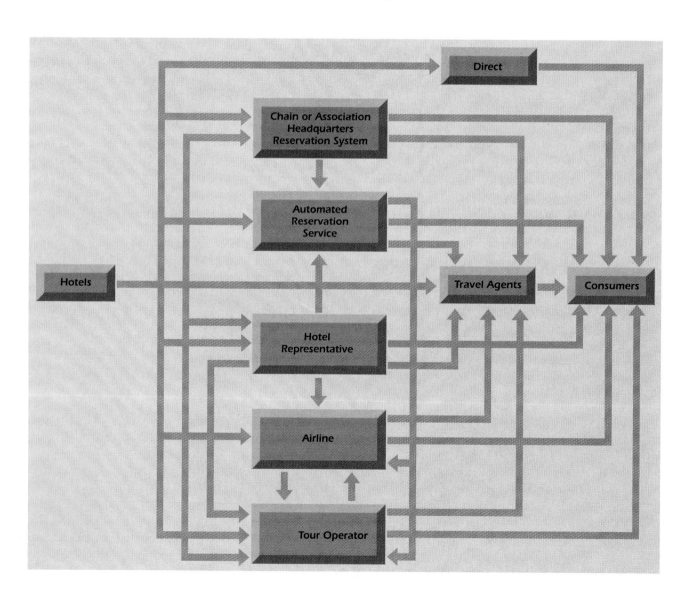

## Wholesaling versus Industrial Distribution

As mentioned previously, wholesaling covers the marketing of goods and services to other organizations and to retailers, who then sell again to consumers. Many of the concepts in this chapter apply to either situation, but you should be aware of some unique aspects of marketing to industrial/commercial customers. The differences can be grouped into two categories:

- *Purchasers themselves use the products.* When the manager of a Winn-Dixie grocery store buys a case of Folger's coffee, he or she wants to know how the store can make money by reselling the exact same case of coffee. In contrast, when the manager of a furniture factory buys a new saw, he or she wants to know how the factory can use that saw to increase furniture sales or decrease production costs. The difference can have profound implications for producers. For instance, the furniture company will want to know about installation, maintenance, repair, training costs, and how long it will take before the new saw will begin to pay for itself. The grocery store, in contrast, wants to know two simple figures: How much do we have to pay for it, and how much can we sell it for?

- *Consumers play an indirect role.* Consumer needs, wants, and tastes directly affect retailers and, consequently, wholesalers. If All Sport starts to take market share away from Gatorade, retailers will expect wholesalers to respond immediately and change the flow of brands. As a result, wholesalers that sell to retailers have to stay on top of the consumer market. In contrast, industrial distributors and their customers are one step removed from the consumer market. The concept of derived demand that you studied in Chapter 5 notes that all industrial/commercial demand is derived from consumer demand, but the effect this has on industrial distribution isn't the same in every case. Let's say that an increase in the number of school-age children increases the demand for notebook paper. Retailers, the wholesalers that supply them with paper, and the paper mills that supply the wholesalers will have to respond immediately. However, this demand shift may have no immediate impact on Beloit, a supplier of paper mill equipment. If the mills can simply increase their output with existing equipment, they won't need to buy any more equipment from Beloit.

Industrial distribution is an area of marketing seldom seen by students or most consumer marketers. However, it continues to be one of the largest employers of marketing specialists and is an important area to consider as you move into the job market.

# CRITERIA FOR SELECTING WHOLESALERS

Both producers and retailers carefully consider the wholesalers they will adopt as channel partners. Because of the crucial role wholesaling plays in many marketing channels, the intermediaries chosen to perform the wholesaling functions have to be competent and reliable, or everyone in the channel will suffer.

## The Producer's Perspective

Producers evaluate wholesalers on the basis of selling capabilities and channel relationships. Selling capabilities start with size, skill, and aggressiveness of sales force, if a sales force is used. Naturally, producers don't want to sign up wholesalers that won't sell their product effectively. The completeness of the selling effort is another key consideration. Manufacturers need to know whether they must supplement the wholesaler's efforts with their own sales force. Also, the total number of lines handled by the wholesaler is an important factor in determining whether a wholesaler will be able to devote enough attention to the manufacturer's products.

When examining a wholesaler's channel relationships, producers can start by seeing how thoroughly the wholesaler can cover the intended market, whether industrial/commercial customers or retailers. For instance, if the producer opts for intensive distribution at the retail level, the wholesaler would do well to have contacts with a large number of retailers. Second, producers look for the quality and continuity of relationships that wholesalers have established with retailers and organizational customers. Also, to ensure the smoothest possible channel situation, producers try to get a feel for the degree to which the wholesaler will cooperate in promotion, pricing, and other channel activities. Finally, producers look into how willing and able the wholesaler is to maintain a long-term relationship with the manufacturer.

## The Retailer's Perspective

From the retail side, wholesalers are selected based on the product lines carried and the variety and level of services offered. Product line criteria include whether the wholesaler carries most or all of the lines and brands required and whether the wholesaler carries sufficient depths in these lines to meet the retailer's needs. Product line depth and breadth includes sizes, colors, quality levels, prices, and other variations that retailers may need to serve all of their customers.

Decisions about a wholesaler's service can start with inventory levels. Retailers don't want to face shortages of products, which result in loss of sales revenue. Next, retailers are concerned with the extent of promotional support, credit, delivery, and special services that they may require from wholesalers. The relationship with the wholesaler's individual salespersons is important as well. Finally, retailers want to be assured that the wholesaler's cost structure will allow selling prices that are low enough to meet the retailer's purchasing needs.[28]

# STRATEGIC WHOLESALING MANAGEMENT

In addition to adeptly managing their own resources, wholesalers depend on one or more channel partners. Given this situation, successful wholesalers have learned to pay close attention to the fundamentals of business strategy, marketing, and channel management. The major managerial decisions facing wholesalers can be divided into questions of marketing strategy and questions of financial performance.

## Marketing Strategy

Like all businesses, wholesalers need a clearly defined marketing strategy that encompasses products, pricing, promotional efforts, and distribution.

- *Product strategy.* A wholesaler's decisions on product strategy center around the breadth and depth of its product offering. Depending on the needs of its customers and the influences of its competitors, a wholesaler can choose a strategy of general merchandise, limited-line, or specialty-line. As part of product strategy, many wholesalers decide on the level of service they'll offer producers, retailers, and organizational customers. When a distributor of electronic products, such as Hall-Mark Electronics, decides to carry personal computers, it decides how much service to offer as well. Hall-Mark's decision to help customers configure their computers, for example, makes their product offering more valuable to customers that need this kind of assistance.
- *Pricing.* Depending on the type of wholesaler involved, pricing ranges from a major decision to no decision at all. A selling agent, for instance, may have total pricing authority, whereas a manufacturers' agent may have little or no say in pricing. Pricing remains a central concern, of course, even if the wholesaler has no control over it. The agent wholesaler whose commission is based on selling price will want the producer to set prices high enough to make commissions attractive without significantly slowing sales volume. The merchant wholesalers caught in

## MANAGING THE LONG-DISTANCE MARKETING CHANNEL

Imagine that you're trying to win the heart of someone you've never actually met. This person lives in another country, probably speaks another language, and may have heard of you before, maybe not. You don't have the time or the money to visit personally, so you hire someone to do the job in your place. However, you can't be sure that the intermediary will say the things you'd say if you were there. Moreover, you'll never be sure whether the intermediary really has your best interests in mind.

Now you have a reasonably accurate idea of how manufacturers feel when they try to reach international markets using agents and other distributors. Doing so involves different languages, time zones, currencies, regulations, and business cultures and practices. Selecting international intermediaries is considered to be one of the most difficult challenges in contemporary marketing. The U.S. Department of Commerce lists insufficient care in selecting international distributors as one of the most common mistakes made by U.S. exporters.

Doing a good job of setting up an international distribution network involves three major steps: (1) locating potential distributors, (2) evaluating and selecting distributors, and (3) negotiating distribution agreements.

**EXPLORING GLOBAL MARKETING**

For the first step, marketers can get names of distributors from industry directories, international marketing consultants, visits to trade shows, and government services such as the U.S. and Foreign Commercial Service (part of the Department of Commerce).

Because your international distributors will play such an important role in your marketing efforts, evaluating potential partners is a vital step. Examine the following factors as they relate to each potential distributor:

- Current status and history, including the credentials of the company managers, stability record, and local reputation
- Resources, including personnel, facilities, and finances
- Sales territory coverage
- Techniques used to introduce products
- References from current U.S. suppliers
- Conflicts with competitive products

- Ability to meet special requirements in customer support, credit arrangements, and so forth

Once you've evaluated all the candidates, you can pick the ones that appear best equipped to move your products.

The third step is negotiating contracts with the distributors you've chosen for your team. The issues that need to be hammered out include pricing, promotion, territory coverage, customer support, product repair, and terms of payment. You may also want to consider confidentiality agreements (in which you agree not to divulge each other's competitive secrets), procedures for handling sales inquiries outside the distributor's territory, and stipulations that the distributor not legally obligate you to anything without your approval.

By identifying the most eligible candidates, evaluating them carefully, and negotiating agreements that allow both of you to win, you're well on your way to success in the international marketplace.

### APPLY YOUR KNOWLEDGE

**1.** What are some potential risks you face when marketing internationally through agents?
**2.** What role do international distributors play in a firm's ability to follow the marketing concept?

---

a price squeeze between producers and retailers will have a keen interest in pricing policies as well.

- *Promotions planning.* Wholesalers engage in promotional activities to differing degrees, depending on the services they've agreed to perform. Two of the major areas of wholesaling promotions are direct sales (to both retailers and organizational customers) and advertising support for retailers. Whatever the level and nature of promotional efforts, wholesalers coordinate promotions with their other channel partners to ensure cost-effectiveness and clear communications.
- *Channel design and management.* Distribution channel strategy is determined by the wholesaler's relationship with producers and the needs of customers (see Exhibit 14.9). For example, when Koley's Medical Supply, a small distributor of hospital supplies, decided to manage its clients' supply inventories for them, it was responding to hospitals' need to reduce inventory costs. A product's stage in the

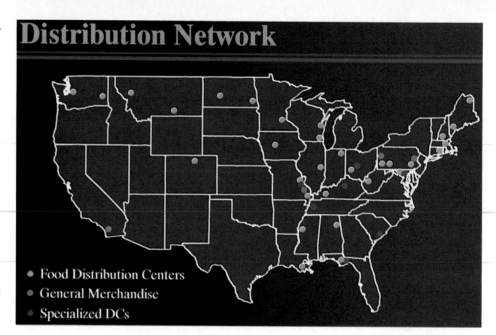

● Food Distribution Centers
● General Merchandise
● Specialized DCs

**Exhibit 14.9
WHOLESALE
DISTRIBUTION
STRATEGIES**
A key decision in wholesaling strategy is determining geographic market coverage. In this map you can see the reach of SuperValu's distribution system, which relies on a number of distribution centers strategically placed across the country.

life cycle also affects a wholesaler's distribution strategy. When a product moves from introduction to growth, for example, wholesalers may be called upon to help the channel shift from selective to intensive distribution. Such a shift might require such changes as expanded inventories or additional warehouses.

## Financial Performance

The management of wholesaling institutions encompasses two components of financial performance. The first is maintaining acceptable profit margins, and the second is ensuring that inventory turns over (sells) fast enough. Net profit in wholesaling operations is usually very sensitive to changes in expense levels, leading successful wholesalers to manage costs very carefully. Improved equipment and automation is one method wholesalers use to keep a lid on costs. Software firms such as Illinois-based Wynstar and the Dutch company Baan International specialize in helping manufacturers and wholesalers automate their distribution processes to keep profits as high as possible. Wynstar's Alliance system, for example, monitors discounts and other trade allowances that can quickly eat up profits if not kept in check.[29]

Unlike manufacturers, merchant wholesalers usually keep a very high proportion of their total assets in inventory; such is the nature of wholesaling. As turnover (the rate at which inventory is sold and replaced) increases, the wholesaler's per unit costs decrease. These costs include warehousing space, property taxes, and insurance.[30] For instance, assume that a wholesaler's costs are $100,000 a year and the firm sells 5,000 units each year. The cost per unit would be $20. Now if sales can be increased to 10,000 units a year without increasing overall costs, the per unit cost will drop to $10, leaving an additional $10 in profit on each unit. Naturally, wholesalers search for product lines that will help them achieve high rates of turnover.

## WHOLESALING TODAY AND TOMORROW

The world of wholesaling is changing and growing more complex. Some wholesalers find themselves competing with new, alternative channels such as warehouse clubs. Others have expanded into retailing. Some have been acquired by or merged with other wholesaling institutions. All these changes are taking place because companies up and down the marketing channel are searching for ways to serve customers and channel partners more competitively. Here's a brief look at the important management and marketing issues facing wholesalers.

# Intermediaries' Share and Comparative Costs

The composition of the wholesaling business has changed in the past half-century, with decreasing share for agents and brokers and with increasing share for manufacturers' own sales offices and branches. The class of merchant wholesalers has grown slightly as well. The share of wholesaling that flows through agents and brokers has dropped by nearly 50 percent in the last 50 years.[31] The desire to control the marketing process in light of increasingly complex products and markets has led many manufacturers to adopt company-owned channels, and this growth has come at the expense of agents and brokers.

As you might expect, the various types of wholesalers discussed in this chapter have different operating expenses. For instance, merchant wholesalers typically have higher costs than agents because they offer a greater range of services. See Exhibit 14.10 for the operating costs of several wholesaling categories, in which a greater range of services implies higher costs. These figures are averages, however, and wholesalers can build competitive advantage by lowering their own operating costs, which decreases the increment they add to the cost seen by final customers. Both producers and retailers naturally seek to do business with wholesaling intermediaries that provide the best combination of service and incremental cost.

Sometimes innovative pricing can help as well. For example, California Hardware and Decatur-Hopkins are two hardware wholesalers that have adopted a pay-per-service pricing policy. This allows them to lower their prices on basic products and then charge retailers for each individual service, such as advertising and in-store merchandising materials. Retailers pay only for the services they need, and this allows them to purchase goods for less in many cases.[32]

## The Changing Composition of the Wholesaling Industry

Despite wholesaling's central role in the economy, wholesaling has historically been an industry of very small organizations. However, the industry has been consolidating at a rapid pace in recent years as the need to operate efficiently at very low profit margins drives wholesalers toward economies of scale. For instance, the Sun Distributors network based in Philadelphia purchased 40 other wholesalers in the span of 14 years, and Sun's owner is still looking for more.[33]

In another example, the number of drug wholesalers in the United States continues to drop, raising concerns about too few companies having too much power. When the number one player (McKesson) tried to buy the number four player (Alco

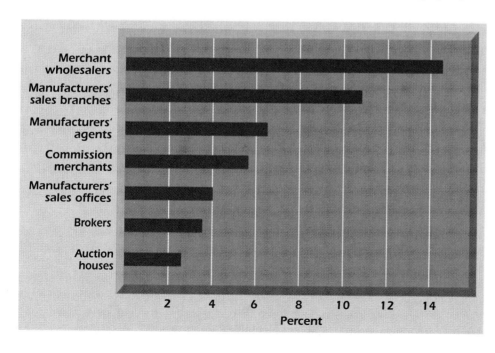

**Exhibit 14.10
COMPARING THE
COSTS OF SELECTED
WHOLESALERS**
Wholesalers' operating costs range from less than 3 percent of sales to over 14 percent, reflecting the various levels of service provided.

Health Services), the Federal Trade Commission stepped in and stopped the deal. It would have reduced competition too far and given McKesson a 90 percent market share in some areas. However, industry observers say that consolidation will happen just as fast as the government will allow. In the words of Charles E. Reiser, Jr., of Cardinal Distributors, it's "gobble or be gobbled."[34]

## The Increasing Use of Technology

Some industry leaders are calling on their academic and business counterparts to increase the attention given to wholesaling, particularly in the area of computers and information management. Computer-integrated systems such as Wynstar's Alliance have the potential to increase customer service capabilities while decreasing operating costs. As the number of players in wholesaling shrinks, those with the best service and best value will be the businesses that survive and succeed.[35] When a consumer buys a pair of Wrangler or Lee jeans from a retailer, computers at VF Corporation (the maker of these and other well-known brands such as Health-Tex) know about it within 24 hours and can respond with stock replenishments.[36]

A clear example of how technology is changing the nature of wholesaling is the growth of so-called service merchandising, which is provided by large merchant wholesalers that now offer the kind of hands-on service previously provided by rack jobbers. These services help retailers maximize their return on limited shelf space and help the grocery retailer in particular deal with nonfood items profitably. For example, by using computers and hand-held scanners, customers of McKesson get faster restocking with fewer slow sellers left sitting on shelves. McKesson will even stock and manage entire sections of retail stores, if retailers desire. With its 26,000 nongrocery items and this kind of service, McKesson has all but driven many traditional rack jobbers out of grocery stores. Retailers appreciate the fact that they can get a high level of service without having to do business with dozens of suppliers.[37]

## The Blurring Distinctions between Wholesalers and Retailers

Another change occurring in wholesaling is the number of firms that have started in retail and grown into wholesaling, or vice versa. For instance, Holiday Companies started about 60 years ago with one general store and is now a diversified, billion-dollar-plus wholesaling and retailing conglomerate. It is a leader in sporting goods retailing, and it owns a food wholesaler, a gasoline distributor, some 34 grocery stores, and about 250 convenience stores. Holiday plans to grow in all these areas, both through internal expansion and through purchase of other wholesale and retail operations.[38]

Such multifunctional companies can gain tremendous power in their channels, but they need to make sure that they aren't inadvertently competing with their own customers. For example, if Holiday wanted to open retail outlets in an area where its wholesaling operation is already serving existing customers, channel conflict would inevitably result. Holiday's management would have to balance the long-term advantages of having its own retail arm against the potential loss of some of the retailing partners currently doing business with the wholesaling operation.

## A Greater Emphasis on Service and Efficiency

**value-added wholesaling**
Wholesaling services that exceed the normal wholesaling functions; applies to anything done by wholesalers to help customers sell more products at lower costs

Producers, retailers, and organizational customers in every segment of the economy are looking for better ways to do business, and many are looking to their wholesaling partners for help. Leading-edge wholesalers are listening, and one important response is known as **value-added wholesaling,** which refers to a wholesaler's ability to go beyond the normal expectations of wholesaling functions to offer services that help customers reduce costs, increase sales, develop skills and knowledge, and improve the management of information. In other words, value-added ser-

## WE'VE MADE A GREAT CASE FOR INCREASING YOUR PROFITS.

PLEN T PAK

**INTRODUCING WRIGLEY'S WHOLESALE CASE.**

**A Special Case For Special Needs**
Wrigley's has created a special case for your unique inventory control and selection needs—a downsized, punch-out, full-faced shipping case that's changing the face of the wholesale gum business.

**Reduces Handling Cost**
Our new punch-out, perforated design makes stocking easier, reduces handling and helps prevent damaged goods. No case-cutting required. Just punch out the face panel and put the case on the shelf.

**Decreases Inventory Cost**
Wrigley's new Wholesale Case provides you with an organized, consistent product layout. What's more, our smaller case size lowers your initial out-of-pocket inventory cost. And that increases ROI.

**Improves Product Visibility And Selection**
This full-faced case with color-coded description improves overall category visibility, and facilitates the selection of sugar, sugarfree and non-stick chewing gums.

Call your Wrigley's representative today for more information about our new innovative inventory control system specially designed to meet the challenges of today's wholesale business.

**Wrigley's Wholesale Case.
A More Profitable Inventory
Management System.**

**Exhibit 14.11
BUILDING RETAILER
LOYALTY**
By helping retailers increase their profits, Wrigley's fosters strong relationships that are vital to its own success.

vices allow wholesalers to make the functions they perform more valuable to their customers.

Koley's Medical Supply illustrates this principle with its program of "stockless distribution." With this system, Koley's basically takes over the function of the traditional stockroom found in hospitals. Rather than making large, general deliveries to the stockroom, the company delivers specific items in just the right quantities directly to the various floors and rooms in the hospital. (This isn't always simple, either. At one hospital, Koley's has to make deliveries to 168 individual receiving points.) Omaha's Bishop Clarkson Memorial Hospital was Koley's first customer under the stockless program, and it managed to reduce annual inventory investment from $500,000 to just $7,000. The remaining $7,000 is used to keep a small stock of critical supplies needed in emergencies. In addition to the direct financial savings, Clarkson also reduced the administrative costs associated with supplies. Through such innovative programs, Koley's manages to serve its customers better and increase its own profitability.[39]

As retailers respond to changing market conditions, the wholesalers that supply them must change as well. For example, Peter J. Schmitt Company, a food wholesaler, works with grocery stores to help them compete against other food stores and alternative sources such as fast-food restaurants. Among the services Schmitt provides are preparation techniques and operation manuals for grocers who want to market prepared carryout foods, salad bars, and other nontraditional items.[40] Helping retailers build their businesses in this manner helps the wholesaler through increased sales and greater customer loyalty (see Exhibit 14.11).

## The Growing Complexity of Target Market Strategies

To effectively respond to changes in their customer bases, many wholesalers are adopting more complex target market strategies. Rather than treating all retailers as one customer type, they're segmenting retailers based on size and other distinguishing variables. Super Food Services, another food wholesaler, realizes that its customers range from 300-square-foot convenience stores to 100,000-square-foot warehouse stores, and it must address the individual needs of each customer segment.

Other wholesalers gain competitive advantage through finding niche markets and serving them better than anybody else. For example, when Wyle, one of the largest distributors of electronic components in the United States, decided to carry a new category of integrated circuits, the company transformed itself from a general merchandise wholesaler to a limited-line wholesaler. The new components, called application-specific integrated circuits, require more engineering expertise and customer support, and Wyle president Charles Clough realized that to be successful the company had to concentrate on fewer markets. This change in strategy gives Wyle a competitive edge because it can meet demanding customer needs better than its general merchandise competitors.[41]

## SUMMARY OF LEARNING OBJECTIVES

### 1. Define the role and importance of wholesalers in the marketing process.

Wholesaling is extremely important simply because of its magnitude: More than $2.5 trillion worth of goods flow through wholesaling intermediaries in the United States every year. Beyond its sheer size, wholesaling is important because of the many ways in which it helps producers, retailers, and customers. Wholesalers provide access to markets for producers and a source of goods to retailers. For both organizational customers and final consumers, wholesaling institutions increase the variety of goods available, and they frequently help to lower the final price because they can move goods through the channel more efficiently.

### 2. Identify the functions performed by wholesaling institutions.

Wholesalers perform a wide range of services for producers and retailers. First, they provide information to producers about market demands and other customer feedback. To retailers, they provide information, advice, and training on products, applications, and various aspects of marketing and management. Second, they can take care of ordering, negotiating, and regrouping tasks to make sure retailers and organizational customers get the right products in the appropriate quantities and at the best possible prices. Third, they frequently handle the storage and transportation tasks needed to move goods from producers to retailers and other businesses. Fourth, some wholesalers take ownership of the products they handle, which removes a burden of risk from producers and retailers. Related to this function is a set of financial services wholesalers can offer, including extending credit and paying for inventory holding costs. Fifth, wholesalers are closely involved with personal selling and other promotional efforts. Sometimes these efforts are directed at a wholesaler's organizational customers, and at other times they help retailers market goods to their final customers. Sixth, wholesalers can perform a group of special services to help producers and retailers, including modifying products for local markets and helping store owners with floor planning and shelf space allocation.

### 3. Distinguish industrial distribution from wholesaling aimed at retailers.

The differences between industrial distribution and wholesaling aimed at retailers can be grouped into two categories. First, the industrial purchasers use the products themselves, whether a piece of production machinery, raw material for a food product, or a business consulting service. The retailer,

on the other hand, buys something with the sole intent of reselling it as quickly as possible. Therefore, the questions the two groups ask before making purchases are different, and marketers need to understand the differences in purchasing behavior. Second, consumers play an indirect role in industrial distribution but a direct role in wholesaling to retailers. In the former, market demand is derived from consumer demand; in the latter, market demand *is* consumer demand, even if the wholesalers don't interact with the eventual consumers.

### 4. Suggest ways in which wholesalers can build competitive advantage.

Building competitive advantage in wholesaling is generally accomplished in two ways: increasing the level of service or decreasing the costs of providing services. Some techniques wholesalers are using to increase service include providing information about product use to retailers and their customers, hooking customers up to computers and arranging for automated ordering, offering advice on store layout and marketing, and arranging stockless distribution. To decrease the costs of providing services, which in turn can lower the commissions or profit margins required, wholesalers have turned to automation, including various computer systems that increase the efficiency of their operations. Also, increasing turnover rates tends to decrease per unit cost of possession.

### 5. Explain the criteria producers and retailers use to select wholesalers.

Producers evaluate wholesalers on the basis of selling capabilities and channel and customer relationships. Selling capabilities include size, skill, and aggressiveness of sales force (if any); completeness of the selling effort; and the total number of lines handled by the wholesaler. Channel relationships include the most thorough coverage of appropriate retail establishments; the quality and continuity of relationships with retailers and organizational customers; the degree to which the wholesaler will cooperate in promotion, pricing, and other channel activities; and the willingness of the wholesaler to maintain long-term relations with the manufacturer.

From the retail side, wholesalers are selected based on the product lines carried and the variety and level of services offered. Product line criteria include whether the wholesaler carries most or all of the lines and brands required and whether the wholesaler carries sufficient depths in these lines to meet the retailer's needs. Service decisions include inventory levels; the extent of promotional support, credit, delivery, and special services that may be required; relationship with the individual salespersons; and whether or not the wholesaler's cost structure will allow selling prices that are low enough to meet the retailer's purchasing price needs.

## 6. Describe the major elements of strategic wholesaling management.

Wholesaling strategy can be viewed in two parts: the marketing mix employed and the financial performance of the wholesaling firm. In the marketing mix, product strategy includes the decisions of depth and breadth of product offerings, together with the levels of service that will be made available to customers. Pricing is often outside the control of wholesalers, but it is naturally a concern of all wholesalers, whether they are compensated through profit margins or commissions. Wholesaling promotions frequently emphasize direct sales to retailers and organizational customers and advertising support for retailers. Distribution strategy is defined largely by the relationship the wholesaler has with producers, retailers, and organizational customers. From the financial perspective, the two variables of expense levels and turnover rate need to be managed carefully to ensure competitive costs and acceptable profit levels.

## 7. Discuss trends in the wholesaling business.

This chapter identified several issues that are likely to shape wholesaling in coming decades. First, companies are consolidating throughout the industry, and some experts predict that as many as 25 percent of the wholesalers now in business won't be by 1995. Second, wholesaling will get increased attention from academic and business leaders as they recognize that wholesaling needs to make strides in terms of technology and information management. Third, developments such as service wholesaling will force wholesalers either to increase the level of service they provide retailers or to risk extinction. Fourth, the line of distinction between retailers and wholesalers is starting to blur as companies on each side expand into the other's arena. Finally, wholesalers will continue to adopt increasingly complex target market strategies that include searching for niche markets, diversifying into different product and market areas, and segmenting their existing customers on the basis of needs and benefits required.

_____ **KEY TERMS** _____

auction houses (435)
cash-and-carry wholesalers (433)
drop shippers (433)
export management companies (EMCs) (436)
full-service merchant wholesalers (432)

general merchandise wholesalers (432)
limited-line wholesalers (432)
limited-service merchant wholesalers (432)
mail-order wholesalers (433)
manufacturers' agents (434)

manufacturers' export agents (MEAs) (436)
merchant wholesalers (432)
rack jobbers (432)
sales branches (430)
sales offices (430)
selling agents (435)
specialty-line wholesalers (432)

trade marts (437)
trade shows (437)
truck wholesalers (433)
value-added wholesaling (444)
wholesalers (429)

_____ **QUESTIONS FOR DISCUSSION** _____

1. As a wholesaler of outdoor sports equipment, what are some special services you could offer the retailers that you supply?
2. For the following products, which of the wholesaling intermediaries described in this chapter would be a good choice? If more than one intermediary might work, list all possibilities.
   a. Used farm equipment
   b. Auto paint sold to home mechanics
   c. Auto paint sold to General Motors
   d. Farm produce
3. Assume you're the marketing manager at Cray Research, a leading maker of supercomputers used in scientific and engineering applications. What are the factors you'll consider when deciding between your own sales force and an outside intermediary, such as a manufacturers' agent?
4. As an operator of a coal mine, would it make sense for you to engage the services of a selling agent? Why?
5. Assume you're a manufacturer of kitchen appliances and have decided to switch your target market from restaurants to consumers. Should your distribution strategy change? If so, how?
6. If you were a grocery wholesaler whose customer base included both convenience stores and large grocery stores, how would you adapt your services to meet the needs of these two groups?
7. As an international agent for a manufacturer of toys, what services could you provide for the manufacturer you represent?
8. As a wholesaler, how would you respond to the suggestion that you should advertise in newspapers and general-interest magazines in order to increase the average consumer's awareness of your company?
9. How could a rack jobber survive the competitive onslaught of "service merchandisers" such as McKesson?
10. As a manufacturer of high-performance racing bicycles, how would you evaluate the services of the wholesalers that carry your products?

### Meeting a Marketing Challenge at SuperValu

SuperValu represents four of the most important trends in contemporary wholesaling. First, it has the power that comes with size. With over $9 billion in sales every year, SuperValu can afford to assign experts to address specific marketing challenges, and it can spend money on both marketing and operational research. Second, it is innovative in terms of technology, research, and store design. Third, it is a leader in customer service. Michael Wright's statement that he wants to make retailers rich is based on a philosophy of being committed to making customers successful. In fact, SuperValu refers to itself not as a wholesaler but as a "retail support company." Fourth, it is growing aggressively by acquiring other wholesale operations.

The company's approach to customer service is summed up well in the statement of philosophy it adopted back in 1974 (long before customer satisfaction became the popular theme it is today): "SuperValu has a total commitment to serving customers more effectively than anyone else could serve them. We believe the pursuit of this meaningful goal is the continuing and overriding responsibility from which every corporate activity must evolve." SuperValu continues to demonstrate that it lives by this philosophy.

As an example of the level of commitment, SuperValu does more than just listen to customers. It becomes the customer, quite literally. To help it understand what retailers face every day, SuperValu also operates some of its own retail stores. These serve as income-generating businesses in their own right and as living laboratories for testing new retailing techniques, store formats, and pioneering technologies. The innovative Cub Foods is a good example of this. SuperValu combined the low-priced warehouse-store concept with elements of high-end retailing to define a new store format that both the company and its franchisees are successful with in 100 stores around the country. A study by the Federal Trade Commission called Cub the most revolutionary development in food retailing in the last two decades.

SuperValu also helps older stores adapt and become more competitive. In one instance, it converted an existing store into a prototype of a new format that combines the speed of a convenience store with the quality of an upscale food store. This provides critical insight for owners of older stores who need to remain competitive but who don't have the room to expand. Without a wholesaler giving this kind of advice, older retail stores in this situation might just fade away in the face of new competition.

To help retailers put the results of this research into practice, SuperValu offers dozens of wholesaling services. These include customized advertising campaigns, consumer research, accounting, and employee training. SuperValu established the Supermarket Directors Institute to train retail store owners and managers. The Institute offers a five-week training program that ranges from analyzing marketing data to developing high-performance employees to making speeches and presentations before community groups. Every major aspect of the store manager's responsibility that could help improve sales is covered.

SuperValu is clearly doing something right. In a business that is notorious for squashing profit margins, SuperValu's profitability is far above that of the competition. Its retailers generate far more revenue per store than those retailers who've aligned themselves with other wholesalers. By keeping customer service as its overriding goal, SuperValu helps its 3,000 retailers meet their formidable competition, and that is the secret to success in contemporary wholesaling. Wright is now expanding the company product focus, from groceries to nonfood items and pharmaceuticals, and actively looking for acquisition targets in dozens of other countries. A recent headline summed up Wright's ambitions clearly: "SuperValu: Tomorrow the World."

**Your mission:** Your dream has come true! You are now running this huge company. Your job is keeping profits up, costs down, and smiles on the faces of 3,000 retailers. How are you going to handle the following situations?

1. Selecting the products you'll carry is obviously a crucial part of wholesaling strategy, but some grocery stores carry tens of thousands of items. So how do you make sure you carry the right ones? Which of these product line research approaches is likely to lead you to the right answer?
   a. A straightforward financial analysis will give you the best product mix. First, set some minimum profitability level for each product in your inventory. Then compute the profit returned by each product; if a product stays above the threshold, keep it; if it falls below the line, drop it. Remember that the cost covers more than just the purchase price and that some products cost more money to ship and support; keep these factors in mind when you're calculating profitability.
   b. It's simple. Listen to those 3,000 retailers. The retailers are in touch with the consumers, so you stay in touch with the retailers. If a retailer requests a certain product, put it in your inventory. No big decision here.
   c. The best approach is to scan the magazines and newspapers that most consumers read, checking for the products that are advertised most frequently. After a month or two of scanning these periodicals, you'll have a good idea of which products are most in demand.
2. SuperValu recently lost one of its larger customers, the Albertson's chain located in the Northwest. This incident represents a temptation that often hits both producers and retailers, particularly larger ones. They look at the wholesalers standing between them and think, "We could do that job and keep the wholesaler's profits for ourselves." Many producers and retailers who try this discover that they are unable to perform the wholesaling function as cheaply as independent wholesaling organizations. However, the temptation remains, and it is a factor in Super-

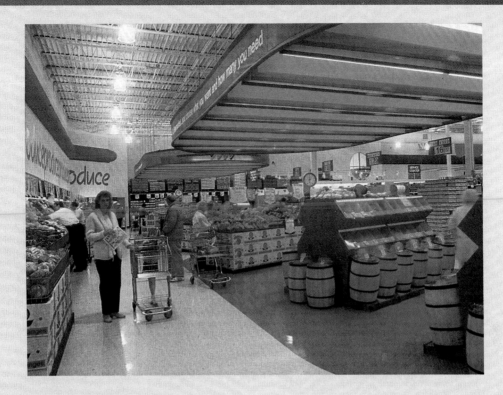

Valu's marketing planning. What should SuperValu do to dissuade producers and retailers from starting their own wholesaling networks?

a. Keep your prices so low that it doesn't make financial sense for retailers to start their own wholesaling operations. If they get restless, immediately open your books and show them what it takes to make a wholesaler profitable. Once they understand your operational and financial details, they'll back off from trying it themselves.

b. Make sure you're performing all the services they need. Sit down with their executives and see what else you can do to help. If they ask you to do something, do it. Big customers are too important to quibble about details or minor profit problems; give them whatever they ask for.

c. Try to meet the needs of every customer, but if you have to lose a few, so be it. It doesn't make sense to hold on to a customer if doing so drives you into financial loss or causes you to divulge competitive secrets. Do the best you can to maintain low prices and solid customer service. As long as you're keeping most of your customers, don't sweat one or two that might get away from you.

3. The box of cornflakes you sell is the same product sold by Scrivner, Fleming, Wetterau, and every other grocery wholesaler. How can you induce grocers to buy that box from you and not from one of your competitors? You can't slash prices all the time because your margins are already painfully thin. You know that superior customer service is one way to add value to the goods you sell and thereby differentiate SuperValu from the competition. What isn't

always so obvious is what it takes to provide superior service to retail operations. Which of the following services do you think would be most valuable to retailers?

a. Pumping promotional money to retailers is the best thing SuperValu could do. Advice is nice, but when you're trying to run a business, there's no substitute for money. The local retailers can handle the planning and execution of their individual advertising programs; just give them the money to run ads.

b. SuperValu should share all it has learned from its various adventures in retailing. The company continues to learn from its retail customers, and in cases where no competitive conflict exists, it should share that knowledge also. Experience has no substitute.

c. Running a retail grocery store is a full-time job and then some. No retailer has the time to deal with a meddling wholesaler that is trying to constantly sell more products. The best thing SuperValu can do is provide a passive answer service; when retailers have a question or problem, they can call in and get advice. Otherwise, SuperValu should just stay out of their way.

4. Let's turn things around for a moment. Put yourself in the place of a small retailer, say with two or three stores in a rural area of Missouri. You realize that several important factors are to be considered when selecting a wholesaler, including depth and number of product lines, inventory levels, cost, credit, and delivery. All the following wholesalers could probably provide the right products, so the choice comes down to services provided. Which of the following three wholesalers would you most like to do business with? *(continued on page 450)*

| Service | Wholesaler A | Wholesaler B | Wholesaler C |
|---|---|---|---|
| Delivery | Slow | Fast, scheduled only | Fast, upon request |
| Sales staff | None | Minimal (computerized ordering only) | Very helpful |
| Inventory | Very deep | Moderate | Shallow |
| Cost | Moderate | High | Low |
| Promotional support | Generous | Limited | Limited |
| Special services | Limited and only by request | Store siting, store layout | None |

a. Wholesaler A would be the best choice because of its very deep inventories and generous promotional sup-port. Advertising is crucial in retailing, and you can't afford to run out of products to sell.

b. Wholesaler B is a good choice for two reasons: First, it offers fast delivery, and that is crucial when you need to get products back on your stores' shelves. Second, the success of retail stores depends in large part on where they're located and designed, and this whole-saler can help you with both.

c. Low cost, fast delivery, and helpful sales staff make wholesaler C the best choice. Profit margins in food re-tailing are very small, and you need all the help you can get from your wholesaler.

## SPECIAL PROJECT

Servicing small, remote stores has always been a problem for grocery wholesalers. The cost of getting the goods deliv-ered, when combined with the small sales volumes, usually means very little profit for the wholesaler, or perhaps no profit at all. However, these stores still need to be serviced. What kind of program could you put together for SuperValu to help these retailers without losing money?[42]

## SHARPEN YOUR MARKETING SKILLS

You've just completed the design work on an innovative en-gine for water-skiing boats. This engine is quieter and gen-erates less water pollution than anything currently on the market. You've got the engineering taken care of, but you have no idea how to get the engine in the hands of customers. A consultant suggests that you let a wholesaling intermedi-ary work with retailers, rather than trying to do so yourself.

**Decision:** Make a brief list of all the services a wholesaler should be able to provide your new company and then pick the type of wholesaler that would be best for you.

**Communication:** Write a one-page letter to a potential wholesaler that you've chosen not to include in your distri-bution system. Explain why you made your decision.

## KEEPING CURRENT IN MARKETING

The nature of wholesaling is changing as companies search for new ways to remain competitive. Find an article that de-scribes an important change made by a wholesaler in the last several years. Here are some suggested topics:

- Application of new technology
- Merger with or acquisition of another wholesaler
- Vertical integration with a retailer
- Innovative services offered to retailers
- Increased efficiency or reduced costs
- Increased emphasis on international business

With the information you've found, answer as many of the following questions as you can:

1. Does this wholesaler serve retailers or organizational cus-tomers? Did customers ask the wholesaler to make the change? How did the wholesaler's customers benefit as a result of the change?

2. What prompted this wholesaler to make the change? How did the wholesaler learn about the opportunity for change? What were the risks involved in making the change? Is the wholesaler in better shape financially as a result? What happened to its position in the market?

3. What effect did the wholesaler's change have on its com-petition? Will other wholesalers adopt the change also? Is this wholesaler an innovator or a follower when it comes to making changes such as this?

## Technology Is Good Medicine for McKesson

Stumble into the control room at McKesson Corporation, and you might think you've stepped into NASA's Mission Control Room in Houston. Computer screens fill the walls with churning data while employees monitor the system to make sure everything proceeds like clockwork. No, it's not NASA. It's the nerve center of the country's largest distributor of pharmaceuticals and personal-care products. The computers help the company manage as many as 5,000 customer orders per hour.

The San Francisco–based McKesson's customers range from the U.S. government to the mighty Wal-Mart to the 3,300 independent drugstores that are members of the Valu-Rite voluntary cooperative. The company has been a pioneer in more ways than one. It is one of the oldest companies in the United States (McKesson began distributing drugs in 1833) and remains a constant innovator in wholesaling and distribution technology.

Information technology expert Jessica Keyes calls McKesson's Economost system "the foremost example of client partnering." Economost is an electronic order entry and customer support system with terminals installed at every pharmacy McKesson serves. The system plays a key role in helping retailers cut their labor and inventory costs and add nonpharmaceutical products in their never-ending battle to compete with the big regional and national chains. You've probably seen drug and grocery store employees walking the aisle with bar-code scanners, reading shelf labels, and noting how many of each item the store needs to reorder. At McKesson's customer sites, these data are transmitted automatically to McKesson's regional distribution centers.

McKesson serves customers through several dozen of these regional centers. The company's 235,000-square-foot center in Atlanta, for instance, supplies customers in Alabama, Georgia, and Tennessee. The warehouses are as high-tech as the information systems. To avoid errors, which are not only disruptive for customers but expensive for McKesson, warehouse workers wear custom-designed technological marvels on their arms. The devices combine a computer, a bar-code scanner, and a two-way radio.

When a warehouse receives an order, the central computer transmits it to an employee, who sees the product list on a three-inch video screen. Not only does the computer tell employees where to go in the warehouse to collect each product, it maps out the fastest way to get there. When employees grab a product, the laser scanner on their arm reads the bar code to confirm a correct choice then radios the central computer that inventory needs updating. The system has cut errors and boosted productivity dramatically.

With profits among the thinnest of any industry in the world, drug and grocery wholesalers must pinch their pennies every way they can. McKesson's technology not only cuts down on labor and error costs, it keeps customers loyal. This can be a major cost savings, as the company doesn't have to spend time and money getting new customers to replace ones that have defected to competitors. Pharmacists who use McKesson save on labor as well, so they are inclined to stay with the company.

In spite of its impressive technology and imposing market share, however, McKesson has had a history of lackluster financial performance. The common thread in its recurring troubles have been efforts to diversify into other business areas. With the company now firmly refocused on distribution and closely related efforts, CEO Alan Seelenfreund is optimistic, though. He believes the company can succeed in the new era of ferocious price competition and an increasing government role in health care. Recent results support his optimism; McKesson reported record sales and profit levels at the end of 1992.

1. Technology has clearly boosted McKesson's ability to compete profitably, but technology itself is never a guarantee of success in business. Can you envision any potential drawbacks to automation this thorough, especially in terms of customer relations?

2. How might a smaller wholesaler, perhaps one that carries only a small portion of the thousands of products McKesson handles, compete with this giant wholesaler? Can you think of competitive angles that smaller wholesalers might be able to exploit?

3. Why would tiny retailers find it attractive to do business with a behemoth like McKesson? Wouldn't they be more comfortable dealing with suppliers more their own size? Explain your answer.

# Retailing

**After studying this chapter, you will be able to**

**1.** Describe the nature and importance of retailing

**2.** Discuss the evolution of retailing and identify current trends

**3.** Explain how factors in target market selection and positioning affect retailing strategies

**4.** Describe the four variables in the retail marketing mix and discuss their implications for the retail marketing strategy

**5.** Identify the seven dimensions for categorizing retailers and explain the importance of understanding the categories

**6.** Explain the concept of nonstore retailing and the reason for its continuing growth

**7.** Describe scrambled merchandising and explain why retailers are often forced to adopt it

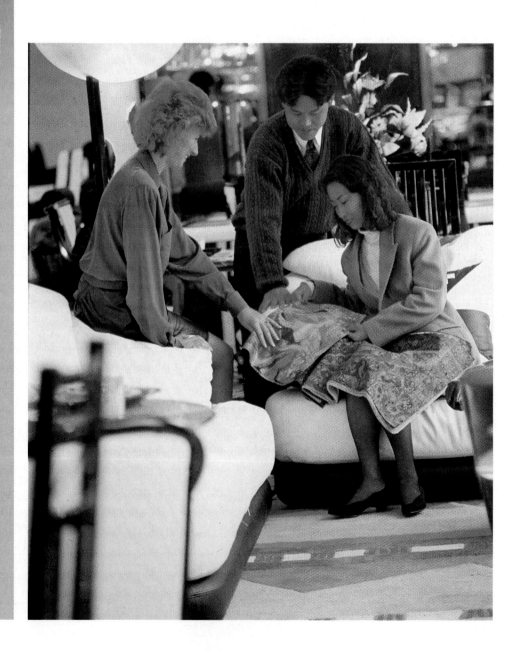

# FACING A MARKETING CHALLENGE AT NORDSTROM

## Service with Style

It all began with just eight shoes. As the twentieth century opened, two partners started Wallin & Nordstrom, a shoe store in downtown Seattle. On their first day, they sold four pairs of shoes, for a total of $12.50. As the twentieth century draws to a close, Nordstrom is ringing up sales of more than $8 million each day. How did the Nordstrom family parlay eight shoes into the fifth largest department store chain in the United States?

The answer lies in John W. Nordstrom's philosophy: "Offer the customer the best service, selection, quality, and value." The story of his retailing rise starts in 1897, when Nordstrom set out for the Klondike to make his fortune in gold mining. He returned to Seattle with enough money to start his own business, and he teamed up with shoemaker Carl F. Wallin to open the first Wallin & Nordstrom store in 1901.

By focusing on service, style, and wide selection, the partners saw sales grow to $80,000 within four years. In 1923 they opened a second store. Not long afterward, Nordstrom retired, selling his share of the business to his three sons. Then just before the Great Depression, Wallin sold his share to the Nordstrom brothers, and the company name was shortened to Nordstrom. After the Depression, the brothers continued to expand the business; by 1959, when they remodeled their main store and stocked it with 100,000 pairs of shoes, the Nordstrom family had built the business into the largest independently owned shoe store retailer in the United States.

However, the saga of the eight shoes didn't stop there. The brothers faced a difficult decision in the early 1960s: Should they expand into California and then move eastward, or should they remain in the Northwest and diversify into apparel retailing? The brothers chose diversifica-

tion, and they bought a northwestern clothing store. In typical Nordstrom fashion, they considered the tastes and needs of shoppers in their market and then stocked their stores with shoes and an assortment of women's apparel priced to appeal to a wide range of customers. Next they added men's and children's apparel to appeal to the customers who were buying men's and children's shoes in their stores. With the firm foundation of service, selection, quality, and value, Nordstrom began to open stores in Alaska, Oregon, Montana, Utah, and California.

John, Bruce, and James Nordstrom, sons of the three Nordstrom brothers, took over in 1970 to become the third generation in the family to run the business. By the early 1990s, they had begun the successful expansion into the midwestern and eastern markets that their predecessors had contemplated. They face sizable challenges in these markets, however. The chain is quickly getting a reputation for selection and service, but the old guard of retailing, including Bloomingdale's, Saks Fifth Avenue, and Lord & Taylor, are already well established with the affluent eastern customers that Nordstrom is targeting. To further complicate matters, Nordstrom's expansion is taking place in a tough retail environment, with consumers pinching pennies and retailers feeling the pressure.

If you were on the Nordstrom leadership team, how would you identify and reach your target markets in the new locations? What would you do to succeed in a market dominated by retail powerhouses that have been serving consumers in the region for decades? How would you apply the elements of the retail marketing mix to help Nordstrom in the East? Which retail marketing strategies would you employ to stay a jump ahead of your competitors?[1]

# CHAPTER OVERVIEW

As the final link in the distribution chain, retailers such as Nordstrom play a vital role in marketing consumer products. Producers rely on retailers to attract the right customers for their products, and customers rely on retailers to offer the right products at the right price. This chapter discusses the importance of retailing in contemporary marketing and gives you an idea of what the world of retailing is all about. It places retailing in a historical context by explaining the evolution of retailing, from old general stores and peddlers to today's hypermarkets and computer-interactive shopping. You'll look at the elements that make up an effective retailing strategy, including target market selection, positioning, and customer service. To help you make sense of the many types of retailers in our economy, the chapter concludes with a discussion of the ways you can categorize retail operations.

# THE NATURE AND IMPORTANCE OF RETAILING

No matter what the hour, somewhere in the United States a retailer is conducting business. Some retailers, like 7-Eleven and Tower Records, have stores open for business 24 hours every day. Others, such as Spiegel, have no stores at all but sell merchandise from a catalog, inviting customers to order by mail, telephone, fax, or computer. In the United States alone, nearly 2 million retail firms ring up well over $1 trillion in sales every year.[2]

Moreover, you're a retail customer nearly every day: when you order a hamburger at McDonald's, call a toll-free number to order the *Rolling Stone* CD collection you saw advertised on television, or have your coat cleaned at the local dry cleaner. Nonprofit organizations ranging from hospitals to public transit authorities engage in retailing as well. In the United States and around the world, retailers are an integral part of everyday life. Retailing is also in the midst of tremendous change today, making it one of the more dynamic and challenging areas in all of marketing. From consumers who'll no longer tolerate high prices to computer systems that eliminate driving, parking, hauling, and the other unpleasant tasks associated with traditional retailing, the rules are changing. Only the strong, the smart, and the fast are likely to survive the new world of retailing in the twenty-first century.[3]

## What Is Retailing?

When you think of retailers, stores such as J. C. Penney, The Gap, and Radio Shack probably come to mind. However, many other types of outlets fit the marketing definition. A retailer is any business that sells products to consumers for their personal use. Restaurants, supermarkets, barbershops, banks, mail-order catalogs, and hotels are all retailers. Without them, buying what you need would be much more difficult because you would have to seek out the manufacturer of every item you wanted. By carrying manufacturers' products at a location close to you, or delivering them to your home, retailing makes it convenient for you to get what you need. **Retailing** is the final connection in the consumer marketing channel that brings goods from manufacturers to consumers.

Goods are not the only side of retailing. Service retailing gives consumers convenient access to personal services such as medical and dental care, hair cutting, laundering, equipment rentals, and insurance. Tax preparation firms such as H&R Block are service retailers, as are Gymboree children's play centers, Budget Rent-A-Car offices, and Aamco Transmission shops. Service retailing is becoming more important as the number of working couples increases and the time available to spend on routine personal and household tasks decreases. The demand for time-saving services (see Exhibit 15.1) continues to grow, making service retailing one of the hottest marketing trends of the 1990s.

**retailing**
The end link in the marketing channel that moves products from manufacturers to consumers

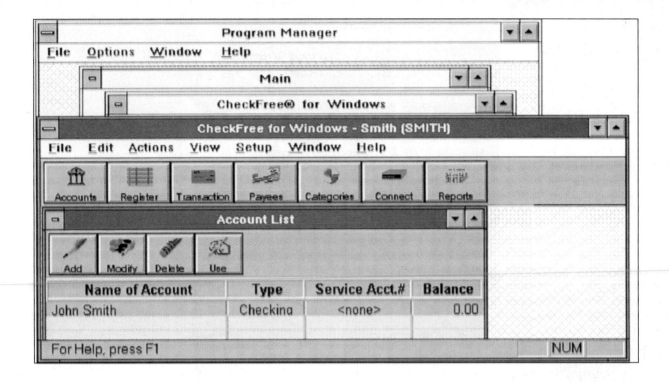

## What Makes Retailing Important?

Retailing is a lot more than simply buying and selling. This distribution link is important to consumers because it creates economic utility. It's important to manufacturers as the major connection in the marketing channel between manufacturers and end users. Retailing is also important because of its contribution to the economy.

RETAILING AND ECONOMIC UTILITY

Retailers add value to the goods and services they sell by creating time, place, possession, and form utilities. Retailers create time utility by stocking goods when consumers need them. Every spring, before beach days arrive, you can shop for bathing suits. Another way that retailers create time utility is by adjusting store hours. During December, Dayton Hudson, Bloomingdale's, The Broadway, and most department stores are open longer hours, providing time utility to busy shoppers.

Retailers create place utility by opening stores in convenient locations. For example, the Wal-Mart chain opened discount stores in small towns across the United States because customers didn't have any large retail outlets nearby.[4] Newsstand operators locate near train and bus stations because these are convenient places for their customers to purchase magazines and newspapers. Retailers also create possession utility when they put products in your hands. You're free to do whatever you want to the product after that.

Retailers add value to their offerings by developing product and form utility. They may alter a product (for example, carpet installation or jewelry engraving) or change the form involved (a caterer cooking food for a picnic, a mechanic repairing a car), and these product and form utilities constitute the basis of the service you are paying for.

RETAILING AS A DISTRIBUTION CHANNEL

To make their products readily available to consumers, manufacturers usually turn to retailers to distribute the goods they produce. As already mentioned, a retailer may be owned by a manufacturer or may be independent of any one manufacturer.

**Exhibit 15.1**
**INNOVATIONS IN SERVICE RETAILING**
The CheckFree bill paying service lets consumers pay bills electronically, without having to write checks or mail envelopes.

**455**

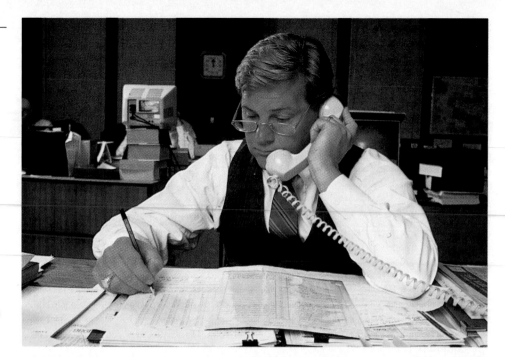

**Exhibit 15.2
RETAILING IS
EVERYWHERE THESE
DAYS**
Although he doesn't have a
store, in the usual sense, this
stockbroker is in fact a re-
tailer.

Manufacturers create a channel of distribution for their goods when they own a retailer. Around the world, Laura Ashley stores are good examples of retail outlets
serving as a distribution channel for clothing and home accessories manufactured
by Laura Ashley. Liz Claiborne, a major women's clothing manufacturer, operates
stores that carry only Liz Claiborne's First Issue label clothing.

However, most retailers are not owned by manufacturers and are therefore able
to distribute products from a variety of sources. In fact, large retailers, such as
D'Agostino Supermarkets in New York, Caldor's discount stores in the Northeast,
and the internationally known Harrods department store in London, stock a mind-
boggling array of products from a huge range of manufacturers. Consider the number of individual products typically carried in each of these retail outlets:

- A supermarket may carry more than 10,000 items
- A discount store may carry more than 50,000 items
- A department store may carry more than 100,000 items

These retailers want to appeal to a large number of shoppers, but so many consumers have varying tastes and requirements that larger stores must carry a vast
number of brands, sizes, and colors, bringing all of these choices to the consumer
from many manufacturers.

By nearly every measure, retailing makes an important contribution to the economy (see Exhibit 15.2). Retailers employ more than one in six U.S. residents, or
over 19 million workers. In fact, retailing is the third largest employer in the United
States, and continues to create job opportunities; government estimates put the number of retail employees as high as 25 million by the year 2005.[5]

## THE EVOLUTION OF RETAILING

Retailing in the United States began at a basic level. In settled areas some 200 years
ago, the general store carried virtually every necessity a colonist might require, plus
some luxury items. Today, general stores are gone from most communities, but they
still survive in some parts of the South and in New England. When the nearest regional shopping center is an hour's drive away, local residents don't always want to
travel that far for a package of nails or a liter of soda. So they shop at places like

the Vermont Country Store, which operates in two locations in Vermont, conducts a mail-order business on the side, and offers basic, reliable products.

Another early form of retailing was peddling. In rural areas, peddlers traveled house to house carrying lines of merchandise such as cooking utensils and sewing materials. This is how Kaufmann's Department Store started in western Pennsylvania. After three years of peddling notions, Jacob Kaufmann opened a 17-by-28-foot store in Pittsburgh. The original business focused on men's tailoring, but soon Kaufmann expanded his stock to include other products. In 1885, Kaufmann's opened a much larger store, The Grand Depot, and advertised that it sold "Everything Under the Sun." More stores followed, and in time the Kaufmann's chain became one of the two leading department stores in Pittsburgh, with 14 locations occupying 3 million square feet.[6] In developments that represent the continual evolution of retailing, Kaufmann's is now owned by May Department Stores and has been merged with Sibley's, a regional chain based in Rochester, New York.[7]

In frontier areas, trading posts were the predominant form of early retailing. Hudson's Bay Company, the nationwide retail powerhouse of Canada, began in the trading post business in Canada and the United States. Adam Gimbel (of the family that established the Gimbel's department stores in Milwaukee, Philadelphia, and New York) began as a peddler covering the fur-trading outposts of the Mississippi River. When he started his first store in Vincennes, Indiana, most of his sales involved barter, not cash; cash was scarce in that area in 1842.[8]

As the U.S. population expanded, demand for additional quantities and types of products put a strain on these early retailers' ability to meet their customers' needs. New merchants opened their doors, new products were offered, and additional services were provided. Just as Jacob Kaufmann moved from peddling to a retail location and then expanded his product line to serve more customers, so other retailers changed their product mix or style of retailing. However, even today, small stores play a key role in the nation's economy. In fact, most of the country's retailers are small, one-store businesses.

As you can see, retailing is a dynamic form of marketing. Some forms of retailing, such as the trading post and the general store, became rare or disappeared; other forms, such as department and discount stores, become commonplace for a time. However, in the past decade, many department stores have merged with giant organizations or have disappeared altogether. At the same time, new retailing formats have arisen, including video stores and shopping via home computer. To help explain this continuous evolution in retailing, several theories have been proposed, including the wheel of retailing, the dialectic process, and the retail life cycle. Keep in mind that these are generic models and that every model has exceptions.

- *The wheel of retailing.* Harvard professor Malcolm P. McNair developed a theory in 1958 to explain the continuous evolution of retailing (see Exhibit 15.3).[9] McNair saw a regular pattern in retail evolution, a pattern he thought was circular. His theory, the **wheel of retailing,** holds that a new retailer enters the marketplace with low prices, low profit margins, and limited product lines.[10] As the innovator succeeds in attracting customers from more established retailers, new competitors arise to copy the innovator. These newer competitors start to take customers away from the original store, putting pressure on the first retailer to trade up by adding more services, expanding product lines, and opening fancier stores. However, in trading up, the innovator becomes more like the established stores it initially challenged. Trading up makes the innovator vulnerable to newcomers because it leaves a gap at the lower end of the marketplace for new competitors. These newer entrants, who are willing to accept lower profits initially, may now challenge the original innovator, and the newest entrants start the wheel of retailing turning once again in a new round of evolution.
- *The dialectic process.* A second theory has been proposed to explain the changes that occur in retailing. According to the **dialectic process,** when a new competitor uses an innovation that gives it an advantage over an established retailer, the established retailer adopts a strategy that brings it closer to that innovation,

**wheel of retailing**
A theory that divides the cyclical patterns in retail evolution into three stages: innovation, trading up, and vulnerability

**dialectic process**
A theory of retail evolution maintaining that established retailers will make changes to adopt the innovations of successful new entrants, resulting in a new retail format that blends the best of the established retailer and the newcomer

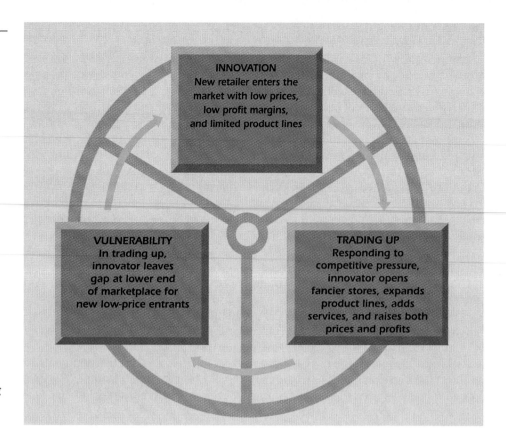

**Exhibit 15.3
THE WHEEL OF
RETAILING**
The wheel of retailing is one
of several theories explaining
the continuous change in retailing.

negating some of the innovator's appeal.[11] The newcomer, in turn, changes its
strategies in a fresh attempt to gain competitive superiority, generally by upgrading, adding product lines, or otherwise modifying the original retail concept.
These changes result in a new type of retailing that blends the best of the established retailers and the newcomers.

• *The retail life cycle.* This theory states that retailers undergo a life cycle divided
into the same four stages as the product life cycle: introduction, growth, maturity,
and decline. In the introduction phase, the store challenges established retailers
through a new competitive advantage, such as price, product line, or service. In
the growth stage, the retailer takes advantage of its competitive advantage and
expands. Maturity comes when growth slows, sales reach a plateau, stores fight
for market share, and may cut prices. Both sales and profits are low in the decline stage of the retail life cycle. Retailers in this stage suffer from a lack of competitive advantage, a condition that can drive the firm into bankruptcy. Some retailing experts believe that the retail life cycle is accelerating, leading to shorter
periods of time between each stage.[12] Exhibit 15.4 shows how quickly more recent retail innovations have moved from introduction to maturity. The latest formats, including warehouse clubs and category killers, have become established
in just a few years.

## RETAIL MARKETING STRATEGIES

Remember when that jewelry store at the mall held its grand opening sale, or when
you got an introductory catalog in the mail from the new compact disk club? Before those retailers started their businesses, they, like all successful businesses, developed a marketing strategy to address two critical issues: identifying the target
market and positioning the retailer to reach that market and to be perceived as being different from competitors. Moreover, retailers must be responsive to survive,
so a retail marketing strategy cannot be a one-shot affair. Good retailers continually

**Exhibit 15.4   ACCELERATION OF RETAIL LIFE CYCLES**

| Institution | Approximate Date of Innovation | Approximate Date of Maturity | Years to Reach Maturity |
|---|---|---|---|
| Downtown department store | 1860 | 1940 | 80 |
| Variety store | 1890 | 1955 | 65 |
| Supermarket | 1930 | 1965 | 35 |
| Discount store | 1950 | 1975 | 25 |
| Home improvement center | 1965 | 1980 | 15 |
| Large specialty retailer | 1980 | 1987 | 7 |

Innovative forms of retailing have been reaching maturity much faster in recent years.

examine their strategies, adjusting their marketing mix and repositioning to keep customers happy and to stay ahead of the competition.

## Target Markets

Like marketers everywhere, retailers start the marketing process by identifying the specific audience for their stores. Retailers generally consider demographic factors such as age, sex, residence, income, and family situation as they focus on one or more narrowly defined customer groups that will become their target market. In addition, psychographic factors (such as lifestyle, interest in shopping, sensitivity to product quality, and concern for fashion) are considered (see Exhibit 15.5). For example, The Limited describes its customers in specific demographic and psychographic terms: "The Limited's target market is the 16- to 35-year-old female. She is educated, affluent, gregarious, fashion-oriented, and more often than not, she is a

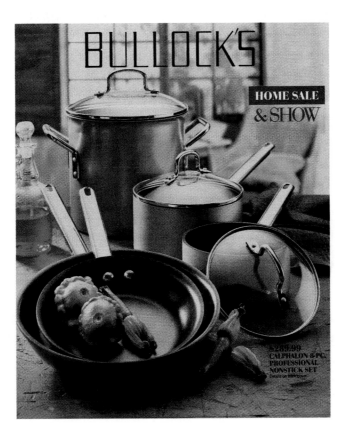

**Exhibit 15.5 RETAILING TARGETS**
Like all retailers, Bullock's tries to target market segments that will respond most favorably to its marketing mix.

working woman who lives in or near a metropolitan area. The Limited is her favorite place to shop because of our fashion and quality."[13]

Other retailers select other target markets. ACA Joe, a menswear chain that started in Mexico, defines its target market as young men aged 18 to 35 who earn between $25,000 and $30,000 in annual income and who have an aversion to shopping.[14] Mickey & Co. stores are targeted toward adults who grew up with Disney cartoon characters. However, target market definition is only the first step in developing a retailing strategy.

## Retail Positioning

Recall that positioning is the process of achieving a certain spot in the minds of customers. The same concept applies in retailing: Marketers position their stores in the minds of customers and potential customers. This involves the basics of the marketing mix, a customer service policy, and a retail image.

### THE RETAIL MARKETING MIX

Retailers face decisions about all four elements of the marketing mix: product, price, distribution, and promotion. Each makes an important contribution to retail positioning, helping to boost customer appeal. In addition, because retailers frequently adopt product, price, distribution, or promotion strategies that are similar to those of competitors, differentiation is a key objective of the retail marketing mix.

PRODUCT When positioning the retail outlet, the choice of product, the depth and number of product lines, and the number and selection of items are important decisions. One way to differentiate a store from other retailers is with the **merchandise assortment,** the array of products you choose to carry in your store (see Exhibit 15.6). For example, 7-Eleven convenience stores carry bread, milk, soft drinks, and a limited selection of food and household products that may be needed between a customer's regular grocery shopping trips. This carefully selected merchandise assortment differentiates 7-Eleven from supermarket competitors. The Reject China Shop in London specializes in imperfect dinnerware and crystal, a merchandise assortment that cannot easily be found elsewhere, clearly differentiating the store from department stores and other retailers that carry only first-quality merchandise. Furniture retailer IKEA invaded the U.S. market from its base in Sweden with

**merchandise assortment**
The unique mix of products offered by one retailer that is not available from any other retailer

**Exhibit 15.6**
**PRODUCT SELECTION IN THE RETAILING MIX**
Having the right mix of products for your target market is a key decision-making challenge in retailing.

ready-to-assemble furniture. Because furniture store competitors often sell furniture made to order for future delivery, IKEA's positioning as a retailer of instant gratification differentiates it in the consumer's mind.[15] These retailers carry unique merchandise assortments carefully geared to the interests and needs of their target markets, using the product mix to differentiate themselves from competitors. The process of product planning in the retail environment is often called **merchandising.** (Merchandising also refers to the way in which products are presented to customers in the store.) The emerging practice of *category management* seeks to maximize profits in each product category. One of the results of category management is often a streamlining of goods offered, meaning that consumers will have fewer product choices to sort through—and fewer manufacturers will be able to reach the public.[16]

**merchandising**
The process of planning the merchandise assortment for a retail store, making sure the right products are available for target customers; also refers to the presentation of products in the retail environment

PRICE    Retailers use price to reach their target markets and to differentiate themselves from other retailers featuring similar merchandise. Common price strategies for retail positioning include full price, discount, off-price, sale price, and everyday low price. FAO Schwarz, for example, sells fancy toys at full price, whereas Toys 'R' Us sells popular name-brand toys at discount prices. Many of their product lines are similar, but they have different price strategies. As a result, they appeal to different target markets that differentiate between these competitors on the basis of price. In Japan, the Daiei chain of grocery stores is causing a stir with its discount prices. Although discount retailing is quite common here in the United States, it is still a rarity in Japan, where consumers are accustomed to spending far more for basic goods than their counterparts in other countries spend.[17]

Similarly, discount pricing allows retailers such as consumer electronics merchant 47th St. Photo (headquartered in New York City) to appeal to customers seeking brand names at lower prices, differentiating the retailer from nearby full-price electronics retailers. Also, Motel 6 uses lower prices to position itself as a lodging chain priced lower than the average hotel or motel to attract budget-conscious travelers. The trend toward everyday low pricing discussed in Chapter 12 is another example of price used as a competitive lever in the marketing mix.

DISTRIBUTION    What are the three most important factors in retailing? Location, location, and location, according to an old retail adage. Simply put, retailers cannot easily survive if their outlets are not located in the right place for their target audiences. For a gasoline dealer like Mobil, place may mean a site on a main street or near a highway exit so that passing motorists have easy access. Hot-dog vendors at baseball games roam the stands, coming right to your seat, the most convenient location. Also, the Pepsi or Coke vending machine in your student activities building makes it easy for you to find a cold drink on campus.

Location choices can have serious consequences. When Bonwit Teller, an elegant store famed for couture fashions, moved from a prime spot on New York's Fifth Avenue to a location around the corner on 57th Street, "Bonwit lost some of its glamour," noted *The Wall Street Journal*.[18] The store also lost some of its clientele, finally closing its New York location in 1990. Customers differentiate between Fifth Avenue retailers that carry top fashion designer clothing and retailers not located on Fifth Avenue. Although location wasn't the only reason for Bonwit's closing, when the retailer moved off Fifth Avenue, it changed its positioning and therefore altered the way customers differentiated between Bonwit and its competitors. Clearly, successful retailers must define location in terms of their target audience's requirements, and they must use location to position themselves in the consumer's mind. Retailing strategists devote considerable time and energy to the process of selecting store sites, using computerized maps, aerial photography, and other tools.

PROMOTION    From the Finast supermarket flier in Sunday's newspaper to the Duane Reade Drugs shopping bag, promotion is a highly visible component of the marketing strategy retailers use to position themselves. Like other marketers, retailers

## TOYS 'R' US STORES PLAY SANTA INTERNATIONALLY

EXPLORING
GLOBAL MARKETING

Imagine 18,000 toys in a 45,000-square-foot toy store—sounds more like Santa's distribution center at the North Pole. Charles Lazarus has put Santa-size Toys 'R' Us stores in over 400 locations around the world. Starting with a single discount store in 1957, the company has grown into an international juggernaut selling over $4 billion worth of toys each year. The first expansion beyond U.S. borders was into Canada in 1984, then in Great Britain in 1985. Today, shoppers in Japan, Singapore, Hong Kong, Germany, and France can also buy dolls, trucks, video games, even disposable diapers at discount prices.

The Toys 'R' Us international marketing strategy combines a clearly defined target market (parents) with unambiguous positioning (the largest possible year-round selection of toys, offered self-service style in a convenient location at discount prices). Toys 'R' Us buyers buy in quantity from manufacturers around the world and tailor the merchandise assortment in each store to local market tastes, which is an important advantage Lazarus uses as he expands globally. Each country's merchandise assortment is fine-tuned individually, with as much as 20 percent of the merchandise geared toward local preferences. In Great Britain, cricket bats are sold alongside Louisville Sluggers. Just because local kids aren't familiar with a particular item doesn't mean it won't sell. Singapore children have learned to play street hockey, thanks to the hockey sticks and pucks available in Toys 'R' Us stores. When Toys 'R' Us buyers toured Germany to research local toy tastes before opening the first stores there, they found wooden toys, trains, and blocks that were so appealing they're now part of the Toys 'R' Us merchandise assortment in the United States.

Toys 'R' Us faces various competitors in each foreign market. Generally, the competition is similar to that in the United States: small neighborhood mom-and-pop toy stores, department stores, and discount and variety chains. However, as the toy superstore concept catches on outside the United States, foreign competitors are challenging Toys 'R' Us head-on. In Britain, for instance, the major competitors are Boots Company, a national drugstore chain, and Woolworth, a variety store chain based in the United States. Both are keenly aware of the Toys 'R' Us invasion and have developed very different competitive strategies. Woolworth is the country's leading toy retailer, and it launched a new chain called Kidstore in 1987. Located in urban areas rather than the suburban free-standing locations that Toys 'R' Us prefers, Kidstore stocks toys in addition to a wide variety of children's goods.

The Lazarus strategy is clearly paying off. The company continues to expand internationally and sales in 1993 were up in every country except Germany, which was stuck in a lingering recession. Toys 'R' Us Stores have sprung up in Belgium, the Netherlands, Switzerland, Portugal, Austria, and Australia. Plans for 1994 include more than 100 new stores for the United States and expansion into Scandinavia. Santa should probably just sell his sleigh and invest the proceeds in Toys 'R' Us stock.

### APPLY YOUR KNOWLEDGE

**1.** What are some of the risks Lazarus would face if he decided to charge higher prices?

**2.** Should Lazarus target higher-income shoppers who may be more interested in high quality and personal service? Why or why not?

need to communicate with their target markets in every way possible. Retail promotions run the gamut from newspaper and television advertising to posters to in-store events to coupons, varied according to each retailer's marketing strategy and how each chooses to position itself.

For example, catalog retailer Lillian Katz began in 1951 by placing ads offering leather goods of her own design in *Seventeen, Redbook,* and *Vogue.* Building on her success with positioning herself through promotion as a retailer of unique leather products, Katz published her first catalog (Lillian Vernon) in 1960, an eight-page booklet featuring black-and-white photos of products for sale. She then branched out beyond leather goods, broadening her positioning to include a wider merchandise assortment, primarily of her own design. Sales are now well over $100 million a year, a result of expanding her promotions to include larger, more colorful catalogs that are mailed more frequently. This strategy differentiates the Lillian Vernon catalog from competing retailers and from specialty catalogs that focus on specific product categories.[19]

When IKEA, the furniture retailer from Sweden, first opened in the Philadelphia area, the store set out to position itself as offering a new concept in furniture retailing: easily assembled and immediately available furniture at a reasonable cost. Because IKEA had no other stores in the country, it needed to differentiate itself from competing furniture retailers and encourage consumers to stop in for a look. IKEA used a variety of promotional tactics to get its name and location in front of potential shoppers, including outdoor billboards, radio and television spots, even ads on city buses. In addition, IKEA mailed nearly 1 million catalogs to local residents, aiming at its target market of consumers 25 to 44 years old. Promotion played up the advantages of furniture that can be taken home the same day and put together in minutes with just a few simple tools. Drawn by the intensive promotion, nearly 100,000 people shopped the new store in its first four days. Subsequent store openings have continued to position IKEA as the furniture retailer selling instant, affordable furniture.[20]

## CUSTOMER SERVICES

To serve or not to serve? That is the question every retailer faces in positioning (see Exhibit 15.7). Some retailers, such as Polo/Ralph Lauren on New York City's Madison Avenue, choose the full-service position, with more than 200 staff members available to serve customers, including 25 tailors for alterations. Retailers positioning themselves as full-service usually use a full-price strategy because they have to cover the high cost of hiring staff to help shoppers. A notable exception to this rule is the Home Depot home improvement chain. Its prices meet or beat those of other low-price competitors, but its service rivals the best full-service hardware stores. The combination of low price and high service is difficult to pull off, but Home Depot did it well enough to become the nation's top home improvement chain.[21]

Other retailers choose self-service; customers select their own merchandise and then head to the cash register to pay for it. Michael Cullen's 1930 vision of a new self-service superstore for food shoppers differentiated his retail establishment from the small, family-operated, full-service grocery stores then prevalent in the United States. His new store, King Kullen, created a fresh position: Shoppers could browse and examine grocery items at their own pace, choosing from a wider selection of lower-priced food products in one location. The concept was so successful that it launched the entire supermarket industry, which today sells nearly $260 billion in food annually.[22]

**Exhibit 15.7
POSITIONING WITH
CUSTOMER SERVICES**
Educating customers about product features and applications is an important aspect of customer service in retailing.

Moreover, retailers can use credit services, return privileges, home delivery, and other services to create positioning strategies that will differentiate their establishments from the competition. For example, whereas most fast-food restaurants position themselves as food only, Arby's has installed automated teller machines in two locations in Indiana, allowing customers to get cash while they're buying roast beef sandwiches.[23]

## RETAILER IMAGE

**retailer image**
The personality of the retailer as perceived by consumers

One of the most powerful components of a retail positioning strategy is **retailer image,** the perception a retailer evokes in the mind of the consumer, or the way in which the store is defined in the consumer's mind.[24] Image includes the physical elements of product, place, price, and promotion, and it goes beyond to include such intangible factors as employee attitude, ease of shopping, and store reputation (see Exhibit 15.8). Defining a retailer's image is a little like describing someone's personality; it involves feelings as well as facts. When retailers examine their positioning strategies and think about how to differentiate themselves from competitors, they must be careful to consider image. A study conducted by the advertising agency BBDO asked shoppers in New York City what they thought of prominent retailers there. The researchers set up a perceptual map that ranged from luxury to thriftiness on the horizontal axis and from tradition to innovation on the vertical axis. As examples, Bergdorf Goodman and Saks Fifth Avenue were strong on luxury and leaned toward tradition. In contrast, Barneys New York scored near the middle of the luxury-thriftiness axis, but strongly in the direction of innovation.[25] As a marketing manager at one of these stores, you could use these positioning insights to build your strength in the marketplace and ward off competitive advances.

**atmosphere**
A part of a retailer's image that is created by a blend of sensory effects intended to create a specific shopping mood

An important part of a retailer's image is **atmosphere,** a combination of sensory effects designed to put the customer in a particular mood. Atmospherics include not only the way a place looks, but the sounds and even the smells (consultants charge up to $50,000 to design a signature scent for upscale retailers).[26] Nordstrom

**Exhibit 15.8
POSITIONING ON
IMAGE**
Galeries Lafayette in Paris positions itself as having a wide range of fashionable consumer products.

positions itself as an upscale retailer by creating a gracious shopping atmosphere, even employing a piano player to serenade patrons.[27] Byerly's is a supermarket in suburban Minneapolis with an atmosphere quite unlike the typical food store. Instead of linoleum and bare fluorescent bulbs, Byerly's features carpeting, fashion wallpaper, and a grand chandelier.[28] Bookstores such as Barnes & Noble and Borders, trying to create a "browser-friendly" atmosphere, have added such amenities as comfortable chairs, classical music, and espresso bars.[29]

At the other end of the atmosphere spectrum is Price/Costco, with its low-price, self-service, no-frills positioning that attracts price-conscious consumers to its Price Club and Costco warehouse stores. The company reinforces its self-service image by stocking merchandise in packing cartons right on the selling floor. By using atmosphere to support its positioning strategy, Price/Costco differentiates itself from discount stores and other competitors. The Sam's Club stores owned by Wal-Mart are another major force in this area of retailing.[30]

# CATEGORIES OF RETAILING

With the wide variety of retail organizations, from drugstores and fast-food restaurants to mail-order merchants and promotional department stores, seeing what retailers have in common is sometimes difficult. Therefore, you might consider classifying retailers according to general descriptive categories such as ownership, product lines, level of service, pricing strategy, size of store, location of store, and method of operation.

Because different types of stores need different types of marketing programs, understanding the nature of a given retail operation is a vital step in creating a successful retailing strategy. Although recognizing the most common types of retailers is important, understanding the categories is perhaps even more important. Understanding the fundamental differences will help you grasp new retailing concepts such as computer-based shopping and interactive television.

## By Ownership

One way to categorize retailers is according to the form of ownership. A retailer may be independent, part of a chain, manufacturer-owned, or a franchise outlet.

Retailers not operated as part of a larger retail chain are **independent retailers.** In the United States and around the world, most retailers are single-location independents, accounting for the majority of retail sales. In the United States, for instance, retail companies with 10 or fewer stores account for nearly 60 percent of all retail sales.[31]

Stores owned and operated as a group by a single corporate organization are called **chain stores.** Centralized buyers purchase merchandise for the entire chain, and other administrative functions are performed by the corporate organization rather than by each store. Examples of chain stores include Safeway Supermarkets, audio-video retailer Circuit City, and Next (a rapidly expanding apparel chain in Great Britain). Each of these retailers operates a central buying and administrative office to support the many store locations in the chain.

A trend is growing toward manufacturers' operating their own retail outlets or catalogs. Hermès in Paris, renowned for its upscale selection of leather goods and clothing, is a good example of a manufacturer-owned retailer. Although Hermès products are sold by other retailers, the manufacturer maintains a Paris showroom and store as well. Other examples include Goodyear Tire & Rubber, Coach Leatherware, and Florsheim Shoes, all operating stores across the United States and featuring products made by their manufacturer-owners. Pepperidge Farm has also joined the trend, selling its cookies and cakes through its own catalogs.

Franchising has become a popular retailing format because it combines many of

**independent retailers**
Retailers that are not part of large retail organizations, but are owned by one person, two or more partners, or a family

**chain stores**
Groups of retail stores owned and operated by corporations that perform centralized buying and administrative functions for all the stores

the advantages of independent business ownership with the name-brand recognition, advertising, and financial muscle of national chains. Examples of franchise retailers include Benetton apparel stores, Baskin-Robbins ice cream stores, and Century 21 real estate offices. The franchisees in these organizations order materials from the parent companies and participate in local advertising campaigns under the franchisors' names. One of the hottest retail franchisors is Blockbuster Video, which dominates the video rental market in many parts of the country.[32] Considering the size of many franchise organizations—McDonald's, Burger King, and Holiday Inns are all franchisors—it should not be surprising that franchise businesses account for more than one-third of all U.S. retail sales.[33]

## By Product Lines

A second way of categorizing retailers is according to the product lines carried. Retailers may stock general merchandise lines, limited lines, or a single line of products. Depending on the depth and number of product lines carried, retailers may be classified according to more specific categories.

### GENERAL MERCHANDISE LINES

**general merchandise retailers**
Retailers offering a wide assortment of product lines

Retailers selling a wide variety of product lines are called **general merchandise retailers.** However, although retailers such as May Company, Woolworth, and J. C. Penney all carry general merchandise lines, each has a unique merchandising strategy that differentiates its stores from competitors.

**department store**
A large general merchandise retailer selling a wide variety of products at full price with full service

A **department store** is a large retailer carrying a broad variety and wide assortment of general merchandise lines plus many in-store services. Department stores such as May Company and J. C. Penney offer their broad array of products at full price with full service, and they supplement their product lines with extra services such as home delivery and store credit. Products are typically displayed in separate areas on the selling floor, grouped by product line or function. For example, you'll usually find shirts and sweaters alongside pants and belts in the men's department of your nearby department store.

**variety stores**
General merchandise retailers that offer fewer product lines and fewer brand choices than discount department stores at low prices in self-service environments

Ben Franklin, Woolworth, and other **variety stores** also offer general merchandise but with less diversity and more limited assortments that are sold at lower prices in a self-service environment. Variety stores are in the decline phase of their life cycle, primarily because consumers perceive the quality to be low, even for the low prices charged. Nevertheless, Woolworth U.K., for example, has successfully repositioned its British variety stores as specialty retailers by offering six distinct departments, limiting the variety of general merchandise, upgrading the quality, and still maintaining low prices.[34] Woolworth is one of the few U.S. retailers to make much of a mark in European retailing, and it plans to continue its success not with general merchandise stores but specialty shops such as its Footlocker chain.[35]

**warehouse club**
A general merchandise retailer selling fewer product lines than discount department stores at very low prices in warehouselike stores

The **warehouse club** is another type of general merchandise retailer. It offers a variety of product lines that are narrower than the lines at discount stores, and it offers deeper discounts with warehouse-size stores and atmosphere (see Exhibit 15.9). When shoppers join the store "club," which usually involves paying a membership fee, they are entitled to even lower prices than nonmembers. San Diego–based Price Club, which launched the category in 1976, generally carries office supplies, apparel, tires, and hardware, in addition to grocery items and appliances. Price Club (which merged with Seattle-based Costco in 1993 to form Price/Costco) and other warehouse operations have carved out a big slice of the retailing industry, with annual sales approaching $40 billion in 1993.[36] Office Depot and Staples are other big players in this segment.

Note that even though this type of store is referred to as a "club," not all stores require shoppers to join. When Office Depot bought out the Office Club chain in 1992, it dropped the requirement that shoppers pay a membership fee. Now all shoppers get the same price.[37]

When retailers carry product lines unrelated to their main merchandise lines,

**Exhibit 15.9**
**WAREHOUSE STORE**
Office Depot is a warehouse store that targets small business owners.

they're practicing **scrambled merchandising.** For example, in its 1,200 drugstores, the Walgreen's chain features food departments as well as such diverse products as computer supplies and audiotape merchandise.[38] Kroger Food Stores, a supermarket chain headquartered in Cincinnati, has also added nonfood products, including school supplies.[39] Both Walgreen's and Kroger use scrambled merchandising to encourage consumers to purchase additional items, which usually have higher profit margins.

**scrambled merchandising**
A retail technique that mixes product lines related and unrelated to the retailer's main merchandise focus

## LIMITED LINES

In contrast to retailers carrying general merchandise lines, **limited-line retailers** carry fewer types of products but stock merchandise in greater depth. For example, supermarkets are generally categorized as limited-line retailers because they usually restrict their product lines to food and related products. In addition to the giant regional supermarket chains such as Ralph's and Winn-Dixie, smaller chains specialize in even more limited lines of merchandise. For example, Mrs. Gooch's is a supermarket in southern California whose seven stores emphasize organically grown produce plus health foods and vitamins.[40]

**limited-line retailers**
Retailers that restrict their product lines to just a few that are carried in great depth

Twenty years ago, another type of limited-line retailer became increasingly popular: the **catalog showroom,** a self-service store where customers select discounted merchandise from a catalog available either through the mail or in the store. Catalog showrooms typically limit merchandise offerings to jewelry, housewares, and gift items. Service Merchandise and Consumers Catalog Showrooms are two large catalog showroom chains. They mail catalogs showing jewelry, household electronics, cameras, and other products that are offered at a discount when purchased by mail or in their nearby retail outlets.

**catalog showroom**
A limited-line discount retailer that offers products from a catalog for purchase by mail or in a self-service store

**Specialty stores** are limited-line retailers that focus on a more narrowly defined product line, carrying even more selections in that narrow line than other limited-line retailers do. For example, Jos. A. Bank Clothiers, a catalog merchant with stores nationwide, is a specialty retailer featuring men's and women's apparel. The store's product line is limited to clothing with a career orientation. Another specialty store chain is HEARx, which limits its product line to merchandise for people with hearing impairment. HEARx operates centers that administer hearing tests and then sell hearing aids to people who require them.[41]

**specialty stores**
Limited-line retailers that carry narrow product assortments in great depth

General merchandise discount stores currently face intense competition from specialty discounters that carry one or perhaps two categories of products, known informally as *category killers* because they set out to dominate a specific product category. In sporting goods, the Kmart-owned chain Sports Authority offers 45,000 items in each of its giant stores.[42] In the book business, superstores such as Barnes & Noble typically stock four times as many titles as their smaller counterparts.[43] Deeper inventories and lower prices at stores like Toys 'R' Us and Circuit City are pulling customers away from Fred Meyer, Kmart, and other broad-line discounters. Some analysts go so far as to predict the demise of most general merchandise discounters. They see a discount landscape in several years populated by a few huge chains like Wal-Mart, with a number of large specialty discounters meeting customer needs in specific product categories such as toys, electronics, and books. In fact, Kmart is responding to the attacks on its turf by buying into category killers itself. In addition to Sports Authority, the company owns the Borders Book Shops, Office Max, and Builders Square chains, all of which are designed as category killers.[44]

## SINGLE LINES

**single-line retailers**
Retailers that carry only one product line in great depth

Retailers that stock only a single product line but in great depth are called **single-line retailers.** The Sock Shop chain in Great Britain, for example, is a single-line retailer of socks and stockings. Tie Rack, also based in Great Britain, sells only ties and scarves from small outlets similar to Sock Shop's. Another single-line retailer is Weathervane Seafood Restaurants & Markets, which serve only inexpensive fish and lobster dinners.[45]

## By Level of Service

A third way to categorize retailers is by level of service provided. As already mentioned, retailers may decide to follow a full-service or self-service strategy. However, retailers also mix their service levels according to product departments, store location, or other factors.

*Full-service* retailers distinguish themselves by providing a wide array of services for their customers, ranging from personal shopping assistance to home delivery (see Exhibit 15.10). The customer service at stores like Nordstrom and Parisian has become legendary. Nordstrom salespeople gift wrap purchases at no charge and have been known to make personal deliveries to customers' homes. Some Nord-

**Exhibit 15.10
THE CLASSIC
DEPARTMENT STORE**
In a traditional department store, consumers can get plenty of help in selecting products; this is not always the case in other types of stores, even though the product may be identical.

strom employees in Alaska even warm up customers' cars while the drivers finish shopping.[46] Nordstrom remains a rare case among department stores, however; consumers don't think much of the service they receive at many so-called full-service retailers. A 1992 survey indicated that nearly two-thirds of U.S. consumers now consider shopping drudgery, and poor service is frequently listed as the main reason.[47]

From supermarkets to fast-food restaurants, discount department stores to catalog showrooms, *self-service* retailers are everywhere. Ordinarily, self-service prices are lower than those at full-service stores. For example, one reason Target can sell a picture frame at a lower price than Bloomingdale's is that Target customers generally select the product without sales assistance. Among the retailers that may be classified as self-service are Fayva Shoe Stores and Toys 'R' Us; at these stores, customers select merchandise without the help of salespeople and carry their choices to the cash register.

Some retailers cannot be categorized as strictly full-service or self-service because they offer various levels of service in various departments or in various locations. For example, many gasoline service stations allow consumers to choose between pumping gas themselves at a self-service price or remaining in the car while the attendant pumps gas at a full-service price. Such gasoline stations practice *mixed-service* retailing. Some of the newer retailers offering services, such as computer-based and television-based shopping, can be included in the mixed-service category; they don't fit or tailor clothes, for instance, but they do deliver right to your doorstep.

## By Pricing Strategy

A fourth way to categorize retailers is according to pricing strategy. As you can see when you look at newspaper ads for retailers, pricing strategies vary considerably. Some retailers sell products at full price, some at off-price, and some at a discount. Of course, some retailers have mixed-pricing strategies, which vary according to local competitive environments, profit objectives, and positioning.

Major department stores such as The Broadway and specialty stores such as Abercrombie & Fitch follow *full-price* strategies, selling high-quality merchandise at market-level prices, or roughly the same price as competitors.[48] Full-price retailers generally achieve a higher profit margin than retailers using other pricing strategies. Because these retailers offer consumers a classy atmosphere with service enhancements such as store credit and home delivery, the full-price strategy can draw a large group of shoppers.

Retailers such as Loehmann's, Filene's Basement, and NBO are **off-price retailers,** pricing merchandise lower than full-price department stores because they offer products later in the season or in limited size or color selection. Off-price retailers generally buy small lots of high-quality merchandise that was never intended to be sold in discount stores. Filene's Basement, for example, buys excess inventory from department stores but also buys directly from manufacturers, receiving new merchandise a few weeks after full-price retailers receive the same merchandise.[49] These buying techniques enable off-price retailers to sell the same high-quality products as full-price retailers, but at lower prices and with a lower profit margin. However, because off-price retailers cannot afford to provide the same luxurious atmosphere as full-price retailers, they often cut down on services such as home delivery and may limit refund and exchange privileges.

In contrast to off-price retailers, **discount retailers** offer a mix of high-quality and low-quality products at lower prices. Discount retailers generally offer two types of products: those that are manufactured specifically for the discount market and those that sell in large numbers when priced at a discount. Because discounters accept a lower profit margin in order to compete more effectively with full-price retailers, discount retailers usually offer few frills. You won't find fashion shows or home delivery in discount stores; you'll also notice these stores project a more spartan image than full-price retailers (see Exhibit 15.11).

Kmart and Wal-Mart are the two largest discount retailers in the United States

**off-price retailers**
Retailers that buy out-of-season or leftover products from manufacturers and large department stores and then offer the merchandise at low prices in self-service environments

**discount retailers**
Retailers that offer both high- and low-quality products at prices lower than full-price retailers in self-service environments

**Exhibit 15.11**
**KEEPING COSTS LOW IN DISCOUNT RETAILING**
This warehouse store in suburban Boston clearly doesn't spend much money on lavish decoration; the savings get passed on to consumers.

(the two largest retailers of any type, in fact). They operate large self-service stores that feature some name-brand merchandise at prices below full-price department store competitors. They also offer products of lesser quality at low prices. Discount retailers typically promote their pricing policies by using slogans such as home-improvement center Pergament's "Everything for your home at the lowest prices—guaranteed!"

## By Size of Store

A fifth way to categorize retailers is by size of store. Sizes range from the smaller boutique stores, some of which may be very small, to larger stores such as supermarkets, superstores, and hypermarkets. Until recently, retailers tended to open ever-larger stores with huge amounts of merchandise. However, with the cost of retail space rising, the latest trend in many markets is toward smaller stores with less merchandise.

When a retailer opens an outlet, its size depends on several factors, including the space available in the desired location, rental costs, and the amount of merchandise planned for that store. Because rental costs can be considerable, merchants think carefully about choosing a small store and offering a limited assortment of products that sell quickly. Woolworth, for example, has been scaling down the size of its variety stores. The retailer is putting the 9,000 best-selling items into Woolworth Express stores, which average 6,000 square feet. Traditional Woolworth stores take up 30,000 square feet and stock 50,000 items. Because the smaller stores are less costly to rent and require less inventory, they are more profitable.[50] Woolworth also uses a small-store format for some of its specialty stores, including Afterthoughts, a chain designed to showcase inexpensive accessories for women in 800-square-foot boutiques.[51]

In contrast, supermarkets, superstores, and hypermarkets are among the largest retail outlets. **Supermarkets** are large retail outlets featuring a wide selection of foods and related merchandise. Michael Cullen's first King Kullen supermarket was a 6,000-square-foot store; today's supermarkets are considerably larger, averaging 31,000 square feet.[52] **Superstores** are a combination of discount store and supermarket, offering a wide variety of both food and nonfood items. The Fred Meyer superstores, headquartered in Portland, Oregon, feature a supermarket on one side and a discount store on the other side. Superstores are generally over 30,000 square

**supermarkets**
Stores that sell primarily food items with selections wide enough to meet most customers' grocery shopping needs

**superstores**
Stores that combine food and nonfood items in large retail locations; larger than supermarkets but smaller than hypermarkets

feet in size, larger than conventional supermarkets.[53] (The term *superstore* is also applied to very large specialty stores, such as Toys 'R' Us and Circuit City; this use is common in the business press.)

**Hypermarkets** are discount superstores that combine food and nonfood products in one gigantic store. Hypermarkets started in France in 1962; the first U.S. hypermarket, Bigg's, opened in Cincinnati in 1984 and was backed by the French hypermarket firm Euromarche. American Fare, Bigg's, and Hypermarket U.S.A. are the major hypermarkets in the United States. Although more than 2,500 hypermarkets have been established across Europe, the concept has had limited success in the United States, which has fewer than 70 hypermarkets ranging in size from 150,000 to 330,000 square feet.[54] The future of hypermarkets in this country appears uncertain, partly because consumers find them overwhelming to shop in.

Retailing formats follow various patterns around the world. In Japan and Hong Kong, for example, the retail industry is dominated by "mom-and-pop" stores, neighborhood shops with limited product selections (see Exhibit 15.12).[55] At the other end of the size spectrum, hypermarkets are popular in France and Germany. They began to appear in Mexico in the mid-1990s, but they never really caught on in the Netherlands, which has a tradition of grocery stores and supermarkets much like the United States. Hong Kong is making the transition from mom-and-pop stores to U.S.-style grocery stores; the number of grocery stores there recently increased sixfold in less than a decade.[56]

## By Location

A sixth way to categorize retailers is according to store location. Generally, retailers establish stores in urban areas, in shopping centers, or in freestanding locations. In fact, most department stores started with downtown stores, then branched out to the suburbs as the urban population expanded beyond the city limits. Today, nationwide chain stores commonly operate outlets in all three locations, depending on

**hypermarkets**
Discount retailers that practice scrambled merchandising by offering food and nonfood products in huge superstore locations; the largest of all retail operations

Retailing formats in other countries have evolved at different rates and in different patterns. In Hong Kong, for instance, large grocery stores were relatively rare until quite recently, when their numbers have begun to increase dramatically.

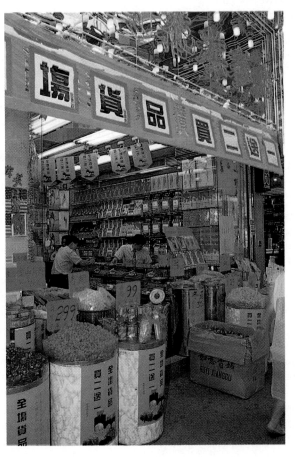

**Exhibit 15.12**
**INTERNATIONAL RETAILING PATTERNS**
This tiny store in Hong Kong is representative of retail stores in many Asian countries.

## Exhibit 15.13  ADVANTAGES AND DISADVANTAGES OF STORE LOCATIONS

| Location | Advantages | Disadvantages |
|---|---|---|
| Urban | Many consumers work or live nearby<br>Mass transit available<br>Other stores in area<br>Downtown revitalization projects | Limited parking<br>Few shoppers in mornings, evenings<br>Population shift to suburbs |
| Shopping center | Large number of stores<br>Anchor stores attract customers<br>Parking available<br>Balanced mix of stores | High rent costs<br>Adherence to mall hours and regulations |
| Freestanding | No competitors nearby<br>Parking available | Difficult to attract customers<br>No other stores to share building or promotion costs |

Retailers must carefully consider the advantages and disadvantages of urban, shopping center, and freestanding locations when deciding where to open a store.

the availability of retail space, the rental costs, and the areas where target consumers live and work. Exhibit 15.13 summarizes the advantages and disadvantages of the three location alternatives.

### URBAN AREAS

Many merchants operate stores in urban areas because of the proximity to consumers who work in the city and the availability of mass transit to bring shoppers from outlying neighborhoods. Department stores traditionally occupy prestigious locations in the heart of the downtown business district and are usually surrounded by smaller specialty stores. For example, Chicago's Miracle Mile on Michigan Avenue is lined with smaller stores such as Crate & Barrel, which is adjacent to Bloomingdale's, Marshall Field's, and other major department stores.

### SHOPPING CENTERS

Shopping centers have become the prime destination for consumers seeking a variety of stores in a single location. Sometimes a shopping center grows up around clusters of stores that open one by one alongside a main street or highway. These sites are usually called *strip malls*. However, since the 1950s, real estate developers have commonly selected the site, constructed the center, and rented space to retail tenants, creating a **planned shopping center,** an organized collection of small and large retailers in one geographic location with consistent architecture and designated parking. Planned shopping centers typically feature one or more **anchor stores,** large department or discount stores that advertise heavily and attract large numbers of consumers to the shopping center. (In 1992 The Gap began building anchorless malls, however, saying it and other specialty stores no longer need the customer draw provided by anchor stores.)[57] Another feature is the unique mixture of retailers, which is balanced by product line to ensure a variety of stores suited to the target audience. Planned shopping centers may be enclosed malls or outdoor areas.

Shopping centers may be large or small, urban or suburban. The Mall of America outside Minneapolis and the West Edmonton Mall (in Edmonton, Alberta,

**planned shopping center**
A carefully conceived cluster of retailers, balanced by size and type of store, organized in one location with an architectural theme and dedicated parking

**anchor stores**
Large department stores or discount stores that serve as the main stores in planned shopping centers because of their strong customer appeal

Canada) are gigantic affairs, with several million square feet of retail space. Smaller and more genteel is New York's Place des Antiquaires, an underground shopping center of fewer than 100 art and antique dealers. In all, nearly 35,000 shopping centers are in the United States, with 4.2 billion square feet of retail space.[58]

Shopping malls, particularly newer, planned developments, are expensive places to do business. As a rule, mall space costs roughly three times as much as comparable space on the street. As mentioned in Chapter 11, one of the problems facing Sears is the high cost of doing business in its hundreds of mall locations. Of course, even if you can afford it, you have no guarantee that you'll get the mall location you want. In an effort to maintain the mall's image and attract a sufficient number of target customers, developers and mall managers are usually particular about which stores they'll allow. However, if you can get the space and pay the rent, mall locations are attractive sites for the right kind of businesses.[59]

In response to the changing retail climate of the 1990s, however, mall developers are beginning to rethink the wisdom of expensive enclosed malls housing high-end department stores and specialty boutiques. With consumers demanding selection and bargain prices, the new retailing stars are Home Depot, Wal-Mart, Burlington Coat Factory, and others that offer attractive prices. To give these stores the advantage of central location that malls offer, developers have established **power centers,** which are giant versions of strip malls; some run up to 800,000 square feet. Rather than a group of smaller stores and one or two larger stores (the typical configuration in both strip malls and enclosed malls), the power center features from 6 to 20 or so big discounters. The United States now has something on the order of 2,000 power centers.[60]

**power centers**
Version of strip malls designed to showcase large "category killer" and other big discounters

## FREESTANDING STORES

A store that is neither part of a planned shopping center nor in the main downtown shopping district is called a **freestanding store.** Freestanding stores may be located along a main road lined with other freestanding retailers, or they may stand alone without neighboring stores. Automobile dealerships, hypermarkets, gasoline stations, and fast-food restaurants, for example, are often freestanding. Tower Records, an international record chain, favors freestanding stores because they become *destination stores,* attracting customers by the very nature of their image and assortment.[61]

**freestanding store**
A retail location that stands alone and unattached to other retailers

The freestanding retailer faces a challenge attracting shoppers. In contrast to planned shopping centers and urban locations where a variety of stores are within walking distance, freestanding stores are generally separated from other stores. This means that customers must make a special trip specifically to shop at the freestanding store, whereas they can visit more than one store on a trip to the mall or the downtown shopping district. However, freestanding retailers that succeed in drawing many customers will frequently attract other stores to open nearby, creating unplanned shopping centers. Toys 'R' Us uses a clever location strategy that yields the best of both worlds: It locates stores near—but not in—popular shopping malls, catching the traffic flowing to the malls without paying mall prices for space.

## By Method of Operation

A seventh way of categorizing retailers is by method of operation. Though we tend to think of retailers as conducting business from a physical store site, other methods of operation exist. **Nonstore retailing** includes direct selling, vending machines, direct mail, telemarketing, television home shopping, and computer-interactive shopping. Some nonstore retailing methods such as direct mail are more than 100 years old; others such as television home shopping are youngsters by comparison. These nonstore formats represent some of the most innovative trends in retailing today. Technology is playing a major role in the evolution of retailing, as marketers use information systems to understand and target their customers. For instance, the tradition of brides registering at a local department store has evolved to include direct-

**nonstore retailing**
A retailing method that creates a marketing channel between producers and consumers without physical stores

mail catalog retailers that offer the same service but with discounted prices. Ross-Simons, one of the leading mail-order players in the bridal market, uses computer databases to locate women aged 45 to 65 who live in affluent neighborhoods. The reason? These women are among the most frequently invited wedding guests.[62]

## DIRECT SELLING

When an Avon representative rings your doorbell, or when you attend a Tupperware party, you are experiencing direct selling. The salesperson brings a catalog to your home or office, often accompanied by samples, and invites orders. Your selections are delivered to your home or office in a week or so, making this method of operation convenient for you as a consumer.

At one time, direct selling was extremely popular. Peddling is a direct-selling method and was one of the first forms of retailing in the United States. In the mid-twentieth century, direct selling became a familiar way to retail baked goods, dairy products, vacuum cleaners, encyclopedias, and personal-care products. For example, Fuller Brush representatives once brought hairbrushes and housewares samples to the door. Today, however, Fuller publishes a catalog and accepts orders by mail only. Direct selling in retail has declined in importance because fewer people are home during the day to buy and because sending sales reps out in person has become increasingly expensive. Still, some retailers, including Mary Kay Cosmetics, operate exclusively through direct selling, targeting people in their offices as well as in their homes.[63]

## VENDING MACHINES

**vending machines**
Customer-operated machines that distribute products automatically upon payment

**Vending machines** are automatic units that dispense products when consumers insert money. Among the products sold through this retail method in the United States are beverages, candy bars, sandwiches, personal-care notions, and detergent. Vending machines may stand alone, as in a gas station, or they may be clustered, as in a snack bar. Sometimes a manufacturer owns the machine—Pepsi machines stock only Pepsi brands, for instance—and sometimes the machines feature products from a variety of manufacturers. Retailers find vending machines a practical method of operation when a salesperson is not required at a particular location. American Greetings has pushed the greeting card business into the vending machine age with its CreataCard System. The machines let consumers select verses and artwork, even adding their own messages, then print the custom cards in full color.[64]

However, because vending machines are unattended, they are vulnerable to vandalism and break-ins and must be secured by retail operators. In Japan, where such crimes are rare, vending machines can be found on nearly every street corner. The range of products sold through Japan's 5 million vending machines is broad, including fresh-brewed coffee, fish bait, socks, razors, records, batteries, bibles, and magazines. Some even dispense information from dating services. In total, the machines pull in more than $40 billion a year. For many Japanese consumers, vending machines are a routine way to shop for anything that's small enough to fit inside the machine.[65]

## DIRECT-MAIL MARKETING

When you order luggage or books from a catalog, that's direct-mail marketing. When you respond to a letter selling insurance or cable television, that's also direct mail. Direct mail is hardly a new invention: Settlers on the western frontier of the late 1800s depended on their Sears, Roebuck catalogs for products large and small, from housewares and apparel to the materials to build their homes. Sears recently shut down its huge but money-losing catalog operation, unable to match the focused product offerings and more effective communications from such firms as Lands' End and L. L. Bean. Many other retailers, including U.S. lingerie retailer Victoria's Secret and England's Next apparel merchants, operate successful direct-mail catalogs in addition to a chain of stores. Still other direct-mail retailers, including GEICO Insurance and American Express, have no stores but offer products exclusively via mail. You can even get catalogs of catalogs, such as the Shop-At-Home Directory featuring over 200 retailers.[66] Direct mail has become a multibillion-dollar business as today's harried consumers look for time-saving convenience.

## TELEMARKETING

Telemarketing is another nonstore method of retail operation. In telemarketing, the retailer's representatives sell products during telephone calls they make to consumers. Insurance, magazine subscriptions, credit cards, books, and records are among the products frequently sold by telemarketing. Telemarketing can also support direct sales efforts; telemarketers make the first contact with potential customers and identify the best prospects for direct salespeople.

Telemarketing retailers enjoy a level of personal contact with their customers, in contrast to direct-mail or computer-interactive retailing, where consumers do not have any contact with a human representative. One of the disadvantages that telemarketing has in common with other nonstore retailing methods is the inability to show the product in person. However, where the product is well known, such as a popular magazine, this disadvantage can be overcome by the retail representative's good sales skills.

Telemarketing retailers do more than flip through a phone book and dial. Many have begun using automated dialing machines, which are programmed to call select telephone numbers, or even telephone numbers at random (this gets around the limitation of unlisted numbers), and then connect a representative when the call is answered. In one variation, the automated dialing machine plays a prerecorded sales message when the consumer answers the phone. Because consumers have complained about automated dialing and taped messages, some states are thinking of restricting or banning these practices, calling them an invasion of the consumer's privacy.

## TELEVISION HOME SHOPPING

Retailers use the **television home shopping** method to display products to television viewers at home, asking consumers to place orders by telephone (see Exhibit 15.14). Fueled by the original discount prices and the variety of products offered, television home shopping has grown into a multibillion-dollar industry.[67] The per-

**television home shopping**
A nonstore retailing technique in which shoppers watch product displays on special television shows and then order products by phone

**Exhibit 15.14**
**THE BOOM IN TELEVISION SHOPPING**
QVC has helped propel television home shopping into a major retailing force.

centage of U.S. shoppers who made a purchase from television shopping shows nearly doubled from 1988 to 1992, and the volume of sales through this channel jumped 30 percent as well. In contrast, sales through regular retail stores dropped by 3 percent during the same period.[68]

One advantage of the television format is the ability to stage a live demonstration of the product's features. Another is the flexibility to spend as many seconds or minutes as needed to describe each product. Also, consumers can sit in their own homes and shop for name-brand goods at their own convenience. One potential drawback, however, is that consumers might get bored and turn away while waiting for merchandise of interest to be displayed. To help solve this problem, some home shopping retailers rotate special shows that feature a specific product line. For example, QVC Network broadcasts separate segments such as "The Cook" and "Craftsman Tools." Among the fastest-selling products are housewares, electronics, fashion, and the most popular line, jewelry.[69] Television shopping is outgrowing its original image as a channel for cheap and tacky goods; some of the most image-conscious retailers in the country (including Nordstrom and Saks Fifth Avenue) are now looking into it as another way to reach today's fragmented consumer audience.[70] The 1993 merger of QVC and Home Shopping Network created a $2.2 billion powerhouse reaching more than 50 million consumers in the United States.[71]

## COMPUTER-INTERACTIVE RETAILING

**computer-interactive retailing**
A nonstore retailing method in which consumers use a computer to learn about products or services and then place orders or use services electronically

One of the recent developments in nonstore retailing is **computer-interactive retailing,** in which the consumer previews products or descriptions on a computer screen and then orders or uses services via a freestanding electronic terminal or a home computer system. Originated in Europe as videotex, where text and graphics are viewed on a computer screen, this concept has been translated by U.S. firms into a retail segment worth $500 million. Key players in the United States include America Online; Prodigy (see Exhibit 15.15), a partnership of IBM and Sears; CompuServe, owned by H&R Block; and GEnie Information Services, part of General Electric.[72]

For a fee, a consumer with a personal computer and a modem (a device that connects the computer to the telephone line) can tap into CompuServe, for example, and browse product offerings from dozens of retailers, including Crabtree & Evelyn, Alamo Rent-A-Car, The Chef's Catalog, and Hammacher Schlemmer. Shoppers order merchandise by typing in the product name or number and method of payment. Computer-interactive retailing is convenient because merchandise is shipped

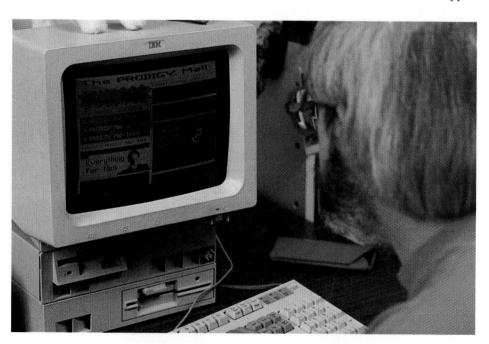

**Exhibit 15.15
INTERACTIVE
RETAILING**
Prodigy was one of the first systems to provide on-line shopping.

## SENDING YOUR COMPUTER OUT TO DO THE SHOPPING

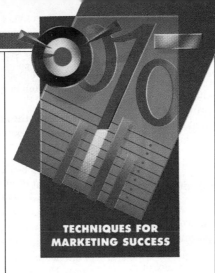

**TECHNIQUES FOR MARKETING SUCCESS**

Television home shopping has blasted its way onto the national retailing scene, becoming a multibillion-dollar business in just a few years. Computer-interactive retailing, however, has gotten off to a much slower start. Even with 70 million personal computers installed in U.S. homes and offices, sales have not grown as fast as some people originally expected.

Perhaps the biggest hurdle is the difficulty of displaying and demonstrating products. If you're checking out a jacket on the QVC shopping channel, the salesperson will point out key features and benefits while the camera pans around and zooms in and out. You can't tell how the garment will fit and feel until it arrives on your doorstep, of course, but you'll have a very good idea of how it looks. Few computers at this point, however, have the necessary horsepower to display high-resolution photos or videotape. Certainly any marketer who wants to reach a wide audience couldn't aim for these few computers. That leaves the promotional channel with just text, very simple graphics, and in some cases, sound.

As with any marketing technique or technology, the key question is how well does it match up with consumer purchase behavior? In its current state, computer-interactive retailing is a great fit in some areas and a weak fit in others. Chapter 4 defined the five general steps of consumer purchasing: recognize a need, search for information, evaluate alternatives, make the purchase, and evaluate the purchase. For some products, computer displays can do a good job of making people aware of products that can solve their needs, provide massive amounts of factual information, help people evaluate alternatives when the decision is based on that factual information, and make purchasing fast and easy. The more consumers know about the products they are trying to purchase—and the more information they can get from the computer—the more likely they are to purchase via computer.

For example, CompuServe offers a shopping feature called the New Car Showroom. As the first step, you can enter your basic purchase parameters, such as your price range, basic body style, transmission type, and so on. The system will then list every car model available in the United States that meets those criteria. Then, for a modest fee, you can get a long list of facts about each model, from the size of the engine to how much the dealer pays for each optional feature. To help you compare and evaluate, you can also get side-by-side listing for two cars. Elsewhere on CompuServe, you can search a database of magazine articles to see what automotive reporters have said about the cars you're considering. Last, although you're not likely to make the actual car purchase by computer, you can purchase thousands of other products on-line.

As much as computers can help in your car purchase, they can't do everything. Obviously, a computer can't test-drive the car or see how comfortable the seats are. Unless you download a graphics file or request an automaker's custom electronic "brochure" (available for only a few cars at present), a computer can't show you what the car looks like or what colors or fabrics you have to choose from. Even if you do get one of the few electronic brochures now available, shopping by computer still won't be the same as looking in person. You'll notice that virtually everything related to the *emotional* side of car buying is not available on the system. You can get all the data in the world from the computer, but you still have to visit a dealer to get a feel for the car.

### APPLY YOUR KNOWLEDGE

**1.** Which of the following products would be most compatible with computer-interactive shopping: cookbooks, produce, swimwear, or computer software? Why?

**2.** Will interactive television do a better job of selling cars than computer systems such as CompuServe? Why or why not?

directly to the consumer's home, plus many consumers like to avoid dealing with salespeople and telemarketers. On-line shopping rang up $750 million in 1992, considered a fast start for a new format.[73] Prodigy even runs on-line advertising, with messages appearing along the bottom of the screen. Interactive television promises to further revolutionize retailing, as more and more consumers opt to shop from home.

Realizing that not all consumers want (or are equipped) to shop by home computer, a company called ScanFone introduced a service in 1992 that lets you shop electronically over the phone. Customers get a bar-code wand that they pass over labels in catalogs, and the system takes care of charging their credit cards and delivering the merchandise.[74]

# SUMMARY OF LEARNING OBJECTIVES

## 1. Describe the nature and importance of retailing.

Retailing is the final link in the marketing channel bringing products and services from producers and providers to consumers. Retailing is important because it creates economic utility, it helps manufacturers reach consumers, and it makes a significant contribution to the economy.

## 2. Discuss the evolution of retailing and identify current trends.

Retailing in the United States has evolved from general stores, trading posts, and peddling to department stores, computer-interactive shopping, and other formats. Three theories help explain the evolution in retailing: the wheel of retailing, the dialectic process, and the retail life cycle. Current trends include an acceleration of the retail life cycle: Retailers move more quickly from introduction and growth into maturity and decline. New forms such as television home shopping have grown to be significant formats just a few years after their introduction.

## 3. Explain how factors in target market selection and positioning affect retailing strategies.

Retailers start by defining their target market according to demographic and psychographic factors. Then they build a retail strategy to attract and retain target market customers, using the retail marketing mix, a customer service policy, and an image to position their companies appropriately.

## 4. Describe the four variables in the retail marketing mix and discuss their implications for the retail marketing strategy.

The retail marketing mix includes the same elements as the general marketing mix: product, price, distribution, and promotion. The mix takes on special meaning in the world of retailing, as companies try to design effective store layouts, choose store locations, and perform other planning tasks not typically found in other industries. Retailers make a variety of decisions about each of the four variables to create a unique retail marketing strategy that will differentiate their business from competitors.

## 5. Identify the seven dimensions for categorizing retailers and explain the importance of understanding the categories.

Retailers can be categorized according to ownership (such as independent or chain stores), product lines (such as general merchandise or limited lines), level of service (such as full-service or self-service), pricing strategy (such as full price or discount), size of store (such as small store or superstore), location of store (such as urban or freestanding), and method of operation (such as direct selling or television home shopping). Understanding the categories is important because successful strategies and tactics vary from one type of retailer to the next, and knowing what kind of store you're running is the first step in designing your marketing programs.

## 6. Explain the concept of nonstore retailing and the reason for its continuing growth.

Nonstore retailing continues to grow because it meets the needs of today's consumers. Customers are looking for easier ways to make purchases, and retailers are looking for innovative and effective ways to reach consumers. Techniques such as computer-interactive shopping can simplify the purchase process for consumers, helping them select the best products for their needs. Television home shopping and other nonstore retailing methods allow customers to make purchases without facing the evils of modern in-store retailing: crowds and traffic.

## 7. Describe scrambled merchandising and explain why retailers are often forced to adopt it.

Retailers practice scrambled merchandising when they carry product lines unrelated to their main merchandise lines. Examples include food stores that carry auto supplies, drugstores that carry office supplies, and toy stores that carry clothing. The reason a retailer adopts scrambled merchandising is to offset the losses incurred when competitors chip away at the retailer's core business.

# A CASE FOR CRITICAL THINKING

## Meeting a Marketing Challenge at Nordstrom

In just three generations, the Nordstrom family built $12.50 worth of shoes into a chain of 60 stores with annual sales of $3 billion. The secret to their success is simple: They pay close attention to what the consumer wants; then they gear the merchandise and service to the needs of customers who shop in each store. In short, since 1901, Nordstrom has been a textbook example of how a retailer should behave to achieve success. However, late in the 1980s, the Nordstrom family began to tackle a new challenge: breaking into the lucrative retail markets east of the Mississippi.

The plan revolved around founder John W. Nordstrom's philosophy of finding and meeting customer needs. Many of Nordstrom's close-knit executive management team are family members who were brought up on the founder's retailing

# KEY TERMS

anchor stores (472)
atmosphere (464)
catalog showroom (468)
chain stores (465)
computer-interactive retailing (476)
department store (466)
dialectic process (457)
discount retailers (469)
freestanding store (473)

general merchandise retailers (466)
hypermarkets (471)
independent retailers (465)
limited-line retailers (467)
merchandise assortment (460)
merchandising (461)
nonstore retailing (473)
off-price retailers (469)

planned shopping center (472)
power centers (473)
retailer image (464)
retailing (455)
scrambled merchandising (467)
single-line retailers (468)
specialty stores (468)
supermarkets (470)

superstores (470)
television home shopping (475)
variety stores (466)
vending machines (474)
warehouse club (467)
wheel of retailing (457)

# QUESTIONS FOR DISCUSSION

1. How can manufacturer-owned retailers compete effectively with retailers that offer merchandise from various manufacturers?
2. How does the catalog showroom exemplify the dialectic process?
3. If you were starting a catalog operation to retail T-shirts with the logos of universities around the world, how would you define your target market?
4. How would the following types of discount retailers use place and product to support a low-price image?
   a. Stereo equipment retailer
   b. Rental car outlet
   c. Fast-food restaurant
   d. Travel agency
5. Assume J. C. Penney is considering changing its price structure from full price with periodic sales to everyday low price. This would position the store's pricing in direct competition with Sears's everyday-low-price strategy. What can J. C. Penney do to differentiate itself in the minds of consumers?
6. Would Kmart be practicing scrambled merchandising if it put snack bars in its discount stores? Why or why not?
7. If you were going to open a record store in your area, would you open a boutique-size outlet or a very large store? What are the advantages and disadvantages of each for you as an independent record retailer?
8. For the following retailers, is the best retail location urban, shopping center, or freestanding? Why?
   a. Major appliance dealer with an extensive selection of merchandise
   b. Accountant specializing in business tax preparation
   c. Small movie theater showing foreign-language films
   d. Boutique offering casual clothing for teenage girls
   e. Large Ford car dealership
   f. Department store branch
9. What are some of the problems Mrs. Fields Cookies would face in using vending machines to retail chocolate chip cookies on campus?
10. Assume Casio is considering nonstore retailing to sell its calculators. Which nonstore methods would be most effective, and why?

philosophy. In addition to John, James, and Bruce Nordstrom, who are all co-chairmen, top managers include John A. McMillan, president, who is a cousin by marriage, and Robert E. Bender, senior vice president and director, who is a friend of the family. Coming up in the ranks are a number of fourth-generation Nordstroms who currently work in a variety of functions. Some are buyers, some are store managers, and one runs the new management training program informally dubbed the University of Nordstrom. So plenty of Nordstroms will be available to keep the family philosophy alive well into the next generation.

Will Nordstrom's combination of service, merchandise, and fashion work back East against highly sophisticated competitors that seem to have a lock on upscale shoppers? The Nordstroms decided to take their unique style of retailing across the country, and they've been trying to keep the focus on local tastes, a policy that has proven successful in the past. Separate buyers for each region stock the local stores

with merchandise that reflects the unique tastes of the region's customers. Like their western counterparts, eastern Nordstrom branches carry almost double the amount of inventory of the typical clothing retailer. Under one Nordstrom roof a customer might find 75,000 pairs of shoes, 5,000 men's dress shirts, 7,000 neckties, and many other products, mostly traditional in styling. With such a vast assortment to choose from, shoppers are able to put together coordinated outfits, including accessories, with the help of Nordstrom's attentive salespeople.

What the Nordstroms won't vary from region to region is the store's commitment to total customer satisfaction. For example, a regular customer once called to say that he had to rush to the airport and needed some clothes for the trip. The Nordstrom employee grabbed the apparel, charged it to the customer's account, and ran out to the curb to be ready when the customer whizzed by. According to another story, one gentleman brought an automobile tire back to a local Nordstrom store and demanded a refund. He reportedly got his money back, even though the store doesn't sell tires.

Pioneering this concept in the East has been the true test of Nordstrom's philosophy. When opening its first eastern store in 1988 in the Tyson's Corner shopping center outside Washington, D.C., Nordstrom wasn't taking any chances. To launch the new store with a ready-made infusion of Nordstrom spirit, 100 employees were transferred from other stores. Another 200 Nordstrom salespeople paid their own moving expenses to be part of the eastern vanguard and help get the new store off on the right foot. In addition, hundreds of local salespeople were hired and trained in the Nordstrom retailing credo. When the doors finally opened, the Tyson's Corner Nordstrom was unlike any other eastern department store: A live piano player serenaded shoppers, employees checked shoppers' coats at the door, and baby-changing tables were available in the ladies' lounge. People flocked in, captivated by the new store. But would they buy? And would they keep buying?

The Nordstroms got their answer at the end of the store's first year in Tyson's Corner. The new store rang up $100 million in sales for 1988, compared to the larger Bloomingdale's, already established as one of the mall's anchor stores, which rang up only $45 million. However, the success wasn't isolated in Tyson's Corner. Competitors were being forced to take notice of another important measure of retail success: sales per square foot. During a year in which the Bloomingdale's chain rang up $287 in sales per square foot, Nordstrom boasted sales of $388 per square foot. This surpassed the record of the number one U.S. department store, J. C. Penney, and the number two chain, Mervyn's. Compared with any of the top 10 department store challengers, Nordstrom stores are far more productive.

Moving toward the twenty-first century, Nordstrom continues to offer premium service as it explores new retailing opportunities. In 1993, its downtown Seattle flagship store opened a large store-within-a-store to promote the Ralph Lauren Polo brand. It was designed to present the most complete collection of menswear in any U.S. department store. Demonstrating a knack for financial strategy, Nordstrom also teamed up with VISA to offer a special Nordstrom/VISA credit card starting in the spring of 1994. Nordstrom has its eyes open to other retailing options, as well. It recently teamed up with the leading French clothing designer Albert Goldberg to open the first U.S. store for his Facconnable line. Looking ahead to the information superhighway, Nordstrom began catalog sales in 1994 as a first step toward interactive television retailing.

**Your mission:** You've been hired by Nordstrom as a part-time salesperson in the women's shoe department, working evenings and weekends during the school year. Now that you have been working for several months, you have been asked to join other employees in a discussion group moderated by Bruce Nordstrom, co-chairman of the board. He is interested in the group's ideas about the store's retail marketing strategies. Using your knowledge of retail marketing, help Nordstrom make decisions that will keep sales growing.

1. Nordstrom operates Nordstrom Rack, a chain of clearance outlets filled with marked-down merchandise from the regular Nordstrom stores. Bruce Nordstrom wants to continue expanding this part of the business. The company's goal is to have one Nordstrom Rack store for every four Nordstrom department stores. At the same time, Nordstrom is concerned that discounting brand name merchandise in the spartan-looking outlet stores will hurt the upscale image that Nordstrom has cultivated for its regular department stores. Your group is challenged to come up with ways to position Nordstrom Rack as a discount chain without hurting Nordstrom's department store business. Which of the following suggestions would you recommend?
   a. Stress first-quality merchandise at discount prices by advertising that Nordstrom Rack stores carry only brand-name merchandise left over after end-of-season sales in regular Nordstrom department stores.
   b. Separate Nordstrom Rack stores from the regular department stores by opening Nordstrom Racks in shopping centers that contain only discount stores.
   c. Supplement the clearance merchandise by buying lower-quality, lower-priced merchandise specifically for the Nordstrom Rack chain.

2. Nordstrom has been looking at various ways to build a strong presence in the new markets. He tells the group that he does not believe in using frequent sales or expensive advertising to entice shoppers. In fact, Nordstrom's advertising expense is extremely low: typically under 2 percent of sales, compared with competitors who spend as much as 3 percent or more. However, he notes that some eastern competitors, three in particular, can match some of Nordstrom's advantages. Saks Fifth Avenue can claim a wide selection of quality merchandise, Lord & Taylor has retrained its salespeople to be friendlier and more helpful, and Bloomingdale's is well known for its upscale clothing. You and your fellow employees must come up with some new ideas to promote Nordstrom while differentiating the store from competitors. Of the following proposals, which do you think would be the most effective?
   a. Insert a notice in the monthly statements going to Nordstrom credit card customers and offer a 10 percent discount during a special "Customer Appreciation Day."
   b. Produce a glamorous Christmas catalog featuring brand-new styles by avant-garde designers and mail it in October to everyone who shops in one of the new branches during July, August, and September.
   c. Have Nordstrom salespeople write thank-you notes to their best customers, offering a $10 gift certificate to each customer who introduces a friend to the store. When the friends buy, they receive a $10 gift certificate toward their next purchase of $100 or more.

3. Nordstrom is considering a plan to spin off specialty stores that will each feature a particular product category in depth. The market research firm hired to examine this issue reports that the Nordstrom name is gaining recognition across the country and would have a positive influence on specialty store shoppers. The research firm conducted focus group interviews with current Nordstrom shoppers and learned that customers are most concerned with personalized service and a wide selection of quality merchandise. Keeping these findings in mind, Nordstrom wants you and the other employees to evaluate the following proposed specialty store ideas. Which would you suggest as a new venture for Nordstrom?
   a. A women's accessory boutique that sells popularly priced belts, scarves, handbags, and costume jewelry.
   b. A self-service discount children's clothing store that stocks all sizes up to preteen.
   c. A full-service men's casual clothing store that features an extensive selection of designer jeans and tops.

4. Because retailers generally ring up a significant portion of the year's sales in the five weeks between Thanksgiving and Christmas, Nordstrom (like all retailers) plans its holiday campaigns very carefully. No aspect of the retail marketing mix is ignored, although the focus may change from year to year. Above all, Nordstrom's holiday campaigns must reinforce the store's positioning and must differentiate the store from competitors while appealing to the target audience. Planning for next year's holiday season has already begun, and Nordstrom asks your group to review the following proposals. Which best fits Nordstrom's positioning and differentiation strategy? Why?
   a. Nordstrom should title its Christmas catalog "Nordstrom's Santa Really Delivers" and emphasize the store's exceptional personal service, speedy home delivery, and extensive selection of apparel and shoes. To continue the theme, have delivery people dress in red suits during November and December.
   b. Nordstrom should place full-page ads in December issues of *GQ, Esquire,* and other magazines that feature men's fashions, and they should show a famous actor in a stylish suit. Include the addresses of all Nordstrom stores across the country so that consumers can look for the outfit in their local stores.
   c. Nordstrom should buy a minivan, paint the store logo on the outside, and fill it with racks of clothing for men and women. The store can then park this minivan on busy downtown street corners during lunch hours and invite people to browse and either buy directly from the minivan or place orders for other sizes and colors to be delivered to the customer's home or office the next day.

## SPECIAL PROJECT

Cooperative marketing efforts have been successful for a number of retailers. These techniques involve two companies teaming up to market their products to a group of target customers. This can be as simple as one company inserting promotional materials in the other company's monthly billing statements. At the other extreme, it can be as complex as opening a combined store. A number of other retailers, in a variety of product categories, have approached Nordstrom with ideas for joint projects. However, the company doesn't have any guidelines for evaluating these proposals. Your task is to draw up a set of guidelines that the company can use to systematically assess each cooperative marketing idea. Remember to consider target customers, positioning, and customer service.[75]

# VIDEO CASE

## Catalog Retailers Leave the Store Behind

Drive down the street in any town's shopping district or walk through a nearby mall, and it's easy to get the impression that all these stores constitute the world of retailing. Open your mail box, of course, and you'll see the other side of the story. Catalog retailing is a huge industry, with annual sales of more than $200 billion. From books and bonsai gardening tools to clothes and coffee, just about every consumer and business product imaginable is available through a catalog. If you're not sure about which catalog to shop from, you can even get catalogs that feature nothing but other catalogs. One of these publications, *The Best Catalogs in the World,* features catalogs from dozens of retailers such as Jos. A. Bank, The Body Shop, and Stash Tea.

The companies highlighted in the accompanying video represent the most significant reasons why catalog retailing is such a big business, and growing every year: precise target marketing, careful merchandise selection, and strong, consistent brand identities.

Precise targeting is one of catalog retailing's most attractive features. Lillian Vernon, a $160 million vendor of home, gardening, and children's accessories, boasts a computer database with 12.5 million names. Five and a half million of these people have made a purchase within the last two years, and the company's marketing specialists track income, family status, educational level, and other key demographic factors that define the company's target market. The database lets the marketers know who is buying what, when they buy, and how much they buy. J. C. Penney uses target marketing to reach Hispanic-Americans, keying in on their spending habits and overall consumption trends. Penney also targets this audience with Spanish-language catalogs, making shopping easier for people who either don't speak English or who prefer to conduct personal affairs in Spanish.

Focused merchandise selection is an outgrowth of knowing a great deal about your customers. For instance, when you know that a young couple has a home and a small child, you can select products that appeal to people in that stage of their lives. In addition, Lillian Ver-

non and most other catalog retailers constantly test-market merchandise to make sure they're providing the products customers want most.

Maintaining a consistent relationship with customers is another hallmark of the successful catalog retailer. Lands' End, Coach Leatherware, and Wayside Gardens all have a clear positioning and meaning to their target customers. A Lands' End shopper, for instance, knows that the catalog will always contain well-made, fairly conservative casual clothes. You won't find exotic designs, fad colors, or poor-quality merchandise in a Lands' End catalog, and regular customers know that.

Tweeds is a good example of why it's not a good idea to make radical changes in either product selection or overall image. The company became one of the hottest new catalog retailers in the late 1980s, with its earthy styles that featured quality fabrics and just enough attitude to stand out from the crowd. Then suddenly, for reasons analysts still can't figure out, the company's Spring 1991 catalog looked completely different. Instead of promoting flowing woolens and other natural fabrics, the catalog was pitching short tube skirts, stretchy short shorts, and neon psychedelic designs in polyester and other synthetic fabrics. To regular customers, the catalog must've looked like it came from another planet. The proof was in the sales reports. As one insider put it, the company lost "millions and millions" as a result and is still trying to recover.

1. Think about the last item you purchased in a store. Would you purchase the same item through a catalog? Why or why not?

2. What are the pros and cons of the traditional printed catalog compared to newer media such as computer-interactive retailing and television shopping shows?

3. Since newness and uniqueness are often the reasons why consumers buy clothes and other personal products, how is a predictable retailer like Lands' End able to succeed year after year?

# SHARPEN YOUR MARKETING SKILLS

To learn more about how retailers differentiate themselves from competitors, visit a department store such as J. C. Penney or Dillard's and a discount department store such as Target or Kmart. Notice the store decor; does it contribute to each store's particular retail image? Find the children's shoe department and look at the variety of shoe styles and prices, the way the shoes are displayed, and the way shoes are actually sold. Which store carries a wider variety of styles and prices? What is each store's customer service policy?

**Decision:** Do you think the discount department store successfully differentiates itself from the department store? What would you do differently?

**Communication:** Pretend you are a retail consultant trying to get new clients. Pick the store that is most in need of your expertise and write the store manager an introductory letter. Explain why the store could benefit from your services.

# KEEPING CURRENT IN MARKETING

Find an article describing an innovation in retailing, used either by one retailer or by a group of retailers in the same category. Recent examples include customers using bank cash (debit) cards instead of cash or credit cards to pay for merchandise; customers using fully automated checkout stations to process, pay for, and bag their own merchandise; large retailers decentralizing their departments, creating separate (often freestanding) stores such as Sears's Brand Central and Furniture stores; telemarketers using automated dialers and computerized voice messages to conduct their campaigns; and customers using interactive video-based catalog shopping at home, in stores, or in public areas of shopping centers.

1. Why is the innovation being introduced? What changes in geographic, demographic, or psychographic circumstances contributed to the decision to launch the innovation?
2. What factors favor consumer acceptance of the innovation? What aspects may temper consumer enthusiasm or result in consumer rejection of the innovation?
3. Consider the trends that resulted in the innovation. If they continue or accelerate, where do you think they'll lead in 10 years? Should your forecast prove true, what steps can management take to ensure optimum results?

# 16

# Physical Distribution

After studying this chapter, you will be able to

**1.** Describe the strategic importance of physical distribution

**2.** Identify the most common objectives of physical distribution

**3.** Discuss the total cost concept in distribution decisions

**4.** Explain why physical distribution is more than trucks, trains, and warehouses

**5.** Discuss the just-in-time inventory management philosophy

**6.** Describe the transportation options available to businesses

**7.** Discuss the storage options available to businesses

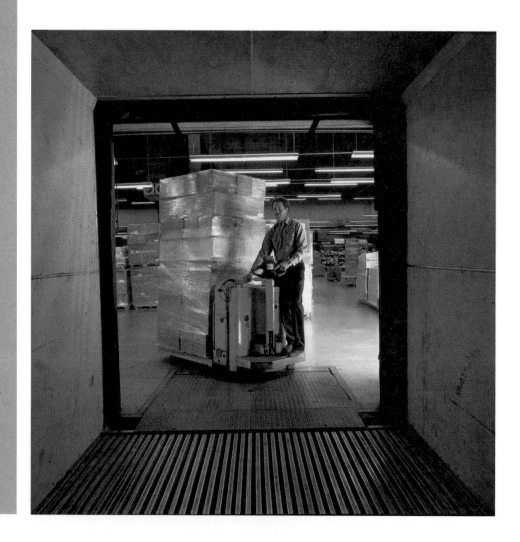

### *Bringing an Old Product to a New Market*

If Sandi Hutsabaut has her way, milk drinkers in Manitoba, Canada, may soon be downing goat's milk with their cookies. Goat's milk has gained a reputation for being beneficial in the treatment of arthritis, skin diseases, and other health problems. People with allergies and digestive problems can digest goat's milk more easily than cow's milk. With more doctors suggesting goat's milk, producers who see an increased demand want to tap these lucrative new markets. In Ontario, British Columbia, and Alberta, large commercial goat dairies have already been set up. However, in Manitoba, Hutsabaut and her fellow producers face hurdles as they work to get their goat's milk flowing into the province's pitchers.

One of 35 goat producers in the area, Hutsabaut has a herd of 12 in Richer, about 50 miles from Winnipeg. She has a few regular customers who make the 100-mile round trip from the city, but more would buy if they could: "It is very frustrating," says Hutsabaut, "because a lot of Winnipeg people request the milk but cannot get it. They lack either the time or a car to drive out here."

The clamor for goat's milk has driven Manitoba producers to ask the provincial government for help in establishing a processing plant. However, because there are few Manitoba producers—and they tend to have small herds—the region may not be able to support the economics of a processing plant. Allan Steinke, a dairy specialist with the Manitoba Department of Agriculture, notes that other Canadian processing plants are supplied by larger groups of commercial producers with herds of 60 to 100 goats per farm, far more than the number in Hutsabaut's herd.

Hutsabaut responds that she is willing to increase her herd, and she has convinced five other producers to do the same. Banded together into a cooperative, these six producers would be able to supply a larger quantity of raw goat's milk for processing and delivery to stores in Winnipeg and nearby areas. Higher output might persuade government officials to provide loans or grants in support of the proposed provincial processing plant.

On behalf of the Manitoba Goatmilk Cooperative, Hutsabaut is pursuing several distribution options. She has met with officials at the University of Manitoba to see whether the school's existing processing plant might be used. An independent creamery in Winnipeg has also expressed interest. Looking beyond milk, Hutsabaut is talking to the Manitoba Research Council about creating recipes that feature goat's milk cheese.

You can imagine how complicated the physical distribution of dairy products can be. First, complete cleanliness must be assured through the entire distribution system. This means stainless steel tanks, special cleaning procedures, and other considerations that add to the cost and effort of moving milk. Second, dairy products must be moved quickly and without mistakes from producer to consumer to ensure freshness. Third, the distribution system must be able to meet the needs of intermediaries and consumers in terms of package sizes and product selection. Retailers are equipped to handle just a few standard sizes of cartons and bottles, and consumers expect to see these packages when they shop.

If you were a member of Hutsabaut's goat's milk cooperative, how would you get your milk processed and stocked on store shelves? How would you select the location of your processing plant? How would you market your product to consumers?[1]

**physical distribution**
The movement of goods from producers to customers; it includes order processing, inventory management, materials handling, warehousing, and transportation

# CHAPTER OVERVIEW

Marketers from Sandi Hutsabaut to the largest corporations in the world all face the challenge of delivering products to customers. In Hutsabaut's case, the challenge is to establish a delivery system where none exists today. Other companies are reexamining physical distribution to look for ways to decrease marketing costs and increase competitive advantage. This chapter discusses the strategic importance of physical distribution and explains why distribution deserves a marketing person's full attention. You'll examine the role of physical distribution in the marketing mix and the various organizations and institutions that make up a physical distribution system. You'll also get a look at just-in-time inventory management, a distribution concept that is transforming the way many companies operate. The chapter concludes with several special issues in physical distribution, including international distribution, and a brief discussion of the future of physical distribution.

# THE STRATEGIC IMPORTANCE OF PHYSICAL DISTRIBUTION

Physical distribution may not sound as exciting as advertising or personal selling, but it can be every bit as important. At the most obvious level, you can't satisfy customers unless you deliver the goods—literally. Just ask Rose Smith, who's in charge of importing clothes for Jordache Enterprises. She says that if she delivers an order even 30 minutes late, her department store customers might refuse it.[2] From a strategic perspective, physical distribution is often one of the biggest influences on a company's success, and managers responsible for distribution are playing a bigger role in their companies.

**Physical distribution** encompasses such activities as order processing, inventory management, materials handling, warehousing, and transportation. It used to be regarded as a necessary evil, a tactical problem in which managers tried to do everything possible to minimize costs and hassles. However, this perception is changing quickly as organizations realize the strategic importance of physical distribution (see Exhibit 16.1). In the beverage industry, for example, company leaders, such as Henry Schimberg of Johnston Coca-Cola Bottling Group in St. Paul, recognize that getting the product on store shelves quickly and efficiently is critical to building competitive advantage in the 1990s.[3]

## Physical Distribution in the Marketing Mix

Even if you put together a clever, aggressive marketing strategy, you won't succeed if your firm's distribution system can't provide the necessary support. Here's a quick look at how physical distribution can affect product design, pricing, and promotional activities.

### PRODUCT DESIGN

Distribution interacts with product design in three areas: physical product attributes, packaging, and competitive differentiation. Physical attributes that affect distribution include weight, size, value, and risk. For instance, a product such as a ready-mix concrete needs specialized delivery equipment (including trucks and pumps) because it is heavy and has a short life span. On the other hand, you can't spend a lot of money delivering cement because it's a product with low differentiation, and customers frequently look for the lowest price. Concrete suppliers usually specify a minimum order size such as 4 or 8 cubic yards because smaller amounts are too expensive to deliver.

Product packaging is an area that demands close cooperation between the marketing and shipping departments. Packaging often plays an important role in promotions, but it must not be at the expense of distribution. The packaging design

**Exhibit 16.1**
**THE STRATEGIC IMPORTANCE OF PHYSICAL DISTRIBUTION**
This automated distribution center helps Lillian Vernon keep costs low and customer service high.

has to provide adequate protection for the product, and it should be compatible with existing delivery and warehouse systems. For example, the size and shape of a package can affect your ability to fill it, stack it, or ship it.

Finally, marketers can use delivery to differentiate their products. The ability to deliver goods quickly or according to a customer-defined schedule is becoming an important means of establishing competitive advantage. Mail-order firms such as Lands' End, for example, use fast, guaranteed delivery to attract last-minute Christmas shoppers. In years past, people who normally preferred to buy gifts from Lands' End would switch to retail stores as Christmas approached, out of worry that gifts wouldn't arrive on time. By using an express package delivery service such as Federal Express, Lands' End now maintains its competitive advantage for many more days in the peak shopping season of the year.[4]

A striking example of the level of service that organizational buyers expect occurred when McNeil Consumer Products used express shipping to help their new drug PediaProfen take the market by storm. "We had a strong sense that our competitors were going to roll out similar products at the same time," said product director Donald Casey, Jr. So the moment the drug received FDA approval, FedEx, in one of its largest one-day bulk shipments ever, carried 2,562 cases and 55,000 samples to pharmacists and doctors across the United States.

"Is it worth spending a significant portion of the brand budget on what was essentially a time advantage?" Casey asked. The initial wave of orders provided a dramatic answer. PediaProfen quickly grabbed two-thirds of the market, indicating that timely delivery can help companies become an overnight success in the marketplace.[5]

## PRICING

One of the basic rules of pricing is that to maximize profits, you do everything you can to minimize costs. In many industries, physical distribution is a big part of these costs. Companies that provide hospital supplies, for example, pay an average of 13.1 percent of their revenues just to get the products to their customers.[6] If a hospital supplier such as Baxter Healthcare Corporation wants to lower its prices to gain competitive advantage, one of the first strings it might try to pull is lowering its distribution costs.

Sweden's IKEA provides a good example of how distribution and pricing can interrelate. IKEA markets Scandinavian-style furniture in Europe and North America, and one of its goals is to offer quality products at moderate prices. However, the transportation and storage costs for bulky items such as tables and bunk beds could drive their prices too high. To overcome this, IKEA's furniture is shipped and warehoused partially assembled. This allows the company to ship a table, for example, in a much smaller, much flatter package. The customer bolts the legs to the table-top after purchase. Because the product is shipped and stored in a smaller package, IKEA minimizes its physical distribution costs.[7]

## PROMOTION

Promotional programs affect physical distribution when they create unexpected or irregular demand. For example, when Kmart offers a limited-time discount on children's clothing, it has to make sure it can supply enough clothes to meet the temporarily increased demand. Similarly, if a manufacturer runs a trade promotion for its distributors or an incentive contest for its sales force, the company's marketing, manufacturing, and distribution staffs need to work together to ensure adequate product supply during the period of increased demand.

On the other hand, marketers sometimes intentionally limit the physical distribution of products, perhaps to increase the prices they're able to charge or to build mystique or to do both. For example, to create an exclusive image for their products, perfume suppliers are increasingly limiting the availability of their products. When Parfums Nina Ricci introduced its new Nina scent, it made the product available only in the Nordstrom department store chain. Such a move increases the market value of Nina because perfume buyers tend to seek out products that are more difficult to obtain.[8]

## Objectives of Physical Distribution

Physical distribution has two major goals: decreasing the cost of delivery and increasing customer satisfaction. (Keep in mind that the customers of physical distribution include other businesses, wholesalers, retailers, and final consumers.) Meeting these goals can be a complex problem that involves technological, marketing, and administrative decisions. Here's a closer look at the objectives of physical distribution.

### TOTAL COST GOALS

**total cost concept**
The practice of considering all the costs associated with distribution in order to attain the best balance among all the cost factors

A physical distribution system encompasses many cost elements, including transportation, storage, materials handling, and the cost of sales lost to inventory shortages. Often these cost elements are inversely related. For example, you can lower the cost of inventory problems by increasing your inventory. However, inventory isn't free, and it costs money to increase your inventory. These competing cost elements present a balancing challenge for management. The **total cost concept** of physical distribution refers to the goal of lowering the overall cost of distribution by striking the best balance among all the individual cost elements. For instance, it might make sense to switch to airfreight delivery (which is usually more expensive but faster), if this lets you cut down on the amount of product held in inventory (which costs money to keep in inventory).

### CUSTOMER SERVICE GOALS

More and more companies are realizing customer service is an integral part of their operations, not a nicety tacked on at the end of the process. One result of this new awareness is increased attention to the role that physical distribution plays in satisfying customers. The customer service goals that are influenced by distribution fall into six categories: time, dependability, communication, convenience, product protection, and accuracy. Exhibit 16.2 lists some examples of customer service standards for physical distribution, and a closer look at each category follows.

TIME    Reducing the time from order to delivery is an important distribution goal for many companies. In this context, time is usually defined as lead time or replenishment time. Both these terms refer to the time it takes a company to deliver a product once a customer places an order. Time is a central issue in the cost-versus-service balance because decreasing delivery time often increases transportation and storage costs. In time-sensitive situations, however, customers are willing to pay the price for fast service.[9] Moreover, as more and more companies speed up deliveries, customer expectations increase. The result is that slower suppliers begin to be less appealing to customers.

Time is a significant issue for international marketers, who not only deal with greater distances, but also with delays at customs when products cross country borders. Efforts such as the reduction in trade barriers between the member nations of the European Union are designed to cut down on these delays and allow companies to deliver goods to their customers in less time.

DEPENDABILITY    Dependability has two meanings in physical distribution. First, it indicates a supplier's ability to deliver products on schedule. Late deliveries to a manufacturing plant, for example, can shut down production lines and cause severe sales problems. On the other hand, early deliveries might sound like a good idea, but they have the potential to upset a customer's inventory system. Second, dependability refers to a supplier's overall consistency. As Robert Wayman of electronics and computer manufacturer Hewlett-Packard notes, "When somebody pays $500,000 for a piece of computer equipment, they are not tolerant of poor delivery. They want it in a timely, complete fashion." Consequently, Hewlett-Packard has increased its attention to providing dependable delivery.[10]

COMMUNICATION    Suppliers and customers depend on communication to ensure efficient physical distribution. Communication must occur in three stages: receiving the order, tracking the delivery while it is in transit, and being able to trace deliveries that don't arrive on time. As customers increasingly demand fast, error-free shipments, communications will become more important. Haggar Apparel is one of a number of manufacturers that have made electronic communication techniques a prerequisite to doing business with the company.[11]

CONVENIENCE    Suppliers can also gain competitive advantage by making distribution more convenient for their customers. For example, Burlington Industries, a leading textile producer, makes life easier for one of its major customers by loading its delivery trucks in a particular sequence. Rather than tossing the rolls of cloth into the truck in random order, Burlington loads them in the reverse order the customer needs to unload them. This allows the customer to immediately unload the cloth and go to work, without reshuffling materials inside its factory.[12]

PRODUCT PROTECTION    Safe and sound delivery relies on both adequate packaging and careful handling while in transit. Companies that control the distribution channel all the way to the final customer have an advantage in this respect because they can directly oversee the handling of goods. However, companies that rely on wholesalers, retailers, or transportation companies need to work with these channel members to make sure products are delivered without damage. Some van lines, for ex-

**Exhibit 16.2    EXAMPLES OF CUSTOMER SERVICE STANDARDS**

| Category | Example Standard |
|---|---|
| Time | 95% of orders are shipped within 24 hours |
| Dependability | All promises are fulfilled |
| Communication | Customers always know status of their orders |
| Convenience | Customers never deal with more than one salesperson |
| Product protection | Fewer than 1% of goods arrive damaged |
| Accuracy | 98% of orders are complete and correct |

Customer service standards require both a category of service and a measurable goal, which must be defined by the customers themselves.

ample, provide specialized trucks for transporting sensitive scientific and engineering equipment.

ACCURACY    Finally, customers demand that suppliers accurately fill and deliver their orders. This involves delivering the right goods to the right location and making sure that orders are complete. Delivering complete orders can be a challenge for companies with widespread manufacturing facilities. If an order will be filled from more than one location, the company should take steps to ensure that shipments are coordinated and that all the pieces arrive simultaneously to minimize disruption at the customer's end.

### COST-SERVICE TRADE-OFFS

As you've probably surmised by now, the two major goals of physical distribution—decreasing costs and increasing customer satisfaction—are often in direct conflict. To achieve the right balance of cost and service, be sure you understand the level of service that customers expect and that competitors deliver. Customers don't always define satisfaction in the same terms as suppliers, and various customers have different standards. In some cases, suppliers spend too much money on physical distribution, incorrectly thinking they must do so to meet customer expectations. In other cases, companies choose the wrong standard or the wrong level to be considered good service.[13]

Flexibility is an important part of this balancing act. Suppliers may want to provide a higher level of service to larger customers. In certain situations, they'll exceed normal standards of service to maintain ongoing customer relationships. Leonard L. McGinty, Jr., president of Torque Quip Corporation in Tampa, Florida, provides a perfect example of taking that extra step in physical distribution. He is a licensed private pilot, and he occasionally jumps into a plane to deliver critical replacement parts himself when customers suffer emergency breakdowns.[14]

# PHYSICAL DISTRIBUTION SYSTEMS

Physical distribution is a lot more than trucks or computers or airlines; it's an integrated collection of information, people, equipment, and organizations. It embraces numerous steps, starting with providing the customer with a means to place an order and ending with putting the product in the customer's hands. Exhibit 16.3 illustrates the major players and processes in physical distribution, including customers, order processing, suppliers, manufacturing, warehouses, information flow, materials handling, and transportation.

## Order Processing

**order processing**
The systems used to receive orders, route them to appropriate supplying functions, and then arrange customer billing

It all starts when a customer places an order. The three main functions of **order processing** are receiving the order, routing it to the proper supplying department, and billing the customer. Depending on the size of a company and its degree of automation, orders are received through the mail, in person, over the telephone, or via a computerized ordering system. Companies with complex channel arrangements need a variety of order entry mechanisms, which can include special terminals for dealers or laptop computers linked via telephone lines for sales personnel. In some cases, customers and suppliers are connected electronically. As one of the fastest-growing retailers in the world, Wal-Mart has established a computerized ordering system between its warehouses and some 300 suppliers.[15]

The next step is directing the order to the right part of the company. This might be as simple as handing it to somebody in the stock room, or it might be as complex as sending an electronic mail message to manufacturing or distribution facilities around the world. When a customer places an order with IBM, GE, or another large multinational manufacturer, the order may have to be sent to multiple factories around the world.

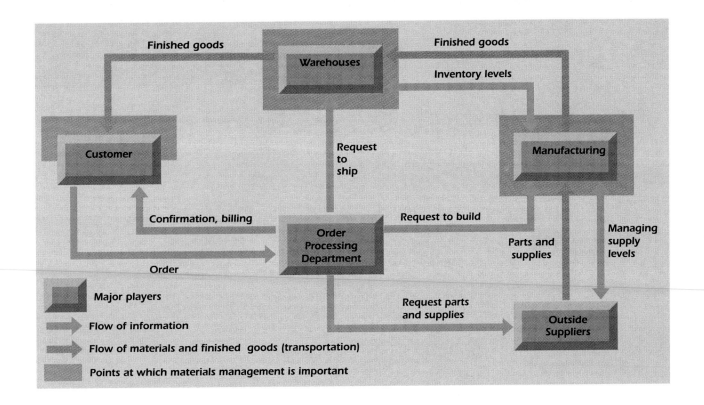

Finished goods

Warehouses

Finished goods

Inventory levels

Customer

Manufacturing

Request to ship

Confirmation, billing

Request to build

Managing supply levels

Parts and supplies

Order Processing Department

Order

Major players

Flow of information

Request parts and supplies

Outside Suppliers

Flow of materials and finished goods (transportation)

Points at which materials management is important

Finally, a shipping method is chosen and the customer is billed. Some companies offer a choice of normal or expedited delivery. For example, Trend-Lines, a Chelsea, Massachusetts, supplier of woodworking equipment and supplies, normally ships orders using United Parcel Service. For an additional charge, Trend-Lines will switch to Federal Express to provide next-day delivery. In either case, the delivery charge is automatically added to the customer's bill.[16]

Although order processing sounds simple enough, an inefficient system can drive down both profits and customer satisfaction. The Air Compressor Group of Ingersoll-Rand, for instance, saved $390,000 a year and improved customer service after installing an integrated order processing system. The new system lowered the cost of inventory, administration, and communications, and it expedited cash flow by getting bills out to customers more quickly.[17]

## Inventory Management

In addition to filling orders quickly, several other reasons for maintaining inventory are crucial to business operations:

- Providing a buffer against interruptions in supply, such as that caused by material shortages or strikes
- Providing a hedge against price increases by suppliers for parts and materials
- Maintaining a reserve of repair parts and supplies to quickly address customer needs in the event of breakdowns
- Providing leverage to get purchasing, transportation, and storage discounts
- Maintaining production levels that ensure optimum use of people and equipment[18]

Clearly, inventory is an important variable in a business operation. However, like the overall distribution system, inventory management is a balancing act. Too little inventory results in a **stockout**, a situation in which a company is unable to fill orders. Too much inventory increases costs, because the money is tied up in products that are finished but not sold. This section examines the various costs involved in inventory and discusses strategies for maintaining a balance between stockouts and excessive costs.

**Exhibit 16.3**
**THE PHYSICAL DISTRIBUTION FLOW**
A physical distribution system encompasses a variety of people, organizations, information, and equipment.

**stockout**
The lack of products to sell, caused by inventory shortages

**491**

## INVENTORY COSTS

The true cost of maintaining inventory can be difficult to identify because inventory is often spread throughout a company. Some of it is found in the work-in-progress and finished-goods inventories in the production department, and more inventory is in storage facilities such as warehouses. Finally, part of a company's inventory is usually in transit, either between two intermediate locations or on its way to customers. Regardless of the location of inventory, companies try to manage three general types of costs associated with inventory: carrying costs, procurement costs, and opportunity costs (different companies assign different names for the specific costs in each category).

- *Carrying costs.* Inventory carrying costs include the expenses involved in product depreciation and obsolescence, taxes on inventory, insurance on the value of the goods held in inventory, and storage resulting either from renting warehouse space or from building and staffing your own warehouse facilities.
- *Procurement costs.* When it's time to create or replenish stocks, inventory managers face a variety of procurement costs (also called ordering costs), such as the labor associated with sending orders and handling the goods when they arrive.
- *Opportunity costs.* Opportunity costs are associated with inventory shortages. When stockouts occur, suppliers face a loss if customers decide to go elsewhere. They can also face a loss because of the cost of back-ordering products, should the customer decide to wait for the product to be restocked.

**safety stock**
Extra inventory kept on hand
to cover unexpected demand
or delays in receiving new
stock

To guard against stockouts, inventory managers sometimes specify a reorder point, which is a certain level of inventory that triggers a reorder to replenish inventories. The reorder point is determined by the rate at which inventory is consumed, the time it takes to get new stock, and the desired level of **safety stock**, which is an extra level of inventory kept on hand to cover unexpected customer demands or delays in receiving new stock.

## JUST-IN-TIME INVENTORY MANAGEMENT

**just-in-time inventory
management**
A technique that seeks to decrease costs by maintaining
lower inventories of parts and
materials

Just-in-time (JIT) inventory management is an increasingly popular method used to manage inventory levels. Manufacturers in a number of industries employ it to help them reduce the amount of production supplies they keep on hand. Manufacturers in Japan, where the system originated, have made great strides in reducing material costs. **Just-in-time inventory management** is a fairly simple concept: Rather than holding massive inventories of parts and materials, manufacturers have suppliers deliver items right before they are needed; in other words, the materials arrive "just in time." A successful JIT implementation requires several elements:

- *Close communication between suppliers and customers.* Suppliers must have sufficient time to deliver needed items. For example, AAA Trucking is a major supplier for Harley-Davidson's assembly plant in York, Pennsylvania. AAA set up an electronic communication system with the Harley plant to allow production schedulers to communicate directly and immediately with the delivery company. This ensures that the JIT process flows without interruption.[19]
- *Attention to quality.* Because there are no backup stocks to replace items found to be defective, parts must be of uniform high quality. Tektronix (an Oregon manufacturer of electronic instruments) dropped its number of suppliers from 100 to 36. The suppliers who made the grade all passed a rigorous certification program to make sure they would provide quality parts.[20]
- *Adequate storage facilities and transportation options.* Suppliers must be able to supply items quickly. The Volvo GM Truck plant in Dublin, Virginia, was experiencing unacceptable delays in the delivery of some parts, which were trucked in after being flown to the Roanoke Airport, 65 miles away. After moving the air-freight drop-off point to an airport only 5 miles away, Volvo GM reduced the delay enough to run a successful JIT operation.[21]

- *Reliable service from suppliers.* Customers have to shut down their production lines if JIT suppliers don't come through. Toyota runs its production lines with only a few hours' parts inventory, so it requires its suppliers to meet down-to-the-minute delivery schedules.[22]

For those manufacturers that can get all the pieces in place, JIT provides an attractive technique for keeping inventory costs down and productivity up. Suppliers of all sizes and shapes need to pay attention to JIT because more and more of their organizational customers are demanding it.

## Warehousing

Warehouses provide a key link in the physical distribution chain, and like other stages of distribution, they're getting close scrutiny from today's business managers. The location, size, and capabilities of warehouses can profoundly affect a company's ability to satisfy its customers and deliver products profitably.

Today's warehouse has come a long way from its dark, dusty ancestor stuffed with piles of merchandise. Modern warehouses are clean, computerized, and efficient, and they are used for a variety of purposes:

- *Storage.* Not surprisingly, companies store things in warehouses. However, storage is more than just goods waiting for delivery to customers; warehouses can also be used for product recalls, aging (as with wines), and blending (coffee beans, for example).
- *Sorting.* Some warehouses take in a stream of different goods and then separate those goods for storage in appropriate areas.
- *Breaking bulk.* To keep transportation costs down, warehouses are often used to break bulk. This happens when a centrally located warehouse receives a large shipment, then breaks it down into smaller shipments intended for local distribution. By limiting the number of shipments made over long distances, breaking bulk takes some of the bite out of transportation costs.
- *Consolidation.* On the other hand, a warehouse can be used to consolidate a number of small shipments to make one large shipment. For example, this is frequently done with overseas transportation to reduce the number of individual shipments.
- *Unitization.* Products are often unitized to make their transportation faster and easier. With **unitization**, companies collect individual products and combine them on one easy-to-transport pallet (a small wooden platform), which allows warehouse employees to handle products more efficiently.
- *Containerization.* The next step up from unitization is **containerization,** collecting goods into large containers for more efficient shipment by truck, train, or ship.

**unitization**
The process of combining individual packages into a larger unit, such as a pallet, for transportation

**containerization**
The process of packing goods in large, rectangular shipping containers

The Caldor's warehouse facility in Newburgh, New York, is a good example of the cutting-edge contemporary warehouse. To keep the company's 140 department stores in the Northeast stocked, the Newburgh operation sorts and ships 35,000 cartons every day. With a price tag of $70 million, the 500,000-square-foot building is large enough to hold nearly nine football fields. Fifty forklifts and motorized carts navigate the aisles, plucking and storing up and down the 40-foot-high shelves.[23]

### TYPES OF WAREHOUSES

Warehouses fall into two general categories, depending on their ownership. **Public warehouses** rent out storage space and associated distribution facilities. Some provide services ranging from inspection to order fulfillment. Atlanta-based Southern Linen, for example, relies on contract warehousing specialist Distribution & Marketing Services for receiving, inspecting, marking, storing, and delivering.[24] Public warehouses often specialize in serving the needs of particular industries. For instance, warehouses designed to handle farm produce provide the temperature-controlled facilities along with the unique equipment needed to handle fruits, vegetables, meat, and dairy products. This is the sort of facility that Sandi Hutsabaut

**public warehouses**
Warehouses that offer storage space to all companies

**field warehouse**
A public warehouse set up at the location of the customer's inventory

**private warehouses**
Warehouses owned by a company for its exclusive use

**distribution center**
A warehouse specially designed to provide the fast transfer of goods from suppliers to retailers or final customers

and the other Manitoba goat's milk producers need. Another specialized public warehouse is the **field warehouse**, which is established at the location of the customer's inventory.

Unlike public warehouses, **private warehouses** are reserved for the exclusive use of their owners. Major retail chains such as Sears and Wal-Mart use private warehouses to move goods between suppliers and retail stores. Companies choose private warehouses when they decide their needs can't be handled well enough by public warehouses or when they need so much storage that it makes financial sense to run their own warehouses. Warehouse facilities can be a major investment, however, so companies make sure they can manage a warehouse effectively and that they'll have sufficient long-term warehousing needs. Exhibit 16.4 summarizes influences on the public-versus-private warehousing decision.

A major advancement in both public and private warehousing is the **distribution center**, a specialized facility designed to rapidly direct goods from suppliers to stores or final customers. These centers use advanced equipment and computers to receive, sort, reload, and reroute tens or hundreds of thousands of packages daily. Wal-Mart is a recognized master at the distribution center concept. It gets as much as 77 percent of its retail merchandise from its own distribution centers, whereas its competitors are forced to use higher-priced outside distributors. As a result, Wal-Mart's distribution costs are 3 percent of its sales, about half that of most chain stores.[25]

Airlines in the United States have gradually adopted a distribution method called the hub-and-spoke system, which is similar to the distribution center concept. Hub-and-spoke uses a small number of major airports to collect passengers and baggage, sort them by destination, then reroute them to a large number of other destinations. (The large centers are the hubs; the paths to final destinations are the spokes.) This technique was designed to feed passengers from smaller cities into larger cities, building enough volume to fill more seats in the larger planes used on hub-to-hub flights. Firms with an interest in high-volume physical distribution have followed the airlines' lead. Federal Express, for instance, uses the airport in Memphis, Tennessee, as one of its hubs to handle hundreds of thousands of packages every day. Hub-and-spoke distribution provides customers with some impressive benefits, including

- More frequent and faster deliveries
- Economies of scale that take advantage of automated facilities at hubs
- Less waste because of greater utilization of distribution capacity[26]

The term *distribution center* also applies to cities and countries that have established themselves as experts in moving goods. To keep up with growing international trade, these global distribution centers are becoming vital. The Netherlands, with one of the world's busiest ports (Rotterdam), one of the busiest airports (Amsterdam), efficient customs clearances, and some of the top trucking companies in Europe, is widely acknowledged as one of the most advanced distribution centers. Experienced marketers also point to Ontario, Hong Kong, Singapore, and Dubai as the other leading centers outside the United States.[27] As with other aspects of physical distribution, marketers in many industries must concern themselves with the nitty-gritty world of global distribution, including knowing the best ways to route goods to their customers.

## WAREHOUSING DECISIONS

Firms that are about to build or rent warehouses make three important decisions: size, location, and number. The final decision is determined by the total cost concept and customer satisfaction goals. For instance, you can serve customers faster by placing warehouses or distribution centers closer to them. However, if your customers are numerous or widespread, this approach requires a lot of warehouses, which drives up your distribution costs. If this is unacceptable, you have to compromise between delivery time and delivery cost.

**Exhibit 16.4  CHOOSING PRIVATE OR PUBLIC WAREHOUSING**

| Factor | Private Warehouse | Public Warehouse |
|---|---|---|
| Initial Investment | Very high | None |
| Cost per unit stored | Inversely related to volume | Low |
| Level of control | High | Low |
| Adequacy for goods stored | High | May or may not be adequate |
| Risk | Yes, due to changes in technologies or demand | Minimal |

When choosing between public and private warehousing, physical distribution managers must consider several factors.

Other factors that play in the location decision include taxes, applicable local laws, access to various transportation facilities, work-force requirements, and the risk of product damage or theft. Consider the example of Lillian Vernon, a fast-growing catalog retailer that was faced with locating a new distribution center. Because the company imports 85 percent of its merchandise, a location close to a major port was crucial. Another major consideration was the huge volume of small packages it sends to customers, estimated at 5 million a year. To accommodate this kind of traffic, the distribution center also needed strong support from a local express package company. Finally, the company's highly seasonal business required a flexible, plentiful work force. After considering these factors, Lillian Vernon chose Virginia Beach, Virginia. It's close to the port at Norfolk, one of the best in the country; the UPS facility and other ground transportation options are sufficient; and the spouses of people stationed at the Norfolk naval facility provide much of the pool of employees.[28]

## Transportation

Now for the most obvious aspect of physical distribution: transportation. The movement of goods between a company's facilities and on to the final customers presents two great opportunities for gaining competitive advantage. First, effective management of transportation costs can help a company increase its profitability. Second, increasing the speed at which they deliver goods allows companies to serve their customers better. The following sections give an overview of the transportation options available to companies and discuss ways to use transportation to gain a competitive edge. This introduces you to the basic terms and issues in transportation, but keep in mind that transportation is a specialized field with details and subtleties that differ from mode to mode.

CLASSES OF CARRIERS

Companies that move freight are called carriers, and they fall into four categories. Common carriers offer their services to the general public. Contract carriers haul freight for selected companies under written contract. Private carriers are company-owned systems that move their own companies' products. Finally, exempt carriers are special cases of common, contract, or private carriers that haul unregulated goods such as unprocessed agricultural products.

Transportation has traditionally been heavily regulated in the United States. However, in 1978 the Interstate Commerce Commission began allowing private trucking companies to act as common or contract carriers. This lets a company make much better use of its private transportation network. As one example, a company can haul its own products to consumers and then pick up another firm's goods for the return. This practice, known as backhauling, doubles the productive use of trans-

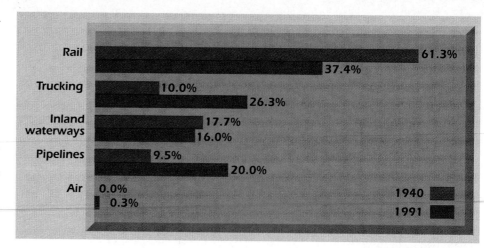

portation equipment. However, backhauling needs to be managed carefully so that incompatible products aren't carried in the same equipment. For instance, in response to contamination of edible oils that had been backhauled in tanker trucks previously used to carry dangerous chemicals such as benzene, the National Institute of Oilseed Products now prohibits its members from backhauling arrangements that might taint food products.[29]

## MODES OF TRANSPORTATION

The five major modes of transportation used for physical distribution are rail, truck, air, water, and pipelines. As seen in Exhibit 16.5, trucks and pipelines have significantly increased their share of the goods moving around inside the United States. On the other hand, inland water transport has decreased slightly, and railroad freight has dropped dramatically. Here's the latest word on all five major modes, plus three special types of transportation providers: package and express shippers, intermodal transport, and freight consolidators.

RAIL    Despite their decline in recent decades, railroads remain the number one method of transporting freight in the United States. (With the exception of oil pipelines, rail is also the most profitable mode.) Rail is the most efficient way to move most bulky commodities such as grain and coal across long distances. There are around 500 railroad companies in this country. Fourteen of these (the "majors" such as Burlington Northern and Southern Pacific) account for more than 90 percent of all rail traffic, but the hundreds of smaller lines (the "short lines") serve as vital links for farmers, manufacturers, and other businesses not located on major lines.[30]

TRUCKING    Trucking is the backbone of transportation in the United States. About two-thirds of all U.S. towns and cities rely on trucks exclusively. Also, many product categories are moved primarily by trucks. For example, 85 percent of furniture and appliance shipments move by trucks, as do 75 percent of all food goods and plastic products. Many larger manufacturers, wholesalers, and retailers maintain their own trucking fleets in addition to using commercial trucking services. Because of trucking's extensive availability, relatively high speed, and dependable service, the industry is able to command comparatively higher prices, and it generates far more revenue than any other mode of transportation.[31]

AIR    Airfreight offers the fastest transportation in most cases, but it's usually the most expensive. In the past, air shipments were most often reserved for critically important or perishable items such as repair parts, seafood, and flowers. For example, air shipments allow flower retailers to sell exotic flowers from the Netherlands, Thailand, and other countries less than 36 hours after they are cut.[32] The realm of air cargo is expanding beyond these industries, however, as more and more companies try to compete in the fast-changing global economy. The Limited stocks its clothing stores using aircraft flying between Hong Kong and a new cargo airport in Columbus, Ohio. Political and business leaders around the country are trying to develop special cargo-only airports to spur the growth in air cargo.[33]

Speed was a major factor in Ampex Corporation's decision to change its international transportation from ocean carriage to airfreight. However, in addition to decreasing its shipment cycle time from an average of 57 days to as low as 70 hours, the audiotape and videotape maker was also able to reduce its international inventories enough to save $1 million in carrying costs. Also, by committing all its business to one airline, Ampex was able to negotiate significantly lower shipping costs. In total, the switch to airfreight has saved the company over $600,000 a year.[34]

WATER    Water transportation includes inland waterways, ocean traffic, and Great Lakes shipping. Inland waterway shipping is typically handled by barges, carrying inexpensive commodity items such as sand, minerals, and grain. Inland shipping is extremely slow, but its low rates are attractive for transporting heavy, bulky, low-value products. Oceangoing ships, on the other hand, carry a wider variety of goods and play a big role in international commerce. This is particularly true for the United States because much of its import-export business involves countries on the other side of the Atlantic and Pacific oceans. Inside this country, ships are also used for transport in the Great Lakes and between ports along both coasts. Canada is the United States's number one trading partner, and Great Lakes shipping plays an important role in that relationship.

PIPELINES    Although you can't move very many products through a pipe, pipelines do carry a large portion of goods sold in this country. More than 213,000 miles of pipelines carry both crude (unrefined) petroleum and refined petroleum products such as gasoline and kerosene. This is an efficient, cost-effective way to move large amounts of material, although at 3 or 4 miles an hour, these liquids don't get anywhere in a big hurry. Some shippers make clever use of pipelines, moving wood chips and coal chips by mixing them with water to help them flow down the pipeline.

PACKAGE AND EXPRESS SHIPPERS    To address the growing need both for shipments of small packages and for high-speed shipments of all sizes, specialized transport companies such as Federal Express, United Parcel Service, and Roadway Package Systems have emerged. These firms offer fast, door-to-door delivery of a wide variety of package types to numerous locations worldwide.

INTERMODAL TRANSPORTATION    A special twist in transportation is called **intermodal transportation** because it takes advantage of more than one major mode (see Exhibit 16.6). For example, logging companies in Oregon and Washington often trans-

**intermodal transportation**
Transportation that uses more than one of the five principal modes

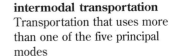

**Exhibit 16.6**
**INTERMODAL TRANSPORTATION**
Intermodal transportation provides the link between trucking, rail, and shipping.

port logs by truck to rail stations; then trains carry the logs on to ports such as Seattle and Tacoma. At the ports, the logs are loaded onto oceangoing freighters for transport to Japan and other countries along the Pacific Rim.

The economies of intermodal transportation make sense only for fairly long distances and when the transition from one mode to the next isn't unduly hampered by regulations, tradition, or technology. This is one of the reasons that intermodal is used much more frequently in the United States than in Europe, for instance. The relatively short distances between countries and major cities, combined with conflicting regulations and such technological hurdles as different sizes of railroad track, make European intermodal challenging at best and impossible at worst.[35]

**freight forwarders**
Transportation firms that specialize in consolidating and sending freight on to its final destination

FREIGHT FORWARDERS   **Freight forwarders**, or freight consolidators, help improve shipping efficiency for many companies by pooling together several small shipments bound for the same general location. Because of the high cost of international air and ocean freight, consolidation is particularly attractive when shipping goods overseas. However, consolidation is playing a bigger role in domestic shipments as well. For example, New Jersey–based Small Parcel Service offers small-package shippers a rate 10 percent below UPS's by combining shipments destined for specific areas of the country.[36]

## FACTORS IN SELECTING TRANSPORTATION MODES

Some transportation mode selections are obvious. You're probably not going to send crude oil by airfreight or put fresh seafood on a slow river barge. However, many choices aren't as clear. Here are several parameters transportation managers consider when selecting modes. Remember that all these factors need to be balanced according to the total cost concept and customer service standards. Exhibit 16.7 rates each mode on these selection factors. Again, keep in mind that transportation can be a complicated issue, and these factors need to be analyzed for each specific case. For instance, airfreight is in fact generally faster, but it's not faster than a truck if you're trying to ship across town.

- *Cost*. Shipping cost is obviously a major factor in the selection of a transportation mode. Air is usually the most expensive mode, except for cases when the faster service it provides allows companies to significantly reduce inventory levels, as in the Ampex example already described. Water is the least expensive mode, but it isn't available or adequate in many cases.
- *Speed*. Delivery time is often an important factor in customer satisfaction. When a customer faces an equipment failure and needs a repair part immediately, computer manufacturers such as Digital Equipment Corporation don't worry too much about cost. DEC will put the part on the next plane out of town, if necessary, in order to get the customer back up and running. Naturally, speed is also of great concern to fresh-food marketers like Sandi Hutsabaut.
- *Access*. Transportation modes aren't much help if customers can't get to them. This is one of the reasons trucking is growing quickly while railroads are suf-

**Exhibit 16.7   SELECTING TRANSPORTATION MODES**

| Factor | Rating | | | | |
|---|---|---|---|---|---|
| | Very High | High | Medium | Low | Very Low |
| Speed | Air | Trucking | Rail | Pipelines | Water |
| Access | Trucking | Air | Rail | Water | Pipelines |
| Dependability | Trucking | Water | Pipelines | Rail | Air |
| Load flexibility | Water | Rail | Trucking | Air | Pipelines |
| Frequency | Trucking | Air | Rail | Water | Pipelines |
| Cost | Air | Trucking | Rail | Pipelines | Water |

The choice of a transportation mode is frequently a compromise, because each mode has its own strengths and weaknesses.

fering. Trucks can be rerouted as customer needs change, and roads go just about anyplace you could want to ship something. However, the supply of railways is much more limited. Obviously, water-based transportation and, to a large extent, airfreight are limited by access in many areas. Increasing access is one of the primary reasons for the birth of intermodal transportation companies. For example, CSX, one of the nation's largest rail companies, purchased Sea-Land, one of the nation's largest container ship operators, so that it could provide customers with better access to transportation.[37]

- *Load flexibility.* Some modes are better able to adapt to various shipping needs. Oceangoing freighters, for instance, can handle a wide variety of products, from cars to the gasoline that powers them. However, at the other end of the flexibility spectrum, pipelines aren't much good at handling anything except liquids and materials that can be combined with liquids.

- *Frequency.* When you're choosing a transportation mode, schedule frequency might be a big concern. Because of their size, freighters offer the lowest frequency; it doesn't make economic sense to raise anchor until the ship is full. Trucks, on the other hand, run fairly often, and pipelines are usually in continual operation.

- *Dependability.* Finally, some modes do a better job of providing reliable transportation. Unreliable service can create huge headaches for customers, so this is often a major selection criterion. Pipelines are considered the most reliable and secure mode; water shipments promise the least reliable service. Trucks generally provide the lowest level of safety among the five major modes.

## Materials Management

**Materials management** is the task of overseeing the systems that move materials around inside warehouses and factories, between a company's facilities, and from the company to its customers. In many organizations it includes the purchasing function as well. Materials handling frequently involves some of the most advanced technologies in the entire distribution system; here's a selection:

- *Automated sorters.* Sorting machines automatically sort and route packages based on size and other attributes.
- *Bar-code scanners.* Companies increasingly use the Universal Product Code (UPC) bars on products and packages, and bar-code scanners let warehouse workers quickly catalog, sort, and store the material they're handling.
- *Automatic guided vehicles.* Following a predetermined path (laid out on the floor with a special tape or programmed by some other technique), automatic guided vehicles deliver parts, finished products, and mail.
- *Radio-linked inventory systems.* By linking inventory systems together with radio communications, warehouse managers are always assured of up-to-date information, even in complex, multifacility storage systems.
- *Computer-controlled shelving.* Computer-controlled shelving brings parts to the operator rather than vice versa, allowing employees to retrieve parts faster and more accurately.

**materials management**
Overseeing the systems that move materials within warehouses and factories, between a company's facilities, and to customers; sometimes also includes the purchasing function

Companies invest in such technologies to increase the speed and accuracy of their materials handling, which in turn reduces cost and increases customer satisfaction.[38]

Ensuring protective packaging is another important element of materials handling (see Exhibit 16.8). Many products need to be protected from rough treatment by workers and machinery. Sensitive or fragile products in particular require close attention to packaging. For example, Wang Laboratories protects the computer assemblies it ships with foam-filled bags that expand up to 200 times their original size. These specially designed cushions protect the expensive electronic components from damage during shipment to Wang's worldwide service centers.[39] In the case of Sandi Hutsabaut's milk distribution challenge, she has to ensure that the product is kept clean and cold, and various packaging and storage techniques are available to do this.

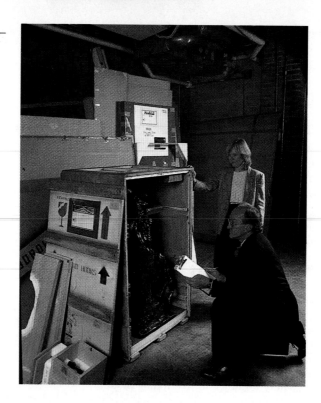

**Exhibit 16.8
PROTECTIVE
PACKAGING**
Protective packaging allows
organizations such as this
Philadelphia art museum to
ship fragile items.

# SPECIAL ISSUES IN PHYSICAL DISTRIBUTION

Now that you have an idea of the basic elements of a physical distribution system, consider some of the emerging issues. More and more companies realize that distribution is a key element of cost control and customer satisfaction, so distribution is receiving a lot more attention than it once did. Here's a summary of the major issues.

## International Physical Distribution

European and Asian companies are looking to the United States to increase worldwide market share. At the same time, U.S. companies that want to expand are going after consumers outside the country in increasing numbers. One result of this increase in global trade is, of course, an increase in international physical distribution.

Several issues confront transportation managers whose companies are shipping overseas. To start with, numerous government regulations in each country must be considered. Conforming to all these regulations means a mountain of paperwork for every international shipment. Moreover, the cost of delivering goods can vary substantially from country to country. For instance, it costs 25 percent more to truck goods onward from the port of Bremerhaven, Germany, than it does from Antwerp, Belgium.[40] Another concern is the general stress and strain of conducting business in a foreign country, dealing with unfamiliar languages, customs, and business practices. The burden of international distribution is too much for some companies, especially for smaller ones. These firms often turn to foreign freight forwarders that specialize in overseas shipping.

## Suboptimization

**suboptimization**
A loss of efficiency or cost controls caused when one of the factors in a system is emphasized at the expense of the total system's performance

The total cost and customer satisfaction goals imply that companies will strike a balance among numerous cost components and customer satisfaction measures. When one component or measure is pursued to such an extent that optimum cost or satisfaction is not achievable, **suboptimization** results. Typical suboptimization situations include too much or too little inventory, fast delivery that is unacceptably ex-

## HIGH-VOLUME INTERNATIONAL DISTRIBUTION? FOLLOW IN NIKE'S FOOTSTEPS

Ever have trouble finding your shoes in the morning? Well, imagine the challenge Carl Davis faces at Nike. As the manager responsible for customs and transportation, he oversees the movement of 80 million pairs of shoes a year. Nike shoes are manufactured in Korea, Indonesia, Taiwan, Thailand, and the People's Republic of China (Nike has Taiwanese representatives handle these manufacturing efforts), and the finished products are marketed all over the world. Davis's job is to get these shoes out of the factories, onto planes or ships, through customs in the country of destination, and on to the next stage of the local marketing channel.

Actually, that's only half of his job. He is also responsible for transporting specially engineered components for Nike's high-end shoes from sources in the United States to those factories in Asia. These components are then integrated with local parts to make shoes for running, tennis, basketball, and fitness. Because he is a critical link in the production system, Davis is constantly on his toes, making sure his shipments don't fall behind schedule.

Davis points to three vital elements that make Nike successful with international physical distribution. These concepts can be applied to nearly any distribution situation, regardless of the products involved. As a first step, Davis advises importers and exporters to learn as much as possible about all the aspects of their businesses so that they understand what is needed for efficient distribution. Various people in different organizations may get in-

**EXPLORING GLOBAL MARKETING**

volved with moving the product along, but the product eventually has to end up in the hands of customers. To make sure it gets there smoothly and efficiently, somebody needs to watch over the entire distribution system. Nike places great importance on meeting customer service standards, and the company has aligned its distribution and delivery policies to maintain those standards.

The second step is to establish an order processing, transportation, and storage network that automates and manages the task for you as much as possible. Nike keeps Davis from going completely crazy with a special order processing method known as a futures ordering system. Customers (distributors and retailers) place orders up to five months before they receive shipments. This system provides benefits in both directions: The customers get guaranteed prices and delivery dates, and Nike is able to keep its production and distribution pipeline full.

To manage the flow of all these shoes (and of the athletic apparel that makes up the other 15 percent of its sales), Nike uses both it own distribution organization and independent distributors. In the United States, the company's own organization usually receives the incoming shipments.

Large orders are shipped directly to customers. In the rest of the world, Nike relies on exclusive distributors to sell to retailers. Some of these are subsidiaries of Nike; others are independent.

Davis's third point is to build close ties with customs officials. This has helped the company in several important ways. First, a close relationship means better communication, so Nike is made aware of potential importation problems before they can disrupt the flow of goods. Second, by doing advance work to ensure smooth shipments, Nike has avoided customs inspections and seizures that have plagued other importers. Finally, the close relationship works to Nike's benefit in its war on counterfeit shoes. With athletic shoes commanding prices up to $150 or more, creating "knockoff" or "backdoor" shoes is a tempting trade for some factories in the Far East. By keeping in touch with customs officials, Nike gets their help in monitoring for these illicit goods.

Clearly, physical distribution plays a big role in Nike's efforts to compete with such firms as Reebok, Adidas, and L. A. Gear. By keeping the flow of both parts and finished goods moving quickly and efficiently, transportation managers like Carl Davis make vital contributions to their companies' success in the global marketplace. The three key points he stresses about international distribution will help any company with its import and export activities.

### APPLY YOUR KNOWLEDGE

**1.** How has Nike used physical distribution to help build competitive advantage in the athletic shoe market?
**2.** How could Nike verify that Carl Davis's efforts toward maintaining customer satisfaction levels are worthwhile?

---

pensive, or excessively long production runs that decrease production costs but increase inventory carrying costs.

Let's say the customer service manager at L. L. Bean, a large catalog clothing and sporting goods retailer, wants to give customers the fastest delivery in the mail-order industry. He recommends using Federal Express's next-morning service, which promises deliveries by 10:30 A.M. but which adds to delivery costs. However,

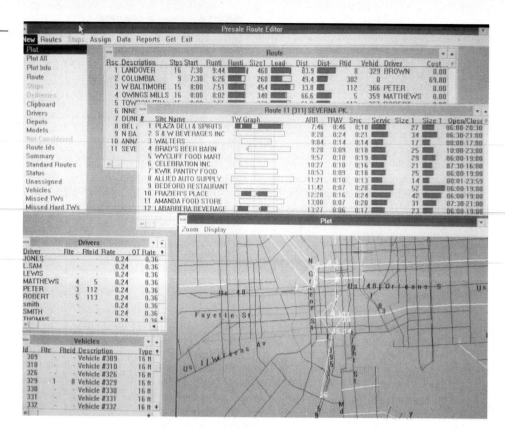

**Exhibit 16.9
OPTIMIZING USING
COMPUTERS**
Route optimization software,
such as the Roadnet package
shown here, helps drivers
pick the fastest, most cost-
effective routes.

the shipping manager wants to keep costs as low as possible. He wants to pile packages up for two weeks, then make huge, consolidated shipments to a handful of distribution centers around the country. Customer orders will take three weeks, the slowest delivery time in the industry, but they won't cost much to deliver. If either of these managers were to get his or her way, the result would be suboptimization. To reach the optimum solution, the marketing manager should step in and decide which compromise best meets the firm's goals of pricing and customer satisfaction. Perhaps she or he will decide to offer second-day delivery or let customers who want next-morning service pay extra for it.

To help companies avoid suboptimization in their distribution systems, software developers are now providing optimization tools. These computer programs assist in such areas as selecting modes of transportation and planning delivery routes (see Exhibit 16.9). Beverage companies such as Anheuser-Busch and PepsiCo, for instance, use route optimization software to make sure they provide the best combination of time, frequency, and cost of delivery.[41]

## Transportation Deregulation

Most modes of transportation have been closely regulated in the United States for decades. Starting in the 1970s and continuing for the next two decades, the federal government has been loosening these restrictions in order to help U.S. companies become more competitive. One result of deregulation is the increased role physical distribution now plays in marketing strategies. With deregulation comes an increase in a company's distribution options. For instance, because of tremendous growth in the number of trucking services companies that use trucking lines have more services to choose from. However, more careful buying decisions are essential because the price and performance of trucking are no longer regulated for consistency.[42]

Deregulation has been an enormous help to the railroading industry. When railroads were granted the freedom to merge, negotiate rates, and close unprofitable lines, they staged a slight comeback in their battle with trucking. Since 1977, for example, operating expenses for the industry have dropped more than 40 percent.

In addition to the ability to negotiate rates with individual customers, this makes railroads much more price competitive than they once were.[43]

Europe has always presented a special headache for international shippers because of the wide variety of transport restrictions, taxes, and administrative procedures. The standardization of trade regulations between member countries of the European Union (which began in 1992 but will take the rest of the decade to be finalized) should make life a lot easier for companies shipping to and through Europe. Some of the benefits of these changes include lower transportation costs, increased speed and reliability of delivery, and increased market potential for products that are less burdened with shipping costs.[44]

## Environmental Impact of Transportation

Transportation has an undeniable effect on the natural and human environments. Its effects range from the noise of aircraft to the wildlife hazards posed by railways in remote areas. We were all given a grim reminder of transportation's potential environmental damage when the *Exxon Valdez* spilled millions of gallons of crude oil in Alaska's Prince William Sound in 1989. Activists responded by calling for tighter regulations on shipping companies, and one change they requested provides a good example of the total cost concept. Double-hulled tankers are less vulnerable to the sort of punctures that caused the *Exxon Valdez* disaster, but they cost substantially more to build. The oil companies would have to pass all or part of this cost on to consumers. Are U.S. consumers ready to pay higher gas prices in order to decrease the risk of oil spills?

Trucking has a sizable cloud on the horizon as well. Trucks rely heavily on the nation's 42,798-mile interstate highway system, and that system is in bad shape. In some states, 30 or 40 percent of the interstate miles are considered deficient. Potholes and other problems plague a system that was designed more than 30 years ago to last only 20 years and to carry only one-third the traffic it now carries. Trucking surely suffers from bad roads, but it also contributes to the problem. The U.S. Transportation Department estimates that one 80,000-pound truck causes as much damage to an interstate as 9,600 automobiles. No wonder proposals to increase the size of truck-trailer combinations are meeting with stiff opposition. Railroads are joining the antitruck protests, and their position is supported by the fact that trucks generate four times as much pollution per ton hauled as railroads.[45]

# THE FUTURE OF PHYSICAL DISTRIBUTION

Because of its strategic importance, physical distribution will continue to get a lot of attention from researchers and managers. Here are quick summaries of some of the major issues that are likely to affect physical distribution in the coming years:

- *Increasing importance of technology.* This includes materials handling technology as well as communications technology. Some of today's most advanced physical distribution systems employ satellite navigation/communication, voice-input computers, machine vision, robots, on-board computer logbooks, planning software relying on artificial intelligence, and electronic data interchange (EDI), in which computers can send and receive orders automatically. Bill Ward, co-founder of OTR Express, a Kansas-based trucking firm, operates the company almost as if it were a giant computer system that just happens to use trucks to get the job done. Trucking is a ferociously competitive business with tight profit margins. By using custom software to track everything from the location of trucks to the best places in the country to buy tires, OTR squeezes impressive profits while keeping the firm's prices competitive.[46]
- *Worldwide messaging standards.* A systems perspective of physical distribution places as much emphasis on information flow as it does on material flow. Unfortunately, this means many distribution systems are drowning in paperwork to

As part of the sweeping economic changes in the European Union, physical distribution between member nations is now simpler, cheaper, and faster.

## MAGIC SHELVES AND ROBOT WORKERS

As the physical distribution function becomes ever more important—in terms of both keeping customers satisfied and driving costs down—marketers at all stages in the distribution chain are looking for answers in advanced technology. For most, adding high-tech gadgets is a competitive necessity, and you can expect technology to play an increasing role in physical distribution.

Imagine standing in front of a wall of warehouse shelves, 10 or 20 feet high and hundreds of feet long. The shelves hold thousands of products. Your job is to move up and down, back and forth, collecting the right set of products to fill each customer order. You can imagine how slow the process is and how many opportunities you would have to make mistakes.

Now imagine that you sit in one location and the shelves come to you. You simply punch a number into your computer terminal, and the correct shelf somehow magically moves right in front of you. You wouldn't have to walk and climb ladders all day, and you'd probably make fewer mistakes. That's the whole idea behind *carousels,* which are computer-controlled shelving systems that bring the product to the person, rather than making the person go find the product. The computer knows which products are stored on which shelves, and when you request a particular item, the shelves rotate (some systems move horizontally, others move vertically) until the right shelf is where the user needs it.

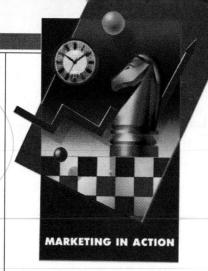

**MARKETING IN ACTION**

When York County Hospital in Newmarket, Ontario, Canada, installed carousels to assist the people who provide the rest of the hospital with supplies and medicines, productivity nearly doubled. Workers no longer spend time walking up and down aisles looking for items; they sit at a workstation and push buttons while the carousel picks out what they need. Moreover, the carousel system does the same work in two-thirds the space occupied by the old manual storage setup, providing another important economic benefit.

Lennox, a major manufacturer of heating and air conditioning systems, found significant customer service advantages in its automated carousels. Its National Parts Center in Urbandale, Iowa, stores 11,000 different parts and supplies more than 60 warehouses serving U.S. and international customers. Lennox prides itself on fast, accurate response to all orders, and you can imagine how important it is for customers to get the right replacement quickly when their heating or air conditioning units are down. Using its carousel system, employees fill 97 percent of orders the same day

they are received. Moreover, in 1992 the center processed 101,155 orders and only 24 errors were reported—an accuracy rate of 99.98 percent.

Warehouse robots usually come into play when companies do need somebody/something to move around a facility but human workers aren't the best choice for one reason or another. Robots can take over tedious, difficult, or dangerous tasks. Stationary robots, working under such names as "pick and place" robots, in fact stay in one place but often use long, multijointed arms to grab materials, stack boxes, and perform other tasks. Robots that move around warehouses don't look much like their science fiction counterparts, however. Some are simply motorized carts that follow wires or special tape on the floor. Others are more advanced, such as driverless forklifts that can read bar codes and make pickups and deliveries in response to instructions from a computer. Whatever they look like mechanically, robots and carousels look like great ways to cut costs and improve customer service in today's warehouses.

### APPLY YOUR KNOWLEDGE

**1.** How might product design affect warehouse automation efforts such as carousels and robots? Pick a product category such as groceries or pharmaceuticals and try to picture the product issues to be considered.
**2.** How might an automated warehouse help a company better serve customers that use JIT manufacturing?

---

move all that information. To address this problem, shippers and customers are pushing for an electronic data interchange method called the International Forwarding and Transportation Message (IFTM). This will allow shippers to replace the paper with electronic messages that carry all the information needed for communicating, routing, scheduling, and billing.[47]

- *Customer-carrier partnerships.* Carriers and the customers they serve will grow closer in many cases. The forces driving them together include just-in-time inventory management and electronic data interchange techniques. These new relationships may involve contractual arrangements or, in some cases, partial ownership of each other's companies.

- *Increasing emphasis on service.* Finally, customers who are affected by physical distribution will continue to increase their calls for better service. Faster service alone is no longer enough. With JIT, for example, you can't be a day late, but you can't be a day early, either. You have to be on time; you have to be dependable. With decreasing inventories comes the need for greater accuracy and for better communication as well. Increasingly, partners in the distribution chain are expected to help out with a variety of value-added services, from marketing research to promotion. As John Morse of meat producer Zenchiku Land and Livestock says rather bluntly, "If you don't add value, we don't need you."[48]

# SUMMARY OF LEARNING OBJECTIVES

## 1. Describe the strategic importance of physical distribution.

Physical distribution includes three elements of importance. First, physical distribution plays a key role in nearly every company's efforts to keep customers satisfied. Second, distribution can be a significant part of a company's costs of doing business; therefore keep distribution costs as low as possible without sacrificing other objectives. Finally, distribution interacts with the other elements of the marketing mix, including product design, pricing, and promotion.

## 2. Identify the most common objectives of physical distribution.

The two general sets of objectives are keeping total costs as low as possible and keeping customers satisfied. Common customer satisfaction objectives include delivery time, dependability, communication with customers about orders, convenience, product protection, and the accuracy with which orders are filled.

## 3. Discuss the total cost concept in distribution decisions.

The total cost concept takes into account all the cost factors that figure in physical distribution. These include transportation, storage, taxes, materials handling, and the cost of sales that are lost because of inventory shortages. The total cost concept seeks the optimum balance among all these factors to achieve lowest overall transportation costs. However, remember that costs always have to be weighed against customer satisfaction goals.

## 4. Explain why physical distribution is more than trucks, trains, and warehouses.

Physical distribution should be viewed as an integrated system that includes equipment, people, organizations, and information as coordinated parts of a cohesive whole. By adopting a perspective that encompasses all the elements, distribution managers and their companies can achieve better efficiency and minimize problems resulting from suboptimization.

## 5. Discuss the just-in-time inventory management philosophy.

JIT seeks to reduce inventory costs and supply problems by tightening the link between customers and their suppliers. Rather than keeping large quantities of parts on hand, a manufacturing facility has its suppliers drop off required parts just before they are needed. Some of the elements required for a successful JIT implementation include close communication, attention to quality, adequate storage and transportation facilities, and reliable service from suppliers.

## 6. Describe the transportation options available to businesses.

Distribution managers can choose from five major modes of transportation: rail, trucking, sea, air, and pipelines. The criteria for making this choice include speed, access, capabilities, reliability, and safety. Two special types of transportation providers are express/package shippers and intermodal carriers.

## 7. Discuss the storage options available to businesses.

Storage options include two general types of warehouses. Public warehouses offer storage space to all companies, although they specialize in servicing selected industries or types of customers. Private warehouses are owned by companies whose primary business is outside the field of distribution, such as retail chains. An important type of private warehouse is the distribution center, which is designed to sort and reship large numbers of products rapidly.

# KEY TERMS

containerization (493)
distribution centers (494)
field warehouse (494)
freight forwarders (498)
intermodal transportation (497)

just-in-time inventory management (492)
materials management (499)
order processing (490)
physical distribution (486)
private warehouses (494)

public warehouses (493)
safety stock (492)
stockout (491)
suboptimization (500)
total cost concept (488)
utilization (493)

## Meeting a Marketing Challenge at the Manitoba Goatmilk Cooperative

Although you might not reach for a nice, frosty glass of goat's milk when you walk in the door on a warm summer's evening, more and more people are doing just that. Drawn by the health benefits—and by the taste—new goat's milk fans are searching their stores for a supply, often coming up empty.

Meanwhile, down on the farm, goat producers are eager to meet this growing demand in a commercial way, which means that the milk must be pasteurized, packaged, stored, handled, and distributed according to exacting requirements.

Today's commercial milk goat has been bred to be a high-output animal, much like a Guernsey cow, and is capable of producing as much as 2 gallons of milk per day. Thus, the output of as few as 40 active goats could be 80 gallons per day; a herd of 500 could give 1,000 gallons, a considerable quantity to bring to a thirsty market.

Right now, no commercial distribution exists specifically for Manitoba's output of goat's milk. Sandi Hutsabaut and her fellow producers have been acting independently of each other and have been unable to develop a market for their product or to create a system to transport, process, package, store, and deliver goat's milk to likely retail outlets throughout Manitoba.

Consider the steps these producers must take. First, they need to increase their herds. Then, in order to collect the raw milk and transport it to the processing plant, they require transportation and handling facilities. Finally, they need a processing plant that is well located.

Transportation of both raw and processed goat's milk calls for careful temperature control and strict cleanliness. Normally, the goatherd delivers raw milk directly from the milking machines to a refrigerated collection tank attached to the milk house. Soon after, the milk is collected by an insulated-tank truck, which delivers it and other milk collected along its route to the processing plant. Each farm's output is recorded at this time.

During transportation the milk is maintained as close to 36° Fahrenheit as possible to avoid souring and the development of undesirable bacterial strains. The milk is also tested for bacterial content and for the presence of penicillin and other antibiotics—and is rejected if the bacteria count is too high or if antibiotic agents are present.

At the processing plant, the milk is pasteurized and homogenized. After fat content is measured to be sure that it meets or exceeds the required minimum for whole milk, the processed milk is packaged.

Deliveries to retail outlets are scheduled according to sales experience in each outlet. Some high-volume stores may receive daily delivery while others are supplied less frequently. Properly processed, fresh milk has a refrigerated shelf life of as much as 28 days, though milk may remain on store shelves for only 7 to 10 days before a dairy accepts its return.

The journey from farm to city store is expensive. Moreover, goat's milk is generally not produced in the same quantities as cow's milk. Where it is available, processed fresh goat's milk usually retails for about four times the price of a comparable quantity of cow's milk.

However, Hutsabaut and the Manitoba Goatmilk Cooperative are determined to milk the market. Sometime soon, if you stop by the dairy case in a Manitoba supermarket, you'll find fresh, wholesome goat's milk waiting for your breakfast cereal or cookie break.

**Your mission:** You have been asked to work with Sandi Hutsabaut to explore the feasibility of several methods for handling the goat's milk as it moves from the Manitoba Goatmilk Cooperative, the point of production, to the ultimate point of sale. Use your expertise as a physical distribution consultant and your experience as a consumer to answer the following questions.

1. The members of the Manitoba Goatmilk Cooperative have decided that their initial target market will be people who are likely to purchase their product for therapeutic reasons—that is, reasons of health. They believe the most likely retail outlets for their output are drugstores and health-food stores. Discussion is now focused on how to place Manitoba Goatmilk in these outlets. Which of the following seems to you to be the most sensible approach?
   a. One member proposes that distribution be handled by an already existing commercial dairy. The product could even be sold under that dairy's brand name, an established one in the province, and trucks from the dairy could deliver goat's milk along with their regular product line.
   b. Another producer favors the co-op's purchasing one or more delivery trucks. She notes that, as far as Manitoba is concerned, goat's milk is a "new" product, so no one knows what kind of delivery schedules are going to work best. She believes that the co-op should control distribution of its product to retailers in order to better achieve its service objective.
   c. A third member advocates simply selling processed milk to drugstore chains in bulk and letting them deliver the product to their own stores. His claim is that doing so would reduce the co-op's costs and allow for a larger margin of profit on each unit sold.
2. If its initial efforts at the commercialization of goat's milk are successful, the Manitoba Goatmilk Cooperative will consider developing other markets for the products of its herds. The products suggested include a variety of cheeses. As an example, feta, the Greek cheese made from goat's milk, is justly famed for its richness and flavor. What might be some of the implications of the decision to expand the product line?

a. Development of new distribution links might be necessary. It is unlikely that the new products will be viewed as therapeutic items.

b. New customers for the products of the co-op would require new approaches to the problem of distribution. After all, cheese and milk have somewhat different uses.

c. If the co-op's milk develops a strong following in the market, a distribution system reaching at least one target segment will be in place. Development of entirely new distribution networks is necessary to bring the co-op's products to new market segments, including ethnic segments like the Greek population.

3. The members of the cooperative have been giving some thought to the idea of direct distribution—delivering goat's milk from the processing plant directly to homes and apartments. Assuming that a processing plant is found or built, which of the following would be most true about such a distribution system?

a. Such a form of distribution is easy to create and operate. You don't have to worry about your product being handled by others, and quality control and dealing with returned goods are entirely in your own hands.

b. This kind of distribution, especially for a fresh-food product, requires widespread demand for the item and a dense population of users. It is a very expensive form of distribution as well, and most commercial cow's milk dairies have abandoned it. It probably won't be possible for a goat's milk co-op to use such a system until goat's milk achieves a high level of consumer acceptance and popularity. Even then, people will probably have to pay a premium for home delivery.

c. This is a more feasible scheme of distribution for rural areas than for the city because getting access to people's homes and apartments in the city is very difficult. Parking the milk truck to service a high-rise could cause real traffic problems. In the country, trips to the store are taken less frequently, but the people drink just as much milk as in the city and would welcome the service.

4. After talking with large supermarkets in Winnipeg, you find they are unenthusiastic about offering goat's milk in addition to cow's milk. Find alternative distribution channels. Which of the following might be good solutions?

a. Open a chain of goat's milk convenience stores. These would be small 500-square-foot stores in Winnipeg residential areas, with early opening hours and late closing hours to allow customers to buy milk and milk products at their convenience.

b. Negotiate with drugstores and health-food stores to set up a small refrigerated section for goat's milk right near the door. This will attract the health-conscious shopper and will give the cooperative control over the stock and merchandising of the section.

c. Outfit refrigerator carts, like those used by ice cream vendors, to offer goat's milk on the streets of Winnipeg. The carts can also be used to offer free samples to passersby, stimulating first-time purchases.

## SPECIAL PROJECT

Sandi Hutsabaut has made some progress: A dairy foods processor in Manitoba has agreed to buy the co-op's goat's milk. This company plans to make and market a variety of goat's milk products, including milk, flavored milks (such as chocolate), ice cream, and cheeses. However, one big hurdle is that the processor operates strictly by just-in-time inventory management and insists that all its suppliers abide by this method. To keep its costs as low as possible, the processor adjusts its production level several times a day to minimize waste and maximize sales. As new orders are received from retailers, the processor increases or decreases its output accordingly.

Hutsabaut wants you to draw up a plan for becoming JIT-compatible. Consider each of the requirements for a successful JIT implementation covered in this chapter, and briefly describe how it would affect the co-op. Summarize your findings by telling the co-op whether or not it should try to go ahead with this deal.[49]

## Hub-and-Spoke Is Wheel of Fortune for Federal Express

Back in the 1960s, Frederick W. Smith was sure that his innovative physical distribution ideas could increase efficiency and decrease the cost of moving packages around the United States. Against the advice of numerous skeptics, he implemented the radical concept of hub-and-spoke distribution, and by 1988 he was flying high with $4 billion in revenues. However, as he continued to expand, Smith faced obstacles that hub-and-spoke couldn't solve: air transport regulations and the challenge of international operations.

The air express industry that Smith envisioned would fly packages from around the country to a central location to be sorted and then shipped to their final destinations. He reasoned that a company using this system would be able to optimize its airplane and trucking resources and provide fast and efficient package handling for shippers anywhere in the country.

Smith chose his hometown, Memphis, as the first hub; it is centrally located and the airport is rarely closed by bad weather. Despite his high hopes, the first night of service was anything but encouraging. Federal Express handled a grand total of eight shipments, seven of which were sent by its own employees to employees in other locations.

One year later, the fledgling company was losing $1 million a month and Smith realized that he needed a new marketing approach to reach organizational buyers. After a couple of false starts, Federal Express aired an ad campaign based on the slogan "When it absolutely, positively has to be there overnight," and sales soared.

By the mid-1980s, Federal Express was delivering nearly half the overnight packages sent within the United States. However, because he knew the market was maturing, Smith began to look beyond U.S. borders for additional growth. In 1985 Federal Express crossed the oceans with a new international service and quickly got caught in the mire of overseas competitors and foreign aviation regulations.

Over a three-year period, Smith lost about $74 million trying to compete internationally. Finally, in 1989 he won government approval to purchase Tiger International, which gave Federal Express access to the Flying Tiger Line air cargo organization, with its 40 years of international experience and well-established routes. Moreover, Smith could now use Tiger's fleet of long-range planes to become a player in the international heavy-freight market. Combining Tiger's strengths with Federal Express's expertise in door-to-door delivery,

Smith thought he had forged a formidable weapon to shake up the global cargo market.

However, FedEx's international hopes didn't pan out quite as successfully as Smith hoped. After pumping millions of dollars into establishing a base of operations throughout Europe, FedEx lost money there for five years in a row. Several factors were at work: Europe is already well served by a number of long-established trucking companies, European businesses didn't take to the overnight urgency message that worked so well in the United States, and the short distances and mountainous paperwork in between countries makes air cargo unacceptably expensive in many cases. Finally in mid-1992, Smith pulled the plug. FedEx retains direct service to 16 European cities, but for service between cities inside Europe, he hands the packages over to competitors for final delivery. In spite of this setback, however, FedEx remains on strong footing in North America and in emerging markets in Latin America and Asia.

1. Although Federal Express has taken on the burden of warehousing inventory for clients of its Business Logistics Services (BLS) division, Smith believes he can add value to this service by expanding its functions. To promote the new service, should he offer to accept inventory returns to the BLS warehouse from his clients' customers, or should he offer to prepare customers' goods with price tags, instruction sheets, and special packaging?

2. Because there are so many competitors in the air express business, imagine that Smith wants to expand into a new area. Should he implement a chain of state-of-the-art public warehouses near the airport in cities with heavy commercial air traffic, or an international water transportation service that would speed containerized goods between major port cities around the world?

3. The Federal Express hub at Memphis airport is virtually unused starting about 4:30 each morning, when planes leave loaded with packages for destinations around the country, until about 11:30 each night, when the planes arrive bearing packages to be sorted for delivery the next day. Smith might want to make the hub more productive during its idle hours. Would you suggest that he make the hub available to passenger airlines during the daytime hours, or would you suggest that he offer a two-day freight consolidation and forwarding service that would utilize the hub during daylight hours only?

# QUESTIONS FOR DISCUSSION

1. What types of companies don't have to worry about physical distribution?
2. What effect would physical distribution have on the marketing mix for the following products?
   a. Bread
   b. Fresh produce
   c. Compact disks
   d. Iron ore
3. How might JIT affect a company's attempts to decrease its total distribution costs?
4. Assume Boeing Commercial Airplanes in Seattle wants to implement JIT inventory management. Many of Boeing's suppliers are local, but some are based in California and Japan. What can Boeing do to make its JIT program successful?
5. Would the following companies be served best by a private or public warehouse? Why?
   a. Distributor of fine wines
   b. Small manufacturer of electric motors
   c. Large mail-order clothes company
   d. Large retail chain
6. Your firm's head office is in Portland, Oregon, and you've recently merged with a firm based in Montreal. Each firm has its own distribution center, but the combined firm clearly needs only one distribution center. What are the variables to examine when you decide which center you'll keep and which one you'll sell?
7. If you were in charge of a railroad, what could you do to be more competitive with trucking?
8. Assume United Airlines has decided to compete with Federal Express in the express package business; what are some of the obstacles United might encounter trying to get into this business?
9. What is the best mode of transportation for each of the following under the circumstances indicated?
   a. Crude oil being moved from wells in Alaska's North Slope to refineries in Anacortes, Washington
   b. Fresh seafood being moved from fishing towns along the Alaskan coast to restaurants in the Midwest
   c. Coal being moved from mines in West Virginia to power plants in the Ohio River valley
   d. Nakamichi stereo equipment being moved from factories in Japan to dealers in Europe
   e. Dreyer's ice cream being moved from production facilities to grocery stores
   f. Replacement parts being moved from the manufacturer to individual hospitals for intensive-care patient monitoring systems
10. What are some of the physical distribution problems you would face trying to import aboriginal artwork and handcrafts from the Australian outback?

# SHARPEN YOUR MARKETING SKILLS

You're part of the management team at Williams-Sonoma, a specialty retailer of housewares based in San Francisco. The mail-order part of your business is plagued by the WISMO monster. WISMO stands for "Where is my order?" You've been getting far too many WISMO calls lately. Customers are upset because their orders arrive late or not at all, and sometimes customers don't receive the right products.

**Decision:** You know that it's important for information to flow back and forth between all the departments involved in the marketing process, including forecasting, promotion, accounting, and shipping. Identify the general types of information that you think a company such as Williams-Sonoma would need in order to distribute products to consumers.

**Communication:** Sketch a diagram that shows the necessary information flow between your various departments and label the type of information that each department needs to receive.

# KEEPING CURRENT IN MARKETING

Select articles that describe in some detail the role of one mode of transportation. You may concentrate further by selecting one carrier company if you like.

1. What criteria favor using this transportation mode or carrier over its competitors? In what way is the mode or carrier unique among its peers?
2. What aspects of the mode or carrier limit its attractiveness? Are these limitations inherent? Do they apply to all goods likely to need transportation services?
3. Comment on the future (next 5 to 10 years) for this mode or carrier. Which trends are in its favor? Which are likely to have an adverse impact? Would you buy stock in companies offering the mode of transportation you've reviewed?

# At Home Depot, Low Prices Don't Compromise Customer Service

"I never had such a positive service experience in my life." Did this person just come from a high-class fashion boutique? A jewelry store that caters to wealthy clientele? One of those $50,000 luxury ocean cruises? No, the customer in question is talking about Home Depot, which specializes in the very down-to-earth business of selling building supplies and materials to consumers who want to fix up their homes. Home Depot is no high-priced supplier, either; it consistently beats other retailers on price, too.

How does Home Depot manage to pull off the impossible, offering both great service and low prices? These two aspects of the chain are part of an integrated strategy that includes carefully chosen locations, customer-focused product assortment, thorough employee training and motivation, and an emphasis on efficiency and cost control.

## Location, Location, Location

Location, of course, is as important to Home Depot as it is to any other retailer. A major market for home-improvement products consists of people who own older homes. Not only do houses typically need more repairs as they age, but their owners often like to replace outdated styles and features with the latest products. For instance, it's not unusual to see a 25- or 50-year-old house with ultramodern kitchen and bathrooms, the latest in home furnishings, and all the trimmings from intercoms to home security systems.

Looking at the United States, Home Depot founders Bernard Marcus and Arthur Blank realized that homes in the Northeast tend to be older than homes in other parts of the country. Knowing that those people would eventually need everything from new paint to new plumbing, Marcus and Blank began by concentrating stores in that area. Concentration is a key word here because isolated stores are more expensive to supply and promote than clusters of stores in a single city or region. If you put a store in Atlanta, another in Ft. Lauderdale, and a third in Nashville, you'd have to run three ad campaigns in local newspapers, for instance. Put all three of them in one city, and you cut your costs significantly.

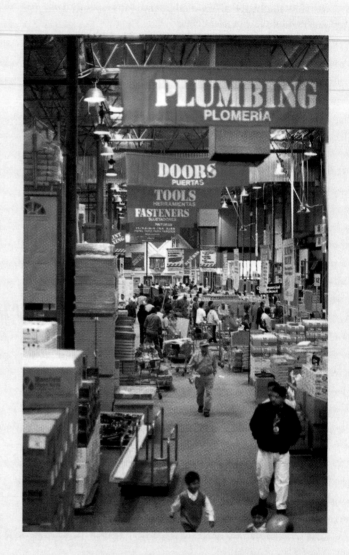

## More of What Customers Look For

Product assortment is one of the key decisions that store managers need to make at Home Depot. Lora Castellanos, the manager in charge of vendor relations, explains that the company wants to focus on product categories where it can dominate in terms of selection. This aspect is crucial in the home-improvement business, where people often shop just looking for ideas and where nobody wants to be locked into a narrow set of choices.

Product categories where Home Depot has expanded its offerings in recent years include kitchen cabinets, bathroom fixtures, and millwork (decorative wood parts used in stair railings, fireplace mantels, and around floors and ceilings). One of the latest expansions is in the garden center arena. Home Depot knows that customers want to have a lot of choice when they are trying to personalize their homes inside and out. Going to a store that offers a huge selection greatly decreases a customer's chances of ending up with an interior or landscaping that looks like everyone else's in the neighborhood.

For all the strategic sophistication, people helping people is one of the keys to Home Depot's success. If you've ever taken on (or watched someone else take on) a major home-repair project, you know how complicated these jobs can be. Home Depot helps these customers by hiring expert, service-oriented employees, then training them extensively (on products and new techniques) and motivating them with stock options and other rewards. Many Home Depot employees worked as plumbers, carpenters, or electricians before they joined the company, so they know how to help homeowners who are trying projects for the first time. With expertise like this on hand, Home Depot has an enormous edge over home centers that employ clerks with no industry background.

## Cost Controls with Generous Compensation

The final element in Home Depot's successful retailing strategy is cost control. The stores themselves look like giant warehouses, both because this sparse decor cuts construction and operating costs and because they in fact function as warehouses, at least to a degree. If Home Depot can store

1,000 light bulbs right on the shelf, it doesn't have to build warehouse space to hold 900 of the bulbs while 100 sit on the retail shelf. Another big cost advantage is Home Depot's ability to buy in much larger quantities than most of its competitors can afford.

This focus on cost control doesn't mean that Home Depot scrimps on salaries, however. Quite the contrary, it pays better than average, on the theory that motivated, satisfied employees will lead to satisfied customers who'll come back for more.

This multipronged strategy puts Home Depot in an enviable position. It can compete with anybody on price, but it doesn't cut corners on service or customer satisfaction. When you can get a competitive price *and* outstanding service and advice from experts, why would you even think about shopping anywhere else?

## Questions

1. What is Home Depot's target market? Think of as many dimensions as you can. Who would be some consumers who aren't in the company target market? How could Home Depot reach its target market with advertising messages?

2. Should Home Depot ignore fast-growing areas of the country where a higher percentage of the houses are new and thus in less need of repair and improvement? Take areas such as the north and east sides of Seattle, where new houses have been built by the thousands in recent years. Would this be a good market for Home Depot? Why or why not?

3. Does Home Depot have an ethical obligation to make sure its customers are successful with the tools and materials they buy? Explain your answer.

4. What are several key market issues Home Depot should research before attempting to build stores in another country?

512

# PART VI
# PROMOTION STRATEGY

# 17

# Promotional Strategies and Processes

**After studying this chapter, you will be able to**

**1.** Explain the role promotion plays in the marketing mix

**2.** Identify the major elements of promotion

**3.** Track a message through the communication process model and identify ways in which communication can break down

**4.** Explain how marketing communication is used to move customers from awareness to purchase to satisfaction

**5.** Define sales objectives and communications objectives and explain why not all promotional efforts can have measurable sales objectives

**6.** List the parameters you need to know about a target audience before designing effective communication programs

**7.** Discuss the relationship between promotion and society, including the criticisms and defenses of promotion

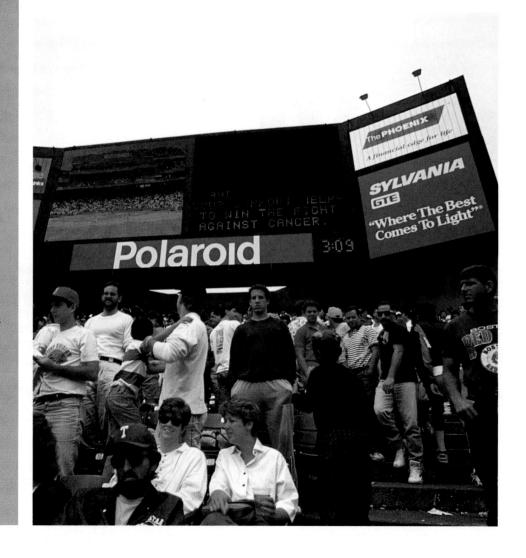

## Driving into a New Chapter in Automotive History

The challenge facing Donald Hudler must rank near the top of the difficulty scale. As vice president of sales, service, and marketing at Saturn, Hudler joined a team of like-minded innovators in what must have seemed to many observers an impossible task: starting a new U.S. car company that could compete successfully with foreign companies. Saturn's parent, General Motors, had lost enormous chunks of the market to Honda, Toyota, and other foreign companies whose import models were considered by many consumers to be better built and more reliable than U.S. cars. Many younger buyers had sworn off U.S. cars entirely.

It hadn't always been that way. In 1965 every second car in the United States was a Chevrolet, a Buick, or one of GM's other brands. At one point, in fact, some suspected the company of intentionally holding down its sales so that it wouldn't catch the eye of governmental antitrust regulators. However, in the last few years, no one has thought of GM as a monopoly; the company has laid off tens of thousands of employees, shut numerous plants, and racked up billions of dollars in losses. GM closed out 1992 with the dubious honor of announcing the largest loss ever experienced by a U.S. corporation: $23.5 billion in the red. That year saw another milestone as well. The import companies' combined share rose to the same level that GM's share had fallen

to; each side finished the year with 35 percent of the market.

GM leaders tried a number of ways to get the magic back, including a massive investment in a new product line and automated factories to produce it. However, the automation and most of the other attempts proved disappointing. The most intriguing effort was the launching of an entirely new car company, one that would be free from the old ways of doing business. Saturn is much more than a new brand name; it's a new way of approaching the automotive business. Consequently, Hudler knew that Saturn needed a new way to approach marketing and advertising as well.

Hudler and his Saturn colleagues were entering a crowded market of more than 40 brands. Although they had several billion dollars in financial backing from GM, they faced a mammoth task: build a better car and then rebuild relationships with the driving public. If you were in Donald Hudler's position at Saturn, what kind of marketing and advertising strategies would you forge? What role would advertising play in your efforts to position Saturn as a viable alternative to the imports? Would your advertising strategy focus on the car itself, the company, or some other element? How would you use advertising to communicate your positioning message and catch the attention of the driving public?[1]

# CHAPTER OVERVIEW

Donald Hudler and the rest of the people at Saturn are acutely aware of the need for promotion and the challenges and opportunities that this branch of marketing offers. This chapter starts by describing the role that promotion plays in the overall marketing effort, from providing information to influencing public behavior. After that, you'll explore the four promotional elements: advertising, sales promotion, public relations, and personal sales. Next, you'll get a look at the communication model that forms the basis for marketing promotions. Then you'll see how to develop a promotional mix, and you'll investigate elements of international, service, and nonprofit marketing. The chapter concludes with a look at the social and economic criticisms leveled at promotion, together with the marketing profession's responses.

# THE ROLE OF PROMOTION

Pretend for a moment that you are the only supplier of surfboards in the world and that every potential customer knows about you, believes in your products, knows where to find them, and is motivated to purchase. In this ideal world, you probably wouldn't need promotion. However, here in the real world, it's a different story. You have ferocious competitors. Many of your prospects have never heard of you or your surfboards. Some of the people who are aware of your products don't like them. Many potential customers don't know where to buy your boards, and others aren't motivated enough to turn off the TV and take up surfing. Now you need promotion (see Exhibit 17.1). Marketers use promotion for a number of reasons:

- *Providing information.* Both buyers and sellers benefit from the informational function that promotion is able to perform. Buyers find out about helpful new products, and sellers can inform prospective customers about goods and services.

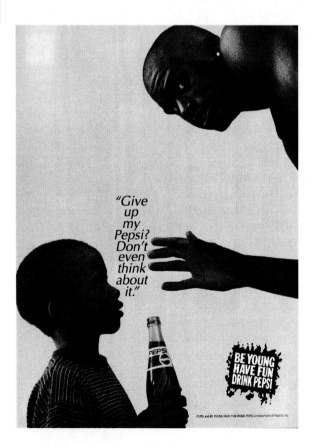

**Exhibit 17.1
PROMOTIONS IN A
CROWDED MARKET**
PepsiCo and Coca-Cola
engage in a multibillion-dollar
ad battle to snare customers
in the hotly competitive soda
market.

"Give up my Pepsi? Don't even think about it."

BE YOUNG HAVE FUN DRINK PEPSI

Clearly, a fine line exists between informing and persuading; education is often used to persuade, but providing information remains an important part of many promotional efforts. For instance, when Chevrolet introduced its new Geo line of imported cars, one of the ads it used emphasized information, telling potential buyers about the cars' vibration-tuned suspension and direct-acting valve train.[2] This approach differs from an ad that shows a car speeding over a mountain road, for instance.

- *Stimulating demand.* One of the most obvious and direct purposes of promotion is to stimulate demand. Marketers want you to buy their bikes or cars or candy bars, and they use promotion to inspire you to such action. You're familiar with demand-stimulation advertising by the big consumer products companies such as Procter & Gamble, McDonald's, Sears, and Reebok, but creative promotion is used all the time by companies you're not likely to run into every day. For instance, Medical SafeTec was frustrated because it couldn't motivate health officials to buy its waste-treatment equipment, which grinds used syringes, gloves, and other medical trash into a plastic confetti. Therefore, the company sent bags of actual treated waste to target customers to show just how effective the equipment can be. As a result, a number of prospects did take action, and Medical SafeTec soon found itself negotiating sales with people who wouldn't even pay attention before the promotion.[3]

- *Differentiating products.* Many organizations try to differentiate themselves and their products through the use of promotions. This is particularly important for products that aren't inherently much different from their competitors. For example, what makes a Sunkist orange different from an ordinary orange? A catchy name and a strong promotional program, that's what. An advertising agency working for the California Fruit Growers Exchange in 1908 came up with the name "Sunkissed," which was soon shortened to its current spelling. By using the Sunkist name in national promotional campaigns, the company took something that grows on trees and turned it into a clearly identifiable national brand that stands apart from all its competitors.[4]

- *Reminding current customers.* Even your existing customers are a good audience for promotional messages. Remind customers of your product's benefits to keep them from switching to competitors when they decide to replace or upgrade.

- *Countering competitors.* Promotions can also be used to counter the marketing efforts of a competitor. For instance, PepsiCo and Coca-Cola have been locked in a competitive promotional battle for years. They run taste tests, ads based on taste tests, and ads that refute each other's taste tests. All these promotional efforts are designed to counter each other's advertising campaigns.

- *Responding to negative news.* Sometimes the competition isn't another company selling similar products. When PepsiCo began to hear reports of syringes and other dangerous objects in cans of Diet Pepsi during the summer of 1993, the company first determined that it was virtually impossible for the syringes to get into the cans in its bottling facilities or for outsiders to tamper with the cans in the store. It then worked with the Food and Drug Administration to follow up on reports that the syringe stories may have in fact been hoaxes. After taking these actions, PepsiCo president Craig Weatherup took to the airwaves on news programs and talk shows to explain the investigations that the company had conducted. PepsiCo integrated this effort with advertising in major newspapers after the investigations, explaining that the company had been the victim of publicity and litigation seekers who had faked their claims.[5]

- *Smoothing demand fluctuations.* Many companies face the challenge of seasonal demand, in which customers buy more during some parts of the year and less during others. For example, the Whistler ski resort in British Columbia can't offer much skiing in the summer, but that doesn't mean the facilities have to sit idle. Whistler uses promotion to tell people about hiking, tennis, horseback riding, and a variety of other fair-weather activities, which helps fill in the "demand gap" during the summer.

**THERE'S ONE
LIFE-SAVING TECHNIQUE
ANYONE CAN PERFORM.**

9 1 1

Help isn't on the way unless
someone calls. So please
teach your child what to do
in case of an emergency.
How to dial 9-1-1. How to give
his or her name, address and
telephone number. And most
importantly, not to hang up.
And please, practice with
the entire family. Because
it's never too soon to start.

To learn more about life-saving techniques,
including those that children can do, call your Red Cross.

American
Red Cross

**Exhibit 17.2
INFLUENCING PUBLIC
BEHAVIOR**
In a compelling example of
the need to influence public
behavior, the American Red
Cross encourages people to
teach children how to dial for
emergency help.

- *Persuading decision makers.* Ever pick up a copy of *The New Republic, Atlantic Monthly,* or similar issues-oriented magazines and see an ad for missile guidance systems or bombers? If so, you probably realized that you're not the target audience for these ads; rather, the advertisers are trying to persuade members of Congress to fund, or continue funding, the projects pictured in the ads. In other cases, the promotion is indirect. For instance, American International Group, a large commercial insurance firm, ran a two-page ad explaining the Earthquake Project. The goal of the project was legislation that would establish a federal earthquake insurance program, but the general public was the primary audience. AIG ended the ad by asking readers to "let your elected officials know what you think of this proposal."[6] This sort of promotion isn't confined to governmental issues. For instance, promotions of some kind are required to get retailers to carry your surfboards before you can start worrying about promotions to final customers. Also, companies frequently use promotions to send messages to stockholders, stock analysts, credit rating services, and others whose decisions can affect the company.
- *Influencing public behavior.* Finally, promotion is used to influence public behavior. Smokey the Bear asks you not to start forest fires. The Partnership for a Drug-Free America begs you to stay away from crack. The U.S. Postal Service would appreciate it if you'd use ZIP codes. These nonprofit organizations have clear goals about the way they would like you to behave, and many nonprofit groups are becoming experts at the art and science of promotion (see Exhibit 17.2).

Actually, the ultimate goal of all promotion is to influence behavior. The plea may not be direct, and the desired action isn't necessarily immediate, but the reason marketers spend time and money on promotion is to get certain people to behave in a certain way. Even ads that appear to be doing nothing more than building an image for a company or educating consumers have the underlying objective of motivating certain actions: buying Wrigley's chewing gum, being more careful with hazardous chemicals, or giving money to build shelters for the homeless. Convincing people to believe something or think a certain way is nice, but until they change their behavior, marketers haven't really accomplished anything.

The techniques of promotion are diverse. Skywriting, lobbying a U.S. senator, painting your name on the side of an ice cream truck, and running a million-dollar TV commercial during the World Cup soccer finals are all examples of promotion. As discussed in Chapter 8, product packaging serves as an important form of promotion, particularly for goods that sit on store shelves. Marketers divide their promotional possibilities into four categories: advertising, sales promotion, public relations, and personal selling.

When you combine two or more promotional elements to pursue a marketing objective, you've created a **promotional mix.** Every industry and every company chooses a unique promotional mix, depending on its objectives, capabilities, and markets. For example, over a billion dollars a year is spent promoting movies, and marketing costs typically equal 25 percent or more of a film's entire production costs. Television advertising eats up the biggest chunk of movie promo budgets, roughly 60 percent. Print ads, particularly in newspaper movie sections, are another important vehicle. Previews, a form of in-theater commercial, are used frequently to "tease" the audience and get them thinking about the upcoming film. Tie-ins and merchandising deals are also important; these are typically done after most of the rest of the promotional money has been spent. They are, of course, significant income generators themselves. Screenings are also vital, particularly with films that don't have immediate popular appeal; reviewers and other opinion leaders can help build awareness and interest. Finally, publicity is as crucial as every other aspect of the mix. For instance, publicists work with the media to get articles written and television pieces filmed about the stars and the movie. Then word-of-mouth advertising takes over, which can make or break a film (and many other products). A final note: The promotional mix often lasts only through the first weekend or two; if the film isn't a hit by then, the marketers often pull the proverbial plug.[7]

All marketers, regardless of the products involved, should develop promotional mixes that allow them to reach target customers in the most effective manner. For example, movie marketers view college students as a key audience and are always searching for new and better ways to reach you and your classmates. Spring break has emerged as one of the best opportunities for movie studios (and a wide variety of other marketers). When you see contests, parties, concerts, dances, and other activities at such favored spring break destinations as Daytona Beach (Florida), Palm Springs (California), and South Padre (Texas), you can be sure that a consumer marketer had a hand in it somehow. For instance, the rock-climbing contests on several beaches in spring 1993 (using an artificial cliff) were sponsored by TriStar Pictures to promote the thriller *Cliffhanger.*[8]

**promotional mix**
A combination of two or more elements of advertising, sales promotion, public relations, and personal selling

## Advertising

Perhaps the most obvious form of promotion, **advertising** is defined as paid, nonpersonal communication with a target market. As you know, advertising shows up on television and radio, in newspapers and magazines, and on T-shirts, race cars, and dozens of other places. People in the United States (and to a growing extent in other countries as well) are subjected to a constant barrage of advertising.[9] You can reach two conclusions based on this. First, businesses must see some benefit in advertising, or they wouldn't do so much of it; and second, any advertising you do is going to compete with hundreds and thousands of messages all vying for the attention of the people you're trying to reach.[10]

Advertising offers some significant advantages over other promotional techniques. The first of these is cost. Some people are shocked when they hear about television commercials that cost thousands of dollars per second, but consider how many viewers these ads reach. For example, if Burger King spends $150,000 for a commercial during a hit prime-time sitcom and reaches 25 million viewers, it is paying just over half a penny to reach each viewer. Contrast this with the most expensive promotional element, personal sales, in which one sales call can cost several

**advertising**
Paid, nonpersonal communication with a target market; advertising media include television, radio, newspapers, magazines, billboards, and direct mail

## SO MANY WAYS TO SPEND MONEY: BALANCING THE PROMOTIONAL MIX

Marketers have developed several techniques for determining how they should assemble and maintain their promotional mixes. Three common techniques are the lead element approach, the hierarchy of effects approach, and the planning sequence approach. Here's a closer look at all three. Keep in mind that companies frequently use a combination of two or even all three approaches.

With the lead element approach, you designate one of the four elements as your main promotional emphasis. You then use the other three to support the lead element. In most cases, either personal selling or

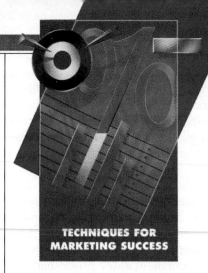

**TECHNIQUES FOR MARKETING SUCCESS**

advertising is the lead element, although some consumer-products marketers rely heavily on sales promotion. In all cases, use public relations to support the lead element.

An important decision with the lead element technique is how you use the supporting elements. For ex-

ample, Northwestern Mutual Life Insurance, which used the lead element approach with personal selling in the lead role, once dropped all its advertising because it could find no correlation between advertising and sales. When the company decided to start advertising once again, it did so with clear objectives for the advertising program: Make customers and agents feel better about being associated with Northwestern and make prospective customers more receptive to personal selling efforts. With this objective as a guide, the advertising became an effective support for the lead element.

The second balancing technique is based on the hierarchy of effects model. With this approach, you assemble a promotional mix targeted at a specific group of prospects who are

hundred dollars in some industries. Advertising's second advantage is ease of repetition, which is often needed to effectively get a message across. You'd get tossed out the door if you called on a customer every day for a week, but you can put your message in a newspaper ad every morning and reach that same customer. Third, advertising seems to be able to get away with a higher level of creative flexibility than other promotional elements. You could use a comedian to speak for your products in a radio commercial, but you might not want to bring that same comedian along on a sales call. Fourth, advertising's impersonal nature can be a big plus if you're marketing sensitive merchandise, such as personal hygiene products. And fifth, many consumers assign some level of prestige to the mass media used in advertising. The simple fact that a product is advertised nationally can add to its image.[11]

Advertising's advantages are balanced with several drawbacks. Ironically, cost is also one of advertising's biggest disadvantages. The fact that Burger King has to spend only half a cent to reach a TV viewer is great, but if the company doesn't have enough money to get on TV in the first place, it's not going to reach anybody. Television has the highest up-front costs of all advertising media, and none of them is particularly cheap. Second, advertising can't provide direct feedback. If your newspaper ad confuses people, you may never get the chance to explain yourself. Third, advertising is difficult to personalize. A salesperson can get to know the likes and dislikes of every customer and prepare individualized presentations, but that is nearly impossible with advertising. Finally, advertising can't always motivate customers to action as effectively as personal selling can.

## Sales Promotion

**sales promotion**
Techniques that are used to stimulate product demand, including special events and activities such as coupons, celebrity appearances, and contests

**Sales promotion** encompasses a variety of promotional activities and events, including coupons, sweepstakes, contests, frequent-flyer programs, sales events, and rebates. Some common goals of sales promotion are convincing people to try new products, encouraging current customers to use a given product more frequently, and moving potential buyers from interest to action. Sales promotion expenditures at a specific stage in the buying process. For instance, a maker of professional woodworking tools could target amateur woodworkers who aren't yet aware of the company's offerings. In this case, the company would design a promotional mix to increase awareness in the target segment. The most efficient methods for doing this are generally mass communication through advertising and public relations. As the segment becomes aware of the company's products, the company could then shift its promotional mix to personal selling and sales promotions to help build preference.

The third method of defining a promotional mix, the planning sequence approach, establishes a plan for addressing each element of the mix in turn. You start with the element that needs the most attention. For instance, your research might indicate that your salespeople aren't as effective as the salespeople in competing companies, and you decide that this is your biggest promotional problem. When using the planning sequence approach, fixing the sales problem would become top priority.

Tayprint used the planning sequence approach when it set out to reverse a decline in market share. The company, which makes tape guns for printed customized labels, figured that poor in-store visibility was its biggest problem. Therefore, the first step was to redesign the package to promote the product more effectively while it was sitting on store shelves. Then Tayprint realized it needed to boost its sales force to make sure retailers kept the tape guns on display year round. Increasing the size of the sales force became the second step in the improvement program. The third step was a series of sales promotions designed to capitalize on the new packaging and larger sales force. Tayprint's carefully planned promotional strategy worked extremely well. Not only did it stop the market share decline, but it raised sales volume 25 percent the first year and 38 percent the second year.

## APPLY YOUR KNOWLEDGE

**1.** What should Tayprint do when it decides that it has fixed all the weak areas in its promotional mix?
**2.** What are some of the difficulties you might face when trying to balance a promotional mix using the hierarchy of effects approach?

---

in the United States now exceed those for advertising.[12] (Not everyone in the marketing world agrees with the numbers in this comparison, however. The sales promotion figure includes $30 billion spent on meetings and conventions, which aren't included in everyone's definition of sales promotion.)[13]

To hang onto the teenage and young adult segment of the television market, MTV runs some rather unusual sales promotions. How about the "I Hate My Miserable Life" contest, in which the winner got a one-way plane ticket to anywhere in the United States and MTV's help in finding a new job and a new place to live? How about the contests that gave away Jon Bon Jovi's boyhood home and a "town" outside Amarillo, Texas? (The town was actually 100 empty acres upon which MTV promised to put a house for the winner.) These contests catch viewers' attention: The Bon Jovi contest prompted 2.5 million phone calls. However, marketers are trying to do more than catch your attention. MTV allows major advertisers to associate with these high-image contests; MTV benefits by building a loyal market of advertising clients, while the advertisers get their names associated with one of the hottest forces in the entertainment industry.[14]

One of the biggest advantages of sales promotions is the ability to generate lots of interest and excitement (see Exhibit 17.3). Because they are by definition something out of the ordinary, sales promotions have the potential to catch the public's attention. For instance, to expand their presence in the Hispanic market, food and household products suppliers such as Continental Baking and Procter & Gamble cooperate with retailers to stage large in-store food festivals.[15] Sales promotion can also build awareness and interest faster than advertising can, and it allows more precise timing than other promotional elements. Some companies even keep special promotional programs ready in case of unexpected sales declines or the introduction of new products from competitors. Finally, sales promotions can be a very effective way to get messages to potential customers when other promotional avenues are cluttered or inaccessible. A common, but controversial, example of this is the sponsorship of sporting events by tobacco companies. These firms are no longer allowed to advertise on television, so they've chosen sporting events as a vehicle to reach young adult audiences.[16] Technology, in the form of checkout scan-

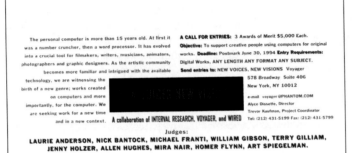

DO NOT ENTER THIS CONTEST IF YOU WANT
HOME SHOPPING, ENCYCLOPEDIAS, AND VIDEO
GAMES TO DEFINE THE INFORMATION
SUPERHIGHWAY.

The personal computer is more than 15 years old. At first it was a number cruncher, then a word processor. It has evolved into a crucial tool for filmakers, writers, musicians, animators, photographers and graphic designers. As the artistic community becomes more familiar and intrigued with the available technology, we are witnessing the birth of a new genre; works created on computers and more importantly, for the computer. We are seeking work for a new time and in a new context.

A CALL FOR ENTRIES: 3 Awards of Merit $5,000 Each.
**Objective:** To support creative people using computers for original works. **Deadline:** Postmark June 30, 1994 **Entry Requirements:** Digital Works, ANY LENGTH ANY FORMAT ANY SUBJECT.
**Send entries to:** NEW VOICES, NEW VISIONS Voyager
578 Broadway Suite 406
New York, NY 10012
e-mail voyager @PHANTOM.COM
Alyce Dissette, Director
Trevor Kaufman, Project Coordinator
Tel: (212) 431-5199 Fax: (212) 431-5799

A collaboration of INTERVAL RESEARCH, VOYAGER, and WIRED

Judges:
LAURIE ANDERSON, NICK BANTOCK, MICHAEL FRANTI, WILLIAM GIBSON, TERRY GILLIAM, JENNY HOLZER, ALLEN HUGHES, MIRA NAIR, HOMER FLYNN, ART SPIEGELMAN.

**Exhibit 17.3
GENERATING
INTEREST AND
EXCITEMENT WITH
CREATIVE SALES
PROMOTIONS**
By co-sponsoring this contest, *Wired* magazine helps raise its awareness and image among people who are likely to subscribe.

ners, has given sales promotion an important boost. Marketers can now closely monitor the effects their sales promotions have on sales levels, giving them greater insight into which promotions work and which don't.

Probably the biggest drawback of sales promotion is its overuse in some industries. Consumers are so accustomed to seeing coupons and rebates for some products that many refuse to buy until the special offers are available. Also, some companies don't like to rely on sales promotion as the primary element in their promotional mixes because of its temporary nature. These companies believe that they need to use long-term advertising programs to keep their place in customers' minds.[17]

## Public Relations

**public relations (PR)**
Promotion that uses nonpaid communication to influence public opinion of a company and its products

Advertising, sales promotion, and personal selling are usually focused on explicit sales messages with an obvious sponsor. In contrast, **public relations (PR),** which is nonpaid communication, encompasses all the other communications that businesses and organizations have with their various audiences. Part of public relations is *corporate PR*; this covers nonsales-oriented topics such as responding to journalists' requests for information, lobbying government leaders, and helping local schools with educational projects. The other side of the public relations effort is **publicity,** also known as *marketing PR*, which seeks to generate significant news coverage about the company or its products and tries to encourage favorable reviews of products in both print (newspapers and magazines) and broadcast (radio and television) media.

**publicity**
News media coverage of a company or its products

A growing number of companies use public events and campaigns both to serve society and help bolster their own images. For instance, S. C. Johnson Wax, maker of Raid and Raid Max roach killer, induced 12,000 New York City residents to pitch in and clean up their neighborhoods. By teaming up with We Care About New York (a nonprofit group trying to motivate people to clean up their city) and the New York Department of Sanitation, the company identified the dirtiest districts in the city and had residents (wearing Raid T-shirts and hats, naturally) join in the Raid Big Block Cleanup. Participants were rewarded with cleaner neighborhoods and a chance at sweepstakes prizes offered by Raid.[18]

Public relations has two major advantages over the other promotional elements. The first is low cost, and in some cases, no cost. (Even though marketers don't pay for public relations directly, they often incur costs when visiting editors, staging public events, and so forth.) The second is the perception of objectivity, which increases the trust people have in the message. If Porsche runs an ad saying its new car is a pleasure to drive, people might respond with "Sure, what else would they say?" But if *Auto Week* reviews the car and its editors say the Porsche is a pleasure to drive, people might respond with "Hmmm, maybe that car is pretty nice."

The biggest disadvantages of public relations are lack of control and short life span. The lack of control can be a particularly nasty problem if a reporter or editor takes a strong dislike to your product and shares that viewpoint with thousands of readers. Just as the positive comments from the media carry a lot of weight with consumers, so do the negative reviews. Moreover, publicity can't be counted on for much more than a short burst of coverage during the introduction phase. Magazines and other media are in the business of selling news, and your six-month-old product is no longer news.

## Personal Selling

The first three promotional elements don't rely primarily on interpersonal contact, although both sales promotion and public relations often involve personal interaction. The fourth element, **personal selling,** is about interpersonal contact exclusively; it is one person making a sales presentation to another person or to a group of potential buyers. The audience for personal selling can be consumers, organizational customers, or marketing intermediaries.

**personal selling**
In-person communication between a seller and one or more potential buyers

Personal selling offers a number of advantages. First, as the only promotional technique that allows immediate, direct feedback, personal selling is about the only way to adapt a presentation to individual customers. This is particularly important when you're selling products that require customization or generate a lot of questions from customers. For example, when salespeople for Merck are presenting a new drug, they can answer doctors' questions about safety, effectiveness, and other factors. Second, it is extremely effective when customers need to see products in action; the salesperson can demonstrate how to use the product and point out its benefits. Third, personal selling is the only easy way to interview customers who are purchasing complex products to make sure you offer the right product or collection of products. Fourth, personal selling can be more effective at inducing people to make a purchase.

The biggest disadvantage of personal selling is cost; in some selling situations a single sales call can cost several hundred dollars. Even for in-store retail sales, staffing a store with salespeople is an expensive endeavor. Consistency can also be a problem with personal sales because you can't be sure that every salesperson will deliver the same message. Nor will each salesperson be consistent from day to day.[19]

## PROMOTION AND THE COMMUNICATION PROCESS

Promotion is first and foremost a process of communication. Whether the message is words or visual images, education or persuasion, what you're trying to do is communicate. To better understand how to do this effectively, look at how human beings communicate.

# How People Communicate

The process of getting an idea from one person's mind into another's is extremely complex. The sender may not verbalize the thought in exactly the same form as it was conceived, and the receiver might reach any of a number of conclusions depending on experience or mood or motivation. In between these two people, the message can be corrupted by "noise" and competing messages from other senders. Exhibit 17.4 is a model of the communication process that shows the elements of successful communication. The following briefly describes each element:[20]

- *Source.* Not surprisingly, the message has to originate somewhere, somehow. The **source** generates the idea to be transmitted and is responsible for encoding it as well. For instance, Saturn is the source of its advertising messages, although it gets help from advertising agencies during encoding.

- *Encoding.* Most of us lack the ability to transmit our thoughts directly to an audience. We have to first convert these thoughts into a form that we can transmit, a process known as **encoding.** Of course, the encoded form must be made up of words and images that both the source and the audience can understand. This mutual understanding will result from shared experience, for the audience will not be able to interpret the message correctly without some common base. At the most obvious level, this means that both the source and the audience must use the same alphabet, language, and so forth. At more subtle levels, encoding can often go awry. For example, you can't communicate effectively by using jokes or historical allusions that are based on experiences the audience doesn't have. Urging your audience to relax by having a yellow, spike-headed cartoon boy say "Don't have a cow, man!" will work if they have seen "The Simpsons," but it might sound pretty silly otherwise.

- *Message.* Once the idea has been encoded into a form acceptable for transmission, it is considered a **message.** Your message might be a particular image, such as a photograph of the product, or it might be a statement like "Buy this and you'll be happy." In many promotional contexts, the message is a combination of words and images.

- *Medium.* The message is carried to your audience by the **medium,** the mode of expression you choose. Typical promotional media include newspapers, magazines, radio, television, signs, packaging, and interpersonal communication. The medium can also be referred to as the *channel.*

- *Decoding.* When people in your audience attempt to extract the idea from your message, they are going through a process called **decoding,** which is the reverse of encoding. For instance, a person looking at a coffee advertisement in a magazine will process the words and the picture of that cup of dark, rich coffee by comparing it with prior experience on this topic. ("Let's see . . . I hate mornings, but I love the smell of fresh coffee; this stuff just might improve the quality of my life.") However, the entire process can fall apart at this stage; in one study of print communications, over 20 percent of the material was miscomprehended.[21] This

**source**
The person or organization that originates and encodes a message

**encoding**
The process of converting an idea into symbols (words and images) to make it compatible with transmission and decoding facilities

**message**
An idea that has been encoded and is capable of being transmitted

**medium**
The channel used to carry a message; this includes sales presentations, newspapers, radio, television, and direct-mail materials

**decoding**
The process an audience goes through to translate a message into an idea with personal meaning; reverse of encoding

**Exhibit 17.4
A MODEL OF THE COMMUNICATION PROCESS**
The communication process is complex and vulnerable to miscommunication at several points.

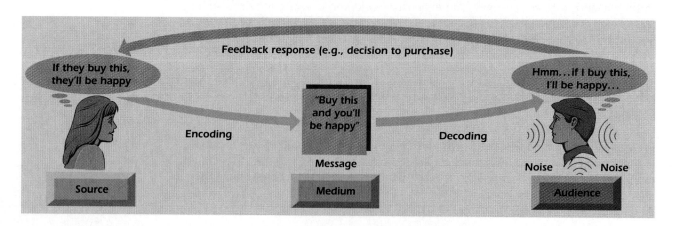

happens for several reasons: The thought wasn't encoded clearly, too much "noise" distorted the message, the medium was inappropriate, or the audience's experience didn't align with the source's. Decoding problems can be amusing—but costly—in international marketing. Chevrolet had sales trouble with its Nova in Spanish-speaking markets until it realized that *no va* is Spanish for "it doesn't go."[22]

- *Audience.* Whether you're sitting across a table from one person or beaming a satellite message to millions, your **audience,** the people receiving your marketing message, play a key role in communication. However, reaching your audience isn't quite that simple: Key tasks are identifying and analyzing members of your audience to find out what they think, feel, and believe.

- *Response and feedback.* After decoding your message, members of your audience will respond according to how well the message was communicated. In the ideal case, they'll interpret your message just as you intended and then take the action you'd like them to take, such as buying a particular product. However, if the message was irrelevant or confusing, they might just ignore you. In the worst possible scenario, your message might prompt them to do just the opposite of what you'd like them to, such as when a TV commercial annoys people so much that they resolve to buy from competitors. All these responses can be considered **feedback,** the response of audience members once they have received and decoded your message. Feedback is usually indirect in marketing situations; the exception is in personal selling, where the audience can respond immediately and directly to the seller.

- *Noise.* From the sender's perspective, anything that interferes with the successful transmission and decoding of the message is **noise.** This noise can be any kind of visual or audio clutter, such as a competitor's advertising or a baby crying during a TV commercial. Try to anticipate noise and find ways to avoid it or overcome it. Advertisers on television, for instance, do this literally by raising the volume during commercials. However, more sophisticated ways of doing this include the creative use of music, sound effects, color, or other elements of the particular medium.

**audience**
The person or persons who are receiving a transmitted message

**feedback**
Communication from the audience back to the source

**noise**
Anything that detracts from the effectiveness of communication, ranging from actual audio noise to competing advertisements

As you can see from this simple model, communication is a precarious process that can fail a lot more easily than it can succeed. Just think of all the times you've spoken face-to-face with a friend who didn't get your point. Now imagine that same problem when you're sending a message to a million people in a radio commercial; at least in face-to-face communication you can ask your audience whether your message got across. With the exception of personal selling, marketers don't have any immediate way of judging the effectiveness of their communication. Even in personal selling situations, only a skilled, experienced communicator can figure out whether the message is really getting across.

The process of communication becomes more complex when your promotions cross cultural or national borders. In addition to making sure that people in other cultures or countries understand an ad, successful marketers make sure those audiences find the style and content of the ad culturally acceptable. For example, a U.S. ad isn't likely to make jokes about death, disease, or drunkenness; any ad that did would offend large portions of the population. In Japan, however, subjects considered taboo in the United States are given humorous treatment in many ads. A good example is a television spot for Gon mothballs, which features an elderly grandfather who pretends he is dead so that he won't have to go shopping.[23]

Whether local or international, this discussion of communication assumes that the audience is paying attention. However, the communication process works only when the audience participates, and people typically ignore most of the promotional messages they are exposed to. If people switch channels when your TV commercial airs, or if they stare at your subway billboard without reading it, they're not participating. Breaking through the clutter in today's information-intensive markets has become a major challenge for most marketers. Doing so requires careful attention to all phases of the communication process.

# How Marketers Communicate

**marketing communications**
The specific use of communication applied to the problem of sending messages to a target market

In the context of marketing, the process of sending messages to your various audiences is called **marketing communications,** sometimes shortened to *marcom.* This starts with the communication fundamentals just described and adds several special topics: the process of moving customers from awareness of your products all the way through purchase to satisfaction, the distinction between mass and personal communications, and the difference between controlled and uncontrolled communication.

## FROM AWARENESS TO SATISFACTION

Successful marketing communicators are aware of a number of distinct phases in the process of communicating with customers. These phases give you insight into the prospect's state of mind as he or she moves toward a purchase.

- *Phase 1: Awareness.* The first step in communicating with a market is to make sure the market is aware of your products. People can't buy things they don't know about.
- *Phase 2: Comprehension.* Once the market is aware, make sure that potential customers understand what you're offering. This usually isn't much of a problem with peanut butter or roofing nails, but it can be a big challenge with computer-aided design software or genetically engineered medicines.
- *Phase 3: Acceptance.* After they understand your product, prospects decide whether or not they accept your product as a solution to their individual problems. Customers reject products for a variety of reasons, ranging from the logical ("this car doesn't have enough room for my family") to the emotional ("I'd feel silly in this car").
- *Phase 4: Preference.* At this stage, buyers consider the products they accept as potential solutions, and they choose a favorite. Be careful here; just because customers prefer your product doesn't mean you've got it made. For instance, what if they can't find it in the stores where they normally shop?
- *Phase 5: Ownership.* Now it's time to get them to reach for their wallets. This is a critical phase in the communication process: motivating buyers to take action. They can sit passively during the first four stages as you funnel them information, but now, if they don't participate, no sale will happen. Marketers pay a lot of attention to the part of an ad or sales presentation that tries to get customers to move. In fact, this section is known as the *call to action.*
- *Phase 6: Satisfaction.* At this point, promotion has done most of its job. However, it can still help you in an important way by increasing customer satisfaction and putting the buyer's mind to rest about making the purchase. One way promotion can do this is by providing useful information that helps customers use your product more effectively, for instance. Perhaps you can send a newsletter to all the people who purchased dogs from your pet store, explaining how to care for them, train them, and so on. Satisfied customers are more likely to buy from you again, and they are more likely to spread positive word-of-mouth advertising for you.

**hierarchy of effects model**
A model of sequential customer responses to promotions; one version of the model starts with awareness and continues with comprehension, acceptance, preference, ownership, and satisfaction

This process is sometimes called the **hierarchy of effects model** because it shows the progressive responses of an audience to your marketing communications.

Why is it important to split communications into so many stages? Consider the two hypothetical shoe brands represented in Exhibit 17.5. The curve for each brand shows where it stands in the market. Eighty percent of the market is aware of Fast Feet, 75 percent comprehend the brand, 50 percent accept it, and so on. You can see that Fast Feet drops off much faster than Super Hoof, which starts off at only 60 percent awareness but ends up with more market share. This graph shows you, among other things, that these two companies face different marketing problems. For example, Super Hoof is doing a good job of converting aware prospects into satisfied customers; it should concentrate on making more people aware. On the other

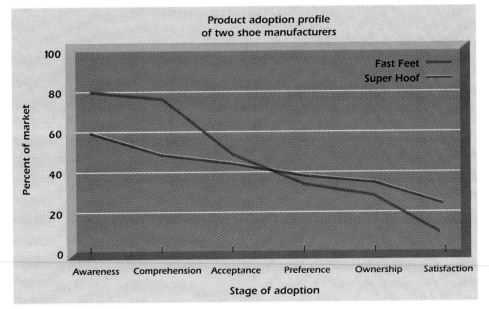

**Product adoption profile of two shoe manufacturers**

Fast Feet ———
Super Hoof ———

Percent of market: 100, 80, 60, 40, 20, 0

Stage of adoption: Awareness, Comprehension, Acceptance, Preference, Ownership, Satisfaction

**Exhibit 17.5
DIAGNOSING
MARKETING
COMMUNICATIONS
PROBLEMS**
These two hypothetical shoe companies face two very different marketing challenges: One aims to build awareness, and the other aims to improve its preference rating.

hand, Fast Feet commands high awareness, but things fall apart after that. A significant portion of the people who comprehend the brand don't accept it; this might be a product problem, a promotion problem, a price problem, or a combination of all three.

Another common communication model is the **AIDA model,** which covers the stages of attention, interest, desire, and action. These four stages describe the psychological progress a buyer must make in order to get to an actual purchase. AIDA is generally used to prepare in-person sales presentations, and as such, it assumes that customers will receive all their information from one source over a limited period of time. This is in contrast to the hierarchy of effects model, which assumes that customers get information from a variety of sources.[24]

Keep in mind that these models are just that, models. They are oversimplifications and generalizations of what happens in real life. Customers don't always buy the product that is objectively "best" for them, nor do they always follow a linear thought process from awareness to action. Much of the mental progress toward a purchase is subconscious; not many people say to themselves, "I'm now at the acceptance stage, so I'd better move ahead to the preference stage." Finally, the process doesn't always flow smoothly or in one direction; customers can be ready to buy one brand, only to become aware of another brand and start the decision-making process all over again. Despite these drawbacks, communication models are still necessary tools for marketers because they provide a framework for studying communication problems and designing effective solutions.

**AIDA model**
An acronym for awareness, interest, desire, and action, which represent the psychological steps a customer goes through on the way toward making a purchase

## INTERPERSONAL VERSUS MASS COMMUNICATION

Promotion involves two very different modes of communication: interpersonal and mass communication. Once you recognize the strengths and limitations of each mode, you can design messages and vehicles that are as effective as possible.

Interpersonal communication is better suited for nonstandard presentations that must be tailored for each audience and for presentations with a lot of technical information. Perhaps most important, interpersonal communication allows you to *listen* as well as talk; this is particularly important when you can't safely assume that you know the buyer's needs and expectations up front. On the minus side, interpersonal communication tends to be expensive and takes a long time to reach a wide audience. Also, it is often poorly suited for sensitive information, such as the promotion of certain health-care products or other goods and services that potential buyers would rather not discuss with anyone else.

On the other hand, mass communication is most effective with simpler messages that must reach a wide audience. Because it reaches multiple listeners, viewers, or readers simultaneously, it is a much faster way to reach a large audience. Another big advantage is consistency; your ads will say the same thing every time, but you can't assume the same about personal sales or most public relations efforts. Of course, mass communication suffers from several drawbacks as well. First, it is essentially passive; it can't be aggressive in the same way that personal selling or some sales promotion events can be. Second, mass communication doesn't offer any mechanism for direct or immediate feedback. You're more likely to get negative feedback when it's too late, in terms of lost sales opportunities. And third, it's impossible to adapt mass communication to the needs and expectations of individual consumers.

## CONTROLLED VERSUS UNCONTROLLED COMMUNICATION

The preceding discussion of promotional elements assumed that you're in control of the communication process. However, you can't control all the messages about your company and its products that reach your customers and prospects. Uncontrolled communication from several sources affects the way people feel about you and your products:

- *The media.* A negative story in *Consumer Reports* or the nightly news can undo a lot of promotional progress you may have made. Sources such as these are viewed as objective, so many customers put substantial faith in what these observers have to say. Even if charges turn out to be baseless, as in PepsiCo's case, the damage can be severe. On the positive side, a good review by someone in the news media can give your sales a tremendous boost. This can be especially beneficial to small companies with strong, innovative products and limited promotional budgets.
- *Other customers.* Word-of-mouth advertising is some of the most powerful promotion your products will ever receive; in some cases it is *the* most powerful. It is so powerful, in fact, that some companies rely on word of mouth as their primary promotional vehicle. (See the video case on Smartfoods at the end of this chapter for a detailed example.) Like media attention, word of mouth can help you or hurt you. For example, General Electric estimates that word of mouth from customers is twice as effective at influencing repurchase intent as the company's

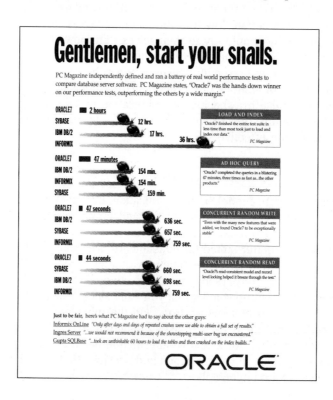

**Exhibit 17.6**
**TAKING ON THE COMPETITION**
Oracle doesn't pull any punches in this competitive ad for computer software.

advertising.[25] Clearly, the best way to ensure the transmission of good news to your future customers is to make sure you keep your current customers happy. Chapter 21 provides a closer look at the word-of-mouth phenomenon and its impact on a company's marketing efforts.

- *Competitors.* Competitors send messages to your current and potential customers through both personal selling and mass communication. An increasing amount of advertising in the United States features direct product comparisons (see Exhibit 17.6), although this type of advertising is closely regulated in some countries and banned in others.[26]

You can see that promotion is a challenging part of the marketing mix. You have lots of ways to reach prospects, but the challenge is to reach them in the presence of your competitors and various other external influences. Developing the optimum blend of advertising, personal selling, public relations, and sales promotion is definitely a balancing act, and that takes planning.

# THE PROMOTIONAL MIX

Developing an effective promotional mix can be one of the more interesting and creative challenges you'll face as a marketer. In the old days of mass-marketed national brands, designing good advertising and buying time on the three networks were fairly simple tasks. However, promotion is more complicated today. Audiences are diverse and fragmented; competitors from across the street and around the world are chasing after your customers; and from blimps to multimedia computers, you have many more promotional vehicles to choose from.

## The Six Steps in Developing a Promotional Mix

The planning and execution of a promotional mix can be divided into six steps: (1) understand your target audience, (2) understand how customers perceive your product, (3) understand the influence of competitors, (4) establish promotional objectives, (5) identify your resources, and (6) create an optimal mix. (Evaluating the effectiveness of promotional efforts is also an important task; this is addressed for each of the four elements in Chapters 18 and 19.)

### STEP 1: UNDERSTAND YOUR TARGET AUDIENCE

Like just about everything else in marketing, planning a promotional mix starts with understanding your market. Customer identification and segmentation are discussed fully in Chapter 7, but several aspects warrant a closer look when you're planning promotions:

- *Geographic distribution.* The location and concentration of your target audience play a major role in the selection of promotional vehicles. If you're trying to sell electric generators to geologists living on Alaska's North Slope, a nationwide television campaign is obviously the wrong answer. Find a way to reach the right customers in the most cost-effective manner.
- *Demographics.* The demographic description of your target customers also influences your choice of promotional vehicles. You can't always reach 10-year-olds with the same medium you'd use to reach senior citizens, nor are you likely to reach physicians through a construction equipment magazine. Of course, demographic insights are important for developing your promotional message as well. For example, you wouldn't promote personal computers to programmers in the same way you promote them to office managers.
- *Customer type.* Whether you're trying to reach consumers, organizational customers, or a balance of both affects promotional choices. Consumers and orga-

nizational customers often look for information in different places, and they're even likely to approach the purchase of identical products in different ways.

- *Needs and expectations.* Identifying potential purchasers by geography, demographics, and customer type is half the answer. The other half is trying to understand their needs and expectations. This is important for two reasons. First, make sure that you're offering the right products to the right people. Second, be sure that you're transmitting the right message. Your chances of success are much better if you understand your audience's lifestyles, personalities, and product use habits. When Columbia Pictures realized it had a hit on its hands with Bill Murray's 1993 *Groundhog Day*, the studio's next question was how to expand beyond the frequent moviegoers. Comedies usually don't fare well with infrequent moviegoers, since they rely on word of mouth among teens and movie buffs. To reach the stay-at-homes, Columbia quickly promoted the film in newspaper ads and scheduled Murray to host "Saturday Night Live." The result was an even bigger hit for a movie that might have slipped out of sight soon after opening.[27]

Another key aspect of understanding customers is to identify their purchase behavior, particularly with respect to the ways they collect and use information. Your promotions should track the six customer phases as closely as possible. To build customer awareness of your offering, advertising is usually a good bet because you want to reach a large audience; personal selling, on the other hand, is probably too slow and too expensive in most cases. Public relations can be crucial at this stage also; mentions in the media can build awareness rapidly. You may have opportunities for sales promotion as well, including trade shows and in-store exhibits.

For some products, you can use the same mix to build comprehension as you used for awareness. However, complicated or substantially new products may require a good deal more information or even some hands-on experience before customers are comfortable with them. This might dictate a shift from advertising to personal selling efforts that involve product demonstrations and in-depth presentations, for instance. Public relations, particularly media coverage of your products, will start to drop in importance if your product is no longer new, mostly because the media aren't terribly interested in covering products that have been on the market for any length of time.

At the acceptance and preference stages, customers' prior experience with the product continues to grow in importance. If customers aren't able to try the product (such as test-driving a new car), your advertising and other promotions will help them vicariously experience ownership as much as possible. One way you can do this is with testimonials, in which satisfied customers do the talking for you. Potential customers will listen to the satisfied customers and (you hope) say to themselves, "Well, it worked for that person, maybe it will work for me, too."

At the critical stage of making the purchase, the importance of all the promotional elements tends to drop. In most cases, it comes down to the customer and the product; only the customer can make the decision to buy. However, in those situations where personal selling was important to begin with, it remains important all the way through the purchase decision, with the salesperson continuing to offer selection advice and other information. In retail environments, sales promotions can still be of some importance, especially if the customer is relying on in-store displays for product information. Both advertising and public relations are substantially less important at this stage.

Once you've made the sale, you may feel like celebrating, but you can't relax yet. Remember that one of the primary uses of promotion is to build customer satisfaction after the purchase. Advertising after the sale can change to product usage information, reassurance, and reminders intended to build repeat purchases. Public relations is seldom important here, except in those instances where uncontrolled negative communication affects customers' perception of the products they've purchased. Sales promotion can be used to foster repeat buys. Personal selling efforts actually increase in some situations, particularly with technical products that require a great deal of installation, training, programming, or other support activities. In other cases, salespeople provide usage information on a more limited basis.[28]

Don't forget about the product itself, which plays an important role throughout this process. In general, as the customer moves closer to purchase, the attributes of the product grow in importance and become critical at the satisfaction stage. Promotion won't (and shouldn't) bring the customer through the purchase process if the product doesn't fit. Selling somebody a product that doesn't have the right features is a great way to ensure dissatisfaction and no repeat purchases.

## STEP 2: UNDERSTAND HOW CUSTOMERS PERCEIVE YOUR PRODUCTS

The attributes of the product you are trying to market also affect promotional decisions. For instance, technically complex products and simple products are promoted differently. Also, shopping products and convenience products require different sales approaches. When considering a product's attributes, the perception that matters is the market's perception, not yours. Saturn and other U.S. carmakers, for instance, continue to battle perceptions that U.S. cars are not as reliable or as desirable as cars from Japan and Europe.

PROMOTION AND THE PRODUCT LIFE CYCLE    The product category's stage in the product life cycle determines to a large extent the nature of the promotional campaign. As Exhibit 17.7 shows, the promotional mix often has to change as the product matures. As with many other topics in marketing, the promotional mixes shown in Exhibit 17.7 are generalizations; individual marketers can always find effective exceptions to the "rules." Moreover, no law of nature insists that all products and product categories must go into the decline phase. In fact, assuming that products are going to decline and then cutting back on promotional expenditures may be a mistake. With effective advertising, some brands have stayed healthy for decades.

Personal computers provide a good example of how the promotion effort must evolve as a product category becomes widely adopted. When PCs first appeared, customers required a lot of technical support and education about computers in gen-

**Exhibit 17.7
PROMOTION AND
THE PRODUCT LIFE
CYCLE**
The promotion mix often has to be changed as a product or a product category progresses through its life cycle. Remember that these are general guidelines only.

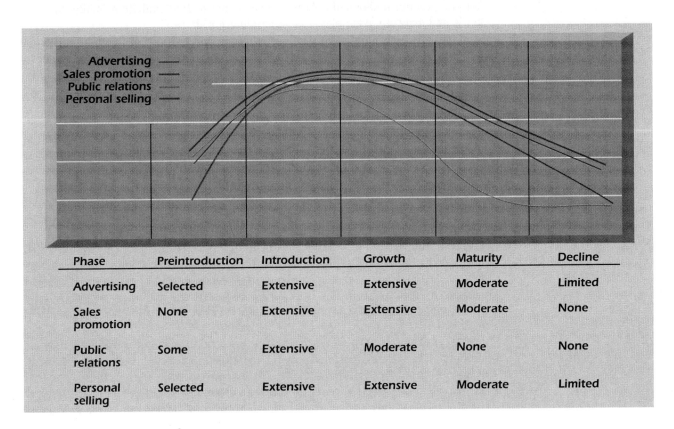

| Phase | Preintroduction | Introduction | Growth | Maturity | Decline |
|---|---|---|---|---|---|
| Advertising | Selected | Extensive | Extensive | Moderate | Limited |
| Sales promotion | None | Extensive | Extensive | Moderate | None |
| Public relations | Some | Extensive | Moderate | None | None |
| Personal selling | Selected | Extensive | Extensive | Moderate | Limited |

eral. Therefore, heavy personal selling and postsales support were required because customers weren't familiar with this new category of hardware and software. It did not make sense for Apple, IBM, and other early suppliers to spend all their time bashing each other before large segments of customers were ready to accept personal computers in general. Once the new gadgets started to catch on, competitors started to behave more like competitors. As customers grew more comfortable with PCs, personal selling continued to decline in importance, and many customers began to buy from mail-order and discount retailers, often giving up technical advice in return for lower prices. Of course, be sure to consider the specific nature of your products, competitors, and markets when adjusting your promotional mix; some general guidelines to follow are available.

Prior to the introduction of a new product, public relations can do a great service for you by preparing your market. For example, if the product you're working on employs some innovative technology, you can write magazine articles to help educate the market before your product is ready. Moreover, appropriate members of the press will be interested in any substantially new product or new way of solving customers' problems. You might also use some selected advertising to alert key customers and opinion leaders in a particular industry about your upcoming product. Also, in some organizational marketing instances, you'll want to start personal selling efforts at this preintroductory stage. Advertising is used less commonly at this stage, but some marketers do choose to advertise early. For example, as the world of interactive, multimedia communications began to heat up in 1993 and 1994, AT&T began running ads depicting things people would be able to do in the future with AT&T services (such as sending faxes from a personal communicator while sitting on a beach).[29]

During the introduction stage, you can use extensive advertising to educate customers, build awareness, and stimulate demand. Strong public relations should continue through this period, as the word about your products is spread far and wide (you hope). Sales promotions can be used to stimulate demand at the consumer level and to increase interest at the wholesaler and retailer levels as well. For instance, Snapple and the other competitors in the fast-growing bottled iced tea market pumped out millions of dollars in advertising in 1992 and 1993. While the market is still growing, each player is scrambling for share.[30]

During the growth stage and into the maturity stage, your promotions will probably have to shift from stimulating primary demand (for the product category) to stimulating selective demand (for your product). Promotions to the trade should focus on supporting the intermediaries you picked up during the introduction stage and on filling the gaps in your channel with new wholesalers and retailers, as required. Public relations will gradually decline in most cases, except for those special events that you stage, such as sports festivals; the news media will be off searching for the next new product somewhere else. Personal selling may become less important as more customers are able to make purchase decisions from advertisements and other nonpersonal sources of information.

During the decline phase, you are primarily interested in keeping profits as high as possible and distractions as low as possible. You'll want to concentrate both time and money on developing new products. Your marketing intermediaries will be looking for the next big opportunity as well, and they won't invest heavily either. You'll probably just use some reminder advertising to let customers know the product is still available. Personal selling will be used as necessary, but keep in mind how expensive it is. Public relations is generally less effective at this stage, particularly press relations, but sales promotion can still be effective at stimulating demand.[31]

CHARACTERISTICS OF YOUR PRODUCT    The perception customers have about your product's features and performance can affect promotional choices. To begin with, if customers perceive some risk in purchasing your product, address these concerns before customers are motivated to buy. Perceived risk can take the form of safety (such as all-terrain vehicles), health (foods with tropical oils), economic loss (innovative manufacturing equipment), social embarrassment (clothes), or frustration (an unreliable model of car). The greater the uncertainty or the poorer the reputation, the more your promotions will have to provide proof of postpurchase satisfaction. This might include testimonials from satisfied users, quotes from reviewers or other perceived experts, demonstrations, or other technical information that seeks to reduce the element of risk. Ads that try to enhance a company's image, on the other hand, probably won't be as effective at reducing the perception of risk.

Another important product factor, somewhat related to risk, is perceived complexity. This includes technically oriented products, products that require custom engineering, and products that require significant postsales support. Customers considering purchase of such products will probably want to see specifications, technical descriptions, contractual arrangements, and other data before they sign. Spur-of-the-moment purchases aren't likely with such products (or with risky products), so using promotional vehicles designed with this objective in mind doesn't make much sense.

Product cost also plays a role in the promotional mix. For example, when CSX buys a new supertanker, it reviews an enormous amount of information from the shipbuilder and spends a lot of time negotiating and arranging details. A television commercial showing a beautiful tanker at sea won't work. In addition to the absolute price of the product, the price as a percentage of the money available is important. For instance, a family that earns $15,000 a year and a family making $75,000 a year will approach the purchase of $50 jeans differently.

## STEP 3: UNDERSTAND THE INFLUENCE OF COMPETITORS

You should always judge the influence of competition before designing and launching a promotional program. What have your competitors been telling the market before you arrived? What issues have they raised? What expectations have they set? You can learn a great deal about competitive influences by listening to potential customers because chances are that customers' perceptions were molded, at least in part, by the competition. Interviews and focus groups with customers can unearth some of these issues. Analyzing competitors' ads is another good technique.

Also, take one step beyond just analyzing the competitors. Predict their potential responses to your promotional efforts. Will your ad campaign annoy a much larger competitor and provoke it into launching a bigger campaign of its own? Will a feisty competitor find something to criticize in your promotions and try to convince the target audience that you're not being completely honest? Will somebody respond to your promotional thrust with a change in another aspect of the marketing mix, such as a price cut? If you consider all the possible competitive reactions, you'll be able to fine-tune your campaign before you launch it, and you'll be ready with counterresponses if required.

## STEP 4: ESTABLISH PROMOTIONAL OBJECTIVES

Clear objectives are an important part of promotions planning. Once you've identified customer and competitor influences, you can define objectives to help guide and control your promotional program. These objectives are linked to your overall marketing objectives. For instance, when the Mexican government set out to increase tourism, it set the specific objective of doubling international arrivals by 1994, an increase of over 6 million tourists.[32] Armed with the goal of 6 million more visitors, Mexico's travel authorities could estimate how many people they needed to reach with radio and television advertising and the various public relations efforts.

Note that this objective includes both a specific target and a completion date. The government didn't just say it wanted to increase tourism; it set specific goals that could be measured and evaluated. While the program is under way, travel officials can monitor their progress against these goals and take corrective action if necessary.

SALES VERSUS COMMUNICATIONS OBJECTIVES   Not every promotional effort can or should be linked directly to sales results, however. The key is whether you can measure the impact on sales; if you can't measure the sales impact, assigning a sales objective makes no sense because you'll never know whether you met that objective. Establishing a sales objective for a particular promotional effort is reasonable only if it meets the following criteria:[33]

- *When it is the only variable in the marketing mix.* What if you set your advertising goal as increasing sales by 10 percent, but then raised the price of your product? If you didn't meet the goal, would it be an advertising failure? Maybe, maybe not. You can't make any significant modifications to the rest of the marketing mix (including other promotions) if you're trying to measure this particular effort's impact on sales.
- *When it is a dominant force in the marketing mix.* The promotional effort has to play a key role in your marketing mix if you want to assign it a sales objective. If 95 percent of your promotional impact comes from television advertising, you can't expect personal sales, coupons, or other efforts to have much of an effect on sales.
- *When it is designed to solicit an immediate response.* Let's say that during the month of January, Saturn runs an ad that focuses on how satisfied customers are with their cars. Would it be reasonable to attribute January's sales to that ad (assuming the first two criteria are met)? What about February's or March's or April's? The more time that elapses between the appearance of an ad and the actual sales transactions, the less reasonable it becomes to assign the ad a sales target. Competitors may have adjusted their marketing mixes or dealers may have increased or decreased their local promotional efforts. Another timing issue is that advertising doesn't always have an immediate effect but may contribute to sales long after a buyer comes in contact with an ad, a phenomenon known as the *carryover effect.*

In addition, some promotional efforts are not designed to stimulate sales directly, but rather to build awareness or acceptance for a company, for instance. To be judged on sales performance, of course, an ad or other effort must be designed to generate sales. Relatively few promotions can meet these criteria completely. The most obvious cases involve direct marketing. For instance, if your primary promotional effort is selling something over the phone (see Exhibit 17.8), it's fairly easy to measure how the effort has affected sales. As long as the phone effort isn't heavily supplemented by other advertising or promotional efforts, you can usually isolate the impact of your advertising, so establishing a sales objective for advertising in such cases can be appropriate. In fact, the ease with which you can measure direct marketing's effects is one of its most attractive aspects.[34]

If you can't measure the direct sales impact of a promotional program and therefore can't reasonably assign a sales objective, you can assign a *communication objective.* When Saturn first appeared on the automotive scene, one of its biggest challenges was simply to make people aware that the cars existed. Hyundai, Kia, and other recent entrants in the U.S. car market faced the same challenge. You can measure how many people are aware of your products before you run your ads and compare that with how many people are aware after you run the ads.

## STEP 5: IDENTIFY YOUR RESOURCES

Few marketers think they have enough money, time, or people to pull off all the promotional programs they'd like to implement. To say that you need a nationwide ad campaign to build awareness for your new product is easy. However, even a tiny ad campaign can cost hundreds of thousands of dollars, and major promotional programs cost millions.

Marketers set promotional budgets in several ways. These are generally applied

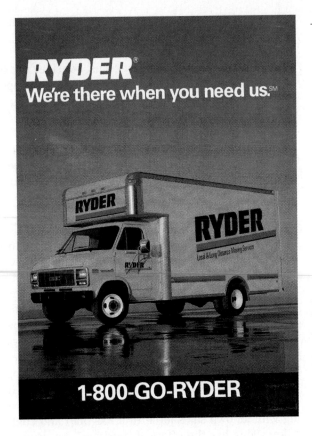

**Exhibit 17.8**
**TRACKING SALES WITH TELEMARKETING**
If advertising is the only place where potential renters are exposed to this toll-free number, Ryder would find it relatively easy to track the advertising's effectiveness.

to advertising, but similar procedures could and should be used for all the promotional elements.

- *Percentage methods.* This covers a wide variety of methods that share one thing: They are all based on some fixed percentage. A common method, for instance, is the share-of-sales approach, in which you allocate a certain percentage of sales revenue to promotions. Another fixed approach is using industry averages or traditional industry standards; you estimate what everyone else in the industry spends and then spend the average amount. A related approach is competitive parity, in which you try to spend as much as your closest competitors. All of these fixed-percentage methods suffer from a severe limitation: They aren't based on any consideration of what you should really spend to meet your marketing objectives. One serious implication of these methods is that it leads you to decrease promotional budgets when sales drop, and you might need to do just the opposite during hard times.

- *Objective and task method.* The big drawback of percentage methods is solved by **objective and task budgeting,** in which you first determine what you are trying to accomplish with your promotions and then figure how much money you need to do it. For instance, if you're trying to gain 10 percent of a 50,000-person market, and your sales promotion convinces 25 percent of the people who see it to purchase your product, you'll need to reach 20,000 people initially ($50,000 \times 0.1 \times 4$). If each sales promotion device costs $1.85, your budget must be $37,000. The tricky part of this method is estimating the effectiveness of the promotional program (the 25 percent sales rate in this example). A combination of research and experience will help you refine these estimates.

- *Other methods.* Other methods are also used to set budgets; some more scientific, some less so. Plain old guesswork, often disguised by such nice labels as "executive opinion," is one of the less rigorous methods. At the other end of the spectrum is the empirical research method, in which you actually implement the promotion on a small scale, measure its effectiveness, and then base your budget on

**objective and task budgeting**
An approach to setting promotional budgets that starts with a clearly defined objective and then derives the budget needed to execute the tasks necessary to meet that objective

this. Quantitative mathematical models are also used to project budget needs based on past promotional programs.[35]

In addition to budgeting concerns, consider the number of people required and the nature of their expertise. Finding enough people with the right skills and personality is often a major challenge facing sales managers. For example, consider the task faced by a pharmaceutical firm such as American Home Products. The salesperson must understand the needs of doctors and nurses, the medications offered for sale, and the purchasing processes of health-care organizations—and must have general selling skills. Finding people who can cover all these bases is not an easy task, and it can have an effect on the balance of your promotional mix.

## STEP 6: CREATE AN OPTIMAL PROMOTIONAL MIX

The first five steps provide the information and insight necessary to create an effective promotional mix and define the goals to strive for. Now as you create the mix that will help you meet those goals, you must make two important decisions. First, are you going to push products through the marketing channel or rely on customers to pull them through? Second, what specific elements of advertising, sales promotion, public relations, and personal selling are you going to use? In addition, consider how to integrate the various elements of your marketing communications.

**push strategy**
A promotional strategy that relies primarily on pushing products through each stage of the marketing channel, from producer to wholesaler to retailer to customer; push strategies can also be used in direct channels, with salespeople presenting products to customers

**pull strategy**
A promotional strategy that primarily builds demand with the final customer and relies on that customer to request the product from the marketing channel; the opposite of a push strategy

SELECTING PUSH VERSUS PULL STRATEGIES    Two opposing methods for stimulating demand in a market are push and pull strategies (see Exhibit 17.9). With a **push strategy,** a manufacturer tries to stimulate demand down through the channel, starting with its own sales force (if it has one) and continuing with wholesalers and retailers. This has the effect of "pushing" the product through the channel. The opposite is a **pull strategy,** in which the manufacturer talks directly to the final customer and relies on the customer to "pull" the product through the channel. Shapeware, makers of the popular Visio graphics-creation program, puts most of its promotional money and energy into building demand at the end-user level. Customers then pull the product through the channel, and distributors and retailers are more than happy to oblige.[36]

Most companies use a combination push and pull strategy; a common technique is using advertising to stimulate demand at the customer level (pulling) while using personal selling in the channel (pushing). This is a particularly powerful combination because advertising can open doors for salespeople by "preparing" customers; ads can introduce the company, the product, and other variables. Note that

**Exhibit 17.9
PUSH AND PULL
STRATEGIES**
Push strategies attempt to push a product through the marketing channel, whereas pull strategies stimulate demand at the customer level and rely on customers to pull products through the channel; many companies use a combined strategy.

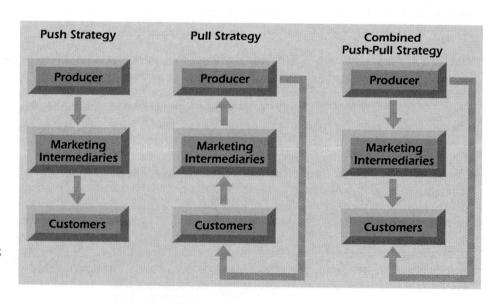

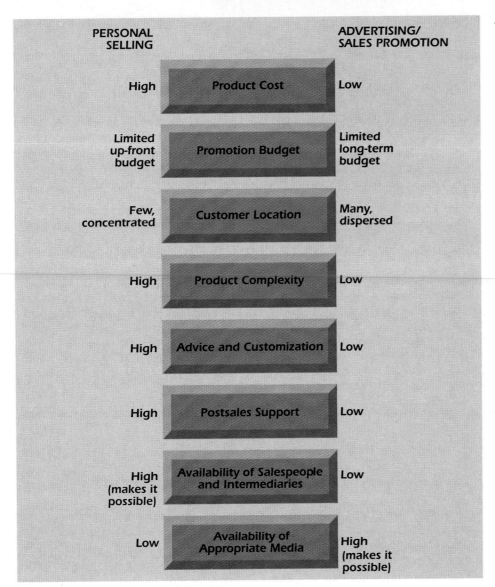

| PERSONAL SELLING | | ADVERTISING/ SALES PROMOTION |
|---|---|---|
| High | **Product Cost** | Low |
| Limited up-front budget | **Promotion Budget** | Limited long-term budget |
| Few, concentrated | **Customer Location** | Many, dispersed |
| High | **Product Complexity** | Low |
| High | **Advice and Customization** | Low |
| High | **Postsales Support** | Low |
| High (makes it possible) | **Availability of Salespeople and Intermediaries** | Low |
| Low | **Availability of Appropriate Media** | High (makes it possible) |

**Exhibit 17.10**
**FINDING THE RIGHT PROMOTIONAL MIX**
You need to consider a number of factors when designing the optimum promotional mix. The factors shown here help you decide whether personal selling, advertising, or sales promotion should be your lead element. You can also use public relations to support the rest of the mix.

the distribution channel is not a passive element in the push-pull decision; wholesalers and retailers have a very large say in what sort of strategy producers can use.[37]

SELECTING THE BEST COMBINATION OF ELEMENTS    Why don't all companies use the same basic promotional mix? For instance, why is it that some companies spend the majority of their promotion budget on advertising, others spend the majority on personal selling, and still others focus on sales promotions? What are the decisions that lead you to a specific promotional mix? You've covered some of the issues already; here's a more comprehensive list. (Exhibit 17.10 shows the choices graphically.) Keep in mind that the promotional mix is usually a compromise of all these elements and that various elements can be used effectively at various stages of the customers' buying process.

- *Product cost.* Generally, the more expensive the product, the more personal selling will be used, rather than advertising or sales promotion.
- *Promotional budget restrictions.* Many advertising and sales promotion efforts require a large budget just to get started, so companies with severe budget restrictions may be stuck with personal selling even though it's not the best choice.

## SHOULD COMPANIES BE ALLOWED TO PROMOTE UNHEALTHY PRODUCTS?

**ETHICAL DILEMMA IN MARKETING**

Tennis and cigarettes. What a combination. One, a sport requiring superb fitness, stamina, and lung power. The other, a product that the U.S. Public Health Service claims is responsible for 300,000 to 350,000 premature deaths a year in the United States. However, Philip Morris, the manufacturer of Virginia Slims cigarettes, sponsored the Virginia Slims tennis tournament for 23 years. Tobacco and alcohol ties are pervasive in sports, from signs in stadiums to advertisements in *Sports Illustrated*.

The growing antismoking sentiment around the country has brought cigarette-sponsored sporting events increasingly under fire. Former Secretary of Health and Human Services Dr. Louis W. Sullivan criticized the tobacco companies, condemning them for "trading death for profits." He said that the link between cigarettes and sports wrongfully implies that smoking is healthful, and that it lures young people (who watch sporting events and emulate athletes as role models) into taking it up. One of the most contentious issues is the Joe Camel cartoon character used to promote Camel cigarettes. Critics assert that the use of a cartoon character is bound to draw in children.

Cigarette manufacturers say their promotions are intended not to entice nonsmokers (and children in particular) but only to persuade current smokers to switch brands. However, the universe of smokers is shrinking. Although there are nearly 60 million smokers in the United States, the proportion of adult smokers has dropped from 42 percent in 1964 to below 30 percent today. In the face of declining sales, cigarette marketers work hard to build and protect their shares of the market.

On the other hand, personal selling is usually more expensive on a per customer basis.

- *Customer location and density.* Reaching a widespread, low-density customer base is difficult to do with personal selling, so such markets are usually addressed through advertising.
- *Product complexity.* Personal selling usually dominates when products or customer applications are complex.
- *Presale selection advice and customization needs.* If customers need technical advice when selecting products, or if the products must be adapted to each customer, personal selling works better than advertising.
- *Postsale support requirements.* Like product complexity, significant postsale support requirements usually lead to promotional mixes that are dominated by personal selling.
- *Availability of salespeople and intermediaries.* Sometimes you simply can't get the right number or right kind of salespeople and intermediaries. This can happen with highly technical products and in competitive situations where established competitors already control the intermediaries. In these cases, you might like to use certain intermediaries but can't; therefore, find other promotional methods.
- *Availability of appropriate media.* If you can't find a cost-effective way to reach your audience through the established media, advertising might not be the best choice. This is usually more of a problem in specialized niche markets.
- *Market expectations.* In addition to the factors shown in Exhibit 17.10, consider the expectations of your target customers. On the one hand, your message might be overlooked or ignored if it comes through an unexpected medium. On the other hand, an unexpected medium can be quite eye-catching. For example, Intel used roadside billboards to promote one of its math co-processors, a highly specialized accessory for personal computers that is normally promoted through technical magazines.

Like most other national consumer-goods companies, cigarette manufacturers find television to be an attractive promotional vehicle. However, the U.S. government banned TV commercials for cigarettes in 1971. Ever since then, cigarette companies have been forced to find other ways to keep their products in front of the public. It's no surprise, then, that Philip Morris's Virginia Slims tournaments and R. J. Reynolds's Winston Cup auto racing both began in 1971 and that Marlboro Cup horse racing was born in 1973. The TV ban spawned countless other cigarette-sponsored sporting events such as the Salem Pro-Sail races, Lucky Strike bowling, and Benson & Hedges on Ice, to name just a few. (Philip Morris stopped sponsoring the Virginia Slims tour in 1993, but might consider sponsoring individual tournaments beginning in 1995.)

Tobacco company profits aren't the only issue here, however. Enough people benefit from cigarette and alcohol marketing revenue to build a coalition of support for these sponsorships and other related advertising, tacit though some of it may be. Top names in women's tennis defended Philip Morris, acknowledging the company's role in raising the status of women's tennis. Publishers like the income from cigarette ads. Furthermore, magazines and other media that refuse tobacco ads might endanger other ad revenues as well, given the conglomerate nature of cigarette ownership. For instance, R. J. Reynolds's holdings include Nabisco, Del Monte, and KFC (Kentucky Fried Chicken). Philip Morris controls 7-Up, Miller Brewing Company, and Kraft General Foods.

Then, perhaps the hardest question of all—what about ice cream, hamburgers, hang gliders, sports cars, and the dozens and dozens of other products that can put life, limb, and arteries at risk? If the public is to be protected from tobacco and alcohol consumption, why not cholesterol and water skiing as well? With so much public sentiment against the tobacco and alcohol marketers, you can see why they sometimes feel unfairly singled out for criticism.

## WHAT'S YOUR OPINION?

**1.** Should the government restrict, or perhaps even ban, advertising for products considered unhealthy?
**2.** How should society determine whether a product is unhealthy enough to warrant advertising restriction?

---

In addition to developing mixes on their own, an increasing number of marketers are teaming up with other marketers to promote two or more products at once. Sometimes these co-promotions involve a smaller marketer "riding piggyback" on a larger company's efforts; in other cases, two or more giants join forces. In soft drinks and athletic shoes, PepsiCo and Reebok have teamed up, and so have Coca-Cola and Nike. During a 1993 campaign, for instance, a PepsiCo promotion featuring Shaquille O'Neal let consumers exchange Pepsi proofs of purchase for a discount on Reebok shoes. You've no doubt seen co-promotions at McDonald's and at the other major fast-food chains, all of which rely on them to stimulate sales. For the 1994 World Cup in soccer, for instance, McDonald's teamed up with Coca-Cola, ITT Sheraton, Adidas, Sprint, and M&M/Mars.[38]

INTEGRATING YOUR MARKETING COMMUNICATIONS   As Chapter 1 pointed out, integrated marketing communications (IMC) is a key aspect of the functional integration that is in turn a cornerstone of the marketing concept. As both markets and marketing have grown more complex in recent years, many marketers in both the organizational and consumer sectors have found themselves with fragmented and confusing promotional programs. When you consider all the ways that audiences can receive marketing messages, the potential for confusion is not all that surprising. Let's say you're in the market for a sports car and have your eye on a new Ford Mustang. You might see a national television ad, a local television ad, a national magazine ad, a local newspaper ad, or some combination of the four. Plus, you'll talk to a salesperson at the dealership and possibly read product review articles in both newspapers and magazines. On top of all that, you might receive a promotional brochure in the mail from Ford. Now, what if all these sources of information told you slightly different stories about the Mustang? It's easy to see how Ford and its dealers could spend a huge amount on promotion and wind up with nothing but confused consumers to show for it.[39]

IMC is the solution to this fragmentation since it coordinates and integrates all of a company's promotional efforts. Properly implemented, IMC promises to increase marketing and promotional effectiveness and decrease marketing costs. However, despite the benefits, most marketers find IMC difficult to implement. The biggest hurdle stems from the manner in which the various elements of communication have been managed in most organizations and in the agencies that support them. For example, look at the separate responsibilities and communication tasks involved when the marketer's sales department takes care of personal selling, the advertising agency prepares print and electronic ads, and the public relations specialist promotes the company's products to the news media. Various company managers oversee these processes and have long-established methods of managing their portions of the marketing mix. Moving to an IMC approach requires new ways of organizing, planning, and managing all marketing functions, and years of habit have created resistance to change.[40] Outside agencies are caught in the commotion as well, as each type of agency tries to sort out its role in an integrated strategy. For example, one of the biggest marketing challenges that consumer-goods marketers face is moving their products through distribution channels. Relatively few advertising agencies have specialized expertise in promoting through distribution channels, but that remains a key marketing problem that needs to be addressed as part of an integrated marketing effort.[41] As difficult as it may be to implement, the potential benefits of IMC are so valuable that the concept is fast becoming standard for everyone in the advertising and marketing professions.[42]

## International Promotional Mixes

Developing promotional mixes for international marketing campaigns involves a few extra steps. Given the complexity of marketing to people in various cultures and the difficulty of maintaining control over worldwide promotional campaigns, experts urge caution and careful planning when entering international markets.

One of the most important steps is to determine the promotional mixes typically used in each country. For instance, radio is a very popular advertising medium in Mexico—so popular, in fact, that most stations carry 24 minutes of commercials every hour. On the other hand, direct-mail advertising is virtually impossible in Chile because the recipient of mail in that country has to pay part of the postage, and people are generally unwilling to help pay for unsolicited advertising. Nineteen African countries have no daily newspaper, one of the most popular vehicles in developed countries.[43]

## Promotional Mixes for Services

Intangibility makes services difficult to promote effectively, for two obvious reasons. First, you can't demonstrate certain services without giving them away. For instance, you can't show customers how well you can cut their hair without actually cutting their hair. Second, advertising depends heavily on graphic images, and you don't have a tangible product to show off. Conveying the power of a Caterpillar tractor in an ad photo is easy, but it's difficult to show the intelligence and experience of your accounting firm. Keep both these problems in mind as you read about the following techniques used to promote services.

Satisfied customers are always a great promotional vehicle, and they can help you overcome the inability to demonstrate your service. Also, the greater the experience and credence qualities of a service and the riskier the purchase, the more important referrals become. You probably won't ask your neighbor to recommend a video store clerk, but you might ask for recommendations about doctors, lawyers, or management consultants.

Because most services are performed by people, personal selling is a key promotional mechanism for service providers. The salesperson and service provider

Each country has its own blend of promotional elements, and some elements are more common than others in each country. In Mexico, for example, radio is an extremely popular advertising medium; nearly half the air time on many stations is filled with commercials.

are frequently one and the same, which presents a special challenge. At some point in the sales process, the person has to switch from sales to service, or customers will start to turn off. Personal selling can be effective in dealing with intangibility. Customers can't see the service, but they can question the salesperson, asking how the service is performed, which other customers have purchased it, and how the benefits of one service compare to those of another service.

Intangibility leads many service providers to use tangible symbols in advertising. One of the most famous is Prudential Insurance's Rock of Gibraltar logo and its ads that promise you "a piece of the rock." It's hard to get much more tangible than a rock, especially a rock the size of Gibraltar. Gibraltar will be around forever—so you're not buying just insurance from this company; you're buying stability, confidence, and security. Another promising technique is to highlight the systems and policies you have for delivering a service. Advertising that your retail store will open additional checkouts when more than three people are standing in line is a good way to communicate the fact that you respond to customer needs.[44]

## Nonprofit Promotional Mixes

As with service marketing, many nonprofit groups base their promotions on symbols. For example, Vandalia, Illinois, successfully attracted business investment by sending corporate leaders photographs of the town's 5,500 residents standing in the two-block downtown area. Along with the picture came the message that the citizens were ready and willing to work hard for any company that would relocate to Vandalia. Instead of one more small town down on its luck, Vandalia became a group of people with a promise.[45] Save the Children achieved success by using pictures of poverty-stricken children in its ads. These pictures personalized the appeal very effectively; donors felt they were helping a specific person with a name and a face. Later ad campaigns that solicited funds for community projects failed because they lacked the powerful symbol of a child.[46]

Events such as concerts and telethons are important promotional vehicles for social marketers. These events frequently depend on the name recognition of celebrities to generate public interest, such as Willie Nelson's Farm Aid concerts and the Band Aid and Live Aid concerts organized by rock singer Bob Geldof.[47] The Easter Seal Telethon is successful year after year, and a key part of its success is a variety of big-name performers.[48]

Nonprofit organizations increasingly use public service announcements (PSAs) to promote goods, services, and ideas. As advertising agencies became more involved in nonprofit marketing, the quality of PSAs increased dramatically. First-class PSAs are important not only for their ability to promote effectively but also because they build the image and credibility of nonprofit organizations.[49]

## PROMOTION AND SOCIETY

This chapter showed you the process for defining a promotional mix and communicating with customers and other audiences. Most businesses have a wide variety of promotional options at their disposal, and a thoughtfully designed promotional mix can be a powerful marketing force indeed. However, some people believe that promotion can be *too* powerful, and they criticize promotion for causing a number of social and economic problems. Advertising is often singled out as the prime culprit, but the following criticisms can apply to promotion in general:

- It makes us buy things we don't need.
- It obscures the truth.
- It trivializes our language through misuse.
- It encourages excessive use of credit.

- It can be offensive or in poor taste.
- It is intrusive and domineering.
- It encourages selfishness and shortsightedness.
- It fosters materialism, waste, and ecological damage.
- It perpetuates social stereotypes.
- It creates a climate of perpetual dissatisfaction.[50]

The writers and thinkers who make these claims are some of the brightest minds in such fields as history, psychology, sociology, education, and linguistics, so it doesn't seem prudent to dismiss their criticisms without giving them serious thought. In addition, the general public is wary of the marketing profession. For example, Opinion Research Corporation of Princeton, New Jersey, has been tracking the public's opinion of advertising since 1964. That year, 54 percent said advertising was a "deceptive persuader," whereas 37 percent said it provided useful information. By 1990, though, only 17 percent said it was useful and 80 percent said it was deceptive.[51]

The most common responses from the marketing world to these complaints are that (1) the power of advertising is exaggerated—it can't do all those things; (2) advertising broadens the choices available to consumers; (3) our society is materialistic to begin with and promotion simply responds to that; (4) promotion is now very closely regulated and scrutinized so that the chance of abuse is much lower than it was in past years; and (5) advertising fees subsidize much of the information and entertainment that we consumers derive from the mass media.[52] In addition, even marketing's critics have to agree that marketing expertise is frequently applied to a variety of social challenges, including drug-abuse education, safe-sex campaigns, and environmental protection.

The controversy surrounding promotion will continue. More research is required to validate both the claims and defenses mentioned here. In any case, marketers should always exercise good judgment, good taste, and honesty in their promotional efforts.

## SUMMARY OF LEARNING OBJECTIVES

### 1. Explain the role promotion plays in the marketing mix.

Promotion plays a vital role in the marketing mix by informing potential customers about a company and its products. The other functions performed by promotion include stimulating demand, differentiating products, countering the promotional efforts of competitors, responding to negative news about the company or its products, smoothing demand fluctuations, persuading decision makers, and influencing public behavior.

### 2. Identify the major elements of promotion.

The major elements of promotion are advertising, sales promotion, public relations, and personal selling. Advertising is paid, nonpersonal communication with a target audience. Sales promotion covers a variety of events and activities designed to stimulate demand and support other promotional efforts. Public relations is nonpaid, nonpersonal communication through the news media and other avenues. Personal

selling occurs when the seller makes a personal presentation to a customer or group of customers.

### 3. Track a message through the communication process model and identify ways in which communication can break down.

Communication starts when the source encodes an idea, thereby creating a message. The message is then transmitted through a medium (such as television, newspaper ads, or personal presentations) to the audience. The audience must then decode the message to extract individual meanings from it. This process can break down at several points. First, if not encoded accurately, the message will not represent the original thought. Second, the message can be distorted or destroyed by noise as it travels through the medium. The message can also be lost if not sent through an appropriate medium. Third, if the audience doesn't have the necessary experience to decode the message as the source intended, the message will be misinterpreted.

**4. Explain how marketing communication is used to move customers from awareness to purchase to satisfaction.**

Phase 1 is awareness; marketing communication starts moving customers toward purchase and satisfaction by first generating awareness of the company and its products. The second phase is comprehension, or helping customers understand what the company is offering. The third phase is acceptance; communication is used to get potential customers to accept the product as a solution. The fourth phase is preference; the company tries to persuade customers to choose its brand over competitive offerings. The fifth phase is ownership; marketing communication plays an important role in prompting potential customers to become actual customers. The sixth stage is satisfaction; communication is used to reaffirm buyers' decisions and to make them feel more confident that they made the right choice.

**5. Define sales objectives and communications objectives and explain why not all promotional efforts can have measurable sales objectives.**

With sales objectives, the goal is to produce a certain number of sales; with communications objectives, the goal is to generate some other effect on the audience (such as awareness). Sales objectives are appropriate only when (a) the promotional effort in question is the only variable being changed in the marketing mix, (b) the effort in question is the dominant force in the entire marketing mix, or (c) the promotion is designed to solicit an immediate response.

**6. List the parameters you need to know about a target audience before designing effective communication programs.**

Before you can design effective communication programs, knowledge of several key parameters about a target audience is essential. The first is simply customers' identity, which encompasses geography, demographics, and whether they are consumers or organizations. Second, be sure to understand their needs and expectations, which are influenced by personality, lifestyle, and product use habits. Third, find out how customers search for and use product information.

**7. Discuss the relationship between promotion and society, including the criticisms and defenses of promotion.**

The relationship of promotion and society is not well understood, but a number of observers do level strong criticisms at promotion, and at advertising in particular. The specific claims are numerous; some prominent examples include accusations that advertising encourages materialism, perpetuates stereotypes, and makes consumers buy things they don't need. Marketers respond to these criticisms by saying that advertising isn't that powerful, that advertising broadens consumers' choices, and that advertising is now so closely regulated as to make the abuses of the past unlikely.

## KEY TERMS

advertising (519)
AIDA model (527)
audience (525)
decoding (524)
encoding (524)
feedback (525)

hierarchy of effects model (526)
marketing communications (526)
medium (524)
message (524)

noise (525)
objective and task budgeting (535)
personal selling (523)
promotional mix (519)
public relations (522)

publicity (522)
pull strategy (536)
push strategy (536)
sales promotion (520)
source (524)

## QUESTIONS FOR DISCUSSION

1. Why would the following organizations use promotion?
   a. The college you're attending
   b. Planned Parenthood
   c. Boeing Military Aircraft Company
   d. Eddie Bauer (a clothing and sporting goods manufacturer and retailer)
2. Would you emphasize personal selling or advertising for a new line of voice-activated home computers? Why?
3. How is the communication model represented in a television commercial for McDonald's? (Identify the elements of the model as they apply to this communication example.)
4. How might communication break down in a radio commercial?
5. How does an automaker such as Toyota use interpersonal and mass communication?
6. Assume you're the sales manager for a local industrial

supply firm that advertises on the radio and sends salespeople out to visit customers who call the company in response to the radio ads. Should the salespeople be held accountable for sales objectives? Explain your answer.
7. You're responsible for promoting a line of sporting goods. What should you learn about your audience first?
8. Consider these two products, both based on laser technology. The first is yet another laser printer that is entering a very competitive, very crowded market; the second is a laser lawn-trimming device that makes conventional lawn mowers obsolete, and it has no direct competition. How would the flavor of their respective promotional mixes differ?
9. How could a bank use promotions to increase customer satisfaction?
10. How would you respond to the criticism that advertising encourages environmental damage?

## Meeting a Marketing Challenge at Saturn

Donald Hudler and his team at Saturn put together a successful marketing and advertising program—and more. *Advertising Age*, the leading trade journal in the advertising industry, calls Saturn "one of the most successful new brands in marketing history." People who want to buy one of Saturn's several models often have to be content to put their name on a waiting list until a car becomes available. Saturn drivers frequently wave at each other as they pass, some even help sell cars in the showrooms, and some have been talking of starting an owners' club. A few owners have actually driven to the factory in Spring Hill, Tennessee, to meet the people who made their cars. Saturn sold over 170,000 cars during its second year (1992) and would've sold even more cars if only it could've made more.

What kind of objectives and strategies created this remarkable success? Hudler defines Saturn's marketing objective as making Saturn "the best-liked car company in America." That's an easy thing to say, but a very difficult goal to achieve. The strategy started with building a reasonably priced car that would satisfy customers, but it didn't stop there. Saturn's strategy included every aspect of the business, from including employees in decision making to setting prices that consumers don't have to haggle over.

Among the many things Hudler and crew did right was to make a sharp departure from traditional automotive advertising strategy. Saturn ads don't talk about technical details or show cars winding over mountain roads. They talk about real people who drive Saturns and the satisfaction those people derive from the cars. This approach not only distinguishes Saturn from the pack but also helps build a strong emotional bond among the public, the product, and the company behind the product.

A good example of Saturn's advertising strategy is a magazine ad that tells the story of New Mexico's Cheryl Silas. Silas was hit from behind while driving her Saturn coupe. The car was totaled, but she walked away unhurt. A police officer at the scene said she was lucky to be alive. The following week, Silas went back to her Saturn retailer and ordered another car. A few days later, so did the police officer. Then one of the officer's friends ordered a Saturn. So did Silas's brother. To top it off, the woman who had run into Silas came in for a test drive. This remarkable story made its way back to Hudler's office and found its way into print as another example of great Saturn advertising.

**Your mission:** Let's say that Donald Hudler has accepted a transfer to GM headquarters, with the mission of infusing the Saturn approach throughout the giant automaker. You take over his job at Saturn and are now responsible for guiding the process of marketing and advertising strategy. Consider the following scenarios and pick solutions that stand the best chance of carrying on Saturn's success and moving the company into profitability.

1. Production slowdowns and a commitment to high-quality cars have resulted in occasional product shortages. In one sense, it's nice to know people are waiting in line to buy your car, but you can't satisfy them until they're behind the wheel of their new Saturns. As in the past, the company must once again run an ad to address this issue. Which of the following concepts would best fit Saturn's overall marketing and advertising strategies?
   a. An ad that apologizes for the delay and explains that problems in the production process are responsible for the shortages. Acknowledge that some people who've ordered their cars but won't receive them for weeks might well be angry; invite them to call their dealers to vent their frustrations.
   b. An ad that apologizes for the delay but that focuses on Saturn's desire to make sure only top-quality cars leave the factory. Feature a Saturn buyer who wrote the company and said that even though it was inconvenient, the car was definitely worth the wait.
   c. An ad that features a Saturn buyer who ordered early and was lucky enough to get a car within a week. The happy buyer would have an impish grin on his or her face while saying something like, "Lucky me, I ordered early and got my Saturn before anyone else in town."
2. One of Saturn's recent ads featured a security guard who drives a phenomenal number of miles every year, several times as much as the average driver. Keeping in mind the issues of lifestyle, product use, and other aspects of identifying your audience, who would be the best target audience for an ad like this?
   a. Anyone who cares about reliability, regardless of the number of miles driven every year.
   b. Anyone who drives 30,000 miles a year or more (assume that most people drive around 10,000 to 15,000 miles a year).
   c. Security guards and other people who use their cars on the job and need to count on them in emergency situations.
3. You'd like to get better data on the effectiveness of Saturn's advertising efforts. You know that the first step is to establish advertising objectives that are as measurable as possible. For the Cheryl Silas ad, which of the following objectives would be most appropriate (focus on the nature of the objectives, not the particular numbers)?

a. Increase Saturn sales by 5 percent over the next six months.

b. Prompt at least 75 percent of the people who read the ad to agree with the following statement: "Saturn is a safe car."

c. Cut into Toyota's market share by 1 percent by the end of this year.

4. Successful advertising nearly always stems from a clear statement of purpose, whether that purpose is to get current customers to buy more or to get new customers to give the brand a try. Based on the list of promotional purposes discussed in the chapter, which of the following could be Saturn's purpose for the Cheryl Silas ad? Be prepared to explain your choice.

a. Reminding current customers

b. Providing information

c. Stimulating demand

## SPECIAL PROJECT

Some members of your marketing staff are having trouble grasping the differences among the six reasons for advertising, and your task is to make sure everyone is clear on this subject. Collect four examples of automobile advertising that you could use to explain the differences. The four examples should be a commercial on network television, a radio commercial, a national magazine ad, and a newspaper ad for a local dealer. (Just write down a description of the television and radio ads.) For each ad, prepare a brief explanation of the reason the ad was created, using one of the six reasons discussed in the chapter.[53]

# Smartfoods Samples Its Way to Snack Success

Shiny black popcorn bags skiing down the mountainside, windsurfing across the water, dancing on billboards—not your ordinary promotional campaign. Of course, the snack inside those shiny black popcorn bags isn't your ordinary junk food, either. Smartfoods is prepopped, preservative-free Kentucky popcorn coated with natural cheddar cheese powder. Catchy name, catchy snack, catchy promotion. Can the same promotional strategy that moved this popcorn treat into the supermarkets and stomachs of New England catapult Smartfoods into the national arena?

Smartfoods began in 1984 when Ann Withey, her husband, Andrew Martin, and their partner, Ken Meyers, were thinking about how to get snack-foods manufacturers interested in a reclosable bag they were pitching. The manufacturers didn't bite, so the three decided to establish their own snack business to showcase the resealable bag technology. They focused on a popcorn-and-cheese concoction because it was healthy, easy to prepare, and inexpensive—and because there was nothing like it on the market. Withey took to the stove and served up batch after batch of cheesy popcorn until they agreed on the best one.

The trio faced decisions about the new product's name, packaging, production, and distribution. The flavored popcorn had no artificial colors or preservatives, so they thought it was a smart alternative to typical junk food and they called it Smartfoods. They created a striking black bag with yellow and green graphics—a virtual scream for attention on store shelves. Then they leased space and bought used corn poppers. By March 1985 Withey, Martin, and Meyers were in business, with the help of independent distributors that agreed to deliver their products to supermarkets and convenience stores throughout New England.

It was time to promote Smartfoods, but because the other expenses had gobbled up most of the capital, money was too scarce for a traditional advertising campaign. The three entrepreneurs wanted to stimulate demand, and their plan was to build a powerful word-of-mouth campaign by giving the product away in an unconventional way. The three founders needed to educate their target audience about this wholesome cheese-flavored popcorn, so they set off in search of crowds to entertain, educate, and amuse.

In the winter, founder Meyers and some friends organized themselves as a ski team. Wearing huge Smartfoods bags, the team skied the slopes of New England and gave away thousands of samples. In the summer, Smartfoods outfitted windsurfing teams with the company logo and dispensed samples at area beaches. Then they turned a used ice cream truck into a roving comedy vehicle that wound through city streets with entertainers standing on the roof and staffers tossing samples to bystanders.

Many firms give away T-shirts, but Smartfoods gives away boxer shorts, too—white shorts emblazoned with their trademark yellow and green cornstalk. "People love them," says Meyers, "especially college kids. Finally, someone's giving them the other half of the underwear ensemble that no one ever gets."

The Smartfoods promotions were fun, they were unusual, and they worked, triggering a sales explosion fueled by word of mouth. First-year sales were $35,000, second-year sales were $550,000, and by 1987, Smartfoods had captured 50 percent of the local market for popped popcorn with sales of $3.5 million. Sales continued to surge, hitting $10 million in 1988, and doubling in 1989 to $20 million. That year, the feisty fledgling agreed to be bought by snack giant Frito-Lay. Only a year later, Frito-Lay's marketing muscle had boosted Smartfoods' sales to $65 million. So far, Frito-Lay hasn't tried to tamper with the Smartfoods formula, and Smartfoods remains the category leader. The spirited promotion program that Meyers calls "field marketing" continues to lead the company in its expansion across the continent.

1. To break into markets far from New England where the popcorn is not well known, assume that Smartfoods has been given the option of piggybacking on promotions developed by Frito-Lay for its other successful snack products or maintaining a separate promotion stance. Which of these options should Ken Meyers choose and why?

2. Store shelves have started to overflow with similar cheese-coated competitors, such as Cape Cod Popcorn, trying to appeal to the same consumers that Smartfoods educated. Now Meyers may have to shift promotional gears, emphasizing preference rather than awareness and acceptance. Should the firm's promotions stress that Smartfoods was first with the great, wholesome taste, or should the promotions lightheartedly tease Smartfoods' competitors about following the leader?

3. Meyers may face an ethical dilemma as the public becomes aware that giant Frito-Lay owns this upstart firm that dares to poke fun at competing snack makers that use preservatives and artificial colors and flavors. Should Smartfoods wear the Frito-Lay logo proudly on its bag and in its promotions? Or should it continue its promotions as if it were a separate company?

Without a doubt, some promotional efforts annoy or offend some people. Collect several examples of promotions that you feel could be offensive. You can bring in ads from magazines and newspapers, write down descriptions and scripts of TV and radio commercials, collect sales promotion materials, or watch for companies' public relations activities.

**Decision:** After you've collected three or four examples, identify why you think they are offensive—and to whom.

**Communication:** Compare notes with your classmates. Do you agree or disagree with their choices? Why? What effect would such disagreements have on a company's promotional plans?

Identify a promotional campaign that uses more than one element of the promotional mix. For example, an automotive company might use a mix that includes TV, radio, and print advertising; personal selling in the dealerships; and a sales promotion such as a rebate program. Study the individual pieces and the overall mix; then answer the following questions.

1. Which promotional element does the company seem to emphasize? Why do you think the company chose that element? Are you accustomed to seeing this kind of promotional mix in this industry?
2. As a consumer, how does the mix work for you? Could the company have reached you more effectively with a different promotional balance? What advice would you give to the company?
3. What sort of promotional mixes do competitors use? Do they mirror this company's efforts, or are they unique? Is there a promotional mix from a competitor that is more effective than the one you've studied?

# 18

# Advertising, Sales Promotion, and Public Relations

**After studying this chapter, you will be able to**

**1.** Identify the major types of advertising

**2.** Describe the steps required to launch an advertising campaign

**3.** List common advertising objectives and advertising appeals

**4.** Explain the strengths and weaknesses of the major advertising media

**5.** Explain the growing attraction of direct mail and other direct-marketing promotional strategies

**6.** Discuss the sales promotion techniques used to stimulate consumer demand

**7.** Describe the functions of public relations that have the closest link to the marketing mix

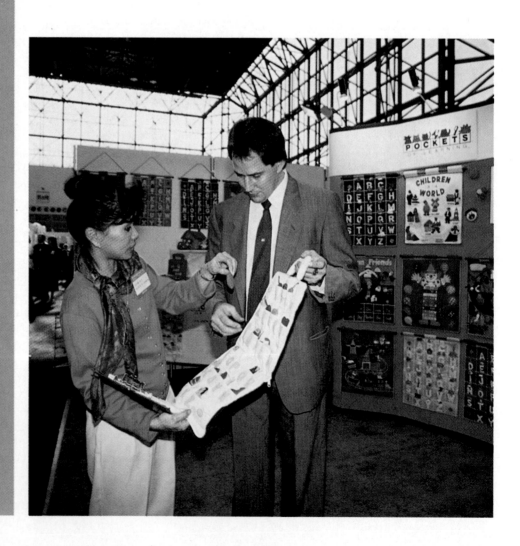

# FACING A MARKETING CHALLENGE AT STARBUCKS COFFEE

## Pouring On the PR for Successful Market Entries

To many people in this country, a cup of coffee is just a cup of coffee, nothing very special. It comes out of a pot, maybe you add cream and sugar, and you down a few cups on the way to work. To Howard Schultz, however, coffee is an all-consuming passion. From tramping through Central American jungles in search of just the right coffee beans to finding precisely the right brewing equipment, Schultz overlooks nothing on the way to a perfect cup of coffee.

Schultz's interest in great coffee extends beyond his personal palate, however. As president and CEO of Seattle-based Starbucks Coffee, Schultz wants everyone to crave premium coffee as much as he does. In Seattle, Portland, and a few other coffee-crazed cities with Starbucks retail stores, people line up every morning to get their favorites, from simple espresso to exotic chocolate concoctions. Schultz isn't content to let Starbucks be a regional brand, however. He views the whole country as his target market and public relations as his key marketing tool.

With more than a decade of coffee retailing experience, Schultz knows that once people get a taste of Starbucks and other premium coffees, they often resist going back to regular coffee. Aficionados think the preground coffee sold in tin cans at the grocery store tastes weak and bitter compared with premium coffees. The key is to get people's attention and interest long enough to give Starbucks a try.

In addition to the taste benefits, premium coffee is a lifestyle issue for many people. Coffee shops and "coffee bars" have replaced traditional bars and taverns for these people, offering patrons all the social benefits of going out with friends and meeting new people without the health and safety risks associated with alcoholic beverages. Caffeine concerns some coffee drinkers, of course, but a wide selection of decaffeinated products allows these people to enjoy coffee without the jittery side effects.

With these trends in mind, Schultz is active in his nationwide expansion, moving both down the West Coast and across to the East Coast. With its millions of inhabitants, Los Angeles represents a key market for just about every consumer product, coffee included. If you were Howard Schultz and wanted to build a strong Starbucks presence in Los Angeles without spending a fortune on advertising, what communication options could you take advantage of? How would you involve the news media to help spread your message? Would you take advantage of the show business aspects of life and business in Los Angeles? What steps could you take to make people feel good about adding premium coffee to their diets and their lifestyles?[1]

# CHAPTER OVERVIEW

Howard Schultz and his colleagues rely on a variety of promotional tools to reach consumers, retailers, and the news media. Chapter 17 introduces the four elements of the promotional mix. This chapter covers three of those elements—advertising, sales promotion, and public relations—in more detail. The fourth element, personal selling, is covered in depth in Chapter 19.

The first part of this chapter differentiates the types of advertising in use today and outlines the reasons companies and organizations use advertising. Next you get a description of the various appeals advertisers use to persuade audiences, including fear, logic, sex, and humor. Once you've decided on the appeal, you determine which media to use, and the major choices are covered in this chapter. After that you'll explore the final steps of an advertising campaign: creating the advertising materials and evaluating their effectiveness. The second part of this chapter examines sales promotions aimed at consumers and at marketing intermediaries. The third part describes how marketers use public relations to help meet business objectives.

# ADVERTISING

If you ever feel like you can't get away from advertising, that's not your imagination; advertisers are constantly searching for new ways to put their messages in front of you (see Exhibit 18.1). Picture yourself at the old ballpark enjoying a baseball game. Some of the players are paid to wear certain brands of shoes, the field is lined with advertising billboards, a blimp might be flying overhead with one or more commercial messages, the program you paid $5 for is full of ads, and you might even buy a hot dog with an ad message imprinted on it.

**Exhibit 18.1
DELIVERING
ADVERTISING
MESSAGES**
The jerseys of bicycle racers
are one of the many
promotional vehicles used by
WordPerfect Corporation.

Who creates all the ads you see every day? That depends on the company or organization in question. Some companies create their own advertisements, buy advertising space and time, and perform some or all of the functions required to put a message in front of you. The groups that perform these services are called **in-house agencies.** Other companies engage the services of **advertising agencies,** companies that specialize in the business of advertising. These agencies range from small firms that offer a limited array of services in selected market areas to huge, international agencies that provide sales promotion and public relations services as well.

## Types of Advertising

Advertising can be categorized in a number of ways, and understanding the particular type you're trying to develop is important. For example, an ad designed to get people to call a toll-free number and subscribe to *Sports Illustrated* is quite different from an ad designed to convince a bicycle dealer to carry Diamond Back cycles. Here's a look at the major types of ads.

### INSTITUTIONAL ADVERTISING

If an organization believes it would benefit from greater awareness and understanding in the marketplace or in the community at large, it may choose to use **institutional advertising,** which focuses on the organization itself rather than on its goods or services. Promoting a positive company image encourages investment, attracts talented employees, eases the attempt to lobby government officials, opens doors for salespeople, counters the effects of negative news coverage, and so on.[2] Smart companies recognize the value of their own reputations and do everything possible to keep their public images polished.

Numerous advertising techniques are used to promote organizations. For instance, to make prospective customers more receptive to salespeople, a company can advertise its technical expertise, number of satisfied customers, or long history. This background work makes personal selling efforts much easier because the prospect already knows the company when the salesperson knocks on the door. Marketers need to be careful with institutional ads, though; many institutional ads focus too much on the institution itself and not enough on the customer.[3]

Some companies choose to promote themselves by supporting public causes. The idea behind these campaigns is to build a good image in the public's mind by helping a good cause. For example, For Members Only, a maker of men's outerwear and sportswear, recently spent its entire advertising budget on antidrug and voter participation campaigns. For Members Only president Herb Goldsmith wanted an advertising strategy that would connect the company with current news stories. The result was a national antidrug marketing campaign that caught on with the news media, politicians, and celebrities. The company helped two worthy causes and garnered a lot of publicity in the process. During a two-year period when the company did no product advertising, its sales increased 20 percent. CEO Ed Wachtel has continued the campaigns into the 1990s. The company alternates antidrug and voter campaigns, racking up millions of dollars in equivalent exposure through press coverage of its efforts.[4]

### PRODUCT ADVERTISING

In contrast to institutional ads, many ads focus directly on specific goods and services, leading to the term **product advertising.** As with institutional ads, product ads can promote a particular image, or they can promote specific features of a good or service. Products that are frequently promoted by their images include clothes, cars, jewelry, and perfume. These ads are definitely about products, but they often don't focus on the physical features of those products. At the other extreme, tech-

**in-house agency**
A department inside a company that performs the complete range of advertising services, from developing ad strategies to buying media space and time

**advertising agencies**
Companies that specialize in providing various levels of advertising services; some agencies focus on specific services or market segments, and others offer a complete range of services covering a wide range of markets

**institutional advertising**
Advertising that promotes the name or image of an organization, rather than its goods or services

**product advertising**
Advertising that promotes specific goods and services while promoting the supplying company to a lesser degree or not at all

nical and industrial product ads often look like little more than lists of features and performance specifications. Many ads combine the image and feature approaches. For instance, a magazine ad for the Jaguar XJ6 might talk about the burled elm dashboard and the 12-cylinder engine while showing the car parked in front of a castle. The reader is supposed to learn something about the car's features while getting the idea that this is a car for royalty and for people who deserve to be treated like royalty.

## COMPETITIVE ADVERTISING

**competitive advertising**
Advertising that tries to promote specific product features that are better than those offered by the competition

**comparative advertising**
A special case of competitive advertising that explicitly compares your product with one or more competitive products

You can argue that all advertising is competitive in nature, but the term **competitive advertising** is applied to those ads that specifically highlight how a product is better than its competitors. The purpose of these ads, of course, is to build selective demand. When two or more products are directly contrasted in an ad, **comparative advertising** is the technique being used. In some countries, comparative ads are tightly regulated and in some cases banned, but that is clearly not the case in the United States. Indeed, the Federal Trade Commission started the ball rolling by encouraging advertisers to use direct product comparisons with the intent of better informing customers. Today 35 to 40 percent of all advertising in this country is comparative.[5]

Comparative advertising is frequently used by competitors with their sights set on the market leader, but it is useful whenever you believe you have some specific product strengths that are important to customers. Burger King used it on McDonald's, PepsiCo used it on Coca-Cola, and Ford finally got tired of getting slammed by Chevrolet truck advertising and decided to fight back with comparative ads. This is bare-knuckle marketing, and when done well, it is effective. However, comparative advertising sometimes ends up getting neutralized by look-alike campaigns from the competition. Analgesics (painkillers) is one category cited as an example of comparative advertising taken too far. So many claims and counterclaims appear in this "ad war" that consumers can no longer keep it all straight.[6] Long-distance telephone service is another intensively advertised category, with AT&T, MCI, and Sprint pounding away on consumers and businesses alike (see Exhibit 18.2).

France is one of several countries that ban comparative advertising; this is in marked contrast to the United States, where comparative ads are common.

Comparative ads can cross legal and ethical boundaries in two ways. First, some ads tout a product's strengths, but they do so selectively, talking about only those areas in which the product beats the competition and ignoring the rest. In the analgesics category, for example, Johnson & Johnson distributed a "safety profile" to doctors, showing that its brand, Tylenol, exhibited fewer side effects than three of its competitors. However, the company didn't list some other possible side effects, including potential liver damage and greater risk of overdose, in which it lost out to the competition. Second, some comparative ads simply overstep the bounds of truth and embellish claims of superiority. For instance, Jartran, a truck rental firm, claimed in its ads that it could "save consumers big money" compared to U-Haul. However, Jartran was promoting a temporary, introductory price, not its normal price. The court determined that the company deliberately tried to deceive customers.[7]

Another potential problem with comparative advertising is unfair portrayal of the quality or characteristics of competitors' products. To help bring an end to this, a U.S. law that went into effect in late 1989 makes such unfair comparisons illegal. Advertisers are now more careful, because victims of unfair ads can sue for damages.[8]

## OTHER CATEGORIES OF ADVERTISING

**direct-action advertising**
Advertising that tries to motivate customers to take action immediately after being exposed to the ad

**indirect-action advertising**
Advertising that tries to influence future purchases and other actions

Ads can be classified in several other ways. One important distinction is the immediacy of the message in the ad. **Direct-action advertising** seeks to motivate the customer to take action *now*. When you see a telephone number or a coupon to clip out and mail, this is direct-action advertising; the company wants you to stop what you're doing and respond. Meanwhile, **indirect-action advertising** tries to convey the right images and information so that people will respond favorably next time

**She came home to
"Friends & Family"® and found
"Friends Around the World"®**

Daniel E. Crawford
President
Network Services

To see why we're a great place for
opportunity and growth, one need
look no further than Patricia A. Davis.
She manages the capital planning
process for the network engineering
side of MCI's business.

Patricia A. Davis
Director
Network Services
Capital Planning

Lucky for us, in 1989, Patricia returned
to her native Washington D.C.
to be among "friends and family".
MCI values Patricia's contributions,
and all the people at MCI who maintain
our friendly, cooperative working
environment focused on responding
to customer needs.

**MCI®**
An Equal Opportunity Employer

**Exhibit 18.2
COMPETING
THROUGH MASSIVE
ADVERTISING**
In one of the world's most
aggressively contested
markets, MCI spends heavily
in its competition with Sprint
and AT&T. The competition
includes vying for the best
employees, the focus of this
MCI ad.

they make a purchase in a given product category. For instance, carmakers know that not everyone is in the market for a new car every day of the year, but they want to continually advertise their products to secure a place in your mind. Then when you are ready to start looking for a car, they've already delivered their message to you.

A product's stage in the product life cycle also suggests a particular type of advertising. When a company introduces a new type of product, it often employs **pioneer advertising,** which tries to build primary demand by educating potential customers about the benefits of this kind of product. These ads might be distinctly uncompetitive; until people have accepted this basic product category, bashing your competitors makes no sense. The ads start to get more competitive as companies try to build selective demand for their own products. As a product slides into the maturity and decline phases, some companies restrict their efforts to **reminder advertising,** which is designed to tell loyal customers that the product is still available and still better than its competition.

**pioneer advertising**
Advertising that tries to build primary, rather than selective, demand

**reminder advertising**
Advertising aimed at existing customers, telling them that products they've adopted are still available

## Organizational versus Consumer Advertising

Companies around the world spend huge sums of money every year on advertising that is never intended to reach final consumers. The targets for this class of advertising are other businesses and marketing intermediaries. Although organizational and consumer advertising are based on the same principles, they require different implementation. Here are some key differences (none of these is a hard-and-fast rule, however):

- Organizational advertising tends to use logical appeals, whereas consumer ads are often based on emotional appeals.
- Organizational ads usually speak to the customer's desire for greater profits; consumer ads usually promise personal satisfaction instead.
- Organizational advertising typically represents a smaller portion of the market-

ing budget than consumer advertising; in addition, organizational ads tend to be a smaller part of the selling process.

• Organizational advertising is usually aimed at specific target markets, whereas consumer ads often try to cover a wide, diverse audience.[9]

Consider three points in the life of a jar of peanut butter. Manufacturers of factory automation equipment advertise their products to the company that buys raw peanuts from the farmers and produces the peanut butter. Next, the producer is likely to advertise its line of products to grocery wholesalers and retailers. Third, both the producer and the retailers probably advertise the product to final consumers. These three instances of advertising are unique because the audience, the available media, and the message are different in each case.

## Advertising Campaigns

Advertising campaigns, defined as a coordinated series of promotional messages distributed over a fixed period of time, vary from small efforts involving a few people and a few thousand dollars (such as a local retailer placing a yellow pages ad) to huge projects costing tens of millions of dollars and employing dozens of people across the country and possibly in other countries as well (such as a TV, radio, and print media campaign by General Motors). Regardless of the cost and complexity, however, all campaigns progress through five basic steps: establish the objective, decide which type of appeal you'll use, select the media, create the advertisement, and evaluate the ad's effectiveness (see Exhibit 18.3). If evaluation reveals performance is not meeting objectives, you can modify the appeal, the advertisement, or the selection and timing of media. Remember, these five steps should be taken only after you've identified the target audience and established the promotional budget, which were discussed in Chapter 17. Here's a closer look at each step.

### STEP 1: ESTABLISH THE ADVERTISING OBJECTIVE

The best advertising objectives are specific and measurable. Saying that you want to make people feel better about your hotel chain is not a good objective because you won't be able to measure your success or failure. A good objective is saying that in the next six weeks you want to make 40 percent of the people in Ohio feel good about your hotel chain. Having an advertising goal that you can measure means you'll always know whether you're spending money effectively. This has never been more true than in today's business environment, with companies trying to justify every dollar they spend. The time frame is an important variable here. Advertising costs money, and most campaigns aren't allowed to run forever; they need to accomplish a specific goal by a specific time. Here are some commonly used advertising objectives:[10]

• *Positioning your company and your products.* A primary objective of all promotional efforts should be to position your company and your products. Even if you are

**Exhibit 18.3
LAUNCHING AN AD CAMPAIGN**
For a local newspaper ad or a $100 million national program, there are five steps you need to follow to launch an ad campaign. If evaluation shows that the ad isn't as effective as it should be, you may have to choose a different appeal, change the ad itself, or select different media or advertising schedules.

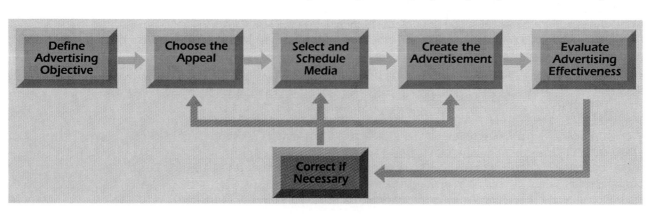

running an ad just to announce a special on lettuce, the way in which you deliver that message will affect your positioning. On the one hand, every time you advertise, you have the opportunity to improve your position in the market. On the other hand, you must always be watchful to make sure you don't hurt your position. For instance, if a local Ferrari dealership runs a shoddy, poor-quality ad, people might react negatively and think a little less of Ferrari as a result. Keep in mind that everything you do affects your position in the market, and as the most visible component of your marketing efforts, advertising is a powerful tool for helping—or hurting—that position.[11]

Consider the example of a Häagen-Dazs ad created under the direction of marketing vice president Beth Bronner. The ad was titled "The Four Food Groups" and featured caviar, a brioche, an artichoke—and Häagen-Dazs. The juxtaposition of Häagen-Dazs with three other rich, luxurious foods helps position Häagen-Dazs as a rich, luxurious product.[12]

- *Increasing use of your products.* A classic technique for increasing sales is to find new ways customers can use existing products and then tell them about it. A great example is Arm & Hammer's baking soda; the company suggests that you keep a box in the refrigerator to absorb food odors, pour a box down your garbage disposal to freshen it up, use it to brush your teeth, and a variety of other uses. All this for a product that is basically a baking ingredient.

- *Increasing the size of orders.* A related objective of advertising is to induce customers to order your products in greater quantities. Not only might this increase your total sales but it also reduces your average cost of sales because you have to process fewer orders.

- *Finding new customers.* When you think current customers are using your product as much as possible, you can set your advertising objective to find new customers. This might involve a broad strategy such as nationwide television commercials, or it might be a strategy of going after selected market niches through ads in specialized magazines.

- *Helping marketing intermediaries.* Producers often establish advertising objectives to help their marketing intermediaries. For instance, Procter & Gamble spends hundreds of millions of dollars every year trying to convince you to pick up some of its products next time you're in your favorite grocery store. This helps P&G, of course, but it also provides an invaluable service to retailers who can't afford the kind of advertising P&G is capable of. Also, manufacturers with their own sales forces often set objectives to introduce the company to prospective customers, which makes personal sales calls easier.

- *Generating sales leads.* Many ad campaigns are based on an objective of generating a certain number of sales leads, which are potential customers who have been identified as having a need for the product, an interest in the product, and the ability to purchase it. Sometimes a sale happens immediately, but other times the lead has to be nurtured and managed for months before the sale can be made.

- *Reaching other decision makers.* In some personal selling situations, the salespeople can't reach everyone who influences the purchase decision. This is particularly true when selling to large organizational customers, who might have a committee of a dozen people making the decision and who might have several layers of management approval on top of that. Advertising extends the reach of the salespeople, getting the message across to decision makers they don't have the time or opportunity to approach in person.

Of course, you have to make these objectives specific to your company's situation. For instance, Quaker Oats might create an informational campaign that explains some uses of its product other than its traditional breakfast role. Its objective might be to "convince another 10 percent of our current customers to try using Quaker Oats in their baking within six months." When you've arrived at a solid objective, the next step is to decide how you're going to appeal to the buyer's motivation.

STEP 2: SELECT THE BASIC APPEAL

Well-designed ads use a carefully planned appeal to whatever motivates the target audience. Naturally, the best appeal to use depends largely on the target audience. By segmenting along lifestyles and other variables, advertisers try to identify which groups of people can be reached with various kinds of appeals.

LOGIC AND EMOTION     One of the most important decisions to make in this regard is whether to use an appeal that is predominantly rational or predominantly emotional. Some ads try to convince you with data; others try to tug at your emotions to get their point across (see Exhibit 18.4). Even with the most unemotional sort of product, however, emotions can play a very big role. Some industrial and high-technology marketers assume that because they're selling to engineers and other technical people, logic is the only way to go. But people are people, and they all have hopes, fears, desires, and dreams, regardless of the job they have or the products they're buying. Even a highly technical ad can appeal to a reader's emotions, if the logic in the story leads to less stress on the job, greater chance of personal success, or some other appealing scenario.

Emotional appeals range from the most syrupy and sentimental to the downright terrifying. Fear has been used to sell a variety of products, from AT&T's phone systems (fear about losing your job if you don't buy an AT&T system) to Campbell's bean and pea soups (fear of getting cancer if you don't eat enough fiber). Personal-care products are often marketed on the basis of fear; after all, you don't want to get rejected because you have dandruff or body odor. Appeals to fear have to be managed carefully, however. Laying it on too thick can anger the audience or even cause them to block out the message entirely.[13]

On the other hand, reducing someone's fear or anxiety, rather than artificially increasing it, can be effective, too. Perrier recognized that some people felt compelled to drink alcoholic beverages in social situations, out of fear of being rejected. To get people to start drinking Perrier in public, the company used advertising that reduced those fears of rejection and sent the message that it's acceptable not to drink alcohol.[14]

Holiday Inn built a global advertising strategy around the realization that all travelers are (1) away from home and out of their personal comfort zones, (2) in different and often unfamiliar surroundings, and (3) subject to the same hassles and hardships. In response to this emotional situation, the company used the dual themes of "Welcome" and "Stay with somebody you know." The strategy and even the visual format of the advertising are the same around the world, although words are translated as needed and variations are made to meet local cultural differences. For example, ads in the United States and Germany feature a businesswoman at the hotel, receiving a faxed drawing from her child. British travelers, however, didn't respond to the heavily sentimental pitch, so the ads there feature a friendly doorman instead.[15]

In contrast to emotional appeals, sometimes the best strategy is simple logic. When it comes to logical appeals, nothing seems more effective than talking about

**Exhibit 18.4**
**EMOTIONAL APPEALS IN ADS**
Officials in San Diego used this billboard near Los Angeles to encourage tourism.

Sure Beats Another Weekend At Home.

SAN DIEGO

value. Appealing to the consumer's sense of value has helped the ad campaigns of some of the nation's biggest retailers, including Wal-Mart, Sears, Kmart, and J. C. Penney.[16] From cars to computer software, value has become a major advertising appeal.

CELEBRITY APPEAL    An increasingly popular ad approach is the use of celebrities. The theory behind these ads is that people will be more inclined to pay attention to the ads and to use products that celebrities use and that some of the star's image, trustworthiness, or other positive qualities will rub off on the products he or she is endorsing. Celebrity endorsement is a popular strategy in both consumer and business-to-business advertising, but it remains something of a theoretical curiosity. On the one hand, it seems like a great way to build visibility and preference for your brand. Experts suggest that, depending on the product, celebrity endorsement can work at three levels: (1) when the star is physically attractive; (2) when the star is trusted by the public (particularly if the star has some legitimate expertise in relation to the product, such as home improvement expert Bob Vila's appearances in advertising for Sears tools); and (3) when the celebrity's image is compatible with the product.

On the other hand, evidence to support the continued and increasing use of the celebrity appeal is hard to find. In one survey, consumers ranked it as the least convincing of all advertising appeals. Does this mean that it is not effective? Not necessarily. James Patterson of the J. Walter Thompson agency argues that many people are simply too embarrassed to admit being influenced by celebrities and that, in spite of what consumers say in surveys, celebrities can indeed build emotional bonds for products. In other words, celebrities might actually persuade consumers more often than consumers would like to admit.[17]

However strong the cases for and against celebrity endorsements, most experts agree on several points: First, it's important to match the celebrity and the product. For a product with a youthful, wholesome image, for instance, you should find a celebrity who always has a youthful wholesome image. Conversely, this same celebrity might not be the best choice for insurance or some other "serious" product.

Second, it's important to remember that celebrities are human beings with public lives outside of their advertising appearances. These public images become associated with their products' public images, so if the star gets in trouble, the brand can suffer—if not in sales, at least in public embarrassment. This is one of the reasons animated cartoon characters such as Bart Simpson are popular as "celebrity" endorsers. An executive at Fox Television, producer of "The Simpsons," put it bluntly: "Bart will never get caught doing crack."[18] The troubles experienced by pop star Michael Jackson in 1993 and 1994 greatly diminished his appeal as an endorser, and led PepsiCo to drop him from its roster of celebrities.[19]

Third, it's not simply a matter of picking celebrities who are well liked by the public. A study from Total Research of Princeton, New Jersey, uncovered some interesting differences between celebrities' likability scores and their effectiveness as product endorsers. In a list of 54 celebrities, singer Paula Abdul ranked twentieth in terms of likability but ninth in terms of endorsement effectiveness. Comedian Bob Hope exhibited the reverse situation, ranking first in likability but eighth in effectiveness. However, in spite of all the confusing and sometimes contradictory evidence, the use of celebrity endorsers is a big part of the advertising business.[20]

SEX APPEAL    Another old standby in the advertising world is selling with sex. The classic technique is to have an attractive, scantily attired model share the page or TV screen with the product. If the model's looks and pose somehow make sense, fine; if they don't, fine. The point is to have the audience associate the product with pleasure. In the United States, this technique went about as far as it could go with sex-drenched ads for Georges Marciano's Guess Jeans and Calvin Klein's Obsession perfume. However, advertisers seem to be pulling away from such extreme measures. A more popular approach today is to keep the clothes on the models and just hint about sex. As *Forbes* magazine put it, advertisers are switching to "fantasy, not flesh." Women are being shown in less passive roles, another big change from previous years. For example, a commercial for Sansabelt men's slacks featured a woman saying, "I always lower my eyes when a man passes to see if he's worth following."[21]

THE POWER OF NOVELTY An approach that has taken hold in recent years is trying to catch the audience's attention by making ads really strange. American Honda Motor Company used this technique with some success when it tried to expand scooter sales in the United States. One of its stranger commercials had questions like these scrawled in white handwriting against a black background: "Who am I? Can dogs think? Am I ugly? Is there truth? Is there any pizza left? Should I buy a vowel?" The commercial concludes with "The new Honda Elite 50. If it's not the answer, at least it's not another question."[22]

Simply making an advertisement off the wall doesn't ensure success, however. Advertising critics and some retailers often pan the stranger ads. The "Reeboks Let U.B.U." campaign was definitely different, with a cast of characters that included a three-legged man and a fairy godmother with a briefcase, and it left some people cold. Nissan's Infiniti division introduced the Infiniti cars with ads that didn't show the car but showed landscapes, seascapes, and other soothing pictures accompanied by an announcer talking about completely unrelated topics. The Infiniti brand scored well in audience recall tests, but sales didn't exactly skyrocket. Getting people to remember your name doesn't mean they'll buy your product.[23] Infiniti sales did start to pick up after the ad strategy was changed to a more traditional approach.

**subliminal advertising**
Advertising that attempts to influence consumer perceptions and behavior through symbols that are not consciously decoded; both the existence and effectiveness of subliminal advertising are open to question, however

SUBLIMINAL ADVERTISING You've probably heard about **subliminal advertising,** ads in which the decoding is supposed to happen subconsciously through the use of visual symbols, subaudio messages, or visual messages shown for a very brief period. A frequently cited example is a movie theater experiment in which the words "Hungry? Eat Popcorn" and "Drink Coca-Cola" were projected on the screen for one three-thousandths of a second. Supposedly, the theater's sales of both popcorn and Coke jumped during the test period, but these impressive results were concocted by the "researcher," who worked for the Subliminal Projection Company. He was trying to drum up business for his firm.[24] However, he caused such an uproar that some states passed laws banning subliminal advertising, and the hunt for hidden persuasion was on.

Beginning in 1973 with the publication of a book called *Subliminal Seduction,* by Wilson Bryan Key, much has been made of nude figures, the word *sex,* and other such things supposedly hidden in product photos and sometimes on products themselves. For example, Key claims that Ritz crackers have the word *sex* embedded on both the top and bottom of the cracker. He says the embedded message even makes the crackers taste better. As incredible as all this sounds, he has been able to generate a significant amount of public mistrust of the advertising profession. However, no one has been able to provide objective evidence of the existence of this sort of trickery. Furthermore, little psychological evidence exists to suggest that it would work even if anyone were doing it.[25]

## STEP 3: SELECT THE MEDIA

**media plan**
A plan that outlines the objectives of an advertising campaign, the target audience, and the specific media vehicles that will be used to reach that audience

As an advertiser, you have a wide variety of vehicles for transmitting your promotional messages. The characteristics of the target audience are a major factor in deciding which of these to use in a given campaign. For instance, you can reach scuba divers through the specialized magazines that cater to that audience, but if you want to reach all consumers in the country, you would use a vehicle with broader distribution, such as television. Exhibit 18.5 shows how U.S. advertisers divide their advertising dollars. You can see that newspapers, direct mail, and television are the dominant categories.

An advertiser's decisions about media are contained in a **media plan,** which out-

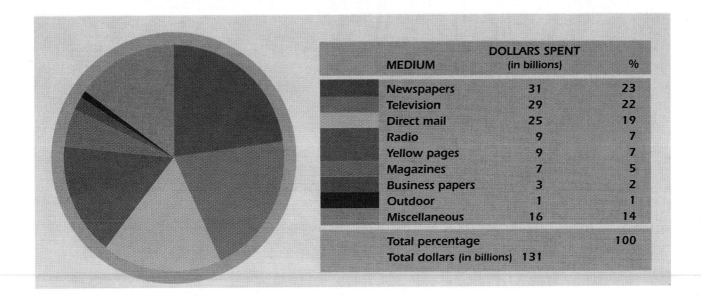

| MEDIUM | DOLLARS SPENT (in billions) | % |
|---|---|---|
| Newspapers | 31 | 23 |
| Television | 29 | 22 |
| Direct mail | 25 | 19 |
| Radio | 9 | 7 |
| Yellow pages | 9 | 7 |
| Magazines | 7 | 5 |
| Business papers | 3 | 2 |
| Outdoor | 1 | 1 |
| Miscellaneous | 16 | 14 |
| Total percentage | | 100 |
| Total dollars (in billions) | 131 | |

lines the media objectives in terms of who is going to be reached and how it will be done. (Just as advertisers create a marketing mix and a promotional mix, they create a *media mix,* which is the collection of media used in an ad campaign.) Beyond the basic advantages and disadvantages of the individual media, advertisers must make two important decisions about coverage and scheduling. The first decision involves **reach,** an advertising term for the number of people who will see an ad, usually expressed as a percentage of the total market. The other variable is **frequency,** which is the average number of times the target audience is exposed to the message. Because ad budgets aren't infinite, you often have to make a compromise between reach and frequency. How many times do you need to run an ad? That depends on the products and the customers. If you have a message about a product that is important to the audience, such as ads for cosmetics or major appliances, you'll probably get the point across the first or second time. For a message about less gripping products, like instant coffee, you'll probably need three or four exposures or more.[26]

Advertisers often talk about buying GRPs, which stands for gross rating points. This number is equal to reach (in percentage points) times frequency. For instance, if Nissan wanted to reach 60 percent of a certain market an average of three times, it would have to buy 180 GRPs. The cost of a GRP depends on the medium. Another common media-buying term is CPM, or cost per thousand, which indicates how much money it takes to reach 1,000 customers.[27]

Picking the advertising schedule can be a difficult task. Ads can be run in many ways, and no single approach works for all products in all markets. The two basic techniques are known as *continuity* and *flighting.* As its name implies, continuity means that ads are run continuously over the duration of the campaign. Flighting, on the other hand, covers a variety of discontinuous approaches. For instance, you might choose to advertise heavily for the first four months of a product's life and then advertise just every other week after that. This is a good way to stretch small ad budgets.[28] See Exhibit 18.6 for a hypothetical media schedule.

When using more than one medium, be sure to keep the various messages consistent. This sounds obvious, but it can be a problem in large companies that split promotions into several departments or with any company that uses more than one outside agency. A lack of coordination dilutes the potential effectiveness of promotional campaigns because you don't get the supporting power from the various media. For example, radio has been shown to be a very effective support mechanism for TV commercials. The message can be sent first via TV and then reinforced with a radio message. This approach can have nearly the same impact as two TV commercials, but it costs less.[29]

**Exhibit 18.5**
**ADVERTISING EXPENDITURES IN THE UNITED STATES**
Newspapers, direct mail, and traditional network television are the leading media choices for U.S. advertisers.

**reach**
A measure of the portion of the target audience that will be reached by an advertisement

**frequency**
A measure of the average number of times that members of the target audience were exposed to an ad during a given period of time

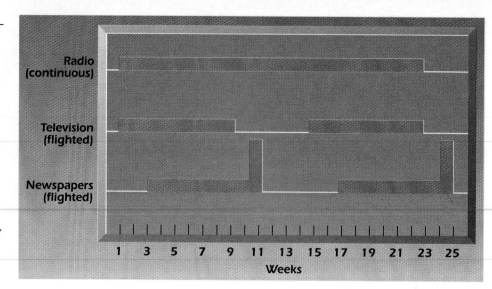

**Exhibit 18.6
A HYPOTHETICAL
MEDIA SCHEDULE**
You can choose from a variety
of scheduling options, including both continuous and
flighting schedules.

**database marketing**
Direct marketing that takes
advantage of comprehensive
information about customers,
including purchase behavior,
demographics, and lifestyle

As you might expect, each medium has distinct advantages and disadvantages. Here is a quick look at the major media, followed by a discussion of emerging and alternative media.

NEWSPAPERS     As the leading advertising medium in this country, newspapers offer some definite strengths, including extensive coverage, low cost, selection of topic areas in which to place ads (sports, home, and so on), and short lead time for placing ads. This short lead time was a big help to Chrysler after the federal government indicted company executives for driving cars without the odometers attached and then selling them as new. The indictment was handed down on a Wednesday; by Sunday the company and its agency had decided how to respond publicly, by Monday morning ads had been designed, and on Wednesday they appeared in major papers nationwide. This kind of fast and vast coverage isn't usually possible with any other type of medium. The downside of newspaper advertising includes short life span, lots of visual competition from other ads, and poor graphic quality.[30]

DIRECT MAIL     Nobody in this country needs to be told that direct mail is on the rise. The reasons are simple: It works, and it is easy to measure. Its advantages include the ability to deliver large amounts of information to narrowly selected audiences. A promising development in audience selection is **database marketing,** in which the advertiser collects, stores, and uses data about each customer's needs, purchase habits, and so on. This allows precise targeting of advertising messages.[31]

In addition to its effectiveness, direct mail (along with other direct techniques such as telemarketing) appeals to marketers because the results are usually measurable. If you have a choice between a $10 million television campaign (where you can't be sure who gets your message and how they respond) and a $10 million direct-mail campaign (where you know the name, address, and probably the purchase habits of every person on your list—and you know who buys and who doesn't), you're likely to take the direct route.

The biggest drawbacks to direct mail are high cost per contact, a generally poor image (it's "junk mail"), and competition from all the other direct-mail pieces in everyone's mailbox. Direct mail is still far less common in other countries, however, so international marketers have an opportunity to take advantage of mail without running into the same mailbox clutter they experience in the United States. A related development is "junk fax." Some advertisers send ads or entire catalogs to businesses' fax machines, although this practice has angered many people and stands a good chance of being banned in some states.

TELEVISION     TV commercials have numerous advantages, starting with the combined impact of sight, sound, and motion. Other strong points include prestige (relative to other media), massive coverage, and the ability to catch people's attention. The downside includes high cost (both initial and ongoing), short message life, general lack of selectivity, and vulnerability to viewers' remote controls. According to some estimates, viewers zap past 10 to 40 percent of TV commercials that air while they're watching (depending on the time of day and programming), although network executives tend to dispute these numbers.[32] Look for continued changes in television advertising as syndication, cable, and pay-per-view systems grow. Also, look for new types of TV advertising, including such infomercial fare as program-length commercials and commercials modeled after talk shows, cooking shows, and other established formats.[33]

RADIO    Radio offers relatively low cost, good local coverage, and the ability to repeat your message frequently. In major metropolitan areas, radio reaches millions of listeners during the morning and afternoon commutes. On the negative side, radio commercials often have a hard time fighting their way into the listener's brain; people don't usually give radio the same degree of attention they give TV or print media. Finally, radio is a completely nonvisual medium; you can't show anything over the radio.

MAGAZINES    Magazines offer some strong benefits, including highly targeted audiences in many cases. Magazines such as *Fine Woodworking* and *Keyboard* go after narrow market niches and are efficient ways to reach specialized audiences. Magazines also provide high-quality production, long message life, and the opportunity to reach multiple readers. The biggest drawbacks to magazines are the long lead time before ads can be placed (up to several months in some cases) and the absence of motion and sound.[34]

OTHER MEDIA    Businesses have many more choices for advertising media, some of which have been around for years and some of which are still in the developmental stage. Outdoor advertising, in the form of billboards, has been used for many years, although it is not always a popular choice in some communities. Transit advertising has long been popular, including ads on buses, subways, taxis, and now the sides of trucks. Also, directories such as the yellow pages and the *Thomas Register of American Manufacturers,* a comprehensive directory used by many industrial firms, help many consumers and organizations find the goods and services they need.

Advertisers continually search for new ways to reach potential customers. Commercials can be included on rented videocassettes and ads can be printed on the rental boxes themselves. Computer-based systems such as Prodigy deliver commercials right to your home-computer screen. Another computer option is disk-based advertisements, in which the ad is contained on a computer disk that is sent to interested customers. Some companies selling expensive or complex products opt to put advertising on videotape, and in some cases they even charge customers for the commercial. In airplane lavatories, on grocery bags, on the backs of ski lift chairs, in special editions of the yellow pages, on parking meters, over in-store radio channels, on restaurant menus, in video screens attached to shopping carts—advertisers and their agencies are looking high and low to find new places to stick promotional messages.[35] Even movies have become a popular advertising medium. In a controversial practice known as **product placement,** companies pay movie producers to work their products or signs into the scenery and to have the stars use or consume a wide variety of products.

**product placement**
The tactic of paying movie producers to promote products in movies; in some cases, products or signs are shown in the scene, and in other cases the stars actually use or consume the products

## STEP 4: CREATE THE ADVERTISEMENT

Once you've decided the best way to approach an audience and selected the best media, the next step is to create the actual advertisement. The specific actions this step requires depend on the media you plan to use, but all ads feature two basic elements. The first is **copy,** which is the verbal part of the ad, and the second is **artwork,** which is the visual part of the ad. In addition, broadcast ads, including

**copy**
The verbal or textual portion of an advertisement

**artwork**
The visual or graphic portion of an advertisement

radio and television commercials, are built around a *script,* and television ads also rely on a *storyboard,* which shows a picture of each scene and the corresponding words that go along with it. This discussion focuses on print media advertisements, but many of the techniques for broadcast commercials are similar.

DEVELOPING COPY    Perhaps you've looked at an ad that has two sentences of copy and then thought to yourself, "That looks easy. Anybody could crank out a couple of sentences." Alas, looks are deceiving. Writing ad copy is part art, part science, and part luck, and few people do it well. Top copywriters are rewarded handsomely for their ability to create effective copy. Following are five fundamental purposes of ad copy:[36]

- *Getting the reader's attention.* It's a funny thing about ads: They work only if somebody reads them. That is one of the biggest challenges facing an advertiser: How do you get somebody to stop flipping through the pages of *Newsweek* long enough to read your ad? The first job of the copywriter is to create a headline that will catch people's attention. This can be done with a few carefully chosen words or an entire sentence (see Exhibit 18.7). David Ogilvy, a widely quoted advertising expert, said this was his best headline: "At 60 miles an hour the loudest noise in the new Rolls-Royce comes from the electric clock."[37]
- *Stimulating interest.* Once you've stopped the reader, you have to give some incentive to keep reading. You do so by stimulating the reader's interest. One powerful way to do this is to let readers know that you understand their situation or their problem and that you've got just the answer. Once you've selected your basic appeal (step 2), whether it's gentle emotions or unyielding logic, you put it to work stimulating interest.
- *Building credibility.* Now that you have the reader's interest, explain how you're able to provide these impressive benefits. This might be based on your company's or product's reputation, some research data, testimonials from satisfied customers, or the endorsement of a recognized expert. Building credibility isn't as easy as you might think; consumers are smarter and better informed about advertising than they've ever been, and they'll usually spot an advertiser who tries to pull a fast one.

Here are some examples from post-*E.T.* films. *Mr. Mom* helped advertise McDonald's, Domino's pizza, Terminex exterminators, Folgers, Lite beer, Jack Daniels, Van Camp's, Ban, Windex, Tide, Spray 'n Wash, Borax, Clorox 2, and Downey. Sylvester Stallone's *Over the Top* displayed three products (Budweiser, Colgate shaving cream, and Michelin tires) before the opening credits even finished. The products don't always just sit there; sometimes they are advertised in the dialogue as well. In *Murphy's Romance,* Sally Field asks for Extra-Strength Tylenol and cheers when the Campbell's soup is ready, calling it by name.

Another controversial aspect about product placement concerns products that fall under television advertising restrictions. You can't run a commercial for distilled spirits (whiskey and the like) or cigarettes on U.S. television any more, but nothing stops you from having celebrities visibly consume these products in movies. As movies make their way to television after their theater lives are over, the once-banned products are right back on TV.

Whether or not the public likes it, product placement is now a sizable industry that shows no signs of subsiding. Companies pay from $25,000 to $50,000 to have a product shown in the background; more involved placements can cost several hundred thousand dollars. For instance, Philip Morris paid $350,000 to have James Bond smoke Larks in *Licence to Kill.* Not only are the dollar figures signif-icant, so are the number of movies involved. Robert Kovoloff, a leading go-between in the placement game, placed products in more than 600 movies in his first five years of business. Over a dozen companies now specialize in product placements.

**WHAT'S YOUR OPINION?**

**1.** Should advertisers be allowed to promote their products through movies and television shows?
**2.** Should movie and TV producers who place products be required to state at the beginning of a program that it contains advertising messages?

- *Heightening desire.* To make customers feel that this product is indeed the answer to their problems, write this material in terms that are meaningful and important to your customer. Too many advertisers waste too much ad money by talking about themselves instead of their customers. Explain how the product will solve the customer's problem. Don't focus on the features of your product; focus on the benefits those features deliver to the customer.
- *Motivating action.* Before readers turn the page, get them to do something. For direct-action advertising, this might be calling a toll-free number and placing an order. For indirect-action ads, the "action" you want them to take might be forming a certain opinion or feeling a certain way.

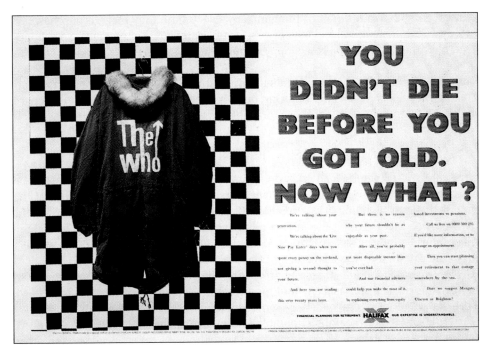

**Exhibit 18.7
THE POWER OF A STRONG HEADLINE**
England's Halifax Financial Services is likely to catch the attention of every person who grew up listening to The Who's "My Generation," which featured the line, "I hope I die before I get old." These people need to start thinking about paying for their retirement years, and Halifax wants their business.

CREATING ARTWORK    Artwork plays a vital role in most ads. In some cases, it is much more prominent than copy, with the visual images conveying most or all of the message. Graphic elements include tables, graphs, drawings, photographs, paintings, and computer-generated images. The arrangement of the copy and artwork in the ad is referred to as the *layout*. Advertising artists work closely with the copywriter to make sure the combined effect of the two basic elements is coherent and powerful.

Visual elements can be based on a variety of themes, including the product's own package, the product in use, product features, humor, before-and-after comparisons, visual comparisons with other products, and testimonials from users or celebrities. For instance, the marketing people behind Maybelline cosmetics want you to get the idea that you too can benefit from the use of their products. So they show the products in use, that is, on the face of their attractive spokesmodel. These photos pack a good one-two punch: You get to see the products in use and thus get the idea that if they work for the model, they might just work for you too.

What makes a good ad? Although you'll find no generic "cookbook" for creating effective ads, many people have developed checklists that help you along the way. The following list highlights the major points for print ads:[38]

- *Visual magnetism.* You have to get the audience's attention right from the start.
- *Clear identification of the target audience.* Sometimes your target will be obvious, but in other cases it might take a word or two of explanation.
- *An invitation to the reader.* The ad's layout should illuminate and dramatize the selling message, and it should invite the reader into the scene.
- *A specific promise.* Your audience needs to know in specific terms how you're going to improve their lives. Vague generalities are easy to write, but they aren't effective.
- *A logical selling presentation.* The layout should leave no question about where to start reading, and it should lead the reader through the selling presentation from beginning to end.
- *Personal style.* People respond best when they are treated in a comfortable manner. Talk to the reader in a casual, informal style.
- *Easy to read.* Too many ads are too hard to read; the audience will give up if reading your ad takes too much energy.
- *Solution orientation.* Good product ads talk about how the product will solve the customer's problem, not how smart the supplier is or how clever the product is.
- *Reflection of the company's character.* Customers buy more than just products; in a way, they buy a little bit of the company every time they make a purchase, so they assign the general feel of your ads to your company. For instance, do a sloppy ad, and they'll think you're a sloppy company.

This list is intended to help you evaluate print ads, but the underlying principles apply to any type of advertising. Figuring out what makes an ad good is the easy part; making it happen is often another story entirely.

## STEP 5: EVALUATE ADVERTISING EFFECTIVENESS

How can you tell whether an ad is doing its job? Evaluating the effectiveness of an ad is not easy, and in some cases, advertisers just have to take it on faith that the money they are spending is worthwhile. Often, so many variables are at work in the marketplace that isolating the impact ads have on sales can be difficult. In spite of these hurdles, however, advertisers, agencies, and academic researchers devote a lot of energy to studying advertising effectiveness.

The two categories of ad testing are **pretesting,** which refers to tests conducted before the advertising is run, and **posttesting,** which is conducted afterward. Pretests range from simply asking representative customers what they think of an ad to utilizing experimental techniques that involve analysis of brainwaves and eye movements (see Exhibit 18.8). Some of these techniques take place in a laboratory

**pretesting**
The practice of testing ads before they are run

**posttesting**
The practice of testing audience reactions and response to ads after they are run

**Exhibit 18.8
ADVERTISING TESTS**
Two miniature cameras track this subject's eyes as he reads through the newspaper. Advertisers can use data from tests such as these to judge the impact of headlines, position on the page, color, and many other aspects of an ad.

setting; others are conducted "in the field." No method works in all cases, but like all good marketing research, thorough pretesting can help reduce the risks involved in business decisions.

Posttesting is often simpler than pretesting. In fact, if the objective of your ad is to generate a certain number of sales, posttesting is quite simple: Just check the cash register. For indirect-action ads and image ads, posttesting is a little more complicated because you aren't always asking for specific, immediate action. Action is fairly easy to measure, but perceptions, feelings, and beliefs aren't. Two common posttest techniques are **aided recall,** in which you show respondents the ad and ask whether they remember it, and **unaided recall,** in which you question the respondents without such prompting.[39]

In addition to pretesting the advertising, you should also pretest the audience's beliefs, behavior, attitude, or whatever variables you are hoping to influence with the ad. This establishes baseline data you can use to measure the ad's effectiveness. For instance, if Mobil Oil wants to see whether an upcoming ad campaign will reduce public suspicion of big business, it should measure those beliefs both before the ads are run and then again after the ads appear. By comparing the pretest and posttest data, Mobil will have a better idea of how well its ads work.

Whether ad testing is needed, or even useful, is a controversial issue. Some people on the creative side (copywriters and artists) say testing tends to produce ho-hum ads that are diluted until they gain the approval of consumer committees. As a result, testing is said to stifle creativity and stop advertisers from taking big risks that might pay off in a big way. On the other hand, many clients and analytic researchers say testing is vital to make sure money isn't wasted. This battle is between creative faith and investment analysis, and it isn't likely to be resolved soon.[40] Another aspect of this issue is whether testing, regardless of how much you do, really helps. Information Resources, a large research firm, recently conducted a study that found "no meaningful relationship between persuasion and recall measures and sales changes." In other words, just because your ad gets high scores in testing doesn't mean your product will get high scores in the marketplace, where it counts.[41]

**aided recall**
A posttesting technique that shows specific ads to people who then answer various questions about them

**unaided recall**
A posttesting technique that, without prompting the audience's memory by showing the ads, asks people about their recall of advertising

## International Advertising

As you might expect, international advertising adds its own special challenges, which range from the obvious (such as language barriers) to the subtle (such as cultural norms regarding graphic symbols). Advertisers have to be careful when taking their campaigns into other countries, both to avoid offending people and to maximize their promotional impact.

The fundamental decision in international advertising is whether to use one standardized campaign worldwide or multiple localized campaigns. Coca-Cola, for example, uses one ad theme worldwide. In addition to being easier to manage, global advertising is less expensive. Coca-Cola saved roughly $90 million over two decades by using a global approach. On the other hand, many companies believe in designing unique advertising for each area of the world. In contrast to Coca-Cola's approach, Levi Strauss creates a number of ad strategies to cover the world. In Britain, Levi's are promoted with a Wild West theme; in continental Europe, the commercials are based on sex appeal; and in Japan, the company goes for a cult hero image using film clips of James Dean and other notable people.[42] In addition to the advertising, marketers consider the rest of the marketing mix as well when selling internationally. This topic is discussed further in Chapter 20.

Now take a closer look at the second element of the promotional mix, sales promotion. Keep in mind that a close relationship often exists between sales promotion efforts and advertising efforts, and coordinate the two elements carefully.

# SALES PROMOTION

As an active consumer in today's retail environment, you've probably come into contact with a wide variety of sales promotions. If you've ever won tickets to a concert, gotten a few cents off on a bag of potato chips, or entered a sweepstakes when subscribing to a magazine, you've had a taste of sales promotion. Sales promotion covers quite a wide range of activities and events, including both pull promotions aimed at consumers and push promotions aimed at marketing intermediaries. Businesses use sales promotion for several reasons: to generate quick sales bursts, to build long-term awareness and market share, and to gain increased shelf space and better in-store display.[43] Consumer marketers spend mightily on sales promotions, far more than they spend on advertising, in fact. In 1992, 45 percent of U.S. consumer-goods marketing allocations went to trade promotions, 28 percent went to consumer promotions, and only 27 percent went to advertising.[44]

## Consumer Promotions

The first category of sales promotions includes those efforts aimed at influencing the final consumer. Such promotions are designed to motivate consumers to immediate (or nearly immediate) action. To accomplish this task, marketers have developed quite a variety of sales promotion techniques. Here are the most common ones:

- *Coupons.* In the United States, companies distribute over 300 billion coupons every year. That's more than 1,000 coupons for every woman, man, and child every year. Consumers redeem only 7 or 8 percent of those 300 billion overall, but most U.S. households redeem at least one coupon a year. Coupons work well in several situations, including stimulating trial of new products, reaching out to nonusers of mature products, encouraging repeat purchases, and reducing the price of products without having to enlist the cooperation of retailers. Coupons have several drawbacks, however. The first is encouraging delayed purchases; some customers won't purchase a product until a coupon is available. The second drawback is wasted advertising and lost profits resulting from delivering coupons to people who would buy the product anyway. Third, coupons have been accused of instilling a bargain-hunting mentality in many consumers, which emphasizes the importance of low prices. Fourth, coupons have a tendency to tarnish the brand's image by making it appear cheap.[45]

- *Premiums.* Remember the little toys you used to dig out of Cracker Jack boxes? That's an example of a **premium,** an item given away with a product to induce you to buy. Well-selected premiums can improve a product's image, increase product trial, and gain customer goodwill. For example, to differentiate Spic and Span cleanser, Procter & Gamble inserted diamonds into some packages. By associating it with precious gemstones, P&G tried to give the product a higher-quality image.[46]

**premium**
Item that is given away with a product as part of a sales promotion

- *Samples.* Sampling is one of the most effective ways of getting people to try new products and to expand the base for established products, and it has been the fastest-growing consumer promotion in recent years. Researchers estimate that 75 percent of the households that receive a sample will try it. Samples can be distributed door-to-door, by mail, or by attaching them to or including them with other products. Sampling can be an effective way to induce people to try a new product because you put some of the product right in their hands for free. The biggest drawback to sampling is cost; it can be the most expensive way to promote a product. Also, be sure that the sample product will be more attractive than customers' current brands or they'll simply switch back to those brands after they consume your sample.[47]

- *Contests and sweepstakes.* Because they have the potential to create interest and excitement, contests and sweepstakes are a good way to draw people toward a brand or an entire company. When service station chain SuperAmerica Group ran a contest in which people got both discount coupons for a high-octane brand of gasoline and a chance to win a new BMW, sales of the brand climbed 227 percent over a four-week period.[48]

- *Point-of-purchase materials.* Displays, window posters, and other advertising materials located right in the store are known as **point-of-purchase (POP) advertising.** Because of its location, point-of-purchase advertising fills that gap between other advertising efforts and the cash register. POP advertising has numerous advantages, starting with the fact that recall isn't a problem. Consumers might forget your TV commercial by the time they get to the store, but they can't forget a display poster that is right in front of them as they reach for products. Many customers make purchase decisions in the store, and POP materials are your last chance to make an impression. Another advantage is stimulating impulse buying; that's why you see the approach to checkout counters stacked with displays of everything from batteries to books. Also, POP advertising is always in the right place at the right time. When customers are in the store looking for a particular product, your message is ready for them (see Exhibit 18.9).[49] One of the biggest problems with POP materials is getting retailer cooperation; store managers

**point-of-purchase (POP) advertising**
Advertising, displays, and other materials that are placed in stores to catch shoppers' attention as they are selecting products

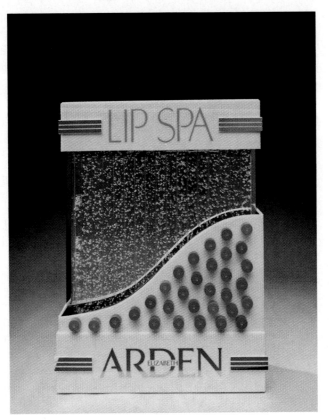

**Exhibit 18.9**
**POINT-OF-PURCHASE ADVERTISING**
This eye-catching Elizabeth Arden display draws shoppers, many of whom will make the purchase decision when they see displays such as this one.

often have to choose among many available displays to fill their limited floor space.

- *Frequency marketing.* The frequent-flyer programs now common in the airline industry are a form of **frequency marketing,** programs that build customer loyalty by providing financial incentives to stay with a product. The programs are also a great way to gather data about customers.[50] Hotels (Marriott and Hilton), department stores (Sears), specialty stores (Waldenbooks and Waldensoft), and many packaged-goods producers (Procter & Gamble, Kraft General Foods, Del Monte) have also adopted frequent-buyer programs. More and more businesses consider frequency marketing programs to be an attractive alternative to endless couponing.[51] However, frequency marketing isn't a great solution for every industry. In fact, a number of hotels began to cut back or eliminate their programs only a couple of years after they started, saying that consumer interest isn't high enough.[52]

## Trade Promotions

Most of the sales promotion devices used with final customers can also be used with the trade (marketing intermediaries). Some additional techniques apply only to the trade, however. For example, allowances and discounts cover a variety of price reduction incentives for wholesalers and retailers. The idea behind these is to increase sales through the channel by offering intermediaries the chance for higher profits. Another trade-oriented promotion is the factory-sponsored in-store demonstration. Retailers can increase store traffic and sales by advertising the appearance of factory experts to demonstrate products and answer consumer questions. Trade shows are another important promotional event in many industries. Cooperative promotions that link the dollars and efforts of producers and intermediaries are also an effective trade promotion tactic. Finally, sales contests for intermediaries with prizes such as vacation packages can be a good way for producers to increase volume through their channels.

## Sales Promotion Strategies

The steps required to plan and implement a sales promotion are quite similar to those in an advertising campaign: understand the target audience, establish objectives, identify resource constraints, select methods and vehicles, and evaluate the program after it is launched. Here are some common objectives for sales promotions:

- Gaining new customers
- Retaining current customers
- Increasing consumption
- Increasing brand awareness
- Increasing shelf space and attention from intermediaries
- Broadening distribution channels

Unlike advertising, sales promotion usually isn't a good way to create an image for a brand, turn around a declining brand or product, or change negative public opinion or consumer attitudes.[53]

Like advertising, however, sales promotion programs should be evaluated to measure their effectiveness at increasing sales, store traffic, product trial, or whatever goal the marketer has established. As mentioned earlier, data from checkout scanners now give marketers fast feedback on the effects of their sales promotions. However, it's always important to remember that multiple forces can be working on product sales, including media advertising, competitive moves, and local retailer efforts. Marketers control the other variables in the marketing mix as tightly as possible to ensure that the effects they see are the result of their sales promotions and not some other factor. Used properly, evaluation data can help cut promotion costs and raise effectiveness. In one study, for instance, researchers found that shoppers in the Northeast responded differently to couponing offers than did shoppers in the Southeast. Such insights help marketers divide their budgets more effectively.[54]

# PUBLIC RELATIONS

Public relations plays a vital role in the success of most companies, and this applies to more than just the marketing of goods and services. Smart businesses maintain positive relations with their communities, investors, industry analysts, government agencies and officials, and the news media. All these activities can fall under the umbrella of public relations. The functions that are most important to examine as part of the marketing mix are press relations, cause-related marketing, and event sponsorship. Much of the visibility of public relations comes from discrete events; however, effective public relations results from continuous, well-managed processes, not from random events.

Public relations is an important element for nonprofit organizations because it can be a good way around the budget limitations frequently faced by these groups. For example, thousands of local news and talk shows are broadcast by television stations across the country, and nonprofit organizations can get a tremendous amount of free promotional exposure on these programs.[55] A representative of a nonprofit hospital could appear on a local show and answer callers' questions about diet and exercise, for instance. This would perform a service for viewers in addition to promoting the hospital. In other cases, hospitals actually deliver some service in conjunction with a public relations event; offering free cholesterol testing at a county fair is a good example.

## Press Relations

Many businesses place heavy emphasis on the coverage they receive in both general and specialized trade media. They pay close attention to **press relations,** the process of communicating with newspapers, magazines, and the broadcast media. In the personal computer industry, for example, manufacturers know that many people look to *PC/Computing, PC Magazine, Byte,* and other computer publications as influential sources of information about new products. Editors and reporters often review new products, pointing out both strengths and weaknesses, and then make recommendations to their readers. Companies roll out the proverbial red carpet for these media figures, treating them to hospitality suites at conventions and arranging factory tours and interviews with company leaders. When introducing products, manufacturers often send review samples to reporters and editors or send representatives to visit the media offices.

**press relations**
The practice of communicating with members of the press about your company, its products, and its people

The standard tools of press relations are the press release, or news release as it is sometimes called, and the press conference, or press briefing. A **press release** is a short memo sent to the media covering topics of potential news interest; some companies send video press releases to television stations. Press releases can announce new products, explain new technologies, introduce new company leaders, describe some community-related activity the company is involved in, or discuss a variety of other topics. A *press kit* can include the publication-ready photos, product samples, background information, and other materials in addition to the press release itself. Unfortunately, press releases are overused and misused, and some editors and reporters are growing impatient with them. To gain a reporter's interest, the press release must contain information that is important to the reporter's audience. The press isn't interested in being a free mouthpiece for a company's marketing department.

**press release**
A short document, also called a news release, that outlines some newsworthy event or activity and that companies send to reporters and editors with the hope of getting press coverage; press releases for television reporters are often done on videotape

**Press conferences** are arranged when companies have significant news to announce. They are used in addition to press releases when the news is of widespread interest, when products need to be demonstrated, or when the company wants to

**press conference**
Bringing media representatives together for an announcement

**TECHNIQUES FOR MARKETING SUCCESS**

# WHEN THE NEWS ISN'T GOOD

Communicating bad news is one of the hardest tasks that business professionals face. It isn't easy to admit that you made a mistake, or that you were caught by surprise, or that something you said last week is no longer true. But there are good ways to spread bad news and bad ways to spread bad news. Smart companies know how to handle rough times and come out more or less unscathed, whereas companies that bungle an announcement of bad news can get hammered by the stock market, the press, and their customers. When bad news breaks, it travels fast, and you must be prepared. Here are six steps you should follow when your company has something unpleasant to announce:

- *First, respond quickly.* Major news events such as company mergers, environmental disasters, and industrial accidents attract a lot of attention, and they attract it in a hurry. When Pepsi was hit with stories about syringes in cans, the company jumped on the problem immediately, telling the public everything it knew.
- *Second, be honest.* Make sure that the public sees you as honest. If you don't tell the truth or don't provide enough information to answer questions, you'll lose credibility that you may never regain. Beyond credibility, however, honesty with the media and the public is simply part of running a business ethically.
- *Third, get top management visibly involved.* People want to see and hear the people in charge.
- *Fourth, coordinate all communica-*

be able to answer reporters' questions. Press conferences can turn into spectacles featuring speeches, videotapes, light shows, and other special effects. Hundreds of people attend press conferences for major announcements from well-known companies, but many press events are smaller. For example, many industrial products are introduced to the press one magazine office at a time, in which case the marketer travels around to visit reporters. If you go to work as a product manager at an electronics firm, for instance, don't be surprised to find yourself carrying a new product around to magazine offices in Boston, New York, and other cities across the country.

## Cause-Related Marketing

**cause-related marketing**
Promotional programs that tie charitable contributions to sales of a specific good or service; the term has been copyrighted by American Express

Marketing efforts and charitable interests cross paths in a recent development called **cause-related marketing,** programs in which a firm offers to contribute a specified amount to a charitable organization when customers buy certain goods or services. The term was copyrighted by American Express, which is credited with popularizing the technique after its successful drive to raise funds for the restoration of the Statue of Liberty. The company continued with such efforts as the Charge Against Hunger campaign in 1993, during which it made a contribution to Share Our Strength (a hunger-relief organization) every time a cardholder charged a purchase.[56] Cause-related marketing is growing because it makes financial sense as well as humanitarian sense; it's a good compromise between a company's need to earn revenue and its desire to help the community. It differs from normal corporate philanthropy because it is more than outright charity; the company also makes money on the deal.

MasterCard International is another organization that found success with cause-related marketing. Its "Choose to Make a Difference" campaign raised millions of dollars for several charities while increasing credit card use and moving MasterCard's image above Visa for the first time in years. One important element of MasterCard's program was allowing cardholders to determine the amount of money that went to each charity. Creating a sense of involvement and promising real progress for the cause in question are key steps in successful cause-related programs.[57]

*tions.* Call a press conference or a public meeting and give everybody one consistent message.

- *Fifth, look for good news to offset the bad.* It isn't always possible to find good news, of course, but you should always try.
- *Sixth, try to avoid bad news in the first place.* This sounds obvious, but more than a few companies have found themselves wishing they had paid more attention to simmering problems before the world found out about them.

Two recent oil spills illustrate the right way and the wrong way to handle a crisis. When the *Exxon Valdez* ran aground in Alaska's Prince William Sound, Exxon had a major PR problem on its hands. The infor-

mation provided by the company during the days following the spill was inadequate and sometimes contradictory. CEO Lawrence Rawl was quiet for six days, and when he did speak he blamed other parties for the slow cleanup. An Exxon executive later said that the company's management couldn't be blamed for the mistakes of a single tanker captain. Public relations experts soundly criticized the way Exxon handled the affair, and the company's reputation suffered greatly.

In contrast, when Ashland Oil spilled a million gallons of diesel fuel in the Monongahela River, CEO John Hall was immediately visible and on the scene. He took responsibility for the company's mistakes and offered to pay for damages. Ashland emerged

from its crisis with the respect of some observers, who appreciated the company's willingness to take responsibility and to do whatever it could to clean up the mess. Ashland received high marks from PR experts for its handling of the crisis.

**APPLY YOUR KNOWLEDGE**

**1.** Should companies publicly apologize when they make mistakes, or should they focus on positive information only?

**2.** Pretend you're the spokesperson for your college. A mysterious disease has put several students in the hospital, but you have no information yet on what it is or how to stop it. What would you tell a reporter who calls asking for comment?

## Event Sponsorship

Another public relations tactic that has gained popularity in recent years is the corporate sponsorship of various athletic and cultural events. Ever wonder why you see so many company names attached to sporting events these days? U.S. companies spend well over several billion dollars sponsoring special events, of which roughly 3,000 in the United States invite corporate support. When people participate in, attend, or view an event on television, the sponsor's name is on display. Coca-Cola is the top sponsoring corporation in the United States, with links to 10 percent of those 3,000 events. Other top sponsors are Anheuser-Busch's Budweiser brand, Miller Brewing, Coors, AT&T, and American Airlines. Coca-Cola's recent five-year, $250 million deal with the National Football League ranks as the biggest sports sponsorship deal ever. Expect to see the various Coke brand names every time you watch NFL games.[58]

A controversy surrounds corporate sponsorship, however, and it concerns tobacco and alcohol companies sponsoring athletic events. The tobacco companies in particular find this to be an effective way to reach the young adult audience, especially since they are shut out of television advertising. However, some observers wonder whether the public interest is served by cigarette manufacturers and beer companies sponsoring sporting events, which are supposed to represent fitness and good health. The "Ethical Dilemma in Marketing" box in Chapter 17 explores this issue in more depth.

## Other Public Relations Functions

Beyond these fundamental marketing mix functions, public relations people are called on to perform a variety of other tasks. One of these is **advocacy advertising,** which is advertising that communicates a company's opinion about various matters. For example, Mobil Oil once ran a newspaper ad to protest what it considered to be censorship by CBS and ABC after those two networks refused to run a Mobil TV commercial.[59] Some companies, including Mobil, use advocacy advertising to shape public opinion on issues ranging from the environment to international competition.

**advocacy advertising**
Nonproduct advertising that promotes a company's viewpoint on a particular issue of public concern

Another important public relations function is investor relations. The people who buy stock in or otherwise have a vested interest in your company want to know how the company is faring. This is usually done through quarterly and annual reports to shareholders, but it can also be done through various forms of advertising. Government relations is another important task. Many companies have staffs dedicated to communicating with public officials and trying to influence legislation in the company's favor. General relations with the community are usually handled by the public relations department as well.

# SUMMARY OF LEARNING OBJECTIVES

### 1. Identify the major types of advertising.

This chapter identified several major types of advertising. One important distinction is the difference between institutional advertising, which promotes the organization, and product advertising, which promotes goods and services. Competitive advertising tries to win customers based on specific product features that are better than the competition's. Comparative advertising takes the extra step of explicitly comparing two or more products. Ads can also be classified by immediacy: Indirect-action ads try to prepare customers for future purchases, whereas direct-action ads want customers to open their wallets immediately. Reminder ads are used later in a product's life to remind customers that the product is still available. Finally, advocacy advertising is nonproduct promotion that airs a company's opinion about a particular issue, such as freedom of speech.

### 2. Describe the steps required to launch an advertising campaign.

Five basic steps are required to launch an advertising campaign. The first is to establish the advertising objectives. Good objectives specify exactly what effect the ad is supposed to have in a given time frame. The second step is deciding what type of appeal the ad will use, including logical, emotional, celebrity, sex, or novelty. Third, select and schedule the various media you'll use. The next step is to create the advertisement itself. The fifth step is evaluation: Was the campaign effective?

### 3. List common advertising objectives and advertising appeals.

This chapter described a number of common advertising objectives. These include increasing the use of existing products, increasing the size of orders from current customers, finding new customers, helping marketing channel partners, generating sales leads, and supporting personal selling efforts by communicating with the decision makers that salespeople are unable to reach in person.

Advertisers try a variety of appeals in their ads. Two common appeals are to logic and to emotion; some ads use a combination of the two. It is important to recognize that even the driest of logic has to have some sort of emotional appeal; people are people, and they all have emotional needs that must be addressed in your advertising. Celebrity endorsements are another common advertising appeal; however, these ads have two potential problems. Unless some logical reason exists for a celebrity to be promoting a product, consumers don't find them terribly convincing. Moreover, the image of the product can become tied to the image of the celebrity so that his or her public and private behavior affects public perception of the product. Sex is a perennial favorite in advertising because companies try to get you to associate pleasure with their products. Finally, novelty is used by some advertisers, primarily as a way to cut through all the ad clutter in today's economy.

### 4. Explain the strengths and weaknesses of the major advertising media.

Each of the major media options has significant strengths and weaknesses. Newspapers offer the advantages of broad coverage, low cost, and short lead times, but they have the disadvantages of poor visual quality, short life span, and extensive clutter. Direct mail's advantages include the ability to deliver a lot of information to a precisely defined audience; its drawbacks are high cost per unit, competition from other direct mail, and a generally unfavorable image. Television provides a powerful platform combining sight, sound, and motion; its other strengths include prestige and extensive coverage. The downside of TV includes high cost, short life, lack of selectivity (in most cases), and vulnerability to zapping. Radio is an answer to the high cost of TV; it also offers good local coverage as well as the chance to repeat messages frequently. On the other hand, radio commercials don't always make a strong impression, because many listeners concentrate on something other than the radio. Of course, radio is a completely nonvisual medium, putting greater creative demands on advertisers who try to describe their products over the radio. Finally, the benefits of magazines include high selectivity in many cases, quality images, and long message life. The disadvantages include long lead times and the absence of motion and sound.

### 5. Explain the growing attraction of direct mail and other direct-marketing promotional strategies.

The two major attractions of direct mail and other direct-marketing techniques are effectiveness and measurability. With database marketing to help identify prospects with precision, marketers can increase the chance that people who get their message will be motivated to buy. Because direct mail identifies every person in the target audience and tracks who buys and who doesn't, marketers have instant and accurate measurements of the effectiveness of their promotions.

**6. Discuss the sales promotion techniques used to stimulate consumer demand.**

The most popular sales promotion technique used to stimulate consumer demand is the coupon, with more than 300 billion distributed every year. Other common devices include premiums, samples, contests, sweepstakes, and point-of-purchase materials. A new development in several market segments is frequency marketing, in which you build customer loyalty by offering incentives for repeat purchases. Frequent-flyer plans are the most prominent form of this promotional technique.

**7. Describe the functions of public relations that have the closest link to the marketing mix.**

Although it can be argued that every aspect of public relations affects the marketing mix, three functions are tied particularly closely. The first is press relations, the practice of communicating with representatives of the media in the hope of obtaining favorable coverage for your organization and its products. The second function with high marketing content is cause-related marketing, promotional programs that link charitable contributions with sales of specified products. The third public relations function is event sponsorship; sporting events are among the most prominent examples.

---

# KEY TERMS

advertising agencies (551)
advocacy advertising (571)
aided recall (565)
artwork (561)
cause-related marketing (570)
comparative advertising (552)
competitive advertising (552)

copy (561)
database marketing (560)
direct-action advertising (552)
frequency (559)
frequency marketing (568)
indirect-action advertising (552)
in-house agency (551)

institutional advertising (551)
media plan (558)
pioneer advertising (553)
point-of-purchase (POP) advertising (567)
posttesting (564)
premium (566)
press conference (569)
press relations (569)

press release (569)
pretesting (564)
product advertising (551)
product placement (561)
reach (559)
reminder advertising (553)
subliminal advertising (558)
unaided recall (565)

---

# QUESTIONS FOR DISCUSSION

1. Assume you're the marketing manager for Harley-Davidson motorcycles. In which ways might you consider using each of the following types of advertising?
   a. Institutional advertising
   b. Product advertising
   c. Advocacy advertising

2. Consider the life cycle of compact disk players, and assume they are eventually replaced by some other technology, such as digital audiotape. As a manufacturer of CD players, how should your advertising change over the time span from the introduction of CDs to their declining years?

3. You're an account executive at an ad agency, and one of your clients presents you with this objective for the next ad campaign: "Quickly and substantially increase consumer awareness of our new line of garden supplies." How should you respond?

4. What type of appeal is each of the following headlines trying to use?
   a. "Make sure your children are safe"
   b. "Increase silicon wafer yield by 10 percent"
   c. "Warning: This perfume will attract those boys your mother always warned you about"
   d. "Roscoe's potato chips: a lot better than eating rocks"

5. What would be some of the pluses and minuses of using a popular singer or rapper as a celebrity endorser for your line of racing bicycles?

6. Which medium would you choose if you needed to reach a wide audience with a message that is highly visual and relies on color? Explain your choice.

7. What's wrong with the following ad copy?
   Schlem-Tech is proud to introduce its Model XRTL/78 correlating hyperbolic transmission system. It is based on years of thorough research by some of the best minds in the scientific and engineering community. Users will be impressed by its numerous technological breakthroughs.

8. Based on what you know about the guidelines for effective advertising, what role should a company's name and logo have in its advertisements?

9. Your manager asks you to develop a sales promotion for a new brand of premium ice cream. She wants you to select either coupons or samples; what are some of the factors you need to consider before making a choice?

10. Which of the following opening sentences from a press release is more likely to catch the interest of a newspaper reporter? Why?
    a. "Compustuff is pleased to announce that its internal tests of disk drive performance prove that Compustuff disk drives are just as fast as everyone else's on the market today."
    b. "The environmental devastation of oil spills can be reduced by using new genetically engineered oil-eating bacteria, just introduced by the Petrobug Corporation."

## Meeting a Marketing Challenge at Starbucks

To ensure a successful entry into the Los Angeles coffee market, Howard Schultz and his team at Starbucks utilized an array of public relations vehicles aimed at several key consumers. With the help of its PR agency, Berkhemer-Kline Golin/Harris, Starbucks created a plan for moving into Los Angeles using no initial advertising at all. The plan had four key elements. First, the PR would be closely integrated with the rest of the marketing program. Second, the initial audience would be trendsetters, people in the area who tended to be among the first to pick up new fashions, new products, and so on. Third, education would be an important part of the PR program, reaching out to chefs and food reporters in the media. Fourth, Starbucks would continue to support and identify itself with social and charitable causes that were important to its target audience.

Integration with the rest of the marketing program was a vital issue because Schultz wanted to build awareness for the products in stages. The first stage involved establishing small Starbucks kiosks in selected area supermarkets. These began to appear in conjunction with the initial PR efforts. Then as awareness and word of mouth began to build in the next three to six months, Starbucks began the next stage, opening its own retail stores, which sell coffeemaking equipment and coffee beans, in addition to a wide variety of coffee beverages ready to drink.

The trendsetters Schultz wanted to reach are the people who dine out frequently and like to experience a wide range of cultural and culinary experiences. Two special events were central to this effort. The first was a preview party for 2,000 members in the singles group associated with the Museum of Contemporary Art. These people, who were likely to tell others about new tastes and trends, got to sample the product and learn more about premium coffee. The second event was an appearance at Taste of the Nation, a fund-raising event that drew other "foodies" and showcased Starbucks alongside the city's finest restaurants and food providers.

Taste of the Nation and other media events and food tastings also played a role in the second element of the PR plan, forging ties with and educating chefs and food editors at local media. Schultz wanted to get these groups on his side early, since they influence the buying behavior of many more people. He also wanted to teach them the difference between the coffee they were used to and the premium product Starbucks would be offering. Moreover, the company's reputation had been built in large part on its quality products, and getting the endorsements of third parties such as chefs is a key part of building a reputation for quality. The events led to numerous stories in local media, and several chefs expressed interest in serving Starbucks in their restaurants.

Since its founding, Starbucks has been an active contributor to and participant in social causes and charitable programs. The company is one of the biggest corporate supporters of CARE, an international relief organization. Through CARE, Starbucks fulfills its commitment to giving something back to the international communities from which it buys coffee beans. The company has funded such CARE projects as a literacy program in Kenya and a health-care program in Guatemala. The news media pick up on these contributions and help position Starbucks as a caring corporation, thereby identifying it with a theme that is important to many consumers in the premium coffee market. On a local level in Los Angeles, Starbucks participated in such events as "Backlot Blowout," a fund-raising party held every summer by the AIDS Project of Los Angeles. This support is not only consistent with its corporate philosophy, but it helps identify the firm with causes that its target audience cares about as well.

The PR program, which continues with special events and other efforts, helped Schultz build a solid foundation in Los Angeles. The *L.A. Times* recently referred to Starbucks as a "role model for budding coffee merchants" and as the "Michael Jordan of the coffee business." Overall, the company's sales have risen ninefold in the past five years. Thoughtful and creative use of public relations continues to be a driving force behind this torrid growth.

**Your mission:** You're now in charge of the marketing effort at Starbucks. Your successful predecessors left some big shoes to fill. Public relations remains the cornerstone of the company's marketing plans, but you've also begun to look at other possibilities as well. Consider the following situations, and make the choices that will best support Starbucks' long-range goal of being the dominant premium coffee producer in the country.

1. Several store managers have suggested that a videotape on making the perfect cup of coffee would be a good promotional tool. What should the primary objective of such a tape be?
   a. To update public perceptions about coffee, explaining what a great cup of premium coffee is all about and how it is made
   b. To promote sales of Starbucks coffees and coffeemaking equipment
   c. To add value to the brand by making it more visible

2. From what you've learned about Starbucks so far, which of the following would be the best slogan to use with respect to community relations efforts?
   a. "Coffee and caring"
   b. "Starbucks cares"
   c. "Premium coffee for a quality lifestyle"
3. If you wanted to demonstrate the taste of Starbucks to some 100 food editors scattered across 15 or 20 states, which of the following would be most sensible to include in a press kit?
   a. A videotape of customers at a Starbucks store, enjoying the coffee
   b. A coffeemaking kit, complete with a low-cost French press (a type of coffeemaker) and a selection of Starbucks coffees
   c. A selection of clippings from newspapers and magazines that have praised Starbucks' taste
4. Starbucks seems like a natural for product placement, since its coffee can be worked unobtrusively into a variety of situations. Which of the following movies would be the best choice for Starbucks?
   a. A thoughtful and classy film on the meaning of life, shot in French with English subtitles
   b. A romantic comedy based on a best-selling novel
   c. A blockbuster action-adventure film

**SPECIAL PROJECT**

You've decided to promote Starbucks through advertising, and the vehicle you've chosen is a television commercial. The commercial's objective is to convince people who haven't yet tried gourmet coffee to give Starbucks a try. You'll feature a toll-free number people can call to get a free sample. Your task now is to design this commercial. How will you get the message across and persuade people to pick up the phone? In two pages or less, describe the visual content of your commercial, provide a draft of the copy, and explain any special effects that you might want to use. Briefly summarize by explaining how the creative choices you've made will help the commercial meet its objective.[60]

# Vistakon Keeps a Close Eye on the Contact Lens Market

Anyone who wears contact lenses knows how important the tiny devices are to one's daily life. However, cleaning and storing them every night was more hassle than a lot of people wanted. When disposable lenses appeared on the market in the late 1980s, millions of consumers were glad to switch, even though disposables tend to cost more than conventional extended-wear lenses. When consumers sign up for disposables, they receive regular shipments of lenses and simply throw out the old ones and replace them with a fresh pair. Users don't have to remove most types of disposables when they sleep, another convenience factor.

The company most responsible for the booming growth in disposables is Vistakon, a unit of the health-care giant Johnson & Johnson. From its innovative plant in Jacksonville, Florida, Vistakon ships lenses to customers all over the world. Its initial disposable, named Acuvue, was the first disposable contact lens approved for sale in the United States.

Success was anything but sure when Vistakon made the bold move to disposables, however. Johnson & Johnson pumped several hundred million dollars into Vistakon with little assurance that the radical new products would catch on with eye doctors or the public. Vistakon also had to contend with two well-established competitors, Bausch & Lomb and Ciba-Geigy.

Under the entrepreneurial hand of president Bernard Walsh, Vistakon spent several years perfecting the manufacturing process and getting a high-volume manufacturing plant ready. The company prepared as quietly as possible, to avoid tipping off the competition. After successful test marketing in Florida in 1987, Walsh and his team quickly established nationwide distribution and advertising. The speed with which they were able to pounce on the U.S. market left Bausch & Lomb and Ciba-Geigy far behind. The two giants were unable to match Vistakon's nationwide presence with the new products for six months. Much of the credit must also go to the corporate culture at Johnson & Johnson, which gives its business units the money and freedom they need to respond quickly to market opportunities.

With any health-related product, establishing a strong relationship with the medical profession is a key step to success. Not only do doctors prescribe and recommend various products, they (along with nurses) serve as an information resource for reporters, stock market analysts, and others who are trying to learn about products and technologies. In a press release announcing a medical conference on the subject of contact lenses, a professor of ophthalmology at Mount Sinai Medical Center in New York City provided the following quote:

Not only is this system a great convenience for wearers, eliminating the need to clean and reuse lenses, but it is also an asset to eye health because there is no buildup of deposits on the lenses over time. Deposit buildup is a problem that some patients have had with extended-wear lenses; this system assures that vision cannot be affected by inadequate cleaning regimens.

Such comments can help build credibility for technologies, product categories, and particular brands, among both the medical community and the public at large. This quote appeared in a press release that discussed the availability and attributes of the original Acuvue product, providing a strong link between medical support and promotional efforts.

Vistakon followed up the one-week Acuvue lenses, first with the two-week Surevue and then in 1993 with the one-day Acuvue. This latest innovation lets consumers start each day with a fresh, sterile set of lenses, reducing the chances of irritation and deposit buildup. The one-day lenses required $100 million and three years of additional research to perfect the design and the manufacturing process. Vistakon supported this introduction with an ad campaign that encouraged consumers to ask their eye doctors for a free 10-day trial kit. Price for the daily disposables is roughly $1.50 a day, which Vistakon pointed out was about what most people spend on coffee and a newspaper every morning. In other words, it's not much to pay for the benefits of new lenses every day.

1. Consider the range of experiences and emotions that contact lens wearers might have, from the self-esteem boost that some people get when they swap their glasses for contacts to the inconvenience and embarrassment of losing a lens during a party or other social event. What kind of advertising appeal would you use to promote daily disposables to people who haven't yet made the switch to contacts? Why?

2. How would you explain the benefits of daily disposables to someone who hasn't experienced any discomfort or irritation with his or her extended-wear lenses?

3. Daily disposables cost roughly 50 percent more than conventional extended-wear contacts (including both the costs of the lenses themselves and the associated care from an eye doctor). How would you persuade people that Acuvue is worth that much more? What would you say in the headline for a magazine ad that would catch the interest of people still using extended-wear lenses?

Most organizations have several audiences for their public relations efforts. Customers are an obvious audience, but companies also have to communicate with employees, investors, stock market analysts, reporters, and government officials. When you prepare information for release to the press, keep all these audiences in mind. Pretend a company you work for has just experienced a dramatic drop in sales because of quality problems.

**Decision:** Making up whatever details you need for this exercise, decide how much you should tell the press. Should you tell all, provide some details, or just announce the drop without explanation?

**Communication:** Write a short press release (one or two paragraphs) that announces the trouble, and think about how each audience will react to the news.

# KEEPING CURRENT IN MARKETING

Find an article about an advertising campaign that was a big success and another article about a campaign that was a failure. A successful campaign is one that met or exceeded the objectives established by the company. A failed campaign, on the other hand, could be one that didn't meet its objectives, confused the audience, annoyed or upset the audience, or caused the target segment to behave in an unanticipated fashion.

1. Why did the successful campaign work? Why did the unsuccessful campaign fail? What did the two campaigns have in common?

2. Could the failure have been avoided? Should the company have done a better job with market research? Was the objective realistic? Did it select an appropriate appeal? Was there a problem with copy, artwork, or media selection?

3. How did the failed campaign affect the company that ran it? Did it lose market share? Did competitors take advantage of the situation? How did customers feel about it? If marketing intermediaries were involved, how did they feel about it?

# 19

# Personal Selling and Sales Management

**After studying this chapter, you will be able to**

**1.** Explain the importance and power of personal selling

**2.** Discuss the seven steps in the personal selling process

**3.** Describe the need-satisfaction approach to selling

**4.** Identify current trends in the sales profession

**5.** Delineate the most common classifications of sales personnel

**6.** Explain three primary aspects of the sales management function

**7.** Analyze common techniques used to motivate salespeople

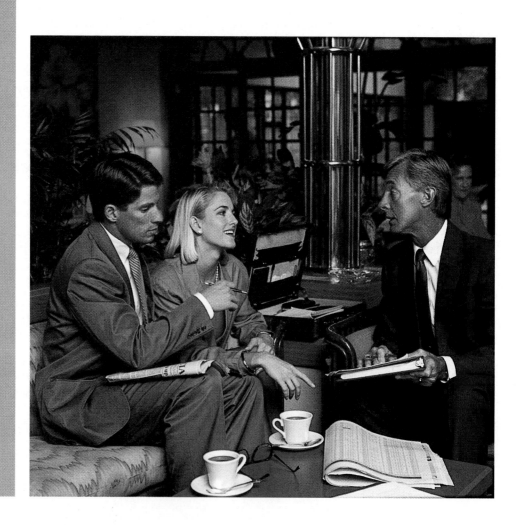

## Copier King Struggles to Duplicate Early Success

The bigger they are, the harder they fall—and few giants have fallen as hard as Xerox. In the early 1960s, the company became the first name in photocopiers, dominating the market with one of the most successful products in history. However, by decade's end, Xerox was headed for trouble, and the company began struggling to reproduce that initial success.

When Xerox founder Joseph Wilson bought the exclusive rights to the xerographic process, he had a vision that would radically change the world of business communications. The Xerox 914 revolutionized the way information was conveyed. Suddenly, a memo that would ordinarily take hours to duplicate again and again on a typewriter could be copied in seconds. Almost overnight, the 914 made it possible to send vital information from the corner office to the corners of the world quickly and inexpensively. This copier's extraordinary success, coupled with the company's entrepreneurial environment, launched Xerox on a course of incredible growth.

Despite continuing success, Wilson felt that Xerox would profit from organizational restructuring, so in 1968 he made C. Peter McColough the company's CEO. The first thing McColough did was give the company a modern management structure; then he filled key posts with executives from big-name corporations. "It was a classic case of doing everything right," says consultant Tom Peters. "They hired people from three of the best-managed companies. But there's nothing harder to deal with than success."

Under McColough's rigid bureaucratic controls, Xerox grew increasingly impersonal and complacent until it was transformed into what has been described as a stodgy organization where corporate politics was more important than creative innovation. Long, expensive delays in prod-uct development led to stagnation, and the competition that didn't exist in 1960 was coming on strong. "We were arrogant enough to think that no one could do anything better than we could," said William Galvin, Xerox vice chairman. That attitude would prove to be costly.

In early 1980, Japan blanketed America with copiers that outperformed Xerox's—at half the price. The company's top managers refused to believe that Japan was capable of manufacturing high-quality copiers until it was too late. By the time it became clear that Xerox needed new leadership, its market share was badly eroded and net income was cut in half.

When David Kearns took over as CEO in 1982, Xerox had a splintered sales force with poor organization, motivation, and leadership. Salespeople representing various Xerox lines often crossed paths trying to reach the same decision maker. This inefficiency confused and annoyed customers and wasted a great deal of time and effort.

Kearns reorganized the sales force from top to bottom and instituted training and incentive programs to give his salespeople a new sense of direction and dedication to goals. The guiding principle behind everything Kearns tried to accomplish was 100 percent fault-free quality in every Xerox product. His goal was to make the company's name synonymous with excellence.

That David Kearns helped revitalize Xerox is certain, but the company has yet to duplicate the success of its early years. If you were in Kearns's place, how would you use personal selling to reposition Xerox in today's marketplace? What kind of incentive, motivation, and compensation programs would you try? What role could telemarketing play in prospecting, customer orientation, and account maintenance?[1]

# CHAPTER OVERVIEW

Like most companies selling capital equipment, Xerox relies on the efforts of sales-people. However, the role of personal selling is not limited to situations like Xerox's; salespeople work in a wide variety of consumer and organizational markets, at the producer, wholesaler, and retailer levels. This chapter explores the importance of personal selling and its role in the promotional mix. Following that, you'll explore the personal selling process, from prospecting for leads to following up after the sale. Then you'll look at important trends in the sales profession, including the increasing role of women and minorities, telemarketing, and a greater emphasis on selling ethics. The final two sections of this chapter address the sales profession, from the perspectives of both the salesperson and sales manager.

# THE IMPORTANCE OF PERSONAL SELLING

For centuries businesses have relied on people to personally sell goods and services. In fact, personal selling has helped achieve the standard of living we enjoy today, and it plays an increasingly significant role in our expanding global economy. If it weren't for the hard work of millions of salespeople over the years, many of our modern-day conveniences might not exist. Even products such as personal computers, photocopiers, and microwave ovens might never have taken off. That means many of us would still be muddling along with typewriters, carbon paper, and cold leftovers for dinner. Not a pleasant thought. Even million-dollar advertising campaigns and sales promotions can't accomplish what a salesperson can when it comes to convincing people to buy.

However, in spite of their positive contribution to society, salespeople have been plagued by an image problem from day one. You may even have had a bad experience or two with a salesperson who deceived you about a product you bought, who "fast-talked" you into buying something you didn't need, or who brazenly gossiped with a co-worker while you waited in line to make a purchase, which probably left you with a bad impression of all salespeople.

Fortunately, a rapidly growing cadre of salespeople are giving the profession a new image (see Exhibit 19.1). Their job is not to push products but to solve problems and help customers make buying decisions. These modern-day sales professionals are well educated, they are well paid, and they use sophisticated techniques and technologies to enhance their selling abilities. They don't disappear after making a sale but continue to provide valuable information and service to their customers. They are also more likely than their predecessors to contribute to other aspects of marketing such as product design, pricing, and distribution. They work hard to advance their own careers, realizing that a position in sales often leads to the executive suite.

Business successes are often credited to superstar products, brilliant leadership, perfect timing, or even luck. Business failures, on the other hand, are often blamed on inferior products, extravagant spending, too much competition, or not enough demand. For many companies, however, success or failure hinges in large part on the effectiveness of the personal selling effort. Most executives recognize this and place a high priority on personal selling.[2]

Although advertising, public relations, and sales promotions may arouse interest in a specific product, few companies would succeed without the promotional power of personal selling. Even if the final customer doesn't interact with a salesperson, personal selling often occurs somewhere in the marketing channel—from producer to wholesaler to retailer. For example, you don't need a salesperson to help you buy a bag of Lay's potato chips, but Frito-Lay depends on salespeople to get those bags of chips into the local stores. Overall, businesses spend more on personal selling than on any other type of promotional method. In the United States alone, companies spend over $125 billion annually on personal selling. The majority of this ex-

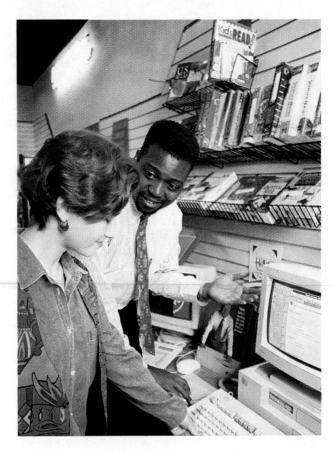

**Exhibit 19.1**
**THE NEW SALES PROFESSIONAL**
Today's professional salespeople are as much problem solvers and consultants as they are "salespeople" in the traditional sense.

penditure pays for salaries and commissions earned by the 7 million to 8 million people who hold sales positions.[3] They include professional sales representatives making six-figure incomes and store clerks making minimum wage.

Certain types of businesses, such as architectural, legal, and accounting firms, may not employ a separate sales force, but that doesn't mean personal selling is unnecessary. The professionals who provide the services have to sell prospective customers on the idea of retaining their firm. Just because someone walks in the door or makes a phone call intending to do business doesn't mean that a buying transaction will follow. Many sales have been lost simply because a potential customer didn't like the attitude of the person handling the sale. Whether a customer is looking for a design for a new home, a divorce lawyer, two dozen fax machines, or a fleet of trucks, personal selling skills often determine which company gets the sale.

## THE PERSONAL SELLING PROCESS

Most everyone has had to become a "salesperson" at some time in life. Even if you've never held an official sales position, perhaps you once ran in a charity marathon and had to sign up sponsors. Maybe you had to participate in school candy sales to raise money for a special project. If so, you may have unknowingly gone through many of the same steps that professional salespeople use in the personal selling process.

Although it may look easy, personal selling is not a simple task. Sure, some sales are made in a matter of minutes. Others can take years to complete. Whether a salesperson spends two hours or two years working on a sale, the selling process consists of seven key steps (as illustrated in Exhibit 19.2): (1) prospecting, (2) preparing, (3) approaching the prospect, (4) making the presentation, (5) handling objections, (6) closing the sale, and (7) following up. The way each step is handled will vary from salesperson to salesperson and from one selling situation to another. Some of the steps may need to be repeated many times before a sale is closed. However, part of what makes this process so effective is its flexibility.

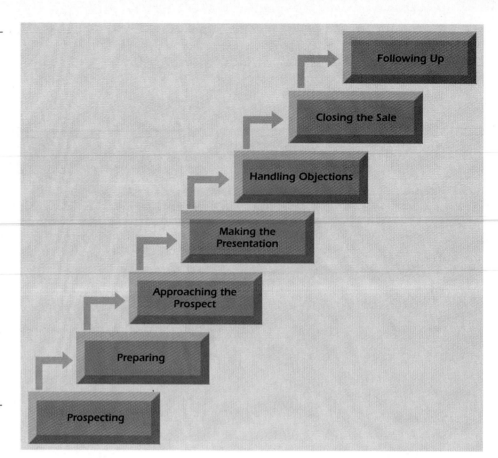

**Exhibit 19.2**
**THE PERSONAL**
**SELLING PROCESS**
Seven key steps define the personal selling process, starting with prospecting and continuing to follow up after the sale.

## Prospecting

Prospecting is the process of finding and qualifying potential customers. When salespeople "qualify" a customer, they check to see whether the customer has an immediate or near-term problem and has the ability to pay for a solution. Although prospecting is one of the most important steps in the personal selling process, it is often one of the most neglected. The reason for the neglect is that prospecting involves tedious, time-consuming work. Like gold prospectors, salespeople have to do a lot of digging, sifting, and testing before they unearth the nuggets of gold.

The amount of time and resources a salesperson invests in prospecting is determined in large part by the nature of the company's business and its specific marketing goals. For example, encyclopedia salespeople rarely make more than one sale per customer and therefore must constantly prospect for new business. On the other hand, a small service business that has an established client base may allocate only a few days a month to prospecting. Some companies like Speedfam, an Illinois machine-tool manufacturer, hire independent marketing firms to do the prospecting for them because they believe specialists are more cost-effective and can do a better job than their own staff.[4]

Most salespeople, however, can learn to develop effective prospecting techniques. The key is to allocate sufficient time on a regular basis and then constantly nurture and refine the process. The prospecting process involves three primary steps: (1) generating sales leads, (2) identifying prospects, and (3) qualifying prospects.

**sales lead**
The name of an individual, organization, or business that might be a likely prospect for the company's product

GENERATING SALES LEADS

A **sales lead** is the name of an individual, organization, or business that *might* be a likely prospect for the company's product. Sources for leads are limited only by a salesperson's imagination and alertness. Exhibit 19.3 includes some of the most common sources for leads. Most salespeople use a variety of sources for generating leads, but they tend to concentrate their efforts on a few key sources that prove to be the most worthwhile for their particular business. For salespeople who handle business-to-business sales, current business publications of all types are often excellent sources for leads.

## IDENTIFYING PROSPECTS

A prospect is a potential customer who indicates a need or a desire for the seller's product. A common technique for identifying prospects is **cold calling**, visiting or telephoning a potential customer when no prior contact has been made. Drop-in visits are generally not the most cost-effective way of selling, but cold calling as part of a telemarketing strategy is quite common in some industries. Stock brokers rely heavily on cold calling over the phone, for instance. As one representative of the industry put it, "Cold-calling is kind of like walking, sleeping, breathing, and getting to the next day. It's just what we do."[5]

Some salespeople identify prospects by writing letters that ask for a specific response. For example, the owner of C. D. West & Company, a Virginia insurance agency, obtained a list of homeowners from the city assessor's office. He then wrote a letter introducing his insurance agency to each homeowner in the highest tax zone. Those who responded become prospects to pursue further.[6]

**cold calling**
Calling on a potential customer by telephone or in person when no previous contact has been made

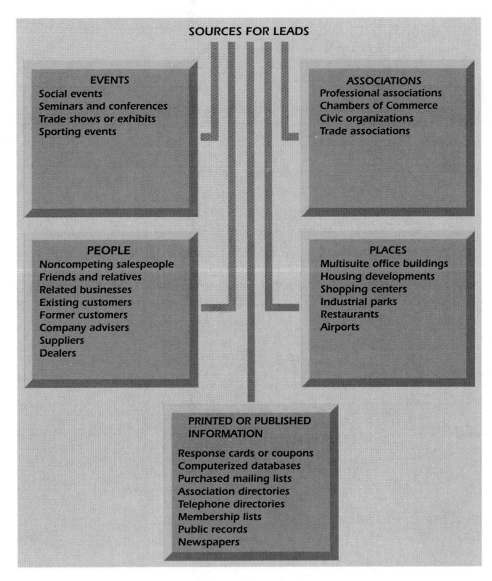

**Exhibit 19.3
WHERE TO FIND LEADS**
Sources for sales leads are limited only by your imagination.

## QUALIFYING PROSPECTS

Not all prospects are worth investing time in. Some may not have the authority to buy or may be considering such a small order that it wouldn't be worth the salesperson's time to pursue them. Others may be unable to afford the purchase. When a salesperson is able to identify a prospect as the decision maker and also as having the financial resources to pay for the product, then the prospect is referred to as a **qualified prospect**. Salespeople can obtain qualifying information by questioning the prospect directly about such things as occupation and place of residence or, in the case of a business, by checking with credit rating services, Dun & Bradstreet, or the company's annual report if one is available.

**qualified prospect**
A prospect who has been identified as being a purchasing decision maker and has the financial resources to pay for the product

When qualifying prospects, successful salespeople record information in an organized and concise manner (see Exhibit 19.4). They also use a ranking system so that they can concentrate their efforts on prospects with the highest potential. Ranking criteria will vary from company to company, but typical factors to consider are the size of the order, the potential for future business, the ease of servicing the account, and the prospect's influence in the marketplace. By applying ranking criteria that are in line with company goals, salespeople avoid wasting valuable time on unprofitable prospects—and good prospects will not slip through the cracks for lack of attention.

**Exhibit 19.4**
**PROSPECT QUALIFICATION FORM**
To facilitate the qualification process, salespeople should record prospect information on a concise, well-organized form. Increasingly, salespeople use computer software for this purpose, not paper forms.

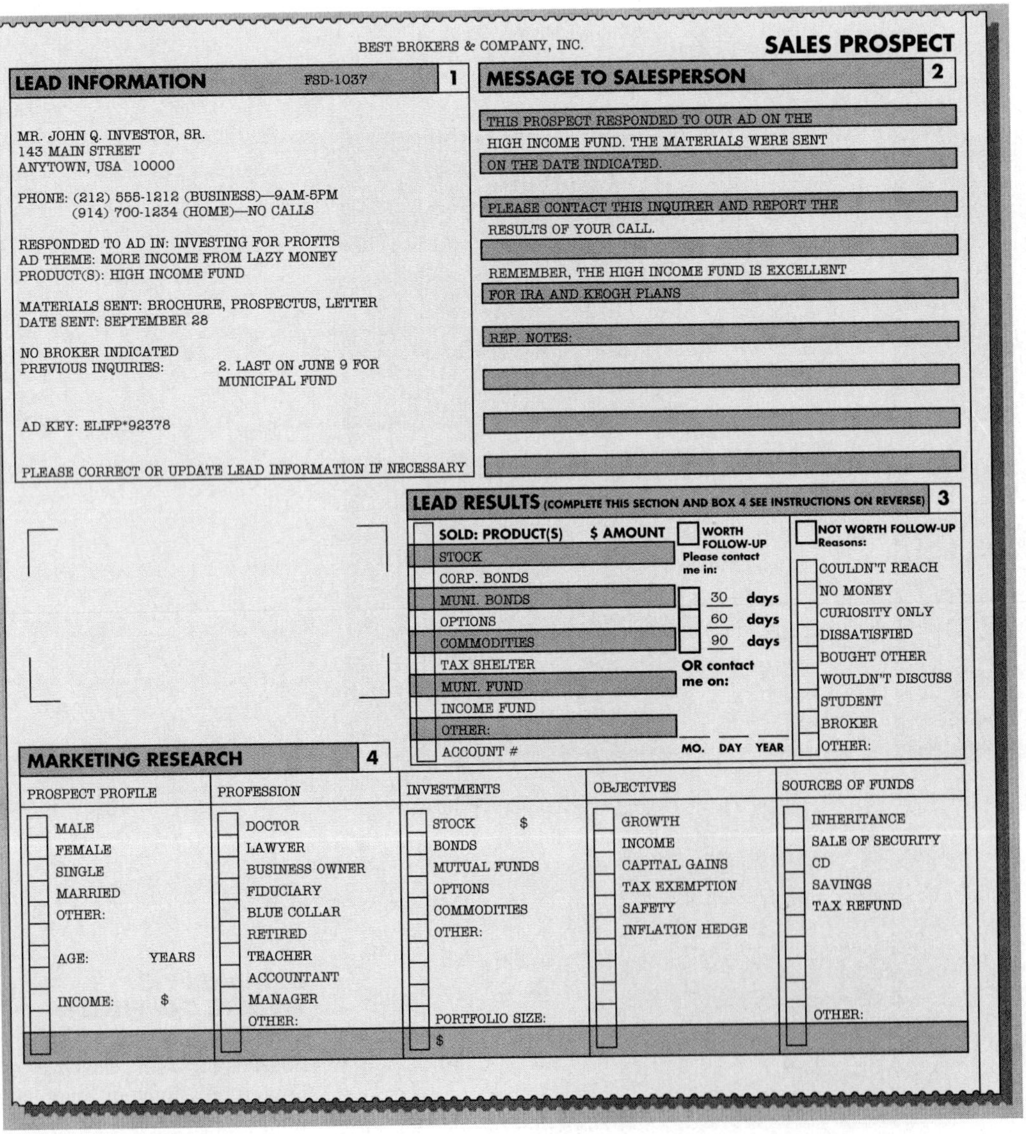
BEST BROKERS & COMPANY, INC.
SALES PROSPECT

LEAD INFORMATION FSD-1037 1

MR. JOHN Q. INVESTOR, SR.
143 MAIN STREET
ANYTOWN, USA 10000

PHONE: (212) 555-1212 (BUSINESS)—9AM-5PM
(914) 700-1234 (HOME)—NO CALLS

RESPONDED TO AD IN: INVESTING FOR PROFITS
AD THEME: MORE INCOME FROM LAZY MONEY
PRODUCT(S): HIGH INCOME FUND

MATERIALS SENT: BROCHURE, PROSPECTUS, LETTER
DATE SENT: SEPTEMBER 28

NO BROKER INDICATED
PREVIOUS INQUIRIES: 2. LAST ON JUNE 9 FOR MUNICIPAL FUND

AD KEY: ELIFP*92378

PLEASE CORRECT OR UPDATE LEAD INFORMATION IF NECESSARY

MESSAGE TO SALESPERSON 2

THIS PROSPECT RESPONDED TO OUR AD ON THE HIGH INCOME FUND. THE MATERIALS WERE SENT ON THE DATE INDICATED.

PLEASE CONTACT THIS INQUIRER AND REPORT THE RESULTS OF YOUR CALL.

REMEMBER, THE HIGH INCOME FUND IS EXCELLENT FOR IRA AND KEOGH PLANS

REP. NOTES:

LEAD RESULTS (COMPLETE THIS SECTION AND BOX 4 SEE INSTRUCTIONS ON REVERSE) 3

SOLD: PRODUCT(S) $ AMOUNT
STOCK
CORP. BONDS
MUNI. BONDS
OPTIONS
COMMODITIES
TAX SHELTER
MUNI. FUND
INCOME FUND
OTHER:
ACCOUNT #

WORTH FOLLOW-UP
Please contact me in:
30 days
60 days
90 days
OR contact me on:
MO. DAY YEAR

NOT WORTH FOLLOW-UP
Reasons:
COULDN'T REACH
NO MONEY
CURIOSITY ONLY
DISSATISFIED
BOUGHT OTHER
WOULDN'T DISCUSS
STUDENT
BROKER
OTHER:

MARKETING RESEARCH 4

| PROSPECT PROFILE | PROFESSION | INVESTMENTS | OBJECTIVES | SOURCES OF FUNDS |
|---|---|---|---|---|
| MALE | DOCTOR | STOCK $ | GROWTH | INHERITANCE |
| FEMALE | LAWYER | BONDS | INCOME | SALE OF SECURITY |
| SINGLE | BUSINESS OWNER | MUTUAL FUNDS | CAPITAL GAINS | CD |
| MARRIED | FIDUCIARY | OPTIONS | TAX EXEMPTION | SAVINGS |
| OTHER: | BLUE COLLAR | COMMODITIES | SAFETY | TAX REFUND |
| | RETIRED | OTHER: | INFLATION HEDGE | |
| AGE: YEARS | TEACHER | | | |
| | ACCOUNTANT | | | |
| INCOME: $ | MANAGER | | | |
| | OTHER: | PORTFOLIO SIZE: $ | | OTHER: |

With a list of hot prospects in hand, the salesperson's next step is to prepare for the sales call. This involves creating a prospect profile, deciding on an approach, establishing objectives, and preparing for the presentation:

- *Create a prospect profile.* Before any sales call, a salesperson should create a profile of the prospect, which includes the names of key people and their role in the decision-making process as well as relevant information such as the prospect's buying needs, motive for buying, current suppliers, income/revenue level, number of employees, and years in business. Numerous resources provide this type of information, including annual reports, newspaper articles, on-line news services, library reference books, credit rating services, trade publications, and advertisements.
- *Decide on an approach.* The second step in preparing for the sales call is to decide how to approach the prospect. Options for a first contact include sending a letter or cold calling in person or by telephone. For an existing customer, the salesperson can either drop by unannounced or call ahead for an appointment, which is generally preferred. The effectiveness of cold calling depends on the nature of the product and on the target market. Ellen Woliner, for example, makes cold calls by telephone to generate leads and identify prospects. During her initial call, Woliner offers to send samples of work done by her New York–based graphic design firm; then she follows up with another phone call asking for a face-to-face meeting. Woliner says her cold-calling efforts have generated a substantial amount of business over the long term.[7]
- *Establish objectives.* Once an appointment is made, you should establish specific objectives to achieve during a sales call. Prospects, particularly in business selling, often give salespeople only a short period of time in which to make a presentation, so having clear objectives is vital for success.
- *Prepare for the presentation.* After outlining the objectives of the sales call, you need to prepare for the presentation. This involves studying available information, developing a presentation strategy, and assembling appropriate materials and visual aids. For expensive goods and services in the business-to-business market, this preparation can be extensive, stretching out over weeks and months.

When you are knowledgeable about the prospect and well prepared for a sales call, you greatly improve the odds of achieving your objectives. Gail Gelber sold two sophisticated data-processing systems for Terminal Applications Group during her first six weeks as a sales representative. Such an impressive performance led to her promotion to vice president of sales for the New York–based firm. Gelber says, "Knowledge is the key. You have to understand the customer's business and how your products will help that business make more money."[8]

## Approaching the Prospect

Perhaps you've heard the saying "You never get a second chance to make a first impression." It certainly holds true when it comes to approaching a prospective customer—whether the approach is by telephone, by letter, or in person. Too often salespeople forge ahead into a sales presentation without first considering how they will approach their prospect. With the right approach you can lay the groundwork for a more successful presentation by getting the prospect's attention, building rapport, and generating interest. The primary considerations in developing an effective approach are appearance, demeanor, and opening lines:

- *Appearance.* The days of plaid polyester suits may be long gone, but salespeople still risk making a bad impression by dressing inappropriately. Although they need not spend a fortune on designer clothes, successful salespeople avoid dressing too casually or too formally for a particular selling environment. Grooming and neatness are also important considerations, including little details such as making sure you don't hand the prospect a smudged or bent business card. When it comes to approaching a prospect by mail, appearance is just as important. For instance, potential customers who receive a letter full of misspelled words and grammatical errors are likely to think that the salesperson is careless.

- *Demeanor.* A salesperson's attitude and behavior can make or break a sale. Even when approaching a prospect by telephone, a salesperson should come across as professional, courteous, and considerate. Avoid gum chewing, smoking, nervous pacing, and tardiness. Maintaining eye contact helps hold the prospect's attention. If you have to go through a secretary or family member to get to the prospect, treat that person with the utmost respect and consideration. After all, you never know who might play a key role in facilitating future communication.

- *Opening lines.* A salesperson's opening lines should include a brief greeting and introduction, followed by a few carefully chosen words that get the prospect's attention and generate interest. The best way to accomplish this is to focus on a benefit to the customer rather than on the product itself. Here's where the salesperson's research on the prospect begins to pay off; the more you know about the customer's problems, the better your chances of striking a responsive chord.

## Making the Presentation

The presentation step in the selling process is the most crucial. Although it can take many forms, the presentation's purpose is always the same: to personally communicate a product message in such a way that it will convince a prospect to buy. For example, a department store salesperson who is helping a customer buy a suit may comment at some point, "I think the gray pinstripe will create the image you're looking for." You can be assured that this is not a casual comment but an important part of the selling process.

For more complex selling situations, an effective presentation should include a detailed description of the product, available options, associated services (such as delivery, installation, maintenance, and warranty), an explanation of how the product will benefit the customer or how it has benefited other customers, and a statement outlining costs. Most salespeople use one of the following two methods to deliver their sales presentation: the canned approach or the need-satisfaction approach.

### THE CANNED APPROACH

**canned approach**
An approach to selling that utilizes a memorized presentation and doesn't take into account individual customer and selling situations

The **canned approach** to selling is based on a memorized presentation. This method of selling was developed during the late 1800s by John H. Patterson of National Cash Register Company. It was used successfully for many years; however, as products and customers became more sophisticated, the canned approach became less effective.

Some of the products typically sold today through a canned approach are encyclopedias, cosmetics, household products, home water purification systems, and vacuum cleaners. The main disadvantage of the canned approach is that it is not designed to accommodate questioning, which can be frustrating for many potential customers. However, this approach can be effective when the product is not highly technical and when the company employs inexperienced salespeople. The canned approach is used most commonly in door-to-door selling and telemarketing programs.

Paul Walton was a commissioned salesperson for US Sprint during its early years, and he used a version of the canned approach to sign up subscribers. He started out working alone from a card table on the San Diego State University campus, but business was so good that he hired subcontractors to do the same thing in major cities throughout the United States. His sales force of 400 clean-cut and articulate college students eventually signed up 600,000 subscribers, making millions of dollars in commissions for Walton.[9]

The **need-satisfaction approach** to selling focuses on identifying the customer's needs and then creating a presentation that addresses those needs. Most professional salespeople today use this approach to selling. Depending on the particular needs of the customer, some salespeople may be able to identify the needs and make an effective presentation all in one meeting. Others may require extensive probing during a series of meetings with a number of people before they have enough information to make an effective presentation.

Your ability to listen and observe while the prospect is speaking is vital to the success of the need-satisfaction approach. Mannie Jackson of Honeywell says that a successful sales presentation is one in which the prospect does 80 percent of the talking.[10] Informal exploratory conversation can reveal important information and clues to the prospect's needs, priorities, interests, and concerns. Michael Franz, of Murata Business Systems, used the need-satisfaction approach to sell 800 fax machines to Sir Speedy. Franz says that when he sells he does more than make a presentation. In the case of Sir Speedy, he looked at all the support requirements Sir Speedy was going to need for its network of franchisees and then took the position of problem solver.[11]

**need-satisfaction approach**
An approach to selling that focuses on identifying the customer's needs and then creating a presentation that addresses those needs

# Handling Objections

No matter how well a presentation is delivered, it doesn't always conclude with an immediate offer from the prospect to buy. Often the prospect will express various types of objections and concerns throughout the presentation. In fact, the absence of objections is often an indication that the prospect is not interested in what the salesperson is selling. Many successful salespeople look at objections as a sign of the prospect's interest and as an opportunity to develop new ideas that will strengthen future presentations.

## IDENTIFYING OBJECTIONS

Alert salespeople try to identify objections before they arise. For instance, information you gather before the presentation may reveal that the prospect's current supplier offers a service that you won't be able to match. To avoid being put on the defensive in this type of situation, you may choose to address and counter the objection before it is raised. However, this approach can sometimes backfire if you bring up a concern the prospect hadn't thought of.

Most objections relate to three primary concerns: price, timing, and competition. Price is the most common objection that prospects raise. Sometimes they really are worried about price, but a price complaint can be a shield for other concerns. For instance, if the prospect doesn't think you are trustworthy but doesn't want to say so to your face, he or she may say the product is too expensive. When you get a price objection, the best plan is to probe, asking questions to see whether some other issue is buried underneath. Timing objections focus on the prospect's need to delay a buying decision, but—like price objections—timing objections are often just a way of covering up another problem. In another case, the prospect really does think the price is too high but won't say so for fear of looking cheap or poor. Objections dealing with competition are more likely to occur with a new customer who is satisfied with the current supplier and doesn't want to change.

## OVERCOMING OBJECTIONS

There are three basic approaches to overcoming objections: Ask the prospect a question, give a response to the objection, or tell the prospect that you will look into the matter and address it later.

For example, if a prospect objects to the price, you might ask the following question: "Why do you feel the price is too high?" The prospect may then point out un-

## WHAT IT TAKES TO CLOSE A BIG-TICKET SALE

"There's no better feeling than making a sale," says Gail DeWitt, and she has plenty to feel good about. As a full-line salesperson for Philips Medical Systems, DeWitt sells big-ticket items to hospitals, at an average price of about $500,000. In one year, she sold $10.8 million worth of medical equipment.

In one recent megadeal, DeWitt waged a year-long campaign to sell a $1.4 million cardiac catheterization unit to New Jersey's Passaic General. To pull it off, she had to sell to the 18 doctors who'd use the equipment, the head technician who'd run it, and the state regulators who had to approve

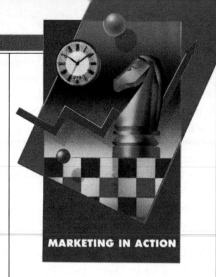

**MARKETING IN ACTION**

it, not to mention the hospital's administration and board of governors. DeWitt attended close to 50 meetings before the deal was done.

When DeWitt first heard that Passaic General was in the market for a cath unit, she knew her company

couldn't beat the competitors on price. However, DeWitt decided she might have a chance by playing on two strengths: the benefits of the product and the powerful company that backed it. She also knew she had to find a powerful advocate inside the hospital who could help her justify the price. So DeWitt tracked down the real power base—Rose Szwed, administrative director of cardiac services.

However, DeWitt didn't go directly to Szwed with her proposition. First, she visited a lab at Passaic General where a similar Philips unit had been installed years earlier. She found problems with the equipment, arranged to have them taken care of, and then used the opportunity to call Szwed to ask if everything was okay. Szwed was impressed with DeWitt's

---

derlying problems or objections that you can address, such as perceived shortcomings the product may have in comparison to a competing product.

When you have a clear understanding of what the client is objecting to, you should respond directly and not be evasive. You can use several techniques, including agreeing with the objection and then offsetting it with a benefit, or mentioning a previous buyer who had the same concern but was completely satisfied after purchasing the product.

Sometimes a prospect raises an objection that you cannot answer without doing some additional research. In this situation, offer to look into the matter and get back to the prospect later. To avoid the situation altogether, salespeople often include technical experts in their sales presentation. This happens more often with industrial products, about which prospects are more likely to ask technical questions that salespeople cannot afford to answer carelessly. Michael Franz of Murata credited much of the success of the Sir Speedy deal to the fact that his salespeople "thought before they spoke."[12]

## Closing

So far, you haven't made a dime. You may have spent weeks or months—years in some cases—to bring the customer to this point, but you don't make any money until the prospect decides to buy. This stage of the selling process, when you persuade the customer to place an order, is referred to as **closing**.

**closing**
The stage in the selling process at which the salesperson gets a purchase commitment from the prospect

When should you ask for the order? Successful sellers try to gauge the prospect's state of mind by doing a *trial close*, which asks for an opinion related to the sale but not for a final decision. For example, you can ask a potential car buyer which options are most important. The manner in which the prospect responds helps you determine whether it is time to ask for the order. You need to move when it's time to move, but trying to force closure before the prospect is ready can backfire.

How should you ask for the order? Of the many closing techniques, here are some of the more popular. The *alternative proposal close* asks the prospect to choose between some minor details, such as method of shipment. With the *assumptive close*,

588

efforts and asked to meet with her. DeWitt learned that what Szwed wanted most was better service. DeWitt lobbied Philips's district service manager to address all of Szwed's complaints and to provide service visits on weekends. Szwed was pleased and DeWitt had her foot in the door.

Soon Szwed asked about inspecting the new Philips equipment in action, which would involve a trip to Los Angeles and Las Vegas. DeWitt gladly arranged every detail of the three-day trip for Szwed as well as the hospital's head technician and head nurse, two cardiologists, and DeWitt's district sales manager. Philips picked up the $5,000 tab.

The trip was a turning point. Everyone relaxed and got to know each other on a more personal level. To be nice, DeWitt made sure the hotel rooms were reserved under Szwed's name and even booked her into a suite. She also talked to Szwed about things that mattered to her, like awaiting the birth of her first grandchild. When it came time to negotiate, Szwed wanted $100,000 worth of extra equipment thrown in free. DeWitt gave in because she knew it was important for Szwed to look good to her bosses.

With Szwed on board everything fell into place. Even when one of the hospital's most influential doctors publicly backed another company, the administration sought out Szwed. She stood behind Philips. Finally, the hospital board of governors gave Philips the nod, and a purchase order was placed 10 months after Szwed announced she was ready to buy.

One final point illustrates DeWitt's savvy when it comes to keeping customers satisfied. When the cath lab was ready for its open house, Szwed called DeWitt and asked whether Philips might foot the bill for food. DeWitt knew that another $2 million cardiac cath lab would eventually be put out for bid, so she petitioned her boss for $250 and paid for the food. It was a small gesture—and she already had the order—but DeWitt realized that small gestures add up to customer satisfaction.

## APPLY YOUR KNOWLEDGE

**1.** What role does customer service play in sales like DeWitt's?
**2.** How would this selling effort have progressed if DeWitt had tried to emphasize low price over every other benefit?

you simply proceed with processing the order, assuming that the prospect has already decided to buy. Another alternative is the *silent close,* in which you finish your presentation and sit quietly, waiting for the customer to respond with his or her buying decision. Finally, many salespeople prefer the *direct close,* in which you just come right out and ask for the order.

These closing techniques might strike you as tricks, and in the hands of unethical salespeople, some closing approaches certainly can be. However, the professional salesperson uses these techniques to make the selling process effective and efficient—not to trick people into buying when they aren't ready.

As important as closing is, many salespeople have trouble making it happen. The reason is simple: When you try to close, hope collides with reality. If you've been hoping you'll get the sale, but the customer has no intention of buying, the bad news will surface when you try to close. To delay the potential rejection, inexperienced salespeople often take a passive stance, waiting for the customer to decide. However, top sellers know that you need to stay in control and guide the prospect all the way through closing.[13] Experienced salespeople tend to feel more comfortable closing because they have learned how to use trial closes to determine when the prospect is ready to make a commitment.

## Following Up

Most salespeople depend on repeat sales, so it's important that they follow up on all sales and not ignore the customer once the first sale is made. During this follow-up stage of the selling process, make sure that the product has been delivered properly and that the customer is satisfied. Inexperienced salespeople may avoid the follow-up stage because they fear facing an unhappy customer. However, an important part of a salesperson's job is to ensure customer satisfaction and build goodwill.

Travel agents, for example, may phone customers who have taken a cruise vacation to welcome them home and find out whether they had any problems during the cruise. Real estate agents often send flowers or have a plant delivered after they sell a home. Many companies that sell a service use a separate team of sales support personnel to service accounts after the initial sale. US West Cellular, for example, has its service representatives place "Welcome Aboard" calls to new subscribers to thank them for their business and to answer questions. The company has found through focus groups that when representatives call customers periodically, the customers perceive improvements in their cellular telephone service—even if there were no improvements.[14]

When you're unable to close a sale, it does not mean the follow-up step should be ignored. Making a follow-up call can sometimes prompt a prospect to reconsider, or it will at least keep the lines of communication open for future prospecting. If a prospect is doing a lot of comparison shopping, the salesperson who makes a follow-up call may be the one who gets the sale. For example, an executive returning from an overseas assignment once needed to buy three new cars for his family. He visited several dealerships and was prepared to spend $40,000, but not one salesperson bothered to follow up.[15]

To improve the odds of keeping a satisfied customer after the sale, salespeople should remember to

- Handle complaints promptly and pleasantly
- Maintain contact with customers
- Keep serving the customer
- Show appreciation[16]

# TRENDS IN PERSONAL SELLING

Personal selling is evolving along with the changing needs of the marketplace. Current trends in the area of personal selling include a greater emphasis on ethics, the increased use of computers, a growth in telemarketing, the growing number of women and minorities in sales, team selling, systems selling, a growing emphasis on selling services, and selling internationally.

## Sales Ethics

Much of the recent emphasis on marketing ethics has focused on ethical sales practices. In many people's eyes, the sales profession has something of a reputation for unethical behavior, a fact that bothers professional salespeople. To counteract the ethics problem, companies are beginning to make ethics a part of their sales-training programs. Typical issues dealt with in such programs include expense accounts, the use of gifts, making promises to the customer about product performance, selling products that customers don't need, and dealing with customers' unethical demands.[17] By clarifying ethical issues and keeping sales reps aware of them, more and more businesses are working to ensure honorable behavior.

Various industries have their own unique sales problems to address, in addition to these general issues. For example, stockbrokers have to make sure they aren't encouraging clients to buy and sell more frequently than is really necessary. This is known as *churning* an account, and every transaction generates additional income for the stockbroker. Automobile dealers, especially in the used-car market, have to watch for unjustified claims of car quality. Sellers of complex products, such as life insurance, factory-automation systems, and financial planning services, have to be sure they're not selling the customer more than is necessary, just because the customer doesn't fully understand the product.

## Computerization

Salespeople are becoming increasingly dependent on computers for all aspects of selling—from prospecting, to organizing their schedules, to giving presentations, to following up with customers after the sale. Dozens of software programs have been written with salespeople in mind (see Exhibit 19.5). In addition to handling admin-

## IS IT A GIFT OR A BRIBE?

When a seller treats a customer or potential customer to a gift, is it really a gift or a bribe? Corporate purchasing agents and managers are responsible for buying everything from pencils to trucks and are therefore in a vulnerable position in terms of gifts. A recent survey by *Purchasing World* magazine revealed that 85 percent of its readers operate under a code of ethics laid down by their companies, but 80 percent accept free lunches and personalized souvenirs. Smaller percentages accept larger gifts: 42 percent accept tickets for sporting events, and 35 percent say that alcoholic beverages are acceptable gifts. One purchasing manager said that gifts serve as a "tie-breaker" if two suppliers offer equal deals. Some rationalize what they're doing as acceptable business practice, whereas others are strict and don't accept any gifts.

Companies' policies vary widely on this question. Pneutronics Corporation represents the extreme case: According to materials manager Patricia Champagne, any buyer will be immediately fired for accepting gifts

**ETHICAL DILEMMA IN MARKETING**

of any kind. Other companies are more lenient. Recreational vehicle manufacturer Travelcraft lets employees accept gifts at Christmas (limited to $25 value), as well as football and baseball tickets.

International marketing presents additional difficulties. For example, some Asian cultures consider the giving and taking of gifts to be an important part of social interaction. In such cases, not accepting a gift is likely to be viewed as a sign of rudeness, not a show of moral fortitude. Just as various individuals approach the gift question from different perspectives, so do various cultures.

To help companies grapple with the ethical ambiguity surrounding

gifts, the National Association of Purchasing Managers offers the following guidelines for accepting or rejecting gifts:

- *Be able to reciprocate.* If a buyer accepts a gift, he or she should be able to return the favor, such as trading lunches.
- *Don't upgrade your lifestyle.* You shouldn't accept anything that enhances the manner in which you live, such as televisions or stereo systems.
- *Ask for advice.* Your boss should be able to offer advice if a potential gift isn't covered by company policy.

Gary Edwards of the Ethics Resource Center poses a simple guideline that might be even more effective: Would you like to read about your decision in tomorrow's newspaper? If you wouldn't be comfortable giving or receiving a gift in public, you shouldn't do it in private, either.

### WHAT'S YOUR OPINION?

**1.** Should lawmakers pass legislation against any type of sales-related gifts?
**2.** In the absence of such laws, what stance should buyers and sellers take on the issue of gifts?

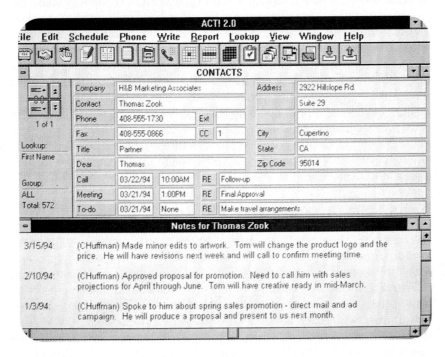

**Exhibit 19.5
SOFTWARE FOR PERSONAL SELLING**
ACT!, one of the leading software packages for lead tracking and contact management, helps boost sales productivity by managing details and taking care of records.

istrative tasks, they also help salespeople with such things as figuring out which type of close will work best with a particular client personality. When it comes to laptop, notebook, and hand-held computers, businesses are buying them by the dozens for their sales forces. The benefits include tighter integration of sales and other business functions, more responsive customer service, better market data, and more effective sales presentations.[18]

Marketers are still learning how to make the best use of all this computing power, however. Falling in love with the latest technology or assuming computers can solve all one's problems are just two of the ways marketers have managed to waste time and money on computerization. Sales automation consultant Allan Levin tells the story of an insurance company that actually decreased the productivity of its sales force by providing the salespeople with complex systems that weren't designed for the task. In contrast, FMC Corporation's Chemical Products Group enjoyed great success with its sales computers. Through careful planning and attention to the needs of the sales force, the company helped sales and marketing staffs work together more closely. The sales force now gets the information to make effective, timely presentations to customers.[19]

## Telemarketing

**telemarketing**
A promotional method utilizing specially trained salespeople to systematically contact a group of prospects or customers by telephone

As the cost of personal sales calls continues to increase, many companies and nonprofit organizations are turning to **telemarketing**—selling over the telephone—to keep costs down. Businesses like telemarketing because they can reach more customers, and many customers like it because it saves them time. Telemarketers now sell everything from investment services to computer systems.[20] Sometimes telemarketing is used by itself; in other cases, it is used in the initial stages of the sales process to find and qualify prospects.

For example, J. Fegely & Son, a Pennsylvania-based distributor of industrial supplies, has attracted 2,000 customers solely from cold calls made by the company's telemarketing staff. Most of the accounts range in size from $4,000 to $12,000, but one telemarketer has built an account as high as $60,000. The telemarketing customers (typically owners of small machine shops) like the idea of not being bothered by salespeople who want to meet with them in person.[21]

Two classes of telemarketing are *outbound telemarketing*, which occurs when companies make cold calls to potential customers who have not requested a sales call, and *inbound telemarketing*, which establishes phone lines for customers to call to place orders. Many consumers and organizational customers enjoy the convenience of inbound telemarketing. On the other hand, outbound telemarketing generates a lot of criticism because it interrupts family or business activities and can even pose a threat to safety by tying up a phone line needed in an emergency. If you've been bothered during dinner or roused from a deep sleep just to answer the phone and listen to someone's sales pitch, you understand the criticism. Perhaps the worst abuse comes from computerized dialing systems that call numbers automatically and send a recorded message. Public pressure is leading some states to consider legislation that would regulate or even ban outbound telemarketing. The Federal Communications Commission has already banned computerized calls to emergency phones and health-care facilities, and many states have regulated computerized calls as well.[22]

## Women and Minorities in Sales

Increasing numbers of women and minorities are being drawn to careers in sales as more opportunities open up and the image of the profession improves. Women have already had a strong presence in retail sales, but they are a growing force in industrial and commercial sales as well. In 1970, women made up less than 7 percent of the U.S. nonretail sales force; in 1993 the figure was 26 percent (although only 13 percent of sales managers are women).[23] Women have proven to be especially successful in real estate sales. For instance, when she immigrated to the United States in 1975, Olivia Hsu Decker decided that real estate was her ticket to the American dream. She eventually became the top luxury-home seller at Merrill Lynch and then left to start her own firm.[24]

Many African-Americans are also achieving outstanding success in sales careers. At Xerox, for example, African-American managers are responsible for 60 percent of the company's sales. Tonya Turner, an African-American saleswoman at Xerox, earns a six-figure income as the company's top seller of facsimile machines. According to Turner, "Sales allows my entrepreneurial spirit to come through."[25]

## Team Selling

Team selling is becoming a necessity in many situations because of the increasing sophistication of both products and buyers. Some companies are beginning to use a team approach simply because it fosters cooperation, not competition, among salespeople. For some marketers, this means the formal equivalent of the industrial buying center you learned about in Chapter 5. The industrial *selling* center has individual roles and responsibilities just as the customer's buying center has. The salesperson is the core of the selling center, and he or she brings in support as needed. This support can come from company executives, production specialists, engineers, or other people with specialized expertise.[26]

In other cases, a sales team can have as few as two people. Carol Nelson and Mary Ann Tighe are among the most successful commercial real estate brokers in New York City. (Real estate brokers help organizations find and negotiate for office and manufacturing space.) Nelson's strength is in getting the selling process rolling, making contact with potential clients and identifying their needs. Tighe's strength is in implementing the transactions and finishing up the deals. By complementing each other's strength, Nelson and Tighe have become highly respected in a tough niche of the sales profession.[27]

## Systems Selling

More companies are turning to **systems selling**, which refers to the concept of selling a coordinated package of goods or services that will meet a customer's needs more effectively than a single product alone. Systems selling requires the salesperson to have extensive knowledge of both the product line and the customer's needs.

**systems selling**
The concept of selling a "package" of goods or services designed to meet a customer's unique needs

For example, computer manufacturers often sell a complete system of hardware, software, and training designed to perform a specific function for a specific customer. The objective of systems selling is not to offer customers a lower price because of the package deal but to better solve the customer's overall problem.

## Selling Services

Sales opportunities in service industries (such as banking, insurance, real estate, transportation, and finance) are growing faster than opportunities in the goods-producing industries. In addition to the growing sales opportunities in service businesses, salespeople in service companies tend to earn more than their counterparts who sell consumer and industrial goods.[28]

Many goods-producing firms now realize that their customers also need a variety of service products to meet their needs. For example, Lexus and Infiniti have established dealer service networks that promote a "total ownership experience" rather than just the automobile itself. In the office equipment industry, companies such Xerox have shifted their sales strategy from selling products to selling total solutions.[29] As a result, more and more salespeople are getting involved with services, even if their primary products are goods.

## International Sales

Sales techniques differ from country to country, and U.S. companies expanding into overseas markets have to be aware of the differences. For example, a salesperson's educational level tends to be more important in some countries than it is in the

United States. Customers in those countries expect a lot of technical expertise from sales reps, and companies try to meet that expectation.[30]

Because of the growing demand for international salespeople, schools and learning centers have developed special international sales-training programs. Although basic sales skills transcend some cultural barriers, certain aspects of selling, such as the style and pace of presentations, negotiations, and contract signing, differ greatly, depending on the location. To successfully sell in foreign countries, salespeople must do more than perfect their selling skills; they must also learn about a country's customs and culture. Many countries have multiple languages, dialects, and subcultures, making the selling task that much more complicated. For example, Belgium is split into areas of French and Flemish origins, and India has as many as 1,000 dialects and subcultures. To navigate these complex markets, U.S. companies often use different selection criteria when hiring international sales personnel.

Belgium, with its separate French and Flemish regions, is an example of the social and cultural diversity that faces salespeople in many countries.

# THE PEOPLE WHO SELL

Among the ranks of successful salespeople are men and women of all races and nationalities, young people and old people, people with Ph.D.s, people still in high school, people who live in million-dollar mansions, and people who live in one-bedroom apartments. When it comes to personality, we often think of salespeople as being outgoing, life-of-the-party types. However, no distinctive personality sets salespeople apart. Although many successful salespeople are fun-loving extroverts, others are just as successful who are no-nonsense introverts. Successful salespeople do, however, seem to share certain attributes that set them apart from the norm.

## Attributes of Successful Salespeople

Successful salespeople have four key attributes in common: empathy, ego drive, service motivation, and ego strength.[31] If salespeople lack even one of these attributes, they are less likely to find success in a sales career over the long term.

**empathy**
The ability to put oneself in another person's place

**Empathy** refers to the ability to put yourself in another person's shoes. This quality is especially important for salespeople because customers often have hidden concerns and agendas. Empathic abilities help you probe and listen effectively in order to determine what will meet the customer's needs. Some people have a greater sense of empathy than others, but everyone can learn to improve his or her empathic abilities.

**ego drive**
The quality that makes a salesperson want to make a sale

**Ego drive** is the quality that makes a salesperson *want* to make a sale. However, when ego drive is not balanced by empathy, a salesperson may appear too "hungry" for a sale and will turn buyers off. To a salesperson, ego drive is like fuel to a car; empathy is what steers it.[32]

**service motivation**
The quality that drives a salesperson to want to provide good service to a customer

**Service motivation** is similar to ego drive, except that the ego-driven salesperson wants a "yes," whereas the service-motivated salesperson wants a "thank you."[33] Although service motivation alone doesn't guarantee success in sales, it is becoming increasingly important as the marketplace continues to place a high priority on the quality of service a company delivers. Through training programs, salespeople can learn to become more service-oriented if that is not their strong point.

**ego strength**
The quality that helps salespeople deal with inevitable rejections

**Ego strength** is what helps salespeople deal with the inevitable rejections that come with the territory. Some salespeople, unfortunately, don't have the ego strength to bounce back from rejections because they take rejection too personally. Encouragement from management helps salespeople develop stronger egos, as does training in techniques for handling rejection.

## Types of Sales Personnel

From the general public's perspective, salespeople are salespeople. However, from a business perspective, various types of salespeople play various roles depending on the size of the company, how it's organized, the type of product it sells, and the nature of its customer base. Because every business has a unique way of operating, salespeople cannot be separated into nice, neat categories that apply to every situation.

Titles commonly assigned to salespeople include sales representative, factory representative, field representative, marketing representative, sales engineer, account executive, account manager, counter salesperson, customer service representative, consultant, counselor, sales assistant, telemarketer, and fund-raiser.

In general, however, salespeople can be categorized according to three broad areas of responsibility: order getting, order taking, and sales support services. Although some salespeople focus primarily on one area of responsibility, others may have broader responsibilities that span several areas.

## ORDER GETTERS

**Order getters** are responsible for generating new sales and for increasing sales to existing customers. Order getters can range from telemarketers selling bottled water and stockbrokers selling securities to engineers selling computers and nuclear physicists selling consulting services. To generate new sales, order getters usually go through the entire seven-step selling process, from prospecting to following up. Sometimes, however, other people in the firm may be responsible for prospecting and will simply give the salesperson leads to follow up on.

Order getting is sometimes referred to as *creative selling,* particularly if the salesperson must invest a significant amount of time determining what the customer needs, devising a strategy to explain how the product can meet those needs, and persuading the customer to buy. This type of creative selling requires a high degree of empathy, with the salesperson taking on the role of consultant in a long-term relationship with the customer.

Both manufacturers and service businesses need creative salespeople. For example, at PPG Industries' Fiber Glass Reinforcement Products division, the salespeople refer to themselves as "consultants to distributors" rather than as salespeople merely calling to get orders.[34] At Jenny Craig Weight Loss Centres, which is primarily a service business, order getters are referred to as "counselors." Their job is to sell tailor-made weight-loss programs to prospective customers. Order getters can be further defined as "outside" or "inside" order getters. *Outside order getters* are also referred to as field salespeople. For instance, the PPG field salespeople who work outside the office calling on prospective and existing distributors are outside order getters. Retail stores selling office supplies also use outside order getters to seek out new accounts by calling on businesses of all types.

*Inside order getters* are people who work at the seller's location, such as the counselors at Jenny Craig Weight Loss Centres. Retail establishments like Sears also use inside order getters to persuade prospective customers to purchase big-ticket items such as major appliances or custom-made draperies. Automobile salespeople are also considered inside order getters.

## ORDER TAKERS

**Order takers** do little creative selling but serve primarily to process orders for existing customers. Unfortunately, the term "order taker" has assumed negative overtones in recent years because salespeople often use it to refer to someone too lazy to prospect or actively close orders, or they use it to refer to someone whose territory is so attractive that he or she can just sit by the phone and wait for orders to roll in. Regardless of how salespeople use the term, order takers in the true sense play an important role in the sales function.

Many companies are even beginning to train their order takers to think more like order getters with the aim of generating additional sales. You've probably noticed, for example, that nearly every time you order a hamburger at McDonald's, the person at the counter will ask, "Would you like an order of french fries to go with that?"

**order getters**
Salespeople responsible for generating new sales and increasing sales to existing customers

**order takers**
Salespeople who primarily process orders for existing customers

Such suggestions can prompt customers to buy something they might not have ordered otherwise.

Standard Process Laboratories, a distributor of nutritional supplements, relies heavily on order takers to process orders that are called in. However, when new owners took over the Southern California distributorship they discovered that the order takers had little knowledge of the product line, and worse, they were actually turning away telephone orders from customers who wouldn't recite their shopping lists in alphabetical order. The owners promptly implemented a training program and incentives to help the order takers develop a new attitude, thereby maximizing their contribution to the company's sales efforts.

Like order getters, order takers can be defined as outside and inside. *Outside order takers* for manufacturers or wholesalers such as Kraft General Foods and Eastman Kodak regularly call on established accounts to inform the customer about new-product offerings, answer questions, and replenish inventory stocks. *Inside order takers* include over-the-counter salespeople at retail stores such as Radio Shack, Sears, and The Gap. Over-the-counter salespeople complete sales by ringing them up on the cash register, accepting payment, and bagging the items purchased. Inside order takers can also include travel agents who book flights for people who are regular customers of the agency.

Order takers are not generally required to have as much expertise or sales talent as order getters; therefore, they don't usually make as much money. However, order takers play an important role in many businesses. If they are poorly trained, less than helpful, indifferent about their responsibilities, or never around when needed, today's more demanding customers will simply take their business elsewhere.

## SALES SUPPORT PERSONNEL

**sales support personnel**
Salespeople who generally facilitate the overall selling effort by providing a variety of services

**Sales support personnel** generally don't sell products, but they facilitate the overall selling effort by providing a variety of services. Their responsibilities can include prospecting, educating prospects and customers, building goodwill, and providing service to customers after the sale. The three most common types of sales support personnel are missionary, technical, and trade salespeople.

**missionary salespeople**
Salespeople who disseminate information about new products to existing customers and who motivate them to resell to their customers

**Missionary salespeople** are employed by manufacturers to disseminate information about new products to existing customers (usually wholesale distributors and retailers) and motivate them to sell the product to their customers. For example, Anacia Perez, a senior account manager at International Paper, is a missionary salesperson. Her objectives include introducing new paper products to distributors' sales forces and motivating them to sell the products to their own customers. Manufacturers of pharmaceuticals and medical supplies also use missionary salespeople to call on doctors and pharmacists. They leave samples and information, answer questions, and persuade doctors to prescribe their products.

**technical salespeople**
Salespeople who contribute technical expertise and assistance to the selling function

**Technical salespeople** contribute technical expertise and assistance to the selling function. They are usually engineers and scientists, or they have received specialized technical training. In addition to providing support services to existing customers, they may also participate in sales calls to prospective customers. Companies that manufacture computers, industrial equipment, and sophisticated medical equipment use technical salespeople to sell their products as well as provide support services to existing customers.

**trade salespeople**
Salespeople who take orders as well as provide support services, such as helping retailers promote the producer's product

**Trade salespeople** sell to and support marketing intermediaries. Hormel, Nabisco, and Sara Lee use trade salespeople to offer samples to customers, set up displays, restock shelves, and obtain more shelf space. Increasingly, producers work to establish lasting, mutually beneficial relationships with their channel partners, and these relationships are built by the trade salespeople.

You can see that salespeople play a wide range of roles in business and that each role is an important part of a company's overall marketing strategy. However, just as important as the efforts of individual salespeople is a company's ability to manage its sales team effectively. With good management, salespeople are more motivated to sell, and that can mean the difference between success and failure for many companies.

# SALES MANAGEMENT

Many salespeople work with a great deal of autonomy (especially outside order getters and outside order takers). They enjoy being self-reliant, having their own territory, and arranging their own schedules. However, even the most autonomous salespeople are still part of a team effort. When the sales team is well managed it can achieve greater results than it could if each member worked independently. Although it is in fact a managerial function, sales management differs from other management jobs in several ways: Job performance is easy to measure (both good and bad performance, that is), everything the sales team does is highly visible, sales managers spend a great deal of time working with people outside the company, and they tend to operate under a great deal of stress.[35] Effective **sales management** involves planning the personal selling effort, organizing the sales personnel, and developing a winning sales team.

**sales management**
Planning the personal selling effort, organizing the sales personnel, and developing a winning sales team

## Planning the Personal Selling Effort

Sales planning is one of the most important responsibilities of sales management. The process of planning involves setting objectives and developing strategies for achieving those objectives. Its purpose is to provide direction for the sales team so that members know where to focus their efforts from year to year. With a clearly defined plan, each member of the team will be pulling in the same direction rather than working at odds with the others.

### SETTING OBJECTIVES

Objectives are statements of what the sales team expects to achieve within a specified period of time. They are generally established for the sales team as a whole, as well as for individual salespeople. The broader objectives for the sales team are linked to objectives that have been established for the entire marketing effort.

The three most common types of sales objectives relate to volume of sales, market share, and profitability. You can define such objectives in several ways, including dollar amount of sales, number of units sold, percentage of increase over the previous year, number of new customers, number of customers retained, and return on funds invested in specific sales activities.

In years past, sales managers had a tendency to set objectives without getting input from their salespeople, but this practice is giving way to a more participative approach to planning. At PPG Industries, for example, setting sales objectives was a one-way, top-down procedure until Kevin Sullivan took over as director of sales for the Fiber Glass Reinforcement Products division. Sullivan discovered that the salespeople were not actively pursuing new sales, so he launched a planning process that got everyone involved. As a result, the salespeople began to see themselves as managers of their own territories rather than as passive order takers.[36]

### FORMULATING STRATEGIES

Strategies are the specific methods used to achieve sales objectives. Sales strategies can focus on a number of areas, including the types and number of salespeople needed, the methods used to identify and call on prospects, the way that sales routes and schedules will be organized, the way existing customers will be managed, and the segments of the market that will be pursued.

For instance, PPG's main sales strategy was to focus on helping its distributors' sales managers and salespeople do a better job of setting goals and planning their own sales activities. The benefit to distributors would be reduced inventories and increased profits. As a result of PPG's sales strategy, its salespeople were able to increase sales to many of their distributors and also pick up new accounts.[37]

**Exhibit 19.6**
**PLANNING SALES TERRITORIES**
Salespeople increasingly turn to mapping software to locate customers and potential customers; this information helps improve the definition of sales territories and the allocation of sales resources.

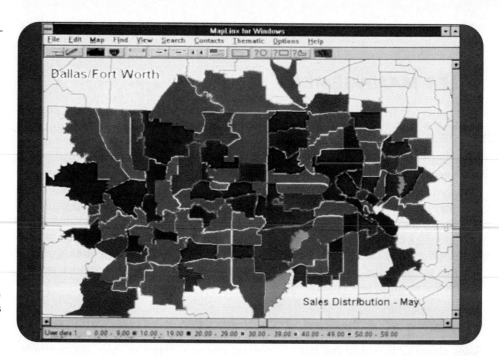

## Organizing the Sales Personnel

Sales personnel can be organized in many ways, depending on the types of salespeople a company requires, its product line, and the nature of its customer base. Some of the most common ways of organizing sales personnel are by geographic territory, product, customer, or a combination of factors (see Exhibit 19.6).

Organizing by *geographic territory* is the simplest and most commonly used method of structuring a sales team. A territory can be as small as a single section of one city or as large as an entire country. One advantage of organizing by territories is that a salesperson can minimize travel time and expense by working from the center of the territory. Another advantage of territories is familiarity; salespeople assigned to one specific region can take the time to learn about that particular market area.

Organizing by *products* allows salespeople to concentrate their efforts on a particular product line, item, or brand. The disadvantage of this approach is that one customer may have to deal with two or three salespeople from the same company.

Organizing by *customers* is often required when members of the customer base have significantly different needs. IBM, for example, uses specialized sales teams for various categories of customers. The main disadvantage of this approach is that selling costs can be high because more than one salesperson may be covering the same geographic area.

Most companies organize their sales personnel by a combination of factors. Large travel agencies, for example, may have separate sales teams for group travel, for corporate travel, and for leisure travel. Each of these sales teams may be organized by geographic location. Then within each geographic territory salespeople may specialize in selling to large accounts or small accounts.

## Developing a Winning Sales Team

With the goals, strategies, and structure in place, the sales manager can concentrate on the most important task of all—developing a winning sales team. To accomplish this, a manager determines the number of salespeople needed, gets the best people, provides effective training, motivates the salespeople, compensates the salespeople, and evaluates performance.

Determining personnel needs is a crucial sales management issue. If a sales manager hires more salespeople than necessary to cover the company's market adequately, profits will be eaten up by the excess costs. On the other hand, if salespeople are spread too thin, morale will suffer, productivity may drop, and sales will decline. The goal is to pinpoint the optimum number of salespeople required to achieve the sales objectives. Two commonly used approaches to determining sales personnel needs are the equalized work load method and the incremental method.

The **equalized work load method** of determining personnel needs is based on the assumption that each salesperson makes approximately the same number of sales calls over a given period of time. If, for example, you estimate that 2,000 current and potential customers will each need to be called on an average of 10 times during the year, that means that 20,000 sales calls must be made in order to adequately cover the market. If the company's average salesperson makes 1,000 sales calls per year, the number of salespeople needed to cover the market would be determined as follows:

**equalized work load method**
A way of determining personnel needs based on the assumption that each salesperson makes approximately the same number of sales calls over a given time period

$$\frac{\text{Total annual sales call requirements}}{\text{Average salesperson calls per year}} = \frac{20,000}{1,000} = 20 \text{ salespeople}$$

Although this method is effective for some companies, it will not be an accurate predictor of personnel needs if a company's customers vary significantly in the number of sales calls they require, or if salespeople vary significantly in the number of calls they can make per year. For example, some salespeople may have to travel farther than others and therefore may not be able to make as many calls as salespeople who spend less time traveling.

The **incremental method** of determining personnel needs is based on the assumption that the addition of a salesperson is justified when the additional sales generated exceed the cost of hiring the salesperson. To apply this method effectively, a manager must be able to accurately estimate future sales and future selling costs.

**incremental method**
A way of determining personnel needs based on the assumption that the addition of a salesperson is justified when the additional sales generated exceed the cost of hiring the salesperson

Most managers cannot rely on one basic method to determine personnel needs. Any formula approach must be weighed against the manager's own subjective opinions on other issues such as industry trends, the nature of the selling tasks, the caliber of the salespeople, and the complexity of customers' needs.

## GETTING THE RIGHT PEOPLE

The people who make up the sales team are a major factor in your company's overall success. Yet some managers seem to do their hiring in a crisis mode. They scramble around looking for someone to fill a vacancy at the last minute, thinking that if the person doesn't work out someone else will always be ready to take his or her place. However, the cost of hiring, training, and retraining a salesperson can run as high as $100,000 or more, so you can't afford to make hiring mistakes.[38]

RECRUITING    Effective sales recruiting is an ongoing process of searching for and obtaining job candidates who are compatible with the company's needs. The objective is to have a constant pool of potentially qualified applicants to select from. However, before recruiting actually begins, management should develop or update job descriptions, qualifications, and salary levels for positions to be filled. These criteria can vary significantly from one sales position to another. Potential sources for sales recruits include the company's own salespeople, suppliers, customers, professional associations, job fairs, employment agencies, advertisements, and colleges and universities (see Exhibit 19.7).

SELECTING    The selection process is often compared to a game of chance—especially when it comes to hiring salespeople. However, the odds of finding the right people can be improved by using a variety of selection tools to screen and select ap-

**Exhibit 19.7**
**RECRUITING SALESPEOPLE**
To attract successful sales professionals, companies try to offer an appealing combination of compensation, job satisfaction, career growth, and other benefits.

plicants. Some of the most common tools are application forms that collect information; personal interviews that evaluate the applicant's qualifications, motivation, desire to succeed, and level of maturity; reference checks; and employment tests that gauge such characteristics as intelligence, knowledge, aptitude, skills, and personality.

Some companies even hire salespeople on a trial basis before making a final selection decision. Moore Business Forms, for example, puts new recruits through a four-week "forward training program," during which 14 tests are given. Recruits are forewarned that if they fail any of the tests, they will be terminated.[39]

## TRAINING SALESPEOPLE

Whether salespeople are young and inexperienced recruits or 30-year veterans, ongoing training will maximize their contribution to the total sales effort. Salespeople themselves are sold on the idea of training: A recent survey revealed that 97 percent of salespeople believe training is important to their success.[40] Through ongoing training, salespeople are kept up-to-date on such matters as product changes and changes in customer needs, in the way territories are organized, and in the way sales functions are handled. Ongoing training also helps reinforce a salesperson's good habits and minimize the development of bad habits.

Although the scope and frequency of sales training vary significantly from one company to another, an increasing number of businesses are providing some type of training for their salespeople. When Avon began selling in China, it brought its Chinese partners to the Philippines to let them observe a functioning Avon sales system in operation. As a whole, U.S. companies spend billions of dollars annually on sales training.[41]

You might think that the majority of training time is spent teaching people how to sell, but in reality most training focuses on teaching salespeople about the products they sell.[42] In addition to product information and selling techniques, other topics of value to salespeople include the company they sell for, the customers, the industry, time management, and forecasting skills.

## MOTIVATING SALESPEOPLE

Motivation is an inner drive that causes people to do something. Although salaries, bonuses, and commissions are usually thought of as the major motivating factors for salespeople, money alone is not enough to motivate salespeople to do their best.

Like all people, they seek emotional, social, and intellectual satisfaction from their jobs. For instance, if salespeople are forced to sell products of poor quality, or if they aren't given the resources to fully support their customers, even a generous compensation package won't overcome the frustration that is sure to result. In addition, closing a sale or solving a customer's problems is an accomplishment that deserves recognition, even if it's nothing more than public mention at a sales meeting or a pat on the back.

Aside from salaries and commissions, other important motivating factors in the sales environment are the manager's leadership style, opportunities for promotion, and recognition for accomplishments. Some managers take a low-key approach; others apply pressure to get results. Frank Pacetta, who manages the Xerox sales force in the Cleveland, Ohio, area, takes the latter approach. As he puts it, "I'll recognize you lavishly, but I expect you to pay the rent. If you don't, you'll face the consequences."[43]

The two motivational tools that probably get the most attention are quotas and sales incentives. Each salesperson has an explicit sales goal, known as a **sales quota.** Quotas can be defined in terms of dollar volume or units sold, depending on how the company tracks sales. Commissions and bonus payments are often based on the percentage of the quota that the salesperson achieves, making the quota an obvious motivational tool. In addition to quotas, salespeople are frequently evaluated by sales-related activities such as the number of calls made per day, the number of new accounts opened, or sales expenses per day.

**Sales incentives** include various types of prizes awarded through sales contests. The objective of the contest is to motivate salespeople to increase their sales. Trips and merchandise are often given as contest prizes. To help ensure that sales contests are effective, management should allow salespeople to participate in developing contest guidelines and prizes.

## COMPENSATING SALESPEOPLE

Financial compensation is one of the sales manager's most important motivational tools. Top salespeople have the potential to reach impressive income levels. However, it is not always easy to develop a compensation program for salespeople (especially field salespeople), because their work is less standardized than the work of other types of employees. The most commonly used methods of compensation are straight salary, straight commission, and salary plus commission.

A **straight salary compensation plan** involves a fixed amount of money paid to the salesperson at regular intervals, just like a normal salary. This is the simplest compensation plan and provides a sense of security to salespeople who like to count on receiving a certain amount of income each month. A straight salary has advantages for the employer, too, because it represents a known, fixed cost.

The primary disadvantage of a straight salary is that it does not provide a strong incentive to achieve specific sales goals. Straight salary programs are more common for missionary salespeople, who do not do any direct selling. Straight salaries are also more likely to be paid to salespeople who work in industries such as aerospace or who sell to the government (because a sale may take years to complete).

A **straight commission compensation plan** pays salespeople a percentage of the sales or of the gross profits they generate. The primary advantage of the straight commission method is that it provides a high degree of motivation. Many salespeople who work only on commission have an entrepreneurial nature and feel like they are in business for themselves. Another advantage, from a management perspective, is that selling costs are always in proportion to sales made.

One company that has done exceptionally well with its straight commission sales force is Re/Max, a multibillion-dollar residential real estate company. Unlike most real estate companies, which split commissions with agents on a 50-50 basis, Re/Max lets its agents keep 100 percent of the commissions earned. In return, agents pay monthly office overhead and franchise fees.[44] Companies like Re/Max that pay only straight commission tend to attract experienced salespeople who are highly confident in their abilities.

**sales quota**
The sales goal established for each salesperson

**sales incentives**
Various types of prizes awarded through sales contests

**straight salary compensation plan**
Payment of a fixed amount of money at regular intervals

**straight commission compensation plan**
Payment of a percentage of the sales or of the gross profits salespeople generate

**salary plus commission compensation plan**
Payment that combines a guaranteed salary with incentive pay

A **salary plus commission compensation plan** combines a guaranteed salary with incentive pay. Most companies use this type of combination compensation plan because it provides the most flexibility. The incentive portion of the compensation can be tied in with specific sales objectives, yet the salesperson has some degree of security with a certain amount of fixed salary each month. The primary disadvantage of the salary plus commission plan is that it is more complicated and costly to administer.

## EVALUATING SALES TEAM PERFORMANCE

Evaluation is the process of assessing the sales team's performance by comparing sales objectives and goals with actual accomplishments. In addition to assessing the performance of the team as a whole, you should assess the performance of individual members. The process of evaluating an individual salesperson's performance is referred to as a *performance appraisal*. When evaluating a salesperson's performance, two types of criteria should be used: quantitative performance criteria and qualitative performance criteria.

*Quantitative performance criteria* relate to objective results, or bottom-line information, such as sales volume, average sales calls per day, new customers obtained, gross profit by product, customer and order size, ratio of selling costs to sales, and number of sales orders. *Qualitative performance criteria* can include specific sales skills, territory management abilities, and personal traits such as attitude, empathy, team spirit, and motivation. These are harder to measure but certainly no less important than quantitative criteria.[45]

One of the most important reasons for conducting performance appraisals is to show salespeople how they're doing. Salespeople, like all employees, tend to become dissatisfied if they never get any feedback on their performance; and when they are dissatisfied, their productivity tends to level off or decline. Performance appraisals provide a framework for developing new goals and motivational strategies. They also help management make decisions concerning compensation and promotions, training needs, and hiring needs.

## SUMMARY OF LEARNING OBJECTIVES

**1. Explain the importance and power of personal selling.**

The importance of personal selling is underscored by the fact that, for centuries, businesses have relied on salespeople to personally sell goods and services. Without the efforts of these salespeople we would not enjoy the standard of living we have today. The power of personal selling is evident in a salesperson's ability to close a sale. Although other promotional methods can generate interest, few businesses would survive without some degree of personal selling.

**2. Discuss the seven steps in the personal selling process.**

The seven steps in the personal selling process are (a) prospecting, which is the process of searching for and qualifying potential customers; (b) preparing for the sales call, which involves creating a prospect profile, deciding how to approach the prospect, establishing sales-call objectives, and preparing for the presentation; (c) approaching the prospect, or making the initial contact by phone, by letter, or in person; (d) making the presentation, which involves personally communicating a product message in such a way that it will convince a prospect to buy; (e) handling objections, which

refers to identifying and overcoming concerns and objections expressed by the prospect about the product; (f) closing the sale, or getting a commitment from the prospect to buy; and (g) following up, or making certain the product was delivered properly and that the customer is satisfied.

**3. Describe the need-satisfaction approach to selling.**

The need-satisfaction approach to selling focuses on identifying the customer's needs and then creating a presentation that addresses those needs. This approach usually requires extensive probing and research to understand the customer's business, as well as a high level of creativity in developing a solution to solve a problem or meet a need.

**4. Identify current trends in the sales profession.**

The sales profession is in the midst of some exciting and important changes. First is an increased emphasis on ethics in personal selling. Salespeople in every industry are becoming more conscious of the ethical foundations of their business transactions, and many companies have instituted ethics training as part of their personnel development programs. Second, salespeople and their managers are relying more and more on computers, for tasks ranging from prospecting to giving presentations. Third, in an effort to control the increasing cost of sales calls, many firms are adopting telemarketing, which allows the salesperson to reach many more prospects than was ever possible in person. Fourth, women and minorities are playing an increasing role in the sales profession. Fifth, as they try to solve customer problems more effectively, many companies are adopting team selling approaches, in which two or more experts join together to maximize customer satisfaction. Sixth, in companies that sell complex products, sales professionals are adopting systems selling to offer complete, fully integrated solutions to customer problems. Seventh, businesses in the service sector continue to rely heavily on personal selling, and the skills of these people are getting increased attention. Eighth, as global marketing becomes a way of life for many companies, international sales will be an increasingly common career path for sales professionals.

### 5. Delineate the most common classifications of sales personnel.

The three most frequently encountered types of sales personnel are (a) order getters, who are responsible for generating new sales and increasing sales to existing customers; (b) order takers, who primarily process the orders from existing customers; and (c) sales support personnel, who facilitate the overall selling effort by providing a variety of services such as prospecting, educating prospects and customers, building goodwill, and providing service to customers after the sale.

### 6. Explain three primary aspects of the sales management function.

Three primary aspects of the sales management function are (a) planning the personal selling effort, which involves setting sales objectives and formulating strategies for achieving those objectives; (b) organizing the sales personnel according to geographic territory, by product, by customer, or by a combination of factors; and (c) developing a winning sales team, which involves determining the number of salespeople needed, getting the best people, providing effective training, motivating the salespeople, developing a compensation plan, and evaluating the performance of salespeople.

### 7. Analyze common techniques used to motivate salespeople.

Two common techniques used to motivate salespeople are (a) quotas, which are sales goals that salespeople are expected to meet within a certain period of time; and (b) sales incentives, or prizes such as cash, merchandise, and trips. If salespeople are not given an opportunity to participate in the setting of quotas, however, they may not be highly motivated to strive for them. Sales incentives also tend to be more effective if salespeople have a say in designing them.

## KEY TERMS

canned approach (586)
closing (588)
cold calling (583)
ego drive (594)
ego strength (594)
empathy (594)
equalized work load method (599)
incremental method (599)

missionary salespeople (596)
need-satisfaction approach (587)
order getters (595)
order takers (595)
qualified prospect (584)
salary plus commission compensation plan (602)

sales incentives (601)
sales lead (582)
sales management (597)
sales quota (601)
sales support personnel (596)
service motivation (594)

straight commission compensation plan (601)
straight salary compensation plan (601)
systems selling (593)
technical salespeople (596)
telemarketing (592)
trade salespeople (596)

## QUESTIONS FOR DISCUSSION

1. If you were an automobile salesperson, how could you determine whether it is worth investing a significant amount of time in a particular prospect?
2. How would you find leads for your marketing consulting firm?
3. If you were planning to make an initial sales call to a prospect who is the purchasing agent for a business in an unfamiliar industry, how would you prepare for that call?
4. How would the challenge of making a good first impression differ for an insurance salesperson and a farm equipment salesperson? Why?
5. If a prospect objects to the price of a suit of clothes you're trying to sell, how might you respond, and why?
6. What type of closing would work best for the following salespeople?
   a. Residential real estate agent
   b. Commercial real estate agent
   c. Computer systems salesperson
   d. Cashier in a gardening supply store
7. How could an office supplies salesperson add value?
8. Should Apple Computer and Nordstrom use the same approach to determining sales staffing requirements? Why or why not?
9. What sort of continuing training might salespeople in the following industries need?
   a. School textbooks
   b. Medical supplies
   c. Commercial aircraft
   d. Clothing
10. Assume two salespeople are having performance problems. One sells telecommunications systems to foreign governments, and the other sells burgers over the counter. Would you solve the problems in the same way? Why or why not?

## Meeting a Marketing Challenge at Xerox

When David Kearns took the helm at Xerox in 1982, the company was foundering like a rudderless ship. Japanese and domestic rivals were seriously challenging the copier giant on price and quality, yet management seemed unconcerned. As Kearns said, "We did not understand the severity of the competition." With sales stagnant and profits plummeting, the new CEO took drastic measures that shook Xerox to its very foundations. He cut staff deeply and reorganized the company's power structure on the theory that by becoming lean and hungry, delegating decisions downward, and staying on top of the competition, Xerox could duplicate its earlier success. Kearns also shifted the company's marketing focus in the belief that by 1995 most of Xerox's sales would come from computers and related products rather than from photocopiers. It was a bold move. Do his customers agree?

Xerox had an image problem. People still insist that Xerox is in the business of "paper output," not "document processing." To alter that perception, Kearns drastically changed the structure and function of his sales force. He reasoned that the same reps who kept Xerox on top in the $10 billion copier business could also sell the company's advanced-technology products in the more complex office automation market.

In 1985 Kearns instituted a five-year plan to make his salespeople more efficient by converting the company's sales specialists into generalists, selling everything—from low-end copiers to expensive document publishing systems—to every prospect. The two-step plan scrapped the existing sales organization and merged 3,500 copier reps with 1,000 reps from other product lines. The new unified sales force was spearheaded by 300 national account managers and 1,000 major account managers who serviced the company's biggest customers. Account reps covered standard commercial customers, and marketing reps called on the rest of the accounts in the company's 80 marketing areas. Kearns also earmarked $20 million for a three-tier training program designed to make each salesperson thoroughly knowledgeable about all Xerox products.

However, Kearns soon discovered that reorganizing a sales force for greater efficiency and inspiring it to peak performance are two separate things. Therefore, various Xerox divisions tried novel approaches to increase productivity. In 1985 Xerox Medical Systems created "Reach Out!"—an incentive program designed to boost sales of its new electrostatic mammography plates. "Reach Out!" was introduced to branch offices by a videotaped "letter" that chronicled a day in the life of a service rep. The four-month program was well received and resulted in a 30 percent sales increase.

A new system called Automated Sales Process (ASP) generated dramatic results by streamlining the way salespeople handle proposals. Xerox was shocked to learn that reps were spending as little as 20 percent of their time with prospects and 50 percent on paperwork. Using ASP at their workstations, reps could finish even complex proposals in a fraction of the time—without ever touching a piece of paper. With so much customer information right at their fingertips, reps were gradually getting better at the fundamentals of sales, including prospecting, preparing, and making proposals.

High-performance sales management is a key part of the Xerox story as well. Frank Pancetta of the Cleveland sales office is a good example of how influential a sales manager can be. In the first year after taking over the office, he and his team raised their performance from bad and getting worse to number four out of 65 districts in the nation. Pancetta's style is a mixture of pushing hard, supporting and rewarding his people, and keeping only those salespeople who can perform at high levels.

Kearns's vision is now in the hands of Paul Allaire, who took over as CEO in 1990. Allaire wants the world to see Xerox as much more than just a vendor of copiers, and he's counting on the productivity of his sales force to help Xerox take its place among the industry leaders. The strategies Xerox employs in the 1990s include extensive team selling and special centers to which they invite key customers for in-depth presentations.

**Your mission:** You're a new sales representative for Xerox, and your manager has asked you to study your territory and determine how you can increase the sales of document-processing equipment, supplies, and services. Your primary assignment is to devise ways to convert promising prospects into new customers. Remember, you are representing Xerox's complete line, so you must carefully explore how each product can be sold without taking sales away from any of the others. In each of the following situations, choose the alternatives that will be most effective in helping you become a productive salesperson.

1. You decide to target companies that process and distribute a large volume of information each day. As you begin researching, your first prospect is the home office of Nationwide Legal Assistance, a publicly held company with offices across the country. Sales records show that Nationwide has never been a regular Xerox customer, so you know that the company must be using a large number of the competition's photocopiers and supplies. However, you're not sure whether they use any computerized office systems like desktop publishing, marketing workstations, or laser printers. What's the first thing you should do to prepare yourself to approach this prospect?
   a. Find out the name of the person in charge of buying office equipment for Nationwide, send out an introductory letter, and then call for an appointment to give your sales presentation.

b. Call the company's public relations department and ask for copies of any available corporate literature (annual report, brochures, newsletters).

c. Send the office manager a "Needs Assessment Form," which asks detailed questions about the number and types of copiers and computer equipment the firm uses. Also ask what the company's future information-processing needs might be.

2. After analyzing the basic research for Nationwide, you make reasonable assumptions about the company's needs and how Xerox can help meet those needs. You state your case in a clear, brief letter to the vice president in charge of office services. He's impressed by the depth of your knowledge, and during your phone conversation, he fills in some of the blanks. You're confident that you now have a firm grip on the company's potential needs. You prepare a cogent sales presentation that clearly states the features and benefits of various Xerox products and services and how they can meet those needs. From a strategic point of view, what's the best way to make your presentation?

a. Position yourself as a problem solver who's chiefly interested in helping the prospect analyze the company's immediate and future needs. When you've reached agreement on which needs are most pressing, suggest a mix of Xerox products and services with the features that will meet those needs best.

b. Begin by giving the prospect an overview of Xerox and its goals for the future. Then, based on your research, present the package of products and services that you feel the prospect needs. Finally, listen carefully to any remarks he makes, answer his questions, and then try to sell him the complete package you've presented.

c. Take the prospect to lunch at an expensive restaurant. Over coffee, give him brochures that describe and explain in detail each of the products and services you recommend for his company. As you leave, shake hands and tell him you'll call with a proposal in a few days.

3. Nationwide's vice president has been very open and communicative during most of your presentation. From the very beginning he's been pleasant, attentive, and rather impressed with the line of Xerox products you've shown him. However, when you begin talking about Xerox's technical support services, you notice that he frowns for a moment. You sense his mood shifting toward the negative. What should you do to get the presentation back on the right track?

a. Ignore the change in mood and keep selling. Perhaps you've misinterpreted his facial expression. Go back and recap the benefits Nationwide Legal Assistance will enjoy by using Xerox's technical services.

b. Ask whether he's had any experience with Xerox tech-
*(continued on page 606)*

nical services. If he's had a problem or heard of any, tell him that you understand his concern and then convince him that Xerox has improved in this area because of the company's renewed commitment to 100 percent fault-free quality.

c. Answer his silent objection with body language of your own, indicating that you understand he has a problem. Shift gears and acknowledge that although Xerox may have had problems with service in the past, that's all changed thanks to the company's dedication to quality control. To prove your point, offer references that he can call.

4. You've handled the vice president's objections, and you sense that he may be reaching the point of making a decision about whether to buy some of the products and services you've discussed. You are now at the moment of truth—you must complete the sale or risk leaving empty-handed. You can close the sale in several ways. In this case, which of the following three closing techniques would be the most effective?

a. The assumptive close. As you end the presentation, you offer choices about specific items that you assume the prospect is going to order. You might say, "Do you think four laser printers will be enough to meet your needs over the next year?"

b. The trial close. At various times toward the end of the presentation you test the prospect's willingness to place an order by asking him to make specific decisions about your products and services. You might ask about possible delivery dates, whether he's interested in yearly service contracts, financing—anything that brings the prospect closer to saying yes.

c. The direct close. After you've finished the presentation and answered all the prospect's questions, you simply ask for the order.

## SPECIAL PROJECT

Devise a strategy for selling Xerox office systems (computers, copiers, faxes, document scanners, and so on) to emerging companies. You can assume a few general facts about these companies: They aren't well known, at least for the time being; they don't have a lot of spare cash to spend on support equipment; they are usually managed by busy, hard-driving entrepreneurs; and they haven't yet established strong ties to particular suppliers. Outline how you'll find prospects, qualify them, and present your sales proposal.[46]

---

## SHARPEN YOUR MARKETING SKILLS

Jelveh Palizban is one of Chicago's rising stars in the import business. Her company, Pari Corporation, represents foreign manufacturers of housewares, and her customers are department stores around the United States. To introduce her first product, Palizban visited at least 200 department stores, demonstrating the product and explaining how it would work well in their product mixes. That first product, the Donvier ice cream maker, launched her company. Pari's sales continued to rise, reaching over $6 million in just four years.

Many factors contribute to Palizban's success, including her extensive use of computers, careful selection of the products to carry, and a strong orientation to establishing and meeting goals. Perhaps most of all, however, her success stems from her abilities as a salesperson. Her sales skills and perseverance got Pari off the ground, and they continue to propel the company.

**Decision:** As her company grows, Palizban will face a situation familiar to all successful sales entrepreneurs: the gradual shift from sales to managerial roles. She can't be everywhere and do everything in a growing company, so she'll have to rely on employees to carry some, or perhaps all, of the sales load. The question is, How can she transfer her selling skills to her employees?

**Communication:** Write an outline (less than one page) for a training plan that will help her train her sales staff.[47]

---

## KEEPING CURRENT IN MARKETING

Find two articles, each profiling a different sales manager. Look for two people who work in distinctly different industries.

1. List the background, experiences, and skills the two people have in common. Identify characteristics that set the two apart. Are the differences you identify important for success in each subject's respective industry?

2. What challenges or accomplishments has each sales manager overcome or achieved that make him or her a standout? What steps were taken to meet the challenge or achieve the accomplishment?

3. Do you believe the two people you've selected and read about could swap jobs and remain successful? Why or why not?

# Avon Finds Opportunity Knocking on Different Doors

Bells are ringing all over the world as Avon's battalion of 1.4 million salespeople fan out to sell cosmetics, gift items, and jewelry. Doorbells are the sound of success; the company now pulls in nearly $4 billion in sales revenue every year. However, the doorbells Avon representatives ring today may not be the same bells they rang just a few years ago. Fewer women are home to answer the door when Avon comes calling. However, ringing doorbells isn't the only way Avon gets sales these days.

Since 1886, when the first rep started selling its perfumes, Avon had been a channel-driven company with marketing strategies geared to door-to-door sales. For decades the company didn't advertise because it was steadily building sales using its winning formula of quality products at reasonable prices sold with the personal touch. During the 26 selling campaigns conducted each year, reps (98 percent of whom are women) canvass their territories, show toiletry items from the latest sales brochure, and record customer orders. When the products arrive from Avon a few days later, the reps personally deliver the merchandise to their customers, and the sales process begins all over again. This simple but effective approach helped Avon break the billion-dollar sales barrier by 1972 and kept sales growing steadily for nearly a decade afterward.

Then changes in American society threatened to slam the door on Avon's domestic sales growth. Avon reps found fewer women at home because they were joining the work force in greater numbers. Even worse, the company had difficulty increasing sales through its traditional method of recruiting additional reps; the women who might have sold Avon products were finding other job opportunities in the workplace. So Avon's army of U.S. reps began to shrink: In 1982 Avon had 440,000 reps, but by 1985 the number of reps was only 375,000. On top of everything else, the U.S. direct sales market wasn't growing in the early 1980s, so Avon had to fight for its share of the market against direct-selling competitors and retail challengers.

Avon needed more than a touch-up. One of the major changes was to shift the focus from ringing home doorbells to ringing company doorbells. More customers were in offices and factories, so Avon reps started to blanket the workplace with brochures and samples. Working women, pressed for time, responded to the convenience, and today one-quarter of Avon's U.S. cosmetics sales are made in the workplace. In fact, roughly 20 percent of Avon's reps sell only in the workplace. Selling at work gives reps access to many more people at one time than they would find by knocking on doors.

Management, first under former CEO Hicks Waldron and now under CEO James Preston, also revived recruiting and improved productivity. Today, reps who attract new recruits are given a bonus of 5 percent of these newcomers' sales. Because fewer than one-fourth of its reps were ringing up $8,000 or more in a year, the company overhauled its training program to underscore productivity. The strategy worked: Trained reps were found to be 23 percent more productive than untrained reps. Moreover, the firm analyzed its sales territories using census data to classify their sales potential. Then Avon's district sales managers matched top-performing reps with the better territories, hiking sales productivity. When recruiting, the company now administers a test called the "success profile" to identify new reps with greater sales drive and assign them to the high-potential territories.

Door-to-door in the home or office is no longer the only promotional channel. Avon now communicates with customers over the phone, by fax, and with infomercials and other advertising efforts. It is even experimenting with retail locations. The firm now has 1.7 million sales reps, due in large part to international expansion. It has 15,000 reps in China, for instance. By responding to demographic changes in its target markets, and by effectively managing its sales force, Avon is now in a position to keep cash registers ringing into the next century.

1. Because persuading women to become Avon representatives is increasingly difficult, Preston might want to consider some new groups. Should he start a recruitment drive to sign up more female college students, or should he increase efforts to attract men as Avon representatives?

2. Preston is concerned about motivating his representatives and is always interested in new ideas about how to get Avon people to do their best. Which of these two plans might be more powerful in motivating representatives: instituting a commission scale that rises with the length of service or instituting an incentive program that awards vacation trips for superior sales results?

3. Many companies are unwilling to let Avon's reps sell during business hours in their business locations, even if the reps are employed by the company. Because door-to-door sales are increasingly unfeasible, Preston needs a plan to persuade these firms to open their doors to Avon reps. Should he offer to give each participating firm a small percentage of the sales generated on its premises, or should he start a public relations campaign aimed at educating companies about the advantages of allowing employees to buy Avon products during their breaks and lunch hours?

## Snapple Is the Old Timer in New Age Beverages

Consumers around the country who discovered Snapple iced teas and fruit drinks in the early and mid-1990s may have thought they had stumbled on the latest overnight success story. The reality, however, is that Snapple has been building its sales slowly but surely over more than two decades. Making any headway in the nonalcoholic beverage market is tough for a newcomer in the face of industry giants PepsiCo and Coca-Cola. Founders Leonard Marsh, Hyman Golden, and Arnold Greenberg are proof that an entrepreneurial company with a quality product and a good promotional strategy can succeed in even the most ferociously competitive industries.

## Drinks Come Naturally to Snapple

Snapple competes in a product category called, for want of anything better, "New Age beverages." (The products aren't connected with New Age music or New Age spiritual movements; the label is just a collective term for new beverages that don't fall into the mainstream carbonated soda pop category.) Snapple offers dozens of flavors, consisting of flavored ice teas, fruit drinks, and a sports beverage called Snapple Sport. The company made its name in iced tea by perfecting a process for bottling real brewed ice tea in a way that doesn't require artificial preservatives.

In fact, an emphasis on naturally good products is the foundation of the company's positioning strategy. Up until 1992, the company behind Snapple drinks was actually called Unadulterated Food Corporation. Now armed with the slogan, "Made from the best stuff on earth," Snapple wants to

spread the word that these are quality, natural beverages that aren't loaded with chemicals or carbonation.

## A Controversial Start to Promotions

Snapple's promotional efforts in the 1980s and early 1990s included hiring two controversial spokespersons: New York "shock jock" disk jockey Howard Stern and conservative radio/television personality Rush Limbaugh. Using endorsers who are disliked by some people as intensely as they are liked by other people is a risky promotional strategy, since it might alienate as many people as it attracts. On the other hand, linking a product with names and faces that are constantly on public display is a cost-effective way for a small company to break through the massive advertising campaigns of giant competitors. Tennis stars such as Ivan Lendl helped balance the stable of endorsers; while not as well known to the general public, he is certainly less controversial.

## Giants Join the Fray

By the early 1990s, Snapple and other drink bottlers had developed the New Age category to the point where it began to interest the world's two beverage giants. PepsiCo decided to enter the market by teaming up with the Lipton division of Unilever, which has been offering canned iced tea for some years. Coca-Cola teamed up with Nestlé, the huge Swiss food company, to market Nestea, which had also been on the market for a while.

The battle with Coca-Cola/Nestlé and PepsiCo/Lipton in the iced tea segment began in 1992. In 1994 Coca-Cola introduced a line of fruit drinks under the Frutopia brand name, giving Snapple new competition in the fruit drink segment as well. Packaged and promoted with a retro-60s and 70s look, Frutopia offers such flavors as Strawberry Passion Awareness and Pink Lemonade Euphoria.

Snapple's first national advertising campaign hit the airwaves in mid-1993. The ads capitalized on the relationship that customers were developing with the brand. Snapple receives thousands of letters from people who write to say how much they enjoy the product. These letters were incorporated into television commercials featuring Wendy Kaufman, a Snapple employee who actually answers the letters.

In one letter, a man from the South wrote that Snapple is the only good thing that ever came out of New York City (where Snapple is based). Snapple responded by sending former mayor Ed Koch to meet with the customer. With cameras rolling, Koch tried to convince the man that New York

had other great things to offer too. The man was unconvinced, but the two agreed that Snapple certainly was good. The commercials had a folksy, real-life feel that set them apart from the high-budget campaigns usually seen in the beverage industry.

A look at Snapple's advertising budgets gives an indication of how the market—and competition—has been growing. From roughly $2.4 million in 1991, to $10 million in 1992, the company spent an estimated $30 million in 1993. By 1994 its budget was in the neighborhood of $65 million, a 2,500 percent increase in just four years.

In addition to battling it out in the U.S. market, Snapple began looking internationally in early 1994. Coca-Cola, PepsiCo, and their partners have sold internationally for decades, so Snapple's challenge is the opposite of the challenge it faced in the United States. While it was the pioneer in the U.S. market, developing consumer demand before the major companies entered the market, it is virtually unknown in other countries. However, given Snapple's persistence and its ability to form relationships with consumers through both its products and its promotions, don't expect it to remain unknown overseas for much longer.

## Questions

1. Will Snapple's low-key, folksy advertising remain a viable strategy as it and the market continue to grow, or will it have to adopt more mainstream beverage advertising (with big productions, celebrity endorsers, and so on)? Explain your answer.

2. PepsiCo and Coca-Cola can easily outspend Snapple, even as Snapple boosts its budget. Why haven't the two big marketers been able to drive Snapple out of the market completely?

3. Do you think "Made from the best stuff on earth" is on solid ground, ethically speaking? Who's to say what the best stuff on earth is, and does Snapple have exclusive use of the best stuff, whatever it is? Take a position on either side of this question and defend it.

4. Consumers in the United States tend to drink much more iced tea than their counterparts in other countries. Tea is a popular beverage worldwide, but outside of this country, most tea is consumed hot, not iced. What sort of promotional strategy would you assemble to persuade consumers in these countries to give iced tea a try?

# PART VII MARKETING IN TODAY'S GLOBAL ECONOMY

# 20

# Intercultural and International Marketing

After studying this chapter, you will be able to

1. Compare intercultural and international marketing

2. Explain how international marketing differs from domestic marketing

3. List and explain five trade issues affecting international marketing

4. Identify the three primary issues to consider when developing an international marketing plan

5. Identify environmental elements that influence activities such as the selection of markets, level of involvement, and marketing strategies

6. Differentiate among the various levels of involvement in international marketing

7. Describe typical product, promotion, distribution, and pricing strategies used in international marketing

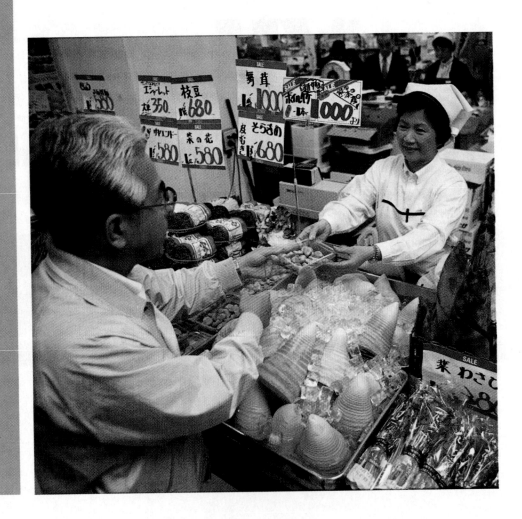

## Sending Invitations across the Globe

Imagine creating an ad for a hotel that draws a mix of both vacationers and business travelers, families and individuals, men and women, and people of diverse ethnic and racial backgrounds. Now imagine creating ads and developing other marketing efforts for nearly 1,700 hotels in more than 50 countries and territories around the world. Such is the challenge faced by Raymond Lewis, vice president of marketing for Holiday Inn Worldwide.

Holiday Inn is an icon of the U.S. highway—its green sign, the words "Holiday Inn" written in script, and a star for emphasis—or so things used to be. Holiday Inn is now Holiday Inn Worldwide, since it was purchased in 1990 by the British conglomerate Bass plc. Business and pleasure travelers can now sleep in any one of 330,000 rooms under the global roof of the Holiday Inn chain. In fact, to keep pace with its new global image, the company is considering changing its logo, its colors, and its signs, as well. It is definitely changing its advertising.

Part of Lewis's job is to monitor and predict changes in the ever-evolving global market. Among the trends he has observed is the increasing similarity between the needs and desires expressed by consumers and businesses around the world, at least in certain product categories such as lodging. On the other hand, he knows that various countries and cultures approach purchases differently and that people in various cultures respond differently to advertising. Therefore, he must figure out how to satisfy both the similar and the diverse needs of his new market.

Travel patterns are another trend that help predict how Holiday Inn should conduct its business. For instance, increasing numbers of North Americans and Europeans are choosing to vacation in Japan, Thailand, Vietnam, and other Asian countries. Some of these travelers are content with traditional Asian lodging, but others have come to expect the more familiar Western-style hotels. Knowing buyer preferences such as this helps advertisers make the right choices when it comes to targeting buyers and communicating advertising messages.

If you were Raymond Lewis, how would you approach the challenge of advertising to this diverse, worldwide audience? Would you use a single strategy for all countries or develop unique strategies for individual countries? Would you use the same visual elements and copy themes in your advertising? How would you handle language and other cultural issues?[1]

**intercultural marketing**
A strategy of recognizing and marketing to specific cultural segments; also called multicultural marketing

**international marketing**
Marketing across national boundaries

# CHAPTER OVERVIEW

As one of the most aggressive international marketers, Holiday Inn knows that it must consider both intercultural and international issues when it markets in other countries. This chapter highlights the unique aspects of marketing across cultures and across national boundaries, and it points out the similarities between intercultural and international marketing. The chapter starts by defining culture and discussing how it affects marketing strategy and tactics in both domestic and international marketing. After that you'll explore the reasons companies choose to market outside their home countries and the international trade issues affecting those marketing efforts. Then you'll take a look at the social elements in international marketing. Following that is an explanation of the various levels at which you can participate in international marketing, ranging from exporting to direct investments in other countries. The chapter concludes with a discussion of how marketing strategies can be adapted for U.S. companies wishing to enter the international marketplace.

# DEFINING INTERCULTURAL MARKETING

Chapter 4 defines *culture* as encompassing a system of beliefs, values, and objects that are shared by a society and passed on to succeeding generations. A look around at your classmates or your community should be enough to convince you that we live in a society composed of many cultures. As competition heats up and countries such as the United States become increasingly diverse, more and more marketers are pursuing a strategy of **intercultural marketing** (also known as *multicultural marketing*), which is a strategy of recognizing and marketing to specific cultural segments. Intercultural marketing can take place inside a single country or between two countries. In contrast, **international marketing** refers generally to any marketing efforts between two or more countries.

Consultant Roger Sennott, who specializes in reaching Hispanic-American markets, refers to intercultural marketing as "international marketing within your own borders."[2] In other words, many of the challenges and opportunities present in international marketing are also present in intercultural marketing. In fact, a close relationship exists between intercultural marketing and international marketing. One of the biggest challenges in international marketing stems from *cultural* differences between countries. Consequently, the better you are at intercultural marketing, the better you'll be at international marketing.

## The Nature of Intercultural Marketing

The United States has always been home to a wide mix of cultures, but marketers are currently stepping up their intercultural efforts for two important reasons. First, the country is becoming even more culturally and ethnically diverse (see Exhibit 20.1). By the year 2000, for instance, people traditionally considered minorities will actually represent more than half the population in California.[3] Second, companies such as Procter & Gamble, Bank of America, Toys 'R' Us, and Coca-Cola have learned that they can increase their marketing effectiveness by targeting particular ethnic and cultural groups.[4] These companies carefully consider cultural issues such as race and nationality, language, and cultural values.

### RACE AND NATIONALITY

Race and national origin can be important factors in consumer marketing. In some cases, the questions and answers are obvious. Because skin color is one of the more visible distinctions of race, for instance, it's not surprising that cosmetics companies are particularly sensitive to this issue. For example, Estée Lauder's Prescriptives

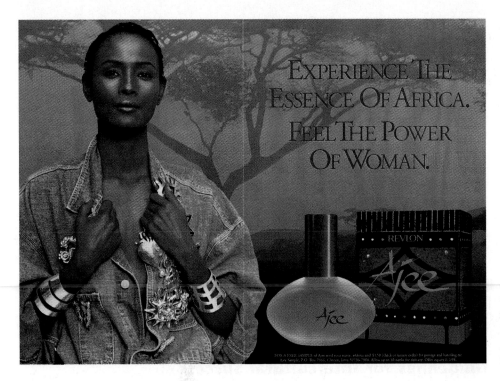

**Exhibit 20.1**
**THE DIVERSE U.S.
POPULATION**
Revlon targets African-
American women in this ad
for Ajee perfume.

Exact Color line reaches out to all major ethnic groups in the United States by including women from each group in its ads and providing shades and hues appropriate for each skin color.[5]

In other cases, the issue of race and nationality is much less clear-cut. Do people from different ethnic and cultural backgrounds buy the same products and make purchases in the same way? Will an ad that works well with African-Americans work just as well with Hispanic-Americans or European-Americans? Questions such as these have prompted increased research into cultural issues and spurred the growth of market service firms that specialize in particular ethnic segments. For instance, the Joseph Jacobs Organization in New York specializes in Jewish markets; Sosa, Bromley, Aguilar, & Asociados in San Antonio specializes in Hispanic-American markets; and Burrell Advertising in Chicago specializes in African-American markets. These agencies and others like them handle intercultural advertising for some of the world's largest advertisers, including Coca-Cola, Volkswagen, and MCI.[6]

Ethnic issues are not just a marketing challenge; they can also be a marketing opportunity. One of the hottest trends in young Japanese society these days is African-American culture. "Black people are so cool," as one Tokyo teenager puts it. Whether it's music, clothes, food, or media, Japanese teens lay out enormous sums of money to buy into their perception of African-American culture.[7]

## LANGUAGE

Say that you're the advertising manager for American Airlines, and you want to reach Hispanic-Americans with your latest ad campaign. Should you write the ad in Spanish or English? It's a tough question with no simple answer. Some Hispanic-Americans rely on Spanish, not English; some are comfortable with both languages; and others don't speak Spanish at all. If you do decide to use Spanish, you then have to decide which version of Spanish. The conventional wisdom maintains that the best way to reach these consumers is in Spanish. Univision, the largest Spanish-language television network in the United States, says that three-quarters of all Hispanic-Americans consider Spanish their dominant language. The English-language magazine *Hispanic,* however, says that advertisers are missing out by not addressing Hispanic-Americans in English. The research firm A. C. Nielsen studied television viewing among Hispanic households in Los Angeles and found that half the television sets were tuned to English-language stations.[8] Similar language issues exist around the United States within groups of people who speak Japanese, Arabic, and a host of other languages.

CULTURAL VALUES

Recognizing the values that a culture considers important is another key aspect of intercultural marketing. You're not likely to see a U.S. ad making jokes about death, disease, or drunkenness, but in Japan subjects considered taboo in the United States are given humorous treatment in many ads. A television commercial for Gon mothballs featured an elderly grandfather who pretends he is dead so that he won't have to go shopping.[9] Nudity in advertising is not uncommon in some European and Latin-American countries (and to a limited degree in the United States), but it is virtually unheard of in much of Asia. India is one of many Asian countries with strict rules about decency in advertising, for example.[10] Islamic cultures also frown on advertising that portrays children as decision makers in the household or that relies on hero worship to make a selling point.[11] These cultural factors that originate in other countries can play a role in your U.S. marketing efforts when immigrants to this country apply the values of their previous cultures to their new roles as U.S. consumers.

## Guidelines for Intercultural Success

You can increase your chances of success by following some commonsense guidelines. First, don't superimpose your own cultural values onto other cultures. Since our values are often so deeply ingrained that we never stop to think about them, we must consciously step outside of our own cultural context when dealing with other cultures.

Second, be sensitive to cultural differences but don't stereotype people. Recognizing that elderly people command a greater degree of respect in some cultures

World Select™ saves in the countries where you call the most.

**Exhibit 20.2**
**WHICH LANGUAGE TO USE?**
Sprint chose to advertise its long-distance services in Spanish in this ad, even though the ad ran in *Hispanic Business,* an English-language magazine.

than in others is being sensitive to cultural differences. Assuming that Asian-Americans are all good at math or that African-Americans are all good at athletics is stereotyping.

Third, when preparing promotional materials, consider the variations that exist in most major languages. English, French, German, Spanish, and Chinese are a few good examples. Each has major regional and cultural dialects, and people who speak one dialect may not necessarily understand or be comfortable using another dialect. In the Hispanic-American market, for example, you can't assume that the Spanish spoken by a recent Puerto Rican immigrant to New York is the same Spanish as that spoken by a third-generation Californian whose family came from Chile. For that matter, you can't assume that people of Hispanic ethnicity even speak Spanish; many U.S.-born Hispanic-Americans speak only English (see Exhibit 20.2).[12]

# DEFINING INTERNATIONAL MARKETING

For many people in this country, the dramatic economic, social, and political changes across the world in recent years have largely taken the form of television reports about other people in other countries. However, for the international marketer such changes are all in a day's work—and an exciting day's work it is. The opening of markets in Eastern Europe, the reunification of Germany, changing trade relations with Canada and Mexico, continued competition with Japan, and the rise of other manufacturing powers in the Far East affect the marketing plans and activities of thousands of U.S. companies.

How does international marketing differ from domestic marketing? In general, international marketing refers to any marketing activities that take place across national boundaries. The concepts and strategies you've learned throughout this book still apply; the biggest difference is that the marketing environment changes from country to country. Marketers have to deal with various cultures, political systems, economic forces, and competitive pressures. In a sense, international marketing starts as a case of market segmentation, where each country is a distinct market segment. Because these segments can differ greatly from one another and from the United States, international marketing is typically more complicated, more expensive, and more challenging—but it can also be interesting and exciting.

## Why Companies Market Internationally

For some companies, international marketing is a matter of opportunity and growth (see Exhibit 20.3). Coca-Cola, for instance, needs to increase global sales because the U.S. market is already drinking as much Coke as could reasonably be expected. McDonald's is another example, going to Moscow to develop a potentially huge market. KFC (Kentucky Fried Chicken) sees "almost unlimited opportunity for growth in Asia."[13] Harley-Davidson enjoys near-cult status in some countries, since consumers will pay dearly for a piece of the Harley mystique.[14]

For other companies, international marketing is a more urgent question of financial survival. Wharton School economist Howard Perlmutter has identified 136 industries in which a company may need to be an international player if it plans to stay in business. These industries include autos, consumer electronics, pharmaceuticals, banking, and publishing. The biggest reason? Markets in the United States are too small for companies in these industries to efficiently produce goods and services. For example, the average cost of developing a new drug has gone from around $16 million in the 1970s to $250 million today, and the process is taking twice as long. There aren't enough customers in a single country to support such enormous product development costs.[15]

Another important reason is increasing competition for sales in the U.S. market. Soft Sheen Products, for example, was slowly being squeezed out of the $1 billion African-American hair-care market by corporate giants such as Revlon and Alberto

*There is only one thing in the world equal to a rigid Samsonite. A flexible Samsonite.*

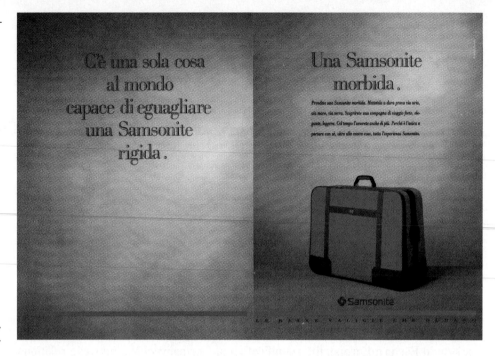

**Exhibit 20.3**
**BRANDS KNOWN THE WORLD OVER**
Samsonite is one of many U.S. brands with global recognition.

Culver. In order to compete, Soft Sheen acquired a London-based manufacturer of similar products so that it could gain access not only to European markets but to African markets as well.[16] For Orion Pictures, it was box office failures that motivated international marketing efforts. The company now depends on profits from foreign markets to help with production costs as well as to compensate for losses on domestic film revenues.[17]

Goods aren't the only products that move across international borders. Hotels, banks, consulting firms, telecommunications, restaurants, and entertainment are some of the important service industries that are part of the international business arena. The import and export of production processes and technical knowledge, another form of services marketing, is also an increasingly common aspect of international marketing.[18]

If one characteristic unites the top corporations today, it's that they view the world—not their home countries—as their marketplace. They know that as big as the United States is (and as big as the top U.S. corporations are), a lot of business goes on outside this country. Furthermore, marketers large and small from other countries pursue the same global markets. What's the largest corporation in the world? General Motors? IBM? Exxon? No, it's Itochu, a Japanese firm with more than $150 billion in annual revenues.[19]

## International Trade Issues

When a company markets across national borders, it is engaging in international *trade* as well as international *marketing*. Therefore, it is important for an international marketer to understand the changing international trade issues.

### FOREIGN EXCHANGE

Foreign exchange refers to the process of balancing accounts in international trade transactions. It is also a generic term referring to a foreign currency and negotiable instruments payable in a foreign currency.[20] The U.S. dollar, for example, is referred to as foreign exchange by international marketers in other countries.

A **foreign exchange rate** is the rate at which one currency can be exchanged for another currency. For instance, the exchange rate for British pounds one day in

**foreign exchange rate**
The rate at which the currency of one country can be exchanged for the currency of another country

late 1993 was 0.6725, which means that one British pound cost about 1.5 U.S. dollars.[21] International marketers are keenly aware of foreign exchange rates because they determine whether products are viewed as affordable by local consumers. They affect the affordability of the physical assets, supplies, labor, and services that a global company purchases in foreign countries. They also affect your ability to make a profit.

Foreign exchange rates are determined in large part by supply and demand in the **foreign exchange market,** which encompasses all the financial institutions and people throughout the world who buy and sell currency. With an estimated turnover of $200 billion a day, the foreign exchange market is the world's largest financial market.[22]

As you can imagine, dynamic foreign exchange rates can create significant financial risks for international marketers. For instance, assume you've agreed to sell 1,000 T-shirts a month to a Japanese wholesaler. You negotiate a price of 650 yen at a time when the yen exchange rate is 130; at this rate, you receive 5 dollars per shirt. However, several months into the contract, the yen rate climbs to 170. The customer is still paying you 650 yen per shirt, but that amount is now worth less than 4 dollars, which might wipe out all your profits.

## BALANCE OF PAYMENTS

In order to assist governments in formulating trade and economic policies, nations that trade internationally must keep track of the value of investments made, products imported and exported, cash payments and receipts, monetary gifts, and vacation and foreign travel. The system that accounts for these international financial transactions is referred to as a nation's **balance of payments.**[23]

One of the most significant aspects of the balance of payments is a nation's import and export activity. To **import** means to purchase goods and raw materials from one country and bring them into another country. To **export** means to sell goods and raw materials to another country. The way imports and exports stack up at the end of each year is referred to as a nation's **balance of trade.** When total imports exceed total exports, a nation has a **trade deficit.** See Exhibit 20.4 for the top 20 regions with which the United States holds trade surpluses and deficits. You can see that U.S. deficit positions are much larger than U.S. surplus positions.

Many people in the United States view our country's trade deficit as a sign of economic weakness. However, others are convinced that a trade deficit is merely a reflection of prices and exchange rates, not a sign of weakness. They maintain that some countries with a trade surplus, such as Brazil, are still considered economically weak, whereas rich countries such as the United States can have a trade deficit and still remain economically strong.[24]

**foreign exchange market**
All the institutions and people throughout the world who buy and sell currency

**balance of payments**
A system that accounts for a nation's international financial transactions

**import**
To purchase goods and raw materials from one country and bring them into another country

**export**
To sell goods and raw materials to another country

**balance of trade**
A nation's total imports in relation to its total exports over a one-year period of time

**trade deficit**
The amount by which a country's imports exceed its exports

## Exhibit 20.4   TRADE DEFICITS AND SURPLUSES

| U.S. Surplus Positions | | U.S. Deficit Positions | |
|---|---|---|---|
| 1. European Union | +9.0 | 1. Japan | −49.6 |
| 2. OECD in Europe | +6.4 | 2. China | −18.3 |
| 3. Western Europe | +6.4 | 3. Taiwan | −9.3 |
| 4. Latin American Republics | +5.9 | 4. Canada | −8.0 |
| 5. LAFTA | +4.6 | 5. Germany | −7.6 |
| 6. Eastern Europe | +2.5 | 6. Nigeria | −4.1 |
| 7. Former Soviet Republics | +2.1 | 7. Malaysia | −3.9 |
| 8. South/Central America | +1.7 | 8. Italy | −3.6 |
| 9. NATO | +1.2 | 9. Thailand | −3.5 |
| 10. Asia-Near East | +1.1 | 10. Saudi Arabia | −3.2 |

Here are the United States' top trade surplus and trade deficit relationships valued in billions of dollars.

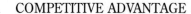

**comparative advantage**
The advantage a nation has when it specializes in exporting products it can produce more cheaply than other nations

**competitive advantage**
In the context of international business, the ability of a nation's industries to innovate and upgrade to the next level of technology and productivity

## COMPETITIVE ADVANTAGE

Perhaps you've noticed how certain industries or products tend to be associated with a specific country, such as Japanese cars, Swiss chocolates, French perfumes, Italian shoes, and Dutch flowers. Traditional explanations for nations achieving international success in particular industries point to the theory of **comparative advantage,** the benefit to nations of specializing in the export of products they can produce more cheaply than others because of their existing natural and human resources.

However, many nations are competing successfully on an international level in industries not dependent on natural resources or huge labor pools. To explain this, business experts now point to the theory of international **competitive advantage,** the ability of a nation's industries to innovate and upgrade to the next level of technology and productivity. A four-year study of 10 important trading nations identified four basic elements of competitive advantage:

- Company strategy, structure, and rivalry—the conditions governing how a nation's businesses are created, organized, and managed, as well as the nature of domestic competition
- Demand conditions—the size of the market, the sophistication of customers, and the media exposure of products
- Related industries—such as clusters of suppliers supporting a certain industry
- Factor conditions—natural resources, education and skill levels, and wage rates[25]

One of the industries studied was the Dutch flower industry. Researchers found that the Dutch are international leaders in cut flowers not because they have an ideal climate; their competitive advantage is achieved through the establishment of innovative research institutions specializing in flower cultivation, packaging, and shipping. The Italian shoe industry, on the other hand, achieves international success because of sophisticated consumer demand and rivalry between family-owned companies. They constantly introduce new designs and improve efficiency in order to remain competitive.[26] In the United States, the concept of international competitiveness has become such an important issue that Congress proclaimed it the country's dominant economic issue for the remainder of this century.[27]

## FREE TRADE VERSUS PROTECTIONISM

The opportunity for companies to compete and trade in open markets benefits not only the companies but also domestic economies by generating more jobs, tax revenues, and investments. However, during the 1930s, the economic benefits of international trade all but disappeared because many countries, including the United States, established protectionist trade policies. The idea was to protect domestic industries from foreign competitors during the Great Depression, but the resulting trade restrictions on imports hurt domestic exporters as well.

To encourage free trade once again and spur economic growth after World War II, 90 nations signed the General Agreement on Tariffs and Trade (GATT). GATT, whose membership has since increased to 117 nations, plays a major role in reducing barriers to trade. The latest round of GATT negotiations concluded in late 1993 and achieved important breakthroughs in three major areas. First, in such areas as agricultural products, governments must begin lowering domestic price supports, which can keep prices artificially high in favor of domestic suppliers. Second, countries must begin to allow access to their own markets in certain industries. Japan, for instance, has long banned rice imports, but under GATT now must allow foreign suppliers access to 8 percent of the Japanese market. An important part of this element is that nontariff barriers must be gradually converted to tariffs. Third, GATT requires reductions in export subsidies. These are essentially government payments to domestic suppliers that allow the suppliers to lower their export prices and thus compete internationally at the expense of suppliers from other countries.[28]

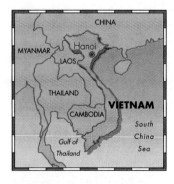

The Vietnamese consumer and industrial markets got a major boost in 1994 when the U.S. government decided to establish trade relations with its one-time enemy.

One of the most important issues in international trade has been the development of economic cooperation within a **multinational market,** which is created when individual countries band together to reduce trade barriers for the economic benefit of participating countries.[29] The most significant multinational markets include the European Union (formerly known as the European Community), and various free-trade areas recently established and currently being negotiated.

THE EUROPEAN UNION    The foremost example of economic cooperation is the **European Union,** referred to as the EU, which aims to improve economic conditions for member nations in two ways: (1) by eliminating internal barriers that impede the flow of goods, services, labor, and capital and (2) by imposing uniform tariffs on imports from nonmembers. The EU was created by the Treaty of Rome in 1957, and its 12 member nations are Belgium, France, Germany, Italy, Luxembourg, the Netherlands, Denmark, Ireland, the United Kingdom, Greece, Portugal, and Spain. Politically, the EU has emerged as the most powerful voice of Europe in international discussions, and it currently negotiates as a single entity in matters of world trade and politics.[30]

The unification of the EU took on new importance with a series of agreements designed to complete the process started by the Treaty of Rome. Known as Europe 1992, this new arrangement is a significant change in the international marketing arena. Although the original plan called for all the new changes to be in place by the end of 1992 (hence the name), the final details will continue falling into place throughout the 1990s.

The economic unification resulting from Europe 1992 will further reduce trade barriers and unite the EU's 325 million consumers, who already form the world's richest market.[31] This multinational market will bring two important changes to international marketing. First, exporters from outside Europe should have an easier time gaining access to various European markets. Second—perhaps more important for some U.S. companies—large, pan-European conglomerates will grow stronger and become even more formidable competitors in the U.S. market. European companies will now find it easier to grow and expand across Europe, giving them economies of scale comparable to the huge corporations in the United States, Japan, and Korea.

The financial impact that Europe 1992 will eventually have on outside trading partners is difficult to predict. However, most experts expect internal competition to increase substantially, resulting in a decrease in consumer prices. If this happens, companies from the United States may find it much more difficult to make a profit in Europe. High-tech companies may be especially vulnerable because of competition from government-subsidized EU firms that are planning to target the same niche markets.[32]

To help more companies in the United States respond to the Europe 1992 challenge, the Commerce Department is providing country- and industry-specific information on the 300 EU regulations affecting everything from agriculture to industrial goods and services.[33] The companies most likely to benefit from Europe 1992 will be those that take time to learn about and prepare for the competition.

FREE-TRADE AREAS    Unlike the EU common market arrangement, a free-trade area does not provide for the flow of labor and capital among member countries or establish common external trade barriers. A **free-trade area** does, however, provide a mass market that encourages the free flow of goods and services between its members. Latin America, for example, has the Latin American Integration Association (LAIA). Europe has the 17-country European Free Trade Association (EFTA), which includes the EU and several other European countries, making it a larger market than the United States and Canada combined.

In 1985 the United States signed a free-trade agreement with Israel, a relatively small but strategically important trading partner. Two years later, Canada and the

**multinational market**
A group of individual countries that band together to reduce trade barriers among participating countries

**European Union**
A multinational European common market created in 1957 to encourage the free flow of goods, services, labor, and capital among member countries and to impose uniform tariffs on imports

**free-trade area**
A multinational market that encourages the free flow of goods and services between member countries but does not provide for the free flow of labor and capital or impose uniform tariffs on imports

United States began negotiating a free-trade agreement that went into effect January 1, 1989, with a 10-year phase-in period. After the signing, industry representatives in Canada observed an almost immediate increase in the level of investment in the country and asked the government to accelerate the implementation of tariff reductions. However, not everyone in Canada is pleased with the arrangement; some people feel that Canada might lose some of its national identity or that large firms will benefit more than small ones.[34] The North American Free Trade Agreement (NAFTA), ratified in late 1993, created a free-trade area spanning Canada, the United States, and Mexico. The eventual effects of NAFTA remain to be seen, but it is likely to position Mexico as an even more attractive market for U.S. goods and services at the possible expense of some lower-paying jobs lost in this country. NAFTA backers hope that the increase in exports will create higher-paying jobs to offset the loss of lower-paying jobs.

## International Marketing Trends

The growing interdependence of nations and similarity of global consumer demand have greatly influenced the ways companies market their goods and services. For example, inward-looking U.S. corporations of the 1960s and 1970s are evolving into global corporations with long-term vision, small exporters are setting up overseas operations, and global corporations are forming joint ventures with their competitors.

### MULTINATIONALS TURN GLOBAL

**multinational corporation**
A corporation that has operations in more than one country, exploits the countries' differences to enhance competitive advantage, and operates primarily from a domestic perspective

A **multinational corporation** has operations in more than one country, exploits the various characteristics of each country, and manages each operation as an independent unit from a single world headquarters. U.S. multinationals of the 1960s and 1970s (such as Ford, RCA, and GE) once dominated the global marketplace. However, even though they had operations in several countries, their marketing decisions tended to be made from a domestic perspective only.

Eventually, foreign competitors with a long-term global perspective started gaining ground. For example, farsighted Asian television manufacturers forced all but one U.S. competitor out of business by selling more reliable compact sets with superior technology. Of the 27 U.S. companies that once competed, Zenith is now the only survivor. To improve the odds of merely staying in the game, Zenith sold off its prosperous computer division and is betting its resources on new TV technologies.[35] In fact, most multinationals are now thinking longer term and are developing a more globalized mentality for survival.

**global corporation**
A corporation that has operations in more than one country, exploits the countries' similarities to enhance competitive advantage, and operates from a one-world, one-market perspective

Today's **global corporation** pursues business objectives by relating world resources to world market opportunities (see Exhibit 20.5). Its managers and directors come from all over the world, and regional headquarters are located wherever the critical action is. A global corporation raises capital, conducts research, buys supplies, and manufactures wherever it can do the job best. To enhance competitive advantage, it exploits the similarities among nations, rather than the differences.[36] Being a global player, however, does not necessarily mean entering foreign markets for the sole purpose of exploiting their immediate profit potential. For example, McDonald's exhibited this new global attitude when it decided to invest in a long-term relationship with Moscow's everyday citizens. The wisdom of that decision was confirmed by one of the 30,000 customers who visited McDonald's on its opening day in Moscow. When he learned his hard-earned money would buy a coveted Big Mac, he proclaimed, "This is my restaurant. This is for me."[37]

### SMALL EXPORTERS ESTABLISH OVERSEAS OPERATIONS

Not to be left out of the global picture, more small exporters are setting up operations overseas, not just shipping their goods abroad. Some of these companies have been around for years; others are start-ups looking to go international soon after

**Exhibit 20.5
COMPANIES WITH
GLOBAL REACH**
AT&T promotes its global
capabilities in this ad that
explains the translation
services that it offers in 140
languages.

they open for business. Many contend that it is essential to staying competitive in
the domestic market because it allows them to gain firsthand knowledge of new
products being introduced by their foreign competitors. In a recent survey, 30 percent of U.S. manufacturers said that three of their top five competitors for the *U.S.
market* are foreign firms.[38]

For example, the Will-Burt Company is a small Ohio-based manufacturer of truck
parts and mobile radio transmission towers. Will-Burt almost lost its parts business
because its main client (Caterpillar) switched to lower-priced Belgian and Brazilian
suppliers. However, Will-Burt eventually won back Caterpillar with more competitive prices by purchasing castings and welded parts from companies in China and
Indonesia. To avoid the same problem with its radio transmission towers, Will-Burt
is planning to shift from exporting solely from Ohio to manufacturing in Ireland
(with a partner to provide the factory and sales force). Will-Burt's chief executive
believes this move will protect the company from foreign competitors that might try
to export towers to the United States during a strong-dollar period.[39]

Many companies are being lured into the global marketplace by low-cost labor
and subsidies from countries eager for investment. For example, the Scottish Development Agency provides as much as 30 percent of the total capital cost of equipment and buildings in Scotland. Singapore gives start-ups low-interest loans and capital for equipment, and it waives taxes for as long as 10 years.[40]

## COMPETITORS FORM JOINT VENTURES

Competitors would seem to make strange bedfellows. Yet in their quest for new markets and technology, competitors around the world are teaming up in record numbers. These arrangements between two or more businesses to collaborate on a specific task or product are referred to as **joint ventures.** In addition to providing
financing for projects that one company might not be able to undertake alone, joint
ventures also offer the opportunity to collaborate on technical and scientific research, new-product development, production, and sales and distribution capabili-

**joint venture**
Collaboration by two or more
companies on a task or product, sharing assets, risks, and
profits

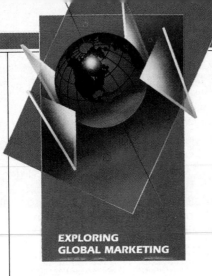
ties. In addition, they can provide credibility for new technologies, concepts, and even new companies.[41]

Fierce competition has spurred hundreds of international alliances, especially among computer companies and among auto manufacturers. In the last few years, major car and truck manufacturers have combined in several hundred joint venture projects. For example, Ford is building a Nissan-designed minivan in Ohio, to be sold by both Nissan and Ford. Mazda designed and built Ford's sporty new Probe. The classic Japanese Toyota Corolla now rolls out of a U.S. plant half-owned by General Motors, and the Corvette, once the epitome of U.S.-made sports cars, now comes with a high-performance transmission built by a German company.[42]

In the competitive aircraft-manufacturing industry, a group of European companies joined forces to establish Airbus Industrie to compete more effectively with industry leader Boeing. With an estimated $10 billion in funding, Airbus was able to move into second place.[43] However, Boeing recently countered Airbus by teaming up with three Japanese companies to manufacture a new jet, the 777, which fills the size gap between Boeing's 767 and 747. The Japanese partners will produce jet parts and provide up to 20 percent of the necessary capital.[44]

## ASSESSING SOCIAL ELEMENTS IN INTERNATIONAL MARKETING

Some of the biggest challenges in international marketing result from the social and cultural differences among peoples of the world. Although many companies open offices in foreign markets so that they can stay closely attuned to the environment, it is possible to learn a great deal about a country's social makeup without even leaving the United States. However, marketers should always keep in mind that any data, whether primary or secondary, must be evaluated carefully for inaccuracies and inconsistencies. The Office of International Trade Administration at the U.S. Department of Commerce has a wealth of information, and so do state trade offices as well as public libraries that have books on foreign countries and international publications such as the *Financial Times of London, The Economist,* and the *Far* velop that can prove critical to the success of the business venture. In some parts of the Third World, businesspeople follow complex visiting patterns established through years of tradition. Everyone knows who they are supposed to visit, when, and why. This doesn't mean that you must constantly host parties, but it may mean adjusting to the idea of drop-in visits. In Third World cultures, drop-in visits are considered communal obligations—although in Western cultures they are often viewed as a violation of personal time or private space.

The third step, after you've had an opportunity to visit and play host, is to do personal or commercial favors without asking for anything in return. This obligates the recipient to repay the favor, which then re-obligates you, which then re-obligates the recipient, and so on. This giving and returning of favors can last a lifetime, and it plays a significant role in Third World culture. It is important that you, as an international marketer, be the first to give, and that you keep giving. By giving, you are showing respect for local custom; as a result, you will gain important allies.

Although the Third World does not yet have markets for many of the products sold in other parts of the world, more companies are beginning to take a serious look at its potential. H. J. Heinz, for example, decided to invest in a joint venture in Zimbabwe after realizing that food consumption in the West was growing by a measly and sluggish 1 percent and that 85 percent of the world's population had never even heard of Heinz. Gillette is patiently promoting the concept of shaving to villagers in Africa and Asia by giving demonstrations in a mobile van equipped with wash basins, towels, and razors. According to Gillette International's assistant general manager, "It's a long process, developing a market."

## APPLY YOUR KNOWLEDGE

**1.** Why would Gillette try to persuade a group of people to start shaving?

**2.** What are the risks involved in educating a market in the same manner as Gillette?

*East Economic Review.* Various international organizations and universities sponsor cross-cultural workshops that are good sources of information on foreign markets.

## Social Organization and Roles

Each country has a unique social organization and a unique way of defining roles within that organization. Organizations and institutions such as the family, racial or ethnic groups, labor unions, special-interest groups, and groups defined by age or gender must be studied in order to answer these basic questions: (1) Who are the relevant peer groups? (2) What constitutes a household? (3) What is the buyer decision-making unit?

For example, teenagers in a given country tend to have more in common with their peers in other countries than they have with their own parents, but some distinct country-by-country attributes exist. McCann-Erickson, a major advertising agency, spent two years surveying 8,000 teenagers in 10 European countries and found that teenagers in Finland, for example, are the most passive and apathetic, French teenagers are the most materialistic, and German teenagers are more keen on environmentalism.[45]

As an international marketer you must be sensitive to the culture of your prospective customers and business counterparts in order to develop effective marketing strategies. For instance, U.S. media companies such as Time Warner realize that television programmers in European countries would like to fill the airwaves with U.S. TV shows. However, these companies also realize that many Europeans resent being bombarded by U.S. culture. In fact, officials in the European Union have agreed among themselves that the majority of European TV programming should be of European origin.[46] This hasn't stopped such powerful U.S. fare as MTV from becoming a top draw on European TV, however.

## Buyer Behavior

Understanding your target customers' lifestyles and habits is vital to international marketing success. You can't assume that consumers everywhere behave like consumers in the United States. Consider the business of food, for example. The average U.S. consumer buys three times as much frozen food as the average Swiss consumer. Italian kitchens have resisted the conversion to microwave convenience (only 3 percent of Italian homes own a microwave oven, compared to 80 percent in the United States). Also, eating habits vary considerably from country to country. Ireland consumes nearly 40 times as much breakfast cereal as Spain (per capita).[47]

Organizational customers behave differently as well. For instance, Japanese companies tend to have highly automated factories, but their offices aren't as highly automated as offices in other countries. Also, business along the Asian side of the Pacific Rim relies heavily on personal contacts. Hong Kong banker David K. P. Li is a good example of a successful Asian business executive. As chairman of the Bank of East Asia, he has contacts throughout the businesses and governments of Hong Kong, China, and Japan, as well as Britain, the United States, Germany, France, Canada, Scotland, and Switzerland. Li says that personal relationships "usually make the difference between success and failure."[48]

## Business Customs

When it comes to adapting to business customs in foreign countries, international marketers still have a lot to learn. Understanding business customs can mean the difference between success and failure. Many businesspeople from the United States have lost potential customers overseas because of cultural blunders involving improper language, dress, seating arrangements, gestures, facial expressions, gifts, timing, suggestions, and etiquette. However, U.S. marketers don't have a monopoly on misunderstanding the ways of foreigners. At a Honda manufacturing plant in the United States, Japanese managers expected U.S. workers to wear company uniforms and sing the company song, but they encountered stiff resistance, not realizing that such practices go against the grain of workers in this country.[49] On the positive side, companies that do take the time to understand business cultures have a significant advantage over their less informed competitors.

One of the most difficult aspects of business to adjust to in a foreign culture is negotiation. The primary reason for the difficulty centers on communication styles. In some cultures, people do not express many of their thoughts verbally but imply or suggest what is on their minds through vague comments or actions. A culture with a preference for this type of implied communication is referred to as a *high-context culture*. In contrast, people in a *low-context culture* tend to be clear and to the point, with nothing implied or hinted in their communication. Exhibit 20.6 shows how several countries rank in terms of low- and high-context cultures. For example, in Germany or the United States, which are low-context cultures, people tend to minimize the small talk and get down to business very quickly. In Japan or one

**Exhibit 20.6
CONTEXTUAL
BACKGROUND OF
VARIOUS COUNTRIES**
Communication is heavily dependent on cultural context. Businesspeople from low-context cultures like to get down to business very quickly, whereas people from high-context cultures like to develop a relationship first.

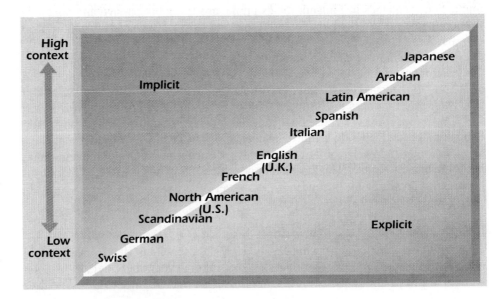

of the Arab countries, which are high-context cultures, people take time to get to know each other and develop a relationship before conducting business.[50]

Even the language in a written contract in many cultures is considered more implicit than explicit. For example, when executives of American Motors signed a contract with the Chinese to establish a joint venture to produce jeeps in Beijing, the American Motors representatives assumed the signing ceremony was the end of negotiations. However, the Chinese saw the signed contract merely as the beginning of a negotiating session that would last as long as the joint venture.[51] Germans, on the other hand, view contracts as explicit documents that should not leave any room for misinterpretation later on. They'll even nail down contract details that U.S. businesspeople might leave to standard trade practice.[52]

Every foreign market has its own unique range of environmental characteristics. Even within a single country, the economic, political, regulatory, and social elements may differ significantly from one region to another. A thorough investigation and ongoing awareness of all environmental elements is essential in determining a company's level of international involvement and in developing effective marketing strategies.

## DETERMINING THE LEVEL OF INTERNATIONAL INVOLVEMENT

Consider several options when deciding how to enter a foreign market. When analyzing the options, keep in mind the nature of the product being sold, the environment of the market being considered, and the financial, physical, and managerial resources your company is willing to commit to the endeavor. Exporting represents the lowest level of commitment; direct investment represents the highest level. Between the extremes are foreign licensing and joint ventures (see Exhibit 20.7).

Manufacturers often enter foreign markets by exporting. This enables them to test a market with small shipments before investing in expanded production capabilities or foreign manufacturing facilities. Service businesses, such as restaurants, hotels, or car rental agencies, usually enter a foreign market through a licensing arrangement, joint venture, or direct investment in foreign facilities.

### Exporting

The low-risk approach to international marketing is exporting, which explains why approximately 100,000 companies in the United States are involved at that level. However, of the 100,000, only 3,600 companies average over 4,400 shipments a year. Around 9,900 companies average approximately 115 shipments a year. The remaining 86,500 average only 9 export shipments a year.[53]

Two basic approaches can be taken to exporting. **Indirect exporting** is handled by intermediaries such as buying or export agents who buy the product directly from the manufacturer and then resell it overseas under their own name. Indirect exporters typically have no contact with customers in their foreign markets. **Direct exporting** is handled directly by the manufacturer and requires a greater commitment of both managerial and financial resources. One of the least risky ways to export indirectly is through an export **trading company,** which buys everything from

**indirect exporting**
Selling goods or services to another country through an intermediary

**direct exporting**
Selling goods or services directly to another country without the use of an intermediary

**trading company**
Company that buys and distributes goods from many countries

**Exhibit 20.7
LEVELS OF INVOLVEMENT IN INTERNATIONAL MARKETING**
A company's level of involvement in international marketing should be based on the nature of the product or service, the market environment, and the financial commitment and risk a company is willing to take on.

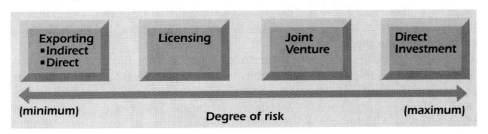

| Exporting<br>■ Indirect<br>■ Direct | Licensing | Joint Venture | Direct Investment |

(minimum)      Degree of risk      (maximum)

manufactured goods to raw materials and then resells these products in foreign markets. The manufacturer receives a guaranteed price, and the trading company assumes all the risk.

However, "to rake in the really big bucks you've got to get involved directly," says James Yoder, president of Beauty Products International (BPI), of Malibu, California. Experts said that the only way to crack the Japanese market was to sell through a large Japanese trading company (or wholesaler). However, Yoder went directly to the retailers and successfully arranged a deal with a major retail chain. The retailer sells BPI's products at a lower price than if it were to buy similar products from a wholesaler, but it still earns nearly double the average profit margin. As a result, BPI products are now selling in over 3,500 Japanese stores, and the retailer has even launched an extensive advertising campaign with national TV commercials.[54]

## Licensing

Licensing provides a way of selling the rights to a patent, brand name, or expertise so that the licensee can produce or market the product in a foreign country. Although licensing does not require large capital outlays, it does mean that the licensing company loses a certain amount of control over how its products are manufactured, marketed, and distributed in a foreign market. However, it does offer a viable alternative for companies to sell internationally with a minimum amount of risk.

For example, Selma Weiser founded Charivari, a chain of avant-garde boutiques on Manhattan's Upper West Side. She licensed the Charivari name to a Japanese manufacturer and retailer that owns 500 menswear stores; in return, Weiser is paid a yearly royalty and a percentage of sales.[55]

One of the fastest-growing forms of international licensing is franchising. There are now over 30,000 franchises in foreign countries for such U.S. companies as KFC and Coca-Cola.[56] Although franchising enables a company to expand quickly in foreign markets, it is not a trouble-free way to market internationally. One problem with international franchising is that it is sometimes more difficult to evaluate potential franchisees in a foreign environment. Another problem is that it can also provide the foreign franchisee with an opportunity to gain valuable expertise that can be used later to compete against the franchising company in the same market.[57] The best way for a franchising company to protect itself is to thoroughly investigate potential franchisees and regularly monitor franchise operations.

## Joint Venture

A joint venture involves shared ownership between a local and foreign company. Because many countries—such as Japan and South Korea—will not allow 100 percent ownership of foreign investment ventures, a joint venture is sometimes the only way for a company to produce and market in a foreign country. Even the National Basketball Association is going international (see Exhibit 20.8). In a recent joint venture with a Japanese partner, the NBA will develop television programming and play basketball games in Japan.[58]

Joint ventures with Japanese and South Korean companies haven't always worked to the benefit of the U.S. companies involved. Two big complaints are that the foreign partner uses the joint venture as a way to learn new technologies and gain access to the U.S. market, not to cooperate in a mutually beneficial manner. However, experts point out that these partnerships can work if U.S. companies pay attention to several important points. First, companies need to understand that partnership in a joint venture should be interpreted as competition, just competition in a new and different form. An overseas partner may still be a competitor, but both companies can benefit if each pursues its strategic goals and doesn't forget the strategic reason for being in the partnership. This also means giving away as much knowledge as the agreement requires, but no more. Second, harmony doesn't always indicate a successful joint venture; the true measure of success is whether both play-

**Exhibit 20.8
EXPANDING
INTERNATIONALLY**
The National Basketball Association has become a major sports marketing force in Europe and other parts of the world.

ers reach their goals. Third, keep in mind that learning from the other company is one other major reason for being in the alliance. If that's not happening, the partnership isn't working.[59]

## Direct Investment

The highest level of involvement in international marketing is **direct investment,** in which companies invest directly in a foreign market to acquire ownership interests in local companies or to establish their own foreign production and marketing facilities—which enables them to maintain maximum control over international operations. U.S. corporations spend billions of dollars building and upgrading factories abroad, and foreign concerns put comparable amounts into their operations in the United States.[60]

**direct investment**
Acquiring ownership interest in a foreign company or investment in foreign production and marketing facilities

From the U.S. government's perspective, one of the problems with direct investment by U.S. companies is that it does nothing to help the nation's trade deficit; goods produced and sold abroad don't enter into trade figures. Nonetheless, many companies are setting up factories abroad in order to avoid import quotas and other trade barriers. Some companies are more concerned about the wide swings in the value of the dollar, and they see direct investment as a way to minimize the risk of locating all their operations in the United States.[61]

Manufacturing concerns are not the only companies buying into foreign markets, however. According to data collected by the United Nations, service businesses account for nearly half of all direct investment in developed countries, and services are the fastest-rising component of investment everywhere.[62] Federal Express, for example, invested in four transport companies in Japan. Even research and development is going international. Several companies, including Upjohn, Du Pont, and Eastman Kodak, recently built R&D centers in Japan so that they can tap the brainpower of Japanese scientists.[63]

Within the last 30 years, worldwide foreign direct investment has increased 50 percent. The Japanese alone have been spending $15 billion or more a year buying real estate and businesses in the United States, although their appetite for investment has been curbed somewhat by tough market conditions in this country. Even though the explosion in direct foreign investment has created more competition for everyone, it has also created an unprecedented expansion of global opportunity.[64]

# DEVELOPING INTERNATIONAL MARKETING STRATEGIES

Pursuing market opportunities in other countries is a good way for U.S. companies to grow and stay healthy. However, the lure of millions of new customers can cause naive entrepreneurs, and even large corporations that should know better, to bumble their way into new foreign markets with products that are totally inappropriate, poorly promoted, inadequately distributed, or overpriced. Such disasters are usually caused by inadequate research, failure to weigh the company's plans against research findings, or simply ignoring the findings altogether.

One U.S. entrepreneur, for instance, tried selling microwaveable popcorn in Moscow—a puzzling proposition since microwave ovens are all but unknown in Russia. Another entrepreneur was seen touting Afro hair-care products to Muscovites.[65] However, don't assume that only small-time operators ignore the obvious. Even Ore-Ida Foods, a unit of giant H. J. Heinz Company, ignored its own market research and decided to sell frozen potatoes in Japan when the demand was only 3 percent of U.S. demand. As a result, the company's marketing strategies didn't have much impact until McDonald's started promoting its breakfast menu with hash-brown potatoes. Soon Japanese consumers took a liking to the idea of potatoes for breakfast, and Ore-Ida finally started ringing up sales. However, without the jump-start from McDonald's hash browns, Ore-Ida could have been in big trouble.[66]

Few companies can afford to rely on luck or deep pockets when launching marketing efforts in a foreign country. The use of market research data to develop appropriate product, promotion, distribution, and pricing strategies will improve the odds of succeeding internationally.

## Product and Promotion Strategies

For companies that already market domestically, existing product and promotion strategies can be duplicated, altered, or disregarded completely when marketing internationally. When companies market in several foreign countries, they often use a different approach for each market. The three basic approaches to developing international product and promotion strategies are the global (or standardized) approach, the customized approach, and the product invention approach (see Exhibit 20.9).

**Exhibit 20.9**
**INTERNATIONAL PRODUCT AND PROMOTION STRATEGIES**
Marketers can use one or more of the alternative strategies to market their products or services internationally.

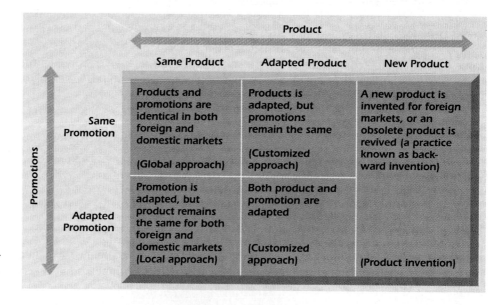

## GLOBAL APPROACH

A **global approach** to international marketing means the product and promotion are both standardized for use around the world, in every country. Companies that successfully use a global marketing strategy include Coca-Cola, Daimler-Benz, American Express, Gillette, Playtex, and Levi Strauss. The advantage of the global approach is that a company can achieve substantial cost savings because of economies of scale in production and marketing activities.

Globalization strategies got a big boost from an article by Harvard's Theodore Levitt entitled "The Globalization of Markets." Levitt said that "instead of adapting to superficial and even entrenched differences within and between nations," the modern global marketer will "seek sensibly to force suitably standardized products and practices on the entire globe."[7] These comments sparked a debate that hasn't subsided yet. Some critics of global marketing contend it doesn't work even under the best of circumstances. Or even if it does, say the critics, its overstandardized products and promotions open the door for competitors offering something with more personality. Carl Spielvogel, chairman of the advertising agency Backer Spielvogel Bates Worldwide, calls global marketing "bunk." He says, "There are about two products that lend themselves to global marketing—and one of them is Coca-Cola."[68]

Levitt did not propose, however, that marketers should disregard country-by-country differences and just bulldoze their way around the world. What he suggested was that companies should focus on and market to the similarities they can find—not the differences. Instead of seeking out and emphasizing differences between countries and cultures, we should look for similarities—and then market to those similarities.[69] This key point is sometimes overlooked when people consider the globalization issue (and when they criticize Levitt's position).

To help ensure that global marketing strategies produce the expected results, remember five key points:

- *Research the marketplace.* Investigate consumer perceptions and preferences, for example.
- *Avoid overstandardization.* Leave room for local innovation.
- *Follow up after kickoff meetings and presentations.* Monitor progress, and solve problems when they first develop.
- *Maintain a broad vision.* Stay open to ideas from local markets and managers.
- *Be flexible about implementation.* Don't force local management to comply with the global strategy if you find stiff resistance. Forced compliance rarely achieves expected results.[70]

**global approach**
Using the same product and promotion strategies in all markets

## CUSTOMIZED APPROACH

The **customized approach** to international marketing involves adapting products and promotions to the distinct characteristics of each market. Within the customized approach are three substrategies: *product adaptation,* which involves altering the product so that it meets the unique needs of foreign markets; *promotion adaptation,* which involves altering the promotion so that foreigners can relate to it more easily; and *dual adaptation,* which involves altering both the product and the promotion.

For example, Remington Products uses the product adaptation approach to sell shavers in Japan. The company's strategy involves redesigning its shavers to accommodate the smaller grip of the Japanese consumer.[71] Campbell Soup experiments with Asian ingredients in its Hong Kong test kitchen, looking for appealing combinations. You won't find pork, fig, or date soups in most U.S. supermarkets, but Campbell knows that these varieties appeal to consumers in other parts of the world.[72]

Sara Lee, which markets the Douwe Egberts brand of coffee throughout Europe, had to allow for such regional consumer preferences as lighter roasted beans in the Netherlands and finer grinds in Greece. Such differences may sound trivial, but they

**customized approach**
Adapting product and promotion strategies to the distinct characteristics of each market

can create sizable production and distribution headaches.[73] Avon uncovered variations in the global fragrance markets as well: Perfumes tend to be light in Asia, full-bodied in Latin America, subtle in Europe, and a "hodgepodge" in the United States.[74]

Companies selling industrial products also use customized international marketing strategies. For instance, Autosplice manufactures machines that provide solderless connections in appliances, computer peripherals, and other electronic devices. However, in order to market outside the United States, Autosplice had to use a dual adaptation approach to its product and promotion strategies. Its Japanese customers demanded a special design for the machine's main shaft that would withstand overtightening, and European customers required the installation of special safety guards. The company's promotional material had to be adapted to include a more detailed analysis of the Autosplice machinery and how it would meet the foreign customer's needs.[75]

### PRODUCT INVENTION

The third approach to developing international product and promotion strategies is product invention, that is, the invention of a completely different product for a foreign market. Quaker Oats, for example, created a cereal called Incaparina for Latin-American consumers. Companies such as Pillsbury, Swift, and Coca-Cola have developed high-protein foods specifically to sell as diet supplements in foreign countries.

**backward invention**
Redesigning and producing a product for specific foreign markets after it is obsolete in industrialized countries

In some cases, U.S. companies enter foreign markets using **backward invention,** which is redesigning and reintroducing products that have become obsolete in the United States and some other countries. For example, Colgate-Palmolive developed an inexpensive manual washing machine for use in homes without electricity, and NCR introduced crank-operated cash registers for customers in developing countries.

## Distribution Strategies

Distribution is one of the most difficult and challenging aspects of a marketing program because it often requires marketers to rely on outside distributors or intermediaries that operate differently from one country to another. To further complicate the international distribution process, marketers must consider two separate aspects of the process, the international distribution channels and the physical distribution of goods.

### INTERNATIONAL DISTRIBUTION CHANNELS

International distribution channels range from direct producer-customer channels to complex systems with several layers of intermediaries in both the home country and the foreign country. As discussed in Chapter 13, two primary types of intermediaries are used to develop marketing channels, agent intermediaries and merchant intermediaries. Here's a quick look at how these two classes of channel partnerships relate to international marketing.

Agent intermediaries work for the producer or manufacturer, usually on a commission basis, and arrange sales of the company's products in the foreign market. They do not actually take title to a product, but they match buyers with sellers. Agents can be individuals acting independently or they can be organizations that also engage in merchant activities. Since agents work on a commission basis, international marketers may be able to exert more control over their selling efforts than those of merchant intermediaries.

Merchant intermediaries buy products and then resell them for the purpose of making a profit for their own firm. Large merchant intermediaries, such as Mitsubishi (a Japanese industrial, trading, and banking conglomerate), buy from companies all over the world and sell billions of dollars' worth of goods each year. Because merchant intermediaries are most concerned with making a profit for their

EXPLORING
GLOBAL MARKETING

## TAKING ADVANTAGE OF THE COUNTERTRADE PHENOMENON

International marketers in the United States tend to think of countertrade and barter as the last resorts in international trade. Perhaps this negative connotation can be traced back to the most famous barter of all time: the purchase of Manhattan Island by Dutch traders for a few dollars' worth of colored glass beads. The U.S. government doesn't forbid companies to participate in countertrade or barter (except for national security reasons), but it doesn't encourage them to pursue such arrangements, either. Its official position is that countertrade is "contrary to an open, free trading system."

Nevertheless, the practice of countertrade is sweeping through the world of international business. As much as 30 percent of all world trade currently results from countertrade transactions. Many of these transactions are so complex that companies such as General Electric, McDonnell Douglas, Rockwell International, Caterpillar, and General Motors have created special departments, or even separate divisions, just to handle countertrade.

Consider Rockwell International's bid to furnish $8 million worth of printing presses to Zimbabwe. Rockwell initially lost out to a French company that offered more favorable financing

subsidized by the French government. However, just before the contract was signed, Rockwell threw in an offer to counterpurchase $8 million worth of ferrochrome and nickel, knowing that Zimbabwe had an oversupply. As a result, Zimbabwe changed the award to Rockwell, which was able to resell the metal it had purchased as part of the deal. A Rockwell executive said his countertrade department at the time was "euphoric, thinking we had found a key to winning every deal. The real world of course was consistently very tough on our bidding later on, but we had at least found one measure that could work in a desperate situation."

Sometimes countertrade transactions can be used to cover financial obligations that clients can no longer meet. N-Ren International, a small engineering and construction firm based in Brussels, expected to receive $60 million for building a fertilizer plant in Madagascar. However, when

the project was about 95 percent complete, Madagascar said it could no longer pay N-Ren because its hard currency had to be used to cover increasing national debt. To compensate for the shortfall, N-Ren agreed to export cloves in a barter arrangement offered by the government of Madagascar. The government provided N-Ren with cloves, and N-Ren got to keep the money it made from selling the spice. Because of its exporting success over the next five years, N-Ren eventually made enough profit to cover the payments not received for the fertilizer plant.

Countertrade and barter arrangements are not without an added measure of risk, however. For example, goods received in trade are sometimes difficult to sell, and facilities set up in other countries can turn into stiff competition later on. Countertrade agreements can also be extremely complex and time consuming to arrange and carry out. However, for international marketers knowledgeable about countertrade and barter, these agreements provide ways to overcome certain trade barriers and to maintain a competitive advantage in the global marketplace.

### APPLY YOUR KNOWLEDGE

**1.** Why would Rockwell even consider countertrade?
**2.** Why would a foreign customer ask for a countertrade arrangement rather than straight barter?

own firm, they do not always represent the best interests of the manufacturer. However, they also bear the majority of the trading risk and provide a valuable service to many companies that could not otherwise afford to export.

International marketers often use complex combinations of agent and merchant intermediaries, depending on what is available or required in order to sell in a particular market. Developing a good relationship with intermediaries is one of the most important aspects of international distribution. In fact, some marketing experts have begun to realize that in order to market successfully in foreign countries, they must view their distributors (not the consumers) as their "real" customers.

Procter & Gamble, for example, had to figure out how to work its way into the tightly knit network of Japanese mom-and-pop wholesalers before it could ever hope to get its products to the consumer. After trying unsuccessfully to compete with or bypass the small wholesalers, P&G decided to build a personal relationship with the distributors, helping them run their businesses, holding elaborate lunches for them, and even attending employee weddings and funerals.[76]

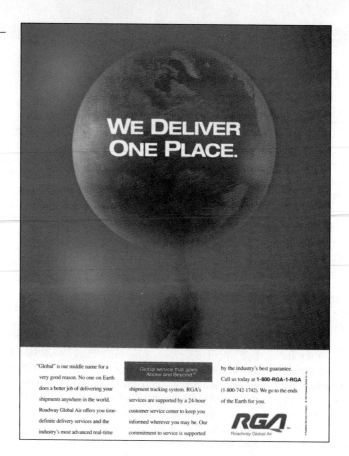

**Exhibit 20.10
INTERNATIONAL
DISTRIBUTION
SERVICES**
International marketers can turn to companies such as Roadway Global Air for help in delivering products to every corner of the planet.

Controlling the results of the marketing channel process is often difficult because of the number of intermediaries involved. However, marketers can maintain greater control at any level of the channel by establishing sales quotas that intermediaries must meet, requiring status reports, and making personal visits to intermediaries.[77]

## PHYSICAL DISTRIBUTION

The physical distribution of goods internationally involves transportation, storage, packaging, materials handling, and inventory control.[78] Many companies rely on foreign-freight forwarders to distribute their products to foreign markets. The forwarder assists with routing and scheduling and advises on shipping rates and related charges, licensing requirements, packaging requirements, and export restrictions. It may also provide shipping insurance, warehouse storage, packing and containerization, and ocean cargo or airfreight space (see Exhibit 20.10).[79]

Once a product is in a foreign country, a marketer must rely on (or work around) the country's existing infrastructure in order to get the products to wholesalers, retailers, consumers, or industrial users in a timely way. Procter & Gamble, for instance, resorted to selling and distributing its products door-to-door in the Philippines because of the country's inadequate transportation system.

The entire distribution process must be carefully planned and orchestrated for a company to achieve sales goals and satisfy customers. It must also enable a company to develop and maintain pricing strategies that make international marketing worthwhile from a profitability standpoint.

## Pricing Strategies

Pricing is becoming an increasingly important element of the marketing mix because of intensified competition in the global marketplace. Even IBM, which never used to negotiate prices for its large computer systems, threw out its mainframe price book and now negotiates prices individually and in secret in order to compete in Europe.[80]

Four factors will influence your international pricing strategy: demand, competition, government regulations, and your company's cost structure and goals. Prices for products sold in foreign markets are usually higher than in the domestic market because of higher costs of transportation, taxes and tariffs, risks associated with financing international production, intermediary fees, supplies, and other costs associated with international marketing activities.

Many companies use a cost-plus pricing strategy that incorporates the additional expenses of international marketing and therefore results in higher prices in foreign markets than at home. However, some companies are willing to accept a lower profit margin on international sales in order to gain market share in new foreign markets. For example, American Express has made significant inroads in Europe with an aggressive international pricing strategy. Although it has gained substantial new revenues, profitability per card is about 40 percent below domestic levels because of greater promotional and operational expenses, which have not been passed on to the customer.[81]

In a few countries, a company's pricing structure is almost meaningless because of blocked currencies, which means the profits from goods sold can't be exchanged for hard currency and must therefore be traded for other goods. If products are exchanged for other products, the transaction is considered a barter arrangement. A related technique becoming increasingly common is the **countertrade,** wherein you agree to buy products from a customer in return for the customer's buying your products. Because of the financial component, countertrade is a slightly different beast from barter.

Countertrade and barter are especially common in Russia, various other Eastern European states, and Latin America. For instance, in order to sell soft drinks to the Russians, Coca-Cola has become involved in the export of Russian Lada cars to Great Britain, where they are sold for hard currency. Coca-Cola has also taken apple juice concentrate as payment for Coca-Cola products. Even Gitano, the New York clothing maker, is taking its Russian profits in cotton poplin cloth that it can use for making shirts in the United States. Tyson Foods recently announced an oil-for-chicken arrangement.[82]

**countertrade**
A trading practice in which the seller agrees to buy products from the customer in exchange for the customer's agreement to buy the seller's products

## SUMMARY OF LEARNING OBJECTIVES

### 1. Compare intercultural and international marketing.

Intercultural and international marketing are closely related, with a couple of key differences. Intercultural marketing concerns doing business across cultures, regardless of whether those cultures are in the same country or not. International marketing, on the other hand, deals strictly with marketing across borders, although a strong element of intercultural marketing is usually involved as well.

### 2. Explain how international marketing differs from domestic marketing.

International marketing refers to marketing activities that take place across national boundaries. It differs from domestic marketing because it involves a greater variety of issues and factors that must be considered and that can be quite different from one foreign market to another. Some of the factors that differ in the international arena are laws and regulations, social and cultural elements, competition, and currency issues.

### 3. List and explain five trade issues affecting international marketing.

The first trade issue of importance to international marketers is foreign exchange, the process of balancing accounts in international trade transactions. Also important is a nation's balance of payments, which can influence a government's monetary, foreign investment, and import and export policies. Another important trade issue is the competitive advantage of nations, which means that some nations have a competitive advantage in certain industries because of their ability to innovate and upgrade to the next level of technology and productivity. Also important to international marketers is the concept of free trade versus protectionism, which refers to markets that are open to trade versus markets that restrict trade. Also significant is the recent development of multinational markets, specifically the European Union and free-trade areas, because they eliminate trade barriers between member nations and spur economic growth.

### 4. Identify the three primary issues to consider when developing an international marketing plan.

The first of these issues is the marketing environment in the countries in which you plan to do business. Many of the environmental elements, including laws, politics, culture, and competition, must be reexamined for international marketing. The second issue is your company's level of involvement in international marketing, which can range from exporting to direct investment. The third issue is the design and implementation of international marketing strategies, which often involves changes in one or more elements of the marketing mix.

## Meeting a Marketing Challenge at Holiday Inn Worldwide

International marketing experts often use Coca-Cola as the point of reference when assessing a company's choice between globalization and localization, since it's one of the best-known and most committed practitioners of the global strategy. The fact that even Coca-Cola executives are impressed with how far Holiday Inn has taken globalization gives you some idea of how passionately Raymond Lewis and his team have embraced the concept.

Lewis bases his globalization strategy on the idea that all travelers, regardless of where they are from or where they are going, share many of the same desires, fears, and expectations when they are traveling. They may not speak the same language or live the same lives while at home, but when they're on the road, all travelers are (1) away from home and out of their personal comfort zones, (2) in different and often unfamiliar surroundings, and (3) subject to the same hassles and hardships.

Thus Holiday Inn's advertising strategy is the same around the world, based on two themes: "Welcome" and "Stay with somebody you know." Although the copy is translated when necessary, even the visual format is the same from country to country. Of course, cultural differences must be accommodated from time to time. For example, travelers in Britain preferred an ad that focused on a friendly doorman; U.S. and German travelers preferred a more sentimental ad showing a businesswoman at the hotel receiving a fax of a drawing from her child.

The inspiration for this global strategy came to Lewis, not surprisingly, while he was traveling. When boarding a plane at Dulles Airport outside of Washington, D.C., he passed a group of Russian teenagers gathered around a guitar player singing "Puff the Magic Dragon," a folk song that was popular in the United States two or three decades ago. This connection between cultures helped convince Lewis that the world's people were alike in many ways, particularly in the field of pleasure and business travel.

It remains to be seen how effective Lewis's strategy will be in the long run. Holiday Inn is one of the few travel-services companies with the global reach needed to pull off such a strategy, but the company is sailing into uncharted waters. At the very least, Lewis is giving the world's advertisers a fascinating real-life study of globalization in action.

**Your mission:** You've joined Holiday Inn as a marketing manager, and you will be helping Ray Lewis put his global plans into action. Your responsibilities include balancing the globalization strategy with the need to adapt to local conditions. In the following scenarios, choose the solutions that will best serve Lewis and Holiday Inn.

1. You're planning a commercial for Swiss television that will reach both German-speaking and French-speaking Swiss; assume that half the audience speaks both. You can afford only one commercial. How should you handle the language issue?
   a. Produce the commercial in one language, and rerecord the spoken words in the other language.
   b. Produce the commercial in English.
   c. Rely on visuals, rather than words, to get your message across. Use a few English words if needed.
2. The movement of women up the corporate ladder is progressing at dramatically different rates in various countries around the world. For instance, women traveling on business is a common sight in North America, somewhat less so in Europe, fairly rare in Asia, and practically unheard of in the Islamic states of the Middle East. If you wanted to reach women business travelers in Asia without offending more conservative travelers, which of the following ad concepts would you use?
   a. Although it runs counter to majority opinion elsewhere in the world, you should go with the flow in Asia and feature only businessmen in your ads.
   b. The traveling businesswoman may be a rare sight in Asia, but it is on the increase. You should feature women in your ad because that will position Holiday Inn as an innovative company.

**5. Identify environmental elements that influence activities such as the selection of markets, level of involvement, and marketing strategies.**

Environmental factors that shape international marketing efforts include the market's level of economic development, infrastructure, currency exchange rate, government stability, trade barriers, legal restrictions, and social and cultural makeup. All these factors must be carefully assessed to help ensure that product, promotion, distribution, and pricing strategies are developed according to the unique characteristics of each foreign market.

**6. Differentiate among the various levels of involvement in international marketing.**

The four primary levels of involvement in international marketing are exporting, licensing, joint ventures, and direct investment. Exporting represents the lowest level of involvement because it does not require an investment in foreign production facilities or the surrender of any rights to the company's product. Licensing is the next step up in international marketing because it involves the selling of rights to a product or to know-how, and it requires careful monitoring to ensure that standards are maintained. A joint venture (or strate-

c. You can't afford to offend either group, so you should focus on the expert hotel staff in your ads, not the guests, and let potential guests of either gender decide that the hotel is for them.

3. Most other international hotel chains have not embraced the globalization approach. Hilton Hotels, in fact, calls it "a waste of time." What should you do if one of the localized competitors starts to take market share from you in a few countries?

   a. Since only a few countries are involved at the moment, study them carefully before doing anything, and then see whether some special attention in those particular markets might solve the problem.

WHO WOULD
KNOW BETTER HOW TO
MAKE YOU FEEL

# WELCOME

IN EUROPE?

Every day, warm, attentive staff welcome guests to Holiday Inn hotels throughout Europe. To spacious and well appointed rooms. To thoughtfully prepared meals. Each Holiday Inn has meeting rooms, and provides fax machines and audio visual equipment to help you keep in touch with colleagues and clients alike. Wherever your business takes you in Europe, that's a welcoming thought.

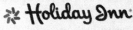

STAY WITH SOMEONE YOU KNOW

FOR RESERVATIONS, CALL US TOLL-FREE THROUGHOUT EUROPE.

AUSTRIA: 660 88 383  FRANCE: 05 903969  ITALY: 1678 77306  SPAIN: 900 99 31 19
BELGIUM: 078 11 88 77  GERMANY: 0130 84133  THE NETHERLANDS: 06 0221155  SWEDEN: 020 793 793
DENMARK: 80 01 6065  IRELAND: 1 800 553355  NORWAY: 050 18333  SWITZERLAND: 155 11 75
FINLAND: 9800 13141                                                        UNITED KINGDOM: 0800 897121
FOR RESERVATIONS FROM OTHER COUNTRIES, CALL (33)-20-69 222 (NOT TOLL-FREE) OR ANY HOLIDAY INN HOTEL.

b. If the competitor is succeeding with localization, your decision to use globalization was obviously a mistake; switch back to localization.

c. Stick with your globalization strategy; it'll pay off in the end.

4. Coordinating and controlling market efforts around the world is always a challenge, particularly when you need the consistency required by a globalized strategy. In Holiday Inn's case, the situation is complicated by the fact that most of its hotels are franchise operations, meaning that an independent businessperson or company actually owns and manages the facility. Convincing all these people to go along with a single global strategy has not been easy. Which of the following managerial approaches would you recommend?

   a. One of the reasons franchising works so well is that local business owners often know their environments better than outsiders; let them decide whether to accept the global campaign.

   b. For a globalized strategy to work, it must have consistency. You should demand agreement and compliance from all franchisees, and in fact, make it a condition of continuing their contracts with Holiday Inn.

   c. You shouldn't try to force people into agreement, nor should you ignore the corporation's strategic direction. Instead, persuade franchisees to buy into the strategy by explaining that it will help them attract more international travelers.

## SPECIAL PROJECT

Choose a country in Asia or the Pacific and assume that Holiday Inn has not yet begun to market its products there. To what degree should the company modify its products and advertising messages? In making your decision, disregard the cost factors that are associated with the adaptation strategies. Although in real life costs play a crucial role in formulating a strategy, the information you would need to help you make your decision based on the cost of each strategy is probably not readily available. Make your decision based on what you know about the country's cultural, physical, economic, and political environment.[83]

gic alliance) goes a step beyond licensing because it involves sharing ownership and risks associated with a foreign venture. The highest level of involvement is direct investment, which refers to the full ownership of production and marketing facilities in a foreign market. Direct investment allows the greatest control over international marketing activities, but it also involves the greatest degree of risk.

**7. Describe typical product, promotion, distribution, and pricing strategies used in international marketing.**

Three primary product and promotion strategies are used by international marketers: a global approach, a customized approach, and product invention. Distribution strategies within a foreign market involve the selection of agent or merchant intermediaries or the use of your own sales and distribution system. Pricing strategies include a cost-plus approach (in which the costs associated with marketing internationally are included in the price) and the extension of domestic price to foreign markets (by absorbing some of the additional costs in order to gain market share). The nature of the target market and the company's products will help shape the product, promotion, distribution, and pricing strategies for each foreign market.

# KEY TERMS

backward invention (632)
balance of payments (619)
balance of trade (619)
comparative advantage (620)
competitive advantage (620)
countertrade (635)
customized approach (631)
direct exporting (627)

direct investment (629)
European Union (621)
export (619)
foreign exchange market (619)
foreign exchange rate (618)
free-trade area (621)
global approach (631)

global corporation (622)
import (619)
indirect exporting (627)
intercultural marketing (614)
international marketing (614)
joint venture (623)

multinational corporation (622)
multinational market (621)
trade deficit (619)
trading company (627)

# QUESTIONS FOR DISCUSSION

1. How would a quick-print service such as Kinko's or PIP have to modify its marketing practices if it chose to go international?
2. Would you market a consumer product to the black population in the United States in the same way you would market it to the black population in England? Explain your answer.
3. Would cultural values be an international advertising issue for a company that makes only industrial products? Why or why not?
4. What effect would a poor infrastructure have on the following products?
   a. *Car & Driver* magazine
   b. Electricity
   c. Panasonic telephones
   d. McKinsey & Company's management consulting services
5. You're considering entering a certain country that has a history of political instability. If you could choose between entering the country to market military equipment or grocery items, which would you choose? Why?

6. Assume you're marketing personal hygiene products internationally, and you're concerned about insulting consumers in your various target markets with inappropriate packaging or advertising. What can you do to avoid such blunders?
7. Why would IBM choose to invest directly in some countries, rather than simply export products from the United States?
8. Which of the following products might be successful with a global marketing approach? Why?
   a. Automobiles
   b. Home appliances
   c. Office furniture
   d. Candy
9. If you were marketing a complex service such as financial consulting, would you choose a direct channel for international markets or align yourself with existing intermediaries? Why?
10. Many companies successfully use humor in their advertising in the United States. Would it be risky to use that same humor in ads in other countries? Why or why not?

# SHARPEN YOUR MARKETING SKILLS

In catalogs or nearby stores, find several products that have been imported into the United States by foreign companies.

**Decision:** How do the advertising and packaging compare to competitive products from U.S. companies? Can you tell the products are imported without close examination?

**Communication:** What would you tell the foreign companies to do differently in order to increase their sales in the United States?

# KEEPING CURRENT IN MARKETING

Scan recent articles describing the experiences of a U.S. company that is attempting, or has recently attempted, to market an established and successful U.S. product outside the country.

1. What goals did the company set out to achieve? How does the marketing strategy reflect those goals? Have the goals changed as experience with the international marketing effort has grown?
2. What cultural or environmental factors did the marketers

identify that would affect their effort? What changes did they make in the product, price, promotion, or distribution strategy to compensate for these factors? Were any unexpected factors encountered? If so, how did the marketer respond?
3. What lessons have been learned that might benefit other marketers, regardless of product? Were lessons learned that apply only to the products involved? How would you characterize the undertaking thus far? Successful? Unsuccessful? Why?

**638**

## Domino's Delivers around the World

From Australia to Venezuela, fresh and hot U.S.-style pizza is only a telephone call away. Domino's Pizza licensees currently deliver fast-food convenience to a hungry worldwide marketplace of more than two dozen countries outside North America, and the list keeps growing. How does Domino's do it?

The answer is dual adaptation. Although every Domino's international licensee uses the same type of superfast ovens, makes pizza from the same basic recipes, and outfits employees in the same type of red, white, and blue uniforms as the original U.S. stores, each localizes the product and the promotion. For an inside look at how one international Domino's licensee cooked up a recipe for local success, consider the experience in Japan.

Domino's granted an exclusive license for Japanese operations to Y. Higa Corp., based in Tokyo, and Ernest M. Higa, executive vice president and son of the company's founder, supervised the national marketing strategy. When he first considered how to introduce Domino's winning formula to the Japanese market, Higa identified several formidable challenges. Pizza was not wildly popular in Japan, as Pizza Hut and other competitors had discovered, and was regarded as more of a snack than a meal. Also, tomato and natural cheese were generally unfamiliar tastes to Japanese palates. Moreover, a dizzying array of noodle vendors, box-lunch caterers, and other food shops already offered doorstep delivery.

To meet these challenges, Higa decided to adapt the product and the promotion. First, he downsized the Domino's pizza to fit Japanese appetites. Rather than offer 12-inch and 16-inch pies like the United States stores, Higa's outlets offer 10-inch and 14-inch pies. Second, he customized toppings to suit local tastes, offering tuna, corn, squid, and other varieties. Next, Higa wondered how he would differentiate Domino's from other food delivery shops and from pizza competitors. He focused on the image projected by other stores as their delivery people darted around the city on aging, unattractive motor scooters and bicycles. Higa believed that Domino's should project a clean, modern image, so he ordered a fleet of new motor scooters, complete with customized roof design and colorful Domino's logo. The Domino's scooter would be an eye-catching promotional tool as it sped through city streets, and it would also be functional: The roof protected the driver from the rainy Japanese weather.

Higa had another key marketing decision to make. Should his outlets adopt the Domino's 30-minute delivery guarantee (which was offered in the United States at the time)? Unlike the U.S. market, many homes in Japanese cities have no street addresses, and buildings are not always sequentially numbered. Moreover, the major urban areas have narrow streets crowded by heavy traffic. If Domino's did not deliver on time, Higa would have to give the customer the equivalent of $3, a severe drain on profits. Because Domino's had built its international reputation on the strength of this guarantee, Higa concluded that he would have to make it work if he wanted to differentiate his pizza outlets and impress customers.

So that his drivers could deliver within 30 minutes, Higa concentrated on populous, affluent neighborhoods of big cities such as Tokyo and Osaka and limited the delivery radius by accepting orders only from customers within a 2-kilometer radius (approximately 1.2 miles). With product and promotion adaptation in place, Higa opened his first Tokyo outlet in September 1985, followed by two more Tokyo stores. Higa's marketing created an instant hit: His first three stores each raked in $1 million in sales before their second anniversary. He aims for more than 100 stores. Domino's has made such an impact in Japan that hundreds of pizza delivery competitors now jam the streets, riding copies of Domino's roofed scooter. Don't look for Higa to slow down anytime soon: He'll need to explore every marketing angle he can to stay ahead of the pack in Japan, a pack that now includes archrival Pizza Hut as well as smaller operators such as Pizza California, Shakey's, and Pizza Station.

1. Once Higa has saturated urban areas with Domino's outlets, should he expand the chain by introducing Domino's to rural areas of Japan? Would he do better by opening near university campuses, industrial complexes, and similar locations?

2. Because Domino's U.S. cachet is important to Higa's marketing success, should he promote the chain's U.S. roots by offering special pricing and toppings on every U.S. holiday? Should he decorate each Domino's store in early American style, complete with a Betsy Ross flag?

3. Imagine that competitors find a way to slice their guaranteed delivery time to 20 minutes. Should Higa respond by introducing a smaller, less expensive personal pizza that will bake faster and can be delivered faster than the competition, or should he differentiate Domino's by diversifying the number and type of toppings to offer varieties that competitors will have difficulty matching?

# 21

# Quality and Customer Service

After studying this chapter, you will be able to

**1.** Express the new meaning of quality

**2.** Clarify the new meaning of customer service

**3.** Explain the importance of delivering quality products and superior customer service

**4.** Examine the effect quality and customer service can have on the marketing mix

**5.** List ways companies can add value to basic goods and services

**6.** Explain marketing's contribution to ensuring product quality

**7.** Describe a plan for delivering superior customer service

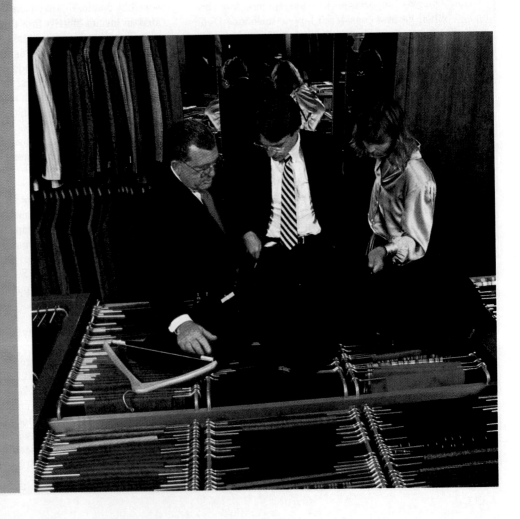

## *Mail-Order Giant Finds Delivering Consistent Quality and Service a Tall Order*

In 1912 Leon Leonwood Bean summed up the philosophy of his new mail-order business when he said, "Sell quality products at a reasonable price, treat your customers as human beings, and they will always come back for more." Come back they did, helping L. L. Bean rack up record sales decade after decade. However, despite the company's commitment to 100 percent customer satisfaction, as its founder grew older, the business fell into disarray. By the early 1960s, lethargic service, outdated catalogs, and a disorganized fulfillment system made busy seasons a nightmare of inefficiency.

Leon Leonwood Bean died in 1967, and his grandson, Leon Gorman, was made president at age 32. Gorman admitted that he was "green as grass" and not much of a sportsman to boot, but he did understand the value of Bean's heritage of quality and service, so he decided to go back to the company's roots and emphasize the basics that built the business. He reasoned that by satisfying current customers, the company would forge solid, trusting relationships and profit from the referrals those relationships helped generate.

Ironically, L. L. Bean has become a little *too* successful, and not only through the mail. Each year thousands of tourists stop at Bean's 24-hour retail outlet in the quaint town center at Freeport, Maine. The enormous store caters to people hunting for Bean's high-quality products and special brand of personalized service. However, Bean's stupendous growth rate has stressed the fabric of the company, leading to compromises in the quality and service that for so long distinguished it from the competition. The company posted spectacular growth figures with yearly increases as high as 40 percent for its trendy outdoor line. This explosive growth seriously taxed Bean's workers and facilities. As Gorman said, "It became apparent to us that all facets of our business were becoming more complicated." The company's quality-control and customer service systems faltered, and as operating units grew larger, customer satisfaction once again became a problem.

Bean struggled mightily to meet customers' expectations, but the company's tremendous growth rate exceeded its ability to deliver faultless quality and service. Despite Herculean efforts, a large number of customers still weren't completely satisfied. In fact, increased mail-order competition made consumers so finicky that in 1988 they returned $82 million worth of goods, or about 14 percent of Bean's $588 million in sales. These returns cost the company $18 million in shipping and handling. The massive returns also cost Bean a chance to win the coveted National Quality Award for service from the Commerce Department.

As he groped for ways to rebuild Bean's reputation for top-quality products and responsive service, Gorman scaled back expansion plans. "We would like to grow at a rate of 5 to 8 percent," Gorman said, trying to catch his breath after a decade of 23 percent annual growth. Even now, he's not sure whether he can keep his customers happy and the competition off his back.

If Gorman *is* sure of one thing, he knows that over the long run a few satisfied customers are worth far more than many who aren't. He also realizes that his company's future success will depend on whether his employees are able to live up to the L. L. Bean tradition of quality workmanship and personalized service.

If you were Leon Gorman, how would you measure and interpret your customers' definition of product quality and customer service? What changes would you make to Bean's policies and procedures to ensure that things are done right the first time? How would you motivate your employees to always put the customer first?[1]

# CHAPTER OVERVIEW

The people at L. L. Bean clearly recognize the value of quality and customer service. They know that quality is more than just a product attribute and that customer service means more than handling complaints. This chapter describes the concepts that quality-service innovators like Bean use to build competitive advantage. You'll explore the new meanings of quality and customer satisfaction, and you'll see why the old meanings are no longer valid. After that, you'll see just how important quality and customer satisfaction are in today's business environment. Next, in a section on quality and customer satisfaction in the marketing mix, you'll find out how you can integrate these concepts with the traditional notions of product, price, promotion, and distribution. Then you'll examine the ways people in the marketing department can contribute to product quality, even though marketing people typically don't make anything. The final section in this chapter takes you through the nine steps needed to establish an effective customer service program.

# WELCOME TO THE NEXT FRONTIER

Chapter 1 explained that a key element of the marketing concept is focusing on customer needs. As more and more companies and nonprofit organizations adopt the marketing concept and manage their businesses accordingly, they are realizing that focusing on customer needs means paying attention to quality and customer service. As a result, these two issues are now at the forefront of contemporary marketing management, and any organization attempting to become customer-oriented is familiar with them.

Quality and service play an important role in the marketing of all products, of course, but they are becoming particularly important in many industries because they are the most effective differentiators for an increasing number of products. Companies that once held commanding market leads based on technology, low price, or just sheer size find themselves competing on quality and customer service (see Exhibit 21.1).

Even though quality and customer service get a lot of attention today, many successful companies have emphasized them for years. Procter & Gamble has relentlessly pursued quality for over 150 years, and IBM has made customer service the cornerstone of its competitive strategy for more than 80 years. Nothing really new lies beneath all the noise and excitement, except for the increased level of concern and attention from management. So if the concepts covered in this chapter strike you as common sense, you're already one step ahead. The only amazing thing is that so few companies seem to recognize and practice the obvious. In the words of *Business Week* magazine: "It seems so simple. Businesses exist to serve customers and should bend over backwards to satisfy their needs. But too many still don't get it. And in the 1990s, more customers are likely to reward the ones that do."[2]

At times, separating the topics of quality and customer service is difficult. Delivering a quality product is part of providing superior customer service, and strong customer support is an important part of many customers' definition of quality. Nonetheless, each topic does have some unique properties and challenges, so they are treated here as separate but closely related. Discussions of quality focus on the basic goods or services a company creates, whereas discussions of customer service emphasize all the activities that companies engage in to add value to their basic products.

## The New Meaning of Quality

With the traditional view of quality, products were evaluated in light of their physical attributes: strength, reliability, and so forth. However, more and more companies are starting to rethink the concept of quality. They now realize that the strongest,

V.O.: K&K Delivery of Hinsdale, are you having more trouble getting faxes through on the first try?

Sherman Reynolds, metal fabricators of Chicago, are you saving less than you'd hoped since leaving AT&T?

*We want you back.* AT&T PRO[R] WATS. A discount plan that gives you very competitive prices. Switch now and get one month of long distance free. Chicago, *WE WANT YOU BACK.* Call 1 800 222–0400.

shiniest product in the world is not ideal if it doesn't satisfy customers' needs, wants, and expectations. The new view of quality takes this into account and leads marketers to define products that offer the right features, the right class of performance, the right level of durability, and so on. Customers will help you define what's right; all you have to do is ask. Furthermore, companies are recognizing that the entire organization must be committed to quality; every employee's job has some effect on quality. All of this leads to a new definition of **quality:** the degree to which a product conforms to customer expectations and specifications.[3] A hair dryer designed to last 100 years has impressive reliability, for instance, but it also has to meet customers' expectations regarding features, styling, price, and performance. **Optimal quality** is a level of quality high enough to meet customer expectations and balanced to avoid adding cost without adding meaningful value. Not all customers want gold-plated quality and service with every purchase; in many cases price is more important.

The new meaning of quality calls for new strategies of organization, implementation, and control. Quality is no longer the exclusive responsibility of a small group of people who monitor service performance or count defects on an assembly line. Every task that an organization performs—writing memos, painting cars, advising clients, sweeping floors—has an element of quality. **Total quality management (TQM)** is an organizational philosophy based on the pursuit of quality and the management practices that lead to total quality. In this sense, quality isn't something that you monitor for or add in at some point in a production process; it is the very essence of the organization.

TQM rode a wave of popularity during the 1980s and into the early 1990s, as one company after another decided it had better improve quality if it wanted to stay in business. By 1992 or 1993, however, a backlash began to build up, with some companies saying that TQM was costing a fortune and not yielding adequate benefits in terms of sales and profits. The problem is not with the concept of quality, but with slavish devotion to programs and processes rather than results. In other words, some companies got caught up in managing their TQM programs instead of using TQM to help manage their businesses.[4] The secret to success with TQM or any quality management program is to use the program in the context of pursuing your marketing and business objectives.

## The New Meaning of Customer Service

When a customer wearing a baseball cap and blue jeans and driving a pickup truck tried to leave the parking lot at a U.S. Bank branch in Spokane, Washington, the parking attendant told him to either cough up the 60 cents for parking or go back inside and get his parking ticket stamped by a teller. The customer then tried to get

**Exhibit 21.1**
**COMPETING ON CUSTOMER SERVICE**
AT&T, which spent decades as a monopoly that didn't have to worry much about competing, now emphasizes customer service as a key competitive advantage.

**quality**
A measure of how closely a product conforms to customers' needs, wants, and expectations

**optimal quality**
The level of quality that meets customer specifications while providing the best balance of satisfaction and cost

**total quality management (TQM)**
A philosophy and management system that bases everything an organization does on the pursuit of quality

his ticket validated, but the teller must've looked at his humble attire and figured he couldn't have been a bank customer. This pushed the customer's patience past the breaking point; as stunned bank personnel looked on, he withdrew his $1 million account from the bank and took it to the competitor next door.[5] The lesson here? It doesn't take much to lose customers—nor does it often take very much to keep them.

Just as quality is getting a new face, so is customer service. Like quality, it's not just some department down in the basement anymore; everybody is (or should be) involved in customer service. Again, from the CEO to the cleaning staff, everyone in a company plays a role in meeting the needs of current and potential customers. Even if a person isn't in a position to support customers directly, he or she will certainly be in a position to support those employees who are servicing customers. Thus, the job traditionally labeled "customer service" is more complex than filling orders, taking returns, or handling complaints.

**customer service**
Actions companies can take to add value to basic goods and services

Based on this perspective, **customer service** encompasses everything a company does to satisfy its customers and help them realize the greatest possible value from the goods and services they are purchasing. This definition is broad enough to cover everything from designing a product that is easy to maintain all the way to helping customers dispose of products that are no longer in use. Note that this definition of customer service does not include the basic good or service you are offering the market; you have to provide that just to play the game. Everything you offer above that is customer service, which you can use to separate your product from the competition.[6] The term **added value** is used in marketing to indicate extensions to a basic product that increase its value to customers. Exhibit 21.2 suggests some of the ways businesses can add value through customer service.

**added value**
Increased worth of a good or service, compared to the basic or expected product

For example, in the airline business, you deliver passengers safely from one city to another. That isn't customer service; it's your basic product. However, when you run a company such as Southwest, which outshines its competitors in terms of on-time performance, fewer canceled flights, and less lost luggage, you can claim to offer superior customer service (see Exhibit 21.3). Southwest enhances the basic product of air travel by making it less of a nuisance than it can be on most other carriers.[7]

**Exhibit 21.2**
**ADDING VALUE THROUGH CUSTOMER SERVICE**
Companies can build competitive advantage by using customer service to add value to basic goods and services.

What about the old customer service department? Some of the companies noted for their superior customer service don't even have one. Their entire organization is devoted to ensuring satisfaction, and their leaders consider this too important to delegate to one department. With customer satisfaction ratings that far exceed those

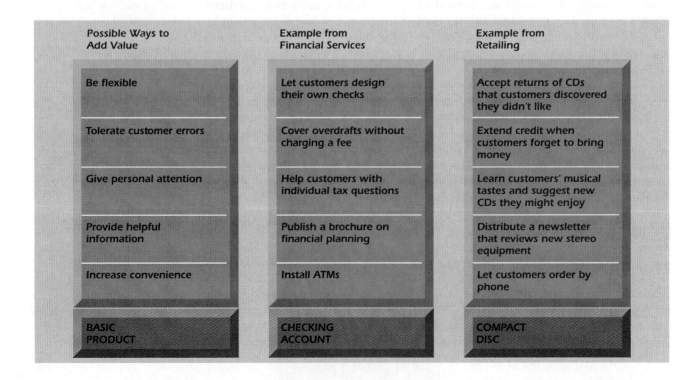

| Possible Ways to Add Value | Example from Financial Services | Example from Retailing |
|---|---|---|
| Be flexible | Let customers design their own checks | Accept returns of CDs that customers discovered they didn't like |
| Tolerate customer errors | Cover overdrafts without charging a fee | Extend credit when customers forget to bring money |
| Give personal attention | Help customers with individual tax questions | Learn customers' musical tastes and suggest new CDs they might enjoy |
| Provide helpful information | Publish a brochure on financial planning | Distribute a newsletter that reviews new stereo equipment |
| Increase convenience | Install ATMs | Let customers order by phone |
| BASIC PRODUCT | CHECKING ACCOUNT | COMPACT DISC |

of other credit card companies, American Express has no customer service department. A former president of American Express Travel Related Services said the entire company is a customer service department.

For many firms, of course, it makes sense to have a function dedicated to answering questions or solving problems. Procter & Gamble, for instance, has a large service organization to answer questions from customers and support its distribution channel partners. However, managers must make sure these customer service departments are really helping customers. Too often, the customer service department becomes a shield to protect the rest of the company from angry customers.[8]

## The Importance of Quality and Customer Service

Satisfied customers are more than a pleasant side effect of your business's effort. Satisfied customers are the source of your profits; they are the reason you are in business (or at least they should be).[9] Unless you hold a monopoly position in a market, you're not going to stay in business if you can't keep customers satisfied. Consistently delivering first–rate quality and customer service allows a company to build a number of important strengths, including competitive barriers, customer loyalty, clearly differentiated products, lower marketing costs, and higher prices. Finally, a simple ethical issue surrounds quality: Customers pay you to meet their expectations, and you have a responsibility to do so.

### BUILDING COMPETITIVE BARRIERS

When we discuss competitive barriers, we normally think in terms of the physical results of strategic investments, such as new plants, distribution centers, or retail facilities. However, a tradition of quality and customer service can present even higher barriers to competition. Just ask any retailer who had to respond to a new Nordstrom store opening in its market. Building a store that looks like a Nordstrom is not terribly difficult, but breathing life into these physical investments as Nordstrom has is an achievement reached by few companies.[10]

Sometimes the answer is to shift investment away from manufacturing capacity or research programs and put the money into customer service. Investors balked when Bruce Smith wanted to sink half of their money into a customer service system for his start-up company, Network Equipment Technologies. Smith reasoned that since he was about to go up against IBM, he'd better be able to beat IBM at its own game. He got his way with the investors and spent the money in two ways: (1) to make NET's products both reliable and easy to repair and (2) to build a **service infrastructure,** which encompasses the people, training, organization, and equipment needed to ensure superior customer service. NET's reliability and responsiveness to customers let it command a 20 percent price premium, which is used to fund and solidify the infrastructure. Not only did NET eat up a big chunk of IBM's market, its service infrastructure now presents a formidable barrier to any hungry potential competitors that might want to join in.[11]

**service infrastructure**
The people, procedures, systems, and equipment that allow a company to provide superior customer service

| RANK | AIRLINE |
|------|---------|
| 1 | Southwest |
| 2 | American |
| 3 | United |
| 4 | Delta |
| 5 | USAir |
| 6 | Northwest |
| 7 | TWA |
| 8 | America West |
| 9 | Continental |

**Exhibit 21.3
CUSTOMER SATISFACTION IN THE AIR TRAVEL INDUSTRY**
Southwest's emphasis on dependable service results in consistently high scores for customer satisfaction. (Although U.S. carriers in general score lower than many of their European and Asian counterparts.)

### ENSURING CUSTOMER LOYALTY

If you ever have the chance to drive around Seattle, home base of the Nordstrom retailing chain, take a look at the license plate frames on the cars around you. Along with the "I'd rather be sailing" and "I'd rather be flying" frames, chances are you'll see quite a number of frames displaying "I'd rather be shopping at Nordstrom." People are so committed to one retailer that they pay money to advertise their allegiance. Nordstrom keeps its customers loyal by providing service that has been labeled as "heroic," including warming up a customer's car on a cold day, meeting a busy customer during a layover at the airport to fit him for a suit, ironing a new shirt for a customer in a hurry for a meeting, and buying merchandise at competing stores and then delivering it when Nordstrom didn't have just what a customer wanted. By solving the particular problems faced by each customer, Nordstrom keeps these people coming back for years.[12]

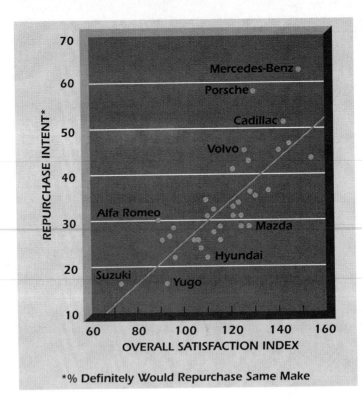

**Exhibit 21.4
SATISFIED
CUSTOMERS ARE
REPEAT CUSTOMERS**
Automobile owners who are
satisfied with their current
cars are more likely than dissatisfied owners to purchase
the same brand next time.

On the other hand, established companies that haven't built a strong reputation
for customer satisfaction can find themselves vulnerable to new competitors that
stress quality and service. For instance, Japanese machine tool manufacturers broke
into the U.S. market by sending waves of engineers to fix problems that appeared
at customer sites. Sometimes a small shift in customer service efforts can change
the competitive balance. When Lincoln Electric, a leading maker of welding equipment and supplies, encouraged its sales force to help customers find welding-related
cost savings, the company increased its share in both domestic and foreign
markets.[13]

Satisfaction and loyalty are related. As Exhibit 21.4 illustrates, automobile buyers
who reported high levels of satisfaction after one year also reported a higher likelihood of purchasing the same brand next time. The correlation holds true at the
other end of the scale also. For example, Peugot, AMC/Renault, and Plymouth
scored lowest in satisfaction, and these three brands scored lowest in repurchase
likelihood. Toyota, on the other hand, scored highest in satisfaction and second in
repurchase likelihood. These data help explain the drop in market share experienced by U.S. automakers; the top nine makes are in a group clearly separate from
the rest of the pack, and no U.S. brand is among them.[14]

Finally, your college or university is a great example of an organization that relies on satisfied customers. Chances are that a favorable review of the school by
someone you trust played at least a small role in your choice.

Efforts by marketers to establish long-term customer loyalty have led to the concept of **relationship marketing,** which focuses on long-term retention of customers,
rather than on making immediate sales. The foundation of this strategy is to become
partners with your customers and to do what is best for them over the long haul.
By doing so you will be rewarded with their loyalty and increased business.

**relationship marketing**
A strategy to build long-term
customer loyalty that is based
on becoming partners with
customers and doing everything possible to contribute to
their success

## DIFFERENTIATING PRODUCTS

A number of business forecasters and observers are issuing warnings about the increasing similarity in a wide variety of products and services. If you're selling a product that looks, feels, and tastes just like the product they're selling across the street,

how can you convince customers to choose you? Customer service is a powerful way to do this; it elevates your offering by adding value to the basic product.

Consider Tasca Lincoln-Mercury in Seekonk, Massachusetts. It doesn't have a polished sales force (*Fortune* magazine said Tasca's salespeople look like sharks) or a striking facility (the building is small and two decades old). Tasca sells the same cars you can buy from any Lincoln dealer anywhere, and yet Tasca sells more Lincolns than any other dealership in the United States. The secret? Tasca's customers give the company unusually high marks for customer service. You can buy a Lincoln anywhere, but you can buy a Lincoln with Tasca service only from Tasca.[15]

Suppliers that raise commonly available products to uncommon levels through superior service lead some business observers to state that no such thing as a commodity exists. Every product, no matter how seemingly simple or mundane, can be differentiated through attention to quality and customer service. Take the humble potato chip. How could you possibly do anything to a potato chip to make it stand apart from the competition? Frito-Lay does it by providing extraordinary service to its customers, the thousands of retail outlets and other establishments that in turn sell the goods to all of us. Frito-Lay will seemingly stop at nothing to keep these channel partners happy, including spending hundreds of dollars to deliver an emergency load of chips worth $30 and helping stores clean up after hurricanes. The reward for Frito-Lay? Two billion dollars in sales, market shares of 70 percent in some areas, and profit margins that are the envy of its competitors.[16]

## DECREASING MARKETING COSTS

Customer service can dramatically lower a company's marketing and selling costs, for three reasons. First, winning a new customer can cost up to five times as much as keeping an existing customer. You spend less time and money on sales presentations, credit checks, and other activities needed to establish new accounts. It just makes better sense financially to hang on to the customers you've already won.

Second, satisfied customers can be your best source of advertising when they tell their family, friends, and colleagues about your company. Because this message comes from real customers, not the company itself, it packs a bigger punch than just about any advertising the company can spend its money on. Potential customers can relate to the experience of actual customers, particularly customers they already know and trust, and this helps reduce the uncertainty of trying a new product or supplier.

The third reason is the reverse of the second: Dissatisfied customers can destroy a business. Customers who aren't happy with the goods and services they purchase will also spread the word. Again, their word-of-mouth advertising will be more effective than your advertising because it also lowers the uncertainty of dealing with your company. Potential buyers who hear about poor service or shoddy products will no longer have to guess what it would be like doing business with you; they have evidence. One widely quoted study estimates that dissatisfied customers are likely to tell from 10 to 20 people about their bad experiences. This is three times higher than the number of people with whom happy customers share their experiences.[17]

The cost savings from improved quality and customer service aren't limited to the marketing department. Experts estimate that 25 to 50 percent of a company's entire operating expenses can be traced to poor quality. These potential cost savings, of course, put a company in a stronger position both to fund its continuing growth and to weather competitive threats.[18]

## INCREASING PRICES

Finally, you can support higher profit margins if customers are satisfied with the quality of your products and customer service. L. L. Bean, for instance, doesn't have to worry about offering rock-bottom prices because customers are willing to pay ex-

## ISO 9000: THE NEW PRICE OF ADMISSION?

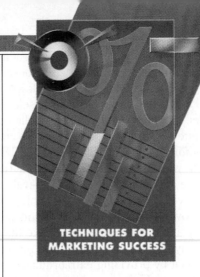

**TECHNIQUES FOR MARKETING SUCCESS**

The Baldrige Award gets most of the media attention these days, but another quality force promises to have a much larger impact on businesses around the globe. A standard of quality management known as ISO 9000 (pronounced "ICE-o-nine thousand") is shaping up to be a standard purchasing requirement. Unlike the Baldrige, which awards a company for performance, ISO 9000 certifies that a company's quality systems are shipshape. Also, unlike the Baldrige, this is not a competition; every company that passes an auditor's test receives the certification. ISO 9000 is administered by the International Organization for Standardization in Geneva, Switzerland, but it has its roots in U.S. military and NATO purchasing procedures.

The essence of ISO 9000 is embodied in 20 subject areas, ranging from management responsibility to the use of appropriate statistical techniques. Other key areas include maintaining a quality procedures manual, ensuring proper testing and inspection of manufactured products, and establishing procedures for correcting quality problems. The intent of all these rules is to make sure companies are doing the things necessary to produce high-quality products.

The value of ISO 9000 certification is a subject of controversy. Baldrige winner Motorola and others say that certification is no guarantee that you'll actually produce quality products. Henry Grimmick of the quality consulting firm Philip Crosby Associates notes that "all ISO 9000 certification ensures is that you're doing the basic things. It doesn't ensure that you're doing them well." Service expert Karl Albrecht goes so far as to say he's sure ISO 9000 will end up in "the management boneyard."

The merits of ISO 9000 may be in some dispute, but no doubt exists that thousands of companies are signing up to be certified. Some companies want certification as a way of monitoring their operations; others are more interested in the perceived marketing value that certification brings. To a growing extent, nearly all are worried that without the ISO 9000 stamp of approval, they'll start to lose business. Maria Huang of S-MOS Systems, a California semiconductor manufacturer, estimates that her firm might've lost 30 percent of its business had it not been certified. Some business customers are going so far as to demand outright that all suppliers pass the ISO test.

The demand for certification is coming primarily from European buyers at this point, but the trend is building in North America and Asia as well. John Yates, in charge of global purchasing for GE's plastics business, is blunt: "There is absolutely no negotiation. If you want to work with us, you have to get it." GE demanded that 340 vendors get certification. In addition, a number of U.S. government agencies (all of whom are major organizational customers) are considering adopting ISO 9000 as a purchase requirement as well.

### APPLY YOUR KNOWLEDGE

**1.** The first few companies in every industry to get ISO 9000 certification might have a short-term marketing advantage, but when the majority of suppliers get it, that advantage will shrink. Assume that you and all of your major competitors have been certified; how would you handle that fact in your promotional communications with customers?

**2.** Would ISO 9000 or any other generalized quality certification serve as a replacement for researching customer needs and perceptions of quality? Why or why not?

---

tra for Bean products and Bean service. Market studies indicate that firms perceived to offer superior customer service can command a 9 to 10 percent price premium over their competitors. Superior service providers average profit margins 12 times greater than those companies at the bottom of the service heap. Similarly, companies whose product quality is in the top one-third of their markets command prices 5 to 6 percent higher than companies in the bottom one-third. With companies pounding and scraping for every fractional percentage of markets and profits, you can see how important the price boost from quality and service can be.[19]

Maytag is a stellar performer in the business of washers, dryers, and dishwashers. The company's objective is to deliver 10 years of trouble-free operation, so the lonely Maytag repairman you see in the TV commercials is lonely for a good reason. Customers who want to avoid the trouble and wasted time surrounding a major home appliance failure reward Maytag's commitment to quality with top market share and prices that are 15 percent higher than the competition's.[20]

Quality and customer service are important influences on the design and management of a company's marketing mix. At the very least, the amount of attention devoted in recent years to these two topics has further sensitized customers. Even if a company is doing nothing different, the perceptions and attitudes of its customers are likely to have changed. Enlightened companies, of course, are doing something about customer satisfaction. This section explains how quality and customer service efforts can potentially affect their marketing mixes.

## Product Factors

It all starts here. Before all the strategies, training, and promotions will have any effect, you've got to offer goods and services that meet the needs and expectations of customers. This advice might seem painfully obvious, but it hasn't always been followed. A great support system and aggressive advertising didn't help Ford sell the Edsel in the 1950s or help Deere sell bicycles in the 1970s. These companies weren't offering products that met customer expectations, and customers sent a clear message by taking their business elsewhere.

Beyond its ability to meet customer needs, a product's design affects other areas of the marketing efforts. First, it can influence the attitude of salespeople. Particularly in markets that require product demonstrations, you've got to make the sales staff successful with the product before they can be successful with customers. In addition, smart salespeople will quickly realize whether or not the product meets users' needs, and this will affect their attempts to sell it. A second area in which product design affects marketing is in advertising and promotions. A product that aligns well with customer expectations is relatively easy to promote, all other things being equal. However, the further a product gets from the customers' ideal, the harder it becomes to promote. If there are restrictions on a product's use, or serious compromises in its design, advertising will have to work around these problems.[21]

### ADDING VALUE TO GOODS AND SERVICES

As noted earlier, customer service can enhance the value of basic goods and services. Tom Vitacco, CEO of PrintMasters, describes the situation in many industries when he says, "The equipment is the same in most print shops. What makes you different in this business is how you treat customers." Vitacco knows that customers can get printing done anywhere, so his people need to add value to the basic product by going the extra mile for customers.[22]

PrintMasters recognizes the distinction between expected products and augmented products. **Expected products,** as the name implies, deliver the basic value that customers expect when they make a purchase. For PrintMasters, the expected value is transforming a customer's original document into a specified number of copies. **Augmented products** enhance the expected product by adding more value; they are also known as extended or enhanced products. Customer service is one of the best ways to augment your products. PrintMasters can create an augmented product by offering delivery, graphic design advice, protective packaging, easy payment plans, and a host of other measures that increase the value received by the customer.

**expected products**
The basic set of values that customers expect in exchange for the price they pay

**augmented products**
The expected products plus all their added value

### DESIGNING PRODUCTS FOR SERVICEABILITY

Another important area where product design and customer service intersect is **serviceability,** the ease with which a product can be maintained, diagnosed, and repaired. Because it's not always the most glamorous issue for a marketing depart-

**serviceability**
A measure of how easily a product can be diagnosed, repaired, and maintained

**Exhibit 21.5
SERVICEABILITY
AFFECTS
SATISFACTION**
Emery Worldwide takes a tongue-in-cheek approach to emphasizing its ability to adapt to customer needs.

ment to address, serviceability often takes a backseat to other development efforts. The results of this lack of attention can cost a business dearly, as it struggles to keep customers satisfied and products repaired (see Exhibit 21.5).

## Price and Profit Factors

In addition to the pricing issues covered in Chapters 11 and 12, customer service throws a new twist into pricing and profit analysis. Many of the actions taken to increase customer satisfaction are free or inexpensive for a company to provide. It doesn't cost much for a front desk clerk in a hotel to smile and offer a pleasant greeting when you approach. However, it does cost the hotel to add a second desk clerk to make sure you don't have to wait in line when you arrive. This second clerk's salary can come from only two places, your pocket or the hotel's profit margin. The hotel can maintain its profit margin if it can generate more bookings or charge higher prices based on its faster service. Otherwise, its profits will drop.

Other service-oriented practices that can cut into a company's margins include a generous, no-questions-asked return policy. If the company can't resell returned goods, the cost of replacement goods must be absorbed either by the company or by its suppliers. Deep inventories are another expensive service investment that customers love. However, some companies go too far in their zeal to please customers. For instance, Indianapolis-based Service Supply Company, a supplier of industrial fasteners (nuts, bolts, and the like), carries an inventory of 74,000 items. It can ship from stock 95 percent of the time, compared with 80 to 85 percent for its competitors. The company's service is so good that *Industrial Distribution* magazine named it the "Distributor of the Century." This is commendable, but Service Supply Company makes very little profit. Unless it can raise its prices, which are already 5 percent above the competition's, or increase its market share and gain some economies of scale, the company's commendable efforts to satisfy customers aren't going to make it much money.[23]

## Promotion Factors

A focus on quality and customer service adds two specific topics to the general concepts and techniques of promotion. The first of these is positioning based on customer service. As noted earlier, customer service can be a powerful tool to enhance the value of any product, no matter how undifferentiated. The degree of customer service value added to the basic product can be a key element in the position a company is trying to establish in a market. The more undifferentiated a product category is, the more important customer service becomes. Exhibit 21.6 shows the worst possible position to be in: a customer service laggard in an undifferentiated market. Companies in this situation are usually headed for oblivion, because customers have no compelling reason to buy from them. About the only option available to such firms is to execute a fundamental shift in service strategy, such as abandoning all but a few segments and concentrating on becoming a service leader in those remaining segments.

Conversely, the best position to be in is to have a market that is still differentiated *and* to be a leader in customer service. Such companies are obviously in a strong position. They do need to keep a close eye on competitors, however, for two reasons: (1) every market tends toward product parity at some point, meaning that all products in that market will start to offer the same level of capabilities, performance, and price; and (2) smart competitors realize that one way to successfully attack a leader is to surpass the accepted norms of customer service. These competitors constantly seek to convince customers that a better way exists.[24]

The second promotional issue to consider is the difficulty a company faces when trying to promote its products based on quality and customer service. In an advertisement, anybody can say "quality" this or "service" that. Just pick up a newspaper or drive down a commercial street and see how many times you can read "Where the customer is king (queen)" or "Your satisfaction comes first." As a result of hearing too many promises and receiving too little satisfaction, people in the United States have grown increasingly immune to advertising messages that deal with quality and customer service. In addition, such messages frequently rely on complex technical terms or intangible concepts, making the promotion that much more difficult. Examples include Yamaha trying to explain that its 18-bit compact disk players produce better sound, when most customers have no idea what those 18 bits do in the first place, or H&R Block trying to persuade taxpayers that its tax preparation service is better than the service offered by the competition, when nobody seems to understand the tax laws.

How can you communicate a convincing message of quality and service? Two common strategies are to provide adequate information and to rely on testimonials from satisfied customers. Information is important because it supports the claims you're making about quality and service. This can be especially significant if the customer's satisfaction hinges on understanding some technical point about your product. Testimonial advertising is also effective because potential customers are more likely to believe someone they can relate to and respect.[25]

No one knows more about customer perceptions of quality than Stan Shih, chairman and CEO of the Acer Group, the largest personal computer manufacturer in Taiwan and one of the largest in the world. Many consumers and businesses in the

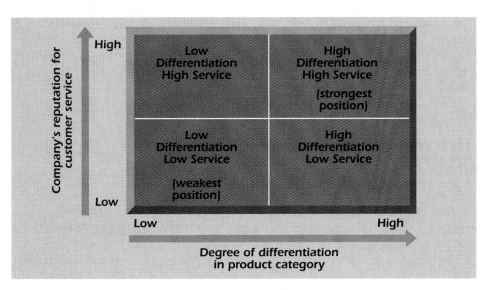

**Exhibit 21.6
CUSTOMER SERVICE
AND PRODUCT
DIFFERENTIATION**
Companies in a highly differentiated market that excel at customer service are in the strongest possible position, whereas those in undifferentiated markets with poor service reputations are in a weak position.

United States and Europe equate "made in Taiwan" with low quality, even though the country boasts state-of-the-art manufacturing technology and is highly respected among industry insiders. In fact, Taiwan already makes 20 percent of the world's PCs, including many that bear the brand names of well-known American and European companies. Some of the biggest names in the industry, including IBM, Apple, Digital Equipment, and Hewlett-Packard, rely on Taiwanese components and systems when building their own products.[26]

To combat the image problem, the Taiwanese government has instituted the Taiwan National Quality Award, modeled after the prestigious (and very difficult to earn) Malcolm Baldrige Award in the United States and the Deming Prize in Japan. However, Shih and other Taiwanese business leaders still have to deal with an image problem left over from the country's days as a fledgling manufacturer of cheap toys and other consumer products. One of the steps Shih has taken is turning Acer into a multinational manufacturer in order to downplay the company's origin in Taiwan. Nevertheless, it will take time to transform the country's image. As an example of the problem Shih faces, Tandy, a U.S. computer company, recently ran an ad in European magazines that showed a healthy-looking man labeled "U.S. made" standing next to a wooden dummy labeled "Taiwan PC." The headline urged readers not to take the risk of buying computers made in Taiwan. The irony is that Tandy itself is a big buyer of Taiwanese computer equipment.[27]

## Distribution Factors

In some cases, distribution can be a company's strongest competitive differentiator. Let's say you want to purchase a Korg electronic keyboard, and you've opted to buy from a mail-order supplier because you value low price more than sales assistance. You flip through a copy of *Keyboard* magazine and find about a dozen mail-order companies that carry Korg. After phoning them all, you learn that the prices are all roughly equal. About the only distinction you can make among these companies is in their distribution. The one that has the best inventory, the safest packaging, and the shortest delivery time is likely to get and keep your business.

Even in cases where some distinction does exist among prices and products, distribution can play an important role in customer satisfaction. If you have to reorder an item because a shipment was lost, or have to drive across town because only one retailer carries what you want, distribution problems have eroded your satisfaction. When companies are putting together programs to ensure customer satisfaction, they must remember some of the pedestrian details involved in distribution so that all aspects of a customer's searching, purchasing, and ownership are satisfying.

Providing your distribution channel partners with superior customer service is also important. Like end customers, wholesalers and retailers will stay loyal to manufacturers that meet their needs and expectations. Deere & Company is an equipment manufacturer that has treated its dealers well for years, and the dealers stay loyal. Deere realized this when it introduced a line of four-wheel-drive tractors plagued with problems. Rather than spend their energy blaming Deere, the dealers worked hard to fix the tractors, and Deere survived its blunder with little loss of market share.[28]

Even though it now has state-of-the-art manufacturing technology and industrial capability to match rivals around the world—and is a major supplier of parts and materials to some of the world's most respected corporations—Taiwan continues to have an image problem when it comes to quality.

## THE MARKETING DEPARTMENT'S CONTRIBUTION TO PRODUCT QUALITY

Although the marketing department doesn't typically manufacture goods or perform services for final customers, it still plays a big role in a company's efforts to create quality products. Marketing people contribute in several important ways: helping everyone in the organization understand customer needs, setting quality standards, and ensuring quality marketing communications. Here's a closer look at each area.

## Understanding Customer Needs

The marketing department frequently takes the lead in understanding a company's customers, particularly when the marketing research function is part of the marketing group. Whoever is in charge of collecting market information makes sure that accurate and meaningful information is collected, appropriate conclusions are drawn, and the information gets to everybody inside the company who needs it. The importance of this task can't be overstated: The cornerstone of providing quality products is understanding the needs, wants, and expectations of the customers one hopes to serve. Also, sales and marketing groups are (or should be) in frequent contact with customers, and it's important for them to channel informal feedback from customers back to the appropriate people inside the company.

## Setting Quality Standards

A task closely related to this information-gathering and distribution process is setting standards for product quality. Understanding customer expectations is important because quality standards frequently involve trade-offs. When Yamaha or another stereo manufacturer decides to gold-plate electrical connections in a compact disk player, it increases reliability but also increases price. Similarly, car manufacturers can spend more time and money in the design stage to improve quality, and this involves trade-offs in both return on investment and time to market. The sales force may want to get the product on the market quickly, the engineers would like to spend as much time as it takes to perfect the product, and the finance department wants to make sure the project meets return-on-investment goals. As a representative of the marketing function, you may be called on to mediate, to make sure that your company delivers the right level of quality while balancing internal financial objectives.

Marketers use two kinds of product quality standards. The first addresses the number of defects. You hear a lot of talk in the business world about "zero defects," which is a rallying cry for many quality-intense manufacturers (see Exhibit 21.7 for an example). The second kind of standard is a measure of overall "goodness." To illustrate the difference, consider an espresso machine made by Krups. On the one

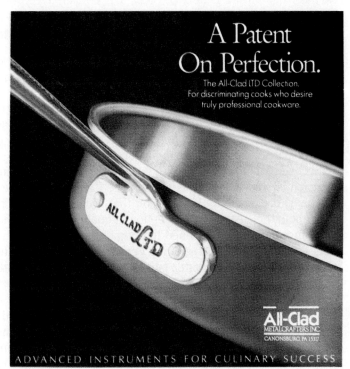

**Exhibit 21.7**
**IN PURSUIT OF PERFECTION**
All-Clad Metalcrafters promotes the idea of totally fault-free quality in this ad.

hand, neither Krups nor its customers want an espresso machine that fails to operate properly. This deals with the number of defects. On the other hand, there are levels of quality above and beyond just the basic operation that allow Krups to add more quality. The steaming cup can be standard or stainless steel, for example. The machine will operate with either grade of steel, but it will last longer and look better with stainless steel.

## Ensuring Quality Marketing Communications

Communications are a big part of quality, in two important ways. First, quality products require quality marketing. This means that everything the marketing department does must support the company's position as a quality supplier. Advertising, sales promotions, seminars, and all other communication-related activities have to reflect a commitment to quality. For instance, you won't see tasteless TV commercials or cheaply printed brochures for Mercedes-Benz; this would detract from customers' perceptions of the manufacturer.

Second, one aspect of quality products is valuable, useful information provided to potential and current customers (see Exhibit 21.8). Particularly with complex products, the quality of information that accompanies the product can profoundly affect both the customer's perception of quality and his or her eventual satisfaction. This information isn't confined to operating manuals or other postsale documentation; marketing groups frequently generate educational materials that are designed to help both before and after purchase. These items include product usage hints, application guides, and newsletters that both educate and promote. The information contained in these documents helps customers make the right purchases, and it contributes to—or potentially detracts from—their satisfaction.

Consider Brüel & Kjaer (B&K), which manufactures instruments for measuring and analyzing sound. B&K faces several major marketing hurdles. First, the field of acoustics is complex, and users tend to avoid suppliers that aren't experts themselves. Second, B&K is located in Denmark, which isn't known around the world as

The answer, obviously enough, was to improve product quality. Motorola embarked on a quest the company calls "Six Sigma." This is a statistical measure that represents 99.9999998 percent perfection. This means that out of every million units produced, Motorola wants to see only 3.4 defects. Six Sigma is practiced and preached as a religion at Motorola, and it applies to more than just the production lines. Clerical workers strive for perfect documents, managers strive for perfect decisions, and marketing communications people strive for perfect advertisements. In addition, any procedure involving customers aims for the same goal. Since the introduction of Six Sigma at the beginning of 1987, both sales and earnings have jumped 20 percent annually. Two examples of its recent success: Motorola is now the world's leading producer of cellular telephones, and it holds the largest share of the personal pager market in Japan.

In recognition of its strides in quality, Motorola was awarded one of the first three Malcolm Baldrige National Quality Awards. Started in 1988, this program subjects entrants to the scrutiny of quality professionals from industry, academia, and government. The screening process is rigorous and thorough; winners are rightly justified in boasting about their success—and boast Motorola does. Its ads now trumpet the company's near-perfect manufacturing and customer service processes, and the Baldrige Award is featured prominently.

By responding to customer dissatisfaction, Motorola was able to rebuild its status in world markets, albeit in some new-product categories. All the attention focused on the company after the Baldrige Award just further strengthens its position as a supplier of very high-quality goods and service. Customers now automatically assume they'll get perfect products from Motorola, which is quite a shift in just 10 years. Oh, by the way: Motorola is working on a method that could reduce defects to two per *billion,* and the company vows not to stop until it does everything with absolute perfection.

## APPLY YOUR KNOWLEDGE

**1.** How could a competitor respond to Motorola's "we won the Baldrige Award" ads?
**2.** What changes should Motorola implement if one of its competitors should happen to win the Baldrige Award?

a center of advanced technology. Third, B&K competes worldwide with several much larger multinational electronics firms. In spite of these difficulties, B&K is one of the leading suppliers in this market segment, and a major reason for its success is the quantity and quality of information it generates. This information positions B&K

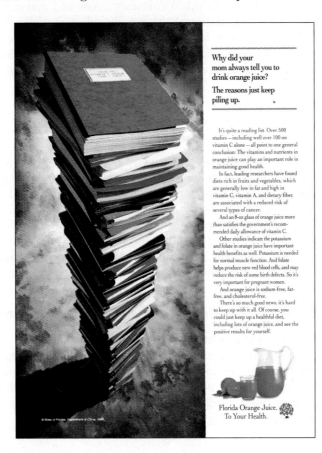

**Exhibit 21.8
THE VALUE OF
INFORMATION**
This ad (from the State of Florida Department of Citrus), provides lots of information to back up the claim that orange juice is good for you.

as the expert supplier and helps it overcome the potential weaknesses of being a small company from a small country.

## Participating in Quality Improvement

Companies around the world have been eagerly adopting new management techniques in the hope of increasing product quality, although as noted earlier regarding TQM, not all these efforts prove fruitful. One of the more popular innovations is the **quality circle,** an informal team of people who meet to analyze problems involving quality and processes and to recommend solutions to management.[29] Thousands of U.S. companies use quality circles involving hundreds of thousands of employees. The benefits start with improved quality, but quality circles can also offer suggestions leading to higher productivity, increased motivation, and greater job satisfaction.

**quality circle**
An informal group of people who meet to diagnose and solve problems with processes and product quality

Quality circles are used most often in manufacturing environments, but they work well with any process that leaves room for improvement. To increase the quality of sales training, for example, you can pull together a team of the trainers, sales staff, and other interested parties. Moreover, quality circles aren't restricted to the production of goods and services. Sometimes they focus on processes rather than on products. A quality circle at Westinghouse Corporation saved the company over $600,000 a year when it suggested that suppliers be forced to stop excessive shipments to Westinghouse factories.[30]

Another quality improvement process that is gaining momentum around the world is **quality function deployment (QFD),** a powerful tool for translating the customer's desires and expectations into products. QFD works by linking customer requirements with engineering and design requirements. For example, if the customer says, "I want fast computer graphics," the QFD methodology will lead you to the technical specifics that produce fast computer graphics. The most important benefit of QFD is that it forces you to systematically think from the customer's perspective. You can't add features to a product because you like them, because your last product had them, or because the competition offers them. QFD links all product attributes to identified customer needs and makes sure the product fulfills the customers' expectations—the new definition of quality.[31]

**quality function deployment (QFD)**
A technique for evaluating customer needs and linking those needs to product features; the result is higher-quality products that do a better job of meeting customers' expectations

Now that you've had a chance to examine the new perspectives on quality and customer service, the following section explains in more detail how companies can establish the necessary systems and environments to deliver superior customer service.

# A PLAN FOR CUSTOMER SERVICE

Companies that score high in customer service share several important characteristics. First, they are obsessive when it comes to listening to customer wants, needs, and expectations. Second, they have a clearly defined and clearly communicated service strategy. Third, the systems put in place to provide service are "customer-friendly," that is, they are designed to treat customers well at each step of the transaction. Fourth, these companies are full of service-oriented people.[32] How can a company develop these traits? This section describes the steps most commonly recommended to increase the customer service capabilities of any organization.

## STEP 1: Understand Customer Expectations

The first and last measure of customer satisfaction is whether you live up to customers' expectations. Therefore, the logical place to start is by understanding just what those expectations are. You can then establish goals to help focus the firm's energy on the areas most important to customers. Naturally, the service goals for a given company depend on its customers' expectations, the competition, and its own service strategy.

Although marketers try to identify the specific standards of customer satisfaction to meet for each market segment, certain universal standards provide a good starting point. Various customers place different priorities on the following attributes, and buyers may not even consider some of them. However, a company should check each one just to be sure.[33]

## VALUE/PRICE RATIO

Of course, customers like to get as much value as possible in return for the prices they pay. The **value/price ratio** measures the value that customers receive as a function of the price they have to pay. You can improve this ratio either by raising the value or by lowering the price. Men's Wearhouse, a Texas-based retail chain, sells some of the same brands as upscale department stores, but it increases its attractiveness by lowering prices.

**value/price ratio**
A measure of how much value customers get in exchange for the price paid

Remember that market segmentation is an important step in setting the correct value/price ratio. Men's Wearhouse doesn't target the same customer segment as Nordstrom, for example, even though the two stores are selling essentially the same products in many cases. Nobody drives a car with license plate frames saying "I'd rather be shopping at Men's Wearhouse." Its customers place more emphasis on price, whereas Nordstrom customers appreciate the atmosphere and prestige associated with that store, and they are willing to pay extra.

## PRODUCT QUALITY

It doesn't matter whether you're buying a space shuttle or a paper clip; you want the product to conform to your expectations. This point can't be emphasized too strongly: All the advertising, discounting, or customer service smiles in the world won't carry the burden of a poor-quality product. Remember, quality must be defined and communicated in terms that are relevant to each customer. Customers don't care whether you're 97 percent perfect in dealing with your customer base overall; they want you to be 100 percent perfect when you're dealing with them specifically.

Assume you're ordering a new winter jacket. You get fast, courteous service when you dial the toll-free number. They have the right jacket in stock, in your size and in your favorite color. The jacket arrives within a few days, just as the person promised. You throw it on and head out the door into a 10-degree January morning, only to discover that the zipper doesn't work. At this point, you don't care that everyone else who has ever bought this jacket received a functioning zipper, or that every other aspect of your transaction was perfect. You're standing outside on a freezing day, and as far as you're concerned, you've got a big quality problem on your hands. To avoid situations like this, the people at L. L. Bean and other top companies work relentlessly, day after day, checking every product in every order, to make sure that product quality problems don't occur and leave you out in the cold.

## FEATURES AND BENEFITS

Every customer has some minimum level of required product features, together with the benefits those features provide. As with product quality, you can't dance around feature and benefit shortcomings: If your product doesn't meet the minimum requirements of your target customers, wrapping a marketing program around it makes no sense. Levi Strauss discovered this when it attempted to expand its product line by introducing a line of men's suits. In addition to problems with the retail channel and other aspects of the marketing mix, the suits weren't designed for custom tailoring, and they carried the Levi's label. In prelaunch research, target customers rejected these two attributes, but Levi's proceeded, on the hope that a massive promotion campaign would overcome customer objections. The plan didn't work, and the company lost millions of dollars on the venture.[34]

## WARRANTIES AND GUARANTEES

Nobody wants to purchase a product without some reassurance that the supplier will make good on promises of performance and quality. A common technique is to offer to refund the purchase price or to replace a defective product in the event that a product fails after purchase. Beyond the legal assurances they give customers, warranties and guarantees give companies a strong message for advertising and sales promotions, and they provide employees with additional encouragement to do the job right the first time.[35]

However, situations come up in which even a 100 percent, no-questions-asked, money-back guarantee is not enough. For instance, such a guarantee doesn't repay the time invested by the customer, nor does it compensate for financial or other losses resulting from use of the good or service in question. This is why medical malpractice has become such a big issue in the health-care industry. Patients want more than a refund for bumbled operations; many ask for millions of dollars to compensate for emotional trauma and personal loss. Finally, even the best money-back guarantee doesn't leave the customer satisfied. As Whirlpool puts it, "Customers don't want their money back. They want a product that works."[36] The best way to ensure this is with product quality and customer service excellence, not by relying on warranties.

## PROBLEM RESOLUTION

As noted earlier, a supplier's response to problem situations is an important point of evaluation for consumers. Smart companies know that a dissatisfied customer presents an opportunity, not a problem. Studies indicate that customers who have a problem and are satisfied with the way you resolve it are likely to be even more loyal than customers who routinely experience your ordinary, trouble-free service. The reason is that when customers come to you with problems, you have their attention and consequently the opportunity to clearly demonstrate your commitment to their satisfaction.[37]

Consider IBM's response to service and quality problems. IBM customers report that when the computer goes down, swarms of technicians arrive on the scene, complete with testing equipment, replacement parts, and profuse apologies for the inconvenience. Other IBM employees get through to the customer on the telephone before the problem is fixed, while the technicians are fixing it, and after they have patched things up and gone home. Some people might consider this much attention to be overkill or a waste of money, but it constantly reinforces in the customer's mind that IBM cares and is willing to do anything to please.[38]

## BUYING EXPERIENCE

Another important measure of customer satisfaction is the experience of selecting and purchasing goods and services. Making the process fast, convenient, trouble-free, and as enjoyable as possible is a powerful way to elevate your products above those from the competition. Conversely, even a strong product can suffer from a buying experience that is slow, unpleasant, and full of hassles. Again, various customers will emphasize different aspects, but nobody wants to be served by grouchy clerks or forced to wait weeks for an order to arrive.

Companies that excel in customer satisfaction recognize the importance of the shopping experience. That's why you'll hear someone playing a grand piano in a Nordstrom store, and you'll rarely hear "Please hold, all our lines are busy" when you call Lands' End. When you shop at Williams-Sonoma, you do more than exchange money for kitchenware: You learn creative new approaches and techniques from people who share your passion for cooking. McDonald's managers have been known to send people out to clean the parking lots of next-door competitors so that McDonald's own customers wouldn't have to look at the messes. Texas-based Dell Computer and New Hampshire–based PC Connection will put a computer or accessory on your doorstep within a day or two of your phone order. Just call and tell them what you need; you needn't waste time sitting in traffic or standing in line. All these companies realize that anybody can sell you most of the products they offer, so they try to differentiate themselves based on the shopping experience.

An unpleasant shopping experience, on the other hand, turns customers off. Six out of ten respondents in a survey by *The Wall Street Journal* indicated they had boycotted stores because of the way they were treated. This percentage increases with a customer's income level. Some of the strategies retailers have employed for years are starting to backfire as customers raise their expectations. For example, many department stores are arranged like big mazes, forcing customers to weave through many short aisles to get to commonly purchased merchandise. The idea is to tempt people into buying more than they came for, but customer researchers say the tactic just irritates many shoppers. Similarly, inventory carrying costs force many stores to keep shallow stocks of goods while trying to appease customers with rain checks. However, more and more buyers are losing patience with stockouts and are responding by transferring their business to companies such as Nordstrom, which is noted for its deep inventories, or are staying out of the stores completely and switching to direct-response retailers.[39]

## STEP 2: Establish Customer Priority

University National Bank & Trust in Palo Alto, California, is cited by experts for excellent customer service. However, if potential customers are worth less than half a million dollars, the bank will do everything it can to drive them away. What's the story here? As much as it might like to be, a company can't be all things to all people, and this is especially true regarding customer service. The bank would spread itself too thin if it attempted to serve both high-income and low-income clients. Thus, rather than serve mediocrity to everybody, University National chose to concentrate on great service for one segment. Federal Express might charter a plane to deliver one package, and IBM will send an army of engineers to fix a computer problem, but they won't do it for just any customer. Of course, service leaders would like to jump through flaming hoops for everybody who walks in the door, but they have to set priorities.

Three general groups are significant when you set priorities. The first is your **core customers,** those people or organizations that buy enough of your products to make it profitable for you to offer them extraordinary service in return. If 20 or 30 percent of the market is going to generate most of your sales, these people are your core customers. You are willing to do almost anything to ensure their satisfaction. The second group is made up of customers whose importance is growing and who have the potential to become core customers. Nurture these up-and-comers as much as possible, without letting this distract you from the core customers. The last group is everybody else. It may not be a pleasant choice, and it will likely make service-oriented employees cringe, but these customers simply can't be allowed to dilute your focus on the core customers. Rather than offer them poor service, it's better not to offer them service at all. University National Bank & Trust, for instance, accomplishes this by requiring high minimum balances that exclude potential customers outside the desired service segment.[40]

Of course, University National's choosing high-income people as its core customers doesn't imply that rich people or big companies should always be your top service priority. Kmart, for instance, focuses on the needs of a different economic group and doesn't bother trying to meet the service expectations of people in higher income brackets.

**core customers**
A company's most important customers, distinguished from the rest by their long-term value to the company

## STEP 3: Define Service Goals

Once you've analyzed customers' expectations and picked the specific customer segments you want to serve, define your customer service goals. For example, Deluxe, the largest check printer in the United States, distilled its service goals into five words: "forty-eight-hour turnaround, zero defects." This is simple but powerful. Deluxe's employees take this statement to heart and figure out what it takes to make it come true every time, for every customer. Meanwhile, customers see this statement as a promise of superior performance, and as such, it draws them to this particular printer. McDonald's service goal is even more concise: "Quality, Service, Value, and Cleanliness."

You won't find any generic cookbook for developing service goals; the choice depends on each firm's unique market situation. However, a statement of service goals should have four attributes:

- It must be a nontrivial statement of the company's intentions.
- It must differentiate the company from its competitors. You wouldn't get too inspired by a statement that read "We strive to offer the same level of service as everybody else in town."
- It must be worded in the customers' language, and it must have value to them. Deluxe's customers care about speed and print quality; that's why the firm's goal statement sounds the way it does.
- It must be achievable. United Airlines, for example, should never promise no delayed flights because it can't control the weather, one of the major causes of flight delays. A firm that promises more than it can deliver will upset its customers and frustrate its employees.[41]

Note that customer service goals are always subject to change. For instance, here are some of the goals that Swissair had in 1989:

- 90 percent of calls are answered within 30 seconds
- 90 percent of passengers are checked in within 3 minutes of arrival
- 80 percent of flights are delayed no more than 15 minutes
- Baggage claim time is only 10 minutes between first and last customer
- Complaints on meals are less than 3 percent
- Complaints on staff are less than 1 percent

Swissair is widely considered one of the world's best airlines in terms of customer service, and these goals represent fairly impressive performance. However, in the face of strong competition and demanding customers, Swissair has "raised the bar" on itself. By 1991, the company was pursuing 100 percent customer satisfaction. Instead of answering 90 percent of calls within 30 seconds, for example, Swissair now strives to answer 100 percent of first-class and business-class reservations within 15 seconds and 100 percent of the calls for general reservations within 30 seconds.[42]

In some cases, anything less than 100 percent conformity to customer expectations is unacceptable. Phil Kelly, a vice president of Motorola, has a strong opinion about quality goals that are anything less than perfect. He offers two stark examples of how bad 99 percent quality could be: The U.S. Postal Service would lose 17,000 pieces of mail every hour, and maternity wards in U.S. hospitals would accidentally drop 30,000 babies a year.[43] Isadore Sharp, founder of the Four Seasons Hotels & Resorts, figured the combination of dissatisfaction and word of mouth this way: If each of his hotels satisfies 99 percent of its guests, and the hotels average 400,000 guests per year, that's 4,000 dissatisfied customers. If each one tells 10 other people, that's 40,000 who know about the problem. Multiply that by 25 hotels in the chain, and you end up with 1 million people who don't want to stay at a Four Seasons property.[44]

## STEP 4: Get Internal Commitment from Top to Bottom

It isn't enough for your company president to be committed to customer service; the president doesn't deliver the services. Likewise, it isn't enough for the frontline employees to be committed; without financial and managerial support, these service providers would be unable to satisfy customers, no matter how hard they try. The answer is that everyone in the organization has to be committed. It takes only one flight attendant, one bank teller, or one delivery person to undo the efforts of everyone else in the company.

Commitment to customer service has to be real. It can't be a slogan or an advertising campaign or something for the frontline people to implement. Macy's found this out when it tried to imitate Nordstrom's superior customer service. Once the king of California retailing, Macy's realized it was losing out every time a Nordstrom moved into the neighborhood. Macy's responded by deepening its inventories, liberalizing its return policy, and even hiring people away from its famous competitor to train Macy's employees in the fine art of taking care of customers. The retailer put all the pieces for success in place, but the effort still flopped. The reason? Senior managers weren't truly committed to customer service. The management team thought the new emphasis on service was the job of the sales staff only and didn't do much to help the frontline people. On top of this, over the years Macy's had developed a culture of rules and procedures in which employees focused on pleasing their bosses, not their customers. Before customer service really takes over at Macy's, the managers and the employees will have to work together to change the culture, and that all starts with true commitment.[45]

## STEP 5: Set Customer Expectations

In one sense, customer satisfaction can be viewed as a simple ratio. If the customer's perception of service received is less than his or her expectations, the result is dissatisfaction. If service matches expectations, the customer is probably relieved but not overjoyed (see Exhibit 21.9). On the other hand, if service exceeds expectations, you've created a satisfied customer. One of the major reasons satisfaction leaders are in that position is that they frequently deliver a little bit more than customers expect.

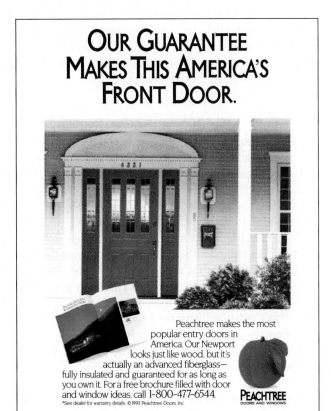

**Exhibit 21.9
CUSTOMER
EXPECTATIONS
OF QUALITY**
Peachtree Doors sets a high level of customer expectation by guaranteeing that its doors will last as long as buyers own their homes.

You can deliver more than your customers expect in two ways: The first is to work harder, spend more, and generally do whatever it takes to pull off miracles. The second way is to carefully manage customers' expectations. The word *carefully* is used here because you don't want to tell your customers to expect terrible service and then surprise them with service that is only slightly horrible. You want to make attractive promises and guarantees that still give you some latitude. If your agency can create an ad by Wednesday, tell the client it'll be done by Thursday. The idea is to estimate the time you need as accurately as possible, and then add a safety margin to cover unexpected delays such as bad weather, mail delays, and so on.

The biggest mistake with customer expectations, obviously, is to set them so high that you can't meet them. United Airlines tried to recapture passenger preference by advertising that it is "rededicated to giving you the service you deserve." If the company can't deliver service now, it gets a double black mark from customers. Not only will customers feel the frustration normally caused by poor service, but they'll feel compounded dissatisfaction because United raised their expectations.

## STEP 6: Establish a Service Infrastructure

Before a company can deliver satisfactory customer service, it has to have the necessary infrastructure in place. For instance, Domino's Pizza couldn't offer speedy delivery if it didn't have the kitchen procedures nailed down, the supplies lined up, and a fleet of delivery vehicles standing by. An infrastructure may be as simple as employees who know how to handle every situation, or it may be a complex international system involving unique diagnostic equipment, teams of engineers and technicians, and delivery mechanisms for spare parts.

## STEP 7: Develop Employees

Customer satisfaction experts are unanimous on this point: The right employees, supported by the right management system, are the key to satisfying customers. This is where all the pieces either fall together or fall apart. When you buy a Big Mac in Boston, it doesn't matter what the McDonald's executives back in Oak Brook, Illinois, are up to at the moment; they aren't delivering the customer service. A relatively low-paid employee, often working strange hours and frequently under intense pressure, is delivering the service. How do companies make sure that service employees can perform? They pay attention to four important fundamentals: selection, training, support, and compensation.

### SELECTION AND TRAINING

Not every employee is a good fit for customer service positions, particularly those jobs that require a lot of customer contact. An employee who just doesn't fit can make an expensive infrastructure meaningless. Because of this, strong service providers take extreme pains to make sure they hire the right people. They realize that human nature is not easily trained, and getting people with the right attitude is the only way to succeed.

Once the right candidates have been selected, they need to be trained both in technical job skills and in the type of behavior the company wants them to exhibit. Training practices vary widely, but here are the highlights from some companies that consistently deliver top-notch customer service:

- *Training takes a lifetime.* Training isn't a one-time event that employees are exposed to when they join a firm. It continues throughout an employee's career, enabling the person to respond to changes in technologies, customers, and job requirements.
- *Untrained employees don't deal with customers.* Putting employees on the front line before they're trained is unfair to the employees, unsatisfying for the customers, and unprofitable for the company. L. L. Bean and Lands' End train their telephone

salespeople for at least a week before they answer calls from customers. Merck, a leading pharmaceuticals producer, trains its salespeople for a year or more before they're allowed to hit the streets and start selling.

- *Training is viewed as an investment.* Like customer service, some traditionalists view training as a necessary evil that a company should spend as little time and money on as possible. Not so with the service leaders; they recognize that training employees is every bit as important as building the stores or buying the airplanes.

## SUPPORT

The Amway Grand Plaza Hotel in Grand Rapids, Michigan, uses an organization chart that puts all the players in the right perspective. Traditional organization charts are pyramid shaped, with the highest-level manager at the top and successively lower-level employees shown at lower levels of the pyramid. Customers are usually not even shown in a typical chart. The Amway Grand Plaza, however, uses a concentric chart, much like a target. Customers are shown at the bull's-eye, the most valuable spot on the target. Surrounding the bull's-eye, at the second most valuable position, are front-line employees who actually deliver the service. Managers are shown in the outermost circle, supporting the employees who support the customers (see Exhibit 21.10). This might seem like a simple piece of paper that anybody could dream up, but it profoundly emphasizes this hotel's commitment to support its employees and satisfy its customers.[46]

Companies that want to deliver customer service must give up some of the traditional managerial controls in order to allow front-line employees to think on their feet and make decisions that best fit each customer. **Employee empowerment** is the term used to indicate the transfer of decision-making authority to those employees on the front line. In other words, it is giving employees the power to solve problems in the way they consider most appropriate for their customers. Implicit in this transfer of power is management's trust and confidence in its employees, who sometimes really have to reach to keep customers happy. For instance, a regional manager at UPS once untangled a misdirected shipment at Christmastime by redirecting two company-owned 727s and hiring an entire train to carry the packages, all before checking with his bosses. If UPS employee policy had forced him to ask

**employee empowerment**
Transferring decision-making power to front-line employees so that they are better able to satisfy customers

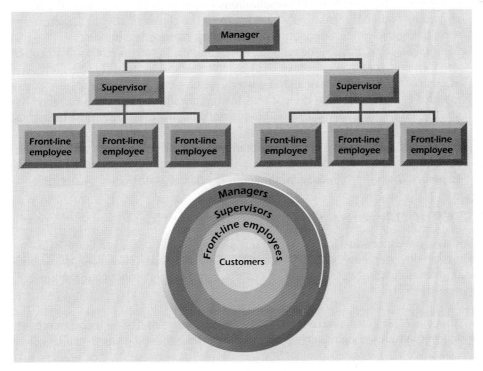

**Exhibit 21.10**
**PUTTING CUSTOMERS, EMPLOYEES, AND MANAGERS IN PERSPECTIVE**
The traditional organization chart is a hierarchy in the shape of a pyramid, with the highest-level managers at the top and the front-line employees, who actually deliver services to customers, at the bottom. The customer-centered organization, on the other hand, puts customers at the center and surrounds them with the front-line employees. Each successive level of management is drawn around the core of customers and front-line employees, indicating that management's role is to support the people who are delivering the service.

permission before taking such extraordinary action, chances are UPS would never have been able to deliver the packages on time. (By the way, he was rewarded by top management for his actions.)[47]

## COMPENSATION

Money is obviously the most important form of compensation, but it isn't the only thing companies should use to motivate employees. Whether you're wiping down tables at Wendy's or designing a skyscraper for a real estate conglomerate, a range of performance is possible in your job. The best way to help you achieve the highest possible performance is to motivate you with the promise of rewards and recognition. This is particularly true in positions with a lot of public contact because these jobs can be particularly frustrating and personally challenging. It takes a special kind of compensation system to motivate employees who have to face extreme pressure.

Even if they don't come under fire from angry customers, service providers are always asked to be pleasant, efficient, sensitive, creative, and productive. Quality and customer satisfaction leaders know that rewards and recognition are the way to motivate employees to perform. Here are some common techniques:

- *Money.* Plain old money is a pretty good motivator for most people. This can be in the form of bonuses, profit sharing, raises, or stock options. LensCrafters' Horizon Club, for example, allows local managers to submit the names of employees who've delivered exceptional service. The top 100 get bonuses of $100, and the top 5 get $1,000.[48]
- *Valuable rewards.* Instead of money, some employers substitute incentives of substantial value. For example, American Airlines and Ryder use vacation travel awards to motivate service employees. Prizes are often considered more valuable if they are exclusive. Both Acura and Southern Bell, a regional telephone company, give away prizes that aren't available any way other than through the companies' motivation programs.
- *Symbolic rewards.* Sometimes it doesn't take money or prizes; the recognition of peers and managers is enough. Money is important to people, of course, but admiration from one's peers can be a powerful reward and motivation as well.
- *Celebration.* LensCrafters, American Express, and Pizza Hut are among the many companies that celebrate the contributions of top performers at annual dinners and other events. By making these employees the center of attention, companies send the signal to the troops that superior performance is a big deal.
- *Meaningful work.* Finally, meaningful work can be a powerful motivator in and of itself. Giving employees a sense of pride and purpose in what they're doing can often accomplish more than all the posters, parties, and slogans. Federal Express founder Fred Smith made it clear that his organization did a lot more than ship stuff when he said, "We do something important. We carry the most important commerce in the history of the world." FedEx employees throughout the company echo Smith's sense of purpose. And people at Walt Disney World don't consider themselves workers at a theme park; they're part of the act, that special performance that goes on every minute of every day at Walt Disney World.[49]

## STEP 8: Measure Customer Satisfaction

Because customer satisfaction determines a company's success or failure, make an effort to discover how satisfied your customers really are. Consider these findings from a comprehensive study of customer satisfaction conducted for the U.S. government:[50]

- About one-third of all households report having been dissatisfied with a purchase.
- Many don't bother complaining because they don't think it's worth the trouble.

- Many of those who complain aren't satisfied with the response.
- Both purchase dissatisfaction and unsatisfactory response result in defections to competitors.
- On the positive side, understanding and responding to customer dissatisfaction can dramatically increase a company's market share and profitability.

Clearly, businesses do whatever they can to get inside the hearts and heads of their customers. When you measure customer satisfaction, look beyond your own customer base. Find out how satisfied your competitors' customers are; maybe you've got what will make them happy. Then again, maybe they're more satisfied than your own customers, in which case you'd better get your act together while you've still got some customers. Also, don't forget about your partners in the various marketing channels. Treat them as customers too, with distinct needs and expectations. The more satisfied you keep the channel, the more it will sell to final customers.

Above all else, keep in mind why you're measuring satisfaction in the first place, and that is to affect the decisions you make in your attempts to keep customers satisfied.[51] Experts caution not to conduct satisfaction surveys if management isn't ready and able to fix any problems that come up; uncovering dissatisfaction, then not doing anything about it will lower employee morale.[52]

## STEP 9: Search for Complainers

In a classic case of not hearing what customers were saying, Donald Burr once claimed in a TV interview that his airline, People Express, had the best service. Interviewer Leslie Stahl challenged him, saying that customers called the airline "People Distress," adding that Burr couldn't possibly claim to offer the best service. Burr repeated that his airline had "absolutely" the best service. Several months later, People Express was in financial trouble and had to merge with Texas Air because, in the words of two customer satisfaction experts, "its abominable service had alienated customers." Yet the airline's chairman felt so confident about the service his company was offering that he boasted about it on national television. How could he have been so wrong?

Burr's mistake provides a stark example of why companies actively search for dissatisfied customers. He relied on complaints filed with the Department of Transportation as the measure of customer satisfaction. Based on the number of complaints filed against People Express, Burr concluded his company was doing just fine. The problem is that very few airline customers ever bother to complain to the federal government. They'll just switch to another airline, and tell all their friends and neighbors along the way.[53]

Researchers estimate that one-quarter of the customers of the average U.S. business are dissatisfied at any given moment. However, only a small portion of these upset customers bother to complain. The overwhelming majority, as many as 95 percent in some cases, will just quietly walk away. Furthermore, in the case of big-ticket products, the intent to repurchase after a dissatisfactory experience drops from over 50 percent (when consumers complain and are satisfied with the response) to less than 10 percent (when they don't bother to complain). Successful marketers figure out why these people aren't satisfied and take steps to correct the problems they uncover.[54]

Finding out what it takes to satisfy customers and then putting the systems in place to make sure they stay satisfied will be the primary challenge for many businesses in the coming years. Competition is getting too intense and customers are getting too frustrated for companies to limp along with poor quality and customer service. Aside from all the technological advantages, breakthroughs in marketing science, and clever promotional tactics, the companies that enter the twenty-first century in a winning position will be those that recognize the value of satisfied customers.

One more thought before ending this chapter. Companies that excel at customer satisfaction talk about the "moment of truth," a term coined by Jan Carlzon, president of Scandinavian Airlines. The moment of truth is the period of time in which the customer comes in contact with the company and is going to come away with either a positive or negative impression. Satisfaction leaders strive to turn every moment of truth with every customer into a winner. As you consider the concepts and techniques presented here, remember that the grand strategies and words of wisdom all come down to people helping people during these moments of truth in order to make quality and customer service real.[55]

# SUMMARY OF LEARNING OBJECTIVES

## 1. Express the new meaning of quality.

Quality is now considered the degree to which a product conforms to customers' specifications. This goes beyond the traditional views of reliability, durability, and so forth, by encompassing the right product definition. Furthermore, it applies to services, ideas, management, administration—to any product or process involved.

## 2. Clarify the new meaning of customer service.

The traditional view held customer service to be a distinct set of tasks, such as order processing, repair, and complaint handling, performed by a department dedicated to these functions. The new view holds that everything companies do to add value and increase customer satisfaction is a part of customer service. Moreover, the customer service function is too important for one department; the entire company must work on it.

## 3. Explain the importance of delivering quality products and superior customer service.

Delivering quality products and superior customer service gives a business several important advantages: competitive barriers, loyal customers, increased differentiation, decreased marketing costs, and increased prices. This is im-

# A CASE FOR CRITICAL THINKING

## Meeting a Marketing Challenge at L. L. Bean

Seems like everybody loves L. L. Bean, and the reason is simple: The company lives to satisfy its customers. Just as L. L. himself once drove a van 500 miles to deliver a canoe, the company's employees often drive to tollbooths on Maine's Interstate 95 to deliver hiking or camping equipment to vacationing customers. That kind of personal service has made Bean one of the world's premier mail-order companies.

However, back in 1912, L. L. Bean was just another avid hunter with cold, wet feet. He figured that others must have the same problem, so he launched his catalog business with a rather improbable product called the Maine Hunting Shoe. The hybrid boots were fashioned from leather uppers and rubber bottoms, and even though they looked preposterous, they did keep Bean's feet dry, so he wrote and mailed fliers advertising the boots. Eventually, he sold 100 pairs; unfortunately, 90 fell apart. True to his word, Bean promptly gave all the dissatisfied customers their money back; from the very beginning, the company has had a 100 percent unconditional guarantee that lets people return any product at any time for a replacement or refund.

Unfazed by his initial failure, Bean borrowed more money to redesign the boots until they were as good as his guarantee, and the Maine Hunting Shoe became an enduring symbol of Bean's credo: Provide customers with uncompromising quality and service, and they'll be yours for life. As the years passed, however, the company's quality and service slipped, and business began to suffer.

When Bean's grandson, Leon Gorman, became president in 1967, he spent a decade revitalizing Bean with innovative programs designed to shore up its sagging quality and service image. With New England's can-do tradition, each division responded enthusiastically to Gorman's challenges. He asked the industrial engineering department to cut turn-around time on tailored trousers, and they devised a system portant in all industries, but it is crucial in situations where the expected products can't be strongly differentiated from the competition. By increasing quality and customer service, marketers increase the value they offer to their customers.

### 4. Examine the effect quality and customer service can have on the marketing mix.

Quality and customer service can affect the marketing mix in several ways. First, product design determines quality both through the traditional measures of goodness and through the new measure of how well a product conforms to customer expectations. Added value and serviceability are also parts of this notion of quality. Second, pricing needs to be reexamined, both from the standpoint of premium pricing and to consider the potential profit squeezes that customer service activities can cause in the short term. Third, quality and customer service can be used to position a company more competitively. However, promoting quality and customer service can be difficult: Customers have heard it all before, and they want proof. Fourth, distribution plays an important role in customer satisfaction; in some cases, it can be the primary determinant of satisfaction.

### 5. List ways companies can add value to basic goods and services.

Among other ways, a company can make purchase and use more convenient, it can be more tolerant of customer errors and more flexible in general, it can personalize the attention given customers, and it can add value by providing helpful information.

### 6. Explain marketing's contribution to ensuring product quality.

The marketing department can contribute to product quality in at least four ways. First, the marketing research function is responsible for making sure that the company gets accurate, timely information about customer needs and expectations. Second, marketing can play a big role in setting quality standards, based on what it knows about customers' needs. Third, marketing is responsible for ensuring quality communications, not only in terms of positioning based on quality and customer service but also in providing value-added information. Fourth, marketing people can be called on to participate in quality improvement efforts such as quality circles and quality function deployment.

### 7. Describe a plan for delivering superior customer service.

Any such plan has nine stages: (a) Understand customer expectations. (b) Prioritize customers based on their long-term value and define a strategy that will drive all your customer service efforts. (c) Define customer service goals. (d) Get commitment from everyone in the company. (e) Set customers' expectations slightly below the level at which you can actually deliver. (f) Establish a service infrastructure so that the company can deliver the necessary service. (g) Develop employees who can deliver the service customers want. (h) Measure customer satisfaction to make sure you're meeting customers' expectations and beating your competition. (i) Search for complainers to uncover reasons for dissatisfaction that can cause defection to competitors.

that trimmed alterations by almost half a day. The operators working the 24-hour telephone lines were trained in communication skills and detailed product knowledge to help them provide great service on every call. Even part-time employees were given nearly two weeks of training to help them maintain Bean's standards during the busy autumn and Christmas seasons. Also, to make sure that complaints and inquiries got handled quickly and correctly, Gorman instituted procedures to track these special cases until they were successfully resolved.

To make buying easier, the company redesigned its catalogs to illustrate that customer satisfaction and comfort were L. L. Bean's primary goals. New items weren't included until they could be extensively field-tested by Bean employees. To support the catalogs, two 24-hour toll-free numbers were added, one for ordering and one for questions and complaints. In addition, the company sent customers free data

sheets that answered questions about outdoor activities and offered suggestions on related clothing and equipment. Bean also made inventory management and fast, accurate order fulfillment two of its highest priorities.

By 1988 it was clear that Leon Gorman's return to Bean's traditional strengths and values was paying off. The company posted almost $600 million in sales and had over 5,000 full- and part-time employees. However, the strain of Bean's spectacular growth rate threatened to undermine much of the progress that had been made, so Gorman launched a new service campaign urging employees to "get it right the first time." He also instituted an 18-month, $36 million program dedicated to improving customer service.

Leon Gorman hopes that the company's rededication to 100 percent customer satisfaction will inspire employees to surpass rather than merely maintain Bean's high standards. Most seem ready to try. As manufacturing division director

Mert Greenleaf said, "We subscribe to L. L. Bean's philosophy. Our reason for existence is to serve our customers. It's the correct way to do business."

As L. L. Bean faces a vigorously competitive mail-order market in the mid-1990s, the company is struggling with another set of problems, including competitors' technological edges and global expansion. Lands' End, for instance, has been investing heavily in a computer system to speed up response times for customers. L. L. Bean has not yet played a major role in the growing mail-order markets in Japan and Europe. The company has figured out how to satisfy customers; now it just needs to compete more vigorously with companies that would love a big slice of its market.

**Your mission:** Leon Gorman, president of L. L. Bean, hired you to be the company's first corporate director of customer satisfaction. As part of your job, Gorman asked you to explore various ways of extending and refining L. L. Bean's commitment to high quality and excellent service wherever feasible throughout the company. As you weigh various possibilities, remember that keeping a current customer satisfied is always much easier and more cost-effective than finding a new one. Also, because Bean was a pioneer in customer service, people will probably expect a higher standard from Bean than from others. With these things in mind, consider each of the following situations, and choose the alternatives that will help you meet Gorman's goals.

1. To begin with, develop a service strategy. Your first step is to decide how much emphasis you're going to give to the key elements in the strategy. With that in mind, which of the following do you think would be most important to customers?
    a. Product quality. All Bean products are made to rigid specifications and offer features that people look for and expect in high-quality clothing.
    b. A 100 percent satisfaction guarantee. Bean customers know that if they're not completely satisfied for any reason, they can return the product at any time for exchange or refund.

## KEY TERMS

c. Value/price ratio. People know that the extra money they pay for Bean products is an investment in clothing that will give them years of rugged wear. That durability, along with the company's ironclad guarantee and legendary customer service, makes each Bean product an unbeatable value.

2. Congratulations! Gorman approved the basic service strategy that you presented to him, so you now have the foundation needed to create a formal customer service plan that can be implemented on a companywide basis. As you write the plan, carefully address the major areas that will have the greatest impact on the way the program actually works. Which one of the following do you think should be your first move?

   a. Establish a service infrastructure. High-quality service doesn't just happen. The company must develop a sophisticated internal service network and train people to work within it effectively.

   b. Set customer expectations—but not too high. It's always best if your customers expect a level of service that's slightly lower than you can actually deliver. This will minimize disappointments, and customers will be delighted when they get more than they expect.

   c. Secure the commitment and support of everyone from the president to the janitor. To be consistent, high-quality service must become a top priority throughout the company. When that happens, it will eventually become part of the corporate culture.

3. As you analyze Bean's various marketing communications, you notice that they all carry a very brief unconditional guarantee. Although the same concise statement has served the company well for decades, you realize that a more comprehensive presentation of Bean's renowned quality and service procedures would help differentiate the company from its competition. You decide to write a new customer service guarantee that codifies and clarifies Bean's policies. Which one of the following do you think would make the best focus for the guarantee?

   a. In an age when brand loyalty has all but disappeared, Bean's steadfast commitment to quality and service has earned it the kind of customer allegiance that makes competitors green with envy.

   b. Bean gives customers more than their money's worth. Each product is built to the highest standard of quality, then field-tested, refined, and priced to be a real value.

   c. Shopping at Bean is an enjoyable experience. The company has made easy ordering and fast fulfillment top priorities, so that customers can begin wearing and using the products they buy as quickly as possible.

4. As you begin to consider the selection, development, and training of employees to carry out your service plan, you realize that the most important customer satisfaction battles must be fought on the front lines by people who are equipped to respond quickly, competently, and efficiently. Rapid response is even more crucial when problems occur; that's why employees must be empowered to act decisively without checking with management. Which of the following alternatives would you recommend as being the single most important step that L. L. Bean could take to truly empower the company's employees?

   a. Institute comprehensive product education and customer service training programs. These steps will give employees the information and self-confidence they need to answer questions, make helpful suggestions, and solve problems.

   b. Encourage management to promote a corporate culture that's so service-oriented that anyone who doesn't go the extra mile to satisfy customers will feel out of place.

   c. Hold regular seminars that deal with the many facets of Bean's unique brand of high-quality service and how to deliver it most effectively. The ultimate goal is to convince employees that they have the ability and autonomy to do whatever it takes to keep customers satisfied.

## SPECIAL PROJECT

During a staff meeting, Gorman points out that smart businesses don't avoid complaints but seek them out. He emphasizes that a dissatisfied customer can damage Bean's reputation for quality and service by complaining to friends and neighbors rather than to the company. In addition, he points out that recent studies have established that a company's most satisfied customers are often those who've had a problem that was resolved quickly and satisfactorily. So customer *dissatisfaction* actually represents an opportunity for a company to win a friend for life.

What disturbs Gorman most is that other studies have shown that many *noncomplainers* may actually be dissatisfied but may never have taken the time to register their complaints. Gorman feels that these people may pose the biggest challenge because you can't fix what doesn't appear to be broken. Gorman asks you to outline how Bean can effectively listen for noncomplainers.[56]

# QUESTIONS FOR DISCUSSION

1. How would you measure the success of the "moment of truth" for an auto insurance company? Explain your answer, and be sure to remember all the opportunities for customer interaction that an insurance company has.

2. Financial services (banking, insurance, and so on) is a notoriously difficult area to compete in because every innovation can be quickly and easily duplicated by competitors. How could you use quality (both perceived and real) to differentiate a financial services firm?

3. Consider a commodity product of the most humble, un-differentiated variety: fill dirt. How could you improve your marketing position with differentiation through superior customer service?
4. What are some of the product attributes that could earn each of the following products a high-quality position in the minds of customers?
   a. Basketball shoes
   b. Scuba gear
   c. Legal services
   d. Diamond earrings
5. What are some potential customer service advantages you could develop for a mail-order compact disk club, such as Columbia House of the Compact Disc Club?
6. Assume you've started a restaurant that will target college students. What are the major customer service standards you'll establish for this business?
7. What are several low-cost ways for a hotel to improve its customer satisfaction rating?
8. What sort of promotional strategy would you put together for a new kind of steel that offers revolutionary strength based on an innovative cold-rolling technique?
9. What personality traits would you look for when hiring an emergency room nurse?
10. What are some steps that an airline could take to empower its employees in the interest of improving customer satisfaction?

## SHARPEN YOUR MARKETING SKILLS

What's the best way to compete in the ultramacho mill-wrighting industry, where a good day's work might include moving a 100-ton cooling system into a factory, hanging a four-story movie screen, or just tooling around in 20-story cranes and trucks the size of railroad cars? Barbara Grogan's secret is to "service the socks off" her clients. Not only is her company, Western Industrial Contractors, a success—it's a success in an industry that is overwhelmingly run by men. (Fewer than a dozen of the nation's 4,600 millwrighting contractors are women.) She also competes with older, larger, better-known companies.

Here's an example of what Grogan means by customer service. She got a call at 6 A.M. from a client whose cement kiln had just been destroyed in an explosion. Three hours later, she had 12 people at the customer's site, and they worked in shifts around the clock for four days repairing the damage. She breaks industry tradition in cases like this by not charging extra when clients are in trouble and need help

fast. As she puts it, "We never take advantage of a client in a bad position." With her enlightened approach to customer service, Barbara Grogan is turning a lot of skeptical companies into committed customers.

**Decision:** Pick an industry that could use some Barbara Grogan–style customer service. Perhaps you're tired of being taken for a ride when you're in trouble, or you'd just like to be treated with respect when you shop. When you've identified a target, list the top three things you'd do to improve customer service in that industry.

**Communication:** Write a one-page (maximum) explanation of how those three things would help a company in the industry improve sales and profits. Pretend you're thinking about buying the company; this document will be included in the loan application that you send to your bank.[57]

## KEEPING CURRENT IN MARKETING

Find an article that describes how a company suffered because of poor quality or unsatisfactory customer service. From the information in the article and your own experience as a consumer, answer as many of the following questions as you can.

1. How are customers responding? Are they exhibiting patience, or are they bolting to the closest alternative source? If they are leaving, do you think they'll come back? How would you summarize the effect that poor quality and customer service have on customer loyalty?

2. How is the company itself responding? How long did the company take to respond? If it is changing the way it does business, what is it doing? How did it handle the issue in public—did it admit mistakes or pretend nothing happened? What happened to the company sales, market share, and profitability? What is the company doing to recapture customers?

3. How are competitors responding? Are they aggressively taking advantage of the company's vulnerability? Do any competitors have obviously superior quality and customer service? Are competitors specifically targeting the company's customers?

# VIDEO CASE

## Leadership through Quality Is Key to Xerox Customer Satisfaction

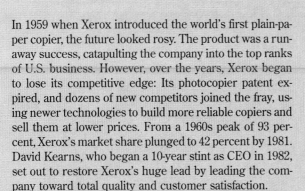

In 1959 when Xerox introduced the world's first plain-paper copier, the future looked rosy. The product was a runaway success, catapulting the company into the top ranks of U.S. business. However, over the years, Xerox began to lose its competitive edge: Its photocopier patent expired, and dozens of new competitors joined the fray, using newer technologies to build more reliable copiers and sell them at lower prices. From a 1960s peak of 93 percent, Xerox's market share plunged to 42 percent by 1981. David Kearns, who began a 10-year stint as CEO in 1982, set out to restore Xerox's huge lead by leading the company toward total quality and customer satisfaction.

Kearns worked with 25 top executives to develop a quality statement to guide the firm's activities. The statement established quality as the basic business principle for Xerox and defined quality as providing external and internal customers with innovative products and services that fully satisfy their requirements. The statement also put the responsibility for quality improvement into the hands of every Xerox employee.

Kearns then implemented a five-point quality strategy dubbed "Leadership through Quality." He worked hard to show his commitment and his senior managers' support for the new focus on quality and service. First, Kearns's team identified appropriate standards and measurements for setting goals and tracking progress. Kearns introduced a nine-step quality-improvement process that helped employees think about the needs of customers and about how to meet those needs.

Second, Kearns had managers study competitors and firms outside the industry to find those with the best way of handling every operation, a technique known as *benchmarking*. For example, Xerox managers identified Federal Express as the model for billing efficiency, Cummins Engine as the model for production scheduling, and other outstanding firms as models for every area within Xerox. The managers then set goals for attaining these high standards, and they continuously evaluated progress toward them. They monitored the accomplishments of competitors in these key areas and set Xerox's goals to meet or exceed those of rivals.

Third, Kearns set up an intensive training program that explained the quality process and the tools to apply it. Xerox employees worldwide were trained, and most took part in problem-solving teams that zeroed in on specific areas of concern.

Fourth, the CEO motivated employees by offering numerous cash awards and staging special events to honor individual achievements. Moreover, Kearns promoted managers who applied the quality process and helped the company move toward customer satisfaction. These people served as role models, and their promotions were evidence of the rewards waiting for those who embraced the company's new values.

Fifth, Xerox launched an ongoing communications effort to spread the quality and service message throughout the organization and showcase the firm's accomplishments to customers. For example, Xerox publishes the magazine *Benchmark* for its customers to show them how the company is working to meet their needs.

During a five-year period, Kearns spent $125 million and devoted 4 million of his employees' work hours to his five-point quality program. He succeeded in mobilizing the entire organization toward better quality and higher customer satisfaction, reducing customer complaints by 60 percent and increasing customer satisfaction by 40 percent. By the time Paul Allaire became CEO in 1991, Xerox had been honored with quality awards in nine countries, including the United States, Australia, Japan, and Mexico. Just as important, Xerox's market share and profits were on the upswing, buoyed by the purchases and loyalty of satisfied customers.

1. Although Xerox has always used a direct channel to sell its products to customers, say that Allaire wants a special distribution strategy to reinforce Xerox's commitment to quality and service. Should he establish a series of well-staffed local showrooms where customers and prospects can view, try, and buy selected Xerox products? Or should he produce a glossy catalog of the entire Xerox line, mail it to customers and to large organizational prospects, and set up a toll-free number for fast service on orders?

2. Because the new Xerox document-handling systems are complex and potentially intimidating to first-time buyers, the company must provide services specifically designed to help customers use this new product more effectively. Should Allaire provide a toll-free number for 24-hour help, or should he provide a free video demonstrating the varied uses of this product?

3. Allaire wants to be sure that Xerox is listening to customer complaints and acting on them to improve customer satisfaction. Should he require his product managers to prepare a yearly report showing the nature of complaints received and the cost of resolution? Or should he include a postage-paid postcard with every product sold and ask customers to address their comments to him so he can examine the nature and importance of the complaints and arrange for fast resolution?

# Marketing Management

**After studying this chapter, you will be able to**

**1.** Link strategic marketing planning with marketing management

**2.** Differentiate between a centralized and decentralized organization structure and list the advantages and disadvantages of each

**3.** Discuss ways of organizing a marketing effort to serve the needs of the company and its customers

**4.** Outline the process of motivating marketing people

**5.** Describe the process of communication within the organization and how information systems fit into this process

**6.** Discuss the task of controlling marketing efforts

**7.** Explain how sales and marketing cost analyses are used to evaluate marketing performance

**8.** Outline the purpose, goals, and use of the marketing audit

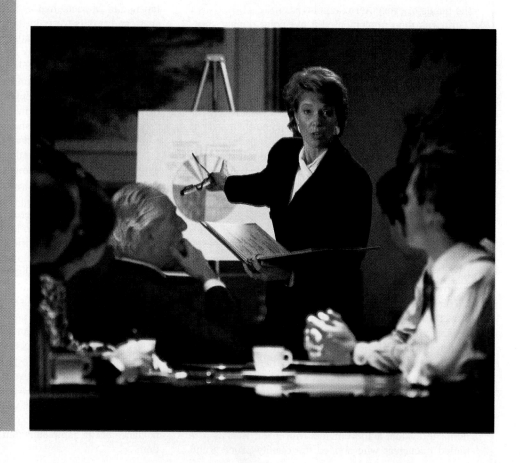

# FACING A MARKETING CHALLENGE AT HEWLETT-PACKARD

## *Keeping a Global Electronics Giant on Track*

People who saw Walt Disney's landmark animated film *Fantasia* also witnessed the birth of a company that is now high on the Fortune 500 list and is a major player in many segments of the international electronics market. Disney's sound effects relied on an innovative signal generator that Bill Hewlett designed as a graduate student at Stanford University. Hewlett teamed up with fellow student Dave Packard, flipped a coin to see whose name would come first, and in 1939 Hewlett-Packard Company was born.

The company now offers thousands of products, from electronic components to computer and instrumentation systems costing hundreds of thousands of dollars. That first signal generator grew into a line of test equipment that can measure just about anything from earth tremors to laser beams. More than half of HP's revenue now comes from computers, printers, and other information-processing equipment.

HP has a reputation for successfully blending attention to product quality with attention to people. Division managers were allowed to run their operations much like independent companies, with their own engineering, marketing, and production facilities. HP gave these managers a great deal of freedom in choosing market segments and designing their marketing mixes. The company was an early proponent of management by objectives (MBO), where employees agreed on their objectives with their managers and then had the freedom to meet those objectives in whatever ways they considered most efficient.

However, as the company grew and diversified, president John Young, Bill and Dave's handpicked successor, realized it was getting harder to maintain the HP culture and satisfy customers in an increasingly complex world marketplace.

He had to balance the desire to give HP people a lot of autonomy with the need to give customers coordinated solutions that combine products from several business units. He had to foster the entrepreneurial spirit that leads to breakthrough products, but he also had to maintain some level of control over the multibillion-dollar company. Young had to make sure that his people stayed in touch with their customers, a diverse collection of government laboratories, small manufacturing firms, multinational conglomerates, hospitals, universities, and a host of others.

Marketing and sales coordination problems can plague any large company, and HP is certainly not immune. In one case, 19 units within the company sold the same type of floppy disks, at prices ranging from $8 to $19. More serious problems were occurring in the sales environment, where salespeople from different parts of the company found themselves calling on the same customers. Marketing communications were inconsistent, with different parts of the company using different strategies, ad agencies, and brochure designs. At one point, the company had more than 50 toll-free numbers for customers to call. The result was inefficiency, missed opportunities, and phone bills that were higher than necessary. From the customer's perspective, these multiple personalities were confusing.

John Young and the people of HP faced a major challenge to keep the company's entrepreneurial culture alive. How would you organize HP to best serve its international customer base? How can the company nurture its collegial atmosphere while competing in the rough-and-tumble global arena? How would you keep the company on track without stifling creativity?[1]

# CHAPTER OVERVIEW

Like many companies in today's challenging markets, Hewlett-Packard realizes that the old way of doing business may no longer be the best way. With such a wide variety of products and customers, Hewlett-Packard carefully considers the way it organizes, implements, and controls its marketing efforts. This chapter starts by linking these three areas with the strategic planning process introduced in Chapter 3. You'll explore an idea that touches on a key point in Hewlett-Packard's thought process: centralized versus decentralized management. After that, you'll investigate the common organizational forms used by today's companies, including organization by function, product, geography, market, and customer. In the next major section, you'll study the implementation of marketing programs, when plans are translated into action. The chapter concludes with a description of marketing control—setting performance standards, evaluating performance, making a marketing audit, and taking corrective action.

# MAKING THINGS HAPPEN IN THE MARKETPLACE

What company invented the personal computer, the laser printer, the computer "mouse," and the copying machine? All four of these breakthrough products were invented by Xerox. Unfortunately, the copying machine is the only one of the four that Xerox was able to turn into a commercial success, and the company's dominance of that market ended when more efficient Japanese producers joined the fray. A lot of companies have benefited from Xerox's work on the other three products, but Xerox wasn't among them.[2] Why should a company that is so brilliant technically have such a hard time making things click commercially?

A company vision that emphasized creative design and engineering excellence gave Xerox a comfortable head start in these product categories, but industry observers say the company was too slow to take advantage of its position. Without effective marketing execution, Xerox's strategy has helped its competitors as much as it has helped Xerox, which highlights one of the most important concepts in this chapter: By itself, strategy is useless. A strategy can't manufacture anything, it can't distribute anything, and it can't sell anything. Nothing happens until you translate marketing strategy into marketing action (see Exhibit 22.1).

How do you make things happen in the marketplace? How do you achieve marketing excellence? Thomas Bonoma, a former Harvard professor and now the head of Benckiser's North American operations (Benckiser is a German consumer-goods company that competes with Procter & Gamble and Unilever), approached this question by breaking the marketing process down into four levels and examining what it takes to succeed at each level:

1. *Fundamentals.* You can't win basketball games if you can't shoot, pass, or dribble. You can't drive a car if you can't steer or brake. And you can't be successful at marketing unless you're good at the fundamentals. Make sure your company is good at selling, advertising, supporting customers, conducting marketing research, and all the other tasks that make things happen in the marketplace. Success—and failure—is often in the details.
2. *Programs.* At the next level up, make sure that the fundamental tasks are conducted as part of coordinated programs. For instance, you can have great advertising and a great sales presentation, but if the two don't support one another, your program might fail anyway.
3. *Systems.* At this level, make sure your monitor-and-control operations help your company. Above the program level, every company has certain systems in place that are designed to monitor and control operations. These systems include the

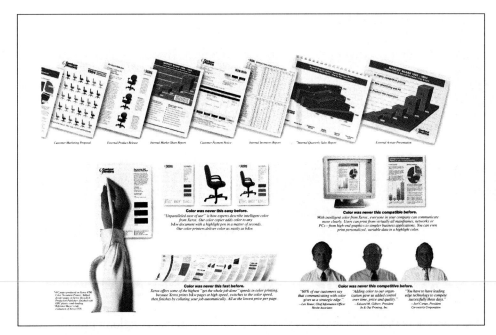

**Exhibit 22.1
TRANSLATING
STRATEGY INTO
ACTION**
By putting new emphasis on marketing and on commercializing its innovative technologies, Xerox is achieving success in new office automation markets.

organizational structure, accounting and budgeting systems, and voice and data communications. Unfortunately, these systems can occasionally hinder, rather than help, the marketing effort. Two examples: an inflexible accounting system that won't let sales managers grant special discounts or an organizational structure that isolates salespeople from the rest of marketing.

4. *Policies.* Be sure your policies and procedures are consistent with your goals. All the written and unwritten guidelines that define a company's culture and direction make up its policies. For example, companies that are famous for good customer service, such as Frito-Lay and American Express, are guided by cultures that emphasize customer service. Whether it's formal employee handbooks or just the general attitude inside the organization, these policies create a climate in which the company can succeed. On the other hand, companies that have unclear or conflicting policies will inadvertently hobble their marketing efforts through confusion and inefficiency. As you might expect, the tone for marketing culture is set by the organization's leaders; poor management rarely leads to marketing excellence. Nucor, a bright spot in an otherwise gloomy U.S. steel industry, gets its marketing orientation from the top down. CEO Ken Iverson makes sure every employee has a marketing orientation, and he makes sure the company has the right policies and procedures in place.[3]

Bonoma's message is that brilliant strategies and creative marketing ideas aren't enough—manage your marketing efforts effectively if you hope to succeed in today's tough markets. Chapter 3 introduced you to the process of strategic marketing planning. Now it's time to complete the process, with the three stages of organizing, implementing, and controlling the marketing effort. As you can see in Exhibit 22.2, the six stages combine to form a continuous loop.

Strategic planning and market management aren't one-time events; they are continuous, dynamic processes, which is why Exhibit 22.2 is constructed as a loop. Strategic planning sets the process in motion; then you implement marketing programs to pursue your objectives. Once the programs are in place, you monitor the results to make sure you'll meet those objectives. If corrective action is required, you reassess the performance of your strategic business units (and perhaps reach different conclusions about your various businesses), reassess your opportunities, change your marketing strategies, or adjust elements of your marketing programs. The first management phase is to organize the people who will make it all happen.

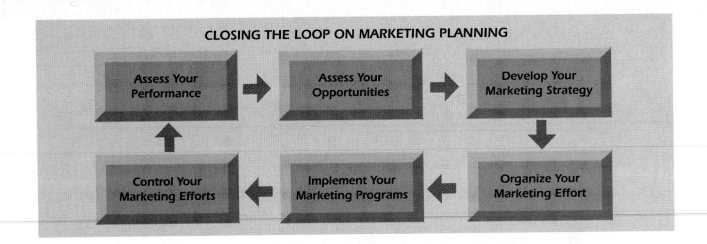

CLOSING THE LOOP ON MARKETING PLANNING

Assess Your Performance → Assess Your Opportunities → Develop Your Marketing Strategy

Control Your Marketing Efforts ← Implement Your Marketing Programs ← Organize Your Marketing Effort

# ORGANIZING THE MARKETING EFFORT

Whether yours is a one-person service firm, a multinational conglomerate, or a non-profit agency, intelligent organization is a prelude to marketing success. An **organizational structure** is a formal plan that defines people's responsibilities and roles in the organization and that gives them the authority to carry out their responsibilities. Marketing is organized differently from firm to firm, depending on the firm's objectives, its marketing mix, and the people who design the organization. Many firms are learning that effective organization can yield competitive advantages, so managers are increasingly concerned about how their firms are organized. Two important issues in marketing organization are the balance of centralization and decentralization and the basic form that the marketing department should have.

## Centralization versus Decentralization

Organizations can be centralized or decentralized to various degrees. A **centralized organization** concentrates authority and responsibility in the hands of relatively few people who are usually located in the same place, such as the home office of the company. A **decentralized organization,** on the other hand, spreads authority and responsibility throughout the organization. Decentralized organizations usually have a number of independent operating units, and each unit has substantial control over its own planning and implementation.

### THE BENEFITS OF CENTRALIZATION

Centralized and decentralized organizations both have advantages and disadvantages. Supporters of the centralized organization claim that this approach allows the firm to take a consistent position toward suppliers, customers, and other groups it must deal with. For example, Eaton Corporation, with over two dozen operating units, decided to centralize marketing communications when it discovered four unrelated ads from four Eaton divisions in the same issue of a magazine.[4] Similarly, Hewlett-Packard found that an extremely decentralized organization causes too many marketing and engineering coordination problems.

Some retailers prefer centralization as a way to provide consistent service. Dillard's, a department store chain headquartered in Little Rock, Arkansas, is an aggressive firm, rapidly growing by buying other chains. Dillard's controls its growth with a strong, centralized organization. The home office wants consistent presentation in each Dillard's store. Newly acquired properties are immediately remodeled and any trace of previous ownership is removed; merchandise assortments are purged of incompatible brands, and the store is made as much like any other Dillard's as possible. Management believes the advantages of consistent presentation and highly similar merchandise assortments in every store outweigh the advantages of treating each city as a separate market segment.[5]

## THE BENEFITS OF DECENTRALIZATION

Critics of centralized structures point out that such arrangements offer little opportunity for lower and middle management to participate in strategic planning. They also observe that, in a growing firm, centralization often means that executives are overloaded. This overload can cause delays in decision making, and costs to the company (as well as the number of unhappy customers) may increase. In addition, employees on the front line often need a great deal of flexibility in order to satisfy customers. Jan Carlzon, former president of Scandinavian Airlines, said that decentralization is especially crucial for service companies because executives don't satisfy customers, frontline employees do. He referred to decentralization as "flattening the pyramid," which means removing some of the layers of hierarchy found in the typical organization.[6] Mazda Motors of America flattened its pyramid in 1993, removing three layers of management in an effort to put the organization closer to its dealers and customers.[7]

One of the biggest pressures to decentralize is the time required to develop products and get them on the market. When engineering and marketing people have the authority to make decisions, they don't spend time asking for approval from endless layers of corporate hierarchy. For instance, Ford, Chrysler, and General Motors discovered that Japanese automakers were cranking out new car designs in three and a half years, compared to five years or more for the U.S. companies. As a result, the Big Three automakers are working to reduce decision-making time during the design cycle.[8] IBM recently opted to give its personal computer business unit free rein to operate as it saw fit. The IBM PC Company responded by increasing its share of the fiercely competitive computer market from 11 percent to 15 percent.[9]

People in favor of decentralization claim that it lets the firm fine-tune its approach to each of its market segments. Decentralized organization recognizes that conditions in one division of a company may not be the same as in another. The people in each division know the strengths and weaknesses of the division better than anyone else, so it makes sense to let the division develop and implement its own programs. One of the most significant moves toward decentralization in recent years occurred at IBM. The computer giant, long noted for its highly centralized structure, broke its operations down into five autonomous groups, each under a general manager.[10] Similarly, Kodak reorganized itself into a *line of business* (LOB) structure when it realized that no single style would fit its diverse business units. Each LOB has its own engineering, production, marketing, and distribution organizations. Furthermore, each LOB makes its own decisions and fails or succeeds according to its own efforts.[11]

The question of centralized versus decentralized control is a big issue for many companies today. Each company must make the decision after examining its challenges and opportunities. According to management expert Rosabeth Moss Kanter, every firm has some periods when centralization is best and others when decentralization is best. She points to the example of GE Medical Systems, where top management provides guidance, support, and long-range stability in strategic planning but gives lower-level people the freedom to act quickly and independently when business conditions dictate.[12]

## Basic Organizational Forms

Whether centrally or decentrally managed, a firm has to have a structure if it is to pursue its goals. This structure can take a number of forms and each has been used at one time or another with success. On the other hand, each has probably been used with poor results as well. Consider the following marketing departments and the conditions under which each works best. (As you read the following descriptions, keep in mind that various organizations use different names for their management positions; the names used here are common but certainly not the only ones in use.)

## THE FUNCTIONAL ORGANIZATION

**functional organization**
An organization structure in which jobs are grouped according to similarity, such as advertising, marketing research, and sales

Functions are jobs that have to be done if marketing is to happen. These jobs can be described and grouped according to purpose. A **functional organization** aligns the marketing department along functional lines, such as product planning, marketing research, advertising, and sales.

Functional organization can be used by small firms or by larger firms with a limited number of offerings in the same market. As Exhibit 22.3 shows, the manager of each department reports to the vice president of marketing. These managers are specialists in the functional areas their departments handle, and this specialization is both a strength and a potential drawback. On the positive side, these specialists can perform their functions better than anybody else. On the other hand, specialists might lose sight of the broader goals of the marketing department. Because of this, the marketing director in a functionally organized firm should take care to coordinate the efforts of these specialists and keep them working toward the marketing department's objectives. As a firm increases in size and its markets become more numerous, keeping the functionally organized marketing department on track can become quite difficult.

## THE PRODUCT-BASED ORGANIZATION

**product-based organization**
An organization structure that uses product managers to handle the marketing mix for each of the products in the firm's marketing portfolio

Also known as brand-management organization, the **product-based organization** adds another managerial position to the organization at the same level as the sales, advertising, marketing research, and product planning managers (see Exhibit 22.4). This *product marketing manager* supervises a group of lower-level executives called *brand managers* or *product managers,* each of whom is responsible for marketing a single product, brand, or product line. Brand/product management is one of the most important jobs in an organization, but it can also be a stressful job when a company operates in uncertain marketing environments.[13]

Procter & Gamble is a pioneering brand-management organization, an arrangement that has worked well for decades. As competition increased worldwide, however, the company realized that it had created too many brand teams, driving up costs in the process. In 1993 the company was reorganized and streamlined in an effort to reduce redundancies and overhead.[14]

The product-based organization makes sense for a company that produces several products (or brands) that appeal to various market segments. If the firm's prod-

**Exhibit 22.3**
**THE FUNCTIONAL ORGANIZATION**

The functional organization is arranged by the various activities that occur in the marketing department.

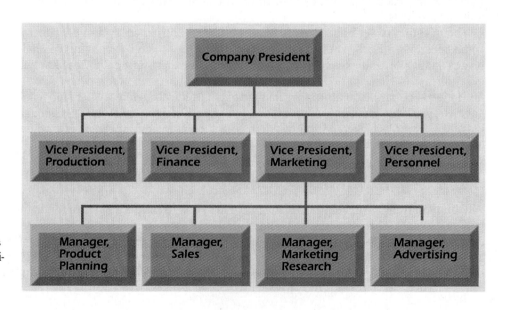

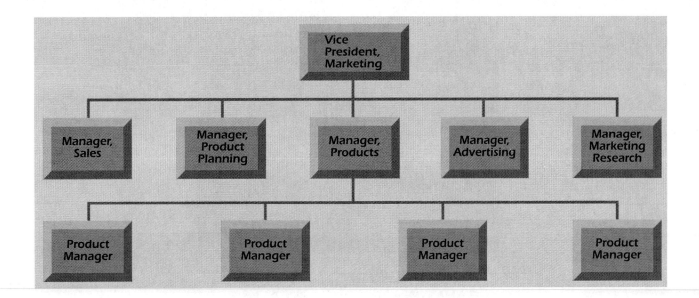

**Exhibit 22.4**
**THE PRODUCT-BASED ORGANIZATION**
The product-based organization expands on the functional organization by adding an executive responsible for all products and a number of product managers responsible for individual products or product lines.

uct mix is large, the organization will include an additional layer of *product group managers* between the product managers and the product marketing manager. Texas Instruments uses a product-based organization. The company's major divisions are the semiconductor group, the defense electronics division, digital products, and metallurgical products. The semiconductor group, for example, is further broken down into specific products.[15] At Texas Instruments, technological similarity and the noncompeting nature of products within a line means each line can be treated like a brand and handled by what amounts to a brand manager.

In the typical product-based organization, placing the responsibility for a specific product or brand in the hands of one person offers several advantages over the functional organization. First, someone takes a personal interest in each product in the firm's product mix. For example, the person in charge of Kraft General Foods' desserts division worries only about Jell-O, Pudding Pops, and related products. This manager doesn't have to worry about Minute Rice, Stove Top Stuffing, Crystal Light, or any of the other Kraft General Foods products that are outside the dessert category.[16] Second, reaction to problems in the marketplace is often more immediate. Managers who can focus on an individual product or a small set of products can often move faster than managers with a large slate of products to worry about. Third, this form of organization is a good training ground for future marketing department managers because they're called on to coordinate the entire range of functional specialties to carry out the plans for their product.

Of course, the advantages of the product-based organization come with some disadvantages. Product managers generally lack the authority to back up their responsibilities and must rely on persuasive interpersonal skills to get the resources they need. Product managers seldom get the opportunity to specialize in any of the functional fields of marketing. Finally, a product orientation can be expensive. For instance, General Electric's major appliance group once had separate marketing, sales, and financial staffs for each product. Realizing that this was costly and inefficient, the company has since merged these staffs into one department.[17]

## THE GEOGRAPHIC ORGANIZATION

The oldest of all the forms of marketing organization is geographic organization. Many companies had this form of organization long before they ever heard of the marketing concept, and the form survives because it allows convenient decentralization of management. **Geographic organization** recognizes that various areas served by the company have different market conditions, and it separates them into geographic territories, assigning a manager to each one.

Geographic organization is useful for a number of reasons. First, population characteristics and customer needs are often different from one geographic region to

**geographic organization**
An organization structure in which jobs are grouped geographically

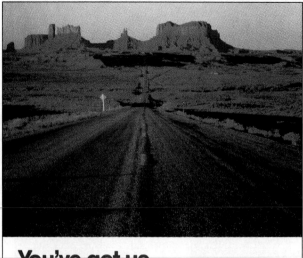

**Exhibit 22.5
INTERNATIONAL
MARKETING
ORGANIZATIONS**
To compete effectively in the transatlantic cargo market, the German carrier Lufthansa set up a marketing organization in the United States to reach customers here.

another. For instance, Apple Computer's regional marketing center in New York City focuses on financial services customers, while its marketing center in Chicago focuses on manufacturing customers.[18] Second, there may be differences in the marketing environment—taxes, transportation systems, regulations, or competition, for example. Third, climate is to some extent a function of geography, and the timing (if not the overall structure) of a company's marketing effort may be affected by this. For example, a Sunkist orange grower in California selling to California customers in the middle of summer has a vastly different problem from an orange grower selling to North Dakota customers in January. The regional approach doesn't always make sense; PepsiCo recently dropped a regional executive structure to focus its programs on a nationwide basis.[19] Humana, one of the nation's largest healthcare companies, uses a form of geographic organization that has been quite successful. In each local market where the company has a hospital, Humana combines the other parts of its business, health insurance and outpatient services, which gives the company a strong presence in each geographic market.[20]

International marketing presents a significant challenge in terms of the marketing organization (see Exhibit 22.5). Marketing specialists in each country can often do the best job of tailoring programs to their individual countries. On the downside, this can be an expensive organizational strategy because you have to duplicate all or part of the marketing department in every country. Hewlett-Packard strikes an affordable balance by using regional marketing centers outside the United States. The company has centers in Amsterdam, Lyon, and Vienna (covering Europe, Africa, and the Middle East); Hong Kong (covering Australia, New Zealand, and most of Asia); and Tokyo (covering Japan). These centers have product and application specialists, as well as product managers responsible for helping customize marketing campaigns for various countries.

**market-based organization**
An organization that directs a unique marketing effort at each market segment in which a firm is active

## THE MARKET-BASED ORGANIZATION

The **market-based organization** recognizes that various segments of the market have different needs and directs a unique marketing effort at each segment in which the firm is active. The management team in charge of each market is responsible for strategic planning, forecasting, and managing the marketing mixes required to satisfy customers.

This form of organization is more often found in firms marketing to industrial customers, but it is catching on with some consumer marketers. In addition to running its Wal-Mart stores, Wal-Mart now operates a chain of DOT deep-discount drugstores, a number of Sam's Wholesale Clubs, three Hypermarket USA stores, and a chain of stores called Helen's aimed at the arts and crafts market. Each of these types of stores aims a distinct marketing mix at a distinct segment of the consumer market, and each has been successful in reaching its segment.[21]

## THE COMBINATION ORGANIZATION

Consider these products: compact disks by Fine Young Cannibals, Def Leppard, and Vladimir Horowitz; the sound and lighting systems at the Olympic Stadium in Barcelona; the 300,000 Magnavox TV sets ordered by Whittle Communications for its Channel One system; the traffic control system for the M25 motorway around London; the vote-counting machine for the Palace of Congresses inside the Kremlin; radar systems for the Brazilian air force; power station equipment in the People's Republic of China; x-ray imaging equipment; and a variety of others ranging from toothbrushes and garage door openers to semiconductors and telephone networks. What do these products have in common? They are all marketed by the Dutch company Philips, or by companies owned by Philips.[22] How could you possibly organize a company to market such a diverse collection of products? How can a company based in a small European country become a major marketing force all over the world? The answer is multiple marketing organizations, each designed for a particular situation.

Firms don't have to organize along only one of the lines presented here. Any or all of these methods can be combined to solve the problems of a particular firm. The resulting hybrid may be functional in some ways, market-based in others, and geographic in others. In cases such as Philips, a variety of organizations can be used.

For instance, the firm represented in Exhibit 22.6 produces four types of products. Each is used differently from the others. Recognizing this, management has decided that a product-based organization will assure that these products are properly handled by the marketing department. On the other hand, management knows that it has two separate markets for its products, each of which differs in its relationships with suppliers. This seems to call for a market-based organization. Therefore, a hybrid organization is created. The product managers of the four products work with the managers of the two markets to create plans suited to the overall needs of their markets. The market managers implement programs that develop market potential over the long term, while the product managers try to maximize

Many U.S. companies establish overseas marketing efforts to help ensure effective marketing efforts in local markets. In addition to sales offices in most countries, Hewlett-Packard maintains regional marketing support centers in five locations around the world.

| | Market Segments | |
| Product Line | Metal products<br>Wholesalers | Hardware<br>Retailers |
| --- | --- | --- |
| Fasteners | Fasteners/Wholesalers | Fasteners/Retailers |
| Sheetgoods | Sheetgoods/Wholesalers | Sheetgoods/Retailers |
| Tubing | Tubing/Wholesalers | Tubing/Retailers |
| Fittings | Fittings/Wholesalers | Fittings/Retailers |

**Exhibit 22.6**
**HYBRID MARKETING ORGANIZATIONS**
Companies with multiple products and multiple markets often find that a hybrid organization is most effective.

sales for their respective products. H. B. Fuller, a manufacturer of adhesives, uses a combination organization to market more than 1,000 products to 100 different industries.[23] Because this type of organization has both horizontal and vertical lines of control, it is often referred to as a *matrix organization*.

## OTHER MARKETING ORGANIZATIONS

Not all marketing efforts emanate from marketing departments inside individual companies. For example, in the luxury hotel segment, very few independent hotels get along all by themselves. Most pool their resources and set up marketing programs that benefit all members. For instance, Preferred Hotels is a marketing system for 75 hotels around the world. By pooling their marketing budgets, members of Preferred Hotels can afford effective advertising and connection to airline reservation systems, among other marketing initiatives. Most important, they gain the freedom to continue operating as distinctive, individual hotels.[24]

Of course, many businesses simply don't have a marketing department. Thousands of small businesses in the United States and around the world get by without a marketing department or with just one or two people dedicated to the marketing function. This places a tremendous burden on business owners and entrepreneurs whose expertise might be in engineering, design, law, or some other profession. Some rely on marketing consultants, some band together in associations, and others try to learn marketing on the fly.

Nonprofit organizations face some special challenges in terms of organization, implementation, and control. To begin with, many nonprofit organizations don't have marketing departments or even a single individual with responsibility for marketing decisions. The other extreme is the organization that believes everyone is responsible for marketing. Some groups believe that formal marketing is inappropriate or not applicable to the nonprofit sector. Others mistakenly equate public relations with marketing and fail to put people in charge of the other marketing functions.[25]

Regardless of the particular structure a marketing organizations uses, a few simple rules apply. First, the organization should produce satisfied customers. Poor communication, unclear responsibilities, and "turf wars" are some of the effects of level of investment. This can work on several levels. If a potential partner in another country already has a key technology, good relationships with important distribution channels, or a strong reputation among customers, you can take advantage of those strengths without investing the time and money needed to develop them on your own. When Electronic Arts, a California video game developer, tried to enter the Japanese market for the second time, it teamed up with Tokyo-based JVC. This partnership gave Electronic Arts such benefits as access to JVC's 500-member sales force. JVC gets to sell the creative products that Electronic Arts is noted for. Such partnerships can be doubly important in fast-moving, competitive markets in which you'll miss strategic windows if you have to develop these strengths on your own.

The third benefit is increased marketing effectiveness, from moving products more efficiently through distribution channels to providing post-sale support to customers. Local businesses already have relationships established with the news media, key customers, retailers, and other entities that are important factors in your success. The faster you can link up with these capabilities, the faster you can start making sales.

Developing successful international partnerships certainly offers some advantages to U.S. marketers, but it is not a fast or easy process. Experts recommend building relationships slowly and carefully in order to minimize the risk of getting stuck in a bad partnership. You can also increase your chances of success by making sure that your potential partners are truly compatible with you before making any commitments.

**APPLY YOUR KNOWLEDGE**

**1.** Why wouldn't Electronic Arts simply choose to establish its own sales force in Japan?

**2.** How might an overseas partnership complicate the process of marketing management?

inappropriate organization that affect customer satisfaction. Second, the structure should promote the efficient use of time, money, and energy. All three of these are precious resources, and if they're being wasted, a clumsy structure is one likely culprit. Third, the organization should encourage the right balance of thought and action. People need enough time to plan and ponder, but in competitive markets, the thinking must usually produce action in a hurry.

## Marketing's Expanding Role in the Organization

The marketing department's role in the company has grown along with the acceptance of the marketing concept. Back when all it did was sell products, marketing's influence on the organization was small. However, the adoption of the marketing concept meant that marketing had to be involved at all levels of the decision-making process. Companies gradually began to modify their organization charts, elevating the marketing manager to a position of equality with the managers of engineering, production, personnel, and finance.

However, being market-driven and being marketing-driven are not the same thing. A market-driven company bases its actions on the needs and expectations of its target markets. On the other hand, a marketing-driven firm is dominated by the marketing department, and this may or may not be the best arrangement for the company and its customers. The marketing department must be an equal partner with research and development, finance, manufacturing, and the other functions in the organization, but it doesn't necessarily have to dominate the company.

A major shift is under way in the marketing departments in many firms, as top managers search for ways to satisfy customers in increasingly complex environments. Some firms have joined with other marketers (even with competitors in some cases) to serve customers better. These *networks* include such innovations as NUMMI, a joint venture between Toyota and General Motors. Among the many implications of these arrangements is a redefinition of the marketing management task. In addition to managing the various marketing functions, marketing executives must also coordinate and control the efforts of other organizations as well (see Exhibit 22.7).[26]

  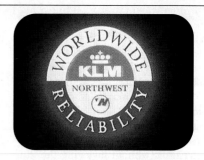

SFX: group singing, "Mr. Sandman, bring me a dream . . ." V.O.: Introducing world business class from the global alliance of KLM and Northwest, a whole new level of service with more choice and the pleasure of your very own video. Best of all, more personal space so you can lie back and stretch out and go to sleep. World business class from KLM and Northwest Airlines. It's what in the world you've been waiting for.

**Exhibit 22.7**
**NEW MARKETING RESPONSIBILITIES**
To complement each other's market coverage, the U.S. airline Northwest teamed up with the Dutch airline KLM to provide more complete global air travel services.

# IMPLEMENTING THE MARKETING EFFORT

Implementation is the process of translating marketing strategy into marketing action. The strategy a firm chooses has an effect on its actions, and those actions have a reciprocal effect on strategy.[27] Successful implementation of marketing strategy depends on skilled management of the firm's marketing effort in both the short and long term.

## Coordinating Marketing Activities

Marketing doesn't exist in a vacuum. Close relationships exist between marketing and research and development, manufacturing, and finance. These relationships must be coordinated through agreement on common objectives, assignment of activities, and creation of schedules. Managing such relationships requires understanding them. Even if each member of every operating unit in a firm is committed to reaching the firm's objectives, they're still going to approach these objectives differently because of differences in their training, aptitudes, and personalities. Research-and-development people, for example, tend to be technically oriented. Some might consider delaying the introduction of a new product, seeking perfection and performance beyond customer expectations before letting the item out of the lab. This attitude can throw the marketing program into turmoil. If the engineers wait long enough, a less exacting competitor may beat them to market with a similar product that satisfies customers sufficiently. Coordination brings together the perfectionists and the pragmatists, helping each group understand how the other thinks. Many organizations promote coordination through the use of *task forces* or *business teams,* which bring together people from various departments to work on projects such as new-product introductions.

## Motivating Marketing People

Success in business depends on how motivated the firm's people are to do what is necessary to succeed. Unfortunately, no one has ever come up with a set of simple, never-fail rules on how to motivate people. The main reason for this is that people are individuals. What you might consider a desirable reward for quality performance might be of little interest to someone else. Creating a program that will motivate everyone in the marketing department to strive for the department's goals is no simple task. Although managers use a wide variety of methods to motivate people, most programs cover these five areas:

- Identifying goals
- Providing the means to attain goals

- Tying rewards to goal achievement
- Being fair
- Providing role models for worker behavior

## Communicating within the Organization

Communication is the key to success in any organization. The objectives adopted by top management must be understood throughout the organization. Information must move from the people who have it to the people who need it. Marketing executives must be able to communicate with top-level management to ensure that the marketing program is directed toward the achievement of the firm's overall objectives. Marketing's communication with other units of the firm is essential to effective implementation of plans. Substantial interdependence exists among marketing, manufacturing, research and development, and finance; communication among these groups is required if they are to carry out their collective tasks.[28]

Effective communication begins with the climate in which the communication system must operate. Such climates range from an open pattern of communication that facilitates the flow of needed information to a closed one in which departments and divisions jealously guard information. When communications are free to flow, goal achievement is made more likely, and unnecessary competition for resources among the firm's own units is minimized.

Interdependence of functions within the business calls for information to flow both horizontally among the units of the firm and vertically, from top to bottom and vice versa. An employee at the lowest rung of the corporate ladder must have access to a communication pathway that reaches the president of the firm if necessary. Similarly, top executives must be able to communicate with all employees through a system of organized vertical and horizontal flows (see Exhibit 22.8). Com-

**Exhibit 22.8**
**COMMUNICATION FLOWS**
Companies need to have communication paths that let information flow freely in both horizontal and vertical directions.

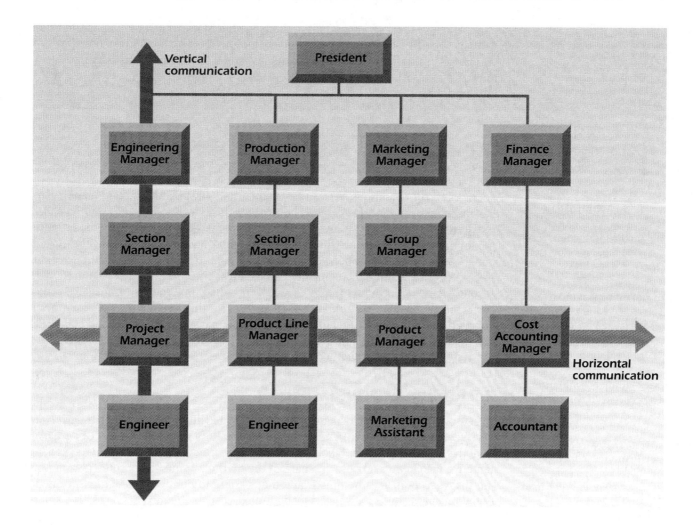

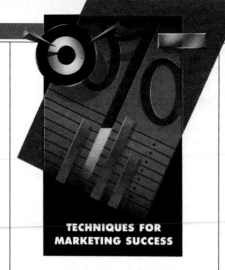
munication originating in one unit of the firm should reach a person in another unit without obstacles. This may seem simple enough, but such communication depends on people in the firm realizing the importance of information and making a commitment to assuring that it is available to every employee who needs it to get the job done.

# CONTROLLING MARKETING EFFORTS

**marketing control**
Reviewing marketing plans and modifying them as market conditions develop and change

Planning is a continuous process, and plans must be reviewed and modified to reflect real-world conditions. As you learned earlier, strategic marketing planning relies on monitoring and feedback. The process of review and modification is called **marketing control,** and it involves three elements (see Exhibit 22.9). The first is **performance standards,** which represent some level of expected performance. For example, if an insurance company sets a goal of selling 1,000 new policies in North America in July, the company has established a performance standard. The second element is **performance evaluation,** which is a means to measure actual performance against performance standards. The third element is **performance correction,** methods for making changes in the marketing system when standards aren't being met. In addition to these *formal controls,* organizations also have various *informal controls,* which include peer pressure and company tradition.

**performance standards**
The expected level of marketing performance; typical standards are specified levels of sales, profit, or market share

**performance evaluation**
The process of comparing actual results with expected performance

## Performance Standards

**performance correction**
Methods for changing a marketing system in order to improve performance

Every plan contains performance standards stated in measurable terms. McDonald's seeks to continue its 15 percent annual earnings growth, whereas General Automotive's aim is to retain 50 percent of the U.S. transit bus market. If General Automotive is to keep a 50 percent share of the market, it must have some idea of how big that market is and the time frame that's going to be the basis of measurement. Should General Automotive worry about next year or the next 10 years? If a single from employee handbooks to executive speeches to television commercials. You're looking for two things here. First, do the materials present a consistent message? For example, does the employee handbook say the same things about quality that your ads say? Second, do the materials communicate in a consistent style? Eaton realized that its independent divisions were presenting an inconsistent picture to the company's numerous markets, so it imposed communications standards as a result of its audit. Dropping the number of ad agencies from 26 to 5 also helped Eaton a great deal.

In the next phase you ask whether the intended messages are getting across. The only sure way to test this is by observing the effect that the materials have on their target audiences. Two common ways of doing this are focus groups and questionnaires. Focus groups help you uncover issues and emotions, giving you a qualitative measure of communications effectiveness. Questionnaires follow up from there, giving you a quantitative measure. For example, a focus group might uncover some confusion about the way Eaton specifies performance for one of its products. You can then take that issue, add it to the survey, and measure how widespread this confusion is in the company's target markets.

Following the external review (or during the external review, if you have enough people helping), analyze the effectiveness of internal communications. This includes internal publications, such as handbooks, newsletters, and memos, as well as the effect that external materials have on the company's own staff. Again, you can use both focus groups and questionnaires to uncover issues and measure effectiveness.

The managers who conducted Eaton's communications audit emphasize an important final point. Get the backing of top management before you start the audit. If the audit uncovers less than ideal communications, your next step will be to make recommendations for change. Also, if you've lined up high-level support before you launch the evaluation, you stand a better chance of making changes happen than if you just show up on the president's doorstep one day with proposed changes.

## APPLY YOUR KNOWLEDGE

**1.** What would you do if you discovered that two divisions of your company were sending conflicting messages to the marketplace?

**2.** What steps would you recommend for a specialized audit of the pricing practices and policies in your marketing department?

year is the measurement base, can the company expect 5,000 or 10,000 or some other number of buses to be sold in this country during the year? In other words, state the standards in meaningful terms so that when they are compared to actual performance, the comparison will yield useful information for decision making.

## Performance Evaluation

When comparisons are made between standards and actual performance, management must be aware of what the company's marketers are doing and what external support organizations are doing to help them. Many businesses use the services of advertising agencies, marketing research firms, and consultants to help with their marketing efforts. The control process calls for monitoring the activities of the

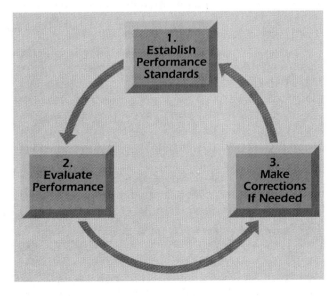

**Exhibit 22.9
THE MARKETING
CONTROL PROCESS**
The process of controlling marketing activities involves setting performance standards, evaluating performance, and taking corrective action if necessary.

firm's own marketing personnel and outside sources of assistance such as advertising agencies. Though it is often difficult to obtain all the needed information, performance can't be measured without it.

Evaluators compare records of actual performance with performance standards and determine whether a difference exists and how large it is. For example, if General Automotive succeeded in selling only 2,000 of the 5,000 transit buses sold during 1991, the difference between the standard and the performance would be significant, and corrective action would be necessary.

Performance evaluation can be particularly difficult for nonprofit organizations. Unlike commercial ventures, nonprofit groups can't look at revenue or earnings to evaluate the success of their marketing activities. For example, groups that press for funding for AIDS research and more humane treatment of AIDS patients can measure one of their goals but not the other. They can easily see whether various government agencies have increased funding for research, but they have more difficulty measuring how kindly the general public is treating people with AIDS.

## SALES ANALYSIS

**sales analysis**
Comparison of current sales with past sales, industry sales, sales by competitors, and forecast sales as a method of evaluating a firm's performance

**Sales analysis** is the use of sales figures to evaluate a firm's current performance. Sales records usually include a lot of information about the products being sold, who's selling them, and to whom they're sold, so writing performance standards in terms of sales is easy. However, sales figures by themselves paint an incomplete picture. Raw information on current sales must be compared with other information, such as your past sales and your competitors' past and present sales. With such comparisons, you gain meaningful information about sales growth, market share, and other parameters.

MEASURING SALES   You can measure sales in several ways. The most basic method is *unit volume,* which measures the number of products sold. You can examine the transaction record of each sale to see what was bought, who sold it, on what terms, and when. This record can be used to analyze sales in terms of any of the items of information. You can look at sales by each representative, sales by product, sales to specific customers, or sales by product description. For example, you can examine sales records to see what proportion of sales on a specific date were credit sales, which sales rep sold the most that day, and what the three most popular items were.

Another measurement basis for many sales analyses is *dollar volume,* the money received from sales. This is convenient because it allows direct comparison of revenue, cost, and profit figures. However, dollar volume can obscure some of the information about what really went on. Since dollar volume is the number of products sold multiplied by their price, if price is increased or decreased and the same number of products is sold, dollar volume will go up or down because of the price change. If inflation or deflation strikes, dollar volume can increase (inflation) or decrease (deflation), but the company's market strength will be unaffected.

Unit volume and dollar volume provide useful data, but they don't tell you how well you're doing relative to your competitors. To learn that, track your market share. If your unit volume is growing but your market share is dropping, your competition is growing faster than you are. At the other extreme, if your unit volume is dropping but your market share is growing, the market is shrinking but you're hanging on better than anybody else.

Exhibit 22.10 demonstrates some of the things you can learn from unit volume, dollar volume, and market share. For instance, at the beginning of the year, you're selling 1,000 units a month at $1.50 each, for a dollar volume of $1,500. The total market size is 5,000 units, so your share in January is 20 percent. In April you raise the price to $1.75, which increases your monthly dollar volume to $1,750. However, the market starts to grow in April while your unit volume stays the same; this causes your market share to drop. By June your share has dropped to 15 percent. You respond in July with a sales promotion that raises unit volume to 1,200 per month.

This temporarily increases your market share, but the market keeps growing, and your share continues to drop until October. In October the market collapses; you respond with a drastic price cut, which keeps your unit and dollar volumes stable while your competitors lose market share. You end the year with 30 percent of the market. You can see from this hypothetical case that monitoring several variables gives you a complete picture of your marketing performance.

ANALYZING SALES   Regardless of whether you use unit volume, dollar volume, market share, or a combination as the measure of performance, choose some basis for sales analysis. If your firm is small and has a very limited product assortment, aggregate sales may be an adequate base. You can compute volume and market share figures across the firm's entire output and make decisions based on what the calculations reveal. Using aggregate figures presents a few problems, however. Sales may not be evenly distributed across product lines, divided equally among customers, or derived from sales territories in equal proportions. Some product lines may contribute small unit volumes to sales but generate higher levels of profits than bigger sellers.

## MARKETING COST ANALYSIS

Marketing is not free. Every aspect of marketing costs money. Selling efforts cost money, advertising costs money, product development costs money, and so does marketing research. **Marketing cost analysis** is an examination of the sources of marketing costs, including why they are incurred, how big or small they are, and

**marketing cost analysis**
Examining marketing costs, their sources, why they are incurred, their size, and their change over time

**Exhibit 22.10**
**TRACKING UNITS, DOLLARS, AND MARKET SHARE**
To get a true picture of your performance, track unit volume, dollar volume, and market share. The text explains the significance of these graphs.

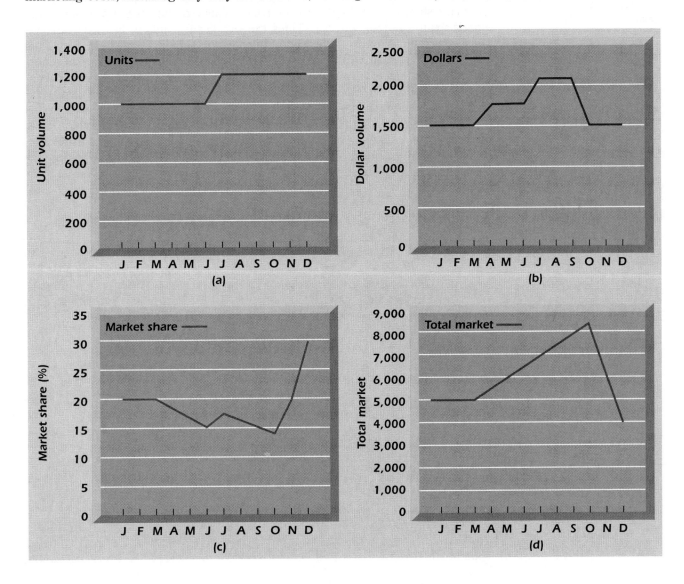

how they change over time. An effective marketing program may not be an efficient one; that is, a marketing program that generates large sales volumes may also create high costs. What you want is an effective program that is also efficient.

A thorough marketing cost analysis system can take a lot of time and energy because some costs (such as an appearance at a trade show or an ad campaign that features an entire line of products) are difficult to assign to specific products. However, it gives you the tools needed to analyze specific elements of the marketing mix in a way that is otherwise impossible. The payoff in better decisions is usually worth the increased accounting complexity.[29]

## The Marketing Audit

**marketing audit**
A comprehensive, systematic, periodic review of a firm's marketing environment, objectives, strategies, and activities

When managers want a complete picture of their marketing performance, they can conduct a **marketing audit,** a comprehensive review of the company's marketing environment, objectives, strategies, and activities. The purpose of the marketing audit is to identify operational weaknesses and strengths and to recommend alterations to the firm's marketing plans and programs. The marketing audit is much broader in scope than sales or cost analysis. A well-designed marketing audit examines current conditions in the marketing environment, the effectiveness of the marketing organization, marketing's productivity, and all the functional relationships within the marketing organization.[30]

Because it is so comprehensive, the marketing audit is an undertaking of major significance, and it must be conducted as systematically as possible. Before the first document is examined, before one employee, customer, or supplier is interviewed, a detailed structure for the audit is prepared. This structure is really a plan of operation for the auditor, and it includes the significant points to be examined, the questions to be asked, and the type of information sought. Exhibit 22.11 outlines such an audit structure. Also, specialized audits can be conducted to measure how well specific areas of a company are doing. For instance, both the product management and marketing communications areas have been subjected to specialized audits in various companies.[31]

Ideally, the marketing audit is conducted by an individual or organization independent of the marketing department. In many cases you'll retain an outside consultant to run the project. This may not always be possible, however, because outside consultants are expensive and don't always possess the exact qualifications the

## Exhibit 22.11   THE MARKETING AUDIT

### Marketing Commitment: Corporate Culture
1. Does the chief executive believe in marketing planning, and is formal planning ingrained with all top managers?
2. Are plans prepared with the participation of functional managers or dictated by the president?
3. Do you have a coordinated marketing program or an isolated sales department?
4. Are you using the computer as a marketing tool, and do your managers understand its capabilities?
5. Do you implement a marketing plan, measure performance, and adjust for deviation?
6. Are all marketing functions under the direction of one executive who reports to the chief executive officer?

### Products: The Reason for Existence
1. Is the product free from deadwood? Do you have a well-defined, continuous program to weed out unprofitable products and add new ones?
2. What is the life cycle stage?
3. How will user demands or trends affect you?
4. Are you a leader in new-product innovation?
5. Do you have a systematic liaison with the research-and-development group?

6. Are inexpensive methods used to establish new-product potentials before considerable amounts are spent on R&D and market introduction?
7. Are new products introduced with forecasts and budgets?
8. Have you investigated possible advantages resulting from new materials or technology?
9. Do you have different quality levels for different markets?
10. Are packages/brochures effective for the products they present?
11. Do you present products in the most appealing formats for markets being served?
12. Are there features or benefits to exploit?
13. Has the safety of the product been brought to a satisfactory level?
14. Is the level of customer service adequate?
15. How are quality and reliability viewed by customers?

### Customer: User Profiles
1. Who is the current and potential customer?
2. Are customers younger or older, on average, than those of competitors?

3. Are there geographic aspects of use: regional, rural, urban?
4. Why do people buy the product; what motivates their preferences?
5. Who makes buying decisions; when, where?
6. What is the frequency and quantity of use?

## Markets: Where Products Are Sold

1. Have you identified and measured major segments?
2. Are you overlooking small but profitable segments of the market in trying to satisfy the tastes of the majority?
3. Are the markets for the products expanding or declining?
4. Should different segments be developed; gaps in penetration?
5. Do segments require marketing differentiation?

## Sales History: Previous Results

1. How do sales break down within the product?
2. Do you know where sales are coming from; segments and customer classification?
3. Are there abnormal cycles or seasonalities; if so, how do you plan for them?
4. Do sales match previous forecasts?
5. Which territories/markets do not yield potential?
6. Are growth and profit trends reflected?

## Competitors: Their Influence

1. Who are the principal competitors, how are they positioned, and where do they seem to be headed?
2. What are their market shares?
3. What features of competitors' products stand out?
4. What are their strengths and weaknesses?
5. Is the market easily entered or dominated?

## Pricing: Profitability Planning

1. What are the objectives of current pricing policy: acquiring, defending, or expanding?
2. Are price limitations inherent in the marketplace?
3. Are price policies set to produce volume or profit?
4. How does pricing compare with competition in similar levels of quality?
5. Do you understand how your prices are set?
6. Is the price list understandable and current?
7. Does cost information show profitability of each item?
8. What is the history of price deals, discounts, and promotions?
9. Are intermediaries making money from the line?
10. Can the product support advertising or promotion programs?
11. Will size or manufacturing process require more volume?
12. Are there cost problems to overcome?
13. Are profitability and marketing cost known by the customer?

## Marketing Channels: Selling Paths

1. Does the system offer the best access to all target markets?
2. Do product characteristics require special channels?
3. Have you analyzed each market with a view toward setting up the most profitable type of presentation: direct vs. reps, master distributors or dealers, and so on?
4. What are the trends in distribution methods?
5. Do you provide cost-effective marketing support, selling aids, and sales tools?

## Sales Administration: Selling Efficiency

1. Have you analyzed communications and designed paperwork or computer programs to provide meaningful management information?
2. Are customers getting coverage in proportion to their potential?
3. Are sales costs properly planned and controlled?
4. Does the compensation plan provide optimum incentive and security at reasonable cost?
5. Is performance measured against potential?
6. Are selling expenses proportionate to results and potentials within markets or territories?
7. Are there deficiencies in recruitment, selection, training, motivation, supervision, performance, promotion, or compensation?
8. Do you provide effective selling aids and sales tools?

## Delivery and Inventory: Physical Performance

1. Are adequate inventories kept in the right mix?
2. Is inventory turnover acceptable?
3. Do orders receive efficient, timely processing?
4. Are shipping schedules and promises kept?
5. Is the product delivered in good condition?
6. Are forecasts for production planning acceptable?
7. How does performance compare with competition?
8. Are warehouses and distribution points properly located?

## Advertising: Media Program

1. Are media objectives and strategies linked to the marketing plan?
2. What are the objectives of the ad program?
3. How is media effectiveness measured?
4. Is advertising integrated with promotion and sales activity?
5. Is the ad agency's effectiveness periodically evaluated?
6. Do you dictate copy theme and content to the agency?
7. Are you spending realistically, in relation to budget?
8. Do you use trade publications effectively?
9. How do you choose the ad agency?

## Promotion: Sales Inducement

1. Does the promotion support a marketing objective?
2. Was it carefully budgeted?
3. Is it integrated with advertising and selling activity?
4. How is it measured for results?
5. What was the reason for its success or failure?
6. Are slogans, trademarks, logos, and brands being used effectively?
7. Is point-of-sale material cost-effective?
8. Do you have satisfactory displays of products?
9. Are you effectively using couponing, tie-ins, incentives, sampling, stuffers, combination offers?
10. How do you evaluate trade shows for effectiveness?

## Public Relations: Prestige Building

1. Do you have a clear idea of the type of company you want people to think you are?
2. Do you have a consistent communications program?
3. What kind of ideas and impressions have you created about your company?
4. Do you really know what your image is on a factual basis, or are you relying on customers' letters, sales reports, and publicity in the press?
5. Does your company name, brand, and logo add to or conflict with the image you want?
6. Are you getting a share of favorable, unpaid publicity in editorials of the media?

The marketing audit is a comprehensive evaluation of a company's products, customers, and marketing processes.

job calls for. Sometimes using in-house talent to prepare the audit is best. Although no one can expect an employee of the company to be totally disinterested in the results of an audit, it is still possible to develop a group within the firm that can do this kind of work professionally and evenhandedly.

Marketing audits are scheduled on a regular basis, at intervals usually greater than one year but not more than five years. If this is done, companies receive relatively few nasty surprises, and corrective action can be taken before conditions grow to crisis proportions. If the firm waits for a crisis before starting a marketing audit, the number of unpleasant surprises may be more than management can handle.

The marketing audit is a tool of planning that goes beyond the day-to-day controlling activities of management. In addition to looking at how well the firm is doing what it's doing, the audit looks at whether the firm is doing what it *should* be doing. The results are sometimes disturbing, especially the first time a marketing audit is conducted. Some audits uncover substantial differences between what everyone in the firm believes to be true about its marketing effort and reality. However, it is better to learn your shortcomings from a friendly auditor than from an angry customer or aggressive competitor.

## Performance Correction

When performance isn't up to expectations, corrective action is called for. Your evaluation of why performance hasn't met standards gives you the information you need to begin correcting the situation. Performance corrections fall into three categories. First, you can change performance standards when it becomes apparent that the standards you've set are no longer realistic. If a competitor introduces a new product or some other change occurs in the marketing environment, you may no longer be able to achieve the sales levels you'd hoped for. Another reason that marketers change performance standards is that it is difficult to forecast sales accurately, and they have to adjust goals once they have some sales history. Second, you can redirect resources. This can mean more salespeople, more advertising coverage, new products, or a host of other marketing initiatives. Sometimes a complete reorganization is called for. Third, you can keep your goals and resource allocations the same and try to stimulate improved performance through better management, employee training, sales contests, more effective promotional materials, or improved products. Examining every element of the marketing mix can help you find opportunities to improve performance.

## _____ SUMMARY OF LEARNING OBJECTIVES _____

### 1. Link strategic marketing planning with marketing management.

Marketing management provides the organization, implementation, and control for the process that was initiated during strategic planning. Organization provides the structure under which the goals established in strategic planning can be achieved. Implementation is the translation of strategy into action; this is the phase during which the plans come to life and the marketing organization goes to work. The control element monitors the progress of marketing programs and provides feedback to managers, allowing them to evaluate performance and take corrective action if necessary.

### 2. Differentiate between a centralized and decentralized organization structure, and list the advantages and disadvantages of each.

A centralized organization structure concentrates authority and responsibility in a few top-level individuals, whereas a decentralized organization spreads authority and responsibility throughout the organization. Supporters of the centralized organization say it allows the firm to take a consistent posture toward suppliers and customers, permits more effective operation, and reduces the time needed to make decisions. Adversaries contend that this structure allows little chance for lower-level executives to participate in planning and overworks executives who do participate, causing delays and lost customers. Centralization can also enforce a rigid approach to marketing all products in all markets, which might not be appropriate in every case.

The decentralized organization, according to its supporters, allows fine-tuning of the firm to the needs of markets and makes it easier for the firm to figure out which of its operations are profitable and which are not. The biggest disadvantage of this form is inconsistencies in policies among the firm's various divisions. The involvement of large numbers of people in decision making is cited as an advantage by some and as a drawback by others.

**3. Discuss ways of organizing a marketing effort to serve the needs of the company and its customers.**

The first way to organize the marketing department is by job function; grouping all the advertising people together, all the research people together, and so on. The second method is by product, in which each brand, product, or product line is overseen by one manager. The third type of organization splits the marketing group along geographic lines. Fourth, you can group marketing people by market segment, such as transportation, aerospace, and mining. The fifth way organizes by customer type, such as those who resell your products versus those who consume them. The sixth method combines two or more of these organizational approaches, such as departments organized by both product and geography.

**4. Outline the process of motivating marketing people.**

Motivation involves getting people to perform by placing the goals of the firm in perspective for them, giving them the means to attain the goals, tying their rewards for performance to the achievement of those goals, being fair to them, and providing them with role models for their activities. Alternative ways of motivating people to perform include job enrichment and implicit bargaining, each of which sets goals for the individual and rewards achievement financially and psychologically.

**5. Describe the process of communication within the organization and how information systems fit into this process.**

The communication climate within the organization may be open, facilitating the free flow of needed data, or closed, with each department jealously guarding its information. An open environment is clearly the better approach because it allows the organization to function more efficiently and effectively.

A communication climate should also have both horizontal and vertical flows. Information systems make it possible to handle more information quicker, and they increase accessibility, giving employees the data and information they need to make informed decisions.

**6. Discuss the task of controlling marketing efforts.**

Marketing efforts are controlled by first establishing performance standards, which are expected levels of performance. Actual performance is compared with the standards in the process of performance evaluation, and if a discrepancy exists, corrective action is taken by changing the standards, reallocating resources, improving actual performance, or using a combination of these three techniques.

**7. Explain how sales and marketing cost analyses are used to evaluate marketing performance.**

Sales analysis gives you insight into how well you're doing compared to your goals and your competition. Three common variables to monitor in sales analysis are unit volume, dollar volume, and market share. Tracking all three of these figures is important if you want a complete picture of your performance in the marketplace. Marketing cost analysis helps you make a marketing program cost-effective by showing you where and why money is being spent.

**8. Outline the purpose, goals, and use of the marketing audit.**

The marketing audit examines the entire marketing program and looks for weaknesses and strengths so that the program can be changed to correct weaknesses and build on strengths. The audit provides information that allows decisions to be made in a reasoned fashion, rather than under crisis conditions.

---

## KEY TERMS

centralized organization (676)
decentralized organization (676)
functional organization (678)
geographic organization (679)

market-based organization (680)
marketing audit (690)
marketing control (686)
marketing cost analysis (689)

organizational structure (676)
performance correction (686)
performance evaluation (686)

performance standards (686)
product-based organization (678)
sales analysis (688)

---

## QUESTIONS FOR DISCUSSION

1. Your firm recently acquired several new divisions, and you were assigned the task of deciding which basic type of organization—centralized or decentralized—each one should use.
   a. A chain of 50 pharmacies, located in the three largest cities in a southeastern state, all operate under the same name, carry basically the same goods, and operate in a similar fashion.

   b. A formerly family-owned company runs 15 building-supply outlets that are scattered across the Southwest. The outlets operate under the same name but are located in a range of climates, which means the demand for products differs from outlet to outlet.
   c. A firm manufactures and distributes food products designed for the Hispanic-American market. The firm's products are distributed primarily in Texas, New

**693**

# A CASE FOR CRITICAL THINKING

## Meeting a Marketing Challenge at Hewlett-Packard

To reach its diverse customer base effectively and efficiently, Hewlett-Packard uses a rather complicated hybrid organizational structure. Depending on the level, Hewlett-Packard's organization is aligned by products, markets, customers, or geography. At the top level of the corporation, the more than 50 manufacturing divisions are grouped into two general areas by market type: technical (engineering-oriented markets) and commercial (business-oriented markets).

At lower levels, different organizational forms are used. For instance, the sales force is divided into three major geographic operations: the United States, Europe (this group also covers Africa and the Middle East), and Intercontinental, which covers the rest of the world. (Japan, one of Hewlett-Packard's largest markets, is covered by Yokogawa Hewlett-Packard, a company jointly owned by Hewlett-Packard and Yokogawa Electric Works.) In each of these three sales operations, markets are subdivided into smaller geographic areas, focusing on countries and regions inside countries. Below that, depending on the products and markets involved, some Hewlett-Packard people specialize in hardware, software applications, and customer types such as government agencies and defense contractors. Selling to large national and global customers requires close coordination between geographic areas, so major account teams with salespeople from different sales regions are often used.

Marketing coordination is another area that has come under the scrutiny of Hewlett-Packard executives in recent years. The 50-plus toll-free numbers have been replaced by one number, which directs calls into the new Customer Information Center (CIC). The CIC handles all the responses to Hewlett-Packard advertising and makes sure that sales reps get leads in a timely fashion. Another aspect of marketing coordination is a standard design for ads and promotional pieces, together with closer alignment of public relations efforts.

One of the biggest hurdles Hewlett-Packard faces is maintaining its culture while competing successfully in a wide variety of markets. The company attracts top engineering talent with promises of entrepreneurial freedom and the opportunity to work with leading-edge technologies. Executives continue to give their people the creative leeway needed to design innovative products and to help customers be successful. At the same time, they have to keep a close eye on marketing efficiency and coordination among Hewlett-Packard's diverse operations. Moves toward centralizing its vast network of divisions have helped improve efficiency; now the company needs to make sure it doesn't lose its unique character.

Hewlett-Packard's future is now in the hands of Lewis Platt, who succeeded John Young in 1992. The company has survived rough price wars in the computer business, shifting global competition, and technology changes that have slowed competitors such as IBM and DEC. Platt continues to stress decentralized independence for HP's divisions, while making sure that coordination takes place when it will benefit the customer.

**Your mission:** You've been called in as a consultant to help Hewlett-Packard with a variety of marketing management issues. As you address the following questions, don't lose sight of the complexity of Hewlett-Packard's marketing situation. More than 50 manufacturing operations are in existence, most with their own marketing groups. Customers are all over the world, ranging from governments to small businesses to consumers. The product offering is quite diverse, and nearly all products are of a highly technical nature.

1. Many of the customers who buy Hewlett-Packard's test and measurement instruments also buy computers to create automated measurement systems. Helping customers with these systems before and after the sale can require a significant degree of knowledge of the customer's application, the instrumentation hardware, the computer hardware, and the computer software. This often adds up to a task that is beyond the training and expertise of any one person. Which of the following arrangements would work best?
   a. Develop specialists who understand the customer's perspective. For example, you could have one team that sells to accounting firms, another that sells to petroleum plants, another that sells to banks, and so forth.
   b. To understand customer needs thoroughly is important, but expertise with your own products is also essential. Therefore, you should organize the selling effort by product specialties.
   c. A solution requires both (a) and (b). Customer needs *and* your own products must be understood. In many cases this will require sending two or more people out to customers to help them choose and implement solutions. It might be more expensive, but it will inevitably lead to satisfied customers.
2. Planning and forecasting are closely tied to a company's organizational form. Centralized companies tend to dictate plans from "on high," and everyone below picks up their orders and goes to work. Decentralized companies, on the other hand, usually let individual operating units make their own plans. Obviously, neither extreme would work, so all companies strike a balance somewhere between the two. Which of the following approaches to planning would work best for Hewlett-Packard?
   a. The tone and overall direction of the company must come from the top. Therefore, start the planning at the top and work down through the organization.
   b. Start planning from the bottom; the people on the front line of the corporation are in daily contact with the market, and they're in a better position to define the plans. Each division should choose the products it wants to offer its markets and the strategies for distributing, promoting, and pricing those products.

c. The company's leaders set goals for the company and then let people in the various parts of the organization draw up their own plans. The people on the front line will know the best way to plan promotions and other elements of the marketing mix. However, at the same time, the various divisions must operate in a coordinated fashion so that they can provide complete solutions for customers.

3. Most of Hewlett-Packard's 50-plus manufacturing divisions have their own marketing departments, where employees perform a wide variety of tasks. The area of helping sales representatives presents an intriguing motivational challenge. When a marketing person assists a sales rep in closing a sale, the sales rep realizes a financial gain (assuming he or she works on a partial or total commission arrangement), but the marketing person doesn't. Which of the following motivational approaches would you use to make sure that marketing people have enough incentive to help the sales reps?

   a. A marketing professional will feel good about a job well done, regardless of the recognition or compensation scheme you have in mind. Don't worry about motivating the marketing department to help with sales.

   b. Arrange a program that allows marketing people to share in the feeling of success when they help with a sale. You can do this in various ways: If you publish a monthly sales report, for instance, you could mention the names of marketing people who've helped the sales force. You could have the sales force elect the "marketing person of the month" or something like that, which would give the marketing staff a target to shoot for.

   c. Arrange a commission-splitting program that gives part of the sales rep's earnings to the marketing person. The two people involved could agree on the percentage each one receives.

4. Not surprisingly, Hewlett-Packard managers want to monitor the company's performance in its various markets. They realize that performance standards can be established in several ways, but they also know that each variable they want to add increases the time and cost of monitoring performance. Which of the following performance monitoring plans presents the best balance of usefulness and cost?

   a. Track unit volume and compare these numbers to your past performance. This system would be easy and inexpensive: Simply total the number of products sold every month by all your manufacturing divisions.

   b. The solution in (a) makes sense but you should also worry about dollar volume. Because you sell to such a wide variety of customers with different discounts and in countries with fluctuating currency exchange rates, you should also track dollar volume to get a better idea of your financial performance.

   c. Tracking market share might be difficult and expensive, but it must be done. Do the best you can with market share estimates, relying on published secondary research data whenever they are available, and making do when they aren't. Track market share wherever you can.

## SPECIAL PROJECT

Diagnosing sales problems can be a tricky process because so many different things can cause a drop in sales. Assume that Hewlett-Packard is experiencing sales troubles with one of its star product lines, the LaserJet printer family. Sales have dropped for several months in a row, but you don't have much information to go on. Identify three steps you could take to start your troubleshooting effort.[32]

Mexico, and Arizona. Some of the products are custom-made for the particular market in which they will be sold. For example, salsas to be sold in Texas are milder and contain less cilantro than those to be sold in New Mexico and Arizona. However, all are made in your plant in San Antonio.

   d. A men's clothing company manufactures, distributes, and sells suits throughout the country. It owns seven plants and markets the suits under five brand names.

2. The Mendocino Manufacturing Company produces several lines of consumer goods targeted at various market segments. Should such a firm be organized functionally or on a product basis? How do you justify your choice?

3. A manufacturer of high-performance minicomputers based in St. Louis has customers throughout the United States and is just starting to build sales in Europe. It hasn't yet moved into other parts of the world. How should it organize its marketing department?

4. Which of the following companies would be most likely to organize its marketing efforts by customer type?
   a. National chain of carpet cleaners
   b. Manufacturer of aircraft used in both commercial and military applications
   c. Publisher of yellow pages directories
   d. Manufacturer of light trucks

5. What type of marketing department would you design for a talent agency whose clients include Cameron Mackintosh, Arrested Development, Spike Lee, Yo-Yo Ma, and Chet Atkins?

6. How might you motivate the concierge in a Nordstrom department store (whose job is to answer customers' questions and direct them to appropriate departments inside the store)?

7. Why would the president of Burger King be interested in what an employee in Charlottesville, Virginia, has to say about the way the business is run?

8. Which of the following are good marketing performance standards and which are not? Why?
   a. Increase sales by 10 percent
   b. Increase dollar volume by 10 percent
   c. Increase dollar volume by 10 percent by the end of the year
   d. Stabilize market share over the next six months

9. Your company is concerned that it may be wasting money evaluating the performance of its sales force. Quarter after quarter, sales force performance exceeds performance standards by a comfortable margin. The company has asked for your opinion. Should you continue to evaluate the performance of the sales force? Why or why not?

10. Your last three marketing audits have shown that few changes in your marketing program were required. You are beginning to think of these audits as a pointless exercise. Should you keep doing them? Why or why not?

## SHARPEN YOUR MARKETING SKILLS

More and more universities are recognizing the value of marketing their services to potential students, donors, and other parties. However, the responsibility for marketing is usually spread across departments that often have different goals and target audiences.

**Decision:** How would you organize the marketing efforts at your college or university? To begin with, does it have a marketing department, or is the responsibility spread out across the admissions department, alumni groups, and so on? What sort of organization would best serve your reaching the school's various audiences, including students, parents, faculty, donors, government agencies, company recruiters, and the local community?

**Communication:** Pair up with a classmate who has reached a different conclusion about the best organizational form, and try to convince each other.

## KEEPING CURRENT IN MARKETING

Find an article that describes a product that has (thus far) failed to sell in its markets but that seems to make perfect sense. Some recent examples include (1) breakaway baseball bases that would reduce injuries from slides; (2) detachable recessed bed frames that support mattress and spring combinations, take up less storage space for merchants than traditional "Hollywood" frames, and don't scrape your legs when you walk near them; and (3) a free magazine targeted at college students.

1. What obstacles account for the intended consumers' rejecting the product? Do the obstacles originate with the product itself? Pricing strategy? Distribution strategy? Promotion? Something else?

2. Was management aware of these obstacles before launching the product? Which could be controlled? Which are beyond management's control?

3. How would you overcome these obstacles to help the product reach its potential? Describe your strategies and why you believe they would work.

# Campbell Soups Up Its Marketing Organization

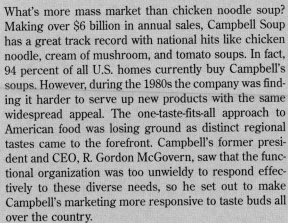

What's more mass market than chicken noodle soup? Making over $6 billion in annual sales, Campbell Soup has a great track record with national hits like chicken noodle, cream of mushroom, and tomato soups. In fact, 94 percent of all U.S. homes currently buy Campbell's soups. However, during the 1980s the company was finding it harder to serve up new products with the same widespread appeal. The one-taste-fits-all approach to American food was losing ground as distinct regional tastes came to the forefront. Campbell's former president and CEO, R. Gordon McGovern, saw that the functional organization was too unwieldy to respond effectively to these diverse needs, so he set out to make Campbell's marketing more responsive to taste buds all over the country.

In two successive restructurings, McGovern moved away from a centralized, functional organization toward a decentralized, geographic organization that could keep track of regional customer needs. First, he sliced up Campbell USA, the division that focused on U.S. operations, to create business units that concentrate on specific groups of Campbell products. Each business unit had its own marketing managers and was encouraged to be more innovative in fulfilling customer needs. Freed from the cumbersome and time-consuming layers of centralized approvals, the business units were able to cook up new products five times as fast as under the previous organization.

Next, McGovern pushed decentralization a step further by dividing the sales organization into 22 regions. Under the old organization, each business unit had its own salespeople who would call on 100 stores apiece and sell only Swanson frozen foods or Campbell's soup, for example. Under the new setup, each sales rep might be responsible for only 10 stores but would now sell the full range of Campbell products.

To better understand regional tastes and needs, McGovern created a new position in every region: the brand sales manager. These managers develop regional and local marketing programs, including sales promotion and advertising campaigns. They also stay on top of demographic trends, changes in food tastes, and competitive movement in their local markets. Of course, brand sales managers can call on the resources of Campbell's national marketing staff, but they tailor national programs to fit the needs of their unique regions.

Herbert M. Baum, president of Campbell USA, shared McGovern's vision of making the new organization work for Campbell, its channel members, and its customers. He believed that regionalization could be im-

plemented down to the production level, so he assigned each of Campbell's domestic manufacturing plants to serve one of five regions. Now the plants are able to gear products and production schedules to fit the needs of their regions. Although this new production organization doesn't come cheap—regional products are as expensive to develop as single mass-market versions—it helps Campbell compete in every market.

The regions aren't completely autonomous, but Baum continues to push in that direction. He evaluated the regions based on sales volume increase compared with money spent per region. Then he gave each region responsibility for its own profits and losses, and he evaluated that. Not every regional plant can supply every product for its region, but that will change as the regions become self-sufficient.

By 1989 the two reorganizations had pushed Campbell's nine-year sales growth over the 9 percent mark. These days, Campbell managers under new CEO David Johnson are looking even closer at restructuring the organization to yield higher profits. Don't be surprised if they stir things up again in the 1990s.

1. Baum wants to keep communication channels open so that marketing activities throughout Campbell USA are coordinated, not duplicated. Should he distribute a calendar every January that reflects the marketing programs going on around the country each day of the coming year? Or should he sponsor monthly meetings that bring together regional marketing people from around the country to exchange their success stories and discuss upcoming events?

2. Suppose that the performance of Campbell's established product line of Home Cookin' ready-to-serve canned soups has started to slip well below Baum's expectations. If he wants to take corrective action to improve the line's sales performance, would you recommend that Baum stimulate improved performance by starting a sales contest that's supported by new point-of-purchase materials? Or would you suggest that Baum change the standards to reflect the lower performance that may indicate uncontrollable changes in the marketing environment?

3. Assume that Campbell's is about to introduce a new gravy product in two regions and plans to take the product national if it succeeds in the initial push. How might the promotional program, distribution, and pricing policies used in the test affect its accuracy and Campbell's ability to project the test results nationally?

## Unilever Pushes for Profits Worldwide

Many of the best-known consumer products sitting on the shelf in U.S. households are marketed by the Anglo-Dutch giant Unilever. If you've purchased a Popsicle, Ragú spaghetti sauce, Lever 2000 bath soap, Aim toothpaste, or Wishbone salad dressing, you're one of Unilever's customers in more than 80 countries worldwide. If you haven't purchased one of those brands, the company has plenty more to offer you, from Q-Tips to Calvin Klein cosmetics.

### A Clean Start

Unilever traces its history back to England in 1885, when James and William Hesketh Lever formed Lever Brothers to market the world's first packaged, branded laundry soap. Called Sunlight, the product is still one of the company's key products, more than a century later. For the next few decades, Lever Brothers expanded around the world. In 1930 the company merged with a Dutch butter and margarine cartel (a combination of independent businesses that join together to regulate production, pricing, and marketing of goods by its members) called the Margarine Union. The new organization was dubbed Unilever, and for tax purposes it maintains headquarters both in London and in Rotterdam, the Netherlands.

Unilever continued to grow through the Great Depression of the 1930s and World War II in the 1940s. Then in 1946, the company ran into its first major obstacle, the new Tide laundry detergent from U.S. rival P & G. Procter & Gamble launched Tide with a vast nationwide advertising program and quickly knocked Unilever out of first place in the U.S. laundry market. From that point on, the U.S. market was a tough arena for Unilever. Finally, in the early 1990s, Unilever turned the tables with its new Lever 2000, which shot to the top of the U.S. bath soap market. (The company's Lux brand

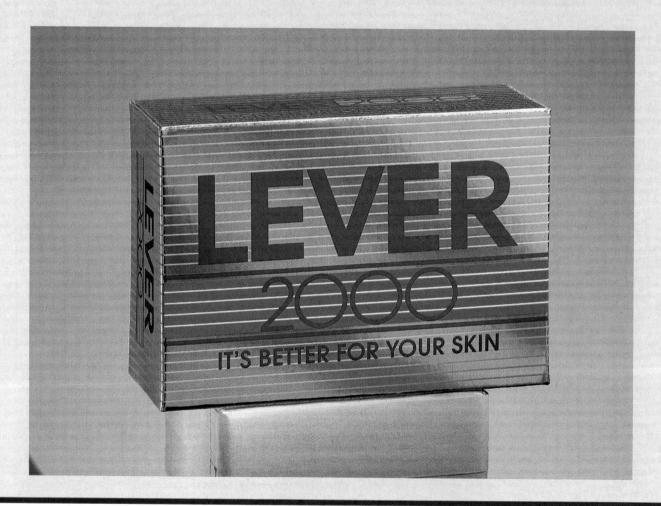

of soap is already the world's top brand.) Acquisitions of Chesebrough Ponds, Fabergé, Elizabeth Arden, and Calvin Klein cosmetics have strengthened Unilever's U.S. presence.

## Standardized versus Customized Marketing

Unilever and P & G approach international marketing in fundamentally different ways. P & G leans toward standardized products and promotions worldwide, whereas Unilever tends to treat each country as a distinct market. Unilever CEO Sir Michael Perry has unabashed disdain for current trends in globalized marketing, which he calls "an incredible amount of pious theory." Instead, Sir Michael and his people concentrate on delivering the most attractive marketing mix for each local market. This is one of the reasons most of the 500-plus companies that Unilever owns worldwide have their own boards of directors who plan product development and marketing in their own markets.

This decentralized, hands-off approach was recently turned on its head in the United States, however. The U.S. household products unit (which operates under the Lever Brothers name) had been operating at below-average performance practically ever since P & G's aggressive move with Tide 50 years ago. One of the key reasons for the troubles up through the 1980s was the unrealistic profit goals set by headquarters back in Europe. Because Unilever doesn't enjoy the dominant position in the United States that it enjoys elsewhere, the only way Lever Brothers could meet the goals was to cut costs wherever possible.

One of the biggest costs in consumer-goods marketing is advertising, and when Lever Brothers cut its advertising, P & G and others charged ahead. Lever's declining sales made it impossible to upgrade and replace older manufacturing plants, leading to a vicious cycle of decreasing sales and increasing production costs (relative to competitors). The result was more than $100 million in losses from 1981 through 1986, prompting Unilever to take drastic action. The chain of command was shortened between U.S. divisions and European headquarters by removing the U.S. top executive level through which the divisions previously reported. The product mix was simplified by getting rid of Lever Brothers products that didn't match Unilever's overall product mix.

## The Benefits of Simplicity

The simpler organization produced benefits quickly. First, expectations were easier to set and to meet because top executives in London and Rotterdam had a better feel for their people in the United States, and vice versa. Second, closer ties to Europe allowed the U.S. unit to take advantage of several very successful European products, including Snuggle fabric softener and Promise Extra Light margarine. In the margarine market, in particular, Van den Burgh Foods jumped from third place to first place in just a few years after the reorganization.

Now with roughly 300,000 employees worldwide, more than $40 billion in annual sales, and a $4 billion promotion budget, Unilever remains a major presence in supermarkets and advertising media worldwide. Sir Michael continues to advocate localized marketing, and so far at least, the results speak for themselves.

## Questions

1. In the late 1980s, Unilever took a popular Swedish shampoo called Timotei across Europe and into Japan with great success. Consumers were attracted by the product's positioning of simple, natural, and pure. Timotei failed to catch on in the United States, however. Why do you think the product didn't sell well in this country? (The answer probably has something to do with timing; if you don't recall the prevailing social attitudes in the United States during the 1980s, consult someone who does or conduct some library research.)

2. What are the risks inherent in Unilever's decentralized strategy of letting managers in each country make many of the decisions involving the products sold in their respective countries? Do you think that in general the benefits outweigh the risks? Explain your answer.

3. Should Unilever and other consumer companies be held responsible for the intentional misuse of their products? For instance, if a consumer uses liquid handsoap in a dishwasher, and the machine is ruined as a result, should Unilever be forced to replace the machine?

4. Assume that Unilever wants to enter a new country in which the quality of the products currently available is lower than the quality of products sold in the United States or most of Europe. Should the company stick with its high quality (and consequently higher prices) in this new market, or should it lower its product quality and match the prices offered by the existing competitors?

# Financial Analysis in Marketing

Sound marketing decisions require an understanding of and an ability to apply a variety of financial concepts. These concepts help you set your financial goals for a particular program or product, plan production and distribution, manage your pricing, and analyze your results. This component chapter introduces some specific techniques of financial analysis that you can use to evaluate your organization's performance and support your future marketing decisions. To set the stage for your financial analysis, start with a look at the elements of a business's income statement.

## THE INCOME STATEMENT

The *income statement* (also called the profit-and-loss statement, the P & L, or the operating statement) shows the financial results over a period of time for a strategic business unit (SBU) or an entire organization. Typically, managers prepare income statements for specific periods (such as every month, every quarter, and every year), and they use these statements to analyze how revenues and expenses contributed to profitability during that period. By comparing the current income statement to statements from previous periods, and by computing various ratios, you can spot sales, expense, and profitability trends, and you can then focus on any problem areas you may find.

## Components of the Income Statement

Exhibit B.1 is a sample income statement for a retail company. The income statement includes eight general sections: the heading, sales revenue, cost of goods

sold, gross profit on sales, operating expenses, income before taxes, taxes, and net income.

- *Heading.* The heading indicates which period of time the income statement covers, as well as the name of the SBU or the organization.
- *Sales revenue.* The sales revenue section accounts for all sales revenue earned during the period. Starting with gross sales, deduct the value of any products returned by customers and the value of any allowances given to customers who claimed a price reduction because of damaged goods or spoilage. The result is your net sales.
- *Cost of goods sold.* This section shows the price paid for products sold during the period, including any inbound transportation costs. In a business such as manufacturing, wholesaling, or retailing, where tangible products are bought and sold, you calculate the cost of goods sold by adding the cost of goods purchased during the period to the cost of goods already in inventory; then you deduct the value of any inventory that remains at the end of the period. Of course, in a service business such as real estate or insurance, you would have no tangible products and therefore no cost of goods sold.
- *Gross profit on sales.* Also known as gross margin, gross profit on sales is computed by deducting the cost of goods sold from the net sales figure.
- *Operating expenses.* The operating expenses shown in this section are divided into three categories: selling expenses, which are expenses related to marketing and sales; administrative expenses, which encompass nonsales salaries and other expenses of running the business; and general expenses, a variety of costs such as telephone and electricity expenses. You allocate promotional expenses and the

**Year Ending December 31, 1995 (in thousands of dollars)**

| | | | |
|---|---|---|---|
| Sales revenue: | | | |
| Sales | | $5,350 | |
| Less: Sales returns and allowances | | $120 | |
| Net sales | | | $5,230 |
| Cost of goods sold: | | | |
| Merchandise in inventory, January 1 (cost) | $1,100 | | |
| Purchases (cost) | $3,450 | | |
| Cost of goods available for sale | | $4,550 | |
| Less: Merchandise in inventory, December 31 (cost) | | $1,650 | |
| Cost of goods sold | | | $2,900 |
| Gross profit on sales | | | $2,330 |
| | | | |
| Operating expenses: | | | |
| Selling expenses | | | |
| Sales salaries | $425 | | |
| Marketing costs | $115 | | |
| Total selling expenses | | $540 | |
| Administrative expenses | | | |
| Administrative salaries | $190 | | |
| Office supplies | $40 | | |
| Total administrative expenses | | $230 | |
| General expenses | | | |
| Utilities (phone and electricity) expense | $90 | | |
| Rent expense | $235 | | |
| Total general expenses | | $325 | |
| Total operating expenses | | | $1,095 |
| Income before taxes | | | $1,235 |
| Taxes | | | $432 |
| Net income (net profit) | | | $803 |

This hypothetical report shows the major elements that make up an income statement. (Note that a number of other items, such as interest income from bank accounts, are not included here.)

salaries and commissions paid to your salespeople to the selling expense category, and you assign other expenses to either the administrative or general expense categories. All expenses are summed to get a figure for total operating expenses.

- *Income before taxes.* This figure is calculated by subtracting total operating expenses from gross profit on sales.
- *Taxes.* Federal income taxes.
- *Net income.* Sometimes called net profit, net income is the amount that remains after taxes have been paid.

## Key Operating Ratios

Understanding the components of the income statement is the first step toward applying financial analysis techniques to marketing situations. Next take a look at the relationships between various figures in the income statement to determine how well your SBU or organization is performing. Once you've calculated these *operating ratios* from income statements covering several months or years, you'll have a clearer picture of your sales, expense, and profit trends, which can help you manage more effectively (and more profitably) in the future.

In addition to monitoring your performance over time, you can also compare your performance with that of a typical firm in your industry and with the performance of your competitors. Dun & Bradstreet and Robert Morris Associates are two organizations that publish detailed financial information about hundreds of product categories. After you've computed your own performance ratios, see how they stack up against the industry standards; your goal is to meet or exceed the competition's performance standard. Also, if you can obtain the annual reports of your competitors, you'll want to calculate their key financial measures and compare them with the numbers from your own firm. If your company's ratios are below the standards of the industry or the performance of competitors, make plans for improvement—and implement your plans as soon as possible. Some of the most commonly used operating ratios are the gross profit ratio, the profit margin on sales ratio, and the operating expense ratio. Here's a closer look at each one:

- *Gross profit ratio.* One ratio that marketers use to examine profitability is the gross profit ratio, also called the gross margin ratio. This is the formula for the gross profit ratio:

$$\text{Gross profit ratio} = \frac{\text{gross profit}}{\text{net sales}}$$

Here is an example of a gross profit ratio calculation, using the figures from Exhibit B.1:

$$\text{Gross profit ratio} = \frac{\text{gross profit}}{\text{net sales}} = \frac{\$2,330,000}{\$5,230,000}$$
$$= 0.445$$
$$= 44.5\%$$

You'll want to compute this ratio for several periods to see whether the trend is upward, downward, or steady. If you look at your gross profits only in terms of dollars or yen, for example, you might be misled by the size of the actual numbers from period to period. However, if you calculate the percentage, you'll be comparing the size of your gross profit to the size of your net sales during the same period. If this ratio changes dramatically from period to period, look more closely at trends in sales, cost of goods sold, and expenses to find your problem.

- *Profit margin on sales ratio.* Another useful calculation is the profit margin on sales ratio, which uses the net income figure from the income statement. Here's the formula:

$$\text{Profit margin on sales} = \frac{\text{net income}}{\text{net sales}}$$

Applying the formula to the figures from Exhibit B.1, you would compute the profit margin as follows:

$$\text{Profit margin on sales} = \frac{\text{net income}}{\text{net sales}} = \frac{\$1,235,000}{\$5,230,000}$$
$$= 0.236$$
$$= 23.6\%$$

To better understand which products and product lines are delivering the best net profits, calculate the net profit on sales for individual products as well as for entire product lines. Remember that your expenses have a direct impact on your net profit, a relationship that is clearly revealed in this ratio. If you see your net profit dropping over a period of time, it may mean that your expenses have been growing while your sales or prices have remained constant. Another explanation might be that you've been maintaining a steady expense base while lowering prices to attract more customers, which also eats into profits.

- *Operating expense ratio.* The operating expense ratio compares the size of the total expense figure to net sales. Here's the formula for the operating expense ratio:

$$\text{Operating expense ratio} = \frac{\text{total operating expenses}}{\text{net sales}}$$

Using the information from Exhibit B.1, you would calculate the operating expense ratio in this way:

$$\text{Operating expense ratio} = \frac{\text{total operating expenses}}{\text{net sales}}$$

$$= \frac{\$1,095,000}{\$5,230,000} = 0.209$$
$$= 20.9\%$$

By computing this ratio over several months or years, you can determine whether your expenses have been rising in relation to your net sales. Also, isolate each expense line individually and calculate its size in relation to net sales if you want to compare the changes in each from period to period. If, for example, your sales have not been growing but expenses have been rising because of higher salaries or a rent increase, consider ways to increase sales or reduce expenses. Unfortunately, runaway expenses can erode your profits in a short time, so this is a key ratio to watch.

## OTHER ANALYTICAL TOOLS

Apart from the operating ratios that can be calculated from the income statement, other financial analysis techniques can be applied to improve your marketing decisions. In particular, you'll want to be able to compute the inventory turnover rate and the return on investment for your business.

### Inventory Turnover Rate

Also called the merchandise turnover rate or the stock turnover rate, this calculation measures the number of times an average inventory turns over (sells out) during a particular period of time. If your business deals with service rather than tangible goods, you won't be able to apply this ratio. Here are two formulas for the inventory turnover rate:

$$\text{Inventory turnover rate} = \frac{\text{cost of goods sold}}{\text{average inventory at cost}}$$

or

$$\text{Inventory turnover rate} = \frac{\text{net units sold}}{\text{average inventory (in units)}}$$

Although the inventory turnover can be calculated in terms of either dollars or units, you'll probably compute this ratio using dollar costs most of the time. To find the inventory turnover rate for a one-year period, for example, start by calculating the average inventory for the year. To do this, (1) add together the cost of inventory on hand at the beginning of the year and the cost of inventory on hand at the end of the year, (2) divide by 2, (3) divide the total cost of goods sold during the year by the average inventory figure for the year, and (4) the result is your inventory turnover rate for that year.

If a plumbing wholesaler started the year with inventory costing $500,000 and ended the year with inventory costing $650,000, the average inventory for the year would be ($500,000 + $650,000)/2, or $575,000. During the year, cost of goods sold totaled $1,800,000, so the inventory turnover rate for that year would have been

$$\text{Inventory turnover rate} = \frac{\text{cost of goods sold}}{\text{average inventory at cost}}$$

$$= \frac{\$1,800,000}{\$575,000}$$

$$= 3.1 \text{ turns}$$

Why is inventory turnover important? It shows how quickly your inventory is selling, and generally the faster you move your products out the door, the healthier your business is. By analyzing the turnover of all the products in your product line on a monthly basis, you can see which sell faster and which sell more slowly, so you can reorder realistically in the future. Also, if your inventory turnover rate is high, it means you're not tying your money up for a long time in inventory that is sitting around waiting to be sold, and you may be able to afford to invest in marketing programs or developing new products. However, if your inventory turnover rate is too high, you may find you're out of stock when customers want to buy particular items. So inventory turnover is a delicate balance between having sufficient stock on hand to satisfy customers and having so much money tied up in slow-moving merchandise that you can't finance all the marketing programs you'd like.

## Return on Investment

Return on investment (ROI) is one of the most important of all the financial ratios because it shows how productively your firm is using the funds it invests in the business. This is the formula for ROI:

$$\text{Return on investment} = \frac{\text{net profit}}{\text{investment}}$$

The term *investment* refers to the money the organization has allocated to the SBU or product you're analyzing. For example, if a new product will cost $320,000 for research and development, production, and marketing, and the net profit before taxes is projected to be $65,000 during the first year, here is how you calculate the ROI for this product:

$$\text{Return on investment} = \frac{\text{net profit}}{\text{investment}} = \frac{\$65,000}{\$320,000}$$

$$= 0.203$$
$$= 20.3\%$$

You won't find the term "investment" on the income statement. However, you can develop an investment figure from the *balance sheet,* an accounting statement of the organization's financial situation at a given time. On the balance sheet you will find the company's assets and liabilities, and you can substitute the total assets figure for the investment number if it's not available. Just be sure to select only assets used in the SBU or product you're analyzing, rather than including assets that are deployed in other business units or products.

You may want to use an alternative method of calculating ROI to get a more detailed look at the numbers and to determine what you can do to improve your return. This is the expanded version of the ROI formula:

$$\text{Return on investment} = \frac{\text{net sales}}{\text{investment}} \times \frac{\text{net income}}{\text{net sales}}$$

The ratio on the right should be familiar: It's the profit margin on sales ratio. The ratio on the left measures the number of times your sales turned over in a given period, compared with the capital you invested in the product or SBU. When you multiply the two together, the result is the equivalent of the shorter ROI formula. However, the advantage of expanding the formula is that you can see the separate impact of your investment, your net sales, and your net income. If you need to raise your ROI, you'll be able to pinpoint which of the components should be adjusted and project what the results will be. An example of the expanded ROI formula is

$$\text{Return on investment} = \frac{\text{net sales}}{\text{investment}} \times \frac{\text{net income}}{\text{net sales}}$$

$$= \frac{\$700,000}{\$400,000} \times \frac{\$50,000}{\$700,000}$$

$$= 1.75 \times 0.07 = 0.12$$
$$= 12\%$$

In this case, you may decide that the ROI doesn't justify such a high investment rate, so you make plans to cut your investment next year. If you now cut next year's investment by $150,000 to $250,000, you'll raise your ROI to 20 percent (2.80 × 0.07 = 0.20). Many corporations set ROI goals that products and product lines must achieve, so marketers proposing new products must calculate the ROI using a variety of investment, net sales, and profit margin scenarios to be sure that they can attain the required ROI.

## Market Share

Over and over again, you've read that increasing market share is an important goal for many marketers. How do you measure market share? You can calculate share in a particular market by units sold or by monetary value:

$$\text{Market share} = \frac{\text{your number of units sold}}{\text{all units sold}}$$

or

$$\text{Market share} = \frac{\text{value of your sales}}{\text{value of all sales}}$$

For example, if you're a manufacturer of remote-controlled model airplanes and you know that 680,000 were sold in South America last year and that your firm sold 425,500 of them, your market share in South America would be 425,500/680,000, or 62.6 percent. To measure your share of the market in terms of value, you divide your dollar sales by the value of all sales of your product type made in the market. So if you sold $285,000 worth of photocopier paper in Denver last year, and your research indicates that total sales of photocopier paper in the city was approximately $4,296,000 that year, your market share in Denver would be $285,000/$4,296,000, or 6.6 percent.

However, when you're marketing a service product, you may not be able to measure units sold the way you would when marketing a tangible product. In that case, you might want to compare your number of customers to the total number of potential customers in the market. To calculate your market share, divide the number of customers you have by the overall number of potential customers in the market. For example, if you're a bank marketer offering special checking accounts for college students, you could measure your market share by dividing the number of college students you have as customers by the number of college students who are in your area.

By calculating market share over a period of time, you can see whether you're gaining or losing ground. Also, keep an eye on the estimated market shares of your competitors to see who is taking share away from whom, and why. Of course, the market potential for a product may expand or contract over time; therefore, update your figures or estimates for all units sold every year, at a minimum.

## WHOLESALE AND RETAIL PRICING CALCULATIONS

Chapter 11 discusses standard markup pricing, a type of cost-plus pricing in which you add a predetermined percentage to your cost to arrive at the selling price. Channel members in wholesaling and retailing frequently use markup pricing (see Exhibit B.2). Although this method doesn't take into account demand, competition, or profit, it is a useful technique for a marketer who must price too many different products to be able to set selling prices individually. Similarly, when retailers hold a sale, they generally lower prices using a percentage formula to keep the calculations manageable. Whether you're setting your initial prices or lowering prices to move your merchandise, these are calculations you'll use again and again.

## Markup Pricing

*Markup pricing,* also called markon pricing, involves adding a percentage (called a markup) to the cost to arrive at a selling price. You can calculate markup pricing in two ways: in terms of the cost and in terms of the selling price. Here are the two formulas:

$$\text{Markup percentage (on cost)} = \frac{\text{markup in dollars}}{\text{cost in dollars}}$$

$$\text{Markup percentage (on selling price)} = \frac{\text{markup in dollars}}{\text{selling price}}$$

Most retailers express markup as a percentage of selling price, but sometimes smaller retailers and wholesalers prefer to express markup as a percentage of cost. With either method you're describing the percentage difference between the selling price and the cost, but each of the two methods will give a different percent-

### Exhibit B.2   MARKUPS IN THE RETAIL DISTRIBUTION CHANNEL

| | Cost | Selling Price to Next Channel Member (or to consumer) | Markup Percentage of Channel Member's Cost | Markup Percentage of Channel Member's Selling Price |
|---|---|---|---|---|
| Manufacturer | $ 8 | $12 | 50% | 33% |
| Wholesaler | $12 | $15 | 25% | 20% |
| Retailer | $15 | $20 | 33% | 25% |

Each channel member adds a markup percentage to the cost to arrive at the selling price the next member in the channel will pay. Although the manufacturer's cost for this product was $8, the consumer will see a selling price of $20 because of the markups in the channel.

## Exhibit B.3  MARKUP PERCENTAGES

| Selling Price | Product Cost | Markup Percentage on Cost | Markup Percentage on Selling Price |
|---|---|---|---|
| $20.00 | $10.00 | 100% | 50% |
| $20.00 | $11.00 | 82% | 45% |
| $20.00 | $12.00 | 67% | 40% |
| $20.00 | $13.00 | 54% | 35% |
| $20.00 | $14.00 | 43% | 30% |
| $20.00 | $15.00 | 33% | 25% |
| $20.00 | $16.00 | 25% | 20% |
| $20.00 | $17.00 | 18% | 15% |
| $20.00 | $18.00 | 11% | 10% |
| $20.00 | $19.00 | 5% | 5% |

This example shows the relationship that product cost has to markup percentages based on cost and on selling price.

age. As an example, assume that you're selling a clock that cost you $15, and you mark it up $5 to a selling price of $20. Here's how the markup percentage would be calculated in terms of cost and in terms of selling price:

$$\text{Markup percentage (on cost)} = \frac{\text{markup in dollars}}{\text{cost in dollars}}$$
$$= \frac{\$5}{\$15}$$
$$= 0.333$$
$$= 33.3\%$$

$$\text{Markup percentage (on selling price)} = \frac{\text{markup in dollars}}{\text{selling price}}$$
$$= \frac{\$5}{\$20}$$
$$= 0.25$$
$$= 25\%$$

Although the dollar amount of the markup is the same in this example, you can see that the markup calculated as a percentage of cost is higher than the markup calculated as a percentage of the selling price.

What if you know the markup on the selling price and want to find out the markup on the cost, or what if you know the markup on the cost and need to figure the markup on the selling price? Exhibit B.3 shows how these values can be converted. However, easy formulas are available to convert from one to the other. Here's the conversion formula to change markup percentage on selling price to markup percentage on cost:

$$\text{Markup percentage (on cost)} = \frac{\text{markup percentage (on selling price)}}{100\% - \text{markup percentage (on selling price)}}$$

Going back to the clock you were selling for $20 in the last example, if your markup percentage on cost is 33 percent, the conversion calculation would look like this:

$$\text{Markup percentage (on cost)} = \frac{25\%}{100\% - 25\%}$$
$$= \frac{25\%}{75\%}$$
$$= 0.333$$
$$= 33.3\%$$

Now suppose you want to convert from the markup percentage on cost to the markup percentage on selling price. You would use this formula:

$$\text{Markup percentage (on selling price)} = \frac{\text{markup percentage (on cost)}}{100\% + \text{markup percentage (on cost)}}$$

To apply this formula, if your markup percentage on cost is 33 percent, you would compute the conversion like this:

$$\text{Markup percentage (on selling price)} = \frac{33.3\%}{100\% + 33.3\%}$$
$$= \frac{33.3\%}{133.3\%}$$
$$= 0.25$$
$$= 25\%$$

When using these formulas, remember that selling price is always considered to be 100 percent, which is why that percentage is shown in the denominator of both formulas. When you use markup percentage on cost, your cost plus the markup added together equals 100 percent; however, when you use markup percentage on selling price, you are adding your markup percentage to the selling price, bringing the total over 100 percent. To demonstrate these relationships, try this computation:

Cost $15 = 100% of cost = 75% of selling price ($15/$20)

\+ Markup $5 = 33.3% of cost = 25% of selling price ($5/$20)

= Selling price $20 = 133.3% of cost = 100% of selling price ($20/$20)

In the last line of this calculation, you can see that adding together the markup and the cost yields $20, which is 133.3 percent of cost—but 100 percent of the selling price.

## Markdown Pricing

When retailers and wholesalers put merchandise on sale, clear out old merchandise, or lower the price on spoiled or damaged merchandise, they use *markdowns* to reduce the original selling price. To calculate the markdown as a percentage of the original selling price, use this formula:

$$\text{Markdown percentage} = \frac{\text{markdown in dollars}}{\text{original selling price in dollars}}$$

To illustrate, assume that your $20 clock isn't selling well and you decide to mark it down by $4 to sell it at $16. You calculate the markdown percentage this way:

$$\text{Markdown percentage} = \frac{\$4}{\$20}$$
$$= 0.20$$
$$= 20\%$$

Most of the time, you'll use markdowns on items that have been in stock and selling for at least several weeks, which means that you've sold some of the items at the original selling price and some at the markdown price. So compute the *markdown ratio,* which will show you the effect of your markdowns on the entire inventory of items sold. This is the markdown ratio formula:

$$\text{Markdown ratio} = \frac{\text{markdowns in dollars}}{\text{total sales in dollars}}$$

As an example, suppose you were able to sell five clocks at the original selling price of $20 and six clocks at the markdown price of $16. You would calculate your markdown ratio in this way:

$$\text{Markdown ratio} = \frac{6 \times \$4}{(5 \times \$20) + (6 \times \$16)}$$
$$= \frac{\$24}{\$100 + \$96}$$
$$= \frac{\$24}{\$196}$$
$$= 0.122$$
$$= 12.2\%$$

As you can see, the markdown ratio for all clocks sold is 12.2 percent, although you took a 20 percent markdown on the six clocks you put on sale. The more merchandise you can sell at the original selling price, the lower your markdown ratio will be. Because markdowns eat into the profit margin that's built into the original selling price, carefully monitor your markdown ratio. The larger retailers compute markdown ratios on a department-by-department basis, and they also consider markdown ratios when evaluating the profit performance of their buyers in a given season and over a longer period of time.

### SHARPEN YOUR MARKETING SKILLS

1. How can you use the income statement to make better marketing decisions? Refer to the sample income statement in Exhibit B.1; explain which sections are of particular importance, and why.
2. From the following information, set up the income statement for this hardware store for the month ending April 30 of this year:

| | |
|---|---|
| Sales | $4,436 |
| Returns, allowances | $ 158 |
| Merchandise on hand, 4/1 | $6,550 |
| Merchandise on hand, 4/30 | $5,902 |
| Goods purchased during April | $2,229 |
| Sales salaries | $ 525 |
| Administrative salaries | $ 223 |
| Marketing costs | $ 48 |
| Utilities expense | $ 27 |
| Rent | $ 125 |
| Taxes | $ 181 |

3. You've just been hired to handle marketing for a book publisher, and you've been given copies of their last two quarterly income statements:

*Book Publisher, January 1–March 31, 1994*

| | |
|---|---|
| Sales | $21,413 |
| Returns, allowances | $ 1,550 |
| Merchandise on hand, 1/1 | $ 2,988 |
| Merchandise on hand, 3/31 | $ 3,615 |
| Goods purchased during 3 months | $16,222 |
| Sales salaries | $ 1,183 |
| Posters, promotion | $ 215 |
| Electricity, telephone expense | $ 369 |
| Administrative salaries | $ 254 |
| Rent | $ 1,005 |
| Taxes | $ 390 |

*Book Publisher, April 1–June 30, 1994*

| | |
|---|---|
| Sales | $23,775 |
| Returns, allowances | $ 1,892 |
| Merchandise on hand, 4/1 | $ 3,615 |
| Merchandise on hand, 6/30 | $ 2,134 |
| Goods purchased during 3 months | $15,229 |
| Sales salaries | $ 1,228 |

| | | |
|---|---|---|
| Posters, promotion | $ | 196 |
| Electricity, telephone expense | $ | 380 |
| Administrative salaries | $ | 223 |
| Rent | $ | 1,005 |
| Taxes | $ | 590 |

a. Calculate for each quarter (1) the gross profit ratio, (2) the profit margin on sales ratio, and (3) the operating expense ratio.

b. Comparing the ratios from the two quarters, do you think the publisher has any problem areas? Explain.

4. The following income statement for an apparel wholesaler is incomplete:

*Income Statement for 12 Months Ending January 31, 1995*

| | |
|---|---|
| Sales revenue: | |
| Sales | $650,600 |
| Returns and allowances | $ X |
| Net sales | $639,800 |
| Cost of goods sold: | |
| Merchandise on hand, 2/1/94 | $188,350 |
| Purchases (at cost) | $466,590 |
| Inbound transportation | $ 27,330 |
| Cost of goods available for sale | $682,270 |
| Merchandise on hand, 1/31/95 | $ X |
| Cost of goods sold | $488,560 |
| Gross profit | $151,240 |
| Operating expenses: | |
| Office manager salary | $ 12,500 |
| Sales salaries | $ 33,515 |
| Utilities expense | $ 8,455 |
| Magazine ads | $ 15,380 |
| Rent | $ 28,610 |
| Office supplies | $ 2,945 |
| Total operating expenses | $101,405 |
| Income before taxes | $ X |
| Taxes | $ 14,590 |
| Net income | $ 35,245 |

Use your knowledge of the relationship between the elements to calculate these elements:
a. Returns and allowances
b. Merchandise in inventory on January 31, 1995
c. Income before taxes

5. In the course of conducting an environmental scan for the video store you've managed for two years, you look at your two main competitors, Store A and Store B.

| | Store A | Store B | Your Store |
|---|---|---|---|
| Goods in stock, 1/1/92 | $125,602 | $139,631 | $105,844 |
| Goods in stock, 12/31/92 | $ 91,926 | $146,221 | $ 88,368 |
| Cost of goods sold, 1/1–12/31 | $396,429 | $339,795 | $299,480 |

a. Use these figures to calculate the annual inventory turnover rate for blank videotapes at your store and at your two competitors' stores.

b. If the average inventory turnover rate for blank videotape sales should be 3.5, how would you rate the performance of your store and your competitors' stores against the industry standard?

c. If your store doesn't achieve 3.5 turns a year, how could you improve your turnover rate?

6. Imagine you're selling apples and you want to keep your inventory turnover rate high enough to sell the apples before they spoil, which happens after a week. You started the month with 228 apples in your bin, you ended the month with 264 in your bin, and you sold 941 apples during the month.

a. Compute your inventory turnover rate for the month.

b. If you didn't achieve your goal of 4 stockturns per month, what should you do to improve your inventory turnover rate?

7. You have only one outlet, but you're considering opening a second branch of your video store. The following table shows the current investment, net sales, and net profits for your current store, and your estimates for the new store:

| | Original Store | New Branch (Estimated) | Combined |
|---|---|---|---|
| Investment | $250,490 | $204,500 | X |
| Net sales | $550,010 | $425,405 | X |
| Net income | $ 49,365 | $ 42,760 | X |
| ROI (%) | X | X | X |

Calculate the return on investment for your original store, for the new branch, and for the combined operation, using the expanded formula.

8. Take another look at the ROI calculations in question 7 and consider whether opening a second store is a good idea.

a. Do you think you should open the second store? Defend your answer.

b. Your goal is to achieve ROI of 21 percent on the combined operation of both stores. What can you do to raise your ROI results to that level?

9. A lighting fixture manufacturer asks you to research its market share for the past three years and report on the trends. By examining the manufacturer's records and reading industry newsletters, you obtain the following information about unit sales of lighting fixtures in your market. What is the manufacturer's market share of units sold in each year?

| | 1993 | 1994 | 1995 |
|---|---|---|---|
| Total number of lighting fixtures sold | 44,605 | 46,400 | 46,800 |
| Number of units sold by manufacturer | 5,630 | 5,685 | 5,710 |

10. The lighting fixture manufacturer has asked you to prepare a report on the results of your market share analysis. What are the marketing implications of the market share trends you see, both for the market overall and for this particular manufacturer?

11. As an appliance dealer, you want to determine your selling prices for the new models of washing machines you've just purchased from Maytag. Your goal for markup percentage on cost is 40 percent; model 1 costs $150, and model 2 costs $175.

a. What selling price should you charge for each model to achieve your markup goal?

b. Calculate the markup on each model in terms of percentage of selling price.

12. Back at the appliance dealership, you're examining your pricing strategy for dishwashers on your sales floor. You've set a 45 percent markup goal on the selling price for the three models in stock. Convert the following markup percentages on cost to markup percentages on selling price. Do all three models meet your goal? Which, if any, are priced too low?
    a. Model A: 67 percent markup on cost
    b. Model B: 150 percent markup on cost
    c. Model C: 233 percent markup on cost

13. Assume you own a greeting card store and you're running a clearance sale on boxes of Christmas cards left over from the holiday season. The original selling price was $12 per box, and you reduce the price to $8 for clearance.
    a. What is the markdown percentage?
    b. If you don't sell all the cards and you lower the price from $8 to $3 per box, what is the new markdown percentage? (Assume that the clearance price of $8 is the selling price in this calculation.)

14. From November 15 to January 10, you were able to sell all your boxed Christmas cards, but at various prices. Before Christmas, you sold 50 boxes at $12 each. From December 26 to December 31, you sold 28 boxes at $8 each.

After January 1, you sold 12 boxes at $3 each. What is your markdown ratio?

15. You've been hired to manage the children's shoe department at the department store in the mall. One of your first tasks is to look at the three product lines you offer to see whether you have a problem with markdowns.

*Sneakers and athletic shoes*
128 sold @ $28 per pair
143 sold @ $22 per pair

*Dress shoes*
87 sold @ $44 per pair
71 sold @ $24 per pair

*Boots*
65 sold @ $18 per pair
33 sold @ $12 per pair

a. Using the information given, compute the markdown ratio for your product lines.

b. Your store manager requires that the markdown ratio be kept at less than 20 percent for each department. If the average of your three lines were to edge over that figure, how would you reduce the ratio?

# C

# Career Planning and Development in Marketing

## EXPLORING MARKETING CAREERS IN THE 1990S AND BEYOND

If you'd like to be part of a stimulating aspect of business that will present plenty of challenges and opportunities in the coming decades, you'll find that marketing is the career for you. As discussed often in this book, marketing encompasses a wide variety of functions, each making an important contribution to the success of the organization. As the age of marketing continues and more companies around the world embrace the marketing concept, you can expect the number of opportunities to expand. In fact, even if you don't start out in a job that's categorized as marketing, you will probably find yourself interacting in some way with the marketing function in your firm. If you take the entrepreneurial route favored by more and more people, you'll definitely have a marketing hat to wear.

This component chapter will help you sort out your options in marketing careers and map some of the steps you can take toward landing a marketing job. The first section describes the organizations that employ marketers, reviews the many flavors of marketing, outlines what life is like for marketers, and then talks about career paths. In the second section, you get a closer look at specific marketing functions and jobs. The third section is all about how to market yourself to prospective employers. The closing section is an overview of sources for further information about marketing careers.

## The Market for Marketers

In the private sector, virtually every company, large or small, needs some form of marketing. In the smallest concerns, the president may be the head marketer, but these companies often hire specialized vendors such as marketing research suppliers and advertising agencies to handle specific marketing tasks. Although the top executive in larger companies generally establishes a vision and direction for the marketing function, these firms can organize their marketing departments in various ways, creating a wide range of openings for people trained in marketing disciplines (see Chapter 22).

Companies in the private sector aren't the only organizations that use marketing talent. Government agencies and nonprofit organizations are adopting the marketing concept. Nonprofit groups now use marketing in a variety of ways, including raising funds, recruiting volunteers, and attracting clients or patients to serve. You'll find lots of opportunities to use your talents in these organizations by working directly for the government or a nonprofit agency or by working for a marketing vendor that handles nonprofit marketing assignments. (Helping nonprofit organizations with their marketing challenges is also a great way to volunteer your services and broaden your own marketing experience.)

Your choices in marketing careers are exceptionally wide: You can market services or goods; you can handle consumer products or industrial products; you can work in the public sector or in the private sector. To narrow your focus and choose among these options, consider your own background and interests. Most of the time, you can transfer skills you learn in one area of marketing to a position in another area of marketing, so don't feel limited by your initial selection.

## On the Job

As the global economy moves toward the year 2000, marketing is a fast-paced arena in which customer needs and changes in the marketing environment affect your everyday marketing decisions. Whether you're a newcomer or a seasoned veteran, you find yourself planning for tomorrow at the same time that you're reacting to today's trends. Because customers are more knowledgeable than ever before (and because they are bombarded by more messages than ever before), you are facing a particular challenge in communicating and persuading. With "junk mail," "junk fax," and even marketing at the movies, consumers are growing weary and wary of the onslaught. To make an impact in this crowded marketplace, you have to think on the run, analyze your products and your markets carefully, and dig into your creative talents for innovative ideas. You also need a strong dose of cross-cultural awareness (to navigate in complex international markets) and a keen sensitivity to environmental concerns.

Because you must work with impressive new technology to access and analyze ever larger marketing databases, to pinpoint your target markets, and to measure your results, computer literacy and quantitative skills (statistics, systems analysis, and so on) are important. New media are available to help you reach your targets, including computerized interactive retailing and international satellite communication. You can also share in the satisfaction of uncovering and fulfilling customer needs through the marketing process, especially in markets such as Eastern Europe, where marketing is a relatively new phenomenon. If you like to travel, or if you have foreign-language skills, note that the global dimensions of the marketing profession are becoming increasingly important. As a professional marketer, you are challenged daily to respond to customer needs, stay on top of the marketing environment, and hone your marketing skills.

## Up the Ladder

Whether you're looking at entry-level or midcareer opportunities, a marketing career promises many exciting paths, including a climb to the very top. Many of the top executives in the largest corporations either started in marketing or had some experience there along the way. Most of the time, the top of the marketing ladder is a position as vice president (or senior vice president) of marketing, guiding all the key marketing functions in an organization. With a number of years of marketing under your belt, you can also con-

sider a consulting career helping organizations that need marketing expertise. Marketing consultants experience the excitement of solving marketing problems for their clients, and they rarely encounter the same problem (or use the same solution) twice in a row. Further, if you think you'll ever have your own business, keep in mind that marketing is critical to the success of any entrepreneurial activity.

## EXAMINING YOUR CAREER OPTIONS

As we move toward the twenty-first century, the types of jobs that were traditional in marketing are evolving, even as new roles have come into existence. These days, you're in marketing whether you're a database manager keeping customer and prospect information up-to-date, a telemarketing representative calling consumers to offer products, or a writer putting together a customer newsletter that features your firm's products.

Many of these new positions have come about because of technological advances; others are the result of changes in the marketing environment. For example, as discussed in Chapter 21, quality and customer service are the new frontiers of marketing, and a variety of jobs are being created to help marketers tame that new frontier. Moreover, an increasing number of companies have set up business teams and task forces to foster a new group-marketing environment, which spreads marketing responsibility beyond the product or brand manager by including representatives from many departments, manufacturing among them. At Procter & Gamble, for example, brand managers still guide the daily progress of each product, but the business-team approach has sped up new-product development and enhanced marketing and manufacturing productivity.

The following sections present the major functional areas in or related to marketing, and they describe selected jobs in each area. Bear in mind that some firms prefer that applicants have an MBA in marketing, management, or a related discipline.

## Product Management

Whether they're marketing consumers or organizational products, most companies rely on the product-based approach to marketing. As discussed in Chapter 22, product managers are totally devoted to the health and welfare of their own products and are not concerned with other products in the firm's product portfolio. Product managers (called brand managers in some firms) develop and implement comprehensive marketing plans for their products, covering all aspects of the marketing mix, from advertising and promotion to packaging and marketing research. They need excellent communication skills to enlist the cooperation and support of other departments with the functional responsibility for performing specific activities such as marketing research, manufacturing, and public relations. They must also have good analytical skills to understand the market, their customers' needs, and the product life cycle. In some firms, product or brand managers are much like internal entrepreneurs because they're the ones in charge, thinking about how to boost their products' profits and how to satisfy customer needs.

Procter & Gamble originated the concept of brand-management. When filling a brand-management position, the company recruits you directly out of college or graduate school, and your entry-level position at P&G is generally brand assistant. Within two years, if all goes well, you can progress to a sales trainee slot in the field, where you concentrate on in-store displays and promotions, working closely with store managers. The next step is away from your original brand and on to a different product as an assistant brand manager. As you gain experience, you'll probably move up to brand manager after several years. At many firms, the next rung on the career ladder is group product manager, and from there, you can advance to vice president–product management or vice president–general manager.

Professionals have found many ways to step onto the brand-management ladder. Some consumer-oriented companies hire people from other disciplines, such as sales or advertising, and put them into product manager roles. Industrial product marketers tend to pull people from the technical ranks (engineers, designers) as well as from the marketing and sales departments for brand management. Just as consumer marketers manage their own brands, such as Crest toothpaste or Jell-O desserts, organizational marketers manage their own brands, such as 3M abrasives or Sikorsky helicopters. In the organizational setting, a typical route to the top might be to start as a salesperson or sales support engineer, move up to a management position in your discipline, cross over to the product manager side, and eventually reach the group product manager level. With the heightened attention that marketing is getting in the organizational end of the business, you might find such a firm a good place to build your marketing career.

## Distribution Management

If you enter distribution management, you'll be in a dynamic field that includes distribution operations, traffic and transportation, order administration, warehouse operations, materials management, and inventory control. Just-in-time delivery is one of the hottest points of differentiation a firm can have today, and distribution is the key to its success. Just-in-time delivery depends on advanced electronic order and inventory control systems, so technical and analytical skills are needed, as is a sensitivity to the delivery requirements of your customers. Both consumer and industrial organizations hire distribution professionals, and you can often transfer your experience from one to the other, so you have some flexibility in your career path.

In distribution operations, you are responsible for supervising and coordinating virtually all the distribution activities of your organization and for staying abreast of any regulatory changes that may affect your distribution network. As a traffic and transportation specialist, you analyze available transportation options for the receipt of your materials and the shipment of your products to customers. By considering the mode of transportation, the routes, the carriers, the schedules, and other variables, your aim is to deliver your products on time while maintaining cost control. If you work in order administration, you deal with customers, process incoming orders, and coordinate delivery with your warehouse and your traffic and transportation specialists.

Warehouse operations cover a variety of functions that relate to receiving, storing, and shipping raw materials and finished products. In this role, you supervise the management of storage facilities for your organization, keeping products and materials secure and accessible. Materials management is another important part of distribution, in which you are charged with the movement of products and parts into or out of warehouses, generally using sophisticated automated systems. If you hold a position in inventory control, you help your organization maintain appropriate levels of products to meet projected and current customer demand. You also coordinate your analysis of stock levels with the production department to ensure that you don't end up with too much or too little product sitting in your warehouse. To become the director or manager of distribution for an organization, you rotate through many if not all of the distribution functions so that you have a thorough understanding of distribution operations.

## Retailing

There's nothing quite as fast-paced or as exciting as working in a retail store during the holiday season. Perhaps you've held a part-time job as a cashier, salesperson, or stock clerk in a local specialty or department store during the holiday rush or summer vacation. If so, then you've experienced the fun and the challenge of marketing goods and services to meet customer needs. It's not all glitter and glamour, of course: Working with the public can be very demanding, and the retail industry is extremely competitive in every aspect of the marketing mix. Therefore, to succeed in retailing, you need a healthy dose of imagination, good analytical skills, and the ability to get along with colleagues, suppliers, and customers.

Depending on the size and type of retailer you join, a wide variety of positions are open to you, offering various ways to get to the top. You can choose from two distinctly different career paths: store management and merchandise management. Store management encompasses such functions as sales, finance and accounting, store credit, in-store and mail-order sales, and facilities management. Merchandise management is an umbrella term for all buying functions, including buyers, group merchandise managers, and divisional merchandise managers.

If you join the management training program of a giant retailer such as Wal-Mart or J. C. Penney, you generally spend time in each of the store management departments, learning the business and interacting with customers. After you've been exposed to a variety of store functions, you move into a sales management assignment, where you are in charge of the sales staff for a particular department. In this role, you prepare sales plans and implement merchandise promotions. You also keep an eye on your inventory level and your profit margin to be sure the store's investment in merchandise is paying off. Finally, you supervise the sales professionals who work in your department. From here, you can progress to higher levels of store management, such as branch management, or you can move into merchandise management.

In merchandise management, the buyer's role is similar to the role of a product or brand manager in a consumer or industrial products company. As a buyer, you are in charge of your own product lines, you arrange to buy or produce merchandise from brand name or private label manufacturers, and then you take care of appropriate packaging, pricing, and promotion. If you succeed, you're in line for a promotion to merchandise manager, where you supervise a number of buyers who buy products in related merchandise areas. Merchandise managers report to group or divisional merchandise managers, who typically oversee the merchandising activities in a broad product category such as menswear. You also have a good shot at the top rung: Many retail CEOs came up through the merchandising route, although a fair number are store management veterans.

## Marketing Communications

Marketing communications is one of the most visible functions in all of marketing. After all, only in marketing communications can you have the opportunity to see your work on national television during a commercial break from the Super Bowl. Although you may never personally experience such a thrill, you can enjoy the satisfaction of knowing that you helped influence customer behavior, whether it's through advertising, sales promotion, direct response, or public relations. All kinds of positions are available in marketing communications if you are creative and have superior communication talents.

To build a career in advertising or sales promotion, you can work either in an ad agency or on the "client side," where you'll manage advertising and sales promotion for a consumer or industrial products firm or a nonprofit organization. Specialized sales promotion agencies do exist, but advertising agencies are increasingly folding this function into their full-service capabilities to serve their clients more efficiently. In an ad agency, you might work in one of the creative services. For example, as a copywriter you would consider the features and benefits of your client's product as you create a set of words and graphics that will produce a powerful message to be projected via magazines, newspapers, television, or new interactive media. Or if you have the talent, you can join the art department, where you'll actually develop the artwork for the ads your agency places. After the copywriting and art departments have worked on an ad, the production specialists take the words and artwork and turn them into storyboards and scripts (for television commercials) or into other formats that are appropriate for the chosen advertising medium.

The media department handles media planning and media buying. As a media planner, you take a close look at the target market and then analyze how various media vehicles will help you reach that target most effectively and efficiently. Media planners often carry the additional responsibility for buying print space for ads. As a media buyer, you buy broadcast time for your ads, to the tune of thousands or millions of dollars. In fact, the media department has become such a critical part of advertising that independent agencies have sprung up, specializing in this function only; some clients want even more control, so they handle media planning and placements themselves.

Another key group within the ad agency is account management, also known as account or client services. Account executives stay in close contact with their clients, learning about their advertising and sales promotion needs and communicating those needs to the creative services people who develop the actual ads. Once the creative side comes up with concepts, the account executive presents them to the client and obtains approval before proceeding with production and placement. To start in this group, you may be assigned as an assistant account executive, working on one client's brand or product, moving up to the account executive's slot after a period of time. This is one of the most demanding jobs in advertising because within the agency you're the voice of the client, keeping your projects on track; within the client's organization, you're the voice of the agency, presenting concepts and media plans. In short, you're at the hub of the wheel, so your communication and persuasion skills had better be top-notch.

On the client side, you may work for a retailer or for a consumer or industrial products firm, directing and coordinating the advertising and sales promotion efforts of your business. Typically, you set goals, supervise the one or more suppliers who handle your advertising and sales promotion activities, and evaluate the results. Sometimes you can move from the agency side to the client side, or you might start on the client side and move to the agency, depending on your particular skills and experience.

An increasing number of firms are using direct-response techniques to reach their target markets, making this a dynamic field. Direct response includes direct mail and telemarketing, and you again have the choice of working on the agency side or on the client side. Working for a supplier, you select from the same categories of jobs you might hold in an ad agency: creative services, account management, and media. If you join the creative services team, you write letter copy or draft telephone scripts, develop the layout and graphics, and consider the impact these elements will have on sales. In the media department, you prepare detailed media plans for each client, track down prospect databases, and if you're handling television or radio direct response, arrange for broadcast time. On the account management end, you are your client's main contact with the agency, staying on top of all the little details that make a direct-response program successful.

Another key role you can play in marketing communications is that of public relations specialist. As discussed in Chapter 18, many organizations—private, public, for-profit, and nonprofit—employ public relations practitioners, and they often hire public relations agencies to handle specific assignments. To do well in this exciting field, you need creative flair and above-average communication skills, both written and oral. As with other functions in the marketing communications world, you can join an agency or work for a client.

On the client side, you might handle projects in public affairs, community relations, media relations, employee relations, or investor relations. At the top of your career ladder is the position of director or vice president of public relations. On the agency side, you might start as an assistant account executive, working with your supervisor on several client accounts in a general area such as sports marketing, health care, or new-product introductions. You can then move up to account executive and on to agency management.

## Sales

In many industries, personal selling is the linchpin around which the marketing program is built. As discussed in Chapter 19, the range of products marketed through personal selling is wide, from highly technical, complex products such as industrial robots to everyday products such as cosmetics or services such as health insurance. Many sales positions offer attractive advantages for the motivated professional, including opportunities for travel, flexibility in setting your work hours, and the freedom to manage your territory in much the same way that an entrepreneur manages a business. To succeed in sales, you need lots of enthusiasm and persistence, well-developed communication skills, and the ability to interact with all types of people. Much of the time, you also need analytical and mathematical abilities, especially if you're working with customers who need solutions to financial or technical problems or if you're following up on customer service questions.

You may want to sell "to the trade," representing manufacturers who sell to wholesalers or retailers (who then resell your products). On the other hand, you may want to sell to end users, such as other businesses and consumers. Like many salespeople, you may start in sales support, playing an important customer service role and providing marketing support to the salespeople on your team. Then you move into a sales role, reporting to a sales manager who sets your sales goals, assigns specific territories, and arranges for training to keep your product and sales skills in tip-top shape. The top job in this area is the director or vice president of sales, directing all the sales activities of your organization.

If you sell to the trade, you are often called on to help your wholesalers and retailers maintain the proper inventory level to meet projected demand, and you may advise your customers on merchandising, pricing, and even advertising. When you sell to end users, you may be meeting with consumers, or you may be meeting with professional purchasing agents who buy for businesses, nonprofit organizations, or government agencies. In either case, you can be an inside or an outside salesperson. The inside salesperson sells by phone to customers and prospects near and far, whereas the outside salesperson meets with customers face-to-face. If you are an outside salesperson, you may have a local or regional territory; in the case of international products, you may be assigned one or more countries to cover.

Sometimes you work from a showroom, where you can display your products, but most often you carry samples or technical literature to educate your customers. Also, nearly every industry has a convention or trade show where hundreds of firms can buy exhibition space. If your firm participates, you may find yourself traveling to a major convention center or large hotel to demonstrate your products for customers and prospects who attend the show. Trade show sales is a lot of work, but it's also fun—and it's rewarding when you write up those big orders. Also keep in mind that your sales career can extend to your own business, whether you are an independent insurance agent, a real estate agent, or involved in some other type of self-employment.

## Marketing Research

Nearly every aspect of marketing relies on marketing research to identify marketing problems and opportunities, consider alternative marketing plans, and monitor performance. Chapter 6 discusses the wide range of marketing research and information systems that marketers use, and in this field, you face exciting challenges every day while you enjoy the satisfaction of helping uncover, measure, and fulfill customer needs. As with many other marketing careers, you can work for a supplier, handling many assignments for various clients, or you can work on the client side, managing marketing research to support only your company's products.

On the client side, you might start as a marketing research assistant, statistician, or junior project director, coordinating the activities of suppliers who handle marketing research for your organization or conducting selected research, statistical, and analytical projects. Your next move up may be to assistant marketing research director or project director, doing more conceptual work in planning large-scale marketing research projects and selecting qualified suppliers; you might also manage research assistants and junior staff. At the top, you can be director or vice president of marketing research, supervising the entire marketing research function for your organization.

On the supplier side, you might begin your career in statistical research or in information systems. An entry-level statistician (or junior analyst) assists with a variety of tasks, including checking research samples and tabulating questionnaires. With experience, you can advance to formulating hypotheses, designing samples, creating questionnaires, and analyzing results, for example. You can work your way up to conducting focus group interviews, supervising direct-mail or telephone research, or handling observational research projects, depending on your firm's specialty. Another entry-level position is in marketing research information systems, working with primary and secondary research data to compile material and reports for the marketing department.

The hierarchy in a marketing research firm is similar to that of an advertising or public relations agency, where you can work in account management or handle marketing research and analysis. In fact, advertising agencies frequently have their own in-house marketing research departments, so you may want to consider that option in addition to the supplier or client side. You'll have opportunities to cross over from supplier or agency to the client side, so don't feel confined by your initial choice.

## ENTERING THE MARKETING WORLD

You've decided to be a marketer. Now you're faced with the most important marketing job of all: marketing yourself. This textbook includes marketing techniques that you can use in your own job search. Just put yourself in the dual role of marketer and product, and you are well on your way to a marketing career. The following sections show you how to start the job search process by considering your skills and your goals, targeting organizations where you'd like to work, and positioning yourself for the jobs you want. Once you're on the job, you have opportunities for further development, and you can be thinking ahead to your next step up the career ladder.

## Taking Inventory: Know Your Skills and Your Goals

The best place to start your job search is by assessing your own talents and setting your personal and professional goals. A lot of excellent books are available on self-assessment to guide you in taking stock of your abilities and interests and to help you match them to your objectives. (See the list of resources at the end of this component.) Consider your educational background and the technical skills you've gained in college. Also, spend time thinking about your strengths and weaknesses, and the kinds of tasks you love (and hate) to do. Look back at the jobs you've held, and consider why some were exciting or challenging and why some seemed dull or monotonous. By evaluating your talents and interests and by understanding why you liked or disliked jobs you've held, you're on your way to narrowing down the world of marketing careers to a handful that make sense and fit with your background. If your abilities don't match up to the careers you're considering, then take some additional courses, look for an internship to gain new skills, or find a job in a related field that gives you the needed experience. Note that in some marketing positions, an MBA is considered desirable, if not necessary. For instance, product/brand management and marketing research positions are typically filled by people with MBAs. Remember, you're the product, so you want to make yourself as marketable as possible.

Next, take the time to consider what you want out of life, personally and professionally. If you want fame or fortune, point yourself in that direction; if you want to help society or save the environment, point yourself in that direction. List the places you'd like to live and work, your salary expectations, and the position you'd like to hold in five years. Although it sounds premature to worry about the future before you even have your first marketing job, setting a career objective with a definite job in mind will help guide you when selecting the organizations to apply to for entry-level spots. Without the personal objectives and future goals, you are a marketer without a target market or a marketing strategy.

## Targeting Organizations

In this phase of the job search, use your marketing research and market segmentation skills to review the market and eliminate career options that are inappropriate or don't interest you; that way you can focus on those you'd really like to pursue. Using some of the sources listed at the end of this component, research the marketing areas you'd like to consider, look for information about the job market in those fields, read about what professionals do on the job, and see how the career paths match up to your five-year goal. If your interest is piqued, make a note of any companies or executives mentioned in these sources so that you can follow up later.

The trade journals and industry associations of the marketing specialties you're investigating can provide valuable information about trends and careers. Some associations have student memberships, giving you a chance to attend professional meetings and mingle with people who work in the field. Ask the staff at your college placement office and at your library about the *Occupational Outlook Handbook,* on-campus recruiting, and other help that's available. Also check one or two of the many excellent career guides for college students. Scan the want ads in the Sunday newspaper to get a feel for job descriptions, requirements, locations, and salary levels and to find the names of companies or employment agencies you can contact. Also, call your state employment office to see whether it has any job listings in marketing fields.

Talk with people you know who work in marketing; ask about the organizations they work for, what they do on the job, and whether they know of job opportunities in marketing. Perhaps some of the people you know can help you arrange an "information interview" with their employers. This type of interview gives you the opportunity to learn more about marketing and the operations of the firm. Even if there's no job immediately available, you'll have the advantage of having a contact if an opening should arise. However, information interviews may not be an accepted practice in your area, so don't overlook other opportunities to get information about your field of choice. You have a wider network than you might think, so ask relatives, friends, classmates, professors, and former employers whether they can help you meet with people who work in the marketing fields you'd like to join. Often, you get your big break through your network rather than through

a classified ad. Build a file of organizations you want to contact in your job search, and use this as your target market.

## Positioning and Marketing Yourself

You've defined your target market; how can you position and market yourself to your audience? The tools in your personal marketing mix include a résumé, cover letter, interview skills, and follow-up communications. Most of the time, you'll start by sending a résumé and a cover letter to the contact names on your list. (See the sample résumé in Exhibit C.1 on page 716 and the cover letter in Exhibit C.2 on page 717, and check the list of resources at the end of this component.)

Your résumé typically consists of a heading, including your name and address; an objective (optional); your educational background, including relevant courses you've taken; your employment experience, including any part-time or volunteer work; any activities and achievements, including community service participation, scholarships, and special language or computer skills; and references (optional).

Your cover letter is another marketing element, designed to catch the reader's attention and to be convincing about your qualifications for the job you're seeking. In most cases, be sure to create a slightly different version of your cover letter in order to position your background and qualifications for various employers and fields. For example, if you're targeting advertising agencies for a copywriting job, you may want to emphasize your work on the college newspaper. However, if you're targeting a marketing research supplier for an analytical job, you may want to emphasize the research project you conducted during your statistics course. Of course, the opening of your letter will vary, depending on whether you're answering an ad, requesting an information interview, or asking for a job interview.

If you've done a good job of positioning yourself, matching your skills and interests to the needs of the organizations in your target market, you'll land a job interview. Prospective employers make their decisions about candidates on the basis of the interview process, so read up on interviews and hone your skills. Come to interviews prepared with background information about the organization and some questions for the interviewer about the job and the firm. Practice answering the standard questions interviewers ask, such as "Why did you choose our company?" and "Why do you want to be in this field?" If you can, have yourself videotaped in a mock interview so that you can get a glimpse of how you look in action and can pinpoint areas for improvement.

Once you've been interviewed, following up and writing a thank-you letter is important. Not only is this good manners but it also gives you another opportunity to market yourself. Whether you are thanking someone for an information interview, a job interview, or a referral to another person or firm, say how much you appreciate the interviewer's time and interest. This follow-up needn't be a long letter, but send it soon after your meeting. If you should run across any items of interest—perhaps one executive mentioned an interest in marathons and you clipped a related article from your campus newspaper—you can keep the dialog going by sending the clipping with a brief personal note. By being personable yet professional, you'll stay on your interviewers' list of active candidates—and, in time, land a job in the field of your choice.

## On the Job

Congratulations! You've successfully launched your career in marketing. Don't stop now—it's never too soon to start thinking about the five-year career objectives you set when you were taking inventory of your skills and background. Watch for opportunities to learn new skills and make professional connections that will prepare you for the next rung on your career ladder. Your employer may offer to send you to a professional training course or technical seminar to introduce you to a new procedure, or you may be asked to assist a senior executive who's presenting a paper to an industry seminar. No matter what the opportunity, you're certain to hear about the latest trends and technology and to meet people from other firms, industries, or disciplines with whom you can exchange ideas.

**Exhibit C.1**
**SAMPLE RÉSUMÉ FOR A MARKETING POSITION**
If you are seeking an entry-level position right after graduation, prepare a functional résumé that emphasizes your areas of competence. Organize the résumé around a list of accomplishments, then identify your employers and academic experiences in the appropriate sections.

```
                          Barbara Holland
                         14014 Oak Boulevard
                        Philadelphia, PA 19111
                          (215) 747-4295

        OBJECTIVE
        * Obtain a position in market research that requires my experience
          in research design and statistical analysis

        RESEARCH DESIGN
        * Developed moderator discussion guides for 14 focus groups
          conducted at the Opinions Unlimited research center, Harrisburg,
          Pennsylvania
        * Created a direct-mail questionnaire to elicit college students'
          reactions to accounts offered by Philadelphia banks
        * Created a telephone interview questionnaire to research students'
          feelings about bank accounts available in Philadelphia

        RESEARCH ANALYSIS
        * Tabulated and analyzed results of direct-mail surveys and
          telephone interviews using SAS computer software
        * Presented findings about students' reactions to Philadelphia-area
          bank products to the Philadelphia Bank Association
        * Summarized and interpreted results of 8 customer-service focus
          group interviews and presented findings to the client

        SECONDARY RESEARCH
        * Researched scholarship funding issues for Temple University
          dean's office, using Dialog computer database
        * Conducted periodicals research for graduate students writing
          theses on marketing topics

        EDUCATION
        * Temple University, Philadelphia, September 1991-May 1995
        * B.A. Marketing (3.7 GPA on 4.0 scale)
        * Advanced workshops included: researching customer satisfaction;
          product concept testing; test marketing; personal interview
          techniques; and research interpretation.

        EXPERIENCE
        * September 1994-May 1995, Research Assistant, Temple University
          Library, Philadelphia, Pennsylvania
        * June 1994-August 1994, Evening Supervisor, Opinions Unlimited,
          Harrisburg, Pennsylvania
        * June 1993-August 1993, Research Intern, Opinions Unlimited,
          Harrisburg, Pennsylvania

        PERSONAL DATA
        * Excellent computer skills; reading knowledge of French

        REFERENCES
        * Leslie Burk, Director, Opinions Unlimited, 539 West Ninth Street,
          Harrisburg, PA 17112; (717) 555-1888
        * Joseph L. Pleasant, Administrator, Temple University Library,
          Philadelphia, PA 19122; (215) 555-9032
```

```
                                        14014 Oak Boulevard
                                        Philadelphia, PA 19111
                                        May 24, 1995

Ms. Theresa Bentley
Vice President, Consumer Research
Pennsylvania Bank of Commerce
6458 River Road
Pittsburgh, PA 15237

Dear Ms. Bentley:

During Temple University's recent Northeast Business symposium,
I met your assistant, John Anderson, who mentioned that you were
seeking to hire two research analysts.  After talking with
Mr. Anderson about the role of market research at Pennsylvania Bank
of Commerce, I believe that my experience in research design and
analysis would be an asset to your group.

In addition to my undergraduate course work in marketing theory
and applications, I have successfully completed a series of five
advanced workshops in market research taught by local practi-
tioners.  I am thoroughly familiar with the latest statistical
analysis computer programs, including SAS and SPSS.

To apply this knowledge, I selected as my senior project an in-
depth analysis of the student bank account market in Philadelphia.
To date, two members of the Philadelphia Bank Association have used
the results of my study to develop new banking products for college
students in the area.

Because your bank is known for customer service excellence, my
background in customer satisfaction research may be beneficial.
For two summers I worked at the Opinions Unlimited focus group
center in Harrisburg, assisting with research projects for two
retail clients.  During the second summer I was promoted to even-
ing supervisor because of my ability to identify potential service
problems and to recommend changes for improving customer relations.

Leslie Burk, director of Opinions Unlimited, will be happy to
confirm my accomplishments and answer any questions you may have
about my research skills.  Please see the enclosed resume for
additional references.

Given my background and interest in financial services, I would
appreciate the opportunity to meet with you to learn about your
department and discuss my qualifications in more detail.  I will
call your office next week to see when we can arrange a convenient
meeting.

                                        Sincerely,

                                        Barbara Holland

                                        Barbara Holland


Enclosure
```

**Exhibit C.2
SAMPLE COVER
LETTER REQUESTING
AN INTERVIEW**
Once you've compiled a list of
organizations to target, send a
letter like this one to ask for
an interview and further information.

Of course, the more skills you gain, the more valuable you are to your organization and the broader your
management perspective is. However, to make your
next move up the ladder, you may find that you need
additional qualifications, such as an MBA or a certificate in a specialized field. If you've identified your five-
year career goals in advance, you are better able to anticipate what you'll need to stay in the race. The more
you learn about your chosen area of marketing expertise, the better you'll be able to pinpoint the specific direction you want your career to take. Therefore, it's a
good idea to review and revise your five-year goals
from time to time to see where you are and to determine whether you want to shift to a different career
path. Welcome to the dynamic world of marketing.

## LOOKING FOR MORE INFORMATION

This section lists selected sources where you can get
additional information about marketing and marketing
careers.

### Professional and Trade Associations

American Advertising Federation
1400 K Street N.W., Suite 1000
Washington, DC 20005
(202) 898-0089

American Association of Advertising Agencies
666 Third Avenue, 13th Floor
New York, NY 10017
(212) 682-2500

American Marketing Association
250 South Wacker Drive, Suite 200
Chicago, IL 60606
(312) 648-0536

American Society of Transportation and Logistics
P.O. Box 33095
Louisville, KY 40232
(502) 451-8150

Association of National Advertisers
144 East 44th Street
New York, NY 10017
(212) 697-5950

Bank Marketing Association
309 West Washington Street
Chicago, IL 60606
(312) 782-1442

Direct Marketing Association
6 East 43d Street
New York, NY 10017
(212) 689-4977

International Advertising Association
342 Madison Avenue, 20th Floor
New York, NY 10017
(212) 557-1133

Life Insurance Marketing and Research Association
P.O. Box 208
Hartford, CT 06141
(203) 677-0033

Marketing Research Association
111 East Wacker Drive, Suite 600
Chicago, IL 60601
(312) 644-6610

Marketing Science Institute
1000 Massachusetts Avenue
Cambridge, MA 02138
(617) 491-2060

National Association for Professional Saleswomen
P.O. Box 2606
Novato, CA 94948
(415) 898-2606

National Association of Purchasing Management
2055 East Centennial Circle
P.O. Box 22160
Tempe, AZ 85282
(602) 752-6276

National Association of Wholesalers and Distributors
1725 K Street N.W.
Washington, DC 20006
(202) 872-0885

National Retail Federation
100 West 31st Street
New York, NY 10001
(212) 244-8780

Point-of-Purchase Advertising Institute
66 N. Van Brunt Street
Englewood, NJ 07631
(201) 894-8899

Public Relations Society of America
33 Irving Place, 3rd Floor
New York, NY 10003
(212) 995-2230

Sales and Marketing Executives International
Statler Office Tower, No. 458
Cleveland, OH 44115
(216) 771-6650

Women in Advertising and Marketing
4200 Wisconsin Avenue N.W., Suite 106–238
Washington, DC 20016
(202) 369-7400

## Career Planning Resources

CAREER PLANNING

Bolles, Richard N., *What Color Is Your Parachute? A Practical Manual for Job Hunters and Career Changers* (Berkeley, Calif.: Ten Speed Press, 1993).

Dumphy, Philip W., ed., *Career Development for the College Student,* 5th ed. (Cranston, R.I.: Carroll Press, 1981).

Fox, Maria, *Put Your Degree to Work: The New Professional's Guide to Career Planning and Job Hunting,* 2d ed. (New York: Wiley, 1988).

Graen, George B., *Unwritten Rules for Your Career: The 15 Secrets for FastTrack Success* (New York: Wiley, 1989).

Henze, Geraldine, *Winning Career Moves: A Guide to Improving Your Work Life* (Homewood, Ill.: Business One Irwin, 1992).

## CAREER GUIDES

*The Career Choices Encyclopedia: A Guide to Entry-Level Jobs* (New York: Walker, 1986).

Greenberg, Jan, *Advertising Careers: The Business and the People* (New York: Henry Holt, 1987).

Lewis, William, and Nancy Schuman, *Fast-Track Careers: A Guide to the Highest-Paying Jobs* (New York: Wiley, 1987).

Lidz, Richard, and Linda Perrin, eds., *Career Information Center,* 3d ed., 13 vols. (New York: Macmillan, 1987).

Porterfield, Jim, *Business Career Planning Guide* (Cincinnati: South-Western, 1993).

Rosenthal, David W., and Michael A. Powell, *Careers in Marketing* (Englewood Cliffs, N.J.: Prentice-Hall, 1984).

U.S. Bureau of Labor Statistics, *Occupational Outlook Handbook* (Washington, D.C.: GPO, 1994).

## Directories for Career Planning

Fry, Ronald W., ed., *Advertising Career Directory* (Hawthorne, N.J.: Career Press, 1990).

Fry, Ronald W., ed., *Marketing & Sales Career Directory,* 3d ed. (Hawthorne, N.J.: Career Press, 1990).

Fry, Ronald W., ed., *Public Relations Career Directory* (Hawthorne, N.J.: Career Press, 1990).

## JOB HUNTING

Beatty, Richard H., *The Complete Job Search Book* (New York: Wiley, 1988).

Beatty, Richard H., *The Perfect Cover Letter* (New York: Wiley, 1989).

Harkavy, Michael David, and the Philip Lief Group, *The 100 Best Companies to Sell For* (New York: Wiley, 1989).

Irish, Richard K., *Go Hire Yourself an Employer,* 3d ed. (Garden City, N.Y.: Doubleday/Anchor Press, 1987).

## RÉSUMÉ PREPARATION

Brett, Pat, *Résumé Writing for Results: A Workbook* (Belmont, Calif.: Wadsworth, 1992).

Corwen, Leonard, *Your Résumé: Key to a Better Job* (Englewood Cliffs, N.J.: Prentice-Hall, 1993).

Eyler, David R., *Résumés That Mean Business* (New York: Random House, 1993).

Jackson, Tom, *Tom Jackson's Résumé Express: The Fastest Way to Write a Winning Résumé* (New York: Random House, 1993).

Smith, Michael H., *The Résumé Writer's Handbook: A Comprehensive, Step-by-Step Writing Guide and Reference Manual for Every Job Seeker* (New York: HarperCollins, 1993).

## INTERVIEWING

Allen, Jeffrey G., *The Complete Q & A Job Interview Book* (New York: Wiley, 1988).

Allen, Jeffrey G., *The Five Hundred Interview Questions and How to Answer Them* (New York: Wiley, 1988).

Medley, H. Anthony, *Sweaty Palms: The Neglected Art of Being Interviewed* (Berkeley, Calif.: Ten Speed Press, 1992).

Shingelton, John, *Successful Interviewing for College Seniors* (Lincolnwood, Ill.: NTC, 1992).

Washington, Tom, *What Now? Interviewing Techniques for Winning in the 90's* (Everett, Wash.: MeyCor Research Institute, 1993). (Video/audio program)

## INTERNSHIPS

Fry, Ronald W., ed., *Internships,* 2 vols. (Hawthorne, N.J.: Career Press, 1990).

*The National Directory of Internships* (Raleigh, N.C.: National Society for Internships and Experimental Education, 1989).

Renetzky, Alvin, ed., *Directory of Internships, Work Experience Programs, and On-the-Job Training Opportunities* (Santa Monica, Calif.: Ready Reference Press, 1986).

# Trade Publications

**Admap**
7-11 St. John's Hill
London SW11 1TE
England

**Advertising Age**
Crain Communications, Inc.
740 North Rush Street
Chicago, IL 60611
(312) 649-5200

**Adweek**
49 East 21st Street
New York, NY 10010
(212) 529-5500

**Asian Advertising & Marketing**
Zindra Limited
31/F Citicorp Centre
18 Whitfield Road
Causeway Bay, Hong Kong

**Brandweek**
49 East 21st Street
New York, NY 10010
(212) 529-5500

**Business Marketing**
Crain Communications, Inc.
740 North Rush Street
Chicago, IL 60611
(312) 649-5200

**Communications Arts**
410 Sherman Avenue
Palo Alto, CA 94303
(415) 326-6040

**Direct Marketing**
224 Seventh Street
Garden City, NY 11530
(516) 746-6700

**DM News: The Newspaper of Direct Marketing**
Mill Hollow Corporation
19 West 21st Street, 8th Floor
New York, NY 10010
(212) 741-2095

**Inside PR**
235 West 48th Street, Suite 34A
New York, NY 10036
(212) 245-8680

**International Archive**
American Showcase
915 Broadway, 14th Floor
New York, NY 10010
(212) 673-6600

**Journal of Advertising Research**
Advertising Research Foundation
3 East 54th Street, 15th Floor
New York, NY 10022
(212) 751-5656

**Journal of Business & Industrial Marketing**
108 Loma Media Road
Santa Barbara, CA 93103

**Journal of Business-to-Business Marketing**
10 Alice Street
Binghamton, NY 13904

**Journal of Consumer Marketing**
108 Loma Media Road
Santa Barbara, CA 93103

**Journal of Direct Marketing**
605 Third Avenue
New York, NY 10022
(212) 850-6000

**Journal of Global Marketing**
10 Alice Street
Binghamton, NY 13904

**Journal of International Consumer Marketing**
10 Alice Street
Binghamton, NY 13904

**Journal of Marketing**
American Marketing Association
250 South Wacker Drive
Chicago, IL 60606
(312) 648-0536

**Journal of Marketing Channels**
10 Alice Street
Binghamton, NY 13904

**Journal of Marketing Research**
American Marketing Association
250 South Wacker Drive
Chicago, IL 60606
(312) 648-0536

*Journal of Product & Brand Management*
60/62 Toller Lane
Bradford, West Yorkshire BDB 9BY
England

*Journal of Promotion Management*
10 Alice Street
Binghamton, NY 13904

*Journal of Services Marketing*
60/62 Toller Lane
Bradford, West Yorkshire BDB 9BY
England

*Marketing*
777 Bay Street
Toronto, ON M5W 1A7
Canada
(416) 596-5858

*Marketing Management*
American Marketing Association
250 South Wacker Drive, Suite 200
Chicago, IL 60606
(312) 648-0536

*Marketing News*
American Marketing Association
250 South Wacker Drive, Suite 200
Chicago, IL 60606
(312) 648-0536

*Marketing Science*
290 Westminster Street
Providence, RI 02903
(401) 274-2525

*Mediaweek*
1515 Broadway
New York, NY 10036

*Promo*
47 Old Ridgefield Road
Wilton, CT 06897
(203) 778-4007

*Public Relations Journal*
Public Relations Society of America
33 Irving Place, 3rd Floor
New York, NY 10003
(212) 995-2230

*PR News*
127 East 80th Street
New York, NY 10021
(212) 879-7090

*Quirk's Marketing Research*
Box 23536
Minneapolis, MN 55423
(612) 861-8051

*Sales & Marketing Management*
633 Third Avenue
New York, NY 10017
(212) 986-4800

*Sales & Marketing Management in Canada*
3500 Dufferin Street, 402
Downsview, ON M3K 1N2
Canada
(416) 633-2020

*Sports Marketing News*
Technical Marketing Group
1460 Post Road East
Westport, CT 06880

*Telemarketing*
Technology Marketing Corp.
One Technology Plaza
Norwalk, CT 06854
(203) 852-6800

# References

References

# REFERENCES

## NOTES

### CHAPTER 1

1. Adapted from Fleming Meeks, "Be Ferocious," *Forbes,* 2 August 1993, 40–41; "A Sense of Cool: Nike's Theory of Advertising," *Harvard Business Review,* July–August 1992, 97; Dori Jones Yang and Robert Buderi, "Step by Step with Nike," *Business Week,* 13 August 1990, 116–117; "The '80s: What a Decade!" *Advertising Age,* 1 January 1990, 25; Kate Fitzgerald, "Nike Flexes Muscle for Kids," *Advertising Age,* 10 July 1989, 51; PRNewswire, computer database, 3 October 1989; "The Billboard Is Back! Nike Captures Award as Decade's Best," PRNewswire, computer database, 5 December 1989; Sheryl Franklin, "The Other Side," *Bank Marketing,* August 1987, 62; "Nike Outdoes Competition in Delivery to Customers," *Global Trade,* March 1988, 8; Ellen Benoit, "Lost Youth," *Financial World,* 20 September 1988, 28–31; Robert F. Hartley, *Marketing Successes, Historical to Present Day: What We Can Learn* (New York: Wiley, 1985), 214–224; Marcy Magiera, "Nike Edges Reebok; L.A. Gear Sprinting," *Advertising Age,* 25 September 1989, 93; Douglas C. McGill, "Nike Is Bounding Past Reebok," *New York Times,* 11 July 1989, sec. d, 1, 4; Barbara Buell, "Nike Catches Up with the Trendy Front-runner," *Business Week,* 24 October 1988, 88; Pat Sloan, "Reebok Runs Harder to Keep Lead," *Advertising Age,* 24 July 1989, 6; G. Christian Hill, "Nike Posts Big Gains in Sales and Profit; Reebok Hopes Pump Will Help It Keep Up," *Wall Street Journal,* 19 December 1989, B10(E), B5(W); Pat Sloan, "Reebok Gets Pumped for 1990," *Advertising Age,* 20 November 1989, 35; Bruce Horovitz, "Athletes Team Up for New Nike Campaign," *Los Angeles Times,* 27 June 1989, sec. 4, 6; Marcy Magiera, "Nike: Bo's Still an All-Star," *Advertising Age,* 20 May 1991, 8; Meg Rottman, "Nike Plans to Put Muscle in Product, Marketing," *Footwear News,* 25 February 1991, 34.

2. "A Job for Romantics," *Los Angeles Times,* 3 July 1989, sec. 4, 1; Carrie Dolan, "Not to Be Immodest, but Isn't It Romantic of Us to Run This Story?" *Wall Street Journal,* 11 July 1989, B1.

3. "AMA Board Approves New Marketing Definition," *Marketing News,* 1 March 1985, 1.

4. Philip Kotler and Sidney J. Levy, "Broadening the Concept of Marketing," *Journal of Marketing,* January 1969, 10–15.

5. Kate Bertrand, "'Creative Deal-Making' Pays Off for Countertrade Unit," *Business Marketing,* August 1986, 24.

6. Advertisement from the Australian Transport Accident Commission.

7. Franklin S. Houston and Jule B. Gassenheimer, "Marketing and Exchange," *Journal of Marketing,* October 1987, 3–18.

8. Michael R. Solomon, *Consumer Behavior* (Needham Heights, Mass.: Allyn & Bacon, 1992), 73.

9. Mark N. Clemente, *The Marketing Glossary* (New York: AMACOM, 1992), 102.

10. Solomon, *Consumer Behavior,* 91–94.

11. *Wireless* catalog, 1993; *Signals* catalog, 1993.

12. Robert Bartels, "Is Marketing Defaulting Its Responsibilities?" *Journal of Marketing,* Fall 1983, 32–35.

13. Robert J. Keith, "The Marketing Revolution," *Journal of Marketing,* January 1960, 35–38.

14. "Pillsbury Promotes Nowell to Vice President and Controller," PRNewswire, 13 October 1993; *Standard & Poor's Corporate Descriptions,* 20 October 1993.

15. Franklin S. Houston, "The Marketing Concept: What It Is and What It Is Not," *Journal of Marketing,* April 1986, 81–87.

16. John A. Howard, "Marketing Theory of the Firm," *Journal of Marketing* 47, no. 4 (Fall 1983): 90–100.

17. William E. Souder, "Managing Relations Between R&D and Marketing in New Product Development Projects," *Journal of Product Innovation Management,* March 1988, 6–19.

18. Allan J. Magrath, "Eight Strategies Engender Teamwork Between Functions," *Marketing News,* 19 June 1989, 12–13.

19. Courtland L. Bovée, John V. Thill, George P. Dovel, and Marian Burk Wood, *Advertising* (New York: McGraw-Hill, 1994).

20. Edwin E. Messikomer, "Du Pont's 'Marketing Community,'" *Business Marketing,* October 1987, 90, 92, 94.

21. George Gendron and Stephen D. Solomon, "The Art of Loving," *Inc.,* May 1989, 35–46.

22. Teri Agins, "Buchman Succeeds by Heeding Shoppers," *Wall Street Journal,* 26 July 1993, B1, B5.

23. Theodore Levitt, "Marketing Myopia," *Harvard Business Review,* July–August 1960, 45–56.

24. Bradley Johnson, "The Marketing 100: Mari Baker," *Advertising Age,* 5 July 1992, S-22.

25. Clemente, *The Marketing Glossary,* 193.

26. Allan J. Magrath, "Born-Again Marketing," *Across the Board,* June 1991, 33–36.

27. David Oates, "Clearer Way Ahead for Dartington," *Director,* April 1988, 92–94.

28. Phyllis Berman, "Is Traveling Well the Best Revenge?" *Forbes,* 8 August 1988, 52–54.

29. Alan Sugar, "The Mind of a Marketing Maverick," *International Management,* October 1987, 104–106.

30. Jason Hand, "They Told Us to Focus," *Forbes,* 31 October 1988, 134–136; Lindsay Brooke, "Take Me Home," *Automotive Industries,* April 1991, 77.

31. David Gelman, Jeanne Gordon, Lisa Drew, Sut Hutchison, and Frank S. Washingon, "Growing Pains for the Shrinks," *Newsweek,* 14 December 1987, 70–72.

32. Rebecca Fannin, "Crunching the Competition," *Marketing & Media Decisions,* March 1988, 70–75.

33. Paula Schnorbus, "B&D Turns On the Power," *Marketing & Media Decisions,* May 1988, 57–58, 62, 64.

34. Walter van Waterschoot and Christophe Van den Bulte, "The 4P Classification of the Marketing Mix Revisited," *Journal of Marketing* 56 (October 1992): 83–93.

35. Joe Cappo, *Future Scope: Success Strategies for the 1990s and Beyond,* as summarized in *Soundview Executive Book Summaries,* January 1990, 1–8; Clemens P. Work, Beth Brophy, Andrea Gabor, Robert F. Black, Mike Tharp, and Alice Z. Cuneo, "The 21st Century Executive," *U.S. News & World Report,* 7 March 1988, 48–51; Marvin J. Cetron, Wanda Rocha, and Rebecca Luckins, "Into the 21st Century," *The Futurist,* July–August 1988, 29–40; Zachary Schiller, "Stalking the New Consumer," *Business Week,* 28 August 1989, 54–62; Pat Ensor, "Prodigy: Bellwether or Pariah?" *Online,* July 1991, 61.

36. Barry Meier, "Products That Are Wrapped in Messages," *New York Times,* 30 March 1991, 36.

37. See note 1.

### CHAPTER 2

1. Adapted from William Glaberson, "After Decade of Big Losses, *USA Today* Has First Profit," *New York Times,* 10 January 1994, sec. c, 1; Dean Foust, "What's Black and White and Blue and Yellow—and Less in the Red?" *Business Week,* 12 July 1993, 30; John Iams, "Soviet Union Distributes *USA Today,*" *Advertising Age,* 13 November 1989, 63; Lindsy Van Gelder, "Can the Chatter, Sweetheart," *Business Month,* February 1989, 50–54; Peter Prichard, *The Making of McPaper: The Inside Story of* USA Today (Kansas City: Andrews, McMeel & Parker, 1987), 7, 79, 80, 88, 93, 95–96, 100, 164, 316, 359–363; Janet Meyers, "*USA Today* Nears Year of Profits," *Advertising Age,* 8 January 1990, 39; Mick O'Leary, "*USA Today* Decisionline Sets 80's Info Trend," *Information Today,* June 1988, 19–23; Al Neuharth, "Confessions of an S.O.B.," *Playboy,* November 1989, 120–121, 126, 178, 180, 182, 186; Gannett Company, Inc., 1989 Annual Report, 12; Wayne Walley and Alison Fahey, "'900' Numbers, Ad Tie-Ins Connect," *Advertising Age,* 5 June 1989, 12, 68; Geraldine Fabrikant, "*USA Today* Enlists Celebrities in Campaign," *New York Times,* 17 April 1989, sec. d, 12.

2. Vicky Cahan, "A Clean-Air Bill Is Easy; Clean Air Is Hard," *Business Week,* 5 November 1990, 50; Richard C. Scherr, Allan G. Smalley, Jr., and Michael E. Norman, "Clean Air Amendments Put Big Burden on Refinery Planners," *Oil and Gas Journal,* 10 June 1991, 35.

3. Rose Gutfeld, "Pure Plays: For Each Dollar Spent on Clean Air Someone Stands to Make a

Buck," *Wall Street Journal,* 29 October 1990, A1, A6.

**4.** Mark Maremon, "Timberland Comes Out of the Woods," *Business Week,* 13 September 1993, 78; Steven Flax, "Boot Camp," *Inc.,* September 1987, 99–100, 103–104; *Moody's Industrial Manual* (New York: Moody's Investors Service, 1989), 6317; Mark Tadeschi, "Timberland's Prize Hikers," *Footwear News,* 15 April 1991, S10.

**5.** Carl P. Zeithaml and Valarie A. Zeithaml, "Environmental Management: Revising the Marketing Perspective," *Journal of Marketing,* Spring 1984, 46–53; Bernie Whalen, "Kotler: Rethink the Marketing Concept," *Marketing News,* 14 September 1984, 1, 22, 24.

**6.** Don Phillips, "Most Flights Become Smoke-Free Sunday," *San Jose Mercury News,* 21 February 1990, sec. a, 1, 12.

**7.** John Williamson, "Telefonica's Aggressive Agenda," *Telephony,* 27 June 1988, 38–39.

**8.** George Rebeck, "The Not So Friendly Skies," *Utne Reader,* November–December 1989, 12–13.

**9.** Jerry M. Rosenberg, *Dictionary of Business and Management,* 2d ed. (New York: Wiley, 1983), 329.

**10.** David Horowitz, *The Business of Business* (New York: Harper & Row, 1989), 217; John Case, "The Disciples of David Birch," *Inc.,* January 1989, 39–45; Kate Bertrand, "Hunting the High Flier," *Business Marketing,* August 1989, 37, 38, 40–42.

**11.** *Statistical Abstract of the United States: 1989* (Washington, D.C.: GPO, 1989), 534; Michael B. Lehmann, *The Dow Jones-Irwin Guide to Using* The Wall Street Journal (Homewood, Ill.: Dow Jones-Irwin, 1990), 312; Geoffrey H. Moore, "Business Cycles, Panics, and Depressions," *Encyclopedia of American Economic History: Studies in the Principal Movements and Ideas* (New York: Scribner, 1980), 151–156.

**12.** Krystal Miller, "Once Prized as Unbeatable Investments, Exotic Sports Cars Crash in Current Value," *Wall Street Journal,* 16 April 1993, B1, B5.

**13.** *Statistical Abstract of the United States: 1989* (Washington, D.C.: GPO, 1989), 534.

**14.** Edward Cundiff and Marye Tharp Hilger, *Marketing in the International Environment,* 2d ed. (Englewood Cliffs, N.J.: Prentice-Hall, 1988), 349–350.

**15.** Thomas A. Stewart, "How to Manage in the New Era," *Fortune,* 15 January 1990, 58–59, 64, 68, 72.

**16.** Mike Brennan, "Business Gets Rainy Day Blues," *The Herald* (Everett, WA), 1 August 1993, B1.

**17.** Jonathan Dahl, "Tourists Will Find Hotels Scarce in Eastern Bloc," *Wall Street Journal,* 11 December 1989, B1; Carlo Wolff, "Managing the New Megachains," *Lodging Hospitality,* February 1991, 48–54; John Parry, "Paying Guests," *International Management,* February 1991, 38–41.

**18.** Celia F. McAllister, ". . . While DEC Is Setting Up Shop in Hungary," *Business Week,* 26 February 1990, 80I; Amal Kumar Nag, "GE to Buy 50% of Hungarian Lighting Firm," *Wall Street Journal,* 16 November 1989, A2, A7.

**19.** Adi Ignatius, "Continental Can Finds Business in China Requires Reading of Political Tea Leaves," *Wall Street Journal,* 9 January 1990, A11.

**20.** Philip R. Cateora, *International Marketing,* 7th ed. (Homewood Ill.: Irwin, 1990), 48.

**21.** Rahul Jacob, "Export Barriers the U.S. Hates Most," *Fortune,* 27 February 1989, 88–89.

**22.** "Coca-Cola to Curtail Practices in Europe; EC Ends Proceedings," *Wall Street Journal,* 10 January 1990, A2.

**23.** Kari Huus, "Look Out, Chinese Love Solution," *Advertising Age International,* 28 September 1992, I-6.

**24.** Richard M. Steuer, *A Guide to Marketing*

*Law: What Every Seller Should Know* (New York: Harcourt Brace Jovanovich, 1986), 4–6.

**25.** Steuer, *A Guide to Marketing Law,* 21, 143, 157.

**26.** "Ma Bell's Family Leaves Home, 1982," *Wall Street Journal,* 1 December 1989, B1; Laura Evenson, "MCI Cuts Intrastate Telephone Call Rates," *San Francisco Chronicle,* 9 January 1990, sec. c. 1, 12.

**27.** Eben Shapiro, "Food Labs Gaze Hungrily at Potential in Labeling Rules," *Wall Street Journal,* 10 December 1992, B2.

**28.** "New TWA Chairman Calls for Price Controls," Prodigy Services Company, 7 July 1993.

**29.** Steuer, *A Guide to Marketing Law,* 131, 143, 155.

**30.** Joann S. Lublin, "FDA Lets Wellcome Cut Dosage of Drug for AIDS, Easing Pressure for Price Cut," *Wall Street Journal,* 17 January 1990, B4.

**31.** Steuer, *A Guide to Marketing Law,* 7.

**32.** Philip Revzin, "European Bureaucrats Are Writing the Rules Americans Will Live By," *Wall Street Journal,* 11 May 1989, A1, A12.

**33.** Michael Siconolfi, "New Rules for Mutual Funds Promise to Usher in a Marketing 'Revolution,'" *Wall Street Journal,* 29 April 1988, 28.

**34.** "Legal Group Opposes Direct-Mail Ads Despite Court Ruling," *Wall Street Journal,* 13 September 1988, 38.

**35.** Cateora, *International Marketing,* 222.

**36.** Susan E. Kuhn, "Eager to Take On the World's Best," *Fortune,* 23 April 1990, 71.

**37.** Syed Tariq Anwar, "How NAFTA Provisions Will Affect Marketers," *Marketing News,* 24 May 1993, 14, 18.

**38.** Cundiff and Hilger, *Marketing in the International Environment,* 217.

**39.** Kate Bertrand, "Politics Pushes to the Marketing Foreground," *Business Marketing,* March 1990, 51–55.

**40.** Mark M. Nelson, "As Shroud of Secrecy Lifts in East Europe, Smog Shroud Emerges," *Wall Street Journal,* 1 March 1990, A1, A13; Mark Maremont, Jonathan Kapstein, and Gail E. Schares, "Eastern Europe's Big Cleanup," *Business Week,* 19 March 1990, 113–115; Peter Fuhrman, "Breathing the Polish Air," *Forbes,* 24 June 1991, 40; James F. Manji, "Cleaning Up in Eastern Europe," *Automation,* May 1991, 20–21.

**41.** William L. Shanklin, "Six Timeless Marketing Blunders," *Journal of Consumer Marketing,* Fall 1986, 31–39; Elizabeth A. Stein, "New Technology Excites, Frustrates Microsoft Chief," *PC Week,* 24 June 1991, 13.

**42.** Anthony Ramirez, "Superconductors Get into Business," *Fortune,* 22 June 1987, 114–116, 118.

**43.** Joseph Pereira, "Toy Makers Are Attacking Video Games with New Dolls, Cars and Movie Tie-ins," *Wall Street Journal,* 15 February 1990, B1, B6.

**44.** Otis Port, "See the Price Tag, Then Ask It a Question," *Business Week,* 15 January 1990, 85.

**45.** "Business Bulletin," *Wall Street Journal,* 25 January 1990, A1.

**46.** Robert Guenther, "Citicorp Skips Computer in New Home-Banking Plan," *Wall Street Journal,* 28 February 1990, B1, B8.

**47.** "The Expanding Focus of Local Camera Shops," *Wall Street Journal,* 26 September 1988, 29.

**48.** Barbara Rudolph, "Food Services Venture Beyond Vanilla Systems," *Computerworld,* 15 January 1990, 66.

**49.** Thomas R. King, "For You, Sally Smith, Coupons and Comedies," *Wall Street Journal,* 22 January 1990, B1; Mollie Neal, "Quaker's Direct Hit," *Direct Marketing,* January 1991, 52.

**50.** U.S. Department of Commerce, *Historical Statistics of the United States: Colonial Times to 1970,* part 1 (Washington, D.C.: GPO, 1975), 49.

**51.** Diane Crispell, Thomas Exter, and Judith Waldrop, "Snapshots of the Nation," *Wall Street Journal,* 9 March 1990, R12–R13.

**52.** Jagdish N. Sheth, "Search for Tomorrow," *Public Relations Journal,* December 1987, 22–25, 28–30, 51.

**53.** Cheryl Russell, "The New Homemakers," *American Demographics,* October 1985, 23–27; "How Working Women Have Changed America: Marketing," *Working Woman,* November 1986, 144, 146.

**54.** John Naisbitt and Patricia Aburdene, "The Growing Power of Women," *San Francisco Chronicle,* 9 January 1990, sec. c. 1, 4, 12.

**55.** U.S. Bureau of the Census, "Projections of the United States, by Age, Sex and Race: 1988–2080," *Current Population Reports,* Series P-25, No. 1018 (Washington, D.C.: GPO, January 1989), 3; U.S. Bureau of the Census, "Projections of the Hispanic Population: 1983–2080," *Current Population Reports,* Series P-25, No. 995 (Washington, D.C.: GPO, November 1986), 2.

**56.** Crispell, Exter, and Waldrop, "Snapshots of the Nation," 43.

**57.** Joel Kotkin, "Selling to the New America," *Inc.,* July 1987, 44–47, 50, 52.

**58.** Matthew Grimm, "KFC Moves from Fryer into the Fire," *Brandweek,* 11 January 1993, 4; David Stipp, "Negative Oat Bran Study May Crimp Marketing Efforts," *Wall Street Journal,* 18 January 1990, B1, B6; Alecia Swasy, "Despite Skepticism, a Once-Lowly Bran Now Aspires to the Level of Oat Cuisine," *Wall Street Journal,* 28 March 1989, B1.

**59.** Walecia Konrad, "If It's Legal, Cigarette Makers Are Trying It," *Business Week,* 19 February 1990, 52, 54.

**60.** Janet Guyon, "Tobacco Companies Race for Advantage in Eastern Europe While Critics Fume," *Wall Street Journal,* 28 December 1992, B1, B5.

**61.** Amanda Bennett, "AIDS Crisis Ends Some Old Taboos on Condom Ads," *Wall Street Journal,* 6 July 1988, 30.

**62.** Robert E. Hite, Joseph A. Bellizzi, and Cynthia Fraser, "A Content Analysis of Ethical Policy Statements Regarding Marketing Activities," *Journal of Business Ethics,* October 1988, 771–776.

**63.** James H. Leigh, Patrick E. Murphy, and Ben M. Enis, "A New Approach to Measuring Socially Responsible Consumption Tendencies," *Journal of Macromarketing,* Spring 1988, 5–20.

**64.** Bill Shaw, "Foreign Corrupt Practices Act: A Legal and Ethical Analysis," *Journal of Business Ethics,* October 1988, 789–795.

**65.** Marilyn Chase, "Burroughs Wellcome Cuts Price of AZT under Pressure from AIDS Activists," *Wall Street Journal,* 19 September 1989, A3, A24; Marilyn Chase, "Pricing Battle: Burroughs Wellcome Reaps Profits, Outrage from Its AIDS Drug," *Wall Street Journal,* 15 September 1989, A1.

**66.** Steven J. Skinner, O. C. Ferrell, and Alan J. Dubinsky, "Organizational Dimensions of Marketing-Research Ethics," *Journal of Business Research* 16 (1988): 209–223.

**67.** Jerry Goodbody, "For More Consumers, Advertising Is the 'Deceptive Persuader,'" *Adweek's Marketing Week,* 5 March 1990, 40.

**68.** "This Industry Leader Means Business," *Sales and Marketing Management,* May 1987, 44; "Probe Scuttled," *Time,* 1 June 1987, 51.

**69.** Margaret A. Stroup, Ralph L. Neubert, and Jerry W. Anderson, Jr., "Doing Good, Doing Better: Two Views of Social Responsibility," *Business*

*Horizons,* March–April 1987, 22–25.

**70.** James F. Engel and Roger D. Blackwell, *Consumer Behavior,* 4th ed. (Hinsdale, Ill.: Dryden Press, 1982), 668.

**71.** Kristen Hannum and Christopher Juniper, "Shades of Green: Consumer Shopping as If the Earth Counted," *Buzzworm: The Environmental Journal,* January–February 1990, 36–41; Connie Koenenn, "Chalk One Up to Impulse," *Los Angeles Times,* 12 November 1990, sec. 3, 1; Jaclyn Fierman, "The Big Muddle in Green Marketing," *Fortune,* 3 June 1991, 91; Martha M. Hamilton, "Big Mac Attacks Trash Problem," *Washington Post,* 17 April 1991, B1.

**72.** Joseph B. White, "GM Says It Plans an Electric Car, but Details Are Spotty," *Wall Street Journal,* 19 April 1990, B1, B4.

**73.** Donald P. Robin and R. Eric Reidenbach, "Social Responsibility, Ethics, and Marketing Strategy: Closing the Gap Between Concept and Application," *Journal of Marketing,* January 1987, 44–58; Robert Lacy, *Ford: The Men and Machine* (Boston: Little, Brown, 1986), 575–583.

**74.** See note 1

## CHAPTER 3

**1.** Adapted from Raymond Roel, "The Power of Nintendo," *Direct Marketing,* September 1989, 24–26, 28–29; Michael Major, "Can Nintendo Bring Video Games Back?" *High-Tech Marketing,* July 1986, 48–49; Joe Mandese, "Power Plays," *Marketing & Media Decisions,* March 1989, 101–103, 106; Stewart Wolpin, "How Nintendo Revived a Dying Industry," *Marketing Communications,* May 1989, 36–38, 40; Carla Lazzareschi, "No Mere Child's Play," *Los Angeles Times,* 16 December 1988, 1–2; Stephen Kreider Yoder, "Nintendo Goes Portable, Stores Go Gaga," *Wall Street Journal,* 4 October 1989, B1; Maria Shao, Amy Dunkin, and Patrick Cole, "There's a Rumble in the Video Arcade," *Business Week,* 20 February 1989, 37; James E. Lalonde, "PCs to Look Beyond Nintendo," *Seattle Times,* 10 December 1989, sec. e, 1–2; Mat Toor, "A Phoenix from the Ashes," *Marketing,* 23 May 1991, 20; "Nintendo Presents Three Essential Rules for Success," *Playthings,* 6 May 1991, 33; "Nintendo of America," *Wall Street Journal,* 28 May 1991, A15.

**2.** John F. Cady and Robert D, Buzzell, *Strategic Marketing* (Boston: Little, Brown, 1986), 13.

**3.** Malcolm H. B. MacDonald, "Ten Barriers to Marketing Planning," *Journal of Product and Brand Management,* Fall 1992, 51–64.

**4.** Mary E. Kulpinski, "The Planning Process—Continuous Improvement," *Journal of Business and Industrial Marketing,* Spring 1992, 71–76.

**5.** Malcolm H. B. MacDonald, "Ten Barriers to Marketing Planning," *Journal of Services Marketing,* Spring 1990, 5–10, 12–18.

**6.** Barbara N. Berkman, "Birth of a Business: AB's Escape Route from Resistors," *Electronic Business,* 6 March 1989, 76, 78.

**7.** The Woodworker's Store, *1994 Catalog,* 2–4.

**8.** Arnold Donald, "Birth of a Business Unit," *Journal of Business Strategy,* May–June 1991, 8–11.

**9.** Lester A. Neidell, *Strategic Marketing Management* (Tulsa: Pennwell Books, 1983), 92.

**10.** Stratford P. Sherman, "The Mind of Jack Welch," *Fortune,* 27 March 1989, 39–50; "Jack Welch Reinvents General Electric—Again," *Economist,* 30 March 1991, 59–60, 62.

**11.** Allan J. Magrath, "Going to Extremes—Not!" *Sales & Marketing Management,* February 1993, 32–33; Brian Dumaine, "Is Big Still Good?" *Fortune,* 20 April 1992, 50–60; Joseph Weber, "How J&J's Foresight Made Contact Lenses Pay," *Business Week,* 4 May 1992, 132.

**12.** Robert D. Buzzell and Bradley T. Gale, *The PIMS Principles: Linking Strategy to Performance* (New York: Free Press, 1987), 4.

**13.** *The Product Portfolio* (Boston: Boston Consulting Group, 1970); *The Experience Curve Reviewed, IV. The Growth Share Matrix of the Product Portfolio* (Boston: Boston Consulting Group, 1973); George S. Day, "Diagnosing the Product Portfolio," *Journal of Marketing,* April 1977, 29–38.

**14.** Robert Jacobson and David A. Aaker, "Is Market Share All That It's Cracked Up to Be?" *Journal of Marketing,* Fall 1985, 11–22; Carolyn Y. Woo and Arnold C. Cooper, "The Surprising Case for Low Market Share," *Harvard Business Review,* November–December 1982, 106–113; Stephen J. Markell, Sue E. Neeley, and Thomas H. Strickland, "Explaining Profitability: Dispelling the Market Share Fog," *Journal of Business Research* 16(1988): 189–196.

**15.** Gael McDonald and Christopher Roberts, "What You Always Wanted to Know About Marketing Strategy . . . But Were Too Confused to Ask," *Management Decision,* vol. 30, no. 7, 54–60.

**16.** Charles W. Hofer and Dan Schendel, *Strategy Formulation: Analytical Concepts* (St. Paul, Minn.: West Publishing, 1978), 32.

**17.** Yoram Wind, Vijay Mahajan, and Donald Swire, "An Empirical Comparison of Standardized Portfolio Models," *Journal of Marketing,* Spring 1983, 89–99.

**18.** Woo and Cooper, "The Surprising Case for Low Market Share," 106–113.

**19.** Theodore Levitt, "Exploit the Product Life Cycle," *Harvard Business Review,* November–December 1965, 45–56.

**20.** Buzzell and Gale, *The PIMS Principles,* 4–5.

**21.** John Schwartz, "Stalking the Youth Market," *Newsweek Special Issue,* Summer–Fall 1990, 34–36.

**22.** Andrew Kupfer, "Success Secrets of Tomorrow's Stars," *Fortune,* 23 April 1990, 77–78, 80, 82, 84.

**23.** Malcolm McDonald and John W. Leppard, *Marketing by Matrix* (Lincolnwood, Ill.: NTC, 1993), 10; H. Igor Ansoff, "Strategies for Diversification," *Harvard Business Review,* November–December 1957, 113–124; H. Igor Ansoff, *Corporate Strategy* (New York: McGraw-Hill, 1965).

**24.** *The Walt Disney World Vacation Guide* (Orlando: Walt Disney World Corporation, 1990), 1–33.

**25.** Timothy K. Smith and Laura Landro, "Profoundly Changed, Coca-Cola Company Strives to Keep On Bubbling," *Wall Street Journal,* 24 April 1986, 1, 22; Greg Prince, "Red and White and Big All Over," *Beverage World,* May 1991, 20–26, 69–71.

**26.** Quaker Oats Company, *Annual Report, 1985;* Denise Gellene, "Ghirardelli Chocolate Co. Put on Block by Quaker," *Los Angeles Times,* 5 January 1989, sec. b, 2; Kara Swisher, "For Fisher-Price, No Joy in Toyland; Parent Unhappy with Offspring's Profits," *Washington Post,* 25 April 1990, sec. g, 1.

**27.** Pankaj Ghemawat, "Sustainable Advantage," *Harvard Business Review,* September–October 1986, 53–58.

**28.** Elaine Underwood, "Just Plane Hot," *Brandweek,* 24 August 1992, 16–17.

**29.** Jay Finegan, "Surviving in the Nike/Reebok Jungle," *Inc.,* May 1993, 98–108.

**30.** Frank Bentayou, "The Car That Wouldn't Die," *Venture,* March 1989, 16–17.

**31.** Derek F. Abell, "Strategic Windows," *Journal of Marketing,* July 1978, 21–26.

**32.** David J. Luck, O. C. Ferrell, and George H. Lucas, Jr., *Marketing Strategy and Plans* (Englewood Cliffs, N.J.: Prentice-Hall, 1989), 72–73.

**33.** Jack Willoughby, "The Last Iceman," *Forbes,* 13 July 1987, 183–204.

**34.** Michael E. Porter, *Competitive Strategy: Techniques for Analyzing Industries and Competitors* (New York: Free Press, 1980), 47–71.

**35.** David A. Aaker, *Strategic Market Management* (New York: Wiley, 1988), 48.

**36.** Philip Kotler and Eduardo L. Roberto, *Social Marketing* (New York: Free Press, 1989), 337.

**37.** Television commercial for Portland General Electric.

**38.** Alex Taylor III, "How to Murder the Competition," *Fortune,* 22 February 1993, 87, 90.

**39.** Brenton R. Schlender, "The Perils of Losing Focus," *Fortune,* 17 May 1993, 100.

**40.** "Marriott Perfects Product Segmentation Strategy," Marriott press release dated 2 October 1989; "Fairfield Inn Opens on Blairwood Road," *Business First–Louisville,* 4 February 1991, 14.

**41.** Christina Dugg, "Fruit's Loom Weaves Some New Threads in Efforts to Shed Underwear-Only Image," *Wall Street Journal,* 28 April 1992, B1, B8.

**42.** George P. Dovel, "Stake It Out: Positioning Success, Step by Step," *Business Marketing,* July 1990, 43–51.

**43.** Lincoln Kaye, "When Small Is Better," *Far Eastern Economic Review (Hong Kong),* 1 June 1989, 60–61.

**44.** Keith H. Hammonds, "It's One Sharp Ad Campaign, but Where's the Blade?" *Business Week,* 5 March 1990, 30.

**45.** Rolph E. Anderson, Joseph F. Hair, and Alan J. Bush, *Professional Sales Management* (New York: McGraw-Hill, 1988), 123.

**46.** Steven P. Schnaars, *Megamistakes: Forecasting and the Myth of Rapid Technological Change* (New York: Free Press, 1989), 11, 14, 15, 24, 28, 133–134.

**47.** E J. Davis, *Practical Sales Forecasting* (London: McGraw-Hill, 1988), 273–274.

**48.** See note 1.

## CHAPTER 4

**1.** Adapted from Robinson G. Clark, "Domino's Franchises Back Decision to Drop Guarantee," *Detroit Free Press,* 24 December 1993, 7B; John P. Cortez, "New Directions for Domino's," *Advertising Age,* 4 January 1993, 3, 34; Marilyn Alva, "Come and Get It," *Restaurant Business,* 10 October 1992, 26; Neal Templin, "Domino's to Deliver Additional Cheese, Toppings on Pizza," *Wall Street Journal,* 29 January 1992, B8; Aimee Stern, "Domino's: A Unique Concept Pays Off," *Dun's Business Month,* May 1986, 51; Raymond Serafin, "Domino's Pizza Takes 'Fresh' Angle," *Advertising Age,* 29 February 1988, 34; Bradley A. Stertz, "Domino's Beefs Up Menu to Keep Pace with Rivals," *Wall Street Journal,* 21 April 1989, B1, B4; Wendy Zellner, "Tom Monaghan: The Fun-Loving Prince of Pizza," *Business Week,* 8 February 1988, 90, 93; Raymond Serafin, "Making Domino's Deliver: How Monaghan Hopes to Get More of the Pie," *Advertising Age,* 28 November 1988, 10, 56; Raymond Serafin, "Domino's Plans Hispanic Push," *Advertising Age,* 15 June 1987, 29; Scott Hume, "Pizza Hut Ads Attack Mac's Test," *Advertising Age,* 7 May 1990, 18; Patricia Sellers, "Getting Customers to Love You," *Fortune,* 13 March 1989, 40; "Pizza Chains Ranked by Top 100 Market Share," *Nation's Restaurant News,* 6 August 1990, 70; Charles Child, "Domino's: 1990 Was 'A Tough Year,'" *Crain's Detroit Business,* 21 January 1991, 5; John P. Cortez, "Grey's Style Drives Domino's Plan," *Advertising Age,* 22 April 1991, 12.

**2.** James F. Engel, Roger D. Blackwell, and Paul W. Miniard, *Consumer Behavior,* 6th ed. (Chicago: Dryden, 1990), 30.

3. Gilles Laurent and Hean-Noel Kapferer, "Measuring Consumer Involvement Profiles," *Journal of Marketing Research,* February 1985, 41–53.

4. Del I. Hawkins, Roger J. Best, and Kenneth A. Coney, *Consumer Behavior: Implications for Marketing Strategy,* 4th ed. (Homewood, Ill.: BPI/Irwin, 1989), 536.

5. Keith Fletcher, "An Analysis of Choice Criteria Using Conjoint Analysis," *European Journal of Marketing* 22 (1988): 25–33.

6. F. G. Crane and J. E. Lynch, "Consumer Selection of Physicians and Dentists: An Examination of Choice Criteria and Cue Usage," *Journal of Health Care Marketing,* September 1988, 16–19.

7. "The 189 Most Important Trends for the 1990s," *Research Alert,* 22 December 1989, 26.

8. Engel, Blackwell, and Miniard, *Consumer Behavior,* 538.

9. "Consumer Complaint Handling in America: An Update Study" (Washington, D.C.: Technical Assistance Research Programs, 1986), Executive Summary, 2.

10. Don Schultz, Stanley Tannebaum, and Robert Lauterborn, "Why People Ignore Facts in Buying Decisions," *Advertising Age,* 4 May 1992, 22; Paul Sherlock, *Rethinking Business to Business Marketing* (New York: Free Press, 1991), 27–30.

11. Abraham Maslow, *Motivation and Personality,* 2d ed. (New York: Harper & Row, 1970), 80.

12. Banwari Mittal, "The Role of Affective Choice Mode in the Consumer Purchase of Expressive Products," *Journal of Economic Psychology* 9 (1988): 499–524.

13. Elizabeth Hirschman and Morris B. Holbrook, "Hedonic Consumption: Emerging Concepts, Methods, and Propositions," *Journal of Marketing* 46 (Summer 1982): 92–101.

14. "Shelter Ads Can Help Deliver 'Big Ideas,'" *Marketing News,* 23 November 1984, 13.

15. J. Jacoby and W. D. Hoyer, "Viewer Miscomprehension of Televised Communication," *Journal of Marketing,* Fall 1982, 12–31.

16. Manager of public relations, Coca-Cola Company, personal communication, 28 June 1990.

17. Leon G. Shiffman and Leslie Lazar Kanuk, *Consumer Behavior* (Englewood Cliffs, N.J.: Prentice-Hall, 1987), 231.

18. Raymond Serafin and Alison Fahey, "New Riney Shop Purrs Like a Kitten," *Advertising Age,* 8 April 1991, 1; Betsy Sharkey, "Agency Executive: Hal Riney," *Adweek's Western Advertising News,* 4 February 1991, CR12.

19. Michael J. Rothschild and William C. Gaidis, "Behavioral Learning Theory: Its Relevance to Marketing and Promotions," *Journal of Marketing* 45 (Spring 1981): 70–78.

20. Paul Farhir, "Selling Shock: Scare Tactics Are the Latest in Advertising," *Washington Post,* 9 November 1989, sec. d, 1.

21. Michael R. Solomon, *Consumer Behavior* (Needham Heights, Mass.: Allyn & Bacon, 1992), 112.

22. Solomon, *Consumer Behavior,* 115–116.

23. Solomon, *Consumer Behavior,* 134.

24. Shiffman and Kanuk, *Consumer Behavior,* 270.

25. "Dutch Women: The Individualization Trend," *Market: Europe,* December 1990, 3–4.

26. Northwest Airlines ad, *Business Week,* 23 July 1990, 7.

27. William O. Beardon, Richard G. Netemeyer, and Jesse E. Teel, "Measurement of Consumer Susceptibility to Interpersonal Influences," *Journal of Consumer Research* 15 (March 1989): 473–481.

28. Frank Farley, "The Big T in Personality," *Psychology Today* 20 (May 1986): 44.

29. M. Joseph Sirgy, "Self-Concept in Consumer Behavior: A Critical Review," *Journal of Consumer Research* 9 (December 1982): 287–300.

30. Russell W. Belk, "Possessions and the Extended Self," *Journal of Consumer Research* 15 (September 1988): 139–165.

31. Hawkins, Best, and Coney, *Consumer Behavior,* 396.

32. Engel, Blackwell, and Miniard, *Consumer Behavior,* 630.

33. "The 189 Most Important Trends," 4.

34. Thia Golson, "Reaching Baby Boomers in Their Prime," *Adweek's Marketing Week,* 22 January 1990, 20–22.

35. "The 189 Most Important Trends," 4.

36. Alvin E. Headen, Jr., "Old Age Is an Opportunity," *Black Enterprise,* March 1993, 47.

37. Hale N. Tongren, "Determinant Behavior Characteristics of Older Consumers," *Journal of Consumer Affairs* 22 (Summer 1988): 136–157.

38. Ken Dychtwald and Greg Gable, "Portrait of a Changing Consumer," *Business Horizons,* January–February 1990, 62–73.

39. "The Gold Plated Consumer," *Marketing Communications,* December 1984, 23–27; "The 189 Most Important Trends," 17–18.

40. Robert B. Settle and Pamela L. Alreck, *Why They Buy* (New York: Wiley, 1989), 279–280.

41. Judith Waldrop, "Spending by Degree," *American Demographics,* February 1990, 23–26.

42. Shiffman and Kanuk, *Consumer Behavior,* 519.

43. Engel, Blackwell, and Miniard, *Consumer Behavior,* 65–66.

44. "The Elusive Euro-Consumer," *The Economist,* reprinted in *World Press Review,* February 1990, 60–61.

45. Eugene L. Mendonsa, "Coming to Terms with Rubber Time," *Business Marketing,* October 1989, 67–68; Stephen Karel, "Learning Culture the Hard Way," *Consumer Markets Abroad,* May 1988, 1, 15.

46. Kinichi Ohmae, "The Triad World View," *Journal of Business Strategy,* Spring 1987, 8–19.

47. Engel, Blackwell, and Miniard, *Consumer Behavior,* 67.

48. "The 189 Most Important Trends," 15.

49. Hawkins, Best, and Coney, *Consumer Behavior,* 97.

50. Cyndee Miller, "Mainstream Marketers Decide Time Is Right to Target Gays," *Marketing News,* 20 July 1992, 8.

51. Fraser P. Seitel, *The Practice of Public Relations,* 5th ed. (New York: Macmillan, 1992).

52. "The 189 Most Important Trends," 6.

53. "The 189 Most Important Trends," 7.

54. Cyndee Miller, "Upwardly Mobile Blacks Keep Strong Sense of Identity," *Marketing News,* 19 February 1990, 10–11; Joseph Cosco, Patricia Orsini, Martha Nolan, Jim Osterman, and Mary Huhn, "African-Americans: In the Era of Nike, Uptown, and Quaker Oats," *Mediaweek,* 21 January 1991, 18.

55. Dan Fost, "Reaching the Hip-Hop Generation," *American Demographics,* May 1993, 15–16; Carrie Goerne, "Retailers Boost Efforts to Target African-American Consumers," *Marketing News,* 22 June 1992, 2.

56. "Black Pride Plays Role in Buying Goods," *Marketing News,* 19 February 1990, 11.

57. Christy Fisher, "Poll: Hispanics Stick to Brands," *Advertising Age,* 15 February 1993, 6.

58. "The 189 Most Important Trends," 40.

59. Joe Schwartz, "Hispanic Opportunities," *American Demographics,* May 1987, 56, 58; Reed E. Bunzel, "Hispanic Reps: Marketing in the Truest Sense," *Broadcasting,* 20 May 1991, 44.

60. Chester A. Swenson, "How to Speak to Hispanics," *American Demographics,* February 1990, 40–41; "Diet Coke Ads Target Hispanics," *Beverage Industry,* March 1991, 67; Christy Fisher, "Coke Taps Latin Beat," *Advertising Age,* 8 April 1991, 57.

61. "The 189 Most Important Trends," 7.

62. "The 189 Most Important Trends," 17.

63. Joel Kotkin, "Selling to the New America," *Inc.,* July 1987, 44–47, 50, 52.

64. Richard P. Coleman, "The Continuing Significance of Social Class to Marketing," *Journal of Consumer Research,* December 1983, 265–280.

65. "The 189 Most Important Trends," 2–3, 5.

66. "Less Than 30 Percent of London Households Have Children," *Market: Europe,* August 1991, 10.

67. Settle and Alreck, *Why They Buy,* 182–183.

68. William O. Beardon and Michael J. Etzel, "Reference Group Influences on Product and Brand Purchase Decisions," *Journal of Consumer Research* 9 (September 1982): 183–194.

69. Adapted from Settle and Alreck, *Why They Buy,* 22–23.

70. Settle and Alreck, *Why They Buy,* 22–23.

71. Barry L. Bayus, "Word of Mouth: The Indirect Effects of Marketing Efforts," *Journal of Advertising Research* 25 (June–July 1985): 31–39.

72. Russell W. Belk, "Situational Variables and Consumer Behavior," *Journal of Consumer Research* 2 (December 1975): 157–164.

73. "The 189 Most Important Trends," 31.

74. See note 1.

75. Adapted from Damon Darlin, "Spree in Seoul: Affluent Koreans Go on a Shopping Binge That Worries Officials," *Wall Street Journal,* 9 February 1990, A1, A6; Jill Lettich, "On the Rim of Success," *Discount Store News,* 6 May 1991, 82; Elliot Zwiebach, "Korea Independents Seek U.S. Style of Distribution," *Supermarket News,* 1 April 1991, 20.

## CHAPTER 5

1. Adapted from Warren Strugatch, "Reliability Is the Buzzword," *Global Trade,* April 1990, 48–51; Jay Gordon, "Zooming to Market: Logistics as a Marketing Weapon," *Distribution,* March 1990, 38–44; Tom Eisenhart, "Spreading the Quality Gospel," *Business Marketing,* February 1990, 34–38; Mary Lu Carnevale, "Ad Notes," *Wall Street Journal,* 6 October 1989, B3; Ty Harrington, "Extremism While Capturing Brand Loyalty Is No Vice," *Wall Street Journal,* 18 September 1989, A16; "Businesses Focus on VCR Users to Push Products," *Marketing News,* 3 July 1989, 8–9; Dean Foust, "Mr. Smith Goes Global," *Business Week,* 3 February 1989, 66–72; "Federal Express Spreads Its Wings," *Journal of Business Strategy,* July–August 1988, 15–20; David J. Dent, "Overnight Sensation," *Black Enterprise,* June 1988, 308–314; "Quality-Based Marketing Needs Bold Communication," *Marketing News,* 25 April 1988, 1; Dean Foust and Resa King, "Why Federal Express Has Overnight Anxiety," *Business Week,* 9 November 1987, 62–66; Marc Beauchamp, "Flying Harder," *Forbes,* 7 September 1987, 65; Carl Williams, "A Company Study: The Challenge of Retail Marketing at Federal Express," *Journal of Services Marketing,* Summer 1987, 25–38; "People Behind the Wonders," *Reader's Digest,* July 1987, 137; "Federal Express's Fred Smith," *Inc.,* October 1986, 35–50; Douglas MacDonald, "Overnight Success (or Failure)," *New England Business,* 21 April 1986, 57–64; Joanne Cleaver, "There's a New Way to Do Business (to Business)," *Advertising Age,* 20 June 1983, M9, M24; "Federal Express Corporation," *Wall Street Transcript,* 15 April 1991, 100680.

2. Michael D. Hutt and Thomas W. Speh, *Indus-*

trial *Marketing Management* (Chicago: Dryden, 1985), 4.

**3.** *Statistical Abstract of the United States 1989* (Washington, D.C.: GPO, 1989), 266, 293, 517, 627; "1988 Survey of Industrial and Commercial Buying Power," *Sales & Marketing Management,* 25 April 1988, 79.

**4.** *Statistical Abstract of the United States 1989,* 726.

**5.** *Statistical Abstract of the United States 1989,* 768.

**6.** *Statistical Abstract of the United States 1989,* 268.

**7.** Steven Burke, "Integrating Systems for Uncle Sam," *PC Week,* 29 January 1990, 121.

**8.** Tim Smart, Pete Engardio, and Geri Smith, "GE's Brave New World," *Business Week,* 8 November 1993, 64–70.

**9.** Philip R. Cateora, *International Marketing* (Homewood, Ill.: Irwin, 1987), 567–569.

**10.** Robert Kearns, "Is Everybody Happy?" *Business Marketing,* December 1989, 30–32, 34, 36.

**11.** Barbara C. Perdue, "Ten Aggressive Bargaining Tactics of Industrial Buyers," *Journal of Business and Industrial Marketing,* Spring 1992, 45–52.

**12.** Michael H. Morris and Jeanne L. Holman, "Source Loyalty in Organizational Markets: A Dyadic Perspective," *Journal of Business Research* 16, no. 2 (1988): 117–131.

**13.** Ernest F. Cooke, "What Is Business and Industrial Marketing?" *Journal of Business and Industrial Marketing,* Fall 1986, 9–17.

**14.** Morris and Holman, "Source Loyalty in Organizational Markets," 118; Cooke, "What Is Business and Industrial Marketing?" 11.

**15.** Haken Hakansson, ed., *International Marketing and Purchasing of Industrial Goods* (New York: Wiley, 1984).

**16.** John G. F. Bonnanzio, "A Partnership Built on Quality," *Industrial Distribution,* January 1989, 21CT–27CT.

**17.** Carl McDaniel, Jr., and William R. Darden, *Marketing* (Boston: Allyn & Bacon, 1987), 167.

**18.** F. Robert Finney, "Reciprocity: Gone but Not Forgotten," *Journal of Marketing,* January 1978, 54–59.

**19.** Frank G. Bingham, Jr., and Barney T. Raffield III, *Business to Business Marketing Management* (Homewood, Ill.: Irwin, 1990), 652.

**20.** Seth Lubove, "Dow's Downer," *Forbes,* 21 June 1993, 58–64.

**21.** William S. Bishop, John L. Graham, and Michael H. Jones, "Volatility of Derived Demand in Industrial Markets and Its Management Implications," *Journal of Marketing,* Fall 1984, 95–103.

**22.** Bishop, Graham, and Jones, "Volatility of Derived Demand in Industrial Markets and Its Management Implications," 97.

**23.** Morry Ghingold, "Testing the 'Buygrid' Buying Process Model," *Journal of Purchasing and Materials Management,* Winter 1986, 30–36.

**24.** Tom Eisenhart, "A Challenging Kind of Guy," *Business Marketing,* August 1989, 10, 12.

**25.** James F. Engel, Roger D. Blackwell, and Paul W. Miniard, *Consumer Behavior,* 5th ed. (Chicago: Dryden, (1986), 567.

**26.** Niren Vyas and Arch G. Woodside, "An Inductive Model of Industrial Supplier Choice Processes," *Journal of Marketing,* Winter 1984, 33.

**27.** Philip L. Dawes, Grahame R. Dowling, and Paul G. Patterson, "Determinants of Pre-Purchase Information Search Effort for Management Consulting Services," *Journal of Business-to-Business Marketing* 1. no. 1 (1993): 31–61.

**28.** Christopher Puto, Wesley E. Patton III, and Ronald H. King, "Risk Handling Strategies in In-dustrial Vendor Selection Decisions," *Journal of Marketing,* Winter 1985, 89–98.

**29.** Roger W. Brucker, "Merchandising: The Hit-and-Run of a Guerrilla Marketing Tactic," *Business Marketing,* April 1987, 76, 78, 80.

**30.** Raydel Tullous and Richard Lee Utecht, "Multiple or Single Sourcing?" *Journal of Business and Industrial Marketing,* Summer 1992, 5–18.

**31.** Mark Treleven, "Single Sourcing: A Management Tool for the Quality Supplier," *Journal of Purchasing and Materials Management,* Spring 1987, 19–24; Susan Avery, "Single Sourcing: The Risks Aren't as Bad as They Seem," *Purchasing,* 16 July 1987, 33.

**32.** "Sole-Sourcing Reduces Costs, Improves Quality and Delivery," *Purchasing,* 9 October 1986, 20–21.

**33.** Eisenhart, "A Challenging Kind of Guy," 10.

**34.** Patrick J. Robinson, Charles W. Faris, and Yoram Wind, *Industrial Buying and Creative Marketing* (Boston: Allyn & Bacon, 1967), 37.

**35.** Vyas and Woodside, "An Inductive Model of Industrial Supplier Choice Processes," 30–45.

**36.** Erin Anderson, Wujin Chu, and Barton Weitz, "Industrial Purchasing: An Empirical Exploration of the Buyclass Framework," *Industrial Purchasing,* July 1987, 71–86.

**37.** Anderson, Chu, and Weitz, "Industrial Purchasing," 83.

**38.** Donald W. Jackson, Jr., Janet E. Keith, and Richard K. Burdick, "Purchasing Agents' Perceptions of Industrial Buying Center Influence: A Situational Approach," *Journal of Marketing,* Fall 1984, 75–83.

**39.** Daniel H. McQuiston, "Novelty, Complexity, and Importance as Causal Determinants of Industrial Buyer Behavior," *Journal of Marketing,* April 1989, 66–79.

**40.** Gary L. Lilien and M. Anthony Wong, "An Exploratory Investigation of the Structure of the Buying Center in the Metalworking Industry," *Journal of Marketing Research,* February 1984, 1–11.

**41.** Wesley L. Johnston and Thomas V. Bonoma, "The Buying Center: Structure and Interaction Patterns," *Journal of Marketing,* Summer 1981, 143–156.

**42.** Johnston and Bonoma, "The Buying Center," 150.

**43.** Thomas V. Bonoma, "Major Sales: Who *Really* Does the Buying?" *Harvard Business Review,* May–June 1982, 111–119.

**44.** Melvin R. Mattson, "How to Determine the Composition and Influence of a Buying Center," *Journal of Marketing Management* 17 (1988): 205–214.

**45.** Gary McWilliams, "Cruising Along in Some Red-Hot Markets," *Business Week,* 5 February 1990, 82D–82E.

**46.** See note 1.

**47.** Adapted from Mary Rowland, "Creating a Plan to Reshape a Business," *Working Woman,* August 1988, 70–72, 74.

## CHAPTER 6

**1.** Cyndee Miller, "U.S. Postal Service Discovers the Merits of Marketing," *Marketing News,* 1 February 1993, 9 18; Rebecca Pirto, *Beyond Mind Games: The Marketing Power of Psychographics* (New York: American Demographics Books, 1991), 135–138; Paul Farhi, "Postal Service Delivers New TV Ad in Campaign to Improve Its Image," *Washington Post,* 28 November 1988, sec. f, 5; Bill McAlister, "Marketing a Public Image: From Mail Delivery to Mining Law, Postal Service Adopts Olympic Theme in Drive for "Pride and Profit,'" *Washington Post,* 25 March 1991, sec. a, 9.

**2.** Aimee Stern, "Do You know What They Want?" *International Business,* March 1993, 102–103.

**3.** Vindu P. Goel and Mary Lu Carnevale, "Devouring the Data," *Wall Street Journal,* 9 March 1990, R30–R31.

**4.** Tim Powell, *Analyzing Your Competition* (New York: Find/SVP, 1992), 8.

**5.** Peter D. Bennett, ed., *Dictionary of Marketing Terms* (Chicago: American Marketing Association,1988), 117.

**6.** Mark N. Clemente, *The Marketing Glossary* (New York: AMACOM, 1992),198.

**7.** Raymond Kaupp, "Avoid Frustration; Use a Good Information System," *Marketing News,* 14 March 1986, 50.

**8.** Dennis Farney, "Inside Hallmark's Love Machine," *Wall Street Journal,* 14 February 1990, B1, B10.

**9.** Tom Eisenhart, "After 10 years of Marketing Decision Support Systems, Where's the Payoff?" *Business Marketing,* June 1990, 46–48, 50–51.

**10.** Thomas C. Kinnear and Ann R. Root, *A Study of the Marketing Research Business,* unpublished study, 1988.

**11.** Stephen Phillips, Amy Dunkin, James B. Treece, and Keith H. Hammonds, "King Customer," *Business Week,* 12 March 1990, 90.

**12.** Pamela G. Hollie, What's New in Market Research," *New York Times,* 15 June 1986, sec. 3, 19.

**13.** David A. Aaker, *Strategic Market Management* (New York: Wiley, 1988), 21.

**14.** Paul L. Riedesel, "Understanding Validity Is Easy Doing Right Research Is Hard," *Marketing News,* 12 September 1986,24.

**15.** Johny K. Johansson and Ikujiro Nonaka, "Market Research the Japanese Way," *Harvard Business Review,* May–June 1987, 16–19.

**16.** Jack J. Honomichl, *Honomichl on Marketing Research* (Lincolnwood, Ill.: NTC Business Books, 1986), 119–121.

**17.** Honomichl, *Honomichl on Marketing Research,* 74–84.

**18.** Alan R. Andreasen, *Cheap but Good Marketing Research* (Homewood, Ill.: Dow Jones-Irwin, 1988), 253–265.

**19.** A. B. Blankenship and George Edward Breen, *State of the Art Marketing Research* (Lincolnwood, Ill.: NTC Business Books, 1993), 295–296.

**20.** Felix Kessler, "High-Tech Shocks in Ad Research," *Fortune,* 7 July 1986, 58.

**21.** Eugene Carlson, "Up for the Count," *Wall Street Journal,* 9 March 1990, R6.

**22.** Robert A. Peterson, *Marketing Researech* (Plano, Tex.: Business Publications, 1982), 338.

**23.** "Store Snooping," *Marketing Management* 2, no. 1 (1993: 6–7; Andreasen, *Cheap but Good Marketing Research,* 112.

**24.** Daniel T. Seymour, "Seeing Is Believing with Systematic Observation," *Marketing News,* 28 August 1987,36.

**25.** Stephen MacDonald, "Eye-Stopping Design in the Supermarket," *Wall Street Journal,* 22 January 1988, 23.

**26.** Bruce Horovitz, "The 'Spy' of Madison Ave.," *Los Angeles Times,* 5 May 1990, sec. d, 10.

**27.** Sally Ringo, "Researchers Can Learn from Ethnography," *Quinn"s Marketing Research Review,* April 1993, 16–43.

**28.** Al Kusada, "Surveys Breathe Life into Market Research," *Wall Street Journal,* 1 February 1988, 26.

**29.** Barbara Marsh, "Polling Picky Eaters to Boost a Restaurant's Popularity," *Wall Street Journal,* 8 May 1990, B2.

**30.** Todd Remington, "Rising Refusal Rates: The Impact of Telemarketing ," *Quirk's Marketing Research Review,* May 1992, 8–15.

**31.** John P. Liefield, "Response Effects in Computer-Administered Questioning," *Journal of Marketing Research* 25 (November 1988): 405–409.

**32.** William M Bulkeley, "More Market Researchers Swear by PC's," *Wall Street Journal,* 15 March 1993, B7.

**33.** Personal communication with Lee Meyer, Hewlett-Packard Lake Stevens Instrument Division, 22 July 1993.

**34.** Alan J. Bush and A. Parasuraman, Mall Intercept Versus Telephone-Interviewing Environment," *Journal of Advertising Research,* April–May 1985, 36–43.

**35.** Donald R. Lehman, *Market Research and Analysis* (Homewood, Ill.: Irwin, 1989),166.

**36.** Jeffrey Durgee, "New Product Ideas from Focus Groups," *Journal of Product and Brand Management,* Summer 1992, 24–32.

**37.** Jeffrey A. Trachtenberg, "Listening, the Old-Fashioned Way," *Forbes,* 5 October 1987, 202,204.

**38.** Lehmann, *Market Research and Analysis,* 145.

**39.** "How to Design and Conduct a Study," *Credit Union Magazine,* October 1983, 36–46.

**40.** Harper W. Boyd, Jr., Ralph Westfall, and Stanley F. Stasch, *Marketing Research: Text and Cases*

**41.** John G. Geer, "What Do Open-Ended Questions Measure?" *Public Opinion Quarterly,* Fall 1988, 365–371.

**42.** Steve Lohr, "Forget Peoria. It's Now: "Will It Play in Tulsa?" *New York Times,* 1 June 1992, A1; Peter M. Chisnall, *Marketing Research* (London: McGraw-Hill, 1986), 198; Peterson, *Marketing Research,*579; Boyd, Westfall, and Stasch, *Marketing Research,* 713.

**43.** Gerry Khermouch, "MarketWare Test Markets sans Messy Test Markets," Brandweek, 5 April 1993, 9; Bruce R. Driesbach, "Marketing: The Key to Successful Research Management," *Marketing News,* 4 January 1985, 3.

**44.** "Caterpillar: Challenging a 'Soft' Market," *Business Marketing,* August 1988, 40,42; Tracy E. Benson, "Caterpillar Wakes Up: Corporate Excavation Uncovers a Hidden Gold Mine," *Industry Week,* 20 May 1991,33.

**45.** "France: Locals Are Formidable," *PC Europa,* May 1993, 5.

**46.** Eugene Carlaosn, "A. C. Nielson Took the Measure of the Crowd," *Wall Street Journal,* 16 May 1989, B2.

**47.** Marsh, "Polling Picky Eaters to Boost a Restaurant's Popularity," B2.

**48.** Jack Honomichl, "three Factors Drive Growth of Top 50 Research Firms," *Marketing News,* 7 June 1993, H2; Philip Barnard, "New Directions in World Research," *Admap,* October 1992, 22.

**49.** Philip R. Cateora, *International Marketing,* 7th ed. (Homewood, Ill.: Irwin, 1990), 372–391.

**50.** Rena Bartos, "International Demographic Data? Incomparable!" *Marketing and Research Today,* November 1989, 205–212.

**51.** Peterson, *Marketing Research,* 651.

**52.** "Marketing Research Council gives Support to ESOMAR Ethics Code," *Marketing News,* 17 August 1992, 14; Peterson *Marketing Research,* 644.

**53.** See note 1.

**54.** Adapted from Jeffrey Rothfeder, Jim Bartimo, Lois Therrien, and Richard Brandt, "How Software Is Making Food Sales a Piece of Cake," *Business Week,* 2 July 1990, 54–55.

## CHAPTER 7

**1.** Adapted from Julie Liesse, "Kellogg Chief to Push Harder for Int'l Growth," *Advertising Age,* 24 August 1992, 4, 26; Julie Liesse, "Kellogg Sees Return of 40% Share as Core Brands Rise," *Advertising Age,* 15 June 1992, 1, 54; Rebecca Fannin, "Crunching the Competition," *Marketing & Media Decisions,* March 1988, 70–75; Patricia Sellers, "How King Kellogg Beat the Blahs," *Fortune,* 29 August 1988, 54–55, 58, 60, 64; Joseph A. Schenk, Dan S. Prickett, and Stanley J. Stough, "The Kellogg Company and the Ready-to-Eat Cereal Industry," *Journal of Management Case Studies,* Fall 1987, 191–214; Richard Gibson, "Fast Fall: Personal 'Chemistry' Abruptly Ended Rise of Kellogg President," *Wall Street Journal,* 28 November 1989, A1, A9; Julie Liesse Erickson, "Cereal Makers Roll More Oats," *Advertising Age,* 6 March 1989, 34; Beth Austin, "Kellogg Opens Superpremium Niche for Cereal," *Advertising Age,* 26 August 1987, 3, 55; Robert J. Samuelson, "The Great Cereal Wars," *Newsweek,* 7 September 1987, 49; Robert Messenger, "No More Blues in Battle Creek," *Prepared Foods,* February 1987, 44–45; Julie Franz, "Cereals Growing Up," *Advertising Age,* 9 February 1987, 22; "Kellogg Readies Oat Cereal to Be Eaten Hot or Cold," *Wall Street Journal,* 25 August 1989, B3; Richard Gibson, "Kellogg Tries to Blunt the Attacks on Cereal Makers' Health Claims," *Wall Street Journal,* 31 August 1989, B6; Julie Liesse Erickson, "Kellogg Pours It On," *Advertising Age,* 28 August 1989, 1, 52; Russell Mitchell, "The Health Craze Has Kellogg Feeling G-r-r-reat," *Business Week,* 30 March 1987, 52–53; William Stockton, "The Energized Cereal Industry," *New York Times,* 30 December 1987, sec. d, 4; Emily DeNitto, "Kellogg Sets Cereal Rollout; Health Claim Debate Renewed," *Supermarket News,* 11 September 1989, 8; David Woodruff, "Winning the War of Battle Creek," *Business Week,* 13 May 1991, 80.

**2.** Ronald Alsop, "Firms Send Brands to College to Cultivate New Consumers," *Wall Street Journal,* 31 July 1986, 25; Joanne Lipman, "Spring Break Sponsors in Florida Find Too Much of a Good Thing," *Wall Street Journal,* 21 March 1989, B1, B7.

**3.** Stan Rapp and Tom Collins, *The Great Marketing Turnaround* (Englewood Cliffs, N.J.: Prentice Hall, 1990), 106–107; Linda Moss, "The Super Story at Barnes & Noble," *Crain's New York Business,* 18 February 1991, 1.

**4.** William H. Davidow, "The Ultimate Marketing Weapon," *Business Marketing,* October 1989, 56–57, 60, 62, 64.

**5.** *Statistical Abstract of the United States 1990* (Washington, D.C.: GPO, 1990), 444; Hank Gilman, "Selling to the Poor: Retailers That Target Low-Income Shoppers Are Growing Rapidly," *Wall Street Journal,* 24 June 1985, 1, 12; Ray Clune, "In Recession Economy: Family Dollar Rings Up Big Bucks," *Daily News Record,* 7 May 1991, 12.

**6.** Rapp and Collins, *The Great Marketing Turnaround,* 100.

**7.** Michael J. McCarthy, "Coke Fields a Sports Drink to Challenge Gatorade's Hold," *Wall Street Journal,* 6 March 1990, B1, B6.

**8.** Robert S. Menchin, *The Mature Market* (Chicago: Probus, 1989), 180; David B. Wolfe, "The Ageless Market," *American Demographics,* July 1987, 26–29, 55–56.

**9.** George Melloan, "Business World: 'White Goods' Makers Seek to Counter the Baby Bust," *Wall Street Journal,* 9 May 1989, A23.

**10.** Alix M. Freedman, "National Firms Find That Selling to Local Tastes Is Costly, Complex," *Wall Street Journal,* 9 February 1987, 17.

**11.** *Statistical Abstract of the United States 1990,* 908, 909, 910, 914.

**12.** *Statistical Abstract of the United States 1990,* 908, 916.

**13.** *Statistical Abstract of the United States 1990,* 908, 914.

**14.** Gerry Khermouch, "Kodak Focuses on 'Life Stages,' " *Brandweek,* 15 February 1993, 4.

**15.** Patricia Sellers, "The ABC's of Marketing to Kids," *Fortune,* 8 May 1989, 114–116, 120; "Gadzooks Caters to Growing Teen Market," *Chain Store Age Executive,* November 1988, 98–101; Brad Edmondson, "Colleges Conquer the Baby Bust," *American Demographics,* September 1987, 26–31, 55; Faye Rice, "Wooing Aging Baby Boomers," *Fortune,* 1 February 1988, 68–69, 72, 76–77; Menchin, *The Mature Market,* 147.

**16.** "Snapshots of the Nation," *Wall Street Journal Reports,* 9 March 1990, R12; Sheila Gadsden, "Toyota Taps Black Buying Power," *Advertising Age,* 14 December 1987, S5–S6; Jose de Cordoba, "More Firms Court Hispanic Consumers—But Find Them a Tough Market to Target," *Wall Street Journal,* 18 February 1988, A25.

**17.** Hans L. Zetterberg, "The Demography of Europe," *Admap,* September 1991, 26–32.

**18.** Michael T. Malloy, "Loblaw Pushes Activist-Endorsed Line Aimed at Issue-Conscious Consumers," *Wall Street Journal,* 1 May 1989, B6.

**19.** Ernest Dichter, "Whose Lifestyle Is It Anyway?" *Psychology & Marketing* 3, no. 3 (Fall 1986): 151–163; Michael J. Weiss, *The Clustering of America* (New York: Harper & Row, 1988), 41.

**20.** Rebecca Piirto, *Beyond Mind Games: The Marketing Power of Psychographics* (New York: American Demographics Books, 1991), 79–90.

**21.** Piirto, *Beyond Mind Games,* 79–90.

**22.** Weiss, *The Clustering of America,* xii; SRI International, "VALS 2: Your Marketing Edge for the 1990s," pamphlet, 1989; Menchin, *The Mature Market,* 20.

**23.** Piirto, *Beyond Mind Games,* 232–233; Weiss, *The Clustering of America,* 10–15.

**24.** Weiss, *The Clustering of America,* 10–15.

**25.** Weiss, *The Clustering of America,* 269, 389.

**26.** Weiss, *The Clustering of America,* 15, 269.

**27.** Piirto, *Beyond Mind Games,* 235.

**28.** Piirto, *Beyond Mind Games,* 237.

**29.** Peter Sleight, "Where They Live," *Admap,* May 1992, 17–22.

**30.** Christine M. Brooks, "Armchair Quarterbacks," *American Demographics,* March 1988, 28–31.

**31.** Michael J. McCarthy, "Royal Crown Cola Shifts Focus of Ads, Aiming for Adults Rather than Teens," *Wall Street Journal,* 5 June 1989, B6; "Small Brands Pack Plenty of Punch," *Beverage Industry,* March 1991, 16.

**32.** Leon G. Schiffman and Leslie Lazar Kanuk, *Consumer Behavior* (Englewood Cliffs, N.J.: Prentice Hall, 1987), 48.

**33.** F. Michael Hruby, "Buyers, Sellers in Business Market Work Best When Working Together," *Marketing News,* 18 December 1989, 8, 16.

**34.** U.S. Bureau of the Census, *Guide to the 1987 Economic Census and Related Statistics* (Washington, D.C.: GPO, 1990), 7, 9; Art Weinstein, *Market Segmentation: Using Niche Marketing to Exploit New Markets* (Chicago: Probus, 1987), 152.

**35.** Benson P. Shapiro and Thomas V. Bonoma, "How to Segment Industrial Markets," *Harvard Business Review,* May–June 1984, 104–110; Robert L. Stewart, "The Mark of a Marketing-Minded Agency: $20 Million in 8 Years!" *Rough Notes,* January 1989, 12–15.

**36.** Philip Kotler and Alan R. Andreasen, *Strategic Marketing for Nonprofit Organizations* (Englewood Cliffs, N.J.: Prentice-Hall, 1987), 117–118.

**37.** Melloan, "Business World: 'White Goods' Makers Seek to Counter the Baby Bust," A23; Debra Goldman, "What Do Women Want?" *Adweek's Marketing Week,* 25 June 1990, 49.

**38.** Jack Willoughby, "The Last Iceman," *Forbes,* 13 July 1987, 183–204.

**39.** "Gymboree Is More than Just Child's Play: Toddler Activity Classes Grow into Lifestyle Concept Retail Stores," *Chain Store Age Executive,* November 1987, 115, 118, 120, 122.

**40.** Rapp and Collins, *The Great Marketing Turnaround,* 97–98.

**41.** Kevin J. Clancy and Mary Lou Roberts, "Toward an Optimal Market Target: A Strategy for Market Segmentation," *Journal of Product and Brand Management,* Winter 1992, 5–13.

**42.** James H. Martin and James M. Daley, "How to Develop a Customer-Driven Positioning Strategy," *Business,* October–December 1989, 11–20.

**43.** Glen L. Urban, John R. Hauser, and Nikhilesh Dholakia, *Essentials of New Product Management* (Englewood Cliffs, N.J.: Prentice Hall, 1987), 110.

**44.** Al R. Ries and Jack T. Trout, *Positioning* (New York: McGraw-Hill, 1986), 58; Judann Dagnoli, "Campbell Stirs Goya Market," *Advertising Age,* 3 August 1987, 58.

**45.** George P. Dovel, "Stake It Out: Positioning Success, Step by Step," *Business Marketing,* July 1990, 43–44, 46, 48–51.

**46.** Philip R. Cateora, *International Marketing* (Homewood, Ill.: Irwin, 1987), 379.

**47.** Roman G. Hiebing, Jr., and Scott W. Cooper, *How to Write a Successful Marketing Plan* (Lincolnwood, Ill.: NTC Business Books, 1990), 119–122.

**48.** Alicia Johnson, "Ernie Townsend: Chipping Out a Niche in Frozen Dinners," *Management Review,* July 1987, 19–22.

**49.** Kotler and Andreasen, *Strategic Marketing for Nonprofit Organizations,* 423.

**50.** Bob Garfield, "Ad Review: Chrysler Agencies Work to Match Ads to Cars," *Advertising Age,* 26 October 1992, 53.

**51.** Product usage suggestion appeared on Jell-O packaging.

**52.** Ad appeared in *Wall Street Journal,* 8 July 1993, A12.

**53.** "S&O Sees Packaging as a Product Repositioning Tool," *Marketing News,* 18 December 1987, 9.

**54.** "The Volvo Marketing Pitch: Be Different, Yet Relevant," *Brandweek,* 31 May 1993.

**55.** "Product Positioning: A Crucial Marketing Strategy," *Small Business Report,* April 1988, 18–22; Dovel, "Stake It Out," 49.

**56.** Dovel, "Stake It Out," 51.

**57.** See note 1.

**58.** Adapted from Bo Burlingham, "This Woman Has Changed Business Forever," *Inc.,* June 1990, 34, 36–38, 41–42, 44–46.

## CHAPTER 8

**1.** Adapted from Brian K. Burton, "Tops in Popcorn: Indiana Is the World's Largest Producer," *Indiana Business,* October 1987, 18–24; Robert Runde, "Fortunes from Scratch: A Popcorn King Who's in the Chips," *Money,* November 1979, 106, 108, 110, 112, 114; Orville Redenbacher, "The Funny-Looking Farmer with the Funny-Sounding Name," *Guideposts,* January 1990, 2–5; Frazier Moore, "A Corn for Connoisseurs," *Madison Avenue,* May 1985, 14, 16–18; Bernice Kanner, "Kernel Knowledge," *New York,* 11 January 1988, 14–15; Lori Kesler, "Personalities Pitching Products," *Advertising Age,* 3 May 1984, M30, M34, M38; Jennie Nash, "Rating the Microwave Popcorn," *Los Angeles Magazine,* February 1991, 16.

**2.** Al Ries and Jack Trout, *Positioning: The Battle for Your Mind* (New York: McGraw-Hill, 1986), 48.

**3.** Ries and Trout, *Positioning,* 16.

**4.** Advertisement for the French Redevelopment Agency, *Electronic Business,* 17 September 1990, 1.

**5.** Patrick E. Murphy and Ben M. Enis, "Classifying Products Strategically," *Journal of Marketing,* July 1986, 26.

**6.** Alison Rogers, "Software to Tell What a Meeting Costs," *Fortune,* 15 November 1993, 16.

**7.** May Beth Regan, "The Sun Shines Brighter on Alternative Energy," *Business Week,* 8 November 1993, 94–95.

**8.** Adrian Room, "The History of Branding," in *Branding: A Key Marketing Tool,* edited by John M. Murphy (New York: McGraw-Hill, 1987), 16.

**9.** "Choosing a Product Name Is a High Stakes Game," Prodigy Services Company, 19 July 1993.

**10.** Howard Schlossberg, "Brand Value Can Be Worth More than Physical Assets," *Marketing News,* 5 March 1990, 6.

**11.** David A. Aaker, *Managing Brand Loyalty* (New York: Free Press, 1991), 19–21.

**12.** S. P. Raj, "Striking a Balance Between Brand 'Popularity' and Brand Loyalty," *Journal of Marketing,* Winter 1985, 53–59.

**13.** Ronald Alsop, "Brand Loyalty Is Rarely Blind Loyalty," *Wall Street Journal,* 19 October 1989, B1, B9.

**14.** Ty Harrington, "Extremism While Capturing Brand Loyalty Is No Vice," *Wall Street Journal,* 18 September 1989, A16.

**15.** Aaker, *Managing Brand Loyalty,* 19.

**16.** Aaker, *Managing Brand Loyalty,* 21.

**17.** David Kiley, "Hyundai. Maybe, Hyandai," *Adweek's Marketing Week,* 17 September 1990, 49.

**18.** Terry Lofton, "How the Big Brands Rank," *Brandweek,* 29 March 1993, 26–30.

**19.** Gabriella Stern, "Cheap Imitation: Perrigo's Knockoffs of Name-Brand Drugs Turn into Big Sellers," *Wall Street Journal,* 15 July 1993, A1, A9; Zachary Schiller, "Procter & Gamble Hits Back," *Business Week,* 19 July 1993, 20–22.

**20.** Patrick Oster, Gabrielle Saveri, and John Templemann, "The Erosion of Brand Loyalty," *Business Week,* 19 July 1993, 22; Yumiko Ono, "The Rising Sun Shines on Private Labels," *Wall Street Journal,* 26 April 1992, B1, B5.

**21.** Eben Shapiro, "Price Lure of Private-Label Products Fails to Hook Many Buyers of Baby Food, Beer," *Wall Street Journal,* 13 May 1993, B1, B8.

**22.** Brian F. Harris and Roger A. Strang, "Marketing Strategies in the Age of Generics," *Journal of Marketing,* Fall 1985, 70–81.

**23.** Walter J. Salmon and Karen A. Cmar, "Private Labels Are Back in Fashion," *Harvard Business Review,* May–June 1987, 99–106.

**24.** Kim Robertson, "Strategically Desirable Brand Name Characteristics," *Journal of Product and Brand Management,* Summer 1992, 62–72; Francine Schwadel, "Spiegel, Crayola Plan Kids' Clothes Line," *Wall Street Journal,* 3 October 1990, B1; "Spiegel Launches Crayola Kids Clothing Line in Fall Catalog," PR Newswire, 26 June 1991.

**25.** Clarke Graham and Mark Peroff, "The Legal Side of Branding," in *Branding,* edited by John M. Henry (New York: McGraw-Hill, 1987), 46–47.

**26.** Frank Delano, "Keeping Your Trade Name or Trademark Out of Court," *Harvard Business Review,* March–April 1982, 72–74.

**27.** Judith Springer Riddle, "Gillette Deodorants Clearly Gel," *Brandweek,* 30 August 1993, 1, 6.

**28.** Ries and Trout, *Positioning,* 116–117.

**29.** Jack Trout, "Brand Extensions . . . Traps and Opportunities," *Boardroom Reports,* 1 October 1987, 8.

**30.** Karen Springen and Annetta Miller, "Sequels for the Shelf," *Newsweek,* 9 July 1990, 42–43.

**31.** "Entertainment Tonight," 15 September 1990.

**32.** "Packaging Plays Starring Role in TV Commercials," *Marketing News,* 30 January 1987, 6.

**33.** Stephen MacDonald, "Toyota Parts Packages: Designed in the U.S.A.," *Wall Street Journal,* 31 March 1988, 25.

**34.** Noreen O'Leary, "Making the Package a Product Benefit," *Adweek Special Report,* 3 October 1988, 18, 20.

**35.** "Cushioning System Saves $1 per Case," *Packaging,* October 1988, 68–69.

**36.** Nancy L. Croft, "Wrapping Up Sales," *Nation's Business,* October 1985, 41–42.

**37.** Laurie Hays, "New Package May Yield Fresher Produce," *Wall Street Journal,* 18 October 1988, B1.

**38.** "Special Packaging Reduces Fire Risk," *Packaging,* March 1988, 72–74.

**39.** Sonia L. Nazario, "Microwave Packages That Add Crunch to Lunch May Also Pose Chemical Risks," *Wall Street Journal,* 1 March 1990, B1, B4.

**40.** Joe Schwartz, "Americans Annoyed by Wasteful Packaging," *American Demographics,* April 1992, 13.

**41.** John Holusha, "New Packaging That Spares the Environment," *New York Times,* 28 March 1990, sec. d, 8.

**42.** "40 Under 40," *Entrepreneur,* October 1990, 113.

**43.** Justin Martin, "It's Green, and It Cleans," *Fortune,* 15 November 1993, 14.

**44.** Paul B. Brown, "Sitting Pretty," *Inc.,* September 1990, 148, 164; Bob Woods, "The Joy of Soy," *Food & Beverage Marketing,* March 1991, 19.

**45.** Lise Heroux, Michel Laroche, and K. Lee McGown, "Consumer Product Label Information Processing: An Experiment Involving Time Pressure and Distraction," *Journal of Economic Psychology,* 1988, 195–214.

**46.** Brown, "Sitting Pretty," 148, 164.

**47.** Elizabeth Lesly, "What's Next, Raiders' Deodorant," *Business Week,* 30 November 1992, 65.

**48.** Elizabeth Conlin, "Prove It!" *Inc.,* October 1990, 25.

**49.** Joseph P. Kahn, "Caddy Shack," *Inc.,* May 1987, 80–82, 87.

**50.** Gail Greco, "Product Liability Bill on Its Way," *Entrepreneur,* October 1990, 192–193.

**51.** Kenneth A. Smalheiser, "Emerging Standards in Information Systems," *Fortune,* 8 October 1990, 168–169, 172–173, 176.

**52.** See note 1.

**53.** Adapted from Ellen Schultz, "The Making of an Entrepreneur," *Savvy,* July 1988, 22–24.

## CHAPTER 9

**1.** Adapted from James A. White, "Japan's Canon Unveils Plain-Paper Copier with Disposable Parts for Personal Market," *Wall Street Journal,* 25 August 1982, 7; Marianne Meyer, "Can Anyone Duplicate Canon's Personal Copiers' Success?" *Marketing & Media Decisions Spring 1985 Special,* 97–101; David M. Kelly, "Canon Catapults Ahead in New Copier Sales," *Marketing & Media Decisions Business to Business Special 1984,* 102–107; Ikujiro Nonaka and Teruo Yamanouchi, "Managing Innovation as a Self-Renewing Process," *Journal of Business Venturing* 4 (September 1989): 299–315; Teruo Yamanouchi, "Breakthrough: The Development of the Canon Personal Copier," *Long-Range Planning* 22, no. 5 (October 1989): 11–21; Richard Cretan, "Brand Management: Copying Success," *Madison Avenue,* March 1985, 25–26; Richard Phalon, "Phototropism," *Forbes,* 3 June 1985, 88–89; Jon Pepper, "Tools for the Office Trade," *Nation's Business,* February 1991, 46.

**2.** William L. Shanklin, *Six Timeless Marketing Blunders* (Lexington, Mass.: Lexington Books, 1989), 111.

**3.** The Walt Disney Company Annual Report, 1989.

4. Glen L. Urban, John R. Hauser, and Nikhilesh Dholakia, *Essentials of New Product Management* (Englewood Cliffs, N.J.: Prentice-Hall, 1987), 287; Rebecca Fannin, "Taking Shape," *Marketing & Media Decisions,* June 1988, 48–53.

5. Elizabeth A. Lesly, "Borden Faces Facts: It's Time to Shed the Flab," *Business Week,* 9 November 1992, 44.

6. Pauline Yoshihashi, "Mattel Shapes a New Future for Barbie," *Wall Street Journal,* 12 February 1990, B1, B5; Anthony Ramirez, "A Radical New Style for Stodgy Old Gillette," *New York Times,* 25 February 1990, sec. f, 5.

7. Anthony Ramirez, "Growth Is Glacial, but the Market Is Big, and So Is the Gross," *New York Times,* 13 May 1990, sec. 3, 11; Alecia Swasy, "Diaper Derby Heats Up as Firms Add Color, Frills," *Wall Street Journal,* 9 May 1989, B1.

8. Robert Johnson and Tananarive Due, "Eatery Chains Pour On Speed at Lunchtime," *Wall Street Journal,* 1 February 1988, 27; Edward Zuckerman, "How Now to Sell a Cow?" *New York Times Magazine,* 29 November 1987, 68–70, 76–78, 91.

9. Richard T. Hise and Michael A. McGinnis, "Product Elimination: Practices, Policies, and Ethics," *Business Horizons,* June 1975, 25–32.

10. Paul B. Carroll, "Americans' Love of IBM Typewriters Outlasts Company's," *Wall Street Journal,* 3 August 1990, A1, A9.

11. Stuart Elliot, "How New Brands Become Too Much of a New Thing," *New York Times,* 2 June 1992, C7.

12. Calvin L. Hodock, "Strategies Behind the Winners and Losers," *Journal of Business Strategy,* September–October 1990, 4; John Small, "Pudding Pops: The Story Behind Their Success," *Prepared Foods,* April 1985, 130, 133.

13. Herbert M. Baum, "New Products—I Can Feel When They're Right," *Journal of Consumer Marketing,* Fall 1987, 41–45; Dan Koeppel, "Powerful Brand 'Families' Key to Growth," *Adweek's Marketing Week Superbrands 1990,* 147–150, 152; Martin Friedman, "New Products: Line Extensions Outnumber the Truly New Wares," *Adweek Special Report,* 14 September 1987, F.P. 33; Steven Flax, "The Big Stretch: How Elastic Is Your Brand?" *The Marketer,* September 1990, 32–35; Borden Annual Report, 1989, 24.

14. Ronald Alsop, "Giving Fading Brands a Second Chance," *Wall Street Journal,* 24 January 1989, B1.

15. Alsop, "Giving Fading Brands a Second Chance," B1.

16. Everett M. Rogers, *Diffusion of Innovation,* 3d ed. (New York: Free Press, 1983), 247.

17. Steve Weiner and Janis Bultman, "Calling Betty Crocker," *Forbes,* 8 August 1988, 88–89.

18. Keith H. Hammonds, "How a $4 Razor Ends Up Costing $300 Million," *Business Week,* 29 January 1990, 62–63; James Cox, "Sensor: Five Million Chins and Counting," *USA Today,* 8 February 1990, 1B; Cathy Taylor, "With Sensor, Gillette Took Lead in 'Orchestration,'" *Adweek,* 3 June 1991, 32; Richard J. Coletti, "Leading Edge: Gillette's Sensor Razor Is a Case Study in How to Marry Engineering Research and Marketing Savvy," *Financial World,* 8 January 1991, 48.

19. "The Marketing 100: Steve Miller," *Advertising Age,* 5 July 1993, 15.

20. Paul B. Brown, "The Eternal Second Act," *Inc.,* June 1988, 119–120.

21. Joshua Hyatt, "Too Hot to Handle," *Inc.,* March 1987, 58.

22. Michael Lev, "As the Craze Cools, a Youth-Based Industry Matures," *New York Times,* 29 April 1990, sec. 3, 10.

23. William Lazer, Mushtaq Luqmani, and Zahir Quraeshi, "Product Rejuvenation Strategies," *Business Horizons,* November–December 1984, 21–28.

24. Ronald Alsop, "Old Chewing-Gum Favorites Find There's Life after Death," *Wall Street Journal,* 11 September 1986, 37.

25. Zachery Schiller and Gail DeGeorge, "What's for Breakfast? Juice Wars," *Business Week,* 5 October 1987, 110–115; Alix M. Freedman, "An Orange Juice War Is Growing as Makers Vie for Fresh Markets," *Wall Street Journal,* 27 April 1988, 30; Michael J. McCarthy, "Squeezing More Life into Orange Juice: Premium Juice Is Focal Point of Fierce Battle," *Wall Street Journal,* 4 May 1989, B1; Dan L. Gunter, "Plentiful Supplies of DCOJ Can Lead You to Higher Profits," *Frozen Food Digest,* April–May 1991, 8.

26. Philip Griswold, "It's the Real Thing?" *Madison Avenue,* July 1984, 30–31; P. R. Nayak and J. M. Kettringham, "The Fine Art of Managing Creativity," *New York Times,* 2 November 1986, sec. 3, 2.

27. "The Rigorous Cultivation of a Natural Drug," *Financial Times,* 27 October 1988, London page 30: S19; "SmithKline Swallows a Bitter Pill," *Financial Times,* 28 July 1988, London page 28: S38; "Ulcer Drug Enjoys 10 Years at the Top," *Financial Times,* 18 November 1986, London page 14: S09.

28. J. Donald LaZerte, "Market Pull/Technology Push: 3M Scotchgard Fabric Protector," *Research-Technology Management,* March–April 1989, 25–27.

29. Philip Kotler and Alan R. Andreasen, *Strategic Marketing for Nonprofit Organizations* (Englewood Cliffs, N.J.: Prentice-Hall, 1987), 423.

30. Kotler and Andreasen, *Strategic Marketing for Nonprofit Organizations,* 386.

31. Robert G. Cooper, *Winning at New Products* (Reading, Mass.: Addison-Wesley, 1986), 103; Tom W. White, "Use Variety of Internal, External Sources to Gather and Screen New Product Ideas," *Marketing News,* 16 September 1983, sec. 2, 12.

32. Robert G. Cooper and Ulrike de Brentani, "Criteria for Screening New Industrial Products," *Industrial Marketing Management* 13 (1984): 149–156; Edward A. Michaels, "New Product Development," *Small Business Reports,* June 1989, 61–66.

33. Tom Gorman, "What Will Our Customers Think of This Product Idea?" *Business Marketing,* September 1987, 76–78, 80.

34. Tom Richman, "The New American Start-Up," *Inc.,* September 1988, 54–66.

35. Suzanne Oliver, "The Shiksa Chef," *Forbes,* 24 May 1993, 66, 68.

36. Rebecca Fannin, "Cream de la Creme," *Marketing & Media Decisions,* March 1989, 59-60, 62.

37. Richman, "The New American Start-Up," 63.

38. William A. Leiva and James W. Obermayer, "Commonsense Product Development," *Business Marketing,* August 1989, 44, 46, 48; "King Customer: At Companies That Listen Hard and Respond Fast, Bottom Lines Thrive," *Business Week,* 12 March 1990, 90; Patricia P. Mishne, "A Passion for Perfection," *Manufacturing Engineering,* November 1988, 46–58; Bruce Nussbaum and John Templeman, "Built to Last—Until It's Time to Take It Apart," *Business Week,* 17 September 1990, 102, 104, 106.

39. John H. Sheridan, "Technology: Manage It as an Asset," *Industry Week,* 21 September 1992, 47–50; Robert Teitelman, "Staying Power," *Financial World,* 4 April 1989, 28–30; David Chandler, "'Open' for Business: AT&T's Standard Effort at UNIX Development," *UNIX Review,* April 1988, 33–41.

40. "Sayett: A Payoff for Kodak's Venture System," *Business Marketing,* July 1987, 48, 50.

41. "It's a Mall World After All," *Chain Store Age Executive,* December 1989, 86; Richard W. Stevenson, "Disney Stores: Magic in Retail?" *New York Times,* 4 May 1990, sec. d, 1, 18; Carrie Goerne, "Nick's Rude 'Ren & Stimpy' Hits It Big with Licensed Goods," *Marketing News,* 9 November 1992, 2, 6.

42. Raymond Goydon, "Easy Numbers," *Forbes,* 23 February 1985, 180–181; Toni Mack, "Let the Computer Do It," *Forbes,* 10 August 1987, 94.

43. Leslie Brennan, "Quick Study: So Fast Are Today's Testing Techniques That Marketers Can Evaluate a Product Before Competitors Get Wise—Usually," *Sales & Marketing Management,* March 1988, 50, 52–53; Nancy Madlin, "Streamlining the Test-Market Process," *Adweek,* 11 November 1985, 10–12.

44. Brennan, "Quick Study," 50, 52.

45. "Caterpillar: Challenging a 'Soft' Market," *Business Marketing,* August 1988, 40, 42.

46. "Six PepsiCo Successes Cited: Spotting Competitive Edges Begets New Product Success," *Marketing News,* 21 December 1984, 4.

47. Calvin Sims, "The Creation of a Hit Product," *New York Times,* 6 June 1986, sec. d, 1, 5.

48. Yoshihashi, "Mattel Shapes a New Future for Barbie," B1.

49. Carroll, "Americans' Love of IBM Typewriters Outlasts Company's," 1.

50. Al Ries and Jack Trout, *Positioning: The Battle for Your Mind* (New York: McGraw-Hill, 1986), 48.

51. Alicia Johnson, "Ernie Townsend: Chipping Out a Niche in Frozen Dinners," *Management Review,* July 1987, 20.

52. Ramirez, "Growth Is Glacial," sec. 3, 11.

53. Johnson, "Ernie Townsend: Chipping Out a Niche in Frozen Dinners," 20.

54. "New Product Success Is Not a Process: It Must Coincide with Corporate Strategies," *Marketing News,* 6 July 1984, 9.

55. Richman, "The New American Start-Up," 54–66; Donald W. Hendon, *Classic Failures in Product Marketing: Marketing Principles Violations and How to Avoid Them* (New York: Quorum Books, 1989), 123.

56. Carl Williams, "The Challenge of Retail Marketing at Federal Express," *Journal of Services Marketing,* Summer 1987, 25–38.

57. Hendon, *Classic Failures in Product Marketing,* 126.

58. Nayak and Kettringham, "The Fine Art of Managing Creativity," sec. 3, 2.

59. Hendon, *Classic Failures in Product Marketing,* 111.

60. Hendon, *Classic Failures in Product Marketing,* 128; Cooper, *Winning at New Products,* 23.

61. Hendon, *Classic Failures in Product Marketing,* 109.

62. Hendon, *Classic Failures in Product Marketing,* 125.

63. David Mahoney, "How the Sparkle Turned to a Fizzle," *Advertising Age,* 7 March 1988, 36, 39.

64. See note 1.

65. Adapted from Walter Coddington, "It's No Fad: Environmentalism Is Now a Fact of Corporate Life," *Marketing News,* 15 October 1990, 7.

## CHAPTER 10

1. Standard & Poor's Corporate Descriptions, November 1993; "WMX Ad Tries High-Powered Approach to Altering Corporate Image," *Business Marketing,* August 1993, 58; Subrata N. Chak-

ravarty, "Dean Buntrock's Green Machine," *Forbes,* 2 August 1993, 96–100.

**2.** James L. Heskett, "Lessons in the Service Sector," *Harvard Business Review,* March–April 1987, 118–126.

**3.** *Statistical Abstract of the United States 1993* (Washington, D.C.: GPO, 1993), 410.

**4.** "The Fitness Market Follows Consumers into Middle Age," *Market: Europe,* November 1991, 8–9.

**5.** *Statistical Abstract of the United States 1990* (Washington, D.C.: GPO, 1990), 380; "Labor Force Status of the Population: 1870 to 1970," *Historical Statistics of the United States: Colonial Times to 1970* (Washington, D.C.: GPO, 1975), part 1, 127–128.

**6.** Lawrence Ingrassia, "Day-Care Business Lures Entrepreneurs," *Wall Street Journal,* 3 June 1988, 17.

**7.** Tony Reynes, "Free-Lance, Computer Graphics Will Be Job Opportunities of the '90s," *Marketing News,* 18 December 1989, 2.

**8.** Alex Taylor III, "The Economy of the 1990s: What the Sober Spenders Will Buy," *Fortune,* 2 February 1987, 35–38.

**9.** Clemens P. Work, "The Flying-Package Trade Takes Off," *U.S. News & World Report,* 2 October 1989, 47, 50.

**10.** Jillian C. Sweeney, Lester W. Johnson, and Robert W. Armstrong, "The Effect of Cues on Service Quality Expectations and Service Selection in a Restaurant Setting," *Journal of Services Marketing,* Fall 1992, 15–22.

**11.** Christopher H. Lovelock, "Classifying Services to Gain Strategic Marketing Insights," *Journal of Marketing,* Summer 1983, 9–20.

**12.** Sally Berger, "Religious Hospitals' Missions Inspire Success," *Modern Healthcare,* 28 April 1989, 40.

**13.** James S. Hirsch, "Airlines Bet That Pampering Passengers Will Build Loyalty, Soften Fare Increases," *Wall Street Journal,* 17 February 1993, B1, B10.

**14.** Richard B. Chase, "Where Does the Customer Fit in a Service Operation?" *Harvard Business Review,* November–December 1978, 137–142.

**15.** Rukeyser, Cooney, and Winslow, *Louis Rukeyser's Business Almanac,* 402.

**16.** Michael J. McCarthy, "Sinking Attendance Leads Baseball Clubs to Come Up with a New Play: Marketing," *Wall Street Journal,* 6 July 1993, B1, B3.

**17.** Rukeyser, Cooney, and Winslow, *Louis Rukeyser's Business Almanac,* 539; "O'Shea: Sellthrough to Outpace Rental by 100% in 1990," *Home Video Publisher,* 19 June 1989, 2–3.

**18.** Christi Harlan, "Lawyers' Groups Debate Sanctity of TV Ads," *Wall Street Journal,* 29 December 1988, B1.

**19.** Mark Bittman, "Professionals Direct Attention to Marketing," *Advertising Age,* 6 March 1986, 26–28.

**20.** Harlan, "Lawyers' Groups Debate Sanctity of TV Ads," 1.

**21.** Rukeyser, Cooney, and Winslow, *Louis Rukeyser's Business Almanac,* 516.

**22.** Gene Bylinsky, "Invasion of the Service Robots," *Fortune,* 14 September 1987, 81–82, 84–86, 88.

**23.** Theodore Levitt, "The Industrialization of Service," *Harvard Business Review,* September–October 1976, 63–74.

**24.** G. Lynn Shostack, "Breaking Free from Product Marketing," *Journal of Marketing,* April 1977, 73–82.

**25.** G. Lynn Shostack, "Service Positioning Through Structural Change," *Journal of Marketing,* January 1987, 34–43.

**26.** James S. Hirsch, "Plain Travel It Ain't; Fancy Services Count for This Tour Agent," *Wall Street Journal,* 12 August 1993, A1, A5.

**27.** William M. Foley, "Selling After the Sale," *Microservice Management,* March 1986, 19–25.

**28.** Christian Grönroos, "A Service Quality Model," *European Journal of Marketing* 18, no. 4 (1984): 36–44.

**29.** Gregg Cebrzynski, "CEOs: Keep 'Service' in Services Marketing," *Marketing News,* 8 November 1985, 11.

**30.** Brad Edmondson, "The Political Sell," *American Demographics,* November 1986, 27–28, 63–66.

**31.** "Ireland Offers Smaller U.S. Companies Trade Access to Europe," press release distributed by the Irish Export Board, October 1989.

**32.** Rick Fleury, "The Most Powerful Icon of the '90s," *Brandweek,* 30 November 1992, 14, 16.

**33.** Sue Kapp, "Uncle Sam's Marketing Man," *Business Marketing,* January 1988, 8, 10, 14.

**34.** William C. Symonds, "Golf: The Ladies Tour Slices into the Rough," *Business Week,* 1 October 1990, 134.

**35.** Philip Kotler and Alan R. Andreasen, *Strategic Marketing for Nonprofit Organizations* (Englewood Cliffs, N.J.: Prentice-Hall, 1987), 14.

**36.** David R. Gourley and Mary E. Moore, "Marketing and Planning in Multihospital Systems," *Hospital and Health Services Administration,* Fall 1988, 331–344.

**37.** See note 1.

## CHAPTER 11

**1.** Adapted from Gregory A. Patterson, "Sears's Makeover into a Department Store Calls for Enhancing the Role of Cosmetics," *Wall Street Journal,* 9 April 1993, B1, B8; Gregory A. Patterson, "Sears Will Re-Establish Base in Malls, Target Middle-of-the-Road Merchants," *Wall Street Journal,* 27 January 1993, A5; Kevin Kelly and Laura Zinn, "Can Ed Brennan Salvage the Sears He Designed?" *Business Week,* 27 August 1990, 34; Brian Bremner, "Now Sears Has Everyday Low Prices, Too," *Business Week,* 21 August 1989, 28; Francine Schwadel, "Sears's Brennan Faces Facts about Costs," *Wall Street Journal,* 10 August 1990, B1; Martha Groves, "Sears Joining Revolution of Stable Pricing Policies," *Los Angeles Times,* 1 March 1989, 1, 16; Francine Schwadel, "The 'Sale' Is Fading as a Retailing Tactic," *Wall Street Journal,* 1 March 1989; B1; Amy Dunkin, David Woodruff, and Dean Foust, "Little Prices Are Looking Good to Big Retailers," *Business Week,* 3 July 1989, 42, 44; Francine Schwadel, "Its Earnings Sagging, Sears Upgrades Line of Women's Apparel," *Wall Street Journal,* 9 May 1990, A1, A4; Kate Fitzgerald, "Sears' Plan on the Ropes," *Advertising Age,* 8 January 1990, 1, 42; William McLoughlin, "Sears' Legendary Move: Shut Down 824 Stores for 42 Hours, Reap $Billion in Free Advertising," *Upscale Discounting,* April 1989, 1, 7; Jube Shiver, Jr., "Shoppers Line Up to Check Out New Low-Pricing Policy at Sears," *Los Angeles Times,* 2 March 1989, sec. 4, 1, 5; Eric N. Berg, "Sears Cutting Prices by as Much as 50% in a Shift of Strategy," *New York Times,* 24 February 1989, sec. a, 1; Tony Lisanti, "Sears Awakes with Vengeance," *Discount Store News,* 20 March 1989, 1, 13, 14, 19; Martha T. Moore, "Slow Start for Pricing Strategy," *USA Today,* 7 September 1989, 1B–2B; Kevin Kerr, "Consumers Are Confused by Sears' New Policy," *Adweek's Marketing Week,* 12 June 1989, 30–31.

**2.** Saeed Samiee, "Pricing in Marketing Strategies of U.S.- and Foreign-Based Companies," *Journal of Business Research* 15 (1987): 17–30; Jon G. Udell, "How Important Is Pricing in Competitive Strategy?" *Journal of Marketing,* January 1964,

44–48; Thomas T. Nagle, *The Strategy and Tactics of Pricing* (Englewood Cliffs, N.J.: Prentice-Hall, 1987), xi.

**3.** John Templeman, "Mercedes Is Downsizing—And That Includes the Sticker," *Brandweek,* 8 February 1993, 38; Terry Lefton, "Amid Rate, Fee and Rebate Squabbles, Sears Finds It Costs to Discover," *Brandweek,* 9 November 1992, 34–35; Faye Rice, "What Intelligent Consumers Want," *Fortune,* 28 December 1992, 56–60; Kathleen Madigan, "The Latest Mad Plunge of the Price Slashers," *Business Week,* 11 May 1992, 36; Krystal Miller, "Jaguar Pulls In Its Car-Pricing Claws," *Wall Street Journal,* 14 October 1992, B1, B11; Michael McCarthy, "Chesebrough and Kimberly Follow P&G into EDLP," *Brandweek,* 5 October 1992, 4.

**4.** Kevin T. Higgins, ". . . By Any Other Name Would Smell as Sweet," *Marketing News,* 17 January 1986, 1, 12; Pat Sloan, "Knock-Offs Deliver Blows to Fragrance Market," *Advertising Age,* 2 March 1987, S-14; Amy Dunkin, "'Obsession' by Any Other Name Sells Sweetly," *Business Week,* 1 June 1987, 97.

**5.** Nitron catalog, Spring 1990, 19.

**6.** Nagle, *The Strategy and Tactics of Pricing,* 5.

**7.** Amy Harmon, "Sticker Shock: High New Car Costs Drive Consumers to Buy Used Vehicles," *Los Angeles Times,* 11 October 1992, D1, D8–D9.

**8.** Michael H. Morris and Mary L. Joyce, "How Marketers Evaluate Price Sensitivity," *Industrial Marketing Management* 17 (1988): 169–176.

**9.** Nagle, *The Strategy and Tactics of Pricing,* 58–70.

**10.** G. Ray Funkhouser, "Using Consumer Expectations as an Input to Pricing Decisions," *Journal of Product and Brand Management,* Spring 1992, 47–53; Michael H. Morris and Gene Morris, *Market Oriented Pricing* (Lincolnwood, Ill.: NTC Business Books, 1992), 58–59.

**11.** "Going, Going, Van Gone," *Time,* 23 November 1987, 57; "Van Gogh Portrait of His Doctor Goes for Record $82.5 Million," *Herald* (Everett, Wash.), 16 May 1990, A3.

**12.** Suzanne Loeffelholz, "The Love Line," *Financial World,* 21 March 1989, 26–28.

**13.** Valarie A. Zeithaml, "Consumer Perceptions of Price, Quality, and Value: A Means-End Model and Synthesis of Evidence," *Journal of Marketing,* July 1988, 2–22.

**14.** Greg Turner, "As Czechoslovakia Modernizes, Its Citizens Show Price Sensitivity," *Market: Europe,* January 1992, 11–16.

**15.** Brenton R. Schlender, "Apple Slashes Macintosh Plus Price 18% in Bid to Reposition Big-Selling Computer," *Wall Street Journal,* 16 March 1988, 5.

**16.** Nagle, *The Strategy and Tactics of Pricing,* 85–96.

**17.** Nagle, *The Strategy and Tactics of Pricing,* 88.

**18.** Nagle, *The Strategy and Tactics of Pricing,* 94.

**19.** Colleen Green, "Strategic Pricing," *Small Business Reports,* August 1989, 27–33.

**20.** Thomas T. Nagle, "Managing Price Competition," *Marketing Management* 2, no. 1, 36–45; Nagle, *The Strategy and Tactics of Pricing,* 100; James P. Woolsey, "Delta Is Ready for Life after Eastern," *Air Transport World,* June 1991, 41.

**21.** Betsy Morris, "Coke and Pepsi Step Up Bitter Price War," *Wall Street Journal,* 10 October 1988, B1; Paul B. Carroll, "Big Blues: Hurt by a Pricing War, IBM Plans Write-Off and Cut of 10,000 Jobs," *Wall Street Journal,* 6 December 1989, A1, A8; Udayan Gupta and Jeffrey A. Tannenbaum, "Casualties in the Fast-Food Price

Wars," *Wall Street Journal,* 23 October 1989, B1.

**22.** Elaine Underwood, "Price-War Payback—$10 Billion in Losses and an Antitrust Suit," *Brandweek,* 4 January 1993, 8.

**23.** Karen Slater, "Home Insurance Gets Cheaper for Many as Competition Heats Up," *Wall Street Journal,* 25 August 1988, 1.

**24.** Scott Kilman, "Market Maze: Why the Price of Milk Depends on Distance from Eau Claire, Wis.," *Wall Street Journal,* 20 May 1991, A1, A5.

**25.** Nagle, *The Strategy and Tactics of Pricing,* 5.

**26.** Andy Pasztor and Larry Reibstein, "Cola Sellers May Have Bottled Up Their Competition," *Wall Street Journal,* 9 December 1987, 6.

**27.** Christine Ammer and Dean S. Ammer, *Dictionary of Business and Economics* (New York: Free Press, 1977), 327.

**28.** Ray O. Werner, ed., "Legal Developments in Marketing: Collusive Practices, United States v. Brown University et al.," *Journal of Marketing,* April 1993, 108–109.

**29.** Underwood, "Price-War Payback—$10 Billion in Losses and an Antitrust Suit," 8.

**30.** Mary Jane Sheffet and Debra L. Scammon, "Resale Price Maintenance: Is It Safe to Suggest Retail Prices?" *Journal of Marketing,* Fall 1985, 82–91.

**31.** Robert A. Garda, "Use Tactical Pricing to Uncover Hidden Profits," *Journal of Business Strategy,* September–October 1991, 17–23; Norton E. Marks and Neely S. Inlow, "Price Discrimination and Its Impact on Small Business," *Journal of Consumer Marketing,* Winter 1988, 31–38.

**32.** James C. Johnson and Kenneth C. Schneider, "Those Who Can, Do—Those Who Can't . . . : Marketing Professors and the Robinson-Patman Act," *Journal of the Academy of Marketing Science,* Summer 1984, 123–138.

**33.** Nagle, *The Strategy and Tactics of Pricing,* 335–336.

**34.** Kent B. Monroe, *Pricing: Making Profitable Decisions,* 2d ed. (New York: McGraw-Hill, 1990), 406.

**35.** Stephen L. Montgomery, *Profitable Pricing Strategies* (New York: McGraw-Hill, 1988), 116.

**36.** Elyse Tanouye and Michael Waldholz, "Senate Study of Drug Prices Could Prove a Bitter Pill for Pharmaceutical Makers," *Wall Street Journal,* 3 February 1993, B1, B6.

**37.** "Lumber Prices Are Soaring on Shortages and Owl Feud," *New York Times,* 11 March 1993, C1, C5.

**38.** Norman V. Carroll, Chanaporn Siridhara, and Jack E. Fincham, "Factors Affecting Market Acceptance of Generic Drug Products: An Examination of Inherent Risk, Price, and Maximum Allowable Cost Coverage," *Akron Business and Economic Review,* Spring 1987, 11–18.

**39.** Fred Williams, "Overnight-Delivery Prices on Rise as Competition Eases," *USA Today,* 22 March 1990, 1B.

**40.** "Pinocchio Awards '89," *Adweek's Marketing Week,* 23 October 1989, 45–46.

**41.** Jonathan Dahl, "Car-Rental Firms Leave Drivers Dazed by Rip-Offs, Opinions, Misleading Ads," *Wall Street Journal,* 1 June 1990, B1, B6.

**42.** Thomas F. O'Boyle and Peter Pae, "The Long View: O'Neill Recasts Alcoa with His Eyes Fixed on a Decade Ahead," *Wall Street Journal,* 9 April 1990, A1, A4; "The Pricing Decision: Part 1—The Cornerstone of the Marketing Plan," *Small Business Report,* May 1985, 71–74, 76–77.

**43.** Barbara J. Coe, "Strategy in Retreat: Pricing Drops Out," *Journal of Business and Industrial Marketing,* Winter–Spring 1990, 5–8, 10, 12–18, 20–25.

**44.** Subrata N. Chakravarty, "Will Toys 'B' Great?" *Forbes,* 22 February 1988, 37–39.

**45.** Jeffrey A. Trachtenberg, "Cocktails at Tiffany," *Forbes,* 6 February 1989, 128–130.

**46.** Schlender, "Apple Slashes Macintosh Plus Price, " 5.

**47.** Kathleen Deveny, "Middle-Price Brands Come Under Siege," *Wall Street Journal,* 2 April 1990, B1, B6.

**48.** Ray Hellstern, "A Pricing Strategy for the U.S. Steel Producer," *Akron Business and Economic Review,* Spring 1987, 45–54.

**49.** See note 1.

## CHAPTER 12

**1.** Adapted from AMR Corporation Annual Report, 1989; Michael Derchin, "Analyzing American's Bold Gambit," *Travel Weekly,* 7 February 1985, 1, 4; Dennis J. H. Kraft, Tae H. Oum, and Michael W. Tretheway, "Airline Seat Management," *Logistics and Transportation Review,* June 1986, 115–130; Jane Levere, "The Pricing Game," *Travel Weekly,* 30 January 1985, 132–133; Bill Poling, "USAir's Malin Hits Airline Pricing System," *Travel Weekly,* 23 January 1986, 70; Jerry Brown, "USAir Official Assails Pricing Departments' Low-Fare Advocates," *Travel Weekly,* 11 April 1988, 17. Note: The yield management system described in this section is a general model based on Kraft et al., and doesn't necessarily reflect the specific practices of American Airlines.

**2.** Benson P. Shapiro, V. Kasturi Rangan, Rowland T. Moriarty, and Elliot B. Ross, "Manage Customers for Profits (Not Just Sales)," *Harvard Business Review,* September–October 1987, 101–108.

**3.** Richard Woodbury, "Prince of Midair," *Time,* 25 January 1993, 55; Suzanne Loeffelholz, "The Love Line," *Financial World,* 21 March 1989, 26–28; "Recriminations Fly Between America West and Southwest," *Aviation Daily,* 8 January 1991, 41.

**4.** Ford S. Worthy, "Japan's Smart Secret Weapon," *Fortune,* 12 August 1991, 72–75.

**5.** Thomas L. Powers, "Breakeven Analysis with Semifixed Costs," *Industrial Marketing Management* 16 (1987): 35–41.

**6.** Powers, "Breakeven Analysis with Semifixed Costs," 35–41.

**7.** "Walt Disney World Magic Kingdom," *Orlando Sentinel,* 7 January 1994; "One Virile Rodent," *Fortune,* 9 May 1988, 6–7.

**8.** Steve Lohr, "Lessons from a Hurricane: It Pays Not to Gouge," *New York Times,* 22 September 1992, C1.

**9.** Alyssa A. Lappen, "Defying the Law of Gravity," *Forbes,* 3 April 1989, 76–77; Jim Seymour, "Value Buying Is Here to Stay for PC Industry," *PC Week,* 17 June 1991, 69; Dan Malovany, "Art of Perception," *Bakery Production and Marketing,* 24 May 1991, 62–64; "Venture Stores Earns $3.7 Million in First Quarter," PR Newswire, 15 May 1991; Richard Martin, "Sizzler Mocks Fast Food with $3.99 Lunch Tactic," *Nation's Restaurant News,* 13 May 1991, 1; "Formats and Products: Charting New Directions," *Supermarket News,* 6 May 1991, 20–22; Carol Casper, "Mexican: Segment Chains Continue Their Eastward Drive," *Restaurant Business Magazine,* 10 April 1991, 147–154; Matthew Grimm, "The Biggest Battle at Burger King," *Adweek's Marketing Week,* 8 April 1991, 20–21; Bruce Horovitz, "Burger King's Chief Is Trying His Own Hand at Cooking Up Sales," *Los Angeles Times,* 16 April 1991, sec. d, 3; Chris Woodyard, "Taco Bell Adding Low-Fat Chicken Items with Ad

Campaign on the Side," *Los Angeles Times,* 11 April 1991, sec. d, 5; Chris Woodyard, "Briefcase: Retail/Leisure," *Los Angeles Times,* 7 February 1991, sec. d, 5; Kevin Maney, "Bargain Hunters' Addiction to Cost Cutting Feeds Slump," *USA Today,* 5 June 1991, sec. b, 1; Cathy Lynn Grossman and Bruce Schwartz, "Leisure Travel," *USA Today,* 24 January 1991, sec. d, 5; "Retailers See Few Signs of an Upturn," *San Jose Mercury News,* 30 May 1991, sec. f, 3; Andrew Leckey, "On Personal Finance—Improving Sales Appear on Fast-Food Menus," *Chicago Tribune,* 31 March 1991, sec. c, 4; Marianne Taylor, "McDonald's Heads into 'Difficult' Year on '90 Sales, Profit Gains," *Chicago Tribune,* 29 January 1991, sec. c, 1; David Mehegan, "Late Shopping Rescues Retailers from Disaster: Price Cutting Did the Trick," *Boston Globe,* 4 January 1991, 61.

**10.** Julie Cohen Mason, "Value: The New Marketing Mania?" *Management Review,* May 1992, 16–21.

**11.** Julie Amparano Lopez, "Cellular Phones Call for Careful Shopping," *Wall Street Journal,* 14 May 1990, B1.

**12.** Tristam H. Englehardt and Michael A. Rie, "Morality for the Medical-Industrial Complex," *New England Journal of Medicine,* 20 October 1988, 1086–1089.

**13.** G. Pascal Zachary, "Microsoft Sells Database Easily, Glitches and All," *Wall Street Journal,* 15 January 1993, B1.

**14.** Eric Mitchell, "AT&T Shows Schizophrenic Tendencies in Pro WATS Ads," *Marketing News,* 24 April 1989, 9, 11; Norman V. Carroll, Chanaporth Siridhara, and Jack E. Fincham, "Factors Affecting Market Acceptance of Generic Drug Products: An Examination of Inherent Risk, Price, and Maximum Allowable Cost Coverage," *Akron Business and Economic Review,* Spring 1987, 11–18.

**15.** Lois Therrien, "Pet Food Moves Upscale—and Profits Fatten," *Business Week,* 15 June 1987, 80, 82.

**16.** Jeffrey H. Birnbaum, "Pricing of Products Is Still an Art, Often Having Little Link to Costs," *Wall Street Journal,* 25 November 1981, 29, 49; Valarie A. Zeithaml, "Consumer Perceptions of Price, Quality, and Value: A Means-End Model and Synthesis of Evidence," *Journal of Marketing,* July 1988, 2–22.

**17.** Thomas T. Nagle, *The Strategy and Tactics of Pricing* (Englewood Cliffs, N.J.: Prentice-Hall, 1987), 249.

**18.** Christina Duff, "Single-Price Stores' Formula for Success: Cheap Merchandise and a Lot of Clutter," *Wall Street Journal,* 30 June 1992, B1, B9.

**19.** "The Customer Is Always Right," *Time,* 7 March 1988, 57.

**20.** Subrata N. Chakravarty, "Will Toys 'B' Great?" *Forbes,* 22 February 1988, 37–39.

**21.** Kevin Gudridge, "Balance Tips Away from Upscale," *Advertising Age,* 2 November 1987, 46.

**22.** George S. Day and Adrian B. Ryans, "Using Price Discounts for a Competitive Advantage," *Industrial Marketing Management* 17 (1988): 1–14; "Panelists Offer Pricing Strategy Advice for Consumer and Industrial Products," *Marketing News,* 1 February 1985, 1, 10.

**23.** James B. Wilcox, Roy D. Howell, Paul Kuzdrall, and Robert Britney, "Price Quantity Discounts: Some Implications for Buyers and Sellers," *Journal of Marketing,* July 1987, 60–70.

**24.** Susan Voyles, "Clever Buyers Leave Firms Holding Bag," *USA Today,* 17 June 1987, 1B.

**25.** Paul B. Carroll, "IBM Establishes a Trade-In Plan for Used PCs," *Wall Street Journal,* 21 June 1988, 44.

**26.** David Kiley, "Automakers and Car Values

Suffer from a Rash of Rebates," *Adweek's Marketing Week,* 15 January 1990, 2; Joann S. Lublin, "Jaguar, Its Sales in U.S. Sagging, Initiates Rebates," *Wall Street Journal,* 14 June 1989, B6; "Many Consumers View Rebates as a Bother," *Wall Street Journal,* 13 April 1989, B1.

**27.** Patricia Sellers, "The Dumbest Marketing Ploy," *Fortune,* 5 October 1992, 88–94.

**28.** Matthew Schifrin, "Arbitraging Dog Food," *Forbes,* 10 May 1993, 78–82; Zachary Schiller, "Not Everyone Loves a Supermarket Special," *Business Week,* 17 February 1992, 64–68.

**29.** Seema Nayyar, "Stores Concede on EDLP with a Slashing Passion," *Brandweek,* 2 November 1992, 1, 6.

**30.** Zachary Schiller, "Procter & Gamble Hits Back," *Business Week,* 19 July 1993, 20–22.

**31.** Richard Gibson, "Broad Grocery Price Cuts May Not Pay," *Wall Street Journal,* 7 May 1993, B1, B4.

**32.** Jon Berry, "So How Is P&G's Share? Lagging, New Study Says," *Brandweek,* 19 April 1993, 16.

**33.** American Machine & Tool Company catalog, Winter 1990.

**34.** Christine Ammer and Dean S. Ammer, *Dictionary of Business and Economics* (New York: Free Press, 1977), 37, 113, 170.

**35.** Gary Karrass, "12 Vital Steps to Raising Prices," *Industrial Distribution,* May 1983, 75.

**36.** Robert A. Garda, "Industrial Pricing: Strategy vs. Tactics," *McKinsey Quarterly,* Winter 1984, 49–63.

**37.** Jack G. Kaikati, "Marketing Without Exchange of Money," *Harvard Business Review,* November–December 1982, 73–74.

**38.** Joseph Kamen, "Price Filtering: Restricting Price Deals to Those Least Likely to Buy Without Them," *Journal of Product and Brand Management,* Summer 1992, 45–51.

**39.** "AMA Cites 'Filtered Pricing' Move Toward Individualization," *Marketing News,* 1 February 1988, 8, 30; Joseph Kamen, "Price Filtering: Restricting Price Deals to Those Least Likely to Buy Without Them," *Journal of Consumer Marketing,* Summer 1989, 37–40, 42.

**40.** Kathleen Deveny, Corie Brown, William J. Hampton, and James B. Treece, "Going for the Lion's Share," *Business Week,* 18 July 1988, 70–72.

**41.** Adapted from Philip Kotler and Alan R. Andreasen, *Strategic Marketing for Nonprofit Organizations* (Englewood Cliffs, N.J.: Prentice-Hall, 1987), 457–462.

**42.** Alex Pham, "Cataloguing Who'll Pay What," *Washington Post,* 3 September 1992, B11, B13.

**43.** See note 1.

## CHAPTER 13

**1.** Adapted from Joseph Weber, "Black & Decker Cuts a Neat Dovetail Joint," *Business Week,* 31 July 1989, 52–53; Janet Meyers, "Black & Decker Ups Share in Hardware," *Advertising Age,* 24 July 1989, 28; Rebecca Fannin and Laura Konrad Jereski, "Black & Decker Powers into Housewares," *Marketing & Media Decisions,* August 1985, 34–40, 109; Bill Kelley, "Black & Decker Rebuilds," *Sales & Marketing Management,* June 1987, 49; Christopher S. Eklund, "How Black & Decker Got Back in the Black," *Business Week,* 13 July 1987, 86, 90; James A. Constantin and Robert F. Lusch, "Discover the Resources in Your Marketing Channel," *Business,* July–September 1986, 19–26; Paula Schnorbus, "B&D Turns On the Power," *Marketing & Media Decisions,* May 1988, 57–58, 62, 64; John Huey, "The New Power in Black & Decker," *Fortune,* 2 January 1989, 89–91, 94; "Winning Turnaround Strategies at Black & Decker," *Jour-*

*nal of Business Strategy,* March–April 1988, 30–33; "Black & Decker to Send Sales Specialists into Industrial and Construction Markets," *Industrial Distribution,* April 1987, 4.

**2.** Louis Rukeyser, John Cooney, and George Winslow, *Louis Rukeyser's Business Almanac* (New York: Simon & Schuster, 1988), 650.

**3.** Definitions of marketing intermediaries adapted from Christine Ammer and Dean S. Ammer, *Dictionary of Business and Economics* (New York: Free Press, 1977), 12, 51, 109, 123, 265, 364, 451.

**4.** Louis W. Stern and Adel I. El-Ansary, *Marketing Channels* (Englewood Cliffs, N.J.: Prentice-Hall, 1988), 7–8.

**5.** *Showcase of Savings* catalog, Early Spring 1990, distributed by L'eggs Brands, Inc., Rural Hall, N.C.

**6.** Caroline E. Mayer, "To Coin a Cuisine," *Washington Post,* 11 November 1992, E1.

**7.** Faridah Hamid, "Direct Sellers Vie for Thai Make-up Market," *Asian Advertising & Marketing,* June 1992, 14–15, 37.

**8.** Karen Blumenthal, "A Few Big Retailers Rebuff Middleman," *Wall Street Journal,* 21 October 1986, 6.

**9.** Information on organizational channels is adapted from Frank G. Bingham, Jr., and Barney T. Raffield III, *Business to Business Marketing Management* (Homewood, Ill.: Irwin, 1990), 334–346.

**10.** James H. Donnelly, Jr., "Marketing Intermediaries in Channels of Distribution for Services," *Journal of Marketing,* January 1976, 55–70.

**11.** Bill Saporito, "Are IBM and Sears Crazy? Or Canny?" *Fortune,* 28 September 1987, 76–80.

**12.** Bob Stone, *Successful Direct Marketing Methods,* 3d ed. (Lincolnwood, Ill.: NTC, 1987), 1.

**13.** Louis W. Stern and Adel El-Ansary, *Management in Marketing Channels* (Englewood Cliffs, N.J.: Prentice-Hall, 1989), 243.

**14.** Andrew J. Sherman, "Building a Sales Network," *Small Business Reports,* October 1991, 57–61.

**15.** Steven Kichen, "Pick a Channel," *Forbes,* 2 March 1992, 108.

**16.** Rowland T. Moriarty and Ursula Moran, *Harvard Business Review,* November–December 1990, 146–155; David Perry, "How You'll Manage Your 1990s 'Distribution Portfolio,'" *Business Marketing,* June 1989, 52, 54, 56.

**17.** Philip R. Cateora, *International Marketing,* 7th ed. (Homewood, Ill.: Irwin, 1990), 587.

**18.** Raymond Roel, "Doubleday Redux," *Direct Marketing,* October 1987, 34–36, 40–42, 44, 46.

**19.** Bert Rosenbloom, *Marketing Channels* (Chicago: Dryden, 1987), 431.

**20.** Robert Hartlein, "Specialty Stores Play Both Ways," *Women's Wear Daily,* 4 November 1987, 9, 13.

**21.** Jeanne Sather, "Egghead Options Point to Retreat from Retail," *Puget Sound Business Journal,* 14, no. 16 (3 September 1993): 1; Hank Gilman, "Learning a New Pitch: Software Retailers Adopt Mainstream Marketing Techniques," *Wall Street Journal,* 30 September 1987, 39.

**22.** "Brushing Up at Fuller," *Newsweek,* 7 September 1987, 44.

**23.** Milind Lele, "Matching Your Channels to Your Product's Life Cycle," *Business Marketing,* December 1986, 61, 64–66, 68–69.

**24.** Frank H. Alpert, Michael A. Kamins, and John L. Graham, "An Examination of Reseller Buyer Attitudes toward Order of Brand Entry," *Journal of Marketing,* July 1992, 25–37.

**25.** Allan J. Magrath, "The Gatekeepers," *Across the Board,* April 1992, 43–46.

**26.** Athletic Supply catalog, 1990, 19.

**27.** Michelle Bekey, "Catching the Wave," *Venture,* April 1988, 29–32.

**28.** Kenneth G. Hardy and Allan J. Magrath, "Ten Ways for Manufacturers to Improve Distribution Management," *Business Horizons,* November–December 1988, 65–69.

**29.** Hardy and Magrath, "Ten Ways for Manufacturers to Improve Distribution Management," 65–69.

**30.** Stern and El-Ansary, *Management in Marketing Channels,* 243.

**31.** Stern and El-Ansary, *Management in Marketing Channels,* 272.

**32.** Polly Lane, "Wal-Mart to Buy Pace Stores," *Seattle Times,* 2 November 1993, D1; Polly Lane, "Kmart May Sell PayLess Units to Thrifty," *Seattle Times,* 1 November 1993, E1; Greg Heberlein, "Price/Costco Trading Begins with Merger Complete, Some Jobs Will Disappear," *Seattle Times,* 22 October 1993, E1.

**33.** Ron Zemke and Dick Schaaf, *The Service Edge* (New York: New American Library, 1989), 364–366.

**34.** Stern and El-Ansary, *Management in Marketing Channels,* 279.

**35.** Stern and El-Ansary, *Management in Marketing Channels,* 279–280.

**36.** Janice Castro, "Franchising Fever," *Time,* 31 August 1987, 36–38; Stern and El-Ansary, *Management in Marketing Channels,* 282–293; Meg Whittemore, "Portrait of a Franchisee," *Inc.,* April 1988, 125–126.

**37.** James A. Narus and James C. Anderson, "Turn Your Industrial Distributors into Partners," *Harvard Business Review,* March–April 1986, 66–71.

**38.** Deirdre Fanning, "Monkey Wrench at Snap-On Tools," *Forbes,* 27 June 1988, 126, 128.

**39.** Matthew Grimm, "Taco Bell Franchisees Want It Hot 'n Later," *Brandweek,* 7 September 1992, 3; Matthew Grimm, "Franchisees Fret over 'Conflict,'" *Brandweek,* 24 August 1992, 1, 6.

**40.** Howard Schlossberg, "Manufacturers Fighting Back with Alternative Retail Outlets," *Marketing News,* 2 August 1992, 9, 11.

**41.** Barbara Marsh, "Franchise Realities: Sandwich-Shop Chain Surges, but to Run One Can Take Heroic Effort," *Wall Street Journal,* 16 September 1992, A1, A10.

**42.** Patricia Sellers, "The Publican at Burger King," *Business Week,* 13 March 1989, 68.

**43.** Allan J. Magrath and Kenneth G. Hardy, "Avoiding the Pitfalls in Managing Distribution Channels," *Business Horizons,* September–October 1987, 29–33; Robert E. Weigand, "Fit Products and Channels to Your Markets," *Harvard Business Review,* January–February 1977, 95–105.

**44.** Mary Connelly, "Auto Dealers Flex Their Muscles," *Advertising Age,* 22 March 1993, S-6; Julie Liesse, "ConAgra 'Chickens Out,'" *Advertising Age,* 7 December 1992, 1, 50.

**45.** Seema Nayyar, "Wal-Mart Move Confirms Shift in Retailer-Marketer Ties," *Brandweek,* 15 February 1993, 8.

**46.** Zachary Schiller, Wendy Zellner, Ron Stodgill II, and Mark Maremount, "Clout! More and More Retail Giants Rule the Marketplace," *Business Week,* 21 December 1992, 66–73.

**47.** Stern and El-Ansary, *Management in Marketing Channels,* 328–334.

**48.** See note 1.

## CHAPTER 14

**1.** Adapted from Steve Weinstein, "SuperValu: Tomorrow the World," *Progressive Grocer,* October 1992, 58–62; Ron Zemke, *The Service Edge* (New York: New American Library, 1989), 338–341; Suzanne Loeffelholz, "Don't Squeeze the Margins," *Financial World,* 15 November 1988, 22–23; Bill Saporito, "SuperValu Does Two Things Well," *Fortune,* 18 April 1983, 114, 116–117; Steve Weinstein, "It's All in the Execution," *Progressive Grocer,* April 1989, 89–96; Jan Parr, "Leader of the Pack," *Forbes,* 8 February 1988, 35–36; Richard Turcsik, "'Old' SuperValu Made into Service Prototype," *Supermarket News,* 22 May 1989, 6, 54.

**2.** Joseph Weber, "It's 'Like Somebody Shot the Postman,'" *Business Week,* 13 January 1992, 82; Louis Rukeyser, John Cooney, and George Winslow, *Louis Rukeyser's Business Almanac* (New York: Simon & Schuster, 1988), 649; Steven P. Galante, "Distributors Switch Strategies to Survive Coming Shakeout," *Wall Street Journal,* 20 July 1987, 21; Bureau of the Census, *Statistical Abstract of the United States* 1989 (Washington, D.C.: GPO, 1989), 779.

**3.** Louis W. Stern and Adel I. El-Ansary, *Management in Marketing Channels* (Englewood Cliffs, N.J.: Prentice-Hall, 1989), 97.

**4.** Stern and El-Ansary, *Management in Marketing Channels,* 109–112.

**5.** Joseph Weber, "Mom and Pop Move Out of Wholesaling," *Business Week,* 9 January 1989, 91; Galante, "Distributors Switch Strategies," 21.

**6.** Stern and El-Ansary, *Management in Marketing Channels,* 104–105.

**7.** Stern and El-Ansary, *Management in Marketing Channels,* 107.

**8.** Robert G. Clifton, "General Line vs. Specialists: Is the Tide Turning?" *Industrial Distribution,* September 1989, 102.

**9.** Stern and El-Ansary, *Management in Marketing Channels,* 116–118.

**10.** Definitions adapted from Christine Ammer and Dean S. Ammer, *Dictionary of Business and Economics* (New York: Free Press, 1977), 451; statistics on wholesaling cooperatives from Laurie A. Shuster, "Wholesaling Today: An Update," *Hardware Age,* October 1988, 55–56, 58, 60, 65.

**11.** Stern and El-Ansary, *Management in Marketing Channels,* 101.

**12.** Ammer and Ammer, *Dictionary of Business and Economics,* 451.

**13.** Stern and El-Ansary, *Management in Marketing Channels,* 102.

**14.** Frank G. Bingham, Jr., and Barney T. Raffield III, *Business to Business Marketing Management* (Homewood, Ill.: Irwin, 1990), 344–345.

**15.** Lois C. DuBois and Roger H. Grace, "The Care and Feeding of Manufacturers' Reps," *Business Marketing,* December 1987, 52, 54, 56–59, 62–64; Harold J. Novick, "Reps Beat the Slow-Growth Catch-22," *Business Marketing,* December 1989, 52, 65–66, 68–69.

**16.** "Ringer Announces Third Quarter Results," PR Newswire, 28 July 1993.

**17.** DuBois and Grace, "The Care and Feeding of Manufacturers' Reps," 52, 54, 56–58.

**18.** Bingham and Raffield, *Business to Business Marketing Management,* 344.

**19.** Ammer and Ammer, *Dictionary of Business and Economics,* 265.

**20.** Ammer and Ammer, *Dictionary of Business and Economics,* 25.

**21.** U.S. Department of Commerce, *A Basic Guide to Exporting* (Lincolnwood, Ill.: NTC, 1989), 17.

**22.** Louis W. Stern and Adel I. El-Ansary, *Marketing Channels* (Englewood Cliffs, N.J.: Prentice-Hall, 1988), 530, 538–539.

**23.** John K. Keitt, Jr., "Pitfalls and Promises of Foreign Distributors," *Management Review,* May 1990, 16–19.

**24.** Lynn Asinof, "Trade Shows Keep Growing, Spawning a Slew of New Convention Centers," *Wall Street Journal,* 21 August 1986, 1.

**25.** National Association of Broadcasters, *NAB '90 Exhibit Directory & Buyers' Guide,* 2, 48, 84–87.

**26.** Kathleen Humphrey, "Challenging Times for European Software Market," *WSA Report,* Summer 1993, 7.

**27.** Chicago Mart Center, *The Mart Center Fact Sheet.*

**28.** Stern and El-Ansary, *Management in Marketing Channels,* 109–112.

**29.** Personal communication with Wynstar International, August 1993.

**30.** Stern and El-Ansary, *Management in Marketing Channels,* 122.

**31.** U.S. Bureau of the Census, *Census of Wholesale Trade 1987* (Washington, D.C.: GPO, 1989), US-9.

**32.** Shuster, "Wholesaling Today," 55–56, 58, 60, 65.

**33.** Weber, "Mom and Pop Move Out of Wholesaling," 91.

**34.** Weber, "Mom and Pop Move Out of Wholesaling," 91.

**35.** Richard J. Sherman, "Look Ahead to Integrated Channels," *Transportation & Distribution,* March 1989, 46.

**36.** Elaine Underwood, "A High-Tech Marketer in Disguise," *Brandweek,* 8 February 1993, 14–17.

**37.** Gail Bronson, "Billion-Dollar Brainstorm," *Forbes,* 19 October 1987, 98.

**38.** Steve Weinstein, "A Diverse Holiday Mix," *Progressive Grocer,* May 1989, 107–108, 110.

**39.** "Changing Markets Demand 'Value-Added Services,'" *Traffic Management,* August 1989, 79, 81, 83, 85.

**40.** "Servicing New Retail Formats," *Supermarket News,* 13 March 1989, 23.

**41.** Marvin Greene, "Why Distributors Don't Strike It Rich with ASICs," *Electronic Business,* 16 April 1990, 85–86.

**42.** See note 1.

## CHAPTER 15

**1.** Adapted from "Nordstrom Opens New Concept Polo Shop," PR Newswire, 20 August 1993; "Nordstrom to Host 'Sneak Peek' of New Factory Direct Store," PR Newswire, 15 June 1993; "Nordstrom Teams with Facconnable to Open New York Store," PR Newswire, 15 June 1993; "Nordstrom to Launch New Visa Card," PR Newswire, 21 July 1993; Debra Prinzing, "One of a Kind: In a Volatile Decade, Nordstrom Reached a New Plateau," *Puget Sound Business Journal,* 23 April 1990, 24–25, 37, 41; Joan Bergmann, "Nordstrom Gets the Gold," *Stores,* January 1990, 44, 56, 67; Joan Bergmann, "How Nordstrom Got There," *Stores,* January 1990, 68, 70; "The Top 100 Department Stores: Mercantile Has Top Profit Ratio," *Stores,* July 1990, 21–23; David P. Schulz, "The Top 100 Department Stores: J. C. Penney Takes Top Spot," *Stores,* July 1990, 9–11; Pauline Yoshihashi, "Nordstrom Moves East with Its Retailing Style," *New York Times,* 27 May 1986, sec. d, 1, 5; Francine Schwadel, "Courting Shoppers: Nordstrom's Push East Will Test Its Renown for the Best in Service," *Wall Street Journal,* 1 August 1989, A1, A4; Kathryn M. Welling, "The Shopping Wars: A Front-Line Observer Sorts Out the Winners from the Losers," *Barron's,* 25 December 1989, 7, 18–20.

**2.** U.S. Department of Commerce, *Census of Retail Trade* (Washington, D.C.: GPO, 1990), 1–3.

**3.** Gretchen Morgenson, "The Fall of the Mall," *Forbes,* 25 May 1993, 106–112.

**4.** Norman M. Miller, "Rural Retailing: The Last Frontier," *Chain Store Age Executive,* March 1986, 18–19, 22.

**5.** *Statistical Abstract of the United States: 1993* (Washington, D.C.: GPO, 1993), 409–410.

**6.** Leon Harris, *Merchant Princes* (New York: Harper & Row, 1977), 92–93.

**7.** David Moin, "May Co. to Consolidate Sibley's into Kaufmann's," *Women's Wear Daily,* 8 January 1990, 2.

**8.** Harris, *Merchant Princes,* 71.

**9.** William R. Davidson, Albert D. Bates, and Stephen J. Bass, "The Retail Life Cycle," *Harvard Business Review,* November–December 1976, 89–96.

**10.** J. Barry Mason, Morris L. Mayer, and Hazel F. Ezell, *Retailing* (Plano, Tex.: Business Publications, 1988), 30.

**11.** Thomas J. Maronick and Bruce J. Walker, "The Dialectic Evolution of Retailing," *Proceedings, Southern Marketing Association,* edited by Burnett Greenburg (Atlanta: Georgia State University, 1974), 147.

**12.** Malcolm P. McNair and Eleanor G. May, "The Next Revolution of the Retailing Wheel," *Harvard Business Review,* September–October 1978, 81–91.

**13.** Roger D. Blackwell and W. Wayne Talarzyk, "Lifestyle Retailing: Competitive Strategies of the 1980s," *Journal of Retailing* 59 (Winter 1983): 7–28.

**14.** Aimee Stern, "Disposable Stores Yield Big Sales with Low Costs," *Adweek's Marketing Week,* 27 October 1986, 20.

**15.** Kevin Maney, "Customers Flood USA IKEA Outlets," *USA Today,* 4 November 1986, 1B.

**16.** Christopher W. Hoyt, "Category Management Is Inevitable, So See Where You Stand," *Brandweek,* 11 January 1993, 19.

**17.** Osamu Katayama, "A Consumer's Piece of Pie," *Look Japan,* January 1993, 18–19.

**18.** Teri Agins, "A Tale of Two Retailers: Bergdorf Rose, Bonwit Fell," *Wall Street Journal,* 26 June 1989, B1.

**19.** "Lillian Vernon Corporation Reports Record Revenues and Earnings," press release dated 3 May 1990; Steven Solomon, *Small Business USA* (New York: Crown Publishers, 1986), 196–197.

**20.** Bill Kelley, "The New Wave from Europe," *Sales & Marketing Management,* November 1987, 46.

**21.** Michael J. McCarthy, "Home Depot's Do-It-Yourself Powerhouse," *Wall Street Journal,* 17 July 1990, B1, B8; Jennet Conant, Janet Huck, and Maggie Malone, "Beautiful Ways to Shop," *Newsweek,* 10 November 1986, 88–90.

**22.** "1989: A Solid, Yet Unspectacular Year," *Progressive Grocer,* Mid-April 1990, 6–9.

**23.** "Fast Food, Fast Credit," *Advertising Age,* 12 March 1990, 12.

**24.** Pierre Martineau, "The Personality of the Retail Store," *Harvard Business Review,* January–February 1958, 47–55.

**25.** Stephanie Strom, "Image and Attitude Are Department Stores' Draw," *New York Times,* 12 August 1993, B1.

**26.** Cyndee Miller, "Scent as a Marketing Tool," *Marketing News,* 18 January 1993, 1, 2.

**27.** "Why Rivals Are Quaking as Nordstrom Heads East," *Business Week,* 15 June 1987, 99–100.

**28.** Leonard L. Berry, "Retail Positioning Strategies for the 1980s," *Business Horizons,* November–December 1982, 45–50.

**29.** Carie Goerne, "Now Book Browsers Can Munch Brownies as They Shop for Browning," *Marketing News,* 6 July 1992, 1, 9.

**30.** Polly Lane, "Wal-Mart to Buy Pace Stores," *Seattle Times,* 2 November 1993, D1; Greg Heberlein, "Price/Costco Trading Begins with Merger Complete; Some Jobs Will Disappear," *Seattle Times,* 22 October 1993, E1; Jack Kaikati, "Don't Discount Off-Price Retailers," *Harvard Business Review,* May–June 1985, 85–92.

**31.** U.S. Bureau of the Census, *Statistical Abstract of the United States 1993,* 113th ed. (Washington, D.C.: GPO, 1993), 777.

**32.** Subrata N. Chakravarty, "Give 'Em Variety," *Forbes,* 2 May 1988, 54–57.

**33.** Alan L. Gilman, "Competitive Growth with Franchising," *Chain Store Age Executive,* January 1990, 160.

**34.** Jeffrey A. Trachtenberg, "You Can't Market Variety," *Forbes,* 27 July 1987, 82–83.

**35.** Carol Cirulli, "U.S. Retailers Develop Aggressive Expansion Plans," *Journal of European Business,* January–February 1993, 55–59.

**36.** Julie Liesse, "Welcome to the Club," *Advertising Age,* 1 February 1993, S3, S6; *Value Line Investment Survey,* 30 November 1990, 1650; Howard C. Gelbtuck, "The Warehouse Club Industry," *Appraisal Journal,* 58 (April 1990): 153–159.

**37.** Office Depot catalog, Fall 1993.

**38.** Bill Keith, "Walgreen, Riding High, Plans 100 New Stores a Year," *Drug Topics,* 6 July 1987, 50, 52.

**39.** Gerald Egyes, "Retailing: A Larger Piece of the Pie," *Marketing Communications,* October 1986, 61.

**40.** Bob Hughes, "Mrs. Gooch's Makes a Fashion Statement with Its Beverly Hills Shop," *Supermarket Business,* May 1988, 70.

**41.** Richard Hoffman, "Doctor Dollar Hears the Call," *Venture,* February 1989, 18–19.

**42.** Gerry Khermouch, "Sports Authority: Category Killing Hits Sporting Goods," *Brandweek,* 8 March 1993, 22.

**43.** Goerne, "Now Book Browsers Can Munch Brownies as They Shop for Browning," 1, 9.

**44.** John P. Cortez, "Kmart Unleashes Its 'Category Killer' Chains," *Advertising Age,* 1 February 1993, S4–S5; Joseph Pereira, "Discount Department Stores Struggle Against Rivals That Strike Aisle by Aisle," *Wall Street Journal,* 19 June 1990, B1, B7; Howard Schlossberg, "Firm That Ignited Superstore Rage Makes Plans to Stay Ahead of Pack," *Marketing News,* 22 January 1990, 2.

**45.** Mark Henricks, "Lobster in the Rough," *Venture,* January 1988, 17–18.

**46.** "Why Rivals Are Quaking," 99.

**47.** Michael Dotson and W. E. Patton III, "Consumer Perceptions of Department Store Service: A Lesson for Retailers," *Journal of Services Marketing,* Spring 1992, 15–28.

**48.** Mason, Mayer, and Ezell, *Retailing,* 359.

**49.** Teri Agins, "Upscale Retailers Head to Enemy Turf," *Wall Street Journal,* 25 August 1989, B1.

**50.** Mary Pembleton, "Specialty Stores Spruce Up Bottom Line," *USA Today,* 26 February 1988, 1B.

**51.** Bill Saporito, "Woolworth to Rule the Malls," *Fortune,* 5 June 1989, 145, 148, 152, 156.

**52.** "Centennial Journal: 100 Years in Business," *Wall Street Journal,* 27 April 1989, B1.

**53.** Mary McCabe English, "Special Report: Grocery Marketing: Chains Cultivating Superstores," *Advertising Age,* 18 April 1985, 17; Michael Garry, "Problem Solving," *Progressive Grocer,* April 1991, 26.

**54.** Anthony Ramirez, "Will American Shoppers Think Bigger Is Really Better?" *New York Times,* 1 April 1990, sec. f, 11.

**55.** Edward Cundiff and Marye Tharp Hilger, *Marketing in the International Environment* (Englewood Cliffs, N.J.: Prentice-Hall, 1988), 449.

**56.** Elisabeth Malkin, "Warehouse Stores Move into Mexico," *Advertising Age,* 18 January 1993, I-3, I-30; Cundiff and Hilger, *Marketing in the International Environment,* 449.

**57.** Ellen Neuborne, "Anchors Away at Gap Specialty Mall," *USA Today,* 28 February 1992, 1B.

**58.** Jennifer Stoffel, "What's New in Shopping Malls: Of Thrills, Spills, Beaches and Department Stores," *New York Times,* 7 August 1988, sec. 3, 11; Alexandra Peers, "Retailing: Art Mall Tries to Be More Than a Still Life," *Wall Street Journal,* 28 March 1990, B1; Michael J. McDermott, "Too Many Malls Are Chasing a Shrinking Supply of Shoppers," *Adweek's Marketing Week,* 5 February 1990, 2–3.

**59.** Eugene Carlson, "New Retailers Face Struggle Getting in Malls," *Wall Street Journal,* 24 July 1990, B1–B2.

**60.** Barbara Solomon, "Power Centers: The New Face of Retailing," *Management Review,* April 1993, 50–53.

**61.** A. Donald Anderson, "King Solomon," *Venture,* April 1987, 72–74, 76.

**62.** Kate Fitzgerald, "Catalog Threat Fuels Database Effort at Stores," *Advertising Age,* 25 January 1993, 28.

**63.** Kate Ballen, "Selling: Get Ready for Shopping at Work," *Fortune,* 15 February 1988, 95, 98.

**64.** Joseph F. McKenna, "From JIT, With Love," *Industry Week,* 17 August 1992, 45–50.

**65.** James Sterngold, "Why Japanese Adore Vending Machines," *New York Times,* 2 January 1992, 1, 12; John Burgess, "Machines in Japan Sell Liquor, Bibles, Fortunes," *Washington Post,* 14 November 1985, sec. a, 33, 38.

**66.** Wayne Curtis, "What's New in Mail Order: For Those Willing to Pay, Catalogues of Catalogues," *New York Times,* 14 May 1989, sec. 3, 15.

**67.** Howard Schlossberg, "Picture Still Looks Bright for TV Shopping Networks," *Marketing News,* 23 October 1989, 8.

**68.** J. Douglas Eldridge, "Non-store Retailing: Planning for a Big Future," *Chain Store Age Executive with Shopping Center Age,* August 1993, 34A–35A.

**69.** Andrew Feinberg, "Picking Up the Pieces in Home Shopping," *New York Times,* 25 September 1988, sec. 3, 4; John M. Higgins, "QVC Has Upbeat End to a Rocky Fiscal Year," *Multichannel News,* 18 March 1991, 48.

**70.** Teri Agins, "Clothing, TV Shopping May Be Tough Fit," *Wall Street Journal,* 31 March 1993, B1, B6.

**71.** Laura Zinn, "Retailing Will Never Be the Same," *Business Week,* 26 July 1993, 54–60.

**72.** "Guerrilla War: Prodigy, Others Fight to Control Videotex Market," *Gannett Westchester Newspapers,* 21 January 1990, H1–H2.

**73.** Morgenson, "The Fall of the Mall," 106–112.

**74.** Morgenson, "The Fall of the Mall," 106–112.

**75.** See note 1.

## CHAPTER 16

**1.** Adapted from Agatha Moir, "To Market, to Market," *Manitoba Business,* February 1985, 43–44; personal communication, Hughes Otnott, director of operations of the Walker-Roemer Dairies, Inc., Metairie, Louisiana, 1990.

**2.** Karen E. Thuermer, "Time to Wake Up," *Global Trade,* November 1992, 13–14.

**3.** R. Deierlein, "Seminar Offers Distribution Solutions to Help Get Competitive Edge," *Beverage World Periscope Edition,* 31 July 1989, 8.

**4.** Francine Schwadel, "Catalog Firms Hope Fast Delivery Mean Holiday Bonus," *Wall Street Journal,* 17 November 1989, B1; "Lands' End Direct Merchants," *Business Journal–Milwaukee,* 20 May 1991, 12.

**5.** Jay Gordon, "Zooming to Market: Logistics as a Marketing Weapon," *Distribution,* March 1990, 38–44.

**6.** Herbert W. Davis, "Physical Distribution Costs: Performance in Selected Industries, 1987," in *Proceedings of the Council of Logistics Management (1987),* 371–379.

**7.** IKEA catalog, Canadian edition, 1988.

**8.** Ronald Alsop, "Exclusive Beginnings Put Perfume in Demand," *Wall Street Journal,* 30 November 1988, B1.

**9.** "Quest for Quality Distribution," *Distribution,* August 1989, 50.

**10.** Jube Silver, Jr., "Critical Flow: Managing Inventories, Timely Deliveries Are Key to Keeping Customers, California Markets Satisfied", *Los Angeles Times,* 9 October 1989, sec. 4, 1.

**11.** "Haggar to Demand Suppliers Go On-Line," *Women's Wear Daily,* 17 May 1989, 18.

**12.** Kate Bertrand, "The Just-in-Time Mandate," *Business Marketing,* November 1986, 44–45, 48, 50, 52–53, 55.

**13.** Robert E. Sabath, "How Much Service Do Customers Really Want?" *Business Horizons,* April 1978, 26–32; William H. Davidow and Bro Uttal, *Total Customer Service: The Ultimate Weapon* (New York: Harper & Row, 1989), 199.

**14.** "Physical Distribution: Delivering the Goods," *Industrial Distribution,* August 1984, 33–36.

**15.** "Wal-Mart Computers Talk to Vendors," *Chain Store Age,* January 1985, 20.

**16.** Trend-Lines catalog, Winter 1989–1990.

**17.** "Compressing Distribution into a Network," *Modern Office Technology,* April 1986, 108, 110, 112.

**18.** Perry A. Trunick, "Cost Control Means Lower Inventories," *Transportation & Distribution,* April 1989, 16–17.

**19.** E. J. Muller, "Harley's Got the Handle on Inbound," *Distribution,* March 1989, 70, 74.

**20.** Arjan T. Sadhwani, M. H. Sarhan, and Dayal Kiringoda, "Just-in-Time: An Inventory System Whose Time Has Come," *Management Accounting,* December 1985, 36–39, 42–44.

**21.** E. J. Muller, "Airfreight Makes Service Levels Soar," *Distribution,* January 1989, 58–63.

**22.** Steven P. Galante, "Distributors Bow to Demands of Just-in-Time Delivery," *Wall Street Journal,* 30 June 1986, 25.

**23.** Susan Scherreik, "New Warehouses: Big, Bright, Efficient," *New York Times,* 30 May 1993, sec. 10, 1, 9.

**24.** "Contract Warehousing Catches On," *Chain Store Age Executive,* October 1989, 108, 110.

**25.** Howard Rudnitsky, "Play It Again, Sam," *Forbes,* 10 August 1987, 48.

**26.** "Breakthroughs via Hub-and-Spoke Marketing," *Marketing News,* 20 June 1986, 1, 18.

**27.** Robert J. Bowman, "Moving the Goods," *World Trade,* May 1993, 145–148.

**28.** "Lillian Vernon Automates Virginia Facility," *Chain Store Age Executive,* June 1989, 39–40, 42.

**29.** "Palm, Coconut Oils Affected: New '89 NIOP Shipping Rules," *Chemical Marketing Reporter,* 13 March 1989, 10–11; Reg Dawson, "Magic Wand Required for Vanishing Trick," *International Freighting Weekly,* 8 April 1991, 4; "Drug Implications in New Backhauling & Device Laws, FDA Advises," *Pharmaceutical Manufacturers Association Newsletter,* 4 February 1991, 1.

**30.** David Warner, "Vital Cogs," *International Business,* January 1993, 30–32; U.S. Department of Commerce, *U.S. Industrial Outlook* (Washington, D.C.: GPO, 1990), sec. 42, 10.

**31.** Gene Bergoffen, "Fleets Contribute to Productivity," *Industry Week,* April 1993, T8, T12; Louis Rukeyser, John Cooney, and George Winslow, *Louis Rukeyser's Business Almanac* (New York: Simon and Schuster, 1988), 637–638.

**32.** Robert J. Bowman, "To Air Is Human . . ." *World Trade,* April 1993, 1110–1114; Steven P.

Galante, "Smaller Flower Retailers Wilt as Competition Grows Intense," *Wall Street Journal,* 4 August 1986, 17.

**33.** Daniel Pearl, "Fields of Dreams: All-Freight Airports, Touted as Way to Lure Firms, Pose Big Risks," *Wall Street Journal,* 2 December 1992, A1, A7.

**34.** Muller, "Airfreight Makes Service Levels Soar," 58–59.

**35.** Robert J. Bowman, "In America Only?" *World Trade,* April 1993, 39–44.

**36.** Robert J. Bowman, "Small Shipment Strategies," *Distribution,* April 1989, 60.

**37.** James Cook, "If It Isn't Profitable, Don't Do It," *Forbes,* 30 November 1987, 54, 56; "CSX Corporation," *Wall Street Transcript,* 10 June 1991, 101428.

**38.** Karen A. Auguston, "Distribution in the 90s: Better Materials Handling, Better Service," *Modern Materials Handling,* August 1989, 44–48.

**39.** "Foam Protection Serves Electronic Parts Well," *Transportation & Distribution,* March 1989, 57–58.

**40.** Graham Sharman, "What 1992 Means for Logistics," *McKinsey Quarterly,* Spring 1989, 104–120.

**41.** Greg Prince, "Accessing Distribution," *Beverage World,* August 1989, 38, 40.

**42.** Bradley Hull, "How to Make a Partnership Work," *Transportation & Distribution,* June 1989, 26–28.

**43.** James Schwartz, "What's New in Freight Trains," *New York Times,* 13 August 1989, sec. 3, 13.

**44.** Sharman, "What 1992 Means for Logistics," 104–120.

**45.** John Yoo, "Bad Trip: As Highways Decay, Their State Becomes Drag on the Economy," *Wall Street Journal,* 30 August 1989, A1, A8; Daniel Machalaba, "Push for Long Trucks Hits Bumpy Road," *Wall Street Journal,* 9 May 1990, B1–B2; Debra Lynn Dadd and Andre Carothers, "A Bill of Goods? Green Consuming in Perspective," *Greenpeace,* May–June 1990, 8–12.

**46.** Edward O. Welles, "Riding the High-Tech Highway," *Inc.,* March 1993, 72–85.

**47.** Tony Seideman, "Worldwide Messaging Standards Inch Closer," *Journal of Commerce,* 17 February 1989, 1A–2A.

**48.** Robert J. Bowman, "Shippers to Carriers: 'Add Value, or Die,'" *World Trade,* July 1992, 70–73.

**49.** See note 1.

## CHAPTER 17

**1.** Carol J. Loomis, "Dinosaurs?" *Fortune,* 3 May 1993, 36–42; Raymond Serafin, "The Saturn Story," *Advertising Age,* 16 November 1992, 1, 8, 13, 16; Fara Warner, "The Marketers of the Year: Donald Hudler," *Brandweek,* 16 November 1992, 21; "Saturn Gears Up Another Blockbuster Ad," *Adweek,* 4 January 1993, 8.

**2.** George E. Belch and Michael A. Belch, *Introduction to Advertising and Promotion Management* (Homewood, Ill.: Irwin, 1990), 479.

**3.** Glenn Ruffenach, "Officials in the Garden State Deny That This Was Really Their Idea," *Wall Street Journal,* 11 November 1988, B1.

**4.** Ruth Stroud, "Sunkist a Pioneer in New Products, Promotions," *Advertising Age,* 9 November 1988, 22, 140.

**5.** Gerry Khermouch, "Pepsi Flack Attack Nips Hoax in the Bud," *Brandweek,* 21 June 1993, 5.

**6.** AIG advertisement, *Atlantic,* June 1990, 58–59.

**7.** Robert Garfield, "Before the Oscars, Somebody Has to Sell Those Movies," *USA Today,* 22 March 1985, 6B; Randall Rothenberg, "Improving Marketing of Movies," *New York Times,* 26 February 1990, sec. d, 9; Betsy Sharkey, "Spotlight Entertainment," *Mediaweek,* 18 March 1991, 31; "Comparative Advertising: Red in Tooth and Claw," *Economist,* 18 May 1991, 79; Michael Lev, "Leo Burnett Makes the Case for the Comparative Method," *New York Times,* 12 April 1991, sec. c, 17.

**8.** Lisa Marie Petersen, "Previews of Coming Attractions," *Brandweek,* 15 March 1993, 22–23.

**9.** "The Advertising Industry," *The Economist,* 9 June 1990, 3–8, 10–18.

**10.** William P. Dommermuth, *Promotion: Analysis, Creativity, and Strategy* (Boston: PWS-Kent, 1989), 42.

**11.** Dommermuth, *Promotion,* 43–44.

**12.** "Sales Promotions—Annual Report 1989: Growing Up & Out," *Marketing & Media Decisions,* July 1990, 20–21.

**13.** Robert Coen, "Sales Promotion: The Data Dilemma," *Marketing & Media Decisions,* June 1989, 122; Russ Bowman, "The Conflict Is Definitions," *Marketing & Media Decisions,* June 1989, 123.

**14.** Michael Lev, "MTV Contests: The Odder the Better," *New York Times,* 12 June 1989, sec. c, 8.

**15.** Joanne Lipman, "Marketers Turn to Promotions to Attract Hispanic Consumers," *Wall Street Journal,* 21 September 1989, B6.

**16.** Edward D. Meyer, "Promotion Magic," *Boardroom Reports,* 1 January 1987, 5; Randall Rothenberg, "Change in Consumer Markets Hurting Advertising Industry," *New York Times,* 3 October 1989, sec. a, 1, sec. d, 23; Dommermuth, *Promotion,* 48.

**17.** Belch and Belch, *Introduction to Advertising and Promotion Management,* 13, 543–544.

**18.** Laurie Petersen, "'Raid' Targets the Inner City with a Block Cleanup," *Adweek's Marketing Week,* 19 February 1990, 53.

**19.** Belch and Belch, *Introduction to Advertising and Promotion Management,* 10.

**20.** Adapted from Scott M. Cutlip, Alan H. Center, and Glen M. Broom, *Effective Public Relations* (Englewood Cliffs, N.J.: Prentice-Hall, 1985), 262.

**21.** Jacob Jacoby and Wayne D. Hoyer, "The Comprehension/Miscomprehension of Print Communication: Selected Findings," *Journal of Consumer Research,* March 1989, 434–443.

**22.** Thomas W. Leigh, Arno J. Rethans, and Tamatha Reichenbach Whitney, "Role Portrayals of Women in Advertising: Cognitive Responses and Advertising Effectiveness," *Journal of Advertising Research,* October–November 1987, 54–63; Barney T. Raffield III, "Marketing across Cultures: Learning from U.S. Corporate Blunders," presented at Eastern Michigan University's Sixth Annual Conference on Languages and Communication for World Business and the Professions, Ann Arbor, Michigan, May 8–9, 1987.

**23.** C. Anthony de Benedetto, Mariko Tamate, and Rajan Chandran, "Developing Creative Strategy for the Japanese Marketplace," *Journal of Advertising Research,* January–February 1992, 39–48.

**24.** Dommermuth, *Promotion,* 434–435.

**25.** William H. Davidow and Bro Uttal, *Total Customer Service* (New York: Harper & Row, 1989), 34.

**26.** Courtland L. Bovée and William F. Arens, *Contemporary Advertising* (Homewood, Ill.: Irwin, 1989), 638.

**27.** Lisa Marie Petersen, "For 'Groundhog,' A One-Week Sequel," *Brandweek,* 22 February 1993, 2.

**28.** This section adapted in part from Dommermuth, *Promotion,* 54.

**29.** AT&T commercials.

**30.** Gerry Khermouch, "Tea Time," *Brandweek,* 22 March 1993, 1, 6.

**31.** Don Sunoo and Lynn Y. S. Lin, "Sales Effects of Promotion and Advertising," *Journal of Advertising Research,* October 1978, 37–40.

**32.** "Mexico Launches Overall Effort to Double Arrivals," *Tour & Travel News,* 20 August 1990, 22.

**33.** Adapted from Russell H. Colley, *Defining Advertising Goals for Measured Advertising Results* (New York: Association of National Advertisers, 1961, reprinted 1984), 12.

**34.** Courtland L. Bovée, John V. Thill, George P. Dovel, and Marian Burk Wood, *Advertising* (New York: McGraw-Hill, 1994).

**35.** Adapted from Bovée and Arens, *Contemporary Advertising,* 242–246.

**36.** Presentation by Bill Bryant, vice president of sales and marketing, Shapeware Corporation, to Washington Software Association, Bellevue, Washington, 12 October 1993.

**37.** Alvin A. Achenbaum and F. Kent Mitchel, "Pulling Away from Push Marketing," *Harvard Business Review,* May–June 1987, 38–40.

**38.** Matthew Grimm, "McDonald's McKicks Off McSoccerFest," *Brandweek,* 1 February 1993, 5; Matthew Grimm, "Reebok Plans Pepsi Approach vs. Possible Nike-Coke Co-Ventures," *Brandweek,* 24 May 1993, 1, 6.

**39.** Bovée et al., *Advertising.*

**40.** Gary Moss and Mark Goldstein, "Integrated Marketing: A Client Task . . . Or Can Agencies Handle It?" *Advertising Age,* 25 January 1993, 19; Don E. Schultz, Stanley I. Tannenbaum, and Robert F. Lauterborn, *Integrated Marketing Communications: Pulling It All Together and Making It Work* (Lincolnwood, Ill.: NTC Business Books, 1993), 157–172.

**41.** Scott Hume, "Integrated Marketing: Who's in Charge Here?" *Advertising Age,* 22 March 1993, 3, 52.

**42.** Bovée et al., *Advertising.*

**43.** Philip R. Cateora, *International Marketing* (Homewood, Ill.: Irwin, 1987), 418, 428, 438.

**44.** Ellen Day, "Conveying Service Quality Through Advertising," *Journal of Services Marketing,* Fall 1992, 53–61.

**45.** Erin Kelly, "Picture Is Worth a Hundred Jobs in Vandalia, Illinois," *USA Today,* 19 August 1985, 7B.

**46.** Dick Wasserman, *"That's Our New Ad Campaign . . .?"* (Lexington, Ky.: Lexington Books, 1988), 75.

**47.** David Zimmerman, "The Outlaw Uses Music to Get Justice," *USA Today,* 10 September 1985, 1D.

**48.** John Garrison, "Telethons—The Positive Story," *Fund Raising Management,* November 1987, 48–52.

**49.** Meryl Davids, "Doing Well by Doing Good," *Public Relations,* July 1987, 17, 39.

**50.** Richard W. Pollay, "The Distorted Mirror: Reflections on the Unintended Consequences of Advertising," *Journal of Marketing,* April 1986, 18–36; Betsy Morris, "Eager to Lend: Banks and Thrifts Aggressively Pitch Personal Loans," *Wall Street Journal,* 9 September 1987, 39.

**51.** Jerry Goodbody, "For More Consumers, Advertising Is the 'Deceptive Persuader,'" *Adweek's Marketing Week,* 5 March 1990, 40.

**52.** Morris B. Holbrook, "Mirror, Mirror, on the Wall, What's Unfair in the Reflections on Advertising?" *Journal of Marketing,* July 1987, 95–103; Francis X. Callahan, "Does Advertising Subsidize Information?" *Journal of Advertising Research,* August 1978, 19–22.

**53.** See note 1.

## CHAPTER 18

**1.** Denise Gellene, "Designer Coffee Is Hot Stuff," *Los Angeles Times,* 14 April 1993, sec. a, 1; "Cool Beans: A Coffee Company with No Bitter Aftertaste Comes to L.A.," *Inside PR,* June 1992, 28–29; Ingrid Abramovitch, "Miracles of Marketing," *Success,* April 1993, 24–27; Debra Prinzing, "Schultz: Grande Designs for Filling Tall Order," *Puget Sound Business Journal,* 25 December 1992, 8; Charles McCoy, "Entrepreneur Smells Aroma of Success in Coffee Bars," *Wall Street Journal,* 8 January 1993, B2; Matt Rothman, "Into the Black," *Inc.,* January 1993, 59–65.

**2.** "To the Winners Belong the Spoils," *Marketing News,* 10 October 1986, 1, 13.

**3.** Thomas F. Garbett, "Look What We're Doing for Humanity," *Across the Board,* May 1989, 45–52.

**4.** "Not for Members Only," *Marketing Management* 1, no. 4 (1993): 6–7; Herb Goldsmith, "Members Only Fashions a Unique Selling Strategy," *Journal of Business Strategy,* May–June 1989, 8–11.

**5.** Janet Neiman, "The Trouble with Comparative Ads," *Adweek's Marketing Week,* 12 January 1987, 4–5.

**6.** Neiman, "The Trouble with Comparative Ads," 4–5; Joseph B. White, "Ford Decides to Fight Back in Truck Ads," *Wall Street Journal,* 28 February 1989, B1, B6.

**7.** Bruce Buchanan and Doron Goldman, "Us vs. Them: The Minefield of Comparative Ads," *Harvard Business Review,* May–June 1989, 38–40, 42, 44, 48, 50.

**8.** Jeffrey A. Trachtenberg, "New Law Adds Risk to Comparative Ads," *Wall Street Journal,* 1 June 1989, B6.

**9.** Frank G. Bingham, Jr., and Barney T. Raffield III, *Business to Business Marketing Management* (Homewood, Ill.: Irwin, 1990), 519.

**10.** Augustino Turner, "Cost-Effective Advertising," *Small Business Reports,* May 1989, 39–46; "Advertising Strategy: Precise Objectives Optimize Investment," *Small Business Report,* October 1986, 70–75.

**11.** George Dovel, "Stake It Out: Positioning Success, Step by Step," *Business Marketing,* July 1990, 43–44, 46, 48–51.

**12.** Jean Sherman, "Building a Better Sundae," *Working Woman,* July 1987, 48; Bill Britt, "Häagen-Dazs Samples Ice Cream Push," *Marketing,* 24 January 1991, 6.

**13.** Paul Duke, Jr., and Ronald Alsop, "Advertisers Beginning to Play Off Worker Concern over Job Security," *Wall Street Journal,* 1 April 1988, 11; Ronald Alsop, "More Food Advertising Plays on Cancer and Cardiac Fears," *Wall Street Journal,* 8 October 1987, 33; George E. Belch and Michael A. Belch, *Introduction to Advertising and Promotion Management* (Homewood, Ill.: Irwin, 1990), 186.

**14.** "Emotions Important for Successful Advertising," *Marketing News,* 12 April 1985, 18.

**15.** Elaine Underwood, "Innkeeper to the World," *Brandweek,* 9 November 1992, 14–19; "Holiday Inn Worldwide Brings Emmy Award-Winning Children's Game Show to Atlanta Halloween Weekend," PR Newswire, 9 October 1992; "Holiday Inn Worldwide Announces Management Changes," PR Newswire, 20 April 1992, "Holiday Inn Worldwide Brand Portfolio Strategy," PR Newswire, 10 March 1992; Megan Rowe, "Asia's Allure," *Lodging Hospitality,* October 1992, 51–52; Megan Rowe, "Holiday Inn: Fat and Sassy to Lean and Mean," *Lodging Hospitality,* July 1992, 24–26.

**16.** Thomas R. King, "Pitches on Value Stick in Consumers' Minds," *Wall Street Journal,* 4 June 1990, B1.

**17.** Grant McCracken, "Who Is the Celebrity Endorser? Cultural Foundations of the Endorsement Process," *Journal of Consumer Research* 16, no. 3 (December 1989): 310–321; Mary Walker, Lynn Langmeyer, and Daniel Langmeyer, "Celebrity Endorsers: Do You Get What You Pay For?" *Journal of Consumer Marketing* 9, no. 2 (1992): 69–76.

**18.** "USA Snapshots: Ads We Find Least Convincing," *USA Today,* 9 March 1988, 1D; Alix Freedman, "Marriages Between Celebrity Spokesmen and Their Firms Can Be Risky Ventures," *Wall Street Journal,* 22 January 1988, 23; Christian Ryssel and Erich Stamminger, "Sponsoring World-Class Tennis Players," *European Research,* May 1988, 110–116.

**19.** "Eyes Are on Revitalizing Carbonated Soft Drinks in '94: Cola Giants Are Designing Ad Campaigns to Jump Start Their Brands," *Beverage Industry,* December 1993, 36.

**20.** Cara Appelbaum, "Signing On: Celebrity Popularity Is No Guaranteed Endorsement," *Adweek's Marketing Week,* 21 October 1991, 6; "USA Snapshots," 1D; Freedman, "Marriages Between Celebrity Spokesmen and Their Firms Can Be Risky Ventures," 23; Joanne Lipman, "Celebrity Pitchmen Are Popular Again," *Wall Street Journal,* 4 September 1991, B5.

**21.** Joshua Levine, "Fantasy, Not Flesh," *Forbes,* 22 January 1990, 118–120.

**22.** Ronald Alsop, "Can Honda Scooter Ads Get Any More Offbeat Than This?" *Wall Street Journal,* 4 June 1987, 25.

**23.** James Cox, "Infiniti's Epiphany," *USA Today,* 15 January 1990, 6B; Joanne Lipman, "Ads of the '80s: The Loved and the Losers," *Wall Street Journal,* 28 December 1989, B1, B4; Ronald Alsop, "Surreal Ads Startle—But Do They Sell?" *Wall Street Journal,* 20 October 1988, B1.

**24.** Mark Crispin Miller, "Hollywood: The Ad," *Atlantic,* April 1990, 41–45, 48–50, 52–54.

**25.** Timothy E. Moore, "Subliminal Advertising: What You See Is What You Get," *Journal of Marketing,* Spring 1982, 38–47; Jack Haberstroh, "Can't Ignore Subliminal Ad Charges," *Advertising Age,* 17 September 1984, 3, 42, 44.

**26.** Linda Keslar, Michele Herman, and Betsy Sharkey, "Studying the Academic Studies," *Adweek,* 7 December 1987, 30–31, 34–35.

**27.** Courtland L. Bovée and William F. Arens, *Contemporary Advertising* (Homewood, Ill.: Irwin, 1989), 379–380, 399.

**28.** Andrea Rothman, "Timing Techniques Can Make Small Ad Budgets Seem Bigger," *Wall Street Journal,* 3 February 1989, B4; Robert Geary, "Advertising Exposure: Flighting or Continuity?" *Business Marketing,* June 1987, 141–142.

**29.** Julie A. Edell and Kevin Lane Keller, "The Information Processing of Coordinated Media Campaigns," *Journal of Marketing Research,* May 1989, 149–163.

**30.** Warren Berger, "We're So Sorry," *Inside Print,* January 1988, 34–36, 38, 40, 44.

**31.** William R. Morrissey, "Gain Competitive Edge with Data-Based Direct Marketing," *Marketing News,* 15 March 1985, 22–23.

**32.** Dennis Kneale, "'Zapping' of TV Ads Appears Pervasive," *Wall Street Journal,* 25 April 1988, 21.

**33.** Stuart Elliott, "'Chameleon' Ads Mimic TV," *USA Today,* 12 June 1989, 5B.

**34.** Paragraphs on media adapted from Belch and Belch, *Introduction to Advertising and Promotion Management,* 311; Tom Eisenhart and Sue Kapp, "Orchestrating Your Media Options," *Business Marketing,* April 1990, 38–41, 44–47.

**35.** Janice Castro, "Invasion of the Yellow Pages," *Time,* 5 October 1987, 52; Anita Manning, "Restaurants' Newest Menu Item: Ads," *USA Today,* 3 January 1990, 1D; Ronald Alsop, "Looking Back at Floppy Ads, Men's Hair Coloring and More," *Wall Street Journal,* 31 December 1987, 9; Ronald Alsop, "More Ads Bombard Airplane Passengers," *Wall Street Journal,* 14 February 1989, B1; "VideOcart Shopping Cart with Computer Screen Creates New Ad Medium That Also Gathers Data," *Marketing News,* 9 May 1988, 1–2; Eileen Norris, "Alternative Media Try to Get Their Feet in the Door," *Advertising Age,* 17 October 1985, 15, 58; James Cox, "Ad Attack: No Place to Escape," *USA Today,* 22 March 1988, 1B–2B; Leslie M. Schultz, "Say It with Video," *Inc.,* June 1985, 123–125; Peter H. Lewis, "And Now, a Word from the Sponsor," *New York Times,* 19 March 1989, sec. 3, 6; Cyndee Miller, "Upscale Consumers Are Even Willing to Pay for Their Ads," *Marketing News,* 20 November 1987, 2; "For These Video Ads, You Don't Need a VCR," *Wall Street Journal,* 9 May 1988, 25.

**36.** Bovée and Arens, *Contemporary Advertising,* 259–261.

**37.** Bovée and Arens, *Contemporary Advertising,* 262.

**38.** Adapted from "Copy Chasers Criteria," *Business Marketing,* January 1988, 117.

**39.** Bovée and Arens, *Contemporary Advertising,* 206, 208.

**40.** Belch and Belch, *Introduction to Advertising and Promotion Management,* 605–608.

**41.** Josh McQueen, "Stimulating Long-Term Brand Growth," *Admap,* April 1992, 43–47.

**42.** Philip R. Cateora, *International Marketing* (Homewood, Ill.: Irwin, 1987), 420, 422.

**43.** Peter H. Engel, "Measuring Promotional Effectiveness," *Adweek's Marketing Week,* 14 March 1988, 14–15; Jeffrey K. McElnea and Michael J. Enzer, "Building Brand Franchise," *Marketing Communications,* April 1986, 42–44.

**44.** "Consumer Promos Gain Favor as Marketing Cut Trade Budgets," *Brandweek,* 5 April 1993, 8.

**45.** Howard Schlossberg, "Coupons Likely to Remain Popular," *Marketing News,* 29 March 1993, 1, 7; Scott Hume, "Coupons Set Record, But Pace Slows," *Advertising Age,* 1 February 1993, 25; Belch and Belch, *Introduction to Advertising and Promotion Management,* 524–526.

**46.** Edward D. Meyer, "Promotion Magic," *Boardroom Reports,* 1 January 1987, 5–6.

**47.** Scott Hume, "Sampling Wins Over More Marketers," *Advertising Age,* 27 July 1992, 12; Belch and Belch, *Introduction to Advertising and Promotion Management,* 519–520.

**48.** "'Win a Beamer' Drives Away with Reggie," *Promo,* April 1992, 16.

**49.** Howard Stumpf and John M. Kawula, "Point-of-Purchase Advertising," in *Handbook of Sales Promotion,* edited by Stanley Ulanoff (New York: McGraw-Hill, 1985), 141–172.

**50.** Brent Houlden, "Come Back Soon," *Small Business Reports,* November 1992, 60–64.

**51.** Meg Cox, "Waldenbooks' Big-Buyer Lure May Mean War," *Wall Street Journal,* 27 February 1990, B12; Michael J. McCarthy, "Rewarding 'Frequent Buyer' for Loyalty," *Wall Street Journal,* 21 June 1989, B1; Lisa H. Towle, "What's New in Frequency Marketing," *New York Times,* 3 December 1989, sec. f, 13.

**52.** Jonathan Dahl, "Hotels Finding 'Frequent-Stay' Plans Don't Fly," *Wall Street Journal,* 5 November 1990, B1.

**53.** William A. Robinson, "Planning a Sales Promotion," in Ulanoff, *Handbook of Sales Promotion,* 394.

**54.** "The Data Daze: Is There an Information Overload?" *Promo,* November 1992, 6–7, 42.

**55.** Philip Kotler and Alan R. Andreasen, *Strategic Marketing for Nonprofit Organizations* (Englewood Cliffs, N.J.: Prentice-Hall, 1987), 586–587.

**56.** *Update,* newsletter to American Express cardholders, October 1993, 1.

**57.** Emily DeNitto, "Marketing with a Conscience," *Marketing Communications,* May 1989, 42–46; P. Rajan Varadarajan and Anil Menon, "Cause-Related Marketing: A Coalignment of Marketing Strategy and Corporate Philanthropy," *Journal of Marketing,* July 1988, 58–74.

**58.** Terry Lefton and Matthew Grimm, "Coca-Cola Cuts \$250 Mil NFL Deal," *Brandweek,* 8 March 1993, 1, 6; "Coke Tops in Backing Big Events," *Advertising Age,* 7 December 1992, 10.

**59.** S. Watson Dunn, *Public Relations* (Homewood, Ill.: Irwin, 1986), 404–405.

**60.** See note 1.

## CHAPTER 19

**1.** Adapted from Marvin A. Jolson, Alan J. Dubinsky, Francis J. Yammarino, and Lucette B. Comer, "Transforming the Salesforce with Leadership," *Sloan Management Review,* Spring 1993, 95–106; Joseph Conlin, "Teaming Up," *Sales & Marketing Management,* October 1993, 98–104; Thayer C. Taylor, "Xerox's Sales Force Learns a New Game," *Sales & Marketing Management,* 1 July 1985, 48–51; Peter Finch, "Xerox Bets All on New Sales Groups," *Business Marketing,* July 1985, 8, 21; Kate Bertrand, "New Twists in the Incentive Game," *Business Marketing,* April 1986, 50, 62; Robert Moskowitz, "Xerox Sets Out in New Directions," *Computer Decisions,* 17 June 1986, 54, 58; John Byrne, "Culture Shock at Xerox," *Business Week,* 22 June 1987, 106, 108, 110; Thayer C. Taylor, "Xerox: Who Says You Can't Be Big and Fast?" *Sales & Marketing Management,* November 1987, 62, 64–65; Regina Eisman, "Xerox Advanced Sales Academy," *Incentive,* August 1989, 56, 58–59; "Have Laptop, Will Sell," *Sales & Marketing Management,* October 1986, 26; Thayer C. Taylor, "S&MM's Survey Results," *Sales & Marketing Management,* May 1987, 50–53; Thayer C. Taylor, "How the Best Sales Forces Use PC's and Laptops," *Sales & Marketing Management,* April 1988, 64–74; Thayer C. Taylor, "Make Way for the Salesman's Best Friend," *Sales & Marketing Management,* February 1988, 53–56; Edward Lawler III, "Reward Systems," in *Improving Life at Work,* edited by J. Richard Hackman and L. Lloyd Suttle (Glenview, Ill.: Scott, Foresman, 1977), 163–226.

**2.** Douglas J. Dalrymple, *Sales Management Concepts and Cases* (New York: Wiley, 1988), 8–9.

**3.** Dalrymple, *Sales Management Concepts and Cases,* 8.

**4.** Richard Manville, "Sales Lead Management That Works," *Business Marketing,* February 1987, 77.

**5.** Carol J. Loomis, "Have You Been Cold-Called?" *Fortune,* 16 December 1991, 109–115.

**6.** C. Dwight West III, "Personal Lines Action Plan Spurs Production," *Rough Notes,* September 1988, 29.

**7.** Dana Shilling, "The Art of the Cold Call," *Working Woman,* December 1987, 52–53.

**8.** Eric Olsen, "Breaking the Sales Barrier," *Success,* May 1990, 48–49.

**9.** Olsen, "Breaking the Sales Barrier," 48–49.

**10.** Iris Randall, "How to Build a Premier Sales Staff," *Black Enterprise,* February 1993, 154–156.

**11.** Liz Murphy, "Building a Million-Dollar Deal at the Last Minute," *Sales & Marketing Management,* April 1988, 36, 38–39, 41; Meg Whittemore, "Quick Printing Turns High-Tech," *Nation's Business,* April 1991, 63.

**12.** Murphy, "Building a Million-Dollar Deal at the Last Minute," 39.

**13.** "Selling at the Top," *Success,* March 1988, 44, 46–47.

**14.** George R. Walther, "Reach Out to Accounts," *Success,* May 1990, 24.

**15.** Dalrymple, *Sales Management Concepts and Cases,* 116.

**16.** Eugene Johnson, David Kurtz, and Eberhard Scheuing, *Sales Management Concepts, Practices, and Cases* (New York: McGraw-Hill, 1986), 81–82.

**17.** Arthur Bragg, "Ethics in Selling, Honest!" *Sales & Marketing Management,* May 1987, 44.

**18.** Tom Eisenhart, "An Interplay of Information," *Business Marketing,* September 1992, 90–92.

**19.** Priscilla C. Brown, "No Quick Fix," *Business Marketing,* September 1992, 91, 98.

**20.** Lynn Asinof, "Telemarketing Makes Rapid Strides at U.S. Corporations," *Wall Street Journal,* 21 July 1988, A1.

**21.** Steve Zurier, "Dialing for Dollars at J. Fegely," *Industrial Distribution,* May 1988, 105, 107.

**22.** "26 Percent of U.S. Salespeople Are Women," *American Salesman,* August 1993, 8–9; Mary Lu Carnevale, "FCC Adopts Rules to Curb Telemarketing," *Wall Street Journal,* 18 September 1992, B1; Mark Land, "On Warpath Against Taped Phone Pitches," *USA Today,* 8 November 1991, 4B.

**23.** Patrick L. Schul and Brent M. Wren, "The Emerging Role of Women in Industrial Selling: A Decade of Change," *Journal of Marketing,* July 1992, 38–54.

**24.** Sarah Stiansen, "Reborn in Real Estate," *Success,* May 1989, 40.

**25.** Michele Block Morse, "Rich Rewards," *Success,* March 1988, 58, 60–61.

**26.** J. Brock Smith and Donald W. Barclay, "Team Selling Effectiveness: A Small Group Perspective," *Journal of Business-to-Business Marketing* 1, no. 2 (1993): 3–32; Cathy Hyatt Hills, "Everybody Sells," *Small Business Reports,* October 1992, 31–40; S. Joe Puri, "Industrial Vendors' Selling Center: Implications for Sales Management," *Journal of Business and Industrial Marketing,* Summer 1992, 59–69.

**27.** Claudia H. Deutsch, "Two Movers in a Tough Market," *New York Times,* 20 December 1992, sec. f, 8.

**28.** William Keenan, Jr., "The Difference in Selling Services," *Sales & Marketing Management,* March 1990, 48–52.

**29.** Keenan, "The Difference in Selling Services," 49–50.

**30.** John S. Hill and Meg Birdseye, "Salesperson Selection in Multinational Corporations: An Empirical Study," *Journal of Personal Selling and Sales Management,* Summer 1989, 39–47.

**31.** Jeanne Greenberg and Herbert Greenberg, "What It Takes to Succeed in Sales," as summarized in *Soundview Executive Book Summaries,* July 1990, 1–8.

**32.** Greenberg and Greenberg, "What It Takes to Succeed in Sales," 1–8.

**33.** Greenberg and Greenberg, "What It Takes to Succeed in Sales," 1–8.

**34.** Kevin F. Sullivan, Richard A. Bobbe, and Martin R. Strasmore, "Transforming the Salesforce in a Maturing Industry," *Management Review,* June 1988, 48.

**35.** Jolson, Dubinsky, Yammarino, and Comer, "Transforming the Salesforce with Leadership," 95–106.

**36.** Sullivan, Bobbe, and Strasmore, "Transforming the Salesforce," 46.

**37.** Sullivan, Bobbe, and Strasmore, "Transforming the Salesforce," 48.

**38.** Paul Faris, "No More Winging It," *Sales & Marketing Management,* August 1986, 88.

**39.** Bob Woods, "Recruiting the Best and the Brightest," *Sales & Marketing Management,* 16 August 1982, 51.

**40.** "Benefits of Sales Training," *Small Business Reports,* July 1990, 12.

**41.** Robert F. McCracken, "Establishing a Market Presence in China: The Avon Experience," *East Asian Executive Reports,* 15 August 1993, 10–11; Siew Meng Leong, Paul S. Busch, and Deborah Roedder John, "Knowledge Bases and Salesperson Effectiveness: A Script-Theoretic Analysis," *Journal of Marketing Research,* May 1989, 164–178.

**42.** Dalrymple, *Sales Management Concepts and Cases,* 326.

**43.** James S. Hirsch, "Sales Force: To One Xerox Man, Selling Photocopiers Is a Gambler's Game," *Wall Street Journal,* 24 September 1991, A1, A9.

**44.** Roger Thompson, "The Rise of Re/Max," *Nation's Business,* April 1990, 29–31; Michael Stremfel, "Re/Max Broker Is Feeling at Home with '90 Sales Commissions Totaling \$1.5 Million," *Los Angeles Business Journal,* 13 May 1991, 14.

**45.** Charles Futrell, *Sales Management* (Chicago: Dryden, 1988), 705.

**46.** See note 1.

**47.** Adapted from Sally Saville Hodge, "Great Rep," *Chicago,* November 1988, 129–130, 132.

## CHAPTER 20

**1.** Elaine Underwood, "Innkeeper to the World," *Brandweek,* 9 November 1992, 14–19; "Holiday Inn Worldwide Brings Emmy Award-Winning Children's Game Show to Atlanta Halloween Weekend," PR Newswire, 9 October 1992; "Holiday Inn Worldwide Announces Management Changes," PR Newswire, 20 April 1992; "Holiday Inn Worldwide Brand Portfolio Strategy," PR Newswire, 10 March 1992; Megan Rowe, "Asia's Allure," *Lodging Hospitality,* October 1992, 51–52; Megan Rowe, "Holiday Inn: Fat and Sassy to Lean and Mean," *Lodging Hospitality,* July 1992, 24–26.

**2.** Richard W. Stevenson, "Catering to Consumers' Ethnic Needs," *New York Times,* 23 January 1993, sec. c, 1, 2.

**3.** Margaret Ambry and Cheryl Russell, *The Official Guide to the American Marketplace* (Ithaca, N.Y.: New Strategist Publications, 1992), 3; Stevenson, "Catering to Consumers' Ethnic Needs," sec. c, 1, 2.

**4.** Stevenson, "Catering to Consumers' Ethnic Needs," sec. c, 1, 2; Dan Koeppel, "P&G Tests Foreign Brands in L.A.," *Adweek's Marketing Week,* 24 June 1991, 4.

**5.** Christy Fisher, "Ethnics Gain Marketing Clout," *Advertising Age,* 5 August 1991, 3, 12.

**6.** Cyndee Miller, "Marketers Say Budgets Hinder Targeting of Asian-Americans," *Marketing News,* 30 March 1990, 2; Jon Berry, "Help Wanted," *Adweek's Marketing Week,* 9 July 1990, 28–34; Stuart Elliot, "Retailers Reach Out to Minorities," *New York Times,* 31 December 1991.

**7.** Yumiko Ono, "Black Is Beautiful in Japanese Shops Selling to Teenagers," *Wall Street Journal,* 23 November 1992, A1, A10.

**8.** Leon W. Wynter, "Choose Your Language for Reaching Hispanics," *Wall Street Journal,* 22 November 1991, B1.

**9.** C. Anthony de Benedetto, Mariko Tamate, and Rajan Chandran, "Developing Creative Strategy for the Japanese Marketplace," *Journal of Advertising Research,* January–February 1992, 39–48.

**10.** "India Moves to Regulate Cable," *Asian Advertising and Marketing,* 13 August 1993, 1.

**11.** Jennifer Clark, "Basta Bare Bottoms in

Blurbs, Say Italos," *Variety,* 18 February 1991, 20, 51; Barbara Sundberg Baudot, *International Advertising Handbook* (Boston: Lexington, 1989), 219–222.

**12.** Judy Yu, "Ethnic Marketing: Asian American Customers," *Women & Minorities Inc.* (Supplement to *Puget Sound Business Journal*), 23 October 1992, 5A; Chester A. Swenson, *Selling to a Segmented Market* (Lincolnwood, Ill.: NTC Business Books, 1990), 88–91.

**13.** Andrew Tanzer, "Hot Wings Take Off," *Forbes,* 18 January 1993, 74.

**14.** Kevin Kelly, "The Rumble Heard Round the World: Harleys," *Business Week,* 24 May 1993, 58–60.

**15.** Jeremy Main, "How to Go Global—And Why," *Fortune,* 28 August 1989, 70.

**16.** Paul S. Besson, "The Guts to Go Global," *Black Enterprise,* June 1988, 192–195.

**17.** Steven Beschloss, "But How Will It Play in Prague?" *New York Times,* 2 April 1989, sec. 3, 9.

**18.** Edward Cundiff and Marye Tharp Hilger, *Marketing in the International Environment* (Englewood Cliffs, N.J.: Prentice-Hall, 1988), 17.

**19.** Tony Spaeth, "Logomania," *Across the Board,* March 1993, 51–53.

**20.** Warren J. Keegan, *Global Marketing Management* (Englewood Cliffs, N.J.: Prentice-Hall, 1989), 214.

**21.** "Currency Trading," *Wall Street Journal,* 17 December 1993, C13.

**22.** Keegan, *Global Marketing Management,* 214.

**23.** Philip R. Cateora, *International Marketing* (Homewood, Ill.: Irwin, 1987), 38–39.

**24.** Herbert Stein, "Don't Worry about the Trade Deficit," *Wall Street Journal,* 16 May 1989, A14.

**25.** Michael E. Porter, "The Competitive Advantage of Nations," *Harvard Business Review,* March–April 1990, 73–93.

**26.** Michael E. Porter, "Why Nations Triumph," *Fortune,* 12 March 1990, 94–95, 98, 102, 104, 108.

**27.** Robert J. Allio, "Formulating Global Strategy," *Planning Review,* March–April 1989, 22–23, 26–28.

**28.** Carol L. Brookins and John A. Schnittker, "Analysts See Short-, Long-Term Benefits in GATT Accord, Question Domestic Policies," *Milling & Baking News,* 28 December 1993; 1+; "GATT Accord Promises Sweeping Changes," *Milling & Baking News,* 21 December 1993, 1+.

**29.** Cateora, *International Marketing,* 258.

**30.** Cateora, *International Marketing,* 270.

**31.** Peter Nulty, "How the World Will Change," *Fortune,* 15 January 1990, 50.

**32.** Robert M. Bryan, "Europe 1992," *Small Business Reports,* January 1990, 30–34, 36–38.

**33.** Peter G. Frederick, "The Blueprint for Change," *Marketing Communications,* March 1989, 22–25.

**34.** Don Del Prete, "Canadians Hopeful, but Fear Ill Effects of Treaty," *Marketing News,* 9 July 1990, 6–7, 19.

**35.** "TV or Not TV," *Time,* 16 October 1989, 58.

**36.** Allio, "Formulating Global Strategy," 23; Main, "How to Go Global," 70.

**37.** Kevin Maney and Dianne Rinehart, "McDonald's in Moscow Opens Today," *USA Today,* 31 January 1990, 1A; Peter Foster, "McDonald's Excellent Soviet Venture?" *Canadian Business* (Canada), May 1991, 51–65; Jeffrey M. Hertzfeld, "Joint Ventures: Saving the Soviets from Perestroika," *Harvard Business Review,* January–February 1991, 80–91.

**38.** John S. McClenahen, "Thinking Globally," *Industry Week,* 21 August 1989, 12–14, 18.

**39.** Louis Uchitelle, "Small Companies Going Global," *New York Times,* 27 November 1989, sec. c, 1, 5.

**40.** Udayan Gupta, "Small Firms Aren't Waiting to Grow Up to Go Global," *Wall Street Journal,* 5 December 1989, B2.

**41.** David Hale, "Strategic Alliances Offer Strong Financial Backing," *San Diego Business Journal,* 28 August 1989, 22.

**42.** Frank Washington and David Pauly, "Driving Toward a World Car?" *Newsweek,* 1 May 1989, 48–49.

**43.** Allio, "Formulating Global Strategy," 28.

**44.** "Boeing Teams with Japanese to Build Jetliner," *San Diego Union,* 14 April 1990, sec. d, 1.

**45.** Barbara Toman, "Looking to 1992, Agencies Rush to Define New Euro-Consumer," *Wall Street Journal,* 27 June 1989, B6; Donald C. Stone, "Assistance to Central and Eastern Europe," *Bureaucrat,* Winter 1990–1991, 7–12.

**46.** David Lieberman, "Keeping Up with the Murdochs," *Business Week,* 20 March 1989, 32–34.

**47.** Joann S. Lublin, "Slim Pickings: U.S. Food Firms Find Europe's Huge Market Hardly a Piece of Cake," *Wall Street Journal,* 15 May 1990, A1, A16.

**48.** Louis Kraar, "Meet 25 People You Ought to Know," *Fortune, Pacific Rim 1989,* 101–102, 104, 106, 108, 110, 112, 114.

**49.** Cateora, *International Marketing,* 125.

**50.** Cateora, *International Marketing,* 140.

**51.** Jim Mann, "One Company's China Debacle," *Fortune,* 6 November 1989, 145, 148, 152.

**52.** Lennie Copeland, "The Art of International Selling," *Business America,* 25 June 1984, 2–7.

**53.** William J. Holstein and Brian Bremner, "The Little Guys Are Making It Big Overseas," *Business Week,* 27 February 1989, 94–96.

**54.** David Weddle, "Jump In!" *World Trade,* February–March 1990, 44.

**55.** Anne-Marie Schiro, "Patterns," *New York Times,* 6 June 1989, sec. b, 4.

**56.** *Statistical Abstract of the United States 1990* (Washington, D.C.: GPO, 1990), 778.

**57.** Cundiff and Hilger, *Marketing in the International Environment,* 70–71.

**58.** "Ideas for the 1990s," *Fortune,* 26 March 1990, 128.

**59.** Gary Hamel, Yves L. Doz, and C. K. Prahalad, "Collaborate with Your Competitors—and Win," *Harvard Business Review,* January–February 1989, 133–139.

**60.** Louis Uchitelle, "Trade Barriers and Dollar Swings Raise Appeal of Factories Abroad," *New York Times,* 26 March 1989, sec. a, 1, 13.

**61.** Uchitelle, "Trade Barriers and Dollar Swings Raise Appeal of Factories Abroad," sec. c, 1, 5.

**62.** Thomas A. Stewart, "How to Manage in the New Era," *Fortune,* 15 January 1990, 58–59, 64, 68, 72.

**63.** Amy Borrus, "Slowly but Surely, the U.S. Is Buying into Japan," *Business Week,* 19 December 1988, 45.

**64.** Nulty, "How the World Will Change," 44–46, 50, 54.

**65.** Lee Smith, "Can You Make Any Money in Russia?" *Fortune,* 1 January 1990, 103.

**66.** Damon Darlin, "Blind Luck, Cartoon Help a U.S. Firm Sell Frozen Potato Products to Japanese," *Wall Street Journal,* 27 May 1987, 26.

**67.** Theodore Levitt, "The Globalization of Markets," in *Global Marketing Perspectives* (Cincinnati: South-Western Publishing, 1989), 2–16.

**68.** Joanne Lipman, "Marketers Turn Sour on Global Sales Pitch Harvard Guru Makes," *Wall Street Journal,* 1 February 1988, 1, 13.

**69.** Keith H. Hammonds, "Ted Levitt Is Back in the Trenches," *Business Week,* 9 April 1990, 82, 84; Levitt, "The Globalization of Markets," 2–16.

**70.** Kamran Kashani, "Beware the Pitfalls of Global Marketing," *Harvard Business Review,* September–October 1989, 91–98.

**71.** Christopher Elias, "A New Razor-Sharp Approach to Old-Fashioned Capitalism," *Insight,* 12 January 1987, 42–43.

**72.** Pete Engardio, "Hmm. Could Use a Little More Snake," *Business Week,* 15 March 1993, 53.

**73.** Patrick Oster, Gabrielle Saveri, and John Templemann, "The Eurosion of Brand Loyalty," *Business Week,* 19 July 1993, 22.

**74.** Martha H. Peak, "Avon's Calling: Now a Full-Service Resource for Women," *Management Review,* February 1993, 30–32.

**75.** H. Garrett DeYoung, "Learning the Ropes," *Inc.,* August 1988, 103–104, 106.

**76.** Brian Dumaine, "P&G Rewrites the Marketing Rules," *Fortune,* 6 November 1989, 34–36, 38, 40, 42, 46, 48.

**77.** Cateora, *International Marketing,* 562.

**78.** Cundiff and Hilger, *Marketing in the International Environment,* 458.

**79.** Cateora, *International Marketing,* 592.

**80.** Thane Peterson, Gail Schares, Maria Shao, and Maria Mallory, "Mike Armstrong Is Improving IBM's Game in Europe," *Business Week,* 20 June 1988, 96–97, 100–101; Jonathon B. Levine and Gail E. Schares, "IBM Europe Starts Swinging Back," *Business Week,* 6 May 1991, 52; Richard L. Hudson, "IBM Again Revamps European Sector," *Wall Street Journal,* 16 April 1991, B3A.

**81.** Donald Shoultz, "American Express Ready to Play Its Cards," *American Banker,* 25 July 1989, 19.

**82.** Lawrence M. Lesser, "Barter Is Best with Cash-Poor Russia," *New York Times,* 16 May 1993, 13; Stephen J. Simurda, "Opening in the East," *Adweek's Marketing Week,* 20 November 1989, 2–4.

**83.** See note 1.

## CHAPTER 21

**1.** Adapted from Phyllis Berman, "Trouble in Bean Land," *Forbes,* 6 July 1992, 42–44; Joseph Pereira, "L. L. Bean Scales Back Expansion Goals to Ensure Pride in Its Service Is Valid," *Wall Street Journal,* 31 July 1989, B3; Beverly Geber, "Training at L. L. Bean," *Training,* October 1988, 85–89; Richard D. Filley, "L. L. Bean's IEs Help Mail-Order Institution Handle Success While Holding onto Tradition," *Industrial Engineering,* June 1983, 46–58; Willis M. Rivinus, "Strength of a Personality Can Increase Prestige, Sales," *Direct Marketing,* January 1982, 54–57; Susan L. Smarr, "The 20th Century Paul Reveres," *Bobbin,* August 1989, 46, 48–50, 52, 54; "Improve Customer Service . . . Or Else," *Target Marketing,* June 1988, 31–32; "Service Makes a Comeback as a Way to Win and Keep Customers," *Profit–Building Strategies,* December 1987, 6–8; Rebecca Fannin, "Bean's Basics," *Marketing & Media Decisions,* July 1987, 20; John Skow, "Using the Old L. L. Bean," *Reader's Digest,* June 1986, 25–26, 29–30; William Henry, "Customer Satisfaction Is Key to Catalog Success," *Direct Marketing,* July 1980, 62–66; "L. L. Bean's Dedication to Service Sets the Standard," *Catalog Age,* September 1989, 127, 129; "L. L. Bean Sporting Specialties Instills Sense of Trust, Authority," *Catalog Age,* September 1989, 128–129; "L. L. Bean's Gold Award Equation: Formula + Reputation = Success," *Catalog Age,* September 1989, 193, 196; James S. Howard, "Quality Taking U.S. Business by Storm," *D&B Reports,* July–August 1985, 31, 42–44.

**2.** Stephen Philips, "King Customer," *Business Week,* 12 March 1990, 88–94.

3. Ron Zemke and Dick Schaaf, *The Service Edge: 101 Companies That Profit from Customer Care* (New York: New American Library, 1989), 50.

4. Cyndee Miller, "TQM's Value Criticized in New Report," *Marketing News,* 9 November 1992, 1, 16; Oren Harari, "Ten Reasons Why TQM Doesn't Work," *Management Review,* January 1993, 33–38; Ken Myers and Ron Ashkenas, "Results-Driven Quality . . . Now!" *Management Review,* March 1993, 40–44; Karl Albrecht, "No Eulogies for TQM," *TQM Magazine,* September–October 1992, 188–190.

5. Peter Glen, "That's Not My Department," *Success,* January–February 1991, 68–70.

6. William H. Davidow and Bro Uttal, *Total Customer Service: The Ultimate Weapon* (New York: Harper & Row, 1989), 21–22.

7. Zemke and Schaaf, *The Service Edge,* 90–91.

8. Davidow and Uttal, *Total Customer Service,* 104–105.

9. Mack Hanan and Peter Karp, *Customer Satisfaction* (New York: AMACOM, 1989), 22.

10. Thomas J. Peters and Robert H. Waterman, Jr., *In Search of Excellence* (New York: Warner Books, 1982), 182; Zemke and Schaaf, *The Service Edge,* 352.

11. David Altany, "The New Bottom Line," *Industry Week,* 22 January 1990, 12–13, 16–18, 20, 22; William H. Davidow, "The Ultimate Marketing Weapon," *Business Marketing,* October 1989, 56–57, 60, 62, 64.

12. Davidow and Uttal, *Total Customer Service,* 88–90.

13. Jerry Flint and William Heuslein, "An Urge to Service," *Forbes,* 18 September 1989, 172, 176.

14. Milind M. Lele, *The Customer Is Key* (New York: Wiley, 1987), 39–41.

15. Davidow and Uttal, *Total Customer Service,* 39.

16. Peters and Waterman, *In Search of Excellence,* 164–165.

17. Davidow and Uttal, *Total Customer Service,* 34–35.

18. Laura A. Liswood, "A New System for Rating Service Quality," *Journal of Business Strategy,* July–August 1989, 42–45.

19. Davidow and Uttal, *Total Customer Service,* 8; Valarie A. Zeithaml, A. Parasuraman, and Leonard L. Berry, *Delivering Quality Service* (New York: The Free Press, 1990), 9.

20. Peters and Waterman, *In Search of Excellence,* 174.

21. Lele, *The Customer Is Key,* 81–88.

22. "Treat Them Right," *Inc.,* October 1989, 131.

23. Davidow and Uttal, *Total Customer Service,* 43.

24. Davidow and Uttal, *Total Customer Service,* 212–213.

25. Hanan and Karp, *Customer Satisfaction,* 84.

26. Janet Endrijonas, "Acer Pres Says Taiwan-Bashing Ended," *Newsbytes,* 27 March 1990; Fred Langa, "Taiwan, the Soviet Union, and You, Part 2," *Byte,* October 1990, 10; "Altos Computer System to Join the Acer Group," *Business Wire,* 5 July 1990.

27. Endrijonas, "Acer Pres Says Taiwan-Bashing Ended"; Jim Dukowitz, "Texas Instruments Wins First Taiwan National Quality Award," *Business Wire,* 2 October 1990; Philip Liu, "Emperor of Taiwan's Computer Industry," *Electronic Business,* 15 October 1988, 96–97.

28. Davidow and Uttal, *Total Customer Service,* 179.

29. Harry Katzan, Jr., *Quality Circle Management* (Blue Ridge Summit, Pa.: Tab Books, 1989), 21.

30. "Quality Circles: Do They Work?" *Incentive,* May 1989, 71–77.

31. D. Keith Denton, "The Service Imperative," *Personnel Journal,* March 1990, 66, 68–71, 74.

32. Zemke and Schaaf, *The Service Edge,* 18.

33. Hanan and Karp, *Customer Satisfaction,* 25–33. These six attributes are a composite of eight attributes identified by Hanan and Karp.

34. "Not by Jeans Alone," video produced by WGBT–TV, Boston, 1981.

35. Linda M. Lash, *The Complete Guide to Customer Service* (New York: Wiley, 1989), 139–140; Charles A. Jaffe, "Guaranteed Results," *Nation's Business,* February 1990, 62–65; Dave Zielinski, "Improving Service Doesn't Require a Big Investment," *Small Business Reports,* February 1991, 15–20.

36. Hanan and Karp, *Customer Satisfaction,* 36–37.

37. Lash, *The Complete Guide to Customer Service,* 154.

38. Michael LeBoeuf, *How to Win Customers and Keep Them for Life* (New York: Putnam, 1987), 56.

39. Francine Schwadel, "Shoppers' Blues: The Thrill Is Gone," *Wall Street Journal,* 13 October 1989, B1–B2.

40. Davidow and Uttal, *Total Customer Service,* 59.

41. Zemke and Schaaf, *The Service Edge,* 39–40.

42. Glenn DeSouza, "Now Service Businesses Must Manage Quality," *Journal of Business Strategy,* May–June 1989, 21–25; personal communication with Richard Wendt, Quality Assurance Manager, Swissair, 1991.

43. Mark Stuart Gill, "Stalking Six Sigma," *Business Month,* January 1990, 42–46.

44. Minda Zetlin, "When 99 Percent Isn't Enough," *Management Review,* March 1993, 49–52.

45. Davidow and Uttal, *Total Customer Service,* 93–94; Godfrey Deeny, James Fallon, Jean MacIntosh, Holly Haber, and Skippy Lawson, "At the Counter," *Women's Wear Daily,* 7 June 1991, F82.

46. Davidow and Uttal, *Total Customer Service,* 104.

47. Zeithaml, Parasuraman, and Berry, *Delivering Quality Service,* 105.

48. Diane Feldman, "Quality Chitchat, Chickens, and Customer Service," *Management Review,* May 1989, 8–9.

49. Zemke and Schaaf, *The Service Edge,* 70–76.

50. Technical Assistance Research Programs Institute, "Consumer Complaint Handling in America: An Update Study," 1 April 1986, executive summary, 2–4.

51. Howard Schlossberg, "Measuring Customer Satisfaction Is Easy to Do—Until You Try It," *Marketing News,* 26 April 1993, 5, 8.

52. Todd M. Helmeke, "Customer Satisfaction Is a Myth for Many Companies," *Marketing News,* 7 June 1993, 4.

53. Davidow and Uttal, *Total Customer Service,* 16.

54. "Consumer Complaint Handling in America: An Update Study," 2–4; Jerry Plymire, "What We Need Are More Complaints," *Business Marketing,* March 1990, 74.

55. Craig Cina, "Creating an Effective Customer Satisfaction Program," *Journal of Consumer Marketing,* Fall 1989, 31–40.

56. See note 1.

57. Adapted from Barbara Wright, "How to Beat Out Big-Name Competition," *Working Woman,* May 1988, 55–57.

## CHAPTER 22

1. Adapted from Tim Clark, "Marketing Key to HP's Battle Plan," *Business Marketing,* May 1993, 15–16; Lance Knobel, "Hewlett-Packard's Culture Shock," *Management Today,* June 1988, 100–106; Jonathan B. Levine, "Mild-Mannered Hewlett-Packard Is Making Like Superman," *Business Week,* 7 March 1988, 110–111, 114; Mike Bucken, "NewWave' Leads Marketing Drive," *Software Magazine,* November 1988, 33; Thayer C. Taylor, "Hewlett-Packard Gives Sales Reps a Competitive Edge," *Sales & Marketing Management,* February 1987, 36–41.

2. Laurence Hooper, "High-Tech Gamble: Xerox Tries to Shed Its Has-Been Image with Big New Machine," *Wall Street Journal,* 20 September 1990, A1, A8.

3. Pack Bryan, "Power Marketing from the Top," *Business Marketing,* March 1993, 22–24; Thomas V. Bonoma, "Making Your Marketing Strategy Work," *Harvard Business Review,* March–April 1984, 69–76.

4. Tom Eisenhart, "Eaton: Clearing the Clutter," *Business Marketing,* January 1989, 36–38.

5. "Dillard's Out to Change New Orleans' Shopping Habits," *New Orleans CitiBusiness,* November 1989, B1.

6. Jan Carlzon, *Moments of Truth* (New York: Harper & Row, 1989), 59–74.

7. Lisa Marie Petersen, "Mazda, Reorganized: Closer to Dealers," *Brandweek,* 31 May 1993, 22–23.

8. John Bussey and Douglas R. Sease, "Manufacturers Strive to Slice Time Needed to Develop Products," *Wall Street Journal,* 23 February 1988, 1, 24.

9. Catherine Arnst and Bart Ziegler, "A Freewheeling Youngster Named IBM," *Business Week,* 3 May 1993, 134–138.

10. John M. Verity and Geoff Lewis, "Big Changes at Big Blue," *Business Week,* 15 February 1988, 92–96.

11. Wilber J. Prezzano, "Kodak Sharpens Its Focus on Quality," *Management Review,* May 1989, 39–41.

12. Rosabeth Moss Kanter, *The Change Masters: Innovation and Entrepreneurship in the American Corporation* (New York: Simon & Schuster, 1984), 172–174.

13. Steven Lysonski, Alan Signer, and David Wilemon, "Coping with Environmental Uncertainty and Boundary Spanning in the Product Manager's Role," *Journal of Product and Brand Management,* Spring 1992, 25–36.

14. Judith S. Riddle, "P&G Mulls Brand Re-Org, Bigtime Cuts, in July," *Brandweek,* 26 April 1993, 1, 6; Judith S. Riddle, "Brand Alert: P&G Mulls Fate of More Big Brands," *Brandweek,* 24 May l993, 1, 6.

15. Valerie Rice, "The Making of a New TI," *Electronic Business,* 17 April 1989, 26–32.

16. Aimee Stern, "General Foods' Strategy for Tomorrow," *Dun's Business Month,* May 1985, 48–49, 52–53.

17. Russell Mitchell and Judith H. Dobrzynski, "Jack Welch: How Good a Manager?" *Business Week,* 14 December 1987, 92–96, 98, 102–103.

18. Rachel Parker, "Apple Reorganizes to Widen Business Appeal," *InfoWorld,* 11 July 1988, 51.

19. Patricia Winters, "Pepsi Refocuses with New Structure," *Advertising Age,* 28 September 1992, 3, 47.

20. Howard Kim, "Growth Through Coordination," *Modern Healthcare,* 21 April 1989, 37–38, 42–43.

21. Joan Bergmann, "The Saga of Sam Walton," *Stores,* January 1988, 129–142.

22. N. V. Philips, Gloeilamfabrieken, Annual Report, 1989.

23. Allan McGrath, "The Management of Mar-

keting Productivity," *Journal of Business and Industrial Marketing,* Fall 1992, 49–54.

**24.** Glenn Withiam, "Unchained Melody: How Independent Hotels Work in Harmony," *Cornell Hotel & Restaurant Administration Quarterly,* August 1987, 77–80.

**25.** Philip Kotler and Alan R. Andreasen, *Strategic Marketing for Nonprofit Organizations* (Englewood Cliffs, N.J.: Prentice-Hall, 1990), 275–276.

**26.** Frederick E. Webster, Jr., "The Changing Role of Marketing in the Corporation," *Journal of Marketing,* October 1992, 1–17.

**27.** Bonoma, "Making Your Marketing Strategy Work," 69–76.

**28.** Robert W. Ruekert and Orville C. Walker, Jr., "Marketing's Interaction with Other Functional Units: A Conceptual Framework and Empirical Evidence," *Journal of Marketing,* January 1987, 1–19.

**29.** Patrick M. Dunne and Harry I. Wolk, "Marketing Cost Analysis: A Modularized Contribution Approach," *Journal of Marketing,* July 1977, 83–94.

**30.** John A. Quelch, Paul W. Farris, and James Olver, "The Product Management Audit: Design and Survey Findings," *Journal of Product and Brand Management,* Spring 1992, 5–18; Philip Kotler, William Gregor, and William Rogers, "The Marketing Audit Comes of Age," *Sloan Management Review,* Winter 1977, 25–43.

**31.** Tom Eisenhart, "You're Talking–But Are They Listening?" *Business Marketing,* January 1989, 30–33, 36–38; John A. Quelch, Paul W. Farris, and James Olver, "The Product Management Audit: Design and Survey Findings," *Journal of Consumer Marketing,* Summer 1987, 45–58; John A. Quelch, Paul W. Farris, and James Olver, "The Product Management Audit," *Harvard Business Review,* March–April 1987, 30, 32, 36.

**32.** See note 1.

## CHAPTER 1

**11 Techniques for Marketing Success:** Pierre Thomas, "Blind Steer the Sighted Along Victory's Path: Braille Sports Car Rally Is Fast, Fun," *Washington Post,* 20 September 1992, sec. b, 3; Fran Jordan, "Summer Camping by Touch," *Washington Post,* 4 May 1993, sec. z, 13; "Lighthouse Flashes with Jobs, New Products," *Puget Sound Business Journal,* 19 December 1988, 1, 22; "Lighthouse for Blind Wins Contract to Sew Sweat Pants for U.S. Army," *San Antonio Business Journal,* 2 April 1990, 8; Michael Conlan, "Marketing for Non-Profit Success," *Fund Raising Management,* August 1988, 48–52. Reprinted with permission of Fund Raising Management Magazine.

**13 Marketing in Action:** Marcy Magiera, "Spike Lee Gets in Front of Camera for Nike," *Advertising Age,* 25 May 1992, 2, 50; Mark Landler, "Spike Lee Does a Lot of Things Right," *Business Week,* 6 August 1990, 62–63; "Hitting the Hot Button: Spike Lee—Artist Who Best Captured the Ethnic Experience in America," *U.S. News and World Report,* 9 July 1990, 52; Richard Gold, "Spike Lee's Latest Does the Lucrative Thing," *Variety,* 5 July 1989, 5.

**26 Video Case:** Adapted from Michael Garry, "Fast Friends," *Progressive Grocer,* March 1993, 10; Milford Prewitt, "McD Rewards, Researches 'Frequent Customers,'" *Nation's Restaurant News,* 1 June 1992, 7, 89; Richard Gibson and Robert Johnson, "Big Mac Plots Strategy to Regain Sizzle," *Wall Street Journal,* 29 September 1989, B1; John F. Love, "Behind the Arches—Author Love Chronicles McDonald's Claim to Fame," *Advertising Age,* 8 December 1986, 41; Brian Bremner, "McDonald's Stoops to Conquer," *Business Week,* 30 October 1989, 120, 124; Brian Bremner, "The Burger Wars Were Just a Warmup for McDonald's," *Business Week,* 8 May 1989, 67, 70; Robert Johnson, "Fast-Food Leader: McDonald's Combines a Dead Man's Advice with Lively Strategy," *Wall Street Journal,* 18 December 1987, 1, 12; "Event Mentality," *Restaurant Hospitality,* May 1989, 174, 176, 177; Dan Koeppel, "Reversing Course, McDonald's Plans Big McChanges," *Adweek's Marketing Week,* 3 December 1990, 4.

## CHAPTER 2

**34 Exhibit 2.4:** Thomas G. Exter, "Baby Boom Incomes." Reprinted with permission. © *American Demographics,* November 1987, 62.

**37 Exhibit 2.6:** Adapted from Warren J. Keegan, *Global Marketing Management* (Englewood Cliffs, N. J.: Prentice-Hall, 1989), 89. Adapted by permission of Prentice-Hall.

**38 Exhibit 2.7:** Adapted from "Where Global Growth Is Going," *Fortune,* 31 July 1989, 92. © 1989 The Time Inc. Magazine Company. All rights reserved.

**40–41 Marketing in Action:** Melanie Rigney, "Matter of Semantics—or of Survival?" *Advertising Age,* 29 June 1992, S-2, S-9; Dennis Chase and Therese Kauchak Smith, "Consumers Keen on Green but Marketers Don't Deliver," *Advertising Age,* 29 June 1992, S-2, S-4; Debra Aho, "Be Precise; Don't Overstate Claims," *Advertising Age,* 29 June 1992, S-6; Michael Parrish, "FTC Issues Guidelines for Green Marketing," *Los Angeles Times,* 29 July 1992, sec. d, 1; "Research Group Says Some Green Marketers Are Only Pretending," *Marketing News,* 20 January 1992, 3; Lynette Lamb, "Eliminating Plastics," *Utne Reader,* November–December 1989, 30; Michael Waldholz, "New Plastic Is Promoted as a Natural," *Wall Street Journal,* 24 January 1990, sec. b, 1, 2; Randolph B. Smith, "Plastics Industry Mulls Campaign to Woo Public," *Wall Street Journal,* 15 January 1990, 5A; Brian Bremner, "A New Sales Pitch: The Environment," *Business Week,* 24 July 1989, 50; Debbie Goldberg, "Du Pont Gets Patent for Freon Substitute That Can Be Used in Existing Machinery," *Wall Street Journal,* 31 January 1989, B4.

**41 Exhibit 2.9:** Eben Shapiro, "Food Labs Gaze Hungrily at Potential in Labeling Rules," *Wall Street Journal,* 10 December 1992, B2; Richard M. Steuer, *A Guide to Marketing Law: What Every Seller Should Know* (New York: Harcourt Brace Jovanovich, 1986), 4–6, 143, 156–157.

**43 Exhibit 2.10:** Kenneth Howe, " 'Reregulation' Is Watchword of '90s," *San Francisco Chronicle,* 2 January 1990, sec. c, 1, 6, 7. © *San Francisco Chronicle.* Reprinted by permission.

**53 Exhibit 2.15:** Introducing Membership Application, American Marketing Association; obtained 16 August 1990. Reprinted by permission.

**54–55 Ethical Dilemma in Marketing:** John A. Byrne, "Can Ethics Be Taught? Harvard Gives It the Old College Try," *Business Week,* 6 April 1992, 34; Jay Halfond, "Should Business Schools Be Sunday Schools?" *Business & Society Review,* Winter 1990, 54–55; George L. Pamental, "The Course in Business Ethics: Can It Work?" *Journal of Business Ethics,* July 1989, 547–551; Jeffrey Gandz and Nadine Hayes, "Teaching Business Ethics," *Journal of Business Ethics,* September 1988, 657–669; Gary A. Luoma, "Can Ethics Be Taught?" *Business & Economic Review,* October–December 1989, 3–5; Derek Bok, "Can Higher Education Foster Higher Morals?" *Business & Society Review,* Summer 1988, 4–12.

**62 Video Case:** Adapted from George Gendron and Stephen D. Solomon, "The Art of Loving," *Inc.,* May 1989, 35–46; Borge Obel, "SAS: Changes in Competition, Strategy, and Organization," *Technovation* 5 (1986): 145–153; Carole A. Shifrin, "Marketing Pacts, Equity Agreements Bring World's Airlines Closer Together," *Aviation Week & Space Technology,* 18 December 1989, 67, 69; Jonathan Kapstein, "Can SAS Keep Flying with the Big Birds?" *Business Week,* 27 November 1989, 142, 146; Karl Albrecht and Ron Zemke, *Service America!* (New York: Warner Books, 1985), 20–27; Jan Carlzon, "We Fly People, Not Planes," *Across the Board,* June 1987, 19–23.

## CHAPTER 3

**71 Exhibit 3.4:** Adapted from *The Product Portfolio* (Boston: Boston Consulting Group, 1970).

**72 Exhibit 3.5:** Adapted from Derek F. Abell and John S. Hammond, *Strategic Market Planning: Problems and Analytical Approaches* (Englewood Cliffs, N.J.: Prentice-Hall, 1979), © 1979, p. 214. Adapted by permission of Prentice-Hall, Englewood Cliffs, New Jersey.

**73 Exhibit 3.6:** Adapted from David J. Luck, O. C. Ferrell, and George H. Lucas, Jr., *Marketing Strategy and Plans* (Englewood Cliffs, N.J.: Prentice-Hall, 1989), 378. From Derek F. Abell and John S. Hammond, *Strategic Market Planning: Problems and Analytical Approaches* (Englewood Cliffs, N.J.: Prentice-Hall, 1979), © 1979, p. 213. Adapted by permission of Prentice-Hall, Englewood Cliffs, New Jersey.

**74 Exhibit 3.7:** Adapted from H. Igor Ansoff, *The New Corporate Strategy* (New York: Wiley, 1988), 83. Reprinted by permission of the author.

**75 Marketing in Action:** Adapted from Edmund O. Lawler, "A Window of Opportunity," *Business Marketing,* January 1991, 16. Reprinted with permission. Copyright © Crain Communications, Inc. All rights reserved.

**84–85 Techniques for Marketing Success:** Adapted from Donald R. Lehman and Russell S. Winer, *Analysis for Marketing Planning* (Homewood, Ill.: BPI Irwin, 1988), 163–165; Pierre Wack, "Scenarios: Uncharted Waters Ahead," *Harvard Business Review,* September–October 1985, 72–89; Pierre Wack, "Scenarios: Shooting the Rapids," *Harvard Business Review,* November–December 1985, 139–150.

**94 Video Case:** Adapted from Carol Kennedy, "How Marriott Corporation Grew Fivefold in Ten Years," *Long Range Planning,* 21 (1988): 10–14; Christopher Muller, "The Marriott Divestment: Leaving the Past Behind," *Cornell Hotel & Restaurant Administration Quarterly,* February 1990, 7–13; Faye Rice, "Hotels Fight for Business Guests," *Fortune,* 23 April 1990, 265–273; Janet Novack, "Tea, Sympathy, and Direct Mail," *Forbes,* 18 September, 1989, 210–211; "New Division Opens to Market Golf Management Services," *Washington Business Journal,* 2 April 1990, 13; Frank E. Camacho, "Meeting the Needs of Senior Citizens Through Lifecare Communities: Marriott's Approach to the Development of a New Service Business," *Journal of Services Marketing,* Winter 1988, 49–53.

## COMPONENT CHAPTER A

**96–101** General information about marketing plans adapted from Roman G. Heibing, Jr., and Scott W. Cooper, *How to Write a Successful Marketing Plan* (Lincolnwood, Ill.: NTC Business Books, 1990), 297–338; David S. Hopkins, *The Marketing Plan* (New York: The Conference Board, 1981), 16–29 (Fidelity Bank example, pp. 63–64). All information related to The Shirt Off My Back is fictional.

**102–103:** Adapted from David Kirkpatrick, "Could AT&T Rule the World?" *Fortune,* 17 May 1993, 54; Gary Slutsker, "The Tortoise and the Hare," *Forbes,* 1 February 1992, 66; Alan Chai, Alta Cambell, and Patrick J. Spain, eds., *Hoover's Handbook of American Business 1992* (Austin, Tex.: The Reference Press, 1992), 104.

## CHAPTER 4

**110 Exhibit 4.3:** Figures adapted from James F. Engel, Roger D. Blackwell, and Paul W. Miniard, *Consumer Behavior,* 6th ed. (Chicago: Dryden, 1990), 474. Copyright © 1990 by The Dryden Press, reproduced by permission of the publisher.

**112 Exhibit 4.5:** Adapted from Leon G. Schiffman and Leslie Lazar Kanuk, *Consumer Behavior* (Englewood Cliffs, N.J.: Prentice-Hall, 1987), 209. Copyright © 1987. Adapted by permission of Prentice-Hall, Englewood Cliffs, New Jersey.

**115 Exhibit 4.6:** Adapted from Abraham H. Maslow, *Motivation and Personality,* 2d ed. (New York: Harper & Row, 1970), 80. Copyright 1954 by Harper & Row, Publishers Inc. Copyright © 1970 by Abraham H. Maslow. Reprinted by permission of HarperCollins Publishers, Inc.

**116 Exhibit 4.7:** Adapted from Del I. Hawkins, Roger J. Best, and Kenneth A. Coney, *Consumer Behavior* (Homewood, Ill.: BPI/Irwin, 1989), 396. Copyright © 1989 Richard D. Irwin, Inc. Reprinted by permission.

**120 Exhibit 4.9:** From Michael R. Solomon, *Consumer Behavior* (Needham Heights, Mass.: Allyn & Bacon, 1992), 115. Copyright © 1992 by Allyn & Bacon. Reprinted by permission.

**126–127 Exploring Global Marketing:** Adapted from Warren Strugatch, "Make Way for the Euroconsumer," *World Trade,* February 1993,

46–50; E. S. Browning, "In Pursuit of the Elusive Euroconsumer," *Wall Street Journal,* 23 April 1992, B1, B9; "European Youth: The Bridge to a Harmonized European Market," *Market: Europe,* Fall 1991, 1–12.

**128 Map:** Adapted from "Dutch Women: The Individualization Trend," *Market: Europe,* December 1990, 3–4.

**130–131 Ethical Dilemma in Marketing:** Adapted from "The Kiddie Marketing Boom," *Kiplinger's Personal Finance Magazine,* April 1993, 17; "Food Makers Hunger for Younger Market," *Insight,* 18 June 1990, 43; Patricia Sellers, "The ABC's of Marketing to Kids," *Fortune,* 8 May 1989, 114–116, 120; David J. Morrow, "Picking Junior's Pocket," *The Marketer,* May 1990, 20–25; Kim Foltz, "Kids as Consumers: Teaching Our Children Well," *Adweek,* 30 November 1987, 40; Noreen O'Leary, "Study Portrays Children as Complex, Savvy Media Mavens," *Adweek,* 30 November 1987, 42; "Selling to Children," *Consumer Reports,* August 1990, 518–521; Susan Dillingham, "The Classroom as a Marketing Tool," *Insight,* 24 September 1990, 40–41.

**133 Exhibit 4.14:** Adapted from Richard P. Coleman, "The Continuing Significance of Social Class to Marketing," *Journal of Consumer Research* 10 (December 1983): 267. Copyright © 1979 by The University of Chicago Press. Reprinted by permission.

**134 Exhibit 4.15:** Adapted from Patrick E. Murphy and William A. Staples, "A Modernized Family Life Cycle," *Journal of Consumer Research,* June 1979, 17. Copyright © 1979 by The University of Chicago Press. Reprinted by permission.

**140 Video Case:** Adapted from Nicholas di Talamo, "Getting U.S. Catalogs into Europe," *Direct Marketing,* December 1992, 21–24; "Database Marketing," *Catalog Age,* May 1988, 85–97; Melissa Della Posta, "Database Marketing: Do You Know Who Your Customers Are?" *Catalog Age,* August 1990, 63; "New Chairman for Russell Hobbs Tower," *Financial Times,* 30 May 1990, 48; Clay Harris, "Man in the News: Living in Shadows of Bright Things in the Past—David Jones," *Financial Times,* 14 April 1990, 6.

## CHAPTER 5

**145 Exhibit 5.1:** Adapted from *Statistical Abstract of the United States 1990* (Washington, D.C.: GPO, 1990), 272, 521.

**146 Exhibit 5.2:** Adapted from *Statistical Abstract of the United States 1990* (Washington, D.C.: GPO, 1990), 741, 1378.

**148–149 Ethical Dilemma in Marketing:** Adapted from Frederick Kempe, "Supplying Saddam: Germans Had Big Role in Helping Iraq Arm, Internal Reports Show," *Wall Street Journal,* 2 October 1990, A1, A18; Peter F. Kalitka, "Export Control: Who's in Charge?" *Security Management,* March 1985, 42–44; W. Seth Carus, "Technology Transfer: Profits vs. Security in Exports to the Third World," *Directors & Boards,* Fall 1989, 43–44.

**154 Techniques for Marketing Success:** Adapted from John R. Graham, "How to Keep Customers Coming Back," *Business Marketing,* June 1989, 96–95. Copyright Crain Communications, Inc. All rights reserved.

**168 Video Case:** Adapted from Stephen Phillips and John W. Verity, "NCR Is Finding Out That No Strategy Works Forever," *Business Week,* 30 January 1989, 80–81; Geoffrey Colvin, "The Wee Outfit That Decked IBM," *Fortune,* 19 November 1990, 165, 168; Maria Mallory, "Will This ATM Team Be a Money Machine?" *Business Week,* 17 September 1990, 142; Robert Bruce Slater, "Cancel the Wake: The Resurrection of the ATM,"

*Bankers Monthly,* March 1988, 52–53; Gary Hoover, Alta Campbell, and Patrick J. Spain, eds., *Hoover's Handbook 1991: Profiles of Over 500 Major Corporations* (Austin, Tex.: The Reference Press, 1990), 397; Gilbert P. Williamson, "At NCR It Is the Sixth Sense That Is Counted On," *Business Month,* April 1989, 104.

## CHAPTER 6

**173 Exhibit 6.1:** Adapted from Harper W. Boyd, Jr., Ralph Westfall, and Stanley F. Stasch, *Marketing Research: Text and Cases* (Homewood, Ill.: Irwin, 1989), 13. Copyright © 1989 Richard D. Irwin, Inc. Reprinted by permission.

**182 Exhibit 6.7:** Adapted from U.S. Bureau of the Census, *Guide to the 1987 Economic Censuses and Related Statistics* (Washington, D.C.: GPO, 1990), 1, 3, 93, 96.

**185 Exhibit 6.10:** Adapted from Harper W. Boyd, Jr., Ralph Westfall, and Stanley F. Stasch, *Marketing Research: Text and Cases* (Homewood, Ill.: Irwin, 1989) 222. Reprinted by permission of Market Facts, Inc., 1989.

**185 Exhibit 6.11:** Adapted from Harper W. Boyd, Jr., Ralph Westfall, and Stanley F. Stasch, *Market Research: Text and Cases* (Homewood, Ill.: Irwin, 1989), 223; Donald R. Lehmann, *Market Research and Analysis* (Homewood, Ill.: Irwin, 1989), 162. Copyright © 1989 Richard D. Irwin, Inc. Reprinted by permission.

**187 Exhibit 6.12:** Courtesy of Hewlett-Packard Company.

**190 Exploring Global Marketing:** Adapted from Jane Rippeteau, "Where's Ft. Wayne When You Need It?" *The Marketer,* July–August 1990, 46–49.

**191 Exhibit 6.13:** Adapted from Thomas C. Kinnear and Ann R. Root, *Survey of Marketing Research 1988* (Chicago: American Marketing Association, 1989), 43. Reprinted by permission of the American Marketing Association.

**192 Exhibit 6.14:** Adapted from Jack Honomichl, "The Jack Honomichl 50," supplement to *Marketing News,* 7 June 1993.

**195 Ethical Dilemma in Marketing:** Adapted from R. C. Baker, Roger Dickinson, and Stanley Hollander, "Big Brother 1994: Marketing Data and the IRS," *Journal of Public Policy & Marketing* 5 (1986): 231; "Is Nothing Private?" *Business Week,* 4 September 1989, 74–82; "Privacy vs. Speech," *Direct Marketing,* May 1989, 42; Robert J. Posch, Jr., "Can We Have à la Carte Constitutional Rights?" *Direct Marketing,* July 1989, 76.

**200 Video Case:** Adapted from Eric Fountain, Ian Parker, and John Samuels, "The Contribution of Research to General Motors' Corporate Communications Strategy in the UK," *Journal of the Market Research Society* 28, no. 1 (January 1986): 25–42; Daniel Ward, "Tough Battle for Top Marques," *Business,* September 1990, 6–7; Gary Hoover, Alta Campbell, and Patrick J. Spain, eds., *Hoover's Handbook 1991: Profiles of Over 500 Major Corporations* (Austin, Tex.: The Reference Press, 1990), 225; Milton Moskowitz, Robert Levering, and Michael Katz, eds., *Everybody's Business* (New York: Doubleday, 1990), 233–236.

## CHAPTER 7

**206 Ethical Dilemma in Marketing:** Adapted from James R. Schiffman, "After Uptown, Are Some Niches Out?" *Wall Street Journal,* 22 January 1990, B1; Michael Specter, "Reynolds Cancels Plan to Market New Cigarette," *Washington Post,* 20 January 1990, A3; Michael Specter, "Sullivan Denounces Reynolds Tobacco," *Washington Post,* 19 January 1990, A1; Judann Dagnoli, "RJR's Dakota Test Faces Counterattack," *Advertising*

*Age,* 12 March 1990, 6; Howard Schlossberg, "Segmenting Becomes Constitutional Issue," *Marketing News,* 16 April 1990, 1–2.

**209 Exhibit 7.3:** Adapted from U.S. Bureau of the Census, *Guide to the 1987 Economic Censuses and Related Statistics* (Washington, D.C.: GPO, 1990), 14–15.

**212 Exhibit 7.4:** From Rebecca Piirto, *Beyond Mind Games: The Marketing Power of Psychographics* (New York: American Demographics Books, 1991), 79–90. Copyright © 1991 American Demographics Books. Reprinted by permission.

**214 Exhibit 7.5:** "America's 40 Neighborhood Types" Michael J. Weiss, from *The Clustering of America* (New York: Harper & Row, Tilden Press, 1988), 4–5. Copyright © 1988 by Michael J. Weiss. Reprinted by permission of HarperCollins Publishers.

**216 Marketing in Action:** Adapted from Winston Williams, "What's New in Marketing Black Colleges: From Oligopoly to Brash Competition," *New York Times,* 13 March 1988, sec. 3, 13; Errol T. Louis, "Marketing Colleges," *Black Enterprise,* November 1986, 24; Mark Russell, "The Push to Make Black Business Competitive," *Black Enterprise,* June 1987, 259–268.

**217 Exhibit 7.6:** Adapted from Art Weinstein, *Market Segmentation: Using Niche Marketing to Exploit New Markets* (Chicago: Probus, 1987), 148. Reprinted by permission of Probus Publishing, Inc.

**218 Exhibit 7.7:** 1987 Standard Industrial Classification Manual, U.S. Office of Management and Budget.

**219 Exhibit 7.8:** Adapted from *The Corporate Technology Directory,* 1989 U.S. edition, published by Corporate Technology Information Services, pages 1–697.

**225 Exhibit 7.11:** Adapted from Glen L. Urban, John R. Hauser, and Nikhilesh Dholakia, *Essentials of New Product Development* (Englewood Cliffs, N.J.: Prentice-Hall, 1987), 105. Adapted by permission of Prentice-Hall.

**232 Video Case:** Adapted from Subrata N. Chakravarty, "A Credit Card Is Not a Commodity," *Forbes,* 16 October 1989, 128–130; "American Express Finds Breakthrough Mail Response," *Direct Marketing,* January 1985, 48–55; Patrick M. Reilly, "Time Cover-Story Ads," *Wall Street Journal,* 20 December 1989, B6; Helene Duffy, "Marketing for Survival: Credit Card Strategies for the '90s," *Bank Management,* April 1990, 47; "American Express Launches Its First Multi-Media Direct Response Campaign Targeted to Small Businesses," PR Newswire, 6 September 1988; Amy Borrus, "The U.S. Is Getting Japan Hooked on Plastic," *Business Week,* 25 May 1987, 100, 104; Jon Friedman and John Meehan, "Can Amex Win the Masses—and Keep Its Class?" *Business Week,* 9 October 1989, 134.

**234–235:** Adapted from Rita Koselka, "A Tight Ship," *Forbes,* 20 July 1992, 141, 144; Amy Barrett and Zachary Schiller, "At Carnation, Nestlé Makes the Very Best . . . Cutbacks," *Business Week,* 22 March 1993, 54; Stan Rapp and Thomas L. Collins, "Nestlé Banks on Databases," *Advertising Age,* 25 October 1993, 16, S7, S10; Alan Chai, Alta Cambell, and Patrick J. Spain, eds., *Hoover's Handbook of World Business 1993* (Austin, Tex.: The Reference Press, 1993), 342–343.

## CHAPTER 8

**244 Exhibit 8.3:** Adapted from Patrick E. Murphy and Ben M. Enis, "Classifying Products Strategically," *Journal of Marketing,* July 1986, 25. Reprinted by permission of the American Marketing Association.

**246 Exhibit 8.4:** Adapted from John M. Murphy, ed., *Branding: A Key Marketing Tool* (New York: McGraw-Hill, 1987), 96. Reprinted by permission of The Macmillan Press Ltd.

**248 Exhibit 8.5:** Reprinted by permission of The Minnesota Orchestra.

**254 Exploring Global Marketing:** Adapted from "Taiwan Cracks Down on Counterfeit Products," *San Jose Mercury News,* 13 December 1987, sec. e, 10; "Fake Software in Taiwan," *New York Times,* 18 October 1990, D10; Philip R. Cateora, *International Marketing* (Homewood, Ill.: Irwin, 1987), 383; Edward Cundiff and Marye Tharp Hilger, *Marketing in the International Environment* (Englewood Cliffs, N.J.: Prentice-Hall, 1988), 422.

**259 Ethical Dilemma in Marketing:** Adapted from Tracy E. Benson, "Product Liability: Deep Waters to Debate," *Industry Week,* 6 August 1990, 46–63; Marisa Manley, "Product Liability: You're More Exposed than You Think," *Harvard Business Review,* September–October 1987, 28–40; "Limits to Liability," *San Diego Union,* 1 October 1990, B6; Marisa L. Manley, "Controlling Product Liability," *Inc.,* February 1987, 103–107; Gail Greco, "Product Liability Bill on Its Way," *Entrepreneur,* October 1990, 192–193.

**264 Video Case:** Adapted from Peter Nulty, "The Bounce Is Back at Goodyear," *Fortune,* 7 September 1992, 70–72; Zachary Schiller, "Goodyear Feels the Heat," *Business Week,* 7 March 1988, 26–28; Subrata N. Chakravarty, "Back to Basics," *Forbes,* 21 September 1987, 40–41; The Goodyear Tire & Rubber Company 1989 Annual Report, 6, 8–10, 18, 36, 47; "Attitude Research Assesses Global Market Potential," *Marketing News,* 1 August 1988, 10; Gregory Stricharchuk, "Michelin, Goodyear Market Share to Rise Sharply with GM in Firestone Phase-Out," *Wall Street Journal,* 8 August 1988, 4; Bob Toth, "Marketing High-Performance Tires," *Modern Tire Dealer,* May 1988, G10–G11; "The OE Connection," *Modern Tire Dealer,* May 1988, G6–G7.

## CHAPTER 9

**272 Marketing in Action:** Adapted from Paul B. Brown, "The Product Is the Message," *Inc.,* June 1990, 104–105. Reprinted with permission, *Inc.* Magazine. Copyright 1990, by Goldhirsh Group, Inc., 38 Commercial Wharf, Boston, MA 02110.

**273 Exhibit 9.4:** Adapted from Charles D. Schewe, *Marketing: Principles and Strategy* (New York: McGraw-Hill, 1987), 294. Reprinted by permission of McGraw-Hill, Inc.

**274–275 Marketing in Action:** Adapted from N. K. Khalla and Sonia S. Yuspeh, "Forget the Product Life Cycle Concept," *Harvard Business Review,* January-February 1976, 102–112. Copyright © 1976 by the President and Fellows of Harvard College; all rights reserved.

**277 Exhibit 9.5:** Adapted from an exhibit from Nariman K. Dhalla and Sonia S. Yuspeh, "Forget the Product Life Cycle Concept," *Harvard Business Review,* January–February 1976, 102–112. Copyright © 1975 by the President and Fellows of Harvard College; all rights reserved. Reprinted by permission of *Harvard Business Review.*

**281 Exhibit 9.8:** Adapted from Robert G. Cooper, *Winning at New Products* (Reading, Mass.: Addison-Wesley, 1986), 103. Copyright © 1986 by Holt, Rinehart and Winston of Canada. Reprinted with permission of Addison-Wesley Publishing Co. Also adapted from Burton V. Dean, *Evaluating Selection and Controlling R&D Project.* Reprinted, by permission of publisher, from *AMA Research Study,* 1968 © 1968. American Management Association, New York. All rights reserved.

**283 Exhibit 9.9:** Adapted from Rodger L. DeRose, "New Products—Sifting Through the Haystack," *Journal of Consumer Marketing,* Summer 1986, 83. Reprinted by permission of Marketing Journals Publishing Co.

**284 Exhibit 9.10:** Adapted from Robert G. Cooper, *Winning at New Products,* 2d ed. (Reading, Mass.: Addison-Wesley, 1993), 156. Copyright © 1993 by Addison-Wesley Publishing Company, Inc. Reprinted by permission of the publishers.

**296 Video Case:** Adapted from Thomas H. Klier, "How Lean Manufacturing Changes the Way We Understand the Manufacturing Sector," *Economic Perspectives,* May–June 1993, 2–9; Alex Taylor III, "New Ecomobiles," *Fortune,* 4 October 1993, 14, 18; Jerry Flint, "Volume Be Damned," *Forbes,* 12 April 1993, 52–53; David Woodruff and Elizabeth Lesly, "Surge at Chrysler; Once Again, It's Roaring Back from Oblivion," *Business Week,* 9 November 1992, 88–96; Brian S. Moskal, "Chrysler's on the Road Again," *Industry Week,* 19 October 1992, 68–76; Wilton Woods, "The World's Top Automakers Change Lanes," *Fortune,* 4 October 1993, 73–75; James Flanagan, "Back from Repair, U.S. Auto-makers Rev in Tune," *Los Angeles Times,* 26 September 1993, D1, D7; Michael K. Ozanian, "Performance Measurement: Chrysler," *FW,* 28 September 1993, 53.

## CHAPTER 10

**304 Ethical Dilemma in Marketing:** Adapted from Matt Rothman, "A Case of Malpractice—In Market Research?" *Business Week,* 10 August 1987, 28–29; "Better Talk Things Over: Panelists Urge Clearer Communications by Researchers, Clients in Light of Lawsuit," *Marketing News,* 4 January 1988, 35; Annetta Miller and Dody Tsiantar, "A Test for Market Research," *Newsweek,* 28 December 1987, 32–33; Ellen Neuborne, "Researchers See 'Chill' from Suit," *Advertising Age,* 20 July 1987, 3, 50.

**306 Exhibit 10.4:** Adapted from an exhibit from James L. Heskett, "Lessons in the Service Sector," *Harvard Business Review,* March–April 1987, 123. Copyright © 1987 by the President and Fellows of Harvard College; all rights reserved. Reprinted by permission of *Harvard Business Review.*

**308 Exhibit 10.6:** Adapted from Christopher Lovelock, *Services Marketing* (Englewood Cliffs, N.J.: Prentice-Hall, 1984), 192. Adapted from Valarie A. Zeithaml, "How Consumer Evaluation Processes Differ between Goods and Services," in James H. Donnelly and William R. George, eds., *Marketing of Services* (Chicago: AMA, 1991). Reprinted by permission of the American Marketing Association.

**313 Exhibit 10.9:** Adapted from G. Lynn Shostack, "Service Positioning through Structural Change," *Journal of Marketing,* January 1987, 41. Reprinted by permission of the American Marketing Association.

**314–315 Marketing in Action:** Adapted from Michael Weisskopf, "Shaking Telephone Tree at the Grass Roots: Huge Senior Citizens' Lobby Answers Call to Fight Health Care Cuts," *Washington Post,* 11 June 1993, sec. a, 1; Bill McAllister, "Nonprofit Mail Discounts: On Route to Cancellation Thousands of Nonprofit Groups Facing Loss of Postage Subsidies," *Washington Post,* 11 May 1993, sec. a, 1; Steven Pearlstein, "The Battle Over 'Generational Equity': Painful Spending, Tax Choices Have the Young Calling for the Old to Get Less," *Washington Post,* 17 February 1993, sec. f, 1; Eric Schurenberg and Lani Luciano, "The Empire Called AARP," *Money,* October 1988, 128–146.

**322 Video Case:** Adapted from Kate Fitzgerald, "H&R Block's New Ads Get 'Neighborly,'" *Adver-tising Age,* 8 January 1990, 3, 42; Stephen D. Solomon and Paul B. Brown, "Taxman Henry Bloch," *Inc.,* December 1987, 35–42; Warren Berger, "Life after Tax Reform," *Adweek's Marketing Week,* 10 April 1989, 32, 34; Kevin Higgins, "Tax Preparation Firms Compete for Customers in a Shrinking Market," *Marketing News,* 15 April 1983, 1, 4.

**324–325:** Adapted from David P. Hamilton and Laura Landro, "Blurred Picture: Sony Loses Services of Visionary Founder at a Critical Juncture," *Wall Street Journal,* 3 December 1993, A1, A5; Alan Chai, Alta Cambell, and Patrick J. Spain, eds., *Hoover's Handbook of World Business 1993* (Austin, Tex.: The Reference Press, 1993), 448–449; Dennis Normile, "Sony Uses Engineers, Marketers to Raise Its Market Share," *R&D Magazine,* July 1992, 23; Brenton R. Schlender, "How Sony Keeps the Magic Going," *Fortune,* 24 February 1992, 76–84; Cyndee Miller, "Sony's Product 'Playground' Yields Insight on Consumer Behavior," *Marketing News,* 3 February 1992, 2, 13.

## CHAPTER 11

**334 Exploring Global Marketing:** Adapted from James Bovard, "The 5th Column: America's Dumping Scandal," *Far Eastern Economic Review,* 25 March 1993, 34; "Dump Dumping—This Protectionist Device Harms Everyone," *Far Eastern Economic Review,* 18 February 1993, 5; Stanley J. Modic, "It's a New World," *Industry Week,* 17 April 1989, 78, 81, 83; Fred Lamesch, "Quota Protection Will Cost Steel Users," *Iron Age,* 20 August 1984, 28; Robert B. Peabody, "Foreign Governments Are Protectionist," *Iron Age,* 20 August 1984, 29; Warren J. Keegan, *Global Marketing Management,* 4th ed. (Englewood Cliffs, N.J.: Prentice-Hall, 1989), 408–410.

**335 Exhibit 11.3:** Adapted from Alan G. Sawyer, Parker M. Worthing, and Paul E. Sendak, "The Role of Laboratory Experiments to Test Marketing Strategies," *Journal of Marketing,* Summer 1979, 60–67. Reprinted by permission of the American Marketing Association.

**343 Marketing in Action:** Adapted from Richard Gibson, "McDonald's Says 'Value Pricing' Helping Business," *Wall Street Journal,* 24 September 1991, B2; Udayan Gupta and Jeffrey A. Tannenbaum, "Casualties in the Fast-Food Price Wars," *Wall Street Journal,* 23 October 1989, B1.

**346 Map:** Kent B. Monroe, *Pricing: Making Profitable Decisions,* 2d ed. (New York: McGraw-Hill, 1990), 406.

**349 Exhibit 11.11:** Adapted from an exhibit from Robert D. Buzzell and Frederick D. Wiersema, "Successful Share-Building Strategies," *Harvard Business Review,* January–February 1981, 137. Copyright © 1981 by the President and Fellows of Harvard College; all rights reserved. Reprinted by permission of *Harvard Business Review.*

**356 Video Case:** Adapted from *Statistical Abstract of the United States 1990* (Washington, D.C.: GPO, 1990), 470; Lewis A. Cosner, Charles Kadushin, and Walter W. Powell, *Books: The Culture and Commerce of Publishing* (New York: Basic Books, 1982), 272–282, 338–341; Curtis G. Benjamin, *A Candid Critique of Book Publishing* (New York: Bowker, 1977), 39, 59, 122.

## CHAPTER 12

**361 Exhibit 12.1:** Adapted from Jim Impoco and Warren Cohen, "Nike Goes to the Full-Court Press," *U.S. News & World Report,* 19 April 1993, 48–50. Reprinted with permission.

**369 Ethical Dilemma in Marketing:** Adapted

from Marilyn Chase, "Pricing Battle: Burroughs Wellcome Reaps Profits, Outrage from Its AIDS Drug," *Wall Street Journal,* 15 September 1989, Al; Marilyn Chase, "Burroughs Wellcome Cuts Price of AZT under Pressure from AIDS Activists," *Wall Street Journal,* 19 September 1989, A3, A24; Jeremy Main, "How to Go Global—and Why," *Fortune,* 28 August 1989, 70.

**378-379 Exploring Global Marketing:** Adapted from Larry Reynolds, "Tough Talk: GATT Round Eight," *Management Review,* May 1993, 49–51; William Drozdiak, "U.S. Rejects EC-Proposed Farm Trade Pact Changes," *Washington Post,* 22 September 1993, F2; William Drozdiak, "French Set for 'Crisis' on Trade; Farmers Press Government to Keep Export Subsidies," *Washington Post,* 16 September 1993, A20; "Guilty on All Counts," *Economist,* 21 August 1993, 51; Sharon LaFraniere, "Move to Eliminate Subsidy Causes Buzz of Confusion," *Washington Post,* 31 August 1993, A17.

**387 Video Case:** Adapted from *British Rail Pocket Timetable 1990/91,* International Edition, rear cover, table 30; "BritRail Launches Speedier Service on Provincial Lines," BritRail Travel International Inc. press release, 4 October 1990, 1–2; "London/Manchester Rail Time to Be Cut in 1994," BritRail Travel International Inc. press release, 31 July 1990, 1–2; BritRail Travel International Inc. press release background information, January 1991, 1–3; "An Engine for Change," *The Economist,* 15 September 1990, 71–72; "The Missing Link," *The Economist,* 9 September 1989, 69–70; "Changing the Signals," *The Economist,* 10 June 1989, 55–56.

**388–389:** Adapted from Stephani Losee, "How Compaq Keeps the Magic Going," *Fortune,* 21 February 1994, 90–92; Rahul Jacob, "Beyond Quality and Value," *Fortune,* Autumn/Winter 1993, 8–11; Mary Beth Grover, "Growth from the Top Down," *Forbes,* 8 November 1993, 358; Stephen Kindel, "Compaq Computer: Earning Power on Screen," *Financial World,* 23 November 1993, 22–24; Michael Fitzgerald, "If at First You Don't Succeed . . ." *Computerworld,* 8 November 1993, 109; Charles Seiter, "New 040 Macs," *Macworld,* December 1993, 92–98; Mary McKenzie Dixon, "From the Office Desk to the Kitchen Table," *Dealerscope Merchandising,* October 1993, 14–23.

## CHAPTER 13

**399 Exhibit 13.3:** Regrouping definitions adapted from Louis W. Stern and Adel I. El-Ansary, *Marketing Channels,* 3d ed. (Englewood Cliffs, N.J.: Prentice-Hall, 1988), 7–8. © 1988. Adapted by permission of Prentice-Hall.

**405 Exhibit 13.8:** Adapted from David Perry, "How You'll Manage Your 1990s 'Distribution Portfolio,'" *Business Marketing,* June 1989, 52, 54, 56. Reprinted with permission of *Business Marketing.* Copyright Crain Communications, Inc. All rights reserved.

**406 Map:** Raymond Roel, "Doubleday Redux," *Direct Marketing,* October 1987, 34–46.

**409 Marketing in Action:** Adapted from Kelly R. Conatser, "Direct Comparisons," *InfoWorld,* 28 June 1993, S80–S92; David C. Huxford, "Windows for Workgroups," *Journal of Financial Planning,* April 1993, 52; Janet Bamford, "The Working Woman 50: America's Top Women Business Owners," *Working Woman,* May 1993, 49–64; "Delivering with a Winning Strategy," *Transportation & Distribution,* March 1993, 26; "PC Connection Tries TV," *Catalog Age,* November 1992, 54; Robert A. Mamis, "Real Service," *Inc.,* May 1989, 80–90. Reprinted with permission, *Inc.* magazine.

Copyright © 1989, by Goldhirsh Group, Inc., 38 Commercial Wharf, Boston, MA 02110.

**417 Ethical Dilemma in Marketing:** Adapted from Gregory Stricharchuk, "Card Makers' Tough Tactics Belie Sweet Verse as Competition Rises," *Wall Street Journal,* 24 December 1987, 11; Denise M. Topolnicki, "Greetings from the Rack Race," *Venture,* February 1988, 44–48; Hallmark Cards press release, 24 October 1988; Michael Booth, "Sweet Talk, Tough Tactics," *New York Times,* 22 January 1989, F6.

**424 Video Case:** Adapted from "20th Annual Report on Black Business," *Black Enterprise,* June 1992, 97–132; Michael Whittaker, "Making a Mark—Beautifully," *Nation's Business,* January 1988, 24; Toni Mack, "Caution + Daring = 82% Returns," *Forbes,* 8 June 1981, 101–103; Thomas Mc-Carroll, "Roar of the Greasepaint," *Black Enterprise,* June 1982, 94, 98; Chip Ricketts, "Comer Cottrell Looks at Issues beyond the Bottom Line," *Dallas Business Journal,* 3 April 1989, 8; Steve Zuckerman, "Pro-Line Looks Abroad to Boost Sagging Sales," *Dallas Business Courier,* 23 June 1986, sec. a, 8; Julie Ryan, "Anticipating a Trend Paid Off for Comer Cottrell," *Dallas,* May 1982, 50.

## CHAPTER 14

**431 Marketing in Action:** Adapted from "Bergen Brunswig Reports Fourth Quarter and Year End Results," PR Newswire, 4 October 1993, 4; Liz Murphy, "Bergen Brunswig Locks in Sales with Service," *Sales & Marketing Management,* June 1987, 48; Ron Zemke, *The Service Edge* (New York: New American Library, 1989), 165–167.

**433 Exhibit 14.4:** Adapted from Louis W. Stern and Adel I. El-Ansary, *Management in Marketing Channels* (Englewood Cliffs, N.J.: Prentice-Hall, 1989), 102. From E. Jerome McCarthy and William D. Perreault, Jr., *Basic Marketing: A Managerial Approach,* 9th ed. (Homewood, Ill.: Irwin, 1987). © 1987, Richard D. Irwin.

**434 Exhibit 14.5:** Adapted from Louis W. Stern and Adel I. El-Ansary, *Management in Marketing Channels* (Englewood Cliffs, N.J.: Prentice-Hall, 1989), 103. From Jerome McCarthy and William D. Perreault, Jr., *Basic Marketing: A Managerial Approach,* 9th ed. (Homewood, Ill.: Irwin, 1987). © 1987, Richard D. Irwin.

**437 Map:** Adapted from John K. Keitt, Jr., "Pitfalls and Promises of Foreign Distributors," *Management Review,* May 1990, 16–19.

**438 Exhibit 14.8::** Adapted from William H. Kaven, "Channels of Distribution in the Hotel Industry," in John M. Rathmell, ed., *Marketing in the Service Sector* (Cambridge, Mass.: Winthrop Publishers, 1974), 118.

**441 Exploring Global Marketing:** Adapted from Warren Strugatch, "No Respect," *World Trade,* August–September 1992, 56–60; Eugene H. Fram, "We Can Do a Better Job of Selecting International Distributors," *Journal of Business and Industrial Marketing,* Spring 1992, 61–70; U.S. Department of Commerce, *A Basic Guide to Exporting* (Lincolnwood, Ill.: NTC, 1989), 85.

**443 Exhibit 14.10:** Data from the U.S. Bureau of the Census, *Census of Wholesale Trade 1987* (Washington, D.C.: GPO, 1989), US-9.

**451 Video Case:** Adapted from Fred Gebhart, "McKesson Reports Third-Quarter Boom in Sales, Earnings," *Drug Topics,* 8 March 1993, 79; Godwin J. Udo, "The Impact of Telecommunications on Inventory Management," *Production & Inventory Management Journal,* 2d Quarter 1993, 32–37; Thayer C. Taylor, "Making the Most of Technology," *Sales & Marketing Management,* July 1993, 22–25; Greg Muirhead, "CPI Purchase Brings New Analytical Tools to McKesson's PCS," *Drug*

*Topics,* 19 April 1993, 90; Myron Magnet, "Who's Winning the Information Revolution," *Fortune,* 30 November 1992, 110–117; Barnaby J. Feder, "McKesson: No. 1 but a Doze on Wall Street," *New York Times,* 17 March 1991, sec. 3, 10.

## CHAPTER 15

**458 Exhibit 15.3:** Adapted exhibit from Avijit Ghosh, *Retail Management* (Chicago: Dryden, 1990), 112. Copyright © 1990 by The Dryden Press, reprinted by permission of the publisher.

**459 Exhibit 15.4:** Adapted from Avijit Ghosh, *Retail Management* (Chicago: Dryden, 1990), 116. Reprinted by permission of *Harvard Business Review.* From an exhibit from William R. Davidson, Albert D. Bates, and Stephen J. Bass, "The Retail Life Cycle," *Harvard Business Review,* November–December 1976. Copyright © 1976 by the President and Fellows of Harvard College; all rights reserved. Reprinted by permission of *Harvard Business Review.*

**462 Exploring Global Marketing:** Adapted from PR Newswire, "Toys 'R' Us Reports Third Quarter Results," 15 November 1993; Kathryn Graven, "For Toys 'R' Us, Japan Isn't Child's Play," *Wall Street Journal,* 7 February 1990, B1; "Toys 'R' Us Goes Overseas—and Finds That Toys 'R' Them, Too," *Business Week,* 26 January 1987, 71–72; Michael Salter, "Big Stores, Bigger Sales: Canada," *McLean's,* 15 December 1986, 42–43; Joseph Pereira, "Toys 'R' Us, Big Kid on the Block, Won't Stop Growing," *Wall Street Journal,* 11 August 1988, B6.

**471 Map:** Edward Cundiff and Marye Tharp Hilger, *Marketing in the International Environment* (Englewood Cliffs, N.J.: Prentice-Hall, 1988), 449.

**472 Exhibit 15.13:** Adapted from J. Barry Mason, Morris L. Mayer, and Hazel F. Ezell, *Retailing* (Plano, Tex.: Business Publications, 1988), 249.

**477 Techniques for Marketing Success:** Adapted from J. Douglas Eldridge, "Non-store Retailing: Planning for a Big Future," *Chain Store Age Executive with Shopping Center Age,* August 1993, 34+; "Prodigy Bounces Unprofitable Merchants," *Communications Daily,* 14 April 1993, 4+; Len Egol, "Beyond the Envelope: Computer Software Can Market Everything from Autos to Groceries," *Direct,* February 1993, S9+.

**482 Video Case:** Adapted from Julie Cohen Mason, "On Target: Lillian Vernon Focuses on Customers," *Management Review,* May 1993, 22–24; Melissa Dowling, "The Ins and Outs of Outlets," *Catalog Age,* July 1993, 151–154; Virginia Simon, "Cataloger of the Year: Fred Hochberg," *Target Marketing,* October 1992, 16–17; Shira Linden, "Usted Habla Español?" *Catalog Age,* January 1991, 65–68; Diane Cyr, "Victim of Success," *Catalog Age,* October 1992, 70–74:

## CHAPTER 16

**495 Exhibit 16.4:** Adapted from Louis W. Stern and Adel I. El-Ansary, *Marketing Channels* (Englewood Cliffs, N.J.: Prentice-Hall, 1988), 158. From Douglas M. Lambert and James R. Stock, *Strategic Physical Distribution Management* (Homewood, Ill.: Irwin, 1982), 211. © Richard D. Irwin, Inc., 1982.

**496 Exhibit 16.5:** Adapted from *Statistical Abstract of the United States 1993* (Washington, D.C.: GPO, 1993), 610; Louis Rukeyser and John Cooney, *Louis Rukeyser's Business Almanac* (New York: Simon and Schuster, 1988), 583. Copyright © 1988 by Louis Rukeyser and John Cooney. Reprinted by permission of Simon & Schuster, Inc.

**498 Exhibit 16.7:** Adapted in part from Louis

W. Stern and Adel I. El-Ansary, *Management in Marketing Channels* (Englewood Cliffs, N.J.: Prentice-Hall, 1989), 158. Adapted by permission of Macmillan College Publishing Company from *Logistical Management*, 3d ed., by Donald J. Bowersox, David J. Closs, and Omar K. Helferich. Copyright © 1986 by Macmillan College Publishing Company, Inc.

**501 Exploring Global Marketing:** Adapted from "Nike Outdoes Competition in Delivery to Customers," *Global Trade*, March 1988, 8. Reprinted by permission of North American Publishing Co.

**503 Map:** Adapted from Graham Sharman, "What 1992 Means for Logistics," *McKinsey Quarterly*, Spring 1989, 107.

**504 Marketing in Action:** Adapted from Christopher Trunk, "Powerful Handling, Control and Ergonomics with Carousels," *Material Handling Engineering*, July 1993, 51+; "Keeping Pace with Demands at Kellogg Canada," *Canadian Packaging*, May 1993, 16+; Adriane B. Miller, "It's the Details That Matter at $200 Million Sun Park," *Baltimore Business Journal*, 4 June 1993, 12+.

**508 Video Case:** Adapted from Mark B. Solomon, "Losses in Europe Left Carrier with Little Choice but to Leave," *Journal of Commerce and Commercial*, 18 March 1992, A1; Douglas MacDonald, "Overnight Success (or Failure)," *New England Business*, 21 April 1986, 57–64; Dean Foust, "Mr. Smith Goes Global," *Business Week*, 13 February 1989, 66–72; "Federal Express Spreads Its Wings," *Journal of Business Strategy*, July–August 1988, 15–19; Carl Williams, "A Company Study: The Challenge of Retail Marketing at Federal Express," *Journal of Services Marketing*, Summer 1987, 25–38; Dean Foust, "Why Federal Express Has Overnight Anxiety," *Business Week*, 9 November 1987, 66; Peter Bradley, "Good Things Come in Small Packages," *Purchasing*, 9 November 1989, 61, 64.

**510–511** Adapted from Michael Treacy and Fred Wiersema, "Customer Intimacy and Other Value Disciplines," *Harvard Business Review*, January–February 1993, 84–93; Patricia Sellers, "Companies That Serve You Best," *Fortune*, 31 May 1993, 74–88; Cyndee Miller, "Big Chains Battle for Market Share in Home Improvement," *Marketing News*, 28 September 1992, 1, 10–11; Leslie Bayor, "Blank Fills Out the Niche for Home Depot Growth," *Advertising Age*, 1 February 1992, S-5; Walecia Konrad, "Cheerleading, and Clerks Who Know Awls from Augers," *Business Week*, 3 August 1992, 51; Steve Wienstein, "Masters of Their Universe," *Progressive Grocer*, September 1992, 95–98.

## CHAPTER 17

**520–521 Techniques for Marketing Success:** Adapted from William P. Dommermuth, *Promotion: Analysis, Creativity, and Strategy* (Boston: PWS-Kent, 1989), 48–57.

**538–539 Ethical Dilemma in Marketing:** Adapted from "Women's Tennis Seeks New Sponsor," *Euromarketing*, 23 March 1993; Daniel Seligman, "Don't Bet Against Cigarette Makers," *Fortune*, 17 August 1987, 70–77; Joanne Lipman, "Decline of Tobacco Sales in Canada Fuels Ad Debate," *Wall Street Journal*, 12 June 1990, B1, B6; "Health Chief Asks Athletes to Shun Tobacco Company 'Blood Money,'" *New York Times*, 24 February 1990, 9; Jason DeParle, "Cigarette Wars Move to a New Arena," *New York Times*, 4 March 1990, sec. e, 5; "Women Tennis Pros Mull Ousting Cigarette Sponsor," *Wall Street Journal*, 20 June 1988, 20; James M. Wall, "Health Hazards at the Old Ballpark," *Christian Century*, 7 March 1990, 235–236; Malcolm Gladwell, "Virginia Slims Tournament Is Backed by 'Blood Money,' Sullivan Charges," *Washington Post*, 24 February 1990, A3; Marlene Cimons, "Tobacco Firms' Sports Ties Assailed," *Los Angeles Times*, 24 February 1990, A23; Jason DeParle, "Warning: Sports Stars May Be Hazardous to Your Health," *Washington Monthly*, September 1989, 34–49; Anthony Lewis, "Merchants of Death," *New York Times*, 19 May 1988, 27; Liz Murphy, "The Controversy Behind Event Marketing," *Sales & Marketing Management*, October 1986, 54–56; Brent Felgner, "Marketers Pursue Special Events for Niche in Consumer Lifestyle," *United States Tobacco and Candy Journal*, 28 December 1987, 16, 18; Wayne Friedman, "No Burnout Here," *Adweek's Marketing Week*, 19 September 1988, SE24–SE25; Joe Agnew, "Alcohol, Tobacco Marketers Battle New Ad Restraints," *Marketing News*, 30 January 1987, 1, 12, 13; Scott Donaton, "Publishers Bracing for Smoke-Free Pages," *Advertising Age*, 12 March 1990, 3.

**540 Map:** Adapted from Philip R. Cateora, *International Marketing* (Homewood, Ill.: Irwin, 1987), 428.

**546 Video Case:** Adapted from "Snack Producers Providing Options," *Milling & Baking News*, 25 June 1991, 19; Ann Malaspina, "Smartfeud," *Boston Magazine*, June 1988, 65–75; Joseph P. Kahn, "The Snack Food That's Eating America," *Inc.*, August 1988, 34–40; Anna M. Warrock, "Popcorn Entrepreneur May Give 'Junk Food' a Good Reputation," *New England Business*, 2 November 1987, 44–48; Judith D. Schwartz, "Smartfoods' Expansion Hasn't Diminished Its Sense of Whimsy," *Adweek's Marketing Week*, 29 January 1990, 34; "A Feud That's Really Popping: Former Partners Square Off in a Popcorn War," *Newsweek*, 24 July 1989, 52; Eileen Ebler, "The Joint Is Poppin'," *Venture*, August 1988, 70.

## CHAPTER 18

**552 Map:** Adapted from Courtland L. Bovée and William F. Arens, *Contemporary Advertising* (Homewood, Ill.: Irwin, 1989), 638.

**559 Exhibit 18.5:** Robert J. Cohen, "Ad Gains Could Exceed 6% This Year," *Advertising Age*, 5 May 1993, 4.

**562–563 Ethical Dilemma in Marketing:** Adapted from Mark Crispin Miller, "Hollywood: The Ad," *Atlantic*, April 1990, 41–45, 48–50, 52–54; Douglas C. McGill, "Questions Raised on Product Placements," *New York Times*, 13 April 1989, sec. c, 18; Joanne Lipman, "Networks Push Program Tie-Ins for Ads," *Wall Street Journal*, 26 October 1988, B1; Randall Poe, "Invasion of the Movie Product-Pushers," *Across the Board*, January 1984, 36–45; Joanne Lipman, "Outcry over Product Placement Worries Movie, Ad Executives," *Wall Street Journal*, 7 April 1989, B6; David Kalish, "Now Showing: Products!" *Marketing & Media Decisions*, August 1988, 28–29.

**570–571 Techniques for Marketing Success:** Adapted from Clare Ansberry, "Oil Spill in the Midwest Provides Case Study in Crisis Management," *Wall Street Journal*, 8 January 1988, 21; Jay Stuller, "When the Crisis Doctor Calls," *Across the Board*, May 1988, 45–51; Stuart Elliott, "Public Angry at Slow Action on Oil Spill," *USA Today*, 21 April 1989, B1–B2; E. Bruce Harrison and Tom Prugh, "Assessing the Damage: Practitioner Perspectives on the *Valdez*," *Public Relations Journal*, October 1989, 40–45; Allanna Sullivan and Amanda Bennett, "Critics Fault Chief Executive of Exxon on Handling of Recent Alaskan Oil Spill," *Wall Street Journal*, 31 March 1989, B1; Tom Eisenhart, "The King of Public Relations Talks Damage Control," *Business Marketing*, September 1990, 86–88; Ben Yagoda, "Cleaning Up a Dirty Image," *Business Month*, April 1990, 48–51; "Cashing In on Corporate Identity" (interview with Clive Chajet), *American Demographics*, July 1990, 42–43; David J. Morrow, "Is Your Corporate Ad Bad?" *The Marketer*, June 1990, 28–33; Lynn Brenner, "Biting the Bullet," *The Marketer*, June 1990, 34–38; Warren Berger, "We're So Sorry," *Inside Print*, January 1988, 34–36, 38, 40, 44.

**576 Video Case:** Adapted from "Disposable Lens Research Findings by Southern California Ophthalmologist," *PR Newswire*, 13 August 1987; "Vistakon Inc. Announces the Acuvue Disposable Contact Lens," *PR Newswire*, 9 March 1988; "Johnson & Johnson Launches 1-Day Acuvue, the World's First Daily Disposable Contact Lens," *PR Newswire*, 16 June 1993; Allan J. Magrath, "Going to Extremes—Not!" *Sales & Marketing Management*, February 1993, 32–33; Brian Dumaine, "Is Big Still Good?" *Fortune*, 20 April 1992, 50–60; Joseph Weber, "How J&J's Foresight Made Contact Lenses Pay," *Business Week*, 4 May 1992, 132.

## CHAPTER 19

**588–589 Marketing in Action:** Adapted from Steve Fishman, "The Longest Sale," *Success*, May 1989, 49–52.

**591 Ethical Dilemma in Marketing:** Adapted from Stanley J. Modic, "Many Purchasers Rationalize Ethics," *Purchasing World*, March 1990, 69–70; Bill Bryan, "A Question for Bankers, Too: Is It a Gift or a Bribe?" *Credit & Financial Management*, March 1986, 35; Jeremy Weir Alderson, "When Does a Gift Become a Bribe?" *Meetings & Conventions*, March 1986, 30–34, 36; Susan Becker Tier, "How to Deal with Xmas Gifts from Distribs," *Electronics Purchasing*, 5 December 1985, 84A31; Amy J. Rogers, "How Purchasing Execs View Taking Gifts from Suppliers," *Purchasing*, 14 February 1985, 23, 25.

**607 Video Case:** Adapted from Robert F. McCracken, "Establishing a Market Presence in China: The Avon Experience," *East Asian Executive Reports*, 15 August 1993, 10–11; Jeffrey A. Trachtenberg, "Avon Wins Over a Longtime Skeptic," *Wall Street Journal*, 1 February 1993, C2; Pat Sloan, "Avon Looks Beyond Direct Sales," *Advertising Age*, 22 February 1993, 32; Seema Naayar, "Avon Calling, by Fax, Phone and Infomercial," *Brandweek*, 22 February 1993, 22, 23; Jeffrey A. Trachtenberg, "Sallie Cook Is One of a Million Reasons Amway Liked Avon," *Wall Street Journal*, 19 May 1989, A1, A4; Denise M. Topolnicki, "Avon's Corporate Makeover: If Women Aren't Home, Avon Goes to the Office," *Working Woman*, February 1988, 57, 59; Kate Ballen, "Get Ready for Shopping at Work," *Fortune*, 15 February 1988, 95, 98; Paul Markovits, "Direct Selling Is Alive and Well," *Sales & Marketing Management*, August 1988, 76–78; "Direct Selling Leaves Home," *New York Times*, 3 September 1985, sec. d, 1.

**608–609:** Adapted from Laurie M. Grossman, "Coca-Cola Launches Fruit-Drink Line Backed by $30 Million Promotional Plan," *Wall Street Journal*, 2 March 1994, B10; Gerry Khermouch, "Snapple Doubles Ad Budget; Seeks Global Agencies," *Brandweek*, 7 February 1994, 1, 6; Greg W. Prince, "It's Only Natural. Marketing for the Love of Snapple," *Beverage World*, 28 February 1993, 19; Joshua Levine, "Watch Out, Snapple!" *Forbes*, 10 May 1993, 142, 146; Patricia Winters, "Ad Storm Near for New Age Drinks," *Advertising Age*, 30 November 1992, 49; Alison Fahey, "Snapple Pours It On," *Advertising Age*, 13 April 1992, 12.

## CHAPTER 20

**624–625 Exploring Global Marketing:** Adapted from Jeffrey A. Fadiman, "Should Smaller Firms Use Third World Methods to Enter Third World Markets: The Project Head as Point Man Overseas," *Journal of Consumer Marketing,* Fall 1989, 15–26; Andrew Kupfer, "How to Be a Global Manager," *Fortune,* 14 March 1988, 58; Christine Vicars, "Bright Future with the Dark Continent," *World Trade,* Spring 1989, 67; Philip R. Cateora, *International Marketing* (Homewood, Ill.: Irwin, 1987), 308.

**626 Exhibit 20.6:** Adapted from Philip R. Cateora, *International Marketing* (Homewood, Ill.: Irwin, 1987), 140. © 1990 Richard D. Irwin, Inc.

**633 Exploring Global Marketing:** Adapted from Matt Schaffer, *Winning the Countertrade War* (New York: Wiley, 1989), 73; Warren J. Keegan, *Global Marketing Management* (Englewood Cliffs, N.J.: Prentice-Hall, 1989), 548; Subrata N. Chakravarty, "How Pepsi Broke into India," *Forbes,* 27 November 1989, 44.

**639 Video Case:** Adapted from Yumiko Ono, "Pizza in Japan Is Adapted to Local Tastes," *Wall Street Journal,* 4 June 1993, B1; Preston Townley, "Going Global in the 1990s," *Vital Speeches,* 15 July 1990, 589–593; Kathryn Graven, "Family in Japan Plays Big Role in Importing Fast Food from U.S.," *Wall Street Journal,* 3 March 1987, 1, 29; "Domino's Pizza International Bucks Current Sales Trend," PR Newswire, 22 April 1991.

## CHAPTER 21

**648 Techniques for Marketing Success:** Adapted from John F. Russell, "The Stampede to ISO 9000," *Electronic Business Buyer,* October 1993, 101–110; Ronald Henkoff, "The Hot New Seal of Quality," *Fortune,* 28 June 1993, 116–120; Sara E. Hagigh, "Obtaining EC Product Approvals after 1992: What American Manufacturers Need to Know," *Business America,* 24 February 1992, 30–33; Todd Spangler, "U.S. Companies Increasingly Look for ISO Label," *Business Marketing,* March 1993, 39.

**651 Exhibit 21.6:** Adapted from William H. Davidow and Bro Uttal, *Total Customer Service: The Ultimate Weapon* (New York: Harper & Row, 1989), 212–213. Copyright © 1989 by William H. Davidow and Bro Uttal. Reprinted by permission of HarperCollins Publishers.

**652 Map:** Janet Endrijonas, "Acer Pres Says Taiwan-Bashing Ended," *Newsbytes,* 27 March 1990; Fred Langa, "Taiwan, the Soviet Union, and You, Part 2," *Byte,* October 1990, 10; "Altos Computer System to Join the Acer Group," *Business Wire,* 5 July 1990.

**654–655 Marketing in Action:** Adapted from Mark Stuart Gill, "Stalking Six Sigma," *Business Month,* January 1990, 42–46; Jeremy Main, "How to Win the Baldrige Award," *Fortune,* 23 April 1990, 101–116.

**671 Video Case:** Adapted from Shari Caudron, "How Xerox Won the Baldrige," *Personnel Journal,* April 1991, 98–102; Lee O. Smith, "The Cuomo Commission's 'New Realism,'" *Challenge,* September–October 1988, 37–43; David Kearns, "Xerox: Satisfying Customer Needs with a New Culture," *Management Review,* February 1989, 61–63; H. Garrett DeYoung, "Back from the Brink: Xerox Redefines Its Notion of Quality," *Electronic Business,* 16 October 1989, 50–54.

## CHAPTER 22

**682–683 Exploring Global Marketing:** Adapted from Dave Savona, "Tackling Japan," *International Business,* December 1992, 122–125; Robert Michelet and Rosemary Remacle, "Forming Successful Strategic Alliances in Europe," *Journal of European Business,* September–October 1992, 11–15.

**686–687 Techniques for Marketing Success:** Adapted from Tom Eisenhart, "You're Talking—But Are They Listening?" *Business Marketing,* January 1989, 30–33, 36–37; Tom Eisenhart, "Eaton: Clearing the Clutter," *Business Marketing,* January 1989, 36–38.

**690–691 Exhibit 22.11:** Adapted from Hal W. Goetsch, "Conduct a Comprehensive Marketing Audit to Improve Marketing Planning," *Marketing News,* 18 March 1983, 14. Reprinted by permission of the American Marketing Association.

**697 Video Case:** Adapted from Amy Barrett, "Hail to the Chef," *FW,* 11 June 1991, 52–54; Gary Hoover, Alta Campbell, and Patrick J. Spain, eds., *Hoover's Handbook 1991: Profiles of Over 500 Major Corporations* (Austin, Tex.: The Reference Press, 1990), 149; Larry Carpenter, "How to Market to Regions," *American Demographics,* November 1987, 44–45; Barbara Hetzer, "Pushing Decisions Down the Line at Campbell Soup," *Business Month,* July 1989, 62–63; Tom Peters, "There Are No Excellent Companies," *Fortune,* 27 April 1987, 341, 344.

**698–699:** Adapted from Noreen O'Leary, "The Hand on the Lever," *Adweek,* 14 December 1992, 22–27; Alan Chai, Alta Cambell, and Patrick J. Spain, eds., *Hoover's Handbook of World Business 1993* (Austin, Tex.: The Reference Press, 1993), 484–485; Laurel Wentz, "Unilever Brands 'Alive, Kicking,' Chairman Assures," *Advertising Age,* 17 May 1993, 39; Bob Hagerty, "Unilever Profit Edged Higher in 2nd Quarter," *Wall Street Journal,* 12 August 1991, B4A; Walecia Conrad, "The New, Improved Unilever Aims to Clean Up in the U.S.," *Business Week,* 29 November 1989, 102, 106.

# PHOTO CREDITS

## CHAPTER 1

**2:** Alan Levenson/Tony Stone.
**4:** Bob Daemmrich/Image Works.
**6:** Courtesy of Continent Bank, Moscow.
**7:** Courtesy of Metropolitan Life Insurance.
**9:** Miro Vintoniv/Stock, Boston.
**13:** AP/Wide World.
**15:** Courtesy of Bentex Watch.
**25:** Courtesy of Nike.

## CHAPTER 2

**28:** Zephyr Pictures.
**33:** Courtesy of Alfa Romeo Distributors of North America.
**34:** Reprinted with permission from Microsoft Corporation.
**39:** Courtesy of AEG.
**41:** Courtesy of Deja Shoe.
**44:** Amy Etra/PhotoEdit.
**49:** Miro Vintovin/Stock, Boston.
**50:** Stacy Pick/Stock, Boston.
**51:** Courtesy of California Department of Public Health.
**60:** Courtesy of New York Vista and Garden Path Florish in the World Trade Center, photo by Danielle Swick, NYC.

## CHAPTER 3

**64:** Pete Saloutos, Zephyr Pictures.
**67:** National Rifle Association.
**77:** Courtesy of New Balance Athletic Shoe.
**79:** Courtesy of Amnesty International.
**81:** Courtesy of SHERPA, Paris, photography Dieter Kiek and Aldin.
**82:** Courtesy of Zeos International.
**92:** Courtesy of Nintendo of America.
**102:** Courtesy of AT&T.

## CHAPTER 4

**106:** Mark Richards/PhotoEdit.
**111:** Courtesy of J. C. Penney.
**119:** Courtesy of Penn Racquet Sports © Gen Corp Polymer Products.
**122:** Courtesy of Toyota Motor Sales U.S.A.
**123:** Courtesy of Aebi/BBDO Zurich.
**125:** Mark Antman/Image Works.
**129:** Chris Jones/The Stock Market.
**139:** Courtesy of Domino's Pizza.

## CHAPTER 5

**142:** Peter Poulides/Tony Stone.
**147:** Courtesy of Catalina Marketing Network.
**150:** Roger Tully/Tony Stone.
**151:** © 1993 Adweek L.P. Used with permission from *Adweek* Superbrands.
**156:** Barrier Rokeach/Image Bank.
**157:** Courtesy Digital Equipment.
**167:** Doane Gregor/Allstock.

## CHAPTER 6

**170:** Rhoda Sidney/PhotoEdit.
**174:** Visionary Shopper was developed by Dr. Raymond R. Burke, Associate Professor of Marketing at the Harvard Business School. It is licensed exclusively by MarketWare Corporation, Norcross, GA.
**178:** Courtesy of Epley Marketing Services.
**179 top:** Courtesy of Focus Suites of Philadelphia.
**179 bottom:** Courtesy of SKIM Market and Policy Research.
**184:** David Young-Wolff/PhotoEdit.
**198:** Courtesy of U.S. Postal Service.

## CHAPTER 7

**202:** Frank Orel/Tony Stone.
**205 top:** Courtesy of General Motors.
**205 bottom:** Courtesy of Sega Genesis.
**220:** Courtesy of Public Broadcasting Service.
**227:** Courtesy of Del Laboratories.
**231:** Courtesy of Kellogg.
**234:** Courtesy of Nestlé France S.A.

## CHAPTER 8

**238:** Melanie Carr/Zephyr Pictures.
**243:** Bob Daemmrich/Stock, Boston.
**248 top:** Courtesy of The Minnesota Orchestra.
**248 bottom:** Bettmann Archive.
**251:** Courtesy of Xerox.
**253:** Tony Freeman/PhotoEdit.
**256:** Courtesy of Calvin Klein.
**258:** Courtesy of Moen.
**260:** Courtesy of Micron Custom Manufacturing Services.
**263:** Courtesy of Orville Redenbacher.

## CHAPTER 9

**266:** John P. Endress/Stock Market.
**268:** Tony Freeman/PhotoEdit.
**271:** Courtesy of Tom's of Maine.
**279:** Courtesy of Polaroid.
**286:** © 1993 Delrina (Washington) Corporation. © 1993 Berkeley Breathed. All Rights Reserved.
**289:** John Coletti/Stock, Boston,
**290:** Courtesy of Sanco.
**294:** Holly Kuper.

## CHAPTER 10

**298:** Lawrence Migdale/Photo Researchers.
**303:** Bob Daemmrich/Image Works.
**307:** Courtesy of Passport Design.
**310:** Courtesy of Dr. Larry Okmin.
**311:** Courtesy of Leo Burnett—Oslo.
**316:** Courtesy of Doyle Advertising & Design Group.
**320:** Robert Brenner/PhotoEdit.
**324:** Courtesy of Sony Electronics.

## CHAPTER 11

**328:** Michael Newman/PhotoEdit.
**331:** Courtesy of Leo Burnett A/S.
**338:** Courtesy of Lotus Approach.
**339:** EPSON is a registered trademark of Seiko EPSON Corp. © 1993 EPSON America, Inc., all company and/or product names are trademarks and/or registered trademarks of their respective manufacturers, including Canon which is registered by Canon Inc. and HP which is registered by Hewlett-Packard.
**341:** Tony Freeman/PhotoEdit.
**345:** Courtesy of K-III Magazine Corporation.
**347:** Robin Landholm.
**353:** Larry Fleming/Image Works.

## CHAPTER 12

**358:** Matthew Neal McVay/Tony Stone.
**361:** Tony Coletti/Stock, Boston.
**367:** David Simson/Stock, Boston.
**371:** Michael Newman/PhotoEdit.
**374:** Courtesy of Miles Laboratories.
**377:** Courtesy of McCann-Erickson, Singapore.
**381:** Courtesy of Michigan Department of Public Health.
**385:** Courtesy of American Airlines.
**388:** Courtesy of Compaq.

## CHAPTER 13

**392:** Jeff Zaruba/Tony Stone.
**394 top:** Steve Benbow/Stock, Boston.
**394 bottom:** Bruce Hands/Stock, Boston.
**400:** Paul Chesley/Tony Stone.
**404:** Courtesy of McCann-Erickson.
**408:** Bruce Zake.
**411:** Felicia Martinez.
**413:** Maggie Porter.
**421:** Courtesy of Black & Decker.

## CHAPTER 14

**426:** Wayne Eastep/Stock Market.
**429 top:** John Elk/Stock, Boston.
**429 bottom:** Courtesy of Delta.
**436:** Courtesy of Wolf's, Cleveland, Ohio.
**437:** Lawrence Migdale/Photo Researchers.
**442:** Courtesy of SuperValu.
**445:** Courtesy of Wm. J. Wrigley Co.
**449:** Courtesy of SuperValu.

## CHAPTER 15

**452:** Don Smetzer/Tony Stone.
**455:** Check Free Corporation.
**456:** David Woo/Stock, Boston.
**459:** Courtesy of Bullock's.
**460:** Chip Henderson/Tony Stone.
**463:** Don Smetzer/Tony Stone.
**464:** R. Stott/Image Works.
**467:** Michael Newman/PhotoEdit.
**468:** Jeff Greenberg/Photo Researchers.
**470:** Donald Dietz/Stock, Boston.
**471:** Sylvain Grandadam/Tony Stone.
**475:** Bob Daemmrich/Image Works.
**476:** Ogust/Image Works.
**480:** Michael Grecco/Stock, Boston.

## CHAPTER 16

**484:** Zephyr Pictures.
**487:** Courtesy of Lillian Vernon Catalog Company, Mt. Vernon, NY.
**497:** Spencer Grant/Stock, Boston.
**500:** Joseph Nettis/Stock, Boston.
**502:** Courtesy of Roadnet Technologies, Inc., a UPS Company.
**507:** Courtesy of Oak Island Acres Goat Dairy.
**510:** Michael Newman/PhotoEdit.

## CHAPTER 17

**514:** John Griffin/Image Works.
**516:** Courtesy of Pepsi-Cola.
**518:** Courtesy of American Red Cross.
**522:** Courtesy of New Voices, New Visions.
**528:** Courtesy of Oracle Corporation.
**535:** Courtesy of Ryder Truck.
**544:** Michael Newman/PhotoEdit.

## CHAPTER 18

**548:** Jeff Isaac Greenberg/Photo Researchers.
**550:** Linc Cornell/Stock, Boston.
**553:** Reprinted with permission from MCI Corporation/John Madere, photographer.
**556:** Courtesy of San Diego Convention & Visitors Bureau.
**563:** Courtesy of Halifax Financial Services and DFSD Bozell, London.
**565:** Reprinted with permission from *Eyes on the News*, copyright © 1991 by The Poynter Institute for Media Studies, St. Petersburg, FL.
**567:** Courtesy of Elizabeth Arden.
**575:** Robin Landholm.

## CHAPTER 19

**578:** Tom McCarthy/PhotoEdit.
**581:** Michael Newman/PhotoEdit.
**591:** Courtesy of Symantec Corporation.
**598:** Courtesy of MapLinx Corporation.
**600:** Courtesy of ACS of Eli Lilly & Company.
**605:** Courtesy of Xerox.
**608:** Courtesy of Snapple Beverage.

## CHAPTER 20

**612:** Charles Gupton/Tony Stone.
**615:** © 1994 Revlon.

**616:** © 1992 Sprint Communications Company Limited Partnership.
**618:** Courtesy of Samsonite.
**623:** Courtesy of AT&T Language Line® Services.
**629:** Courtesy of National Basketball Association.
**634:** Courtesy of Roadway Global Air.
**637:** Courtesy of Holiday Inn Worldwide.

## CHAPTER 21

**640:** Peter Menzel/Stock, Boston.
**643:** Courtesy of AT&T and McCann-Erickson.
**650:** Courtesy of Consolidated Freightways.

**653:** Courtesy of All-Clad Metalcrafters.
**655:** © State of Florida, Dept. of Citrus, 1994.
**661:** Courtesy of Peachtree Windows and Doors.
**668:** Courtesy of L. L. Bean.

## CHAPTER 22

**672:** Bruce Ayres/Tony Stone.
**675:** Courtesy of Xerox.
**680:** Courtesy of Lufthansa.
**684:** Courtesy of Northwest Airlines and KLM.
**695:** Courtesy of Hewlett-Packard.
**698:** Courtesy of Lever Brothers.

# Glossary

# GLOSSARY

## A

**Acceleration principle** The idea that a small change in consumer demand can lead to a major change in organizational demand

**Accumulating** Gathering individual homogeneous supplies into one large heterogeneous supply

**Added value** Increased worth of a good or service, compared to the basic or expected product

**Administered marketing system** A type of VMS in which one player has control by way of influence and agreement but not through explicit ownership or contractual arrangement

**Advertising** Paid, nonpersonal communication with a target market; advertising media include television, radio, newspapers, magazines, billboards, and direct mail

**Advertising agencies** Companies that specialize in providing various levels of advertising services; some agencies focus on specific services or market segments, and others offer a complete range of services covering a wide range of markets

**Advocacy advertising** Nonproduct advertising that promotes a company's viewpoint on a particular issue of public concern

**Agents** Intermediaries who assist with the marketing of goods and services but who don't assume ownership of products; agents, unlike brokers, usually work long term for producers

**AIDA model** An acronym for awareness, interest, desire, and action, which represent the psychological steps a customer goes through on the way toward making a purchase

**Aided recall** A posttesting technique that shows specific ads to people who then answer various questions about them

**Allocating** Breaking accumulated supplies into smaller units that are easier for later intermediaries and customers to handle

**Allowances** Indirect reductions from list price in which part of the list price is effectively returned to the customers, such as with a rebate

**Anchor stores** Large department stores or discount stores that serve as the main stores in planned shopping centers because of their strong customer appeal

**Artwork** The visual or graphic portion of an advertisement

**Assorting** As the final step in the regrouping process, assorting creates the particular mix of goods required by target customers

**Atmosphere** A part of a retailer's image that is created by a blend of sensory effects intended to create a specific shopping mood

**Attitude** Enduring positive or negative inclinations toward objects, people, ideas, or products in a particular way

**Auction houses** Facilities designed to bring buyers and sellers together for the purpose of selling products to the highest bidder

**Audience** The person or persons who are receiving a transmitted message

**Augmented products** The expected products plus all their added value

**Average fixed cost** The amount of fixed cost attributed to each unit produced; equal to total fixed costs divided by the number of units

**Average total cost** The sum of average total and average variable costs; represents the average expenses required to make one unit

**Average variable cost** The amount of variable cost attributed to each unit produced; equal to variable costs divided by the number of units

## B

**Baby boom** The increase in births that started in 1945, when World War II ended, and extended into the early 1960s

**Baby boomers** The generation of people who were born in the United States between 1946 and 1964

**Backward invention** Redesigning and producing a product for specific foreign markets after it is obsolete in industrialized countries

**Balance of payments** A system that accounts for a nation's international financial transactions

**Balance of trade** A nation's total imports in relation to its total exports over a one-year period of time

**Barriers to entry** Competitive conditions that make it expensive, illegal, or otherwise difficult to enter a market as a competitor

**Barter** An exchange that is not based on monetary prices

**Basing-point pricing** A form of delivered pricing that sets shipping charges based on delivery from one or more locations, even if the shipment never actually moved through those locations

**Behavioral segmentation** A way of dividing large markets into smaller groupings according to consumer behavior

**Benefit segmentation** A form of behavioral segmentation that divides the market according to benefits sought by consumers

**Brand** A name, term, phrase, design, symbol, or any combination of these chosen by an individual or organization to distinguish a product from competing products

**Brand awareness** A measure of the percentage of the target market that is aware of a brand name

**Brand equity** The overall strength of a brand in the marketplace and its value to the company that owns it; composed of brand loyalty, brand awareness, perceived quality, brand associations, and other proprietary brand assets

**Brand extension** Assigning an existing brand name to a new product in the same product line or in a different product line

**Brand licensing** A type of licensing arrangement in which one company sells others the right to use one or more of its brand names

**Brand loyalty** The level of commitment that customers feel toward a given brand, as represented by their continuing purchase of that brand

**Brand mark** The portion of a brand that cannot be expressed verbally, such as a graphic design or symbol

**Brand name** The portion of a brand that can be expressed verbally, including letters, words, or numbers

**Breakeven analysis** A profit analysis technique that identifies the sales volume at which total cost is equal to total revenue; you'll make a profit if sales exceed this level and suffer a loss if they don't reach this level

**Breakeven point** The sales volume at which a company breaks even

**Breaking bulk** Breaking accumulated supplies into smaller units that are easier to handle; synonymous with allocating

**Brokers** Intermediaries who assist with the marketing of goods and services but who don't assume ownership of products; brokers typically have short-term relationships with producers

**Bundle pricing** The practice of including several products together for one price; the objective is to persuade buyers to buy more by offering an attractive price for a group of products

**Business cycle** A predictable economic fluctuation that gives rise to four stages: prosperity, recession, depression, and recovery

**Business-to-business marketing** The process of marketing goods and services to nonconsumer customers

**Buyclasses** Types of organizational buying situations, including straight rebuys, modified rebuys, and new-task purchases

**Buyers' markets** Market conditions in which supply exceeds demand

**Buying center** The group of individuals involved in making a particular buying decision within an organization

**Buying center roles** Roles assumed by various members of the buying center, including initiator, influencer, decision maker, gatekeeper, purchaser, and user

**Buying power** The consumer's ability to purchase products

**Buying power index (BPI)** A measure of various geographic regions' collective purchasing power, based on population, effective buying income, and retail sales

# C

**Canned approach** An approach to selling that utilizes a memorized presentation and doesn't take into account individual customer and selling situations

**Cannibalization** A situation in which a new product steals sales or market share from other products in the existing product line

**Capital equipment** Industrial machinery, office and store equipment, or transportation vehicles that are purchased infrequently and are used to produce goods, provide a service, or support the day-to-day operation of an organization

**Cash discount** A discount given in return for paying a bill within a certain number of days

**Cash-and-carry wholesalers** Limited-service merchant wholesalers that traditionally require customers to pay cash and then carry goods away themselves; however, some of these intermediaries are expanding their service offerings with credit, delivery, and other forms of assistance

**Catalog showroom** A limited-line discount retailer that offers products from a catalog for purchase by mail or in a self-service store

**Causal research** Research that helps marketers identify a specific factor that causes an effect in the marketplace

**Cause-related marketing** Promotional programs that tie charitable contributions to sales of a specific good or service; the term has been copyrighted by American Express

**Census** A survey of every person or item in the population

**Centralized organization** An organization in which authority and responsibility are concentrated in the hands of relatively few people, usually the higher levels of management

**Chain stores** Groups of retail stores owned and operated by corporations that perform centralized buying and administrative functions for all the stores

**Channel captains** The dominant players in a given marketing channel who have power over other channel members

**Channel power** The ability of the channel captain to influence or control the behavior of the rest of the channel

**Classical conditioning** Learning to associate a stimulus with a response

**Closing** The stage in the selling process at which the salesperson gets a purchase commitment from the prospect

**Cold calling** Calling on a potential customer by telephone or in person when no previous contact has been made

**Commercialization** The part of the product development process in which the new product is launched beyond the test markets into the full target market and is supported by the preferred marketing mix

**Comparative advantage** The advantage a nation has when it specializes in exporting products it can produce more cheaply than other nations

**Comparative advertising** A special case of competitive advertising that explicitly compares your product with one or more competitive products

**Competition** The rivalry among sellers trying to increase sales, profits, or market share while addressing the same set of customers

**Competitive advantage** In the context of international business, the ability of a nation's industries to innovate and upgrade to the next level of technology and productivity

**Competitive advertising** Advertising that tries to promote specific product features that are better than those offered by the competition

**Competitor intelligence** The systematic collection and analysis of data about a firm's competitors, with the goals of understanding the competitors' positions in the market and of formulating strategies in response

**Computer-interactive retailing** A nonstore retailing method in which consumers use a computer to learn about products or services and then place orders or use services electronically

**Concentrated marketing** A strategy in which you target a single market segment with a single product or limited line of products

**Concept testing** A type of marketing research in which marketers describe a new product and ask consumers to react to the concept

**Consumer behavior** Selecting, seeking, purchasing, using, and disposing of goods and services

**Consumer buying behavior** Deciding what goods or services to buy and then obtaining them

**Consumer decision process** A five-step process consumers go through when making a purchase

**Consumer learning** The way people acquire the knowledge and experience they apply to consumer behavior

**Consumerism** A social, economic, and political movement that seeks to protect the safety and rights of consumers

**Containerization** The process of packing goods in large, rectangular shipping containers

**Contractual marketing system** A VMS in which contracts explicitly spell out the roles and responsibilities of all members in the channel

**Controllable elements** Internal factors over which marketers have a high degree of control, specifically their own pricing, promotion, distribution, and product selection

**Convenience products** Relatively inexpensive products that buyers or users choose frequently with a minimum of thought and effort

**Copy** The verbal or textual portion of an advertisement

**Core customers** A company's most important customers, distinguished from the rest by their long-term value to the company

**Core values** Pervasive and enduring values within a culture

**Corporate marketing system** A type of VMS (vertical marketing system) in which one company owns every player in the channel

**Correlation analysis** A forecasting method that predicts the sales of an item on the basis of the sale, use, or availability of one or more other items

**Cost of ownership** The total cost of acquiring and owning a product; it includes the search costs, the purchase price, and any other expenses related to installation, maintenance, service, and replacement

**Cost-plus pricing** A simple pricing technique that calculates price by adding an acceptable profit level to average total costs

**Countertrade** A trading practice in which the seller agrees to buy products from the customer in exchange for the customer's agreement to buy the seller's products

**Credence qualities** Product attributes that cannot be evaluated, even after consumption

**Culture** The beliefs, values, and objects shared by a group and passed on to succeeding generations

**Customer orientation** A management philosophy in which the customer is central to everything the company does

**Customer service** Actions companies can take to add value to basic goods and services

**Customized approach** Adapting product and promotion strategies to the distinct characteristics of each market

**Cycle analysis** A time-series correction technique that adjusts forecasts for movements in the overall economy

# D

**Data** The statistics, facts, and opinions that market researchers record and store

**Database** A computerized system that stores and retrieves a variety of data

**Database marketing** Direct marketing that takes advantage of comprehensive information about customers, including purchase behavior, demographics, and lifestyle

**Dealer** Basically the same type of intermediary as a distributor, although some people distinguish dealers as those intermediaries that sell only to final customers, not to other intermediaries

**Decentralized organization** An organization characterized by widespread distribution of authority and responsibility

**Deceptive pricing** Pricing and promotional tactics that disguise the true price customers must pay for a good or service

**Decline phase** The fourth phase in a product's life cycle when both sales and profits decline

**Decoding** The process an audience goes through to translate a message into an idea with personal meaning; reverse of encoding

**Delivered pricing** A class of geographic pricing in which shipping charges are included in the selling price

**Delphi technique** A forecasting method that uses the averaged opinions of inside and outside experts who are allowed to change their predictions after learning the overall results of a first-round forecast; the revised estimate becomes the final forecast

**Demand** The degree to which potential customers have an interest in, and the financial ability to buy, a product or class of products

**Demand curve** A graph that plots the relationship between demand and price; it indicates the sensitivity of buyers to various selling prices

**Demand-backwards pricing** An approach that starts with a price the market will support and backs up through the marketing channel, subtracting the profits and fees needed by retailers and wholesalers, until it arrives at the price the manufacturer can charge

**Demographic segmentation** A way to divide large markets into smaller groupings according to the elements of size, composition, and distribution of the population

**Demographics** A system of describing a population's objective attributes such as age, income, education, and marital status

**Department store** A large general merchandise retailer selling a wide variety of products at full price with full service

**Dependent variable** The marketplace factor that is affected when another factor is changed

**Depression** A more intense form of recession in which unemployment peaks, buying power drops dramatically, and consumers lose faith in the economy

**Derived demand** The fact that the demand for organizational products is driven by the demand for consumer products

**Descriptive research** A type of preliminary research that allows marketers to better describe the marketing problem

**Dialectic process** A theory of retail evolution maintaining that established retailers will make changes to adopt the innovations of successful new entrants, resulting in a new retail format that blends the best of the established retailer and the newcomer

**Differentiated marketing** A strategy in which you offer many products or product variations aimed at specific segments, using marketing mixes adapted for each segment

**Direct channels** Marketing channels that lack intermediaries, in which producers and customers interact directly

**Direct exporting** Selling goods or services directly to another country without the use of an intermediary

**Direct investment** Acquiring ownership interest in a foreign company or investment in foreign production and marketing facilities

**Direct marketing** An interactive system of marketing in which producers or intermediaries communicate directly and individually with target customers

**Direct selling** Selling in which individual sellers communicate through direct contact with individual buyers

**Direct-action advertising** Advertising that tries to motivate customers to take action immediately after being exposed to the ad

**Discount retailers** Retailers that offer both high- and low-quality products at prices lower than full-price retailers in self-service environments

**Discounts** Direct reductions from the list price

**Discrepancies of assortment** Situations in which the assortment of products available doesn't match the assortment desired

**Discrepancies of quantity** Situations in which the quantity available doesn't match the quantity desired

**Discretionary income** The portion of disposable income the consumer retains after paying for food, shelter, and other necessities

**Discrimination** The ability to distinguish between similar stimuli

**Disposable income** Income the consumer retains after paying taxes

**Distinctive competencies** Things you do better than everyone else in the market, such as customer service or product design

**Distribution** The process of moving products from the producer to the consumer, which may involve seversl steps and the participation of multiple companies

**Distribution center** A warehouse specially designed to provide the fast transfer of goods from suppliers to retailers or final customers

**Distributor** A general term usually applied in organizational markets to intermediaries that perform the equivalent functions of both wholesalers and retailers

**Diversification** A broad growth approach in which a firm enters new markets with new products

**Drop shippers** Limited-service wholesalers that assume ownership of large shipments but don't take physical possession

**Dual distribution** Channel systems in which more than one channel is used

**Dumping** The combination of price discrimination and predatory pricing in international marketing situations; this occurs when a company tries to sell products below cost to customers in another country

**Durable goods** Goods that are used or consumed over a long period of time, usually at least several years; examples include houses and automobiles

# E

**Economic elements** Factors in the marketing environment that are shaped by, or are part of, the economic climate, such as consumer wealth, buying power, and income

**Effective buying income (EBI)** The consumer's total income after taxes

**Ego drive** The quality that makes a salesperson want to make a sale

**Ego strength** The quality that helps salespeople deal with inevitable rejections

**Elastic demand** A price-demand relationship in which a decrease in price increases total revenue

**Empathy** The ability to put oneself in another person's place

**Employee empowerment** Transferring decision-making power to frontline employees so that they are better able to satisfy customers

**Encoding** The process of converting an idea into symbols (words and images) to make it compatible with transmission and decoding facilities

**Environmental analysis** The interpretation of data generated in environmental scanning

**Environmental scanning** The process of gathering data on the marketing environment from people and publications

**Equalized work load method** A way of determining personnel needs based on the assumption that each salesperson makes approximately the same number of sales calls over a given time period

**Equipment-based services** Services that are delivered primarily by equipment

**European Union** A multinational European common market created in 1957 to encourage the free flow of goods, services, labor, and capital among member countries and to impose uniform tariffs on imports

**Everyday low pricing (EDLP)** A strategy of keeping prices at consistent levels, day in and day out, rather than setting a comparatively high price and running frequent sales

**Evoked set** The group of alternatives that a consumer actually considers before making a choice

**Exchange** The transfer between two or more parties of tangible or intangible items of value

**Exclusive dealing agreements** A contract that prohibits an intermediary from carrying competing contracts; it is illegal in some circumstances

**Exclusive distribution** An extreme case of selective distribution in which only one outlet in a market territory is allowed to carry a product or product line

**Exclusive territory** A sales territory granted to one intermediary; granting exclusive territories can be illegal if it restrains competition

**Expected products** The basic set of values that customers expect in exchange for the price they pay

**Experience qualities** Product attributes that can be evaluated only after consumption of the product

**Experiment** Research in which one or more variables are changed while others are kept constant so that the results can be measured

**Exploratory research** A type of research conducted to clarify the problem definition and prepare for additional research to prove or disprove the hypothesis

**Exponential smoothing** A time-series analysis method that assigns weights to the sales data used in the forecast; you can give newer data either a high or low weighting, depending on how much you want to emphasize them

**Export** To sell goods and raw materials to another country

**Export management companies (EMCs)** Firms that act as the international marketing arms of the manufacturers they represent; EMCs frequently operate under the names of those manufacturers in international markets

**Extensive problem solving (EPS)** Complex evaluation of a number of alternatives

# F

**Facilitating agents** People and organizations that assist with the flow of products and information in marketing channels, including banking and insurance functions

**Family brand** A brand assigned to an entire line of product items

**Feedback** Communication from the audience back to the source

**Field experiment** An experiment conducted in the real world rather than in a laboratory

**Field warehouse** A public warehouse set up at the location of the customer's inventory

**Filtered pricing** A strategy of variable pricing that tries to restrict discounts and allowances to only those customers who probably won't buy without them

**Fixed costs** The portion of a company's production and marketing costs that remains constant regardless of the level of production

**Focus group interview** A personal survey technique that involves interaction between a small group of people and a moderator

**Foreign exchange market** All the institutions and people throughout the world who buy and sell currency

**Foreign exchange rate** The rate at which the currency of one country can be exchanged for the currency of another country

**Form utility** The value created by shaping raw materials and components into products

**Franchise** A business entity licensed to use the trademarks, operations, and other attributes of a business

**Free-trade area** A multinational market that encourages the free flow of goods and services between member countries but does not provide for the free flow of labor and capital or impose uniform tariffs on imports

**Freestanding store** A retail location that stands alone and unattached to other retailers

**Freight forwarders** Transportation firms that specialize in consolidating and sending freight on to its final destination

**Freight-absorption pricing** A form of delivered pricing in which the seller agrees to return freight costs to the buyer in the form of a discount

**Frequency** A measure of the average number of times that members of the target audience were exposed to an ad during a given period of time

**Frequency marketing** Programs that reward customers for repeat purchases of specific goods and services

**Full-service merchant wholesalers** Those merchant wholesalers that offer a wide variety of marketing services, including providing information, ordering, negotiating, regrouping, storing and transporting, financing, taking risks, promoting, and offering various specialized services

**Functional intermediaries** Intermediaries that, unlike merchants, do not assume ownership of the products they are selling

**Functional organization** An organization structure in which jobs are grouped according to similarity, such as advertising, marketing research, and sales

# G

**General merchandise retailers** Retailers offering a wide assortment of product lines

**General merchandise wholesalers** Full-service merchant wholesalers that carry a variety of product lines; they are distinguished more by the breadth of their offerings than by the depth

**Generalization** The tendency to respond in the same way to similar stimuli

**Generic brand** A nonbranded product that is identified only by its product category

**Geodemographic segmentation** A segmentation approach in which you average demographic data inside geographic segments; the resulting profiles can be remarkably accurate predictors of values and lifestyles

**Geographic organization** An organization structure in which jobs are grouped geographically

**Geographic segmentation** A way to separate large markets into smaller groupings according to country, region, state, city, community, or block divisions

**Global approach** Using the same product and promotion strategies in all markets

**Global corporation** A corporation that has operations in more than one country, exploits the countries' similarities to enhance competitive advantage, and operates from a one-world, one-market perspective

**Goods** Tangible products that customers can evaluate by touching, seeing, tasting, or hearing

**Goods-dominant products** Products for which the main benefits to customers are derived from goods

**Government market** Federal, state, local, and foreign governments that buy goods and services

**Growth phase** The second phase of a product's life cycle when sales increase rapidly and profits peak and begin declining

**Growth/share matrix** A portfolio analysis technique developed by the Boston Consulting Group that categorizes SBUs for investment based on their current market share and the prospects for growth of their market

**Guarantee** An assurance, written or implied, that a product is as represented and will perform satisfactorily

# H

**Hedonic needs** Needs for pleasure or personal expression

**Heterogeneity** The inconsistency in the performance of services that causes variations in quality

**Heterogeneous market** A market in which people or organizations have differing characteristics

**Hierarchy of effects model** A model of sequential customer responses to promotions; one version of the model starts with awareness and continues with comprehension, acceptance, preference, ownership, and satisfaction

**High-contact services** Services in which customers experience a high degree of involvement with the service providers

**Homogeneous market** A market in which people or organizations have similar characteristics

**Horizontal integration** The integration of intermediaries in one level of the marketing process, such as retail outlets

**Household** All the people who occupy a housing unit

**Hypermarkets** Discount retailers that practice scrambled merchandising by offering food and nonfood products in huge superstore locations; the largest of all retail operations

**Hypothesis** The marketer's untested assumption about the probable solution to the marketing problem

# I

**Ideas** Concepts, philosophies, or images that can be exchanged in the marketplace

**Import** To purchase goods and raw materials from one country and bring them into another country

**Import quota** A monetary or quantity limit placed on a product coming into a country

**In-house agency** A department inside a company that performs the complete range of advertising services, from developing ad strategies to buying media space and time

**Income** The consumer's financial gain from all sources, usually specified over some time interval

**Incremental method** A way of determining personnel needs based on the assumption that the addition of a salesperson is justified when the additional sales generated exceed the cost of hiring the salesperson

**Independent retailers** Retailers that are not part of large retail organizations, but are owned by one person, two or more partners, or a family

**Independent variable** The marketplace factor that, when manipulated, affects a dependent variable

**Indirect channels** Marketing channels that rely on intermediaries to move products from producers to customers

**Indirect exporting** Selling goods or services to another country through an intermediary

**Indirect-action advertising** Advertising that tries to influence future purchases and other actions

**Individual brand** A separate brand assigned to an individual product item within a product line

**Industrial/commercial market** The portion of the organizational market made up of companies that produce goods and services to be sold to other businesses or to consumers

**Industrialization of services** The application of technology and manufacturing techniques to services

**Inelastic demand** A price-demand relationship in which a decrease in price decreases total revenue

**Information** Data that are useful in a specific marketing situation to help marketers make a decision

**Infrastructure** A nation's energy (gas and electric utilities), transportation, and communication systems

**Inseparability** The attribute of services that denotes the inability to separate production from consumption

**Institutional advertising** Advertising that promotes the name or image of an organization, rather than its goods or services

**Intangibility** The characteristic of services that prevents customers from evaluating products according to sensory criteria

**Integrated marketing communications (IMC)** A strategy in which marketers try to coordinate and integrate all of their communications and promotions efforts with customers

**Intensive distribution** A channel strategy that seeks to make products available in as many appropriate places as possible

**Interactive marketing** Marketing situations in which the customer is actively involved in the production/performance and delivery of products

**Intercultural marketing** A strategy of recognizing and marketing to specific cultural segments; also called multicultural marketing

**Intermodal transportation** Transportation that uses more than one of the five principal modes

**International marketing** Marketing across national boundaries

**Introduction phase** The first phase of a product's life cycle when sales growth is slow and profits are low or nonexistent

**Intuition** The personal beliefs, experiences, and views of a marketer

**Involvement** The degree of personal importance or relevance a decision has for a consumer

# J

**Joint venture** Collaboration by two or more companies on a task or product, sharing assets, risks, and profits

**Jury of executive opinion** A method of forecasting that averages the predictions of top executives of the firm to create a sales forecast

**Just-in-time inventory management** A technique that seeks to decrease costs by maintaining lower inventories of parts and materials

# K

**Knowledge structure** An arrangement of related bits of information in a consumer's mind

# L

**Labor-based services** Services that are delivered primarily by people

**Laboratory experiment** An experiment set in an environment where all the factors can be controlled

**Leader pricing** The strategy of pricing one or more products at attractively low prices (and usually with low profit as well), with the purpose of attracting customers; the intent is to sell a mix of other products in addition to your leaders so that your overall profit picture remains acceptable

**Lifestyle** A person's interests, activities, likes and dislikes, and consumption patterns

**Limited problem solving (LPS)** Choosing between a small number of alternatives using only a few criteria

**Limited-line retailers** Retailers that restrict their product lines to just a few that are carried in great depth

**Limited-line wholesalers** Full-service merchant wholesalers that carry only a few lines; however, they typically carry deeper selections in their lines than do general merchandisers

**Limited-service merchant wholesalers** Those merchant wholesalers that perform fewer marketing channel functions than their full-service counterparts

**List price** The "official" price of a product, even if the product is sold at that price only occasionally

**Logo** A unique symbol that represents a specific firm or organization, or a brand name written in a distinctive type style

**Loss leader** In an extreme case of leader pricing, this is a product that is sold at negative profit

**Low-contact services** Services in which customers experience a low degree of involvement with the service providers

# M

**Mail-order wholesalers** Limited-service merchants that operate in the same manner as mail-order retailers but focus on retailers and organizational customers rather than consumers

**Make/buy decision** The choice organizations (and consumers) face between making a product themselves and buying it from an outside supplier

**Manufacturer brand** A brand that is designated, owned, and used by the manufacturer of the product

**Manufacturers' agents** Independent firms that perform a variety of marketing functions, including personal selling, on behalf of the manufacturers they represent; they are paid on commission, don't assume ownership, and rarely take physical possession

**Manufacturers' export agents (MEAs)** Firms that perform services similar to those of export management companies, except that they operate under their own names and don't always maintain long-term relationships with producers

**Marginal analysis** A method of cost analysis that identifies maximum potential profit by showing when marginal cost is equal to marginal revenue

**Marginal cost** The expense required to produce one more unit; the incremental cost of increasing production by one unit

**Marginal revenue** The revenue generated by selling one additional unit; this figure is used in marginal analysis to help identify maximum potential profit

**Market** The customers and potential customers who want or need a product and who are willing and able to exchange something for it

**Market attractiveness/business position model** Developed by General Electric and the consulting firm of McKinsey & Company, this portfolio analysis model evaluates market attractiveness and business position in terms of multiple criteria

**Market development strategy** A growth strategy that involves entering new markets with existing products

**Market penetration strategy** A growth strategy based on increasing the intensity of the firm's marketing effort in its current markets with current products

**Market potential** The amount of product, in dollars or units, that a firm's entire industry can be expected to sell during some specified future period

**Market price** The actual price at which a product sells (to consumers and organizational customers other than resellers); equal to list price minus discounts and allowances

**Market segmentation** A way of dividing a large market into smaller groupings of consumers or organizations in which each subset has a common characteristic such as needs, wants, or behavior

**Market segmentation matrix** A grid that illustrates the marketing segments formed when two or more segmentation variables are applied to a market

**Market share** An organization's portion of the total sales in a given market, expressed as a percentage

**Market-based organization** An organization that directs a unique marketing effort at each market segment in which a firm is active

**Marketing** The process of developing and exchanging ideas, goods, and services that satisfy customer and organizational needs, using the principles of pricing, promotion, and distribution

**Marketing audit** A comprehensive, systematic, periodic review of a firm's marketing environment, objectives, strategies, and activities

**Marketing channel** A system designed to move goods and services from producers to customers, which consists of people and organizations supported by various facilities, equipment, and information resources

**Marketing communications** The specific use of communication applied to the problem of sending messages to a target market

**Marketing concept** The idea of maximizing long-term profitability while integrating marketing with other parts of the company and meeting customer needs and wants

**Marketing control** Reviewing marketing plans and modifying them as market conditions develop and change

**Marketing cost analysis** Examining marketing costs, their sources, why they are incurred, their size, and their change over time

**Marketing culture** A corporate culture geared toward customer satisfaction through marketing concepts and procedures

**Marketing database** A computerized system to store and retrieve data as needed by marketers

**Marketing decision support system (MDSS)** A computerized system of accessing and handling MIS data and other data so that marketers can apply analysis and modeling methods and immediately see the results

**Marketing environment** The general atmosphere in which marketers operate and are influenced by such external elements as competitors, economics, nature, politics, regulations, technology, and society

**Marketing era** The period that began in the 1950s and continues today, during which companies formed marketing departments, began to pay attention to customer wants and needs, and started to implement the marketing concept

**Marketing ethics** The moral sensibility that guides marketing choices and activities

**Marketing information system (MIS)** An established series of procedures and methods to collect, sort, analyze, store, and distribute marketing information on an on-going basis

**Marketing intelligence** Information on trends and forces in the marketing environment

**Marketing intermediaries** People or organizations that assist in the flow of products in a marketing channel

**Marketing mix** The four key elements of marketing strategy: product, promotion, distribution, and price

**Marketing myopia** Product orientation without regard for customer benefits

**Marketing plan** A formal document that details your objectives, your situation analysis, your marketing strategy, and the elements of your marketing mix

**Marketing research** The systematic collecting, recording, and analyzing of information to support marketing decision making

**Marketing strategy** The overall plan for marketing a product that includes selecting and analyzing a target market and creating and maintaining a marketing mix

**Mass marketing** The practice of covering an entire market with one marketing mix

**Materials management** Overseeing the systems that move materials within warehouses and factories, between a company's facilities, and to customers; sometimes also includes the purchasing function

**Maturity phase** The third phase in a product's life cycle when sales level off and profits decline

**Media plan** A plan that outlines the objectives of an advertising campaign, the target audience, and the specific media vehicles that will be used to reach that audience

**Medium** The channel used to carry a message; this includes sales presentations, newspapers, radio, television, and direct-mail materials

**Merchandise assortment** The unique mix of products offered by one retailer that is not available from any other retailer

**Merchandising** The process of planning the merchandise assortment for a retail store, making sure the right products are available for target customers; also refers to the presentation of products in the retail environment

**Merchant wholesalers** Independent businesses that buy products from producers and then resell them to retailers and organizational customers

**Merchants** Intermediaries that assume ownership of the goods they sell to customers or other intermediaries; merchants usually take physical possession of the goods they sell

**Message** An idea that has been encoded and is capable of being transmitted

**Microculture** A group of people who share beliefs, values, and customs different from those of the larger culture

**Middleman** An outdated term that is synonymous with marketing intermediary—a person or organization that helps producers move products through marketing channels

**Missionary salespeople** Salespeople who disseminate information about new products to existing customers and who motivate them to resell to their customers

**Modeling** Learning behaviors by observing others

**Modified rebuy** An organizational buying situation in which the purchaser considers a limited number of choices before making a decision

**Monopolistic competition** A competitive structure in which many marketers compete to sell similar products and in which marketing strategies typically emphasize product differentiation

**Monopoly** A competitive structure in which one marketer controls the supply of a product that has no direct substitutes

**Motives** Internal factors that activate and direct behavior toward some goal

**Moving average** A forecasting method that averages inside a moving window of fixed duration; for instance, a three-month moving average averages three months of data at a time and then adds the newest month and discards the oldest month to compute the next data point

**MRO items** Consumable industrial supplies categorized specifically as maintenance, repair, and operating supplies

**Multilevel marketing (MLM)** A hierarchical distribution system in which independent distributors sell products and recruit other distributors to work for them

**Multinational corporation** A corporation that has operations in more than one country, exploits the countries' differences to enhance competitive advantage, and operates primarily from a domestic perspective

**Multinational market** A group of individual countries that band together to reduce trade barriers among participating countries

**Multiple-zone pricing** A modification of single-zone pricing that uses more than one zone and calculates an average shipping charge for each zone

# N

**Natural elements** Factors in the marketing environment that are not human-made, such as natural resources, weather, and geologic and astronomical events

**Need-satisfaction approach** An approach to selling that focuses on identifying the customer's needs and then creating a presentation that addresses those needs

**Needs** Differences between customers' actual conditions and their desired conditions; the driving forces behind all purchases

**New-task purchase** An organizational buying situation in which the purchaser is unfamiliar with the product and must use an extensive decision-making process to arrive at a choice

**Noise** Anything that detracts from the effectiveness of communication, ranging from actual audio noise to competing advertisements

**Nondurable goods** Goods that are used or consumed over a short period of time or after one or a few uses; examples include food and office supplies

**Nonprice competition** Competition that occurs on factors other than price, such as quality, image, convenience of distribution, and performance

**Nonprobability samples** Samples in which items are selected from the population according to convenience, a quota, or the researcher's judgment

**Nonprofit marketing** Marketing with objectives that don't involve financial return; includes the marketing of ideas, causes, places, persons, and organizations, as well as goods and services sold without profit motives

**Nonprospects** Consumers or organizations that are not potential customers

**Nonstore retailing** A retailing method that creates a marketing channel between producers and consumers without physical stores

# O

**Objective and task budgeting** An approach to setting promotional budgets that starts with a clearly defined objective and then derives the budget needed to execute the tasks necessary to meet that objective

**Observation** The recording of consumer actions or marketplace events as they occur

**Odd-even pricing** A pricing technique that uses specific numbers chosen for their supposed psychological effect on customers; the most common approach is prices that end in 9, just below a round number

**Off-peak pricing** The practice of using lower prices to stimulate demand during times of low demand

**Off-price retailers** Retailers that buy out-of-season or leftover products from manufacturers and large department stores and then offer the merchandise at low prices in self-service environments

**Oligopoly** A competitive structure in which a small number of competitors control the market

**Operational planning** Planning that is engaged in by supervisory managers and that focuses on activities of narrow scope and short duration

**Opinion leaders** Individuals who exert influence on consumer decisions through word of mouth

**Optimal quality** The level of quality that meets customer specifications while providing the best balance of satisfaction and cost

**Order getters** Salespeople responsible for generating new sales and increasing sales to existing customers

**Order processing** The systems used to receive orders, route them to appropriate supplying functions, and then arrange customer billing

**Order takers** Salespeople who primarily process orders for existing customers

**Organizational buying process** The steps that organizations go through to purchase goods and services

**Organizational market** Group that buys goods and services for use in its operations, for resale, or as raw materials or components for other products

**Organizational mission** A statement of the firm's desired role in its sphere of business, often stated in terms of long-term goals and objectives

**Organizational structure** A formal definition of people's responsibilities and the allocation of authority in a company

**Origin-point pricing** A class of geographic pricing that doesn't include shipping charges in the selling price; also called FOB pricing

# P

**Penetration pricing** A value-pricing technique in which you set prices aggressively low in order to gain as much market share as possible; the opposite of skim pricing

**Perceived risk** Uncertainty about a purchase decision and concern about the potential losses from making the wrong choice

**Perception** Reception and interpretation of sensory stimuli

**Perceptual map** A diagram that shows how customers perceive products in the market according to the most important attributes

**Perfectly elastic demand** The case when changes in demand have no effect on price; the opposite of perfectly inelastic demand

**Perfectly inelastic demand** The most extreme case of inelastic demand, in which changes in price have no effect on demand; this applies to products that people can't or won't live without

**Performance correction** Methods for changing a marketing system in order to improve performance

**Performance evaluation** The process of comparing actual results with expected performance

**Performance standards** The expected level of marketing performance; typical standards are specified levels of sales, profit, or market share

**Peripheral services** Services performed by a company in support of its core service offering

**Perishability** The quality of services that prevents the creation or storage of inventory

**Personal selling** In-person communication between a seller and one or more potential buyers

**Personality** A person's evaluation of a product, person, place, idea, or issue

**Physical distribution** The movement of goods from producers to customers; it includes order processing, inventory management, materials handling, warehousing, and transportation

**Pioneer advertising** Advertising that tries to build primary, rather than selective, demand

**Place utility** The value of providing products where customers want them

**Planned shopping center** A carefully conceived cluster of retailers, balanced by size and type of store, organized in one location with an architectural theme and dedicated parking

**Point-of-purchase (POP) advertising** Advertising, displays, and other materials that are placed in stores to catch shoppers' attention as they are selecting products

**Political elements** Factors in the marketing environment related to domestic and international politics and governmental policies

**Population** The universe of people, places, or things to be investigated in a specific research study

**Portfolio analysis** One of several techniques for categorizing a firm's SBUs for purposes of investment, development, or divestiture

**Position** The spot that a product holds in the minds of current and potential customers, relative to competitive products

**Positioning** The process of achieving a desired spot in the minds of customers and potential customers; you can position your company, your products, your technologies, or any other entity that commands customer attention

**Possession utility** The value of owning a product and controlling its use

**Postpurchase dissonance** A feeling of discomfort or doubt following a purchase

**Posttesting** The practice of testing audience reactions and response to ads after they are run

**Power centers** Version of strip malls designed to showcase large "category killer" and other big discounters

**Predatory pricing** The practice of lowering prices to a point where they inflict financial damage on competitors: the extreme case of predatory pricing seeks to drive competitors out of business entirely and is illegal

**Premium** Item that is given away with a product as part of a sales promotion

**Press conference** Bringing media representatives together for an announcement

**Press relations** The practice of communicating with members of the press about your company, its products, and its people

**Press release** A short document, also called a news release, that outlines some newsworthy event or activity and that companies send to reporters and editors with the hope of getting press coverage; press releases for television reporters are often done on videotape

**Prestige pricing** A technique that attempts to use a high price to establish an image of quality or exclusivity

**Pretesting** The practice of testing ads before they are run

**Price** The value, usually in monetary terms, that sellers ask in exchange for the products they are offering

**Price discrimination** The practice of offering attractive discounts to some customers but not to others for the same product; usually illegal

**Price elasticity of demand** The measure of price sensitivity, expressed as the ratio of percentage change in demand to percentage change in price

**Price fixing** An illegal collaboration between two or more competitors who agree on the prices they'll charge for products in the same category

**Price leadership** The position in a given market held by the company that takes the lead in raising or lowering prices

**Price lining** The establishment of a limited number of price levels that cover an entire product line

**Price sensitivity** An indication of the effect price has on buyers' intentions to purchase a given product or class of product; if buyers are considered price sensitive, changes in price will cause definite changes in their buying behavior

**Price war** A market situation in which competitors constantly try to beat each other's prices; a frequent result is that prices are driven down so low that companies sell at a loss

**Primary data** Data that are gathered directly from the subjects or through on-site research for a specific marketing research program

**Private brand** A brand that is designated, owned, and used by a wholesaler or retailer

**Private warehouses** Warehouses owned by a company for its exclusive use

**Proactive marketing** An approach to marketing in which you try to anticipate changes in the marketing environment and perhaps even try to influence future changes

**Probability samples** Samples in which every member of the population has a known, nonzero chance of being chosen to be surveyed

**Problem definition** A clear description of the marketing problem being researched

**Product** A good, service, or idea for which customers will exchange money or something else of value

**Product advertising** Advertising that promotes specific goods and services while promoting the supplying company to a lesser degree or not at all

**Product development strategy** A growth strategy that improves present products or develops new ones for the firm's current markets

**Product diffusion process** The acceptance of new products by various segments of a market

**Product liability** A product's capacity to cause damage or injury for which the producer or manufacturer is held responsible

**Product life cycle** A model that describes the stages that a product or a product category passes through, from its introduction to its removal from the market

**Product line** A group of closely related product items

**Product line depth** The number of products in each product line

**Product line extension** A method of adding products to the product mix by introducing products into an existing product line

**Product line width** The number of product lines in a company's product mix

**Product mix** A company's complete assortment of product lines and items

**Product placement** The tactic of paying movie producers to promote products in movies; in some cases, products or signs are shown in the scene, and in other cases the stars actually use or consume the products

**Product portfolio** A combination of products and product lines balanced to achieve the company's profitability goals and satisfy the needs of the target market

**Product value** A measure of the value that products represent to customers; equal to the benefits a product provides minus the costs of acquiring and owning it

**Product-based organization** An organization structure that uses product managers to handle the marketing mix for each of the products in the firm's marketing portfolio

**Production era** The period extending from the Industrial Revolution to about 1930, during which companies focused on perfecting their manufacturing techniques

**Profit Impact on Marketing Strategy (PIMS)** A database developed by the Strategic Planning Institute that is used to compare strategies with marketplace performance and thereby isolate reasons for marketing success

**Profit margin** The amount of profit left over after expenses have been accounted for, expressed as a percentage of revenue

**Promotion** A variety of techniques, including advertising, sales promotion, public relations, and personal selling, that are used to communicate with customers and potential customers

**Promotional discounts** Discounts given as part of promotional programs, such as when products are put on sale to increase traffic in a retail store

**Promotional mix** A combination of two or more elements of advertising, sales promotion, public relations, and personal selling

**Prospects** Consumers or organizations that are potential customers

**Prosperity** The stage of the business cycle in which consumers enjoy high income, willingness to spend, and low unemployment

**Protectionism** A country's attempt to protect its own industries by imposing high tariffs on competitive imported goods

**Psychographic segmentation** A way of dividing large markets into smaller groupings according to consumer lifestyles, activities, opinions, and beliefs

**Psychological influences** Characteristics within the individual that influence consumer behavior

**Psychological pricing** A general term encompassing all techniques that attempt to evoke a certain reaction based on price; applies both to prestige and to odd-even pricing

**Public relations (PR)** Promotion that uses nonpaid communication to influence public opinion of a company and its products

**Public warehouses** Warehouses that offer storage space to all companies

**Publicity** News media coverage of a company or its products

**Pull strategy** A promotional strategy that primarily builds demand with the final customer and relies on that customer to request the product from the marketing channel; the opposite of a push strategy

**Pure competition** The ideal competitive structure in which many marketers compete to sell the same undifferentiated product

**Push strategy** A promotional strategy that relies primarily on pushing products through each stage of the marketing channel, from producer to wholesaler to retailer to customer; push strategies can also be used in direct channels, with salespeople presenting products to customers

# Q

**Qualified prospect** A prospect who has been identified as being a purchasing decision maker and has the financial resources to pay for the product

**Quality** A measure of how closely a product conforms to customers' needs, wants, and expectations

**Quality circle** An informal group of people who meet to diagnose and solve problems with processes and product quality

**Quality function deployment (QFD)** A technique for evaluating customer needs and linking those needs to product features; the result is higher-quality products that do a better job of meeting customers' expectations

**Quantity discount** A discount based on the number of products purchased or on the total value of the purchase

# R

**Rack jobbers** Specialty-line wholesalers that own and stock racks of selected products, such as food and kitchen accessories, on location for their retailer customers

**Random factor analysis** Analysis of unexplained differences between predicted and actual sales behavior; usually due to such random occurrences as strikes, wars, and factory fires

**Reach** A measure of the portion of the target audience that will be reached by an advertisement

**Reactive marketing** An approach to marketing in which you view environmental forces as uncontrollable and simply try to adjust to changes after they occur

**Recession** The stage of the business cycle in which unemployment rises and consumer buying power drops

**Reciprocity** The practice of buying products from one's own customers; it is illegal if the arrangement restricts competition

**Recovery** The stage of the business cycle in which the economy moves from depression or recession toward prosperity

**Reference group** A group that has an influence on a particular consumer

**Regrouping activities** Four functions (sorting out, accumulating, allocating, and assorting) that eliminate discrepancies of quantity or assortment

**Regulatory elements** Factors in the marketing environment, specifically laws and regulations, that govern pricing, distribution, promotion, and product decisions

**Reinforcement** Strengthening behavior as a result of rewards

**Relationship marketing** A strategy to build long-term customer loyalty that is based on becoming partners with customers and doing everything possible to contribute to their success

**Reliability** One of the aspects of the scientific method requiring repeated studies to produce the same result every time

**Reminder advertising** Advertising aimed at existing customers, telling them that products they've adopted are still available

**Repositioning** An attempt to change the way existing products are perceived by consumers; the term is also applied to one marketer's efforts to change the perceived position of a competitor's product

**Request for proposal (RFP)** A document sent to potential suppliers, outlining requirements and requesting bids

**Resale price maintenance** The effort of manufacturers to suggest and potentially influence the prices charged by retailers carrying their products

**Resellers** Establishments in the organizational market that help move goods and services from producers to consumers

**Retailer cooperative** A voluntary contractual marketing system led by a group of retailers

**Retailer image** The personality of the retailer as perceived by consumers

**Retailers** Intermediaries that sell to final customers; they purchase goods from wholesalers, or in some cases, directly from producers

**Retailing** The end link in the marketing channel that moves products from manufacturers to consumers

**Return on equity** A measure of profitability that is similar to ROI but indicates profit as a percentage of the owner's equity in the company

**Return on investment (ROI)** A measure of profitability; specifically, the ratio of profits to overall investment

**Routine problem solving (RPS)** Automatic buying behavior

# S

**Safety stock** Extra inventory kept on hand to cover unexpected demand or delays in receiving new stock

**Salary-plus-commission compensation plan** Payment that combines a guaranteed salary with incentive pay

**Sales analysis** Comparison of current sales with past sales, industry sales, sales by competitors, and forecast sales as a method of evaluating a firm's performance

**Sales branches** Manufacturer-owned selling locations that perform a variety of marketing functions; distinguished from sales offices by the fact that they carry inventory and usually fill orders from stock

**Sales era** The period from approximately 1930 to 1950, during which companies focused on promoting and distributing their products

**Sales forecast** An estimate of a firm's sales volume in dollars or units for a specified future period

**Sales incentives** Various types of prizes awarded through sales contests

**Sales lead** The name of an individual, organization, or business that might be a likely prospect for the company's product

**Sales management** Planning the personal selling effort, organizing the sales personnel, and developing a winning sales team

**Sales offices** Manufacturer-owned selling locations that are similar in many respects to sales branches, except that sales offices don't carry inventory

**Sales promotion** Techniques that are used to stimulate product demand, including special events and activities such as coupons, celebrity appearances, and contests

**Sales quota** The sales goal established for each salesperson

**Sales support personnel** Salespeople who generally facilitate the overall selling effort by providing a variety of services

**Sample** A portion of a population that represents the whole in a research study

**Sampling error** A measure of the discrepancy between the results of surveying a sample and the expected results of surveying the entire population

**Scientific method** The process of methodically gathering and organizing data in an objective way

**Scrambled merchandising** A retail technique that mixes product lines related and unrelated to the retailer's main merchandise focus

**Search qualities** Product attributes that can be objectively evaluated prior to purchase

**Seasonality** The effect exhibited by recurring annual fluctuations in sales data; seasonality is caused by such events as school schedules, weather cycles, holidays, and crop-growing seasons

**Secondary data** Data that have been collected for other purposes, not specifically for the research being conducted

**Selective attention** Choosing to attend to only a small portion of the stimuli to which you are exposed

**Selective distribution** A channel strategy that limits availability of products to a few carefully selected outlets in a given market area

**Self-concept** Your perceptions, beliefs, and feelings about yourself

**Self-regulation** A form of nongovernmental regulation in which industry groups or leaders promote specific marketing approaches

**Sellers' markets** Market conditions in which the demand for products exceeds the supply, giving sellers an advantage in the exchange process

**Selling agents** Agent intermediaries that go beyond manufacturers' agents by taking control of promotion, pricing, and distribution; they are used by producers that don't want to get involved in the marketing of their own products

**Service capacity management** The process of smoothing demand fluctuations and responding to fluctuations that cannot be smoothed

**Service infrastructure** The people, procedures, systems, and equipment that allow a company to provide superior customer service

**Service mark** A trademark that represents a service rather than a tangible good

**Service motivation** The quality that drives a salesperson to want to provide good service to a customer

**Service sector** That portion of the economy whose output is services, as opposed to goods

**Service-dominant products** Products for which the main benefits to customers are derived from services

**Serviceability** A measure of how easily a product can be diagnosed, repaired, and maintained

**Services** Intangible products that offer financial, legal, medical, recreational, or other benefits to the consumer

**Shopping products** Products that are more costly and involve more risk than convenience products, thereby causing buyers and users to invest more time and effort when making the selection

**Signaling** Sending a message to competitors about your pricing intentions; this includes both genuine messages and "bluffs"

**Simulated test marketing** A forecasting method that gathers data for predicting a product's likely market performance by marketing it in artificial settings

**Single sourcing** Using only a single supplier for a particular product

**Single-line retailers** Retailers that carry only one product line in great depth

**Single-source data** A technique of gathering and storing data about product and brand sales, coupon redemption, and television advertising, in a single database

**Single-zone pricing** Delivered pricing that charges each customer an average shipping charge based on the seller's total shipping expenses; customers end up paying more or less than the actual shipping cost

**Situational influences** Factors within a particular time or place that influence consumer behavior

**Skim pricing** A variation of value pricing for new products in which you attempt to recover a high level of profit for a limited period of time, based on the unique value that you're offering the market

**Slotting allowance** A specific example of the sort of power retailers can exert over producers, in which retailers refuse to grant shelf space to a product unless the producers give them some promotional money first

**Social classes** Stratified groups in society made up of people with similar values, lifestyles, interests, and behaviors

**Social elements** Factors in the marketing environment that correlate with social trends, including changes in consumer values and tastes

**Social marketing** Nonprofit marketing that aims to change attitudes and behaviors on various social and personal issues

**Social responsibility** Marketers' duty to enhance the welfare of customers and the general public through their products

**Societal marketing concept** An expanded view of marketing urging companies and organizations to act in ways that contribute to society's well-being

**Sorting out** Dividing one heterogeneous supply into separate, homogeneous supplies

**Source** The person or organization that originates and encodes a message

**Source loyalty** An organizational customer's commitment to continue buying from its current suppliers

**Specialty products** Products that are the most costly and that are unique or so specialized that buyers and users are willing to expend great effort to seek out and acquire them

**Specialty stores** Limited-line retailers that carry narrow product assortments in great depth

**Specialty-line wholesalers** Full-service merchant wholesalers with the narrowest product line selection of all; they typically offer only a few products, but they provide high levels of expertise in product application and market knowledge

**Standard Industrial Classification (SIC)** A system devised by the U.S. government that assigns codes to industries based on various product categories

**Standard markup pricing** A version of cost-plus pricing in which you assign a predetermined markup to average total cost in order to arrive at the selling price

**Statistical interpretation** Using statistical methods to learn how some data differ from the study's averages and how some data are similar to the study's averages, and the reasons for these deviations

**Stockout** The lack of products to sell, caused by inventory shortages

**Straight commission compensation plan** Payment of a percentage of the sales or of the gross profits salespeople generate

**Straight rebuy** An organizational buying situation in which the purchaser automatically reorders the same item from the same supplier

**Straight salary compensation plan** Payment of a fixed amount of money at regular intervals

**Strategic business unit (SBU)** A unit of the firm that can be considered a separate entity for planning purposes; it may be a single product, a product line, a division, or the entire company

**Strategic marketing planning** The process of exploring marketing opportunities, investing time and money to pursue those opportunities, and predicting the outcome of those investments

**Strategic window** A limited period of time during which the characteristics of a market and the distinctive competencies of a firm fit together well and reduce the risks of seizing a particular market opportunity

**Subliminal advertising** Advertising that attempts to influence consumer perceptions and behavior through symbols that are not consciously decoded; both the existence and effectiveness of subliminal advertising are open to question, however

**Suboptimization** A loss of efficiency or cost controls caused when one of the factors in a system is emphasized at the expense of the total system's performance

**Supermarkets** Stores that sell primarily food items with selections wide enough to meet most customers' grocery shopping needs

**Superstores** Stores that combine food and nonfood items in large retail locations; larger than supermarkets but smaller than hypermarkets

**Survey** A method of gathering data directly from consumers via a questionnaire

**Syndicated data services** Marketing research firms that regularly collect data on a variety of issues by following a standardized format

**Systems selling** The concept of selling a "package" of goods or services designed to meet a customer's unique needs

# T

**Tabulating** Calculating the answers to survey questions and then summarizing for interpretation

**Tactical planning** Planning typically undertaken by middle management to examine the performance over a relatively short period of time of specific products in a firm's marketing portfolio

**Target market** The market you've selected as the focus of your marketing program; it covers the potential customers you think are most likely to need or want your product

**Target marketing** The practice of identifying desirable segments in a market and developing special marketing mixes to meet the needs of those segments

**Tariff** A tax imposed by a government on goods entering its borders

**Technical salespeople** Salespeople who contribute technical expertise and assistance to the selling function

**Technology** The result of applying scientific and engineering knowledge to practical problems

**Technology licensing** A type of licensing arrangement in which one company sells its technology to other companies

**Telemarketing** A promotional method utilizing specially trained salespeople to systematically contact a group of prospects or customers by telephone

**Television home shopping** A nonstore retailing technique in which shoppers watch product displays on special television shows and then order products by phone

**Test marketing** Field experiments in which markets select a geographic area in which to try a new product and measure sales or usage results

**Time utility** The value of providing products when customers want them

**Time-series analysis** A collection of forecasting methods that predict future sales by analyzing historical sales patterns

**Total cost** The sum of variable costs and fixed costs; represents all the expenses required to make a specified number of units

**Total cost concept** The practice of considering all the costs associated with distribution in order to attain the best balance among all the cost factors

**Total quality management (TQM)** A philosophy and management system that bases everything an organization does on the pursuit of quality

**Trade deficit** The amount by which a country's imports exceed its exports

**Trade discounts** Discounts at which products are sold to wholesalers and retailers; trade discounts allow these marketing intermediaries to recover their costs and generate profits

**Trade marts** Permanent facilities where wholesalers and retailers can shop for various goods, such as furniture and computer equipment; if they sell to final customers, those customers are charged higher prices

**Trade name** The business name under which an organization operates

**Trade salespeople** Salespeople who take orders as well as provide support services, such as helping retailers promote the producer's product

**Trade shows** Exhibitions that feature a specific industry's products and bring together buyers and sellers for a short period of time; many industries use trade shows as forums for technical, political, and other issues as well

**Trademark** A brand or portion of a brand that is legally registered with the U.S. government for exclusive use by the owner of the brand

**Trading company** Company that buys and distributes goods from many countries

**Trend analysis** A time-series forecasting method that creates an equation to describe the expected behavior of sales in the future using sales data accumulated over some period in the past

**Truck wholesalers** Limited-service wholesalers that sell directly from trucks and other vehicles; they are common in tools and perishable foods

**Tying contracts** Contracts specifying that other products must be purchased along with the central product in a transaction; in most cases such arrangements are illegal

# U

**Unaided recall** A posttesting technique that, without prompting the audience's memory by showing the ads, asks people about their recall of advertising

**Uncontrollable elements** External factors such as currency exchange rates, consumer tastes, and political shifts, over which the marketer has no control (although some elements may be subject to influence)

**Undifferentiated marketing** A strategy in which you sell only one product or product line and offer it to all customers in a single marketing mix; another name for mass marketing

**Uniform pricing** An extreme case of price lining in which all products are sold for one price

**Unit pricing** Prices that are calculated in terms of some common standard of measurement, such as ounces, to make price comparisons easier for consumers

**Unitization** The process of combining individual packages into a larger unit, such as a pallet, for transportation

**Universal product code (UPC)** A type of bar code assigned to products, which indicates price, weight, and inventory number and can be read by optical scanners at store checkout counters

**Utilitarian needs** Needs that fulfill a functional purpose

**Utility** The ability of a product to satisfy the customer's wants or needs

# V

**Validity** The ability to design marketing research that will measure specifically what researchers need to know

**Value analysis** A comparison of the cost of a potential purchase and the benefits it promises

**Value pricing** A somewhat vague term often used to describe the practice of adopting a lower price while maintaining the product's basic value

**Value-added reseller (VAR)** Intermediaries that buy basic products from producers, add value by modifying or expanding the products, then resell them to final customers

**Value-added wholesaling** Wholesaling services that exceed the normal wholesaling functions; applies to anything done by wholesalers to help customers sell more products at lower costs

**Value/price ratio** A measure of how much value customers get in exchange for the price paid

**Values** Beliefs about what is good or desirable

**Variable costs** The portion of a company's production and marketing costs that are dependent on the level of production

**Variety stores** General merchandise retailers that offer fewer product lines and fewer brand choices than discount department stores at low prices in self-service environments

**Vending machines** Customer-operated machines that distribute products automatically upon payment

**Vendor analysis** Formal evaluation of suppliers

**Vertical integration** The process of developing a marketing system that includes both the source of production and the distribution capabilities; the result of vertical integration is called a vertical marketing system

**Vertical marketing system (VMS)** A channel that is integrated from producer down to final intermediary

# W

**Wants** The particular choices (including the type of product and the specific brands) that people make to satisfy their needs

**Warehouse club** A general merchandise retailer selling fewer product lines than discount department stores at very low prices in warehouselike stores

**Warranty** A statement specifying what the producer of a product will do to compensate the buyer if the product does not live up to its promised level of performance

**Wealth** Total financial resources accumulated over time

**Wheel of retailing** A theory that divides the cyclical patterns in retail evolution into three stages: innovation, trading up, and vulnerability

**Wholesaler-sponsored voluntary chain** A type of contractual marketing system that is led by one or more wholesalers

**Wholesalers** Intermediaries that perform a variety of marketing channel functions to move goods and services through the channel to retailers and organizational customers

**Word-of-mouth communication** Transmission of consumer information from person to person

# Indexes

# Author Index

Coleman, Richard P., R-4
Coletti, Richard J., R-8
Colley, Russell H., R-14
Collins, Tom, R-6, R-7
Comer, Lucette B., R-16
Conant, Jennet, R-12
Coney, Kenneth A., R-4,
Conlin, Elizabeth, R-7
Conlin, Joseph, R-16
Connelly, Mary, R-11
Constantin, James A., R-11
Cook, James, R-14
Cooke, Ernest F., R-5
Cooney, John, R-9, R-11, R-12, R-13
Cooper, Arnold C., R-3
Cooper, Robert G., R-8
Cooper, Scott W., R-7
Copeland, Lennie, R-17
Cortez, John P., R-3, R-13
Corwen, Leonard, 719
Cosco, Joseph, R-4
Cox, James, R-8, R-15
Cox, Meg, R-15
Crane, F. G., R-4
Cretan, Richard, R-7
Crispell, Diane, R-2
Croft, Nancy L., R-7
Cundiff, Edward, R-2, R-13, R-17
Cuneo, Alice Z., R-1
Curtis, Wayne, R-13
Cutlip, Scott M., R-14

Dadd, Debra Lynn, R-14
Dagnoli, Judann, R-7
Dahl, Jonathan, R-2, R-10, R-15
Daley, James M., R-7
Dalrymple, Douglas J., R-16
Darden, William R., R-5
Darlin, Damon, R-4, R-17
Davidow, William H., R-6, R-13, R-14, R-18
Davids, Meryl, R-14
Davidson, William R., R-12
Davis, E. J., R-3
Davis, Herbert W., R-13
Dawes, Philip L., R-15
Dawson, Reg, R-13
Day, Ellen, R-14
Day, George S., R-3, R-10
de Benedetto, C. Anthony, R-14, R-16
de Brentani, Ulrike, R-8
de Cordoba, Jose, R-6
Deeny, Godfrey, R-18
DeGeorge, Gail, R-8
Deierlein, R., R-13
Del Prete, Don, R-17
Delano, Frank, R-7
DeNitto, Emily, R-6, R-16
Dent, David J., R-4
Denton, D. Keith, R-18
Derchin, Michael, R-10
DeSouza, Glenn, R-18
Deutsch, Claudia H., R-16
Deveny, Kathleen, R-10, R-11
DeYoung, H. Garrett, R-17
Dholakia, Nikhilesh, R-7, R-8
Dichter, Ernest, R-6
Dobrzynski, Judith H., R-18
Dolan, Carrie, R-1
Dommermuth, William P., R-14
Donald, Arnold, R-3
Donnelly, James H., Jr., R-11
Dotson, Michael, R-13
Dovel, George P., R-1, R-3, R-7, R-14, R-15, R-40
Dowling, Grahame R., R-5
Doz, Yves L., R-17

Driesbach, Bruce R., R-6
Drew, Lisa, R-1
Dubinsky, Alan J., R-2, R-16
DuBois, Lois C., R-12
Due, Tananarive, R-8
Duff, Christina, R-10
Dugg, Christina, R-3
Duke, Paul, Jr., R-15
Dukowitz, Jim, R-18
Dumaine, Brian, R-3, R-17
Dumphy, Philip W., 718
Dunkin, Amy, R-3, R-5, R-9
Dunn, S. Watson, R-16
Dunne, Patrick M., R-19
Durgee, Jeffrey, R-6
Dychtwald, Ken, R-4

Edell, Julie A., R-15
Edmondson, Brad, R-6, R-9
Egyes, Gerald, R-13
Eisenhart, Tom, R-4, R-5, R-15, R-16, R-18, R-19
Eisman, Regina, R-16
Eklund, Christopher S., R-11
El-Ansary, Adel I., R-11, R-12
Eldridge, J. Douglas, R-13
Elias, Christopher, R-17
Elliott, Stuart, R-8, R-15, R-16
Endrijonas, Janet, R-18
Engardio, Pete, R-5, R-17
Engel, James F., R-3, R-4, R-5
Engel, Peter H., R-15
Englehardt, Tristam H., R-10
English, Mary McCabe, R-13
Enis, Ben M., R-2, R-7
Ensor, Pat, R-1
Enzer, Michael J., R-15
Erickson, Julie Liesse, R-6
Etzel, Michael J., R-4
Evenson, Laura, R-2
Exter, Thomas, R-2
Eyler, David R., 719
Ezell, Hazel F., R-12, R-13

Fabrikant, Geraldine, R-1
Fahey, Alison, R-1, R-4
Fallon, James, R-18
Fannin, Rebecca, R-1, R-6, R-8, R-11, R-17
Fanning, Deirdre, R-11
Farhi, Paul, R-5
Farhir, Paul, R-4
Faris, Charles W., R-5
Faris, Paul, R-16
Farley, Frank, R-4
Farney, Dennis, R-5
Farris, Paul W., R-19
Feinberg, Andrew, R-13
Feldman, Diane, R-18
Ferrell, O. C., R-2, R-3
Fierman, Jaclyn, R-3
Filley, Richard D., R-17
Finch, Peter, R-16
Fincham, Jack E., R-10
Finegan, Jay, R-3
Finney, F. Robert, R-5
Fisher, Christy, R-4, R-16
Fitzgerald, Kate, R-1, R-9, R-13
Flax, Steven, R-2, R-8
Fletcher, Keith, R-4
Fleury, Rick, R-9
Flint, Jerry, R-18
Foley, William M., R-9
Fost, Dan, R-4
Foster, Peter, R-17
Foust, Dean, R-1, R-4, R-9

Fox, Maria, 718
Franklin, Sheryl, R-1
Franz, Julie, R-6
Fraser, Cynthia, R-2
Frederick, Peter G., R-17
Freedman, Alix M., R-6, R-8, R-15
Friedman, Martin, R-8
Fry, Ronald W., 719
Fuhrman, Peter, R-2
Funkhouser, G. Ray, R-9
Futrell, Charles, R-16

Gable, Greg, R-4
Gabor, Andrea, R-1
Gadsden, Sheila, R-6
Gaidis, William C., R-4
Galante, Steven P., R-12, R-13
Gale, Bradley T., R-3
Garbett, Thomas F., R-15
Garda, Robert A., R-10, R-11
Garfield, Bob, R-7
Garfield, Robert, R-14
Garrison, John, R-14
Garry, Michael, R-2, R-13
Gassenheimer, Jule B., R-1
Geary, Robert, R-15
Geber, Beverly, R-17
Geer, John G., R-6
Gelbtuck, Howard C., R-13
Gellene, Denise, R-3, R-15
Gelman, David, R-1
Gendron, George, R-1
Ghemawat, Pankaj, R-3
Ghingold, Morry, R-5
Gibson, Richard, R-2, R-6, R-11
Gill, Mark Stuart, R-18
Gilman, Alan L., R-13
Gilman, Hank, R-6, R-11
Glaberson, William, R-1
Glen, Peter, R-18
Goel, Vindu P., R-5
Goerne, Carrie, R-4, R-8, R-12, R-13
Goldman, Debra, R-6
Goldman, Doron, R-15
Goldsmith, Herb, R-15
Goldstein, Mark, R-14
Golson, Thia, R-4
Goodbody, Jerry, R-2, R-14
Gordon, Jay, R-4, R-13
Gordon, Jeanne, R-1
Gorman, Tom, R-8
Gourley, David R., R-9
Goydon, Raymond, R-8
Grace, Roger H., R-12
Graen, George B., 718
Graham, Clarke, R-7
Graham, John L., R-5, R-11
Greco, Gail, R-7
Green, Colleen, R-9
Greenberg, Herbert, R-16
Greenberg, Jan, 719
Greenberg, Jeanne, R-16
Greenburg, Burnett, R-12
Greene, Marvin, R-12
Gregor, William, R-19
Grimm, Matthew, R-2, R-10, R-11, R-14, R-16
Griswold, Philip, R-8
Grönroos, Christian, R-9
Grossman, Cathy Lynn, R-10
Groves, Martha, R-9
Gudrige, Kevin, R-10
Guenther, Robert, R-2
Gunter, Dan L., R-8
Gupta, Udayan, R-9, R-17
Gutfeld, Rose, R-1
Guyon, Janet, R-2

Liu, Philip, R-18
Loeffelholz, Suzanne, R-9, R-10, R-11
Lofton, Terry, R-7
Lohr, Steve, R-6, R-10
Loomis, Carol J., R-14, R-16
Lopez, Julie Amparano, R-10
Lovelock, Christopher H., R-9
Lublin, Joann S., R-2, R-11, R-17
Lubove, Seth, R-5
Lucas, George H., Jr., R-3
Luck, David J., R-3
Luckins, Rebecca, R-1
Luqmani, Mushtaq, R-8
Lusch, Robert F., R-11
Lynch, J. E., R-4
Lysonski, Steven, R-18

McAlister, Bill, R-5
McAllister, Celia F., R-2
McCarthy, Michael, R-9
McCarthy, Michael J., R-6, R-8,
    R-9, R-12, R-15
McClenahen, John S., R-17
McCoy, Charles, R-15
McCracken, Grant, R-15
McCracken, Robert F., R-16
McDaniel, Carl, Jr., R-5
McDermott, Michael J., R-13
MacDonald, Douglas, R-4
McDonald, Gael, R-3
McDonald, Malcolm, R-3
MacDonald, Malcolm H. B., R-3
MacDonald, Stephen, R-5, R-7
McElnea, Jeffrey K., R-15
McGill, Douglas C., R-1
McGinnis, Michael A., R-8
McGown, K. Lee, R-7
McGrath, Allan, R-18
Machalaba, Daniel, R-14
MacIntosh, Jean, R-18
Mack, Toni, R-8
McKenna, Joseph F., R-13
McLoughlin, William, R-9
McNair, Malcolm P., R-12
McQueen, Josh, R-15
McQuiston, Daniel H., R-5
McWilliams, Gary, R-5
Madigan, Kathleen, R-9
Madlin, Nancy, R-8
Magiera, Marcy, R-1
Magrath, Allan J., R-1, R-3, R-11
Mahajan, Vijay, R-3
Mahoney, David, R-8
Main, Jeremy, R-17
Major, Michael, R-3
Malkin, Elisabeth, R-13
Mallory, Maria, R-17
Malloy, Michael T., R-6
Malone, Maggie, R-12
Malovany, Dan, R-10
Mandese, Joe, R-3
Maney, Kevin, R-10, R-12, R-17
Manji, James F., R-2
Mann, Jim, R-17
Manning, Anita, R-15
Manville, Richard, R-16
Maremount, Mark, R-2, R-11
Markell, Stephen J., R-3
Marks, Norton E., R-10
Maronick, Thomas J., R-12
Marsh, Barbara, R-5, R-6, R-11
Martin, James H., R-7
Martin, Justin, R-7
Martin, Richard, R-10
Martineau, Pierre, R-12
Maslow, Abraham, R-4
Mason, J. Barry, R-12, R-13

Mason, Julie Cohen, R-10
Mattson, Melvin R., R-5
May, Eleanor G., R-12
Mayer, Caroline E., R-11
Mayer, Morris L., R-12, R-13
Medley, H. Anthony, 719
Meeks, Fleming, R-1
Mehegan, David, R-10
Meier, Barry, R-1
Melloan, George, R-6
Menchin, Robert S., R-6
Mendonsa, Eugene L., R-4
Menon, Anil, R-16
Messenger, Robert, R-6
Messikomer, Edwin E., R-1
Meyer, Edward D., R-14, R-15
Meyer, Lee, R-6
Meyer, Marianne, R-7
Meyers, Janet, R-1, R-11
Michaels, Edward A., R-8
Miller, Annetta, R-7
Miller, Cyndee, R-4, R-5, R-12, R-15, R-16, R-18
Miller, Krystal, R-2, R-9
Miller, Mark Crispin, R-15
Miller, Norman M., R-12
Miniard, Paul W., R-3, R-4, R-5
Mishne, Patricia P., R-8
Mitchel, F. Kent, R-14
Mitchell, Eric, R-10
Mitchell, Russell, R-6, R-18
Mittal, Banwari, R-4
Moin, David, R-12
Moir, Agatha, R-13
Monroe, Kent B., R-10
Montgomery, Stephen L., R-10
Moore, Frazier, R-7
Moore, Geoffrey H., R-2
Moore, Martha T., R-9
Moore, Mary E., R-9
Moore, Timothy E., R-15
Moran, Ursula, R-11
Morgenson, Gretchen, R-12, R-13
Moriarity, Rowland T., R-10, R-11
Morris, Betsy, R-9, R-14
Morris, Gene, R-9
Morris, Michael H., R-5, R-9
Morrissey, Wiliam R., R-15
Morse, Michele Block, R-16
Moskowitz, Robert, R-16
Moss, Gary, R-14
Moss, Linda, R-6
Muller, E. J., R-13, R-14
Murphy, John M., R-7
Murphy, Liz, R-16
Murphy, Patrick E., R-2, R-7
Myers, Ken, R-18

Nag, Amal Kumar, R-2
Nagle, Thomas T., R-9, R-10
Naisbitt, John, R-2
Narus, James A., R-11
Nash, Jennie, R-7
National Association of Broadcasters, R-12
Nayak, P. R., R-8
Nayyar, Seema, R-11
Nazario, Sonia L., R-7
Neal, Mollie, R-2
Neeley, Sue E., R-3
Neidell, Lester A., R-3
Neiman, Janet, R-15
Nelson, Mark M., R-2
Netemeyer, Richard G., R-4
Neubert, Ralph L., R-2
Neuborne, Ellen, R-13
Neuharth, Al, R-1
Nolan, Martha, R-4
Nonaka, Ikujiro, R-5, R-7

Norman, Michael E., R-1
Norris, Eileen, R-15
Novick, Harold J., R-12
Nulty, Peter, R-17
Nussbaum, Bruce, R-8

Oates, David, R-1
Obermayer, James W., R-8
O'Boyle, Thomas F., R-10
Ohmae, Kinichi, R-4
O'Leary, Mick, R-1
O'Leary, Noreen, R-7
Oliver, Suzanne, R-8
Olsen, Eric, R-16
Olver, James, R-19
Ono, Yumiko, R-7, R-16
Orsini, Patricia, R-4
Oster, Patrick, R-7, R-17
Osterman, Jim, R-4
Oum, Tae H., R-10

Pae, Peter, R-10
Parasuraman, A., R-6, R-18
Parker, Rachel, R-18
Parr, Jan, R-12
Parry, John, R-2
Pasztor, Andy, R-10
Patterson, Gregory A., R-9
Patterson, Paul G., R-5
Patton, W. E., III, R-13
Patton, Wesley E., III, R-5
Pauly, David, R-17
Peak, Martha, R-17
Pearl, Daniel, R-14
Peers, Alexandra, R-13
Pembleton, Mary, R-13
Pepper, Jon, R-7
Perdue, Barbara C., R-5
Pereira, Joseph, R-2, R-13, R-17
Peroff, Mark, R-7
Perrin, Linda, 719
Perry, David, R-11
Peters, Thomas J., R-18
Petersen, Laurie, R-14
Petersen, Lisa Marie, R-14, R-18
Peterson, Robert A., R-5, R-6
Peterson, Thane, R-17
Phalon, Richard, R-7
Pham, Alex, R-11
Philips, N. V., R-18
Philips, Stephen, R-17
Phillips, Don, R-2
Phillips, Stephen, R-5
Pirto, Rebecca, R-5, R-6
Plymire, Jerry, R-18
Poling, Bill, R-10
Pollay, Richard W., R-14
Port, Otis, R-2
Porter, Michael E., R-3, R-17
Porterfield, Jim, 719
Powell, Michael A., 719
Powell, Tim, R-5
Powers, Thomas L., R-10
Prahalad, C. K., R-17
Prezzano, Wilber J., R-18
Prichard, Peter, R-1
Prickett, Dan S., R-6
Prince, Greg, R-3, R-14
Prinzing, Debra, R-12, R-15
Puri, S. Joe, R-16
Puto, Christopher, R-5

Quelch, John A., R-19
Quraeshi, Zahir, R-8

Raffield, Barney T., III, R-5, R-11,
    R-12, R-14, R-15

Raj, S. P., R-7
Ramirez, Anthony, R-2, R-8, R-13
Randall, Iris, R-16
Rangan, V. Kasturi, R-10
Rapp, Stan, R-6, R-7
Rebeck, George, R-2
Redenbacher, Orville, R-7
Regan, May Beth, R-7
Reibstein, Larry, R-10
Reidenbach, R. Eric, R-3
Remington, Todd, R-6
Renetzky, Alvin, 719
Rethans, Arno J., R-14
Revzin, Philip, R-2
Reynes, Tony, R-9
Rice, Faye, R-6, R-7, R-9
Rice, Valerie, R-18
Richman, Tom, R-8
Riddle, Judith Springer, R-7, R-18
Rie, Michael A., R-10
Riedesel, Paul L., R-5
Ries, Al, R-7, R-8
Rinehart, Dianne, R-17
Ringo, Sally, R-5
Rivinus, Willis M., R-17
Roberto, Eduardo L., R-3
Roberts, Christopher, R-3
Roberts, Mary Lou, R-7
Robertson, Kim, R-7
Robin, Donald P., R-3
Robinson, Patrick J., R-5
Robinson, William A., R-15
Rocha, Wanda, R-1
Roel, Raymond, R-3, R-11
Rogers, Alison, R-7
Rogers, Everett M., R-8
Rogers, William, R-19
Room, Adrian, R-7
Root, Ann R., R-5
Rosenberg, Jerry M., R-2
Rosenbloom, Bert, R-11
Rosenthal, David W., 719
Ross, Elliot B., R-10
Rothenberg, Randall, R-14
Rothfeder, Jeffrey, R-6
Rothman, Andrea, R-15
Rothman, Matt, R-15, R-24
Rothschild, Michael J., R-4
Rottman, Meg, R-1
Rowe, Megan, R-15, R-16
Rowland, Mary, R-5
Rudnitsky, Howard, R-13
Rudolph, Barbara, R-2
Ruekert, Robert W., R-19
Ruffenach, Glenn, R-14
Rukeyser, Louis, R-9, R-11, R-12, R-13
Runde, Robert, R-7
Russell, Cheryl, R-2, R-16
Ryans, Adrian B., R-10
Ryssel, Christian, R-15

Sabath, Robert E., R-13
Sadhwani, Arjan T., R-13
Salmon, Walter J., R-7
Samiee, Saeed, R-9
Samuelson, Robert J., R-6
Saporito, Bill, R-11, R-12, R-13
Sarhan, M. H., R-13
Sather, Jeanne, R-11
Saveri, Gabrielle, R-7, R-17
Scammon, Debra L., R-10
Schaaf, Dick, R-11, R-18
Schares, Gail E., R-2, R-17
Schendel, Dan, R-3
Schenk, Joseph A., R-6
Scherr, Richard C., R-1
Scherreik, Susan, R-13

Scheuing, Eberhard, R-16
Schiffman, Leon G., R-6
Schifrin, Matthew, R-11
Schiller, Zachery, R-1, R-7, R-8, R-11
Schiro, Anne-Marie, R-17
Schlender, Brenton R., R-3, R-9, R-10
Schlossberg, Howard, R-7, R-11, R-13,
    R-15, R-18
Schnaars, Steven P., R-3
Schneider, Kenneth C., R-10
Schnittker, John A., R-17
Schnorbus, Paula, R-1, R-11
Schul, Patrick L., R-16
Schultz, Don E., R-4, R-14
Schultz, Ellen, R-7
Schultz, Leslie M., R-15
Schulz, David P., R-12
Schuman, Nancy, 719
Schwadel, Francine, R-7, R-9, R-12, R-13, R-18
Schwartz, Bruce, R-9
Schwartz, James, R-14
Schwartz, Joe, R-4, R-7
Schwartz, John, R-3
Sease, Douglas R., R-18
Seideman, Tony, R-14
Seitel, Fraser P., R-4
Sellers, Patricia, R-3, R-6, R-11
Serafin, Raymond, R-3, R-4, R-14
Settle, Robert B., R-4
Seymour, Daniel T., R-5
Seymour, Jim, R-10
Shanklin, William L., R-2, R-7
Shao, Maria, R-3, R-17
Shapiro, Benson P., R-6, R-10
Shapiro, Eben, R-2, R-7
Sharkey, Betsy, R-4, R-14, R-15
Sharman, Graham, R-14
Shaw, Bill, R-2
Sheffet, Mary Jane, R-10
Sheridan, John H., R-8
Sherlock, Paul, R-4
Sherman, Andrew J., R-11
Sherman, Jean, R-15
Sherman, Richard J., R-12
Sherman, Stratford P., R-3
Sheth, Jagdish N., R-2
Shiffman, Leon G., R-4
Shilling, Dana, R-16
Shingelton, John, 719
Shiver, Jube, Jr., R-9, R-13
Shostack, G. Lynn, R-9
Shoultz, Donald, R-17
Shuster, Laurie A., R-12
Siconolfi, Michael, R-2
Signer, Alan, R-18
Sims, Calvin, R-8
Simurda, Stephen J., R-17
Sirgy, M. Joseph, R-4
Siridhara, Chanaporn, R-10
Skinner, Steven J., R-2
Skow, John, R-17
Slater, Karen, R-10
Sleight, Peter, R-6
Sloan, Pat, R-1, R-9
Smalheiser, Kenneth A., R-7
Small, John, R-8
Smalley, Allan G., Jr., R-1
Smarr, Susan L., R-17
Smart, Tim, R-5
Smith, Geri, R-5
Smith, J. Brock, R-16
Smith, Lee, R-17
Smith, Michael H., 719
Smith, Timothy K., R-3
Solomon, Barbara, R-13
Solomon, Michael R., R-1, R-4
Solomon, Stephen D., R-1

Solomon, Steven, R-12
Souder, William E., R-1
Spaeth, Tony, R-17
Speh, Thomas W., R-4
Springen, Karen, R-7
Stamminger, Erich, R-15
Stasch, Stanley F., R-6
Stein, Elizabeth A., R-2
Stein, Herbert, R-17
Stern, Aimee, R-3, R-5, R-12, R-18
Stern, Gabriella, R-7
Stern, Louis W., R-11, R-12
Sterngold, James, R-13
Stertz, Bradley A., R-3
Steuer, Richard M., R-2
Stevenson, Richard W., R-8, R-16
Stewart, Robert L., R-6
Stewart, Thomas A., R-2, R-17
Stiansen, Sarah, R-16
Stipp, David, R-2
Stockton, William, R-6
Stodgill, Ron, II, R-11
Stoffel, Jennifer, R-13
Stone, Bob, R-11
Stone, Donald C., R-17
Stough, Stanley J., R-6
Strang, Roger A., R-7
Strasmore, Martin R., R-16
Stremfel, Michael, R-16
Strickland, Thomas H., R-3
Strom, Stephanie, R-12
Stroud, Ruth, R-14
Stroup, Margaret A., R-2
Strugatch, Warren, R-4
Stumpf, Howard, R-15
Sugar, Alan, R-1
Sullivan, Kevin F., R-16
Sunoo, Don, R-14
Suttle, L. Lloyd, R-16
Swasy, Alecia, R-2, R-8
Sweeney, Jillian C., R-9
Swenson, Chester A., R-4, R-17
Swire, Donald, R-3
Swisher, Kara, R-3
Symonds, William C., R-9

Tadeschi, Mark, R-2
Talarzyk, W. Wayne, R-12
Tamate, Mariko, R-14, R-16
Tannenbaum, Jeffrey A., R-9
Tannenbaum, Stanley L., R-4, R-14
Tanouye, Elyse, R-10
Tanzer, Andrew, R-17
Taylor, Alex, III, R-3, R-9
Taylor, Cathy, R-8
Taylor, Marianne, R-10
Taylor, Thayer C., R-16, R-18
Teel, Jesse E., R-4
Teitelman, Robert, R-8
Templeman, John, R-7, R-8, R-9, R-17
Templin, Neal, R-3
Tharp, Mike, R-1
Therrien, Lois, R-6, R-10
Thill, John V., R-1, R-14
Thompson, Roger, R-16
Thuermer, Karen E., R-13
Toman, Barbara, R-17
Tongren, Hale N., R-4
Toor, Mat, R-3
Towle, Lisa H., R-15
Trachtenberg, Jeffrey A., R-6, R-10, R-13, R-15
Treece, James B., R-5, R-11
Treleven, Mark, R-5
Tretheway, Michael W., R-10
Trout, Jack T., R-7, R-8
Trunick, Perry A., R-13
Tullous, Raydel, R-5

# Subject Index

Idea/cause marketing, 10
Ideas, 5, 6
    new product, 281–282
    screening, 282, 283
Identifying suppliers and obtaining bids, 156–157
Imperfect information, acting on, 114
Import, 619
Import quota, 39–40
Importance in buying situations, 160
In-house agency, 551
In-market testing, 382
Inbound telemarketing, 592
Income, 34–35
    buying behavior and, 125–126
Income statement, 700–701
Incremental method, 599
Independent retailers, 465
Independent variable, 180
India, 37, 83, 147, 380, 616
Indirect-action advertising, 552–553
Indirect channels, 401
Indirect exchange, 317
Indirect exporting, 627
Individual brand, 252
Individualized marketing, 223
Indonesia, 147, 623
    culture and, 128
Industrial/commercial market, 144–145
Industrial distribution versus wholesaling, 439
Industrial market, 144
Industrial marketers, 20
Industrialization of services, 311
Inelastic demand, 336
Inert set, 112
Influencer role, 162
Informal controls, 686
Informal reciprocity, 152
Information, 173
    acting on imperfect, 114
    defined, 173
    providing, 516–517
    search for, 111–112, 156–157
Infrastructure, 38
Initiator role, 162
Inseparability, 302
Inside order getters, 595
Inside order takers, 596
Inspection buying method, 163
Installations, 245
Institutional advertising, 551
Intangibility, 301–302
Intangible products, 6, 240, 241
Integrated marketing channels, 412–415
    horizontal, 412–413
    vertical, 413–415
Integrated marketing communications (IMC),
    14, 539–540
Intensive distribution, 411
Interactive marketing, 312
Intercultural marketing, 614–617
    defined, 614
    guidelines for success, 616–617
    nature of, 614–616
        cultural values, 616
        language, 615–616
        race and nationality, 614–615
Intermodal transportation, 497–498
International brokers and agents, 436
International Forwarding and Transportation
    Message (IFTM), 504
International marketing, 617–639
    antidumping regulation, 334, 346
    branding and, 254
    channels for, 405–406
    countertrade and barter, 633, 635
    defined, 614, 617
    demographic segmentation and, 211

determining the level of, 627–630
    direct investment, 629–630
    exporting, 627–628
    joint venture, 628–629
    licensing, 628
distribution strategies, 632–634
    international, 632–634
    physical distribution, 634
at Domino's, 639
geographic segmentation and, 210
global consumer, 126–127
at Holiday Inn, 613, 636–637
issues in, 618–622
    balance of payments, 619
    competitive advantage, 620
    foreign exchange, 618–619
    free trade versus protectionism, 620
    multinational markets, 621–622
pricing strategies, 634–635
product and promotion strategies for, 630–632
    customized approach, 631–632
    global approach, 631
    product invention, 632
reasons companies engage in, 617–618
social elements in, 624–627
    business customs, 626–627
    buyer behavior, 625–626
    social organization and roles, 625
test marketing and, 190
Third World markets, 624–625
trends in, 622–624
    global corporations, 622
    joint ventures, 623–624
    multinational corporations, 622
    small exporters establishing overseas opera-
        tions, 622–623
International Organization for Standardization,
    648
International physical distribution, 500
    high-volume, 501
International pricing, 380
International regulatory elements, 45–46
    host-nation law, 46
    international treaties and agreements, 46
    U.S. law, 45–46
International sales, 593–594
Interpersonal communication, 527
Interpretation, perception and, 117–118
Interviews (see Personal surveys)
Introduction phase, 274
    strategies for, 276–278
Intuition, 176
Inventory management, 491–493
    costs of, 492
    just-in-time (JIT), 492–493
    reasons for, 491
    safety stock and, 492
    stockout and, 491
Inventory turnover rate, 702–703
Investor relations, 572
Involvement, 109, 153
Iran, 148
Iraq, 148–149
Ireland, 621, 626
Islamic cultures, 616
ISO 9000, 648
Israel, 621
Italy, 405–406, 619, 620, 621, 626
    culture and, 127

Japan, 124, 128, 249–250, 254, 334, 346, 461, 462,
    525, 566, 680, 682, 683
    government subsidies and, 379
    international marketing and, 615–633, 639
    marketing in, 21
    quality control in, 654
    strategic marketing objectives in, 67

vending machines in, 400, 474
Joint ventures, 628–629
    competitors forming, 623–624
    presence in desirable markets and, 682–683
"Junk fax," 560
"Junk mail," 560
Jury of executive opinion, 85
Just-in-time (JIT) inventory management, 492

Knowledge structure, 120

Labeling, 255–257
    design considerations, 257
    information for buyers and intermediaries, 256
    as promotional support, 256
    regulatory compliance and, 256–257
Labor-based services, 305–306
Laboratory experiment, 189–190
Language and intercultural marketing, 615–616
Lanham Act of 1946, 251
Late majority, 276
Latin America, 226, 616, 632, 635
Latin American Integration Association (LAIA),
    621
Layout, 564
Leader pricing, 372
Learning (see Consumer learning)
Legitimate power, 418
Licensing:
    brand, 286
    international marketing, 628
    technology, 285
Lifestyle, 123
    segmentation by, 211–213
Limited-line retailers, 467–468
Limited-line wholesalers, 432
Limited problem solving (LPS), 109, 110
Limited-service merchant wholesalers, 432–433
Line of business (LOB) structure, 677
Linear regression analysis, 87
List price, 373
Living standards, 38
Location of stores, 471–473
Logical appeals, 556–557
Logo, 247
    international marketing and, 254
Long-term profitability, 13–14
Loss leader, 372
Love, need for, 116
Low-contact services, 306
Low-context culture, 626–627
Luxembourg, 621

Madagascar, 633
Magazine advertising, 561
Mail-order wholesalers, 433
Mail surveys, 185
Make/buy decision, 156
Malaysia, 619
Malcolm Baldrige National Quality Award, 648,
    652, 655
Mall intercepts, 186
Management by objectives (MBO), 673
Managerial objectives and marketing channels,
    410
Manufacturer brand, 249
Manufacturers' agents, 434–435
Manufacturer's export agents (MEAs), 436
Manufacturers' wholesalers, 430–431
Manufacturing:
    distribution of U.S., 145, 146
    entering foreign markets, 627
Marginal analysis, 363–364
Marginal costs, 362–364
Marginal revenue, 363–364
Markdown pricing, 706
Markdown ratio, 706

Marketing research (*continued*)
    collect data (*see* Data collection)
    design of research (*see* Research design)
       presentation, 193
       problem definition, 176–177
    systems for managing data, 174–175
    at the U.S. Postal Service, 171, 198–199
Marketing strategy, 16–21
    developing a, 80–83
       developing a marketing mix, 83
       selecting a target market, 80–81
       staking out a market position, 81–83
    elements of, 17
    marketing mix (*see* Marketing mix)
Markup pricing, 704–706
Maslow's needs hierarchy, 115, 116
Mass communication, 528
Mass marketing, 21, 204, 222
Materials management, 499
Matrix organization, 681–682
Mature market, 124–125
Maturity phase, 274–275
    strategies for, 278–279
Media, 528
    selection of, in advertising campaigns,
       558–561
Media mix, 559
Media plan, 558–559
Medium, 524
Memory and consumer behavior, 120
Merchandise assortment, 460
Merchandising, 461
Merchant intermediaries for international mar-
    keting, 632–634
Merchant wholesalers, 432–433
Merchants, 396
Message, 524
Metropolitan statistical areas (MSAs), 209, 210
Mexico, 147, 254, 257, 471, 540, 617, 622
Microculture, 129–132
    African-Americans, 130–131
    Asian-Americans, 132
    defined, 129
    Hispanic-Americans, 131–132
Middle East, 680
Middlemen, 395
Minorities in sales, 592–593
Minority groups (*see* Microculture)
Mission statement, 79–80
Missionary salespeople, 596
Mixed-service retailing, 469
Modeling, 119
Modified rebuy, 159
Modifying products, 270–271
Molded circuit boards (MCBs), 67–68
Monopolistic competition, 33
Monopoly, 32
Morale of employees, 303
Motivation:
    of marketers, 684–685
    of salespeople, 600–601
Motives, 115
    consumer and organizational purchases and,
      150–151
Moving average, 87–88
MRO items, 244
Multicultural marketing (*see* Intercultural mar-
    keting)
Multilevel marketing (MLM), 404
Multinational corporation, 622
Multinational markets, 621–622
Multiple buying influence, 152
Multiple-choice questions, 189
Multiple marketing channels, 404–405
Multiple-zone pricing, 376

National brands, 249

National Laboratories Employment Act, 43
National Quality Award, 641
Nationality and intercultural marketing, 614–615
Natural elements, 38
Natural environment:
    government regulation and, 30–31
    packaging and, 255
Need recognition:
    customer buying process and, 110–111
    organizational buying process and, 155–156
Need-satisfaction approach, 587
Needs, 8–9, 115–116
Negotiated contracts, 163
Negotiated pricing, 377
"Neighborhoods," 213, 214
Netherlands, the, 128, 462, 471, 494, 496, 620,
    621, 631, 681
Networks, 683, 684
New products, 272–273
    at Chrysler, 296
    developing, 280–288
       commercialization, 287–288
       concept testing, 282–285
       developing the product, 285–286
       generating ideas, 281–282
       screening ideas, 282, 283
       test marketing, 286–287
    in existing markets, 75–76
    failure of, 290–291
    in new markets, 76
    success of, 288–290
       marketing environment, 290
       positioning or marketing mix, 289
       product, 288
       product development process, 289–290
New-task purchase, 159
New Zealand, 320, 346, 680
Newspapers, advertising in, 560
Nigeria, 619
Noise, 525
Nondurable goods, 241–242
Nonfinancial exchanges, 317
Nongovernmental regulation, 45
Nonprice competition, 347
Nonprobability samples, 183–184
Nonprofit marketing, 9–10, 315–318
    decision making in, 114–115
    importance of, 316–317
    organizing and, 682
    pricing strategies for, 380–381
    segmentation for, 220
    success in, 11
    unique aspects of, 317–318
Nonprofit organizations as customers, 148
Nonprospects, 221
Nonstore retailing, 473
North American Free Trade Agreement
    (NAFTA), 46, 622
Northern Ireland, 190
Norway, 331, 346
Novelty:
    appeal of, 558
    in buying situations, 159–160
Nutrition Labeling and Education Act of 1990,
    41, 43, 44, 74

Objective and task budgeting, 535
Objectives:
    pricing (*see* Pricing objectives)
    setting, 79–80
Observation, 184–185
Odd-even pricing, 370
Off-peak pricing, 312
Off-price retailers, 469
Oligopoly, 32–33
Open-ended questions, 188
Opening lines, personal selling and, 586

Operating expense ratio, 702
Operating expenses, 700–701
Operating ratios, 701–702
Operational planning, 68
Operational segmentation, 219–220
Opinion leaders, 135
    organizational purchasing and, 154
Opportunistic pricing, 340
Opportunities, assessment of, 73–80
    analyzing the environment, 74–76
    recognizing your capabilities, resources, and
      limitations, 76–77
    setting objectives, 79–80
    weighing the risks and rewards, 77–79
Opportunity costs, 492
Optimal quality, 643
Order getters, 595
Order processing, 490–491
Order takers, 595–596
Organizational advertising, 553–554
Organizational buying process, 155–160
    buying situations, 158–160
    complexity of, 160, 161
    evaluating alternatives, 157–158
    evaluating product and supplier performance,
      158
    identifying suppliers and obtaining bids,
      156–157
    influences on, 160–164
      buying center, 160–163
      buying methods, 163
      operational and situational, 163–164
    making the purchase, 158
    recognizing a need, 155–156
    setting specifications, 156
Organizational goods, marketing channels for,
    402–403
Organizational market, 144–148
    characteristics of, 149–153
      buyer-seller relationship, differences in,
       151–152
      nature of organizational demand, 152–153
      products and purchasing differences in,
       149–151
    Federal Express and, 143, 166–167
    government market, 146–148
    industrial/commercial market, 144–145
    manufacturing and service businesses, 145,
      146
    marketing channels and, 407
    NCR and, 168
    nonprofit sector, 148
    resellers market, 145–146, 147
    segmentation in, 215–220
      demographic, 217–219
      geographic, 216–217
      operational, 219–220
    in the U.S., 145
Organizational mission, 79–80
Organizational products, 149–150, 243–245
Organizational structure, 676
    (*See also* Marketing management, organizing)
Origin-point pricing, 375
Outbound telemarketing, 592
Outdoor advertising, 561
Outside order getters, 595
Outside order takers, 596
Ownership phase of communication, 526, 527

Package and express shippers, 497
Packaging, 252–255
    cost of, 255
    distribution and, 253–254
    environmental impact of, 255
    promotion and, 252–253
    safety and, 255
Peddling, 457, 474

# Name/Organization/Brand/ Company Index

222, 393, 420, 476, 490, 528, 622, 633, 648, 679
General Foods, 189, 226, 227, 269, 270, 273, 291
General Mills, 20, 203, 269, 291, 682
General Motors (GM), 57, 66, 84, 146, 152, 200, 204, 205, 213, 245, 260, 264, 396, 399–400, 492, 515, 554, 624, 633, 677, 683
General Motors Acceptance Corporation, 396
General Services Administration, 45
GEnie Information Services, 476
Geo, 517
Georges Marciano, 557
Georgia Pacific, 367
Gerber, 250
Geritol, 246
Gibson Greetings, 417
Gillette, 83, 252, 270, 277, 625, 631
Gimbel, Adam, 457
Gimbel's, 457
Gitano, 635
Glass, David, 418
Glass, Stephanie, 255
Glaxo, 175, 285
GM Card, 205
Godfather's Pizza, 245
Gold Card, 135, 232
Goldberg, Albert, 480
Goldberg, Stanley, 435
Golden, Hyman, 608
Golden Gate Bridge, 381
Goldsmith, Herb, 551
Golub, Harvey, 232
Gon Moth Balls, 525, 616
Good & Plenty, 274, 275
Good News, 270
Goodrich, 341
Goodyear Go Centers, 411
Goodyear Tire and Rubber Company, 74, 249, 264, 341, 411, 465
Goofy, 286
Gorman, Leon, 641, 666–669
Gotcha Sportswear, 410
*Gourmet,* 213
Government Service Adminstration, 147
*GQ,* 481
Grand Cherokee, 296
Grand Depot, The, 457
Grand Metropolitan, 12, 416
Granucci, Leo, 431
Granville Island Public Market, 935
Grattan, 140
Great British Kettles, 285
Great Starts, 172
Greenberg, Arnold, 608
Greenleaf, Mert, 668
Gretzky, Wayne, 24, 232
Grimmick, Henry, 648
Grönroos, Christian, 314
*Groundhog Day,* 530
Group Health Insurance Program, 314
Guess Jeans, 557
Guy's, 273
Gymboree, 223, 454

H&R Block, 110, 322, 454, 476, 651
H. B. Fuller, 682
H. J. Heinz, 130, 156, 398, 625, 630
Häagen-Dazs, 335–336, 555
Haggar Apparel, 489
Haigler, T. E., Jr., 55
Halifax Financial Services, 563
Hall, David, 409
Hall, John, 571
Hall-Mark Electronics, 440
Hallmark Cards, 174, 249, 251, 417
Hallmark Circuits, 251
Hallmark Financial Services, 251

Hamilton Standard, 151
Hammacher Schlemmer, 476
Harley-Davidson, 114, 492, 617
Harman, Karen, 15
Harrods, 332, 456
Harvard University, 344
Hasbro, 280
Hawkins, Gus, 424
Hayes, 260
Head and Shoulders, 246
Head Start, 79
Health-Tex, 444
Hearst Magazines, 222–223
Heartwise, 230
Hearty Fruit Muffins, 286
HEARx, 467
Heath English Toffee Bar, 274
Henckel, 32
Hercules, 254
Hermes, 332, 465
Herrschners, 76
Hershey Foods, 289
Hershey's, 248, 562
Hertz, 19
Hewlett, Bill, 673
Hewlett-Packard (HP), 20, 22, 73, 147, 186, 187, 377, 410, 489, 652, 673, 674, 676, 680, 681, 694–695
Hi C, 254
Higa, Ernest M., 139, 639
Hills Brothers, 234
Hilton Hotels, 568, 637
Hirayama, Tomoshi, 325
Hires, 247
*Hispanic,* 615
*Hispanic Business,* 616
History Book Club, 406
Ho, Kenny, 42
Holiday Companies, 444
Holiday Inn, 210, 466, 613, 614, 636
Holiday Inn Worldwide, 613, 636–637
Hollywood Brands, 274
Homa, Kenneth, 420
Home Cookin', 226, 697
Home Depot, 26, 367, 463, 473, 510–511
Home Shopping Network, 476
Homefurnishings Mart, 437
Honda, 122, 296, 515, 558, 626, 654
Honeywell, 285, 587
Hope, Bob, 557
Horizon Club, 664
Hormel, 283, 596
Hostess, 395
Hot 'n Now, 416
Hot Shoppe, 94
Hot Wheels, 270
Hotel Lotte, 307
Hotpoint, 222
Hoult, Peter, 206
*House Beautiful,* 222
House Subcommittee on Transportation of Hazardous Materials, 206
Howard, William, 43
Huang, Maria, 648
Hudler, Donald, 515, 544
Hudson's Bay Company, 395, 457
Huffy, 278
Huggies, 270
Humana, 680
Hunt-Wesson, 262–263, 272
Hussein, Saddam, 148–149
Hutsabaut, Sandi, 485, 486, 493–494, 498, 506, 507
Hypermarket U.S.A., 471, 681
Hyundai, 249, 348, 534

"I Hate My Miserable Life," 521
Iaccoca, Lee, 296

IBM, 14, 20, 21, 82, 143, 168, 220, 247, 272, 288, 374, 388, 389, 403, 405, 406, 409, 476, 490, 532, 598, 634, 642, 645, 652, 658, 659, 677, 682
IBM PC Company, 677
Ibuku, Masaru, 324–325
IDS Financial Services, 232
IGA, 418
IKEA, 460–461, 463, 487–488
Illinois Tool Works (ITW), 404
*Inc.,* 132, 295
*Industrial Distribution,* 650
Infiniti, 17, 81–83, 331, 418, 558, 593
Infocel, 147
Information Resources Inc. (IRI), 181, 308, 565
Information Services Company, 232
Ingersoll-Rand, 491
Innovators, 276
Intergraph, 400
Internal Revenue Service (IRS), 316, 322
*International Electronics Directory: Guide to European Manufacturers, Agents, and Applications,* 219
International Exhibitors Association, 437
International Franchising Association (IFA), 45
International Organization for Standardization, 648
International Paper, 596
International Playtex, 275
Interstate Commerce Commission, 418, 495
Intrepid, 296
Intuit, 16
Irish Export Board, 316
Irish Spring, 215
Itochu, 618
ITT Sheraton, 539
Iverson, Ken, 675
Ivy League, 344

J. C. Penney, 25, 111, 130, 354, 454, 466, 480, 482, 557, 712
J. Fegely & Son, 592
J. Walter Thompson, 557
Jack Daniels, 563
Jack-in-the-Box, 133
Jackson, Mannie, 587
Jackson, Mary Anne, 283–285, 289
Jackson, Michael, 424, 557
Jackson Hewitt, 322
Jaguar, 33, 331, 374, 398, 410, 552
James Bond, 563
*Japan Trade Journal,* 219
Jartran, 552
JCB card, 232
Jeep, 296
Jell-O, 227, 679, 711
Jell-O Pudding Pops, 273
Jenny Craig Weight Loss Centers, 303, 595
Jimmy'z, 410
Jockey, 249
Joe Camel, 538
Johnson, David, 697
Johnson & Johnson, 32, 57, 70, 552, 575
Johnson Products, 424
Johnson Wax, S. C., 282, 283, 522
Johnston Coca-Cola Bottling Group, 486
Jolly Green Giant, 12
Jolly Time, 262
Jones, David C., 140
Jordache Enterprises, 486
Jordan, Michael, 13, 24
Jos. A. Bank Clothiers, 76, 467, 482
Joseph Jacobs Organization, 615
Joy de Jean Patou, 332
Juanarena, Douglas, 435
*Jungle Fever,* 13
Juran, Joseph, 654

Piaget, 19
Pierre Audoin Conseil, 192
Pillsbury, Charles A., 10
Pillsbury, 10, 11, 12, 286, 416, 632
Pine Bros., 274
Pink Lemonade Euphoria, 609
Pinto, 57
Pitney Bowes, 292
Pizza California, 639
Pizza Hut, 45, 138, 245, 270, 288, 343, 639, 664
Pizza Station, 639
Place des Antiquaires, 473
Platinum Card, 135, 232
Platinum Software, 528
Platt, Lewis, 694
Playtex, 631
Plaza Research, 192
Pleasure Island, 76
Plymouth, 204, 646
Pneutronics Corporation, 591
Poland Spring, 234
Polaroid, 279
Polaroid Cool Cam, 130
Polo/Ralph Lauren, 463, 480
PolyGram, 361–362
Pontiac, 204
Popsicle, 698
Population Development Associates of Thailand, 241
Porsche, 121, 207, 523
Portland General Electric, 80
*Portrait of Dr. Gachet,* 337, 339
Potential Rating Index by Zip Markets (PRIZM), 213
Powell, Tim, 172
Power Test Corporation, 77
PowerAde, 208
PPG Industries, 595, 597
Practical Peripherals, 260
Preference, 19
Preferred Hotels, 682
Prego, 286
Premier, 408
*Premiere,* 345
Prescriptives Exact Color, 614–615
Presley, Elvis, 171
Preston, James, 607
Prestone, 119
Price Club, 465, 466
Price/Costco, 412, 465, 466
Price Waterhouse, 34, 245, 312
Princeton University, 344
PrintMasters, 649
Pro-Grain, 203
Pro-Line, 424
PRO WATS, 643
PROBE (Epley), 178
Probe (Ford), 624
Procter & Gamble (P&G), 32, 40, 50, 249, 270, 309, 331, 416, 430, 517, 521, 555, 566, 568, 614, 633, 634, 642, 645, 674, 678, 698, 699, 710, 711
Prodigy, 21, 403, 476, 477, 561
Product 19, 247
*Professional Builder,* 20
Promise Extra Light, 699
Protege, 204
Prudential Insurance, 541
PS/2, 374
Public Broadcasting System (PBS), 220
Pudding Pops, 679
Puma, 3, 24
Pump, The, 24, 245
*Purchasing World,* 591
Purdue University, 239
Purk, Mary, 375

Q-Tips, 698
Quaker Oats, 48, 76, 368, 555, 632
*Qualified Remodeler,* 20
Quicken, 16
Quicksilver, 410
Quinlan, Michael R., 26
QVC Network, 475, 476, 477

R. J. Reynolds Tobacco (RJR), 206, 539
Radio Corporation of America (RCA), 70
Radio Shack, 454, 596
Ragú, 698
Raid, 522, 523
Raid Max, 522
Raider candy bar, 126
Rain Blo, 274
Raisin Bran, 230–231
Raisin Squares, 203
Ralph Lauren, 249, 332, 463, 480
Ralph's, 467
Ramada, 350
Rand McNally, 61
Range Rover, 8, 9, 17
"Rapid Refund," 322
Rapp, Gregg, 257
Rapp, Stan, 223
Rawl, Lawrence, 571
RCA, 622
Re/Max, 601
"Reach Out," 604
*Reader's Digest,* 61
ReaLemon, 190, 246
Red Bow, 239, 262
Red Cross, 220, 250, 254, 316, 518
*Redbook,* 462
Redenbacher, Orville, 239–240, 247, 252, 262–263
Reebok, 3, 13, 24, 77, 245, 246, 254, 398, 501, 517, 539, 558
Reese's Pieces, 562
Regina Corporation, 345
*Register,* 218
Reid, Sir Bob, 387
Reiser, Charles E., Jr., 444
Reject China Shop, 460
Remington Arms Company, 259
Remington Products, 631
Ren & Stimpy, 286
Renaissance, 350
Residence Inn, 81
Revlon, 615, 617
RGA, 634
Ribbon Project, 316
Rice Krispies, 252
Richardson-Vicks, 275
Riddell, 410
Riese, Murray, 343
Right Guard ClearGel, 252
Riney, Hal, 118
Ring, Leonard M., 259
Ringer Corporation, 435
Ritz Crackers, 558
Roadshow, 502
Roadway Package Systems, 497
Robert Morris Associates, 701
Robins, A. H., 374
Robinson, F. George, Jr., 272
Robinson Brick, 272
Robitussin, 374
Rock of Gibraltar, 541
Rockwell International, 633
Rodeway Inns, 350
Rolex, 254, 332
Rolls-Royce, 332, 562
Ross-Simons, 474
Routing Technology Software, 502
Rowitch, Jerome, 371

Roy Rogers, 94, 343
Royal Crown Cola, 215, 224
Royal Dutch/Shell, 85
Rubbermaid, 268
Russell Stover Candies, 344
Rust International, 320
RX-7, 264
Ryder, 535, 664

S-MOS Systems, 648
Saab, 120
Sa'ad, 16, 148
Saatchi & Saatchi, 304
Sable, 285
Safeway Supermarkets, 372, 398, 399, 465
Saks Fifth Avenue, 464, 476, 481
Salada, 230
Salem, 206, 539
Salem Pro-Sail, 539
*Sales & Marketing Management's Survey of Industrial and Commercial Buying Power,* 218
Sally Hansen, 227
Salvation Army, 117
Sam's Club, 465, 681
Samsonite, 337, 618
Samuelson, Joan Benoit, 24
San Diego, California, 556
SANCO, 290
Sansabelt, 558
Sara Lee, 252, 274, 286, 596, 631
Sargent & Strong, 313
*Saturday Night Live,* 530
Saturn, 118, 515, 516, 524, 531, 534, 544–545
Save the Children, 541
Sayett Technology, 285
Scandinavian Airlines System (SAS), 15, 62, 666, 677
ScanFone, 477
Schaefer, Paul, 220
Schering-Plough, 285
Schimberg, Henry, 486
Schlage dead bolts, 115
Schulthess, 123
Schultz, Howard, 549, 550, 574
Scotchgard, 282
Scott, Willard, 60
Scott, 252
Scottish Development Agency, 623
Scrivner, 449
Sculpture Gardens, 371
Sea-Land, 499
Sealwrap, 246
Sears, 21, 25, 130, 232, 249, 352–355, 401, 403, 408, 414, 473, 474, 475, 476, 494, 517, 557, 568, 595, 596
Seaton, W. B., 46
Seelenfreund, Alan, 451
See's Candies, 118
Sega, 92, 93, 205, 278
Selective Service Administration, 195
Selectric, 272, 288
*Selling to the Military,* 147
Semiconductor Specialists, 432
Sennott, Roger, 614
Sensor, 83, 270, 277
Service Merchandise, 467
Service Supply Company, 650
ServiceMaster, 245
7-Eleven, 211, 395, 399, 454, 460
747, 624
767, 624
777, 624
*Seventeen,* 462
Seven-Up, 130, 539
Sewell Village Cadillac, 257–258
Shake 'N Bake, 291